Philosophy of Religion: An Anthology

Third Edition

L O U I S   P.   P O J M A N

U.S. Military Academy, West Point

Wadsworth Publishing Company

I(T)P® **An International Thomson Publishing Company**

Belmont, CA • Albany, NY • Bonn • Boston • Cincinnati • Detroit • Johannesburg • London • Madrid
Melbourne • Mexico City • New York • Paris • Singapore • Tokyo • Toronto • Washington

Dedicated to the memory of my father and mother, Louis A. and Helen Pojman

Philosophy Editor: Peter Adams
Assistant Editor: Kerri Abdinoor
Editorial Assistant: Kelly Bush
Marketing Manager: Dave Garrison
Production: The Book Company
Print Buyer: Stacy Weinberger
Permissions Editor: Robert Kauser
Designer: Lois Stanfield, Al Burkhardt
Copy Editor: Jane Townsend
Cover Design: Bill Stanton
Compositor: Kachina Typesetting
Printer: Maple-Vail Book Manufacturing

This book is printed on acid-free recycled paper.

Printed in the United States of America
 4 5 6 7 8 9 10

For more information, contact Wadsworth Publishing Company, 10 Davis Drive, Belmont, CA 94002, or electronically at http://www.wadsworth.com/wadsworth.html

International Thomson Publishing Europe
Berkshire House 168-173
High Holborn
London, WC1V7AA, England

Thomas Nelson Australia
102 Dodds Street
South Melbourne 3205
Victoria, Australia

Nelson Canada
1120 Birchmount Road
Scarborough, Ontario
Canada M1K 5G4

International Thomson Publishing GmbH
Königswinterer Strasse 418
53227 Bonn, Germany

International Thomson Editores
Campos Eliseos 385, Piso 7
Col. Polanco
11560 México D.F. México

International Thomson Publishing Asia
221 Henderson Road
#05-10 Henderson Building
Singapore 0315

International Thomson Publishing Japan
Hirakawacho Kyowa Building, 3F
2-2-1 Hirakawacho
Chiyoda-ku, Tokyo 102, Japan

International Thomson Publishing Southern Africa
Building 18, Constantia Park
240 Old Pretoria Road
Halfway House, 1685 South Africa

Library of Congress Cataloging-in-Publication Data

Philosophy of religion : an anthology / [edited by]
Louis P. Pojman. -
  - 3rd ed.
    p. cm.
  Includes bibliographical references.
  ISBN 0-534-52956-9
  1. Religion—Philosophy.   I. Pojman, Louis P.
BL51.P532 1998
210—dc21   97-18435

Contents

PART **I**   **TRADITIONAL ARGUMENTS FOR THE EXISTENCE OF GOD**   **1**

PART **II**   **THE ARGUMENT FROM RELIGIOUS EXPERIENCE**   **99**

---

*An asterisk indicates a more challenging article.

PART **VII** FAITH AND REASON   373

PART **VIII** RELIGIOUS PLURALISM   507

PART **IX** RELIGION AND ETHICS   561

Preface

I am grateful for the wide use the first two editions of *Philosophy of Religion* received and am delighted for the opportunity of bringing out an improved, up-dated edition. Many instructors and students over the past eleven years sent me helpful suggestions for a future edition, and many have been incorporated here. There are ten new articles (plus additions to old ones) for a total of seventy-three.

Here are some of the additions: In Part One, I have added two articles by William Lane Craig on the Kalām Cosmological Argument together with a new critique by Paul Draper. I have added J. N. Findlay's Negative Ontological Argument, where he argues that the ontological argument actually shows that God's existence is impossible. In Part II, I have added Freud's analysis of religion as wish-fulfillment, a projection of the father-image. For Part III, Paul Draper has written a paper on "Evolution and the Problem of Evil" wherein he outlines a cumulative case against theism, linking the problem of evil and evolutionary theory. In Part VII, I have added my article, "Faith Without Belief?" exploring the possibility that other propositional attitudes besides belief are adequate for religious faith. Part VIII on Religious Pluralism has been enhanced by David Basinger's "Hick's Religious Pluralism and Reformed Epistemology—A Middle Ground" and Joseph Runzo's "God, Commitment and Other Faiths: Pluralism Versus Relativism" in which he argues for religious relativism. In addition, several selections have been revised. For example, I have added

sections to the selections by James's "The Will to Believe" and Leibniz's "Theodicy: A Defense of Theism." I believe these additions greatly strengthen this anthology and hope that they will prove challenging and useful to you, the instructors and students.

The same general format of general introductions followed by individual classic and contemporary readings has been continued, and the basic topics are treated: traditional arguments for the existence of God, the argument from religious experience, the problem of evil, the attributes of God, miracles and revelation, death and immortality, faith and reason, and religion and ethics. To these eight topics, a ninth, religious pluralism, has been added.

There are individual introductions to each reading and the more advanced or difficult readings have been marked in the table of contents by an asterisk (*). These more difficult readings are intended for advanced students and graduate students. I am gratified that this book is used both in undergraduate and graduate courses.

I am also pleased that Wadsworth Publishing Company has two excellent single-author textbooks that may serve as an accompaniment to this anthology: William Rowe's *Philosophy of Religion: An Introduction* (2nd ed 1992) and William Wainwright's *Philosophy of Religion* (1988). I have used both of these with good success.

I would like to express my thanks to all the reviewers who offered me helpful advice in shaping this work: Michael Awalt, Belmont College;

Keith De Rose, New York University; John Donnelly, University of San Diego; Frederick Ferre, University of Georgia; Ted Klein, Texas Christian University; George Mavrodes, University of Michigan; Richard Purtill, Western Washington University; William Rowe, Purdue University; W. Jay Wood, Wheaton College; Keith Yandell, University of Wisconsin; and especially, Edward Wierenga, University of Rochester.

Reviewers who offered helpful suggestions for the second edition are M. Jamie Ferreira, University of Virginia; Robert C. Good, Rider College; Noa Latham, Barnard College; George Mavrodes, University of Michigan; Robert M. Timko, Mansfield University of Pennsylvania; Edward Wierenga, University of Rochester; and Linda Zagzebski, Loyola Marymount University.

Thanks also, to reviewers of the third edition: Kenton Machina, Illinois State University; Wesley Morrison, University of Colorado at Boulder; Michael Myers, Washington State University; and Patrick O'Neil, Broome Community College.

Peter Adams, the Philosophy Editor for Wadsworth, enthusiastically supported this project at every stage, and Dusty Davidson, the Production Editor, did a marvelous job bringing the work into production.

This book was and remains dedicated to the memory of my father and mother, one an agnostic, who searched for truth and deeply pondered issues of religion, the other a devout Christian. Among my earliest childhood memories are discussion of questions about religion, a sense of wonder of the cosmos (which inspired an adolescent mysticism), a longing for knowledge of God, a Dostoevskian agony over the problem of evil, debates over the necessity of religion for morality. All this in the context of love and mutual respect was a patrimony that I would bequeath to those who read and reflect on the essays contained in this work.

Louis P. Pojman
U.S. Military Academy
West Point, N.Y.
July 19, 1997

Introduction

No other subject has exercised as profound a role in human history as religion. Offering a comprehensive explanation of the universe and of our place in it, religion offers us a cosmic map and shows us our place on the map; through its sacred books, it provides lessons in cosmic map reading, enabling us to find our way through what would otherwise be a labyrinth of chaos and confusion. Religion tells where we came from, where we are, where we are going, and how we can get there. In this regard, religion legitimizes social mores, rituals, and morals. All have a coherent place on reality's map.

Moreover, religion is value-laden. It typically gives us a sense of dignity and self-worth. "We hold these truths to be self-evident," wrote Thomas Jefferson in the Declaration of Independence, "that all men are created equal, that they are endowed by their Creator with certain unalienable rights, that among these are life, liberty and the pursuit of happiness." The notions of equal worth and dignity were originally religious notions, derived from the idea of a benevolent Supreme Being creating humans in his own image, and become problematic apart from a religious framework.

Religion offers comfort in sorrow, hope in death, courage in danger, and spiritual joy in the midst of despair. It tells us that this world is not a mere impersonal materialist conundrum but a friendly home, provided for us by our heavenly Father. As William James says, if religion is true, "the universe is no longer a mere *It* to us, but a *Thou*, and any relation that may be possible from person to person might be possible here."

The sacred tomes of the religions of the world—the Vedas, the Bhagavad Gītā, the Bible, the Koran, the Dhammapada—are literary classics in their own right. In the Western tradition, who has not marveled at the elegance of the Creation story in Genesis 1 or the stories of Joseph's brothers selling him into slavery, Moses leading the children of Israel out of bondage in Egypt, the birth of Jesus, the Sermon on the Mount, or the parable of the good Samaritan?

Religion has inspired millions in every age: Its architecture—from the pyramids to the Parthenon, from the Hindu Juggernaut to the cathedral at Chartres—rises as a triumph of the human hope; its art from the Muslim mosaics in Grenada to Michelangelo's Sistine Chapel is without peer; its music from Hindu chants through Bach's cantata and Handel's *Messiah* to thousands of hymns and spirituals has lit the hearts in weal and in woe of people in all times and almost all places. Every time we date a letter, a check, or a contract, we pay homage to the founder of Christianity, dividing the calendar into BC and AD (anno domini).

Religion holds a power over humanity like nothing else. Saints and martyrs have been created in its crucible, reformations and revolutions ignited by its flame, and outcasts and criminals have been catapulted to a higher level of existence by its propulsion. Auschwitz survivor Olga Lengyel writes that almost the only people to keep their dignity in the Nazi concentration camp were people animated by faith—"priests and nuns in the camp [who] proved that they had real strength of character." When I worked with the poor in Bedford-Stuyvesant, Brooklyn, the work of the pentecostal Christian David Wilkerson astounded the civil authorities, for drug addicts who were considered incorrigible suddenly would "kick the habit cold-turkey" upon being converted. Such is the power of religion.

Nonetheless, despite its enormous dynamics, religion's power and influence are no guarantees of truth. It could be that the impact of religion in human affairs only shows that humans are myth-making and myth-craving animals. We need a Big Myth to help us make it through the darkness of existence, whether it be a religion, Nazism, Marxism, or astrology. And it could be that humanity will someday "come of age," outgrow religion and stand on its own as an autonomous adult. There is a dark side to religion, too—its bigotry, wars, and intolerance—which should give us pause in evaluating its merits.

Sigmund Freud, in *The Future of an Illusion*, said that religion is an illusion, a projection of the father image. Little children grow up thinking their parents, often their father, are godlike and very powerful. They stand in reverent awe of his grandeur and look to him for providential support. When they become teens, they realize that their fathers are also mortal and not especially powerful, but they still have this inclination to worship the kind of being that they revered as small children—hence, the projection on the empty skies of the father image, thus worshiping a God. Religion, as illusory, would evaporate when people became autonomous and didn't need myths.

Similarly, Karl Marx viewed religion as the misplaced longings of alienated people:

Religion . . . is the self-conscious and self-feeling of the man who either has not yet found himself, or else (having found himself) has lost himself once more. But man is not an abstract being. . . . Man is the world of men, the State, society. This State, this society, produces religion, produces a perverted world consciousness, because they are a perverted world. . . .

Religion is the sigh of the oppressed creature, the feelings of a heartless world, just as it is the spirit of unspiritual conditions. It is the opium of the people.

The people cannot be really happy until it has been deprived of illusory happiness by the abolition of religion. The demand that the people should shake itself free of illusion as to its own condition is the demand that it should abandon a condition which needs illusion.*

Are Freud and Marx correct in treating religion as an illusion? The jury is still out on this. It could be that Freudianism and Marxism, both comprehensive worldviews—rivals to religious views—have the defect of imposing their own controversial assumptions onto religion. For example, why should one automatically assume religion is an illusion just because belief in God is (partially?) caused by our relation as children to our more powerful and benevolent parents? Could that not be the medium by which God prepares us for a trusting relationship with himself? Many would argue that Freudianism itself, together with Freud's thesis in *The Future of an Illusion*, is the "illusion of the future," and Marxism has been criticized as a mistaken attempt to reduce all human experience to class struggle and economic conditions. You will have to decide the relative merits of these theories.

What is the truth about religion? We want to know if religion, one at least, is true. We want to assess the evidence and arguments for and against its claims in an impartial, judicious, and open-minded manner. And this is what we will endeavor to do in this part of our work.

The key notion of most religions is the idea of a God, an all-powerful, benevolent, and providential being who created the universe and all therein. Questions connected with the existence of God may be the most important that we can ask and try to answer. If God exists, then it is of the utmost importance that we come to know that fact and as much as possible about God and his plan. Implica-

*"Introduction to a Critique of the Hegelian Philosophy of Right," in K. Marx and F. Engels, *Collected Works*, Vol. 3 (London: Lawrence & Wishart, 1975).

tions follow that affect our understanding of the world and ourselves. If God exists, the world is not accidental, a product of mere chance and necessity, but a home that has been designed for rational and sentient beings, a place of personal purposefulness. We are not alone in our struggle for justice but are working together with One whose plan is to redeem the world from evil. Most importantly, there is Someone to whom we are responsible and to whom we owe absolute devotion and worship. Other implications follow for our self-understanding, the way we ought to live our lives and prospects for continued life after death. In short, if there is a God, we ought to do everything possible to discover this fact, including using our reason in the discovery itself or as a means to test the validity of claims of such a discovery.

On the other hand, it may be that a supreme, benevolent being does not exist. If there is no God, we want to know this too. Whether we believe in God or not will make a difference in the way we view the universe and in the way we live.

Many people have lived well without believing in God. Pierre Simon Laplace, when asked about his faith, is reported to have replied, "I have no need of that hypothesis." But the testimony of humankind is against him. Millions have needed and been inspired by this notion. So great is the inspiration issuing from the idea of God that we could say that if God doesn't exist, the idea is the greatest invention of the human mind. What are all the world's works of literature, art, music, drama, architecture, science, and philosophy compared to this simple concept?

To quote Anthony Kenny,

> If there is no God, then God is incalculably the greatest single creation of the human imagination. No other creation of the imagination has been so fertile of ideas, so great an inspiration to philosophy, to literature, to painting, sculpture, architecture, and drama. Set beside the idea of God, the most original inventions of mathematicians and the most unforgettable characters in drama are minor products of the imagination: Hamlet and the square root of minus one pale into insignificance by comparison.*

The field of philosophy of religion documents the history of humanity's quest for a supreme being.

Even if God does not exist, the arguments centering on this quest are interesting in their own right for their ingenuity and subtlety, even apart from their possible soundness. It can be argued that the Judeo-Christian tradition has informed our self-understanding to such a degree that it is imperative for every person who would be well informed to come to grips with the arguments and counterarguments surrounding its claims. Hence, even if one rejects the assertions of religion, it is important to understand what is being rejected and why.

In this work, we will examine the major problems in philosophy of religion whether God exists, the significance of religious and mystical experience, the attributes of God, the problem of evil, miracles, survival after death, faith and reason, the possibility that all (or many) religions point to the same truth, and religion and ethics.

I can only hope that the passion and vitality of the debate that has lasted over 2000 years will ignite your hearts and minds in coming to grips with these issues.

---

*Faith and Reason (New York: Columbia University Press, 1983), 59.

PART I

TRADITIONAL ARGUMENTS FOR THE EXISTENCE OF GOD

Can the existence of God be demonstrated or made probable by argument? The debate between those who believe that reason can demonstrate that God exists and those who do not has an ancient lineage, going back to Protagoras (ca. 450 BC) and Plato (427–347 BC). The Roman Catholic church has traditionally held that the existence of God is demonstrable by human reason. The strong statement of the First Vatican Council (1870) indicates that human reason is adequate to arrive at a state of knowledge:

> If anyone says that the one and true God, our creator and Lord, cannot be known with certainty with the natural light of human reason by means of the things that have been made: let him be anathema.

Many others, including theists of various denominations, among them Catholics, have denied that human reason is adequate to arrive at knowledge or demonstrate the existence of God.

Arguments for the existence of God divide into two main groups: a priori and a posteriori arguments. An *a posteriori argument* is based on premises that can be known only by means of experience of the world (e.g., that there is a world, events have causes, and so forth). An *a priori argument,* on the other hand, rests on premises that can be known to be true independently of experience of the world. One need only clearly conceive of the proposition in order to see that it is true.

In this work we consider two types of a posteriori arguments for the existence of God and one a priori argument. The a posteriori arguments are the cosmological argument and the teleological argument. The a priori argument is the ontological argument; we offer two forms of that argument type.

The question before us in this part of our work is, What do the arguments for the existence of God establish? Do any of them demonstrate beyond reasonable doubt the existence of a supreme being or deity? Do any of them make it probable (given the evidence at hand) that such a being exists?

I.A The Cosmological Argument for the Existence of God

Asking people why they believe in God is likely to evoke something like the following response. "Well, things just didn't pop up out of nothing. Someone, a pretty powerful Someone, had to cause the universe to come into existence. You just can't have causes going back forever. God must have made the world. Nothing else makes sense."

All versions of the cosmological argument begin with the a posteriori assumptions that the universe exists and that something outside the universe is required to explain its existence. That is, it is *contingent*, depending on something outside of itself for its existence. That "something else" is logically prior to the birth of the universe. It constitutes the reason for the existence of the universe. Such a being is God.

One version of the cosmological argument is called the "first-cause argument." From the fact that some things are caused, we may reason to the existence of a first cause. The Catholic monk St. Thomas Aquinas (1225–1274) gives a version of this argument in our first reading. His "second way" is based on the idea of causation:

We find that there is among material things a regular order of causes. But we do not find, nor indeed is it possible, that anything is the cause of itself, for in that case it would be prior to itself, which is impossible. Now it is not possible to proceed to infinity in causes. For if we arrange in order all causes, the first is the cause of the intermediate, and the intermediate the cause of the last, whether the intermediate be many or only one. But if we remove a cause the effect is removed; therefore, if there is no *first* among causes, neither will there be a last or an intermediate. But if we proceed to infinity in causes there will be no first cause, and thus there will be no ultimate effect, nor any intermediate causes, which is clearly false. Therefore it is necessary to suppose the existence of some first cause, and this men call God.

The general outline, focusing on the second argument, goes something like this:

1. There exist things that are caused.
2. Nothing can be the cause of itself.
3. There cannot be an infinite regress of causes.
4. Therefore, there exists an uncaused first cause.
5. The word *God* means uncaused first cause.
6. Therefore, God exists.

What can we say of this argument? Certainly the first premise is true—some things have causes. Indeed, we generally believe that every event has a cause that explains why the event happened. The second premise seems correct, for how could something that didn't exist cause anything, let alone its own existence? Note that premise 2 and premise 4 are not contradictions. There is nothing obviously incoherent about the idea that something or someone existed from eternity and so is uncaused, whereas there is something incoherent about the idea that something nonexistent caused itself to come into being.

One difficulty with the argument is premise 3: There cannot be an infinite regress of causes. Why can't there be such a regress? You might object that there are an infinite regress of numbers, so why can't there be an infinite regress of causes?

One response to this objection is that there is a significant difference between numbers and events and persons. Numbers are just abstract entities, whereas events and persons are concrete, temporal entities, the sort of things that need to be brought into existence. Numbers exist in all possible worlds. They are eternal, but Napoleon, Mt. Everest, and you are not eternal but need a causal explanation. The child asks, "Mommy, who made me?" and the mother responds, "You came from my womb." The child persists, "Mommy, who made you and your womb?" The mother responds that she came from a fertilized egg in her mother's womb, but the child persists in the query until the mother is forced to admit that she doesn't know the answer or perhaps says, "God made the world and all that is in it."

God may be one explanatory hypothesis, answering the question why the world came to be, but the question is, Does the argument from first cause, even if it is valid, give us a full-blown proof of the existence of God?

In our second reading, the eighteenth-century philosopher Samuel Clarke sets forth a different version of the cosmological argument, the argument from contingency (Aquinas's third way). Clarke, like Aquinas before him, identifies the independent and necessary being with God. We are dependent, or contingent, beings. Reducing the argument to the bare bones, the argument from contingency is this:

1. Every being that exists is either contingent or necessary.
2. Not every being can be a contingent.
3. Therefore, there exists a necessary being upon which the contingent beings depend.
4. A necessary being on which all contingent beings exist is what we mean by *God*.
5. Therefore, God exists.

A necessary being is self-existing, independent, and has the explanation of its existence in itself, whereas contingent beings do not have the reason for their existence in themselves but depend on other beings and, ultimately, depend on a necessary being.

In our third reading, Paul Edwards separates the two versions of the cosmological argument. He argues that the first version commits the fallacy of composition, that of erroneously attributing properties of individuals to the groups they constitute (e.g., each person in the group has a mind, but the group doesn't have a mind), and the second version fails to recognize that the universe may be a brute fact.

Next, William Rowe examines the cosmological argument, and especially versions like the argument from contingency based on the *principle of sufficient reason* (PSR), the thesis that everything must have an explanation to account for it. He points out problems connected with this principle.

In our fifth reading, William Lane Craig defends two versions of the *kalām* cosmological argument, an argument first set forth by Arab Islamic scholars, al-Kindi and al-Ghazali, in the Middle Ages. This argument purports to show that the universe must have a cause. Craig goes on to argue that scientific investigation corroborates this conclusion.

In our final reading, Paul Draper analyzes Craig's versions of the *kalām* argument and claims that, enticing as this argument is, it rests on an equivocation of the idea of "beginning to exist," which undermines its soundness.

I.A.1 The Five Ways

THOMAS AQUINAS

The Dominican monk Thomas Aquinas (1225–1274) is considered by many to be the greatest theologian in Western religion. The five ways of showing the existence of God given in this selection

are versions of the cosmological argument; put simply, their strategies are as follows: The first way concerns the fact that there is change (or motion) and argues that there must be an Unmoved Mover that originates all change but itself is not moved. The second way is from the idea of causation and argues that there must be a first cause to explain the

Reprinted from *Summa Theologica*, translated by Anton C. Pegis. By permission of the A. Pegis estate.

existence of cause. The third way is from the idea of contingency. It argues that because there are dependent beings (e.g., humans), there must be an independent or necessary being on whom the dependent beings rely for their subsistence. The fourth way is from excellence, and it argues that because there are degrees of excellence, there must be a perfect being from whence cometh all excellences. The final way is from the harmony of things. There is a harmony of nature, which calls for an explanation. The only sufficient explanation is that there is a divine designer who planned this harmony.

Objection 1. It seems that God does not exist; because if one of two contraries be infinite, the other would be altogether destroyed. But the name God means that He is infinite goodness. If, therefore, God existed, there would be no evil discoverable; but there is evil in the world. Therefore God does not exist.

Objection 2. Further, it is superfluous to suppose that what can be accounted for by a few principles has been produced by many. But it seems that everything we see in the world can be accounted for by other principles, supposing God did not exist. For all natural things can be reduced to one principle, which is nature; and all voluntary things can be reduced to one principle, which is human reason, or will. Therefore there is no need to suppose God's existence.

On the contrary, It is said in the person of God: *I am Who am* (Exod. iii. 14).

I answer that, The existence of God can be proved in five ways.

The first and most manifest way is the argument from motion. It is certain, and evident to our senses, that in the world some things are in motion. Now whatever is moved is moved by another, for nothing can be moved except it is in potentiality to that towards which it is moved; whereas a thing moves inasmuch as it is in act. For motion is nothing else than the reduction of something from potentiality to actuality. But nothing can be reduced from potentiality to actuality, except by something in a state of actuality. Thus that which is actually hot, as fire,

makes wood, which is potentially hot, to be actually hot, and thereby moves and changes it. Now it is not possible that the same thing should be at once in actuality and potentiality in the same respect, but only in different respects. For what is actually hot cannot simultaneously be potentially hot; but it is simultaneously potentially cold. It is therefore impossible that in the same respect and in the same way a thing should be both mover and moved, i.e., that it should move itself. Therefore, whatever is moved must be moved by another. If that by which is moved be itself moved, then this also must needs be moved by another, and that by another again. But this cannot go on to infinity, because then there would be no first mover, and, consequently, no other mover, seeing that subsequent movers move only inasmuch as they are moved by the first mover; as the staff moves only because it is moved by the hand. Therefore it is necessary to arrive at a first mover, moved by no other; and this everyone understands to be God.

The second way is from the nature of efficient cause. In the world of sensible things we find there is an order of efficient causes. There is no case known (neither is it, indeed, possible) in which a thing is found to be the efficient cause of itself: for so it would be prior to itself, which is impossible. Now in efficient causes it is not possible to go on to infinity, because in all efficient causes following in order, the first is the cause of the intermediate cause, and the intermediate is the cause of the ultimate cause, whether the intermediate cause be several, or one only. Now to take away the cause is to take away the effect. Therefore, if there be no first cause among efficient causes, there will be no ultimate, nor any intermediate, cause. But if in efficient causes it is possible to go on to infinity, there will be no first efficient cause, neither will there be an ultimate effect, nor any intermediate efficient causes; all of which is plainly false. Therefore it is necessary to admit a first efficient cause, to which everyone gives the name of God.

The third way is taken from possibility and necessity, and runs thus. We find in nature things are possible to be and not to be, since they are found to be generated, and to be corrupted, and consequently, it is possible for them to be and not to be.

But it is impossible for these always to exist, for that which can not-be, at some time is not. Therefore if everything can not-be then at one time there was nothing in existence. Now if this were true, even now there would be nothing in existence, because that which does not exist begins to exist only through something already existing. Therefore, if at one time nothing was in existence, it would have been impossible for anything to have begun to exist; and thus even now nothing would be in existence—which is absurd. Therefore, not all beings are merely possible, but there must exist something the existence of which is necessary. But every necessary thing either has its necessity caused by another, or not. Now it is impossible to go on to infinity in necessary things which have their necessity caused by another, as has been already proved in regard to efficient causes. Therefore we cannot but admit the existence of some being having of itself its own necessity, and not receiving it from another, but rather causing in others their necessity. This all men speak of as God.

The fourth way is taken from the gradation to be found in things. Among beings there are some more and some less good, true, noble and the like. But *more* and *less* are predicted of different things according as they resemble in their different ways something which is the maximum, as a thing is said to be hotter according as it more nearly resembles that which is hottest; so that there is something which is truest, something best, something noblest, and consequently, something which is most being, for those things that are greatest in truth are greatest in being, as it is written in *Metaph.* ii. Now the maximum in any genus is the cause of all in that genus, as fire, which is the maximum of heat, is the cause of all hot things, as is said in the same book. Therefore there must also be something which is to all beings the cause of their being, goodness, and every other perfection; and this we call God.

The fifth way is taken from the governance of the world. We see that things which lack knowledge, such as natural bodies, act for an end, and this is evident from their acting always, or nearly always, in the same way, so as to obtain the best result. Hence it is plain that they achieve their end, not fortuitously, but designedly. Now whatever lacks knowledge cannot move towards an end, unless it be directed by some being endowed with knowledge and intelligence; as the arrow is directed by the archer. Therefore some intelligent being exists by whom all natural things are directed to their end; and this being we call God.

Reply Objection 1. As Augustine says: *Since God is the highest good, He would not allow any evil to exist in His works, unless His omnipotence and goodness were such as to bring good even out of evil.* This is part of the infinite goodness of God, that He should allow evil to exist, and out of it produce good.

Reply Objection 2. Since nature works for a determinate end under the direction of a higher agent, whatever is done by nature must be traced back to God as to its first cause. So likewise whatever is done voluntarily must be traced back to some higher cause other than human reason and will, since these can change and fail; for all things that are changeable and capable of defect must be traced back to an immovable and self-necessary first principle, as has been shown.

I.A.2   The Argument from Contingency

SAMUEL CLARKE

Samuel Clarke (1675–1729), an English philosopher and Anglican minister, one of the first to appreciate the work of Isaac Newton, here sets forth a version of the argument from contingency. It is based on the idea that if some beings are dependent, or contingent, there must of necessity be an independent being upon which all other beings are dependent.

There has existed from eternity some one unchangeable and independent being. For since something must needs have been from eternity; as hath been already proved, and is granted on all hands: either there has always existed one unchangeable and *independent* Being, from which all other beings that are or ever were in the universe, have received their original; or else there has been an infinite succession of changeable and *dependent* beings, produced one from another in an endless progression, without any original cause at all: which latter supposition is so very absurd, that tho' all atheism must in its account of most things (as shall be shown hereafter) terminate in it, yet I think very few atheists ever were so weak as openly and directly to defend it. For it is plainly impossible and contradictory to itself. I shall not argue against it from the supposed impossibility of infinite succession, *barely and absolutely considered in itself;* for a reason which shall be mentioned hereafter: but, if we consider such an infinite progression, as *one*

entire endless *series of dependent* beings; 'tis plain this whole *series* of beings can have no cause *from without,* of its existence; because in it are supposed to be included *all things* that are or ever were in the universe: and 'tis plain it can have no reason *within itself,* of its existence; because no one being in this infinite succession is supposed to be self-existent or *necessary* (which is the only ground or reason of existence of any thing, that can be imagined *within the thing itself,* as will presently more fully appear), but every one *dependent* on the foregoing: and where *no part* is necessary, 'tis manifest *the whole* cannot be necessary; absolute necessity of existence, not being an outward, relative, and accidental determination; but an inward and essential property of the nature of the thing which so exists. An infinite succession therefore of merely *dependent beings,* without any original independent cause; is a *series* of beings, that has neither necessity nor cause, nor any reason *at all* of its existence, neither *within itself* nor *from without:* that is, 'tis an express contradiction and impossibility; 'tis a supposing *something to be caused,* (because it's granted in every one of its stages of succession, not to be necessary and from itself); and yet that in the whole it is caused *absolutely by nothing:* Which every man knows is a contradiction to be done *in time;* and because duration in this case makes no difference, 'tis equally a contradiction to suppose it done from eternity: And consequently there must *on the contrary,* of necessity have existed from eternity, *some one* immutable and *independent* Being: Which, what it is, remains in the next place to be inquired.

Reprinted from *A Discourse Concerning Natural Religion* (1705).

I.A.3   A Critique of the Cosmological Argument

PAUL EDWARDS

Paul Edwards (1923–   ) until his recent retirement was professor of philosophy at Brooklyn College and is the author of several works in philosophy. He is the editor of The Encyclopedia of Philosophy *(1967).*

In this article, Edwards distinguishes two versions of the cosmological argument, the causal argument and the argument from contingency, and argues against both versions. Regarding the first version, he makes an important distinction between a cause in fieri (a cause that brought its effect into existence) and a cause in esse (a cause that sustains its effect, ensuring its continued existence) and shows how they bear on the argument.

I

The so-called "cosmological proof" is one of the oldest and most popular arguments for the existence of God. It was forcibly criticized by Hume, Kant, and Mill, but it would be inaccurate to consider the argument dead or even moribund. Catholic philosophers, with hardly any exception, appear to believe that it is as solid and conclusive as ever. Thus Father F. C. Copleston confidently championed it in his Third Programme debate with Bertrand Russell, and in America, where Catholic writers are more sanguine, we are told by a Jesuit professor of physics that "the existence of an intelligent being as the First Cause of the universe can be established by *rational scientific inference.*"[1]

I am absolutely convinced [the same writer continues] that any one who would give the same consideration to that proof (the cosmological argument), as outlined for example in William Brosnan's *God and*

Reason, as he would give to a line of argumentation found in *Physical Review* or the *Proceedings of the Royal Society* would be forced to admit that the cogency of this argument for the existence of God far outstrips that which is found in the reasoning which Chadwick uses to prove the existence of the neutron, which today is accepted as certain as any conclusion in the physical sciences.

Mild theists like the late Professor Dawes Hicks and Dr. [A. C.] Ewing, who concede many of Hume's and Kant's criticisms, nevertheless contend that the argument possesses a certain core of truth. In popular discussions it also crops up again and again—for example, when believers address atheists with such questions as "You tell me where the universe came from!" Even philosophers who reject the cosmological proof sometimes embody certain of its confusions in the formulation of their own position. In the light of all this, it may be worth while to undertake a fresh examination of the argument with special attention to the fallacies that were not emphasized by the older critics.

II

The cosmological proof has taken a number of forms, the most important of which are known as the "causal argument" and "the argument from contingency," respectively. In some writers, in Samual Clarke for example, they are combined, but it is best to keep them apart as far as possible. The causal argument is the second of the "five ways" of Aquinas and roughly proceeds as follows: we find that the things around us come into being as the result of the activity of other things. These causes are themselves the result of the activity of other things. But such a causal series cannot "go back to infinity." Hence there must be a first member, a member which is not itself caused by any preceding member—an uncaused or "first" cause.

Reprinted from *The Rationalist Annual,* 1959, edited by Hector Hawton. Reprinted by permission of Paul Edwards. Foodnotes edited.

It has frequently been pointed out that even if this argument were sound it would not establish the existence of *God*. It would not show that the first cause is all-powerful or all-good or that it is in any sense personal. Somebody believing in the eternity of atoms, or of matter generally, could quite consistently accept the conclusion. Defenders of the causal argument usually concede this and insist that the argument is not in itself meant to prove the existence of God. Supplementary arguments are required to show that the first cause must have the attributes assigned to the deity. They claim, however, that the argument, if valid, would at least be an important step towards a complete proof of the existence of God.

Does the argument succeed in proving so much as a first cause? This will depend mainly on the soundness of the premise that an infinite series of causes is impossible. Aquinas supports this premise by maintaining that the opposite belief involves a plain absurdity. To suppose that there is an infinite series of causes logically implies that nothing exists now; but we know that plenty of things do exist now; and hence any theory which implies that nothing exists now must be wrong. Let us take some causal series and refer to its members by the letters of the alphabet:

$$A \rightarrow B \ldots W \rightarrow X \rightarrow Y \rightarrow Z$$

Z stands here for something presently existing, e.g. Margaret Truman. Y represents the cause or part of the cause of Z, say Harry Truman. X designates the cause or part of the cause of Y, say Harry Truman's father, etc. Now, Aquinas reasons, whenever we take away the cause, we also take away the effect: if Harry Truman had never lived, Margaret Truman would never have been born. If Harry Truman's father had never lived, Harry Truman and Margaret Truman would never have been born. If A had never existed, none of the subsequent members of the series would have come into existence. But it is precisely A that the believer in the infinite series is "taking away." For in maintaining that the series is infinite he is denying that it has a first member; he is denying that there is such a thing as a first cause; he is in other words denying the existence of A. Since without A, Z could not have existed, his

position implies that Z does not exist now; and that is plainly false.

This argument fails to do justice to the supporter of the infinite series of causes. Aquinas has failed to distinguish between the two statements:

(1) A did not exist, and
(2) A is not uncaused.

To say that the series is infinite implies (2), but it does not imply (1). The following parallel may be helpful here: Suppose Captain Spaulding had said, "I am the greatest explorer who ever lived," and somebody replied, "No, you are not." This answer would be denying that the Captain possessed the exalted attribute he had claimed for himself, but it would not be denying his existence. It would not be "taking him away." Similarly, the believer in the infinite series is not "taking A away." He is taking away the privileged status of A; he is taking away its "first causiness." He does not deny the *existence* of A or of any particular member of the series. He denies that A or anything else *is the first member* of the series. Since he is not taking A away, he is not taking B away, and thus he is also not taking X, Y, or Z away. His view, then, does not commit him to the absurdity that nothing exists now, or more specifically, that Margaret Truman does not exist now. It may be noted in this connection that a believer in the infinite series is not necessarily denying the existence of supernatural beings. He is merely committed to denying that such a being, if it exists, is uncaused. He is committed to holding that whatever other impressive attributes a supernatural being might possess, the attribute of being a first cause is not among them.

The causal argument is open to several other objections. Thus, even if otherwise valid, the argument, would not prove a *single* first cause. For there does not seem to be any good ground for supposing that the various causal series in the universe ultimately merge. Hence even if it is granted that no series of causes can be infinite the possibility of a plurality of first members has not been ruled out. Nor does the argument establish the *present* existence of the first cause. It does not prove this, since experience clearly shows that an effect may exist long after its cause has been destroyed.

III

Many defenders of the causal argument would contend that at least some of these criticisms rest on a misunderstanding. They would probably go further and contend that the argument was not quite fairly stated in the first place—or at any rate that if it was fair to some of its adherents it was not fair to others. They would in this connection distinguish between two types of causes—what they call "causes *in fieri*" and what they call "causes *in esse*." A cause *in fieri* is a factor which brought or helped to bring an effect into existence. A cause *in esse* is a factor which "sustains" or helps to sustain the effect "in being." The parents of a human being would be an example of a cause *in fieri*. If somebody puts a book in my hand and I keep holding it up, his putting it there would be the cause *in fieri,* and my holding it would be the cause *in esse* of the book's position. To quote Father [G. H.] Joyce:

> If a smith forges a horse-shoe, he is only a cause *in fieri* of the shape given to the iron. That shape persists after his action has ceased. So, too, a builder is a cause *in fieri* of the house which he builds. In both cases the substances employed act as causes *in esse* as regards the continued existence of the effect produced. Iron, in virtue of its natural rigidity, retains in being the shape which it has once received; and similarly, the materials employed in building retain in being the order and arrangement which constitute them into a house.[2]

Using this distinction, the defender of the argument now reasons in the following way. To say that there is an infinite series of causes *in fieri* does not lead to any absurd conclusions. But Aquinas is concerned only with causes *in esse* and an infinite series of *such* causes is impossible. In the words of the contemporary American Thomist, R. P. Phillips:

> Each member of the series of causes possesses being solely by virtue of the actual present operation of a superior cause. . . . Life is dependent, *inter alia,* on a certain atmospheric pressure, this again on the continual operation of physical forces, whose being and operation depends on the position of the earth in the solar system, which itself must endure relatively unchanged, a state of being which can only be continuously produced by a definite—if unknown—constitution of the material universe. This constitution, however, cannot be its own cause. That a thing should cause itself is impossible: for in order that it may cause it is necessary

for it to exist, which it cannot do, on the hypothesis, until it has been caused. So it must *be* in order to cause itself. Thus, not being uncaused nor yet its own cause, it must be caused by another, which produces and preserves it. It is plain, then, that as no member of this series possesses being except in virtue of the actual present operation of a superior cause, if there be no first cause actually operating none of the dependent causes could operate either. We are thus irresistibly led to posit a first efficient cause which, while itself uncaused, shall impart causality to a whole series. . . .

> The series of causes which we are considering is not one which stretches back into the past; so that we are not demanding a beginning of the world at some definite moment reckoning back from the present, but an actual cause now operating, to account for the present being of things.[3]

Professor Phillips offers the following parallel to bring out his point:

> In a goods train each truck is moved and moves by the action of the one immediately in front of it. If then we suppose the train to be infinite, i.e. that there is no end to it, and so no engine which starts the motion, it is plain that no truck will move. To lengthen it out to infinity will not give it what no member of it possesses of itself, viz. the power of drawing the truck behind it. If then we see any truck in motion we know there must be an end to the series of trucks which gives causality to the whole.[4]

Father Joyce introduces an illustration from Aquinas to explain how the present existence of things may be compatible with an infinite series of causes *in fieri* but not with an infinite series of causes *in esse.*

> When a carpenter is at work, the series of efficient causes on which his work depends is necessarily limited. The final effect, e.g. the fastening of a nail is caused by a hammer: the hammer is moved by the arm: and the motion of his arm is determined by the motor-impulses communicated from the nerve centres of the brain. Unless the subordinate causes were limited in number, and were connected with a starting-point of motion, the hammer must remain inert; and the nail will never be driven in. If the series be supposed infinite, no work will ever take place. But if there is question of causes on which the work is not essentially dependent, we cannot draw the same conclusion. We may suppose the carpenter to have broken an infinite number of hammers, and as often to have replaced the broken tool by a fresh one. There is nothing in such a supposition which excludes the driving home of the nail.

The supporter of the infinite series of causes, Joyce also remarks, is

> . . . asking us to believe that although each link in a suspended chain is prevented from falling simply because it is attached to the one above it, yet if only the chain be long enough, it will, taken as a whole, need no support, but will hang loose in the air suspended from nothing.

This formulation of the causal argument unquestionably circumvents one of the objections mentioned previously. If *Y* is the cause *in esse* of an effect, *Z*, then it must exist as long as *Z* exists. If the argument were valid in this form it would therefore prove the present and not merely the past existence of a first cause. In this form the argument is, however, less convincing in another respect. To maintain that all "natural" or "phenomenal" objects—things like tables and mountains and human beings—require a cause *in fieri* is not implausible, though even here Mill and others have argued that strictly speaking only *changes* require a causal explanation. It is far from plausible, on the other hand, to claim that all natural objects require a cause *in esse*. It may be granted that the air around us is a cause *in esse* of human life and further that certain gravitational forces are among the causes *in esse* of the air being where it is. But when we come to gravitational forces or, at any rate, to material particles like atoms or electrons it is difficult to see what cause *in esse* they require. To those not already convinced of the need for a supernatural First Cause some of the remarks by Professor Phillips in this connection appear merely dogmatic and question-begging. Most people would grant that such particles as atoms did not cause themselves, since, as Professor Phillips observes, they would in that event have had to exist before they began existing. It is not at all evident, however, that these particles cannot be uncaused. Professor Phillips and all other supporters of the causal argument immediately proceed to claim that there is something else which needs no cause *in esse*. They themselves admit thus, that there is nothing self-evident about the proposition that everything must have a cause in esse. Their entire procedure here lends substance to Schopenhauer's gibe that supporters of the cosmological argument treat the law of universal causation like "a hired cab which we dismiss when we have reached our destination."

But waiving this and all similar objections, the restatement of the argument in terms of causes *in esse* in no way avoids the main difficulty which was previously mentioned. A believer in the infinite series would insist that his position was just as much misrepresented now as before. He is no more removing the member of the series which is supposed to be the first cause *in esse* than he was removing the member which had been declared to be the first cause *in fieri*. He is again merely denying a privileged status to it. He is not denying the reality of the cause *in esse* labelled *"A."* He is not even necessarily denying that it possesses supernatural attributes. He is again merely taking away its "first causiness."

The advocates of the causal argument in either form seem to confuse an infinite series with one which is long but finite. If a book, *Z*, is to remain in its position, say 100 miles up in the air, there must be another object, say another book, *Y*, underneath it to serve as its support. If *Y* is to remain where it is, it will need another support, *X*, beneath it. Suppose that this series of supports, one below the other, continues for a long time, but eventually, say after 100,000 members, comes to a first book which is not resting on any other book or indeed on any other support. In that event the whole collection would come crashing down. What we seem to need is a first member of the series, a first support (such as the earth) which does not need another member as *its* support, which in other words is "self-supporting."

This is evidently the sort of picture that supporters of the First Cause argument have before their minds when they rule out the possibility of an infinite series. But such a picture is not a fair representation of the theory of the infinite series. A *finite* series of books would indeed come crashing down, since the first or lowest member would not have a predecessor on which it could be supported. If the series, however, were infinite this would not be the case. In that event every member *would* have a predecessor to support itself on and there would be no crash. That is to say: a crash can be avoided either by a finite series with a first self-supporting member or by an infinite series. Similarly, the present existence of motion is equally compatible with the theory of a first unmoved mover and with the theory of an infinite series of moving objects; and the present existence of causal activity is compatible with the theory of a first cause *in esse* as much as with the theory of an infinite series of such causes.

The illustrations given by Joyce and Phillips are hardly to the point. It is true that a carpenter would not, *in a finite time-span,* succeed in driving in a nail if he had to carry out an infinite number of movements. For that matter, he would not accomplish this goal in a finite time if he broke an infinite number of hammers. However, to make the illustrations relevant we must suppose that he has infinite time at his disposal. In that case he would succeed in driving in the nail even if he required an infinite number of movements for this purpose. As for the goods train, it may be granted that the trucks do not move unless the train has an engine. But this illustration is totally irrelevant as it stands. A relevant illustration would be that of engines, each moved by the one in front of it. Such a train would move if it were infinite. For every member of this series there would be one in front capable of drawing it along. The advocate of the infinite series of causes does not, as the original illustration suggests, believe in a series whose members are not really causally connected with one another. In the series he believes in every member is genuinely the cause of the one that follows it.

IV

No staunch defender of the cosmological argument would give up at this stage. Even if there were an infinite series of causes *in fieri* or *in esse,* he would contend, this still would not do away with the need for an ultimate, a first cause. As Father Copleston put it in his debate with Bertrand Russell:

Every object has a phenomenal cause, if you insist on the infinity of the series. But the series of phenomental causes is an insufficient explanation of the series.

Therefore, the series has not a phenomenal cause, but a transcendent cause. . . .

An infinite series of contingent beings will be, to my way of thinking, as unable to cause itself as one contingent being.

The demand to find the cause of the series as a whole rests on the erroneous assumption that the series is something over and above the members of which it is composed. It is tempting to suppose this, at least by implication, because the word "series" is a noun like "dog" or "man." Like the expression "this dog" or "this man" the phrase "this series" is easily taken to designate an individual object. But reflection shows this to be an error. If we have explained the individual members there is nothing additional left to be explained. Supposing I see a group of five Eskimos standing on the corner of Sixth Avenue and 50th Street and I wish to explain why the group came to New York. Investigation reveals the following stories:

- Eskimo No. 1 did not enjoy the extreme cold in the polar region and decided to move to a warmer climate.
- No. 2 is the husband of Eskimo No. 1. He loves her dearly and did not wish to live without her.
- No. 3 is the son of Eskimos 1 and 2. He is too small and too weak to oppose his parents.
- No. 4 saw an advertisement in the *New York Times* for an Eskimo to appear on television.
- No. 5 is a private detective engaged by the Pinkerton Agency to keep an eye on Eskimo No. 4.

Let us assume that we have now explained in the case of each of the five Eskimos why he or she is in New York. Somebody then asks: "All right, but what about the group as a whole; why is *it* in New York?" This would plainly be an absurd question. There is no group over and above the five members, and if we have explained why each of the five members is in New York we have *ipso facto* explained why the group is there. It is just as absurd to ask for the cause of the series as a whole as distinct from asking for the causes of individual members.

V

It is most unlikely that a determined defender of the cosmological line of reasoning would surrender even here. He would probably admit that the series is not a thing over and above its members and that it does not make sense to ask for the cause of the series if the cause of each member has already been found. He would insist, however, that when he asked for the explanation of the entire series, he was not asking for its *cause.* He was really saying that a series, finite or infinite, is not "intelligible" or "explained" if it consists of nothing but "contingent" members. To quote Father Copleston once more:

What we call the world is intrinsically unintelligible apart from the existence of God. The infinity of the series of events, if such an infinity could be proved, would not be in the slightest degree relevant to the situation. If you add up chocolates, you get chocolates after all, and not a sheep. If you add up chocolates to infinity, you presumably get an infinite number of chocolates. So, if you add up contingent beings to infinity, you still get contingent beings, not a necessary being.

This last quotation is really a summary of the "contingency argument," the other main form of the cosmological proof and the third of the five ways of Aquinas. It may be stated more fully in these words: All around us we perceive contingent beings. This includes all physical objects and also all human minds. In calling them "contingent" we mean that they might not have existed. We mean that the universe can be *conceived* without this or that physical object, without this or that human being, however certain their actual existence may be. These contingent beings we can trace back to other contingent beings—e.g. a human being to his parents. However, since these other beings are also contingent, they do not provide a real or full explanation. The contingent beings we originally wanted explained have not yet become intelligible, since the beings to which they have been traced back are no more necessary than they were. It is just as true of our parents, for example, as it is of ourselves, that they might not have existed. We can then properly explain the contingent beings around us only by tracing them back ultimately to some necessary

being, to something which exists necessarily, which has "the reason for its existence within itself." The existence of contingent beings, in other words, implies the existence of a necessary being.

This form of cosmological argument is even more beset with difficulties than the causal variety. In the first place, there is the objection, stated with great force by Kant, that it really commits the same error as the ontological argument in tacitly regarding existence as an attribute or characteristic. To say that there is a necessary being is to say that it would be a self-contradiction to deny its existence. This would mean that at least one existential statement is a necessary truth; and this in turn presupposes that in at least one case existence is contained in a concept. But only a characteristic can be contained in a concept and it has seemed plain to most philosophers since Kant that existence is not a characteristic, that it can hence never be contained in a concept, and that hence no existential statement can ever be a necessary truth. To talk about anything "existing necessarily" is in their view about as sensible as to talk about round squares, and they have concluded that the contingency-argument is quite absurd.

It would lead too far to discuss here the reasons for denying that existence is a characteristic. I will assume that this difficulty can somehow be surmounted and that the expression "necessary being," as it intended by the champions of the contingency-argument, might conceivably apply to something. There remain other objections which are of great weight. I shall try to state these by first quoting again from the debate between Bertrand Russell and Father Copleston:

Russell: . . . it all turns on this question of sufficient reason, and I must say you haven't defined "sufficient reason" in a way that I can understand—what do you mean by sufficient reason? You don't mean cause?

Copleston: Not necessarily. Cause is a kind of sufficient reason. Only contingent being can have a cause. God is his own sufficient reason; and he is not cause of himself. By sufficient reason in the full sense I mean an explanation adequate for the existence of some particular being.

Russell: But when is an explanation adequate? Suppose I am about to make a flame with a match. You may say that the adequate explanation of that is that I rub it on the box.

Copleston: Well for practical purposes—but theoretically, that is only a partial explanation. An adequate explanation must ultimately be a total explanation, to which nothing further can be added.

Russell: Then I can only say that you're looking for something which can't be got, and which one ought not to expect to get.

Copleston: To say that one has not found it is one thing; to say that one should not look for it seems to me rather dogmatic.

Russell: Well, I don't know. I mean, the explanation of one thing is another thing which makes the other thing dependent on yet another, and you have to grasp this sorry scheme of things entire to do what you want, and that we can't do.

Russell's main point here may be expanded in the following way. The contingency- argument rests on a misconception of what an explanation is and does, and similarly on what it is that makes phenomena "intelligible." Or else it involves an obscure and arbitrary redefinition of "explanation," "intelligible," and related terms. Normally, we are satisfied that we have explained a phenomenon if we have found its cause or if we have exhibited some other uniform or near-uniform connection between it and something else. Confining ourselves to the former case, which is probably the most common, we might say that a phenomenon, Z, has been explained if it has been traced back to a group of factors, *a, b, c, d,* etc., which are its cause. These factors are the full and real explanation of Z, quite regardless of whether they are pleasing or displeasing, admirable or contemptible, necessary or contingent. The explanation would not be adequate only if the factors listed are not really the cause of Z. If they are the cause of Z, the explanation would be adequate, even though each of the factors is merely a "contingent" being.

Let us suppose that we have been asked to explain why General Eisenhower won the elections of 1952. "He was an extremely popular general,"

we might answer, "while Stevenson was relatively little known; moreover there was a great deal of resentment over the scandals in the Truman Administration." If somebody complained that this was only a partial explanation we might mention additional antecedents, such as the widespread belief that the Democrats had allowed communist agents to infiltrate the State Department, that Eisenhower was a man with a winning smile, and that unlike Stevenson he had shown the good sense to say one thing on race relations in the North and quite another in the South. Theoretically, we might go further and list the motives of all American voters during the weeks or months preceding the elections. If we could do this we would have explained Eisenhower's victory. We would have made it intelligible. We would "understand" why he won and why Stevenson lost. Perhaps there is a sense in which we might make Eisenhower's victory even more intelligible if we went further back and discussed such matters as the origin of American views on Communism or of racial attitudes in the North and South. However, to explain the outcome of the election in any ordinary sense, loose or strict, it would not be necessary to go back to prehistoric days or to the amoeba or to a first cause, if such a first cause exists. Nor would our explanation be considered in any way defective because each of the factors mentioned was a "contingent" and not a necessary being. The only thing that matters is whether the factors were really the cause of Eisenhower's election. If they were, then it has been explained although they are contingent beings. If they were not the cause of Eisenhower's victory, we would have failed to explain it even if each of the factors were a necessary being.

If it is granted that, in order to explain a phenomenon or to make it intelligible, we need not bring in a necessary being, then the contingency-argument breaks down. For a series, as was already pointed out, is not something over and above its members; and every contingent member of it could in that case be explained by reference to other contingent beings. But I should wish to go further than this and it is evident from Russell's remarks that he would do so also. Even if it were granted, both that the phrase "necessary being" is meaningful and that all explanations are defective unless the phenomena to be explained are traced back to a necessary being, the conclusion would still not have been established. The conclusion follows from this premise together with the additional premsie that *there are* explanations of phenomena in the special sense just mentioned. It is this further premise which Russell (and many other philosophers) would question. They do not merely question, as Copleston implies, whether human beings can ever obtain explanations in this sense, but whether they *exist*. To assume without further ado that phenomena have explanations or an explanation in this sense is to beg the very point at issue. The use of the same word "explanation" in two crucially different ways lends the additional premise a plausibility it does not really possess. It may indeed be highly plausible to assert that phenomena have explanations, whether we have found them or not, in the ordinary sense in which this usually means that they have causes. It is then tempting to suppose, because of the use of the same word, that they also have explanations in a sense in which this implies dependence on a necessary being. But this is a gross *non sequitur*.

VI

It is necessary to add a few words about the proper way of formulating the position of those who reject the main premise of the cosmological argument, in either of the forms we have considered. It is sometimes maintained in this connection that in order to reach a "self-existing" entity it is not necessary to go beyond the universe: the universe itself (or "Nature") is "self-existing." And this in turn is sometimes expanded into the statement that while all individual things "within" the universe are caused, the universe itself is uncaused. Statements of this kind are found in Büchner, Bradlaugh, Haeckel, and other free-thinkers of the nineteenth and early twentieth century. Sometimes the assertion that the universe is "self-existing" is elaborated to mean that *it* is the "necessary being." Some eighteenth-century unbelievers, apparently accepting the view that

there is a necessary being, asked why Nature or the material universe could not fill the bill as well or better than God.

"Why," asks one of the characters in Hume's *Dialogues*, "may not the material universe be the necessarily existent Being? . . . We dare not affirm that we know all the qualities of matter; and for aught we can determine, it may contain some qualities, which, were they known, would make its nonexistence appear as great a contradiction as that twice two is five."

Similar remarks can be found in Holbach and several of the Encyclopedists.

The former of these formulations immediately invites the question why the universe, alone of all "things," is exempted from the universal sway of causation. "The strong point of the cosmological argument," writes Dr. Ewing, "is that after all it does remain incredible that the physical universe should just have happened . . . It calls out for some further explanation of some kind." The latter formulation is exposed to the criticism that there is nothing any more "necessary" about the existence of the universe or Nature as a whole than about any particular thing within the universe.

I hope some of the earlier discussions in this article have made it clear that in rejecting the cosmological argument one is not committed to either of these propositions. If I reject the view that there is a supernatural first cause, I am not thereby committed to the proposition that there is a *natural* first cause, and even less to the proposition that a mysterious "thing" called "the universe" qualifies for this title. I may hold that there is no "universe" over and above individual things of various sorts; and, accepting the causal principle, I may proceed to assert that all these things are caused by other things, and these other things by yet other things, and so on, *ad infinitum*. In this way no arbitrary exception is made to the principle of causation. Similarly, if I reject the assertion that God is a "necessary being," I am not committed to the view that the universe is such an entity. I may hold that it does not make sense to speak of anything as a "necessary being" and that even if there were such a thing as the universe it could not be properly considered a necessary being.

However, in saying that nothing is uncaused or that there is no necessary being, one is not committed to the view that everything, or for that matter anything, is merely a "brute fact." Dr. Ewing laments that "the usual modern philosophical views opposed to theism do not try to give any rational explanation of the world at all, but just take it as a brute fact not to be explained." They thus fail to "rationalize the universe. Theism, he concedes, cannot completely rationalize things either since it does not show "how God can be his own cause or how it is that he does not need a cause." Now, if one means by "brute fact" something for which there *exists* no explanation (as distinct from something for which no explanation is in our possession), then the theists have at least one brute fact on their hands, namely God. Those who adopt Büchner's formulation also have one brute fact on their hands, namely "the universe." Only the position I have been supporting dispenses with brute facts altogether. I don't know if this is any special virtue, but the defenders of the cosmological argument seem to think so.

Notes

1. J. S. O'Connor, "A Scientific Approach to Religion," *The Scientific Monthly* (1940), p. 369; my italics.
2. *The Principles of Natural Theology*, p. 58.
3. *Modern Thomistic Philosophy*, Vol. II, pp. 284–85.
4. Ibid., p. 278.

I.A.4   An Examination of the Cosmological Argument

WILLIAM ROWE

William Rowe (1931–   ) is professor of philosophy at Purdue University and the author of several works in philosophy of religion, including Philosophy of Religion: An Introduction *(1978), from which this selection is taken. Rowe begins by distinguishing between a priori and a posteriori arguments and setting the cosmological argument in historical perspective. Next, he divides the argument into two parts: that which seeks to prove the existence of a self-existent being and that which seeks to prove that this self-existent being is the God of theism. He introduces the principle of sufficient reason: "There must be an explanation (a) of the existence of any being, and (b) of any positive fact whatever" and shows its role in the cosmological argument. In the light of this principle, he examines the argument itself and four objections to it.*

Reprinted from William Rowe, *Philosophy of Religion* (Wadsworth Publishing Co., 1978), by permission.

Stating the Argument

Arguments for the existence of God are commonly divided into *a posteriori* arguments and *a priori* arguments. An *a posteriori* argument depends on a principle or premise that can be known only by means of our experience of the world. An *a priori* argument, on the other hand, purports to rest on principles all of which can be known independently of our experience of the world, by just reflecting on and understanding them. Of the three major arguments for the existence of God—the Cosmological, the Teleological, and the Ontological—only the last of these is entirely *a priori*. In the Cosmological Argument one starts from some simple fact about the world, such as that it contains things which are caused to exist by other things. In the Teleological Argument a somewhat more complicated fact about the world serves as a starting point, the fact that the world exhibits order and design. In the Ontological Argument, however, one begins simply with a concept of God.

Before we state the Cosmological Argument itself, we shall consider some rather general points about the argument. Historically, it can be traced to the writings of the Greek philosophers, Plato and Aristotle, but the major developments in the argument took place in the thirteenth and in the eighteenth centuries. In the thirteenth century Aquinas put forth five distinct arguments for the existence of God, and of these, the first three are versions of the Cosmological Argument.[1] In the first of these he started from the fact that there are things in the world undergoing change and reasoned to the conclusion that there must be some ultimate cause of change that is itself unchanging. In the second he started from the fact that there are things in the world that clearly are caused to exist by other things and reasoned to the conclusion that there must be some ultimate cause of existence whose own existence is itself uncaused. And in the third argument he started from the fact that there are things in the world which need not have existed at all, things which do exist but which we can easily imagine might not, and reasoned to the conclusion that there must be some being that had to be, that exists and could not have failed to exist. Now it might be objected that even if Aquinas' arguments do prove beyond doubt the existence of an unchanging changer, an uncaused cause, and a being that could not have failed to exist, the arguments fail to prove the existence of the theistic God. For the theistic God, as we saw, is supremely good, omnipotent, omniscient, and creator of but separate from and independent of the world. How do we know, for example, that the unchanging changer isn't evil or slightly ignorant? The answer to this objection is that the Cosmological Argument has two parts. In the first part the effort is to prove the existence of a special sort of being, for example, a being that could not have failed to exist, or a being that causes change in other things but is itself unchanging. In the second part of the argument the effort is to prove that the special sort of being whose existence has been established in the first part has, and must have, the features—perfect goodness, omnipotence, omniscience, and so on—which go together to make up the theistic idea of God. What this means, then, is that Aquinas' three arguments are different ver-

sions of only the first part of the Cosmological Argument. Indeed, in later sections of his *Summa Theologica* Aquinas undertakes to show that the unchanging changer, the uncaused cause of existence, and the being which had to exist are one and the same being and that this single being has all of the attributes of the theistic God.

We noted above that a second major development in the Cosmological Argument took place in the eighteenth century, a development reflected in the writings of the German philosopher, Gottfried Leibniz (1646–1716), and especially in the writings of the English theologian and philosopher, Samuel Clarke (1675–1729). In 1704 Clarke gave a series of lectures, later published under the title *A Demonstration of the Being and Attributes of God.* These lectures constitute, perhaps, the most complete, forceful, and cogent presentation of the Cosmological Argument we possess. The lectures were read by the major skeptical philosopher of the century, David Hume (1711–1776), and in his brilliant attack on the attempt to justify religion in the court of reason, his *Dialogues Concerning Natural Religion,* Hume advanced several penetrating criticisms of Clarke's arguments, criticisms which have persuaded many philosophers in the modern period to reject the Cosmological Argument. In our study of the argument we shall concentrate our attention largely on its eighteenth-century form and try to assess its strengths and weaknesses in the light of the criticisms which Hume and others have advanced against it.

The first part of the eighteenth-century form of the Cosmological Argument seeks to establish the existence of a self-existent being. The second part of the argument attempts to prove that the self-existent being is the theistic God, that is, has the features which we have noted to be basic elements in the theistic idea of God. We shall consider mainly the first part of the argument, for it is against the first part that philosophers from Hume to Russell have advanced very important objections.

In stating the first part of the Cosmological Argument we shall make use of two important concepts, the concept of a *dependent being* and the concept of a *self-existent being*. By *a dependent being* we mean *a being whose existence is ac-*

counted for by the causal activity of other things. Recalling Anselm's division into the three cases: "explained by another," "explained by nothing," and "explained by itself," it's clear that a dependent being is a being whose existence is explained by another. By a *self-existent being* we mean *a being whose existence is accounted for by its own nature*. This idea . . . is an essential element in the theistic concept of God. Again, in terms of Anselm's three cases, a self-existent being is a being whose existence is explained by itself. Armed with these two concepts, the concept of a dependent being and the concept of a self-existent being, we can now state the first part of the Cosmological Argument.

1. Every being (that exists or ever did exist) is either a dependent being or a self-existent being.
2. Not every being can be a dependent being.

Therefore,

3. There exists a self-existent being.

Deductive Validity

Before we look critically at each of the premises of this argument, we should note that this argument is, to use an expression from the logician's vocabulary, *deductively valid*. To find out whether an argument is deductively valid, we need only ask the question: If its premises were true, would its conclusion have to be true? If the answer is yes, the argument is deductively valid. If the answer is no, the argument is deductively invalid. Notice that the question of the validity of an argument is entirely different from the question of whether its premises are in fact true. The following argument is made up entirely of false statements, but it is deductively valid.

1. Babe Ruth is the President of the United States.
2. The President of the United States is from Indiana.

Therefore,

3. Babe Ruth is from Indiana.

The argument is deductively valid because even though its premises are false, if they were true its conclusion would have to be true. Even God, Aquinas would say, cannot bring it about that the prem-

ises of this argument are true and yet its conclusion is false, for God's power extends only to what is possible, and it is an absolute impossibility that Babe Ruth be the President, the President be from Indiana, and yet Babe Ruth not be from Indiana.

The Cosmological Argument (that is, its first part) is a deductively valid argument. If its premises are or were true, its conclusion would have to be true. It's clear from our example about Babe Ruth, however, that the fact that an argument is deductively valid is insufficient to establish the truth of its conclusion. What else is required? Clearly that we know or have rational grounds for believing that the premises are true. If we know that the Cosmological Argument is deductively valid, and can establish that its premises are true, we shall thereby have proved that its conclusion is true. Are, then, the premises of the Cosmological Argument true? To this more difficult question we must now turn.

PSR and the First Premise

At first glance the first premise might appear to be an obvious or even trivial truth. But it is neither obvious nor trivial. And if it appears to be obvious or trivial, we must be confusing the idea of a self-existent being with the idea of a being that is not a dependent being. Clearly, it is true that any being is either a dependent being (explained by other things) or it is not a dependent being (not explained by other things). But what our premise says is that any being is either a dependent being (explained by other things) or it is a self-existent being (explained by itself). Consider again Anselm's three cases.

a. explained by another
b. explained by nothing
c. explained by itself

What our first premise asserts is that each being that exists (or ever did exist) is either of sort *a* or of sort *c*. It denies that any being is of sort *b*. And it is this denial that makes the first premise both significant and controversial. The obvious truth we must not confuse it with is the truth that any being is either of sort *a* or not of sort *a*. While this is true it is neither very significant nor controversial.

Earlier we saw that Anselm accepted as a basic principle that whatever exists has an explanation of its existence. Since this basic principle denies that any thing of sort *b* exists or ever did exist, it's clear that Anselm would believe the first premise of our Cosmological Argument. The eighteenth-century proponents of the argument also were convinced of the truth of the basic principle we attributed to Anselm. And because they were convinced of its truth, they readily accepted the first premise of the Cosmological Argument. But by the eighteenth century, Anselm's basic principle had been more fully elaborated and had received a name, the *Principle of Sufficient Reason.* Since this principle (PSR, as we shall call it) plays such an important role in justifying the premises of the Cosmological Argument, it will help us to consider it for a moment before we continue our enquiry into the truth or falsity of the premises of the Cosmological Argument.

The Principle of Sufficient Reason, as it was expressed by both Leibniz and Samuel Clarke, is a very general principle and is best understood as having two parts. In its first part it is simply a restatement of Anselm's principle that there must be an explanation of the *existence* of any being whatever. Thus if we come upon a man in a room, PSR implies that there must be an explanation of the fact that that particular man exists. A moment's reflection, however, reveals that there are many facts about the man other than the mere fact that he exists. There is the fact that the man in question is in the room he's in, rather than somewhere else, the fact that he is in good health, and the fact that he is at the moment thinking of Paris, rather than, say, London. Now, the purpose of the second part of PSR is to require an explanation of these facts, as well. We may state PSR, therefore, as the principle that *there must be an explanation (a) of the existence of any being, and (b) of any positive fact whatever.* We are now in a position to study the role this very important principle plays in the Cosmological Argument.

Since the proponent of the Cosmological Argument accepts PSR in both its parts, it is clear that he will appeal to its first part, PSRa, as justification for the first premise of the Cosmological Argument. Of course, we can and should enquire into the deeper question of whether the proponent of the argument is rationally justified in accepting PSR itself. But we shall put this question aside for the moment. What we need to see first is whether he is correct in thinking that *if* PSR is true then both of the premises of the Cosmological Argument are true. And what we have just seen is that if only the first part of PSR, that is, PSRa, is true, the first premise of the Cosmological Argument will be true. But what of the second premise of the argument? For what reasons does the proponent think that it must be true?

The Second Premise

According to the second premise, not every being that exists can be a dependent being, that is, can have the explanation of its existence in some other being or beings. Presumably, the proponent of the argument thinks there is something fundamentally wrong with the idea that every being that exists is dependent, that each existing being was caused by some other being which in turn was caused by some other being, and so on. But just what does he think is wrong with it? To help us in understanding his thinking, let's simplify things by supposing that there exists only one thing now, A_1, a living thing perhaps, that was brought into existence by something else, A_2, which perished shortly after it brought A_1, into existence. Suppose further that A_2 was brought into existence in similar fashion some time ago by A_3, and A_3 by A_4, and so forth back into the past. Each of these beings is a *dependent* being, it owes its existence to the preceding thing in the series. Now if nothing else ever existed but these beings, then what the second premise says would not be true. For if every being that exists or ever did exist is an *A* and was produced by a preceding *A,* then every being that exists or ever did exist would be dependent and, accordingly, premise two of the Cosmological Argument would be false. If the proponent of the Cosmological Argument is correct there must, then, be something wrong with the idea that every being that exists or did exist is an *A* and that they form a causal series. A_1 caused by A_2, A_2 caused by A_3, A_3 caused by A_4, . . . A_n caused by A_{n+1}. How does the proponent of the Cosmological Argument propose to show us that there is something wrong with this view?

A popular but mistaken idea of how the proponent tries to show that something is wrong with the view, that every being might be dependent, is that he uses the following argument to reject it.

1. There must be a first being to start any causal series.
2. If every being were dependent there would be no *first* being to start the causal series.

Therefore,

3. Not every being can be a dependent being.

Although this argument is deductively valid, and its second premise is true, its first premise overlooks the distinct possibility that a causal series might be *infinite,* with no first member at all. Thus if we go back to our series of *A* beings, where each *A* is dependent, having been produced by the preceding *A* in the causal series, it's clear that if the series existed it would have no first member, for every *A* in the series there would be a preceding *A* which produced it, *ad infinitum.* The first premise of the argument just given assumes that a causal series must stop with a first member somewhere in the distant past. But there seems to be no good reason for making that assumption.

The eighteenth-century proponents of the Cosmological Argument recognized that the causal series of dependent beings could be infinite, without a first member to start the series. They rejected the idea that every being that is or ever was is dependent not because there would then be no first member to the series of dependent beings, but because there would then be no explanation for the fact that there are and have always been dependent beings. To see their reasoning let's return to our simplification of the supposition that the only things that exist or ever did exist are dependent beings. In our simplification of that supposition only one of the dependent beings exists at a time, each one perishing as it produces the next in the series. Perhaps the first thing to note about this supposition is that there is no individual *A* in the causal series of dependent beings whose existence is unex-

plained —A_1 is explained by A_2, A_2 by A_3, and A_n by A_{n+1}. So the first part of PSR, PSRa, appears to be satisfied. There is no particular being whose existence lacks an explanation. What, then, is it that lacks an explanation, if every particular A in the causal series of dependent beings has an explanation? it is the *series itself* that lacks an explanation, Or, as I've chosen to express it, *the fact that there are and have always been dependent beings.* For suppose we ask why it is that there are and have always been As in existence. It won't do to say that As have always been producing other As—we can't explain why there have always been As by saying there always have been As. Nor, on the supposition that only As have ever existed, can we explain the fact that there have always been As by appealing to something other than an A—for no such thing would have existed. Thus the supposition that the only things that exist or ever existed are dependent things leaves us with a fact for which there can be no explanation; namely, the fact that there are and have always been dependent beings.

Questioning the Justification of the Second Premise

Critics of the Cosmological Argument have raised several important objections against the claim that if every being is dependent the series or collection of those beings would have no explanation. Our understanding of the Cosmological Argument, as well as of its strengths and weaknesses, will be deepened by a careful consideration of these criticisms.

The first criticism is that the proponent of the Cosmological Argument makes the mistake of treating the collection or series of dependent beings as though it were itself a dependent being, and, therefore, requires an explanation of its existence. But, so the objection goes, the collection of dependent beings is not itself a dependent being any more than a collection of stamps is itself a stamp.

A second criticism is that the proponent makes the mistake of inferring that because each member of the collection of dependent beings has a cause, the collection itself must have a cause. But, as

Bertrand Russell noted, such reasoning is as fallacious as to infer that the human race (that is, the collection of human beings) must have a mother because each member of the collection (each human being) has a mother.

A third criticism is that the proponent of the argument fails to realize that for there to be an explanation of a collection of things is nothing more than for there to be an explanation of each of the things making up the collection. Since in the infinite collection (or series) of dependent beings, each being in the collection does have an explanation—by virtue of having been caused by some preceding member of the collection—the explanation of the collection, so the criticism goes, has already been given. As David Hume remarked, "Did I show you the particular causes of each individual in a collection of twenty particles of matter, I should think it very unreasonable, should you afterwards ask me, what was the cause of the whole twenty. This is sufficiently explained in explaining the cause of the parts."[2]

Finally, even if the proponent of the Cosmological Argument can satisfactorily answer these objections, he must face one last objection to his ingenious attempt to justify premise two of the Cosmological Argument. For someone may agree that if nothing exists but an infinite collection of dependent beings, the infinite collection will have no explanation of its existence, and still refuse to conclude from this that there is something wrong with the idea that every being is a dependent being. Why, he might ask, should we think that everything has to have an explanation? What's wrong with admitting that the fact that there are and have always been dependent beings is a *brute fact,* a fact having no explanation whatever? Why does everything have to have an explanation anyway? We must now see what can be said in response to these several objections.

Responses to Criticism

It is certainly a mistake to think that a collection of stamps is itself a stamp, and very likely a mistake to think that the collection of dependent beings is itself

a dependent being. But the mere fact that the proponent of the argument thinks that there must be an explanation not only for each member of the collection of dependent beings but for the collection itself is not sufficient grounds for concluding that he must view the collection as itself a dependent being. The collection of human beings, for example, is certainly not itself a human being. Admitting this, however, we might still seek an explanation of why there is a collection of human beings, of why there are such things as human beings at all. So the mere fact that an explanation is demanded for the collection of dependent beings is no proof that the person who demands the explanation must be supposing that the collection itself is just another dependent being.

The second criticism attributes to the proponent of the Cosmological Argument the following bit of reasoning.

1. Every member of the collection of dependent beings has a cause or explanation.

Therefore,

2. The collection of dependent beings has a cause or explanation.

As we noted in setting forth this criticism, arguments of this sort are often unreliable. It would be a mistake to conclude that a collection of objects is light in weight simply because each object in the collection is light in weight, for if there were many objects in the collection it might be quite heavy. On the other hand, if we know that each marble weighs more than one ounce, we could infer validly that the collection of marbles weighs more than an ounce. Fortunately, however, we don't need to decide whether the inference from 1 to 2 is valid or invalid. We need not decide this question because the proponent of the Cosmological Argument need not use this inference to establish that there must be an explanation of the collection of dependent beings. He need not use this inference because he has in PSR a principle from which it follows immediately that the collection of dependent beings has a cause or explanation. For according to PSR, every positive fact must have an explanation. If it is a fact that there exists a collection of dependent beings then, according to PSR, that fact too must have an explanation. So it is PSR that the proponent of the Cosmological Argument appeals to in concluding that there must be an explanation of the collection of dependent beings, and not some dubious inference from the premise that each member of the collection has an explanation. It seems, then, that neither of the first two criticisms is strong enough to do any serious damage to the reasoning used to support the second premise of the Cosmological Argument.

The third objection contends that to explain the existence of a collection of things is the same thing as to explain the existence of each of its members. If we consider a collection of dependent beings where each being in the collection is explained by the preceding member which caused it, it's clear that no member of the collection will lack an explanation of its existence. But, so the criticism goes, if we've explained the existence of every member of a collection, we've explained the existence of the collection—there's nothing left over to be explained. This forceful criticism, originally advanced by David Hume, has gained considerable support in the modern period. But the criticism rests on an assumption that the proponent of the Cosmological Argument would not accept. The assumption is that to explain this existence of a collection of things it is *sufficient* to explain the existence of every member in the collection. To see what is wrong with this assumption is to understand the basic issue in the reasoning by which the proponent of the Cosmological Argument seeks to establish that not every being can be a dependent being.

In order for there to be an explanation of the existence of the collection of dependent beings, it's clear that the eighteenth-century proponents would require that the following two conditions be satisfied:

C1. There is an explanation of the existence of each of the members of the collection of dependent beings.

C2. There is an explanation of why there are any dependent beings.

According to the proponents of the Cosmological Argument, if every being that exists or ever did exist is a dependent being—that is, if the whole of reality consists of nothing more than a collection of dependent beings—C1 will be satisfied, but C2 will not be satisfied. And since C2 won't be satisfied, there will be no explanation of the collection of dependent beings. The third criticism, therefore, says in effect that if C1 is satisfied, C2 will be satisfied, and, since in a collection of dependent beings each member will have an explanation in whatever it was that produced it, C1 will be satisfied. So, therefore, C2 will be satisfied and the collection of dependent beings will have an explanation.

Although the issue is a complicated one, I think it is possible to see that the third criticism rests on a mistake: the mistake of thinking that if C1 is satisfied C2 must also be satisfied. The mistake is a natural one to make for it is easy to imagine circumstances in which if C1 is satisfied C2 also will be satisfied. Suppose, for example that the whole of reality includes not just a collection of dependent beings but also a self-existent being. Suppose further that instead of each dependent being having been produced by some other dependent being, every dependent being was produced by the self-existent being. Finally, let us consider both the possibility that the collection of dependent beings is finite in time and has a first member, and the possibility that the collection of dependent beings is infinite in past time, having no first member. Using *G* for the self-existent being, the first possibility may be diagramed as follows:

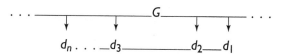

G, we shall say, has always existed and always will. We can think of d_1 as some presently existing dependent being, d_2, d_3, and so forth as dependent beings that existed at some time in the past, and d_n as the first dependent being to exist. The second possibility may be portrayed as follows:

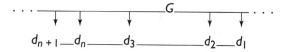

On this diagram there is no first member of the collection of dependent beings. Each member of the infinite collection, however, is explained by reference to the self-existent being G which produced it. Now the interesting point about both these cases is that the explanation that has been provided for the members of the collection of dependent beings carries with it, at least in part, an answer to the question of why there are any dependent beings at all. In both cases we may explain why there are dependent beings by pointing out that there exists a self-existent being that has been engaged in producing them. So once we have learned that the existence of each member of the collection of dependent beings has its existence explained by the fact that G produced it, we have already learned why there are dependent beings.

Someone might object that we haven't really learned why there are dependent beings until we also learn *why G* has been producing them. But, of course, we could also say that we haven't really explained the existence of a particular dependent being, say d_3, until we also learn not just that G produced it but *why G* produced it. The point we need to grasp, however, is that once we admit that every dependent being's existence is explained by G, we must admit that the fact that there are dependent beings has also been explained. So it is not unnatural that someone should think that to explain the existence of the collection of dependent beings is nothing more than to explain the existence of its members. For, as we've seen, to explain the collection's existence is to explain each member's existence and to explain why there are any dependent beings at all. And in the examples we've considered, in doing the one (explaining why each dependent being exists) we've already done the other (explained why there are any dependent beings at all). We must now see, however, that on the supposition that the whole of reality consists *only* of a collection of dependent beings, to give an explanation of each member's existence is not to provide an explanation of why there are dependent beings.

In the examples we've considered, we have gone outside of the collection of dependent beings in order to explain the members' existence. But if the only beings that exist or ever existed are de-

pendent beings then each dependent being will be explained by some other dependent being, ad infinitum. This does not mean that there will be some particular dependent being whose existence is unaccounted for. Each dependent being has an explanation of its existence; namely, in the dependent being which preceded it and produced it. So C1 is satisfied: there is an explanation of the existence of each member of the collection of dependent beings. Turning to C2, however, we can see that it will not be satisfied. We cannot explain why there are (or have ever been) dependent beings by appealing to all the members of the infinite collection of dependent beings. For if the question to be answered is why there are (or have ever been) any dependent beings at all, we cannot answer that question by noting that there always have been dependent beings, each one accounting for the existence of some other dependent being. Thus on the supposition that every being is dependent, it seems there will be no explanation of why there are dependent beings. C2 will not be satisfied. Therefore, on the supposition that every being is dependent there will be no explanation of the existence of the collection of dependent beings.

The Truth of PSR

We come now to the final criticism of the reasoning supporting the second premise of the Cosmological Argument. According to the criticism, it is admitted that the supposition that every being is dependent implies that there will be a *brute fact* in the universe, a fact, that is, for which there can be no explanation whatever. For there will be no explanation of the fact that dependent beings exist and have always been in existence. It is this brute fact that the proponents of the argument were describing when they pointed out that if every being is dependent, the series or collection of dependent beings would lack an explanation of *its* existence. The final criticism asks what is wrong with admitting that the universe contains such a brute, unintelligible fact. In asking this question the critic challenges the fundamental principle, PSR, on which the Cosmological Argument rests. For, as we've seen, the first premise of the argument denies that there exists a being whose existence has no explanation. In support of this premise the proponent appeals to the first part of PSR. The second premise of the argument claims that not every being can be dependent. In support of this premise the proponent appeals to the second part of PSR, the part which states that there must be an explanation of any positive fact whatever.

The proponent reasons that if every being were a dependent being, then although the first part of PSR would be satisfied—every being would have an explanation—the second part would be violated; there would be no explanation for the positive fact that there are and have always been dependent beings. For first, since every being is supposed to be dependent, there would be nothing outside of the collection of dependent beings to explain the collection's existence. Second, the fact that each member of the collection has an explanation in some other dependent being is insufficient to explain why there are and have always been dependent beings. And, finally, there is nothing about the collection of dependent beings that would suggest that it is a self-existent collection. Consequently, if every being were dependent, the fact that there are and have always been dependent beings would have no explanation. But this violates the second part of PSR. So the second premise of the Cosmological Argument must be true: Not every being can be a dependent being. This conclusion, however, is no better than the principle, PSR, on which it rests. And it is the point of the final criticism to question the truth of PSR. Why, after all, should we accept the idea that every being and every positive fact must have an explanation? Why, in short, should we believe PSR? These are important questions, and any final judgment of the Cosmological Argument depends on how they are answered.

Most of the theologians and philosophers who accept PSR have tried to defend it in either of two ways. Some have held that PSR is (or can be) known *intuitively* to be true. By this they mean that if we fully understand and reflect on what is said by PSR we can see that it must be true. Now, undoubtedly, there are statements which are known intuitively to be true. "Every triangle has

exactly three angles" or "No physical object can be in two different places in space at one and the same time" are examples of statements whose truth we can apprehend just by understanding and reflecting on them. The difficulty with the claim that PSR is intuitively true, however, is that a number of very able philosophers fail to apprehend its truth, and some even claim that the principle is false. It is doubtful, therefore, that many of us, if any, know intuitively that PSR is true.

The second way philosophers and theologians who accept PSR have sought to defend it is by claiming that although it is not known to be true, it is, nevertheless, a presupposition of reason, a basic assumption that rational people make, whether or not they reflect sufficiently to become aware of the assumption. It's probably true that there are some assumptions we all make about our world, assumptions which are so basic that most of us are unaware of them. And, I suppose, it might be true that PSR is such an assumption. What bearing would this view of PSR have on the Cosmological Argument? Perhaps the main point to note is that even if PSR is a presupposition we all share, the premises of the Cosmological Argument could still be false. For PSR itself could still be false. The fact, if it is a fact, that all of us *presuppose* that every existing being and every positive fact has an explanation does not imply that no being exists, and no positive fact obtains, without an explanation. Nature is not bound to satisfy our presuppositions. As the American philosopher William James once remarked in another connection, "In the great boarding house of nature, the cakes and the butter and the syrup seldom come out so even and leave the plates so clear."

Our study of the first part of the Cosmological Argument has led us to the fundamental principle on which its premises rest, the Principle of Sufficient Reason. Since we do not seem to know that PSR is true, we cannot reasonably claim to know that the premises of the Cosmological Argument are true. They might be true. But unless we do know them to be true they cannot *establish* for us the conclusion that there exists a being that has the explanation of its existence within its own nature. If it were shown, however, that even though we do not *know* that PSR is true we all, nevertheless, *presuppose* PSR to be true, then, whether PSR is true or not, to be consistent we should accept the Cosmological Argument. For, as we've seen, its premises imply its conclusion and its premises do seem to follow from PSR. But no one has succeeded in *showing* that PSR is an assumption that most or all of us share. So our final conclusion must be that although the Cosmological Argument might be a *sound* argument (valid with true premises), it does not provide us with good rational grounds for believing that among these beings that exist there is one whose existence is accounted for by its own nature. Having come to this conclusion, we may safely put aside the second part of the argument. For even if it succeeded in showing that a self-existent being would have the other attributes of the theistic God, the Cosmological Argument would still not provide us with good rational grounds for belief in God, having failed in its first part to provide us with good rational grounds for believing that there is a self-existent being.

Notes

1. See St. Thomas Aquinas, *Summa Theologica,* 1a. 2, 3.
2. David Hume, *Dialogues Concerning Natural Religion,* Part IX, ed. H. D. Aiken (New York: Hafner Publishing Company, 1948), pp. 59–60.

I.A.5   The *Kalām* Cosmological Argument

WILLIAM LANE CRAIG

William Lane Craig is a research professor of philosophy at Biola University in Los Angeles. He received his Ph.D. in philosophy from the University of Birmingham (England) and a Th.D from the University of Munich (Germany). He is the author of several works in philosophy of religion, including The Kalām Cosmological Argument *(1979) and* Reasonable Faith *(1994), from which the following selection is taken. The* kalām *argument refers to a version of the cosmological argument developed by Arab Islamic scholars, al-Kindi and al-Ghazali, in the Middle Ages. The Arabic word* kalām *means "argument." In this article Craig develops two versions of the* kalām *argument, both aiming to prove that the universe must have a cause of its existence.*

existence of God. In particular, I find the *kalām* cosmological argument for a temporal first cause of the universe to be one of the most plausible arguments for God's existence. The argument shows that the universe began to exist. Anything that begins to exist must have a cause that brings it into being. So the universe must have a cause. Philosophical analysis reveals that such a cause must have several of the principal theistic attributes.

The argument may be formulated in three simple steps.

1. Whatever begins to exist has a cause.
2. The universe began to exist.
3. Therefore, the universe has a cause.

The logic of the argument is valid and very simple; the argument has the same logical structure as the argument: "All men are mortal; Socrates is a man; therefore, Socrates is mortal." So the question is, are there good reasons to believe that each of the steps is true? I think there are.

Defense of the *Kalām* Argument

I find quite a number of proffered theistic arguments to be sound and persuasive and together to constitute a powerful cumulative case for the

Reprinted from *Reasonable Faith* (Crossway, 1994) by permission of William Lane Craig. Endnotes deleted.

Whatever Begins to Exist Has a Cause

The first step is so intuitively obvious that I think scarcely anyone could sincerely believe it to be false. I therefore think it somewhat unwise to argue in favor of it, for any proof of the principle is likely to be less obvious than the principle itself. And as Aristotle remarked, one ought not to try to prove the obvious via the less obvious. The old axiom "out of nothing, nothing comes" remains as obvious today as ever. When I first wrote *The Kalām Cosmological Argument,* I remarked that I found it an attractive feature of this argument that it allows the atheist a way of escape: he can always deny the first premise and assert that the universe sprang into existence uncaused out of nothing. I figured that few would take this option, since I believed they would thereby expose themselves as persons interested only in an academic refutation of the argument and not in really discovering the truth about the universe. To my surprise, however, atheists seem to be increasingly taking this route. For example, Quentin Smith, commenting that philosophers are too often adversely affected by Heidegger's dread of "the nothing," concludes that "the most reasonable belief is that we came from nothing, by nothing, and for nothing"—a nice ending of a sort of Gettysburg Address of atheism, perhaps.

Similarly, the late J. L. Mackie, in refuting the *kalām* cosmological argument, turns his main guns on this first step: "there is *a priori* no good reason why a sheer origination of things, not determined by anything, should be unacceptable, whereas the existence of a god [*sic*] with the power to create something out of nothing is acceptable." Indeed, he believes *creatio ex nihilo* raises problems: (i) If God began to exist at a point in time, then this is as great a puzzle as the beginning of the universe. (ii) Or if God existed for infinite time, then the same arguments would apply to his existence as would apply to the infinite duration of the universe. (iii) If it be said that God is timeless, then this, says Mackie, is a complete mystery.

Now notice that Mackie never *refutes* the principle that whatever begins to exist has a cause. Rather, he simply demands what good reason there is *a priori* to accept it. He writes, "As Hume pointed out, we can certainly conceive an uncaused beginning-to-be of an object; if what we can thus conceive is nevertheless in some way impossible, this still requires to be shown." But, as many philosophers have pointed out, Hume's argument in no way makes it plausible to think that something could really come into being without a cause. Just because I can imagine an object, say a horse, coming into existence from nothing, that in no way proves that a horse really could come into existence that way. The defender of the *kalām* argument is claiming that it is *really* impossible for something to come uncaused from nothing. Does Mackie sincerely believe that things can pop into existence uncaused, out of nothing? Does anyone in his right mind really believe that, say, a raging tiger could suddenly come into existence uncaused, out of nothing, in this room right now? The same applies to the universe: if prior to the existence of the universe, there was absolutely nothing—no God, no space, no time—how could the universe possibly have come to exist?

In fact, Mackie's appeal to Hume at this point is counterproductive. For Hume himself clearly believed in the causal principle. In 1754 he wrote to John Stewart, "But allow me to tell you that I never asserted so absurd a Proposition as *that anything might arise without a cause.* I only maintain'd, that our Certainty of the Falsehood of that Proposition proceeded neither from Intuition nor Demonstration, but from another source." Even Mackie confesses, "Still this [causal] principle has some plausibility, in that it is constantly confirmed in our experience (and also used, reasonably, in interpreting our experience)." So why not accept the truth of the causal principle as plausible and reasonable—at the very least more so than its denial?

Because, Mackie thinks, in this particular case the theism implied by affirming the principle is even more unintelligible than the denial of the principle. It makes more sense to believe that the universe came into being uncaused out of nothing than to believe that God created the universe out of nothing.

But is this really the case? Consider the three problems Mackie raises with *creatio ex nihilo*. Certainly, the proponent of the *kalām* argument would not hold (i) that God began to exist or (ii) that God has existed for an infinite number of, say, hours, or any other unit of time. But what is wrong with (iii), that God is, without creation, timeless? I would argue that God exists timelessly without creation and in time subsequent to creation. This may be "mysterious" in the sense of "wonderful" or "awe-inspiring," but it is not, so far as I can see, unintelligible; and Mackie gives us no reason to think that it is. Moreover, there is also an alternative which Mackie failed to consider: (iv) prior to creation God existed in an undifferentiated time in which hours, seconds, days, and so forth simply do not exist. Because this time is undifferentiated, it is not incompatible with the *kalām* argument that an infinite regress of events cannot exist. It seems to me, therefore, that Mackie is entirely unjustified in rejecting the first step of the argument as not being intuitively obvious, plausible, and reasonable.

The Universe Began to Exist

If we agree that whatever begins to exist has a cause, what evidence is there to support the crucial second step in the argument, that the universe began to exist? I think that this step is supported by both philosophical arguments and scientific confirmation of those arguments.

Philosophical Arguments: (1) Argument from the Impossibility of an Actually Infinite Number of Things

An actually infinite number of things cannot exist because this would involve all sorts of absurdities, which I'll illustrate in a moment. And if the universe never had a beginning, then the series of all past events is actually infinite. That is to say, an actually infinite number of past events exists. Because an actually infinite number of things cannot exist, then an actually infinite number of past events cannot exist. The number of past events is finite; therefore, the series of past events had a beginning. Since the history of the universe is identical to the series of all past events, the universe must have begun to exist. This argument can also be formulated in three steps:

1. An actually infinite number of things cannot exist.
2. A beginningless series of events in time entails an actually infinite number of things.
3. Therefore, a beginningless series of events in time cannot exist.

Let's examine each step individually.

1. *An actually infinite number of things cannot exist.* In order to understand this first step, we need to understand what an actual infinite is. There is a difference between a potential infinite and an actual infinite. A potential infinite is a collection that is increasing toward infinity as a limit but never gets there. Such a collection is really indefinite, not infinite. For example, any finite distance can be subdivided into potentially infinitely many parts. You can just keep on dividing parts in half forever, but you will never arrive at an actual "infinitieth" division or come up with an actually infinite number of parts. By contrast, an actual infinite is a collection in which the number of members really is infinite. The collection is not growing toward infinity; it *is* infinite, it is "complete." This sort of infinity is used in set theory to designate sets that have an infinite number of members, such as {1, 2, 3 . . . }. Now I am arguing, not that a potentially infinite number of things cannot exist, but that an actually infinite number of things cannot exist. For if an actually infinite number of things could exist, this would spawn all sorts of absurdities.

Perhaps the best way to bring this home is by means of an illustration. Let me use one of my favorites, Hilbert's Hotel, a product of the mind of the great German mathematician David Hilbert. Let's imagine a hotel with a finite number of rooms. Suppose, furthermore, that all the rooms are full. When a new guest arrives asking for a room, the proprietor apologizes, "Sorry, all the rooms are full." But now let us imagine a hotel with an infinite number of rooms and suppose once more that *all the rooms are full.* There is not a single vacant room throughout the entire infinite hotel. Now suppose a new guest shows up, asking for a room. "But of course!" says the proprietor, and he immediately shifts the person in room #1 into room #2, the person in room #2 into room #3, the person in room

#3 into room #4, and so on, out to infinity. As a result of these room changes, room #1 now becomes vacant and the new guest gratefully checks in. But remember, before he arrived, all the rooms were full!

Equally curious, according to the mathematicians, there are now no more persons in the hotel than there were before: the number is just infinite. But how can this be? The proprietor just added the new guest's name to the register and gave him his keys—how can there not be one more person in the hotel than before? But the situation becomes even stranger. For suppose an infinity of new guests show up at the desk, asking for a room. "Of course, of course!" says the proprietor, and he proceeds to shift the person in room #1 into room #2, the person in room #2 into room #4, the person in room #3 into room #6, and so on out to infinity, always putting each former occupant into the room number twice his own. Because any natural number multiplied by two always equals an even number, all the guests wind up in even-numbered rooms. As a result, all the odd-numbered rooms become vacant, and the infinity of new guests is easily accommodated. And yet, before they came, all the rooms were full! And again, strangely enough, the number of guests in the hotel is the same after the infinity of new guests check in as before, even though there were as many new guests as old guests. In fact, the proprietor could repeat this process *infinitely many times* and yet there would never be one single person more in the hotel than before.

But Hilbert's Hotel is even stranger than the German mathematician made it out to be. For suppose some of the guests start to check out. Suppose the guest in room #1 departs. Is there not now one less person in the hotel? Not according to the mathematicians—but just ask the woman who makes the beds! Suppose the guests in rooms #1, 3, 5 . . . check out. In this case an infinite number of people have left the hotel, but according to the mathematicians, there are no less people in the hotel—but don't talk to that laundry woman! In fact, we could have every other guest check out of the hotel and repeat this process infinitely many times, and yet there would never be any less people in the hotel.

Now suppose the proprietor doesn't like having a half-empty hotel (it looks bad for business). No matter! By shifting occupants as before, but in reverse order, he transforms his half-vacant hotel into one that is jammed to the gills. You might think that by these manoeuvres the proprietor could always keep this strange hotel fully occupied. But you would be wrong. For suppose that the persons in rooms #4, 5, 6. . . checked out. At a single stroke the hotel would be virtually emptied, the guest register would be reduced to three names, and the infinite would be converted to finitude. And yet it would remain true that the *same* number of guests checked out this time as when the guests in rooms #1, 3, 5 . . . checked out! Can anyone believe that such a hotel could exist in reality?

Hilbert's Hotel is absurd. As one person remarked, if Hilbert's Hotel could exist, it would have to have a sign posted outside: NO VACANCY—GUESTS WELCOME. The above sorts of absurdities show that it is impossible for an actually infinite number of things to exist. There is simply no way to avoid these absurdities once we admit the possibility of the existence of an actual infinite. Students sometimes react to such absurdities as Hilbert's Hotel by saying that we really don't understand the nature of infinity and, hence, these absurdities result. But this attitude is simply mistaken. Infinite set theory is a highly developed and well-understood branch of mathematics, so that these absurdities result precisely because we *do* understand the notion of a collection with an actually infinite number of members.

William J. Wainwright has suggested that we could reduce the force of these absurdities by translating them into mathematical terms; for example, an actually infinite set has a proper subset with the same cardinal number as the set itself. But this amounts only to a way of *concealing* the absurdities; it was to bring out the paradoxical character of these mathematical concepts that Hilbert came up with his illustration in the first place. And the whole purpose of philosophical analysis is to bring out what is entailed by unanalyzed notions and not to leave them at face value.

But does the possibility of an actual infinite really *entail* that such absurdities are possible, or could an actual infinite be possible, as Wainwright suggests, without thereby implying that such absurdities are possible? The answer to that question is simple: the possibility of the existence of an actual infinite *entails*, that is, necessarily implies, that such absurdities could exist. Hilbert's illustration merely serves to bring out in a practical and vivid way what the mathematics necessarily implies; for if an actually infinite number of things is possible, then a hotel with an actually infinite number of rooms must be possible. Hence, it logically follows that if such a hotel is impossible, then so is the real existence of an actual infinite.

These considerations also show how superficial Mackie's analysis of this point is. He thinks that the absurdities are resolved by noting that for infinite groups the axiom that *the whole is greater than its part* does not hold, as it does for finite groups. But far from being the solution, this is precisely the problem. Because in infinite set theory this axiom is denied, one gets all sorts of absurdities, like Hilbert's Hotel, when one tries to translate that theory into reality. And the contradictions that result when guests check out of the hotel are not even *prima facie* resolved by Mackie's analysis. (In trans-finite arithmetic, subtraction is against the rules because it leads to contradictions; but in reality, you can't stop people from checking out of the hotel if they want to!) Hence, I conclude that an actually infinite number of things cannot exist.

2. *A beginningless series of events in time entails an actually infinite number of things.* This second point is pretty obvious. If the universe never began to exist, then the series of events would be infinite. If the universe never began to exist, then prior to the present there have existed an actually infinite number of previous events. Thus, a beginningless series of events in time entails an actually infinite number of things, namely, events.

3. *Therefore, a beginningless series of events in time cannot exist.* If the above two premises are true, then the conclusion follows logically. The series of past events must be finite and have a beginning. Since, as I said, the universe is not distinct from the series of events, the universe therefore began to exist.

Philosophical Arguments: (2) Argument from the Impossibility of Forming an Actually Infinite Collection of Things by Adding One Member After Another

It is very important to note that this argument is distinct from the foregoing argument, for it does not deny that an actually infinite number of things can exist. It denies that a collection containing an actually infinite number of things can be *formed* by adding one member after another. Basically, the argument goes like this: you cannot form an actually infinite collection of things by adding one member after another, because it would be impossible to get to infinity. The series of past events is a collection that has been formed by adding one event after another. Therefore, the series of past events up till now can only be finite, not infinite. Otherwise, it would be an actually infinite collection formed by adding one member after another. This argument, too, can be formulated in three steps:

1. The series of events in time is a collection formed by adding one member after another.
2. A collection formed by adding one member after another cannot be actually infinite.
3. Therefore, the series of events in time cannot be actually infinite.

Let's take a look at each step.

1. *The series of events in time is a collection formed by adding one member after another.* This is rather obvious. The past did not spring into being whole and entire but was formed sequentially, one event occurring after another. Notice, too, that the direction of this formation is "forward," in the sense that the collection grows with time. Although we sometimes speak of an "infinite regress" of events, in reality an infinite past would be an "infinite progress" of events with no beginning and its end in the present.

2. *A collection formed by adding one member after another cannot be actually infinite.* This is the crucial step. It's important to realize that this impossibility has nothing to do with the amount of time available: no matter how much time one has available, an actual infinite cannot be formed. No matter

how many numbers you count, you can always add one more before arriving at infinity.

Now someone might say that while an infinite collection cannot be formed by beginning at a point and adding members, nevertheless an infinite collection could be formed by never beginning but ending at a point, that is to say, ending at a point after having added one member after another from eternity. But this method seems even more unbelievable than the first method. If one cannot count to infinity, how can one count down from infinity? If one cannot traverse the infinite by moving in one direction, how can one traverse it by moving in the opposite direction?

Indeed, the idea of a beginningless series ending in the present seems absurd. To give just one illustration: suppose we meet a man who claims to have been counting from eternity and who is now finishing: . . , –3, –2, –1, 0. We could ask, why didn't he finish counting yesterday or the day before or the year before? By then an infinite time had already elapsed, so that he should already have finished. Thus, at no point in the infinite past could we ever find the man finishing his countdown, for by that point he should already be done! In fact, no matter how far back into the past we go, we can never find the man counting at all, for at any point we reach he will already have finished. But if at no point in the past do we find him counting, this contradicts the hypothesis that he has been counting from eternity. This illustrates that the formation of an actual infinite by never beginning but reaching an end is as impossible as beginning at a point and trying to reach infinity.

Hence, set theory has been purged of all temporal concepts; as Russell says, "classes which are infinite are given all at once by the defining properties of their members, so that there is no question of 'completion' or of 'successive synthesis.'" The only way an actual infinite could come to exist in the real world would be by being created all at once, simply in a moment. It would be a hopeless undertaking to try to form it by adding one member after another.

Mackie's objections to this step are off the target. He thinks that the argument illicitly assumes an infinitely distant starting point in the past and then pronounces it impossible to travel from that point to today. If we take the notion of infinity "seriously," he says, we must say that in the infinite past there would be no starting point whatever, not even an infinitely distant one. Yet from any given point in the past, there is only a finite distance to the present.

Now I know of no proponent of the *kalām* argument who assumed that there was an infinitely distant starting point in the past. On the contrary, the beginningless character of the series of past events only serves to underscore the difficulty of its formation by adding one member after another. The fact that there is *no beginning at all,* not even an infinitely distant one, makes the problem worse, not better. It is not the proponent of the *kalām* argument who fails to take infinity seriously. To say the infinite past could have been formed by adding one member after another is like saying someone has just succeeded in writing down all the negative numbers, ending at –1. And, we may ask, how is Mackie's point that from any given moment in the past there is only a finite distance to the present even relevant to the issue? The defender of the *kalām* argument could agree to this without batting an eye. For the issue is how the *whole* series can be formed, not a finite portion of it. Does Mackie think that because every *finite* segment of the series can be formed by adding one member after another the whole *infinite* series can be so formed? That is as logically fallacious as saying because every part of an elephant is light in weight, the whole elephant is light in weight. Mackie's point is therefore irrelevant. It seems that this step of the argument, that an actually infinite collection cannot be formed by adding one member after another, remains unrefuted.

3. *Therefore, the series of events in time cannot be actually infinite.* Given the truth of the premises, the conclusion logically follows. If the universe did not begin to exist a finite time ago, then the present moment would never arrive. But obviously it has arrived. Therefore, we know that the universe is finite in the past and began to exist.

We thus have two separate arguments to prove that the universe began to exist, one based on the impossibility of an actually infinite number of things and one on the impossibility of forming an actually infinite collection by successive addition. If one wishes to deny the beginning of the universe, he must refute, not one, but both of these arguments.

I.A.6 Scientific Confirmation of the Cosmological Argument

WILLIAM LANE CRAIG

William Lane Craig is a research professor at Biola University in Los Angeles and is the author of several works in philosophy of religion. In this essay Craig describes the evidence from astronomy for the kalām cosmological argument for the existence of God. He argues that evidence for the Big Bang confirms the thesis that the universe began to exist and so, must have had a cause. Toward the end of the article Craig introduces "the anthropic principle," which states that "if the universe were in fact different in any significant way from the way it is, we wouldn't be here to wonder why it is" (a definition given by Dewey Schwatzenburg). Finally, Craig argues that there is good reason to believe, on the basis of the anthropic principle, that the First Cause is the Personal Creator of Theism.

Some people find philosophical arguments difficult to follow. They prefer empirical evidence. So I now turn to an examination of [a] remarkable scientific confirmation of the conclusion already reached by philosophical argument alone. This evidence comes from what is undoubtedly one of the most exciting and rapidly developing fields of science: astronomy and astrophysics.

Reprinted from *Reasonable Faith* (Crossway, 1994) by permission of William Lane Craig. Endnotes deleted.

Confirmation from the Big Bang Model of the Universe

Prior to the 1920's, scientists had always assumed that the universe was stationary. But in 1929 an alarming thing happened. An astronomer named Edwin Hubble discovered that the light from distant galaxies appears to be redder than it should. The startling conclusion to which Hubble was led was that the light is redder because the universe is *growing apart;* it is expanding! The light from the galaxies is affected because they are moving away from us. But this is the interesting part: Hubble not only showed that the universe is expanding, but that *it is expanding the same in all directions.*

To get a picture of this, imagine a balloon with buttons glued on its surface. As you blow up the balloon, the buttons get farther and farther apart. Now those but- tons are just like the galaxies in space. Everything in the universe is expanding outward. The staggering implication of this is that at some point in the past *the entire known universe was contracted down to a single mathematical point,* from which it has been expanding ever since. The further back one goes in the past, the denser the universe becomes, so that one finally reaches a point of infinite density called the singularity from which the universe began to expand. That initial event has come to be known as the "Big Bang."

How long ago did the Big Bang occur? In a very important series of nine articles published over the course of three decades, two scientists, Allan Sandage and G. A. Tammann, estimated that the Big Bang occurred about 15 billion years ago. Therefore, according to the Big Bang theory the universe began to exist with a great explosion from a state of infinite density about 15 billion years ago. Four of the world's most famous astronomers describe that event in these words:

> The universe began from a state of infinite density. . . . Space and time were created in that event and so was all the matter in the universe. It is not meaningful to ask what happened before the Big Bang; it is like asking what is north of the North Pole. Similarly, it is not sensible to ask where the Big Bang took place. The point-universe was not an object isolated in space; it was the entire universe, and so the only answer can be that the Big Bang happened everywhere.

Thus, the term "Big Bang" and the terminology associated with an explosion can be misleading, because it is not correct to suppose that the expansion can be visualized from the outside. There is no external vantage point from which the expansion could be observed because what is expanding is the entire universe. Space itself is expanding in the sense that the separation between any two galaxies grows with time.

The event that marked the beginning of the universe becomes all the more amazing when one reflects on the fact that it implies the origin of the universe out of nothing. As the British physicist P.C.W. Davies explains,

> If we extrapolate this prediction to its extreme, we reach a point when all distances in the universe have shrunk to zero. An initial cosmological singularity therefore forms a past temporal extremity to the universe. We cannot continue physical reasoning, or even the concept of spacetime, through such an extremity. For this reason most cosmologists think of the initial singularity as the beginning of the universe. On this view the big bang represents the creation event; the creation not only of all the matter and energy in the universe, but also of spacetime itself.

Similarly, another pair of physicists conclude, "At this singularity, space and time came into existence; literally nothing existed before the singularity, so, if the Universe originated in such a singularity, we would truly have a creation *ex nihilo*." Thus, as astronomer Fred Hoyle points out, the Big Bang theory requires the creation of the universe from nothing. This is because as one goes back in time, one reaches a point at which, in Hoyle's words, the

universe was "shrunk down to nothing at all." So what the Big Bang model implies is that the universe had a beginning and was created out of nothing.

Now some people were deeply disturbed with the idea that the universe began from nothing. Einstein wrote privately, "This circumstance of an expanding universe irritates me. . . . To admit such possibilities seems senseless." Another scientist, Arthur Eddington, wrote, "I have no axe to grind in this discussion, but the notion of a beginning is repugnant to me. . . . I simply do not believe that the present order of things started off with a bang. . . . The expanding universe is preposterous . . . incredible. . . . It leaves me cold." The German chemist Walter Nernst declared, "To deny the infinite duration of time would be to betray the very foundations of science." Phillip Morrison of the Massachusetts Institute of Technology said, "I find it hard to accept the Big Bang theory; I would like to reject it, but I have to face the facts."

Alternative models. But if one rejects the Big-Bang model, the alternatives are not very convincing. Let's examine the major kinds of competing theories.

The *steady state model* holds that the universe never had a beginning, but has always existed in the same state. As the galaxies mutually recede, new matter comes into existence in the voids left by the retreating galaxies, so that the overall state of the universe remains the same. Ever since this model was first proposed in 1948, it has never been very convincing. According to S. L. Jaki, this theory never secured "a single piece of experimental verification." It always seemed to be trying to explain away the facts rather than explain them. According to Jaki, the proponents of this model were actually motivated by "openly anti-theological, or rather anti-Christian motivations."

Against this theory is the fact that a count of galaxies emitting radio waves indicates that there were once more radio sources than there are today. Therefore, the universe is not in a steady state after all. But the theory was decisively discredited when in 1965 two scientists working for the Bell Telephone Laboratory, A. A. Penzias and R. W. Wilson, discovered that the entire universe is bathed with a background of microwave radiation. This radiation background shows that the universe was once in a very hot and very dense state. In the steady state model no such state could have existed, since the universe is supposed to have been the same from eternity. Therefore, the steady state model has been abandoned by virtually everyone. According to Ivan King, "The steady-state theory has now been laid to rest, as a result of clear-cut observations of how things have changed with time."

A second alternative model is the *oscillating model.* John Gribbin describes this model:

> The biggest problem with the Big Bang theory of the origin of the universe is philosophical—perhaps even theological—what was there before the bang? This problem alone was sufficient to give a great initial impetus to the steady state theory; but with that theory now sadly in conflict with the observations, the best way round this initial difficulty is provided by a model in which the universe expands, collapses back again, and repeats the cycle indefinitely.

According to this model, the universe is sort of like a spring, expanding and contracting from eternity. This model became a sort of "Great White Hope" for atheistic scientists, who terribly wanted it to be true so as to avoid an absolute beginning of the universe. You may have seen Carl Sagan, for example, in his popular "Cosmos" program on public television propounding this model and reading from the Hindu scriptures about cyclical Brahman years in order to illustrate the oscillating universe.

There are, however, at least two very well-known difficulties with the oscillating model, which Sagan did not mention. First, the oscillating model is physically impossible. That is to say, for all the talk about such a model, the fact remains that it is only a *theoretical* possibility, not a *real* possibility. You can draft such models on paper, but they cannot be descriptive of the real universe, because they contradict the known laws of physics. As the late Professor Tinsley of Yale explains, in oscillating models "even though the mathematics *says* that the universe oscillates, there is no known physics to reverse the collapse and bounce back to a new expansion. The physics seems to say that those models start from the Big Bang, expand, collapse, then end." More recently, four other scientists, themselves obviously in sympathy with the oscillat-

ing model, admitted, in describing the contraction of the universe, "there is no understanding of how a bounce can take place. . . . We have nothing to contribute to the question of whether and/or how the universe bounces." In order for the oscillating model to be correct, the known laws of physics would have to be revised.

Second, the observational evidence is contrary to the oscillating model. Let me explain two respects in which the observational evidence does not support the oscillating model. The first is that there is no way to account for the observed even distribution of matter in the universe on the basis of an oscillating model. This is because as the universe contracts, black holes begin to suck everything up, so that matter becomes very unevenly distributed. But when the universe (supposedly) rebounds from its contracting phase, there is no mechanism to "iron out" these lumps and make the distribution smooth. Hence, the scientists cited above confess that even if there is some unknown mechanism that could cause the universe to bounce back to a new expansion, it is still not clear that it would prevent the unevenness that would result from the black holes formed during the contraction phase. The present evenness of matter distribution simply cannot be explained by using models in which the universe begins with matter unevenly distributed. The oscillating model therefore cannot satisfactorily account for the presently observed evenness of the distribution of matter in the universe.

A second respect in which the observational evidence is contrary to the oscillating model concerns the question of whether the universe will someday re-contract or continue to expand forever. If the first alternative is correct, the expansion will reach a certain point, halt, and then gravity will pull everything back together again. But if the second alternative is right, the force of the expansion is greater than the force of gravity so that the expansion will never stop but will just go on and on forever.

An illustration of this difference concerns the escape velocity needed by a rocket to escape earth's gravity. If a certain speed is not attained, the force of gravity will pull the ship back to earth again. But if the rocket attains or exceeds escape velocity, then the force of the earth's gravity cannot prevent its flying off into space. Similarly, if the universe is expanding, so to speak, at escape velocity or faster, then it will overcome the internal pull of its own gravity and will expand forever. Now clearly, the oscillating model, even in order to be a *possibility,* must posit a closed universe, one that is expanding slower than escape velocity. But is it?

The crucial factor in answering that question is the density of the universe. For density determines the gravitational force of an object. Scientists have estimated that if there are more than about three hydrogen atoms per cubic meter on the average throughout the universe, then the universe will re-contract. Now that may not sound like very much, but remember that most of the universe is just empty space. I won't go into all the technicalities of how scientists measure the density of the universe, but let me simply report their conclusions. If all matter were luminous, visible matter associated with galaxies, then the universe would possess only a trifling 1% of the density necessary to bring about re-contraction. But undoubtedly there is dark, non-luminous matter surrounding the galaxies and galactic structures and perhaps in inter-galactic space. Repeated measurements on ever-widening scales of the effects of this dark matter on galactic motion and of the constraints placed on it by the abundance of the lightest elements in the universe (which would not have been produced were the universe too dense) vindicate earlier estimates that even taking all luminous and non-luminous matter together, the density of the universe is still only about 10% of what is necessary for re-contraction. In order for the universe to recontract, 99% of the matter in the universe would have to be invisible, which is, as Sandage muses, "a bizarre requirement."

Theoretical physicists bent on finding the "missing" 90% have proposed that it may take the form of exotic matter rather than ordinary matter. Two scenarios have been proposed. *Hot Dark Matter* theories hold that subatomic particles like neutrinos (particles which have no electrical charge, no rest mass, and which travel at the speed of light) may have a mass after all and exist in sufficient quantities to bring the density up to the 100% necessary for

re-contraction. These scenarios have now been widely abandoned because the evidence supports the traditional picture of neutrinos as massless, and especially because such scenarios predict a large-scale structure of the universe which is completely at odds with what is observed.

The *Cold Dark Matter* theories postulate the existence of unknown particles of weakly interacting matter (facetiously called WIMPs) which exist in sufficient abundance to make the universe re-contract. But there is no evidence that WIMPs even exist; theorists have to simply invent such particles and their masses. Worse still, Cold Dark Matter scenarios have to say that this exotic matter exists mainly in intergalactic space, so as not to disrupt the measured motion of galaxies. But the existence of vast amounts of exotic matter in intergalactic space is incompatible with the recent measurements by the COBE satellite of the primordial fluctuations in the microwave background radiation. The fact is that nobody knows where the so-called "missing mass" of 90% is supposed to come from. Astronomer Joseph Silk reflects, "If the hidden mass is completely unobservable, anything is permissible. Suggestions for the missing mass have ranged from snowflakes to rocks, planets, black holes, even to excess issues of the *Astrophysical Journal*." ". . . in the absence of observable evidence, any suggestions must lack credibility."

The observational evidence thus supports a low density universe destined to indefinite expansion. Sandage and Tammann conclude: "Hence, we are forced to decide that . . . it seems inevitable that the Universe will expand forever." This conclusion may be strengthened. For Sandage and Tammann in a later discussion go on to point out that in order to fit the observational evidence, even high density universes (which are typically thought to re-contract) may also have to expand forever. They conclude, "Hence, the one certain conclusion is that in all models of either high or low density, . . . the Universe will not stop its expansion. *This means it has happened only once. The creation event was unique.*"

The oscillating model, therefore, is seriously flawed. It contradicts both the known laws of physics and the current observational evidence. It therefore provides no plausible escape from the beginning of the universe.

In recent years theoretical cosmology has become increasingly speculative, obscuring the boundary between physics and metaphysics. The marriage of the General Theory of Relativity (upon which the Big Bang model is based) to Quantum Theory (sub-atomic physics) has resulted in the conception of a third alternative to the standard Big Bang model: *quantum models* of the universe. One should say the "would-be marriage," for the fact is that these two great theories of modern physics are mutually inconsistent, and nobody knows how to reconcile them. Quantum models grow out of the attempt at one such reconciliation. Prior to 10^{-43} second after the Big Bang (that's .00000000-000000000000000000000000000000001 of a second) quantum physics must be employed to describe the universe, and the goal of the union of Relativity Theory and Quantum Theory is to describe this brief moment. Unfortunately, this period is so poorly understood that one commentator has compared it with the regions on the maps of ancient cartographers marked "Here there be dragons!"—it can be filled with all sorts of fantasies. The fact is that these theories are as much speculation as science.

The first class of models appealing to quantum effects to explain the origin of the universe were *vacuum fluctuation models.* These theories hold that what we have thus far taken to be the expansion of the *whole* universe is really only the expansion of a *part* of it, or, in other words, that our observable universe is just a tiny part of a wider Universe-as-a-whole. The Universe-as-a-whole is itself a vacuum in a steady state. But throughout this vacuum sub-atomic energy fluctuations are conceived to be occurring, by means of which material particles are created out of the energy contained in the vacuum. These then grow into separate mini-universes within the whole. All we can observe is the expansion of our mini-universe, and we have no knowledge whatsoever of what is going on in other similar mini-universes.

Our universe thus never went back to an initial singularity, but emerged by an uncaused fluctuation from the vacuum of a wider background space—a view that is often expressed by saying that the universe is a "free lunch" because in this case we got something for nothing.

Such a congenial way of talking is, however, completely misleading. In popular presentations of these models it is often not explained that they require the postulation of some sort of specially fine-tuned, background space on the analogy of a quantum mechanical vacuum from which the universe emerges via a fluctuation. Thus, the origin of the observable universe out of this wider space-time is not at all a free lunch, but requires an elaborately set table in advance.

Such models face formidable theoretical difficulties which are so severe that even some of the original proponents of these models have now abandoned them. Brout and Spindel, for example, have moved beyond such models, commenting that the theoretical foundations of the particle production mechanisms as well as the instability of the background space to fluctuations "are flimsy at best."

In any case such models have been shown to be incompatible with observational cosmology. On such scenarios, there is no way to specify exactly when and where a fluctuation in the primordial vacuum will occur which will grow into a universe. Within any finite interval of time there is a positive probability of such a fluctuation occurring at any point in space. It follows that given infinite past time, universes will spring into being at every point in the vacuum and, as they expand, will begin to collide and coalesce with one another. But we do not observe anything of this sort happening in nature.

Isham comments that this problem is "fairly lethal" to vacuum fluctuation models and that they therefore "have not found wide acceptance." About the only way to avoid the difficulty of colliding universes is to postulate that the background vacuum space is itself expanding—but then we're forced to posit some origin of the wider Universe itself, and we're right back where we started from.

I mentioned that vacuum fluctuation models have been abandoned as plausible accounts of the origin of the universe by some of their original expositors and to that extent are already somewhat passé. Brout and Spindel now contend that an explanation of the origin of the universe "must await the yet-to-come quantum theory of gravity." That brings us to the second class of quantum models.

In addition to vacuum fluctuation models, there are also *quantum gravity models.* The particular quantum gravity model of the origin of the universe which has drawn the most attention in recent years is the Hartle-Hawking model, popularized by Stephen Hawking, the brilliant mathematical theorist of Cambridge University, who has received wide publicity of his views in the popular press. One of the most interesting features of Hawking's best-selling *Brief History of Time,* in which he expounds his views, is its overtly theological orientation. Although Hawking does not deny the existence of God, he does deny that there is a Creator in the sense of a temporal First Cause of the origin of the universe.

In discussing whether a Creator exists, Hawking admits that if the universe began to exist, then one could identify the Big Bang as the instant at which God created the universe. In fact, he thinks that a number of attempts to avoid the Big Bang were probably motivated by the feeling that a beginning of time "smacks of divine intervention." Although it is not clear if Hawking shares this same motivation, he does tout his model as preferable to the Big Bang, because there would be no edge of space-time at which one "would have to appeal to God."

Hawking's theory is perhaps most easily understood by contrasting it to the standard Big Bang model. In the standard model, the universe sprang from an initial singularity which marked the origin of all matter and energy, indeed, of physical space and time themselves. Nothing existed before this point; hence, the singularity cannot have any natural cause.

Hawking hopes that by introducing quantum physics into the description of the earliest stage of the universe, prior to 10^{-43} seconds after the Big Bang, one can eliminate the singularity. In order to accomplish this, however, Hawking must introduce imaginary numbers for the time variable in his equations, that is to say, numbers like $\sqrt{-1}$. Since any real number squared always equals a positive

number, it is evident that there can be no real number which is the square root of –1. Therefore, mathematicians call such numbers "imaginary."

By using imaginary numbers for the time variable, one eliminates the singularity all right, but one also thereby eliminates the difference between time and space in the equations describing the universe. As Hawking says, ". . . the distinction between time and space disappears completely." This is a very peculiar feature of the model, since in both the Special and General Theories of Relativity, time and space are distinct in virtue of their variables' having different mathematical signs (+ or –) in the equations. But in Hawking's model, this difference in sign disappears, because he is using imaginary numbers for the time variable. By means of this device, Hawking proposes a model in which time becomes imaginary prior to 10^{-43} second, so that the singularity is rounded off. Space-time in this early region is geometrically the four-dimensional analogue of the two-dimensional surface of a sphere. Any point on a sphere which one chooses to be an "initial" or "beginning" point, such as the North Pole, is really just like every other point on the sphere's surface. In particular, it does not constitute an edge or boundary to that surface. Thus, on Hawking's model, the past is finite, but boundless. Moreover, since imaginary time is not distinguishable from space, it would be improper to regard any point on this sphere-like surface as actually *earlier* than any other point on that surface, just as it would be improper to think of any point on the surface of a ball as earlier than any other similar point. Hawking comments,

> There would be no singularities at which the laws of science broke down and no edge of space-time at which one would have to appeal to God or some new law to set the boundary conditions for space-time. . . . The universe would be completely self-contained and not affected by anything outside itself. It would be neither created nor destroyed. It would just BE.

In saying that the universe on his theory would not begin to exist, but would just BE, Hawking expresses the timeless existence of this four-dimensional space-time in which time is imaginary. He is not at all reluctant to draw theological conclusions from his model:

The idea that space and time may form a closed surface without boundary . . . has profound implications for the role of God in the affairs of the universe. . . . So long as the universe had a beginning, we could suppose it had a creator. But if the universe is really completely self-contained, having no boundary or edge, it would have neither beginning nor end. What place, then, for a creator?

In assessing Hawking's proposed model, one could criticize it effectively merely on the physical level alone. It is on the face of it highly speculative, and, according to Isham, it is most unlikely that it is even mathematically consistent. Moreover, it is now generally recognized that the Hartle-Hawking approach fails to predict uniquely our universe; consequently, why this universe exists rather than one of an infinite number of alternatives cannot be explained.

But I prefer to leave such criticisms aside; perhaps better, more consistent models can be devised. Rather my objections strike much deeper, at the philosophical or metaphysical foundations of such theories. Hawking's quantum cosmology is rife with unexamined philosophical assumptions which are, at best, unproven and, at worst, false. Given his claim to have eliminated the need for a Creator, it's evident that Hawking does not take his theory to be merely some mathematical model which is useful for facilitating scientific predictions but which makes no pretense to be a realistic description of the world. Such a non-realist (or instrumentalist) understanding of the theory would not be incompatible with the claim that in actual fact the universe began to exist in real time and was created. Hawking's model would in that case be a sort of symbolic description of the real origin of the universe using the mathematical formalism of quantum physics. The fact that there is no beginning of the universe *in the model* would do nothing to eliminate the beginning of the universe *in reality.* Since Hawking wants to avoid a beginning of the universe and the attendant need for a Creator, he must (and does) take his model to be a realistic description of the early universe. But this is precisely where the problems arise. It seems quite evident that Hawking faces acute difficulties in commending his theory as a realistic account of the origin of the universe.

Take just one example: his use of so-called "imaginary time." Two problems arise in connection with this notion. First, it is physically unintelligible. If he is to commend his theory as a realistic description of the universe, then Hawking has the burden to explain what "imaginary time" means. Otherwise it is a meaningless combination of words. But it is no more evident what an imaginary interval of time is anymore than, say, the imaginary volume of a box or the imaginary area of a field or the imaginary number of people in a room. Hawking insists that imaginary time is "a well-defined mathematical concept." But that's not the question; rather the question is whether that mathematical concept corresponds to any physical reality. The fact that something can be defined mathematically is no guarantee that any physical reality corresponds to it, as the late Sir Herbert Dingle so vividly illustrated:

Suppose we want to find the number of men required for a certain job under certain conditions. Every schoolboy knows such problems, and he knows that he must begin by saying: "Let x = the number of men required." But that substitution introduces a whole range of possibilities that the nature of the original problem excludes. The mathematical symbol x can be positive, negative, integral, fractional, irrational, imaginary, complex, zero, infinite, and whatever else the fertile brain of the mathematician may devise. The number of men, however, must be simply positive and integral. Consequently, when you say, "Let x = the number of men required" you are making a quite invalid substitution, and the result of the calculation, though entirely possible for the symbol, might be quite impossible for the men.

Every elementary algebra book contains such problems that lead to quadratic equations, and these have two solutions, which might be 8 and –3, say. We accept 8 as the answer and ignore –3 because we know from experience that there are no such things as negative men, and the only alternative interpretation—that we could get the work done by subtracting three men from our gang—is obviously absurd. . . .

So we just ignore [one] of the mathematical solutions, and quite overlook the significance of that fact—namely, that in the language of mathematics we can tell lies as well as truths, and *within the scope of mathematics itself there is no possible way of telling one from the other.* We can distinguish them *only by experience* or *by reasoning outside the mathematics,* applied to the possible relation between the mathematical solution and its supposed physical correlate.

The point is that a "well-defined mathematical concept" may in fact be a metaphysical impossibility and that the only way to determine this is by getting outside the mathematics to consult what experience or extra-mathematical reasoning tells us reality is like. Time is one of those aspects of reality with which we are most intimately acquainted by experience and which has received extensive philosophical analysis as well. We simply have no comprehension of what it would be for time to be "imaginary" in the mathematical sense. Putting in imaginary numbers for the time variable appears to make no more sense than using negative numbers for the number of men required to do a job. It is a mere mathematical artifice.

Such a use of imaginary numbers for the time coordinate is nothing new. Already in 1920, Sir Arthur Eddington said that readers who found it difficult to understand curved space-time could evade the difficulty by using the "dodge" of imaginary numbers. But, he said, it is "not very profitable" to speculate on the implications of this, because "it can scarcely be regarded as anything more than an analytical device." Imaginary time was only an illustrative tool, "which certainly does not correspond to any physical reality."

Imaginary numbers are useful as mathematical devices which help in the computation of certain equations; but one always converts back to real numbers at the end in order to have some physically meaningful result. Hawking himself admits, "As far as everyday quantum mechanics is concerned, we may regard our use of imaginary time . . . as a merely mathematical device (or trick) to calculate answers about real space-time." But Hawking in his model simply declines to take the final step of re-converting to real numbers. When you do that, the singularity suddenly reappears. Hawking states,

> Only if we could picture the universe in terms of imaginary time would there be no singularities. . . . When one goes back to the real time in which we live, however, there will still appear to be singularities.

Thus, Hawking does not really eliminate the singularity; he only conceals it behind the physically unintelligible artifice of imaginary time.

Secondly, the use of imaginary numbers for the time variable makes time a spatial dimension, which is just bad metaphysics. Space and time are essentially different. Space is ordered by a relation of *betweenness*: for three points x, y, and z on a spatial line, y is between x and z. But time is ordered in addition by a unique relation of *earlier/later than*: for two moments t_1 and t_2 in time, t_1 is earlier than t_2, and t_2 is later than t_1. Spatial points are not related by any such relation; but this relation is essential to the nature of time, as the philosopher George Schlesinger points out: "The relations "before" and "after" have generally been acknowledged as being the most fundamental temporal relations, which means that time deprived of these relations would cease to be time." Thus, it is impossible for time to be a dimension of space. Moreover, time is also ordered by the relations *past/future* with respect to the present. For example, my eating breakfast this morning was once present; but now it is past. There is nothing even remotely similar to this relation among points in space. Thus, space and time are essentially distinct.

But perhaps Hawking can be interpreted as holding, not that time in the earliest stage of the universe is a dimension of space, but that as one goes back in time, time ceases to exist and is replaced by a spatial dimension. But such an interpretation makes no sense. It would mean that the early history of the universe was timeless. But this assertion is contradictory to the claim that this era existed *before* the point that time began. For *before/after* is precisely a temporal relation, as we have seen. Thus, to say that this timeless segment existed *before* time is to presuppose a time before time, which is self-contradictory.

Hawking seems to realize the impossibility of having two successive stages of the universe, one timeless and the other temporal, and so he is driven to the position that our universe's existing in real time is just an illusion! He asserts,

> This might suggest that the so-called imaginary time is really the real time, and that what we call real time is just a figment of our imaginations. In real time, the universe has a beginning and an end at singularities that form a boundary to spacetime and at which the laws of science break down. But in imaginary time, there are

no singularities or boundaries. So maybe what we call imaginary time is really more basic, and what we call real is just an idea that we invent to help us describe what we think the universe is like.

But as Smith points out, such an interpretation is "preposterous . . . at least observationally, since it is perfectly obvious that the universe in which we exist lapses in real rather than imaginary time." If Hawking were right, we could not even correctly say, for example, that Lincoln's assassination occurred after his birth, since this is to assert a temporal relation between these two events.

Significantly, this philosophical critique applies not to the Hartle-Hawking model alone, but to all quantum gravitational models, since they all share the common feature of having real space-time originate in a quantum mechanical region which is a four-dimensional space involving imaginary time. The metaphysical inadequacy of such scenarios is not a deficiency which can be solved through scientific advance precisely because the deficit is metaphysical, not physical. Of course, if some such model is interpreted non-realistically, then no metaphysical objection arises. On a non-realist interpretation, the real beginning of the universe at an initial singularity can be re-described in the language of quantum physics as a non-singular point existing in imaginary time. But the advance here is scientific (in the instrumental sense), not metaphysical. Such a model would not abrogate the fact the universe really began to exist.

It seems evident, therefore, that quantum models of the origin of the universe avoid the beginning of the universe only at the expense of making enormous and unjustified metaphysical assumptions about reality, assumptions which in the end deny the reality of time and temporal becoming and thus vitiate the models based on them as realistic descriptions of the universe. Thus, it appears that none of the alternatives to the Big Bang model of the origin of the universe is plausible. The best scientific evidence available confirms that the universe began to exist. . . .Therefore, on the basis of both philosophical argument and scientific evidence, I think we are justified in accepting our second premiss, that the universe began to exist.

Therefore, the Universe Has a Cause of Its Existence

From the first premiss—that *whatever begins to exist has a cause*—and the second premiss—that *the universe began to exist*—it follows logically that *the universe has a cause.* This conclusion ought to stagger us, to fill us with awe, for it means that the universe was brought into existence by *something* which is greater than and beyond it.

But what is the nature of this first cause of the universe? It seems to me quite plausible that it is a personal being who created the universe. This thesis is supported by both philosophical argument and scientific confirmation.

Philosophical Argument

Consider the following puzzle: we've concluded that the beginning of the universe was the effect of a first cause. By the nature of the case that cosmic cause cannot have any beginning of its existence nor any prior cause. Nor can there have been any changes in this cause, either in its nature or operations, prior to the beginning of the universe. It just exists changelessly without any beginning, and a finite time ago it brought the universe into existence. Now this is exceedingly odd. The cause is in some sense eternal and yet the effect which it produced is not eternal, but began to exist a finite time ago. How can this be? If the necessary and sufficient conditions for the production of the effect are eternal, then why isn't the effect eternal? How can all the causal conditions sufficient for the production of the effect be changelessly existent and yet the effect not also be existent along with the cause? How can the cause exist without the effect?

Let me illustrate what I mean: Let's say the cause of water's freezing is sub-zero temperatures. Whenever the temperature falls below zero degrees Centigrade, the water freezes. Once the cause is given, the effect must follow, and if the cause exists from eternity, the effect must also exist from eternity. If the temperature were to remain below zero degrees from eternity, then any water around would be frozen from eternity. But this seems to imply that if the cause of the universe existed eternally, the universe would also have existed eternally. And this we know to be false.

One might say that the cause came to exist or changed in some way just prior to the first event. But then the cause's beginning or changing would be the first event, and we must ask all over again for its cause. And this cannot go on forever, for we know that a beginningless series of events cannot exist. There must be an absolutely first event, before which there was no change, no previous event. We know that this first event must have been caused. The question is: How can a first event come to exist if the cause of that event exists changelessly and eternally? Why isn't the effect as co-eternal as the cause?

It seems that there is only one way out of this dilemma, and that is to infer that the cause of the universe is a personal agent who chooses to create a universe in time. Philosophers call this type of causation "agent causation," and because the agent is free, he can initiate new effects by freely bringing about conditions which were not previously present. For example, a man sitting from eternity could will to stand up; thus, a temporal effect arises from an eternally existing agent. Similarly, a finite time ago a Creator endowed with free will could have willed to bring the world into being at that moment. In this way, God could exist changelessly and eternally but choose to create the world in time. By "choose" one need not mean that the Creator changes His mind about the decision to create, but that He freely and eternally intends to create a world with a beginning. By exercising his causal power, He therefore brings it about that a world with a beginning comes to exist. So the cause is eternal, but the effect is not. In this way, then, it is possible for the temporal universe to have come to exist from an eternal cause: through the free will of a personal Creator.

The Anthropic Principle

This purely philosophical argument for the personhood of the cause of the origin of the universe receives powerful scientific confirmation from the observed fine-tuning of the universe, which bespeaks intelligent design. Without wanting to go into a discussion of the teleological argument, let me simply say that in recent years the scientific community has been stunned by its discovery of how complex and sensitive a balance of initial conditions must be given in the Big Bang in order for the universe to permit the origin and evolution of intelligent life on Earth. The universe appears, in fact, to have been incredibly fine-tuned from the moment of its inception for the production of intelligent life on Earth at this point in cosmic history.

The incredibly complex and delicately balanced nexus of initial conditions necessary for intelligent life seems to be most plausibly explained if that nexus is the product of intelligent design, that is to say, if the cause of the beginning of the universe is a personal Creator. The scientific evidence thus serves to underscore the conclusion to which philosophical argument has led us. More than that, however: the evidence also suggests a special relationship between the Creator and human beings. For man truly is the crown of creation. Though diminutive in size in comparison with the cosmos, a human being is nonetheless the most complex structure in the universe. After listing a minimum of ten crucial steps in the evolution of *Homo sapiens,* each of which is so improbable that the sun would have ceased to be a main sequence star and so incinerated the Earth before it would occur, Barrow and Tipler estimate that the odds against the assembly of the human genome are between $4^{-180(110,000)}$ and $4^{-360(110,000)}$! They also point out that far from showing the unimportance of human life, the vast size of the universe is a prerequisite of the natural production of just those elements which are necessary to life: ". . . for there to be enough time to construct the constituents of living beings, the Universe must be at least ten billion years old and therefore, as a consequence of its expansion, at least ten billion light years in extent." That the entire universe should thus be so designed as to culminate in man as its most marvelous creation is highly suggestive of some special care of the Creator for human creatures in particular. Indeed, the Creator might be properly understood to be a Cosmic Parent of whom we are the children. The contemporary debate surrounding the Anthropic Principle thus not only confirms the personhood of the Creator, but is also quite suggestive theologically.

So we have both good philosophical and scientific reasons for regarding the cause of the universe as a personal Creator. What more can be known about his nature? On the basis of our philosophical arguments for the beginning of the universe, we know that He must be uncaused and changeless (since an infinite regress of events is impossible). Even if God was causally active prior to the creation of the universe in some sort of metaphysical time (say, creating spiritual realms), there must still be a beginning point to His activity and, hence to change; otherwise, one would have an infinite regress of events, which is impossible. Since we know nothing about God's having been active prior to physical creation, we may assume for simplicity's sake that time (or at least differentiated time) begins at creation and that God without creation is changeless. Since He is changeless without creation, He must be either timeless without creation, or at least "relatively timeless," to borrow the expression of one philosopher; that is, He exists in an undifferentiated time prior to creation. Since He is causally related to the world, He must be in time subsequent to creation (given that the "flow" of time is in some sense real). Since He is changeless without creation, He must be immaterial, since matter inherently involves change. Being immaterial, He must be spaceless as well as timeless. Since He created the universe from nothing, we know that He must be enormously powerful, if not omnipotent. Since He brought the universe into being without any antecedently determining conditions and fine-tuned it with a precision that literally defies comprehension, He must be both free and unimaginably intelligent, if not omniscient. Moreover, the fact that the entire known universe, from the smallest elementary particles to the most distant stars, was designed in such a way as to be a suitable environment for the existence of human life on Earth suggests the astounding conclusion that He may have some special concern for us. These properties constitute the central core of what theists mean by "God."

The book of Genesis declares, "In the beginning God created the heavens and the earth." For thousands of years, muses Robert Jastrow, people who have believed this statement have known the truth which scientists have discovered only within the last fifty years. For the rationalistic scientist (and, we may add, philosopher), the story ends, smiles Jastrow, like a bad dream:

> He has scaled the mountains of ignorance; he is about to conquer the highest peak; as he pulls himself over the final rock, he is greeted by a band of theologians who have been sitting there for centuries.

The beginning of the universe—declared by revelation, established by philosophy, and confirmed by science—thus points beyond itself to God, its Personal Creator.

Objections. Now certain thinkers have objected to the intelligibility of this conclusion. For example, Adolf Grünbaum, a prominent philospher of space and time and a vociferous critic of theism, has marshaled a whole troop of objections against inferring God as the Creator of the universe.[80] As these are very typical, a brief review of his objections should be quite helpful. Grünbaum's objections fall into three groups. Group I seeks to cast doubt upon the concept of "cause" in the argument for a cause of the universe. (1) When we say that everything has a cause, we use the word "cause" to mean something that transforms previously existing materials from one state to another. But when we infer that the universe has a cause, we must mean by "cause" something that creates its effect out of nothing. Since these two meanings of "cause" are not the same, the argument is guilty of equivocation and is thus invalid. (2) It does not follow from the necessity of there being a cause that the cause of the universe is a conscious agent. (3) It is logically fallacious to infer that there is a *single* conscious agent who created the universe.

But these objections do not seem to present any insuperable difficulties: (1) The univocal concept of "cause" employed throughout the argument is the concept of something which brings about or produces its effects. Whether this production involves transformation of already existing materials or creation out of nothing is an incidental question. Thus, the charge of equivocation is groundless. (2) The personhood of the cause does not follow from the cosmological argument proper, but from an analysis of the notion of a first cause of the beginning of the universe, confirmed by Anthropic considerations. (3) The inference to a single cause of the origin of the universe seems justified in light of the principle, commonly accepted in science, that one should not multiply causes beyond necessity. One is justified in inferring only causes such as are necessary to explain the effect in question; positing any more would be gratuitous. Since the universe is a single effect originating in the Big Bang event, we have no grounds for inferring a plurality of causes.

The objections of Group II relate the notion of causality to the temporal series of events: (1) Causality is logically compatible with an infinite, beginningless series of events. (2) If everything has a cause of its existence, then the cause of the universe must also have a cause of its existence.

Both of these objections, however, seem to be based on misunderstandings. (1) It is not the concept of causality which is incompatible with an infinite series of past events. Rather the incompatibility, as we have seen, is between the notion of an actually infinite number of things and the series of past events. That causality has nothing to do with it may be seen by reflecting on the fact that the philosophical arguments for the beginning of the universe would work even if the events were all spontaneous, causally non-connected events. (2) The argument does not presuppose that everything has a cause. Rather the operative causal principle is that *whatever begins to exist has a cause.* Something that exists eternally and, hence, without a beginning would not need to have a cause. This is not special pleading for God, since the atheist has always maintained the same thing about the universe: it is beginningless and uncaused. The difference between these two hypotheses is that the atheistic view has been shown to be untenable.

Group III objections are aimed at the alleged claim that creation from nothing surpasses all un-

derstanding: (1) If creation out of nothing is incomprehensible, then it is irrational to believe in such a doctrine. (2) An incomprehensible doctrine cannot explain anything.

But with regard to (1), creation from nothing is not incomprehensible in Grünbaum's sense. By "incomprehensible" Grünbaum appears to mean "unintelligible" or "meaningless." But the statement that a finite time ago a transcendent cause brought the universe into being out of nothing is clearly a meaningful statement, not mere gibberish, as is evident from the very fact that we are debating it. We may not understand *how* the cause brought the universe into being out of nothing, but then it is even more incomprehensible, in this sense, how the universe could have popped into being out of nothing without *any* cause, material or productive. One cannot avert the necessity of a cause by positing an absurdity. (2) The doctrine, being an intelligible statement, obviously does constitute a purported explanation of the origin of the universe. It may be a metaphysical rather than a scientific explanation, but it is no less an explanation for that.

Grünbaum has one final objection against inferring a cause of the origin of the universe: the cause of the Big Bang can be neither *after* the Big Bang (since backward causation is impossible) nor *before* the Big Bang (since time begins at or after the Big Bang). Therefore, the universe's beginning to exist cannot have a cause. But this argument pretty clearly confronts us with a false dilemma. For why couldn't God's creating the universe be *simultaneous* (or coincident) with the Big Bang? On the view I've defended, God may be conceived to be timeless or relatively timeless without creation and in time at and subsequent to the first moment of creation.

None of Grünbaum's objections, therefore, seems to undermine the credibility of our argument for God as the Personal Creator of the universe.

Hence, amazing as it may seem, the most plausible answer to the question of why something exists rather than nothing is that God exists.

I.A.7   A Critique of the *Kalām* Cosmological Argument

PAUL DRAPER

Paul Draper is associate professor of philosophy at Florida International University in Miami and the author of several essays in philosophy of religion. In this article he analyzes William Lane Craig's two versions of the cosmological argument: the argument from contingency and the kalām *argument (selection I.A.5). Draper argues that the argument rests on an equivocation of the phrase "begins to exist," and that this fallacy undermines its force.*

Epistemology begins in doubt, ethics in conflict, and metaphysics in *wonder.*

In a recent book,[1] William Lane Craig offers a philosophical and scientific defense of a very old and very wonderful argument: the *kalām* cosmological argument. Unlike other cosmological arguments, the *kalām* argument bases its conclusion that the universe has a cause of its existence on the premise that the universe began to exist a finite time ago. Craig calls it the "*kalām*" cosmological argument because "*kalām*" is the name of a theological movement within Islam that used reason, including this argument, to defend the Muslim faith against philosophical objections. After being fully developed by Arab thinkers like al-Kindi and al-Ghazali, the argument eventually made its way to the West, where it was rejected by St. Thomas Aquinas and defended by St. Bonaventure.[2] My focus in this paper will be on Craig's philosophical defense of the argument. I will try to show that this defense fails, both because it fails to establish that the universe had a beginning and because it commits the fallacy of equivocation.

Compare the following two cosmological arguments, each of which concludes that the universe has a cause of its existence:

(1) Every contingent thing (including things that are infinitely old) has a cause of its existence.
(2) The universe is contingent.
(3) Therefore, the universe has a cause of its existence.

(1) Everything that begins to exist has a cause of its existence.
(2) The universe began to exist.
(3) Therefore, the universe has a cause of its existence.

The first of these arguments is sometimes called the argument from contingency. It was suggested by Aristotle, clearly formulated by Arabic philosophers like ibn Sina, and later championed in the West by St. Thomas Aquinas. I find it completely unpersuasive. For although the second premise is clearly true (so long as "contingent" means "logically contingent"), I do not find the first premise appealing at all. If something is infinitely old, then it has always existed, and it's hard to see why something that has always existed requires a cause of its existence, even if it is logically possible that it not have existed. (Indeed, it's not even clear that something that has always existed *could* have a cause of its existence.)

The second of these arguments is the *kalām* cosmological argument. This argument avoids the weakness of the argument from contingency by denying that the universe is infinitely old and maintaining that the universe needs a cause, not because it is contingent, but rather because it had a beginning. In other words, it replaces the weak premise that every contingent thing needs a cause of its existence with the compelling premise that everything that begins to exist needs a cause of its existence. Of course, a price must be paid for strengthening the first premise: the second premise—that the universe began to exist—is not by a long shot as unquestionably true as the claim that the universe is contingent.

Craig, however, provides a spirited and plausible defense of this premise. He offers four arguments in support of it, two of which are philosophical (armchair cosmology at its best) and two of which are scientific (but still interesting). Both philosophical arguments depend on a distinction between a potential infinite and an actual infinite. A potential infinite is a series or collection that can increase forever without limit but is always finite (e.g., the set of events that have occurred since the birth of my daughter or the set of completed years after 1000 BCE). An actual infinite is a set of distinct things (real or not) whose number is actually infinite (e.g., the set of natural numbers). The first philosophical argument claims that there can't be an infinite regress of events, because actual infinites cannot exist in reality. According to the second argument, an infinite regress of events is impossible because, even if actual infinites could exist in reality, they could not be formed by successive addition.

The first scientific argument is based on the evidence for the Big Bang theory, which seems to many scientists to support the view that the universe had a beginning. The second scientific argument appeals to the Second Law of Thermodynamics. According to this law, the amount of energy available to do mechanical work always decreases in a closed system. Thus, since the universe as a whole is a closed system with a finite amount of such energy, an infinitely old universe is incompatible with the fact that we have not yet run out of such energy—the universe has not yet reached its "equilibrium end state." Since I'm no scientist, I will focus my attention on Craig's philosophical arguments, beginning with the second one.

As Craig himself points out, his second philosophical argument is very similar to the argument that Immanuel Kant uses to support the thesis of his first antinomy:

If we assume that the world has no beginning in time, then up to every given moment an eternity has elapsed and there has passed away in the world an infinite series of successive states of things. Now the infinity of a series consists in the fact that it can never be completed through successive synthesis. It thus follows that it is impossible for an infinite world-series to have passed away, and that a beginning of the world is therefore a necessary condition of the world's existence.[3]

Craig formulates the argument as follows:

(i) The temporal series of events is a collection formed by successive addition.
(ii) A collection formed by successive addition cannot be an actual infinite.
(iii) Thus, the temporal series of events cannot be an actual infinite. (from i and ii)
(iv) Therefore, the temporal regress of events is finite. (from iii)[4]

This argument is closely related to Zeno's paradoxes, which depend on the claim that one cannot complete an infinite series of tasks one at a time since that would imply an infinitieth member of the series. As it stands, the argument is unconvincing. For while it is true that one cannot start with a finite collection and then by adding one new member at a time turn it into an infinite collection (no matter how much time one has available), nothing of the sort is required in order for the past to be infinite. For if the temporal regress of events is infinite, then the universe has never had a finite number of past events. Rather, it has always been the case that the collection of past events is infinite. Thus, if the temporal regress of events is infinite, then the temporal series of events is not an infinite collection formed by successively adding to a finite collection. Rather, it is a collection formed by successively adding to an infinite collection. And surely it is not impossible to form an infinite collection by successively adding to an already infinite collection.

One might object that, if the temporal regress of events is infinite, then there must be some event E separated from the birth of my daughter by an infinite number of intermediate events, in which case the collection containing E and all those intermediate events would have to be an actually infinite collection formed by successively adding to a finite collection of events, namely the collection containing E as its only member. This objection fails because it is simply not true that, if the temporal regress of events is infinite, then there must be two events separated by an infinite number of intermediate events. For consider the set of natural numbers. It is actually infinite, yet every member of it is such that there is a finite number of members between it and its first member.[5]

Craig's first philosophical argument is, I believe, much more promising than his second. It bases its conclusion that the temporal regress of physical events must be finite—there must have been a first physical event—on the premises that an actual infinite cannot exist in reality and an infinite temporal regress of events is an actual infinite.[6] From this and the further claim that a first physical event could not have been preceded by an eternal absolutely quiescent physical universe, the conclusion is drawn that the physical universe had a beginning. The first stage of this argument can be formulated as follows:

(a) No set of real things is actually infinite.
(b) If there was no first event, then the set of all real events occurring prior to the birth of my daughter is actually infinite.
(c) Therefore, there was a first event.

Craig defends premise (a) of this argument by pointing out that the assumption that a set of real things is actually infinite has paradoxical implications.[7] For example, it implies that we could have a library consisting of infinitely many black books (each might be assigned an even number). We could then add infinitely many red books (each might be assigned an odd number) and yet not increase the number of books in the library by a single volume. Indeed, we could add infinitely many different colors of books with infinitely many books of each color (the red books could be assigned rational numbers between 0 and 1, the black books rational numbers between 1 and 2, and so on) and not increase our collection by a single volume.

These paradoxes arise because the following three statements constitute an inconsistent triad:

S1: A set has more members than any of its proper subsets.
S2: If the members of two sets can be placed in one-to-one correspondence, then neither set has more members than the other.
S3: There are actually infinite sets.

For example, since the set of even numbers has one-to-one correspondence with the set of natural numbers and even with the set of rational numbers, S2 implies that one could add infinitely many red books or infinitely many books of each of infinitely many different colors to the library without increasing the size of that library's collection. (One need only make sure that the additions are *denumerably* infinite.) But of course S1 implies that any such addition would increase the size of the collection since the set of even numbers is a proper subset both of the set of natural numbers and of the set of rational numbers. Thus, two intuitively appealing principles together imply a contradiction on the assumption that there can be an actually infinite collection of books. One way to avoid this contradiction is to reject the assumption that there can be an actually infinite collection of books. So the underlying argument in defense of the claim that no collection of real things is actually infinite is simply that, since S1 and S2 are both true of collections of real things, it follows that S3 is not true of such collections—no collections of real things are actually infinite.

Craig claims that Georg Cantor's theory of transfinite numbers is consistent because it rejects the first member of the triad. But this member is not rejected because it can be proven false about actually infinite sets nor is the second member accepted because it can be proven that if a one-to-one correspondence between the elements of two actually infinite sets can be established then the sets are equivalent. Rather, equivalent sets are simply defined as sets having one-to-one correspondence. Thus, while Cantor's theory is a consistent mathematical system, there is, according to Craig, no reason to think that it has any interesting ontological implications. In particular, it does not provide any reason to think that S1 is false about actually infinite sets and hence provides no justification for thinking that actual infinites can exist in reality.[8]

Notice that, if Craig is right that past events are real but future events are not, then his argument for a first event does not commit him to the position that there is a last event. For consider the following parallel argument for the conclusion that there will be a last event:

(a) No set of real things is actually infinite.

(d) If there will be no last event, then the set of all real events occurring after the birth of my daughter is actually infinite.

(e) Therefore, there will be a last event.

Since future events are not real, the second premise of this argument is false. If there is no last event, then the set of all real events occurring after the birth of my daughter is merely potentially infinite—not actually infinite. This collection can increase in size indefinitely, but it will always be finite. Past events, on the other hand, are all real. So if there is no first past event, then the set of all real past events is actually infinite, not potentially infinite. Craig concludes that, although there may be no last event, there must be a first event, and hence, since matter cannot exist without events occurring, it follows that the universe has not always existed—it began to exist.

Although this fascinating argument for the second premise of the *kalām* argument may be sound, Craig has not given us adequate reason to believe it is. The problem concerns the inconsistent triad mentioned above. What Craig needs to do is to show that, when it comes to collections of real things, we should reject the third member of the triad instead of S1 or S2. But he has not shown this. S1 and S2 are certainly true for finite collections. But it's far from clear that they are true for all collections. Allow me to explain why.

Consider S1, which says that a set has more members than any of its proper subsets. If "more" means "a greater number," then the claim that S1 is true for actually infinite sets requires us to make sense of claiming that actually infinite sets have a *number* of members. But an actually infinite set doesn't have a natural number of members or a rational number of members or a real number of members, so one such set can't have a greater natural or rational or real number of members than another. Of course, an actually infinite set does have a transfinite number of members. But transfinite numbers are what Cantor defines them to be. And given his definition, it simply isn't true that actually infinite sets have a greater transfinite number of members than all of their proper subsets. We

could say that an actually infinite set has a greater "infinite number" of members than all of its proper subsets, but Craig gives us no theory of infinite numbers that would justify that claim.

Of course, Craig might claim that no such theory is necessary, that we don't even need to make use of the word *number* here; for it's just obvious that, in some sense of the word *more,* any set that has every member that another set has and some members it doesn't have has more members than the other set. I agree this is obvious, but in the case of infinite sets, this is obvious only because "more" can just mean "has every member the other set has and some members it doesn't have." If, however, we grant Craig that S1 is true on these grounds, then why accept S2? Why not claim instead that actually infinite collections of real objects are possible, but the fact that two of them have one-to-one correspondence is not a good reason to believe that neither has "more" members than the other? Why, for example, is it more reasonable to believe that actually infinite libraries are impossible than to believe that, although they are possible, one such library can have "more" books than a second despite the fact that the books in the first can be placed in one-to-one correspondence with the books in the second? Craig provides no good answer to these questions. Obviously he cannot all of a sudden appeal to Cantor's theory to justify accepting S2. For that would commit him to rejecting S1. And since, when infinite sets are compared, the word *more* cannot mean what it does when finite sets are compared, the fact that S2 is true for finite sets is not by itself a good reason to believe that it is true for all sets.

So Craig fails to show that S1 and S2 are both true of all collections of real objects, and hence he fails to show that actually infinite collections of real objects are impossible. Therefore, his first philosophical argument, like his second, fails to establish that an infinite regress of events is impossible and so fails to establish that the universe began to exist. This leaves us with Craig's scientific arguments. Since I lack the expertise to evaluate these arguments, let's assume, for the sake of arguments, that they succeed and hence that the universe did begin to exist. Must we then conclude that the *kalām* argument succeeds? This would be a profound result. Granted, this argument doesn't get all the way to God's existence. But accepting its conclusion does require rejecting naturalism—since nothing can be a cause of its own existence, a cause outside the natural world would be required.

As wonderful as this conclusion is, I do not believe that Craig's defense of the *kalām* argument justifies accepting it, even assuming that his scientific arguments are sound. This is because Craig commits the fallacy of equivocation. The verb "to begin" has a narrow or strict sense and a broad or loose sense. In the narrow sense, "to begin" means "to begin within time." When used in this way, "x begins to exist" implies that there was a time at which x did not exist and then a later time at which x exists. But "to begin" can also mean "to begin either within or with time." When used in this way, "x begins to exist" does not imply that there was a time at which x did not exist, because the past may itself be finite in which case something that begins to exist at the first moment in time is such that there never was a time at which it did not exist—it begins with time rather than within time. Now consider the two premises of the *kalām* argument in the light of this distinction.

The second premise is that the universe began to exist. All of Craig's arguments in favor of this premise, including his scientific ones, would be unsound if one interpreted "began to exist" in the second premise as meaning "began to exist within time." For nothing in these arguments counts against a relational view of time. And on a relational view of time, a first temporal event is simultaneous with a first moment in time. This would mean that, if the temporal series of past events is finite, then the universe began to exist with time. Indeed, if anything, the arguments in favor of the second premise support a beginning with time. For if an infinite regress of events is an actual infinite and for that reason impossible, then it would seem that an infinite past would be an actual infinite and for that reason impossible. Moreover, one of Craig's scientific arguments appeals to an interpretation of the Big Bang Theory according to which time did not exist "before" the big bang. So the most that Craig

has established is that the universe began to exist either within or with time.

The first premise is that anything that begins to exist has a cause of its existence. What does "begins to exist" mean here? Craig defends this premise by claiming that it is an "empirical generalisation enjoying the strongest support experience affords."[9] But experience only supports the claim that anything that begins to exist *within* time has a cause of its existence. For we have no experience whatsoever of things beginning to exist with time.[10] Such things would require timeless causes. And even if it is conceptually possible for a temporal event to have a timeless cause, we certainly have no experience of this. Of course, Craig also claims that premise (1) is intuitively obvious—that it needs no defense at all. But it is far from obvious that a universe that begins to exist with time needs a cause of its existence. Like an infinitely old universe, a universe that begins to exist with time has always existed—for any time t, the universe existed at t. And once again, it's far from obvious that something that has always existed requires a cause for its existence. It's not even clear that such a thing *could* have a cause of its existence.

So in order to be justified in believing both of the premises of the argument—justified, that is, solely on the basis of Craig's defense of those premises—we would need to equivocate on the meaning of "begins to exist." We would need to use this term in the narrow sense in the first premise and in the broad sense in the second premise. But then the conclusion of the argument would not follow from its premises. Thus, Craig commits the fallacy of equivocation.[11]

Do my objections to Craig's defense of the *kalām* argument prove that it is doomed? I don't think so. The argument remains promising. Perhaps, for example, it could be shown that an absolute theory of time is correct, and that such a theory, together with scientific or new philosophical evidence against an infinitely old universe, implies a beginning of the universe within time. Or perhaps it could be shown that the universe began to exist with time and that even something that begins to exist with time requires a cause of its existence. So my conclusion is not that the *kalām* argument should be dismissed. It is just that it has not yet been adequately defended. I still *wonder* whether the argument is a good one.

Notes

1. William Lane Craig, *The Kalām Cosmological Argument* (New York: Harper & Row Publishers), 1979.

2. For a brief but interesting history of the argument, see Craig, Part I.

3. Immanuel Kant, *Critique of Pure Reason*, trans. Norman Kemp Smith (London: Macmillan & Co., 1929), p. 396. Quoted by Craig on p. 189.

4. Craig, p. 103.

5. Cf. Quentin Smith, "Infinity and the Past," in *Theism, Atheism, and Big Bang Cosmology,* ed. William Lane Craig and Quentin Smith (Oxford: Clarendon Press, 1993), pp. 78–83; Antony Flew, "The Case for God Challenged," in *Does God Exist?: The Great Debate,* ed. J. P. Moreland and Kai Nielsen (Nashville: Thomas Nelson Publishers, 1990), p. 164; and Keith Parsons, "Is There a Case for Christian Theism?" in *Does God Exist?: The Great Debate,* p. 187.

6. Craig, p. 69.

7. Craig, pp. 82–87.

8. Craig, pp. 94–95.

9. Craig, p. 145. Craig also suggests here that premise (1) could be defended by appealing to an a priori category of causality. Such Kantian maneuvering does not seem very promising in this context. For in order to reconcile it with the realism presupposed by the *kalām* argument, one would need to claim that the causal principle must, as a necessary precondition of thought, hold without exception in the noumenal world!

10. Cf. Quentin Smith, "The Uncaused Beginning of the Universe," in *Theism, Atheism, and Big Bang Cosmology,* p. 123.

11. In "The Caused Beginning of the Universe" (in *Theism, Atheism, and Big Bang Cosmology*) Craig denies that his inference is equivocal on the grounds that "our conviction of the truth of the causal principle is not based upon an inductive survey of existents in space-time, but rather upon the metaphysical intuition that something cannot come out of nothing" (p. 147). Of course, he did appeal to such a survey in his book, but Craig claims that this was just "a last-ditch defence of the principle designed to appeal to the hard-headed empiricist who resists the metaphysical intuition that properly grounds our conviction of the principle" (p. 147, note 13). This response to the charge of equivocation is not at all convincing. For metaphysical intuitions about contingent matters are notoriously unreliable—that's why so many contemporary philosophers are, quite justifiably, "hard-headed empiricists." Further, at the risk of committing the genetic fallacy, it is worth pointing out that it is probably our experience of things beginning to exist within time that causes some of us to have the metaphysical intuition that something cannot come out of nothing.

I.B The Teleological Argument for the Existence of God

The teleological argument for the existence of God begins with the premise that the world exhibits intelligent purpose or order, and it proceeds to the conclusion that there must be or probably is a divine intelligence, a supreme designer, to account for the observed or perceived intelligent purpose or order. Although the argument has been cited in Plato, in the Bible (Rom. 1), and in Cicero, the clearest sustained treatment of it is found in William Paley's *National Theology* (1802). In his opening chapter, included here as our first selection, he offers his famous "watch" argument, which begins as follows:

> In crossing a heath, suppose I pitched my foot against a stone, and were asked how the stone came to be there, I might possibly answer, that for anything I knew to the contrary, it had lain there forever; nor would it, perhaps, be very easy to show the absurdity of this answer. But suppose I found a watch upon the ground, and it should be inquired how the watch happened to be in that place, I should hardly think of the answer which I had before given—that, for anything I knew, the watch might have always been there. Yet why should not this answer serve for the watch as well as for the stone? Why is it not as admissible in the second case, as in the first?

Paley argues that just as we infer an intelligent designer to account for the purpose-revealing watch, we must analogously infer an intelligent grand designer to account for the purpose-revealing world. "Every indication of contrivance, every manifestation of design, which existed in the watch, exists in the works of nature; with the difference, on the side of nature, of being greater and more, and that in a degree which exceeds all computation." The skeleton of the argument looks like this:

1. Human artifacts are products of intelligent design (purpose).
2. The universe resembles these human artifacts.
3. Therefore, the universe is (probably) a product of intelligent design (purpose).
4. But the universe is vastly more complex and gigantic than a human artifact.
5. Therefore, there probably is a powerful and vastly intelligent designer who designed the universe.

Ironically, Paley's argument was attacked even before Paley had set it down, for David Hume (1711–1776) had long before written his famous *Dialogues Concerning Natural Religion* (published posthumously in 1779), the classic critique of the teleological argument. Paley seems to have been unaware of it. A selection from the *Dialogue* is included as our second reading. In it, the natural theologian, Cleanthes, debates the orthodox believer, Demea, and the skeptic or critic, Philo, who does most of the serious arguing.

Hume, through Philo, attacks the argument from several different angles. He argues first of all that the universe is not sufficiently like the productions of human design to support the argument. Philo puts it as follows:

> But can you think, Cleanthes, that your usual phlegm and philosophy have been preserved in so wide a step as you have taken, when you compare to the universe, houses, ships, furniture, machines and from their similarity in some circumstances infer a similarity in their causes? . . . But can a conclusion, with any propriety, be transferred from the parts to the whole? Does not the great disproportion bar all comparison and inferences? From observing the growth of a hair, can we learn anything concerning the generation of a man?

We cannot argue from the parts to the whole. You, the reader, will want to test this judgment with some possible counterexamples.

Philo's second objection is that the analogy from artifact to divine designer fails because you have no other universe with which to compare this one. We would need to make such a comparison in order to decide if it were the kind of universe that was designed or simply the kind that developed on its own. As C. S. Peirce put it, "Universes are not as plentiful as blackberries." Since there is only one of them, we have no standard of comparison by which to judge it. Paley's answer to this would be that if we could find one clear instance of purposiveness in nature (e.g., the eye), it would be sufficient to enable us to conclude that there is probably an intelligent designer. Hume makes several other points against the design argument, which you will want to examine on your own.

A modern objection to the argument, one that was anticipated by Hume, is that based on Darwinian evolution, which has cast doubt upon the notion of teleological explanation altogether. In his *Origin of Species* (1859) Darwin claimed that the process of development from simpler organisms to more complex ones took place gradually over millions of years through an apparently nonpurposive process of trial and error, of natural selection and survival of the fittest. As Julian Huxley put it, the evolutionary process

results immediately and automatically from the basic property of living matter—that of self-copying, but with occasional errors. Self-copying leads to multiplication and competition; the errors in self-copying are what we call mutations, and mutations will inevitably confer different degrees of biological advantage or disadvantage on their possessors. The consequence will be differential reproduction down the generations—in other words, natural selection.*

As important as Darwin's contribution is in offering us an alternative model of biological development, it doesn't altogether destroy the argument from design. The theist can still argue that the process of natural selection is the *way* an ultimate designer is working out his purpose for the world. The argument from design could still be used as an argument to the best explanation.

Such an argument is set forth in the third and final reading in this section, "The Argument from Design," excerpted from Richard Swinburne's *The*

---

*Evolution as Process (New York: Harper & Row, 1953), 4.

Existence of God (1979). Swinburne, a modern Cleanthes, rejects all deductive forms of arguments for the existence of God, but in their place he sets a series of inductive arguments: versions of the cosmological argument, the teleological argument, the argument from religious experience, and others. Although none of these alone proves the existence of God or shows it to be more probable than not, each adds to the probability of God's existence. Together they constitute a cumulative case for theism. There is something crying for an explanation: Why does this grand universe exist? Together the arguments for God's existence provide a plausible explanation of the existence of the universe, of why we are here, of why there is anything at all and not just nothing.

Swinburne's arguments are set in terms of confirmation theory. He distinguishes arguments that are "P-inductive" (in which the premises make the conclusion probable) from those that are "C-inductive" (in which the premises confirm the probability of the conclusion or make it more probable than it otherwise would be—although without showing the conclusion to be more probable than not). The cosmological and teleological arguments are, according to Swinburne, good C-inductive arguments. Since there is no counterargument to theism (note that Swinburne believes he can successfully meet the argument from evil; see Part 3) and since religious experience offers "considerable evidential force" in favor of theism, the cumulative effect is "sufficient to make theism all over probable."

The chapter on teleological arguments in Swinburne's book contains the essential structure of the confirmation argument used in the rest of his arguments. From it you should be able to figure out the kind of case he makes for those other arguments. A few notes are crucial to an understanding of Swinburne's essay. First of all, Swinburne believes that scientific, purely deterministic accounts—what he calls the Hempel account—are not the only type of explanatory theory. We can also explain things in terms of rational intentions or agency. Indeed, a full explanation often demands such an account. Theism makes use of such a personal explanatory account.

Secondly, Swinburne puts a great deal of weight on the notion of simplicity. All things being equal, if theory *A* is simpler than theory *B*, theory *A* is to be accepted as the better explanatory account. This is a version of Occam's Razor, which counsels us not to multiply entities unnecessarily. You will want to think through this principle and decide whether or to what degree it applies to the teleological argument. Does Swinburne's account get more mileage from such a principle than is warranted?

Finally, Swinburne uses Bayes's theorem to sustain his argument: Let h = a theory or hypothesis; let e = the evidential phenomena; and let k = our background knowledge. Then $P(h/k)$ repre-sents the prior probability of h, and $P(e/h,k)$ represents the probability of the phenomena occurring given our hypothesis and our background knowledge. $P(h/e,k)$ represents the probability of h being true given the available evidence and our background knowledge. You do not need to understand the intricacies of Bayes's theorem in order to follow Swinburne's reasoning, but you should beware of his use of k, the background knowledge. What does it come to? What is our background knowledge (minus the evidence in question) with regard to the hypothesis that God exists?

We turn now to the readings.

I.B.1   The Watch and the Watchmaker

WILLIAM PALEY

William Paley (1743–1805), Archdeacon of Carlisle, was a leading evangelical apologist. His most important work is Natural Theology, or Evidences of the Existence and Attributes of the Deity Collected from the Appearances of Nature *(1802), the first chapter of which is reprinted here. Paley argues that just as we infer an intelligent designer to account for the purpose-revealing watch, so likewise we must infer an intelligent Grand Designer to account for the purpose-revealing world.*

Statement of the Argument

In crossing a heath, suppose I pitched my foot against a stone, and were asked how the stone came to be there, I might possibly answer, that, for anything I knew to the contrary, it had lain there for ever; nor would it, perhaps, be very easy to show the absurdity of this answer. But suppose I found a watch upon the ground, and it should be inquired how the watch happened to be in that place, I should hardly think of the answer which I had given—that, for anything I knew, the watch might have always been there. Yet why should not this answer serve for the watch as well as for the stone? why is it not as admissible in the second case as in the first? For this reason, and for no other; viz., that, when we come to inspect the watch, we perceive (what we could not discover in the stone) that its several parts are framed and put together for a purpose, e.g. that they are so formed and adjusted as to produce motion, and that motion so regulated as to point out the hour of the day; that, if the different parts had been differently shaped from what they are, if a different size from what they are, or placed after any other manner, or in any other order than that in which they are placed, either no motion at all would have been carried on in the machine, or none which would have answered the use that is now served by it. To reckon up a few of the plainest of these parts, and of their offices, all tending to one result:—We see a cylindrical box containing a coiled elastic spring, which, by its

From William Paley, *Natural Theology, or Evidences of the Existence and Attributes of the Deity Collected from the Appearances of Nature* (1802).

endeavor to relax itself, turns round the box. We next observe a flexible chain (artificially wrought for the sake of flexure) communicating the action of the spring from the box to the fusee. We then find a series of wheels, the teeth of which catch in, and apply to, each other, conducting the motion from the fusee to the balance, and from the balance to the pointer, and, at the same time, by the size and shape of those wheels, so regulating that motion as to terminate in causing an index, by an equable and measured progression, to pass over a given space in a given time. We take notice that the wheels are made of brass, in order to keep them from rust; the springs of steel, no other metal being so elastic; that over the face of the watch there is placed a glass, a material employed in no other part of the work, but in the room of which, if there had been any other than a transparent substance, the hour could not be seen without opening the case. This mechanism being observed, (it requires indeed an examination of the instrument, and perhaps some previous knowledge of the subject, to perceive and understand it; but being once, as we have said, observed and understood,) the inference, we think, is inevitable, that the watch must have had a maker; that there must have existed, at some time, and at some place or other, an artificer or artificers who formed it for the purpose which we find it actually to answer; who comprehended its construction, and designed its use.

I. Nor would it, I apprehend, weaken the conclusion, that we had never seen a watch made; that we had never known an artist capable of making one; that we were altogether incapable of executing such a piece of workmanship ourselves, or of understanding in what manner it was performed; all this being no more than what is true of some exquisite remains of ancient art, of some lost and to the generality of mankind, of the more curious productions of modern manufacture. Does one man in a million know how oval frames are turned? Ignorance of this kind exalts our opinion of the unseen and unknown artist's skill, if he be unseen and unknown, but raises no doubt in our minds of the existence and agency of such an artist, at some former time, and in some place or other. Nor can I perceive that it varies at all the inference, whether

the question arise concerning a human agent, or concerning an agent of a different species, or an agent possessing, in some respect, a different nature.

II. Neither, secondly, would it invalidate our conclusion, that the watch sometimes went wrong, or that it seldom went exactly right. The purpose of the machinery, the design, and the designer, might be evident, and, in the case supposed, would be evident, in whatever way we accounted for the irregularity of the movement, or whether we could account for it or not. It is not necessary that a machine be perfect, in order to show with what design it was made; still less necessary, where the only question is, whether it were made with any design at all.

III. Nor, thirdly, would it bring any uncertainty into the argument, if there were a few parts of the watch, concerning which we could not discover, or had not yet discovered, in what manner they conduced to the general effect; or even some parts, concerning which we could not ascertain whether they conduced to that effect in any manner whatever. For, as to the first branch of the case, if by the loss, or disorder, or decay of the parts in question, the movement of the watch were found in fact to be stopped, or disturbed, or retarded, no doubt would remain in our minds as to the utility or intention of these parts, although we should be unable to investigate the manner according to which, or the connection by which, the ultimate effect depended upon their action or assistance; and the more complex is the machine, the more likely is this obscurity to arise. Then, as to the second thing supposed, namely, that there were parts which might be spared without prejudice to the movement of the watch, and that he had proved this by experiment, these superfluous parts, even if we were completely assured that they were such, would not vacate the reasoning which we had instituted concerning other parts. The indication of contrivance remained, with respect to them, nearly as it was before.

IV. Nor, fourthly, would any man in his senses think the existence of the watch, with its various machinery, accounted for, by being told that it was one out of possible combinations of material forms; that whatever he had found in the place where he found the watch, must have contained some internal configuration or other; and that this configuration might be the structure now exhibited, viz., of the works of a watch, as well as a different structure.

V. Nor, fifthly, would it yield his inquiry more satisfaction, to be answered, that there existed in things a principle of order, which had disposed the parts of the watch into their present form and situation. He never knew a watch made by the principle of order; nor can he even form to himself an idea of what is meant by a principle of order, distinct from the intelligence of the watchmaker.

VI. Sixthly, he would be surprised to hear that the mechanism of the watch was no proof of contrivance, only a motive to induce the mind to think so:

VII. And not less surprised to be informed, that the watch in his hand was nothing more than the result of the laws of *metallic* nature. It is a perversion of language to assign any law as the efficient, operative cause of anything. A law presupposes an agent; for it is only the mode according to which an agent proceeds; it implies a power; for it is the order according to which that power acts. Without this agent, without this power, which are both distinct from itself, the *law* does nothing, is nothing. The expression, "the law of metallic nature," may sound strange and harsh to a philosophic ear; but it seems quite as justifiable as some others which are more familiar to him such as "the law of vegetable nature," "the law of animal nature," or, indeed, as "the law of nature" in general, when assigned as the cause of phenomena in exclusion of agency and power, or when it is substituted into the place of these.

VIII. Neither, lastly, would our observer be driven out of his conclusion, or from his confidence in its truth, by being told that he knew nothing at all about the matter. He knows enough for his argument: he knows the utility of the end: he knows the subserviency and adaptation of the means to the end. These points being known, his ignorance of other points, his doubts concerning other points, affect not the certainty of his reasoning. The consciousness of knowing little need not beget a distrust of that which he does know. . . .

Application of the Argument

Every indication of contrivance, every manifestation of design, which existed in the watch, exists in the works of nature; with the difference, on the side of nature, of being greater and more, and that in a degree which exceeds all computation. I mean that the contrivances of nature surpass the contrivances of art, in the complexity, subtilty, and curiosity of the mechanism; and still more, if possible, do they go beyond them in number and variety; yet in a multitude of cases, are not less evidently mechanical, not less evidently contrivances, not less evidently accommodated to their end, or suited to their office, than are the most perfect productions of human ingenuity.

I.B.2   A Critique of the Design Argument

DAVID HUME

From David Hume, *Dialogues Concerning Natural Religion* (1779).

The Scottish empiricist and skeptic David Hume (1711–1776) is one of the most important philosophers who ever lived. The Dialogues Concerning Natural Religion *(published posthumously in 1779) contains the classic critique of the argument from design. Our reading is from Parts 2 and 5 of this dialogue. Cleanthes, who opens our selection, is a natural theologian, the Paley of his time, who opposes both the orthodox believer, Demea, and the skeptic, Philo. It is Philo who puts forth the major criticisms against the argument from design.*

Cleanthes: Look round the world: Contemplate the whole and every part of it: You will find it to be nothing but one great machine, subdivided into an infinite number of lesser machines, which again admit of subdivisions to a degree beyond what human senses and faculties can trace and explain. All these various machines, and even their most minute parts, are adjusted to each other with an accuracy which ravishes into admiration all men who have ever contemplated them. The curious adapting of means to ends, throughout all nature, resembles exactly, though it much exceeds, the productions of human contrivance; of human design, thought, wisdom, and intelligence. Since therefore the effects resemble each other, we are led to infer, by all the rules of analogy, that the causes also resemble, and that the Author of Nature is somewhat similar to the mind of man, though possessed of much larger faculties, proportioned to the grandeur of the work which he has executed. By this argument a *posteriori*, and by this argument alone, do we prove at once the existence of a Deity and his similarity to human mind and intelligence.

Demea: I shall be so free, *Cleanthes,* said *Demea,* as to tell you that from the beginning I could not approve of your conclusion concerning the similarity of the Deity to men; still less can I approve of the mediums by which you endeavor to establish it. What! No demonstration of the Being of God! No abstract arguments! No proofs a *priori*! Are these which have hitherto been so much insisted on by philosophers all fallacy, all sophism? Can we reach no farther in this subject than experience and probability? I will say not that this is betraying the cause of a Deity; but surely, by this affected candor, you give advantages to atheists which they never could obtain by the mere dint of argument and reasoning.

Philo: What I chiefly scruple in this subject, said *Philo,* is not so much that all religious arguments are by *Cleanthes* reduced to experience, as that they appear not to be even the most certain and irrefragible of that inferior kind. That a stone will fall, that

fire will burn, that the earth has solidity, we have observed a thousand and a thousand times; and when any new instance of this nature is presented, we draw without hesitation the accustomed inference. The exact similarity of the cases gives us a perfect assurance of a similar event, and a stronger evidence is never desired nor sought after. But wherever you depart, in the least, from the similarity of the cases, you diminish proportionably the evidence; and may at last bring it to a very weak *analogy,* which is confessedly liable to error and uncertainty. After having experienced the circulation of the blood in human creatures, we make no doubt that it takes place in *Titius* and *Maevius*; but from its circulation in frogs and fishes it is only a presumption, though a strong one, from analogy that it takes place in men and other animals. The analogical reasoning is much weaker when we infer the circulation of the sap in vegetables from our experience that the blood circulates in animals; and those who hastily followed that imperfect analogy are found, by more accurate experiments, to have been mistaken.

If we see a house, *Cleanthes,* we conclude, with the greatest certainty, that it had an architect or builder because this is precisely that species of effect which we have experienced to proceed from that species of cause. But surely you will not affirm that the universe bears such a resemblance to a house that we can with the same certainty infer a similar cause, or that the analogy is here entire and perfect. The dissimilitude is so striking that the utmost you can here pretend to is a guess, a conjecture, a presumption concerning a similar cause; and how that pretension will be received in the world, I leave you to consider.

Cleanthes: It would surely be very ill received, replied *Cleanthes;* and I should be deservedly blamed and detested did I allow that the proofs of a Deity amounted to no more than a guess or conjecture. But is the whole adjustment of means to ends in a house and in the universe so slight a resemblance? The economy of final causes? The order, proportion, and arrangement of every part? Steps of a stair are plainly contrived that human legs may use them in mounting; and this inference is certain and infallible. Human legs are also contrived for walking and mounting; and this inference, I allow, is not altogether so certain because of the dissimilarity which you remark; but does it, therefore, deserve the name only of presumption or conjecture?

Demea: Good God! cried *Demea,* interrupting him, where are we? Zealous defenders of religion allow that the proofs of a Deity fall short of perfect evidence! And you, *Philo,* on whose assistance I depended in proving the adorable mysteriousness of the Divine Nature, do you assent to all these extravagant opinions of *Cleanthes?* For what other name can I give them? or, why spare my censure when such principles are advanced, supported by such an authority, before so young a man as *Pamphilus?*

Philo: You seem not to apprehend, replied *Philo,* that I argue with *Cleanthes* in his own way, and, by showing him the dangerous consequences of his tenets, hope at last to reduce him to our opinion. But what sticks most with you, I observe, is the representation which *Cleanthes* has made of the argument *a posteriori;* and, finding that that argument is likely to escape your hold and vanish into air, you think it so disguised that you can scarcely believe it to be set in its true light. Now, however much I may dissent, in other respects, from the dangerous principle of *Cleanthes,* I must allow that he has fairly represented that argument, and I shall endeavor so to state the matter to you that you will entertain no further scruples with regard to it.

Were a man to abstract from everything which he knows or has seen, he would be altogether incapable, merely from his own ideas, to determine what kind of scene the universe must be, or to give the preference to one state or situation of things above another. For as nothing which he clearly conceives could be esteemed impossible or implying a contradiction, every chimera of his fancy would be upon an equal footing; nor could he assign any just reason why he adheres to one idea or system, and rejects the others which are equally possible.

Again, after he opens his eyes and contemplates the world as it really is, it would be impossible for him at first to assign the cause of any one event, much less of the whole of things, or of the universe.

He might set his fancy a rambling, and she might bring him in an infinite variety of reports and representations. These would all be possible; but, being all equally possible, he would never of himself give a satisfactory account for his preferring one of them to the rest. Experience alone can point out to him the true cause of any phenomenon.

Now, according to this method of reasoning, *Demea,* it follows (and is, indeed, tacitly allowed by *Cleanthes* himself) that order, arrangement, or the adjustment of final causes, is not of itself any proof of design, but only so far as it has been experienced to proceed from that principle. For aught we can know *a priori,* matter may contain the source or spring of order originally within itself, as well as mind does; and there is no more difficulty in conceiving that the several elements, from an internal unknown cause, may fall into the most exquisite arrangement, than to conceive that their ideas, in the great universal mind, from a like internal unknown cause, fall into that arrangement. The equal possibility of both these suppositions is allowed. But, by experience, we find, according to *Cleanthes,* that there is a difference between them. Throw several pieces of steel together, without shape or form; they will never arrange themselves so as to compose a watch. Stone and mortar and wood, without an architect, never erect a house. But the ideas in a human mind, we see, by an unknown, inexplicable economy, arrange themselves so as to form the plan of a watch or house. Experience, therefore, proves that there is an original principle of order in mind, not in matter. From similar effects we infer similar causes. The adjustment of means to ends is alike in the universe, as in a machine of human contrivance. The causes, therefore, must be resembling.

I was from the beginning scandalized, I must own, with this resemblance which is asserted between the Deity and human creatures, and must conceive it to imply such a degradation of the Supreme Being as no sound theist could endure. With your assistance, therefore, *Demea,* I shall endeavor to defend what you justly call the adorable mysteriousness of the Divine Nature, and shall refute this reasoning of *Cleanthes,* provided he allows that I have made a fair representation of it.

When *Cleanthes* had assented, *Philo,* after a short pause, proceeded in the following manner.

That all inferences, *Cleanthes,* concerning fact are founded on experience, and that all experimental reasonings are founded on the supposition that similar causes prove similar effects, and similar effects similar causes, I shall not at present much dispute with you. But observe, I entreat you, with what extreme caution all just reasoners proceed in the transferring of experiments to similar cases. Unless the cases be exactly similar, they repose no perfect confidence in applying their past observation to any particular phenomenon. Every alteration of circumstances occasions a doubt concerning the event; and it requires new experiments to prove certainly that the new circumstances are of no moment or importance. A change in bulk, situation, arrangement, age, disposition of the air, or surrounding bodies; any of these particulars may be attended with the most unexpected consequences. And unless the objects be quite familiar to us, it is the highest temerity to expect with assurance, after any of these changes, an event similar to that which before fell under our observation. The slow and deliberate steps of philosophers here, if anywhere, are distinguished from the precipitate march of the vulgar, who, hurried on by the smallest similitude, are incapable of all discernment or consideration.

But can you think, *Cleanthes,* that your usual phlegm and philosophy have been preserved in so wide a step as you have taken when you compared to the universe houses, ships, furniture, machines; and, from their similarity in some circumstances, inferred a similarity in their causes? Thought, design, intelligence, such as we discover in men and other animals, is no more than one of the springs and principles of the universe, as well as heat or cold, attraction or repulsion, and a hundred others which fall under daily observation. It is an active cause by which some particular parts of nature, we find, produce alterations on other parts. But can a conclusion, with any propriety, be transferred from parts to the whole? Does not the great disproportion bar all comparison and inference? From observing the growth of a hair, can we learn anything concerning the generation of a man? Would the manner of a leaf's blowing, even through perfectly known, afford us any instruction concerning the vegetation of a tree?

But allowing that we were to take the *operations* of one part of nature upon another for the foundation of our judgment concerning the *origin* of the whole (which never can be admitted), yet why select so minute, so weak, so bounded a principle as the reason and design of animals is found to be upon this planet? What peculiar privilege has this little agitation of the brain which we call "thought", that we must thus make it the model of the whole universe? Our partiality in our own favor does indeed present it on all occasions, but sound philosophy ought carefully to guard against so natural an illusion.

So far from admitting, continued *Philo,* that the operations of a part can afford us any just conclusion concerning the origin of the whole, I will not allow any one part to form a rule for another part if the latter be very remote from the former, is there any reasonable ground to conclude that the inhabitants of other planets possess thought, intelligence, reason, or anything similar to these faculties in men? When nature has so extremely diversified her manner of operation in this small globe, can we imagine that she incessantly copies herself throughout so immense a universe? And if thought, as we may well suppose, be confined merely to this narrow corner, and has even there so limited a sphere of action, with what propriety can we assign it for the original cause of all things? The narrow view of a peasant who makes his domestic economy the rule for the government of kingdoms is in comparison a pardonable sophism.

But were we ever so much assured that a thought and reason resembling the human were to be found throughout the whole universe, and were its activity elsewhere vastly greater and more commanding than it appears in this globe; yet I cannot see why the operations of a world constituted, arranged, adjusted, can with any propriety be extended to a world which is in its embryo state, and is advancing towards that constitution and arrangement. By observation we know somewhat of the economy, action, and nourishment of a finished animal; but we must transfer with great caution that observation to the growth of a fetus in the womb, and still more to the formation of an animalcule in the loins of its male parent. Nature, we find, even from our limited experience, possesses an infinite number of springs and principles which incessantly discover themselves on every change of her position and situation. And what new and unknown principles would actuate her in so new and unknown a situation as that of the formation of a universe, we cannot, without the utmost temerity, pretend to determine.

A very small part of this great system, during a very short time, is very imperfectly discovered to us; and do we thence pronounce decisively concerning the origin of the whole?

Admirable conclusion! Stone, wood, brick, iron, brass, have not, at this time, in this minute globe of earth, an order or arrangement without human art and contrivance; therefore, the universe could not originally attain its order and arrangement without something similar to human art. But is a part of nature a rule for another part very wide of the former? Is it a rule for the whole? Is a very small part a rule for the universe? Is nature in one situation a certain rule for nature in another situation vastly different from the former?

And can you blame me, *Cleanthes,* if I here imitate the prudent reserve of *Simonides,* who, according to the noted story, being asked by *Hiero, What God was?* desired a day to think of it, and then two days more; and after that manner continually prolonged the term, without ever bringing in his definition or description? Could you even blame me if I had answered, at first, *that I did not know,* and was sensible that this subject lay vastly beyond the reach of my faculties? You might cry out skeptic and raillier, as much as you pleased; but, having found in so many other subjects much more familiar the imperfections and even contradictions of human reason, I never should expect any success from its feeble conjectures in a subject so sublime and so remote from the sphere of our observation. When two species of objects have always been observed to be conjoined together, I can *infer,* by custom, the existence of one wherever I see the existence of the other; and this I call an argument from experience. But how this argument can have place where the objects, as in the present case, are single, individ-

ual, without parallel or specific resemblance, may be difficult to explain. And will any man tell me with a serious countenance that an orderly universe must arise from some thought and art like the human because we have experience of it? To ascertain this reasoning it were requisite that we had experience of the origin of worlds; and it is not sufficient, surely, that we have seen ships and cities arise from human art and contrivance. . . .

Philo: But to show you still more inconveniences, continued *Philo,* in your anthropomorphism, please to take a new survey of your principles. *Like effects prove like causes.* This is the experimental argument; and this, you say too, is the sole theological argument. Now it is certain that the liker the effects are which are seen and the liker the causes which are inferred, the stronger is the argument. Every departure on either side diminishes the probability and renders the experiment less conclusive. You cannot doubt of the principle; neither ought you to reject its consequences.

All the new discoveries in astronomy which prove the immense grandeur and magnificence of the works of nature are so many additional arguments for a Deity, according to the true system of theism; but, according to your hypothesis of experimental theism, they become so many objections, by removing the effect still farther from all resemblance to the effects of human art and contrivance. For if *Lucretius,* even following the old system of the world, could exclaim:

> Who is strong enough to rule the sum, who to hold in hand and control the mighty bridle of the unfathomable deep? who to turn about all the heavens at one time, and warm the fruitful worlds with ethereal fires, or to be present in all places and at all times.[1]

If Tully[2] esteemed this reasoning so natural as to put it into the mouth of his Epicurean:

> What power of mental vision enabled your master Plato to descry the vast and elaborate architectural process which, as he makes out, the deity adopted in building the structure of the universe? What method of engineering was employed? What tools and levers and derricks? What agents carried out so vast an understanding? And how were air, fire, water, and earth enabled to obey and execute the will of the architect?

If this argument, I say, had any force in former ages, how much greater must it have at present when the bounds of nature are so infinitely enlarged and such a magnificent scene is opened to us? It is still more unreasonable to form our idea of so unlimited a cause from our experience of the narrow productions of human design and invention.

The discoveries by microscopes, as they open a new universe in miniature, are still objections, according to you; arguments, according to me. The farther we push our researches of this kind, we are still led to infer the universal cause of all to be vastly different from mankind, or from any object of human experience and observation.

And what say you to the discoveries in anatomy, chemistry, botany? . . . *Cleanthes:* These surely are no objections, replied *Cleanthes;* they only discover new instances of art and contrivance. It is still the image of mind reflected on us from innumerable objects. *Philo:* Add a mind *like the human,* said *Philo. Cleanthes:* I know of no other, replied *Cleanthes, Philo:* And the liker, the better, insisted *Philo. Cleanthes:* To be sure, said *Cleanthes.*

Philo: Now, *Cleanthes,* said *Philo,* with an air of alacrity and triumph, mark the consequences. First, by this method of reasoning you renounce all claim to infinity in any of the attributes of the Deity. For, as the cause ought only to be proportioned to the effect, and the effect, so far as it falls under our cognizance, is not infinite: What pretensions have we, upon your suppositions, to ascribe that attribute to the Divine Being? You will still insist that, by removing him so much from all similarity to human creatures, we give in to the most arbitrary hypothesis, and at the same time weaken all proofs of his existence.

Secondly, you have no reason, on your theory, for ascribing perfection to the Deity, even in his finite capacity; or for supposing him free from every error, mistake, or incoherence, in his undertakings. There are many inexplicable difficulties in the works of Nature which, if we allow a perfect author to be proved *a priori,* are easily solved, and become only seeming difficulties from the narrow capacity of man, who cannot trace infinite relations. But according to your method of reasoning, these difficulties become all real; and, perhaps, will be insisted on as new instances of likeness to human art and contrivance. At least, you must acknowledge that it is impossible for us to tell, from our limited views, whether this system contains any great faults or deserves any considerable praise if compared to other possible and even real systems. Could a peasant, if the *Aeneid* were read to him, pronounce that poem to be absolutely faultless, or even assign to it its proper rank among the productions of human wit, he who had never seen any other production?

But were this world ever so perfect a production, it must still remain uncertain whether all the excellences of the work can justly be ascribed to the workman. If we survey a ship, what an exalted idea must we form of the ingenuity of the carpenter who framed so complicated, useful, and beautiful a machine? And what surprise must we feel when we find him a stupid mechanic who imitated others, and copied an art which, through a long succession of ages, after multiplied trials, mistakes, corrections, deliberations, and controversies, had been gradually improving? Many worlds might have been botched and bungled, throughout an eternity, ere this system was struck out; much labor lost; many fruitless trials made; and a slow but continued improvement carried on during infinite ages in the art of world-making. In such subjects, who can determine where the truth, nay, who can conjecture where the probability lies, amidst a great number of hypotheses which may be proposed, and a still greater which may be imagined?

And what shadow of an argument, continued Philo, can you produce from your hypothesis to prove the unity of the Deity? A great number of men join in building a house or ship, in rearing a city, in framing a commonwealth; why may not several deities combine in contriving and framing a world? This is only so much greater similarity to human affairs. By sharing the work among several, we may so much further limit the attributes of each, and get rid of that extensive power and knowledge which must be supposed in one deity, and which, according to you, can only serve to weaken the proof of his existence. And if such foolish, such vicious creatures as man can yet often unite in framing and executing one plan, how much more those deities or demons, whom we may suppose several degrees more perfect?

To multiply causes without necessity is indeed contrary to true philosophy, but this principle applies not to the present case. Were one deity antecedently proved by your theory who were possessed of every attribute requisite to the production of the universe, it would be needless, I own (though not absurd), to suppose any other deity existent. But while it is still a question whether all these attributes are united in one subject or dispersed among several independent beings; by what phenomena in nature can we pretend to decide the controversy? Where we see a body raised in a scale, we are sure that there is in the opposite scale, however concealed from sight, some counterpoising weight equal to it; but it is still allowed to doubt whether that weight be an aggregate of several distinct bodies or one uniform united mass. And if the weight requisite very much exceeds anything which we have ever seen conjoined in any single body, the former supposition becomes still more probable and natural. An intelligent being of such vast power and capacity as is necessary to produce the universe, or, to speak in the language of ancient philosophy, so prodigious an animal, exceeds all analogy and even comprehension.

But further, *Cleanthes,* men are mortal, and renew their species by generation; and this is common to all living creatures. The two great sexes of male and female, says *Milton,* animate the world. Why must this circumstance, so universal, so essential, be excluded from those numerous and limited deities? Behold, then, the theogony of ancient times brought back upon us.

And why not become a perfect anthropomorphite? Why not assert the deity or deities to be corporeal, and to have eyes, a nose, mouth, ears, etc.? *Epicurus* maintained that no man had ever seen reason but in a human figure; therefore, the gods must have a human figure. And this argument, which is deservedly so much ridiculed by *Cicero,* becomes, according to you, solid and philosophical.

In a word, *Cleanthes,* a man who follows your hypothesis is able, perhaps, to assert or conjecture that the universe sometime arose from something like design: But beyond that position he cannot ascertain one single circumstance, and is left afterwards to fix every point of his theology by the utmost license of fancy and hypothesis. This world, for aught he knows, is very faulty and imperfect, compared to a superior standard; and was only the first rude essay of some infant deity who afterwards abandoned it, ashamed of his lame performance: It is the work only of some dependent, inferior deity, and is the object of derision to his superiors: It is the production of old age and dotage in some superannuated deity; and ever since his death has run on at adventures, from the first impulse and active force which it received from him. . . . You justly give signs of horror, *Demea,* at these strange suppositions; but these, and a thousand more of the same kind, are *Cleanthes'* suppositions, not mine. From the moment the attributes of the Deity are supposed finite, all these have place. And I cannot, for my part, think that so wild and unsettled a system of theology is, in any respect, preferable to none at all.

Cleanthes: These suppositions I absolutely disown, cried *Cleanthes:* They strike me, however, with no horror, especially when proposed in that rambling way in which they drop from you. On the contrary, they give me pleasure when I see that, by the utmost indulgence of your imagination, you never get rid of the hypothesis of design in the universe, but are obliged at every turn to have recourse to it. To this concession I adhere steadily; and this I regard as a sufficient foundation for religion.

Notes

1. *On the Nature of Things,* II, 1096–1099 (trans. by W. D. Rouse).

2. Tully was a common name for the Roman lawyer and philosopher, Marcus Tullius Cicero, 106–43 BC. The excerpt is from *The Nature of the Gods,* I, viii, 19 (trans. by H. Rackham).

I.B.3   The Argument from Design

RICHARD SWINBURNE

Richard Swinburne (1934–   ) is the Nolloth professor of philosophy of religion at Oxford University. He has written several articles on the traditional arguments for the existence of God. The following selection is from The Existence of God *(1979), in which he rejects all deductive forms of arguments for the existence of God but, in their place, sets a series of inductive arguments. In this selection, he presents an inductive version of the argument from design. His strategy is to show that several of the arguments, though only minimally suggestive when taken in isolation, together make a cumulative case for the truth of theism.*

I understand by an argument from design one which argues from some general pattern of order in the universe or provision for the needs of conscious beings to a God responsible for these phenomena. An argument from a general pattern of order I shall call a teleological argument. In the definition of 'teleological argument' I emphasize the words 'general pattern'; I shall not count an argument to the existence of God from some particular pattern of order manifested on a unique occasion as a teleological argument.

Two Forms of Teleological Argument

I begin with the distinction between spatial order and temporal order, between what I shall call regularities of co-presence and regularities of succession. An example of a regularity of co-presence would be a town with all its roads at right angles to each other, or a section of books in a library arranged in alphabetical order of authors. Regularities

of succession are simple patterns of behaviour of objects, such as their behavior in accordance with the laws of nature—for example, Newton's laws.

Many of the striking examples of order in the universe evince an order which is due both to a regularity of co-presence and to a regularity of succession. A working car consists of many parts so adjusted to each other that it follows the instructions of the driver delivered by his pulling and pushing a few levers and buttons and turning a wheel, to take passengers whither he wishes. Its order arises because its parts are so arranged at some instant (regularity of co-presence) that, the laws of nature being as they are (regularity of succession) it brings about the result neatly and efficiently. The order of living animals and plants likewise results from regularities of both types.

Men who marvel at the order of the universe may marvel at either or both of the regularities of co-presence and of succession. The thinkers of the eighteenth century to whom the argument from design appealed so strongly were struck almost exclusively by the regularities of co-presence. They marveled at the order in animals and plants; but since they largely took for granted the regularities of succession, what struck them about the animals and plants, as to a lesser extent about machines made by men, was the subtle and coherent arrangement of their millions of parts. Paley's *Natural Theology* dwells mainly on details of comparative anatomy, on eyes and ears and muscles and bones arranged with minute precision so as to operate with high efficiency, and in the *Dialogues* Hume's Cleanthes produces the same kind of examples: 'Consider, anatomize the eye, survey its structure and contrivance, and tell me from your own feeling, if the idea of a contriver does not immediately flow in upon you with a force like that of sensation.'

The eighteenth-century argument from spatial order seems to go as follows. Animals and plants have the power to reproduce their kind, and so, given the past existence of animals and plants, their present existence is to be expected. But what is vastly surprising is the existence of animals and plants at all. By natural processes they can only come into being through generation. But we know that the world has not been going on for ever, and so the great puzzle is the existence of the first animals and plants in 4004 BC or whenever exactly it was that animals and plants began to exist. Since they could not have come about by natural scientific processes, and since they are very similar to the machines, which certain rational agents, viz. men, make, it is very probable that they were made by a rational agent—only clearly one much more powerful and knowledgeable than men.

In the *Dialogues,* through the mouth of Philo, Hume made some classical objections to the argument in this form, some of which have some force against all forms of the argument; I shall deal with most of these as we come to appropriate places in this chapter. Despite Hume's objections, the argument is, I think, a very plausible one—given its premises. But one of its premises was shown by Darwin and his successors to be clearly false. Complex animals and plants can be produced through generation by less complex animals and plants— species are not eternally distinct; and simple animals and plants can be produced by natural processes from inorganic matter. This discovery led to the virtual disappearance of the argument from design from popular apologetic—mistakenly, I think, since it can easily be reconstructed in a form which does not rely on the premises shown to be false by Darwin. This can be done even for the argument from spatial order.

We can reconstruct the argument from spatial order as follows. We see around us animals and plants, intricate examples of spatial order in the ways which Paley set out, similar to machines of the kind which men make. We know that these animals and plants have evolved by natural processes from inorganic matter. But clearly this evolution can only have taken place, given certain special natural laws. These are first, the chemical laws stating how under certain circumstances inorganic molecules combine to make organic ones, and organic ones combine to make organisms. And secondly,

there are the biological laws of evolution stating how organisms have very many offspring, some of which vary in one or more characteristics from their parents, and how some of these characteristics are passed on to most offspring, from which it follows that, given shortage of food and other environmental needs, there will be competition for survival, in which the fittest will survive. Among organisms very well fitted for survival will be organisms of such complex and subtle construction as to allow easy adaptation to a changing environment. These organisms will evince great spatial order. So the laws of nature are such as, under certain circumstances, to give rise to striking examples of spatial order similar to the machines which men make. Nature, that is, is a machine-making machine. In the twentieth century men make not only machines, but machine-making machines. They may therefore naturally infer from nature which produces animals and plants, to a creator of nature similar to men who make machine-making machines.

This reconstructed argument is now immune to having some crucial premises shown false by some biologist of the 1980s. The facts to which its premises appeal are too evident for that—whatever the details, natural laws are clearly such as to produce complex organisms from inorganic matter under certain circumstances. But although this is so, I do not find the argument a very strong one, and this is because of the evident paucity of organisms throughout the universe. The circumstances under which nature behaves as a machine-making machine are rare. For that reason nature does not evince very strongly the character of a machine-making machine and hence the analogies between the products of natural processes on the one hand and machines on the other are not too strong. Perhaps they give a small degree of probability to the hypothesis that a rational agent was responsible for the laws of evolution in some ways similar to the rational agents who make machines, but the probability is no more than that.

I pass on to consider a form of teleological argument which seems to me a much stronger one—the teleological argument from the temporal order of the world. The temporal order of the universe is, to the man who bothers to give it a moment's thought, an overwhelmingly striking fact about it. Regularities of succession are all-pervasive. For simple laws govern almost all successions of events. In books of physics, chemistry, and biology we can learn how almost everything in the world behaves. The laws of their behavior can be set out by relatively simple formulae which men can understand and by means of which they can successfully predict the future. The orderliness of the universe to which I draw attention here is its conformity to formula, to simple, formulable, scientific laws. The orderliness of the universe in this respect is a very striking fact about it. The universe might so naturally have been chaotic, but it is not—it is very orderly.

That the world has this very peculiar characteristic may be challenged in various ways. It may be said of the order which we seem to see in the universe that we impose the order on the world, that it is not there independently of our imposition. Put another way, all that this temporal order amounts to, it might be said, is a coincidence between how things have been so far in the world and the patterns which men can recognize and describe, a coincidence which is itself susceptible of an explanation in terms of natural selection. In fact, however, the temporal order of the world is something deeper than that. The premise of a good teleological argument is not that so far (within his life or within human history) things have conformed to a pattern which man can recognize and describe. The premiss is rather that things have and will continue to conform to such a pattern however initial conditions vary, however men interfere in the world. If induction is justified, we are justified in supposing that things will continue to behave as they have behaved in the kinds of respect which scientists and ordinary people recognize and describe. I assume that we are justified in believing that the laws of gravity and chemical cohesion will continue to hold tomorrow—that stones will fall, and desks hold together tomorrow as well as today—however initial conditions vary, however men interfere in the world. It may of course be doubted whether philosophers have given a very satisfactory account of what makes such beliefs justified (hence 'the problem of induction'); but I assume the common-sense

view that they are justified. So the teleologist's premiss is not just that there has been in nature so far an order which men can recognize and describe; but there has been and will continued to be in nature an order, recognizable and describable by men certainly, but one which exists independently of men. If men are correct in their belief that the order which they see in the world is an order which will hold in the future as in the past, it is clearly not an imposed or invented order. It is there in nature. For man cannot make nature conform subsequently to an order which he has invented. Only if the order is there in nature is nature's future conformity to be expected.

An objector may now urge that although the order of the universe is an objective matter, nevertheless, unless the universe were an orderly place, men would not be around to comment on the fact. (If there were no natural laws, there would be no regularly functioning organisms, and so no men.) Hence there is nothing surprising in the fact that men find order—they could not possibly find anything else. This conclusion is clearly a little too strong. There would need to be quite a bit of order in and around our bodies if men are to exist and think, but there could be chaos outside the earth, so long as the earth was largely unaffected by that chaos. There is a great deal more order in the world than is necessary for the existence of humans. So men could still be around to comment on the fact even if the world were a much less orderly place than it is. But quite apart from this minor consideration, the argument still fails totally for a reason which can best be brought out by an analogy. Suppose that a madman kidnaps a victim and shuts him in a room with a card-shuffling machine. The machine shuffles ten packs of cards simultaneously and then draws a card from each pack and exhibits simultaneously the ten cards. The kidnapper tells the victim that he will shortly set the machine to work and it will exhibit its first draw, but that unless the draw consists of an ace of hearts from each pack, the machine will simultaneously set off an explosion which will kill the victim, in consequence of which he will not see which cards the machine drew. The machine is then set to work, and to the amazement and relief of the victim the machine exhibits an ace of hearts drawn from each pack. The victim thinks that this extraordinary fact needs an explanation in terms of the machine having been rigged in some way. But the kidnapper, who now reappears, casts doubt on this suggestion. 'It is hardly surprising', he says, 'that the machine draws only aces of hearts. You could not possibly see anything else. For you would not be here to see anything at all, if any other cards had been drawn.' But of course the victim is right and the kidnapper is wrong. There is indeed something extraordinary in need of explanation in ten aces of hearts being drawn. The fact that this peculiar order is a necessary condition of the draw being perceived at all makes what is perceived no less extraordinary and in need of explanation. The teleologist's starting-point is not that we perceive order rather than disorder, but that order rather than disorder is there. Maybe only if order is there can we know what is there, but that makes what is there no less extraordinary and in need of explanation.

So the universe is characterized by vast, all-pervasive temporal order, the conformity of nature to formula, recorded in the scientific laws formulated by men. Now this phenomenon, like the very existence of the world, is clearly something 'too big' to be explained by science. If there is an explanation of the world's order it cannot be a scientific one, and this follows from the nature of scientific explanation. For, in scientific explanation we explain particular phenomena as brought about by prior phenomena in accord with scientific laws; or we explain the operation of scientific laws in terms of more general scientific laws (and perhaps also particular phenomena). Thus we explain the operation of Kepler's laws in terms of the operation of Newton's laws (given the masses, initial velocities, and distances apart of the sun and planets); and we explain the operation of Newton's laws in terms of the operation of Einstein's field equations for space relatively empty of matter. Science thus explains particular phenomena and low-level laws in terms partly of high-level laws. But from the very nature of science it cannot explain the highest-level laws of all; for they are that by which it explains all other phenomena.

At this point we need to rephrase our premises in terms of the powers-and-liabilities account of science, which we have seen reason for preferring to the Hempelian account. On this account what the all-pervasive temporal order amounts to is the fact that throughout space and time there are physical objects of various kinds, every such object having the powers and liabilities which are described in laws of nature—e.g. the power of attracting each other physical object in the universe with a force of $\gamma mm^1/r^2$ dynes (where γ is the gravitational constant) the liability always to exercise this power, and the liability to be attracted by each other body in the universe with a force of $\gamma mm^1/r^2$ dynes and so on. From the fact that it has such general powers it follows that an object will have certain more specific powers, given the kind of object that it is. For example, given that it has a mass of I gram, it will follow that it has the power of attracting each other body in the universe with a force of $\gamma m^1/r^2$ dynes. This picture allows us to draw attention to one feature of the orderliness of the universe which the other picture makes it easy to ignore. Unlike the feature to which I have drawn attention so far, it is not one of which men have always known; it is one which the atomic theory of chemistry strongly suggested, and the discovery of fundamental particles confirmed. It is this. The physical objects scattered throughout space and time are, or are composed of, particles of a few limited kinds, which we call fundamental particles. Whether the protons and electrons which we suppose to be the fundamental particles are in fact fundamental, or whether they are composed of yet more fundamental particles (e.g. quarks) which are capable of independent existence is not altogether clear—but what does seem clear is that if there are yet more fundamental particles, they too come in a few specific kinds. Nature only has building-blocks of a few kinds. Each particle of a given kind has a few defining properties which determine its behaviour and which are specific to that kind. Thus all electrons have a mass of $1/2 MeV/c^2$, a charge of –I, a spin of $1/2$, etc. All positions have other properties the same as electrons, but a charge of +I. All protons have a mass of $938 \, MeV/c^2$, a charge of +I, and a spin of $1/2$. And so on. There are innumerably many particles which belong to each of a few kinds, and no particles with characteristics intermediate between those of two kinds. The properties of fundamental kinds, that is, which give specific form to the general powers which all objects have, belong to a small class; and the powers and liabilities of large-scale objects are determined by those of their fundamental components. Particles have constant characteristics over time; they only change their characteristics, or are destroyed or converted into other particles by reason of their own liabilities (e.g. to decay) or the action of other particles acting in virtue of their powers.

Put in these terms then, the orderliness of nature is a matter of the vast uniformity in the powers and liabilities of bodies throughout endless time and space, and also in the paucity of kinds of components of bodies. Over centuries long, long ago and over distances distant in millions of light years from ourselves the same universal orderliness reigns. There are, as we have seen, explanations of only two kinds for phenomena—scientific explanation and personal explanation. Yet, although a scientific explanation can be provided of why the more specific powers and liabilities of bodies hold (e.g. why an electron exerts just the attractive force which it does) in terms of more general powers and liabilities possessed by all bodies (put in Hempelian terms—why a particular natural law holds in terms of more general natural laws), science cannot explain why all bodies do possess the same very general powers and liabilities. It is with this fact that scientific explanation stops. So either the orderliness of nature is where all explanation stops, or we must postulate an agent of great power and knowledge who brings about through his continuous action that bodies have the same very general powers and liabilities (that the most general natural laws operate); and, once again, the simplest such agent to postulate is one of infinite power, knowledge, and freedom, i.e. God. An additional consideration here is that it is clearly vastly simpler to suppose that the existence and the order of the world have the same cause, and the considerations which lead us to postulate a being of infinite power, knowledge, and freedom as the cause of the former reinforce the

considerations which lead us to postulate such a cause for the latter.

In the *Dialogues* Hume made the objection—why should we not postulate many gods to give order to the universe, not merely one? 'A great number of men join in building a house or a ship, in rearing a city, in framing a commonwealth, why may not several deities combine in framing a world?' Hume again is aware of the obvious counter-objection to his suggestion. 'To multiply causes without necessity is . . . contrary to true philosophy.' He claims, however, that the counter-objection does not apply here, because (in my terminology) although the supposition that there is one god is a simpler supposition than the supposition that there are many, in postulating many persons to be responsible for the order of the universe we are postulating persons more like to men in power and knowledge—that is we are putting forward a hypothesis which fits in better with our background knowledge of what there is in the world. That may be. But Hume's hypothesis is very complicated—we want to ask about it such questions as why are there just 333 deities (or whatever the number is), why do they have powers of just the strength which they do have, and what moves them to cooperate as closely as obviously they do; questions of a kind which obtrude far less with the far simpler and so less arbitrary theistic hypothesis. Even if Hume were right in supposing that the prior probability of his hypothesis were as great as that of theism (because the fit with background knowledge of the former cancels out the simplicity of the latter) (and I do not myself think that he is right), the hypothesis of theism nevertheless has greater explanatory power than the Humean hypothesis and is for that reason more more probable. For theism leads us to expect that we will find throughout nature one pattern of order. But if there were more than one deity responsible for the order of the universe, we would expect to see characteristic marks if the handiwork of different deities in different parts of the universe, just as we see different kinds of workmanship in the different houses of a city. We would expect to find an inverse square of law of gravitation obeyed in one part of the universe, and in another part a law which was just short of being an inverse square law—without the difference being explicable in terms of a more general law. It is enough to draw this absurd conclusion to see how wrong the Humean objection is.

So I shall take as the alternatives—the first, that the temporal order of the world is where explanation stops, and the second, that the temporal order of the world is due to the agency of God; and I shall ignore the less probable possibilities that the order is to be explained as due to the agency of an agent or agents of finite power. The proponent of the teleological argument claims that the order of nature shows an orderer—God.

The Force of the Second Form of Teleological Argument

The teleological argument, whether from temporal or spatial order, is, I believe, a codification by philosophers of a reaction to the world deeply embedded in the human consciousness. Men see the comprehensibility of the world as evidence of a comprehending creator. The prophet Jeremiah lived in an age in which the existence of a creator-god of some sort was taken for granted. What was at stake was the extent of his goodness, knowledge, and power. Jeremiah argued from the order of the world that he was a powerful and reliable god, that god was God. He argued to the power of the creator from the extent of the creation—'The host of heaven cannot be numbered, neither the sand of the sea measured'; and he argued that its regular behaviour showed the reliability of the creator, and he spoke of the 'covenant of the day and night' whereby they follow each other regularly, and 'the ordinances of heaven and earth',[1] and he used their existence as an argument for the trust-worthiness of the God of Jacob. The argument from temporal order has been with us ever since.

You get the argument from temporal order also in Aquinas's fifth way, which runs as follows:

The fifth way is based on the guidedness of nature. An orderedness of actions to an end is observed in all bodies obeying natural laws, even when they lack awareness. For their behaviour hardly ever varies, and will practically always turn out well; which shows that they truly tend to a goal, and do not merely hit it by accident. Nothing however that lacks awareness tends to a goal, except under the direction of someone with awareness and with understanding; the arrow, for example requires an archer. Everything in nature, therefore is directed to its goal by someone with understanding and this we call 'God'.[2]

Aquinas argues that the regular behaviour of each inanimate thing shows that some animate being is directing it (making it move to achieve some purpose, attain some goal); and from that he comes—rather quickly—to the conclusion that one 'being with understanding' is responsible for the behaviour of all inanimate things.

It seems to me fairly clear that no argument from temporal order—whether Aquinas's fifth way or any other argument can be a good deductive argument. For although the premiss is undoubtedly correct—a vast pervasive order characterizes the world—the step from premiss to conclusion is not a valid deductive one. Although the existence of order may be good evidence of a designer, it is surely compatible with the non-existence of one—it is hardly a logically necessary truth that all order is brought about by a person. And although, as I have urged, the supposition that one person is responsible for the orderliness of the world is much simpler and so more probable than the supposition that many persons are, nevertheless, the latter supposition seems logically compatible with the data—so we must turn to the more substantial issue of whether the argument from the temporal order of the world to God is a good inductive argument. We had reached the conclusion that either the vast uniformity in the powers and liabilities of bodies was where explanation stopped, or that God brings this about by his continuous action, through an intention constant over time.

Let us represent by *e* this conformity of the world to order, and let *h* be the hypothesis of theism. It is not possible to treat a teleological argument in complete isolation from the cosmological argument. We cannot ask how probable the premiss of the teleological argument makes theism, independently of the premiss of the cosmological argument, for the premiss of the teleological argument entails in part the premiss of the cosmological argument. That there is order of the kind described entails at least that there is a physical universe. So let *k* be now, not mere tautological evidence, but the existence of a complex physical universe (the premiss of the version of the cosmological argument to which I devoted most attention). Let us ask how much more probable does the orderliness of such a universe make the existence of God than does the mere existence of the universe.

With these fillings, we ask whether $P(h/e.k) > P(h/k)$ and by how much. As we have seen $P(h/e.k)$ will exceed $P(h/k)$ if and only if $P(e/h.k) > P(e/ \sim h.k)$. Put in words with our current fillings for *h*, *e*, and *k*, the existence of order in the world confirms the existence of God if and only if the existence of this order in the world is more probable if there is a God than if there is not. We saw in Chapter 6 that where *h* is the hypothesis that there is a God $P(e/h.k)$ may exceed $P(e/ \sim h.k)$, either because *e* cannot be explained in any other way and is very unlikely to occur uncaused or because God has character such that he is more likely to bring about *e* than alternative states. With respect to the cosmological argument, I suggested that its case rested solely on the first consideration. Here I shall suggest that again the first consideration is dominant, but that the second has considerable significance also.

Let us start with the first consideration. *e* is the vast uniformity in the powers and liabilities possessed by material objects—$P(e/ \sim h.k)$ is the probability that there should be that amount of uniformity in a God-less world, that this uniform distribution of the powers of things should be where explanation terminates, that they be further inexplicable. That there should be material bodies is strange enough; but that they should all have such similar powers which they inevitably exercise, seems passing strange. It is strange enough that physical objects should have powers at all—why should they not just be, without being able to make a difference to the world? But that they should all, throughout infinite time and space, have some general powers identical to those of all other objects (and they all be made of components of very few fundamental kinds, each component of a given kind being identical in all characteristics with each other such component) and yet there be no cause of this at all

seems incredible. The universe is complex as we urged, in the last chapter, in that there are so many bodies of different shapes, etc., and now we find an underlying orderliness in the identity of powers and paucity of kinds of components of bodies. Yet this orderliness, if there is no explanation of it in terms of the action of God, is the orderliness of coincidence—the fact that one body has certain powers does not explain the fact that a second body has—not the simplicity of a common underlying explanation. The basic complexity remains in the vast number of different bodies in which the orderliness of identical powers and components is embodied. It is a complexity too striking to occur unexplained. It cries out for explanation in terms of some single common source with the power to produce it. Just as we would seek to explain all the coins' of the realm having an identical pattern in terms of their origin from a common mould, or all of many pictures' having a common style in terms of their being painted by the same painter, so too should we seek to explain all physical objects' having the same powers in terms of their deriving them from a common source. On these grounds alone $P(e/h.k) \gg P(e/k)$, and so $P(h/e.k) \gg P(h/k)$.[3]

I think, however, that we can go further by bringing in considerations from God's character—we saw in Chapter 6 that God will bring about a state of affairs if it is over all a good thing that he should, he will not bring about a state of affairs if it is over all a bad thing that he should, and that he will only bring about a state of affairs if it is in some way a good thing that he should. Put in terms of reasons—he will always act on overriding reasons and cannot act except for a reason. Now there are two reasons why human beings produce order. One is aesthetic—beauty comes in the patterns of things, such as dances and songs. Some sort of order is a necessary condition of phenomena having beauty; complete chaos is just ugly—although of course not any order is beautiful. The second reason why a human being produces order is that when there is order he or other rational agents can perceive that order and utilize it to achieve ends. If we see that there is a certain pattern of order in phenomena we can then justifiably predict that that order will continue, and that enables us to make predictions about the future on which we can rely. A librarian puts books in an alphabetical order of authors in order that he and users of the library who come to know that the order is there may subsequently be able to find any book in the library very quickly (because, given knowledge of the order, we can predict whereabouts in the library any given book will be).

God has similar reasons for producing an orderly, as opposed to a chaotic universe. In so far as some sort of order is a necessary condition of beauty, and it is a good thing—as it surely is—that the world be beautiful rather than ugly, God has reason for creating an orderly universe. Secondly, I shall argue in Chapter 10 that it is good that God should make finite creatures with the opportunity to grow in knowledge and power. Now if creatures are going consciously to extend their control of the world, they will need to know how to do so. There will need to be some procedures which they can find out, such that if they follow those procedures, certain events will occur. This entails the existence of temporal order. There can only be such procedures if the world is orderly, and, I should add, there can only be such procedures ascertainable by men if the order of the world is such as to be discernible by men. To take a simple example, if hitting things leads to them breaking or penetrating other things, and heating things leads to them melting, men can discover these regularities and utilize them to make artefacts such as houses, tables, and chairs. They can heat iron ore to melt it to make nails, hammers, and axes, and use the latter to break wood into the right shapes to hammer together with nails to make the artefacts. Or, if light and other electro-magnetic radiation behave in predictable ways comprehensible by men, men can discover those ways and build telescopes and radio and television receivers and transmitters. A world must evince the temporal order exhibited by laws of nature if men are to be able to extrapolate from how things have behaved in the past, to how they will behave in the future, which extrapolation is necessary if men are to have the knowledge of how things will behave in the future, which they must have in order to be able to extend their control over the world. (There would not need to be complete determinism—agents themselves could be exempt from the full rigors of determinism, and there might be violations of natural laws from time to time. But basically the world has to be governed by laws of nature if agents are consciously to extend their control of the world.) If I am right in supposing that God has reason to create finite creatures with the opportunity to grow in knowledge and power, then he has reason to create temporal order. So I suggest that God has at least these two reasons for producing an orderly world. Maybe God has reasons for not making creatures with the opportunity to grow in knowledge and power, and so the second reason for his creating an orderly universe does not apply. But with one possible, and, I shall show, irrelevant qualification, the first surely does. God may choose whether or not to make a physical universe, but if he does, he has reason for making a beautiful and so an orderly one. God has reason, if he does make a physical universe, not to make a chaotic or botched-up one. The only reason of which I can think why God should make the universe in some respects ugly would be to give to creatures the opportunity to discover the aesthetic merits of different states of affairs and through cooperative effort to make the world beautiful for themselves. But then the other argument shows that if they are to be able to exercise such an opportunity the world will need to be orderly in some respects. (There will have to be predictable regularities which creatures may utilize in order to produce beautiful states of affairs.) So, either way, the world will need to be orderly. It rather looks as if God has overriding reason to make an orderly universe if he makes a universe at all. However, as I emphasized, human inquiry into divine reasons is a highly speculative matter. But it is nevertheless one in which men are justified in reaching tentative conclusions. For God is postulated to be an agent like ourselves in having knowledge, power, and freedom, although to an infinitely greater degree than we have. The existence of the analogy legitimizes us in reaching conclusions about his purposes, conclusions which must allow for the quantitative difference, as I have tried to do.

So I suggest that the order of the world is evidence of the existence of God both because its occurrence would be very improbable *a priori* and also because, in virtue of his postulated character, he has very good, apparently overriding, reason for making an orderly universe, if he makes a universe at all. It looks as if $P(e/h.k)$ equals I. For both reasons $P(e/h.k) \gg P(e/\sim h.k)$ and so $P(h/e.k) \gg P(h/k)$. I conclude that the teleological argument from temporal order is a good C-inductive argument to the existence of God.[†]

Let us look at the argument from a slightly different angle. It is basically an argument by analogy, an analogy between the order in the natural world (the temporal order codified in laws of nature) and the patterns of order which men often produce (the ordered books on library shelves, or the temporal order in the movements of a dancer or the notes of a song). It argues from similarity between phenomena of two kinds B and B^* to similarity between their causes A and A^*. In view of the similarities between the two kinds of order B and B^*, the theist postulates a cause (A^*) in some respects similar to A (men); yet in view of the dissimilarities the theist must postulate a cause in other respects different. All arguments by analogy do and must proceed in this way. They cannot postulate a cause in all respects similar. They postulate a cause who is such that one would expect him to produce phenomena similar to B in the respects in which B^* are similar to B and different from B in the respects in which B^* are different from B.

All argument from analogy works like this. Thus various properties of light and sound were known in the nineteenth century, among them that both light and sound are reflected, refracted, diffracted, and show interference phenomena. In the case of sound these were known to be due to disturbance of the medium, air, in which it is transmitted. What could one conclude by analogy about the cause of the reflection, etc., of light? One could conclude that the propagation of light was, like the propagation of sound, the propagation of a wave-like disturbance in a medium. But one could not conclude that it was the propagation of a disturbance in the

same medium—air, since light passed through space empty of air. Scientists had to postulate a separate medium—aether, the disturbance of which was responsible for the reflection, etc., of light. And not merely does all argument by analogy proceed like this, but all inductive inference can be represented as argument by analogy. For all inductive inference depends on the assumption that in certain respects things continue the same and in other respects they differ. Thus that crude inference from a number of observed swans all having been white to the next swan's being white is an argument by analogy. For it claims that the next swan will be like the observed swans in one respect—color, while being unlike them in other respects.

In our case the similarities between the temporal order which men produce and the temporal order in nature codified in scientific laws mean postulating as cause of the latter a person who acts intentionally. The dissimilarities between the kinds of order include the world-wide extent of the order in nature in comparison with the very narrow range of order which men produce. This means postulating as cause of the former a person of enormous power and knowledge. Now, as we saw in Chapter 2, a person has a body if there is a region of the world under his direct control and if he controls other regions of the world only by controlling the former and by its movements having predictable effects on the outside world. Likewise he learns about the world only by the world having effects on this region. If these conditions are satisfied, the person has a body, and the stated region is that body. But if a person brings about directly the connections between things, including the predictable connections between the bodies of other persons and the world, there is no region of the world, goings-on in which bring about those connections. The person must bring about those connections as a basic action. His control of the world must be immediate, not mediated by a body. So the dissimilarities between the two kinds of order necessarily lead to the postulation of a non-embodied person (rather than an embodied person) as cause of the temporal order in nature.

These considerations should suffice to rebut that persistent criticism of the argument from design

---

[†] Earlier in the book Swinburne distinguishes a P-inductive argument from a C-inductive argument. A P-inductive argument is one in which the premises make the conclusion probable. A C-inductive argument is one in which the premises *add* to the probability of the conclusion (i.e., make it more probable than it would otherwise be).

which we have heard ever since Hume that, taken seriously, the argument ought to be postulating an embodied god, a giant of a man. 'Why not', wrote Hume, 'become a perfect anthropomorphite? Why not assert the deity or deities to be corporeal, and, to have eyes, a nose, mouth, ears, etc.?' The answer is the simple one that dissimilarities between effects lead the rational man to postulate dissimilarities between causes, and that this procedure is basic to inductive inference.

It is true that the greater the dissimilarities between effects, the weaker is the argument to the existence of a similar cause; and it has been a traditional criticism of the argument from design represented as an argument by analogy that the analogy is weak. The dissimilarities between the natural world and the effects which men produce are indeed striking; but the similarities between these are also, I have been suggesting, striking—in both there is the conformity of phenomena to a simple pattern of order detectable by men. But although the dissimilarities are perhaps sufficiently great to make the argument not a good P-inductive argument, this chapter suggests that it remains a good C-inductive argument. The existence of order in the universe increases significantly the probability that there is a God, even if it does not by itself render it probable.

The Argument from Beauty

We saw that God has reason, apparently overriding reason, for making, not merely any orderly world (which we have been considering so far) but a beautiful world—at any rate to the extent to which it lies outside the control of creatures. (And he has reason too, I would suggest, even in whatever respects the world does lie within the control of creatures, to give them experience of beauty to develop, and perhaps also some ugliness to annihilate.) So God has reason to make a basically beautiful world, although also reason to leave some of the beauty or ugliness of the world within the power of creatures to determine; but he would seem to have overriding reason not to make a basically ugly world beyond the powers of creatures to improve. Hence, if there is a God there is more reason to expect a basically beautiful world than a basically ugly one—by the principles of Chapter 6. *A priori*, however, there is no particular reason for expecting a basically beautiful rather than a basically ugly world. In consequence, if the world is beautiful, that fact would be evidence for God's existence. For, in this case, if we let k be 'there is an orderly physical universe', e be 'there is a beautiful universe', and h be 'there is a God', $P(e/h.k)$ will be greater than $P(e/k)$; and so by our previous principles the argument from e to h will be another good C-inductive argument.

Few, however, would deny that our universe (apart from its animal and human inhabitants, and aspects subject to their immediate control) has that beauty. Poets and painters and ordinary men down the centuries have long admired the beauty of the orderly procession of the heavenly bodies, the scattering of the galaxies through the heavens (in some ways random, in some ways orderly), and the rocks, sea, and wind interacting on earth, 'The spacious firmament on high, and all the blue aethereal sky', the water lapping against 'the old eternal rocks', and the plants of the jungle and of temperate climates, contrasting with the desert and the Arctic wastes. Who in his senses would deny that here is beauty in abundance? If we confine ourselves to the argument from the beauty of the inanimate and plant worlds, the argument surely works.

Notes

1. Jer. 33: 20f. and 25f.
2. St. Thomas Aquinas, Summa Theologiae, 1a, 2.3, trans. T. McDermott, OP (London, 1964).
3. '$\gg$' means 'is much greater than', '$\ll$' means 'is much less than'.

I.C The Ontological Argument for the Existence of God

The ontological argument for the existence of God is the most intriguing of all the arguments for theism. It is one of the most remarkable arguments ever set forth. First devised by Anselm (1033–1109), Archbishop of Canterbury in the eleventh century, the argument has continued to puzzle and fascinate philosophers ever since. Let the testimony of the agnostic philosopher Bertrand Russell serve as a typical example here:

> I remember the precise moment, one day in 1894, as I was walking along Trinity Lane [at Cambridge University where Russell was a student], when I saw in a flash (or thought I saw) that the ontological argument is valid. I had gone out to buy a tin of tobacco; on my way back, I suddenly threw it up in the air, and exclaimed as I caught it: "Great Scott, the ontological argument is sound!"*

The argument is important not only because it claims to be an a priori proof for the existence of God but also because it is the primary locus of such philosophical problems as whether existence is a property and whether the notion of necessary existence is intelligible. Furthermore, it has special religious significance because it is the only one of the traditional arguments that clearly concludes to the necessary properties of God, that is, his omnipotence, omniscience, omnibenevolence, and other great-making properties.

Although there are many versions of the ontological argument and many interpretations of some of these, most philosophers agree on the essential form of Anselm's version in the second chapter of his *Proslogium*. Anselm believes that God's existence is so absolutely certain that only a fool would doubt or deny it. Yet he desires understanding to fulfill his faith. "And so, Lord, do thou, who dost give understanding to faith, give me, so far as thou knowest it to be profitable, to understand that thou art as we believe; and that thou art that which we believe. And indeed, we believe that thou art a being than which nothing greater can be conceived. Or is there no such nature, since the fool hath said in his heart, there is no God?"

The argument that follows may be treated as a reductio ad absurdum argument. That is, it begins with a supposition (S: suppose that the greatest conceivable being exists in the mind alone) that is contradictory to what one desires to prove. One then goes about showing that (S) together with other certain or self-evident assumptions (A_1 and A_2) yields a contradiction, which in turn demonstrates that the contradictory of (S) must be true: A greatest possible being must exist in reality. You, the reader, can work out the details of the argument.

A monk named Gaunilo, a contemporary of Anselm's, sets forth the first objection to Anselm's argument. Accusing Anselm of pulling rabbits out of hats, he tells the story of a delectable lost island, one that is more excellent than all lands. Since it is better that such a perfect island exist in reality than simply in the mind alone, this Isle of the Blest must necessarily exist. Anselm's reply is that the analogy fails, for unlike the greatest possible being, the greatest possible island can be conceived as not existing. Recently, Alvin Plantinga has clarified Anselm's point. There simply are some properties that have intrinsic maximums and some properties that do not. No matter how wonderful we make the Isle of the Blest, we can conceive of a more wonderful island. The greatness of islands is like the greatness of numbers in this respect. There is no greatest natural number, for no matter how large the number we choose, we can always conceive of one twice as large. On the other hand, the properties of God have intrinsic maximums. For example, perfect knowledge has an intrinsic maximum: For any proposition, an omniscient being knows whether it is true or false.

Autobiography of Bertrand Russell (New York: Little, Brown & Co., 1967).

Our next reading is the critique by Immanuel Kant (1724–1804), who accused the proponent of the argument of defining God into existence. Kant claims that Anselm makes the mistake of treating 'existence' or 'being' as a first-order predicate like 'blue' or 'great.' When we say that the castle is blue, we are adding a property (viz., blueness) to the idea of a castle, but when we say that the castle *exists,* we are not adding anything to the concept of a castle. We are saying only that the concept is exemplified or instantiated. In Anselm's argument 'existence' is treated as a first-order predicate, which adds something to the concept of an entity and makes it *greater.* This, according to Kant, is the fatal flaw in the argument.

In our third reading, "The Ontological Argument," Alvin Plantinga analyzes Anselm's argument, defends it against Kant's criticism, and then constructs a modal version of the argument. That is, the argument is set forth in terms of the modes of possibility and necessity or in terms of possible and necessary existence. The key premise, number (29) in this essay, is this: "There is a possible world in which maximal greatness is instantiated." Plantinga explicates and defends this premise, which rests on the premise that a being has maximal excellence in every possible world and which therefore entails the existence of God. Plantinga believes that this version of the ontological argument is sound, but he doesn't claim that it proves that God exists (for the argument works only if (29) is true, and it may not be). But there is nothing irrational about believing (29). His argument "establishes not the truth of theism, but its rational acceptability."

Following Plantinga's article is William Rowe's explication of how modal versions of the ontological argument work. Specifically, Rowe analyzes and critiques Plantinga's version. Appreciating the subtlety and validity of the argument itself, he argues that Plantinga's assessment of what his modal version of the argument does is inaccurate. Plantinga claims that the argument shows that one can rationally accept theism, but Rowe thinks that all he has shown is that one may not be foolish to accept it.

In our final reading, J. N. Findlay tries to turn the ontological argument on its head, arguing that the idea of a necessary being, while necessary for theism, is impossible. Hence, necessarily, a necessary being, so that God does not and cannot exist.

There are many other considerations involved in the ontological argument that are not dealt with in our readings. For a clear discussion of the wider issues involved in this argument, see William Rowe's introductory work, *Philosophy of Religion* (chapter 3, "The Ontological Argument"). However, the readings before you will most likely provide more than enough to whet your appetite.

I.C.1   The Ontological Argument

ST. ANSELM

St. Anselm (1033–1109), Abbot of Bec and later Archbishop of Canterbury, is the originator of one of the most intriguing arguments ever devised by the human mind, the ontological argument for the existence of a supremely perfect being. After the short selection from Anselm's Proslogium, *there follows a brief selection from Gaunilo's reply,* In Behalf of the Fool, *and a counterresponse by Anselm.*

Reprinted from *Anselm's Basic Writings,* translated by S. W. Deane, 2d ed. (La Salle, Ill.: Open Court Publishing Company, 1962), by permission of the publisher.

St. Anselm's Presentation

*Truly there is a God, although the fool hath
said in his heart, There is no God.*

And so, Lord, do thou, who dost give understanding to faith, give me, so far as thou knowest it
to be profitable, to understand that thou art as we
believe; and that thou art that which we believe.
And, indeed, we believe that thou art a being than
which nothing greater can be conceived. Or is there
no such nature, since the fool hath said in his heart,
there is no God? (Psalms xiii, 1). But, at any rate,
this very fool, when he hears of this being of which
I speak—a being than which nothing greater can be
conceived—understands what he hears, and what
he understands is in his understanding; although he
does not understand it to exist.

For, it is one thing for an object to be in the
understanding, and another to understand that the
object exists. When a painter first conceives of what
he will afterwards perform, he has it in his understanding, but he does not yet understand it to be,
because he has not yet performed it. But after he
has made the painting, he both has it in his understanding, and he understands that it exists, because
he has made it.

Hence, even the fool is convinced that something exists in the understanding, at least, than
which nothing greater can be conceived. For, when
he hears of this, he understands it. And whatever
is understood, exists in the understanding. And assuredly that, than which nothing greater can be conceived, cannot exist in the understanding alone. For,
suppose it exists in the understanding alone: then
it can be conceived to exist in reality; which is
greater.

Therefore, if that, than which nothing greater
can be conceived, exists in the understanding
alone, the very being, than which nothing greater
can be conceived, is one, than which a greater can
be conceived. But obviously this is impossible.
Hence, there is no doubt that there exists a being,
than which nothing greater can be conceived, and
it exists both in the understanding and in reality.

*God cannot be conceived not to exist.—God
is that, than which nothing greater can be conceived.—That which can be conceived not to
exist is not God.*

And it assuredly exists so truly, that it cannot be
conceived not to exist. For, it is possible to conceive
of a being which cannot be conceived not to exist;
and this is greater than one which can be conceived
not to exist. Hence, if that, than which nothing
greater can be conceived, can be conceived not to
exist, it is not that, than which nothing greater can
be conceived. But this is an irreconcilable contradiction. There is, then, so truly a being than which
nothing greater can be conceived to exist, that it
cannot even be conceived not to exist; and this
being thou art, O Lord, our God.

So truly, therefore, dost thou exist, O Lord, my
God, that thou canst not be conceived not to exist;
and rightly. For, if a mind could conceive of a being
better than thee, the creature would rise above the
Creator; and this is most absurd. And, indeed, whatever else there is, except thee alone, can be
conceived not to exist. To thee alone, therefore,
it belongs to exist more truly than all other beings,
and hence in a higher degree than all others. For,
whatever else exists does not exist so truly, and
hence in a less degree it belongs to it to exist.
Why, then, has the fool said in his heart, there is
no God (Psalms xiii, 1), since it is so evident, to
a rational mind, that thou does exist in the highest
degree of all? Why, except that he is dull and a
fool?

*How the fool has said in his heart what cannot
be conceived.—A thing may be conceived in
two ways: (1) when the word signifying it is
conceived: (2) when the thing itself is understood. As far as the word goes, God can be
conceived not to exist; in reality he cannot.*

But how has the fool said in his heart what he
could not conceive; or how is it that he could not
conceive what he said in his heart? since it is the
same to say in the heart, and to conceive.

But, if really, nay, since really, he both conceived, because he said in his heart; and did not say in his heart, because he could not conceive; there is more than one way in which a thing is said in the heart or conceived. For, in one sense, an object is conceived, when the word signifying it is conceived; and in another, when the very entity, which the object is, is understood.

In the former sense, then, God can be conceived not to exist; but in the latter, not at all. For no one who understands what fire and water are can conceive fire to be water, in accordance with the nature of the facts themselves, although this is possible according to the words. So, then, no one who understands what God is can conceive that God does not exist; although he says these words in his heart, either without any or with some foreign, signification. For, God is that than which a greater cannot be conceived. And he who thoroughly understands this, assuredly understands that this being so truly exists, that not even in concept can it be non-existent. Therefore, he who understands that God so exists, cannot conceive that he does not exist.

I thank thee, gracious Lord, I thank thee; because what I formerly believed by thy bounty, I now so understand by thine illumination, that if I were unwilling to believe that thou dost exist, I should not be able not to understand this to be true.

Gaunilo's Criticism*

For example: it is said that somewhere in the ocean is an island, which, because of the difficulty, or rather the impossibility, of discovering what does not exist, is called the lost island. And they say that this island has an inestimable wealth of all manner of riches and delicacies in greater abundance than is told of the Islands of the Blest; and that having no owner or inhabitant, it is more excellent than all other countries, which are inhabited by mankind, in the abundance with which it is stored.

Now if some one should tell me that there is such an island, I should easily understand his words, in which there is no difficulty. But suppose that he went on to say, as if by a logical inference: "You can no longer doubt that this island which is more excellent than all lands exists somewhere, since you have no doubt that it is in your understanding. And since it is more excellent not to be in the understanding alone, but to exist both in the understanding and in reality, for this reason it must exist. For if it does not exist, any land which really exists will be more excellent than it; and so the island already understood by you to be more excellent will not be more excellent."

If a man should try to prove to me by such reasoning that this island truly exists, and that its existence should no longer be doubted, either I should believe that he was jesting, or I know not which I ought to regard as the greater fool: myself, supposing that I should allow this proof; or him, if he should suppose that he had established with any certainty the existence of this island. For he ought to show first that the hypothetical excellence of this island exists as a real and indubitable fact, and in no wise as any unreal object, or one whose existence is uncertain, in my understanding.

St. Anselm's Rejoinder

A criticism of Gaunilo's example, in which he tries to show that in this way the real existence of a lost island might be inferred from the fact of its being conceived.

But, you say, it is as if one should suppose an island in the ocean, which surpasses all lands in its fertility, and which, because of the difficulty, or rather the impossibility, of discovering what does not exist, is called a lost island; and should say that there can be no doubt that this island truly exists in reality, for this reason, that one who hears it described easily understands what he hears.

Now I promise confidently that if any man shall devise anything existing either in reality or in concept alone (except that than which a greater cannot be conceived) to which he can adapt the sequence

---

*Gaunilo, a monk, was a contemporary of St. Anselm's.

of my reasoning, I will discover that thing, and will give him his lost island, not to be lost again.

But it now appears that this being than which a greater is inconceivable cannot be conceived not to be, because it exists on so assured a ground of truth; for otherwise it would not exist at all.

Hence, if any one says that he conceives this being not to exist, I say that at the time when he conceives of this either he conceives of a being than which a greater is inconceivable, or he does not conceive at all. If he does not conceive, he does not conceive of the non-existence of that of which he does not conceive. But if he does conceive, he certainly conceives of a being which cannot be even conceived not to exist. For if it could be conceived not to exist, it could be conceived to have a beginning and an end. But this is impossible.

He, then, who conceives of this being conceives of a being which cannot be even conceived not to exist; but he who conceives of this being does not conceive that it does not exist; else he conceives what is inconceivable. The non-existence, then, of that than which a greater cannot be conceived is inconceivable.

I.C.2 A Critique of the Ontological Argument

IMMANUEL KANT

The German philosopher Immanuel Kant (1724–1804) in his remarkable work Critique of Pure Reason *(1781), from which our selection is taken, set forth a highly influential critique of the ontological argument. Essentially, the objection is that "existence is not a predicate," whereas the opposite is assumed to be true in the various forms of the ontological argument. That is, when you say that Mary is my mother, you are noting some property that describes or adds to who Mary is. But when you say, "Mary, my mother, exists," you are not telling us anything new about Mary; you are simply affirming that the concepts in question are exemplified. 'Existence' is a second-order predicate or property, not to be treated as other first-order, normal predicates or properties are.*

The Impossibility of an Ontological Proof of the Existence of God

It is evident from what has been said, that the conception of an absolutely necessary being is a

From *Kant's Critique of Pure Reason,* translated by J. M. D. Meiklejohn (New York: Colonial Press, 1900). I have revised the translation.

mere idea, the objective reality of which is far from being established by the mere fact that it is a need of reason. On the contrary, this idea serves merely to indicate a certain unattainable perfection, and rather limits the operations than, by the presentation of new objects, extends the sphere of the understanding. But a strange anomaly meets us at the very threshold; for the inference from a given existence in general to an absolutely necessary existence, seems to be correct and unavoidable, while the conditions of the *understanding* refuse to aid us in forming any conception of such a being.

Philosophers have always talked of an *absolutely necessary* being, and have nevertheless declined to take the trouble of conceiving whether—and how—a being of this nature is even cogitable, not to mention that its existence is actually demonstrable. A verbal definition of the conception is certainly easy enough; it is something, the non-existence of which is impossible. But does this definition throw any light upon the conditions which render it impossible to cogitate the non-existence of a thing—conditions which we wish to ascertain, that we may discover whether we think anything in the conception of such a being or not? For the mere fact that I throw away, by means of the word *Unconditioned,* all the conditions which the understanding habitually requires in order to regard anything as necessary, is very far from making clear whether by means of the conception of the unconditionally necessary I think of something, or really of nothing at all.

Nay, more, this chance-conception, now become so current, many have endeavored to explain by examples, which seemed to render any inquiries regarding its intelligibility quite needless. Every geometrical proposition—a triangle has three angles—it was said, is absolutely necessary; and thus people talked of an object which lay out of the sphere of our understanding as if it were perfectly plain what the conception of such a being meant.

All the examples adduced have been drawn, without exception, from *judgments,* and not from *things.* But the unconditioned necessity of a judgment does not form the absolute necessity of a thing. On the contrary, the absolute necessity of a judgment is only a conditioned necessity of a thing, or of the predicate in a judgment. The proposition above-mentioned, does not enounce that three angles necessarily exist, but, upon condition that a triangle exists, three angles must necessarily exist—in it. And thus this logical necessity has been the source of the greatest delusions. Having formed an à priori conception of a thing, the content of which was made to embrace existence, we believed ourselves safe in concluding that, because existence belongs necessarily to the object of the conception (that is, under the condition of my positing this thing as given), the existence of the thing is also posited necessarily, and that it is therefore absolutely necessary—merely because its existence has been cogitated in the conception.

If, in an identical judgment, I annihilate the predicate in thought, and retain the subject, a contradiction is the result; and hence I say, the former belongs necessarily to the latter. But if I suppress both subject and predicate in thought, no contradiction arises; for there *is nothing* at all, and therefore no means of forming a contradiction. To suppose the existence of a triangle and not that of its three angles, is self-contradictory; but to suppose

the non-existence of both triangle and angles is perfectly admissible. And so is it with the conception of an absolutely necessary being. Annihilate its existence in thought, and you annihilate the thing itself with all its predicates; how then can there be any room for contradiction? Externally, there is nothing to give rise to a contradiction, for a thing cannot be necessary externally; nor internally, for, by the annihilation or suppression of the thing itself, its internal properties are also annihilated. God is omnipotent—that is a necessary judgment. His omnipotence cannot be denied, if the existence of a Deity is posited—the existence, that is, of an infinite being, the two conceptions being identical. But when you say, *God does not exist,* neither omnipotence nor any other predicate is affirmed; they must all disappear with the subject, and in this judgment there cannot exist the least self-contradiction.

You have thus seen, that when the predicate of a judgment is annihilated in thought along with the subject, no internal contradiction can arise, be the predicate what it may. There is no possibility of evading the conclusion—you find yourselves compelled to declare: There are certain subjects which cannot be annihilated in thought. But this is nothing more than saying: There exist subjects which are absolutely necessary—the very hypothesis which you are called upon to establish. For I find myself unable to form the slightest conception of a thing which, when annihilated in thought with all its predicates, leaves behind a contradiction; and contradiction is the only criterion of impossibility, in the sphere of pure à priori conceptions.

Against these general considerations, the justice of which no one can dispute, one argument is adduced, which is regarded as furnishing a satisfactory demonstration from the fact. It is affirmed, that there is one and only one conception, in which the non-being or annihilation of the object is self-contradictory, and this is the conception of an *ens realissimum.** It possesses, you say, all reality, and you feel yourselves justified in admitting the possibility of such a thing. (This I am willing to grant for the present, although the existence of a conception which is not self-contradictory, is far from being sufficient to prove the possibility of an object.[1]) Now the notion of all reality embraces in it that of

---

*Latin: "most real being."

existence; the notion of existence lies, therefore, in the conception of this possible thing. If this thing is annihilated in thought, the internal possibility of the thing is also annihilated, which is self-contradictory.

I answer: It is absurd to introduce—under whatever term disguised—into the conception of a thing, which is to be cogitated solely in reference to its possibility, the conception of its existence. If this is admitted, you will have apparently gained the day, but in reality have enounced nothing but a mere tautology. I ask, is the proposition, *this or that thing* (which I am admitting to be possible) *exists,* an analytical or a synthetical proposition? If the former, there is no addition made to the subject of your thought by the affirmation of its existence; but then the conception in your minds is identical with the thing itself, or you have supposed the existence of a thing to be possible, and then inferred its existence from its internal possibility—which is but a miserable tautology. The word *reality* in the conception of the thing, and the word *existence* in the conception of the predicate, will not help you out of the difficulty. For, supposing you were to term all positing of a thing, reality, you have thereby posited the thing with all its predicates in the conception of the subject and assumed its actual existence, and this you merely repeat in the predicate. But if you confess, as every reasonable person must, that every existential proposition is synthetical, how can it be maintained that the predicate of existence cannot be denied without contradiction—a property which is the characteristic of analytical propositions, alone.

I should have a reasonable hope of putting an end forever to this sophistical mode of argumentation, by a strict definition of the conception of existence, did not my own experience teach me that the illusion arising from our confounding a logical with a real predicate (a predicate which aids in the determination of a thing) resists almost all the endeavors of explanation and illustration. A *logical predicate* may be what you please, even the subject may be predicated of itself; for logic pays no regard to the content of a judgment. But the determination of a conception is a predicate, which adds to and enlarges the conception. It must not, therefore, be contained in the conception.

Being is evidently not a real predicate, that is, a conception of something which is added to the conception of some other thing. It is merely the positing of a thing, or of certain determinations in it. Logically, it is merely the copula of a judgment. The proposition, *God is omnipotent,* contains two conceptions, which have a certain object or content; the word *is,* is no additional predicate—it merely indicates the relation of the predicate to the subject. Now, if I take the subject (God) with all its predicates (omnipotence being one), and say, *God is,* or *There is a God,* I add no new predicate to the conception of God, I merely posit or affirm the existence of the subject with all its predicates—I posit the *object* in relation to my *conception.* The content of both is the same; and there is no addition made to the conception, which expresses merely the possibility of the object, by my cogitating the object—in the expression, it *is*—as absolutely given or existing. Thus the real contains no more than the possible. A hundred real dollars contain no more than a hundred possible dollars. For, as the latter indicate the conception, and the former the object, on the supposition that the content of the former was greater than that of the latter, my conception would not be an expression of the whole object, and would consequently be an inadequate conception of it. But in reckoning my wealth there may be said to be more in a hundred real dollars, than in a hundred possible dollars—that is, in the mere conception of them. For the real object—the dollars—is not analytically contained in my conception, but forms a synthetical addition to my conception (which is merely a determination of my mental state), although this objective reality—this existence—apart from my conception, does not in the least degree increase the aforesaid hundred dollars.

It does not matter which predicates or how many of them we may think a thing possesses, I do not make the least addition to it when we further declare that this thing exists. Otherwise, it would not be the exact same thing that exists, but something more than we had thought in the idea or concept; and hence, we could not say that the exact object of my thought exists. On the contrary, it exists with the same defect with which I have thought it, since otherwise what exists would be something different from what I thought. So when I think of a being as the highest reality, without any imperfection, the question still remains whether or not this being exists. For although, in my idea, nothing may be lacking in the possible real content of a thing in general, something is still lacking in its relation to my mental state; that is, I am ignorant of whether the object is also possible *à posteriori*. It is here we discover the core of our problem. If the question regarded an object of sense merely, it would be impossible for me to confuse the idea of a thing with its existence. For the concept of the object merely enables me to think of it according to universal conditions of experience; while the existence of the object permits me to think of it within the context of actual experience. However, in being connected with the content of experience as a whole, the concept of the object is not enlarged. All that has happened is that our thought has thereby acquired another possible perception. So it is not surprising that, if we attempt to think existence through the pure categories alone, we cannot specify a single mark distinguishing it from mere possibility.

Whatever be the content of our conception of an object, it is necessary to go beyond it, if we wish to predicate existence of an object. In the case of sensuous objects, this is attained by their connection according to empirical laws with some one of my perceptions; but when it comes to objects of pure thought, there is no means whatever of knowing of their existence, since it would have to be known in a completely *à priori* manner. But all our knowledge of existence (be it immediately by perception or by inferences connecting some object with a perception) belongs entirely to the sphere of experience—which is in perfect unity with itself—and although an existence out of this sphere cannot be absolutely declared to be impossible, it is a hypothesis the truth of which we have no means of discovering.

The idea of a supreme being is in many ways a very useful idea; but for the very reason that it is an idea, it is incapable of enlarging our knowledge with regard to the existence of things. It is not even sufficient to instruct us as to the possibility of a being which we do not know to exist. The analytical criterion of possibility, which consists in the absence of contradiction in propositions, cannot be denied it. But the connection of real properties in a thing is a synthesis of the possibility of which an *à priori* judgment cannot be formed, because these realities are not presented to us specifically; and even if this were to happen, a judgment would still be impossible, because the criterion of possibility of synthetical cognitions must be sought for in the world of experience, to which the object of an idea cannot belong. And thus the celebrated Leibniz has utterly failed in his attempt to establish upon *à priori* grounds the possibility of this sublime ideal being.

The celebrated ontological or Cartesian argument for the existence of a Supreme Being is therefore insufficient; and we may as well hope to increase our stock of knowledge by the aid of mere ideas, as the merchant to increase his wealth by adding a few zeros to his bank account.

Note

1. A conception is always possible, if it is not self-contradictory. This is the logical criterion of possibility, distinguishing the object of such a conception from the *nihil negativum*. But it may be, notwithstanding, an empty conception, unless the objective reality of this synthesis, by which it is generated, is demonstrated; and a proof of this kind must be based upon principles of possible experience, and not upon the principle of analysis or contradiction. This remark may be serviceable as a warning against concluding, from the possibility of a conception—which is logical, the possibility of a thing—which is real.

I.C.3 The Ontological Argument

ALVIN PLANTINGA

Alvin Plantinga (1932–   ) is a professor of philosophy at the University of Notre Dame and one of the leading philosophers of religion today. In this reading, Plantinga analyzes Anselm's argument, defends it against Kant's criticism, and then constructs a modal version of the argument. That is, the argument is set forth in terms of the modes of possibility and necessity or in terms of possible and necessary existence. The key premise becomes "There is a possible world in which maximal greatness is instantiated." Plantinga explicates and defends this premise, which rests on the premise that a being has maximal excellence in every possible world and which therefore entails the existence of God. Plantinga believes that this version of the ontological argument is sound, but he doesn't claim that it proves that God exists (for the argument works only if (29) is true, and it may not be). But there is nothing irrational about believing (29). His argument "establishes not the truth of theism, but its rational acceptability."

The third theistic argument I wish to discuss is the famous "ontological argument" first formulated by Anselm of Canterbury in the eleventh century. This argument for the existence of God has fascinated philosophers ever since Anselm first stated it. Few people, I should think, have been brought to belief in God by means of this argument; nor has it played much of a role in strengthening and confirming religious faith. At first sight Anselm's argument is remarkably unconvincing if not downright irritating; it looks too much like a parlor puzzle or word magic. And yet nearly every major philosopher from the time of Anselm to the present has had something to say about it; this argument has a long and illustrious line of defenders extending to the

Reprinted from Alvin Plantinga, *God, Freedom and Evil* (New York: Harper & Row, 1974) by permission of the author.

present. Indeed, the last few years have seen a remarkable flurry of interest in it among philosophers. What accounts for its fascination? Not, I think, its religious significance, although that can be underrated. Perhaps there are two reasons for it. First, many of the most knotty and difficult problems in philosophy meet in this argument. Is existence a property? Are existential propositions—propositions of the form *x exists*—ever necessarily true? Are existential propositions about what they seem to be about? Are there, in any respectable sense of "are," some objects that do not exist? If so, do they have any properties? Can they be compared with things that do exist? These issues and a hundred others arise in connection with Anselm's argument. And second, although the argument certainly looks at first sight as if it ought to be unsound, it is profoundly difficult to say what, exactly, is wrong with it. Indeed, I do not believe that any philosopher has ever given a cogent and conclusive refutation of the ontological argument in its various forms. . . .

At first sight, [Anselm's] argument smacks of trumpery and deceit; but suppose we look at it a bit more closely. Its essentials are contained in these words:

> And assuredly that, than which nothing greater can be conceived, cannot exist in the understanding alone. For suppose it exists in the understanding alone; then it can be conceived to exist in reality; which is greater.
> Therefore, if that, than which nothing greater can be conceived, exists in the understanding alone, the very being, than which nothing greater can be conceived, is one, than which a greater can be conceived. But obviously this is impossible. Hence there is no doubt that there exists a being, than which nothing greater can be conceived, and it exists both in the understanding and in reality.

How can we outline this argument? It is best construed, I think, as a *reductio ad absurdum* argument. In a *reductio* you prove a given proposition *p* by showing that its denial, *not-p*, leads to (or more strictly, entails) a contradiction or some other kind of absurdity. Anselm's argument can be seen as an attempt to deduce an absurdity from the proposition that there is no God. If we use the term "God" as an abbreviation for Anselm's phrase "the being than which nothing greater can be conceived," then the argument seems to go approximately as follows: Suppose

(1) God exists in the understanding but not in reality.

(2) Existence in reality is greater than existence in the understanding alone. (premise)

(3) God's existence in reality is conceivable. (premise)

(4) If God did exist in reality, then He would be greater than He is. [from (1) and (2)]

(5) It is conceivable that there is a being greater than God is. [(3) and (4)]

(6) It is conceivable that there be a being greater than the being than which nothing greater can be conceived. [(5) by the definition of "God"]

But surely (6) is absurd and self-contradictory; how could we conceive of a being greater than the being than which none greater can be conceived? So we may conclude that

(7) It is false that God exists in the understanding but not in reality

It follows that if God exists in the understanding, He also exists in reality; but clearly enough He *does* exist in the understanding, as even the fool will testify; therefore, He exists in reality as well.

Now when Anselm says that a being *exists in the understanding,* we may take him, I think, as saying that someone has *thought of* or thought about that being. When he says that something *exists in reality,* on the other hand, he means to say simply that the thing in question really does exist. And when he says that a certain state of affairs is *conceivable,* he means to say, I believe, that this state of affairs is possible in our broadly logical sense, there is a possible world in which it obtains. This means that step (3) above may be put more perspicuously as

(3′) It is possible that God exists

and step (6) as

(6′) It is possible that there be a being greater than the being than which it is not possible that there be a greater.

An interesting feature of this argument is that all of its premises are *necessarily* true if true at all. (1) is the assumption from which Anselm means to deduce a contradiction. (2) is a premise, and presumably necessarily true in Anselm's view; and (3) is the only remaining premise (the other items are consequences of preceding steps); it says of some *other* proposition (*God exists*) that it is possible. Propositions which thus ascribe a modality—possibility, necessity, contingency—to another proposition are themselves either necessarily true or necessarily false. So all the premises of the argument are, if true at all, necessarily true. And hence if the premises of this argument are true, then [provided that (6) is really inconsistent] a contradiction can be deduced from (1) together with necessary propositions; this means that (1) entails a contradiction and is, therefore, necessarily false. . . .

1. Kant's Objection

The most famous and important objection to the ontological argument is contained in Immanuel Kant's *Critique of Pure Reason.* Kant begins his criticism as follows:

If, in an identical proposition, I reject the predicate while retaining the subject, contradiction results; and I therefore say that the former belongs necessarily to the latter. But if we reject the subject and predicate alike, there is no contradiction; for nothing is then left that can be contradicted. To posit a triangle, and yet to reject its three angles, is self-contradictory, but there is no contradiction in rejecting the triangle together with its three angles. The same holds true of the concept of an absolutely necessary being. If its existence is rejected, we reject the thing itself with all its predicates; and no question of contradiction can then arise. There is nothing outside it that would then be contradicted, since the necessity of the thing is not supposed to be derived from anything external; nor is there anything internal that would be contradicted, since in rejecting the thing itself we have at the same time rejected all its internal properties. "God is omnipotent" is a necessary judgment. The omnipotence cannot be rejected if we posit a Deity, that is, an infinite being; for the two concepts are identical. But if we say "There is no God," neither the omnipotence nor any other of its predicates is given; they are one and all rejected together with the subject, and there is therefore not the least contradiction in such a judgment. . . .

For I cannot form the least concept of a thing which, should it be rejected with all its predicates, leaves behind a contradiction.

One characteristic feature of Anselm's argument, as we have seen, is that if successful, it establishes that *God exists* is a *necessary* proposition. Here Kant is apparently arguing that no *existential* proposition—one that asserts the existence of something or other—is necessarily true; the reason, he says, is that no *contra-existential* (the denial of an existential) is contradictory or inconsistent. But in which of our several senses of inconsistent? What he means to say, I believe, is that no existential proposition is necessary in the broadly logical sense. And this claim has been popular with philosophers ever since. But why, exactly, does Kant think it's true? What is the argument? When we take a careful look at the purported reasoning, it looks pretty unimpressive; it's hard to make out an argument at all. The conclusion would apparently be this: if we deny the existence of something or other, we can't be contradicting ourselves; no existential proposition is necessary and no contra-existential is impossible. Why not? Well, if we say, for example, that God does not exist, then says Kant, "There is nothing outside it (i.e., God) that would then be contradicted, since the necessity of the thing is not supposed to be derived from anything external; nor is there anything internal that would be contradicted, since in rejecting the thing itself we have at the same time rejected all its internal properties."

But how is this even *relevant?* The claim is that *God does not exist* can't be necessarily false. What could be meant, in this context, by saying that there's nothing "outside of" God that would be contradicted if we denied His existence? What would contradict a proposition like *God does not exist* is some other proposition—*God does exist,* for example. Kant seems to think that if the proposition in question *were* necessarily false, it would have to contradict, not a proposition, but some *object* external to God—or else contradict some internal part

or aspect or property of God. But this certainly looks like confusion; it is *propositions* that contradict each other; they aren't contradicted by objects or parts, aspects or properties of objects. Does he mean instead to be speaking of *propositions* about things external to God, or about His aspects or parts or properties? But clearly many such propositions do contradict *God does not exist;* an example would be *the world was created by God.* Does he mean to say that no *true* proposition contradicts *God does not exist?* No, for that would be to affirm the *nonexistence* of God, an affirmation Kant is by no means prepared to make.

So this passage is an enigma. Either Kant was confused or else he expressed himself very badly indeed. And either way we don't have any argument for the claim that contra-existential propositions can't be inconsistent. This passage seems to be no more than an elaborate and confused way of *asserting* this claim.

The heart of Kant's objection to the ontological argument, however, is contained in the following passage.

"Being" is obviously not a real predicate; that is, it is not a concept of something which could be added to the concept of a thing. It is merely the positing of a thing, or of certain determinations, as existing in themselves. Logically, it is merely the copula of a judgment. The proposition "God is omnipotent" contains two concepts, each of which has its object—God and omnipotence. The small word "is" adds no new predicate, but only serves to posit the predicate in its relation to the subject. If, now, we take the subject (God) with all its predicates (among which is omnipotence), and say "God is," or "There is a God," we attach no new predicate to the concept of God, but only posit it as an object that stands in relation to my concept. The content of both must be one and the same; nothing can have been added to the concept, which expresses merely what is possible, by my thinking its object (through the expression "it is") as given absolutely. Otherwise stated, the real contains no more than the merely possible. A hundred real thalers do not contain the least coin more than a hundred possible thalers. For as the latter signify the concept and the former the object and the positing of the concept, should the former contain more than the latter, my concept would not, in that case, express the whole object, and would not therefore be an adequate concept of it. My financial position, however, is affected very differently by a hundred real thalers than it is by the mere concept of them (that is, of the possibility). For the object, as it actually exists, is not analytically contained in my concept, but is added to my concept (which is a determination of my state) synthetically; and yet the conceived hundred thalers are not themselves in the least increased through thus acquiring existence outside my concept.

By whatever and by however many predicates we may think a thing—even if we completely determine it—we do not make the least addition to the thing when we further declare that this thing is. Otherwise it would not be exactly the same thing that exists, but something more than we had thought in the concept: and we could not, therefore, say that the object of my concept exists. If we think in a thing every feature of reality except one, the missing reality is not added by my saying that this defective thing exists.

Now how, exactly is all this relevant to Anselm's argument? Perhaps Kant means to make a point that we could put by saying that it's not possible to *define things into existence.* (People sometimes suggest that the ontological argument is just such an attempt to define *God* into existence.) And this claim is somehow connected with Kant's famous but perplexing *dictum* that *being* (or existence) is not a real predicate or property. But how shall we understand Kant here? What does it mean to say that existence isn't (or is) a real property?

Apparently Kant thinks this is equivalent to or follows from what he puts variously as "the real *contains* no more than the merely possible"; "the *content* of both (i.e., concept and object) must be one and the same"; "being is not the concept of something that could be *added to* the concept of a thing," and so on. But what does all this mean? And how does it bear on the ontological argument? Perhaps Kant is thinking along the following lines. In defining a concept—*bachelor*, let's say, or *prime number*—one lists a number of properties that are *severally necessary* and *jointly sufficient* for the concept's applying to something. That is, the concept applies to a given thing only if that thing has each of the listed properties, and if a thing does have them all, then the concept in question applies to it. So, for example, to define the concept *bachelor* we list such properties as *being unmarried, being male, being over the age of twenty-five,* and the like. Take any one of these properties: a thing is a bachelor only if it has it, and if a thing has all of them, then it follows that it is a bachelor.

Now suppose you have a concept *C* that has application *contingently* if at all. That is to say, it is not necessarily true that there are things to which this concept applies. The concept *bachelor* would be an example; the proposition *there are bachelors,* while *true,* is obviously not necessarily true. And suppose $P_1, P_2 \ldots, P_n$ are the properties jointly sufficient and severally necessary for something's falling under *C*. Then *C* can be defined as follows:

■   A thing x is an instance of *C* (i.e., *C* applies to x) if and only if x has $P_1, P_2 \ldots, P_n$.

Perhaps Kant's point is this. There is a certain kind of mistake here we may be tempted to make. Suppose $P_1, \ldots, P_n$ are the defining properties for the concept *bachelor.* We might try to define a new concept *superbachelor* by adding *existence* to $P_1, \ldots, P_n$. That is, we might say

■ x is a superbachelor if and only if x has $P_1, P_2, \ldots, P_n$, and x exists.

Then (as we might mistakenly suppose) just as it is a necessary truth that bachelors are unmarried, so it is a necessary truth that superbachelors exist. And in this way it looks as if we've defined superbachelors into existence.

But of course this is a mistake, and perhaps that is Kant's point. For while indeed it is a necessary truth that bachelors are unmarried, what this means is that the proposition

(8)   Everything that is a bachelor is unmarried

is necessarily true. Similarly, then,

(9)   Everything that is a superbachelor exists

will be necessarily true. But obviously it doesn't follow that there *are* any superbachelors. All that follows is that

(10)   All the superbachelors there are *exist* which is not really very startling. If it is a contingent truth, furthermore, that there are bachelors, it will be equally contingent that there are superbachelors. We can see this by noting that the defining properties of the concept *bachelor* are included among those of *superbachelor;* it

is a necessary truth, therefore, that every superbachelor is a bachelor. This means that

(11) There are some superbachelors

entails

(12) There are some bachelors.

But then if (12) is contingent, so is (11). Indeed, the concepts *bachelor* and *superbachelor* are equivalent in the following sense: it is impossible that there exists an object to which one but not the other of these two concepts applies. We've just seen that every superbachelor must be a bachelor. Conversely, however, every bachelor is a superbachelor: for every bachelor exists and every existent bachelor is a superbachelor. Now perhaps we can put Kant's point more exactly. Suppose we say that a property or predicate P is *real* only if there is some list of properties P_1 to P_n such that the result of adding P to the list does not define a concept equivalent (in the above sense) to that defined by the list. It then follows, of course, that existence is not a real property or predicate. Kant's point, then, is that one cannot *define things into existence* because *existence* is not a real property or predicate in the explained sense.

2. The Irrelevance of Kant's Objection

If this is what he means, he's certainly right. But is it relevant to the ontological argument? Couldn't Anselm thank Kant for this interesting point and proceed merrily on his way? Where did he try to define God into being by adding existence to a list of properties that defined some concept? According to the great German philosopher and pessimist Arthur Schopenhauer, the ontological argument arises when "someone excogitates a conception, composed out of all sorts of predicates, among which, however, he takes care to include the predicate actuality or existence, either openly or wrapped up for decency's sake in some other predicate, such as perfection, immensity, or something of the kind." If this were Anselm's procedure—if he

had simply added existence to a concept that has application contingently if at all—then indeed his argument would be subject to the Kantian criticism. But he didn't, and it isn't.

The usual criticisms of Anselm's argument, then, leave much to be desired. Of course, this doesn't mean that the argument is successful, but it does mean that we shall have to take an independent look at it. What about Anselm's argument? Is it a good one? The first thing to recognize is that the ontological argument comes in an enormous variety of versions, some of which may be much more promising than others. Instead of speaking of *the* ontological argument, we must recognize that what we have here is a whole family of related arguments. (Having said this I shall violate my own directive and continue to speak of *the* ontological argument.)

3. The Argument Restated

Let's look once again at our initial schematization of the argument. I think perhaps it is step (2)

(2) Existence in reality is greater than existence in the understanding alone

that is most puzzling here. Earlier we spoke of the properties in virtue of which one being is greater, just as a being, than another. Suppose we call them *great-making properties*. Apparently Anselm means to suggest that *existence* is a great-making property. He seems to suggest that a nonexistent being would be greater than in fact it is, if it did exist. But how can we make sense of that? How could there be a nonexistent being anyway? Does that so much as make sense?

Perhaps we can put this perspicuously in terms of possible worlds. You recall that an object may exist in some possible worlds and not others. There are possible worlds in which you and I do not exist; these worlds are impoverished, no doubt, but are not on that account impossible. Furthermore, you recall that an object can have different properties in different worlds. In the actual world Paul J. Zwier is not a good tennis player; but surely there are worlds in which he wins the Wimbledon Open. Now if a person can have different properties in different worlds, then he can have different degrees of greatness in different worlds. In the actual world Raquel Welch has impressive assets; but there is a world RW, in which she is fifty pounds overweight and mousy. Indeed, there are worlds in which she does not so much as exist. What Anselm means to be suggesting, I think, is that Raquel Welch enjoys very little greatness in those worlds in which she does not exist. But of course this condition is not restricted to Miss Welch. What Anselm means to say, more generally, is that for any being x and worlds W and W', if x exists in W but not in W', then x's greatness in W exceeds x's greatness in W'. Or, more modestly, perhaps he means to say that if a being x does not exist in a world W (and there is a world in which x does exist), then *there is at least one world* in which the greatness of x exceeds the greatness of x in W. Suppose Raquel Welch does not exist in some world W. Anselm means to say that there is at least one possible world in which she has a degree of greatness that exceeds the degree of greatness she has in that world W. (It is plausible, indeed, to go much further and hold that she has *no greatness at all* in worlds in which she does not exist.)

But now perhaps we can restate the whole argument in a way that gives us more insight into its real structure. Once more, use the term "God" to abbreviate the phrase "the being than which it is not possible that there be a greater." Now suppose

(13) God does not exist in the actual world

Add the new version of premise (2):

(14) For any being x and world W, if x does not exist in W, then there is a world W' such that the greatness of x in W' exceeds the greatness of x in W.

Restate premise (3) in terms of possible worlds:

(15) There is a possible world in which God exists.

And continue on:

(16) If God does not exist in the actual world, then there is a world W' such that the greatness of God in W' exceeds the greatness of God in the actual world. [from (14)]

(17) So there is a world W' such that the greatness of God in W' exceeds the greatness of God in the actual world. [(13) and (16)]

(18) So there is a possible being x and a world W' such that the greatness of x in W' exceeds the greatness of God in actuality. [(17)]

(19) Hence it's possible that there be a being greater than God is. [(18)]

(20) So it's possible that there be a being greater than the being than which it's not possible that there be a greater. [(19)], replacing "God" by what it abbreviates

But surely

(21) It's not possible that there be a being greater than the being than which it's not possible that there be a greater.

So (13) [with the help of premises (14) and (15)] appears to imply (20), which, according to (21), is necessarily false. Accordingly, (13) is false. So the actual world contains a being than which it's not possible that there be a greater—that is, God exists.

Now where, if anywhere, can we fault this argument? Step (13) is the hypothesis for *reductio*, the assumption to be reduced to absurdity, and is thus entirely above reproach. Steps (16) through (20) certainly look as if they follow from the items they are said to follow from. So that leaves only (14), (15), and (20). Step (14) says only that it is possible that God exists. Step (15) also certainly seems plausible: if a being doesn't even *exist* in a given world, it can't have much by way of greatness in that world. At the very least it can't have its *maximum* degree of greatness—a degree of greatness that it does not excel in any other world—in a world where it doesn't exist. And consider (20): surely it has the ring of truth. How could there be a being greater than the being than which it's not possible that there be a greater? Initially, the argument seems pretty formidable.

4. Its Fatal Flaw

But there is something puzzling about it. We can see this if we ask what sorts of things (14) is supposed to be *about*. It starts off boldly: "For any being *x* and world *W*, . . ." So (14) is talking about worlds and beings. It says something about each world-being pair. And (16) follows from it, because (16) asserts of *God* and *the actual world* something that according to (14) holds of every being and world. But then if (16) follows from (14), God must be a *being*. That is, (16) follows from (14) only with the help of the additional premise that God is a being. And doesn't this statement—that God is a being—imply that *there is* or *exists* a being than which it's not possible that there be a greater? But if so, the argument flagrantly begs the question; for then we can accept the inference from (14) to (16) only if we already know that the conclusion is true.

We can approach this same matter by a slightly different route. I asked earlier what sorts of things (14) was *about*; the answer was: beings and worlds. We can ask the same or nearly the same question by asking about the *range* of the *quantifiers*—"for any being," "for any world"—in (14). What do these quantifiers range over? If we reply that they range over possible worlds and beings—*actually existing* beings—then the inference to (16) requires the additional premise that God is an actually existing being, that there *really is* a being than which it is not possible that there be a greater. Since this is supposed to be our conclusion, we can't gracefully add it as a *premise*. So perhaps the quantifiers don't range just over actually existing beings. But what else is there? Step (18) speaks of a *possible being*—a thing that may not in fact exist, but *could* exist. Or we could put it like this. A possible being is a thing that exists in some possible world or other; a thing *x* for which there is a world *W*, such that if *W* had been actual, *x* would have existed. So (18) is really about worlds and *possible beings*. And what it says is this: take any possible being *x* and any possible world *W*. If *x* does not exist in *W*, then there is a possible world *W'* where *x* has a degree of greatness that surpasses the greatness that it has in *W*.

And hence to make the argument complete perhaps we should add the affirmation that God is a *possible being*.

But *are* there any possible beings—that is, *merely* possible beings, beings that don't in fact exist? If so, what sorts of things are they? Do they have properties? How are we to think of them? What is their status? And what reasons are there for supposing that there are any such peculiar items at all?

These are knotty problems: Must we settle them in order even to consider this argument? No. For instead of speaking of *possible beings* and the worlds in which they do or don't exist, we can speak of *properties* and the worlds in which they do or don't *have instances,* are or are not *instantiated* or *exemplified.* Instead of speaking of a possible being named by the phrase, "the being than which it's not possible that there be a greater," we may speak of the property *having an unsurpassable degree of greatness*—that is, *having a degree of greatness such that it's not possible that there exist a being having more.* And then we can ask whether this property is instantiated in this or other possible worlds. Later on I shall show how to restate the argument this way. For the moment please take my word for the fact that we can speak as freely as we wish about possible objects; for we can always translate ostensible talk about such things into talk about properties and the worlds in which they are or are not instantiated.

The argument speaks, therefore, of an unsurpassably great being—of a being whose greatness is not excelled by any being in any world. This being has a degree of greatness so impressive that no other being in any world has more. But here we hit the question crucial for this version of the argument. *Where* does this being have that degree of greatness? I said above that the same being may have different degrees of greatness in different worlds; in which world does the possible being in question have the degree of greatness in question? All we are really told, in being told that God is a possible being, is this: among the possible beings there is one that in some world or other has a degree of greatness that is nowhere excelled.

And this fact is fatal to this version of the argument. I said earlier that (21) has the ring of truth; a closer look (listen?) reveals that it's more of a dull thud. For it is ambiguous as between

(21') It's not possible that there be a being whose greatness surpasses that enjoyed by the unsurpassably great being *in the worlds where its greatness is at a maximum*

and

(21") It's not possible that there be a being whose greatness surpasses that enjoyed by the unsurpassably great being *in the actual world.*

There is an important difference between these two. The greatest possible being may have different degrees of greatness in different worlds. Step (21') points to the worlds in which this being has its maximal greatness; and it says, quite properly, that the degree of greatness this being has in those worlds is nowhere excelled. Clearly this is so. The greatest possible being is a possible being who in some world or other has unsurpassable greatness. Unfortunately for the argument, however, (21') does not contradict (20). Or to put it another way, what follows from (13) [together with (14) and (15)] is not the denial of (21'). If that *did* follow, then the *reductio* would be complete and the argument successful. But what (20) says is not that there is a possible being whose greatness exceeds that enjoyed by the greatest possible being *in a world where the latter's greatness is at a maximum;* it says only that there is a possible being whose greatness exceeds that enjoyed by the greatest possible being *in the actual world*—where, for all we know, its greatness is *not* at a maximum. So if we read (21) as (21'), the *reductio* argument falls apart.

Suppose instead we read it as (21"). Then what it says is that there couldn't be a being whose greatness surpasses that enjoyed by the greatest possible being in Kronos, the actual world. So read, (21) does contradict (20). Unfortunately, however, we have no reason, so far, for thinking that (21") is true at all, let alone necessarily true. If, among the possible beings, there is one whose greatness *in some world or other* is absolutely maximal—such

that no being in any world has a degree of greatness surpassing it—then indeed there couldn't be a being that was greater than *that*. But it doesn't follow that this being has that degree of greatness in the *actual* world. It has it *in some world or other* but not necessarily in Kronos, the actual world. And so the argument fails. If we take (21) as (21'), then it follows from the assertion that God is a possible being; but it is of no use to the argument. If we take it as (21"), on the other hand, then indeed it is useful in the argument, but we have no reason whatever to think it true. So this version of the argument fails.

5. A Modal Version of the Argument

But of course there are many other versions; one of the argument's chief features is its many-sided diversity. The fact that *this* version is unsatisfactory does not show that *every* version is or must be. Professors Charles Hartshorne and Norman Malcolm claim to detect two quite different versions of the argument in Anselm's work. In the first of these versions *existence* is held to be a perfection or a great-making property; in the second it is *necessary existence*. But what could *that* amount to? Perhaps something like this. Consider a pair of beings A and B that both do in fact exist. And suppose that A exists in every other possible world as well—that is, if any other possible world has been actual, A would have existed. On the other hand, B exists in only some possible worlds; there are worlds W such that had any of *them* been actual, B would not have existed. Now according to the doctrine under consideration, A is so far greater than B. Of course, *on balance* it may be that A is not greater than B; I believe that the number seven, unlike Spiro Agnew, exists in every possible world; yet I should be hesitant to affirm on that account that the number seven is greater than Agnew. Necessary existence is just one of several great-making properties, and no doubt Agnew has more of some of these others than does the number seven. Still, all this is compatible with saying that necessary existence is a great-making property. And given this notion, we can restate the argument as follows:

(22) It is possible that there is a greatest possible being.

(23) Therefore, there is a possible being that in some world *W'* or other has a maximum degree of greatness—a degree of greatness that is nowhere exceeded.

(24) A being *B* has the maximum degree of a greatness in a given possible world *W* only if *B exists in every possible world.*

(22) and (24) are the premises of this argument; and what follows is that if *W'* had been actual, *B* would have existed in every possible world. That is, if *W'* had been actual, *B*'s nonexistence would have been impossible. But logical possibilities and impossibilities do not vary from world to world. That is to say, if a given proposition or state of affairs is impossible in at least one possible world, then it is impossible in every possible world. There are no propositions that in fact are possible but could have been impossible; there are none that are in fact impossible but could have been possible. Accordingly, *B*'s nonexistence is impossible in every possible world; hence it is impossible in *this* world; hence *B* exists and exists necessarily.

6. A Flaw in the Ointment

This is an interesting argument, but it suffers from at least one annoying defect. What it shows is that if it is possible that there be a greatest possible being (if the idea of a greatest possible being is coherent) and if that idea includes necessary existence, then in fact there is a being that exists in every world and in *some* world has a degree of greatness that is nowhere excelled. Unfortunately it doesn't follow that the being in question has the degree of greatness in question in Kronos, the actual world. For all the argument shows, this being might *exist* in the actual world but be pretty insignificant here. In some world or other it has maximal greatness; how does this show that it has such greatness in Kronos?

But perhaps we can repair the argument. J. N. Findlay once offered what can only be called an ontological *disproof* of the existence of God. Findlay begins by pointing out that God, if He exists, is

an "adequate object of religious worship." But such a being, he says, would have to be a *necessary* being; and, he adds, this idea is incredible "for all who share a contemporary outlook." "Those who believe in necessary truths which aren't merely tautological think that such truths merely connect the *possible* instances of various characteristics with each other; they don't expect such truths to tell them whether there *will* be instances of any characteristics. This is the outcome of the whole medieval and Kantian criticism of the ontological proof." I've argued above that "the whole medieval and Kantian criticism" of Anselm's argument may be taken with a grain or two of salt. And certainly most philosophers who believe that there are necessary truths, believe that some of them *do* tell us whether there will be instances of certain characteristics; the proposition *there are no married bachelors* is necessarily true, and it tells us that there will be no instances whatever of the characteristic *married bachelor.* Be that as it may what is presently relevant in Findlay's piece is this passage:

> Not only is it contrary to the demands and claims inherent in religious attitudes that their object should *exist* "accidentally"; it is also contrary to these demands that it should *possess its various excellences* in some merely adventitious manner. It would be quite unsatisfactory from the religious stand point, if an object merely *happened* to be wise, good, powerful, and so forth, even to a superlative degree. . . . And so we are led on irresistibly, by the demands inherent in religious reverence, to hold that an adequate object of our worship must possess its various excellences *in some necessary manner.*

I think there is truth in these remarks. We could put the point as follows. In determining the greatness of a being *B* in a world *W*, what counts is not merely the qualities and properties possessed by *B* in *W*; what *B* is like in *other* worlds is also relevant. Most of us who believe in God think of Him as a being than whom it's not possible that there be a greater. But we don't think of Him as a being who, had things been different, would have been powerless or uninformed or of dubious moral character. God doesn't *just happen* to be a greatest possible being; He couldn't have been otherwise.

Perhaps we should make a distinction here between *greatness* and *excellence.* A being's excellence in a given world *W*, let us say, depends only upon the properties it has in *W*; its greatness in *W* depends upon these properties but also upon what it is like in other worlds. Those who are fond of the calculus might put it by saying that there is a function assigning to each being in each world a degree of excellence; and a being's *greatness* is to be computed (by someone unusually well informed) by integrating its excellence over all possible worlds. Then it is plausible to suppose that the maximal degree of greatness entails *maximal excellence in every world*. A being, then, has the maximal degree of *greatness* in a given world *W* only if it has *maximal excellence in every possible world*. But *maximal excellence* entails *omniscience, omnipotence,* and *moral perfection*. That is to say, a being *B* has maximal excellence in a world *W* only if *B* has omniscience, omnipotence, and moral perfection in *W*—only if *B* would have been omniscient, omnipotent, and morally perfect if *W* had been actual.

7. The Argument Restated

Given these ideas, we can restate the present version of the argument in the following more explicit way.

(25) It is possible that there be a being that has maximal greatness.

(26) So there is a possible being that in some world *W* has maximal greatness.

(27) A Being has maximal greatness in a given world only if it has maximal excellence in every world.

(28) A being has maximal excellence in a given world only if it has omniscience, omnipotence, and moral perfection in that world.

And now we no longer need the supposition that necessary existence is a perfection; for obviously a being can't be omnipotent (or for that matter omniscient or morally perfect) in a given world unless it *exists* in that world. From (25), (27), and (28) it follows that there actually exists a being that is omnipotent, omniscient, and morally perfect; this being, furthermore, exists and has these qualities in

every other world as well. For (26), which follows from (25), tells us that there is a possible world *W'*, let's say, in which there exists a being with maximal greatness. That is, had *W'* been actual, there would have been a being with maximal greatness. But then according to (27) this being has maximal excellence in every world. What this means, according to (28), is that in *W'* this being has omniscience, omnipotence, and moral perfection *in every world*. That is to say, if *W'* had been actual, there would have existed a being who was omniscient and omnipotent and morally perfect and who would have had these properties in every possible world. So if *W'* had been actual, it would have been *impossible* that there be no omnipotent, omniscient, and morally perfect being. But while *contingent* truths vary from world to world, what is logically impossible does not. Therefore, in every possible world *W* it is impossible that there be no such being; each possible world *W* is such that if it had been actual, it would have been impossible that there be no such being. And hence it is impossible in the *actual* world (which is one of the possible worlds) that there be no omniscient, omnipotent, and morally perfect being. Hence there really does exist a being who is omniscient, omnipotent, and morally perfect and who exists and has these properties in every possible world. Accordingly these premises, (25), (27), and (28), entail that God, so thought of, exists. Indeed, if we regard (27) and (28) as consequences of a *definition*—a definition of maximal greatness—then the only premise of the argument is (25).

But now for a last objection suggested earlier. What about (25)? It says that there is a *possible being* having such and such characteristics. But what *are* possible beings? We know what *actual* beings are—the Taj Mahal, Socrates, you and I, the Grand Teton—these are among the more impressive examples of actually existing beings. But what is a *possible* being? Is there a possible mountain just like Mt. Rainier two miles directly south of the Grand Teton? If so, it is located at the same place as the Middle Teton. Does that matter? Is there another such possible mountain three miles east of the Grand Teton, where Jenny Lake is? Are there possible mountains like this all over the world? Are there also possible oceans at all the places where there are possible mountains? For any place you mention, of course, it is *possible* that there be a mountain there; does it follow that in fact *there is* a possible mountain there?

These are some questions that arise when we ask ourselves whether there are merely possible beings that don't in fact exist. And the version of the ontological argument we've been considering seems to make sense only on the assumption that there are such things. The earlier versions also depended on that assumption; consider for example, this step of the first version we considered:

(18) So there is a possible being *x* and a world *W'* such that the greatness of *x* in *W'* exceeds the greatness of God in actuality.

This possible being, you recall, was God Himself, supposed not to exist in the actual world. We can make sense of (18), therefore, only if we are prepared to grant that there are possible beings who don't in fact exist. Such beings exist in other worlds, of course; had things been appropriately different, they would have existed. But in fact they don't exist, although nonetheless there *are* such things.

I am inclined to think the supposition that there are such things—things that are possible but don't in fact exist—is either unintelligible or necessarily false. But this doesn't mean that the present version of the ontological argument must be rejected. For we can restate the argument in a way that does not commit us to this questionable idea. Instead of speaking of *possible beings* that do or do not exist in various possible worlds, we may speak of *properties* and the worlds in which they are or are not *instantiated*. Instead of speaking of the possible fat man in the corner, noting that he doesn't exist, we may speak of the property *being a fat man in the corner,* noting that it isn't instantiated (although it could have been). Of course, the *property* in question, like the property *being a unicorn,* exists. It is a perfectly good property which exists with as much equanimity as the property of equininity, the property of being a horse. But it doesn't happen to apply to anything. That is, in *this* world it doesn't apply to anything; in other possible worlds it does.

8. The Argument Triumphant

Using this idea we can restate this last version of the ontological argument in such a way that it no longer matters whether there are any merely possible beings that do not exist. Instead of speaking of the possible being that has, in some world or other, a maximal degree of greatness, we may speak of *the property of being maximally great* or *maximal greatness.* The premise corresponding to (25) then says simply that maximal greatness is possibly instantiated, i.e., that

(29) There is a possible world in which maximal greatness is instantiated.

And the analogues of (27) and (28) spell out what is involved in maximal greatness:

(30) Necessarily, a being is maximally great only if it has maximal excellence in every world

and

(31) Necessarily, a being has maximal excellence in every world only if it has omniscience, omnipotence, and moral perfection in every world.

Notice that (30) and (31) do not imply that there are possible but nonexistent beings—any more than does, for example,

(32) Necessarily, a thing is a unicorn only if it has one horn.

But if (29) is true, then there is a possible world *W* such that if it had been actual, then there would have existed a being that was omnipotent, omniscient, and morally perfect; this being, furthermore, would have had these qualities in every possible world. So it follows that if *W* had been actual, it would have been *impossible* that there be no such being. That is, if *W* had been actual,

(33) There is no omnipotent, omniscient, and morally perfect being

would have been an impossible proposition. But if a proposition is impossible in at least one possible world, then it is impossible in every possible world; what is impossible does not vary from world to world. Accordingly (33) is impossible in the *actual* world, i.e., impossible *simpliciter*. But if it is impossible that there be no such being, then there actually exists a being that is omnipotent, omniscient, and morally perfect; this being, furthermore, has these qualities essentially and exists in every possible world.

What shall we say of this argument? It is certainly valid; given its premise, the conclusion follows. The only question of interest, it seems to me, is whether its main premise—that maximal greatness *is* possibly instantiated—is *true*. I think it *is* true; hence I think this version of the ontological argument is sound.

But here we must be careful; we must ask whether this argument is a successful piece of natural theology, whether it *proves* the existence of God. And the answer must be, I think, that it does not. An argument for God's existence may be

sound, after all, without in any useful sense proving God's existence. Since I believe in God, I think the following argument is sound:

- Either God exists or 7 + 5 = 14
- It is false that 7 + 5 = 14
- Therefore God exists.

But obviously this isn't a *proof*; no one who didn't already accept the conclusion, would accept the first premise. The ontological argument we've been examining isn't just like this one, of course, but it must be conceded that not everyone who understands and reflects on its central premise—that the existence of a maximally great being is *possible*—will accept it. Still, it is evident, I think, that there is nothing *contrary to reason* or *irrational* in accepting this premise. What I claim for this argument, therefore, is that it establishes, not the *truth* of theism, but its rational acceptability. And hence it accomplishes at least one of the aims of the tradition of natural theology.

I.C.4 Modal Versions of the Ontological Argument

WILLIAM ROWE

William Rowe is professor of philosophy at Purdue University. In this essay he critically analyzes Plantinga's version of the ontological argument, appreciating its brilliance but leveling some objections at what it claims to have accomplished.

It has sometimes been thought that two distinct ontological arguments can be found in chapters 2 and 3 of Anselm's *Proslogium*. It is clear that in chapter 2 Anselm intended to set forth an argument for God's existence. He there introduces his con-

cept of God as a being than which none greater is possible, and he advances the principle that existence in reality contributes to the greatness of a being. He then argues that God, as conceived by him, exists in reality—for otherwise a being greater than the greatest possible being would be possible.[1] Having satisfied himself that God's existence has been established, in chapter 3 Anselm turns to consider the mode or way in which God exists. Some things, like cabbages and kings, exist only *contingently*. It is possible that they should not have existed at all. Put in the language of possible worlds, we might say that the possible world that happens to be actual contains cabbages and kings.[2] Other possible worlds, however, do not contain them; and

This article was written specifically for the first edition of this volume.

had one of those worlds been the actual world, cabbages and kings would not have existed.

Does God exist only contingently? Anselm thought not, for a being would be greater if it existed in such a way that it logically could not fail to exist. Put in the language of possible worlds, a being would be greater if it is contained in *every* possible world rather than in just some possible worlds. So if God exists contingently, it would be possible for God to be greater than he is. Since it is not possible for God to be greater than he is, God must exist *necessarily.*

As I have interpreted Anselm, he did not intend in chapter 3 to be offering a further argument for God's existence. Instead, he wanted to determine whether God, whose existence he had already established in chapter 2 exists contingently or necessarily. But whatever his intentions may have been, it is not difficult to see in chapter 3 the makings of a distinct argument for God's existence. For chapter 3 presents us with the principle that *necessary existence*, no less than the *existence in reality* of chapter 2, contributes to the greatness of a being. If it is possible for Anselm's God to possess necessary existence, then that is the sort of existence he does possess—otherwise it would be possible for God to be greater.

Reflection on chapter 3 of Anselm's *Proslogium* has led philosophers to create various modal versions of the ontological argument. Among the most interesting versions is one set forth by Alvin Plantinga. Plantinga's version has the merit of extraordinary simplicity. By defining the concept of maximal greatness in a certain manner, Plantinga is able to boil down his version of the argument to the assertion of a single premise: that there is a possible world in which the property of maximal greatness is instantiated. Another merit of Plantinga's version is that it makes use of the idea of possible worlds, thus reducing the logic of the modal argument to its most intuitive level. Before we consider his version, however, let's prepare ourselves for some of the questions we need to raise by examining two quite simple ontological arguments that are suggested by the reasoning in chapters 2 and 3 of Anselm's *Proslogium.*

Consider two distinct concepts of God that I will call G_1 and G_2. We shall define G_1 as follows:

> G_1 = the concept of an omnipotent, omniscient, wholly good being who is such that he exists with these perfections in the actual world.

G^2 is defined as follows:

> G_2 = the concept of an omnipotent, omniscient, wholly good being who is such that he exists with these perfections in every possible world.

Let us say that a *normal* concept C of a being or kind of being is *satisfied* in a given possible world just in case, were that world actual, that being or a being of that kind would exist. Thus the concept *elephant* is satisfied in our world, but the concept *unicorn* is not. For our world is actual and elephants do exist, but unicorns do not. In some other possible world, however, just the reverse is true—the concept *unicorn* is satisfied, but the concept *elephant* is not. For if that world were actual, at least one unicorn would exist, but no elephants would exist. Armed with this idea of what it is for a normal concept of a being (or kind of being) to be *satisfied* in a possible world, let's consider our two concepts of God introduced above.

With a little reflection, I think we can see that our first concept, G_1, may not be a *normal* concept. To ask whether the normal concept *unicorn* is satisfied in w is simply to ask whether a unicorn would exist if w were actual. Where w is some possible world other than the possible world that is in fact actual, the question of whether the concept *unicorn* is satisfied in w has nothing to do with whether unicorns, elephants, cabbages, or kings exist in the actual world. But this is not so with G_1. Whether G_1 is satisfied in w depends in part on what sorts of beings *actually exist*, what sorts of beings exist in the actual world. It is not enough that w contains an omnipotent, omniscient, wholly good being. For unless *that being* exists in the actual world with just those perfections, G_1 is not satisfied in w. The important point to grasp here is that the satisfaction of G_1 in any possible world depends on the *actual existence* of an omnipotent, omniscient, wholly good being.[3]

The following argument is suggested by the reasoning of *Proslogium 2*:

(1) There is a possible world in which G_1 is satisfied.

Therefore,

(2) There exists an omnipotent, omniscient, wholly good being.

This argument is logically valid. Is its premise true? Well, that depends, as we've seen, on what beings are contained in the actual world. If every existing being has some moral defect, then there is no possible world in which G_1 is *in fact* satisfied.

For an argument to be a *proof* of its conclusion we must know its premise(s) to be true without basing that knowledge on a prior knowledge of its conclusion. Is it logically possible for some human being to know (1) to be true without basing that knowledge on knowing (2) to be true? It would be rash to answer no to this question. For it is difficult to draw *logical* limits to the ways in which human beings might come to know that a certain proposition is true. But perhaps we can say this much. It is exceedingly difficult to see how some human being would in fact come to a knowledge of (1) independently of knowing (2). So it is more than likely true that this argument is not a proof of its conclusion for any human being.

G_2 is a more far-reaching concept than is G_1. For G_1's being satisfied in a possible world w requires that the actual world contain an omnipotent, omniscient, wholly good being but allows that many other possible worlds lack such a being. G_2, however, is satisfied in a possible world w only if *every* possible world (including the actual world) contains an omnipotent, omniscient, wholly good being. In the spirit of *Proslogium 3*, if not the letter, we can construct the following argument:

(3) There is a possible world in which G_2 is satisfied.

Therefore,

(4) There necessarily exists an omnipotent, omniscient, wholly good being.

Once we realize that the satisfaction of G_2 in *any* possible world requires the existence of an omnipotent, omniscient, wholly good being in *every* possible world, we can appreciate the extraordinary difficulty of viewing this argument as a *proof* of its conclusion. Perhaps if we know that the actual world contains an omnipotent, omniscient, wholly good being, we might begin to ponder whether this being holds forth in all or just some possible worlds. But it is difficult to see how merely reflecting on the concept G_2 can enable us to know that it is satisfied in some possible world. For, as we've noted, its satisfaction in *any* possible world depends on what is contained in *every* possible world. But again, it would be unwise to declare that it is logically impossible for someone to come to know (3) independently of knowing (4), or even (2). But few, I believe, would be inclined to view this argument as a *proof* of its conclusion.

For reasons we need not consider here, Plantinga prefers to state his modal version of the ontological argument in terms of whether a certain property—the property of being maximally great—is instantiated in any possible world. For a property to be instantiated in a world w is for it to be true that if w were actual some thing would exist having that property. Thus the property of being an elephant is instantiated in our possible world, but the property of being a unicorn is not. Plantinga's property of being maximally great, however, is vastly different from such pedestrian properties as being an elephant or being a unicorn. The question of whether these two properties are instantiated in some possible but nonactual world w doesn't at all depend on whether the actual world contains elephants or unicorns. But Plantinga's property of being maximally great can be instantiated in some possible world w only if the actual world contains a being that is omnipotent, omniscient, and morally perfect. And even this is not enough. Not only must the actual world contain an omnipotent, omniscient, and morally perfect being, but *every* possible world must contain a being having these marvelous attributes, and it must be the *same* being who has these attributes in all these different worlds. Once we understand all this, we can see what an extraordinary property it is to which Plantinga has drawn our attention. If any possible world whatever happens to lack an omnipotent, omniscient, and morally perfect being, then Plantinga's extraordinary property is an impossible property and is instantiated in no possible world.

Analogous to our argument concerning concept G_2, the following argument is valid:

(5) There is a possible world in which maximal greatness is instantiated.

Therefore,

(6) There necessarily exists an omnipotent, omniscient, and morally perfect being.

And, for reasons given in connection with our two earlier arguments, it is extremely unlikely that this argument is a *proof* of its conclusion.

Consider the property of being in less than perfect company, where it is understood that a person has that property in a world *w* just in case every person in *w* (human and nonhuman) has some degree of imperfection, however slight. It may be that we enjoy (or are burdened with) this property in the actual world. But even if we are not, surely, one would think, it is *possible* that this property be instantiated. Surely there is some possible world in which every person has some imperfection, however slight. But if so, then Plantinga's extraordinary property is impossible; there is no possible world in which it is instantiated. If either of these properties is instantiated in some world *w*, then the other is uninstantiated in *w* and in every other possible world. Since only one can be instantiated, which, if either, might it be? The instantiation of Plantinga's extraordinary property in a possible world *w* is *dependent* on what every other possible world contains—every possible world must contain an omnipotent, omniscient, and morally perfect being. The instantiation in *w* of the property of being in less than perfect company requires only that each person *in w* have some flaw, however slight. If you know nothing else relevant to your decision and had to bet on which property is possibly instanti-

ated, knowing that both cannot be, which would you bet on?

Although Plantinga accepts the version of the ontological argument that he sets forth, he acknowledges that it is not a *proof* of its conclusion. It does not, he notes, establish the truth of theism. What then does the argument do? It establishes, Plantinga claims, the *rational acceptability* of theism. It does this, Plantinga argues, because the premise of the argument, proposition (5), is something that can be believed without violating any rule of reason concerning what we may or may not believe. Since we do no wrong in accepting (5), and since we acknowledge that (5) entails the truth of theism, we do no wrong in accepting the truth of theism. If it is not wrong for me to believe a proposition, then that proposition is rationally acceptable for me.

Perhaps the first point to note about Plantinga's claim is that in his view the premise of an argument may be rationally acceptable and may thus establish the rational acceptability of the argument's conclusion, even though one doesn't know the premise to be true, and even though the truth of the premise is a matter of significant controversy. After all, some who reflect on the amount of tragic evil in our world are committed to the view that the property of being in less than perfect company is instantiated in our world. Others, including a number who believe that there exists an omnipotent, omniscient, and morally perfect being, would insist that there is some possible world in which the property of being in less than perfect company is instantiated. Both groups, therefore, are committed to the denial of Plantinga's premise that there is some possible world in which maximal greatness is instantiated. Still others may hold that there is simply no way of telling whether maximal greatness is possibly instantiated. So the premise of Plantinga's argument is denied by many and held in question by others. Moreover, Plantinga offers no argument for his premise and acknowledges that reflecting on it does not enable us to somehow see that it must be true; he does not claim that after sufficient reflection the inquiring mind somehow comes to find his premise *self-evident*.

What, then, does Plantinga claim for his premise? He claims, as we've seen, that it is not *irrational* to accept it, that in accepting it one does not violate any rules concerning what we may or may not believe. Of course, if it were a rule that one must not accept a premise unless one can prove it or has some good evidence for it, Plantinga would be unjustified in accepting his premise. But the "rule" just mentioned is difficult to defend. Perhaps what Plantinga holds is this: There are circumstances in which it is *permissible* to believe a proposition even though you cannot prove it and don't have good evidence for it. What are these circumstances? Well, one circumstance, surely, is that you have no good reason to think the proposition false. (Some think that the idea of a maximally great being is like the idea of a largest integer—an impossible object. But this may well be wrong. It might be that we have no good reason to think Plantinga's premise false.) The other circumstances that must obtain are difficult to specify. But if we agree with Plantinga about this, then I think we can say that it *may* be permissible for someone to believe Plantinga's premise. Plantinga says something much stronger. He says it is "evident" that believing his premise is permissible. This claim, I believe, is excessive. We need to be much clearer about the circumstances that must obtain for Plantinga's premise to be acceptable before we declare its acceptability with the unabashed assurance Plantinga here expresses.

Some philosophers declare that the ontological argument in all its versions commits some gross fallacy or contains some obviously false premise. Plantinga's careful work on the argument helps us to see that we can confidently reject such criticisms. But when the argument is set forth with care and rigor, we can see, I believe, how very difficult it is to know or establish the truth of its premise(s). (Indeed, in some versions one has great difficulty in even imagining how one might know the premise(s) without basing such knowledge on a prior knowledge of the conclusion.) I think Plantinga sees this as well. Anselm's high hope of discovering an ar-

gument that would conclusively establish God's existence remains unfulfilled, even in Plantinga's skillful hands. As a consolation prize, Plantinga proposes a weak sense of rational acceptability that he claims is satisfied by the premise of his modal version of the argument. Anselm thought that if we really understood the argument it would be obvious that it is a sound demonstration of the existence of God. To reject the argument, therefore, is to be foolish. Plantinga makes no such claim. He holds only that it is clear that one is not foolish to accept it. If I am right, all that has been shown is that it may not be foolish to accept it. To *establish* that it is not foolish requires that we become clear that its premise satisfies all the circumstances (whatever they are) that are required for it to be permissible to believe a proposition even though we cannot prove it and don't have good evidence for it.

Notes

1. This argument has fascinated philosophers and theologians for centuries. For an exposition of the argument and the major objections to it, see my essay, "The Ontological Argument," in my *Philosophy of Religion* (Belmont, Calif.: Wadsworth, 1978).

2. The idea of *possible worlds* is explained briefly and clearly in Alvin Plantinga's *God, Freedom and Evil* (New York: Harper & Row, 1974), 34–39.

3. G_1 is an *abnormal* concept if there is a possible world in which no perfect being exists. For in that case, G_1's being satisfied in w depends in part upon *which* possible world is actual. Suppose possible world w^* contains an omnipotent, omniscient, wholly good being, but possible world w^{**} does not. If w^* is the actual world, then depending on what w contains, G_1 may be satisfied in w. But if w^{**} is the actual world, then no matter what w contains, G_1 is not satisfied in w. G_2, although a more far-reaching concept than G_1, is, however, a *normal* concept. Although its being satisfied in w depends upon what is contained in every other possible world, its being satisfied in w does not depend on *which* possible world is actual.

I.C.5 God's Existence Is Necessarily Impossible

J. N. FINDLAY

J. N. Findlay (1903–   ), a British philosopher, taught for many years at King's College, London University, before coming to Boston University. In this essay Findlay attempts to turn the ontological argument on its head, arguing that rather than prove that God necessarily exists, the argument actually demonstrates that God necessarily does not exist.

The course of philosophical development has been full of attempted proofs of the existence of God. Some of these have sought a basis in the bare necessities of thought, while others have tried to found themselves on the facts of experience. And, of these latter, some have founded themselves on *very general facts*, as that something exists, or that something is in motion, while others have tried to build on *highly special facts*, as that living beings are put together in a purposive manner, or that human beings are subject to certain improbable urges and passions, such as the zeal for righteousness, the love for useless truths and unprofitable beauties, as well as the many specifically religious needs and feelings. The general philosophical verdict is that none of these 'proofs' is truly compelling. The proofs based on the necessities of thought are universally regarded as fallacious: it is not thought possible to build bridges between mere abstractions and concrete existence. The proofs based on the general facts of existence and motion are only felt to be valid by a minority of thinkers, who seem quite powerless to communicate this sense of validity to others. And while most thinkers would accord weight to arguments resting on the special facts we have mentioned, they wouldn't think such arguments successful in ruling out a vast range of counter-possibilities. Religious people have, in fact,

come to acquiesce in the total absence of any cogent proofs of the Being they believe in: they even find it positively satisfying that something so far surpassing clear conception should also surpass the possibility of demonstration. And non-religious people willingly mitigate their rejection with a tinge of agnosticism: they don't so much deny the existence of a God, as the existence of good reasons for believing in him. We shall, however, maintain in this essay that there isn't room, in the case we are examining, for all these attitudes of tentative surmise and doubt. For we shall try to show that the Divine Existence can only be conceived, in a religiously satisfactory manner, if we also conceive it as something inescapable and necessary, whether for thought or reality. From which it follows that our modern denial of necessity or rational evidence for such an existence amounts to a demonstration that there cannot be a God.

Before we develop this argument, we must, however, give greater precision to our use of the term 'God.' For it is possible to say that there are nearly as many 'Gods' as there are speakers and worshippers, and while existence may be confidently asserted or denied of *some* of them, we should feel more hesitant in the case of others. It is one thing, plainly, to pronounce on God's existence, if he be taken to be some ancient, shapeless stone, or if we identify him with the bearded Father of the Sistine ceiling, and quite another matter, if we make of him an 'all-pervasive, immaterial intelligence,' or characterize him in some yet more negative and analogical manner. We shall, however, choose an indirect approach, and pin God down for our purposes as the 'adequate object of religious attitudes.' Plainly we find it possible to gather together, under the blanket term 'religious,' a large range of cases of possible action, linked together by so many overlapping[1] affinities that we are ready to treat them as the varying 'expressions' of a single 'attitude' or 'policy.' And plainly we find

Reprinted from *New Essays in Philosophical Theology* by Antony Flew and Alasdair MacIntyre (Macmillan Publishing Company, 1955).

it possible to indicate the character of that attitude by a number of descriptive phrases which, though they may err individually by savoring too strongly of particular cases, nevertheless permit us, in their totality, to draw a rough boundary round the attitude in question. Thus we might say, for instance, that a religious attitude was one in which we tended to abase ourselves before some object, to defer to it wholly, to devote ourselves to it with unquestioning enthusiasm, to bend the knee before it, whether literally or metaphorically. These phrases, and a large number of similar ones, would make perfectly plain the sort of attitude we were speaking of, and would suffice to mark it off from cognate attitudes which are much less unconditional and extreme in their tone. And clearly similar phrases would suffice to fix the boundaries of religious *feeling*. We might describe religious frames of mind as ones in which we felt ready to abase ourselves before some object, to bend the knee before it, and so forth. Here, as elsewhere, we find ourselves indicating the *felt* character of our attitudes, by treating their inward character as, in some sense, a concentrated and condensed substitute for appropriate lines of action, a way of speaking that accords curiously with the functional significance of the inward.[2] But not only do we incorporate, in the meanings of our various names for attitudes, a reference to this readiness for appropriate lines of action: we also incorporate in these meanings a reference to *the sorts of things or situations to which these attitudes are the normal or appropriate responses.* For, as a matter of fact, our attitudes are not indifferently evoked in *any* setting: there is a range of situations in which they normally and most readily occur. And though they may at times arise in circumstances which are not in this range, they are also readily dissipated by the consciousness that such circumstances *are* unsuitable or unusual. Thus fear is an attitude very readily evoked in situations with a character of menace or potential injury, and it is also an attitude very readily allayed by the clear perception that a given situation isn't really dangerous. And anger, likewise, is an attitude provoked very readily by perverse resistance and obstructive difficulty in some object, and is also very readily dissipated, even in animals, by the consciousness that a given object is innocent of

offense. All attitudes, we may say, *presume* characters in their objects, and are, in consequence, strengthened by the discovery that their objects *have* these characters, as they are weakened by the discovery that they really haven't got them. And not only do we find this out empirically: we also incorporate it in the *meanings* of our names for attitudes. Thus attitudes are said to be 'normal,' 'fully justified' and so forth, if we find them altered in a certain manner (called 'appropriate') by our knowledge of the actual state of things, whereas we speak of them as 'queer' or 'senseless' or 'neurotic,' if they aren't at all modified by this knowledge of reality. We call it abnormal, from this point of view, to feel a deep-seated fear of mice, to rage maniacally at strangers, to greet disasters with a hebephrenic giggle, whereas we think it altogether normal to deplore deep losses deeply, or to fear grave dangers gravely. And so an implicit reference to some standard object—which makes an attitude either normal or abnormal—is part of what we ordinarily mean by all our names for attitudes, and can be rendered explicit by a simple study of usage. We can consider the circumstances in which ordinary speakers would call an attitude 'appropriate' or 'justified.' And all that philosophy achieves in this regard is merely to push further, and develop into more considered and consistent forms, the implications of such ordinary ways of speaking. It can inquire whether an attitude would still seem justified, and its object appropriate, after we had reflected long and carefully on a certain matter, and looked at it from every wonted and unwonted angle. And such consideration may lead philosophers to a different and more reasoned notion of the appropriate objects of a given attitude, than could be garnered from our unreflective ways of speaking. And these developments of ordinary usage will only seem unfeasible to victims of that strange modern confusion which thinks of attitudes exclusively as hidden processes 'in our bosoms,' with nothing but an adventitious relation to appropriate outward acts and objects.

How then may we apply these notions to the case of our religious attitudes? Plainly we shall be following the natural trends of unreflective speech if we say that religious attitudes presume *superiority* in their objects, and such superiority, moreover, as reduces us, who feel the attitudes, to comparative nothingness. For having described a worshipful attitude as one in which we feel disposed to bend the knee before some object, to defer to it wholly, and the like, we find it natural to say that such an attitude can only be fitting where the object reverenced *exceeds* us very vastly, whether in power or wisdom or in other valued qualities. And while it is certainly possible to worship stocks and stones and articles of common use, one does so usually on the assumption that they aren't merely stocks and stones and ordinary articles, but the temporary seats of 'indwelling presences' or centers of extraordinary powers and virtues. And if one realizes clearly that such things *are* merely stocks and stones or articles of common use, one can't help suffering a total vanishing or grave abatement of religious ardor. To feel religiously is therefore to presume surpassing greatness in some object: so much characterizes the attitudes in which we bow and bend the knee, and enters into the ordinary meaning of the word 'religious .' But now we advance further— in company with a large number of theologians and philosophers, who have added new touches to the portrait of deity, pleading various theoretical necessities, but really concerned to make their object worthier of our worship—and ask whether it isn't wholly anomalous to worship anything *limited* in any thinkable manner. For all limited superiorities are tainted with an obvious relativity, and can be dwarfed in thought by still mightier superiorities, in which process of being dwarfed they lose their claim upon our worshipful attitudes. And hence we are led on irresistibly to demand that our religious object should have an *unsurpassable* supremacy along all avenues, that it should tower *infinitely* above all other objects. And not only are we led to demand for it such merely quantitative superiority: we also ask that it shouldn't stand surrounded by a world of *alien* objects, which owe it no allegiance, or set limits to its influence. The proper object of religious reverence must in some manner be *all-comprehensive*: there mustn't be anything capable of existing, or of displaying any virtue, without owing all of these absolutely to this single source. All these, certainly, are difficult requirements, in-

volving not only the obscurities and doubtful significance of the infinite, but also all the well-worn antagonisms of the immanent and transcendent, of finite sinfulness and divine perfection and preordination, which centuries of theological brooding have failed to dissipate. But we are also led on irresistibly to a yet more stringent demand, which raises difficulties which make the difficulties we have mentioned seem wholly inconsiderable: we can't help feeling that the worthy object of our worship can never be a thing that merely *happens* to exist, nor one on which all other objects merely *happen* to depend. The true object of religious reverence must not be one, merely, to which no *actual* independent realities stand opposed: it must be one to which such opposition is totally *inconceivable*. God mustn't merely cover the territory of the actual, but also, with equal comprehensiveness, the territory of the possible. And not only must the existence of *other* things be unthinkable without him, but his own non-existence must be wholly unthinkable in any circumstances. There must, in short, be no conceivable alternative to an existence properly termed 'divine': God must be wholly inescapable, as we remarked previously, whether for thought or reality. And so we are led on insensibly to the barely intelligible notion of a Being in whom Essence and Existence lose their separateness. And all that the great medieval thinkers really did was to carry such a development to its logical limit.

We may, however, approach the matter from a slightly different angle. Not only is it contrary to the demands and claims inherent in religious attitudes that their object should *exist* 'accidentally': it is also contrary to those demands that it should *possess its various excellences* in some merely adventitious or contingent manner. It would be quite unsatisfactory from the religious standpoint, if an object merely *happened* to be wise, good, powerful and so forth, even to a superlative degree, and if other beings had, *as a mere matter of fact*, derived their excellences from this single source. An object of this sort would doubtless deserve respect and admiration, and other quasireligious attitudes, but it would not deserve the utter self-abandonment peculiar to the religious frame of mind. It would deserve the δουλεία canonically accorded to the saints, but not the λατρεία that we properly owe to God. We might respect this object as the crowning instance of most excellent qualities, but we should incline our head before the qualities and not before the person. And wherever such qualities were manifested, though perhaps less eminently, we should always be ready to perform an essentially similar obeisance. For though such qualities might be intimately characteristic of the Supreme Being, they still wouldn't be in any sense inalienably his own. And even if other beings had, in fact, derived such qualities from this sovereign source, they still would be *their own* qualities, possessed by them in their own right. And we should have no better reason to *adore* the author of such virtues, than sons have reason to adore superior parents, or pupils to adore superior teachers. For while these latter may deserve deep deference, the fact that we are coming to *participate* in their excellences renders them unworthy of our *worship*. Plainly a being that possesses and imparts desirable qualities—which other things might nevertheless have manifested though this source were totally absent—has all the utter inadequacy as a religious object which is expressed by saying that it would be *idolatrous* to worship it. Wisdom, kindness and other excellences deserve respect wherever they are manifested, but no being can appropriate them as its personal perquisites, even if it does possess them in a superlative degree. And so we are led on irresistibly, by the demands inherent in religious reverence, to hold that an adequate object of our worship must possess its various qualities *in some necessary manner.* These qualities must be intrinsically incapable of belonging to anything except in so far as they belong primarily to the object of our worship. Again we are led on to a queer and barely intelligible Scholastic doctrine, that God isn't merely good, but is in some manner indistinguishable from his own (and anything else's) goodness.

What, however, are the consequences of these requirements upon the possibility of God's existence? Plainly, (for all who share a contemporary outlook), they entail not only that there isn't a God, but that the Divine Existence is either senseless[3] or impossible. The modern mind feels not the faintest axiomatic force in principles which trace contin-

gent things back to some necessarily existent source, nor does it find it hard to conceive that things should display various excellent qualities without deriving them from a source which manifests them supremely. Those who believe in necessary truths which aren't merely tautological, think that such truths merely connect the *possible* instances of various characteristics with each other: they don't expect such truths to tell them whether there *will* be instances of any characteristics. This is the outcome of the whole medieval and Kantian criticism of the Ontological Proof. And, on a yet more modern view of the matter, necessity in propositions merely reflects our use of words, the arbitrary conventions of our language. On such a view the Divine Existence could only be a necessary matter if we had made up our minds to speak theistically *whatever the empirical circumstances might turn out to be.* This, doubtless, would suffice for some, who speak theistically, much as Spinoza spoke monistically, merely to give expression to a particular way of looking at things, or of feeling about them. And it would also suffice for those who make use of the term 'God' to cover whatever tendencies towards righteousness and beauty are actually included in the make-up of our world. But it wouldn't suffice for the full-blooded worshipper, who can't help finding our actual world anything but edifying, and its half-formed tendencies towards righteousness and beauty very far from adorable. The religious frame of mind seems, in fact, to be in a quandary; it seems invincibly determined both to eat its cake and have it. It desires the Divine Existence both to have that inescapable character which can, on modern views, only be found where truth reflects an arbitrary convention, and also the character of 'making a real difference' which is only possible where truth doesn't have this merely linguistic basis. We may accordingly deny that modern approaches allow us to remain agnostically poised in regard to God: they force us to come down on the atheistic side. For if God is to satisfy religious claims and needs, he must be a being in every way inescapable, One whose existence and whose possession of certain excellences we cannot possibly conceive away. And modern views make it self-evidently absurd (if they don't make it ungrammatical) to speak of such a Being and attribute existence to him. It was indeed an ill day for Anselm when he hit upon his famous proof. For on that day he not only laid bare something that is of the essence of an adequate religious object, but also something that entails its necessary non-existence.[4]

The force of our argument must not, however, be exaggerated. We haven't proved that there aren't beings of all degrees of excellence and greatness, who may deserve attitudes approximating indefinitely to religious reverence. But such beings will at best be instances of valued qualities which we too may come to exemplify, though in lesser degree. And not only would it be idolatrous for us to worship them, but it would also be monstrous for them to exact worship, or to care for it. The attitude of such beings to our reverence would necessarily be deprecating: they would prefer cooperative atheists to adoring zealots. And they would probably hide themselves like royal personages from the anthems of their worshippers, and perhaps the fact that there are so few positive signs of their presence is itself a feeble evidence of their real existence. But whether such beings exist or not, they are not divine, and can never satisfy the demands inherent in religious reverence. And the effect of our argument will further be to discredit generally such forms of religion as attach a uniquely sacred meaning to existent things, whether these things be men or acts of institutions or writings.

But there are other frames of mind, to which we shouldn't deny the name 'religious,' which acquiesce quite readily in the non-existence of their objects. (This non-existence might, in fact, be taken to be the 'real meaning' of saying that religious objects and realities are 'not of this world.') In such frames of mind we give ourselves over unconditionally and gladly to the task of indefinite approach toward a certain imaginary focus where nothing actually is, and we find this task sufficiently inspiring and satisfying without demanding (absurdly) that there should be something actual at that limit. And the atheistic religious attitude we have mentioned has also undergone reflective elaboration by such philosophers as Fichte and Erigena and Alexander. There is, then, a religious atheism which takes full stock of our arguments, and we may be glad that this is so. For since the religious spirit is one of reverence before things greater than ourselves, we should be gravely impoverished and arrested if this spirit ceased to be operative in our personal and social life. And it would certainly be better that this spirit should survive, with all its fallacious existential trimmings, than that we should cast it forth merely in order to be rid of such irrelevances.

Notes

1. This word is added to avoid the suggestion that there must be *one* pervasive affinity linking together all the actions commonly called 'religious.'

2. Whatever the philosophical 'ground' for it may be, this plainly is the way in which we do describe the 'inner quality' of our felt attitudes.

3. I have included this alternative, of which I am not fond, merely because so many modern thinkers make use of it in this sort of connection.

4. Or 'non-significance,' if this alternative is preferred.

Bibliography for Part I

General

Hick, John. *Arguments for the Existence of God.* London: Macmillan, 1971. A clearly written, insightful examination of the central arguments.

Mackie, J. L. *The Miracle of Theism.* Oxford, Eng.: Oxford Univ. Press, 1982. A lively discussion of the proofs for the existence of God and other issues by one of the ablest atheist philosophers of our time.

Martin, Michael. *Atheism.* Philadelphia: Temple Univ. Press, 1990. The most comprehensive attack on theism in the English language. Clearly set forth.

Peterson, Michael, William Hasker, Bruce Reichenbach, and David Basinger. *Reason and Religious Belief.* New York: Oxford Univ. Press, 1991. A clearly written, helpful book from a theist point of view.

Rowe, William. *Philosophy of Religion: An Introduction.* Belmont, Calif.: Wadsworth, 1978. A readable, reliable introductory work by a first-rate scholar.

Swinburne, Richard. *The Existence of God.* Oxford, Eng.: Oxford Univ. Press, 1979. Perhaps the most sustained and cogent defense of theism in the literature.

Tomberlin, James, ed. *Philosophical Perspectives, 5. Philosophy of Religion 1991.* Atascadero, Calif.: Ridgeview Publishing Co., 1991. Contains important, recent articles on several issues in philosophy of religion.

Wainwright, William J. *Philosophy of Religion.* Belmont, Calif.: Wadsworth, 1988. A careful, well-argued text from a theistic perspective.

The Cosmological Argument

(All the books listed above also have important chapters on the cosmological argument.)

Craig, William. *The Cosmological Argument from Plato to Leibniz.* New York: Barnes & Noble, 1980. A good survey of the history of the argument.

———. *The Kalām Cosmological Argument.* New York: Harper & Row, 1980.

Gale, Richard. *On the Nature and Existence of God.* Cambridge, Eng.: Cambridge Univ. Press, 1992. Chapter 7 is an excellent discussion of the argument.

Moreland, J. P., and Kai Nielsen, eds. *Does God Exist?: The Great Debate.* Nashville: Thomas Nelson Publishers, 1990.

Rowe, William. *The Cosmological Argument.* Princeton, N.J.: Princeton Univ. Press, 1971. A thorough and penetrating study.

Taylor, Richard. *Metaphysics.* Englewood Cliffs, NJ.: Prentice Hall, 1983.

The Teleological Argument

McPherson, Thomas. *The Argument from Design.* London: Macmillan, 1972. A good introduction to the various forms of the argument.

Salmon, Wesley. "Religion and Science. A New Look at Hume's Dialogue." *Philosophical Studies* 33 (1978):145.

Swinburne, Richard. "The Argument from Design." *Philosophy* 43 (1968):199–212. A detailed response to Hume.

———. "The Argument from Design—A Defence." *Religious Studies* 8 (1972):193–205.

Tennant, R. R. *Philosophical Theology.* Cambridge, Eng.: Cambridge Univ. Press, 1928–30. A classic post-Humean version of the teleological argument.

The Ontological Argument

Barnes, Jonathan. *The Ontological Argument.* London: Macmillan, 1972. A good general discussion of the argument.

Plantinga, Alvin, ed. *The Ontological Argument from St. Anselm to Contemporary Philosophers.* Garden City, N.Y.: Doubleday, 1965.

THE ARGUMENT FROM RELIGIOUS EXPERIENCE

There was not a mere consciousness of something there, but fused in the central happiness of it, a startling awareness of some ineffable good. Not vague either; not like the emotional effect of some poem, or scene, or blossom, or music, but the sure knowledge of the close presence of a sort of mighty person, and after it went, the memory persisted as the one perception of reality. Everything else might be a dream, but not that.

AN ANONYMOUS MYSTIC cited by William James in *Varieties of Religious Experience*, 1902.

The heart of religion is and always has been experiential. Encounters with the supernatural, a transcendent dimension, the Wholly Other are at the base of every great religion. Abraham hears a Voice calling him to leave his family in Haran and venture out into a broad unknown, thus becoming the father of Israel. Abraham's grandson Jacob wrestles all night with an angel and is transformed, gaining the name "Israel," "prince of God." While tending his father-in-law's flock, Moses has a vision of "I am that I am" (Yahweh) in the burning bush and is ordered to deliver Israel out of slavery into a land flowing with milk and honey. Isaiah has a vision of the Lord "high and exalted, and the train of his robe filled the temple" of heaven. In the New Testament, John, James, and Peter behold Jesus gloriously transformed on the Mount of Transfiguration and are themselves transformed by the experience. After the death of Jesus, Saul is traveling to Damascus to persecute Christians, when he is met by a blazing light and hears a Voice, asking him why he is persecuting the Lord. Changing his name to Paul, he becomes the leader of the Christian missionary movement. The Hindu experiences the Atman (soul) as the Brahman (God), "That art Thou," or beholds the glories of Krishna. The Advaitian Hindu merges with the One, as a drop of water merges with the vast ocean. The Buddhist merges with Nirvana or beholds a vision of the Buddha. Allah reveals his holy word, the Koran, to Mohammed. Joan of Arc hears voices calling on her to save her people, and Joseph Smith has a vision of the Angel Moroni, calling him to do a new work for God.

Saints, mystics, prophets, ascetics, and common believers of every creed, of every race, in every land, and throughout recorded history have undergone esoteric experiences that are hard to explain but impossible to dismiss as mere nonsense. Common features appear to link these otherwise disparate experiences to one another, resulting in a common testimony to this Otherness, a *consensus mysticum*. Rudolf Otto characterizes the religious (or "numinal" spiritual) dimension in all these experiences as the "mysterium tremendum et fascinans." Religion is an unfathomable mystery: *tremendum* ("to be trembled at"), awe-inspiring, and *fascinans* ("fascinating"), magnetic. To use a description from Søren Kierkegaard, religious experience is a "sympathetic antipathy and an antipathetic sympathy" before a deep unknown. Like looking into an abyss, it both repulses and strangely attracts.

What, then, is the problem with religious experience? If I say that I hear a pleasant tune, and you listen and say, "Yes, I hear it now too," we have no problem; but if you listen carefully and don't hear it, you might well wonder whether I am really hearing sounds or only imagine that I am. Perhaps we could bring in others to check out the matter. If they agree with me, well and good; but if they agree with you and don't hear the sounds, then we have a problem. Perhaps, we could bring in an audiometer to measure the decibels in the room. If the meter confirms my report, then it is simply a case of my having better hearing than you and the rest of the witnesses; but if the meter doesn't register at all, then, assuming that it is in working order, we would have good evidence that I am only imagining the sounds. Perhaps I need to change my claim and say, " Well, I seem to be hearing a pleasant tune."

One problem is that religious experience is typically private. You have the sense of God forgiving you or an angel speaking to you, but I, who am in the same room with you, neither hear, nor see, nor feel anything unusual. You are praying and suddenly feel transported by grace and sense the unity of all reality. I, who am sitting next to you, wonder at the strange expression on your face and ask you if something is wrong. Perhaps your brain is experiencing an altered chemical or electrical state?

Yet, as noted above, religious experiences of various varieties have been reported by numerous people, from dairymaids like Joan of Arc to mystics like Teresa of Avila and St. John of the Cross. They cannot be simply dismissed without serious analysis.

There are two levels of problem here: (1) To what degree, if any, is the subject of a religious experience justified in inferring from the psychological experience (the subjective aspect) to the existential or ontological reality of that which is the object of the experience (the objective aspect)? (2) To what degree, if any, does the cumulative witness of those undergoing religious experience justify the claim that there is a God or transcendent reality?

Traditionally, the argument from religious experience has not been one of the "proofs" for God's existence. At best, it has confirmed and made existential what the proofs conveyed with icy logic. Some philosophers, such as C.

D. Broad (1887–1971), as well as contemporary philosophers such as Richard Swinburne and Gary Gutting, believe that the common experience of mystics is *strong justification* or evidence for all of us for the existence of God. Others, such as William James (1842–1910), believe that religious experience is sufficient evidence for the subject himself or herself for the existence of a divine reality, but only constitutes a possibility for the nonexperiencer. That is, religious experience grants us only *weak justification*. Religious skeptics, like Walter Stace (1886–1967) and Wallace Matson (see the fifth reading), doubt this and argue that a subjective experience by itself never warrants making an existential claim (of an object existing outside oneself). It is a fallacy to go from the psychological experience of *X* to the reality of *X*.

There are two main traditions regarding religious experience. One, which we can call *mystical*, posits the unity of all reality or the unity of the subject with its object (the mystic is absorbed in God, becomes one with God, etc.). The second type of religious experience can be called simply *religious experience* in order to distinguish it from the mystical. It does not conflate the subject with the object but is a numinal experience wherein the believer (or subject) experiences the presence of God or an angel or Christ or the Holy Spirit, either speaking or appearing to the experient or forgiving him or her. While in prayer, believers often experience a sense of the presence of God or the Holy Spirit.

Now, there are many psychological explanations of religious experience that cast doubt on its validity. One of the most famous is the Freudian interpretation set forth in our third reading. Sigmund Freud (1856–1939) said that it was the result of the projection of the father image within oneself. The progression goes like this. When you were a child, you looked upon your father as a powerful hero who could do everything, meet all your needs, and overcome the normal obstacles, which hindered your way at every step. When you grew older, you sadly realized that your father was fallible and very finite, indeed. But you still had the need of the benevolent, all-powerful father. So, subconsciously you projected your need for that long lost parent onto the empty heavens and invented a god for yourself. Because this is a common phenomenon, all of us who have successfully "projected daddy onto the big sky" go to church or synagogue or mosque or whatever and worship the illusion on our favorite holy day. But it is a myth. The sky is empty, and the sooner we realize it, the better for everyone.

This is one explanation of religious experience and religion in general. It is not a disproof of God's existence, simply an hypothesis. Even if it is true psychologically that we tend to think of God like a powerful and loving parent, it could still be the case that the parental relationship is God's way of teaching us about himself—by analogy.

Another explanation of religious experience is naturalism. According to this theory, all reality can be explained by reference to physical processes, so there is no need to bring in mysterious spiritual entities. There is no soul or spiritual reality, although there are values and consciousnesses that are explained with reference to functions of physical states. Consciousness, or mind, is a function of brain states, nothing more or less. The brain processes spatiotemporal experiences communicated to it through the senses. All learning is produced in this way. The mechanisms of the brain modify and coordinate the experiences, but there is no good reason to believe that the brain has access to extraphysical reality. There are problems with this version of naturalism, but it is a coherent explanatory theory that rivals theism. In our readings, Wallace Matson defends this point of view.

We begin with four selections of religious experience from four different traditions, the Jewish, the Christian, the Hindu, and the Buddhist.

Our first full reading (the second reading) is an excerpt from William James's classic study *The Varieties of Religious Experience* (1902). In this selection, James describes mystical experience, which he considers to be the deepest kind of religious experience. It is something that transcends our ordinary, sensory experience and that cannot be described in terms of our normal concepts and language. It is 'ineffable experience.' The subject realizes that the experience "defies expression, that no adequate report of its content can be given in words," James writes. "It follows from this that its quality must be directly experienced; it cannot be imparted or transferred to others." And yet it contains a 'noetic quality,' a content. It purports to convey truth about the nature of reality, namely, that there is a unity of all things and that that unity is spiritual, not material. It is antinaturalistic, pantheistic, and optimistic. Further, mystical states are *transient*—that is, they cannot be sustained for long—and they are *passive*—that is, the mystic is acted upon by divine deliverance. We may prepare ourselves for the experience, but it is not something that we do; it is something that happens to us.

James is cautious about what can be deduced from mystical experience. Although mystic states are and ought to be absolutely authoritative for the individuals to whom they come, "no authority emanates from them which should make it a duty for those who stand outside of them to accept their revelations uncritically." But their value for us, James argues, is that they show us a valid alternative to the "non-mystical rationalistic consciousness, based on understanding and the senses alone. They open up the possibility of other orders of truth, in which, so far as anything in us vitally responds to them, we may freely continue to have faith."

Our third selection, from Freud's *Future of an Illusion*, has already been discussed.

Our fourth selection is C. D. Broad's important article, "The Argument from Religious Experience" (1953), in which he considers the extent to which we can infer from religious experience to the existence of God. Broad likens the religious sense to an ear for music. There are a few people on the negative end who are spiritually tone deaf and a few on the positive end who are the founders of religions, the Bachs and Beethovens. In between are the ordinary followers of religion, who are like the average musical listeners, and above them are the saints, who are likened to those with a very fine ear for music.

The chief difference is that religion, unlike music, says something about the nature of reality. Is what it says true? And does religious experience lend any support to the truth claims of religion? Is religious experience *veridical*? Are the claims about "the nature of reality which are an integral part of the experience true or probable?" Broad considers the argument from mystical agreement, which goes as follows:

(1) There is an enormous unanimity among the mystics concerning the spiritual nature of reality.
(2) When there is such unanimity among observers as to what they believe themselves to be experiencing, it is reasonable to conclude that their experiences are veridical (unless we have good reason to believe that they are deluded).
(3) There are no positive reasons for thinking that mystical experiences are delusory.
(4) Therefore it is reasonable to believe that mystical experiences are veridical.

The weak premise is (3), for there is evidence that mystics are neuropathic or sexually repressed. In considering these charges, Broad admits some plausibility in them but suggests that they are not conclusive. Regarding the charge of neuropathology, he urges that "one might need to be slightly 'cracked' in order to have some peep-holes into the super-sensible world." With regard to sexual abnormality, it could simply be the case that no one who was "incapable of strong sexual desires and emotions could have anything worth calling religious experience."

His own guarded judgment is that, given what we know about the origins of religious belief and emotions, there is no reason to think that religious experience is "specially likely to be delusive or misdirected." On the other hand, the evidence suggests that the concepts and beliefs of even the best religions are "extremely inadequate to the facts which they express; that they are highly confused and are mixed up with a great deal of positive error and sheer nonsense; and that, if the human race goes on and continues to have religious experiences and to reflect on them, they will be altered and improved almost out of recognition."

Our fifth reading on religious experience is a section from Wallace Matson's book *The Existence of God* (1965). Matson first presents a brief analysis of perception. He then applies it to the notion of certifying the experience of a god. He notes that there are several conditions that must be fulfilled in normal perceptual reports, such as corroboration and publicity, that are not fulfilled in religious experiences. By itself, therefore, the testimony of the subject cannot be used to persuade others of its veridicality (unless we have independent evidence for the existence of a god, in which case we should expect such experiences).

Matson grants even less authority to experiences that are *unlike* ordinary perceptions. Even if the mystics are sane, their experiences have no authority for us. Their seeming authority comes from analogy with other esoteric knowledge. For example, physicists tell us that pi-mesons exist and that with an appropriate amount of study of mathematics and physics (i.e., by becoming physicists), most of us (but not all of us) could eventually come to learn how to confirm this belief. Similarly, mystics tell us that through prayer and meditation we could become mystics and have the chance of experiencing what they report. Of course, there is no guarantee that the process will succeed, any more than there is that we will master the material necessary to verify the existence of pi-mesons. Matson contends that this argument fails because of several disanalogies: (1) Physicists can still talk with one another without difficulty, but the mystic has no way of discussing the ineffable even with other mystics. (2) There is an agreed curriculum of study for the physicist but not for the mystic. (3) There is no need for faith in the process of physics as there is in mystical experience.

Matson compares the mystic to a seer among the blind who describes the sun's influence in bringing warmth. He argues that just as it would be unreasonable for the blind to believe such seers unless they could check out their reports in some way, so likewise it is reasonable for the "non-mystic to believe the mystic only if the mystic makes some checkable statements that show him to have a power of directly experiencing what the non-mystic knows about only indirectly."

In the sixth essay I distinguish between a strong and a weak justification for religious belief. A strong justification would make it rationally obligatory for everyone to believe in the conclusion of an argument. A weak justification would provide rational support only for those who had an "of-God" experience (or already accepted the worldview that made such experiences likely). I argue against philosophers, such as Gary Gutting, who believe that they have provided a strong justification for religious belief, showing that the best one can offer is a weak justification. At the end of my essay, I raise the question of why religious experience does not yield ways of checking the accuracy of its content or predictions that would confirm it.

In the last reading in this part, "Religious Experience and Religious Belief," William Alston argues that religious experience can provide grounds for religious belief. Comparing the epistemology of Christian religious experience with the epistemology of perceptual experience, Alston shows that although perceptual practices include more stringent requirements than religious practices, there are good reasons why the two should be different. Whereas the criteria for valid perceptual experiences include verifiability and predictability, God's being wholly other may preclude those criteria from applying to religious experience. One question that you may want to put to Alston's argument is that even though God's nature may preclude our being able to find regularities in his behavior, might not God, if he exists, be able to give us confirming data, signs to encourage and convince the seeker after truth?

II.1 Selections of Mystical Experiences

An Old Testament Selection: The Call of Isaiah

In the year of King Uzziah's death I saw the Lord seated on a throne, high and exalted, and the skirt of his robe filled the temple. About him were attendant seraphim, and each had six wings; one pair covered his face and one pair his feet, and one pair was spread in flight. They were calling ceaselessly to one another,

> Holy, holy, holy is the LORD of Hosts:
> the whole earth is full of his glory.

And, as each one called, the threshold shook to its foundations, while the house was filled with smoke. Then I cried,

> Woe is me! I am lost,
> for I am a man of unclean lips
> and I dwell among a people of unclean lips;
> yet with these eyes I have seen the King, the
> LORD of Hosts.

Then one of the seraphim flew to me carrying in his hand a glowing coal which he had taken from the altar with a pair of tongs. He touched my mouth with it and said,

> See, this has touched your lips;
> your iniquity is removed,
> and your sin is wiped away.

Then I heard the Lord saying, Whom shall I send? Who will go for me? And I answered, Here am I; send me. He said, Go and tell this people:

> You may listen and listen, but you will not un-
> derstand.
> You may look and look again, but you will
> never know.
> This people's wits are dulled,

their ears are deafened and their eyes blinded,
so that they cannot see with their eyes
nor listen with their ears
nor understand with their wits,
so that they may turn and be healed.

ISAIAH, Chapter 6, *New English Bible*

The Christian Mystic, St. Teresa of Avila

One day when I was at prayer . . . I saw Christ at my side—or, to put it better, I was conscious of Him, for I saw nothing with the eyes of the body or the eyes of the soul (the imagination). He seemed quite close to me and I saw that it was He. As I thought, He was speaking to me. Being completely ignorant that such visions were possible, I was very much afraid at first, and could do nothing but weep, though as soon as He spoke His first word of assurance to me, I regained my usual calm, and became cheerful and free from fear. All the time Jesus Christ seemed to be at my side, but as this was not an imaginary vision I could not see in what form. But I most clearly felt that He was all the time on my right, and was a witness of everything that I was doing . . . if I say that I do not see Him with the eyes of the body or the eyes of the soul, because this is no imaginary vision, how then can I know and affirm that he is beside me with greater certainty than if I saw Him? If one says that one is like a person in the dark who cannot see someone though he is beside him, or that one is like somebody who is blind, it is not right. There is some similarity here, but not much, because a person in the dark can perceive with the other senses, or hear his neighbor speak or move, or can touch him. Here this is not so, nor is there any feeling of darkness. On the contrary, He appears to the soul by a knowledge brighter than the sun. I do not mean that any sun is seen, or any brightness, but there is a light which, though unseen, illuminates the understanding.

> J. M. COHEN, trans. *The Life of St. Teresa of Avila*, London: Penguin, 1957

A Hindu Example

The Ego has disappeared. I have realized my identity with Brahman and so all my desires have melted away. I have arisen above my ignorance and my knowledge of this seeming universe. What is this joy I feel? Who shall measure it? I know nothing but joy, limitless, unbounded! The treasure I have found there cannot be described in words. The mind cannot conceive of it. My mind fell like a hailstone into that vast expanse of Brahman's ocean. Touching one drop of it, I melted away and became one with Brahman. Where is this universe? Who took it away? Has it merged into something else? A while ago, I beheld it—now it exists no longer. Is there anything apart or distinct from Brahman? Now, finally and clearly, I know that I am the Atman [the soul identified with Brahman], whose nature is eter-

nal joy. I see nothing, I hear nothing, I know nothing that is separate from me.

> SWAMI PRABHAVANDANDA trans. *Shankara's Crest Jewel of Discrimination*, New York: Mentor Books, 1970

A Buddhist Meditation

Of one who has entered the first trance the voice has ceased; of one who has entered the second trance reasoning and reflection have ceased; of one who has entered the third trance joy has ceased; of one who has entered the fourth trance the inspiration and expiration have ceased; of one who has entered the realm of the infinity of space the perception of form has ceased; of one who has entered the realm of the infinity of consciousness the perception of the realm of the infinity of space has ceased; of one who has entered the realm of nothingness the perception of the realm of the infinity of consciousness has ceased.

> HENRY WARREN, ed. *Samyutta-Nikaya*, in *Buddhism in Translation*, New York: Atheneum, 1973

II.2 Mysticism

WILLIAM JAMES

William James (1842–1910), American philosopher and psychologist, was one of the most influential thinkers of his time. He taught at Harvard University and is considered, along with C. S. Peirce, one of the fathers of pragmatism. The Varieties of Religious Experience (1902) is his classic

study of religious experience. In this selection James describes mystical experience which he considers to be the deepest kind of religious experience. It is something that transcends our ordinary, sensory experience and that cannot be described in terms of our normal concepts and language.

From William James, *The Varieties of Religious Experience* (New York: Longman, Green & Co., 1902). Some footnotes deleted.

Over and over again in these lectures I have raised points and left them open and unfinished until we should have come to the subject of Mysticism. Some of you, I fear, may have smiled as you noted my reiterated postponements. But now the hour has come when mysticism must be faced in good earnest, and those broken threads wound up together. One may say truly, I think, that personal religious experience has its root and centre in mystical states of consciousness; so for us, who in these lectures are treating personal experience as the exclusive subject of our study, such states of consciousness ought to form the vital chapter from which the other chapters get their light. Whether my treatment of mystical states will shed more light or darkness, I do not know, for my own constitution shuts me out from their enjoyment almost entirely, and I can speak of them only at second hand. But though forced to look upon the subject so externally, I will be as objective and receptive as I can; and I think I shall at least succeed in convincing you of the reality of the states in question, and of the paramount importance of their function.

First of all, then, I ask, What does the expression "mystical states of consciousness" mean? How do we part off mystical states from other states?

The words "mysticism" and "mystical" are often used as terms of mere reproach, to throw at any opinion which we regard as vague and vast and sentimental, and without a base in either facts or logic. For some writers a "mystic" is any person who believes in thought-transference, or spirit-return. Employed in this way the word has little value: there are too many less ambiguous synonyms. So, to keep it useful by restricting it, I will do what I did in the case of the word "religion," and simply propose to you four marks which, when an experience has them, may justify us in calling it mystical for the purpose of the present lectures. In this way we shall save verbal disputation, and the recriminations that generally go therewith.

1. *Ineffability.*—The handiest of the marks by which I classify a state of mind as mystical is negative. The subject of it immediately says that it defies expression, that no adequate report of its contents can be given in words. It follows from this that its quality must be directly experienced; it cannot be imparted or transferred to others. In this peculiarity mystical states are more like states of feeling than like states of intellect. No one can make clear to another who has never had a certain feeling, in what the quality or worth of it consists. One must have musical ears to know the value of a symphony; one must have been in love one's self to understand a lover's state of mind. Lacking the heart or ear, we cannot interpret the musician or the lover justly, and are even likely to consider him weak-minded or absurd. The mystic finds that most of us accord to his experiences an equally incompetent treatment.

2. *Noetic quality.*—Although so similar to states of feeling, mystical states seem to those who experience them to be also states of knowledge. They are states of insight into depths of truth unplumbed by the discursive intellect. They are illuminations, revelations, full of significance and importance, all inarticulate though they remain; and as a rule they carry with them a curious sense of authority for aftertime.

These two characters will entitle any state to be called mystical, in the sense in which I use the word. Two other qualities are less sharply marked, but are usually found. These are:—

3. *Transiency.*—Mystical states cannot be sustained for long. Except in rare instances, half an hour, or at most an hour or two, seems to be the limit beyond which they fade into the light of common day. Often, when faded, their quality can but imperfectly be reproduced in memory; but when they recur it is recognized; and from one recurrence to another it is susceptible of continuous development in what is felt as inner richness and importance.

4. *Passivity.*—Although the oncoming of mystical states may be facilitated by preliminary voluntary operations, as by fixing the attention, or going through certain bodily performances, or in other ways which manuals of mysticism prescribe; yet when the characteristic sort of consciousness once has set in, the mystic feels as if his own will were in abeyance, and indeed sometimes as if he were grasped and held by a superior power. This latter peculiarity connects mystical states with certain definite phenomena of secondary or alternative personality, such as prophetic speech, automatic

writing, or the mediumistic trance. When these latter conditions are well pronounced, however, there may be no recollection whatever of the phenomenon, and it may have no significance for the subject's usual inner life, to which, as it were, it makes a mere interruption. Mystical states, strictly so-called, are never merely interruptive. Some memory of their content always remains, and a profound sense of their importance. They modify the inner life of the subject between the times of their recurrence. Sharp divisions in this region are, however, difficult to make, and we find all sorts of gradations and mixtures.

These four characteristics are sufficient to mark out a group of states of consciousness peculiar enough to deserve a special name and to call for careful study. Let it then be called the mystical group.

Our next step should be to gain acquaintance with some typical examples. Professional mystics at the height of their development have often elaborately organized experiences and a philosophy based thereupon. But you remember what I said in my first lecture: phenomena are best understood when placed within their series, studied in their germ and in their over-ripe decay, and compared with their exaggerated and degenerated kindred. The range of mystical experience is very wide, much too wide for us to cover in the time at our disposal. Yet the method of serial study is so essential for interpretation that if we really wish to reach conclusions we must use it. I will begin, therefore, with phenomena which claim no special religious significance, and end with those of which the religious pretensions are extreme.

The simplest rudiment of mystical experience would seem to be that deepened sense of the significance of a maxim or formula which occasionally sweeps over one. "I've heard that said all my life," we exclaim, "but I never realized its full meaning until now." "When a fellow-monk," said Luther, "one day repeated the words of the Creed: 'I believe in the forgiveness of sins,' I saw the Scripture in an entirely new light; and straightway I felt as if I were born anew. It was as if I had found the door of paradise thrown wide open." This sense of deeper significance is not confined to rational

propositions. Single words, and conjunctions of words, effects of light on land and sea, odors and musical sounds, all bring it when the mind is tuned aright. Most of us can remember the strangely moving power of passages in certain poems read when we were young, irrational doorways as they were through which the mystery of fact, the wildness and the pang of life, stole into our hearts and thrilled them. The words have now perhaps become mere polished surfaces for us; but lyric poetry and music are alive and significant only in proportion as they fetch these vague vistas of a life continuous with our own, beckoning and inviting, yet ever eluding our pursuit. We are alive or dead to the eternal inner message of the arts according as we have kept or lost this mystical susceptibility. . . .

. . . .

[An] incommunicableness of the transport is the keynote of all mysticism. Mystical truth exists for the individual who has the transport, but for no one else. In this, as I have said, it resembles the knowledge given to us in sensations more than that given by conceptual thought. Thought, with its remoteness and abstractness, has often enough in the history of philosophy been contrasted unfavorably with sensation. It is a commonplace of metaphysics that God's knowledge cannot be discursive but must be intuitive, that is, must be constructed more after the pattern of what in ourselves is called immediate feeling, than after that of proposition and judgment. But *our* immediate feelings have no content but what the five senses supply; and we have seen and shall see again that mystics may emphatically deny that the senses play any part in the very highest type of knowledge which their transports yield.

In the Christian church there have always been mystics. Although many of them have been viewed with suspicion, some have gained favor in the eyes of the authorities. The experiences of these have been treated as precedents, and a codified system of mystical theology has been based upon them, in which everything legitimate finds its place. The basis of the system is "orison" or meditation, the methodical elevation of the soul towards God. Through the practice of orison the higher levels of mystical experience may be attained. It is odd that Protestantism, especially evangelical Protestantism, should seemingly have abandoned everything methodical in this line. Apart from what prayer may lead to, Protestant mystical experience appears to have been almost exclusively sporadic. It has been left to our mind-curers to reintroduce methodical meditation into our religious life.

The first thing to be aimed at in orison is the mind's detachment from outer sensations for these interfere with its concentration upon ideal things. Such manuals as Saint Ignatius's *Spiritual Exercises* recommend the disciple to expel sensation by a graduated series of efforts to imagine holy scenes. The acme of this kind of discipline would be a semi-hallucinatory mono-ideism—an imaginary figure of Christ, for example, coming fully to occupy the mind. Sensorial images of this sort, whether literal or symbolic, play an enormous part in mysticism. But in certain cases imagery may fall away entirely, and in the very highest raptures it tends to do so. The state of consciousness becomes then insusceptible of any verbal description. Mystical teachers are unanimous as to this. Saint John of the Cross, for instance, one of the best of them, thus describes the condition called the "union of love," which, he says, is reached by "dark contemplation." In this the Deity compensates the soul, but in such a hidden way that the soul—

finds no terms, no means, no comparison whereby to render the sublimity of the wisdom and the delicacy of the spiritual feeling with which she is filled. . . . We receive this mystical knowledge of God clothed in none of the kinds of images, in none of the sensible representations, which our mind makes use of in other circumstances. Accordingly in this knowledge, since the senses and the imagination are not employed, we get neither form nor impression, nor can we give any account or furnish any likeness, although the mysterious and sweet-tasting wisdom comes home so clearly to the inmost parts of our soul. Fancy a man seeing a certain kind of thing for the first time in his life. He can understand it, use and enjoy it, but he cannot apply a name to it, nor communicate any idea of it, even though all the while it be a mere thing of sense. How much greater will be his powerlessness when it goes beyond the senses! This is the peculiarity of the divine language. The more infused, intimate, spiritual, and supersensible it is, the more does it exceed the senses, both inner and outer, and impose silence upon them.

. . . The soul then feels as if placed in a vast and profound solitude, to which no created thing has access, in an immense and boundless desert, desert the more delicious the more solitary it is. There, in this abyss of wisdom, the soul grows by what it drinks in from the wellsprings of the comprehension of love, . . . and recognizes, however sublime and learned may be the terms we employ, how utterly vile, insignificant, and improper they are, when we seek to discourse of divine things by their means.

I cannot pretend to detail to you the sundry stages of the Christian mystical life. Our time would not suffice, for one thing; and moreover, I confess that the subdivisions and names which we find in the Catholic books seem to me to represent nothing objectively distinct. So many men, so many minds; I imagine that these experiences can be as infinitely varied as are the idiosyncrasies of individuals.

The cognitive aspects of them, their value in the way of revelation, is what we are directly concerned with, and it is easy to show by citation how strong an impression they leave of being revelations of new depths of truth. Saint Teresa is the expert of experts in describing such conditions, so I will turn immediately to what she says of one of the highest of them, the "orison of union."

In the orison of union (says Saint Teresa) the soul is fully awake as regards God, but wholly asleep as regards things of this world and in respect of herself. During the short time the union lasts, she is as it were deprived of every feeling, and even if she would, she could not think of any single thing. Thus she needs to employ no artifice in order to arrest the use of her understanding: it remains so stricken with inactivity that she neither knows what she loves, nor in what manner she loves, nor what she wills. In short, she is utterly dead to the things of the world and lives solely in God. . . . I do not even know whether in this state she has enough life left to breathe. It seems to me she has not; or at least that if she does breathe, she is unaware of it. Her intellect would fain understand something of what is going on within her, but it has so little force now that it can act in no way whatsoever. So a person who falls into a deep faint appears as if dead. . . .

Thus does God, when he raises a soul to union with himself, suspend the natural action of all her faculties. She neither sees, hears, nor understands, so long as she is united with God. But this time is always short, and it seems even shorter than it is. God establishes himself in the interior of this soul in such a way, that when she returns to herself, it is wholly impossible for her to doubt that she has been in God, and God in her.

This truth remains so strongly impressed on her that, even though many years should pass without the condition returning, she can neither forget the favor she received, nor doubt of its reality. If you, nevertheless, ask how it is possible that the soul can see and understand that she has been in God, since during the union she has neither sight nor understanding, I reply that she does not see it then, but that she sees it clearly later, after she has returned to herself, not by any vision, but by a certitude which abides with her and which God alone can give her. I knew a person who was ignorant of the truth that God's mode of being in everything must be either by presence, by power, or by essence, but who, after having received the grace of which I am speaking, believed this truth in the most unshakable manner. So much so that, having consulted a half-learned man who was as ignorant on this point as she had been before she was enlightened, when he replied that God is in us only by "grace," she disbelieved his reply, so sure she was of the true answer; and when she came to ask wiser doctors, they confirmed her in her belief, which much consoled her. . . .

But how, you will repeat, *can* one have such certainty in respect to what one does not see? This question, I am powerless to answer. These are secrets of God's omnipotence which it does not appertain to me to penetrate. All that I know is that I tell the truth; and I shall never believe that any soul who does not possess this certainty has ever been really united to God.

The kinds of truth communicable in mystical ways, whether these be sensible or supersensible, are various. Some of them relate to this world—visions of the future, the reading of hearts, the sudden understanding of texts, the knowledge of distant events, for example; but the most important revelations are theological or metaphysical.

Saint Ignatius confessed one day to Father Laynez that a single hour of meditation at Manresa had taught him more truths about heavenly things than all the teachings of all the doctors put together could have taught him. . . . One day in orison, on the steps of the choir of the Dominican church, he saw in a distinct manner the plan of divine wisdom in the creation of the world. On another occasion, during a procession, his spirit was ravished in God, and it was given to him to contemplate, in a form and images fitted to the weak understanding of a dweller on the earth, the deep mystery of the holy Trinity. This last vision flooded his heart with such sweetness, that the mere memory of it in after times made him shed abundant tears.

Similarly with Saint Teresa.

One day, being in orison (she writes), it was granted me to perceive in one instant how all things are seen and contained in God. I did not perceive them in their proper form, and nevertheless the view I had of them was of a sovereign clearness, and has remained vividly impressed upon my soul. It is one of the most signal of all the graces which the Lord has granted me. . . . The view was so subtle and delicate that the understanding cannot grasp it.

She goes on to tell how it was as if the Deity were an enormous and sovereignly limpid diamond, in which all our actions were contained in such a way their full sinfulness appeared evident as never before. On another day, she relates, while she was reciting the Athanasian Creed—

Our Lord made me comprehend in what way it is that one God can be in three persons. He made me see it so clearly that I remained as extremely surprised as I was comforted, . . . and now, when I think of the holy Trinity, or hear It spoken of, I understand how the three adorable Persons form only one God and I experience an unspeakable happiness.

On still another occasion it was given to Saint Teresa to see and understand in what wise the Mother of God had been assumed into her place in Heaven.

The deliciousness of some of these states seems to be beyond anything known in ordinary consciousness. It evidently involves organic sensibilities, for it is spoken of as something too extreme to be borne, and as verging on bodily pain. But it is too subtle and piercing a delight for ordinary words to denote. God's touches, the wounds of his spear, references to ebriety and to nuptial union have to figure in the phraseology by which it is shadowed forth. Intellect and senses both swoon away in these highest states of ecstasy. "If our understanding comprehends," says Saint Teresa, "it is in a mode which remains unknown to it, and it can understand nothing of what it comprehends. For my own part, I do not believe that it does comprehend, because, as I said, it does not understand itself to do so. I confess that it is all a mystery in which I am lost." In the condition called *raptus* or ravishment by theologians, breathing and circulation are so depressed that it is a question among the doctors whether the soul be or be not temporarily dissevered from the body. One must read Saint Teresa's descriptions and the very exact distinctions which she makes, to persuade one's self that one is dealing, not with imaginary experiences, but with phenomena which, however rare, follow perfectly definite psychological types.

To the medical mind these ecstasies signify nothing but suggested and imitated hypnoid states, on an intellectual basis of superstition, and a corporeal one of degeneration and hysteria. Undoubtedly these pathological conditions have existed in many and possibly in all the cases, but that fact tells us nothing about the value for knowledge of the consciousness which they induce. To pass a spiritual judgment upon these states, we must not content ourselves with superficial medical talk, but inquire into their fruits for life.

Their fruits appear to have been various. Stupefaction, for one thing, seems not to have been altogether absent as a result. You may remember the helplessness in the kitchen and schoolroom of poor Margaret Mary Alacoque. Many other ecstatics would have perished but for the care taken of them by admiring followers. The "other-worldliness" encouraged by the mystical consciousness makes this over-abstraction from practical life peculiarly liable to befall mystics in whom the character is naturally passive and the intellect feeble; but in natively strong minds and characters we find quite opposite results. The great Spanish mystics, who carried the habit of ecstasy as far as it has often carried, appear for the most part to have shown indomitable spirit and energy, and all the more so for the trances in which they indulged.

Saint Ignatius was a mystic, but his mysticism made him assuredly one of the most powerfully practical human engines that ever lived. Saint John of the Cross, writing of the intuitions and "touches" by which God reaches the substance of the soul, tells us that—

They enrich it marvelously. A single one of them may be sufficient to abolish at a stroke certain imperfections of which the soul during its whole life had vainly tried to rid itself, and to leave it adorned with virtues and loaded with supernatural gifts. A single one of these intoxicating consolations may reward it for all the labors undergone in its life—even were they numberless. Invested with an invincible courage, filled with an impassioned desire to suffer for its God, the soul then is seized with a strange torment—that of not being allowed to suffer enough.

Saint Teresa is as emphatic, and much more detailed. You may perhaps remember a passage I quoted from her in my first lecture. There are many similar pages in her autobiography. Where in literature is a more evidently veracious account of the formation of a new centre of spiritual energy, than is given in her description of the effects of certain ecstasies which in departing leave the soul upon a higher level of emotional excitement?

Often, infirm and wrought upon with dreadful pains before the ecstasy, the soul emerges from it full of health and admirably disposed for action . . . as if God had willed that the body itself, already obedient to the soul's desires, should share in the soul's happiness. . . . The soul after such a favor is animated with a degree of courage so great that if at that moment its body should be torn to pieces for the cause of God, it would feel nothing but the liveliest comfort. Then it is that promises and heroic resolutions spring up in profusion in us, soaring desires, horror of the world, and the clear perception of our proper nothingness. . . . What empire is comparable to that of a soul who, from this sublime summit to which God has raised her, sees all the things of earth beneath her feet, and is captivated by no one of them? How ashamed she is of her former attachments! How amazed at her blindness! What lively pity she feels for those whom she recognizes still shrouded in the darkness! . . . She groans at having ever been sensitive to points of honor, at the illusion that made her ever see as honor what the world calls by that name. Now she sees in this name nothing more than an immense lie of which the world remains a victim. She discovers, in the new light from above, that in genuine honor there is nothing spurious, that to be faithful to this honor is to give our respect to what deserves to be respected really, and to consider as nothing, or as less than nothing, whatsoever perishes and is not agreeable to God. . . . She laughs when she sees grave persons, persons of orison, caring for points of honor for which she now feels profoundest contempt. It is suitable to the dignity of their rank to act thus, they pretend, and it makes them more useful to others. But she knows that in despising the dignity of their rank for the pure love of God they would do more good in a single day than they would effect in ten years by preserving it. . . . She laughs at herself that there should ever have been a time in her life when she made any case of money, when she ever desired it. . . . Oh! if human beings might only agree together to regard it as so much useless mud, what harmony would then reign in the world! With what friendship we would all treat each other if our interest in honor and in money could but disappear from earth! For my own part, I feel as if it would be a remedy for all our ills.

Mystical conditions may, therefore, render the soul more energetic in the lines which their inspiration favors. But this could be reckoned an advantage only in case the inspiration were a true one. If the inspiration were erroneous, the energy would be all the more mistaken and misbegotten. So we stand once more before the problem of truth which confronted us at the end of the lectures on saintliness. You will remember that we turned to mysticism precisely to get some light on truth. Do mystical states establish the truth of those theological affections in which the saintly life has its root?

In spite of their repudiation of articulate self-description, mystical states in general assert a pretty distinct theoretic drift. It is possible to give the outcome of the majority of them in terms that point in definite philosophical directions. One of these directions is optimism, and the other is monism. We pass into mystical states from out of ordinary consciousness as from a less into a more, as from a smallness into a vastness, and at the same time as from an unrest to a rest. We feel them as reconciling, unifying states. They appeal to the yes-function more than to the no-function in us. In them the unlimited absorbs the limits and peacefully closes the account. Their very denial of every adjective you may propose as applicable to the ultimate truth—He, the Self, the Atman, is to be described by "No! no!": only, say the Upanishads—though it seems on the surface to be a no-function, is a denial made on behalf of a deeper yes. Whoso calls the Absolute anything in particular, or says that it is *this,* seems implicitly to shut it off from being *that*—it is as if he lessened it. So we deny the "this," negating the negation which it seems to us to imply, in the interests of the higher affirmative attitude by which we are possessed. The fountainhead of Christian mysticism is Dionysius the Areopagite. He describes the absolute truth by negatives exclusively.

The cause of all things is neither soul nor intellect; nor has it imagination, opinion, or reason, or intelligence; nor is it reason or intelligence; nor is it spoken or thought. It is neither number, nor order, nor magnitude, nor littleness, nor equality, nor inequality, nor similarity, nor dissimilarity. It neither stands, nor moves, nor rests. . . . It is neither essence, nor eternity, nor time. Even intellectual contact does not belong to it. It is neither science nor truth. It is not even royalty or

wisdom; not one; not unity; not divinity or goodness; nor even spirit as we know it (etc., *ad libitum*).

But these qualifications are denied by Dionysius, not because the truth falls short of them, but because it so infinitely excels them. It is above them. It is *super*-lucent, *super*-splendent, *super*-essential, *super*-sublime, *super* everything that can be named. Like Hegel in his logic, mystics journey towards the positive pole of truth only by the "Methode der Absoluten Negativität."

Thus comes the paradoxical expressions that so abound in mystical writings. As when Eckhart tells of the still desert of the Godhead, "where never was seen difference, neither Father, Son, nor Holy Ghost, where there is no one at home, yet where the spark of the soul is more at peace than in itself." As when Boehme writes of the Primal Love, that "it may fitly be compared to Nothing, for it is deeper than any Thing, and is as nothing with respect to all things, forasmuch as it is not comprehensible by any of them. And because it is nothing respectively, it is therefore free from all things, and is that only good, which a man cannot express or utter what it is, there being nothing to which it may be compared, to express it by." Or as when Angelus Silesius sings:—

["God is pure Nothing. Neither Now
nor Here affects Him.
But the more you grasp him,
the more He disappears"]   (Ed. trans.)

To this dialectical use, by the intellect, of negation as a mode of passage towards a higher kind of affirmation, there is correlated the subtlest of moral counterparts in the sphere of the personal will. Since denial of the finite self and its wants, since asceticism of some sort, is found in religious experience to be the only doorway to the larger and more blessed life, this moral mystery intertwines and combines with the intellectual mystery in all mystical writings.

Love (continues Boehme) [is Nothing, for] when thou art gone forth wholly from the Creature and from that which is visible, and art become Nothing to all that is Nature and Creature, then thou art in that eternal One, which is God himself, and then thou shalt feel within thee the highest virtue of Love. . . . The treasure of treasures for the soul is where she goeth out of the Somewhat into that Nothing out of which all things may be made. The soul here saith, *I have nothing,* for I am utterly stripped and naked; *I can do nothing,* for I have no manner of power, but am as water poured out; *I am nothing,* for all that I am is no more than an image of Being, and only God is to me I AM; and so, sitting down in my own Nothingness, I give glory to the eternal Being, and *will nothing* of myself, that so God may will all in me, being unto me my God and all things.

In Paul's language, I live, yet not I, but Christ liveth in me. Only when I become as nothing can God enter in and no difference between his life and mine remain outstanding.

This overcoming of all the usual barriers between the individual and the Absolute is the great mystic achievement. In mystic states we both become one with the Absolute and we become aware of our oneness. This is the everlasting and triumphant mystical tradition, hardly altered by differences of clime or creed. In Hinduism, in Neoplatonism, in Sufism, in Christian mysticism, in Whitmanism, we find the same recurring note, so that there is about mystical utterances an eternal unanimity which ought to make a critic stop and think, and which brings it about that the mystical classics have, as has been said, neither birthday nor native land. Perpetually telling of the unity of man with God, their speech antedates languages, and they do not grow old.

"That are Thou!" says the Upanishads, and the Vedantists add: "Not a part, nor a mode of That, but identically That, that absolute Spirit of the World." "As pure water poured into pure water remains the same, thus, O Gautama, is the Self of a thinker who knows. Water in water, fire in fire, ether in ether, no one can distinguish them: likewise a man whose mind has entered into the self." "'Everyman,' says the Sufi Gulshan-Râz, whose heart is no longer shaken by any doubts, knows with certainty that there is no being save only One. . . . In his divine majesty the *me,* and *we,* the *thou,* are not found, for in the One there can be no distinction. Every being who is annulled and entirely separated from himself, hears resound outside of him this voice and this echo: *I am God*: he has an eternal way of existing, and is no longer subject to death.'" In the vision of God, says Plotinus, "what sees is not our reason, but

something prior and superior to our reason. . . . He who thus sees does not properly see, does not distinguish or imagine two things. He changes, he ceases to be himself, preserves nothing of himself. Absorbed in God, he makes but one with him, like a centre of a circle coinciding with another centre." "Here," writes Suso, "the spirit dies, and yet is all alive in the marvels of the Godhead . . . and is lost in the stillness of the glorious dazzling obscurity and of the naked simple unity. It is in this modeless *where* that the highest bliss is to be found." ["I am as great as God,"] sings Angelus Silesius again, ["He is as small as I. He cannot be above me, nor I under Him."] (Ed. trans.)

In mystical literature such self-contradictory phrases as "dazzling obscurity," "whispering silence," "teeming desert," are continually met with. They prove that not conceptual speech, but music rather, is the element through which we are best spoken to by mystical truth. Many mystical scriptures are indeed little more than musical compositions.

He who would hear the voice of Nada, "the Soundless Sound," and comprehend it, he has to learn the nature of Dhârana. . . . When to himself his form appears unreal, as do on waking all the forms he sees in dreams; when he has ceased to hear the many, he may discern the ONE—the inner sound which kills the outer. . . . For then the soul will hear, and will remember. And then to the inner ear will speak THE VOICE OF THE SILENCE . . . And now thy *Self* is lost in SELF, *thyself* unto THYSELF, merged in that SELF from which thou first didst radiate. . . . Behold! thou hast become the Light, thou hast become the Sound, thou art thy Master and thy God. Thou art THYSELF the object of thy search: the VOICE unbroken, that resounds throughout eternities, exempt from change, from sin exempt, the seven sounds in one, the VOICE OF THE SILENCE. *Om tat Sat.*

These words, if they do not awaken laughter as you receive them, probably stir chords within you which music and language touch in common. Music gives us ontological messages which non-musical criticism is unable to contradict, though it may laugh at our foolishness in minding them. There is a verge of the mind which these things haunt; and whispers therefrom mingle with the operations of our understanding, even as the waters of the infinite ocean send their waves to break among the pebbles that lie upon our shores.

> Here begins the sea that ends not till the world's end. Where we stand,
> Could we know the next high sea-mark set beyond these waves that gleam,
> We should know what never man hath known, nor eye of man hath scanned.
> . . .
> Ah, but here man's heart leaps, yearning towards the gloom with venturous glee,
> From the shore that hath no shore beyond it, set in all the sea.

That doctrine, for example, that eternity is timeless, that our "immortality," if we live in the eternal, is not so much future as already now and here, which we find so often expressed to-day in certain philosophical circles, finds its support in a "hear, hear!" or an "amen," which floats up from that mysteriously deeper level. We recognize the passwords to the mystical region as we hear them, but we cannot use them ourselves; it alone has the keeping of "the password primeval."

I have now sketched with extreme brevity and insufficiency, but as fairly as I am able in the time allowed, the general traits of the mystic range of consciousness. *It is on the whole pantheistic and optimistic, or at least the opposite of pessimistic. It is anti-naturalistic, and harmonizes best with twice-bornness and so-called other-wordly states of mind.*

My next task is to inquire whether we can invoke it as authoritative. Does it furnish any *warrant for the truth* of the twice-bornness and super-naturality and pantheism which it favors? I must give my answer to this question as concisely as I can.

In brief my answer is this—and I will divide it into three parts:—

(1) Mystical states, when well developed, usually are, and have the right to be, absolutely authoritative over the individuals to whom they come.
(2) No authority emanates from them which should make it a duty for those who stand outside of them to accept their revelations uncritically.
(3) They break down the authority of the non-mystical or rationalistic consciousness, based upon the understanding and the senses alone. They show it to be only one kind of consciousness. They open out the possibility of other orders of truth, in which, so far as anything in us vitally responds to them, we may freely continue to have faith.

I will take up these points one by one.

1. As a matter of psychological fact, mystical states of a well-pronounced and emphatic sort *are* usually authoritative over those who have them. They have been "there," and know. It is vain for rationalism to grumble about this. If the mystical truth that comes to a man proves to be a force that he can live by, what mandate have we of the majority to order him to live in another way? We can throw him into a prison or a madhouse, but we cannot change his mind—we commonly attach it only the more stubbornly to its beliefs. It mocks our utmost efforts, as a matter of fact, and in point of logic it absolutely escapes our jurisdiction. Our own more "rational" beliefs are based on evidence exactly similar in nature to that which mystics quote for theirs. Our senses, namely, have assured us of certain states of fact; but mystical experiences are as direct perceptions of fact for those who have them as any sensations ever were for us. The records show that even though the five senses be in abeyance in them, they are absolutely sensational in their epistemological quality, if I may be pardoned the barbarous expression—that is, they are face to face presentations of what seems immediately to exist.

The mystic is, in short, *invulnerable*, and must be left, whether we relish it or not, in undisturbed enjoyment of his creed. Faith, says Tolstoy, is that by which men live. And faith-state and mystic state are practically convertible terms.

2. But I now proceed to add that mystics have no right to claim that we ought to accept the deliverance of their peculiar experiences, if we are ourselves outsiders and feel no private call thereto. The utmost they can ever ask of us in this life is to admit that they establish a presumption. They form a consensus and have an unequivocal outcome; and it would be odd, mystics might say, if such a unan-

imous type of experience should prove to be altogether wrong. At bottom, however, this would only be an appeal to numbers, like the appeal of rationalism the other way; and the appeal to numbers has no logical force. If we acknowledge it, it is for "suggestive," not for logical reasons: we follow the majority because to do so suits our life.

But even this presumption from the unanimity of mystics is far from being strong. In characterizing mystic states as pantheistic, optimistic, etc., I am afraid I over-simplified the truth. I did so for expository reasons, and to keep the closer to the classic mystical tradition. The classic religious mysticism, it now must be confessed, is only a "privileged case." It is an *extract*, kept true to type by the selection of the fittest specimens and their preservation in "schools." It is carved out from a much larger mass; and if we take the larger mass as seriously as religious mysticism has historically taken itself, we find that the supposed unanimity largely disappears. To begin with, even religious mysticism itself, the kind that accumulates traditions and makes schools, is much less unanimous than I have allowed. It has been both ascetic and antinomianly self-indulgent within the Christian church. It is dualistic in Sankhya, and monistic in Vedanta philosophy. I called it pantheistic; but the great Spanish mystics are anything but pantheists. They are with few exceptions non-metaphysical minds, for whom "the category of personality" is absolute. The "union" of man with God is for them much more like an occasional miracle than like an original identity. How different again, apart from the happiness common to all, is the mysticism of Walt Whitman, Edward Carpenter, Richard Jefferies, and other naturalistic pantheists, from the more distinctively Christian sort. The fact is that the mystical feeling of enlargement, union, and emancipation has no specific intellectual content whatever of its own. It is capable of forming matrimonial alliances with material furnished by the most diverse philosophies and theologies, provided only they can find a place in their framework for its peculiar emotional mood. We have no right, therefore, to invoke its prestige as distinctively in favor of any special belief, such as that in absolute idealism, or in the absolute monistic identity, or in the absolute

goodness, of the world. It is only relatively in favor of all these things—it passes out of common human consciousness in the direction in which they lie.

So much for religious mysticism proper. But more remains to be told, for religious mysticism is only one half of mysticism. The other half has no accumulated traditions except those which the textbooks on insanity supply. Open any one of these and you will find abundant cases in which "mystical ideas" are cited as characteristic symptoms of enfeebled or deluded states of mind. In delusional insanity, paranoia, as they sometimes call it, we may have a *diabolical* mysticism, a sort of religious mysticism turned upside down. The same sense of ineffable importance in the smallest events, the same texts and words coming with new meanings, the same voices and visions and leadings and missions, the same controlling by extraneous powers; only this time the emotion is pessimistic: instead of consolations we have desolations; the meanings are dreadful; and the powers are enemies to life. It is evident from the point of view of their psychological mechanism, the classic mysticism and these lower mysticisms spring from the same mental level, from that great subliminal or transmarginal region of which science is beginning to admit the existence, but of which so little is really known. That region contains every kind of matter: "seraph and snake" abide there side by side. To come from thence is no infallible credential. What comes must be sifted and tested, and run the gauntlet of confrontation with the total context of experience, just like what comes from the outer world of sense. Its value must be ascertained by empirical methods, so long as we are not mystics ourselves.

Once more, then, I repeat that non-mystics are under no obligation to acknowledge in mystical states a superior authority conferred on them by their intrinsic nature.

3. Yet, I repeat once more, the existence of mystical states absolutely overthrows the pretension of non-mystical states to be the sole and ultimate dictators of what we may believe. As a rule, mystical states merely add a supersensuous meaning to the ordinary outward data of consciousness. They are excitements like the emotions of love or ambition, gifts to our spirit by means of which facts

already objectively before us fall into a new expressiveness and make a new connection with our active life. They do not contradict these facts as such, or deny anything that our senses have immediately seized. It is the rationalistic critic rather who plays the part of denier in the controversy, and his denials have no strength, for there never can be a state of facts to which new meaning may not truthfully be added, provided the mind ascend to a more enveloping point of view. It must always remain an open question whether mystical states may not possibly be such superior points of view, windows through which the mind looks out upon a more extensive and inclusive world. The difference of the views seen from the different mystical windows need not prevent us from entertaining this supposition. The wider world would in that case prove to have a mixed constitution like that of this world, that is all. It would have its celestial and its infernal regions, its tempting and its saving moments, its valid experiences and its counterfeit ones, just as our world has them; but it would be a wider world all the same. We should have to use its experiences by selecting and subordinating and substituting just as is our custom in this ordinary naturalistic world; we should be liable to error just as we are now; yet the counting in of that wider world of meanings, and the serious dealing with it, might, in spite of all the perplexity, be indispensable stages in our approach to the final fullness of the truth.

In this shape, I think, we have to leave the subject. Mystical states indeed wield no authority due simply to their being mystical states. But the higher ones among them point in directions to which the religious sentiments even of non-mystical men incline. They tell of the supremacy of the ideal, of vastness, of union, of safety, and of rest. They offer us *hypotheses*, hypotheses which we may voluntarily ignore, but which as thinkers we cannot possibly upset. The supernaturalism and optimism to which they would persuade us may, interpreted in one way or another, be after all the truest of insights into the meaning of this life.

"Oh, the little more, and how much it is; and the little less, and what worlds away!" It may be that possibility and permission of this sort are all that our religious consciousness requires to live on. In my last lecture I shall have to try to persuade you that this is the case. Meanwhile, however, I am sure that for many of my readers this diet is too slender. If supernaturalism and inner union with the divine are true, you think, then not so much permission, as compulsion to believe, ought to be found. Philosophy has always professed to prove religious truth by coercive argument; and the construction of philosophies of this kind has always been one favorite function of the religious life, if we use this term in the large historic sense. But religious philosophy is an enormous subject, and in my next lecture I can only give that brief glance at it which my limits will allow.

Conclusions on Religious Experience

Let us agree, then, that Religion, occupying herself with personal destinies and keeping thus in contact with the only absolute realities which we know, must necessarily play an eternal part in human history. The next thing to decide is what she reveals about those destinies, or whether indeed she reveals anything distinct enough to be considered a general message to mankind. We have done as you see, with our preliminaries, and our final summing up can now begin. . . .

Both thought and feeling are determinants of conduct, and the same conduct may be determined either by feeling or by thought. When we survey the whole field of religion, we find a great variety in the thoughts that have prevailed there; but the feelings on the one hand and the conduct on the other are almost always the same, for Stoic, Christian, and Buddhist saints are practically indistinguishable in their lives. The theories which Religion generates, being thus variable, are secondary; and if you wish to grasp her essence, you must look to the feelings and the conduct as being the more constant elements. It is between these two elements that the short circuit exists on which she carries on her principal business, while the ideas and symbols and other institutions form loop-lines which may be perfections and improvements, and may even some day all be united into one harmonious system, but which are not to be regarded as organs with an indispensable function, necessary at all times for religious life to go on. This seems to me the first conclusion which we are entitled to draw from the phenomena we have passed in review.

The next step is to characterize the feelings. To what psychological order do they belong?

The resultant outcome of them is in any case what Kant calls 'sthenic' affection, an excitement of the cheerful, expansive, 'dynamogenic' order which, like any tonic, freshens our vital powers. In almost every lecture, but especially in the lectures on Conversion and on Saintliness, we have seen how this emotion overcomes temperamental melancholy and imparts endurance to the Subject, or a zest, or a meaning, or an enchantment and glory to the common objects of life. The name of 'faith-state,' by which Professor Leuba designates it, is a good one. It is a biological as well as a psychological condition, and Tolstoy is absolutely accurate in classing faith among the forces *by which men live.* The total absence of it, anhedonia, means collapse.

The faith-state may hold a very minimum of intellectual content. We saw examples of this in those sudden raptures of the divine presence, or in such mystical seizures as Dr. Bucke described. It may be a mere vague enthusiasm, half spiritual, half vital, a courage, and a feeling that great and wondrous things are in the air.

When, however, a positive intellectual content is associated with a faith-state, it gets invincibly stamped in upon belief, and this explains the passionate loyalty of religious persons everywhere to the minutest details of their so widely differing creeds. Taking creeds and faith-state together, as forming 'religions,' and treating these as purely subjective phenomena, without regard to the question of their 'truth,' we are obliged, on account of their extraordinary influence upon action and endurance, to class them amongst the most important biological functions of mankind. Their stimulant and anaesthetic effect is so great that Professor Leuba, in a recent article, goes so far as to say that so long as men can *use* their God, they care very little who he is, or even whether he is at all. "The truth of the matter can be put," says Leuba, "in this way: *God is not known, he is not understood; he is used*—sometimes as meat-purveyor, sometimes as

moral support, sometimes as friend, sometimes as an object of love. If he proves himself useful, the religious consciousness asks for no more than that. Does God really exist? How does he exist? What is he? are so many irrelevant questions. Not God, but life, more life, a larger, richer, more satisfying life is, in the last analysis, the end of religion. The love of life, at any and every level of development, is the religious impulse."

At this purely subjective rating, therefore, Religion must be considered vindicated in a certain way from the attacks of her critics. It would seem that she cannot be a mere anachronism and survival, but must exert a permanent function, whether she be with or without intellectual content, and whether, if she have any, it be true or false.

We must next pass beyond the point of view of merely subjective utility, and make inquiry into the intellectual content itself.

First, is there, under all the discrepancies of the creeds, a common nucleus to which they bear their testimony unanimously?

And second, ought we to consider the testimony true?

I will take up the first question first, and answer it immediately in the affirmative. The warring gods and formulas of the various religions do indeed cancel each other, but there is a certain uniform deliverance in which religions all appear to meet. It consists of two parts:—

1. An uneasiness; and
2. Its solution.

1. The uneasiness, reduced to its simplest terms, is a sense that there is *something wrong about us* as we naturally stand.
2. The solution is a sense that *we are saved from the wrongness* by making proper connection with the higher powers.

In those more developed minds, which alone we are studying, the wrongness takes a moral character, and the salvation takes a mystical tinge. I think we shall keep well within the limits of what is common to all such minds if we formulate the essence of their religious experience in terms like these:—

The individual, so far as he suffers from his wrongness and criticises it, is to that extent consciously beyond it, and in at least possible touch with something higher, if anything higher exist. Along with the wrong part there is thus a better part of him, even though it may be but a most helpless germ. With which part he should identify his real being is by no means obvious at this stage; but when stage 2 (the stage of solution or salvation) arrives, the man identifies his real being with the germinal higher part of himself; and does so in the following way. *He becomes conscious that this higher part is conterminous and continuous with a MORE of the same quality, which is operative in the universe outside of him, and which he can keep in working touch with, and in a fashion get on board of and save himself when all his lower being has gone to pieces in the wreck.*

It seems to me that all the phenomena are accurately describable in these very simple general terms. They allow for the divided self and the struggle; they involve the change of personal centre and the surrender of the lower self; they express the appearance of exteriority of the helping power and yet account for our sense of union with it; and they fully justify our feelings of security and joy. There is probably no autobiographic document, among all those which I have quoted, to which the description will not well apply. One need only add such specific details as will adapt it to various theologies and various personal temperaments, and one will then have the various experiences reconstructed in their individual forms.

So far, however, as this analysis goes, the experiences are only psychological phenomena. They possess, it is true, enormous biological worth. Spiritual strength really increases in the subject when he has them, a new life opens for him, and they seem to him a place of conflux where the forces of two universes meet; and yet this may be nothing but his subjective way of feeling things, a mood of his own fancy, in spite of the effects produced. I now turn to my second question: What is the objective 'truth' of their content?

The part of the content concerning which the question of truth most pertinently arises is that 'MORE of the same quality' with which our own higher self appears in the experience to come into harmonious working relation. Is such a 'more' merely our own notion, or does it really exist? If so, in what shape does it exist? Does it act, as well as exist? And in what form should we conceive of that 'union' with it of which religious geniuses are so convinced?

It is in answering these questions that the various theologies perform their theoretic work, and that their divergencies most come to light. They all agree that the 'more' really exists; though some of them hold it to exist in the shape of a personal god or gods, while others are satisfied to conceive it as a stream of ideal tendency embedded in the eternal structure of the world. They all agree, moreover, that it acts as well as exists, and that something really is effected for the better when you throw your life into its hands. It is when they treat of the experience of 'union' with it that their speculative differences appear most clearly. Over this point pantheism and theism, nature and second birth, works and grace and karma, immortality and reincarnation, rationalism and mysticism, carry on inveterate disputes.

At the end of my lecture on Philosophy I held out the notion that an impartial science of religions might sift out from the midst of their discrepancies a common body of doctrine which she might also formulate in terms to which physical science need not object. This, I said, she might adopt as her own reconciling hypothesis, and recommend it for general belief. I also said that in my last lecture I should have to try my own hand at framing such an hypothesis.

The time has now come for this attempt. Who says 'hypothesis' renounces the ambition to be coercive in his arguments. The most I can do is, accordingly, to offer something that may fit the facts so easily that your scientific logic will find no plausible pretext for vetoing your impulse to welcome it as true.

The 'more,' as we called it, and the meaning of our 'union' with it, form the nucleus of our inquiry. Into what definite description can these words be translated, and for what definite facts do they stand? It would never do for us to place ourselves offhand at the position of a particular theology, the Christian theology, for example, and proceed immediately to define the 'more' as Jehovah, and the 'union' as his imputation to us of the righteousness of Christ. That would be unfair to other religions, and from our present standpoint at least, would be an over-belief.

We must begin by using less particularized terms; and, since one of the duties of the science of religions is to keep religion in connection with the rest of science, we shall do well to seek first of all a way of describing the 'more,' which psychologists may also recognize as real. The *subconscious self* is nowadays a well-accredited psychological entity; and I believe that in it we have exactly the mediating term required. Apart from all religious considerations, there is actually and literally more life in our total soul than we are at any time aware of. The exploration of the transmarginal field has hardly yet been seriously undertaken, but what Mr. Myers said in 1892 in his essay on the Subliminal Consciousness is as true as when it was first written: "Each of us is in reality an abiding psychical entity far more extensive than he knows—an individuality which can never express itself completely through any corporeal manifestation. The Self manifests through the organism; but there is always some part of the Self unmanifested; and always, as it seems, some power of organic expression in abeyance or reserve." Much of the content of this larger background against which our conscious being stands out in relief is insignificant. Imperfect memories, silly jingles, inhibitive timidities, 'dissolutive' phenomena of various sorts, as Myers calls them, enter into it for a large part. But in it many of the performances of genius seem also to have their origin; and in our study of conversion, of mystical experiences, and of prayer, we have seen how striking a part invasions from this region play in the religious life.

Let me then propose, as an hypothesis, that whatever it may be on its *farther* side, the 'more' with which in religious experience we feel ourselves connected is on its *hither* side the subconscious continuation of our conscious life. Starting thus with a recognized psychological fact as our basis, we seem to preserve a contact with 'science' which the ordinary theologian lacks. At the same time the theologian's contention that the religious man is moved by an external power is vindicated, for it is one of the peculiarities of invasions from the subconscious region to take on objective appearances, and to suggest to the Subject an external control. In the religious life the control is felt as 'higher'; but since on our hypothesis it is primarily the higher faculties of our own hidden mind which are controlling, the sense of union with the power beyond us is a sense of something, not merely apparently, but literally true.

This doorway into the subject seems to me the best one for a science of religions, for it mediates between a number of different points of view. Yet it is only a doorway, and difficulties present themselves as soon as we step through it, and ask how far our transmarginal consciousness carries us if we follow it on its remoter side. Here the over-beliefs begin: here mysticism and the conversion-rapture and Vedantism and transcendental idealism bring in their monistic interpretations and tell us that the finite self rejoins the absolute self, for it was always one with God and identical with the soul of the world. Here the prophets of all the different religions come with their visions, voices, raptures, and other openings, supposed by each to authenticate his own peculiar faith.

Those of us who are not personally favored with such specific revelations must stand outside of them altogether and, for the present at least, decide that, since they corroborate incompatible theological doctrines, they neutralize one another and leave no fixed result. If we follow any one of them, or if we follow philosophical theory and embrace monistic pantheism on non-mystical grounds, we do so in the exercise of our individual freedom, and build out our religion in the way most congruous with our personal susceptibilities. Among these susceptibilities intellectual ones play a decisive part. Although the religious question is primarily a question of life, of living or not living in the higher union which opens itself to us as a gift, yet the spiritual excitement in which the gift appears a real one will often fail to be aroused in an individual until certain particular intellectual beliefs or ideas which, as we say, come home to him, are touched. These ideas will thus be essential to that individual's religion;— which is as much as to say that over-beliefs in various directions are absolutely indispensable, and that we should treat them with tenderness and tolerance so long as they are not intolerant themselves. As I have elsewhere written, the most interesting and valuable things about a man are usually his over-beliefs.

Disregarding the over-beliefs, and confining ourselves to what is common and generic, we have in *the fact that the conscious person is continuous with a wider self through which saving experiences come*, a positive content of religious experience which, it seems to me, *is literally and objectively true as far as it goes*. If I now proceed to state my own hypothesis about the farther limits of this extension of our personality, I shall be offering my own over-belief—though I know it will appear a sorry under-belief to some of you—for which I can only bespeak the same indulgence which in a converse case I should accord to yours.

The further limits of our being plunge, it seems to me, into an altogether other dimension of existence from the sensible and merely 'understandable' world. Name it the mystical region, or the supernatural region, whichever you choose. So far as our ideal impulses originate in this region (and most of them do originate in it, for we find them possessing us in a way for which we cannot articulately account), we belong to it in a more intimate sense than that in which we belong to the visible world, for we belong in the most intimate sense wherever our ideals belong. Yet the unseen region in question is not merely ideal, for it produces effects in this world. When we commune with it, work is actually done upon our finite personality, for we are turned into new men, and consequences in the way of conduct follow in the natural world upon our regenerative change. But that which produces effects within another reality must be termed a reality itself, so I feel as if we had no philosophic excuse for calling the unseen or mystical world unreal.

God is the natural appellation, for us Christians at least, for the supreme reality, so I will call this higher part of the universe by the name of God. We and God have business with each other; and in opening ourselves to his influence our deepest destiny is fulfilled. The universe, at those parts of it which our personal being constitutes, takes a turn genuinely for the worse or for the better in propor-

tion as each one of us fulfills or evades God's demands. As far as this goes I probably have you with me, for I only translate into schematic language what I may call the instinctive belief of mankind: God is real since he produces real effects.

The real effects in question, so far as I have as yet admitted them, are exerted on the personal centres of energy of the various subjects, but the spontaneous faith of most of the subjects is that they embrace a wider sphere than this. Most religious men believe (or 'know,' if they be mystical) that not only they themselves, but the whole universe of beings to whom the God is present, are secure in his parental hands. There is a sense, a dimension, they are sure, in which we are *all* saved, in spite of the gates of hell and all adverse terrestrial appearances. God's existence is the guarantee of an ideal order that shall be permanently preserved. This world may indeed, as science assures us, some day burn up or freeze; but if it is part of his order, the old ideals are sure to be brought elsewhere to fruition, so that where God is, tragedy is only provisional and partial, and shipwreck and dissolution are not the absolutely final things. Only when this farther step of faith concerning God is taken, and remote objective consequences are predicted, does religion, as it seems to me, get wholly free from the first immediate subjective experience, and bring a *real hypothesis* into play. A good hypothesis in science must have other properties than those of the phenomenon it is immediately invoked to explain, otherwise it is not prolific enough. God, meaning only what enters into the religious man's experience of union, falls short of being an hypothesis of this more useful order. He needs to enter into wider cosmic relations in order to justify the subject's absolute confidence and peace.

That the God with whom, starting from the hither side of our own extra-marginal self, we come at its remoter margin into commerce should be the absolute world-ruler, is of course a very considerable over-belief. Over-belief as it is, though, it is an article of almost every one's religion. Most of us pretend in some way to prop it up upon our philosophy, but the philosophy itself is really propped upon this faith. What is this but to say that Religion, in her fullest exercise of function, is not a mere illumination of facts already elsewhere given, not a mere passion, like love, which views things in a rosier light. It is indeed that, as we have seen abundantly. But it is something more, namely, a postulator of new *facts* as well. The world interpreted religiously is not the materialistic world over again, with an altered expression; it must have, over and above the altered expression, a *natural constitution* different at some point from that which a materialistic world would have. It must be such that different events can be expected in it, different conduct must be required.

This thoroughly 'pragmatic' view of religion has usually been taken as a matter of course by common men. They have interpolated divine miracles into the field of nature, they have built a heaven out beyond the grave. It is only transcendentalist metaphysicians who think that, without adding any concrete details to Nature, or subtracting any, but by simply calling it the expression of absolute spirit, you make it more divine just as it stands. I believe the pragmatic way of taking religion to be the deeper way. It gives it body as well as soul, it makes it claim, as everything real must claim, some characteristic realm of fact as its very own. What the more characteristically divine facts are, apart from the actual inflow of energy in the faith-state and the prayer-state, I know not. But the over-belief on which I am ready to make my personal venture is that they exist. The whole drift of my education goes to persuade me that the world of our present consciousness is only one out of many worlds of consciousness that exist, and that those other worlds must contain experiences which have a meaning for our life also; and that although in the main their experiences and those of this world keep discrete, yet the two become continuous at certain points, and higher energies filter in. By being faithful in my poor measure to this over-belief, I seem to myself to keep more sane and true. I *can*, of course, put myself into the sectarian scientist's attitude, and imagine vividly that the world of sensations and of scientific laws and objects may be all. But whenever I do this, I hear that inward monitor of which W. K. Clifford once wrote, whispering the word 'bosh!' Humbug is humbug, even though it bear the scientific name, and the total expression of human experience, as I view it objectively, invincibly urges me beyond the narrow 'scientific' bounds. Assuredly, the real world is of a different temperament,—more intricately built than physical science allows. So my objective and my subjective conscience both hold me to the over-belief which I express. Who knows whether the faithfulness of individuals here below to their own poor over-beliefs may not actually help God in turn to be more effectively faithful to his own greater tasks? . . .

Note

1. The word 'truth' is here taken to mean something additional to bare value for life, although the natural propensity of man is to believe that whatever has great value for life is thereby certified as true.

II.3 The Future of an Illusion

SIGMUND FREUD

Reprinted from Sigmund Freud, *The Future of an Illusion*, trans. James Strachey (W. W. Norton Publishing Co., 1961) by permission of the publisher. Translation © 1961 by James Strachey, renewed by Alex Strachey.

Sigmund Freud (1856–1939), an Austrian psychologist, is considered the father of psychoanalysis. His works include Beyond the Pleasure Principle, Civilization and Its Discontents, *and* The Complete Introductory Lectures on Psychoanalysis. *Our selection is from* The Future of an Illusion *(1927), in which Freud argues that religion is a projection of the father image onto the heavens. It is an "infantile neurosis" that is in need of a cure so that the individual can become a healthy, mature adult.*

When we are children, the father fulfills our needs, protecting us from danger, attributing value to our being, and providing food and shelter. He seems omnipotent, omniscient, and omnibenevolent. When we grow up, we become aware of the fallibility and vulnerability of our fathers but the need for protection remains. So humanity has created the idea of a Divine Father to take the place of the human father. This is why we have religious experiences. They are the unconscious internalizations of our primordial need for relief from the insecurity and tragedy of existence. However, we need to grow up and become responsible for ourselves. In order to do this we must renounce the obsessional neurosis of religion and substitute reason and autonomy.

In what does the peculiar value of religious ideas lie?

We have spoken of the hostility to civilization which is produced by the pressure that civilization exercises, the renunciations of instinct which it demands. If one imagines its prohibitions lifted—if, then, one may take any woman one pleases as a sexual object, if one may without hesitation kill one's rival for her love or anyone else who stands in one's way, if, too, one can carry off any of the other man's belongings without asking leave—how splendid, what a string of satisfactions one's life would be! True, one soon comes across the first difficulty: everyone else has exactly the same wishes as I have and will treat me with no more consideration than I treat him. And so in reality only one person could be made unrestrictedly happy by such a removal of the restrictions of civilization, and he would be a tyrant, a dictator, who had seized all the means to power. And even he would have every reason to wish that the others would observe at least one cultural commandment: 'thou shalt not kill.'

But how ungrateful, how short-sighted after all, to strive for the abolition of civilization! What would then remain would be a state of nature, and that would be far harder to bear. It is true that nature would not demand any restrictions of instinct from us, she would let us do as we liked; but she has her own particularly effective method of restricting us. She destroys us—coldly, cruelly, relentlessly, as it seems to us, and possibly through the very things that occasioned our satisfaction. It was precisely because of these dangers with which nature threatens us that we came together and created civilization, which is also, among other things, intended to make our communal life possible. For the principal task of civilization, its actual *raison d'être*, is to defend us against nature.

We all know that in many ways civilization does this fairly well already, and clearly as time goes on it will do it much better. But no one is under the illusion that nature has already been vanquished; and few dare hope that she will ever be entirely subjected to man. There are the elements, which seem to mock at all human control: the earth, which quakes and is torn apart and buries all human life and its works; water, which deluges and drowns everything in a turmoil; storms, which blow everything before them; there are diseases, which we have only recently recognized as attacks by other organisms; and finally there is the painful riddle of death, against which no medicine has yet been found, nor probably will be. With these forces nature rises up against us, majestic, cruel and inexorable; she brings to our mind once more our weakness and helplessness, which we thought to escape through the work of civilization. One of the few gratifying and exalting impressions which mankind can offer is when, in the face of an elemental catastrophe, it forgets the discordancies of its civilization and all its internal difficulties and animosities, and recalls the great common task of preserving itself against the superior power of nature.

For the individual, too, life is hard to bear, just as it is for mankind in general. The civilization in which he participates imposes some amount of privation on him, and other men bring him a measure of suffering, either in spite of the precepts of his civilization or because of its imperfections. To this are added the injuries which untamed nature—he calls it Fate—inflicts on him. One might suppose that this condition of things would result in a permanent state of anxious expectation in him and a severe injury to his natural narcissism. We know already how the individual reacts to the injuries which civilization and other men inflict on him: he develops a corresponding degree of resistance to the regulations of civilization and of hostility to it. But how does he defend himself against the superior powers of nature, of Fate, which threaten him as they threaten all the rest?

Civilization relieves him of this task; it performs it in the same way for all alike; and it is noteworthy that in this almost all civilizations act alike. Civilization does not call a halt in the task of defending man against nature, it merely pursues it by other means. The task is a manifold one. Man's self-regard, seriously menaced, calls for consolation; life and the universe must be robbed of their terrors; moreover his curiosity, moved, it is true, by the strongest practical interest, demands an answer.

A great deal is already gained with the first step: the humanization of nature. Impersonal forces and destinies cannot be approached; they remain eternally remote. But if the elements have passions that rage as they do in our own souls, if death itself is not something spontaneous but the violent act of an evil Will, if everywhere in nature there are Beings around us of a kind that we know in our own society, then we can breathe freely, can feel at home in the uncanny and can deal by psychical means with our senseless anxiety. We are still defenceless, perhaps, but we are no longer helplessly paralysed; we can at least react. Perhaps, indeed, we are not even defenceless. We can apply the same methods against these violent supermen outside that we employ in our own society; we can try to adjure them, to appease them, to bribe them, and, by so influencing them, we may rob them of a part of their power. A replacement like this of natural science by psychology not only provides immediate relief, but also points the way to a further mastering of the situation.

For this situation is nothing new. It has an infantile prototype, of which it is in fact only the continuation. For once before one has found oneself in a similar state of helplessness: as a small child, in relation to one's parents. One had reason to fear them, and especially one's father; and yet one was sure of his protection against the dangers one knew. Thus it was natural to assimilate the two situations. Here, too, wishing played its part, as it does in

dream-life. The sleeper may be seized with a presentiment of death, which threatens to place him in the grave. But the dream-work knows how to select a condition that will turn even that dreaded event into a wish-fulfilment: the dreamer sees himself in an ancient Etruscan grave which he has climbed down into, happy to find his archaeological interests satisfied.[1] In the same way, a man makes the forces of nature not simply into persons with whom he can associate as he would with his equals—that would not do justice to the overpowering impression which those forces make on him—but he gives them the character of a father. He turns them into gods, following in this, as I have tried to show,[2] not only an infantile prototype but a phylogenetic one.

In the course of time the first observations were made of regularity and conformity to law in natural phenomena, and with this the forces of nature lost their human traits. But man's helplessness remains and along with it his longing for his father, and the gods. The gods retain their threefold task: they must exorcize the terrors of nature, they must reconcile men to the cruelty of Fate, particularly as it is shown in death, and they must compensate them for the sufferings and privations which a civilized life in common has imposed on them.

But within these functions there is a gradual displacement of accent. It was observed that the phenomena of nature developed automatically according to internal necessities. Without doubt the gods were the lords of nature; they had arranged it to be as it was and now they could leave it to itself. Only occasionally, in what are known as miracles, did they intervene in its course, as though to make it plain that they had relinquished nothing of their original sphere of power. As regards the apportioning of destinies, an unpleasant suspicion persisted that the perplexity and helplessness of the human race could not be remedied. It was here that the gods were most apt to fail. If they themselves cre-

---

[1][This was an actual dream of Freud's reported in Chapter VI (G) of *The Interpretation of Dreams* (1900a), *Standard Ed.*, **5**, 454–5.]

[2][See Section 6 of the fourth essay in *Totem and Taboo* (1912–13), *Standard Ed.*, **13**, 146 ff.]

ated Fate, then their counsels must be deemed inscrutable. The notion dawned on the most gifted people of antiquity that Moira [Fate] stood above the gods and that the gods themselves had their own destinies. And the more autonomous nature became and the more the gods withdrew from it, the more earnestly were all expectations directed to the third function of the gods—the more did morality become their true domain. It now became the task of the gods to even out the defects and evils of civilization, to attend to the sufferings which men inflict on one another in their life together and to watch over the fulfilment of the precepts of civilization, which men obey so imperfectly. Those precepts themselves were credited with a divine origin; they were elevated beyond human society and were extended to nature and the universe.

And thus a store of ideas is created, born from man's need to make his helplessness tolerable and built up from the material of memories of the helplessness of his own childhood and the childhood of the human race. It can clearly be seen that the possession of these ideas protects him in two directions—against the dangers of nature and Fate, and against the injuries that threaten him from human society itself. Here is the gist of the matter. Life in this world serves a higher purpose; no doubt it is not easy to guess what that purpose is, but it certainly signifies a perfecting of man's nature. It is probably the spiritual part of man, the soul, which in the course of time has so slowly and unwillingly detached itself from the body, that is the object of this elevation and exaltation. Everything that happens in this world is an expression of the intentions of an intelligence superior to us, which in the end, though its ways and byways are difficult to follow, orders everything for the best—that is, to make it enjoyable for us. Over each one of us there watches a benevolent Providence which is only seemingly stern and which will not suffer us to become a plaything of the overmighty and pitiless forces of nature. Death itself is not extinction, is not a return to inorganic lifelessness, but the beginning of a new kind of existence which lies on the path of development to something higher. And, looking in the other direction, this view announces that the same moral laws which our civilizations have set up

govern the whole universe as well, except that they are maintained by a supreme court of justice with incomparably more power and consistency. In the end all good is rewarded and all evil punished, if not actually in this form of life then in the later existences that begin after death. In this way all the terrors, the sufferings and the hardships of life are destined to be obliterated. Life after death, which continues life on earth just as the invisible part of the spectrum joins on to the visible part, brings us all the perfection that we may perhaps have missed here. And the superior wisdom which directs this course of things, the infinite goodness that expresses itself in it, the justice that achieves its aim in it—these are the attributes of the divine beings who also created us and the world as a whole, or rather, of the one divine being into which, in our civilization, all the gods of antiquity have been condensed. The people which first succeeded in thus concentrating the divine attributes was not a little proud of the advance. It had laid open to view the father who had all along been hidden behind every divine figure as its nucleus. Fundamentally this was a return to the historical beginnings of the idea of God. Now that God was a single person, man's relations to him could recover the intimacy and intensity of the child's relation to his father. But if one had done so much for one's father, one wanted to have a reward, or at least to be his only beloved child, his Chosen People. . . .

I THINK we have prepared the way sufficiently for an answer to both these questions. It will be found if we turn our attention to the psychical origin of religious ideas. These, which are given out as teachings, are not precipitates of experience or end-results of thinking: they are illusions, fulfilments of the oldest, strongest and most urgent wishes of mankind. The secret of their strength lies in the strength of those wishes. As we already know, the terrifying impression of helplessness in childhood aroused the need for protection—for protection through love—which was provided by the father; and the recognition that this helplessness lasts throughout life made it necessary to cling to the existence of a father, but this time a more powerful one. Thus the benevolent rule of a divine Providence allays our fear of the dangers of life; the establishment of a moral world-order ensures the fulfilment of the demands of justice, which have so often remained unfulfilled in human civilization; and the prolongation of earthly existence in a future life provides the local and temporal framework in which these wish-fulfilments shall take place. Answers to the riddles that tempt the curiosity of man, such as how the universe began or what the relation is between body and mind, are developed in conformity with the underlying assumptions of this system. It is an enormous relief to the individual psyche if the conflicts of its childhood arising from the father-complex—conflicts which it has never wholly overcome—are removed from it and brought to a solution which is universally accepted.

When I say that these things are all illusions, I must define the meaning of the word. An illusion is not the same thing as an error; nor is it necessarily an error. Aristotle's belief that vermin are developed out of dung (a belief to which ignorant people still cling) was an error; so was the belief of a former generation of doctors that *tabes dorsalis* is the result of sexual excess. It would be incorrect to call these errors illusions. On the other hand, it was an illusion of Columbus's that he had discovered a new sea-route to the Indies. The part played by his wish in this error is very clear. One may describe as an illusion the assertion made by certain nationalists that the Indo-Germanic race is the only one capable of civilization; or the belief, which was only destroyed by psycho-analysis, that children are creatures without sexuality. What is characteristic of illusions is that they are derived from human wishes. In this respect they come near to psychiatric delusions. But they differ from them, too, apart from the more complicated structure of delusions. In the case of delusions, we emphasize as essential their being in contradiction with reality. Illusions need not necessarily be false—that is to say, unrealizable or in contradiction to reality. For instance, a middle-class girl may have the illusion that a prince will come and marry her. This is possible; and a few such cases have occurred. That the Messiah will come and found a golden age is much less likely. Whether one classifies this belief as an illusion or as something analogous to a delusion will depend on one's personal attitude. Examples of illusions which have proved true are not easy to find, but the illusion of the alchemists that all metals can be turned into gold might be one of them. The wish to have a great deal of gold, as much gold as possible, has, it is true, been a good deal damped by our present-day knowledge of the determinants of wealth, but chemistry no longer regards the transmutation of metals into gold as impossible. Thus we call a belief an illusion when a wish-fulfilment is a prominent factor in its motivation, and in doing so we disregard its relations to reality, just as the illusion itself sets no store by verification.

Having thus taken our bearings, let us return once more to the question of religious doctrines. We can now repeat that all of them are illusions and insusceptible of proof. No one can be compelled to think them true, to believe in them. Some of them are so improbable, so incompatible with everything we have laboriously discovered about the reality of the world, that we may compare them—if we pay proper regard to the psychological differences—to delusions. Of the reality value of most of them we cannot judge; just as they cannot be proved, so they cannot be refuted. We still know too little to make a critical approach to them. The riddles of the universe reveal themselves only slowly to our investigation; there are many questions to which science to-day can give no answer. But scientific work is the only road which can lead us to a knowledge of reality outside ourselves. It is once again merely an illusion to expect anything from intuition and introspection; they can give us nothing but particulars about our own mental life, which are hard to interpret, never any information about the questions which religious doctrine finds it so easy to answer. It would be insolent to let one's own arbitrary will step into the breach and, according to one's personal estimate, declare this or that part of the religious system to be less or more acceptable. Such questions are too momentous for that; they might be called too sacred.

At this point one must expect to meet with an objection. 'Well then, if even obdurate sceptics admit that the assertions of religion cannot be refuted by reason, why should I not believe in them, since they have so much on their side—tradition, the agreement of mankind, and all the consolations they offer?' Why not, indeed? Just as no one can be forced to believe, so no one can be forced to disbelieve. But do not let us be satisfied with deceiving ourselves that arguments like these take us along the road of correct thinking. If ever there was a case of a lame excuse we have it here. Ignorance is ignorance; no right to believe anything can be derived from it. In other matters no sensible person will behave so irresponsibly or rest content with such feeble grounds for his opinions and for the line he takes. It is only in the highest and most sacred things that he allows himself to do so. In reality these are only attempts at pretending to oneself or to other people that one is still firmly attached to religion, when one has long since cut oneself loose from it. Where questions of religion are concerned, people are guilty of every possible sort of dishonesty and intellectual misdemeanour. Philosophers stretch the meaning of words until they retain scarcely anything of their original sense. They give the name of 'God' to some vague abstraction which they have created for themselves; having done so they can pose before all the world as deists, as believers in God, and they can even boast that they have recognized a higher, purer concept of God, notwithstanding that their God is now nothing more than an insubstantial shadow and no longer the mighty personality of religious doctrines. Critics persist in describing as 'deeply religious' anyone who admits to a sense of man's insignificance or impotence in the face of the universe, although what constitutes the essence of the religious attitude is not this feeling but only the next step after it, the reaction to it which seeks a remedy for it. The man who goes no further, but humbly acquiesces in the small part which human beings play in the great world—such a man is, on the contrary, irreligious in the truest sense of the word.

To assess the truth-value of religious doctrines does not lie within the scope of the present enquiry. It is enough for us that we have recognized them as being, in their psychological nature, illusions. But we do not have to conceal the fact that this discovery also strongly influences our attitude to the question which must appear to many to be the most important of all. We know approximately at what periods and by what kind of men religious doctrines were created. If in addition we discover the motives which led to this, our attitude to the problem of religion will undergo a marked displacement. We shall tell ourselves that it would be very nice if there were a God who created the world and was a benevolent Providence, and if there were a moral order in the universe and an after-life; but it is a very striking fact that all this is exactly as we are bound to wish it to be. And it would be more remarkable still if our wretched, ignorant and downtrodden ancestors had succeeded in solving all these difficult riddles of the universe.

II.4 The Argument from Religious Experience

C. D. BROAD

C. D. Broad (1887–1971) was a professor of philosophy at Cambridge University who wrote prolifically on philosophy of mind, philosophy of religion, and psychical research. In his article "The Argument from Religious Experience" (1953), he considers the extent to which we can infer from religious experience to the existence of God. Broad likens the religious sense to an ear for music. There are a few people on the negative end who are spiritually tone deaf and a few on the positive end who are the founders of religions, the Bachs and Beethovens. In between are the ordinary followers of religion, who are like the average musical listeners, and above them are the saints, who are likened to those with a very fine ear for music.

The chief difference is that religion, unlike music, says something about the nature of reality. Is what it says true? And does religious experience lend any support to the truth claims of religion? Is religious experience veridical? Are the claims about "the nature of reality which are an integral part of the experience true or probable?" Broad carefully considers these questions.

I shall confine myself in this article to specifically religious experience and the argument for the existence of God which has been based on it.

This argument differs in the following important respect from the other two empirical types of argument. The Argument from Design and the arguments from ethical premises start from facts which are common to every one. But some people seem to be almost wholly devoid of any specifically religious experience; and among those who have it the differences of kind and degree are enormous. Founders of religions and saints, e.g., often claim to

Reprinted from C. D. Broad, *Religion, Philosophy and Psychical Research* (London: Routledge & Kegan Paul PLC, 1930), by permission of the publisher.

have been in direct contact with God, to have seen and spoken with Him, and so on. An ordinary religious man would certainly not make any such claim, though he might say that he had had experiences which assured him of the existence and presence of God. So the first thing that we have to notice is that capacity for religious experience is in certain respects like an ear for music. There are a few people who are unable to recognize and distinguish the simplest tune. But they are in a minority, like the people who have absolutely no kind of religious experience. Most people have some light appreciation of music. But the differences of degree in this respect are enormous, and those who have not much gift for music have to take the statements of accomplished musicians very largely on trust. Let us, then, compare tone-deaf persons to those who have no recognizable religious experience at all; the ordinary followers of a religion to men who have some taste for music but can neither appreciate the more difficult kinds nor compose; highly religious men and saints to persons with an exceptionally fine ear for music who may yet be unable to compose it; and the founders of religions to great musical composers, such as Bach and Beethoven.

This analogy is, of course, incomplete in certain important respects. Religious experience raises three problems, which are different though closely interconnected. (i) What is the *psychological analysis* of religious experience? Does it contain factors which are present also in certain experiences which are not religious? Does it contain any factor which never occurs in any other kind of experience? If it contains no such factor, but is a blend of elements each of which can occur separately or in non-religious experiences, its psychological peculiarity must consist in the characteristic way in which these elements are blended in it. Can this peculiar structural feature of religious experience be indicated and described? (ii) What are the *genetic and causal conditions* of the existence of religious experience? Can we trace the origin and development of the disposition to have religious experiences (*a*) in the human race, and (*b*) in each individual? Granted that the disposition is present in nearly all individuals at the present time, can we discover and state the variable conditions which call it into activity on certain occasions and leave it in abeyance on others? (iii) Part of the content of religious experience is alleged knowledge or well-founded belief about the nature of reality, e.g., that we are dependent on a being who loves us and whom we ought to worship, that values are somehow conserved in spite of the chances and changes of the material world at the mercy of which they seem *prima facie* to be, and so on. Therefore there is a third problem. Granted that religious experience exists, that it has such-and-such a history and conditions, that it seems vitally important to those who have it, and that it produces all kinds of effects which would not otherwise happen, is it *veridical*? Are the claims to knowledge or well-founded belief about the nature of reality, which are an integral part of the experience, *true or probable*? Now, in the case of musical experience, there are analogies to the psychological problem and to the genetic or causal problem, but there is no analogy to the epistemological problem of validity. For, so far as I am aware, no part of the content of musical experience is alleged knowledge about the nature of reality; and therefore no question of its being veridical or delusive can arise.

Since both musical experience and religious experience certainly exist, any theory of the universe which was incompatible with their existence would be false, and any theory which failed to show the connexion between their existence and the other facts about reality would be inadequate. So far the two kinds of experience are in exactly the same position. But a theory which answers to the condition that it allows of the existence of religious experience and indicates the *connexion* between its existence and other facts about reality may leave the question as to its *validity* quite unanswered. Or, alternatively it may throw grave doubt on its cognitive claims, or else it may tend to support them. Suppose, e.g., that it could be shown that religious experience contains no elements which are not factors in other kinds of experience. Suppose further

it could be shown that this particular combination of factors tends to originate and to be activated only under certain conditions which are known to be very commonly productive of false beliefs held with strong conviction. Then a satisfactory answer to the questions of psychological analysis and causal antecedents would have tended to answer the epistemological question of validity in the negative. On the other hand, it might be that the only theory which would satisfactorily account for the origin of the religious disposition and for the occurrence of actual religious experiences under certain conditions was a theory which allowed some of the cognitive claims made by religious experience to be true or probable. Thus the three problems, though entirely distinct from each other, may be very closely connected; and it is the existence of the third problem in connexion with religious experience which puts it, for the present purpose, in a different category from musical experience.

In spite of this essential difference the analogy is not to be despised, for it brings out at least one important point. If a man who had no ear for music were to give himself airs on that account, and were to talk [disdainfully] about those who can appreciate music and think it highly important, we should regard him, not as an advanced thinker, but as a self-satisfied Philistine. And, then if he did not do this but only propounded theories about the nature and causation of musical experience, we might think it reasonable to feel very doubtful whether his theories would be adequate or correct. In the same way, when persons without religious experience regard themselves as being *on that ground* superior to those who have it, their attitude must be treated as merely silly and offensive. Similarly, any theories about religious experience constructed by persons who have little or none of their own should be regarded with grave suspicion. (For that reason it would be unwise to attach very much weight to anything that the present writer may say on this subject.)

On the other hand, we must remember that the possession of a great capacity for religious experience, like the possession of a great capacity for musical appreciation and composition, is no guarantee of high general intelligence. A man may be a saint or a magnificent musician and yet have very little common sense, very little power of accurate introspection or of seeing causal connexions, and scarcely any capacity for logical criticism. He may also be almost as ignorant about other aspects of reality as the non-musical or non-religious man is about musical or religious experience. If such a man starts to theorize about music or religion, his theories may be quite as absurd, though in a different way, as those made by persons who are devoid of musical or religious experience. Fortunately it happens that some religious mystics of a high order have been extremely good at introspecting and describing their own experiences. And some highly religious persons have had very great critical and philosophical abilities. St. Teresa is an example of the first, and St. Thomas Aquinas of the second.

Now I think it must be admitted that, if we compare and contrast the statements made by religious mystics of various times, races, and religions, we find a common nucleus combined with very great differences of detail. Of course the interpretations which they have put on their experiences are much more varied than the experiences themselves. It is obvious that the interpretations will depend in a large measure on the traditional religious beliefs in which various mystics have been brought up. I think that such traditions probably act in two different ways.

(i) The tradition no doubt affects the theoretical interpretation of experiences which would have taken place even if the mystic had been brought up in a different tradition. A feeling of unity with the rest of the universe will be interpreted very differently by a Christian who has been brought up to believe in a personal God and by a Hindu mystic who has been trained in a quite different metaphysical tradition.

(ii) The traditional beliefs, on the other hand, probably determine many of the details of the experience itself. A Roman Catholic mystic may have visions of the Virgin and the saints, whilst a Protestant mystic pretty certainly will not.

Thus the relations between the experiences and the traditional beliefs are highly complex. Presumably the outlines of the belief are determined by the experience. Then the details of the belief are fixed for a certain place and period by the special peculiarities of the experiences had by the founder of a certain religion. These beliefs then become traditional in that religion. Thenceforth they in part determine the details of the experiences had by subsequent mystics of that religion, and still more do they determine the interpretations which these mystics will put upon their experiences. Therefore, when a set of religious beliefs has once been established, it no doubt tends to produce experiences which can plausibly be taken as evidence for it. If it is a tradition in a certain religion that one can communicate with saints, mystics of that religion will seem to see and to talk with saints in their mystical visions; and this fact will be taken as further evidence for the belief that one can communicate with saints.

Much the same double process of causation takes place in sense-perception. On the one hand, the beliefs and expectations which we have at any moment largely determine what *interpretation* we shall put on a certain sensation which we should in any case have had then. On the other hand, our beliefs and expectations do to some extent determine and modify some of the sensible characteristics of the *sensa themselves*. When I am thinking only of diagrams a certain visual stimulus may produce a sensation of a sensibly flat sensum; but a precisely similar stimulus may produce a sensation of a sensibly solid sensum when I am thinking of solid objects.

Such explanations, however, plainly do not account for the first origin of religious beliefs, or for the features which are common to the religious experiences of persons of widely different times, races, and traditions.

Now, when we find that there are certain experiences which, though never very frequent in a high degree of intensity, have happened in a high degree among a few men at all times and places; and when we find that, in spite of differences in detail which we can explain, they involve certain fundamental conditions which are common and peculiar to them; two alternatives are open to us. (i) We may suppose that these men are in contact with an aspect of reality which is not revealed to ordinary persons in their everyday experience. And we may suppose that the characteristics which they agree in ascribing to reality on the basis of these experiences probably do belong to it. Or (ii) we may suppose that they are all subject to a delusion from which other men are free. In order to illustrate these alternatives it will be useful to consider three partly analogous cases, two of which are real and the third imaginary.

(a) Most of the detailed facts which biologists tells us about the minute structure and changes in cells can be perceived only by persons who have had a long training in the use of the microscope. In this case we believe that the agreement among trained microscopists really does correspond to facts which untrained persons cannot perceive. (b) Persons of all races who habitually drink alcohol to excess eventually have perceptual experiences in which they seem to themselves to see snakes or rats crawling about their rooms or beds. In this case we believe that this agreement among drunkards is merely a uniform hallucination. (c) Let us now imagine a race of beings who can walk about and touch things but cannot see. Suppose that eventually a few of them developed the power of sight. All that they might tell their still blind friends about colour would be wholly unintelligible to and unverifiable by the latter. But they would also be able to tell their blind friends a great deal about what the latter would feel if they were to walk in certain directions. These statements would be verified. This would not, of course, *prove* to the blind ones that the unintelligible statements about colour correspond to certain aspects of the world which they cannot perceive. But it would show that the seeing persons had a source of additional information about matters which the blind ones could understand and test for themselves. It would not be unreasonable then for the blind ones to believe that probably the seeing ones are also able to perceive other aspects of reality which they are describing correctly when they make their unintelligible statements containing colour-names. The question then is whether it is reasonable to regard the agreement between the experiences of religious mystics as more like the agreement among trained microscopists about the minute structure of cells, or as more like the agreement among habitual drunkards about

the infestation of their rooms by pink rats or snakes, or as more like the agreement about colours which the seeing men would express in their statements to the blind men.

Why do we commonly believe that habitual excess of alcohol is a cause of a uniform delusion and not a source of additional information? The main reason is as follows. The things which drunkards claim to perceive are not fundamentally different in kind from the things that other people perceive. We have all seen rats and snakes, though the rats have generally been grey or brown and not pink. Moreover the drunkard claims that the rats and snakes which he sees are literally present in his room and on his bed, in the same sense in which his bed is in his room and his quilt is on his bed. Now we may fairly argue as follows. Since these are the sort of things which we could see if they were there, the fact that we cannot see them makes it highly probable that they are not there. Again, we know what kinds of perceptible effect would generally follow from the presence in a room of such things as rats or snakes. We should expect fox-terriers or mongooses to show traces of excitement, cheese to be nibbled, corn to disappear from bins, and so on. We find that no such effects are observed in the bedrooms of persons suffering from *delirium tremens*. It therefore seems reasonable to conclude that the agreement among drunkards is a sign, not of a revelation, but of a delusion.

Now the assertions in which religious mystics agree are not such that they conflict with what we can perceive with our senses. They are about the structure and organization of the world as a whole and about the relations of men to the rest of it. And they have so little in common with the facts of daily life that there is not much chance of direct collision. I think that there is only one important point on which there is conflict. Nearly all mystics seem to be agreed that time and change and unchanging duration are unreal or extremely superficial, whilst these seem to plain men to be the most fundamental features of the world. But we must admit, on the one hand, that these temporal characteristics present very great philosophical difficulties and puzzles when we reflect upon them. On the other hand, we may well suppose that the mystic finds it impossible to state clearly in ordinary language what it is that he experiences about the facts which underlie the appearance of time and change and duration. Therefore it is not difficult to allow that what we experience as the temporal aspect of reality corresponds in some sense to certain facts, and yet that these facts appear to us in so distorted a form in our ordinary experience that a person who sees them more accurately and directly might refuse to apply temporal names to them.

Let us next consider why we feel fairly certain that the agreement among trained microscopists about the minute structure of cells expresses an objective fact, although we cannot get similar experiences. One reason is that we have learned enough, from simpler cases of visual perception, about the laws of optics to know that the arrangement of lenses in a microscope is such that it will reveal minute structure, which is otherwise invisible, and will not simply create optical delusions. Another reason is that we know of other cases in which trained persons can detect things which untrained people will overlook, and that in many cases the existence of these things can be verified by indirect methods. Probably most of us have experienced such results of training in our own lives.

Now religious experience is not in nearly such a strong position as this. We do not know much about the laws which govern its occurrence and determine its variations. No doubt there are certain standard methods of training and meditation which tend to produce mystical experiences. These have been elaborated to some extent by certain Western mystics and to a very much greater extent by Eastern Yogis. But I do not think that we can see here, as we can in the case of microscopes and the training which is required to make the best use of them, any conclusive reason why these methods should produce veridical rather than delusive experiences. Uniform methods of training and meditation would be likely to produce more or less similar experiences, whether these experiences were largely veridical or wholly delusive.

Is there any analogy between the facts about religious experience and the fable about the blind men some of whom gained the power of sight? It might be said that many ideals of conduct and ways of life, which we can all recognize now to be good and useful, have been introduced into human history by the founders of religions. These persons have made actual ethical discoveries which others can afterwards recognize to be true. It might be said that this is at least roughly analogous to the case of the seeing men telling the still blind men of facts which the latter could and did verify for themselves. And it might be said that this makes it reasonable for us to attach some weight to what founders of religions tell us about things which we cannot understand or verify for ourselves; just as it would have been reasonable for the blind men to attach some weight to the unintelligible statements which the seeing men made to them about colours.

I think that this argument deserves a certain amount of respect, though I should find it hard to estimate how much weight to attach to it. I should be inclined to sum up as follows. When there is a nucleus of agreement between the experiences of men in different places, times, and traditions, and when they all tend to put much the same kind of interpretation on the cognitive content of these experiences, it is reasonable to ascribe this agreement to their all being in contact with a certain objective aspect of reality *unless* there be some positive reason to think otherwise. The practical postulate which we go upon everywhere else is to treat cognitive claims as veridical unless there be some positive reason to think them delusive. This, after all, is our only guarantee for believing that ordinary sense-perception is veridical. We cannot *prove* that what people agree in perceiving really exists independently of them; but we do always assume that ordinary waking sense-perception is veridical unless we can produce some positive ground for thinking that it is delusive in any given case. I think it would be inconsistent to treat the experiences of religious mystics on different principles. So far as they agree they should be provisionally accepted as veridical unless there be some positive ground for thinking that they are not. So the next question is whether there is any positive ground for holding that they are delusive.

There are two circumstances which have been commonly held to cast doubt on the cognitive claims of religious and mystical experience. (i) It is alleged that founders of religions and saints have nearly always had certain neuropathic symptoms or certain bodily weaknesses, and that these would be likely to produce delusions. Even if we accept the premises, I do not think that this is a very strong argument. (*a*) It is equally true that many founders of religions and saints have exhibited great endurance and great power of organization and business capacity which would have made them extremely successful and competent in secular affairs. There are very few offices in the cabinet or in the highest branches of the civil service which St. Thomas Aquinas could not have held with conspicuous success. I do not, of course, regard this as a positive reason *for* accepting the metaphysical doctrines which saints and founders of religions have based on their experiences; but it is relevant as a *rebuttal* of the argument which we are considering. (*b*) Probably very few people of extreme genius in science or art are perfectly normal mentally or physically, and some of them are very crazy and eccentric indeed. Therefore it would be rather surprising if persons of religious genius were completely normal, whether their experiences be veridical or delusive. (*c*) Suppose, for the sake of argument, that there is an aspect of the world which remains altogether outside the ken of ordinary persons in their daily life. Then it seems very likely that some degree of mental and physical abnormality would be a necessary condition for getting sufficiently loosened from the objects of ordinary sense-perception to come into cognitive contact with this aspect of reality. Therefore the fact that those persons who claim to have this peculiar kind of cognition generally exhibit certain mental and physical abnormalities is rather what might be anticipated if their claims were true. One might need to be slightly 'cracked' in order to have some peep-holes into the super-sensible world. (*d*) If mystical experience were veridical, it seems quite likely that it would *produce* abnormalities of behaviour in those who had it strongly. Let us suppose, for the sake of argument, that those who have religious experience are in frequent contact with an aspect of reality of which most men get only rare and faint glimpses. Then such persons are, as it were, living in two

worlds, while the ordinary man is living in only one of them. Or, again, they might be compared to a man who has to conduct his life with one ordinary eye and another of a telescopic kind. Their behaviour may be appropriate to the aspect of reality which they alone perceive and think all-important; but, for that very reason, it may be inappropriate to those other aspects of reality which are all that most men perceive or judge to be important and on which all our social institutions and conventions are built.

(ii) A second reason which is commonly alleged for doubt about the claims of religious experience is the following. It is said that such experience always originates from and remains mixed with certain other factors, e.g., sexual emotion, which are such that experiences and beliefs that arise from them are very likely to be delusive. I think that there are a good many confusions on this point, and it will be worth while to begin by indicating some of them.

When people say that B 'originated from' A, they are liable to confuse at least three different kinds of connexion between A and B. (i) It might be that A is a necessary but insufficient condition of the existence of B. (ii) It might be that A is a necessary and sufficient condition of the existence of B. Or (iii) it might be that B simply *is* A in a more complex and disguised form. Now, when there is in fact evidence only for the first kind of connexion, people are very liable to jump to the conclusion that there is the third kind of connexion. It may well be the case, e.g., that no one who was incapable of strong sexual desires and emotions could have anything worth calling religious experience. But it is plain that the possession of a strong capacity for sexual experience is not a *sufficient* condition of having a religious experience; for we know that the former quite often exists in persons who show hardly any trace of the latter. But, even if it could be shown that a strong capacity for sexual desire and emotion is *both* necessary and sufficient to produce religious experience, it would not follow that the latter is just the former in disguise. In the first place, it is not at all easy to discover the exact meaning of this metaphorical phrase when it is applied to psychological topics. And, if we make use of physical analogies, we are not much helped. A mixture of oxygen and hydrogen in presence of a spark is necessary and sufficient to produce water accompanied by an explosion. But water accompanied by an explosion is not a mixture of oxygen and hydrogen and a spark 'in a disguised form,' whatever that may mean.

Now I think that the present rather vaguely formulated objection to the validity of the claims of religious experience might be stated somewhat as follows. 'In the individual, religious experience originates from, and always remains mixed with, sexual desires and emotions. The other generative factor of it is the religious tradition of the society in which he lives, the teachings of his parents, nurses, schoolmasters, etc. In the race religious experience originated from a mixture of false beliefs about nature and man, irrational fears, sexual and other impulses, and so on. Thus the religious tradition arose from beliefs which we now recognize to have been false and from emotions which we now recognize to have been irrelevant and misleading. It is now drilled into children by those who are in authority over them at a time of life when they are intellectually and emotionally at much the same stage as the primitive savages among whom it originated. It is, therefore, readily accepted, and it determines beliefs and emotional dispositions which persist long after the child has grown up and acquired more adequate knowledge of nature and of himself.'

Persons who use this argument might admit that it does not definitely *prove* that religious beliefs are false and groundless. False beliefs and irrational fears in our remote ancestors *might* conceivably be the origin of true beliefs and of an appropriate feeling of awe and reverence in ourselves. And, if sexual desires and emotions be an essential condition and constituent of religious experience, the experience *may* nevertheless be veridical in important respects. We might merely have to rewrite one of the beatitudes and say 'Blessed are the *impure* in heart, for they shall see God.' But, although it is logically possible that such causes should produce such effects, it would be said that they are most unlikely to do so. They seem much more likely to produce false beliefs and misplaced emotions.

It is plain that this argument has considerable plausibility. But it is worth while to remember that modern science has almost as humble an ancestry as contemporary religion. If the primitive witch-smeller is the spiritual progenitor of the Archbishop of Canterbury, the primitive rain-maker is equally the spiritual progenitor of the Cavendish Professor of Physics. There has obviously been a gradual refinement and purification of religious beliefs and concepts in the course of history, just as there has been in the beliefs and concepts of science. Certain persons of religious genius, such as some of the Hebrew prophets and the founders of Christianity and of Buddhism, do seem to have introduced new ethico-religious concepts and beliefs which have won wide acceptance, just as certain men of scientific genius, such as Galileo, Newton, and Einstein, have done in the sphere of science. It seems somewhat arbitrary to count this process as a continual approximation to true knowledge of the material aspect of the world in the case of science, and to refuse to regard it as at all similar in the case of religion. Lastly, we must remember that all of us have accepted the current common-sense and scientific view of the material world on the authority of our parents, nurses, masters, and companions at a time when we had neither the power nor the inclination to criticize it. And most of us accept, without even understanding, the more recondite doctrines of contemporary physics simply on the authority of those whom we have been taught to regard as experts.

On the whole, then, I do not think that what we know of the conditions under which religious beliefs and emotions have arisen in the life of the individual and the race makes it reasonable to think that they are *specially* likely to be delusive or misdirected. At any rate any argument which starts from that basis and claims to reach such a conclusion will need to be very carefully handled if its destructive effects are to be confined within the range contemplated by its users. It is reasonable to think that the concepts and beliefs of even the most perfect religions known to us are extremely inadequate to the facts which they express; that they are highly confused and are mixed up with a great deal of positive error and sheer nonsense; and that, if the human race goes on and continues to have religious experiences and to reflect on them, they will be altered and improved almost out of recognition. But all this could be said, *mutatis mutandis*, of scientific concepts and theories. The claim of any particular religion or sect to have complete or final truth on these subjects seems to me to be too ridiculous to be worth a moment's consideration. But the opposite extreme of holding that the whole religious experience of mankind is a gigantic system of pure delusion seems to me to be almost (though not quite) as far-fetched.

II.5   Skepticism on Religious Experience

WALLACE MATSON

Wallace Matson is professor of philosophy at the University of California at Berkeley. This selection is from his book The Existence of God *(1965). Matson first offers a brief analysis of perception. He then applies it to the notion of certifying the experience of a god. He notes that there are several conditions that must be fulfilled in normal perceptual reports, such as corroboration and publicity, that are not fulfilled in religious experiences. By itself, therefore, the testimony of the subject cannot be used to persuade others of its veridicality (unless we have independent evidence for the existence of a god, in which case we should expect such experiences).*

Experience

Now we can begin to consider reasons, offered as justifying belief in gods, that are at least on their face of the same sort as reasons granted by everyone to be good reasons in other contexts.

One kind of good reason for believing in the existence of X is that one has perceived X, one has had experience of X. To be sure, philosophers sometimes question, or write as if they were questioning, the cogency of such reasons. Some theorists of knowledge profess to find many difficulties

in justifying belief in the existence of a tree "in reality," "out there," "independent of the perceiver" merely on the ground that normal persons truthfully report that they see, smell, kick, climb in, or cut down a tree. I shall, however, ignore all such skeptical cavils and take it for granted that seeing or smelling a tree is normally a good reason for believing that an "objective" tree exists ("normally" meaning: in the absence of special positive reasons for doubt, such as ingestion of drugs, paresis, crazy-house context, hypnotist in vicinity, etc.); that a certain recognizable and distinguishable taste—the "taste of gin"—is normally a good reason for believing there to be gin in the punch; that objects roughly similar to ourselves in appearance and behavior are also like us in possessing consciousnesses with roughly similar contents; in a word, I shall assume, naively if you like, that perception is in general valid ground for claiming knowledge, at the same time remaining aware, as everyone must, of the existence of illusions and delusions, and of the difficulty, in some cases, of distinguishing the veridical from the illusory.

Perception

. . . Perception is analyzable into a conscious experience (CE) of a perceiver (P), the object (O) perceived, and a relation (R) between the object and the perception. The CE must reveal characters that the O really has. To defend this statement, or even to explain it fairly fully, would involve us in unnecessary complications. An example may help to convey the bearing of this requirement: a tomato really is red. Someone looks at a tomato in a darkroom (under a red light). If he follows our recommendations, he will not say, "I saw a white tomato," but rather, "I seemed to see a white tomato," or "The tomato looked white," i.e., "The experience I had was like what I would have had if, in normal illumination, I had seen a tomato that really was white."

R is a causal relation. O causes CE or is an indispensable part of the cause. If I have my eyes closed and experience a hallucination of a tomato in a dish, I am not perceiving a tomato, even if there happens to be a tomato in a dish in front of me.

To sum up these points, perception, as we shall use the word, requires a real object. This is the important distinction between it and two other kinds of conscious experiences: feelings and fantasies. "Feelings" are experiences which do not, in and of themselves, reveal any features of the outside world, and which are such that no one is tempted to suppose that they do: aches and pains, joy, anger are some examples. Of course it is not denied that one is often led to infer features of the outside world from feelings; and such inferences are often justified. From "seeing stars" we may infer a lump on the head; but "seeing stars" is not perceiving a lump on the head, any more than it is perceiving stars, or perceiving anything at all. "Fantasies" will here be employed as a general term for all conscious experiences that are similar (in form and content) to perceptions, and that it is natural to describe in the "It seemed as if I were perceiving . . . " locution, or in terms limited in their application to such experiences: "I dreamed that . . . ," "I pictured to myself the . . . ," "I imagined myself to be . . . ," etc. We subdivide fantasies into the subclasses of imaginings, those fantasies which the subject does not confuse with perception; and delusions, which the subject mistakes for perception.

Nothing is a perception that does not fulfill our conditions of revelation and causality. It is of course one of the major traditional problems of philosophy to develop criteria for knowing that these conditions are satisfied—for distinguishing, and knowing that one has distinguished, between perceptions and delusions. This is another morass that we shall skirt. Or at any rate we shall not wade in it more deeply than we have to.

Visions and Voices

We now return to our main problem, that of trying to determine what sort of experience might suffice to certify the existence of a god.

Experiences that might possibly accomplish this will either be like ordinary experiences or unlike them. Let us consider the former class first.

A god-certifying experience might be like a perception; indeed, it might even *be* a perception. Let us assume that someone is known to have perceived some person and the perceiver claims, on the basis of this experience, to have knowledge of the existence of a god.

The claim, if reasonable, must be based either on some reasons advanced by the allegedly divine personage perceived or on the character of the personage. We have already considered the latter case, and we have only to repeat our conclusion: very extraordinary behavior by the personage might confer some probability on the claim; but there is no convincing evidence of this ever having happened. The evidential value (if any) of such epiphanies is in confirming beliefs otherwise established, whether in the first instance rationally or not; but if the original belief was not based on rational considerations, the appearance cannot confer reasonableness on it.

But is not something more than superfluous corroboration to be expected from an appearance of a well-known personage of religion? For surely this would show that the personage in question was real, not merely mythical. Suppose that belief in god X is based on an ancient document, which among other assertions minutely describes Y, the immortal messenger of X. Suppose now that a being of precisely this description (there is not and could not be any mistake about it) appears out of nowhere and announces that he is Y, sent by X; after performing various miracles, he vanishes upward. Would this not confirm the claims of the document?

Of course it would. To say so, however, is not to concede any more than we have already admitted in discussing miracles. The tremendous, if not insuperable, difficulties of ruling out the possibility of hallucination would remain. The evidential value of an epiphany would be greatly increased if Y appeared to someone who had never heard of him or of the document in question. It is safe to say that there is no reason to suppose that any such Y (or X, for that matter) has ever appeared to anyone who had not previously heard of Y or X. There are famous instances of apparitions to *nonbelievers*, but this does not alter the case: the psychology of such phenomena is well enough understood. So far from anyone *knowing* that someone has perceived a supernatural personage, there is no reason to believe that it has ever occurred. For the ordinary tests for distinguishing perceptions from fantasies turn on the publicity of the phenomena. (It will be noted that no publicity requirement has been incorporated into our definition of perception.) If P reports that he sees or hears something of a size or loudness such that ordinary persons normally see and hear such things, and no one else in the vicinity sees it or hears it, the claim of perception is dismissed without further ado. A certain degree of corroboration by others, however, may be attained without validating the claim, because of the well-known phenomena of mass delusion. What is needed is that several persons, of normal eyesight, hearing, and intelligence, not predisposed to believe reports of the phenomenon, and so insulated from one another that the effects of suggestibility can be ruled out, should corroborate the apparition. There may be some reason to believe that such corroboration has been achieved for some "paranormal" manifestations investigated by psychical researchers. However, such evidence does not seem to be available to support any claim for the existence of a god, except at most a very inferior sort of deity (poltergeists and such). We can imagine what the evidence would be like that would support the sort of claim that we are interested in; but in fact such evidence does not exist. This is not to say that it may not be discovered in future; I am inclined to agree with C. D. Broad that theologians should be more interested in psychical research than they are.

To be sure, failure of publicity tests does not disprove the claim that an apparition of a god or his messenger is a perception. We have defined "perception" in such a way that if experience reveals certain characters of a being, and that being really exists and has those characters, and, furthermore, the being causes the subject to have the experience, then the experience is a perception. Publicity is only the most usual and reliable way in which we test whether the experience is of this nature. But as we have just pointed out, an experience may pass the test and still not be a perception; equally it might fail the test and still really be a perception. This possibility has to be seriously considered in the religious context, and perhaps in no other. For a god—a nature-controller, hence a perception-controller—might see fit to reveal himself selectively: just to the believer, or to the virtuous, or to the infidel in need of shock therapy; never to those whose hearts he had hardened or to those beyond some pale or other. Indeed, we can even imagine that such behavior might not be a matter of choice on the part of the god; it might be a law of nature or of supernature that a god of limited power could not "get through" except to those already somehow attuned to him. Such hypotheses would explain why A sees him and B does not, compatibly with A's really seeing him.

If that is the way some god chooses to behave, however, he does so at the price of depriving his epiphanies of evidential value. He really appears to A, we suppose; even so, A cannot know that he has been favored with a theophany, for in the absence of confirmation from fellow men, the hypothesis that the appearance is delusory must have greater probability than that it is veridical. And even if A somehow did know (was rationally convinced of) the reality of the phenomenon, there still could be no reason for B to accept A's testimony concerning it.

The case is different if there is independent evidence for the existence of a god. In that case, there might be some probability, on that evidence, that the god would manifest himself, perhaps privately; and there could be ways of distinguishing genuine manifestations from spurious ones. To perceive the god, or his messengers, would then be to have confirmatory evidence for the existence of that god. But it seems equally clear that no such phenomena—no visions or voices—could ever of themselves establish, or confer the slightest degree of probability on, the existence of a god, either for the recipient of the visitation or for anyone else. (We have noted the one possible exception to this verdict: manifestation to someone utterly ignorant of the supposed existence of the god in question.) Unless the existence of the god is first established by some other means, there is not and cannot be any reason to believe that a private appearance of that god is not a delusion.

Mystical Experience

We must now see how the case stands with experience unlike ordinary perceptions. At the outset it may seem clear that if epiphanies cannot establish the existence of gods, then experiences not involving personal appearances must be of even less evidential value. For an experience unlike a perception must either be a feeling—and we need not labor the point that a mere feeling or hunch, not confirmed or substantiated by something else, is without evidential value according to the ordinary canons of evidence—or else it must be something altogether unlike any ordinary experience. Now one trouble with apparitions is their privacy; but at least the nature of the experience can be communicated to others. One can say, "The being was such and such form and figure, and he spake thus and so." But if an experience is utterly unlike any that one's audience has undergone, then one cannot even describe it intelligibly. It is hard to imagine what evidential value an indescribable encounter might have to others.

To others. . . . But what about to the person who has it? We must consider these two cases separately.

Let us try to rid ourselves of prejudices. Let us try to determine in advance and in a vacuum, so to speak, what a direct experience of a god should be like; what would be the most "natural" (in some sense) form for such an encounter to take; and let us try to forget what we have heard already on this score.

Now God is totally unlike any object of our ordinary experience; and if it is allowable to speak of God as a sort of limiting case that finite deities might more or less approximate, then insofar as a deity approaches to the character of God just to that extent the deity moves farther and farther from the orbit of worldly doings. Just to that extent, also, the deity becomes interesting as a religious object, a fit object of worship. But likewise, just to the extent to which a deity is unlike an everyday object, so one should expect in advance that an encounter with him would be unlike an everyday encounter. Hence the presumption is that an immediate experience of God, or of any august deity, would be so very strange as to be partly or wholly indescribable.

Of course religious persons of a certain degree of sophistication realize this; that is why, if they put any credence at all in epiphanies, they take it for granted that the appearance is only of a messenger (*angellos*) of the god, not of the god himself. On the other hand, it is equally clear that the mere occurrence of an indescribable experience cannot be regarded, in advance, as evidence for the existence of a god or of anything else. And it is hard to see how one indescribable experience can be distinguished from another—at all events by one who only hears tell of such occurrences. It looks then as if an experience, to be evidence for the existence of a god, must be indescribable; but an indescribable experience cannot be evidence for anything; therefore no experience can be evidence for the existence of a god.

It is, however, only the spectator who is at this impasse. Possibly the man who has the experience is not thus embarrassed, and perhaps there is some way in which he can communicate something of evidential value to the spectator.

Experiences of a unique and indescribable sort, which are taken by their subjects to be revelatory of a god, are not very common; but they are common enough to have a name, "mystical experiences"; and they are reported in nearly all cultures. We shall use the term "mystic" to refer to the subject of such an experience. This usage should not be confused with the vaguer, usually derogatory, popular sense.

Although the content of the mystical experience is indescribable, this does not mean that the experience itself cannot be characterized. William James lists four properties:

1. *Ineffability* . . . The subject of it immediately says that it defies expression, that no adequate report of its contents can be given in words. . . .
2. *Noetic quality.*—Although so similar to states of feeling, mystic states seem to those who experience them to be also of knowledge. They are states of insight into depths of truth unplumbed by the discursive intellect. They are illuminations, revelations, full of significance and importance, all inarticulate though they remain; and as a rule they carry with them a curious sense of authority for aftertime. . . .
3. *Transiency.*—Mystical states cannot be sustained for long. Except in rare instances, half an hour, or at most an hour or two, seems to be the limit beyond which they fade into the light of common day. . . .
4. *Passivity.*—Although the oncoming of mystical states may be facilitated by preliminary voluntary operations . . . when the characteristic sort of consciousness once has set in, the mystic feels as if his own will were in abeyance, and indeed sometimes as if he were grasped and held by a superior power.[1]

The ineffability of the mystical experience has not prevented the creation of a vast and fascinating mystical literature, in which mystics attempt to convey the feel of their experiences, and to state those insights into the nature of things that they say have been revealed to them.

First, mystics pretty generally agree that their experiences reveal the reality of an order of being distinct from, and in some sense higher than, the world perceived through the senses. Commonly the world of the senses is inferred to be mere confused appearance of this higher reality, or at any rate dependent on it.

Second, reality is revealed to be one; at all events, it is more accurately described as one than as many, though no description is quite right. In any case, reality is emphatically not the "one damned thing after another" that the average sensual man

supposes it to be. Moreover, the unity of all things is a tighter unity than any mere regularity or fitting together of parts that science may discover. The unity revealed to the mystics (we are told) transcends the categories of subject and object altogether. The mystic, in his rapture, does not contemplate the unity of all things; he is absorbed into it.

Third, reality is perfect. All that is ultimately valuable is somehow embedded in it; all that is evil is somehow excluded, as "mere appearance" or what you will. Optimism seems to be universal among mystics—even among the Oriental mystics, whose view of the world of the senses is gloomy indeed. And that is just as one would expect: for whatever religion may be, certainly it is supposed to offer us some sort of deliverance from, compensation for, or means of coming to terms with the uneasinesses and horrors that permeate the ordinary condition of man in nature.

Finally, the human soul is identical with, or at least akin to, the supersensible reality. Whatever may be the status of the material world, the soul, or at least some part or aspect of it, is of the same stuff as ultimate reality. Hence it is capable of shuffling off its mortal coil, of escaping from its fleshly prison, and of experiencing the ultimate bliss of reabsorption into the Infinite. The mystical experience itself is usually interpreted as a temporary foretaste of the heavenly state.

These four insights seem to comprise the principal points of agreement found in mystics of different cultures. Within a particular culture or religious tradition, a more specific consensus may obtain, for instance, concerning the reality of the Holy Trinity; and such conclusions may be different from, even incompatible with, what mystics of other religious antecedents infer from their ecstasies. From this fact some critics are led to deny that there is any mystical unanimity, hence to explain away mystical experience as delusion, in effect the heroic degree of wishful thinking. Now certainly mystics do agree on some points and disagree on others; to a certain extent it is an arbitrary matter whether one emphasizes the agreements and explains away the disagreements or vice versa. But it is too much to expect that thousands of human beings, vastly separated in space and time, each with his own cultural and religious heritage, each being the subject of an experience of such a nature as not to be describable in any ordinary language, let alone translatable into all the others—it is too much to expect that all these men should agree on every plank of a metaphysical platform, that their separate interpretations of their separate experiences should be unmixed with circumambient ideas. Rather, any substantial agreement at all will take on an extraordinary and striking importance.

That many mystics, probably a majority, are in substantial agreement on the four points that we have sketched, seems to be a fact; at any rate we shall assume that it is. This is a fact, then, to be explained. The agreement goes very far toward canceling the suspicions otherwise aroused by the private and ineffable nature of the experience. One hypothesis to explain the agreement—a hypothesis that it would be sheer dogmatism to dismiss with no consideration—is that the mystics happen to be right.

Is it our business, however, to investigate the claims of mystics? For our study is of reasons for believing that there is a god; and mystics are not in agreement on the proposition. The existence of God, as an Infinite Personal Intelligence, is not part of the mystical consensus, which seems to point to a view that is more akin to pantheism than to the personal theism that we are scrutinizing. Mystical ecstasy is often described as union with a something—call it X; but more often than not this X is described as impersonal (or superpersonal, if that is different), as something identical with the whole of reality.

However, the relation of God to the world is a nice point in any theology; and it surely is not our business to dwell on the subtleties of that relation. Moreover, our study will be naive and trivial unless we emancipate ourselves from the crudities of anthropomorphism; yet one of the prices of the emancipation is the giving up of any comfortable, intuitive notion of personality, as the term is to be applied to God. All that clearly remains is some abstract notion of unity; and mysticism is surely not wanting in such a notion. In any case, many mystics (suspiciously, those reared in theistic cultures) agree that the experience reveals the existence of God, in

a more or less orthodox sense of the proposition. We cannot therefore excuse ourselves from the task of looking into the bearing of their experience on our question.

It will simplify our study if we make certain assumptions. Let us assume that all the mystics we are to consider are unanimous in asserting that God—an infinitely powerful, wise, and good Being, the source and support of all creation—exists. When asked for their reasons, they tell us that they know this with absolute certainty because the mystical experience has revealed it to them in such a manner that no doubt whatever is admissible. But when pressed further, they lapse into silence and only smile.

The nonmystic is put into an exasperating situation. Here he is being solicited to adopt an exotic metaphysic, on no better evidence than the say-so of certain persons who claim to have reasons, but who decline altogether to produce them, saying that language—which is adequate enough to describe quantum theory and relativity—is incapable of expressing those reasons. It is understandable if the nonmystic's reaction is to complain that the mystic is crazy. And evidence tending to support this conclusion is not difficult to find. The claim to possess a profound but inexpressible insight is characteristic of many psychotic states. The austerities and mortifications practiced by many mystics in order to "facilitate the oncoming of mystical states" might be interpreted as systematic methods for driving oneself out of one's mind. The mystic ecstasy itself, as far as an outsider can judge, bears a sinister resemblance to intoxications that can be induced by drugs known to be deleterious to the higher nervous functions. It is well known that in many cultures drug-induced hallucinations are ritually cultivated; and it is not clear how, or even whether, these states are to be distinguished from true mystic ecstasy. It is somehow unseemly that the secret of the universe should be unveiled via eating mushrooms.

The mystic retorts that it is outrageous to suppose that men like Plato, St. Paul, Plotinus, and Pascal, and women like St. Teresa, were simply demented. In rebuttal the skeptic speaks of the proverbial thin line and points out that no one with even a superficial acquaintance with the great of the world, particularly the intellectually great, is under the illusion that they are as a class paradigms of mental health. The counterrebuttal is that the great mystics were great poets, philosophers, scientists, even administrators, because of their mysticism and not in spite of it. The beatific vision is a source of strength as well as of joy. Counter-counterterrebuttal: various neuroses (if not psychoses) often have the effect of making their sufferers into most energetic and creative persons.

And so it goes. It might appear that the controversy could be resolved if more detailed clinical material were collected. There is, however, a more fundamental difficulty. Sanity must presumably be defined in terms of adjustment to reality; and the question here is, precisely, what *is* reality? If it is the everyday world, and only that, then pretty clearly the mystic is insane, temporarily or permanently. But to decide the issue this way would obviously beg the question.

We shall just leave the matter up in the air. Mysticism, for all we know, may be lunacy; and the ravings of lunatics, we may assume, are of no evidential value for any purpose except diagnosis. It is not unreasonable to suspect that mysticism is insanity. What is unreasonable is to conclude, in the present state of our knowledge, that it must be. In consequence, we are obliged to explore the hypothesis that mystics are sane.

In that case, their conviction must be taken seriously, as the firm belief of reasonable men arrived at on the basis of evidence available to them. And if they are being reasonable in believing, is it not reasonable for the nonmystics to share their belief on trust?

It may seem at this point that our answer must be negative, because the situation is identical with that of the absolute authority, which we have already rejected as a source of rational belief. But it is not, though the difference is subtle. The absolute authority urges us to believe him just because he is who he is, and for no other reason. The mystic, however, urges us to believe him because his belief is grounded in satisfactory evidence—though he cannot tell us what the evidence is. There is a real difference here, because if the existence of evi-

dence is not even mentioned, then the question of possible access to it does not arise. But when the assertion is made that some kind of evidence exists, then it may after all prove possible to get access to it: the nonmystic may be given directions for becoming a mystic; or failing this, there may be some indirect method of establishing, by ordinary means, the existence and relevance of the evidence.

Physicists tell us that pi-mesons exist. This kind of assertion, and the evidence offered for it, may be taken as a paradigm case of objective existence ("out there"), public verifiability, inferences drawn from undoubted facts in accordance with impeccable canons of scientific procedure, and all the rest that the nonmystic charges the mystic with ignoring. For all that, the evidence for the existence of the pi-meson is in fact inaccessible to the author of this book and very likely to most of its readers. Indeed, the meaning of the sentence "There are pi-mesons" is not understood. The author takes it on faith that this sentence has a meaning to those who concern themselves with such matters and that evidence of its truth is available to them.

It is surely reasonable for me (and for you) to do this. It would be impertinent for us to say: "The alleged evidence for pi-mesons is the property of a small confraternity, who make no pretense of communicating it to anyone outside their clique. What imposture!" For the physicists' retort is unanswerable: "To be sure, the evidence for pi-mesons is in fact inaccessible to you—meaning that if it were before you in your present condition, you could not make anything of it. However, if you are of slightly higher than moderate intelligence, and are willing to devote a rather large amount of time and effort to the study of mathematics and physics, you can be put in a position to understand the evidence and judge for yourself. That is: you can become a physicist. To say that the evidence for the pi-meson is publicly verifiable does not mean that it is easy to comprehend, that it is available right now to the general public; it only means that someone who follows a stated procedure can arrive at comprehension."

The mystic's argument is parallel: "You refuse to believe anything not 'publicly verifiable,' as you put it? Very well. You say that physics is publicly verifiable, though admitting that to understand physics one must become a physicist. Surely then it cannot be unreasonable for us mystics to tell you that the way to understand mysticism is to become a mystic. Now here is the way you do it: fifteen minutes of contemplation the first day, increasing fifteen minutes a day for six weeks; the following breathing exercises . . . ; fasting . . . ; mortifications, etc., etc. After this, your chance of being illuminated will be a fair one. . . . Too difficult? Why should it be easier to penetrate the secret of the universe than to understand the pi-meson? You ask whether we guarantee success if the regimen is followed? Of course we don't! But then, what physicist ever guaranteed that everybody could become a physicist?"

The analogy is plausible. But there are disanalogies:

Item: Physicists, if they cannot talk to laymen, can still talk to one another without difficulty. But there is no technical vocabulary of mysticism enabling mystics to converse about their experiences in a precise manner even among themselves.

Item: There is an agreed curriculum for the study of physics. There is no agreed road to mystical illumination. The manuals vary in their prescriptions, and whole sects of mystics reject set procedures altogether.

Item: The discipline required of the would-be physicist is entirely intellectual. At no point in the proceedings is it made a condition of progress that he "have faith," reform his morals, or anything of that sort. It is otherwise with the mystic path.

Here we have a very serious objection. To lay it down that one must "believe in order to understand" is nothing less than to refuse to play the rational game. So-called evidence that counts as evidence only to believers is just not evidence at all in any recognizable sense of the word. It would be hardly less objectionable to claim that the evidence can be vouchsafed only to the "pure"—and practically it would amount to the same thing, since religions tend to make belief an indispensable condition of "purity." In plain language, what is being said is just this: "Unless you can manage somehow to believe without evidence, you cannot get any

evidence." "Unless you really believe in fairies, you will never see any."

Only two considerations prevent this last objection from being fatal to the mystics' claim to rationality. The first is that we probably malign the mystics in complaining that they *always* make faith an antecedent condition of illumination. Perhaps there have been cases of unbelievers being converted all at once by an unsought-for and unexpected ecstasy: St. Paul on the road to Damascus (though that was a vision rather than a rapture). If not, even so the mystic might say that it *could* happen were it not for the lamentable fact that unbelievers, because of their unbelief, are unwilling to tread the rocky path. (Unbelievers in pi-mesons seldom bother to learn physics.) Second, it is after all conceivable that there should really be fairies, who are, however, too shy, or uninterested in proselytizing, to display themselves to vulgar cavilers; similarly, it is conceivable that the believer, and only the believer, is favored by evidence that would convert an unbeliever if it were presented to him—but there is a "law of supernature" that such pearls are not to be cast before swine. We may say if we like that such additional saving hypotheses become somewhat strained, besides being repugnant to our sense of what is fair in the rational game.

It seems fair to conclude, however, that while "But you can become a mystic" may have some force against the flat denial of evidential value to mystical experience, the question is not to be settled this way. For the rejoinder is not enough like "But you can become a physicist" and too much like "But you can become a telepathist." It behooves us all the more, therefore, to appraise the contention that mystical experience is not really different, in those respects that bear on its adequacy as evidence, from ordinary experience; and that, in consequence, people who do not have it ought to listen to people who do have it, for the same excellent reason that the blind should pay attention to the sighted.

Mystics often argue that the privacy and incommunicability of their experiences are characteristics shared by all experiences; the only reason they are noticed in the case of mysticism, but unnoticed about drunkenness, is that mysticism is rarer than drunkenness. But it is absurd to make mere rarity into an incurable evidential defect.

Some philosophers say that every experience is private and incommunicable. What is meant by this paradox is that the quality of the experience—"how it feels," roughly speaking—cannot be put into language. We can communicate its form—how long it takes, what brings it on, how it affects one's blood pressure, etc.; and we can say what it feels *like*. That is all.

When we describe what an experience is like, we do so via assumptions about antecedent experiences of our hearers and about their qualitative similarity to ours.

A: "What does the pudding taste like?" B: "It must have bananas in it." Such an interchange is as successful as any communication could be. If A has not been told all about the pudding, he knows something anyway: he can anticipate the taste of it, and when he tastes it he will not be surprised; he can use the information to decide whether he wants to order a portion for himself; and so on.

The communication is successful only because B can assume that A already knows how a banana tastes. Such an assumption is a reasonable one to make of an adult twentieth-century English-speaking person. Bananas are discriminable physical objects. I bite one; a certain taste-experience ensues. This experience I name "banana-taste." I see someone else bite a banana; I assume that some experience then occurs in him. By the rules of language this experience, whatever its quality, its feel, will be named "banana-taste" likewise. I assume furthermore that the quality of his experience is similar to mine.

A philosopher might challenge this assumption: "How do you know that his banana-taste isn't like your carrot-taste, or even quite unlike any experience you have ever had? All you know, and all you can know, is that he has taken a bite from the banana. What happens then is private to him; there is no conceivable way for you to find out what the quality of his experience is. You mustn't be deceived by the identity of name into supposing you know it in its innerness."

One could meet this challenge by pointing to the publicly observable similarity of his banana to my banana, the similarity of his physiology to mine, and the principle "same cause same effect." If the philosopher is not satisfied by this reasoning, the only thing to do is to say to him: "It doesn't matter. He has some sort of experience when he bites a banana. Whatever its quality, that quality is repeated, so he tells us, whenever he bites any banana. Now, when I tell him the pudding tastes as if it has banana mashed up in it, I succeed in conveying the only kind of information that could be called for in the circumstances: I give him a basis for expecting that repeatable quality (whatever its innerness may be) to be repeated yet once more if he tastes the pudding."

We have touched here on a point of some importance: success in communicating does not depend on knowledge shared by the communicators of the respective feels of their experiences. As far as language is concerned, the banana-taste simply is the experience one has when one bites a banana. To be sure, I believe, I think reasonably, that the quality or content of your banana-taste experience is like mine. But if this were not true—indeed even if I knew that it was not true—I should go on talking about bananas in just the same way. We can sum this up by saying that language conveys the structure of experience but not its content.

Let us illustrate further. If someone reports that bananas taste just like oranges to him, then we know that his experience is *not* like ours; but what we know in this case is that the structures of our experiences differ: he fails to make a discrimination that we make. This is how we tell that some persons are color-blind. But as long as his discriminations correlate with the differences in the stimuli in the same way that ours do, there is no way we can tell whether the private experiential basis of his discriminations—the qualities, feels, contents of his experiences—are like ours or not.

Nor does language even attempt to describe contents as distinguished from structures, as is indicated by the clumsy and artificial vocabulary we have just had to employ in trying to talk about this distinction. If we suppose that it does, that is because we make a same-structure-same-contents assumption. (I am not questioning that assumption, only pointing it out.)

Another way of making this point is by analyzing what happens when one is asked to describe an experience to someone who has never had it. The same banana will do, if we suppose we lived a hundred years earlier, when bananas were uncommon in the northern hemisphere. You have never tasted a banana. I have. You ask me to describe its taste to you. All I can do is say that it tastes more like *this* than like *that* (where *this* and *that* are things you have tasted), though not *quite* the same as *this*. If I am clever enough, it may occur to me (as it did to one Victorian) to describe it as "a sort of pineapple-flavoured marrow."

The more disparate the experience I try to describe is from any my hearer has gone through, the greater the difficulties. "What does straight whisky taste like?" "Well, it is aromatic, and bitter-sweet— more sweet than bitter—and it burns on the way down." "Like very hot sweetened coffee, then?" "No, no, not that kind of bitter-sweet, and certainly not that kind of burn."

The climax is reached when one struggles to describe the experiences of one sense modality to a person deprived of that sense: "To describe colors to a blind man." One can say something meaningful and suggestive even here: somehow scarlet really is more like a trumpet blast than aquamarine is, and busy wallpaper is rather like walking over gravel; but this is not much help. If it is any help at all, that is because there is some remote similarity between seeing a tomato and hearing a trumpet. Even so, only the person with sight can know this; the blind man must take it on faith.

To return now to the mystic and his defense: the ineffability of mystic ecstasy is just this same ineffability of content that is met in every experience, no matter how commonplace. When the mystic speaks to the nonmystic haltingly, in puzzling metaphors, the same sort of thing is occurring as when a man with sight tries to describe vision to a blind man. The only difference is that mystic experience, not being sensory at all, lacks even that tenuous analogy to our other senses that sight has to hearing.

All that is very well, the nonmystic replies; but those who can see have a rich and precise vocabulary in which they can communicate with one another about their visual experiences; whereas, we must repeat, there is no analogous vocabulary shared by the mystics with which they can communicate among themselves. They talk to one another in the same puzzling metaphors that they address to the general public.

It is not too difficult for the mystic to counter this objection. The reason there is a rich vocabulary of visual terms is that visual experience is structurally complex: there are all sorts of different things to see, and all of them have names. The same is true, though in less degree, of other sense modalities. Mystic ecstasy, on the other hand, is absolutely simple structurally: there is just one object (if it is permissible to use this word) of the experience. Suppose there were just one visible object: say, the sun. Then men of vision would have very little to say to each other: "Have you seen *it* today?" would be about the extent of this talk. They would probably not even have such a word as "bright," since there would be nothing dim to contrast it with; only the total darkness of everything else, wholly other than the sun. Perhaps they would attempt to convey their experience to the blind by saying that the sun is "loud": it comes closer to the mark to describe the sun as loud than as soft, though of course one should not suppose that it has the same kind of loudness that a thunderclap has. (The burn of whisky is not the same kind of burn as that of hot coffee.) But all these difficulties notwithstanding, they really would be seeing the sun, which really would be "out there"; moreover, they could explain why noonday is warmer than midnight, etc.

This analogy goes a long way toward vindicating mysticism against the ineffability objection. Let us see how far it can be stretched.

Our supposition must be that the sun is the only thing visible and that very few persons are able to see at all. Our question is: Would it be reasonable for the sightless majority to believe in the existence of the sun on the basis of what the few visionaries told them? Our supposition does not answer the question of itself; a belief can be true without being reasonable.

The question of reasonableness, here as always, turns on the question of what kind of evidence in support of the assertion could be produced by the sighted to the blind. We have already suggested that the sighted could explain why noonday is warmer than midnight. Let us follow this out.

The blind people are already aware of two warmth cycles, one of twenty-four hours, the other of 365 days. These cycles are for them brute facts; the visionaries explain them by the movements of the sun, the "source" of warmth. The blind people know that tomatoes will not grow inside wooden structures, but will grow outdoors or in glass houses. The men with sight explain that this is because wood obscures ("stops the sound of"?) the sun, whereas glass does not. The blind men, by endless fiddling with a convex lens, occasionally succeed in setting tinder on fire; the men with sight accomplish this every time straight off.

Now in such circumstances it would be reasonable for the blind men to believe the seers, precisely because the blind men would already have inferred the existence and properties of the sun! The seer would explain the daily cycle of warmth by saying: "There is a big fire up above that moves from east to west." But the blind men, familiar with the warming properties of terrestrial fire, would already have suspected the existence of a moving fiery object, and would have confirmed their hypothesis by various methods: the simplest to describe would perhaps be a convex lens, the position of which was governed by a heat-sensitive servomechanism. Blind men could learn for themselves, simply by feeling, the differential properties of wood and glass with respect to passage of the sun's rays. These men would therefore conclude, correctly, that the seers possessed the ability to perceive directly what "ordinary men" could know only indirectly, via apparatus and associated theory—as if someone were to arise among us who could "hear" radio waves, or see" electrons making quantum jumps.

It is not to the point to object that our suppositious case is fantastic, that a race of blind men could not stay alive, much less contrive heat-sensitive servomechanisms. We have been talking about what is possible in principle; and it should be fairly easy to see that a blind man could know all of physics—not in the trivial sense of taking on credit what men with sight told him, but by having conducted the fundamental experiments and made the inferences from them. As far as knowing the structure of the physical world is concerned—and that is what physics is solely concerned with—sight is in principle a dispensable sense.

These assertions may be unconvincing, however, and justifying them would take us too far afield. Well then, let us suppose, if you prefer, a more plausible race of blind men—men incapable of building any sort of physicists' apparatus, quite unacquainted with technology. And suppose, now, that the seers appear. Then the brute fact of the warmth cycles is "explained" by the existence and travels of the sun. Really, however, this would be no explanation at all; one brute fact known to the blind would be correlated with another brute fact known to the seer. There would be no reason for the blind man to believe in the seer's fact, first, because there would be no way for him to check up on it; second, because there would be no way of connecting the two facts.

We can now conclude this excursion into the land of the blind. If seers arose among the blind, the blind would have reason to believe what the seers told them only insofar as the seers' assertions were amenable to checking procedures that could be carried out by the blind men themselves , or at least were of the same general nature as checkable assertions. The qualification is necessary because, for example, it would be reasonable for the blind to believe seers' descriptions of sunspots, even if the blind had no independent means of verifying their existence—if the seers had first established their credibility by making a sufficient number of checkable statements. The main point is that it would not be reasonable for the blind to believe in the sun solely on the testimony of the seers. And we must not be misled by the fact that what the seers reported would be true.

If we now apply this analogy to the case of the mystic in relation to the nonmystic, it is easy to see what conclusion we must come to. At best, it is reasonable for the nonmystic to believe the mystic only if the mystic makes some checkable statements that show him to have a power of directly experiencing what the nonmystic knows about only indirectly—but nonetheless knows about independently of the mystic. In other words, the mystic, just like the seer of visions, could confirm and to some degree extend the nonmystic's knowledge of God—but his testimony could not be sufficient in itself to establish that knowledge in the first instance on a rational basis.

Mystics might object to the application of this analogy, on the ground that the blind-man-and-seer case refers only to what can be reasonably believed about facts in the realm of nature, whereas the mystic claims access to facts (if that is not a misleading word) about supernature. The mystic will tell us that he does not claim a "sixth sense" or anything like a sense; hence conclusions about the circumstances in which we should credit someone with having an extra sense are simply irrelevant.

Actually, however, we have given the mystic more than a run for his money. It must be harder to establish the possession of a faculty of intuition totally unlike a sense, for seeing into a realm totally unlike nature, than to present reasons for believing that one has some mode like the ordinary five senses of apprehending facts in some ways like those of ordinary experience.

II.6   A Critique of the Argument from Religious Experience

LOUIS P. POJMAN

Louis Pojman is the editor of this anthology and professor of philosophy at the United States Military Academy, West Point, New York. In this article he analyzes religious experience, distinguishing a strong and a weak justification for religious belief based on religious experience: A strong justification would make it rationally obligatory for everyone to believe in the conclusion of an argument. A weak justification would provide rational support only for those who had had an "of-God" experience (or already accepted the worldview that made such experiences likely). Pojman argues that only the weak version is plausible. Furthermore, the fact that religious experience fails in not being confirmable in the way perceptual experience is makes it highly problematic even for those who have had religious experiences.

The Ego has disappeared. I have realized my identity with Brahman and so all my desires have melted away. I have arisen above my ignorance and my knowledge of this seeming universe. What is this joy I feel?

Reprinted from *Philosophy: The Pursuit of Wisdom* (Wadsworth Publishing Co., 1994). Copyright © 1994 Wadsworth, Inc..

Who shall measure it? I know nothing but joy, limitless, unbounded! The treasure I have found there cannot be described in words. The mind cannot conceive of it. My mind fell like a hailstone into that vast expanse of Brahman's ocean. Touching one drop of it, I melted away and became one with Brahman. Where is this universe? Who took it away? Has it merged into something else? A while ago, I beheld it—now it exists no longer. Is there anything apart or distinct from Brahman? Now, finally and clearly, I know that I am the Atman [the soul identified with Brahman], whose nature is eternal joy. I see nothing, I hear nothing, I know nothing that is separate from me.[1]

Encounters with God

The heart of religion is and always has been experiential. Encounters with the supernatural, a transcendent dimension, the Wholly Other are at the base of every great religion. Abraham hears a Voice that calls him to leave his family in Haran and venture out into a broad unknown, thus becoming the father of Israel. Abraham's grandson, Jacob, wrestles all night with an angel and is transformed, gaining the name "Israel, prince of God." While tending his father-in-law's flock, Moses is appeared to by "I am that I am" (Yahweh) in the burning bush and ordered to deliver Israel out of slavery into a land flowing with milk and honey. Isaiah has a vision of the Lord "high and exalted, and the train of his robe filled the temple" of heaven. In the New Testament, John, James, and Peter behold Jesus gloriously transformed on the Mount of Transfiguration and are themselves transformed by the experience. After the death of Jesus, Saul is traveling to Damascus to persecute Christians, when he is met by a blazing light and hears a Voice, asking him why he is persecuting the Lord.[2] Changing his name to Paul, he becomes the leader of the Christian missionary movement. The Hindu experiences the Atman (soul) as the Brahman (God), "That art Thou," or beholds the glories of Krishna. The Advaitian Hindu merges with the One, as a drop of water merges with the vast ocean. The Buddhist merges with Nirvana or beholds a vision of the Buddha.[3] Allah reveals his holy word, the Koran, to Mohammed. Joan of Arc hears voices calling on her to save her people, and Joseph Smith has a vision of the angel Moroni calling him to do a new work for God.

Saints, mystics, prophets, ascetics, and common believers—of every creed, of every race, in every land, and throughout recorded history—have undergone esoteric experiences that are hard to explain but impossible to dismiss as mere nonsense. Common features appear to link these otherwise disparate experiences to one another, resulting in a common testimony to this Otherness, a *consensus mysticum*. Rudolf Otto characterizes the religious (or "numinal" spiritual) dimension in all of these experiences as the "mysterium tremendum et fascinans."[4] Religion is an unfathomable mystery, *tremendum* ("to be trembled at"), awe-inspiring, *fascinans* ("fascinating"), and magnetic. To use a description from Søren Kierkegaard, religious experience is a "sympathetic antipathy and an antipathetic sympathy" before a deep unknown.[5] Like looking into an abyss, it both repulses and strangely attracts.

An Analysis of Religious Experience

What, then, is the problem with religious experience? If I say that I hear a pleasant tune, and you

listen and say, "Yes, I hear it now too," we have no problem; but if you listen carefully and don't hear it, you might well wonder whether I am really hearing sounds or only imagining that I am. Perhaps we could bring in others to check out the matter. If they agree with me, well and good; but if they agree with you and don't hear the sounds, then we have a problem. Perhaps, we could bring in an audiometer to measure the decibels in the room. If the meter confirms my report, then it is simply a case of my having better hearing than you and the rest of the witnesses; but if the meter doesn't register at all, assuming that it is in working order, we would then have good evidence that I am only imagining the sounds. Perhaps, I need to change my claim and say, "Well, I seem to be hearing a pleasant tune."

One problem is that religious experience is typically private. You have the sense of God forgiving you or an angel speaking to you, but I, who am in the same room with you, neither hear, nor see, nor feel anything unusual. You are praying and suddenly feel transported by grace and sense the unity of all reality. I, who am sitting next to you, wonder at the strange expression on your face and ask you if something is wrong. Perhaps your brain is experiencing an altered chemical or electrical state?

Yet, religious experiences of various types have been reported by numerous people, from dairymaids like Joan of Arc to mystics like Teresa of Avila and St. John of the Cross. They cannot be simply dismissed without serious analysis.

There are two levels of problem here: (1) To what degree, if any, is the subject of a religious experience justified in inferring from the psychological experience (the subjective aspect) to the existential or ontological reality of that which is the object of the experience (the objective aspect)? (2) To what degree, if any, does the cumulative witness of those undergoing religious experience justify the claim that there is a God or transcendent reality?

Traditionally, the argument from religious experience has not been one of the "proofs" for God's existence. At best, it has confirmed and made existential what the proofs conveyed with icy logic. Some philosophers, such as C. D. Broad (1887–1971), as well as contemporary philosophers, such as Richard Swinburne and Gary Gutting, believe that the common experience of mystics is *strong justification* or evidence for all of us for the existence of God.[6] Others, such as William James (1842–1910), believe that religious experience is sufficient evidence for the subject himself or herself for the existence of a divine reality, but only constitutes a possibility for the nonexperiencer. That is, religious experience grants us only *weak justification*. Religious skeptics, like Walter Stace (1886–1967) and Bertrand Russell (1872–1970), doubt this and argue that a subjective experience by itself is never a sufficient warrant for making an existential claim (of an object existing outside oneself). It is a fallacy to go from the psychological experience of *X* to the reality of *X*.

There are two main traditions regarding religious experience. One, which we can call *mystical*, posits the unity of all reality or the unity of the subject with its object (the mystic is absorbed in God, becomes one with God, etc.). The second type of religious experience can be called simply *religious experience* in order to distinguish it from the mystical. It does not conflate the subject with the object but is a numinal experience wherein the believer (or subject) experiences the presence of God or an angel or Christ or the Holy Spirit, either speaking to or appearing to the experient or forgiving him or her. While in prayer, believers often experience a sense of the presence of God or the Holy Spirit.

Many psychological explanations of religious experience cast doubt on its validity. One of the most famous is the Freudian interpretation. Sigmund Freud said that it was the result of the projection of the father image within oneself. The progression goes like this. When you were a child, you looked upon your father as a powerful hero who could do everything, meet all your needs, and overcome the normal obstacles that hindered your way at every step. When you grew older, you sadly realized that your father was fallible and very finite, indeed, but you still had the need of the benevolent, all-powerful father. So, subconsciously you projected your need for that long-lost parent onto the empty heavens and invented a god for yourself. Because this is a common phenomena, all of us who have successfully "projected daddy onto the big sky" go to church or synagogue or mosque or whatever and worship the illusion on our favorite holy day. But it is a myth. The sky is empty, and the sooner we realize it, the better for everyone.

This is one explanation of religious experience and religion in general. It is not a disproof of God's existence, simply an hypothesis. Even if it is psychologically true that we tend to think of God like a powerful and loving parent, it could still be the case that the parental relationship is God's way of teaching us about himself—by analogy.

In his classic on the subject, *Varieties of Religious Experience* (1902), James describes what he considers the deepest kind of religious experience, mystical experience, a type of experience that transcends our ordinary, sensory experience and that cannot be described in terms of our normal concepts and language. It is "ineffable experience." The experient realizes that the experience "defies expression, that no adequate report of its content can be given in words. It follows from this that its quality must be directly experienced; it cannot be imparted or transferred to others."[7] And yet it contains a *noetic quality*, a content. It purports to convey truth about the nature of reality, namely, that there is a unity of all things and that unity is spiritual, not material. It is antinaturalistic, pantheistic, and optimistic. Two other characteristics are predicated to this state. Mystical states are *transient*—that is, they cannot be sustained for long—and they are *passive*—that is, the mystic is acted upon by divine deliverance, grace. We can prepare ourselves for the experience, but it is something that happens to us, not something that we do.

James is cautious about what can be deduced from mystic experience. Although mystic states are and ought to be absolutely authoritative over the individuals to whom they come, "no authority emanates from them which should make it a duty for those who stand outside of them to accept their revelations uncritically." But their value is that they provide us a valid alternative to the "non-mystical rationalistic consciousness, based on understanding and the senses alone. They open up the possibility of other orders of truth, in which, so far as anything in us vitally responds to them, we may freely continue to have faith."

Broad goes even further than James. In his book *Religion, Philosophy, and Psychical Research* (1930), he likens the religious sense to an ear for music. There are a few people on the negative end who are spiritually tone deaf and a few on the positive end who are the founders of religion, the Bachs and Beethovens. In between are the ordinary followers of religion, who are like the average musical listener, and above them are the saints, who are likened to those with a very fine ear for music.

The chief difference is that religion, unlike music, says something about the nature of reality. Is what it says true? Does religious experience lend any support to the truth claims of religion? Is religious experience "veridical," and are the claims about "the nature of reality which are an integral part of the experience, true or probable?" Broad considers the argument from mystical agreement:

1. There is an enormous unanimity among the mystics concerning the spiritual nature of reality.
2. When there is such unanimity among observers as to what they take themselves to be experiencing, it is reasonable to conclude that their experiences are veridical (unless we have good reason to believe that they are deluded).
3. There are no positive reasons for thinking that mystical experiences are delusive.
4. ∴ It is reasonable to believe that mystical experiences are veridical.

Premise 3 is weak, for there is evidence that mystics are neuropathic or sexually repressed. Broad considers these charges, admits some plausibility in them, but suggests that they are not conclusive. Regarding the charge of neuropathology, he urges that "one might need to be slightly 'cracked' in order to have some peep-holes into the supersensible world"; with regard to sexual abnormality, it could simply be the case that no one who was "incapable of strong sexual desires and emotions could have anything worth calling religious experience."

His own guarded judgment is that, given what we know about the origins of religious belief and emotions, there is no reason to think that religious experience is "specially likely to be delusive or misdirected," so that religious experience can be said to offer us strong justification for a transcendent reality.

Gutting develops Broad's strong-justification thesis further, arguing that religious experience "establishes the existence of a good and powerful being concerned about us, and [this] justifies a central core of religious belief."[8] On this basis, he argues that the essential validity of religion is vindicated. However, like Broad, he finds that this sort of justified belief "falls far short of the claims of traditional religions and that detailed religious accounts are nearly as suspect as nonreligious accounts. The heart of true religious belief is a realization that we have *access* to God but only minimal reliable *accounts* of his nature and relation to us." Gutting develops three criteria that veridical religious experiences must meet: They must be repeatable, be experienced by many in many diverse climes and cultures, and issue forth in morally better lives.

However, in arguing for the strong-justification thesis, Gutting seems to me to have gone too far. A strong justification makes it rationally obligatory for everyone to believe in the conclusion of an argument, in this case, that God exists. A weak justification only provides rational support for those who have an "of-God" experience (or already accept the worldview that made such experiences likely). Gutting believes that he has given a strong justification for religious belief, sufficient to establish the existence of God, but there are reasons to suppose that the argument from religious experience offers, at best, only weak justification.

A Critique of the Strong-Justification Thesis

Three criticisms of the strong thesis are the following:

1. Religious experience is too amorphous and disparate for us to generalize from in the way Gutting would have us do. That is, there are many varieties of religious experiences, which seem mutually contradictory or vague, so that it is not clear whether we can give the proper criteria necessary to select "of-God" experiences as veridical or having privileged status.
2. Justification of belief in the veridicality of religious experience is circular, so that the belief in it will rest on premises that are not self-evident to everyone. In effect, all assessment of the veridicality of such experience depends on background beliefs.
3. When taken seriously as a candidate for veridical experience, religious experience has the liability of not being confirmed in the same way that perceptual experience is. That is, although religious experience may sometimes be veridical, it cannot be checked like ordinary perceptual experience, nor can we make predictions on account of it. This indicates that it cannot be used as an argument for the existence of God in the way that Gutting uses it.

Let us look closer at these counterarguments.

Religious Experience Is Amorphous and Varied

Religious experience is amorphous and too varied to yield a conclusion with regard to the existence of God. Consider the various types of religious experiences, most of which can be documented in the literature:

1. S senses himself absorbed into the One, wherein the subject-object distinction ceases to hold.
2. One senses the unity of all things and that she is nothing at all.
3. The Buddhist monk who is an atheist senses the presence of the living Buddha.
4. One senses the presence of God, the Father of our Lord Jesus Christ.
5. The Virgin Mary appears to S (in a dream).
6. The Lord Jesus appears to Paul on the road one afternoon, though no one else realizes it but him.
7. One senses the presence of Satan, convincing him that Satan is the highest reality.
8. Achilles is appeared to by the goddess Athene, whom he believes to be descended from Zeus's head. She promises that he will win the battle on the morrow.
9. Allah appears to S and tells him to purify the land by executing all infidels (e.g., Jews and Christians) whose false worship corrupts the land.
10. A guilt-ridden woman senses the presence of her long-deceased father, assuring her that he has forgiven her of her neglect of him while he was aging and dying.
11. A mother senses the presence of the spirit of the river, telling her to throw back her deformed infant because it belongs to the river and not to her.
12. One senses the presence of the Trinity and understands how it could be that the three persons are one God, but he cannot tell others.
13. One senses the presence of the demiurge who has created the universe but makes no pretense to be omnipotent or omnibenevolent.
14. An atheist senses a deep infinite gratitude for the life of his son without in the least believing that a god exists (George Nakhnikian's personal example).
15. An atheist has a deep sense of nothingness in which she is absolutely convinced that the universe has manifested itself to her as a deep void.

The problem for those who would strongly justify the practice of religious experience—that is, show that we are rationally obligated to believe the content of the experience—is to differentiate the valid interpretations from the invalid. Which of these experiences are valid? That is, do any of these guarantee the truth of the propositions contained in the experience? For the believer or experient, each is valid for him or her, but why should the nonexperient accept any of these reports? And why should the experient continue to believe the content of the report himself after it is over and after he notes that there are other possible interpretations of it or that others have had mutually contradictory experiences? It would seem that they cancel each other out. Note the disparity of different types of "nonphysical" or religious experiences in the preceding list. There is not even any consensus that there is one supreme being, who is benevolent. Experiences 1 through 3 do not involve a divine being at all. Contrary to what Gutting says about the virtual universality of god experiences, the branches of Buddhism and Hinduism (in experiencing Nirvana) have religious experiences without experiencing a god. Furthermore, experience 7 supposes that the supreme being is evil, and experience 13 denies omnibenevolence. Experiences 14 and 15 have all the self-authenticating certainty of a religious experience but involve a conviction that no God exists. Do we understand how to distinguish genuine religious experiences from "spiritually" secular ones like experience 14? Why should we believe that the testimony of "of-God" experients is veridical, but not the other types (e.g., 1–3, 7–9, 11, 13, and 15) that are inconsistent with it? The very *private* nature of religious experience should preclude our being hasty in inferring from the psychological state to the reality of the object of the experience.

Gutting recognizes the diversity of religious experiences but fails to realize how troublesome this is for his thesis. He tries to find a core in these experiences to the effect that there is a "good and powerful non-human being who cares about us."[9] Gutting admits that we can't derive very much from "of-God" experiences, only that there is a being who is more powerful than us, very powerful and very good. But even if his argument were to show this, would it be sufficient as a definition of "God?" What would be the difference between this and experience 13, Plato's finite demiurge, or experience 10, the guilt-ridden woman's sense of her father, who presumably was both mentally and physically more powerful than she? (He was Arthur Conan Doyle, a genius and pugilist.) How would this show that there is a God, whom we should worship? How would this differ from ancestor worship or polytheism? Or a visitor from outer space? All of these could be "powerful, good, nonhuman, and caring for us." Why should we prefer the "of-God" experiences to the "of-a-supreme-devil" experiences? Gutting rejects the notion of self-authentication as the guarantee for the veridicality of these religious experiences,[10] but if this is so, how does the experient tell the difference between the nonhuman being who cares for her and one who only pretends to care? And how does one reidentify the being who has appeared to him in a nonsensory form?

Religious Experience Is Circular

Justification of belief in religious experience is circular, so that the belief in it will rest on premises that are not self-evident to everyone. If I am right about the difficulties in singling out "of-God" experiences from other deeply felt experiences, it would seem that we can only justify belief in the content of religious experience through circular reasoning, by setting forth hypothetical assumptions that we then take as constraints on the experience itself. For example, we suppose that God's ways are mysterious and beyond finding out, and so we are ready to accept our fellow believer's testimony of a deep "of-God" experience. A polytheist in East Africa already believes that the hippopotamus-god appears to women with deformed children in dreams, asking for them back and so credits his wife with a veridical experience when she reports that she has had such an encounter in a dream.

It would seem, then, that whether or not our interpretations of religious experience are justified depends on our background beliefs and expectations. Our beliefs appear to form a network, or web, in which all our beliefs are variously linked and supported by other beliefs. Some beliefs (call them "core beliefs"—e.g., my belief that $2 + 2 = 4$ or that there are other minds or that I am not now dreaming) are more centrally located and interconnected than other beliefs. If our core beliefs fall, our entire noetic structure is greatly affected, whereas some beliefs are only loosely connected to our noetic structure (e.g., my belief that the Dodgers will win the pennant this year or that it is better to have an IBM PC computer than a Macintosh). Similarly, religious people and nonreligious people often differ by having fundamentally different propositions at or near the center of their noetic structure. The religious person already is predisposed to have theistic-type religious experiences, whereas the nonreligious person is not usually so disposed (in the literature, Christians have visions of Jesus; Hindus, of Krishna; Buddhists, of Buddha; ancient Greeks, of Athene and Apollo; etc.). If you had been brought up in a Hindu culture, wouldn't you be more likely to have Hindu religious experiences than a Christian type? Would there be enough in common for you to decide that both really converged to a common truth?

All experiencing takes place within the framework of a worldview. Certain features of the worldview may gradually or suddenly change in importance, thus producing a different total picture, but there is no such thing as neutral evaluation of the evidence. As we have noted, what we see depends to some degree on our background beliefs and expectations. The farmer, real estate dealer, and the artist looking at the same field do not see the *same* field. Neither do the religious person and the atheist see the same thing when evaluating other people's religious experience.

It might be supposed that we could agree on some criteria of assessment in order to arrive at the best explanatory theory regarding religious experience, and there are, of course, competing explanations. There are Freudian, Marxian, and naturalist accounts that, suitably revised, seem to be as internally coherent as the sophisticated theist account. For one account to win our allegiance, it would be necessary for that account to win out over all others. To do this, we would have to agree on the criteria to be met by explanatory accounts. But it could turn out that there are competing criteria, so that theory A would fulfill criteria 1 and 2 better than theories B and C; but B would fulfill criteria 3 and 4 better than the others, whereas C might have the best

overall record without fulfilling any of the criteria best of all. It could be a close second in all of them. At this point, it looks like the very formulation and preference of the criteria of assessment depend on the explanatory account that one already embraces. The theist may single out *self-authentication* of the "of-God" experience, but why should that convince the atheist who suspects that criterion in the first place? It seems that there is no unambiguous, noncircular consensus of a hierarchy of criteria.

Gutting is confident of a core content that would be experienced (1) repeatedly, (2) by many, and (3) in such a way that these will be led to live better moral lives.[11] But why should this convince a naturalist who already has a coherent explanation of this phenomena? Plato's "noble lie" (a lie that is useful to achieve social harmony) presumably would have had the same effect, but it still is a lie. Even if we took a survey and discovered that the "of-God" experiences were common to all people, what would that in itself prove? We might still have grounds to doubt its veridicality. As Richard Gale notes, mere unanimity or agreement among observers is not a sufficient condition for the truth of what is experienced:

> Everybody who presses his finger on his eyeball will see double, everybody who stands at a certain spot in the desert will see a mirage, etc. The true criterion for objectivity is the Kantian one: An experience is objective if its contents can be placed in a spatiotemporal order with other experiences in accordance with scientific laws.[12]

Gale may go too far in limiting objectivity to that which is accessible to scientific laws, but his negative comments about unanimity are apposite.

Let me illustrate this point in another way. Suppose Timothy Leary had devised a psychogenic pill that had this result: Everyone taking it had a "deep religious experience" exactly similar to that described by the Western theistic mystics. Would this be good evidence for the existence of God? Perhaps some would be justified in believing it to be. We could predict the kinds of religious experience atheists would have upon taking the pill. But suppose, further, that upon taking *two* of the same pills, everyone had a deep religious experience common only to a remote primitive tribe: sensing the presence of a pantheon of gods, one being a three-headed hippopotamus who created the lakes and rivers of the world but didn't care a bit about people. The fact that there was complete agreement about what was experienced in these states hardly *by itself* can count for strong evidence for the truth of the existential claims of the experience. It would be likely that theists took the experience to be veridical until they had a double dosage, and it would be likely that the tribes people believed the double dosage to be veridical until they took a single dosage. Doesn't this indicate that it is our accepted background beliefs that predispose us to accept or reject that which fits or doesn't fit into our worldview?

Religious Experience Cannot Be Confirmed

When taken seriously as candidates of veridical experience, religious experience fails in not being confirmed in the same way that perceptual experience is. There is, however, one criterion of assessment that stands out very impressively in the minds of all rational people (indeed, it is one of the criteria of rationality itself) but that is unduly ignored by proponents of the argument from religious experience, like Gutting. It is the Achilles' heel (if anything is) of those who would place too much weight on religious experience as *evidence* for the content of religion. This is the complex criterion of *checkability–predictability* (I link them purposefully). The chemist who says that Avogadro's law holds (i.e., equal volumes of different gases at the same temperature and pressure contain an equal number of molecules) predicts exactly to what degree the inclusion of certain gases will increase the overall weight of a gaseous compound. Similarly, if, under normal circumstances, we heat water to 100°C, we can predict that it will boil. If you doubt my observation, check it out yourself. After suitable experiment, we see these propositions confirmed in such a way as to leave little room for doubt in our minds about their truth. After studying some chemistry, we see that they play a role in a wider network of beliefs that are mutually supportive. The perceptual beliefs force themselves on us.

This notion of predictability can be applied to social hypotheses as well. For instance, an orthodox Marxist states that if his theory is true, capitalism will begin to collapse in industrialized countries. If it doesn't, we begin to doubt Marxism. Of course, the Marxist may begin to revise her theory and bring in **ad hoc** hypotheses to explain why what was expected didn't occur, but the more ad hoc hypotheses she has to bring to bear in order to explain why the general thesis isn't happening, the weaker the hypothesis itself becomes. We come to believe many important propositions through experiment, either our own or those of others whom we take as authoritative (for the moment at least). With regard to authority, the presumption is that we could check out the propositions in question if we had time or need to do so.

How do we confirm the truth of religious experience? Does it make any predictions that we could test now in order to say, "Look and see, the fact that *X* occurs shows that the content of the religious experience is veridical?" How do we check on other people's religious experiences, especially if they purport to be nonsensory perceptions?

The checkability factor is weak in Gutting's account. He claims that we have a duty to believe simply on the report of others, not on the basis of our own experience or any special predictions that the experient would be able to make. But, if the Bible is to be believed, this wasn't always the case, nor should it be today. We read in 1 Kings 18 that to convince the Israelites that Yahweh, and not Baal, was worthy of being worshipped, Elijah challenged the priests of Baal to a contest. He proposed that they prepare a bullock and call on Baal to set fire to it. Then he would do the same with Yahweh. The priests failed, but Elijah succeeded. Convincing evidence! Similarly, at the end of Mark, we read of Jesus telling his disciples that "signs shall follow them that believe; in my name shall they cast out devils; they shall speak with new tongues; they shall take up serpents; and if they drink any deadly thing, it shall not hurt them; they shall lay hands on the sick, and they shall recover" (Mark 16:17, 18). Some believers doubt whether this text is authentic, and others seek to explain it away (e.g., "Jesus only meant his apostles and was referring to the apostolic age"), but if a religion is true, we might well expect some outward confirmation of it, such as we find in Elijah's actions at Mt. Carmel or in Jesus' miracles. The fact that religious experience isn't testable and doesn't yield any nontrivial predictions surely makes it less reliable than perceptual experience.

Not only doesn't religious experience usually generate predictions that are confirmed, but it sometimes yields false predictions. An example is an incident that happened to me as a student in an evangelical Christian college. A group of students believed that the Bible is the inerrant Word of God and cannot contain an untruth. Now the Gospel of Matthew 18:19 records Jesus as saying that "if two of you shall agree on earth as touching anything that they shall ask, it shall be done for them of my Father which is in heaven," and Matthew 17:20 tells of faith being able to move mountains: "Nothing shall be impossible for you." Verses in Mark confirm this, adding that God will answer our prayer if we pray in faith and do not doubt. So, one night several believers prayed through the entire night for the healing of a student who was dying of cancer. They prayed for her in childlike faith, believing that God would heal her. As morning broke, they felt the presence of God among them, telling them that their prayer had been answered. As they left rejoicing and were walking out of the room, they received the news that the woman had just died.

It is interesting to note that none of the participants lost faith in God over this incident. Some merely dismissed it as one of the mysteries of God's ways, others concluded that the Bible wasn't to be taken literally, and still others concluded that they hadn't prayed hard enough or with enough faith. But as far as the argument for the veridicality of the content of religion is concerned, this has to be taken as part of the total data. How it weighs against empirically successful prayers or times when the content of the experience was confirmed, I have no idea, and I think Gutting hasn't either. But unless we do, it is hard to see how the argument from religious experience could be used as strong evidence for the existence of God *to anyone else except those who had the experiences.* As James concludes about mystical states (one form of religious experience), whereas those having the experi-

ence have a right to believe in their content, "no authority emanates from them which should make it a duty for those who stand outside of them to accept their revelations uncritically."

Let me close with an illustration of what might be a publicly verifiable experience of God, one that would be analogous to the kind of perceptual experience by which we check scientific hypotheses. What if tomorrow morning (8 AM CST) there were a loud trumpet call and all over North America people heard a voice speak out, saying, "I am the Lord, your God, speaking. I have a message for you all. I am deeply saddened by the violence and lack of concern you have for one another. I am calling upon all nations to put aside nuclear weapons. This same message is being delivered to all other nations of Earth at different times today. I want you to know that I will take all means necessary to prevent a nuclear war and punish those nations who persist on the mad course on which they are now embarked. I love each one of you. A few signs will confirm this message. Later today, while speaking to Israel and the Arab states, I will cause an island, which is intended as a homeland for the Palestinians, to appear west of Lebanon in the Mediterranean. I will also cause the Sahara desert to become fruitful in order to provide food for the starving people in that area. But I will have you know that I will not intervene often in your affairs. I'm making this exception simply because it is an emergency situation."

Imagine that all over the world the same message is conveyed during the next twenty-four hours and the predictions fulfilled. Would your religious faith be strengthened by such an event? The question is, Why don't religious experiences like this happen? If there is a God, why does he seem to hide from us? Why doesn't God give us more evidence? I leave this question for you to reflect on.

Summary

Religious experience is at the core of the religious life. Throughout the ages, in virtually every culture, people have reported deeply religious, even mystical, experiences that have confirmed their beliefs and added meaning to their lives. Yet problems surround the phenomena: There are discrepancies between accounts, they tend to be amorphous and varied, and they seldom are verified.

Notes

1. *Shankara's Crest Jewel of Discrimination,* trans. Swami Prabhavandanda (New York: Mentor Books, 1970), 103–104.

2. "Now as he journeyed, Saul approached Damascus, and suddenly a light from heaven flashed about him. And he fell to the ground and heard a voice saying to him, 'Saul, Saul, why do you persecute me?' And he said, 'Who are you, Lord?' And he said, 'I am Jesus whom you are persecuting; but rise and enter the city, and you will be told what you are to do.' The men traveling with him stood speechless, hearing the voice but seeing no one. Saul arose from the ground; and when his eyes were opened, he could see nothing; so they led him into Damascus" (Acts 9).

3. Here is an illustration of Buddhist meditation:

Of one who has entered the first trance the voice has ceased; of one who has entered the second trance reasoning and reflection have ceased; of one who has entered the third trance joy has ceased; of one who has entered the fourth trance the inspiration and expiration have ceased; of one who has entered the realm of the infinity of space the perception of form has ceased; of one who has entered the realm of the infinity of consciousness the perception of the realm of the infinity of space has ceased; of one who has entered the realm of

nothingness the perception of the realm of the infinity of consciousness has ceased. [*Samyutta-Nikaya* 36:115, in *Buddhism in Translation,* ed. Henry C. Warren (New York: Atheneum, 1973), 384.]

4. Rudolf Otto, *The Idea of the Holy* (Oxford: Oxford University Press, 1958).

5. Søren Kierkegaard, *The Concept of Dread* (Princeton, NJ: Princeton University Press, 1939).

6. C. D. Broad, *Religion, Philosophy, and Psychical Research* (London: Routledge & Kegan Paul, 1930); Richard Swinburne, *The Existence of God* (Oxford: Clarendon Press, 1979); and Gary Gutting, *Religious Belief and Religious Skepticism* (Notre Dame, IN: University of Notre Dame Press, 1982).

7. James, op. cit., 371. Here is another testimony reported by James:

I remember the night, and almost the very spot on the hilltop, where my soul opened out, as it were, into the Infinite, and there was a rushing together of the two worlds, the inner and the outer. I stood alone with Him who had made me, and all the beauty of the world, and love, and sorrow, and even temptation. I did not seek Him, but felt the perfect unison of my spirit with His. The darkness held a presence that was all the more felt because it was not seen. I could not any more have doubted that He was there than that I was. I felt myself to be, if possible, the less real of the two. (p. 67)

8. Gutting, op. cit.

9. Ibid., 113.

10. Ibid., 145.

11. Ibid., 152.

12. Richard Gale, "Mysticism and Philosophy," *Journal of Philosophy* (1960).

II.7 Religious Experience and Religious Belief

WILLIAM P. ALSTON

In the last reading in this part, "Religious Experience and Religious Belief," William Alston (1921–   ), professor of philosophy at Syracuse University and editor of Faith and Philosophy, *argues that religious experience can provide grounds for religious belief. Comparing the epistemology of Christian religious*

experience with the epistemology of perceptual experience, Alston shows that although perceptual practices include more stringent requirements than religious practices, there are good reasons why the two should be different. Whereas the criteria for valid perceptual experience include verifiability and predictability, God's being wholly other may preclude those criteria from applying to religious experience. Do not be intimidated by Alston's use of symbols; they are simply a convenient shorthand.

Reprinted by permission of the author and of the editor of *NOÛS,* Vol. 16 (1982):3–12. Footnotes deleted.

For example, one of Alston's central theses is as follows: "CP will be J_{nw} for S provided S has no significant reason for regarding it as unreliable." Parsed out, this reads, "Christian practices are justified in the weak, normative sense for a person (S = subject) provided that the person has no significant reason for regarding that practice as unreliable."

I

Can religious experience provide any ground or basis for religious belief? Can it serve to justify religious belief, or make it rational? This paper will differ from many others in the literature by virtue of looking at this question in the light of basic epistemological issues. Throughout we will be comparing the epistemology of religious experience with the epistemology of sense experience.

We must distinguish between experience directly, and indirectly, justifying a belief. It indirectly justifies belief B_1 when it justifies some other beliefs, which in turn justify B_1. Thus I have learned indirectly from experience that Beaujolais wine is fruity, because I have learned from experience that this, that, and the other bottle of Beaujobis is fruity, and these propositions support the generalization. Experience will directly justify a belief when the justification does not go through other beliefs in this way. Thus, if I am justified, just by virtue of having the visual experiences I am now having, in taking what I am experiencing to be a typewriter situated directly in front of me, then the belief that there is a typewriter directly in front of me is directly justified by that experience.

We find claims to both direct and indirect justification of religious beliefs by religious experience. Where someone believes that her new way of relating herself to the world after her conversion is to be explained by the Holy Spirit imparting supernatural graces to her, she supposes her belief that *the Holy Spirit imparts graces to her* to be indirectly justified by her experience. What she directly learns from experience is that she sees and reacts to things differently; this is then taken as a reason for suppos-

ing that the Holy Spirit is imparting graces to her. When, on the other hand, someone takes himself to be experiencing the presence of God, he thinks that his experience justifies him in supposing that God is *what* he is experiencing. Thus, he supposes himself to be directly justified by his experience in believing God to be present to him.

In this paper I will confine myself to the question of whether religious experience can provide direct justification for religious belief. This has implications for the class of experiences we shall be considering. In the widest sense 'religious experience' ranges over any experiences one has in connection with one's religious life, including any joys, fears, or longings one has in a religious context. But here I am concerned with experiences that could be taken to *directly* justify religious beliefs, i.e. experiences that give rise to a religious belief and that the subject takes to involve a direct awareness of what the religious belief is about. To further focus the discussion, let's confine ourselves to beliefs to the effect that God, as conceived in theistic religions, is doing something that is directed to the subject of the experience—that God is speaking to him, strengthening him, enlightening him, giving him courage, guiding him, sustaining him in being, or just being present to him. Call these "M-beliefs" ('M' for 'manifestation').

Note that our question concerns what might be termed a general "epistemic practice," the accepting of M-beliefs on the basis of experience, rather than some particular belief of that sort. I hold that practices, or habits, of belief formation are the primary subject of justification and that particular beliefs are justified only by issuing from a practice (or the activation of a habit) that is justified. The following discussion of concepts of justification will provide grounds for that judgment.

Whether M-beliefs can be directly justified by experience depends, *inter alia*, on what it is to be justified in a belief. So let us take a look at that.

First, the justification about which we are asking is an "epistemic" rather than a "moral" or "prudential" justification. Suppose one should hold that the practice in question is justified because it makes us feel good. Even if this is true in a sense, it has no bearing on epistemic justification. But why not? What makes a justification *epistemic*? Epistemic justification, as the name implies, has something to do with knowledge, or, more broadly, with the aim at attaining truth and avoiding falsity. At a first approximation, I am justified in believing that *p* when, from the point of view of that aim, there is something O.K., all right, to be approved, about that fact that I believe that *p*. But when we come to spell this out further, we find that a fundamental distinction must be drawn between two different ways of being in an epistemically commendable position.

On the one hand there is what we may call a "normative" concept of epistemic justification (J_n), "normative" because it has to do with how we stand *vis-a-vis* norms that specify our intellectual obligations, obligations that attach to one *qua* cognitive subject, *qua* truth-seeker. Stated most generally, J_n consists in one's not having violated one's intellectual obligations. We have to say "not having violated" rather than "having fulfilled" because in all normative spheres, *being justified* is a negative status; it amounts to one's behavior not being in violation of the norms. If belief is under direct voluntary control, we may think of intellectual obligations as attaching directly to believing. Thus one might be obliged to refrain from believing in the absence of adequate evidence. But if, as it seems to me, belief is not, in general, under voluntary control, obligations cannot attach directly to believing. However, I do have voluntary control over moves that can influence a particular belief formation, e.g., looking for more evidence, and moves that can affect my general belief forming habits or tendencies e.g., training myself to be more critical of testimony. If we think of intellectual obligations as attaching to activities that are designed to influence belief formation, we may say that a certain epistemic practice is normatively justified provided it is not the case that the practitioner would not have engaged in it had he satisfied intellectual obligations to engage in activities designed to inhibit it. In other words, the practice is justified if and only if the practitioner did not fail to satisfy an obligation to inhibit it.

However epistemologists also frequently use the term 'justified' in such a way that it has to do not with how the subject stands *vis-a-vis* obligations, but rather with the strength of her epistemic position in believing that *p*, with how likely it is that a belief of that sort acquired or held in that way is true. To say that a practice is justified in this, as I shall say, "evaluative" sense, (J_e) is to say that beliefs acquired in accordance with that practice, in the sorts of circumstances in which human beings typically find themselves, are generally true. Thus we might say that a practice is J_e if and only if it is reliable.

One further complication in the notion of J_n remains to be canvassed. What is our highest reasonable aspiration for being J_n in accepting a belief on the basis of experience? Being J_n no matter what else is the case? A brief consideration of sense perception would suggest a negative answer. I may be justified in believing that there is a tree in front of me by virtue of the fact that I am currently having a certain kind of sense experience, but this will be true only in "favorable circumstances." If I am confronted with a complicated arrangement of mirrors, I may not be justified in believing that there is an oak tree in front of me, even though it looks for all the world as if there is. Again, it may look for all the world as if water is running uphill, but the general improbability of this greatly diminishes the justification the corresponding belief receives from that experience.

What this shows is that the justification provided by one's experience is only defeasibly so. It is inherently liable to be overridden, diminished, or cancelled by stronger considerations to the contrary. Thus the justification of beliefs about the physical environment that is provided by sense experience is a defeasible or, as we might say, *prima facie* justification. By virtue of having the experience, the subject is in a position such that she will be adequately justified in the belief *unless* there are strong enough reasons to the contrary.

It would seem that direct experiential justification for *M*-beliefs, is also, at most, *prima facie*. Beliefs about the nature and ways of God are often used to override *M*-beliefs, particularly beliefs concerning communications from God. If I report that God told me to kill all phenomenologists, fellow Christians will, no doubt, dismiss the report on the grounds that God would not give me any such injunction as that. I shall take it that both sensory experience and religious experience provide, at most, *prima facie* justification.

One implication of this stand is that a particular experiential epistemic practice will have to include some way of identifying defeaters. Different theistic religions, even different branches of the same religion, will differ in this regard, e.g., with respect to what sacred books, what traditions, what doctrines are taken to provide defeaters. We also find difference of this kind in perceptual practice. For example, with the progress of science new defeaters are added to the repertoire. Epistemic practices can, of course, be individuated with varying degrees of detail. To fix our thoughts with regard to the central problem of this paper let's think of a "Christian epistemic practice" (*CP*) that takes its defeaters from the Bible, the classic creeds, and certain elements of tradition. There will be differences between sub-segments of the community of practitioners so defined, but there will be enough commonality to make it a useful construct. My foil to *CP*, the practice of forming beliefs about the physical environment on the basis of sense-experience, I shall call "perceptual practice" (*PP*).

Actually it will prove most convenient to think of each of our practices as involving not only the formation of beliefs on the basis of experience, but also the retention of these beliefs in memory, the formation of rationally self-evident beliefs, and various kinds of reasoning on the basis of all this. *CP* will be the richer complex, since it will include the formation of perceptual beliefs in the usual way, while *PP* will not be thought of as including the distinctive experiential practice of *CP*.

One final preliminary note. J_n is relative to a particular person's situation. If practice P_1 is quite unreliable, I may still be J_n in engaging in it either because I have no way of realizing its unreliability or because I am unable to disengage myself: while you, suffering from neither of these disabilities, are not J_n. When we ask whether a given practice is J_n,

we shall be thinking about some normal, reasonably well informed contemporary member of our society.

II

Let's make use of all this in tackling the question as to whether one can be justified in *CP* and in *PP*. Beginning with J_n, we will first have to determine more precisely what one's intellectual obligations are *vis-a-vis* epistemic practices. Since our basic cognitive aim is to come into possession of as much truth as possible and to avoid false beliefs, it would seem that one's basic intellectual obligation *vis-a-vis* practices of belief formation would be to do what one can (or, at least, do as much as could reasonably be expected of one) to see to it that these practices are as *reliable* as possible. But this still leaves us with an option between a stronger and a weaker view as to this obligation. According to the stronger demand one is obliged to refrain (or try to refrain) from engaging in a practice unless one has adequate reasons for supposing it to be reliable. In the absence of sufficient reasons for considering the practice reliable, it is not justified. Practices are guilty until proved innocent. While on the more latitudinarian view one is justified in engaging in a practice provided one does not have sufficient reasons for regarding it to be unreliable. Practices are innocent until proved guilty. Let's take J_{ns} as an abbreviation for 'justified in the normative sense on the stronger requirement,' and 'J_{nw}' as an abbreviation for 'justified in the normative sense on the weaker requirement.'

Now consider whether Mr. Everyman is J_{nw} in engaging in *PP*. It would seem so. Except for those who, like Parmenides and Bradley, have argued that there are ineradicable inconsistencies in the conceptual scheme involved in *PP*, philosophers have not supposed that we can show that sense perception is not a reliable guide to our immediate surroundings. Sceptics about *PP* have generally confined themselves to arguing that we can't show that perception is reliable; i.e., they have argued that *PP* is not J_{ns}. I shall assume without further ado that *PP* is J_{nw}.

J_{ns} and J_e can be considered together. Although a practice may actually be reliable without my having adequate reasons for supposing so, and *vice versa*, still in considering whether a given practice is reliable, we will be seeking to determine whether there are adequate reasons for supposing it reliable, that is whether Everyman *could* be possessed of such reasons. And if we hold, as we shall, that there are no such reasons, the question of whether they are possessed by one or another subject does not arise.

I believe that there are no adequate noncircular reasons for the reliability of *PP* but I will not be able to argue that point here. If I had a general argument I would unveil it, but, so far as I can see, this thesis is susceptible only of inductive support, by unmasking each pretender in turn. And since this issue has been in the forefront of the Western philosophical consciousness for several centuries, there have been many pretenders. I do not have time even for criticism of a few representative samples. Instead I will simply assume that *PP* is not J_{ns}, and then consider what bearing this widely shared view has on the epistemic status of *CP*.

If J_{nw} is the most we can have for perceptual practice, then if *CP* is also J_{nw} it will be in at least as strong an epistemic position as the former. (I shall assume without argument that *CP* can no more be noncircularly shown to be reliable than can *PP*.) And *CP* will be J_{nw} for *S*, provided *S* has no significant reasons for regarding it as unreliable. Are there any such reasons? What might they be? Well, for one thing, the practice might yield a system that is ineradically internally inconsistent. (I am not speaking of isolated and remediable inconsistencies that continually pop up in every area of thought and experience.) For another, it might yield results that come into ineradicable conflict with the results of other practices to which we are more firmly committed. Perhaps some fundamentalist Christians are engaged in an epistemic practice that can be ruled out on such grounds as these. But I shall take it as obvious that one *can* objectify certain stretches of one's experience, or indeed the whole of one's experience, in Christian terms without running into such difficulties.

III

One may grant everything I have said up to this point and still feel reluctant to allow that *CP* is J_{nw}. *CP* does differ from *PP* in important ways, and it may be thought that some of these differences will affect their relative epistemic status. The following features of *PP*, which it does not share with *CP*, have been thought to have this kind of bearing.

1. Within *PP* there are standard ways of checking the accuracy of any particular perceptual belief.
2. By engaging in *PP* we can discover regularities in the behavior of the objects putatively observed, and on this basis we can, to a certain extent, effectively predict the course of events.
3. Capacity for *PP*, and practice of it, is found universally among normal adult human beings.
4. All normal adult human beings, whatever their culture, use basically the same conceptual scheme in objectifying their sense experience.

If *CP* includes *PP* as a proper part, as I ruled on above, how can it lack these features? What I mean is that there is no analogue of these features for that distinctive part of *CP* by virtue of which it goes beyond *PP*. The extra element of *CP* does not enable us to discover extra regularities, e.g., in the behavior of God, or increase our predictive powers. *M*-beliefs are not subject to interpersonal check in the same way as perceptual beliefs. The practice of forming *M*-beliefs on the basis of experience is not engaged in by all normal adults. And so on.

Before coming to grips with the alleged epistemic bearing of these differences, I want to make two preliminary points. (1) We have to engage in *PP* to determine that this practice has features 1.–4., and that *CP* lacks them. Apart from observation, we have no way of knowing that, e.g., while all cultures agree in their way of cognizing the physical environment they differ in their ways of cognizing the divine, or that *PP* puts us in a position to predict while *CP* doesn't. It might be thought that this is loading the dice in favor of my opponent. If we are to use *PP*, rather than some neutral source, to determine what features it has, shouldn't the same courtesy of self-assessment be accorded *CP*? Why should *it* be judged on the basis of what we learn about it from another practice, while that other practice is allowed to grade itself? To be sure, this is a serious issue only if answers to these questions *are* forthcoming from *CP* that differ from those we arrive at by engaging in *PP*. Fortunately, I can avoid getting involved in these issues by ruling that what I am interested in here is how *CP* looks from the standpoint of *PP*. The person I am primarily concerned to address is one who, like all the rest of us, engages in *PP*, and who, like all of us except for a few outlandish philosophers, regards it as justified. My aim is to show this person that, on his own grounds, *CP* enjoys basically the same epistemic status as *PP*. Hence it is consonant with my purposes to allow *PP* to determine the facts of the matter with respect to both practices. (2) I could quibble over whether the contrast is as sharp as is alleged. Questions can be raised about both sides of the putative divide. On the *PP* side, is it really true that all cultures have objectified sense experience in the same way? Many anthropologists have thought not. And what about the idea that all *normal* adult human beings engage in the same perceptual practice? Aren't we loading the dice by taking participation in what we regard as standard perceptual practice as our basic criterion for normality? On the *CP* side, is it really the case that this practice reveals no regularities to us, or only that they are very different from regularities in the physical world? What about the point that God is faithful to His promises? Or that the pure in heart will see God? However, I believe that when all legitimate quibbles have been duly registered there will still be very significant differences between the two practices in these respects. So rather than contesting the factual allegations, I will concentrate on the *de jure* issue as to what bearing these differences have on epistemic status.

How could the lack of 1.–4. prevent *CP* from being *J*$_{nw}$? Only by providing an adequate ground for a judgment of unreliability. And why suppose that? Of course, the lack of these features implies that we lack certain reasons we might conceivably have had for regarding *CP* as reliable. If we could ascertain that *PP* has those features, without using *PP* to do so, that would provide us with strong reasons for judging *PP* to be reliable. And the parallel possibility is lacking for *CP*. This shows that we cannot have *certain* reasons for taking *CP* to be reliable, but it doesn't follow that we have reasons for unreliability. That would follow only if we could also premise that a practice is reliable *only if* (as well as *if*) it has 1.–4. And why suppose that?

My position is that it is a kind of parochialism that makes the lack of 1.–4. appear to betoken untrustworthiness. The reality *CP* claims to put us in touch with is conceived to be vastly different from the physical environment. Why should the sorts of procedures required to put us in effective cognitive touch with this reality not be equally different? Why suppose that the distinctive features of *PP* set an appropriate standard for the cognitive approach to God? I shall sketch out a possible state of affairs in which *CP* is quite trustworthy while lacking 1.–4., and then suggest that we have no reason to suppose that this state of affairs does not obtain.

Suppose, then, that

(A) God is too different from created beings, too "wholly other," for us to be able to grasp any regularities in His behavior.

Suppose further that

(B) for the same reason we can only attain the faintest, sketchiest, and most insecure grasp of what God is like.

Finally, suppose that

(C) God has decreed that a human being will be aware of His presence in any clear and unmistakable fashion only when certain special and difficult conditions are satisfied.

If all this is the case, then it is the reverse of surprising that *CP* should lack 1.–4, even if it does involve a genuine experience of God. It would lack 1.–2. because of (A). It is quite understandable that it should lack 4. because of (B). If our cognitive powers are not fitted to frame an adequate conception of God, it is not at all surprising that there should be wide variation in attempts to do so. This is what typically happens in science when investigators are grappling with a phenomenon no one really understands. A variety of models, analogues, metaphors, hypotheses, hunches are propounded, and it is impossible to secure universal agreement. 3. is missing because of (C). If very difficult conditions are set it is not surprising that few are chosen. Now it is compatible with (A)–(C) that

(D) religious experience should, in general, constitute a genuine awareness of the divine.

and that

(E) although any particular articulation of such an experience might be mistaken to a greater or lesser extent, indeed even though all such articulations might miss the mark to some extent, still such judgments will, for the most part, contain some measure of truth; they, or many of them, will constitute a useful approximation of the truth;

and that

(F) God's designs contain provision for correction and refinement, for increasing the accuracy of the beliefs derived from religious experience. Perhaps as one grows in the spiritual life one's spiritual sight becomes more accurate and more discriminating; perhaps some special revelation is vouchsafed under certain conditions; and there are many other conceivable possibilities.

If something like all this were the case then *CP* would be trustworthy even though it lacks features 1.–4. This is a conceivable way in which *CP* would constitute a road to the truth, while differing from *PP* in respects 1.–4. Therefore unless we have adequate reason for supposing that no such combination of circumstances obtains, we are not warranted in taking the lack of 1.–4. to be an adequate reason for a judgment of untrustworthiness.

Moreover it is not just that A.–C. constitute a bare possibility. In the practice of *CP* we seem to learn that this is the way things are. As for (A) and (B) it is the common teaching of all the higher religions that God is of a radically different order of being from finite substances and, therefore, that we cannot expect to attain the grasp of His nature and His doings that we have of worldly objects. As for (C), it is a basic theme in Christianity, and in other religions as well, that one finds God within one's experience, to any considerable degree, only as one progresses in the spiritual life. God is not available for *voyeurs*. Awareness of God, and understanding of His nature and His will for us, is not a purely cognitive achievement; it requires the involvement of the whole person; it takes a practical commitment and a practice of the life of the spirit, as well as the exercise of cognitive faculties.

Of course these results that we are using to defend *CP* are derived from that same practice. But in view of the fact that the favorable features of *PP*, 1.–4., are themselves ascertained by engaging in *PP*, our opponent is hardly in a position to fault us on this score. However I have not forgotten that I announced it as my aim to show that even one who engaged only in *PP* should recognize that *CP* is J_{nw}. For this purpose, I ignore what we learn in *CP* and revert to the point that my opponent has no basis for ruling out the conjoint state of affairs A.–F., hence has no basis for taking the lack of 1.–4. to show *CP* to be untrustworthy, and hence has no reason for denying that *CP* is J_{nw}.

I conclude that *CP* has basically the same epistemic status as *PP* and that no one who subscribes to the latter is in any position to cavil at the former.

Bibliography for Part II

Alston, William. *Perceiving God*. Ithaca, N.Y.: Cornell Univ. Press, 1991. An important recent work on the epistemology of religious experience.

Freud, Sigmund. *The Future of an Illusion*. New York: Norton, 1961. Contains his famous theory that religion is the outgrowth of the projection of the father image.

Gale, Richard. "Mysticism and Philosophy." *Journal of Philosophy* 57 (1960). A clear analysis and cogent critique of some key concepts and arguments related to mystical experience. (Republished in *Contemporary Philosophy of Religion*, ed. Steven M. Cahn and David Shatz. Oxford, Eng.: Oxford Univ. Press, 1982.)

————. *On the Nature and Existence of God*. Cambridge, Mass.: Cambridge Univ. Press, 1991. Chapter 8 contains a penetrating critique.

Gutting, Gary. *Religious Belief and Religious Skepticism*. Notre Dame, Ind.: Univ. of Notre Dame Press, 1982. A well-argued contemporary discussion.

James, William. *Varieties of Religious Experience*. New York: Modern Library, 1902. This marvelous treatise is the definitive work on the subject.

Martin, C. B. "A Religious Way of Knowing." *Mind* 61 (1952). A watershed article. (Reprinted and expanded in his book *Religious Belief*. Chap. 5. Ithaca, N.Y.: Cornell Univ. Press, 1959.)

Mavrodes, George. *Belief in God*. Chap. 3. New York: Random House, 1970. A good analysis.

Otto, Rudolf. *The Idea of the Holy*, trans. J. W. Harvey. Oxford, Eng.: Oxford Univ. Press, 1923. A classic study of religious experience.

Rowe, William. *Philosophy of Religion*. Belmont, Calif.: Wadsworth, 1978. A valuable commentary on some of the major work in the field.

Stace, Walter T. *Time and Eternity*. Princeton, N.J.: Princeton Univ. Press, 1952. An important study.

————, ed. *The Teaching of the Mystics*. New York: New American Library, 1960. Contains useful material, especially the article by Stace himself.

Swinburne, Richard. *The Existence of God*. Chap. 13. Oxford, Eng.: Clarendon Press, 1979. Contains a cogently reasoned defense for the veridicality of religious experience.

Wainwright, William. "Mysticism and Sense Perception." *Religious Studies* 9 (1973). Perhaps the best modern analysis of mysticism.

————. *Mysticism*. Madison: Univ. of Wisconsin Press, 1981. A comprehensive and sympathetic study of mysticism.

THE PROBLEM OF EVIL

Is he willing to prevent evil, but not able? then he is impotent. Is he able, but not willing? then he is malevolent. Is he both able and willing? whence then is evil?

E P I C U R U S (341–270 BC)

We have been looking at arguments in favor of God's existence. The agnostic and atheist usually base their case on the *absence* of evidence for God's existence. But they have one arrow in their own quiver, an argument for disbelief. It is the problem of evil. From it the "atheologian" (one who argues against the existence of God) hopes either to neutralize any positive evidence for God's existence, based on whatever in the traditional arguments survives their criticism, or to demonstrate that it is unreasonable to believe in God.

The problem of evil arises from the paradox of an omnibenevolent, omnipotent deity's allowing the existence of evil. The Judeo-Christian tradition has affirmed these three propositions:

1. God is all-powerful (his powers include omniscience).
2. God is perfectly good.
3. Evil exists.

But if he is perfectly good, why does he allow evil to exist? Why didn't he create a better world, if not one without evil, at least one with substantially less evil than this world? Many have contended that this paradox, first articulated by Epicurus, is not just a paradox but an implicit contradiction, for it contains premises that are inconsistent with one another. They argue something like the following:

4. If God (an all-powerful, omniscient, omnibenevolent being) exists, there would be no (or no unnecessary) evil in the world.
5. There is evil (or unnecessary evil) in the world.
6. Therefore, God does not exist.

You will want to examine each of these premises carefully. A few words about them are in order. Generally, Western thought has distinguished between two types of evil: moral and natural. 'Moral evil' covers all those bad things for which humans are morally responsible. 'Natural evil' or 'surd evil' includes those terrible events that occur in nature of their own accord, such as hurricanes, tornadoes, earthquakes, volcano eruptions, natural diseases, and so on, that cause suffering to humans and animals. However, some defenses of theism affirm that all evil is essentially moral evil, with the devil brought in as the cause of natural evil.

The main defense of theism in the light of evil is the free will defense, going back as far as St. Augustine (354–430) and receiving modern treatment in the work of John Hick, Alvin Plantinga, and Richard Swinburne. The free will defense adds a fourth premise to Epicurus's paradox in order to show that premises 1–3 are consistent and not contradictory:

7. It is logically impossible for God to create free creatures and guarantee that they will never do evil.

Since it is a good thing to create free creatures who are morally responsible agents, there is no assurance that they will not also do evil.

This defense assumes a libertarian view of freedom of the will. That is, humans are free to choose between good and evil acts. They are not caused (though they may be influenced) to do one deed rather than the other; they are causally underdetermined. Given two identical situations with identical causal antecedents, an agent could do act *A* at one time and *B* at the other. This view is opposed to determinism as well as compatibilism (a view that tries to reconcile freedom of action with determinism). If you are committed to compatibilism or determinism, the free will defense will not be effective against the argument from evil. This matter is well treated in chapter 9 of J. L. Mackie's *The Miracle of Theism*.

Proponents of the free will defense claim that all moral evil derives from creatures' freedom of will. But how does the theist account for natural evil? There are two different ways. The first one, suggested by Alvin Plantinga (see Part 3 Bibliography), is to attribute natural evil, such as disease and tornadoes, to the work of the devil and his angels. The second way, favored by Swinburne, argues that natural evil is part and parcel of the nature of things, resulting from the combination of deterministic physical laws that are necessary for consistent action and the responsibility given to humans to exercise their freedom.

There is one further distinction necessary to work through this problem. Some theists attempt to answer the charge of inconsistency by simply showing that there is no formal contradiction in propositions 1–3; thus the nontheists haven't proved their point. But others want to go beyond this negative function and offer a plausible account of evil. These latter are called "theodicists," for they attempt to justify the ways of God before humankind. They endeavor to show that God allows the temporary evil in order to bring out greater good. Gottfried Leibniz, and John Hick, included in our readings, are theodicists.

Let me outline the main points of the readings that follow. The eight readings included here constitute three separate debates. The first two readings are classic formulations of opposite positions. In the first reading, "The Argument from Evil," David Hume argues through his persona Philo that not merely the fact of evil but the enormous amount of evil make it dubious that a deity exists. It is arguable that there is actually more evil than good in the world, so it is hard to see how one can harmonize the crucial propositions. In the second reading, "Theodicy: A Defense of Theism," Gottfried Leibniz (1646–1716) argues that the fact of evil in no way refutes theism, and he answers the kinds of objections made by Hume. He contends that God permitted evil to exist in order to bring about greater good and that Adam's fall was a *felix culpa* ("happy sin") because it led to the incarnation of the Son of God, raising humanity to a higher destiny than would otherwise have been the case. He argues that although God can foresee the future, humans are still free, in that they act voluntarily.

We come to contemporary formulations. Our third reading, John Hick's "Evil and Soul-Making," is an example of a theodicy argument that is based on the free will defense. Theodicies can be of two different types depending on how they justify the ways of God in the face of evil. The Augustinian position is that God created humans without sin and set them in a sinless, paradisical world. However, humanity fell into sin through misuse of its free will. God's grace will save some of us, but others will perish everlastingly. In this division God's goodness is manifested, for his mercy redeems some and his justice is served on the rest. But there is another theory of theodicy, stemming from Irenaeus (120–202), in the tradition of the Greek Church. The Irenaean tradition views Adam not as a free agent rebelling against God but as a child. The fall is humanity's first faulty step in the direction of freedom. God is still working with humanity in order to bring it from undeveloped life (*bios*) to a state of self-realization in divine love, spiritual life (*zoe*). This life is viewed as the "vale of soul-making." Spiritual development requires obstacles and the opportunity to fail as well as to succeed. Hick declares that those who are opposed to the challenge that our freedom grants us are looking for a hedonistic paradise in which every desire is gratified and we are treated by God as pet animals rather than autonomous agents. On the other hand, those who accept the challenge of freedom consider themselves to be coworkers with God in bringing forth the kingdom of God.

In the fourth reading, "A Critique of Hick's Theodicy," Edward H. Madden and Peter H. Hare attack Hick's theory. They ask whether the amount of evil in the world is necessary for soul-making and accuse Hick of three fallacies, called "all or nothing," "it could be worse," and "slippery slope."

The *all or nothing* fallacy involves the idea that what we have is desirable because not having it at all would be far worse. "The erroneous assumption," wrote Madden and Hare, "is that we must have this thing either in its present form and amount or not at all. But it is often the case that only *some* amount of the thing in *some* form is necessary to the achievement of a desirable end." Hick concedes that there is an appalling amount of evil in the world but insists that the alternative is for humans to be mere puppets or pets. We may object to this set of extreme alternatives because we can easily imagine intermediate states where there is still great good but much less evil. Taking away Auschwitz or the Gulag Archipelago doesn't seem to leave the world any worse off.

It could be worse is the claim that "something is not really bad because it will be followed by all manner of desirable things." But this overlooks the fact that things could also be better. Hick seems to ignore the fact that although it is true that we can imagine the world's being a worse place than it is, we can also imagine it to be a far better place. The question is, Why hasn't God created this far better place?

The *slippery slope* fallacy states that if God once started eliminating evil from the world, he could not stop short of a perfect world. This notion overlooks the fact that humanity could be shown by God why a certain proportion of good to evil is ideal.

In our fifth essay, J. L. Mackie argues that the problem of evil constitutes an incoherent set of beliefs. Consider the propositions:

1. There is a God who is omnipotent, omniscient, and perfectly good.
2. Evil exists.
3. A good being always eliminates evil as far as it can.

Mackie argues that because propositions 1–2 are held by theists, they are guilty of a logical inconsistency and so should recognize that their belief in God is irrational.

Alvin Plantinga in our sixth essay argues that Mackie is wrong in thinking that the problem of evil constitutes a logical inconsistency. He argues that proposition 3 is not necessarily correct, for God may have a sufficient reason for permitting some evil.

Plantinga's defense, unlike Leibniz's and Hick's earlier essays in this section, is not a theodicy—not an argument that the ways of God are justified, let alone that this is the best of all possible worlds. Rather, he aims to defeat the arguments set forth by the atheologian, a person who argues that belief in God is irrational given the reality of evil. Plantinga's arguments rest on the free will defense. God didn't have to create a universe (as far as we know), but once having decided to do so, he could not make humans free and guarantee that they not sin. Plantinga sets forth the hypothesis of *transworld depravity,* defined as the condition that humans go wrong in every possible world. If this hypothesis is true, God could not create a world where no evil obtained. So, it could be the case that God could not have created a world with a significantly better balance of good over evil than obtains in our world.

In our seventh reading William Rowe argues that while Plantinga is correct in arguing that the deductive argument from evil against the existence of God fails, an inductive argument from evil succeeds. Whether Rowe is successful must be left to you to decide.

In the final reading Paul Draper argues that a cumulative case against theism can be made by combining the problem of evil with a naturalist explanation for human existence based evolution. We now turn to our readings.

III.1 The Argument from Evil

DAVID HUME

In his Dialogues Concerning Natural Religion, *David Hume (1711–1776) argues through his persona Philo that not merely the fact of evil but the enormous amount of evil make it dubious that a deity exists. It is arguable that there is actually more evil than good in the world, so it is hard to see how one can harmonize the crucial propositions.*

Part X

It is my opinion, I own, replied Demea, that each man feels, in a manner, the truth of religion within his own breast, and, from a consciousness of his imbecility and misery rather than from any reasoning, is led to seek protection from that Being on whom he and all nature is dependent. So anxious or so tedious are even the best scenes of life that futurity is still the object of all our hopes and fears. We incessantly look forward and endeavour, by prayers, adoration, and sacrifice, to appease those unknown powers whom we find, by experience, so able to afflict and oppress us. Wretched creatures that we are! What resource for us amidst the innumerable ills of life did not religion suggest some methods of atonement, and appease those terrors with which we are incessantly agitated and tormented?

I am indeed persuaded, said Philo, that the best and indeed the only method of bringing everyone to a due sense of religion is by just representations of the misery and wickedness of men. And for that purpose a talent of eloquence and strong imagery is more requisite than that of reasoning and argument. For is it necessary to prove what everyone feels within himself? It is only necessary to make us feel it, if possible, more intimately and sensibly.

The people, indeed, replied Demea, are sufficiently convinced of this great and melancholy truth. The miseries of life, the unhappiness of man, the general corruptions of our nature, the unsatisfactory enjoyment of pleasures, riches, honours—these phrases have become almost proverbial in all languages. And who can doubt of what all men declare from their own immediate feeling and experience?

In this point, said Philo, the learned are perfectly agreed with the vulgar; and in all letters, *sacred* and *profane*, the topic of human misery has been insisted on with the most pathetic eloquence that sorrow and melancholy could inspire. The poets, who speak from sentiment, without a system, and whose testimony has therefore the more authority, abound in images of this nature. From Homer down to Dr. Young, the whole inspired tribe have ever been sensible that no other representation of things would suit the feeling and observation of each individual.

As to authorities, replied Demea, you need not seek them. Look round this library of Cleanthes. I shall venture to affirm that, except authors of particular sciences, such as chemistry or botany, who have no occasion to treat of human life, there is scarce one of those innumerable writers from whom the sense of human misery has not, in some passage or other, extorted a complaint and confession of it. At least, the chance is entirely on that side; and no one author has ever, so far as I can recollect, been so extravagant as to deny it.

There you must excuse me, said Philo: Leibniz has denied it, and is perhaps the first[1] who ventured upon so bold and paradoxical an opinion; at least, the first who made it essential to his philosophical system.

And by being the first, replied Demea, might he not have been sensible of his error? For is this a subject in which philosophers can propose to make discoveries especially in so late an age? And can

Reprinted from David Hume, *Dialogues Concerning Natural Religion:* (1779; London: Longmans Green, 1878).

any man hope by a simple denial (for the subject scarcely admits of reasoning) to bear down the united testimony of mankind, founded on sense and consciousness?

And why should man, added he, pretend to an exemption from the lot of all other animals? The whole earth, believe me, Philo, is cursed and polluted. A perpetual war is kindled amongst all living creatures. Necessity, hunger, want stimulate the strong and courageous; fear, anxiety, terror agitate the weak and infirm. The first entrance into life gives anguish to the new-born infant and to its wretched parent; weakness, impotence, distress attend each stage of that life, and it is, at last, finished in agony and horror.

Observe, too, says Philo, the curious artifices of nature in order to embitter the life of every living being. The stronger prey upon the weaker and keep them in perpetual terror and anxiety. The weaker, too, in their turn, often prey upon the stronger, and vex and molest them without relaxation. Consider that innumerable race of insects, which either are bred on the body of each animal or, flying about, infix their stings in him. These insects have others still less than themselves which torment them. And thus on each hand, before and behind, above and below, every animal is surrounded with enemies which incessantly seek his misery and destruction.

Man alone, said Demea, seems to be, in part, an exception to this rule. For by combination in society he can easily master lions, tigers, and bears, whose greater strength and agility naturally enable them to prey upon him.

On the contrary, it is here chiefly, cried Philo, that the uniform and equal maxims of nature are most apparent. Man, it is true, can, by combination, surmount all his *real* enemies and become master of the whole animal creation; but does he not immediately raise up to himself *imaginary* enemies, the demons of his fancy, who haunt him with superstitious terrors and blast every enjoyment of life? His pleasure, as he imagines, becomes in their eyes a crime; his food and repose give them umbrage and offence; his very sleep and dreams furnish new materials to anxious fear; and even death, his refuge from every other ill, presents only the dread of endless and innumerable woes. Nor does the wolf molest more the timid flock than superstition does the anxious breast of wretched mortals.

Besides, consider, Demea: This very society by which we surmount those wild beasts, our natural enemies, what new enemies does it not raise to us? What woe and misery does it not occasion? Man is the greatest enemy of man. Oppression, injustice, contempt, contumely, violence, sedition, war, calumny, treachery, fraud—by these they mutually torment each other, and they would soon dissolve that society which they had formed were it not for the dread of still greater ills which must attend their separation.

But though these external insults, said Demea, from animals, from men, from all the elements, which assault us form a frightful catalogue of woes, they are nothing in comparison of those which arise within ourselves, from the distempered condition of our mind and body. How many lie under the lingering torment of diseases? Hear the pathetic enumeration of the great poet.

> Intestine stone and ulcer, colic-pangs,
> Demoniac frenzy, moping melancholy,
> And moon-struck madness, pining atrophy,
> Marasmus, and wide-wasting pestilence.
> Dire was the tossing, deep the groans:
>> *Despair*
> Tended the sick, busiest from couch to
>> couch.
> And over them triumphant *Death* his dart
> Shook: but delay'd to strike, though oft
>> invok'd
> With vows, as their chief good and final
>> hope.[2]

The disorders of the mind, continued Demea, though more secret, are not perhaps less dismal and vexatious. Remorse, shame, anguish, rage, disappointment, anxiety, fear, dejection, despair—who has ever passed through life without cruel inroads from these tormentors? How many have scarcely ever felt any better sensations? Labour and poverty, so abhorred by everyone, are the certain lot of the far greater number; and those few privileged persons who enjoy ease and opulence never reach contentment or true felicity. All the goods of life united would not make a very happy man, but all the ills united would make a wretch indeed; and any one of them almost (and who can be free from every one?), nay, often the absence of one good (and who can possess all?) is sufficient to render life ineligible.

Were a stranger to drop on a sudden into this world, I would show him, as a specimen of its ills, an hospital full of diseases, a prison crowded with malefactors and debtors, a field of battle strewed with carcases, a fleet foundering in the ocean, a nation languishing under tyranny, famine, or pestilence. To turn the gay side of life to him and give him a notion of its pleasures—whither should I conduct him? To a ball, to an opera, to court? He might justly think that I was only showing him a diversity of distress and sorrow.

There is no evading such striking instances, said Philo, but by apologies which still further aggravate the charge. Why have all men, I ask, in all ages, complained incessantly of the miseries of life? . . . They have no just reason, says one: these complaints proceed only from their discontented, repining, anxious disposition. . . . And can there possibly, I reply, be a more certain foundation of misery than such a wretched temper?

But if they were really as unhappy as they pretend, says my antagonist, why do they remain in life? . . .

Not satisfied with life, afraid of death—

this is the secret chain, say I, that holds us. We are terrified, not bribed to the continuance of our existence.

It is only a false delicacy, he may insist, which a few refined spirits indulge, and which has spread these complaints among the whole race of mankind. . . . And what is this delicacy, I ask, which you blame? Is it anything but a greater sensibility to all the pleasures and pains of life? And if the man of a delicate, refined temper, by being so much more alive than the rest of the world, is only so much more unhappy, what judgment must we form in general of human life?

Let men remain at rest, says our adversary, and they will be easy. They are willing artificers of their own misery. . . . No! reply I: an anxious langour

follows their repose; disappointment, vexation, trouble, their activity and ambition.

I can observe something like what you mention in some others, replied Cleanthes, but I confess I feel little or nothing of it in myself, and hope that it is not so common as you represent it.

If you feel not human misery yourself, cried Demea, I congratulate you on so happy a singularity. Others, seemingly the most prosperous, have not been ashamed to vent their complaints in the most melancholy strains. Let us attend to the great, the fortunate emperor, Charles V, when, tired with human grandeur, he resigned all his extensive dominions into the hands of his son. In the last harangue which he made on that memorable occasion, he publicly avowed *that the greatest prosperities which he had ever enjoyed had been mixed with so many adversities that he might truly say he had never enjoyed any satisfaction or contentment.* But did the retired life in which he sought for shelter afford him any greater happiness? If we may credit his son's account, his repentance commenced the very day of his resignation.

Cicero's fortune, from small beginnings, rose to the greatest lustre and renown; yet what pathetic complaints of the ills of life do his familiar letters, as well as philosophical discourses, contain? And suitably to his own experience, he introduces Cato, the great, the fortunate Cato protesting in his old age that had he a new life in his offer he would reject the present.

Ask yourself, ask any of your acquaintance, whether they would live over again the last ten or twenty years of their life. No! but the next twenty, they say, will be better:

> And from the dregs of life, hope to receive
> What the first sprightly running could not
>   give.[3]

Thus, at last, they find (such is the greatness of human misery, it reconciles even contradictions) that they complain at once of the shortness of life and of its vanity and sorrow.

And is it possible, Cleanthes, said Philo, that after all these reflections, and infinitely more which might be suggested, you can still persevere in your anthropomorphism, and assert the moral attributes of the Deity, his justice, benevolence, mercy, and rectitude, to be of the same nature with these virtues in human creatures? His power, we allow, is infinite; whatever he wills is executed; but neither man nor any other animal is happy; therefore, he does not will their happiness. His wisdom is infinite; he is never mistaken in choosing the means to any end; but the course of nature tends not to human or animal felicity; therefore, it is not established for that purpose. Through the whole compass of human knowledge there are no inferences more certain and infallible than these. In what respect, then, do his benevolence and mercy resemble the benevolence and mercy of men?

Epicurus' old questions are yet unanswered.

Is he willing to prevent evil, but not able? then is he impotent. Is he able, but not willing? then is he malevolent. Is he both able and willing? whence then is evil?

You ascribe, Cleanthes, (and I believe justly) a purpose and intention to nature. But what, I beseech you, is the object of that curious artifice and machinery which she has displayed in all animals—the preservation alone of individuals, and propagation of the species? It seems enough for her purpose, if such a rank be barely upheld in the universe, without any care or concern for the happiness of the members that compose it. No resource for this purpose: no machinery in order merely to give pleasure or ease; no fund of pure joy and contentment; no indulgence without some want or necessity accompanying it. At least, the few phenomena of this nature are overbalanced by opposite phenomena of still greater importance.

Our sense of music, harmony, and indeed beauty of all kinds, gives satisfaction, without being absolutely necessary to the preservation and propagation of the species. But what racking pains, on the other hand, arise from gouts, gravels, megrims, toothaches, rheumatisms, where the injury to the animal machinery is either small or incurable? Mirth, laughter, play, frolic seem gratuitous satisfactions which have no further tendency; spleen, melancholy, discontent, superstition are pains of the same nature. How then does the Divine benevolence display itself, in the sense of you anthropomorphites?

None but we mystics, as you were pleased to call us, can account for this strange mixture of phenomena, by deriving it from attributes infinitely perfect but incomprehensible.

And have you, at last, said Cleanthes smiling, betrayed your intentions, Philo? Your long agreement with Demea did indeed a little surprise me, but I find you were all the while erecting a concealed battery against me. And I must confess that you have now fallen upon a subject worthy of your noble spirit of opposition and controversy. If you can make out the present point, and prove mankind to be unhappy or corrupted, there is an end at once of all religion. For to what purpose establish the natural attributes of the Deity, while the moral are still doubtful and uncertain?

You take umbrage very easily, replied Demea, at opinions the most innocent and the most generally received, even amongst the religious and devout themselves; and nothing can be more surprising than to find a topic like this—concerning the wickedness and misery of man—charged with no less than atheism and profaneness. Have not all pious divines and preachers who have indulged their rhetoric on so fertile a subject, have they not easily, I say, given a solution of any difficulties which may attend it? This world is but a point in comparison of the universe; this life but a moment in comparison of eternity. The present evil phenomena, therefore, are rectified in other regions, and in some future period of existence. And the eyes of men, being then opened to larger views of things, see the whole connection of general laws, and trace, with adoration, the benevolence and rectitude of the Deity through all the mazes and intricacies of his providence.

No! replied Cleanthes, no! These arbitrary suppositions can never be admitted, contrary to matter of fact, visible and uncontroverted. Whence can any cause be known but from its known effects? Whence can any hypothesis be proved but from the apparent phenomena? To establish one hypothesis upon another is building entirely in the air; and the utmost we ever attain by these conjectures and fictions is to ascertain the bare possibility of our opinion, but never can we, upon such terms, establish its reality.

The only method of supporting Divine benevolence—and it is what I willingly embrace—is to deny absolutely the misery and wickedness of man. Your representations are exaggerated; your melancholy views mostly fictitious; your inferences contrary to fact and experience. Health is more common than sickness; pleasure than pain; happiness than misery. And for one vexation which we meet with, we attain, upon computation, a hundred enjoyments.

Admitting your position, replied Philo, which yet is extremely doubtful, you must at the same time allow that, if pain be less frequent than pleasure, it is infinitely more violent and durable. One hour of it is often able to outweigh a day, a week, a month of our common insipid enjoyments; and how many days, weeks, and months are passed by several in the most acute torments? Pleasure, scarcely in one instance, is ever able to reach ecstasy and rapture; and in no one instance can it continue for any time at its highest pitch and altitude. The spirits evaporate, the nerves relax, the fabric is disordered, and the enjoyment quickly degenerates into fatigue and uneasiness. But pain often, good God, how often! rises to torture and agony; and the longer it continues, it becomes still more genuine agony and torture. Patience is exhausted, courage languishes, melancholy seizes us, and nothing terminates our misery but the removal of its cause or another event which is the sole cure of all evil, but which, from our natural folly, we regard with still greater horror and consternation.

But not to insist upon these topics, continued Philo, though most obvious, certain, and important, I must use the freedom to admonish you, Cleanthes, that you have put the controversy upon a most dangerous issue, and are unawares introducing a total scepticism into the most essential articles of natural and revealed theology. What! no method of fixing a just foundation for religion unless we allow the happiness of human life, and maintain a continued existence even in this world, with all our present pains, infirmities, vexations, and follies, to be eligible and desirable! But this is contrary to everyone's feeling and experience; it is contrary to an authority so established as nothing can subvert. No decisive proofs can ever be produced against this authority; nor is it possible for you to compute, estimate, and compare all the pains and all the pleasures in the lives of all men and of all animals; and thus, by your resting the whole system of religion on a point which, from its very nature, must forever be uncertain, you tacitly confess that that system is equally uncertain.

But allowing you what never will be believed, at least, what you never possibly can prove, that animal or, at least, human happiness in this life exceeds its misery, you have yet done nothing; for this is not, by any means, what we expect from infinite power, infinite wisdom, and infinite goodness. Why is there any misery at all in the world? Not by chance, surely. From some cause then. Is it from the intention of the Deity? But he is perfectly benevolent. Is it contrary to his intention? But he is almighty. Nothing can shake the solidity of this reasoning, so short, so clear, so decisive, except we assert that these subjects exceed all human capacity, and that our common measures of truth and falsehood are not applicable to them—a topic which I have all along insisted on, but which you have, from the beginning, rejected with scorn and indignation.

But I will be contented to retire still from this intrenchment, for I deny that you can ever force me in it. I will allow that pain or misery in man is *compatible* with infinite power and goodness in the Deity, even in your sense of these attributes: what are you advanced by all these concessions? A mere possible compatibility is not sufficient. You must *prove* these pure, unmixed, and uncontrollable attributes from the present mixed and confused phenomena, and from these alone. A hopeful undertaking! Were the phenomena ever so pure and unmixed, yet, being finite, they would be insufficient for that purpose. How much more, where they are also so jarring and discordant!

Here, Cleanthes, I find myself at ease in my argument. Here I triumph. Formerly, when we argued concerning the natural attributes of intelligence and design, I needed all my sceptical and metaphysical subtilty to elude your grasp. In many views of the universe and of its parts, particularly the latter, the beauty and fitness of final causes strike us with such irresistible force that all objections appear (what I believe they really are) mere cavils and sophisms; nor can we then imagine how it was ever possible for us to repose any weight on them. But there is no view of human life or of the condition of mankind from which, without the greatest violence, we can infer the moral attributes or learn that infinite benevolence, conjoined with infinite power and infinite wisdom, which we must discover by the eyes of faith alone. It is your turn now to tug the labouring oar, and to support your philosophical subtilties against the dictates of plain reason and experience.

Notes

1. That sentiment had been maintained by Dr. King and some few others before Leibniz, though by none of so great fame as that German philosopher.
2. Milton: *Paradise Lost,* Bk. XI.
3. John Dryden, *Aureng-Zebe*, Act IV, sc. 1.

III.2   Theodicy: A Defense of Theism

GOTTFRIED LEIBNIZ

Gottfried Wilhelm Leibniz (1646–1716) was a German idealist who tried to set forth a thorough-going theodicy, a justification of the ways of God. In this selection he argues that the fact of evil in no way refutes theism, and he answers the kinds of objections made by Hume. He contends that God permitted evil to exist in order to bring about greater good and that Adam's fall was a felix culpa *(a "happy sin") because it led to the incarnation of the Son of God, raising humanity to a higher destiny than would otherwise have been the case. He argues that although God can foresee the future, humans are still free in that they act voluntarily.*

Some intelligent persons have desired that this supplement be made [to the Theodicy], and I have the more readily yielded to their wishes as in this way I have an opportunity again to remove certain difficulties and to make some observations which were not sufficiently emphasized in the work itself.

1. *Objection.* Whoever does not choose the best is lacking in power, or in knowledge, or in goodness.

Reprinted from Gottfried Leibniz, *The Theodicy: Abridgement of the Argument Reduced to Syllogistic Form* (1710).

God did not choose the best in creating this world.

Therefore, God has been lacking in power, or in knowledge, or in goodness.

Answer. I deny the minor, that is, the second premise of this syllogism; and our opponent proves it by this.

Prosyllogism. Whoever makes things in which there is evil, which could have been made without any evil, or the making of which could have been omitted, does not choose the best.

God has made a world in which there is evil; a world, I say, which could have been made without any evil, or the making of which could have been omitted altogether.

Therefore, God has not chosen the best.

Answer. I grant the minor of this prosyllogism; for it must be confessed that there is evil in this world which God has made, and that it was possible to make a world without evil, or even not to create a world at all, for its creation has depended on the free will of God; but I deny the major, that is, the first of the two premises of the prosyllogism, and I might content myself with simply demanding its proof; but in order to make the matter clearer, I have wished to justify this denial by showing that the best plan is not always that which seeks to avoid evil, since it may happen that *the evil is accompanied by a greater good.* For example, a general of an army will prefer a great victory with a slight wound to a condition without wound and without victory. We have proved this more fully in the large work by making it clear, by instances taken from mathematics and elsewhere, that an imperfection in the part may be required for a greater perfection in the whole. In this I have followed the opinion of St. Augustine, who has said a hundred times, that God has permitted evil in order to bring about good, that is, a greater good; and that of Thomas Aquinas (in libr. II. sent. dist. 32, qu. I, art. 1), that the permitting of evil tends to the good of the universe. I have shown that the ancients called Adam's fall *felix culpa,* a happy sin, because it had been retrieved with immense advantage by the incarnation of the Son of God, who has given to the universe something nobler than anything that ever would have been among creatures except for it. For the sake of a clearer understanding, I have added, following many good authors, that it was in accordance with order and the general good that God allowed to certain creatures the opportunity of exercising their liberty, even when he foresaw that they would turn to evil, but which he could so well rectify; because it was not fitting that, in order to hinder sin, God should always act in an extraordinary manner. To overthrow this objection, therefore, it is sufficient to show that a world with evil might be better than a world without evil; but I have gone even farther, in the work, and have even proved that this universe must be in reality better than every other possible universe.

II. *Objection.* If there is more evil than good in intelligent creatures, then there is more evil than good in the whole work of God.

Now, there is more evil than good in intelligent creatures.

Therefore, there is more evil than good in the whole work of God.

Answer. I deny the major and the minor of this conditional syllogism. As to the major, I do not admit it at all, because this pretended deduction from a part to the whole, from intelligent creatures to all creatures, supposes tacitly and without proof that creatures destitute of reason cannot enter into comparison nor into account with those which possess it. But why may it not be that the surplus of good in the non-intelligent creatures which fill the world, compensates for, and even incomparably surpasses, the surplus of evil in the rational creatures? It is true that the value of the latter is greater; but, in compensation, the others are beyond comparison the more numerous, and it may be that the proportion of number and quantity surpasses that of value and of quality.

As to the minor, that is no more to be admitted; that is, it is not at all to be admitted that there is more evil than good in the intelligent creatures. There is no need even of granting that there is more evil than good in the human race, because it is possible, and in fact very probable, that the glory and the perfection of the blessed are incomparably greater than the misery and the imperfection of the damned, and that here the excellence of the total good in the smaller number exceeds the total evil in the greater number. The blessed approach the Divinity, by means of a Divine Mediator, as near as may suit these creatures, and make such progress in good as is impossible for the damned to make in evil, approach as nearly as they may to the nature of demons. God is infinite, and the devil is limited; the good may and does go to infinity, while evil has its bounds. It is therefore possible, and is credible, that in the comparison of the blessed and the damned, the contrary of that which I have said might happen in the comparison of intelligent and non-intelligent creatures, takes place; namely, it is possible that in the comparison of the happy and the unhappy, the proportion of degree exceeds that of number, and that in the comparison of intelligent and non-intelligent creatures, the proportion of number is greater than that of value. I have the right to suppose that a thing is possible so long as its impossibility is not proved; and indeed that which I have here advanced is more than a supposition.

But in the second place, if I should admit that there is more evil than good in the human race, I have still good grounds for not admitting that there is more evil than good in all intelligent creatures. For there is an inconceivable number of genii, and perhaps of other rational creatures. And an opponent could not prove that in all the City of God, composed as well of genii as of rational animals without number and of an infinity of kinds, evil exceeds good. And although in order to answer an objection, there is no need of proving that a thing is, when its mere possibility suffices; yet, in this work, I have not omitted to show that it is a consequence of the supreme perfection of the Sovereign of the universe, that the kingdom of God is the most perfect of all possible states or governments, and that consequently the little evil there is, is required for the consummation of the immense good which is found there.

III. *Objection.* If it is always impossible not to sin, it is always unjust to punish.

Now, it is always impossible not to sin; or, in other words, every sin is necessary.

Therefore, it is always unjust to punish.

The minor of this is proved thus:

1. *Prosyllogism.* All that is predetermined is necessary.

Every event is predetermined.

Therefore, every event (and consequently sin also) is necessary.

Again this second minor is proved thus:

2. *Prosyllogism.* That which is future, that which is foreseen, that which is involved in the causes, is predetermined.

Every event is such.

Therefore, every event is predetermined.

Answer. I admit in a certain sense the conclusion of the second prosyllogism, which is the minor of the first; but I shall deny the major of the first prosyllogism, namely, that every thing predetermined is necessary; understanding by the *necessity* of sinning, for example, or by the impossibility of not sinning, or of not performing any action, the necessity with which we are here concerned, that is, that which is essential and absolute, and which destroys the morality of an action and the justice of punishments. For if anyone understood another necessity or impossibility, namely, a necessity which should be only moral, or which was only hypothetical (as will be explained shortly); it is clear that I should deny the major of the objection itself. I might content myself with this answer and demand the proof of the proposition denied; but I have again desired to explain my procedure in this work, in order to better elucidate the matter and to throw

more light on the whole subject, by explaining the necessity which ought to be rejected and the determination which must take place. That *necessity* which is contrary to morality and which ought to be rejected. and which would render punishment unjust, is an insurmountable necessity which would make all opposition useless, even if we should wish with all our heart to avoid the necessary action, and should make all possible efforts to that end. Now, it is manifest that this is not applicable to voluntary actions, because we would not perform them if we did not choose to. Also their prevision and predetermination are not absolute, but presuppose the will: if it is certain that we shall perform them, it is not less certain that we shall choose to perform them. These voluntary actions and their consequences will not take place no matter what we do or whether we wish them or not; but, *through* that which we shall do and through that which we shall wish to do, which leads to them. And this is involved in prevision and in predetermination, and even constitutes their ground. And the necessity of such an event is called conditional or hypothetical, or the necessity of consequence, because it supposes the will, and the other *requisites;* whereas the necessity which destroys morality and renders punishment unjust and reward useless, exists in things which will be whatever we may do or whatever we may wish to do, and, in a word, is in that which is essential; and this is what is called an absolute necessity. Thus it is to no purpose, as regards what is absolutely necessary, to make prohibitions or commands, to propose penalties or prizes, to praise or to blame; it will be none the less. On the other hand, in voluntary actions and in that which depends upon them, precepts armed with power to punish and to recompense are very often of use and are included in the order of causes which make an action exist. And it is for this reason that not only cares and labors but also prayers are useful; God having had these prayers in view before he regulated things and having had that consideration for them which was proper. This is why the precept which says *ora et labora* (pray and work), holds altogether good; and not only those who (under the vain pretext of the necessity of events) pretend that the care which business demands may be neglected, but also those who reason against prayer, fall into what the ancients even then called the *lazy sophism*. Thus the predetermination of events by causes is just what contributes to morality instead of destroying it, and causes incline the will, without compelling it. This is why the *determination* in question is not a necessitation—it is certain (to him who knows all) that the effect will follow this inclination; but this effect does not follow by a necessary consequence, that is, one the contrary of which implies contradiction. It is also by an internal inclination such as this that the will is determined, without there being any necessity. Suppose that one has the greatest passion in the world (a great thirst, for example), you will admit to me that the soul can find some reason for resisting it, if it were only that of showing its power. Thus, although one may never be in a perfect indifference of equilibrium and there may be always a preponderance of inclination for the side taken, it, nevertheless, never renders the resolution taken absolutely necessary.

IV. *Objection.* Whoever can prevent the sin of another and does not do so, but rather contributes to it although he is well informed of it, is accessory to it.

God can prevent the sin of intelligent creatures; but he does not do so, and rather contributes to it by his concurrence and by the opportunities which he brings about, although he has a perfect knowledge of it.

Hence, etc.

Answer. I deny the major of this syllogism. For it is possible that one could prevent sin, but ought not, because he could not do it without himself committing a sin, or (when God is in question) without performing an unreasonable action. Examples have been given and the application to God himself has been made. It is possible also that we contribute to evil and that sometimes we even open the road to it, in doing things which we are obliged to do; and, when we do our duty or (in speaking of God) when, after thorough consideration, we do that which reason demands, we are not responsible for the results, even when we foresee them. We do not desire these evils; but we are willing to permit them for the sake of a greater good which we cannot reasonably help preferring to other considerations.

And this is a *consequent* will, which results from *antecedent* wills by which we will the good. I know that some persons, in speaking of the antecedent and consequent will of God, have understood by the *antecedent* that which wills that all men should be saved; and by the *consequent*, that which wills, in consequence of persistent sin, that some should be damned. But these are merely illustrations of a more general idea, and it may be said for the same reason that God, by his antecedent will, wills that men should not sin; and by his consequent or final and decreeing will (that which is always followed by its effect), he wills to permit them to sin, this permission being the result of superior reasons. And we have the right to say in general that the antecedent will of God tends to the production of good and the prevention of evil, each taken in itself and as if alone (*particulariter et secundum quid*, Thom. I, qu. 19, art. 6), according to the measure of the degree of each good and each evil; but that the divine consequent or final or total will tends toward the production of as many goods as may be put together, the combination of which becomes in this way determined, and includes also the permission of some evils and the exclusion of some goods, as the best possible plan for the universe demands. Arminius, in his *Anti-perkinsus*, has very well explained that the will of God may be called consequent, not only in relation to the action of the creature considered beforehand in the divine understanding, but also in relation to other anterior divine acts of will. But this consideration of the passage cited from Thomas Aquinas, and that from Scotus (I. dist. 46, qu. XI), is enough to show that they make this distinction as I have done here. Nevertheless, if anyone objects to this use of terms let him substitute *deliberating* will, in place of antecedent, and *final* or decreeing will, in place of consequent. For I do not wish to dispute over words.

V. *Objection.* Whoever produces all that is real in a thing, is its cause.

God produces all that is real in sin.

Hence, God is the cause of sin.

Answer. I might content myself with denying the major or the minor, since the term *real* admits of interpretations which would render these propositions false. But in order to explain more clearly, I will make a distinction. *Real* signifies either that which is positive only, or, it includes also privative beings: in the first case, I deny the major and admit the minor; in the second case, I do the contrary. I might have limited myself to this, but I have chosen to proceed still farther and give the reason for this distinction. I have been very glad therefore to draw attention to the fact that every reality purely positive or absolute is a perfection; and that imperfection comes from limitation, that is, from the privative: for to limit is to refuse progress, or the greatest possible progress. Now God is the cause of all perfections and consequently of all realities considered as purely positive. But limitations or privations result from the original imperfection of creatures, which limits their receptivity. And it is with them as with a loaded vessel, which the river causes to move more or less slowly according to the weight which it carries: thus its speed depends upon the river, but the retardation which limits this speed comes from the load. Thus in the *Theodicy*, we have shown how the creature, in causing sin, is a defective cause; how errors and evil inclinations are born of privation; and how privation is accidentally efficient; and I have justified the opinion of St. Augustine (lib. I, ad Simpl. qu. 2) who explains, for example, how God makes the soul obdurate, not by giving it something evil, but because the effect of his good impression is limited by the soul's resistance and by the circumstances which contribute to this resistance, so that he does not give it all the good which would overcome its evil. *Nec* (inquit) *ab illo erogatur aliquid quo homo fit deterior, sed tantum quo fit melior non erogatur.* But if God had wished to do more, he would have had to make either other natures for creatures or other miracles to change their natures, things which the best plan could not admit. It is as if the current of the river must be more rapid than its fall admitted or that the boats should be loaded more lightly, if it were necessary to make them move more quickly. And the original limitation or imperfection of creatures requires that even the best plan of the universe could not receive more good, and could not be exempt from certain evils, which, however, are to result in a greater good. There are certain disorders in the parts which marvelously enhance the beauty

of the whole; just as certain dissonances, when properly used, render harmony more beautiful. But this depends on what has already been said in answer to the first objection.

VI. *Objection.* Whoever punishes those who have done as well as it was in their power to do, is unjust.

God does so.

Hence, etc.

Answer. I deny the minor of this argument. And I believe that God always gives sufficient aid and grace to those who have a good will, that is, to those who do not reject this grace by new sin. Thus, I do not admit the damnation of infants who have died without baptism or outside of the church; nor the damnation of adults who have acted according to the light which God has given them. And I believe that if *any one has followed the light which has been given him*, he will undoubtedly receive greater light when he has need of it, as the late M. Hulseman, a profound and celebrated theologian at Leipzig, has somewhere remarked; and if such a man has failed to receive it during his lifetime he will at least receive it when at the point of death.

VII. *Objection.* Whoever gives only to some, and not to all, the means which produces in them effectively a good will and salutary final faith, has not sufficient goodness.

God does this.

Hence, etc.

Answer. I deny the major of this. It is true that God could overcome the greatest resistance of the human heart; and does it, too, sometimes, either by internal grace, or by external circumstances which have a great effect on souls; but he does not always do this. Whence comes this distinction? it may be asked, and why does his goodness seem limited? It is because, as I have already said in answering the first objection, it would not have been in order always to act in an extraordinary manner, and to reverse the connection of things. The reasons of this connection, by means of which one is placed in more favorable circumstances than another, are hidden in the depths of the wisdom of God; they depend upon the universal harmony. The best plan of the universe, which God could not fail to choose, made it so. We judge from the event itself; since

God has made it, it was not possible to do better. Far from being true that this conduct is contrary to goodness, it is supreme goodness which led him to it. This objection with its solution might have been drawn from what was said in regard to the first objection; but it seemed useful to touch upon it separately.

VIII. *Objection.* Whoever cannot fail to choose the best, is not free.

God cannot fail to choose the best.

Hence, God is not free.

Answer. I deny the major of this argument; it is rather true liberty, and the most perfect, to be able to use one's free will for the best, and to always exercise this power, without ever being turned aside either by external force or by internal passions, the first of which causes slavery of the body, the second, slavery of the soul. There is nothing less servile, and nothing more in accordance with the highest degree of freedom, than to be always led toward the good, and always by one's own inclination, without any constraint and without any displeasure. And to object therefore that God had need of external things, is only a sophism. He created them freely; but having proposed to himself an end, which is to exercise his goodness, wisdom has determined him to choose the means best fitted to attain this end. To call this a need, is to take that term in an unusual sense which frees it from all imperfection, just as when we speak of the wrath of God.

Seneca has somewhere said that God commanded but once but that he obeys always, because he obeys laws which he willed to prescribe to himself: *semel jussit, semper paret.* But he might better have said that God always commands and that he is always obeyed; for in willing, he always follows the inclination of his own nature, and all other things always follow his will. And as this will is always the same, it cannot be said that he obeys only that will which he formerly had. Nevertheless, although his will is always infallible and always tends toward the best, the evil, or the lesser good, which he rejects, does not cease to be possible in itself; otherwise the necessity of the good would be geometrical (so to speak), or metaphysical, and altogether absolute; the contingency of things would be destroyed, and there would be no choice. But this sort of necessity, which does not destroy the possibility of the contrary, has this name only by analogy; it becomes effective, not by the pure essence of things, but by that which is outside of them, above them, namely, by the will of God. This necessity is called moral, because, to the sage, *necessity* and *what ought to be* are equivalent things; and when it always has its effect, as it really has in the perfect sage, that is, in God, it may be said that it is a happy necessity. The nearer creatures approach to it, the nearer they approach to perfect happiness. Also this kind of necessity is not that which we try to avoid and which destroys morality, rewards and praise. For that which it brings, does not happen whatever we may do or will, but because we will it so. And a will to which it is natural to choose well, merits praise so much the more; also it carries its reward with it, which is sovereign happiness. And as this constitution of the divine nature gives entire satisfaction to him who possesses it, it is also the best and the most desirable for the creatures who are all dependent on God. If the will of God did not have for a rule the principle of the best, it would either tend toward evil, which would be the worst; or it would be in some way indifferent to good and to evil, and would be guided by chance: but a will which would allow itself always to act by chance, would not be worth more for the government of the universe than the fortuitous concourse of atoms, without there being any divinity therein. And even if God should abandon himself to chance only in some cases and in a certain way (as he would do, if he did not always work entirely for the best and if he were capable of preferring a lesser work to a greater, that is, an evil to a good, since that which prevents a greater good is an evil), he would be imperfect, as well as the object of his choice; he would not merit entire confidence; he would act without reason in such a case, and the government of the universe would be like certain games, equally divided between reason and chance. All this proves that this objection which is made against the choice of the best, perverts the notions of the free and of the necessary, and represents to us the best even as evil: which is either malicious or ridiculous.

III.3   Evil and Soul-Making

JOHN HICK

*John Hick (1922–   ) was for many years profes-
sor of theology at the University of Birmingham in
England and, until his recent retirement, was professor of philosophy at Claremont Graduate School.
His book* Evil and the God of Love *(1966), from
which the following selection is taken, is considered one of the most thorough treatises on the
problem of evil. "Evil and Soul-Making" is an example of a theodicy argument that is based on the
free will defense. Theodicies can be of two differing
types depending on how they justify the ways of
God in the face of evil. The Augustinian position is
that God created humans without sin and set them
in a sinless, paradisical world. However, humanity
fell into sin through misuse of its free will. God's
grace will save some of us, but others will perish
everlastingly. The second type of theodicy stems
from the thinking of Irenaeus (120–202), of the
Greek Church. The Irenaean tradition views Adam
not as a free agent rebelling against God but as a
child. The fall is humanity's first faulty step in the
direction of freedom. God is still working with
humanity in order to bring it from undeveloped life
(bios) to a state of self-realization in divine love,
spiritual life (zoe). This life is viewed as the "vale of
soul-making." Hick favors this version and develops it in this reading.*

Fortunately there is another and better way. As well
as the "majority report" of the Augustinian tradition,
which has dominated Western Christendom, both
Catholic and Protestant, since the time of Augustine
himself, there is the "minority report" of the
Irenaean tradition. This latter is both older and
newer than the other, for it goes back to Sr. Irenaeus
and others of the early Hellenistic Fathers of the

Pp. 253–261 from *Evil and the God of Love,* revised edition, by
John Hick. Copyright © 1966, 1977 by John Hick. Reprinted by
permission of Harper & Row, Publishers, Inc. Footnotes edited.

Church in the two centuries prior to St. Augustine,
and it has flourished again in more developed forms
during the last hundred years.

Instead of regarding man as having been created
by God in a finished state, as a finitely perfect being
fulfilling the divine intention for our human level of
existence, and then falling disastrously away from
this, the minority report sees man as still in process
of creation. Irenaeus himself expressed the point in
terms of the (exegetically dubious) distinction between the "image" and the "likeness" of God referred to in Genesis i.26: "Then God said, Let us
make man in our image, after our likeness." His
view was that man as a personal and moral being
already exists in the image, but has not yet been
formed into the finite likeness of God. By this "likeness" Irenaeus means something more than personal existence as such; he means a certain valuable quality of personal life which reflects finitely
the divine life. This represents the perfecting of man,
the fulfillment of God's purpose for humanity, the
"bringing of many sons to glory," the creating of
"children of God" who are "fellow heirs with
Christ" of his glory.

And so man, created as a personal being in the
image of God, is only the raw material for a further
and more difficult stage of God's creative work. This
is the leading of men as relatively free and autonomous persons, through their own dealings with life
in the world in which He has placed them, towards
that quality of personal existence that is the finite
likeness of God. The features of this likeness are
revealed in the person of Christ, and the process of
man's creation into it is the work of the Holy Spirit.
In St. Paul's words, "And we all, with unveiled
faces, beholding the glory of the Lord, are being
changed into his likeness (εἰκών) from one degree
of glory to another; for this comes from the Lord
who is the Spirit";[1] or again, "For God knew his own
before ever they were, and also ordained that they
should be shaped to the likeness (εἰκών) of his

Son."[2] In Johannine terms, the movement from the image to the likeness is a transition from one level of existence, that of animal life (*Bios*), to another and higher level, that of eternal life (*Zoe*), which includes but transcends the first. And the fall of man was seen by Irenaeus as a failure within the second phase of this creative process, a failure that has multiplied the perils and complicated the route of the journey in which God is seeking to lead mankind.

In the light of modern anthropological knowledge some form of two-stage conception of the creation of man has become an almost unavoidable Christian tenet. At the very least we must acknowledge as two distinguishable stages the fashioning of *homo sapiens* as a product of the long evolutionary process, and his sudden or gradual spiritualization as a child of God. But we may well extend the first stage to include the development of man as a rational and responsible person capable of personal relationship with the personal Infinite who has created him. This first stage of the creative process was, to our anthropomorphic imaginations, easy for divine omnipotence. By an exercise of creative power God caused the physical universe to exist, and in the course of countless ages to bring forth within it organic life, and finally to produce out of organic life personal life; and when man had thus emerged out of the evolution of the forms of organic life, a creature had been made who has the possibility of existing in conscious fellowship with God. But the second stage of the creative process is of a different kind altogether. It cannot be performed by omnipotent power as such. For personal life is essentially free and self-directing. It cannot be perfected by divine fiat, but only through the uncompelled responses and willing co-operation of human individuals in their actions and reactions in the world in which God has placed them. Men may eventually become the perfected persons whom the New Testament calls "children of God," but they cannot be created ready-made as this.

The value-judgement that is implicitly being invoked here is that one who has attained to goodness by meeting and eventually mastering temptations, and thus by rightly making responsible choices in concrete situations, is good in a richer and more valuable sense than would be one created *ab initio* in a state either of innocence or of virtue. In the former case, which is that of the actual moral achievements of mankind, the individual's goodness has within it the strength of temptation overcome, a stability based upon an accumulation of right choices, and a positive and responsible character that comes from the investment of costly personal effort. I suggest, then, that it is an ethically reasonable judgment, even though in the nature of the case not one that is capable of demonstrative proof, that human goodness slowly built up through personal histories of moral effort has a value in the eyes of the Creator which justifies even the long travail of the soul-making process.

The picture with which we are working is thus developmental and teleological. Man is in process of becoming the perfected being whom God is seeking to create. However, this is not taking place—it is important to add—by a natural and inevitable evolution, but through a hazardous adventure in individual freedom. Because this is a pilgrimage within the life of each individual, rather than a racial evolution, the progressive fulfillment of God's purpose does not entail any corresponding progressive improvement in the moral state of the world. There is no doubt a development in man's ethical situation from generation to generation through the building of individual choices into public institutions, but this involves an accumulation of evil as well as of good. It is thus probable that human life was lived on much the same moral plane two thousand years ago or four thousand years ago as it is today. But nevertheless during this period uncounted millions of souls have been through the experience of earthly life, and God's purpose has gradually moved towards its fulfillment within each one of them, rather than within a human aggregate composed of different units in different generations.

If, then, God's aim in making the world is "the bringing of many sons to glory," that aim will naturally determine the kind of world that He has created. Antitheistic writers almost invariably assume a conception of the divine purpose which is contrary to the Christian conception. They assume that the purpose of a loving God must be to create a hedonistic paradise; and therefore to the extent that the world is other than this, it proves to them that God is either not loving enough or not powerful enough to create such a world. They think of God's relation to the earth on the model of a human being building a cage for a pet animal to dwell in. If he is humane he will naturally make his pet's quarters as pleasant and healthful as he can. Any respect in which the cage falls short of the veterinarian's ideal, and contains possibilities of accident or disease, is evidence of either limited benevolence or limited means, or both. Those who use the problem of evil as an argument against belief in God almost invariably think of the world in this kind of way. David Hume, for example, speaks of an architect who is trying to plan a house that is to be as comfortable and convenient as possible. If we find that "the windows, doors, fires, passages, stairs, and the whole economy of the building were the source of noise, confusion, fatigue, darkness, and the extremes of heat and cold" we should have no hesitation in blaming the architect. It would be in vain for him to prove that if this or that defect were corrected greater ills would result: "still you would assert in general, that, if the architect had had skill and good intentions, he might have formed such a plan of the whole, and might have adjusted the parts in such a manner, as would have remedied all or most of these inconveniences.[3]

But if we are right in supposing that God's purpose for man is to lead him from human *Bios,* or the biological life of man, to that quality of *Zoe,* or the personal life of eternal worth, which we see in Christ, then the question that we have to ask is not, Is this the kind of world that an all-powerful and infinitely loving being would create as an environment for his human pets? or, Is the architecture of the world the most pleasant and convenient possible? The question that we have to ask is rather, Is this the kind of world that God might make as an environment in which moral beings may be fashioned, through their own free insights and responses, into "children of God"?

Such critics as Hume are confusing what heaven ought to be, as an environment for perfected finite beings, with what this world ought to be, as an environment for beings who are in process of be-

coming perfected. For if our general conception of God's purpose is correct the world is not intended to be a paradise, but rather the scene of a history in which human personality may be formed towards the pattern of Christ. Men are not to be thought of on the analogy of animal pets, whose life is to be made as agreeable as possible, but rather on the analogy of human children, who are to grow to adulthood in an environment whose primary and overriding purpose is not immediate pleasure but the realizing of the most valuable potentialities of human personality.

Needless to say, this characterization of God as the heavenly Father is not a merely random illustration but an analogy that lies at the heart of the Christian faith. Jesus treated the likeness between the attitude of God to man, and the attitude of human parents at their best towards their children, as providing the most adequate way for us to think about God. And so it is altogether relevant to a Christian understanding of this world to ask, How does the best parental love express itself in its influence upon the environment in which children are to grow up? I think it is clear that a parent who loves his children, and wants them to become the best human beings that they are capable of becoming, does not treat pleasure as the sole and supreme value. Certainly we seek pleasure for our children, and take great delight in obtaining it for them; but we do not desire for them unalloyed pleasure at the expense of their growth in such even greater values as moral integrity, unselfishness, compassion, courage, humour, reverence for the truth, and perhaps above all the capacity for love. We do not act on the premise that pleasure is the supreme end of life; and if the development of these other values sometimes clashes with the provision of pleasure, then we are willing to have our children miss a certain amount of this, rather than fail to come to possess and to be possessed by the finer and more precious qualities that are possible to the human personality. A child brought up on the principle that the only or the supreme value is pleasure would not be likely to become an ethically mature adult or an attractive or happy personality. And to most parents it seems more importantly to try to foster quality and strength of character in their children than to fill their lives at all times with the utmost possible degree of pleasure. If, then, there is any true analogy between God's purpose for his human creatures, and the purpose of loving and wise parents for their children, we have to recognize that the presence of pleasure and the absence of pain cannot be the supreme and overriding end for which the world exists. Rather, this world must be a place of soul-making. And its value is to be judged, not primarily by the quantity of pleasure and pain occurring in it at any particular moment, but by its fitness for its primary purpose, the purpose of soul-making.

In all this we have been speaking about the nature of the world considered simply as the God-given environment of man's life. For it is mainly in this connection that the world has been regarded in Irenaean and in Protestant thought. But such a way of thinking involves a danger of anthropocentrism from which the Augustinian and Catholic tradition has generally been protected by its sense of the relative insignificance of man within the totality of the created universe. Man was dwarfed within the medieval worldview by the innumerable hosts of angels and archangels above him—unfallen rational natures which rejoice in the immediate presence of God, reflecting His glory in the untarnished mirror of their worship. However, this higher creation has in our modern world lost its hold upon the imagination. Its place has been taken, as the minimizer of men, by the immensities of outer space and by the material universe's unlimited complexity transcending our present knowledge. As the spiritual environment envisaged by Western man has shrunk, his physical horizons have correspondingly expanded. Where the human creature was formerly seen as an insignificant appendage to the angelic world, he is now seen as an equally insignificant organic excrescence, enjoying a fleeting moment of consciousness on the surface of one of the planets of a minor star. Thus the truth that was symbolized for former ages by the existence of the angelic hosts is today impressed upon us by the vastness of the physical universe, countering the egoism of our species by making us feel that this immense prodigality of existence can hardly all exist for the sake of man—though, on the other hand, the very realization that it is not all for the sake of man may itself be salutary and beneficial to man!

However, instead of opposing man and nature as rival objects of God's interest, we should perhaps rather stress man's solidarity as an embodied being with the whole natural order in which he is embedded. For man is organic to the world; all his acts and thoughts and imaginations are conditioned by space and time; and in abstraction from nature he would cease to be human. We may, then, say that the beauties and sublimities and powers, the microscopic intricacies and macroscopic vastnesses, the wonders and the terrors of the natural world and of the life that pulses through it, are willed and valued by their Maker in a creative act that embraces man together with nature. By means of matter and living flesh God both builds a path and weaves a veil between Himself and the creature made in His image. Nature thus has permanent significance; for God has set man in a creaturely environment, and the final fulfilment of our nature in relation to God will accordingly take the form of an embodied life within "a new heaven and a new earth." And as in the present age man moves slowly towards that fulfillment through the pilgrimage of his earthly life, so also "the whole creation" is "groaning in travail," waiting for the time when it will be "set free from its bondage to decay."

And yet however fully we thus acknowledge the permanent significance and value of the natural order, we must still insist upon man's special character as a personal creature made in the image of God; and our theodicy must still centre upon the soul-making process that we believe to be taking place within human life.

This, then, is the starting-point from which we propose to try to relate the realities of sin and suffering to the perfect love of an omnipotent Creator. And as will become increasingly apparent, a theodicy that starts in this way must be eschatological in its ultimate bearings. That is to say, instead of looking to the past for its clue to the mystery of evil, it looks to the future, and indeed to that ultimate future to which only faith can look. Given the conception of a divine intention working in and through human time towards a fulfilment that lies in its completeness beyond human time, our theodicy must find the meaning of evil in the part that it is made to play in the eventual outworking of that purpose; and must find the justification of the whole process in the magnitude of the good to which it leads. The good that outshines all ill is not a paradise long since lost but a kingdom which is yet to come in its full glory and permanence.

Notes

1. II Corinthians iii. 18.
2. Romans viii. 29. Other New Testament passages expressing a view of man as undergoing a process of spiritual growth within God's purpose are: Ephesians ii. 21, iii. 16; Colossians ii. 19; I John iii. 2; II Corinthians iv. 16.
3. *Dialogues Concerning Natural Religion*, pt. xi. Kemp-Smith's ed. (Oxford: Clarendon Press, 1935), p. 251.

III.4   A Critique of Hick's Theodicy

EDWARD H. MADDEN and PETER H. HARE

Edward H. Madden (1925–   ) and Peter H. Hare (1935–   ) teach philosophy at the State University of New York at Buffalo. In this selection, they attack Hick's theory. They ask whether the amount of evil in the world is necessary for soul-making and accuse Hick of three fallacies, called "all or nothing," "it could be worse," and "slippery slope."

The intellectual honesty of John Hick is impressive. Unlike the majority of Christian apologists he does not try to find safety in the number of solutions but instead searchingly criticizes and disowns many of the favorite solutions. He concludes, nevertheless, the apologetics reduced to fighting trim is all the more effective. He believes that a sophisticated combination of the character-building and free-will solutions will serve. They show evil to serve God's purpose of "soul-making."

Earlier we pointed out the difficulties involved in the usual formulations of the character-building and free-will solutions. We shall consider here how successful Hick is in avoiding these difficulties.

Reprinted from Edward H. Madden and Peter H. Hare, *Evil and the Concept of God* (1968), 83–90, 102–103. Courtesy of Charles C. Thomas, Publisher, Springfield, Illinois. Footnotes deleted.

According to Hick,

man, created as a personal being in the image of God, is only the raw material for a further and more difficult stage of God's creative work. This is the leading of men as relatively free and autonomous persons through their own dealings with life in the world in which he has placed them, towards that quality of personal existence that is the finite likeness of God.

The basic trouble, he says, with antitheistic writers is that "they assume that the purpose of a loving God must be to create a hedonistic paradise." He concedes that evil is not serving any, even remote, hedonistic end, but insists that it is serving the end of the development of moral personalities in loving relation to God. It is logically impossible to do this either by the forcing them to love him or by forcing them always to act rightly. A creature *forced* to love would not be genuinely loving and a creature *forced* to do the right would not be a moral personality. Only through freedom, suffering, and initial remoteness from God ("epistemic distance") can the sort of person God is looking for come about.

Before we discuss in detail the difficulties involved in Hick's position we will briefly describe three informal fallacies Hick adroitly uses in his solution. They are all fallacies which have been used in one form or another throughout the history of Christian apologetics, and we have had occasion to mention them in our discussion of other writers in the previous chapter. However, it will be convenient in discussing Hick's skillful and elaborate use of them to describe and label clearly these arguments: "All or nothing," "It could be worse," and "slippery slope."

All or nothing. This is the claim that something is desirable because its complete loss would be far worse than the evil its presence now causes. The erroneous assumption is that we must have this thing either in its present form and amount or not at all. But it is often the case that only *some* amount of the thing in *some* form is necessary to the achievement of a desirable end.

It could be worse. This is the claim that something is not really bad because it will be followed by all manner of desirable things. The erroneous assumption here is that showing that having these later desirable things is a great boon also shows that the original evil is a necessary and not gratuitous one. Actually it only shows that the situation would be still worse if the desirable things did not follow. To show that it could be worse does not show that it could not be better.

Slippery slope. This is the claim that if God once started eliminating evils of this world he would have no place to stop short of a "perfect" world in which only robots and not men were possible. The erroneous assumption is that God would have no criterion to indicate where on the slippery slope to stop and no ability to implement it effectively. The same argument is used in human affairs and the answer is equally clear. "Once we venture, as we sometimes must, on a dangerous course which may lead to our salvation in a particular situation but which may also be the beginning of our path to perdition, the only answer we can give to the question 'Where will you stop?' is 'Wherever our intelligence tells us to stop!'"

Hick's use of the free-will solution is an example of the "all or nothing" fallacy. He concedes that there is an appalling amount of moral evil in the world but insists that it would be logically impossible for God to achieve his purpose of soul-making

by creating puppets who always acted rightly. This is a position we have criticized elsewhere and we must show here how the same criticism applies to Hick.

Hick says that the difficulty with criticisms of the free-will solution has been that they suppose God would have done better to create man as a "pet animal" in a cage, "as pleasant and healthful" as possible. Undeniably critics of the free-will solution have often made this mistake, but it is a mistake easily avoided. We are prepared to grant that a better world would not have been created by making men as pet animals. However, the damaging question is whether God had only two alternatives: to create men with the unfortunate moral inclinations they have at present or to create men as pet animals. There are clearly other alternatives. There are, after all, many different ways for a parent to guide his child's moral growth while respecting his freedom.

Perhaps an analogy will be helpful. God, as Hick views him, might be described as headmaster to a vast progressive school where the absolute freedom of the students is sacred. He does not want to force any children to read textbooks because, he feels, that will only produce students who are more motivated by fear of punishment than by love of knowledge for its own sake. Every student must be left to educate himself as much as possible. However, it is quite unconvincing to argue that because rigid regulation has horrible consequences, almost no regulation is ideal—there are dangers in either extreme. And it is just as much of a mistake to argue that because the possibility of God's creation of men as pet animals is ghastly to contemplate. God's creation of men with the sort of freedom they have now is the best possible choice.

One of Hick's more unfortunate uses of the "all or nothing" argument appears in his justification of man's "initial epistemic distance" from God. He suggests that God has deliberately refrained from giving much knowledge of himself to men for fear that it would jeopardize the development of "authentic fiduciary attitudes" in men. God is fearful (in our analogy) that "spoon-feeding" his creatures will prevent them from developing genuine intellectual curiosity. Because he thinks that constant and thorough spoon-feeding will ruin their intellects, he advocates contact between schoolboy and teacher only once a year.

But we are being too kind in our analogy. God does not even think it wise to deliver a matriculation address to each student. Almost all students must be content with meager historical records of a matriculation address in the distant past and a hope of a commencement speech in the future. It is no wonder there have been student riots. The countless generations before Christ were especially destitute of faculty-student contact. And even now the vast amount of humanity in non-Christian parts of the world find it difficult to be admitted to the soul-making school at all.

Sometimes Hick feels the weakness of the "all or nothing" argument and accordingly shifts to the "it could be worse" strategy. "Christian theodicy must point forward to that final blessedness, and claim that this infinite future good will render worth while all the pain and travail and wickedness that has occurred on the way to it." To be sure, we should be grateful to God for not tormenting us for an eternity, but the question remains of why he is torturing us at all. However, this strategy is beside the point. Hick must still show us how all the suffering in this world is the most efficient way of achieving God's goal. Merely to assure the student who is threatening riot that in his old age he will somehow come to regard the indignities of his student days as rather unimportant is not to explain why those indignities must be visited upon him at all.

Although Hick does not himself feel confident that in the Kingdom of God all men will completely forget their earthly sufferings, he suggests that, if such a loss of memory were to occur, it would help solve the problem of evil. However, we can concede complete heavenly amnesia and this concession does not move us any closer to a solution. If a man were to torture his wife, and afterwards somehow to remove completely the memory of the torture from her mind so that she returned to her earlier love of him, this would certainly be better than retaining the painful memory, but it still would not explain the necessity of torturing her in the first place.

Hick, however, candidly admits to a feeling that neither of the two strategies discussed above is completely effective in the last analysis and realizes that he must face "excessive or dysteleologically suffering." Consequently he moves on to the "slippery slope" argument.

> Unless God eliminated all evils whatsoever there would always be relatively outstanding ones of which it would be said that He should have secretly prevented them. If, for example, divine providence had eliminated Hitler in his infancy, we might now point instead to Mussolini. . . . There would be nowhere to stop, short of divinely arranged paradise in which human freedom would be narrowly circumscribed.

He claims, in other words, that there would be no way of eliminating some evils without removing all of them with the effect of returning us to the "all or nothing" situation.

This argument fails because the erroneous assumption is made that in the process of removing evils God would not be able precisely to calculate the effect of each removal and stop at exactly the point at which soul-making was most efficiently achieved. Presumably at that point men would still suffer and complain about their suffering, but it would be possible to offer them an explanation of the necessity of this amount of suffering as a means to the end of soul-making. In the analogy we used earlier, no matter how much is done to increase faculty-student contact there will still be some student complaints, but presumably it is possible to reach a point at which such students can be shown how the present amount of faculty-student contact is precisely the right amount to maximize creative intellectual activity.

Hick even comes to admit that this third strategy is no more effective than the first two. He appears to be like a man flourishing toy weapons before an assailant, knowing that in the last analysis they cannot be effective, but hoping that the assailant will be scared off before he comes close enough to see that they are not genuine weapons. In the last analysis he must appeal to mystery. "I do not now have an alternative theory to offer that would explain in any rational or ethical way why men suffer as they do. The only appeal left is to mystery."

Hick's use of mystery is not the usual appeal to mystical experience or commitment so often made by theists. He suggests that mystery, too, contributes to soul-making. Here again he uses the "all or nothing" argument and asks us to imagine a world which contained no unjust, excessive, or apparently unnecessary misery, a world in which suffering could always be seen to be either punishment justly deserved or a part of moral training.

In such a world human misery would not evoke deep personal sympathy or call forth organized relief and sacrificial help or service. For it is presupposed in these compassionate reactions both that the suffering is not deserved and that it is *bad* for the sufferer.

There are at least three ways of criticizing this strategy:

(a) It is quite possible to feel intense compassion for someone even though his suffering is understood to be an unavoidable means to an end, desirable both to the sufferer and to oneself. A husband may feel convinced that his wife's labor pains are a necessary means to a highly desirable end and at the same time feel great compassion. One can even feel compassion for the pain suffered by a criminal being punished in a way that one thinks is deserved.

(b) Even if some undeserved and unnecessary suffering is necessary to make possible compassion, it is obvious that a minute percentage of the present unnecessary suffering would do the job adequately.

(c) One must remember that while unjust suffering may increase compassion, it also creates massive resentment. This resentment often causes individuals indiscriminately to lash out at the world. The benefits of compassion are probably more than offset by the damage done by resentment.

However, Hick thinks that there is still one last justification for unjust suffering. He asks us to consider what would happen if all unjust suffering were eliminated. In such a world reward would be the predictable result of virtue and punishment the predictable outcome of wickedness. But in such a world doing right simply for its own sake—what Kant called the good will—would be impossible "for whilst the possibility of the good will by no means precludes that right action shall in fact eventually lead to happiness, and wrong action to misery, it does preclude this happening so certainly, instantly, and manifestly that virtue cannot be separate in experience and thought from its reward, or vice from its punishment."

This solution, itself a sign that the end is near at hand, can be rejected with confidence for the following reasons.

(a) This effort to solve the problem of evil does not do justice to the good sense God presumably would have were he to exist. God would certainly have sense enough to administer rewards and punishments in view of *motives* and not simply in view of what an agent *does*. It would already be an unjust response if God rewarded an agent for doing what is objectively right on prudential grounds alone.

(b) This effort misfires psychologically as well as theologically. If God usually rewarded men when they sincerely performed an act solely because it was right, this could only have a beneficial effect on human morality. If a parent regularly rewards the child who performs a good act only because he thinks it right more than he rewards a child performing the same act only to curry favor with the parent, this can only tend to reinforce the tendency to act virtuously.

(c) Even if completely regular rewarding of right-behavior would tend to undermine the good will, there is still every reason to believe that an enormous amount of the present unjust punishment could be eliminated without jeopardizing the possibility of acting from a sense of duty. The "all-or-nothing" fallacy is omnipresent in theistic arguments and its presence here at the end, after it had been supposedly rejected, comes as no surprise.

III.5   Evil and Omnipotence

J. L. MACKIE

John L. Mackie (1917–1981) was born in Australia and taught at Oxford University until his death. He made important contributions to the fields of metaphysics, epistemology, ethics, and philosophy of religion. Among his works are The Cement of the Universe *(1974),* Ethics: Inventing Right and Wrong *(1977), and* The Miracle of Theism *(1982). In this essay, Mackie argues that the argument from evil demonstrates the incoherence of theism. If there is a God who is all-powerful and completely good, he will be able and willing to eliminate all evil in the world. But there is evil, so no God exists.*

The traditional arguments for the existence of God have been fairly thoroughly criticised by philosophers. But the theologian can, if he wishes, accept this criticism. He can admit that no rational proof of God's existence is possible. And he can still retain all that is essential to his position, by holding that God's existence is known in some other, non-rational way. I think, however, that a more telling criticism can be made by way of the traditional problem of evil. Here it can be shown, not that religious beliefs lack rational support, but that they are positively irrational, that the several parts of the essential theological doctrine are inconsistent with one another, so that the theologian can maintain his position as a whole only by a much more extreme rejection of reason than in the former case. He must now be prepared to believe, not merely what cannot be proved, but what can be *disproved* from other beliefs that he also holds.

The problem of evil, in the sense in which I shall be using the phrase, is a problem only for someone who believes that there is a God who is both omnipotent and wholly good. And it is a logical problem, the problem of clarifying and reconciling a number of beliefs: it is not a scientific problem that might be solved by further observations, or a practical problem that might be solved by a decision or an action. These points are obvious; I mention them only because they are sometimes ignored by theologians, who sometimes parry a statement of the problem with such remarks as "Well, can you solve the problem yourself?" or "This is a mystery which may be revealed to us later" or "Evil is something to be faced and overcome, not to be merely discussed."

In its simplest form the problem is this: God is omnipotent; God is wholly good; and yet evil exists. There seems to be some contradiction between these three propositions, so that if any two of them were true the third would be false. But at the same time all three are essential parts of most theological positions: the theologian, it seems, at once *must* adhere and *cannot consistently* adhere to all three. (The problem does not arise only for theists, but I shall discuss it in the form in which it presents itself for ordinary theism.)

However, the contradiction does not arise immediately; to show it we need some additional premises, or perhaps some quasi-logical rules connecting the terms 'good,' 'evil,' and 'omnipotent.' These additional principles are that good is opposed to evil, in such a way that a good thing always eliminates evil as far as it can, and that there are no limits to what an omnipotent thing can do. From these it follows that a good omnipotent thing eliminates evil completely, and then the propositions that a good omnipotent thing exists, and that evil exists, are incompatible.

A. Adequate Solutions

Now once the problem is fully stated it is clear that it can be solved, in the sense that the problem will not arise if one gives up at least one of the proposi-

From *Mind*, Vol. LXIV, No. 254 (1955). Reprinted by permission of Oxford University Press.

tions that constitute it. If you are prepared to say that God is not wholly good, or not quite omnipotent, or that evil does not exist, or that good is not opposed to the kind of evil that exists, or that there are limits to what an omnipotent thing can do, then the problem of evil will not arise for you.

There are, then, quite a number of adequate solutions of the problem of evil, and some of these have been adopted, or almost adopted, by various thinkers. For example, a few have been prepared to deny God's omnipotence, and rather more have been prepared to keep the term 'omnipotence' but severely to restrict its meaning, recording quite a number of things that an omnipotent being cannot do. Some have said that evil is an illusion, perhaps because they held that the whole world of temporal, changing things is an illusion, and that what we call evil belongs only to this world, or perhaps because they held that although temporal things *are* much as we see them, those that we call evil are not really evil. Some have said that what we call evil is merely the privation of good, that evil in a positive sense, evil that would really be opposed to good, does not exist. Many have agreed with Pope that disorder is harmony not understood, and that partial evil is universal good. Whether any of these views is *true* is, of course, another question. But each of them gives an adequate solution of the problem of evil in the sense that if you accept it this problem does not arise for you, though you may, of course, have *other* problems to face.

But often enough these adequate solutions are only *almost* adopted. The thinkers who restrict God's power, but keep the term 'omnipotence,' may reasonably be suspected of thinking, in other contexts, that his power is really unlimited. Those who say that evil is an illusion may also be thinking, inconsistently, that this illusion is itself an evil. Those who say that "evil" is merely privation of good may also be thinking, inconsistently, that privation of good is an evil. (The fallacy here is akin to some forms of the "naturalistic fallacy" in ethics, where some think, for example, that "good" is just what contributes to evolutionary progress, and that evolutionary progress is itself good.) If Pope meant what he said in the first line of his couplet, that "disorder" is only harmony not understood, the

"partial evil" of the second line must, for consistency, mean "that which, taken in isolation, falsely appears to be evil," but it would more naturally mean "that which, in isolation, really is evil." The second line, in fact, hesitates between two views, that "partial evil" isn't really evil, since only the universal quality is real, and that "partial evil" is really an evil, but only a little one.

In addition, therefore, to adequate solutions, we must recognise unsatisfactorily inconsistent solutions, in which there is only a half-hearted or temporary rejection of one of the propositions which together constitute the problem. In these, one of the constituent propositions is explicitly rejected, but it is covertly re-asserted or assumed elsewhere in the system.

B. Fallacious Solutions

Besides these half-hearted solutions, which explicitly reject but implicitly assert one of the constituent propositions, there are definitely fallacious solutions which explicitly maintain all the constituent propositions, but implicitly reject at least one of them in the course of the argument that explains away the problem of evil.

There are, in fact, many so-called solutions which purport to remove the contradiction without abandoning any of its constituent propositions. These must be fallacious as we can see from the very statement of the problem, but it is not so easy to see in each case precisely where the fallacy lies. I suggest that in all cases the fallacy has the general form suggested above: in order to solve the problem one (or perhaps more) of its constituent propositions is given up, but in such a way that it appears to have been retained, and can therefore be asserted without qualification in other contexts. Sometimes there is a further complication: the supposed solution moves to and fro between, say, two of the constituent propositions, at one point asserting the first of these but covertly abandoning the second, at another point asserting the second but covertly abandoning the first. These fallacious solutions often turn upon some equivocation with the words 'good' and 'evil,' or upon some vagueness about the way in which good and evil are opposed to one another, or about how much is meant by 'omnipotence.' I propose to examine some of these so-called solutions, and to exhibit their fallacies in detail. Incidentally, I shall also be considering whether an adequate solution could be reached by a minor modification of one or more of the constituent propositions, which would, however, still satisfy all the essential requirements of ordinary theism.

(1) "Good cannot exist without evil" or "Evil is necessary as a counterpart to good."

It is sometimes suggested that evil is necessary as a counterpart to good, that if there were no evil there could be no good either, and that this solves the problem of evil. It is true that it points to an answer to the question "Why should there be evil?" But it does so only by qualifying some of the propositions that constitute the problem.

First, it sets a limit to what God can do, saying that God *cannot* create good without simultaneously creating evil, and this means either that God is not omnipotent or that there are *some* limits to what an omnipotent thing can do. It may be replied that these limits are always presupposed, that omnipotence has never meant the power to do what is logically impossible, and on the present view the existence of good without evil would be a logical impossibility. This interpretation of omnipotence may, indeed, be accepted as a modification of our original account which does not reject anything that is essential to theism, and I shall in general assume it in the subsequent discussion. It is, perhaps, the most common theistic view, but I think that some theists at least have maintained that God can do what is logically impossible. Many theists, at any rate, have held that logic itself is created or laid down by God, that logic is the way in which God arbitrarily chooses to think. (This is, of course, parallel to the ethical view that morally right actions are those which God arbitrarily chooses to command, and the two views encounter similar difficulties.) And *this* account of logic is clearly inconsistent with the view that God is bound by logical necessities—unless it is possible for an omnipotent being to bind himself, an issue which we shall consider later, when we come to the Paradox of Omnipo-

tence. This solution of the problem of evil cannot, therefore, be consistently adopted along with the view that logic is itself created by God.

But, secondly, this solution denies that evil is opposed to good in our original sense. If good and evil are counterparts, a good thing will not "eliminate evil as far as it can." Indeed, this view suggests that good and evil are not strictly qualities of things at all. Perhaps the suggestion is that good and evil are related in much the same way as great and small. Certainly, when the term 'great' is used relatively as a condensation of 'greater than so-and-so,' and 'small' is used correspondingly, greatness and smallness are counterparts and cannot exist without each other. But in this sense greatness is not a quality, not an intrinsic feature of anything; and it would be absurd to think of a movement in favour of greatness and against smallness in this sense. Such a movement would be self-defeating, since relative greatness can be promoted only by a simultaneous promotion of relative smallness. I feel sure that no theists would be content to regard God's goodness as analogous to this—as if what he supports were not the *good* but the *better,* and if he had the paradoxical aim that all things should be better than other things.

This point is obscured by the fact that 'great' and 'small' seem to have an absolute as well as a relative sense. I cannot discuss here whether there is absolute magnitude or not, but if there is, there could be an absolute sense for 'great,' it could mean of at least a certain size, and it would make sense to speak of all things getting bigger, of a universe that was expanding all over, and therefore it would make sense to speak of promoting greatness. But in *this* sense great and small are not logically necessary counterparts: either quality could exist without the other. There would be no logical impossibility in everything's being small or in everything's being great.

Neither in the absolute nor in the relative sense, then, of 'great' and 'small' do these terms provide an analogy of the sort that would be needed to support this solution of the problem of evil. In neither case are greatness and smallness *both* necessary counterparts *and* mutually opposed forces or possible objects for support and attack.

It may be replied that good and evil are necessary counterparts in the same way as any quality and its logical opposite: redness can occur, it is suggested, only if non-redness also occurs. But unless evil is merely the privation of good, they are not logical opposites, and some further argument would be needed to show that they are counterparts in the same way as genuine logical opposites. Let us assume that this could be given. There is still doubt of the correctness of the metaphysical principle that a quality must have a real opposite: I suggest that it is not really impossible that everything should be, say, red, that the truth is merely that if everything were red we should not notice redness, and so we should have no word 'red'; we observe and give names to qualities only if they have real opposites. If so, the principle that a term must have an opposite would belong only to our language or to our thought, and would not be an ontological principle, and correspondingly, the rule that good cannot exist without evil would not state a logical necessity of a sort that God would just have to put up with. God might have made everything good, though *we* should not have noticed it if he had.

But, finally, even if we concede that this *is* an ontological principle, it will provide a solution for the problem of evil only if one is prepared to say, "Evil exists, but only just enough evil to serve as the counterpart of good." I doubt whether any theist will accept this. After all, the ontological requirement that non-redness should occur would be satisfied even if all the universe, except for a minute speck, were red, and, if there were a corresponding requirement for evil as a counterpart to good, a minute dose of evil would presumably do. But theists are not usually willing to say, in all contexts, that all the evil that occurs is a minute and necessary dose.

(2) "Evil is necessary as a means to good."

It is sometimes suggested that evil is necessary for good not as a counterpart but as a means. In its simple form this has little plausibility as a solution of the problem of evil, since it obviously implies a severe restriction of God's power. It would be a *causal* law that you cannot have a certain end without a certain means, so that if God has to introduce evil as a means to good, he must be subject to at least some causal laws. This certainly conflicts with what a theist normally means by omnipotence. This view of God as limited by causal laws also conflicts with the view that causal laws are themselves made by God, which is more widely held than the corresponding view about the laws of logic. This conflict would, indeed, be resolved if it were possible for an omnipotent being to bind himself, and this possibility has still to be considered. Unless a favourable answer can be given to this question, the suggestion that evil is necessary as a means to good solves the problem of evil only by denying one of its constituent propositions, either that God is omnipotent or that 'omnipotent' means what it says.

(3) "The universe is better with some evil in it than it could be if there were no evil."

Much more important is a solution which at first seems to be a mere variant of the previous one, that evil may contribute to the goodness of a whole in which it is found, so that the universe as a whole is better as it is, with some evil in it, than it would be if there were no evil. This solution may be developed in either of two ways. It may be supported by an aesthetic analogy, by the fact that contrasts heighten beauty, that in a musical work, for example, there may occur discords which somehow add to the beauty of the work as a whole. Alternatively, it may be worked out in connection with the notion of progress, that the best possible organization of the universe will not be static, but progressive, that the gradual overcoming of evil by good is really a finer thing than would be the eternal unchallenged supremacy of good.

In either case, this solution usually starts from the assumption that the evil whose existence gives rise to the problem of evil is primarily what is called physical evil, that is to say, pain. In Hume's rather half-hearted presentation of the problem of evil, the evils that he stresses are pain and disease, and those who reply to him argue that the existence of pain and disease makes possible the existence of sympathy, benevolence, heroism, and the gradually successful struggle of doctors and reformers to overcome these evils. In fact, theists often seize the opportunity to accuse those who stress the problem of evil of taking a low, materialistic view of good and evil, equating these with pleasure and pain, and of ignoring the more spiritual goods which can arise in the struggle against evils.

But let us see exactly what is being done here. Let us call pain and misery 'first order evil' or 'evil (1).' What contrasts with this, namely, pleasure and happiness, will be called 'first order good' or 'good (1),' Distinct from this is 'second order good' or 'good (2)' which somehow emerges in a complex situation in which evil (1) is a necessary component—logically not merely causally, necessary. (Exactly *how* it emerges does not matter: in the crudest version of this solution good (2) is simply the heightening of happiness by the contrast with misery, in other versions it includes sympathy with suffering, heroism in facing danger, and the gradual decrease of first order evil and increase of first order good.) It is also being assumed that second order good is more important than first order good or evil, in particular that it more than outweighs the first order evil it involves.

Now this is a particularly subtle attempt to solve the problem of evil. It defends God's goodness and omnipotence on the ground that (on a sufficiently long view) this is the best of all logically possible worlds, because it includes the important second order goods, and yet it admits that real evils, namely first order evils, exist. But does it still hold that good and evil are opposed? Not, clearly, in the sense that we set out originally: good does not tend to eliminate evil in general. Instead, we have a modified, a more complex pattern. First order good (*e.g.* happiness) *contrasts with* first order evil (*e.g.* misery): these two are opposed in a fairly mechanical way; some second order goods (*e.g.* benevolence) try to maximize first order good and minimize first order evil; but God's goodness is not this, it is rather the will to maximize *second* order good. We might, therefore, call God's goodness an example of a third order goodness, or good (3). While this account is different from our original one, it might well be held to be an improvement on it, to give a more accurate description of the way in which good is opposed to

evil, and to be consistent with the essential theist position.

There might, however, be several objections to this solution.

First, some might argue that such qualities as benevolence—and *a fortiori* the third order goodness which promotes benevolence—have a merely derivative value, that they are not higher sorts of good, but merely means to good (1), that is, to happiness, so that it would be absurd for God to keep misery in existence in order to make possible the virtues of benevolence, heroism, etc. The theist who adopts the present solution must, of course, deny this, but he can do so with some plausibility, so I should not press this objection.

Secondly, it follows from this solution that God is not in our sense benevolent or sympathetic: he is not concerned to minimize evil (1), but only to promote good (2); and this might be a disturbing conclusion for some theists.

But, thirdly, the fatal objection is this. Our analysis shows clearly the possibility of the existence of a *second* order evil, an evil (2) contrasting with good (2) as evil (1) contrasts with good (1). This would include malevolence, cruelty, callousness, cowardice, and states in which good (1) is decreasing and evil (1) increasing. And just as good (2) is held to be the important kind of good, the kind that God is concerned to promote, so evil (2) will, by analogy, be the important kind of evil, the kind which God, if he were wholly good and omnipotent, would eliminate. And yet evil (2) plainly exists, and indeed most theists (in other contexts) stress its existence more than that of evil (1). We should, therefore, state the problem of evil in terms of second order evil, and against this form of the problem the present solution is useless.

An attempt might be made to use this solution again, at a higher level, to explain the occurrence of evil (2); indeed the next main solution that we shall examine does just this, with the help of some new notions. Without any fresh notions, such a solution would have little plausibility: for example, we could hardly say that the really important good was a good (3), such as the increase of benevolence in proportion to cruelty, which logically required for its occurrence the occurrence of some second order evil. But even if evil (2) could be explained in this way, it is fairly clear that there would be third order evils contrasting with this third order good: and we should be well on the way to an infinite regress, where the solution of a problem of evil, stated in terms of evil (*n*), indicated the existence of an evil (*n* + 1), and a further problem to be solved.

(4) "Evil is due to human free will."

Perhaps the most important proposed solution of the problem of evil is that evil is not to be ascribed to God at all, but to the independent actions of human beings, supposed to have been endowed by God with freedom of the will. This solution may be combined with the preceding one: first order evil (*e.g.* pain) may be justified as a logically necessary component in second order good (*e.g.* sympathy) while second order evil (*e.g.* cruely) is not *justified*, but is so ascribed to human beings that God cannot be held responsible for it. This combination evades my third criticism of the preceding solution.

The free will solution also involves the preceding solution at a higher level. To explain why a wholly good God gave men free will although it would lead to some important evils, it must be argued that it is better on the whole that men should act freely, and sometimes err, than that they should be innocent automata, acting rightly in a wholly determined way. Freedom that is to say, is now treated as a third order good, and as being more valuable than second order goods (such as sympathy and heroism) would be if they were deterministically produced, and it is being assumed that second order evils, such as cruelty, are logically necessary accompaniments of freedom, just as pain is a logically necessary precondition of sympathy.

I think that this solution is unsatisfactory primarily because of the incoherence of the notion of freedom of the will: but I cannot discuss this topic adequately here, although some of my criticisms will touch upon it.

First I should query the assumption that second order evils are logically necessary accompaniments of freedom. I should ask this: if God has made men such that in their free choices they sometimes prefer what is good and sometimes what is evil, why could he not have made men such that they always freely choose the good? If there is no logical impossibility in a man's freely choosing the good on one, or on several, occasions, there cannot be a logical impossibility in his freely choosing the good on every occasion. God was not, then, faced with a choice between making innocent automata and making beings who, in acting freely, would sometimes go wrong: there was open to him the obviously better possibility of making beings who would act freely but always go right. Clearly, his failure to avail himself of this possibility is inconsistent with his being both omnipotent and wholly good.

If it is replied that this objection is absurd, that the making of some wrong choices is logically necessary for freedom, it would seem that 'freedom' must here mean complete randomness or indeterminacy, including randomness with regard to the alternatives good and evil, in other words that men's choices and consequent actions can be "free" only if they are not determined by their characters. Only on this assumption can God escape the responsibility for men's actions; for if he made them as they are, but did not determine their wrong choices, this can only be because the wrong choices are not determined by men as they are. But then if freedom is randomness, how can it be a characteristic of *will*? And, still more, how can it be the most important good? What value or merit would there be in free choices if these were random actions which were not determined by the nature of the agent?

I conclude that to make this solution plausible two different senses of 'freedom' must be confused, one sense which will justify the view that freedom is a third order good, more valuable than other goods would be without it, and another sense, sheer randomness, to prevent us from ascribing to God a decision to make men such that they sometimes go wrong when he might have made them such that they would always freely go right.

This criticism is sufficient to dispose of this solution. But besides this there is a fundamental difficulty in the notion of an omnipotent God creating men with free will, for if men's wills are really free this must mean that even God cannot control them, that is, that God is no longer omnipotent. It may be objected that God's gift of freedom to men does not mean that he *cannot* control their wills, but that he always *refrains* from controlling their wills. But why, we may ask, should God refrain from controlling evil wills? Why should he not leave men free to will rightly, but intervene when he sees them beginning to will wrongly? If God could do this, but does not, and if he is wholly good, the only explanation could be that even a wrong free act of will is not really evil, that its freedom is a value which outweighs its wrongness, so that there would be a loss of value if God took away the wrongness and the freedom together. But this is utterly opposed to what theists say about sin in other contexts. The present solution of the problem of evil, then, can be maintained only in the form that God has made men so free that he *cannot* control their wills.

This leads us to what I call the Paradox of Omnipotence: can an omnipotent being make things which he cannot subsequently control? Or, what is practically equivalent to this, can an omnipotent being make rules which then bind himself? (These are practically equivalent because any such rules could be regarded as setting certain things beyond his control, and *vice versa*.) The second of these formulations is relevant to the suggestions that we have already met, that an omnipotent God creates the rules of logic or causal laws, and is then bound by them.

It is clear that this is a paradox: the questions cannot be answered satisfactorily either in the affirmative or in the negative. If we answer "Yes," it follows that if God actually makes things which he cannot control, or makes rules which bind himself, he is not omnipotent once he has made them: there are *then* things which he cannot do. But if we answer "No," we are immediately asserting that there are things which he cannot do, that is to say that he is already not omnipotent.

It cannot be replied that the question which sets this paradox is not a proper question. It would make perfectly good sense to say that a human mechanic has made a machine which he cannot control: if there is any difficulty about the question it lies in the notion of omnipotence itself.

This, incidentally, shows that although we have approached this paradox from the free will theory, it is equally a problem for a theological determinist.

No one thinks that machines have free will, yet they may well be beyond the control of their makers. The determinist might reply that anyone who makes anything determines its ways of acting, and so determines its subsequent behaviour: even the human mechanic does this by his *choice* of materials and structure for his machine, though he does not know all about either of these: the mechanic thus determines, though he may not foresee, his machine's actions. And since God is omniscient, and since his creation of things is total, he both determines and foresees the ways in which his creatures will act. We may grant this, but it is beside the point. The question is not whether God *originally* determined the future actions of his creatures, but whether he can *subsequently* control their actions, or whether he was able in his original creation to put things beyond his subsequent control. Even on determinist principles the answers "Yes" and "No" are equally irreconcilable with God's omnipotence.

Before suggesting a solution of this paradox, I would point out that there is a parallel Paradox of Sovereignty. Can a legal sovereign make a law restricting its own future legislative power? For example, could the British parliament make a law forbidding any future parliament to socialise banking, and also forbidding the future repeal of this law itself? Or could the British parliament, which was legally sovereign in Australia in, say, 1899, pass a valid law, or series of laws, which made it no longer sovereign in 1933? Again, neither the affirmative nor the negative answer is really satisfactory. If we were to answer "Yes," we should be admitting the validity of a law which, if it were actually made, would mean that parliament was no longer sovereign. If we were to answer "No," we should be admitting that there is a law, not logically absurd, which parliament cannot validly make, that is, that parliament is not now a legal sovereign. This paradox can be solved in the following way. We should distinguish between first order laws, that is laws governing the actions of individuals and bodies other than the legislature, and second order laws, that is laws about laws, laws governing the actions of the legislature itself. Correspondingly, we should distinguish two orders of sovereignty, first order sovereignty (sovereignty (1)) which is unlimited authority to make first order laws, and second order sovereignty (sovereignty (2)) which is unlimited authority to make second order laws. If we say that parliament is sovereign we might mean that any parliament at any time has sovereignty (1), or we might mean that parliament has both sovereignty (1) and sovereignty (2) at present, but we cannot without contradiction mean both that the present parliament has sovereignty (2) and that every parliament at every time has sovereignty (1), for if the present parliament has sovereignty (2) it may use it to take away the sovereignty (1) of later parliaments. What the paradox shows is that we cannot ascribe to any continuing institution legal sovereignty in an inclusive sense.

The analogy between omnipotence and sovereignty shows that the paradox of omnipotence can be solved in a similar way. We must distinguish between first order omnipotence (omnipotence (1)), that is unlimited power to act, and second order omnipotence (omnipotence (2)), that is unlimited power to determine what powers to act things shall have. Then we could consistently say that God all the time has omnipotence (1), but if so no beings at any time have powers to act independently of God. Or we could say that God at one time had omnipotence (2), and used it to assign independent powers to act to certain things, so that God thereafter did not have omnipotence (1). But what the paradox shows is that we cannot consistently ascribe to any continuing being omnipotence in an inclusive sense.

An alternative solution of this paradox would be simply to deny that God is a continuing being, that any times can be assigned to his actions at all. But on this assumption (which also has difficulties of its own) no meaning can be given to the assertion that God made men with wills so free that he could not control them. The paradox of omnipotence can be avoided by putting God outside time, but the free will solution of the problem of evil cannot be saved in this way, and equally it remains impossible to hold that an omnipotent God *binds himself* by causal or logical laws.

Conclusion

Of the proposed solutions of the problem of evil which we have examined, none has stood up to criticism. There may be other solutions which require examination, but this study strongly suggests that there is no valid solution of the problem which does not modify at least one of the constituent propositions in a way which would seriously affect the essential core of the theistic position.

Quite apart from the problem of evil, the paradox of omnipotence has shown that God's omnipotence must in any case be restricted in one way or another, that unqualified omnipotence cannot be ascribed to any being that continues through time. And if God and his actions are not in time, can omnipotence, or power of any sort, be meaningfully ascribed to him?

III.6   The Free Will Defense

ALVIN PLANTINGA

Alvin Plantinga is professor of philosophy at the University of Notre Dame and the author of several works in metaphysics, epistemology, and the philosophy of religion, including God and Other Minds *(1967),* The Nature of Necessity *(1974), and* God, Freedom and Evil *(1974) from which this selection is taken.*

Plantinga argues that Mackie and other atheologians (those who argue against the existence of God) are mistaken in thinking that the problem of evil constitutes a demonstration or even good reason to reject the thesis that a perfectly good and powerful God exists. He formulates an argument to show that no logical inconsistency need occur in the free will defense for the existence of God despite the reality of evil.

1. On the Alleged Contradiction in Theism

In a widely discussed piece entitled "Evil and Omnipotence" John Mackie makes this claim:

> I think, however, that a more telling criticism can be made by way of the traditional problem of evil. Here it can be shown, not that religious beliefs lack rational support, but that they are positively irrational, that the several parts of the essential theological doctrine are *inconsistent* with one another. . . .[1]

Is Mackie right? Does the theist contradict himself? But we must ask a prior question: just what is being claimed here? That theistic belief contains an inconsistency or contradiction, of course. But what, exactly, is an inconsistency or contradiction? There are several kinds. An *explicit* contradiction is a *proposition* of a certain sort—a conjunctive proposition, one conjunct of which is the denial or negation of the other conjunct. For example:

> Paul is a good tennis player, and it's false that Paul is a good tennis player.

(People seldom assert explicit contradictions.) Is Mackie charging the theist with accepting such a contradiction? Presumably not; what he says is

> In its simplest form the problem is this: God is omnipotent; God is wholly good; yet evil exists. There seems to be some contradiction between these three propositions, so that if any two of them were true the third would be false. But at the same time all three are essential parts of most theological positions; the theologian, it seems, at once *must* adhere and *cannot consistently* adhere to all three.

According to Mackie, then, the theist accepts a group or set of three propositions; this set is inconsistent. Its members, of course, are

(1)   God is omnipotent
(2)   God is wholly good

and

(3)   Evil exists.

Call this set *A*; the claim is that *A* is an inconsistent set. But what is it for a *set* to be inconsistent or contradictory? Following our definition of an explicit contradiction, we might say that a set of propositions is explicitly contradictory if one of the members is the denial or negation of another member. But then, of course, it is evident that the set we are discussing is not explicitly contradictory; the denials of (1), (2), and (3), respectively, are

(1′)   God is not omnipotent (or it's false that God is omnipotent)
(2′)   God is not wholly good

and

(3′)   There is no evil

none of which is in set *A*.

From *God, Freedom, and Evil* by Alvin Plantinga (Harper & Row, 1974). Reprinted by permission of the author. Footnotes edited.

Of course many sets are pretty clearly contradictory, in an important way, but not *explicitly* contradictory. For example, set *B*:

(4) If all men are mortal, then Socrates is mortal
(5) All men are mortal
(6) Socrates is not mortal.

This set is not explicitly contradictory; yet surely *some* significant sense of that term applies to it. What is important here is that by using only the rules of ordinary logic—the laws of propositional logic and quantification theory found in any introductory text on the subject—we can deduce an explicit contradiction from the set. Or to put it differently, we can use the laws of logic to deduce a proposition from the set, which proposition, when added to the set, yields a new set that is explicitly contradictory. For by using the law *modus ponens* (if *p*, then *q*; *p*; therefore *q*) we can deduce

(7) Socrates is mortal

from (4) and (5). The result of adding (7) to *B* is the set {(4), (5), (6), (7)}. This set, of course, is explicitly contradictory in that (6) is the denial of (7). We might say that any set which shares this characteristic with set *B* is *formally* contradictory. So a formally contradictory set is one from whose members an explicit contradiction can be deduced by the laws of logic. Is Mackie claiming that set *A* is formally contradictory?

If he is, he's wrong. No laws of logic permit us to deduce the denial of one of the propositions in *A* from the other members. Set *A* isn't formally contradictory either.

But there is still another way in which a set of propositions can be contradictory or inconsistent. Consider set *C*, whose members are

(8) George is older than Paul
(9) Paul is older than Nick

and

(10) George is not older than Nick.

This set is neither explicitly nor formally contradictory; we can't, just by using the laws of logic, deduce the denial of any of these propositions from the others. And yet there is a good sense in which it is consistent or contradictory. For clearly it is *not possible* that its three members all be true. It is *necessarily true* that

(11) If George is older than Paul, and Paul is older than Nick, then George is older than Nick.

And if we add (11) to set *C*, we get a set that is formally contradictory; (8), (9), and (11) yield, by the laws of ordinary logic, the denial of (10).

I said that (11) is *necessarily true*; but what does *that* mean? Of course we might say that a proposition is necessarily true if it is impossible that it be false, or if its negation is not possibly true. This would be to explain necessity in terms of possibility. Chances are, however, that anyone who does not know what necessity is, will be equally at a loss about possibility, the explanation is not likely to be very successful. Perhaps all we can do by way of explanation is to give some examples and hope for the best. In the first place many propositions can be established by the laws of logic alone—for example,

(12) If all men are mortal and Socrates is a man, then Socrates is mortal.

Such propositions are truths of logic; and all of them are necessary in the sense of question. But truths of arithmetic and mathematics generally are also necessarily true. Still further, there is a host of propositions that are neither truths of logic nor truths of mathematics but are nonetheless necessarily true; (11) would be an example, as well as

(13) Nobody is taller than himself
(14) Red is a color
(15) No numbers are persons
(16) No prime number is a prime minister

and

(17) Bachelors are unmarried.

So here we have an important kind of necessity—let's call it "broadly logical necessity." Of course there is a correlative kind of *possibility*: a proposition *p* is possibly true (in the broadly logical sense) just in case its negation or denial is not necessarily true (in that same broadly logical sense).

This sense of necessity and possibility must be distinguished from another that we may call *causal* or *natural* necessity and possibility. Consider

(18) Henry Kissinger has swum the Atlantic.

Although this proposition has an implausible ring, it is not necessarily false in the broadly logical sense (and its denial is not necessarily true in that sense). But there is a good sense in which it is impossible: it is *causally* or *naturally* impossible. Human beings, unlike dolphins, just don't have the physical equipment demanded for this feat. Unlike Superman, furthermore, the rest of us are incapable of leaping tall buildings at a single bound or (without auxiliary power of some kind) traveling faster than a speeding bullet. These things are *impossible* for us—but not *logically* impossible, even in the broad sense.

So there are several senses of necessity and possibility here. There are a number of propositions, furthermore, of which it's difficult to say whether they are or aren't possible in the broadly logical sense; some of these are subjects of philosophical controversy. Is it possible, for example, for a person never to be conscious during his entire existence? Is it possible for a (human) person to exist *disembodied?* If that's possible, is it possible that there be a person who *at no time at all* during his entire existence has a body? Is it possible to see without eyes? These are propositions about whose possibility in that broadly logical sense there is disagreement and dispute.

Now return to set *C*. . . . What is characteristic of it is the fact that the conjunction of its members—the proposition expressed by the result of putting "and's" between (8), (9), and (10)—is necessarily false. Or we might put it like this: what characterizes set *C* is the fact that we can get a formally contradictory set by adding a necessarily true proposition—namely (11). Suppose we say that a set is *implicitly contradictory* if it resembles *C* in this respect. That is, a set *S* of propositions is implicitly contradictory if there is a necessary proposition *p* such that the result of adding *p* to *S* is a formally contradictory set. Another way to put it: *S* is implicitly contradictory if there is some necessarily true proposition *p* such that by using just the laws of ordinary logic, we can deduce an explicit contradiction from *p* together with the members of *S*. And when Mackie says that set *A* is contradictory, we may properly take him, I think, as holding that it is implicitly contradictory in the explained sense. As he puts it:

> However, the contradiction does not arise immediately; to show it we need some additional premises, or perhaps some quasi-logical rules connecting the terms "good" and "evil" and "omnipotent." These additional principles are that good is opposed to evil, in such a way that a good thing always eliminates evil as far as it can, and that there are no limits to what an omnipotent thing can do. From these it follows that a good omnipotent thing eliminates evil completely, and then the propositions that a good omnipotent thing exists, and that evil exists, are incompatible.[2]

Here Mackie refers to "additional premises"; he also calls them "additional principles" and "quasilogical rules"; he says we need them to show the contradiction. What he means, I think, is that to get a formally contradictory set we must add some more propositions to set *A*; and if we aim to show that set *A* is implicitly contradictory, these propositions must be necessary truths—"quasi-logical rules" as Mackie calls them. The two additional principles he suggests are

(19) A good thing always eliminates evil as far as it can

and

(20) There are no limits to what an omnipotent being can do.

And, of course, if Mackie means to show that set *A* is implicitly contradictory, then he must hold that (19) and (20) are not merely *true* but *necessarily true.*

But, are they? What about (20) first? What does it mean to say that a being is omnipotent? That he is *all-powerful*, or *almighty*, presumably. But are there no limits *at all* to the power of such a being? Could he create square circles, for example, or married bachelors? Most theologians and theistic philosophers who hold that God is omnipotent, do not hold that He can create round squares or bring it about that He both exists and does not exist. These theologians and philosophers may hold that there are no *nonlogical* limits to what an omnipotent being can do, but they concede that not even an omnipotent being can bring about logically impossible states of affairs or cause necessarily false propositions to be true. Some theists, on the other hand—Martin Luther and Descartes, perhaps—have apparently thought that God's power is unlimited even by the laws of logic. For these theists the question whether set *A* is contradictory will not be of much interest. As theists they believe (1) and (2), and they also, presumably, believe (3). But they remain undisturbed by the claim that (1), (2), and (3) are jointly inconsistent—because, as they say, God can do what is logically impossible. Hence He can bring it about that the members of set *A* are all true, even if that set is contradictory (concentrating very intensely upon this suggestion is likely to make you dizzy). So the theist who thinks that the power of God isn't limited *at all*, not even by the laws of logic, will be unimpressed by Mackie's argument and won't find any difficulty in the contradiction set *A* is alleged to contain. This view is not very popular, however, and for good reason; it is quite incoherent. What the theist typically means when he says that God is omnipotent is not that there are *no* limits to God's power, but at most that there are no nonlogical limits to what He can do; and given this qualification, it is perhaps initially plausible to suppose that (20) is necessarily true.

But what about (19), the proposition that every good thing eliminates every evil state of affairs that it can eliminate? Is that necessarily true? Is it true at all? Suppose, first of all, that your friend Paul unwisely goes for a drive on a wintry day and runs out of gas on a deserted road. The temperature dips to −10°, and a miserably cold wind comes up. You are sitting comfortably at home (twenty-five miles from Paul) roasting chestnuts in a roaring blaze. Your car is in the garage; in the trunk there is the full five-gallon can of gasoline you always keep for emergencies. Paul's discomfort and danger are certainly an evil, and one which you could eliminate. You don't do so. But presumably you don't thereby forfeit your claim to being a "good thing"—you simply didn't know of Paul's plight. And so (19) does not appear to be necessary. It says that every good thing has a certain property—the property of eliminating every

evil that it can. And if the case I described is possible—a good person's failing through ignorance to eliminate a certain evil he can eliminate—then (19) is by no means necessarily true.

But perhaps Mackie could sensibly claim that if you *didn't know* about Paul's plight, then in fact you were *not*, at the time in question, able to eliminate the evil in question; and perhaps he'd be right. In any event he could revise (19) to take into account the kind of case I mentioned:

(19a) Every good thing always eliminates every evil that *it knows about* and can eliminate.

{(1), (2), (3), (20), (19a)}, you'll notice is not a formally contradictory set—to get a formal contradiction we must add a proposition specifying that God *knows about* every evil state of affairs. But most theists do believe that God is omniscient or all-knowing; so if this new set—the set that results when we add to set *A* the proposition that God is omniscient—is implicitly contradictory then Mackie should be satisfied and the theist confounded. (And, henceforth, set *A* will be the old set *A* together with the proposition that God is omniscient.)

But is (19a) necessary? Hardly. Suppose you know that Paul is marooned as in the previous example, and you also know another friend is similarly marooned fifty miles in the opposite direction. Suppose, furthermore, that while you can rescue one or the other, you simply can't rescue both. Then each of the two evils is such that it is within your power to eliminate it; and you know about them both. But you can't eliminate *both*; and you don't forfeit your claim to being a good person by eliminating only one—it wasn't within your power to do more. So the fact that you don't doesn't mean that you are not a good person. Therefore (19a) is false; it is not a necessary truth or even a truth that every good thing eliminates every evil it knows about and can eliminate.

We can see the same thing another way. You've been rock climbing. Still something of a novice, you've acquired a few cuts and bruises by inelegantly using your knees rather than your feet. One of these bruises is fairly painful. You mention it to a physician friend, who predicts the pain will leave of its own accord in a day or two. Meanwhile, he says, there's nothing he can do, short of amputating your leg above the knee, to remove the pain. Now the pain in your knee is an evil state of affairs. All else being equal, it would be better if you had no such pain. And it is within the power of your friend to eliminate this evil state of affairs. Does his failure to do so mean that he is not a good person? Of course not; for he could eliminate this evil state of affairs only by bringing about another, much worse evil. And so it is once again evident that (19a) is false. It is entirely possible that a good person fail to eliminate an evil state of affairs that he knows about and can eliminate. This would take place, if, as in the present example, he couldn't eliminate the evil without bringing about a *greater* evil.

A slightly different kind of case shows the same thing. A really impressive good state of affairs *G* will *outweigh* a trivial *E*—that is, the conjunctive state of affairs *G* and *E* is itself a good state of affairs. And surely a good person would not be obligated to eliminate a given evil if he could do so only by eliminating a good that outweighed it. Therefore (19a) is not necessarily true; it can't be used to show that set *A* is implicitly contradictory.

These difficulties might suggest another revision of (19); we might try

(19b) A good being eliminates every evil *E* that it knows about and that it can eliminate without either bringing about a greater evil or eliminating a good state of affairs that outweighs *E*.

Is this necessarily true? It takes care of the second of the two difficulties afflicting (19a) but leaves the first untouched. We can see this as follows. First, suppose we say that a being *properly eliminates* an evil state of affairs if it eliminates that evil without either eliminating an outweighing good or bringing about a greater evil. It is then obviously possible that a person find himself in a situation where he could properly eliminate an evil *E* and could also properly eliminate another evil *E'*, but couldn't properly eliminate them *both*. You're rock climbing again, this time on the dreaded north face of the Grand Teton. You and your party come upon Curt and Bob, two mountaineers stranded 125 feet apart on the face. They untied to reach their ciga-

rettes and then carelessly dropped the rope while lighting up. A violent, dangerous thunderstorm is approaching. You have time to rescue one of the stranded climbers and retreat before the storm hits; if you rescue both, however, you and your party and the two climbers will be caught on the face during the thunderstorm, which will very likely destroy your entire party. In this case you can eliminate one evil (Curt's being stranded on the face) without causing more evil or eliminating a greater good; and you are also able to properly eliminate the other evil (Bob's being thus stranded). But you can't properly eliminate them *both*. And so the fact that you don't rescue Curt, say, even though you could have, doesn't show that you aren't a good person. Here, then, each of the evils is such that you can properly eliminate it; but you can't properly eliminate them both, and hence can't be blamed for failing to eliminate one of them.

So neither (19a) nor (19b) is necessarily true. You may be tempted to reply that the sort of counterexamples offered—examples where someone is able to eliminate an evil *A* and also able to eliminate a different evil *B*, but unable to eliminate them both—are irrelevant to the case of a being who, like God, is both omnipotent and omniscient. That is, you may think that if an omnipotent and omniscient being is able to eliminate each of two evils, it follows that he can eliminate them *both*. Perhaps this is so; but it is not strictly to the point. The fact is the counterexamples show that (19a) and (19b) are not necessarily true and hence can't be used to show that set *A* is implicitly inconsistent. What the reply does suggest is that perhaps the atheologian will have more success if he works the properties of omniscience and omnipotence into (19). Perhaps he could say something like

(19c) An omnipotent and omniscient good being eliminates every evil that it can properly eliminate.

And suppose, for purposes of argument, we concede the necessary truth of (19c). Will it serve Mackie's purposes? Not obviously. For we don't get a set that is formally contradictory by adding (20) and (19c) to set *A*. This set (call it *A'*) contains the following six members:

(1) God is omnipotent
(2) God is wholly good
(2′) God is omniscient
(3) Evil exists
(19c) An omnipotent and omniscient good being eliminates every evil that it can properly eliminate

and

(20) There are no nonlogical limits to what an omnipotent being can do.

Now if *A′* were formally contradictory, then from any five of its members we could deduce the denial of the sixth by the laws of ordinary logic. That is, any five would *formally entail* the denial of the sixth. So if *A′* were formally inconsistent, the denial of (3) would be formally entailed by the remaining five. That is, (1), (2), (2′), (19c), and (20) would formally entail

(3′) There is no evil.

But they don't; what they formally entail is not that there is no evil *at all* but only that

(3″) There is no evil that God can properly eliminate.

So (19c) doesn't really help either—not because it is not necessarily true but because its addition [with (20)] to set *A* does not yield a formally contradictory set.

Obviously, what the atheologian must add to get a formally contradictory set is

(21) If God is omniscient and omnipotent, then he can properly eliminate every evil state of affairs.

Suppose we agree that the set consisting in *A* plus (19c), (20), and (21) is formally contradictory. So if (19c), (20), and (21) are all necessarily true, then set *A* is implicitly contradictory. We've already conceded that (19c) and (20) are indeed necessary. So we must take a look at (21). Is this proposition necessarily true?

No. To see this let us ask the following question. Under what conditions would an omnipotent being be unable to eliminate a certain evil *E* without

eliminating an outweighing good? Well, suppose that *E* is *included in* some good state of affairs that outweighs it. That is, suppose there is some good state of affairs *G* so related to *E* that it is impossible that *G* obtain or be actual and *E* fail to obtain. (Another way to put this: a state of affairs *S* includes *S′* if the conjunctive state of affairs *S* but not *S′* is impossible, or if it is necessary that *S′* obtains if *S* does.) Now suppose that some good state of affairs *G* includes an evil state of affairs *E* that it outweighs. Then not even an omnipotent being could eliminate *E* without eliminating *G*. But *are* there any cases where a good state of affairs includes, in this sense, an evil that it outweighs? [3] Indeed there are such states of affairs. To take an artificial example, let's suppose that *E* is Paul's suffering from a minor abrasion and *G* is your being deliriously happy. The conjunctive state of affairs, *G and E*—the state of affairs that obtains if and only if both *G* and *E* obtain—is then a good state of affairs: it is better, all else being equal, that you be intensely happy and Paul suffer a mildly annoying abrasion than that this state of affairs not obtain. So *G and E* is a good state of affairs. And clearly *G and E* includes *E*: obviously it is necessarily true that if you are deliriously happy and Paul is suffering from an abrasion, then Paul is suffering from an abrasion.

But perhaps you think this example trivial, tricky, slippery, and irrelevant. If so, take heart; other examples abound. Certain kinds of values, certain familiar kinds of good states of affairs, can't exist apart from evil of some sort. For example, there are people who display a sort of creative moral heroism in the face of suffering and adversity—a heroism that inspires others and creates a good situation out of a bad one. In a situation like this the evil, of course, remains evil; but the total state of affairs—someone's bearing pain magnificently, for example—may be good. If it is, then the good present must outweigh the evil; otherwise the total situation would not be *good*. But, of course, it is not possible that such a good state of affairs obtain unless some evil also obtain. It is a necessary truth that if someone bears pain magnificently, then someone is in pain.

The conclusion to be drawn, therefore, is that (21) is not necessarily true. And our discussion thus far shows at the very least that it is no easy matter to find necessarily true propositions that yield a formally contradictory set when added to set A.[4] One wonders, therefore, why the many atheologians who confidently assert that this set is contradictory make no attempt whatever to *show* that it is. For the most part they are content just to *assert* that there is a contradiction here. Even Mackie, who sees that some "additional premises" or "quasi-logical rules" are needed, makes scarcely a beginning towards finding some additional premises that are necessarily true and that together with the members of set A formally entail an explicit contradiction.

3. Can We Show That There Is No Inconsistency Here?

To summarize our conclusions so far: although many atheologians claim that the theist is involved in contradiction when he asserts the members of set A, this set, obviously, is neither *explicitly* nor *formally* contradictory; the claim, presumably, must be that it is *implicitly* contradictory. To make good this claim the atheologian must find some necessarily true proposition p (it could be a conjunction of several propositions) such that the addition of p to set A yields a set that is formally contradictory. No atheologian has produced even a plausible candidate for this role, and it certainly is not easy to see what such a proposition might be. Now we might think we should simply declare set A implicitly consistent on the principle that a proposition (or set) is to be presumed consistent or possible until proven otherwise. This course, however, leads to trouble. The same principle would impel us to declare the atheologian's claim—that set A is inconsistent—possible or consistent. But the claim that a given set of propositions is implicitly contradictory, is itself either necessarily true or necessarily false; so if such a claim is *possible*, it is not necessarily false and is, therefore, true (in fact, necessarily true). If we followed the suggested principle, therefore, we should be obliged to declare set A implicitly consistent (since it hasn't been shown to be otherwise), but we should have to say the same

thing about the atheologian's claim, since we haven't shown *that* claim to be inconsistent or impossible. The atheologian's claim, furthermore, is necessarily true if it is possible. Accordingly, if we accept the above principle, we shall have to declare set A both implicitly consistent and implicitly inconsistent. So all we can say at this point is that set A has not been shown to be implicitly inconsistent.

Can we go any further? One way to go on would be to try to *show* that set A is implicitly consistent or possible in the broadly logical sense. But what is involved in showing such a thing? Although there are various ways to approach this matter, they all resemble one another in an important respect. They all amount to this: to show that a set S is consistent you think of a *possible state of affairs* (it needn't *actually obtain*) which is such that if it were actual, then all of the members of S would be true. This procedure is sometimes called *giving a model of S*. For example, you might construct an axiom set and then show that it is consistent by giving a model of it; this is how it was shown that the denial of Euclid's parallel postulate is formally consistent with the rest of his postulates.

There are various special cases of this procedure to fit special circumstances. Suppose, for example, you have a pair of propositions p and q and wish to show them consistent. And suppose we say that a proposition p_1 *entails* a proposition p_2 if it is impossible that p_1 be true and p_2 false—if the conjunctive proposition p_1 and not p_2 is necessarily false. Then one way to show that p is consistent with q is to find some proposition r whose conjunction with p is both possible, in the broadly logical sense, and entails q. A rude and unlettered behaviorist, for example, might hold that thinking is really nothing but movements of the larynx; he might go on to hold that

P Jones did not move his larynx after April 30

is inconsistent (in the broadly logical sense) with

Q Jones did some thinking during May.

By way of rebuttal, we might point out that P appears to be consistent with

R While convalescing from an April 30 laryngo-
tomy, Jones whiled away the idle hours by
writing (in May) a splendid paper on Kant's
Critique of Pure Reason.

So the conjunction of *P* and *R* appears to be consistent; but obviously it also entails *Q* (you can't write
even a passable paper on Kant's *Critique of Pure
Reason* without doing some thinking); so *P* and *Q*
are consistent.

We can see that this is a special case of the
procedure I mentioned above as follows. This
proposition *R* is consistent with *P*; so the proposition
P and R is possible, describes a possible state of
affairs. But *P and R* entails *Q*; hence if *P and R* were
true, *Q* would also be true, and hence both *P* and
Q would be true. So this is really a case of producing
a possible state of affairs such that, if it were actual,
all the members of the set in question (in this case
the pair set of *P* and *Q*) would be true.

How does this apply to the case before us? As
follows, let us conjoin propositions (1), (2), and (2')
and henceforth call the result (1):

(1)   God is omniscient, omnipotent, and wholly
      good.

The problem, then, is to show that (1) and (3) (evil
exists) are consistent. This could be done, as we've
seen, by finding a proposition *r* that is consistent
with (1) and such that (1) and (*r*) together entail (3).
One proposition that might do the trick is

(22)   God creates a world containing evil and has a
       good reason for doing so.

If (22) is consistent with (1), then it follows that (1)
and (3) (and hence set A) are consistent. Accordingly, one thing some theists have tried is to show
that (22) and (1) are consistent.

One can attempt this in at least two ways. On
the one hand, we could try to apply the same
method again. Conceive of a possible state of affairs
such that, if it obtained, an omnipotent, omniscient,
and wholly good God would have a good reason
for permitting evil. On the other, someone might try
to specify *what God's reason is* for permitting evil
and try to show, if it is not obvious, that it is a good
reason. St. Augustine, for example, one of the greatest and most influential philosopher-theologians of
the Christian Church, writes as follows:

> . . . some people see with perfect truth that a crea-
> ture is better if, while possessing free will, it remains al-
> ways fixed upon God and never sins; then, reflecting
> on men's sins, they are grieved, not because they con-
> tinue to sin, but because they were created. They say:
> He should have made us such that we never willed to
> sin, but always to enjoy the unchangeable truth.
>   They should not lament or be angry. God has not
> compelled men to sin just because He created them
> and gave them the power to choose between sinning
> and not sinning. There are angels who have never
> sinned and never will sin.
>   Such is the generosity of God's goodness that He
> has not refrained from creating even that creature
> which He foreknew would not only sin, but remain in
> the will to sin. As a runaway horse is better than a
> stone which does not run away because it lacks self-
> movement and sense perception, so the creature is
> more excellent which sins by free will than that which
> does not sin only because it has no free will.[5]

In broadest terms Augustine claims that God could
create a better, more perfect universe by permitting
evil than He could by refusing to do so:

> Neither the sins nor the misery are necessary to the
> perfection of the universe, but souls as such are neces-
> sary, which have the power to sin if they so will, and
> become miserable if they sin. If misery persisted after
> their sins had been abolished, or if there were misery
> before there were sins, then it might be right to say that
> the order and government of the universe were at fault.
> Again, if there were sins but no consequent misery, that
> order is equally dishonored by lack of equity.[6]

Augustine tries to tell us *what God's reason is* for
permitting evil. At bottom, he says, it's that God can
create a more perfect universe by permitting evil. A
really top-notch universe requires the existence of
free, rational, and moral agents; and some of the
free creatures He created went wrong. But the
universe with the free creatures it contains and the
evil they commit is better than it would have been
had it contained neither the free creatures nor this
evil. Such an attempt to specify God's reason for
permitting evil is what I earlier called a *theodicy;*
in the words of John Milton it is an attempt to "justify
the ways of God to man," to show that God is just
in permitting evil. Augustine's kind of theodicy
might be called a Free Will Theodicy, since the idea

of rational creatures with free will plays such a prominent role in it.

A theodicist, then, attempts to tell us why God permits evil. Quite distinct from a Free Will Theodicy is what I shall call a Free Will Defense. Here the aim is not to say what God's reason *is,* but at most what God's reason *might possibly be.* We could put the difference like this. The Free Will Theodicist and Free Will Defender are both trying to show that (1) is consistent with (22), and of course if so, then set *A* is consistent. The Free Will Theodicist tries to do this by finding some proposition *r* which in conjunction with (1) entails (22); he claims, furthermore, that this proposition is true, not just consistent with (1). He tries to tell us what God's reason for permitting evil *really is.* The Free Will Defender, on the other hand, though he also tries to find a proposition *r* that is consistent with (1) and in conjunction with it entails (22), does *not* claim to know or even believe that *r* is true. And here, of course, he is perfectly within his rights. His aim is to show that (1) is consistent with (22); all he need do then is find an *r* that is consistent with (1) and such that (1) and (*r*) entail (22); whether *r* is *true* is quite beside the point.

So there is a significant difference between a Free Will Theodicy and a Free Will Defense. The latter is sufficient (if successful) to show that set *A* is consistent; in a way a Free Will Theodicy goes beyond what is required. On the other hand, a theodicy would be much more satisfying, if possible to achieve. No doubt the theist would rather know what God's reason *is* for permitting evil than simply that it's possible that He has a good one. But in the present context (that of investigating the consistency of set *A*), the latter is all that's needed. Neither a defense or a theodicy, of course, gives any hint to what God's reason for some *specific* evil—the death or suffering of someone close to you, for example—might be. And there is still another function—a sort of pastoral function[7]—in the neighborhood that neither serves. Confronted with evil in his own life or suddenly coming to realize more clearly than before the *extent* and *magnitude* of evil, a believer in God may undergo a crisis of faith. He may be tempted to follow the advice of Job's "friends"; he may be tempted to "curse God and die." Neither a Free Will Defense nor a Free Will Theodicy is designed to be of much help or comfort to one suffering from such a storm in the soul (although in a specific case, of course, one or the other could prove useful). Neither is to be thought of first of all as a means of pastoral counseling. Probably neither will enable someone to find peace with himself and with God in the face of the evil the world contains. But then, of course, neither is intended for that purpose.

4. The Free Will Defense

In what follows I shall focus attention upon the Free Will Defense. I shall examine it more closely, state it more exactly, and consider objections to it; and I shall argue that in the end it is successful. Earlier we saw that among good states of affairs there are some that not even God can bring about without bringing about evil: those goods, namely, that *entail* or *include* evil states of affairs. The Free Will Defense can be looked upon as an effort to show that there may be a very different kind of good that God can't bring about without permitting evil. These are good states of affairs that don't include evil; they do not entail the existence of any evil whatever; nonetheless God Himself can't bring them about without permitting evil.

So how does the Free Will Defense work? And what does the Free Will Defender mean when he says that people are or may be free? What is relevant to the Free Will Defense is the idea of *being free with respect to an action*. If a person is free with respect to a given action, then he is free to perform that action and free to refrain from performing it; no antecedent conditions and/or causal laws determine that he will perform the action, or that he won't. It is within his power, at the time in question, to take or perform the action and within his power to refrain from it. Freedom so conceived is not to be confused with unpredictability. You might be able to predict what you will do in a given situation even if you are free, in that situation, to do something else. If I know you well, I may be able to predict what action you will take in response to a certain set of conditions; it does not follow that you are not free with respect to that action. Secondly, I shall say that an action is *morally significant,* for a given person, if it would be wrong for him to perform the action but right to refrain or *vice versa.* Keeping a promise, for example, would ordinarily be morally significant for a person, as would refusing induction into the army. On the other hand, having Cheerios for breakfast (instead of Wheaties) would not normally be morally significant. Further, suppose we say that a person is *significantly free,* on a given occasion, if he is then free with respect to a morally significant action. And finally we must distinguish between *moral evil* and *natural evil.* The former is evil that results from free human activity; natural evil is any other kind of evil.[8]

Given these definitions and distinctions, we can make a preliminary statement of the Free Will Defense as follows. A world containing creatures who are significantly free (and freely perform more good than evil actions) is more valuable, all else being equal, than a world containing no free creatures at all. Now God can create free creatures, but He can't *cause* or *determine* them to do only what is right. For if He does so, then they aren't significantly free after all; they do not do what is right *freely.* To create creatures capable of *moral good,* therefore, He must create creatures capable of moral evil; and He can't give these creatures the freedom to perform evil and at the same time prevent them from doing so. As it turned out, sadly enough, some of the free creatures God created went wrong in the exercise of their freedom; this is the source of moral evil. The fact that free creatures sometimes go wrong, however, counts neither against God's omnipotence nor against His goodness; for He could have forestalled the occurrence of moral evil only by removing the possibility of moral good.

I said earlier that the Free Will Defender tries to find a proposition that is consistent with

(1)   God is omniscient, omnipotent, and wholly good

and together with (1) entails that there is evil. According to the Free Will Defense, we must find this proposition somewhere in the above story. The heart of the Free Will Defense is the claim that it is *possible* that God could not have created a universe containing moral good (or as much moral good as this world contains) without creating one that also contained moral evil. And if so, then it is possible that God has a good reason for creating a world containing evil.

Now this defense has met with several kinds of objections. For example, some philosophers say that *causal determinism* and *freedom,* contrary to what we might have thought, are not really incompatible.[9] But if so, then God could have created free creatures who were free, and free to do what is wrong, but nevertheless were causally determined to do only what is right. Thus He could have created creatures who were free to do what was wrong, while nevertheless preventing them from ever performing any wrong actions—simply by seeing to it that they were causally determined to do only what is right. Of course this contradicts the Free Will Defense, according to which there is inconsistency in supposing that God determines free creatures to do only what is right. But is it really possible that all of a person's actions are causally determined while some of them are free? How could that be so? According to one version of the doctrine in question, to say that George acts freely on a given occasion is to say only this: *if George had chosen to do otherwise, he would have done otherwise.* Now George's action A is causally determined if some event E—some event beyond his control—has already occurred, where the state of affairs consisting in E's occurrence conjoined with Geroge's *refraining* from performing A, is a causally impossible state of affairs. Then one can consistently hold both that all of a man's actions are causally determined and that some of them are free in the above sense. For suppose that all of a man's actions are causally determined and that he *couldn't,* on any occasion, have made any choice or performed any action different from the ones he did make and perform. It could still be true that if he *had* chosen to do otherwise, he would have done otherwise. Granted, he couldn't have chosen to do otherwise; but this is consistent with saying that *if* he had, things would have gone differently.

This objection to the Free Will Defense seems utterly implausible. One might as well claim that being in jail doesn't really limit one's freedom on the grounds that if one were *not* in jail, he'd be free to come and go as he pleased. So I shall say no more about this objection here.[10]

A second objection is more formidable. In essence it goes like this. Surely it is possible to do only what is right, even if one is free to do wrong. It is *possible,* in that broadly logical sense, that there would be a world containing free creatures who always do what is right. There is certainly no *contradiction* or *inconsistency* in this idea. But God is omnipotent; his power has no nonlogical limitations. So if it's possible that there be a world containing creatures who are free to do what is wrong but never in fact do so, then it follows that an omnipotent God could create such a world. If so, however, the Free Will Defense must be mistaken in its insistence upon the possibility that God is omnipotent but unable to create a world containing moral good without permitting moral evil. J. L. Mackie . . . states this objection:

> If God has made men such that in their free choices they sometimes prefer what is good and sometimes what is evil, why could he not have made men such that they always freely choose the good? If there is no logical impossibility in a man's freely choosing the good on one, or on several occasions, there cannot be a logical impossibility in his freely choosing the good on every occasion. God was not, then, faced with a choice between making innocent automata and making beings who, in acting freely, would sometimes go wrong; there was open to him the obviously better possibility of making beings who would act freely but always go right. Clearly, his failure to avail himself of this possibility is inconsistent with his being both omnipotent and wholly good.[11]

Now what, exactly, is Mackie's point here? This. According to the Free Will Defense, it is possible both that God is omnipotent and that He was unable to create a world containing moral good without creating one containing moral evil. But, replies Mackie, this limitation on His power to create is inconsistent with God's omnipotence. For surely it's *possible* that there be a world containing perfectly virtuous persons—persons who are significantly

free but always do what is right. Surely there are *possible worlds* that contain moral good but no moral evil. But God, if He is omnipotent, can create any possible world He chooses. So it is *not* possible, contrary to the Free Will Defense, both that God is omnipotent and that He could create a world containing moral good only by creating one containing moral evil. If He is omnipotent, the only limitations of His power are *logical* limitations; in which case there are no possible worlds He could not have created.

This is a subtle and important point. According to the great German philosopher G. W. Leibniz, *this* world, the actual world, must be the best of all possible worlds. His reasoning goes as follows. Before God created anything at all, He was confronted with an enormous range of choices; He could create or bring into actuality any of the myriads of different possible worlds. Being perfectly good, He must have chosen to create the best world He could; being omnipotent, He was able to create any possible world He pleased. He must, therefore, have chosen the best of all possible worlds; and hence *this* world, the one He did create, must be the best possible. Now Mackie, of course, agrees with Leibniz that God, if omnipotent, could have created any world He pleased and would have created the best world he could. But while Leibniz draws the conclusion that this world, despite appearances, must be the best possible, Mackie concludes instead that there is no omnipotent, wholly good God. For, he says, it is obvious enough that this present world is not the best of all possible worlds.

The Free Will Defender disagrees with both Leibniz and Mackie. In the first place, he might say, what is the reason for supposing that *there* is such a thing as the best of all possible worlds? No matter how marvelous a world is—containing no matter how many persons enjoying unalloyed bliss—isn't it possible that there be an even better world containing even more persons enjoying even more unalloyed bliss? But what is really characteristic and central to the Free Will Defense is the claim that God, though omnipotent, could not have actualized just any possible world He pleased.

5. Was It Within God's Power to Create Any Possible World He Pleased?

This is indeed the crucial question for the Free Will Defense. If we wish to discuss it with insight and authority, we shall have to look into the idea of *possible worlds*. And a sensible first question is this: what sort of thing is a possible world? The basic idea is that a possible world is a *way things could have been*; it is a *state of affairs* of some kind. Earlier we spoke of states of affairs, in particular of good and evil states of affairs. Suppose we look at this idea in more detail. What sort of thing is a state of affairs? The following would be examples:

Nixon's having won the 1972 election
7 + 5's being equal to 12
All men's being mortal

and

Gary, Indiana's, having a really nasty pollution problem.

These are *actual* states of affairs: states of affairs that do in fact *obtain*. And corresponding to each such actual state of affairs there is a true proposition—in the above cases, the corresponding propositions would be *Nixon won the 1972 presidential election, 7 + 5 is equal to 12, all men are mortal,* and *Gary, Indiana, has a really nasty pollution problem.* A proposition *p corresponds* to a state of affairs *s,* in this sense, if it is impossible that *p* be true and *s* fail to obtain and impossible that *s* obtain and *p* fail to be true.

But just as there are false propositions, so there are states of affairs that do *not* obtain or are *not* actual. *Kissinger's having swum the Atlantic* and *Hubert Horatio Humphrey's having run a mile in four minutes* would be examples. Some states of affairs that do not obtain are *impossible:* e.g., *Hubert's having drawn a square circle, 7 + 5's being equal to 75,* and *Agnew's having a brother who was an only child.* The propositions corresponding to these states of affairs, of course, are necessarily false. So there are states of affairs that *obtain* or *are actual* and also states of affairs that

don't obtain. Among the latter some are *impossible* and others are possible. And a possible world is a possible state of affairs. Of course not every possible state of affairs is a possible world; *Hubert's having run a mile in four minutes* is a possible state of affairs but not a possible world. No doubt it is an *element* of many possible worlds, but it isn't itself inclusive enough to be one. To be a possible world, a state of affairs must be very large—so large as to be *complete* or *maximal.*

To get at this idea of completeness we need a couple of definitions. As we have already seen . . . a state of affairs *A includes* a state of affairs *B* if it is not possible that *A* obtain and *B* not obtain or if the conjunctive state of affairs *A but not B*—the state of affairs that obtains if and only if *A* obtains and *B* does not—is not possible. For example, *Jim Whittaker's being the first American to climb Mt. Everest* includes *Jim Whittaker's being an American.* It also includes *Mt. Everest's being climbed, something's being climbed, no American's having climbed Everest before Whittaker did,* and the like. *Inclusion* among states of affairs is like *entailment* among propositions; and where a state of affairs *A* includes a state of affairs *B,* the proposition corresponding to *A* entails the one corresponding to *B.* Accordingly, *Jim Whittaker is the first American to climb Everest* entails *Mt. Everest has been climbed, something has been climbed,* and *no American climbed Everest before Whittaker did.* Now suppose we say further that a state of affairs *A precludes* a state of affairs *B* if it is not possible that *both* obtain, or if the conjunctive state of affairs *A and B* is impossible. Thus *Whittaker's being the first American to climb Mt. Everest* precludes *Luther Jerstad's being the first American to climb Everest,* as well as *Whittaker's never having climbed any mountains.* If *A* precludes *B,* than *A*'s corresponding proposition entails the denial of the one corresponding to *B.* Still further, let's say that the *complement* of a state of affairs is the state of affairs that obtains just in case *A* does not obtain. [Or we might say that the complement (call it $\overline{A}$) of *A* is the state of affairs corresponding to the *denial* or *negation* of the proposition corresponding to *A.*] Given these definitions, we can say what it is for a state of affairs to be *complete: A* is a complete state of affairs if and only if for every state of affairs *B*, either *A* *includes B* or *A* *precludes B*. (We could express the same thing by saying that if *A* is a complete state of affairs, then for every state of affairs *B*, either *A* includes *B* or *A* includes $\overline{B}$ the complement of B.) And now we are able to say what a possible world is: a possible world is any possible state of affairs that is complete. If *A* is a possible world, then it says something about everything; every state of affairs *S* is either included in or precluded by it.

Corresponding to each possible world *W*, furthermore, there is a set of propositions that I'll call the book on *W*. A proposition is in the book on *W* just in case the state of affairs to which it corresponds is included in *W*. Or we might express it like this. Suppose we say that a proposition *P* *is true in a world W* if and only if *P would have been true if W had been actual*—if and only if, that is, it is not possible that *W* be actual and *P* be false. Then the book on *W* is the set of propositions true in *W*. Like possible worlds, books are *complete*; if *B* is a book, then for any proposition *P*, either *P* or the denial of *P* will be a member of *B*. A book is a *maximal consistent set* of propositions; it is so large that the addition of another proposition to it always yields an explicitly inconsistent set.

Of course, for each possible world there is exactly one book corresponding to it (that is, for a given world *W* there is just one book *B* such that each member of *B* is true in *W*); and for each book there is just one world to which it corresponds. So every world has its book.

It should be obvious that exactly one possible world is actual. At *least* one must be, since the set of true propositions is a maximal consistent set and hence a book. But then it corresponds to a possible world, and the possible world corresponding to this set of propositions (since it's the set of *true* propositions) will be actual. On the other hand there is at *most* one actual world. For suppose there were two: *W* and *W'*. These worlds cannot include all the very same states of affairs; if they did, they would be the very same world. So there must be at least one state of affairs *S* such that *W* includes *S* and *W'* does not. But a possible world is maximal; *W'*, therefore, includes the complement *S* of *S*. So if both *W* and *W'* were actual, as we have supposed, then

both *S* and $\overline{S}$ would be actual—which is impossible. So there can't be more than one possible world that is actual.

Leibniz pointed out that a proposition *p* is necessary if it is true in every possible world. We may add that *p* is possible if it is true in one world and impossible if true in none. Furthermore, *p entails q* if there is no possible world in which *p* is true and *q* is false, and *p is consistent with q* if there is at least one world in which both *p* and *q* are true.

A further feature of possible worlds is that people (and other things) *exist* in them. Each of us exists in the actual world, obviously; but a person also exists in many worlds distinct from the actual world. It would be a mistake, of course, to think of all of these worlds as somehow "going on" at the same time, with the same person reduplicated through these worlds and actually existing in a lot of different ways. This is not what is meant by saying that the same person exists in different possible worlds. What is meant, instead, is this: a person Paul exists in each of those possible worlds *W* which is such that, if *W had been actual,* Paul would have existed—actually existed. Suppose Paul had been an inch taller than he is, or a better tennis player. Then the world that does in fact obtain would not have been actual; some other world—*W'*, let's say—would have obtained instead. If *W'* had been actual, Paul would have existed; so Paul exists in *W'*. (Of course there are still other possible worlds in which Paul does not exist—worlds, for example, in which there are no people at all.) Accordingly, when we say that Paul exists in a world *W*, what we mean is that Paul *would have* existed had *W* been actual. Or we could put it like this: Paul exists in each world *W* that includes the state of affairs consisting in Paul's existence. We can put this still more simply by saying that Paul exists in those worlds whose books contain the proposition *Paul exists*.

But isn't there a problem here? *Many* people are named "Paul": Paul the apostle, Paul J. Zwier, John Paul Jones, and many other famous Pauls. So who goes with "Paul exists"? Which Paul? The answer has to do with the fact that books contain *propositions*—not sentences. They contain the sort of thing sentences are used to express and assert. And the same sentence—"Aristotle is wise," for example— can be used to express many different propositions. When Plato used it, he asserted a proposition predicating wisdom of his famous pupil; when Jackie Onassis uses it, she asserts a proposition predicating wisdom of her wealthy husband. These are distinct propositions (we might even think they differ in truth value); but they are expressed by the same sentence. Normally (but not always) we don't have much trouble determining which of the several propositions expressed by a given sentence is relevant in the context at hand. So in this case a given person, Paul, exists in a world W if and only if W' book contains the proposition that says that he— that particular person—exists. The fact that the sentence we use to express this proposition can also be used to express *other* propositions is not relevant.

After this excursion into the nature of books and worlds we can return to our question. Could God have created just any world He chose? Before addressing the question, however, we must note that God does not, strictly speaking, *create* any possible worlds or states of affairs at all. What He creates are the heavens and the earth and all that they contain. But He has not created states of affairs. There are, for example, the state of affairs consisting in God's existence and the state of affairs consisting in His nonexistence. That is, there is such a thing as the state of affairs consisting in the existence of God, and there is also such a thing as the state of affairs consisting in the nonexistence of God, just as there are the two propositions *God exists* and *God does not exist*. The theist believes that the first state of affairs is actual and the first proposition true, the atheist believes that the second state of affairs is actual and the second proposition true. But, of course, both propositions *exist*, even though just one is true. Similarly, there are two states of affairs here, just one of which is actual. So both states of affairs *exist*, but only one *obtains*. And God has not created either one of them since there never was a time at which either did not exist. Nor has he created the state of affairs consisting in the earth's existence; there was a time when *the earth* did not exist, but none when the state of affairs consisting in the earth's existence didn't exist. Indeed, God did not bring into existence any states of affairs at all.

What He did was to perform actions of a certain sort—creating the heavens and the earth, for example—which resulted in the *actuality* of certain states of affairs. God *actualizes* states of affairs. He actualizes the possible world that does in fact obtain; He does not create it. And while He has created Socrates, He did not create the state of affairs consisting in Socrates' existence.[12]

Bearing this in mind, let's finally return to our question. Is the atheologian right in holding that if God is omnipotent, then he could have actualized or created any possible world He pleased? Not obviously. First, we must ask ourselves whether God is a *necessary* or a *contingent* being. A *necessary* being is one that exists in every possible world—one that would have existed no matter which possible world had been actual; a contingent being exists only in some possible worlds. Now if God is not a necessary being (and many, perhaps most, theists think that He is not), then clearly enough there will be many possible worlds He could not have actualized—all those, for example, in which He does not exist. Clearly, God could not have created a world in which He doesn't even exist.

So, if God is a contingent being then there are many possible worlds beyond His power to create. But this is really irrelevant to our present concerns. For perhaps the atheologian can maintain his case if he revises his claim to avoid this difficulty; perhaps he will say something like this: if God is omnipotent, then He could have actualized any of these possible worlds *in which He exists*. So if He exists and is omnipotent, He could have actualized (contrary to the Free Will Defense) and of those possible worlds in which He exists and in which there exist free creatures who do no wrong. He could have actualized worlds containing moral good but no moral evil. Is this correct?

Let's begin with a trivial example. You and Paul have just returned from an Australian hunting expedition: your quarry was the elusive double-wattled cassowary. Paul captured an aardvark, mistaking it for a cassowary. The creature's disarming ways have won it a place in Paul's heart; he is deeply attached to it. Upon your return to the States you offer Paul $500 for his aardvark, only to be rudely turned down. Later you ask yourself, "What would he have done if I'd offered him $700?" Now what is it, exactly, that you are asking? What you're really asking in a way is whether, under a *specific set of conditions*, Paul would have sold it. These conditions include your having offered him $700 rather than $500 for the aardvark, everything else being as much as possible like the conditions that did in fact obtain. Let *S'* be this set of conditions or state of affairs. *S'* includes the state of affairs consisting in your offering Paul $700 (instead of the $500 you did offer him); of course it does not include his *accepting* your offer, and it does not include his *rejecting* it; for the rest, the conditions it includes are just like the ones that did obtain in the actual world. So, for example, *S'* includes Paul's being free to accept the offer and free to refrain; and if in fact the going rate for an aardvark was $650, then *S'* includes the state of affairs consisting in the going rate's being $650. So we might put your question by asking which of the following conditionals is true:

(23) If the state of affairs *S'* had obtained, Paul would have accepted the offer

(24) If the state of affairs *S'* had obtained, Paul would not have accepted the offer.

It seems clear that at least one of these conditionals is true, but naturally they can't both be; so exactly one is.

Now since *S'* includes neither Paul's accepting the offer not his rejecting it, the antecedent of (23) and (24) does not entail the consequent of either. That is,

(25) *S'* obtains

does not entail either

(26) Paul accepts the offer

or

(27) Paul does not accept the offer.

So there are possible worlds in which both (25) and (26) are true, and other possible worlds in which both (25) and (27) are true.

We are now in a position to grasp an important fact. Either (23) or (24) is in fact true; and either way there are possible worlds God could not have actualized. Suppose, first of all, that (23) is true. Then it was beyond the power of God to create a world in which (1) Paul is free to sell his aardvark and free to refrain, and in which the other states of affairs included in *S'* obtain, and (2) Paul does not sell. That is, it was beyond His power to create a world in which (25) and (27) are both true. There is at least one possible world like this, but God, despite His omnipotence, could not have brought about its actuality. For let *W* be such a world. To actualize *W*, God must bring it about that Paul is free with respect to this action, and that the other states of affairs included in *S'* obtain. But (23), as we are supposing, is true; so if God had actualized *S'* and left Paul *free* with respect to this action, he would have sold: in which case *W* would not have been actual. If, on the other hand, God had *brought it about* that Paul didn't sell or had *caused him* to refrain from selling, then Paul would not have been free with respect to this action; then *S'* would not have been actual (since *S'* includes Paul's being free with respect to it), and *W* would not have been actual since *W* includes *S'*.

Of course if it is (24) rather than (23) that is true, then another class of worlds was beyond God's power to actualize—those, namely, in which *S'* obtains and Paul *sells* his aardvark. These are the worlds in which both (25) and (26) are true. But either (23) or (24) is true. Therefore, there are possible worlds God could not have actualized. If we consider whether or not God could have created a world in which, let's say, both (25) and (26) are true, we see that the answer depends upon a peculiar kind of fact; it depends upon what Paul would have freely chosen to do in a certain situation. So there are any number of possible worlds such that it is partly up to Paul whether God can create them.[13]

That was a past tense example. Perhaps it would be useful to consider a future tense case, since this might seem to correspond more closely to God's situation in choosing a possible world to actualize. At some time *t* in the near future Maurice will be free with respect to some insignificant action—having freeze-dried oatmeal for breakfast, let's say. That is, at time *t* Maurice will be free to have oatmeal but also free to take something else—shredded wheat, perhaps. Next, suppose we consider *S'*, a state of affairs that is included in the actual world and includes Maurice's being free with respect to taking oatmeal at time *t*. That is, *S'* includes Maurice's being free at time *t* to take oatmeal and free to reject it. *S'* does not include Maurice's taking oatmeal, however; nor does it include his rejecting it. For the rest *S'* is as much as possible like the actual world. In particular there are many conditions that do in fact hold at time *t* and are *relevant* to his choice—such conditions, for example, as the fact that he hasn't had oatmeal lately, that his wife will be annoyed if he rejects it, and the like; and *S'* includes each of these conditions. Now God no doubt knows what Maurice will do at time *t*, if *S* obtains; He knows which action Maurice would freely perform if *S* were to be actual. That is, God knows that one of the following conditionals is true:

(28) If *S'* were to obtain, Maurice will freely take the oatmeal

or

(29) If *S'* were to obtain, Maurice will freely reject it.

We may not know which of these is true, and Maurice himself may not know; but presumably God does.

So either God knows that (28) is true, or else He knows that (29) is. Let's suppose it is (28). Then there is a possible world that God, though omnipotent, cannot create. For consider a possible world *W'* that shares *S'* with the actual world (which for ease of reference I'll name "Kronos") and in which Maurice does *not* take oatmeal. (We know there is such a world, since *S'* does not include Maurice's taking the oatmeal.) *S'* obtains in *W'* just as it does in Kronos. Indeed, everything in *W'* is just as it is in Kronos up to time *t*. But whereas in Kronos Maurice takes oatmeal at time *t*, in *W'* he does not. Now *W'* is a perfectly possible world; but it is not within God's power to create it or bring about its actuality. For to do so He must actualize *S'*. But (28) is in fact true. So if God actualizes *S'* (as He must to create *W'*) and leaves Maurice free with respect to the action in question, then he will take the oatmeal; and then, of course, *W'* will not be actual.

If, on the other hand, God causes Maurice to *refrain* from taking the oatmeal, then he is not *free* to take it. That means, once again, that *W'* is not actual; for in *W'* Maurice is free to take the oatmeal (even if he doesn't do so). So if (28) is true, then this world *W'* is one that God can't actualize, it is not within His power to actualize it even though He is omnipotent and it is a possible world.

Of course, if it is (29) that is true, we get a similar result; then too there are possible worlds that God can't actualize. These would be worlds which share *S'* with Kronos and in which Maurice *does* take oatmeal. But either (28) or (29) *is* true; so either way there is a possible world that God can't create. If we consider a world in which *S'* obtains and in which Maurice freely chooses oatmeal at time *t*, we see that whether or not it is within God's power to actualize it depends upon what Maurice would do if he were free in a certain situation. Accordingly, there are any number of possible worlds such that it is partly up to Maurice whether or not God can actualize them. It is, of course, up to God whether or not to create Maurice and also up to God whether or not to make him free with respect to the action of taking oatmeal at time *t*. (God could, if He chose, cause him to succumb to the dreaded *equine obsession,* a condition shared by some people and most horses, whose victims find it *psychologically impossible* to refuse oats or oat products.) But if He creates Maurice and creates him free with respect to this action, then whether or not he actually performs the action is up to Maurice—not God.[14]

Now we can return to the Free Will Defense and the problem of evil. The Free Will Defender, you recall, insists on the possibility that it is not within God's power to create a world containing moral good without creating one containing moral evil. His atheological opponent—Mackie, for example—agrees with Leibniz in insisting that *if* (as the theist holds) God is omnipotent, then it *follows* that He could have created any possible world He pleased. We now see that this contention—call it "Leibniz' Lapse"—is a mistake. The atheologian is right in holding that there are many possible worlds containing moral good but no moral evil; his mistake lies in endorsing Leibniz' Lapse. So one of his premises—that God, if omnipotent, could have actualized just any world He pleased—is false.

6. Could God Have Created a World Containing Moral Good but No Moral Evil?

Now suppose we recapitulate the logic of the situation. The Free Will Defender claims that the following is possible:

(30) God is omnipotent, and it was not within His power to create a world containing moral good but no moral evil.

By way of retort the atheologian insists that there are possible worlds containing moral good but no moral evil. He adds that an omnipotent being could have actualized any possible world he chose. So if God is omnipotent, it follows that He could have actualized a world containing moral good but no moral evil, hence (30), contrary to the Free Will Defender's claim, is not possible. What we have seen so far is that his second premise—Leibniz' Lapse—is false.

Of course, this does not settle the issue in the Free Will Defender's favor. Leibniz' Lapse (appropriately enough for a lapse) is false; but this doesn't show that (30) is possible. To show this latter we must demonstrate the possibility that among the worlds God could not have actualized are all the worlds containing moral good but no moral evil. How can we approach this question?

Instead of choosing oatmeal for breakfast or selling an aardvark, suppose we think about a morally significant action such as taking a bribe. Curley Smith, the mayor of Boston, is opposed to the proposed freeway route; it would require destruction of the Old North Church along with some other antiquated and structurally unsound buildings. L. B. Smedes, the director of highways, asks him whether he'd drop his opposition for $1 million. "Of course," he replies. "Would you do it for $2?" asks Smedes. "What do you take me for?" comes the indignant reply. "That's already established," smirks Smedes; "all that remains is to nail down

your price." Smedes then offers him a bribe of $35,000; unwilling to break with the fine old traditions of Bay State politics, Curley accepts. Smedes then spends a sleepless night wondering whether he could have bought Curley for $20,000.

Now suppose we assume that Curley was free with respect to the action of taking the bribe—free to take it and free to refuse. And suppose, furthermore, that he would have taken it. That is, let us suppose that

(31) If Smedes had offered Curley a bribe of $20,000, he would have accepted it.

If (31) is true, then there is a state of affairs S' that (1) includes Curley's being offered a bribe of $20,000; (2) does not include either his accepting the bribe or his rejecting it; and (3) is otherwise as much as possible like the actual world. Just to make sure S' includes every relevant circumstance, let us suppose that it is a *maximal world segment.* That is, add to S' any state of affairs compatible with but not included in it, and the result will be an entire possible world. We could think of it roughly like this: S' is included in at least one world W in which Curley takes the bribe and in at least one world W' in which he rejects it. If S' is a maximal world segment, then S' is what remains of W when *Curley's taking the bribe* is deleted; it is also what remains of W' when *Curley's rejecting the bribe* is detected. More exactly, if S' is a maximal world segment, then every possible state of affairs that includes S', but isn't included by S', is a possible world. So if (31) is true, then there is a maximal world segment S' that (1) includes Curley's being offered a bribe of $20,000; (2) does not include either his accepting the bribe or his rejecting it; (3) is otherwise as much as possible like the actual world—in particular, it includes Curley's being free with respect to the bribe; and (4) is such that if it were actual then Curley would have taken the bribe. That is,

(32) if S' were actual, Curley would have accepted the bribe is true.

Now, of course, there is at least one possible world W' in which S' is actual and Curley does not take the bribe. But God could not have created

W'; to do so, He would have been obliged to actualize *S'*, leaving Curley free with respect to the action of taking the bribe. But under these conditions Curley, as (32) assures us, would have accepted the bribe, so that the world thus created would not have been *S'*.

Curley, as we see, is not above a bit of Watergating. But there may be worse to come. Of course, there are possible worlds in which he is significantly free (i.e., free with respect to a morally significant action) and never does what is wrong. But the sad truth about Curley may be this. Consider *W'*, any of these worlds: in *W'* Curley is significantly free, so in *W'* there are some actions that are morally significant for him and with respect to which he is free. But at least one of these actions—call it *A*—has the following peculiar property. There is a maximal world segment *S'* that obtains in *W'* and is such that (1) *S'* includes Curley's being free *re A* but neither his performing *A* nor his refraining from *A*; (2) *S'* is otherwise as much as possible like *W'* and (3) if *S'* had been actual, Curley would have gone wrong with respect to *A*.[15] (Notice that this third condition holds in fact, in the actual world; it does not hold in that world *W'*.)

This means, of course, that God could not have actualized *W'*. For to do so He'd have been obliged to bring it about that *S'* is actual; but then Curley would go wrong with respect to *A*. Since in *W'* he always does what is right, the world thus actualized would not be *W'*. On the other hand, if God *causes* Curley to go right with respect to *A* or *brings it about that* he does so, then Curley isn't free with respect to *A*; and so once more it isn't *W'* that is actual. Accordingly God cannot create *W'*. But *W'* was just any of the worlds in which Curley is significantly free but always does only what is right. It therefore follows that it was not within God's power to create a world in which Curley produces moral good but no moral evil. Every world God can actualize is such that if Curley is significantly free in it, he takes at least one wrong action.

Obviously Curley is in serious trouble. I shall call the malady from which he suffers *transworld depravity*. (I leave as homework the problem of comparing transworld depravity with what Calvin-ists call "total depravity.") By way of explicit definition:

(33) A person *P* suffers from transworld depravity if and only if the following holds: for every world *W* such that *P* is significantly free in *W* and *P* does only what is right in *W*, there is an action *A* and a maximal world segment *S'* such that

    (1) *S'* includes *A*'s being morally significant for *P*

    (2) *S'* includes *P*'s being free with respect to *A*

    (3) *S'* is included in *W* and includes neither *P*'s performing *A* nor *P*'s refraining from performing *A*

and

(4) If *S'* were actual, *P* would go wrong with respect to *A*.

(In thinking about this definition, remember that (4) is to be true in fact, in the actual world—not in that world *W*.)

What is important about the idea of transworld depravity is that if a person suffers from it, then it wasn't within God's power to actualize any world in which that person is significantly free but does no wrong—that is, a world in which he produces moral good but no moral evil.

We have been here considering a crucial contention of the Free Will Defender: the contention, namely, that

(30) God is omnipotent, and it was not within His power to create a world containing moral good but no moral evil.

How is transworld depravity relevant to this? As follows. Obviously it is possible that there be persons who suffer from transworld depravity. More generally, it is possible that *everybody* suffers from it. And if this possibility were actual, then God, though omnipotent, could not have created any of the possible worlds containing just the persons who do in fact exist, and containing moral good but no moral evil. For to do so He'd have to create persons who were significantly free (otherwise there would be no moral good) but suffered from transworld depravity. Such persons go wrong with respect to at least one action in any world God could have actualized and in which they are free with respect to morally significant actions; so the price for creating a world in which they produce moral good is creating one in which they also produce moral evil.

Notes

1. John Mackie, "Evil and Omnipotence," in *The Philosophy of Religion*, ed. Basil Mitchell (London: Oxford University Press, 1971), p. 92.[See previous reading.]

2. Ibid., p. 93. [*Philosophy of Religion: Selected Readings,* Second Edition, p. 224.]

3. More simply, the question is really just whether any good state of affairs includes an evil; a little reflection reveals that no good state of affairs can include an evil that it does *not* outweigh.

4. In Plantinga, *God and Other Minds* (Ithaca, N.Y.: Cornell University Press, 1967), chap. 5, I explore further the project of finding such propositions.

5. *The Problem of Free Choice*, Vol. 22 of *Ancient Christian Writers* (Westminster, Md.: The Newman Press, 1955), bk. 2, pp. 14–15.

6. Ibid., bk. 3, p. 9.

7. I am indebted to Henry Schuurman (in conversation) for helpful discussion of the difference between this pastoral function and those served by a theodicy or a defense.

8. This distinction is not very precise (how, exactly, are we to construe "results from"?), but perhaps it will serve our present purposes.

9. See, for example, A. Flew, "Divine Omnipotence and Human Freedom," in *New Essays in Philosophical Theology*, eds. A. Flew and A. MacIntyre (London: SCM, 1955), pp. 150–53.

10. For further discussion of it see Plantinga, *God and Other Minds,* pp. 132–35.

11. Mackie, in *The Philosophy of Religion*, pp. 100–101.

12. Strict accuracy demands, therefore, that we speak of God as *actualizing* rather than creating possible worlds. I shall continue to use both locutions, thus sacrificing accuracy to familiarity. For more about possible worlds see my book *The Nature of Necessity* (Oxford: The Clarendon Press, 1974), chaps. 4–8.

13. For a fuller statement of this argument see Plantinga, *The Nature of Necessity*, chap. 9, secs. 4–6.

14. For a more complete and more exact statement of this argument see Plantinga, *The Nature of Necessity,* chap. 9, secs. 4–6.

15. A person goes wrong with respect to an action if he either wrongfully performs it or wrongfully fails to perform it.

III.7   The Inductive Argument from Evil Against the Existence of God

WILLIAM ROWE

William Rowe argues that an inductive or probabilistic version of the argument from evil justifies atheism. He concedes that deductive arguments against the existence of God on the basis of evil, such as J. L. Mackie uses (reading III.5), do not succeed. Nevertheless, it is reasonable to believe that there is evil in the form of pointless suffering which a God, if He existed, would prevent. So it is reasonable to believe that there is no God. In the last part of his essay Rowe defines his position as "friendly atheism," since he admits that a theist may be justified in rejecting the probabilistic argument from evil.

Reprinted from "The Problem of Evil and Some Varieties of Atheism," *American Philosophical Quarterly* 16 (1979) by permission. Footnotes edited.

This paper is concerned with three interrelated questions. The first is: Is there an argument for atheism based on the existence of evil that may rationally justify someone in being an atheist? To this first question I give an affirmative answer and try to support that answer by setting forth a strong argument for atheism based on the existence of evil.[1] The second question is: How can the theist best defend his position against the argument for atheism based on the existence of evil? In response to this question I try to describe what may be an adequate rational defense for theism against any argument for atheism based on the existence of evil. The final question is: What position should the informed atheist take concerning the rationality of theistic belief? Three different answers an atheist may give to this question serve to distinguish three varieties of atheism: unfriendly atheism, indifferent atheism, and friendly atheism. In the final part of the paper I discuss and defend the position of friendly atheism.

Before we consider the argument from evil, we need to distinguish a narrow and a broad sense of the terms 'theist.' 'atheist,' and 'agnostic.' By a 'theist' in the narrow sense I mean someone who believes in the existence of an omnipotent, omniscient, eternal, supremely good being who created the world. By a 'theist' in the broad sense I mean someone who believes in the existence of some sort of divine being or divine reality. To be a theist in the narrow sense is also to be a theist in the broad sense, but one may be a theist in the broad sense—as was Paul Tillich—without believing that there is a supremely good, omnipotent, omniscient, eternal being who created the world. Similar distinctions must be made between a narrow and a broad sense of the terms 'atheist' and 'agnostic.' To be an atheist in the broad sense is to deny the existence of any sort of divine being or divine reality. Tillich was not an atheist in the broad sense. But he was an atheist in the narrow sense, for he denied that there exists a divine being that is all-knowing, all-powerful and perfectly good. In this paper I will be using the terms 'theism,' 'theist,' 'atheism,' 'atheist,' 'agnosticism,' and 'agnostic' in the narrow sense, not in the broad sense.

I

In developing the argument for atheism based on the existence of evil, it will be useful to focus on some particular evil that our world contains in considerable abundance. Intense human and animal suffering, for example, occurs daily and in great plenitude in our world. Such intense suffering is a clear case of evil. Of course, if the intense suffering leads to some greater good, a good we could not have obtained without undergoing the suffering in question, we might conclude that the suffering is justified, but it remains an evil nevertheless. For we must not confuse the intense suffering in and of itself with the good things to which it sometimes leads or of which it may be a necessary part. Intense human or animal suffering is in itself bad, an evil, even though it may sometimes be justified by virtue of being a part of, or leading to, some good which is unobtainable without it. What is evil in itself may sometimes be good as a means because it leads to something that is good in itself. In such a case, while remaining an evil in itself, the intense human or animal suffering is, nevertheless, an evil which someone might be morally justified in permitting.

Taking human and animal suffering as a clear instance of evil which occurs with great frequency in our world, the argument for atheism based on evil can be stated as follows:

1. There exist instances of intense suffering which an omnipotent, omniscient being could have prevented without thereby losing some greater good or permitting some evil equally bad or worse.[2]
2. An omniscient, wholly good being would prevent the occurrence of any intense suffering it could, unless it could not do so without thereby losing some greater good or permitting some evil equally bad or worse.
3. There does not exist an omnipotent, omniscient, wholly good being.

What are we to say about this argument for atheism, an argument based on the profusion of one sort of evil in our world? The argument is valid; therefore, if we have rotational grounds for accepting its premises, to that extent we have rational grounds for accepting atheism. Do we, however, have rational grounds for accepting the premises of this argument?

Let's begin with the second premise. Let s_1 be an instance of intense human or animal suffering which an omniscient, wholly good being could prevent. We will also suppose that things are such that s_1 will occur unless prevented by the omniscient, wholly good (*OG*) being. We might be interested in determining what would be a *sufficient* condition of *OG* failing to prevent s_1. But, for our purpose here, we need only try to state a necessary condition for *OG* failing to prevent s_1. That condition, so it seems to me, is this:

Either
(i)   there is some greater good, *G*, such that *G* is obtainable by *OG* only if *OG* permits s_1,
or
(ii)   there is some greater good, *G*, such that *G* is obtainable by *OG* only if *OG* permits either s_1 or some evil equally bad or worse,
or
(iii) s_1 is such that it is preventable by *OG* only if *OG* permits some evil equally bad or worse.

It is important to recognize that (iii) is not included in (i). For losing a good greater than s_1 is not the same as permitting an evil greater than s_1. And this because the *absence* of a good state of affairs need not itself be an evil state of affairs. It is also important to recognize that s_1 might be such that it is preventable by *OG without* losing *G* (so condition (i) is not satisfied) but also such that if *OG* did prevent it, *G* would be lost *unless OG* permitted some evil equal to or worse than s_1. If this were so, it does not seem correct to require that *OG* prevent s_1. Thus, condition (ii) takes into account an important possibility not encompassed in condition (i).

Is it true that if an omniscient, wholly good being permits the occurrence of some intense suffering it could have prevented, then either (i) or (ii) or (iii) obtains? It seems to me that it is true. But if it is true then so is premise (2) of the argument for atheism. For that premise merely states in more compact form what we have suggested must be true if an omniscient, wholly good being fails to prevent some intense suffering it could prevent. Premise (2) says that an omniscient, wholly good being would prevent the occurrence of any intense suffering it could, unless it could not do so without thereby losing some greater good or permitting some evil equally bad or worse. This premise (or something not too distant from it) is, I think, held in common

by many atheists and nontheists. Of course, there may be disagreement about whether something is good, and whether, if it is good, one would be morally justified in permitting some intense suffering to occur in order to obtain it. Someone might hold, for example, that no good is great enough to justify permitting an innocent child to suffer terribly. Again, someone might hold that the mere fact that a given good outweighs some suffering and would be lost if the suffering were prevented, is not a morally sufficient reason for permitting the suffering. But to hold either of these views is not to deny (2). For (2) claims only that *if* an omniscient, wholly good being permits intense suffering *then* either there is some greater good that would have been lost, or some equally bad or worse evil that would have occurred, had the intense suffering been prevented. (2) does not purport to describe what might be a *sufficient* condition for an omniscient, wholly good being to permit intense suffering, only what is a *necessary* condition. So stated, (2) seems to express a belief that accords with our basic moral principles, principles shared by both theists and nontheists. If we are to fault the argument for atheism, therefore, it seems we must find some fault with its first premise.

Suppose in some distant forest lightning strikes a dead tree, resulting in a forest fire. In the fire a fawn is trapped, horribly burned, and lies in terrible agony for several days before death relieves its suffering. So far as we can see, the fawn's intense suffering is pointless. For there does not appear to be any greater good such that the prevention of the fawn's suffering would require either the loss of that good or the occurrence of an evil equally bad or worse. Nor does there seem to be any equally bad or worse evil so connected to the fawn's suffering that it would have had to occur had the fawn's suffering been prevented. Could an omnipotent, omniscient being have prevented the fawn's apparently pointless suffering? The answer is obvious, as even the theist will insist. An omnipotent, omniscient being could have easily prevented the fawn from being horribly burned, or, given the burning, could have spared the fawn the intense suffering by quickly ending its life, rather than allowing the fawn to lie in terrible agony for several days. Since the fawn's intense suffering was preventable and, so far as we can see, pointless, doesn't it appear that premise (1) of the argument is true, that there do exist instances of intense suffering which an omnipotent, omniscient being could have prevented without thereby losing some greater good or permitting some evil equally bad or worse?

It must be acknowledged that the case of the fawn's apparently pointless suffering does not prove that (1) is true. For even though we cannot see how the fawn's suffering is required to obtain some greater good (or to prevent some equally bad or worse evil), it hardly follows that it is not so required. After all, we are often surprised by how things we thought to be unconnected turn out to be intimately connected. Perhaps, for all we know, there is some familiar good outweighing the fawn's suffering to which that suffering is connected in a way we do not see. Furthermore, there may well be unfamiliar goods, goods we haven't dreamed of, to which the fawn's suffering is inextricably connected. Indeed, it would seem to require something like omniscience on our part before we could lay claim to *knowing* that there is no greater good connected to the fawn's suffering in such a manner than an omnipotent, omniscient being could not have achieved that good without permitting that suffering or some evil equally bad or worse. So the case of the fawn's suffering surely does not enable us to *establish* the truth of (1).

The truth is that we are not in a position to prove that (1) is true. We cannot know with certainty that instances of suffering of the sort described in (1) do occur in our world. But it is one thing to *know* or *prove* that (1) is true and quite another thing to have *rational grounds* for believing (1) to be true. We are often in the position where in the light of our experience and knowledge it is rational to believe that a certain statement is true, even though we are not in a position to prove or to know with certainty that the statement is true. In the light of our past experience and knowledge it is, for example, very reasonable to believe that neither Goldwater nor McGovern will ever be elected President, but we are scarcely in the position of knowing with certainty that neither will ever be elected President. So, too, with (1), although we cannot know with cer-

tainty that it is true, it perhaps can be rationally supported, shown to be a rational belief.

Consider again the case of the fawn's suffering. Is it reasonable to believe that there is some greater good so intimately connected to that suffering that even an omnipotent, omniscient being could not have obtained that good without permitting that suffering or some evil at least as bad? It certainly does not appear reasonable to believe this. Nor does it seem reasonable to believe that there is some evil at least as bad as the fawn's suffering such that an omnipotent being simply could not have prevented it without permitting the fawn's suffering. But even if it should somehow be reasonable to believe either of these things of the fawn's suffering, we must then ask whether it is reasonable to believe either of these things of *all* the instances of seemingly pointless human and animal suffering that occur daily in our world. And surely the answer to this more general question must be no. It seems quite unlikely that *all* the instances of intense suffering occurring daily in our world are intimately related to the occurrence of greater goods or the prevention of evils at least as bad; and even more unlikely, should they somehow all be so related, that an omnipotent, omniscient being could not have achieved at least some of those goods (or prevented some of those evils) without permitting the instances of intense suffering that are supposedly related to them. In the light of our experience and knowledge of the variety and scale of human and animal suffering in our world, the idea that none of this suffering could have been prevented by an omnipotent being without thereby losing a greater good or permitting an evil at least as bad seems an extraordinary absurd idea, quite beyond our belief. It seems then that although we cannot *prove* that (1) is true, it is, nevertheless, altogether *reasonable* to believe that (1) is true, that (1) is a *rational* belief.

Returning now to our argument for atheism, we've seen that the second premise expresses a basic belief common to many theists and nontheists. We've also seen that our experience and knowledge of the variety and profusion of suffering in our world provides *rational support* for the first premise. Seeing that the conclusion, 'There does not exist an omnipotent, omniscient, wholly good being' follows from these two premises, it does seem that we have *rational support* for atheism, that it is reasonable for us to believe that the theistic God does not exist.

II

Can theism be rationally defended against the argument for atheism we have just examined? If it can, how might the theist best respond to that argument? Since the argument from (1) and (2) to (3) is valid, and since the theist, no less than the nontheist, is more than likely committed to (2), it's clear that the theist can reject this atheistic argument only by rejecting its first premise, the premise that states that there are instances of intense suffering which an omnipotent, omniscient being could have prevented without thereby losing some greater good or permitting some evil equally bad or worse. How, then, can the theist best respond to this premise and the considerations advanced in its support?

There are basically three responses a theist can make. First, he might argue not that (1) is false or probably false, but only that the reasoning given in support of it is in some way *defective.* He may do this either by arguing that the reasons given in support of (1) are *in themselves* insufficient to justify accepting (1), or by arguing that there are other things we know which, when taken in conjunction with these reasons, do not justify us in accepting (1). I suppose some theists would be content with this rather modest response to the basic argument for atheism. But given the validity of the basic argument and the theist's likely acceptance of (2), he is thereby committed to the view that (1) is false, not just that we have no good reasons for accepting (1) as true. The second two responses are aimed at showing that it is reasonable to believe that (1) is false. Since the theist is committed to this view, I shall focus the discussion on these two attempts, attempts which we can distinguish as 'the direct attack' and 'the indirect attack.'

By a direct attack, I mean an attempt to reject (1) by pointing out goods, for example, to which suffering may well be connected, goods which an omnipotent, omniscient being could not achieve without permitting suffering. It is doubtful, however, that the direct attack can succeed. The theist may point out that some suffering leads to moral and spiritual development impossible without suffering. But it's reasonably clear that suffering often occurs in a degree far beyond what is required for character development. The theist may say that some suffering results from free choices of human beings and might be preventable only by preventing some measure of human freedom. But, again, it's clear that much intense suffering occurs not as a result of human free choices. The general difficulty with this direct attack on premise (1) is twofold. First, it cannot succeed, for the theist does not know what greater goods might be served, or evils prevented, by each instance of intense human or animal suffering. Second, the theist's own religious tradition usually maintains that in this life it is not given to us to know God's purpose in allowing particular instances of suffering. Hence, the direct attack against premise (1) cannot succeed and violates basic beliefs associated with theism.

The best procedure for the theist to follow in rejecting premise (1) is the indirect procedure. This procedure I shall call 'the G. E. Moore shift', so-called in honor of the twentieth century philosopher, G. E. Moore, who used it to great effect in dealing with the arguments of the skeptics. Skeptical philosophers such as David Hume have advanced ingenious arguments to prove that no one can know of the existence of any material object. The premises of their arguments employ plausible principles, principles which many philosophers have tried to reject directly, but only with questionable success. Moore's procedure was altogether different. Instead of arguing directly against the premises of the skeptic's arguments, he simply noted that the premises implied, for example, that he (Moore) did not know of the existence of a pencil. Moore then proceeded indirectly against the skeptic's premises by arguing:

> I do know that this pencil exists.
> If the skeptic's principles are correct I cannot know of the existence of this pencil.
> ∴ The skeptic's principles (at least one) must be incorrect.

Moore then noted that his argument is just as valid as the skeptic's, that both of their arguments contain the premise 'If the skeptic's principles are correct Moore cannot know of the existence of this pencil,' and concluded that the only way to choose between the two arguments (Moore's and the skeptic's) is by deciding which of the first premises it is more rational to believe—Moore's premise 'I do know that this pencil exists' or the skeptic's premise asserting that his skeptical principles are correct. Moore concluded that his own first premise was the more rational of the two.

Before we see how the theist may apply the G. E. Moore shift to the basic argument of atheism, we should note the general strategy of the shift. We're given an argument: *p, q,* therefore, *r.* Instead of arguing directly against *p,* another argument is constructed not-*r, q,* therefore, not-*p*—which begins with the denial of the conclusion of the first argument, keeps its second premise, and ends with the denial of the first premise as its conclusion. Compare, for example, these two:

I. *p*   II. not-*r*
   q   *q*
   r   not-*p*

It is a truth of logic that if I is valid II must be valid as well. Since the arguments are the same so far as the second premise is concerned, any choice between them must concern their respective first premises. To argue against the first premise (*p*) by constructing the counter argument II is to employ the G. E. Moore shift.

Applying the G. E. Moore shift against the first premise of the basic argument for atheism, the theist can argue as follows:

not-3. There exists an omnipotent, omniscient, wholly good being.
　2.　An omniscient, wholly good being would prevent the occurrence of any intense suffering it could, unless it could not do so without thereby losing some greater good or permitting some evil equally bad or worse.

therefore,

not-1. It is not the case that there exist instances of intense suffering which an omnipotent, omniscient being could have prevented without thereby losing some greater good or permitting some evil equally bad or worse.

We now have two arguments: the basic argument for atheism from (1) and (2) to (3), and the theist's best response, the argument from (not-3) and (2) to (not-1). What the theist then says about (1) is that he has rational grounds for believing in the existence of the theistic God (not-3), accepts (2) as true, and sees that (not-1) follows from (not-3) and (2). He concludes, therefore, that he has rational grounds for rejecting (1). Having rational grounds for rejecting (1), the theist concludes that the basic argument for atheism is mistaken.

III

We've had a look at a forceful argument for atheism and what seems to be the theist's best response to that argument. If one is persuaded by the argument for atheism, as I find myself to be, how might one best view the position of the theist? Of course, he will view the theist as having a false belief, just as the theist will view the atheist as having a false belief. But what position should the atheist take concerning the *rationality* of the theist's belief? There are three major positions an atheist might take, positions which we may think of as some varieties of atheism. First, the atheist may believe that no one is rationally justified in believing that the theistic God exists. Let us call this position 'unfriendly atheism'. Second, the atheist may hold no belief concerning whether any theist is or isn't rationally justified in believing that the theistic God exists. Let us call this view 'indifferent atheism'. Finally, the atheist may believe that some theists are rationally justified in believing that the theistic God exists. This view we shall call 'friendly atheism'. In this final part of the paper I propose to discuss and defend the position of friendly atheism.

If no one can be rationally justified in believing a false proposition then friendly atheism is a paradoxical, if not incoherent position. But surely the truth of a belief is not a necessary condition of someone's being rationally justified in having that belief. So in holding that someone is rationally justified in believing that the theistic God exists, the friendly atheist is not committed to thinking that the theist has a true belief. What he is committed to is that the theist has rational grounds for his belief, a belief the atheist rejects and is convinced he is rationally justified in rejecting. But is this possible? Can someone, like our friendly atheist, hold a belief, be convinced that he is rationally justified in holding that belief, and yet believe that someone else is equally justified in believing the opposite? Surely this is possible. Suppose your friends see you off on a flight to Hawaii. Hours after take-off they learn that your plane has gone down at sea. After a twenty-four hour search, no survivors have been found. Under these circumstances they are rationally justified in believing that you have perished. But it is hardly rational for you to believe this, as you bob up and down in your life vest, wondering why the search planes have failed to spot you. Indeed, to amuse yourself while awaiting your fate, you might very well reflect on the fact that your friends are rationally justified in believing that you are now dead, a proposition you disbelieve and are rationally justified in disbelieving. So, too, perhaps an atheist may be rationally justified in his atheistic belief and yet hold that some theists are rationally justified in believing just the opposite of what he believes.

What sort of grounds might a theist have for believing that God exists? Well, he might endeavor to justify his belief by appealing to one or more of the traditional arguments: Ontological, Cosmological, Teleological, Moral, etc. Second, he might appeal to certain aspects of religious experience, perhaps even his own religious experience. Third, he might try to justify theism as a plausible theory in terms of which we can account for a variety of phenomena. Although an atheist must hold that the theistic God does not exist, can he not also believe, and be justified in so believing, that some of these 'justifications of theism' do actually rationally justify some theists in their belief that there exists a supremely good, omnipotent, omniscient being? It seems to me that he can.

If we think of the long history of theistic belief and the special situations in which people are sometimes placed, it is perhaps as absurd to think that no one was ever rationally justified in believing that the theistic God exists as it is to think that no one was ever justified in believing that human beings would never walk on the moon. But in suggesting that friendly atheism is preferable to unfriendly atheism, I don't mean to rest the case on what some human beings might reasonably have believed in the eleventh or thirteenth century. The more interesting question is whether some people in modern society, people who are aware of the usual grounds for belief and disbelief and are acquainted to some degree with modern science, are yet rationally justified in accepting theism. Friendly atheism is a significant position only if it answers this question in the affirmative.

It is not difficult for an atheist to be friendly when he has reason to believe that the theist could not reasonably be expected to be acquainted with the grounds for disbelief that he (the atheist) possesses. For then the atheist may take the view that some theists are rationally justified in holding to theism, but would not be so were they to be acquainted with the grounds for disbelief—those grounds being sufficient to tip the scale in favor of atheism when balanced against the reasons the theist has in support of his belief.

Friendly atheism becomes paradoxical, however, when the atheist contemplates believing that the theist has all the grounds for atheism that he, the atheist, has, and yet is rationally justified in maintaining his theistic belief. But even so excessively friendly a view as this perhaps can be held by the atheist if he also has some reason to think that the grounds for theism are not as telling as the theist is justified in taking them to be.

In this paper I've presented what I take to be a strong argument for atheism, pointed out what I think is the theist's best response to that argument, distinguished three positions an atheist might take concerning the rationality of theistic belief, and made some remarks in defense of the position called 'friendly atheism'. I'm aware that the central points of the paper are not likely to be warmly received by many philosophers. Philosophers who are atheists tend to be tough minded—holding that there are no good reasons for supposing that theism is true. And theists tend either to reject the view that the existence of evil provides rational grounds for atheism or to hold that religious belief has nothing to do with reason and evidence at all. But such is the way of philosophy.

Notes

1. Some philosophers have contended that the existence of evil is *logically inconsistent* with the existence of the theistic God. No one, I think, has succeeded in establishing such an extravagant claim. Indeed, granted incompatibilism, there is a fairly compelling argument for the view that the existence of evil is logically consistent with the existence of the theistic God. (For a lucid statement of this argument see Alvin Plantinga, *God, Freedom, and Evil* (New York, 1974), 29–59.) There remains, however, what we may call the *evidential* form—as opposed to the *logical* form—of the problem of evil; the view that

the variety and profusion of evil in our world, although perhaps not logically inconsistent with the existence of the theistic God, provides, nevertheless, *rational support* for atheism. In this paper I shall be concerned solely with the evidential form of the problem, the form of the problem which, I think, presents a rather severe difficulty for theism. William L. Rowe, 'The Problem of Evil and Some Varieties of Atheism', first published in *American Philosophical Quarterly*, 16 (1979), pp. 335–41. Used with permission.

2. If there is some good, *G*, greater than any evil, (1) will be false for the trivial reason that no matter what evil, *E*, we pick the conjunctive good state of affairs consisting of *G* and *E* will outweigh *E* and be such that an omnipotent being could not obtain it without permitting *E*. (See Alvin Plantinga, *God and Other Minds* (Ithaca, 1967), 167.) To avoid this objection we may insert 'unreplaceable' into our premises (1) and (2) between 'some' and 'greater'. If *E* isn't required for *G*, and *G* is better than *G* plus *E*, then the good conjunctive state of affairs composed of *G* and *E* would be *replaceable* by the greater good of *G* alone. For the sake of simplicity, however, I will ignore this complication both in the formulation and discussion of premises (1) and (2).

III.8 Evolution and the Problem of Evil

PAUL DRAPER

Paul Draper is associate professor of philosophy at Florida International University in Miami and the author of several essays in philosophy of religion. *In this article he notes that traditionally the problem of evil has been, with few exceptions, the only atheological argument against the existence of God. In this essay Draper argues that the naturalistic account of evolution can provide a cogent alternative to theism and that by combining that with the problem of evil, one can begin to build a cumulative case against theism.*

I. Introduction

Naturalism and theism are powerful and popular worldviews. They suggest very different conceptions of the nature of human beings, our relationship to the world, and our future. Though I hope that theism is true, I believe that it faces a number of evidential problems, problems that prevent my hope from becoming belief. In this paper I will examine two of those problems: evolution and evil. I will use certain known facts about the origin of complex life and the pattern of pain and pleasure in the world to construct a powerful *prima facie* case against theism.

By "theism" I mean the hypothesis[1] that God is the creator of the physical universe. I take the word "God" to be a title that, by definition, can be borne only by a perfect supernatural person. To claim that

God is a "person" is to claim that God performs actions and has beliefs and purposes. "Supernatural" persons are not natural—they are neither a part nor a product of the physical universe—and yet they can affect natural objects. A "perfect" person is, among other things, perfect in power (omnipotent), perfect in knowledge (omniscient), and perfect in moral goodness (morally perfect). While some have dismissed this conception of God as religiously insignificant, I am convinced that, for millions of Jews, Christians, and Muslims, factual belief in a perfect supernatural person is essential for making sense of their forms of worship. By "naturalism" I mean the hypothesis that the physical universe is a "closed system" in the sense that nothing that is neither a part nor a product of it can affect it. So naturalism entails the nonexistence of all supernatural beings, including the theistic God.

Arguments against theism can be divided into two main types. *Logical* arguments attempt to show that theism is either self-contradictory or logically inconsistent with some known fact. *Evidential* arguments attempt to show that certain known facts that are (at least so far as we can tell) consistent with theism nevertheless provide evidence against it.[2] The arguments in this paper will be evidential. I will show that certain known facts support the hypothesis of naturalism over the hypothesis of theism because we have considerably more reason to expect them to obtain on the assumption that naturalism is true than on the assumption that theism is true. This is a threat to theism because naturalism and theism are alternative hypotheses—they cannot both be true. Thus, if (after considering all of the evidence) naturalism turns out to be more probable than theism, then theism is probably false.

II. Evolution

Ever since the publication of Darwin's *On the Origin of Species,* countless theologians, philosophers, and scientists have pointed out that evolution could be the means by which God has chosen to create human beings and the rest of the living world. This is thought to show that, while the truth of evolution does refute the biblical story of creation as told in the book of Genesis, it in no way threatens the more general belief that the universe was created by God. In other words, it provides no reason to doubt theism. The plausibility of this argument is reflected by the fact that many scientists are both evolutionists and theists. Commenting on this fact, Stephen Jay Gould says:

> Unless at least half my colleagues are dunces, there can be—on the most raw and direct empirical grounds—no conflict between science and religion. I know hundreds of scientists who share a conviction about the fact of evolution, and teach it in the same way. Among these people I note an entire spectrum of religious attitudes—from devout daily prayer and worship to resolute atheism. Either there's no correlation between religious belief and confidence in evolution—or else half these people are fools.[3]

What Gould neglects to mention is that many well-educated people, including many of Gould's colleagues on the irreligious end of the spectrum, reject theism precisely because they believe in evolution. For example, William B. Provine, a leading historian of science, maintains that those who retain their religious beliefs while accepting evolution "have to check [their] brains at the church-house door."[4]

So who is correct? Is it compatibilists like Gould and the liberal preacher Henry Ward Beecher, who claimed in 1885 that evolution "will change theology, but only to bring out the simple temple of God in clearer and more beautiful lines and proportions"[5]? Or is it incompatibilists like Provine and the fundamentalist preacher William Jennings Bryan, who once defined "theistic evolution" as "an anesthetic which deadens the patient's pain while atheism removes his religion"[6]? My own position, as my introductory remarks suggest, lies somewhere between the view that theistic evolution is a happy marriage and the view that it must end in divorce. I agree with the compatibilists that theism and evolution are logically consistent. What I disagree with is the compatibilist's inference from no inconsistency to no conflict. For while consistency implies that the truth of evolution does not disprove theism—that there is no good *logical* argument from evolution against theism just as there is no good logical argument from evil against theism—it does not imply that the truth of evolution is no evidence at all against theism. My position is that evolution is evidence favoring naturalism over theism. There is, in other words, a good *evidential* argument from evolution against theism.

By "evolution," I mean the conjunction of two theses. The first, which I will call "the genealogical thesis," asserts that evolution did in fact occur—complex life did evolve from relatively simple life. Specifically, it is the view that all multicellular organisms and all (relatively) complex unicellular organisms on earth (both present and past) are the (more or less) gradually modified descendents of a small number of relatively simple unicellular organisms. The second thesis, which I will call "the genetic thesis," addresses the issue of how evolution occurred. It states that all evolutionary change in populations of complex organisms either is or is the result of trans-generational genetic change (or, to be more precise, trans-generational change in nucleic acids). It is important to distinguish this claim about the mechanisms by which evolution takes place from the much more specific claim that natural selection operating on random genetic mutation is the principal mechanism driving evolutionary change (or the principal mechanism driving the evolutionary change that results in increased complexity). Let's call this more specific claim "Darwinism" and its conjunction with evolution "Darwinian evolution."

Many evolutionary arguments against theism appeal to Darwinian evolution rather than just to evolution. I believe that such arguments overestimate the strength of the evidence for Darwinism. Darwinism may be highly probable on the assumption that naturalism is true. But it is far less probable on the assumption that theism is true, because on theism it is a real possibility that God has guided evolution by directly causing various genetic changes to occur. Thus, any argument against theism that is based on the truth of Darwinism is at best question-begging. This is why my argument appeals only to evolution rather than to Darwinian evolution. It is my belief (which I won't defend here) that the evidence for evolution, unlike the evidence for Darwinian evolution, is overwhelming—so overwhelming that evolution can legitimately be taken

as fact rather than mere theory for the purpose of arguing against theism.

The specific claim I wish to defend is the following:

> Antecedently, evolution is much more probable on the assumption that naturalism is true than on the assumption that theism is true.

By "antecedently" I mean "independent of the observations and testimony that together constitute the primary evidence upon which what we know about evolution, as well as the connection between pain and pleasure and reproductive success, is based." Thus, I intend to abstract from our information about selective breeding and other changes within populations of animals, as well as what we know about the geographical distribution of living things, homologies, the fossil record, genetic and biochemical evidence, imperfect adaptations, and vestigial organs. The additional abstraction concerning pain and pleasure is necessary because eventually I will combine my argument concerning evolution with an argument concerning the systematic connection between pain and pleasure and reproductive success. The claim will be made that evolution and this connection are, taken together, antecedently much more likely on naturalism than on theism. One last point. No other abstraction from what we know is intended. For example, I do not intend to abstract from our knowledge that complex life of various forms exists nor from our knowledge that this life has not always existed. It is an interesting and difficult question whether these facts are evidence favoring theism over naturalism, but that issue is beyond the scope of this paper.

Let "T," "N," and "E" stand for theism, naturalism and evolution, let "Pr(p)" stand for the antecedent probability of p being true, and let "Pr(p/q)" stand for the antecedent probability of p being true on the assumption that q is true. Finally, let ">!" stand for "is much greater than." The claim I wish to defend can now be restated as follows:

$$Pr(E/N) >! Pr(E/T)$$

My strategy for proving this claim requires one more symbol and one more definition. Let "S" stand for special creationism, by which I mean the statement that some relatively complex living things did not descend from relatively simple single-celled organisms but rather were independently created by a supernatural person. (The use of the word "independently" here signifies not just that the creation in question violates genealogical continuity, but also that it involves the direct intervention of the deity in the natural order.) Since evolution entails that special creationism is false, some basic theorems of the probability calculus give us:

Pr(E/N) >! Pr(E/T) if and only if Pr(~S/N) × Pr(E/~S&N) >! Pr(~S/T) × Pr(E/~S&T)[7]

My strategy for establishing that Pr(E/N) >! Pr(E/T) will be to show both that Pr(~S/N) >! Pr(~S/T) and that Pr(E/~S&N) ≥ Pr(E/~S&T). In other words, I will show both that special creationism is antecedently much more likely to be false on naturalism than on theism and that, even on the assumption that special creationism is false, evolution is still antecedently at least as likely to be true on naturalism as it is on theism.

Since naturalism entails that no supernatural beings exist, it entails that special creationism is false. Thus, the falsity of special creationism is antecedently certain on naturalism: Pr(~S/N) = 1. But on theism special creationism might, for all we know antecedently, be true: Pr(~S/T) < 1. Thus, the falsity of special creationism is antecedently more probable on naturalism than on theism, which implies that the falsity of special creationism is some evidence favoring naturalism over theism—it raises the ratio of the probability of naturalism to the probability of theism. But how strong is this evidence? Is the falsity of special creationism *much* more probable on naturalism than on theism? I will show that ~S is at least twice as probable antecedently on naturalism as it is on theism, which implies that it at least doubles the ratio of the probability of naturalism to the probability of theism.[8] Since Pr(~S/N) = 1, my task is to show that Pr(~S/T) ≤ 1/2, which is to say that Pr(S/T) ≥ 1/2—that, independent of the evidence for evolution, special creationism is at least as likely as not on the assumption that theism

is true. To defend this claim, I will first evaluate some antecedent reasons for believing that God, assuming he exists, did not create any complex living things independently. Then I will show that we have a very strong antecedent reason for believing that God, assuming he exists, did specially create.

At first glance, it seems that the evidence for evolution is the only strong reason theists have for believing that God is not a special creator (which is to say that we don't have any strong *antecedent* reasons for believing this). After all, for all we know antecedently, God might have chosen to create in a variety of different ways. For example, while he might have created life in a way consistent with genealogical continuity, he might also have created each species independently. Or he might have created certain basic types independently, allowing for evolutionary change, including change resulting in new species, within these types. Or he might have independently created only a few species or even only a single species, humans perhaps. Antecedently—that is, independent of the evidence for evolution—it appears we have no reason at all to think that an omnipotent, omniscient, and morally perfect creator would prefer evolution or any other "naturalistic" approach to one of these forms of special creation.

Some theists, however, are quite confident on purely *a priori* grounds that God is not a special creator. According to Diogenes Allen and Howard J. Van Till, for example, special creationism was implausible even before the evidence for evolution was discovered, because it is an implication of God's "rationality" or his status as creator rather than as "member of the universe" that God "creates a universe with members that are coherently connected."[9] This coherence precludes God's intervening in the natural order and hence precludes any sort of special creation, including the creation of those first simple life forms from which all subsequent life has evolved. Thus, according to these theists, the only sort of explanations of natural phenomena that theistic scientists should look for are ones that are consistent with naturalism. In short, these theists are committed methodological naturalists.

I don't find these arguments at all convincing. What possible justification could be given for thinking that if God were the immediate cause of a natural event that would reduce God's status from creator to "member of the universe"? Also, what does God's rationality have to do with this? Perhaps the idea is that, just as a perfectly rational car manufacturer would produce a car that never needed its gas tank filled or its air filter replaced, a perfectly rational creator would make a universe that ran on its own. But such a car would be preferable because filling up with gas or replacing parts has a cost in terms of time, energy, and so on. An omnipotent and omniscient creator wouldn't have such worries. In general, what counts as a rational or perfect or defective universe depends on the creator's goals. What goal or plan of God would be better served by a universe in which God never intervenes? Of course, human freedom may place limitations on the amount and type of God's interventions. But it doesn't rule out special creation. For all we know, God may have some goal that is furthered by the laws of nature we have, but those laws are such that they will not by themselves produce the sort of complex life God wants. If this were the case, then God would independently create that life. Surely such intervention in the course of nature would not conflict with God's status as creator or with his rationality. Nor would it imply that the universe is in some way defective or inferior to universes in which God never intervenes.

Another theist who holds that we have antecedent reasons for believing that God would not perform any special creative acts is the philosopher Ernan McMullin. In response to Alvin Plantinga's defense of special creationism, McMullin says that "from the theological and philosophical standpoints, such intervention is, if anything, antecedently *improbable*."[10] McMullin claims that "the eloquent texts of *Genesis, Job, Isaiah,* and *Psalms*" support his position, because "The Creator whose powers are gradually revealed in these texts is omnipotent and all-wise, far beyond the reach of human reckoning. His Providence extends to all His creatures; they are all part of His single plan, only a fragment of which we know, and that darkly."[11] But how this is supposed to support his position is never explained. It seems to do the opposite, since any claim to know that God would never intervene in the natural order will be difficult to justify if we are as much in the dark about God's plans as these texts suggest.[12]

Incidentally, I find it interesting that, when confronted with arguments against theism based on the idea that it is antecedently unlikely that God would permit heinous evil, theistic philosophers are quick to suggest that, since God is omniscient, humans are not in a position to make such a judgment. Yet, if we are to believe Allen and Van Till (McMullin has his doubts), then humans are in a position to judge that it is antecedently unlikely that God would create any life forms independently! Personally, I find the claim that the torturing of innocent children is antecedently improbable on theism vastly more plausible than the claim that special creationism is antecedently improbable on theism.

The problem with the theistic objections to special creationism considered so far is that they all involve *a priori* theological or philosophical speculation, the direction of which is influenced far too much by the conclusion desired.[13] Indeed, these attempts to make special creation seem incompatible with theism are no more objective and no more plausible than William B. Provine's attempt to make evolution seem incompatible with theism. While Allen, Van Till, and McMullin claim that God would never intervene in nature to create life, Provine claims that the idea of a God who "works through the laws of nature" is "worthless" and "equivalent to atheism."[14] How convenient!

A more serious attempt to show that special creationism is antecedently unlikely on theism is *a posteriori* in nature. We know by past experience that God, if he exists, has at least latent deistic tendencies. Teleology was, after all, eliminated from the physical sciences well before Darwin wrote *On the Origin of Species*. And even independent of the evidence for evolution there is considerable evidence that various biological processes work quite well without divine intervention. In general, even independent of the evidence on which evolution is based, the history of science is a history of success for naturalistic explanations and failure for supernaturalistic ones. Thus, we have a good antecedent *a posteriori* reason to believe that, assuming theism is true, God does not intervene in nature.

I believe that the past success of naturalistic science does provide some reason for theists to believe that God is not a special creator. But it is easy to overestimate the strength of this reason, especially for intellectual theists who must admit to living in a "post-mythological" era or else risk being held personally responsible for the plight of Galileo. But putting scientific propaganda aside, it is important to remember how little we actually know about the causal history of the universe! Were it not for the evidence for evolution, our sample of successful naturalistic explanations seems to me to be much too small to justify great confidence in the claim that, *assuming God exists*, God is not a special creator. Of course, it is worth mentioning that, if I am underestimating how successful the search for naturalistic explanations has been, then theists hardly escape unscathed. For if the search for such explanations has been so successful that any supernaturalistic explanation of a natural phenomenon is implausible even on the assumption that theism is true, then that would be powerful evidence against theism. For such extraordinary success would be antecedently much more likely on naturalism—which entails that all supernaturalistic explanations are false—than it would on theism.

More to the point, however, I believe theists have a very strong antecedent reason for believing that God did create at least some complex life independently. For the division between conscious and nonconscious life is enormously significant if theism is true. Theism implies an extreme metaphysical dualism—a mind existed prior to the physical world and was responsible for its existence. Thus, on the assumption that theism is true, it is antecedently likely that minds are fundamentally nonphysical entities and hence that conscious life is fundamentally different from nonconscious life. But this in turn makes it likely that conscious living things are not just the genetically modified descendents of nonconscious living things—that conscious life was created independently. And since special creationism is defined as the position that at least some complex life was created independently,

it follows that, on the assumption that theism is true, it is antecedently likely that special creationism is true.

The dualism inherent in theism may explain why so many theists were drawn to the idea of special creationism before (and in many cases even after) the evidence for evolution was discovered. For this dualism supports a dualistic view of human nature—a view that must have made the idea that we are the effect of altering the nucleic acids of single-celled organisms seem ludicrous. Offspring don't have to be identical to their parents, but surely genetic change can't result in fundamental metaphysical lines being crossed! Thus, even if we know by past experience that God, assuming he exists, generally doesn't intervene in nature, the sort of metaphysics presupposed by theism makes it antecedently likely that God did intervene in the physical world in order to create a mental world within it. So it's hardly surprising that, before Darwin, many theists were special creationists. They had a good reason and we have a good *antecedent* reason to believe that God, assuming he or she exists, performed at least one special creative act. Thus, $Pr(S/T) \geq 1/2$. And this implies that the falsity of special creationism is at least twice as probable antecedently on naturalism as it is on theism: $Pr(\sim S/N) \geq 2 \times Pr(\sim S/T)$.

Recall that, in order to show that $Pr(E/N) >!$ $Pr(E/T)$, it is sufficient to show first that $Pr(\sim S/N) >!$ $Pr(\sim S/T)$ and second that $Pr(E/\sim S\&N) \geq Pr(E/\sim S\&T)$. I have completed the first of these two tasks. Turning to the second, we are now assuming that special creationism is false and asking how likely evolution is on naturalism and on theism. Of course, naturalism entails that special creationism is false, so the denial of special creationism conjoined with naturalism ($\sim S\&N$) just is naturalism (N). I will call the denial of special creationism conjoined with theism ($\sim S\&T$) "regular theism." So my task is to show that evolution is antecedently at least as probable on naturalism as it is on regular theism.

It is important to recognize that the probabilities in question are to be assessed relative to the background knowledge that various complex life forms do exist. Thus, the issue is not whether complex life together with the evolutionary mechanisms that produce it are more surprising on theism or on naturalism. (Again, whether or not there is a good anthropic design argument supporting theism is beyond the scope of this paper.) Given that complex life exists, what makes evolution so likely on naturalism is the lack of plausible naturalistic alternatives to evolution. On naturalism, it is antecedently much more likely that all complex organisms descended from a small number of relatively simple organisms than that complex life descended from a large number of relatively simple single-celled organisms all of which arose independently from nonliving matter or that complex life arose directly from nonliving matter. Furthermore, given the genealogical thesis, it is antecedently likely on naturalism that all evolutionary change in complex life is or results from one basic sort of change like genetic change. On regular theism, alternatives to evolution are somewhat more likely, simply because there is less reason to assume that the complex must arise from the simple. When one starts with omnipotence and omniscience, so much is possible!

Even if the regular theist grants that these considerations favor naturalism, she might counter that it has never been proven that naturalistic evolution is biologically possible. Perhaps evolution could not have produced complex life without supernatural assistance. For example, it might be argued that, without some intelligent being guiding genetic change, such magnificent ordered systems as the human eye would never have evolved. The stronger the evidence for this, the lower the antecedent probability of evolution on naturalism. I do not believe, however, that the evidence for this is very strong. Admittedly, no one can describe in detail exactly how the eye or any other complex organic system could have come about without supernatural assistance. And it's hard to see how anyone could prove that evolution could produce complex life in a naturalistic universe. But neither has anyone provided good reason for thinking that it couldn't either. (Some special creationists have tried, but their arguments are very weak.[15]) This is not to say that there are no real difficulties for naturalistic evolution. (For example, it's notoriously difficult to explain how sexual reproduction evolved.) It's just

to say that no one has given a good reason to believe that naturalistic solutions to these problems will not be found. Indeed, the fact that plausible solutions have been found to some of these problems (e.g., the problem of altruistic behavior) gives the naturalist reason for optimism. So any advantage that the problems faced by naturalistic evolution give to regular theism is more than offset by the considerations favoring naturalism mentioned above. All things considered, then, the modest conclusion that evolution is at least as probable antecedently on naturalism as it is on regular theism is justified. Therefore, since the falsity of special creationism is antecedently much more probable on naturalism than on theism, it follows for the reasons explained earlier that evolution is antecedently much more probable on naturalism than on theism.

III. Pain and Pleasure

It is true by definition that a morally perfect God would permit an instance of pain only if he or she had a morally sufficient reason to do so. (By "pain" I mean any suffering, physical or mental.) Thus, the "logical" problem of pain is the problem of whether or not God's being both omnipotent and omniscient is logically compatible with God's having a morally sufficient reason to permit all of the suffering in the world. No one has been able to demonstrate an incompatibility because not even an omnipotent being can do the logically impossible and it might, for all we know or can prove, be logically impossible to bring about certain important goods without at least risking the existence of the suffering we find in our world. So demonstrative logical arguments from pain have been unsuccessful. And nondemonstrative or probabilistic logical arguments from pain have been challenged on the grounds that they involve questionable inductive generalizations, questionable inferences from there being no *known* morally sufficient reasons for an omnipotent and omniscient being to permit certain instances of suffering to their probably being no such morally sufficient reasons. But these discussions of the logical problem of pain leave unsettled the issue of whether or not the suffering in our world is evidence against theism or evidence favoring naturalism over theism. In other words, the failure of logical arguments from evil, including probabilistic ones, does not preclude a successful evidential argument from evil.

I do not, however, wish to consider suffering in isolation. Instead, I will address the issue of whether the pattern of both pain and pleasure in the world is evidence favoring naturalism over theism. The more common strategy of focusing only on evil, indeed only on a few particularly heinous evils, has its advantages. I choose not to pursue this strategy because the theist might counter such an argument by pointing out a few particularly glorious goods and plausibly claiming that they are equally strong evidence favoring theism over naturalism. So my argument will be based on both pain and pleasure. There may, of course, be other intrinsic evils and intrinsic goods besides pain and pleasure, but the issue of whether or not there are, and whether or not, if there are, their existence is evidence against theism, will not be addressed in this paper.

There are many facts about pain and pleasure that might provide the resources for an evidential argument against theism. Because I wish to explore how our knowledge of evolution affects the problem of evil, I will focus on the fact that much of the pain and pleasure we find in the world is systematically connected (in a variety of often complex ways) to reproductive success. For example, it is no accident that we find a warm fire on a cold night pleasurable and lying naked in a snowbank painful. Maintaining a constant body temperature increases our chances of (temporary) survival and thereby increases our chances of reproducing. Of course, the connections are not all this obvious or this direct. For example, children enjoy playing, which promotes the development of various physical, social, and intellectual skills, which in turn increases children's chances of surviving and reproducing. Even less obviously and less directly, adults find play pleasurable (though typically not as much as children do), which may or may not promote reproductive success, but which results from our capacity to enjoy play as children, which, as we have seen, does promote reproductive success. I could give countless other examples, but the connection

between pain and pleasure and reproductive success and the systematic nature of that connection is so striking that additional examples aren't really needed. Instead, I will now turn to the task of showing that, antecedently, this connection is much more probable on evolutionary naturalism than it is on evolutionary theism. I will offer a two-part argument for this position, and then reply to two objections.

The first part of my argument appeals to natural selection. I suggested earlier that Darwinism is much more likely to be true if evolutionary naturalism is true than if evolutionary theism is true. Allow me to explain why. Darwinism is likely on evolutionary naturalism both because it explains the increase in the complexity of life over time better than other naturalistic mechanisms and, most importantly for our purposes, it solves an explanatory problem for naturalism: the problem of explaining teleological or "means–end" order in organic systems. Since evolutionary theism can explain teleological order in terms of God's conscious purposes, it wouldn't be at all surprising on theism if the principal mechanisms driving evolution themselves displayed teleological order—if, for example, organisms had built-in mechanisms that would produce precisely those genetic changes needed to solve a problem arising because of some environmental change. (Such mechanisms would have made William Paley a happy evolutionist!) On naturalism, natural selection is just the sort of process one would expect to drive evolution: a simple "blind" process that can explain the extremely complex teleological order in the living world without itself displaying such order. Notice also that, contrary to popular belief, natural selection does not generally promote the good of individual animals. Variations that result in reproductive success will be favored, regardless of the other consequences— good or bad—of the variation. For example, if walking upright gave our distant ancestors a reproductive advantage (e.g., by allowing them to carry tools while they walked), then this trait was selected despite the foot, back, heart, and numerous other ailments that resulted from it. Further, natural selection requires competition for scarce resources and thus entails that many living things will not flourish.

So the claim that natural selection is the principal mechanism driving evolutionary change is much more probable on evolutionary naturalism than on evolutionary theism.

Of course, if natural selection is the principal mechanism driving evolution, then it is likely on evolutionary naturalism that it played a significant role in the evolution of pain and pleasure and so it is likely on evolutionary naturalism that pain and pleasure will, like anything produced by natural selection, be systematically connected to reproductive success. Thus, the fact that natural selection is antecedently much more likely to have governed the evolution of pain and pleasure if evolutionary naturalism is true than if evolutionary theism is true supports my position that the systematic connection between reproductive success and the pain and pleasure we find in the world is antecedently much more likely on evolutionary naturalism than on evolutionary theism.

This position is further supported by our antecedent knowledge that many other parts of organic systems are systematically connected to reproductive success. This gives us much more reason to believe that pain and pleasure will also be so connected if we assume that evolutionary naturalism is true than if we assume that evolutionary theism is true. To see why, consider the inductive inference from a sample consisting of other physical and mental parts of organic systems that are systematically connected to reproductive success to the conclusion that pain and pleasure are also systematically connected to reproductive success. Although a good number of parts of organic systems lack such a connection, this inference is potentially quite strong given the suitability of pain and pleasure for promoting reproductive success. But the assumption that evolutionary theism is true undermines this inference, while the assumption that evolutionary naturalism is true does not. To see why, notice that this inference is an inductive inference from a sample to another member of a population, and the strength of any such inference depends on how much reason one has to believe that this other member is relevantly different from the members of the sample. Now pain and pleasure are strikingly different from other parts of organic

systems in one way: They have a specific sort of moral significance that other parts lack. (Other parts of organic systems may have moral significance, but not of the same sort.) But is this a relevant difference? We have much more reason to believe it is on the assumption that evolutionary theism is true than on the assumption that evolutionary naturalism is true. For the biological goal of reproductive success does not provide an omnipotent omniscient creator with a morally sufficient reason for permitting humans and animals to suffer in the ways they do or for limiting their pleasure to the sorts and amounts we find. Thus, on evolutionary theism, pain and pleasure would be systematically connected to the biological goal of reproductive success only if this goal and some unknown justifying moral goal happened to coincide in such a way that each could be simultaneously satisfied. Such a coincidence is (to say the least) antecedently far from certain. So on the assumption that evolutionary theism is true, the inference to the conclusion that pain and pleasure are systematically connected to reproductive success from the premise that other parts of organic systems are so connected is very weak. This inference is much stronger on the assumption that evolutionary naturalism is true because evolutionary naturalism entails nothing that would undermine the inference—on evolutionary naturalism the moral significance of pain and pleasure provides no antecedent reason at all to doubt that they will resemble other parts of organic systems by being systematically connected to reproductive success. Therefore, our antecedent knowledge that pain and pleasure have a certain sort of moral significance adds further support to my position that the systematic connection between pain and pleasure and reproductive success is antecedently much more probable on evolutionary naturalism than on evolutionary theism.

One might object that my argument ignores the many instances of pain and pleasure that are, so far as we can tell, disconnected from the biological goal of reproductive success. For example, some aesthetic pleasures seem to have at most a very remote connection to reproductive success. But neither the existence of such pain and pleasure, nor the fact that, in general, such pain and pleasure is more common in animals that are psychologically complex, is at all surprising on evolutionary naturalism. For the greater the complexity of a system, the more likely that some of its characteristics will be epiphenomenal. Also, much biologically gratuitous pain and pleasure is pathological—it results from the failure of an organic system to function properly. And the existence of this sort of pain and pleasure is also unsurprising on evolutionary naturalism. So on evolutionary naturalism, what we know about biologically gratuitous pain and pleasure is not surprising, while on evolutionary theism, the excess pleasure is perhaps to be expected, but this advantage is offset by the limited amount of such pleasure, by the existence of biologically gratuitous pain, and by the fact that a significant amount of biologically gratuitous pleasure and pain is pathological.

One might also object that theodicies undermine my argument; for theodicies make certain facts about pain antecedently more likely than they would otherwise be. The problem with existing theodicies, however, is that they explain certain facts at the price of making others even more mysterious. That is, they make certain facts more likely only by making others less likely. For example, if one of God's reasons for permitting pain is to punish sinners, then why do the innocent suffer as much as the guilty? Or, if we assume that God wants to use pain to build moral character, then pain (and pleasure) that is demoralizing becomes even more surprising. If, instead of focusing on a few isolated cases, one looks at the overall pattern of pain and pleasure in the world, one cannot help but be struck by its apparent moral randomness. Pain and pleasure do not systematically promote justice or moral virtue. Nor are moral agents treated all that differently from nonmoral agents. Nonhuman animals suffer in many of the ways humans suffer (the more similar the animal, the more similar the suffering), despite the fact that such suffering cannot play a moral role in their lives, since they are not moral agents.

All of these facts, which might be summed up by saying that pain and pleasure do not systematically promote any discernible moral ends, are ex-

actly what one would expect on evolutionary naturalism. For on evolutionary naturalism, the causes of good and evil are morally indifferent. Thus, on the assumption that evolutionary naturalism is true, it would be surprising in the extreme if pain and pleasure appeared to be anything but morally random. But a discernible moral pattern would be less surprising on theism even if, given the cognitive distance between humans and an omniscient being, it should not be expected. Notice that I am not claiming that the apparent moral randomness of pain and pleasure is antecedently unlikely on evolutionary theism. I'm just claiming that it is antecedently less likely on evolutionary theism than on evolutionary naturalism. And it seems to me that this is obvious. But that means that this apparent randomness adds to the evidence favoring evolutionary naturalism over evolutionary theism. It may not add a lot, but it certainly offsets any advantage evolutionary theism has as a result of the moral roles that pain and pleasure admittedly do play in human lives.

IV. Conclusion

I have argued both that evolution is antecedently much more probable on naturalism than on theism and that the systematic connection between pain, as well as pleasure, and reproductive success is antecedently much more probable on evolutionary naturalism than on evolutionary theism. This entails that the conjunction of evolution and the statement that pain and pleasure are systematically connected to reproductive success is antecedently very much more probable on naturalism than on theism. And since neither the truth nor falsity of naturalism or theism is certain, it follows that this conjunction substantially raises the ratio of the probability of naturalism to the probability of theism. Of course, if naturalism were far less plausible than theism (or if it were compatible with theism), then this sort of evidence would be worthless. But naturalism is a very serious alternative to theism. Neither evolution nor anything about pain and pleasure is built into it in an *ad hoc* way. (It is not as if I were claiming, for example, that *evolution* is antecedently more probable on *evolutionary* naturalism than on theism.) Also, naturalism doesn't deny the existence of all nonnatural beings—it only denies the existence of supernatural beings. And surely this is no less plausible than asserting the existence of a very specific sort of supernatural being. So naturalism is at least as plausible as theism.

Therefore, it follows from my arguments concerning evil and evolution that, other evidence held equal, naturalism is very much more probable than theism. And since naturalism and theism are alternative hypotheses—they cannot both be true—this implies that, other evidence held equal, it is highly likely that theism is false. So the evidence discussed in this paper provides a powerful *prima facie* case against theism. To put it another way, if one looks only at the evidence discussed here—evolution, the ability of natural selection to explain complex biological order without purpose, the systematic connection between pain and pleasure and reproductive success, and the apparent moral randomness of pain and pleasure—then Hume's words ring true: "The whole presents nothing but the idea of a blind nature, impregnated by a great vivifying principle, and pouring forth from her lap, without discernment or parental care, her maimed and abortive children."[16,17]

Appendix

My argument in this paper is based on the following two theorems of the probability calculus:

$$\text{A:} \quad \frac{\Pr(N/E\&P)}{\Pr(T/E\&P)} = \frac{\Pr(N)}{\Pr(T)} \times \frac{\Pr(E\&P/N)}{\Pr(E\&P/T)}$$

$$\text{B:} \quad \frac{\Pr(E\&P/N)}{\Pr(E\&P/T)} = \frac{\Pr(E/N)}{\Pr(E/T)} \times \frac{\Pr(P/E\&N)}{\Pr(P/E\&T)}$$

In using these two equations, I assume that neither naturalism nor theism is certainly true or certainly false.

$\Pr(N/E\&P)$ is the antecedent probability of naturalism given the conjunction of evolution and the statement (P) that pain and pleasure are systematically connected to reproductive success. In other words, it is the probability of naturalism, all things considered. (I assume here that the "given E&P"

puts back everything of significance that the "antecedent" takes out.) Similarly, $\Pr(T/E\&P)$ is the probability of theism, all things considered. So the left side of equation A is the ratio of the probability of naturalism to the probability of theism. If this ratio is greater than 1, then naturalism is more probable than theism and hence theism is probably false.

Now consider the right side of equation A. The main purpose of my paper was to evaluate the second ratio here: The ratio of the antecedent probability of evolution conjoined with P given naturalism to the antecedent probability of this conjunction given theism. This ratio was evaluated using equation B. The first of the two ratios on the right side of B is the ratio of the antecedent probability of evolution given naturalism to the antecedent probability of evolution given theism. And the second is the ratio of the antecedent probability of P given evolutionary naturalism to the antecedent probability of P given evolutionary theism. I argued that each of these two ratios is much greater than 1. From this it follows (using equation B) that the ratio of $\Pr(E\&P/N)$ to $\Pr(E\&P/T)$ is very much greater than 1.

Now look at the first ratio on the right side of equation A. $\Pr(N)$ is the antecedent probability of naturalism. In other words, it is the probability of naturalism independent of our knowledge of E&P. And $\Pr(T)$ is the probability of theism independent of our knowledge of E&P. So the first ratio on the right side of equation A depends on the plausibility of naturalism and theism as well as on other evidence (propositional or nonpropositional) for and against naturalism and theism (e.g., the existence of life on earth, the success of science, religious experiences, immorality, etc.). I argued very briefly that considerations of plausibility do not give us any reason to believe that this ratio is less than one. But I did not, of course, evaluate all of the other relevant evidence for and against theism and naturalism. So I did not come to any conclusion about this first ratio. This is why my case against theism is a *prima facie* one. I am entitled to conclude only that, *other evidence held equal*, the ratio on the left side of equation A is very much greater than 1. And this implies that, other evidence held equal, it is highly probable that theism is false.

The following summarizes my argument:

(1) Evolution is antecedently much more probable on the assumption that naturalism is true than on the assumption that theism is true [i.e., Pr(E/N) >! Pr(E/T)].

(2) The statement that pain and pleasure are systematically connected to reproductive success is antecedently much more probable on the assumption that evolutionary naturalism is true than on the assumption that evolutionary theism is true [i.e., Pr(P/E&N) >! Pr(P/E&T)].

(3) Therefore, evolution conjoined with this statement about pain and pleasure is antecedently very much more probable on the assumption that naturalism is true than on the assumption that theism is true [i.e., Pr(E&P/N) >!! Pr(E&P/T)]. (From 1 and 2)

(4) Naturalism is at least as plausible as theism [i.e., other evidence held equal, Pr(N) ≥ Pr(T)].

(5) Therefore, other evidence held equal, naturalism is very much more probable than theism [i.e., other evidence held equal, Pr(N/E&P) >!! Pr(T/E&P)]. (From 3 and 4)

(6) Naturalism entails that theism is false.

(7) Therefore, other evidence held equal, it is highly probable that theism is false [i.e., other evidence held equal, Pr(T/E&P) <!! 1/2. (From 5 and 6)

Notes

1. By "hypothesis" I mean a statement that is neither certainly true nor certainly false.

2. It is worth noting that, although "probabilistic" arguments from evil are usually classified as evidential, many such arguments are logical—they attempt to show that theism is probably inconsistent with some known fact about evil.

3. "Darwinism Defined: The Difference Between Fact and Theory," *Discover*, Jan. 1987, p. 70. Quoted in James Rachels, *Created from Animals: The Moral Implications of Darwinism* (Oxford University Press, 1990), p. 100.

4. Quoted in Phillip E. Johnson, *Darwin on Trial* (InterVarsity Press, 1993), p. 126.

5. "The Two Revelations," in Gail Kennedy, *Evolution and Religion* (D. C. Heath and Company, 1957), p. 20. Also quoted on p. xiv.

6. Quoted in Kennedy, p. xiv.

7. Proof: Since E entails ~S, E is logically equivalent to ~S&E. Thus, since it is a theorem of the probability calculus that logically equivalent statements are equally probable, it follows that Pr(E/N) >! Pr(E/T) if and only if Pr(~S&E/N) >! Pr(~S&E/T). But it is also a theorem of the probability calculus that Pr(p&q/r) = Pr(p/r) × Pr(q/p&r). Therefore, Pr(E/N) >! Pr(E/T) if and only if Pr(~S/N) × Pr(E/ ~S&N) >! Pr(~S/T) × Pr(E/ ~S&T).

8. Of course, whether this strong evidence is also significant depends on what the ratio of the probability of naturalism to the probability of theism is prior to considering the fact that special creationism is false. If it is extremely high or low, then the falsity of special creationism will not be significant evidence favoring naturalism. If, on the other hand, the other evidence is nearly balanced and both hypotheses are plausible, then this evidence will be significant. For example, if theism starts out twice as probable as naturalism, then the two hypotheses will end up being equally probable.

9. Diogenes Allen, *Christian Belief in a Postmodern World* (Westminster: John Knox Press, 1989), p. 59. Quoted with approval in Howard J. Van Till, "When Faith and Reason Cooperate," *Christian Scholar's Review* 21.1 (1991), p. 43.

10. "Plantinga's Defense of Special Creation," *Christian Scholar's Review* 21.1 (1991), p. 74. Plantinga refers to McMullin's position as "semi-deism." McMullin complains that this terminology is loaded, yet he describes his own position as believing in "the integrity of the natural order." It would seem then that Christians have a dilemma. No good Christian wants to be called a "deist," but no good Christian would want to deny that God's creation has "integrity"!

11. Ibid., p. 75.

12. For additional criticisms of the positions of Van Till and McMullin, see Alvin Plantinga, "Evolution, Neutrality, and Antecedent Probability: A Reply to Van Till and McMullin," *Christian Scholar's Review* 21.1 (1991), pp. 80–109.

13. Cf. Plantinga, p. 100.

14. Review of "Trial and Error: The American Controversy over Creation and Evolution", *Academe* 73.1 (1987), 50–52. Quoted in McMullin, p. 58.

15. For an excellent defense of evolution against special creationist objections, see Philip Kitcher, *Abusing Science: The Case Against Creationism* (Cambridge, Massachusetts: The MIT Press, 1982).

16. *Dialogues Concerning Natural Religion*, ed. Norman Kemp Smith (Macmillan Publishing Co., 1947), p. 211.

17. I am grateful to Kai Draper, Daniel Howard-Snyder, James Keller, George Mavrodes, Wes Morriston, William L. Rowe, Michael Tooley, and Stephen J. Wykstra for helpful comments on earlier versions of this paper.

Bibliography for Part III

Adams, Marilyn McCord, and Robert Merrihew Adams, eds. *The Problem of Evil*. Oxford, Eng.: Oxford Univ. Press, 1990. The best collection of contemporary articles on the subject, containing essays by J. L. Mackie, Nelson Pike, Alvin Plantinga, William Rowe, Robert M. Adams, John Hick, and others.

Draper, Paul. "Pain and Pleasure: An Evidential Problem for Theists," *Nous* 23 (1989). An intricate and well-crafted challenge to theists.

Gale, Richard. *On the Nature and Existence of God*. Cambridge, Eng.: Cambridge Univ. Press, 1991. Contains a careful analysis of the problem of evil and the free will defense.

Hick, John. *Evil and the God of Love*. London: Macmillan, 1966. A classic defense of theodicy.

Howard-Snyder, Daniel, ed. *The Evidential Argument from Evil*. Bloomington, IN: Indiana University Press, 1996. Contains the most contemporary arguments of any anthology.

Lewis, C. S. *The Problem of Pain*. London: Geoffrey Bles, 1940. Clearly and cogently written.

Mackie, J. L. "Evil and Omnipotence." *Mind* 64 (1955):200–12. One of the earlier contemporary attacks on the existence of God from the argument from evil, used in many anthologies.

———. *The Miracle of Theism*. Chap. 9. Oxford, Eng.: Oxford Univ. Press, 1982. An insightful and well-argued chapter from an atheist's point of view.

McCloskey, H. J. "God and Evil." *The Philosophical Quarterly* 10 (1960):97–114. A sharp attack on theism, arguing that given the problem of evil theism is indefensible.

Pike, Nelson. "Human on Evil." *The Philosophical Review* 72 (1963):180–97. A trenchant criticism of Hume's position.

Plantinga, Alvin. *The Nature of Necessity*. Chap. 9. Oxford, Eng.: Clarendon Press, 1974. An excellent article developing in detail a version of the free will defense. In this version all evil is reduced to moral evil, with the devil being held accountable for natural evil. (A more accessible version of this argument is found in Plantinga's work *God, Freedom and Evil*. New York: Harper & Row, 1974.

Schlesinger, George N. "Suffering and Evil." In *Contemporary Philosophy of Religion*, edited by Steven M. Cahn and David Schatz. Oxford, Eng.: Oxford Univ. Press, 1982. Schlesinger argues that when a complaint applies to every situation, it applies to none. Hence, because one could always complain that God could have created a better world, one cannot complain that this one could be better.

Swinburne, Richard. *The Existence of God*. Chap. 11. Oxford, Eng.: Oxford Univ. Press, 1978. This contains a fuller defense than is presented in the reading included in this volume.

———. "Natural Evil." *American Philosophical Quarterly* 15 (1978):295–301. A detailed response to the charge that natural evil undermines theism.

Wainwright, William J. "God and the Necessity of Physical Evils." *Sophia* 11 (1972):16–19.

Wykstra, Stephen J. "The Humean Obstacle to Evidential Arguments from Suffering: On Avoiding the Evils of 'Appearance.' " *International Journal of Philosophy of Religion* 16 (1984).

PART IV

THE ATTRIBUTES OF GOD

In the Judeo-Christian tradition God is viewed as having attributes that set him apart from other beings as supreme. Traditionally, some of these attributes have been omnibenevolence (being perfectly good), timelessness (eternity), immutability (changelessness), omnipotence (being all-powerful), and omniscience (being all-knowing). From time to time each of these attributes have been challenged, and some philosophers and theologians have suggested that there are problems with all of them. The problem of evil casts doubt on benevolence and omnipotence. The notion of timeless eternity gives rise to problems in transitivity. The notion of immutability seems inconsistent with the biblical idea that God loves, forgives, and acts. The notion of omnipotence gives rise to such puzzles as whether God can create a stone heavier than he can lift and whether he can sin, and the notion of omniscience leads to the possibility of eliminating free will in humans.

In the last few decades, the assault on these attributes has come from within the theistic community as well as from without. Process theologians, such as Charles Hartshorne, have denied all but the first attribute, omnibenevolence, arguing that the other four are holdovers from ancient Greek philosophy and are not found in the Bible at all. For them, God need not be all-powerful and all-knowing in order to be the Creator of the Universe and our loving savior; and since God, like other persons, grows in wisdom and insight, he must be able to change and, consequently, be in time rather than timeless. On the other hand, all of the above attributes have had their defenders. In this part of our work we examine the three most controversial of God's attributes—his eternity, his omniscience, and his omnipotence—and present arguments on both sides of these issues.

IV.A Time and Eternity

Thy years do not come and go; while these years of ours do come and go, in order that they all may come. All Thy years stand together [and in one nonextended instant], for they stand still, nor are those going away cut off by those coming, for they do not pass away, but these years of ours shall all be when they are all no more. Thy years are but one day, and Thy day is not a daily recurrent, but today. Thy present day does not give place to tomorrow nor, indeed, does it take the place of yesterday. Thy present day is eternity.*

All theists agree that God exists as an eternal being. The question is how to interpret this notion. Does God's eternality put him outside of time, or may he still be inside? That is, is his eternity *timeless* or does it have *temporal duration* (sometimes such words as *everlasting* or *temporally eternal* indicate the second position). The notion of the eternal as timelessness first appears in Parmenides' poem "The Way to Truth," in which he says of the One, "It neither was at any time nor will be since it is now all at once a single whole." He and his disciple, Zeno, denied the reality of time. The concept of the eternal was further developed by Plato in the *Timaeus*, in which it is glorified as infinitely superior to the temporal. The *Timaeus* deeply influenced the early Church, and through Augustine and Boethius the doctrine of eternity (as timelessness) made its way into Christian thought, becoming the dominant position in mainstream Christianity. In the Middle Ages and the Reformation period it was embraced by Anselm, Aquinas, Luther, Calvin, and the vast majority of theologians but challenged by Duns Scotus and William of Ockham. In recent times Anthony Kenny, Nelson Pike, and Nicholas Wolterstorff, among others, have argued that the notion of timelessness is unbiblical and incoherent

and should be replaced with the notion of everlastingness.

In our readings, Hugh McCann defends the traditional timeless notion of God's eternity, and Stephen T. Davis argues that the notion of *temporally eternal* should be substituted for the timeless notion. In the first reading, Davis sets forth the contrasting ideas of "timeless eternity" and "temporal eternity." The former posits a God who is outside time and lacks both temporal location and extension. All events are simultaneously present to God. Temporal eternity, on the other hand, posits a God who has both temporal location and extension. Davis offers three arguments in favor of temporal eternity: (1) The concept of God's creative activity makes far more sense if we accept the notion that he exists in time. For if God creates a given temporal thing, his act of creation itself must be temporal. (2) A timeless being cannot be the personal, caring, involved God of the Bible. (3) The notion of simultaneity of timeless eternity seems to result in absurd consequences with regard to time; for if events in 3021 BC are no earlier than the events of 1986 for God, then time must be illusory. But there is no good reason to deem time illusory. Hence the notion of timeless eternity seems incoherent. This point is stated with elegance by Anthony Kenny:

> Indeed, the whole concept of a timeless eternity, the whole of which is simultaneous with every part of time, seems to be radically incoherent. For simultaneity as ordinarily understood is a transitive relation. If *A* happens at the same time as *B*, and *B* happens at the same time as *C*, then *A* happens at the same time as *C*. If the BBC programme and the ITV programme both start when Big Ben strikes ten, then they both start at the same time. But in St. Thomas' view, my typing of this paper is simultaneous with the whole of eternity. Again, on this view, the great fire of Rome is simultaneous with the whole of eternity. Therefore, while I type these very words, Nero fiddles heartlessly on.*

---

*St. Augustine, *Confessions*, bk. 11, chap. 13, translated by V. J. Bourke, in *The Fathers of the Church* (New York: Catholic University of America Press, 1953), 342f.

*"Divine Foreknowledge and Human Freedom," in *Aquinas: A Collection of Critical Essays*, edited by Anthony Kenny (New York: Doubleday, 1969), 264.

Davis answers several objections to his view, concluding that the concept of temporal eternity is more coherent than the notion of timeless eternity.

In his contribution, "The God Beyond Time," McCann argues just the opposite. He examines objections to the atemporal notion of God and tries to answer them, beginning with Davis's first argument, that the concept of God's creative *activity* makes far more sense if we accept the notion that he exists in time (for if God creates a given temporal thing, his act of Creation must be temporal). McCann argues that although things may be said to be brought about at some *time*, this does not entail that God must *exist at some time* in order to bring them about. He contends that it is coherent to talk about temporal differences from our point of view but not from God's. Hence, the idea of timelessness is coherent. The whole of Creation is one eternal fiat.

Furthermore, McCann argues, the notion of an atemporal God makes better sense of God's sovereignty and omniscience without creating problems for human freedom.

You, the reader, will decide which view is more plausible.

IV.A.1 Temporal Eternity

STEPHEN T. DAVIS

Stephen T. Davis is professor of philosophy at Claremont McKenna College. In his article, he sets forth the contrasting ideas of "timeless eternity" and "temporal eternity." The former posits a God who is outside time and lacks both temporal location and extension, and the latter posits a God who has both temporal location and extension. Davis offers three arguments in favor of temporal eternity: (1) The concept of God's creative activity makes far more sense if we accept the notion that he exists in time. For if God creates a given temporal thing, his act of creation itself must be temporal. (2) A timeless being cannot be the personal, caring, involved God of the Bible. (3) The notion of simultaneity of timeless eternity seems to result in absurd consequences with regard to time; for if events in 3021 BC are no earlier than the events of 1986 for God, then time must be illusory. But there is no good reason to deem time illusory. Hence the notion of timeless eternity seems incoherent.

One divine property that we will deal with early in the book is God's eternality. It will be best if we discuss it here because one's opinion on this subject is likely to affect opinions one has about several other divine properties, especially omnipotence, omniscience and immutability. Thus we must now raise the thorny question of God's relation to time.

It is part of the Judeo-Christian tradition that God is eternal.

> Lord, thou has been our dwelling place in all
>   generations.
> Before the mountains were brought forth, or
>   ever thou hadst formed the earth and the
>   world, from everlasting to everlasting
>   thou art God.
> Thou turnest man back to the dust, and
>   sayeth, 'Turn back, O children of man!'
> For a thousand years in thy sight are but as
>   yesterday when it is past, or as a watch in
>   the night. (Ps. 90:1–4)
> Of old thou didst lay the foundation of the
>   earth, and the heavens are the work of
>   thy hands.

Reprinted from Stephen T. Davis, *Logic and the Nature of God.* (Grand Rapids, Mich.: Eerdmans, 1983), by permission of the author. Copyright © Stephen T. Davis. Footnotes edited.

They will perish, but thou dost endure; they
    will all wear out like a garment.
Thou changest them like raiment, and they
    pass away; but thou art the same and thy
    years have no end. (Ps. 102:25–7)
I am the Alpha and the Omega, the first and
    the last, the beginning and the end. (Rev.
    22:13)

But what does it mean to say that God is eternal? Jews and Christians agree that God's eternality entails that he has always existed and always will exist, that he has no beginning and no end. But from this central point there are two routes that might be taken. One is to say that God is *timelessly eternal* and the other is to say that he is *temporally eternal.*

Let us first consider the view that God is timelessly eternal or 'outside of time'. There are a variety of reasons a Christian might be tempted by this thesis. One might be to emphasize God's transcendence over his creation as much as possible. Another might be to reconcile divine foreknowledge and human freedom. (Boethius and others have argued that human beings can be free despite God's knowledge of what they will do in their future because God's knowledge is timeless.) Another might be to retain consistency with other things one says about God, for example that he is immutable. (And it certainly does seem true that a timeless being—to be defined below—must be immutable.)

Whatever the reasons, a variety of Christian theologians and philosophers have claimed that God is timeless. For example, Anselm graphically depicts God's relation to time as follows:

Thou wast not, then, yesterday, nor wilt thou be tomorrow; but yesterday and today and tomorrow thou art; or, rather, neither yesterday; nor today nor tomorrow thou art; but, simply, thou art, outside all time. For yesterday and today and tomorrow have no existence, except in time; but thou, although nothing exists without thee, nevertheless dost not exist in space or time, but all things exist in thee.[1]

That God is timeless was also claimed by Augustine and Boethius before Anselm, and was also held after him, notably by Aquinas and Schleiermacher. In a famous definition, Boethius called eternity 'the complete possession all at once of illimitable life';

it is a kind of 'now that stands still'. (Notice that Boethius is using 'eternal' as a synonym for 'timeless', which I am not.) Since God is eternal, he lives in what might be called an 'everlasting present'; he has an infinity of movable time—past, present and future—all at once everlastingly present to him. Boethius is perhaps most clear on this point when he speaks of divine foreknowledge:

Wherefore since . . . God hath always an everlasting and present state, his knowledge also surpassing all motions of time, remaineth in the simplicity of his presence, and comprehending the infinite spaces of that which is past and to come, considereth all things in his simple knowledge, as though they were now in doing. So that, if thou wilt weigh his foreknowledge with which he discerneth all things, thou wilt more rightly esteem it to be the knowledge of a never fading instant than a foreknowledge as of a thing to come.[2]

Following Boethius, Aquinas stressed that for God there is no past, present and future, and no before and after, that all is 'simultaneously whole' for him.[3]

These statements are not easy to understand. What precisely is meant by the term 'timeless' or 'timeless being'? Following Nelson Pike, let us say that a given being is timeless if and only if it:

(1) lacks temporal location
and
(2) lacks temporal extension.[4]

A being lacks temporal location if it does not make sense to say of it, for example, that it existed before the French Revolution or that it will exist on Jimmy Carter's seventieth birthday. Thus, if God is timeless, statements like these cannot meaningfully be made about him. A being lacks temporal extension if it has no duration, i.e. if it makes no sense to say of it, for example, that it has lived for eighty years or that it was alive during the entire period of the Truman administration.

It is not easy to feel that one has fully grasped the notion of a timeless being. Perhaps this is in part because it is difficult to see precisely what criteria (1) and (2) imply. Very possibly they imply another characteristic of a timeless being, one which is also difficult to state and explicate precisely:

(3) Temporal terms have no significant application to him.

What is a 'temporal term'? Without wishing to suggest that my list is exhaustive, let me stipulate that a temporal term is one like those included in the following list: 'past', 'present', 'future', 'before', 'after', and other similar terms like 'simultaneous', 'always', 'later', 'next year', 'forever', 'at 6:00 p.m.', etc. Now there appears to be a sense in which temporal terms cannot meaningfully be predicated of a being that lacks temporal location and temporal extension. Neither the timeless being itself, nor its properties, actions or relations with other beings can be significantly modified by temporal terms. Thus if God is a timeless being, the following sentences are either meaningless or necessarily false:

- God existed before Moses.
- God's power will soon triumph over evil.
- Last week God wrought a miracle.
- God will always be wiser than human beings.

Does this imply that time as we understand it is unreal, a kind of illusion? If the timeless being in question is God, the ultimate reality of the universe, the creator of the heavens and the earth, one might well push the argument in this way: if from God's point of view there is no past, present and future, and no before and after, then—it might well be argued—there is no ultimately real past, present and future, and no ultimately real relationship of before and after. Thus time as we experience it is unreal.

But the argument need not be pushed in this direction. Even if God is a timeless being, it can be argued that time is real and that our temporal distinctions are apt just because God created time (for us to live 'in'). Perhaps an analogy from space will help. Just because God is spaceless (he has no spatial location or extension) no one wants to say that space is unreal. It is just that God does not exist in space as we do. Similarly, he does not exist 'in' time, but time is still real, both for us and for God. Well then—one might want to ask at this point—if God is timeless is it or is it not meaningful to say that 'God existed before Moses' or that 'God will always be wiser than human beings'? The answer is that it depends on who you are: for us these statements are meaningful and true; for God they are meaningless or at least necessarily false.

Is the doctrine of divine timelessness coherent? I do not know. I suspect it is possible for a philosopher to lay out a concept of divine timelessness which I am unable to refute, i.e. prove incoherent. I will discuss one such attempt later in this chapter. However, throughout this book, for reasons I will presently explain, I do not propose to assume that God is timeless. In fact, I plan to make and argue for the assumption that God is 'temporally eternal'. In my view, this is a far simpler procedure, with far fewer theological dangers, as I will explain. For the fact is that every notion of divine timelessness with which I am familiar is subject to difficulties which, at the very least, seem serious.

I will argue against the doctrine of divine timelessness on two counts: first, that a timeless being cannot be the Christian God; and second, that the notion of a timeless being is probably incoherent. The first point has been convincingly argued by both Nelson Pike and Richard Swinburne.[5] I will not mention all of the traditional attributes of God they claim timelessness rules out; I will instead concentrate on just two: the claim that God is the creator of the universe, and the claim that God is a personal being who acts in human history, speaking, punishing, warning, forgiving, etc. Both notions are obviously crucial to Christianity; if timelessness really does rule them out this will constitute a very good reason for a Christian to reject the doctrine.

Notice the following argument:

(5) God creates x.
(6) x first exists at T.
(7) Therefore, God creates x at T.

If this argument is valid, it seems to rule out the possibility of a timeless God creating anything at all, the universe or anything in it, for 'x' here is a variable ranging over anything at all about which it is logically possible that it be created. The reason the argument rules out the doctrine that God is creator is that (7) cannot be true if God lacks temporal location. For we saw earlier that no temporal term like 'at T' can meaningfully be applied to a being or to the actions of a being that lacks temporal location and temporal extension. God is not the creator Christians have traditionally believed in if he is not the creator of things like me and the eucalyptus tree outside my office. But no timeless being can be the creator of such things since they came into existence at various points in time. Thus timelessness is inconsistent with the Christian view of God as creator.

But cannot God, so to speak, timelessly create something temporal? Aquinas, at least, argued that he can. God may create something at a certain point in time (say, create me in the year 1940), but it does not follow from this, Aquinas would say, that God's act of creating occurred at that point in time (or indeed at any point in time); his creating may well be based on changeless and eternal aspects of his will. Thus Aquinas says:

> God's act of understanding and willing is, necessarily, His act of making. Now, an effect follows from the intellect and the will according to the determination of the intellect and the command of the will. Moreover, just as the intellect determines every other condition of the thing made, so does it prescribe the time of its making; for art determines not only that this thing is to be such and such, but that it is to be at this particular time, even as a physician determines that a dose of medicine is to be drunk at such a particular time. So that, if his act of will were of itself sufficient to produce the effect, the effect would follow anew from his previous decision, without any new action on his part. Nothing, therefore, prevents our saying that God's action existed from all eternity, whereas its effect was not present from eternity, but existed at that time when, from all eternity, He ordained it.[6]

Thus—so Aquinas would say—(5) and (6) in the above argument do not entail (7) after all.

Is Aquinas correct? It depends on what he means by 'eternity' in the above lines. If he means temporal eternity I believe he is correct. It may well be true that God can, so to speak, 'from all eternity create x at T'. I have no wish to deny this, at any rate. A temporally eternal being apparently can eternally (that is, at all points in time) will that a given temporal being come to exist at a certain point in time. Of course, this case is not precisely parallel to the case of Aquinas's physician at a given point in time willing that a dosage be taken at a later point in time. But nevertheless, as concerns temporal eternality, Aquinas appears to be correct: as it stands, the (5)–(7) argument is invalid.

But Aquinas's argument, which in my opinion successfully applies to temporally eternal things, does not apply to timeless things. (Notice that the physician in his example is not timeless.) Even if it is true that I was created in 1940 not because of a choice God made in 1940 (or at some other time) but because of a temporally eternal divine choice, this does not make the choice *timeless* in the sense of lacking temporal location and extension. Temporally eternal things certainly do have temporal extention. It would still make sense and quite possibly be true to say, 'God willed in 1940 that Davis exist' (although it would also be meaningful and perhaps equally true to make the same statement with 3469 B.C. or A.D. 2610 or any other date substituted for 1940). Equally, if all God's decisions and actions are temporally eternal they are *simultaneous* with each other; and statements like 'x's desire to create a and x's decision to do b are simultaneous' cannot, as we saw, meaningfully be made about a timeless being.[7] This too is to apply a temporal term—'simultaneous'—to it.

Of course, nothing prevents a defender of timelessness from simply insisting that an action (e.g. the causing of something to exist) can be timeless and the effect (e.g. its coming into existence) temporal. Such a person can ask why the temporality of the effect requires that the cause be temporal. But to anticipate a point I will make in more detail later, the answer to this is that we have on hand no acceptable concept of atemporal causation, i.e. of what it is for a timeless cause to produce a temporal effect. Surely, as Nelson Pike argues, in all the cases of causation with which we are familiar, a temporal relationship obtains between an action and its effect. We are in no position to deny that this need always be the case unless we are armed with a usable concept of atemporal causation, which we are not.

Let us return to the argument mentioned above:

(5) God creates x.
(6) x first exists at T.
(7) Therefore, God creates x at T.

What we need to notice is that (7) is ambiguous between (7a) and (7b):

(7a) God, at T, creates x.

(7b) God creates x, and x first exists at T.

Now (7a) clearly cannot be true of God if God is timeless—a being that performs some action at a certain point in time is temporal. So (7b) is the interpretation of (7) that will be preferred by the defender of divine timelessness. Notice that (7b) is simply the conjunction of (5) and (6), and accordingly is indeed entailed by (5) and (6). But can (7b) be true of God if God is timeless? Only if we have available a usable concept of atemporal causation, which, as I say, we do not have. Therefore, we are within our rights in concluding that (5) and (6) entail that God is temporal, i.e. that a timeless being cannot be the creator of the universe.

Accordingly, it is not clear how a timelessly eternal being can be the creator of this temporal universe. If God creates a given temporal thing, then God's act of creation is itself temporal (though it may be temporally eternal). If God is timelessly eternal in the sense defined earlier, he cannot create temporal things.

Second, a timeless being cannot be the personal, caring, involved God we read about in the Bible. The God of the Bible is, above all, a God who cares deeply about what happens in history and who acts to bring about his will. He makes plans. He responds to what human beings, do, e.g. their evil deeds or their acts of repentance. He seems to have temporal location and extension. The Bible does not hesitate to speak of God's years and days (see Psalm 102:24, 27; Hebrews 1:12). And God seems to act in temporal sequences—first he rescues the children of Israel from Egypt and later he gives them the Law; first he sends his son to be born of a virgin and later he raises him from the dead. These are generalizations meant to be understood as covering the whole Bible rather than specific passages; nevertheless here are two texts where such points seem to be made:

If you obey the commandments of the Lord your God . . . by loving the Lord your God, by walking in his ways, and by keeping his commandments and his statutes and his ordinances, then you shall live and multiply, and the Lord your God will bless you . . . . But if your heart turns away, and you will not hear, but are drawn away to worship other gods and serve them, I de-

clare to you this day, that you shall perish. (Deut. 30:16–18)

In many and various ways God spoke of old to our fathers by the prophets; but in these last days he has spoken to us by a Son. (Heb. 1:1–2)

But the obvious problem here is to understand how a timeless being can plan or anticipate or remember or respond or punish or warn or forgive. All such acts seem undeniably temporal.[8] To make plans is to formulate intentions about the future. To anticipate is to look forward to what is future. To remember is to have beliefs or knowledge about what is past. To respond is to be affected by events that have occurred in the past. To punish is to cause someone to suffer because of something done in the past. To warn is to caution someone about dangers that might lie in the future. To forgive someone is to restore a past relationship that was damaged by an offense.

On both counts, then, it is difficult to see how a timeless being can be the God in which Christians have traditionally believed. It does not seem that there is any clear sense in which a timeless being can be the creator of the universe or a being who acts in time.

The other and perhaps more important argument against divine timelessness is that both the notion of a timeless being per se and the notion of a timeless being who is also omniscient are probably incoherent. The incoherence of the notion per se can be seen by considering carefully the Boethius-Anselm-Aquinas claim that for God all times are simultaneously present. Events occurring at 3021 B.C., at 1982, and at A.D. 7643, they want to say, are all 'simultaneously present' to God. If this just means that at any point in time God knows in full and complete detail what happens at any other point in time, I can (and do) accept it. But it clearly means something different and much stronger than this, and in this stronger sense (whatever precisely it comes to) the claim does not seem possibly true.[9]

That is, if the doctrine of timelessness requires us to say that the years 3021 B.C. and A.D. 7643 are simultaneous, then the doctrine is false, for the two are not simultaneous. They may of course be simultaneous in some sense if time is illusory. But since I see no good reason to affirm that time is illusory and every reason to deny that it is illusory, I am within my rights in insisting that the two indicated years are not simultaneous and that the doctrine of divine timelessness is accordingly probably false.

Suppose an event that occurred yesterday is the cause of an event that will occur tomorrow, e.g. suppose your having thrown a banana peel on the pavement yesterday will cause me to trip and break a bone tomorrow. How can the throwing of the banana peel and the breaking of the bone be simultaneous? Surely if the first caused the second the first must be temporally prior to the second; and if so, they are not simultaneous. (Perhaps some causes are simultaneous with their effects, but not causes of events of this sort.)

But the following objection might be raised: 'Any argument for the conclusion that timeless beings cannot exist must be mistaken for the simple reason that timeless beings do exist'. It has been seriously suggested, for example, that numbers are timeless beings. Thus William Kneale says:

An assertion such as 'There is a prime number between five and ten' can never be countered sensibly by the remark 'You are out of date: things have altered recently.' And this is the reason why the entities discussed in mathematics can properly be said to have a timeless existence. To say only that they have a sempiternal or omnitemporal existence (i.e., an existence at all times) would be unsatisfactory because this way of talking might suggest that it is at least conceivable that they should at some time cease to exist, and that is an absurdity we want to exclude.[10]

Is the number seven, for example, timeless? I do not think so. (I agree that it is eternal and that it would be absurd to suggest that it might not exist; it is, in short, a sort of 'necessary being'.) But if the number seven is not just eternal but timeless, then on our earlier definition of 'timeless', the following statements cannot meaningfully be made:

- The number seven existed on 27 July 1883.
- The number seven was greater than the number six during the whole of the Punic wars.
- The number seven existed yesterday and will exist tomorrow.

But the number seven is not a timeless being; all three of these sentences, in my opinion, are not only meaningful but true. (The fact that the first might be taken by someone to suggest that the number seven might not exist at some time other than 27 July 1883 is only an interesting psychological fact about the person who misreads it in this way. The statement implies nothing of the sort.)

But defenders of divine timelessness can raise an objection to this argument that their notion is incoherent. They can say something like this:

Of course talk about 'eternal present', 'simultaneously whole', etc. seems incoherent to us. This is because such talk is at best a stumbling way of understanding a mystery—the mystery of God's transcendence over time—that we cannot really understand. Statements like 'my nineteenth birthday occurred before my twentieth' only seem indubitable to us because, unlike God, our minds are limited. If we had God's intellectual prowess, if we understood temporal reality as he does, we would see that this statement is false or inadequate or misleading. We would then see time correctly.

There may be some sense in which the claims being made here are true. I will not deny them, at any rate. . . . God's consciousness of time may indeed so far transcend ours that the best way we have of expressing it is by making apparently incoherent statements. But whether or not these claims are true, I am quite sure that we have no good reason to believe them. Like it or not, we are stuck with these limited minds of ours; if we want to be rational we have no choice but to reject what we judge to be incoherent. It may be true, in some sense, that some statements we presently consider true (like 'my nineteenth birthday occurred before my twentieth') are really false or inadequate or misleading when understood in some way which we cannot now understand. But it is irrational for us now to affirm that this is true. . . .

We have been discussing the notion of timelessness as an attempt to understand the Christian tradition that God is eternal. It can now be seen why I find the notion inadequate and why I much prefer the other alternative, which is to say that God is temporally eternal. Let us say that a temporally eternal being is (1) eternal in the sense that there never was or will be a moment when it does not exist, (2) temporal in the sense that it has both temporal location and temporal extension, and (3) temporal in the sense that the distinctions among past, present and future, and between before and after, can meaningfully be applied to it. If God is such a temporally eternal being, there are still several ways of understanding his relation to time.

Perhaps the simplest way is to say that time has always existed alongside God. This is difficult to state coherently—'Time has always existed' reduces to the tautology 'There is no moment of time in which time does not exist'. Perhaps it is better to state this view as the simple claim that time is not a contingent, created thing like the universe.

A second possibility is espoused by Augustine. He says that time was created by God, exists, and then will cease to exist. Before the creation of the universe and after the universe ceases to exist there exists not time but timeless eternity. Thus God has control over time—he created it and can presumably destroy it whenever he wants. While this view has some attractions—time or at least our consciousness of it does seem in some sense dependent on the existence of mutable things—a possible problem is that the notion of timeless eternity before the creation of the universe and after it ceases to exist may be just as difficult to understand as the doctrine of timeless eternity itself. This problem may well be solvable, however. In timeless eternity there will presumably be no appearance of temporal succession, i.e. of events occurring before or after each other, which is at least one of the fundamental problems connected with regarding God as timeless at the same time that we live in a world of apparent temporal succession.

A third possibility was suggested by the eighth-century church father John of Damascus. Time has always existed, John appears to say, yet is only measurable when things like the sun and moon exist. Thus before the creation there existed non-measurable time, and after the end of the heavens and the earth non-measurable time will again exist. Measurable time is what exists from the point of creation of the world to the point of its destruction.

Since it is probably the simplest, and since I see no danger in it for Christianity (as I will argue below), I will adopt the first alternative: time was

not created; it necessarily exists (like numbers); it depends for its existence on nothing else. Time, perhaps, is an eternal aspect of God's nature rather than a reality independent of God. But the point is that God, on this view, is a temporal being. Past, present and future are real to him; he has simultaneity and succession in his states, acts and knowledge. He knows statements like 'Today is 24 April' and 'My nineteenth birthday occurred before my twentieth'. He has temporal location. It makes good sense to say: 'God exists today' and 'God was omniscient on Napoleon's birthday'. And he has temporal extension. It makes good sense to say 'God existed during the entire period of the Punic wars' and to ask, 'How long has God existed?' The answer to the latter is: forever.

The three main motives for the theory of timeless eternity, I suggested, were to reconcile human freedom and divine foreknowledge, to retain consistency with other things one says about God, and to exalt God's transcendence as much as possible. As to the first, I believe foreknowledge and freedom can be reconciled without appealing to any doctrine of timelessness. . . . As to the second, I do not believe that anything I say about God in this book (or indeed anything said about God in the Bible) logically requires that he be timeless. And as to the third, I feel no need to exalt God's transcendence in every possible way. What Christians must do, I believe, is emphasize God's transcendence over his creation in the ways that scripture does and in ways that seem essential to Christian theism. And I do not believe that the Bible teaches, implies or presupposes that God is timeless. Nor do I feel any theological or philosophical need to embrace timelessness.

Nor is there any reason to doubt that a temporal God who is 'in' time just as we are is everything the Judeo-Christian God is traditionally supposed to be. He can still be an eternal being, i.e. a being without beginning or end. He can still be the creator of the universe. He can still be immutable in the sense of remaining ever true to his promises and purposes and eternally retaining his essential nature. (But he cannot be immutable in other stronger senses.) He can still have complete knowledge of all past, present and future events. (If he 'transcends time', it is only in the sense that he has this power—a power no other being has.) He can still be the loving, omnipotent redeemer Christians worship.

Some might still wish to object to this as follows: 'Surely God must be free of all temporal limitations if he is truly God. But a temporal God is not so free. Thus God must be timeless'. The answer to this is that a temporally eternally God such as I have described is free of certain temporal limitations, e.g. he is free of our inability to remember things that happened hundreds of years ago. Furthermore, not even a timelessly eternal God is free of all temporal limitations, for he is actually unable to experience 'before' or 'after'. His nature limits him; he is unable to experience such things, for if he did experience them he would be temporal. There is temporal limitation whichever view we take. It appears that however we look at it, the doctrine of divine temporal eternity is greatly preferable to timeless eternity. So it is the former that I will embrace.

Notes

1. Anselm, *St Anselm: Basic Writings* (LaSalle, Illinois: Open Court Publishing Company, 1958) p. 25.

2. Boethius, *The Theological Treatises and the Consolation of Philosophy* (Loeb Classical Library, London: William Heinemann, 1918) pp. 403–5; cf. also pp. 21–3, 401–5.

3. *The Summa Theologica of St Thomas Aquinas* (London: Burns, Oates and Washbourne, 1920) Pt. I, Q. X, Arts. 2 and 4.

4. These points are taken from Nelson Pike's *God and Timelessness* (New York: Schocken Books, 1970) p. 7. Pike's work is an outstanding study of this subject and has influenced me at several points.

5. Ibid., pp. 97–118, 125–8; Richard Swinburne, *The Coherence of Theism* (Oxford University Press, 1977) pp. 221–2.

6. Thomas Aquinas, *Summa Contra Gentiles,* trans A.C. Pegis (Notre Dame, Indiana: University of Notre Dame Press, 1975) II, 35.

7. This has been argued by Nicholas Wolterstorff in his 'God Everlasting'. See *God and the Good,* ed. Clifton J. Orlebeke and Lewis B. Smedes (Grand Rapids, Michigan: William B. Eerdmans, 1975) pp. 181–203.

8. See Pike, *God and Timelessness,* pp. 128–9; Swinburne, *The Coherence of Theism* pp. 220–1.

9. See Swinburne, *The Coherence of Theism* pp. 220–1.

10. William Kneale, 'Time and Eternity in Theology', *Proceedings of the Aristotelian Society,* vol. 61 (1961) p. 98.

IV.A.2 The God Beyond Time

HUGH J. McCANN

Hugh J. McCann is professor of philosophy at Texas A&M University and the author of several articles in metaphysics and philosophy of action. *In this essay, he opposes the position of the last essay (Stephen Davis's "Temporal Eternity") and defends the classical doctrine that God is atemporal (i.e., exists in eternity outside of time). He argues that attributing timeless eternity to God makes better sense of His sovereignty and omniscience, and it satisfies the classic view that God's essence is to exist. McCann labels the opposing position, that God is temporal, sempiternalism (that is, God endures constantly and continuously, and is everlasting).*

McCann answers the sempiternalist's charges that their temporal notion of God is closer to the biblical view of deity and that an atemporal God cannot create a world or providentially enter into human events or know tensed propositions. To the contrary, he contends, it is the temporalist who has difficulty explaining how God can be in time but not in space and can be ominiscient.

This essay was commissioned for the first edition of this anthology. This is a revised version.

By both tradition and common agreement, God is supposed to be eternal. But the agreement is today more apparent than real, for there is profound conflict over how this claim is to be understood. Traditional theologians, for the most part, took it to mean that God is completely outside of time, and is in fact the Creator of it. Only such a God, they reasoned, could justly be called the Creator of heaven and earth, could have full knowledge of what for us is the future, and could have the sovereignty and immutability appropriate to the divine essence. More recently, however, all of this has come into dispute. It is argued that only a God who is in time could create anything at all, and that only a temporal God could be the loving father Scripture describes, who periodically intervenes in nature and history for our sake. Furthermore, a timeless God's knowledge would be woefully inadequate: Being outside of time, he would be unable to know what is true *now,* and hence unable to know *any* tensed proposition, not just certain ones about the future. Hence, it is claimed, God's eternity must be understood as *sempiternity*. He is an everlasting God, one who always was and will be, but who is otherwise subject to temporal passage just like you and me. Such a God may not match the ideal of eternalists, but he has as much sovereignty as a God can have, and knows all that a God can know. And if he is not unchanging in knowledge and action, he can still be unchanging in character and temperament.

In what follows I want to defend the first of the above conceptions. I shall argue that there is no reason to think a timelessly eternal God cannot create, or act so as to alter the course of events in the world, and that only a timeless creator can exercise rational and complete sovereignty over creation. As for knowledge, I will claim it is, if anything, a timebound God whose knowledge of tensed propositions must be limited, whereas a timeless God's knowledge of them is complete. I want to begin by getting clear on the two notions of eternity at stake in the dispute, and giving some reasons why God was traditionally understood as timelessly eternal.

I. Sempiternity Versus Timelessness

The more familiar of these two concepts is that of sempiternity or everlastingness. Under this conception God is a temporally persistent or enduring entity just like you and me.[1] He is located within time, and subject to the restrictions of tense and temporal passage. So like us, he has a history and a future; he remembers and anticipates, presumably observes the course of the universe, and acts at his pleasure to produce change in the world he has created. The difference is that God's career extends through all of time, which on this sort of view is usually taken to be without beginning or end. He always was, is now, and always will be. On this conception of eternity, it makes sense to say of God that he always knew you would be reading this sentence at this moment, that he knows now that you are doing so, and that he will always know hereafter that you did. In short, but for its being unbounded at either end, the life and experience of an everlasting God need not in principle be much different from yours and mine.

The conception of God as timelessly eternal is less familiar, and radically different. On this view God, unlike you and I, is not located within time, and tense and related temporal conceptions have no application to him whatever. Strictly speaking, therefore, it is false to say of God that he ever has existed, that he exists now, or that he ever will exist. At best, such claims are a clumsy way of indicating what we who are within time can always truthfully *assert.* And that is simply this: that God exists—where the verb, though in the grammatical present, signifies nothing of temporal presentness, but rather a reality that stands completely outside of time, untouched by becoming or transition of any kind. God exists timelessly on this account, and his life and experience, while they may concern the world of change, are themselves unchanging. So it would also be wrong to say God ever has known or will know about your reading this or any other sentence. Yet, it would be true that he knows, timelessly, that you are reading this sentence—even, if he is omniscient, that you are reading it now. God knows this, and everything else as well, in a single, timeless act of awareness that encompasses all of heaven and earth, in its complete history. His action as Creator is from the same vantage point. There is no time at which he creates the universe, for time itself is an aspect of the world of change and that is what God creates. In a single *fiat* he produces the entire universe, in all of its history, all of it with equal directness and absolute control. This does not prevent its being the case that from our perspective within time, not everything does, or even could, occur at once. But that is tensed talk, which does not apply to God. From his perspective, the production of all that, as we would say, ever was or will be, occurs in a single, unified act, in timeless eternity.

Timeless eternity is, to say the least, not familiar to us, and the conception of it is not easy to grasp. One may wonder, therefore, how it gained ascendancy in accounts of God's nature. Scripture, it is fair to say, leans heavily in the opposite direction. The God of the Bible creates the world over a six-day period, and then desists from his labors on the seventh (Gen. 1:1–2:2). At intervals, he speaks to Moses and the prophets, and he intervenes repeatedly in his people's history to save them from disaster. Above all, he is portrayed as *reacting* to the behavior of humankind; he adjusts his behavior to our own, as when he desists from his plan to destroy Nineveh (Jon. 3:10). Obviously, this is not a God who is remote from the world. His involvement in it is deep, and his actions as a loving father are attuned to the needs of each situation.

There is no denying that such an interactive God is more easily understood as temporal. As always with the reading of Scripture, however, one must be cautious, for too much literalism leads straight into trouble. Indeed, the very first phrase of the entire Bible tells us that the God about to be described as creating the world in six days did so "in the beginning." How could this be if time had no beginning? Furthermore, this same God is presented as a spatial being: as having a head, hands and feet, as dwelling in cities and tabernacles, as moving from place to place. If it is fair to take this kind of talk as metaphorical, then surely passages that portray God as temporal can in principle be so taken as well. Finally, the Bible contains clear hints of a much more sophisticated conception. The name God gives himself from the burning bush, "I am" (Exod. 3:14), becomes entirely unimpressive when taken to mean only that he existed at that moment. Or consider the sudden shift to the grammatical present in such passages as, "Before the mountains

were born, or thou didst give birth to the earth and the world, even from everlasting to everlasting, thou art God" (Ps. 90:2), or, "I say to you, before Abraham was born, I am" (John 8:58). It is not unreasonable to think passages like this aim at an atemporal conception. Finally, despite his seeming change of mind about the Ninevites, the Bible is at points fairly decisive in claiming that in God there is no change, not even a shadow of it (Mal. 3:6, James 1:17).

This kind of conflict is familiar. It has been said that the Bible is a book not of theology but of life, and so cannot be expected to offer a unified and seamlessly consistent theory of the divine nature. That is the work of philosophers and theologians, who have usually aimed at an account that respects the rigors of metaphysics as well as the content of faith. And from a metaphysical perspective, it is not surprising that some theories would call for a timeless God. The view that ultimate reality is timeless is as old as Parmenides, and its association with theories of the divine nature was probably inevitable. But there are reasons for the alliance. Both in Scripture and in cosmological proofs for the existence of God, he is portrayed as the Creator of everything but himself and as ruling the universe with complete power and authority. But if God is in time, his sovereignty is restricted: There is something other than himself that he did not create—namely, time itself—and his experience and action are made subject to the limitations of opportunity. Better, then, if possible, to have a God who in creating the world creates time, but whose own being lies beyond it. A second consideration, of which we will see more below, has to do with human freedom. If it is true that God gives us wills that escape the reach of causal determination, then to treat him as temporal is to threaten his omniscience. How could he know today what I will do tomorrow if I have not yet decided? A timelessly eternal God, by contrast, should be able to know as much about tomorrow as he does about today: everything, presumably.

But perhaps the deepest running argument for a timelessly eternal God is that the divine essence, as well as we are able to understand it, seems incompatible with any sort of change. A thing changes either by coming to have a characteristic it previously lacked, or by losing a characteristic it previously had. Thus an apple might change colors by ceasing to be green and becoming red; or it may fall to the earth, thereby exchanging its position at the end of a branch for one on the ground. Now the characteristics with respect to which a thing changes must be accidental rather than essential ones, at least if the thing is to continue existing, for the essential properties of a thing are by definition characteristics without which it cannot continue in being. An apple may change its color or position, but it cannot cease to be colored or positioned at all and remain in existence, for color and position are essential to apples. The same considerations apply to God. If he is to undergo change without ceasing to be, it must be by gaining or losing accidental features. Perhaps he comes to have a thought he previously did not, or to act in a new way. It turns out, however, that unlike created beings, God cannot have accidental features.

The reason for this is that if God does have accidental properties, his authority over the universe has to be limited. It is fair to demand that any accidental properties God has will have a sufficient explanation. Otherwise, his having them would be arbitrary and not in accordance with the concept of a perfect being. But unfortunately, the explanation for the presence of an accidental property in a thing can never arise entirely from the thing's own nature. If it did, the property would be entailed by the entity's essence, and so be essential rather than accidental. But if it is essential, then it is not a property with respect to which the thing could change after all. So the accidental properties of a thing must always be explained at least in part from without: The color of the apple will depend in part on its environment, and its location will hinge on the forces to which it is subject. And the same applies to God. If his thought and activity change from time to time, there will have to be an explanation, and the explanation will have to invoke things other than the divine nature. Perhaps what he is thinking will be explained by the events of the moment, or his activity by the opportunity they present. But whatever the explanation is, it will have to invoke something extrinsic to the divine nature, and it cannot do so without introducing depen-

dence and passivity into God. His experience will depend on the stage of world history, and he will have to await his chances to redirect it. For traditional theology at least, that is not what one expects of the Sovereign Lord of heaven and earth.

A perfectly sovereign God cannot, then, have accidental properties; and of course a being that cannot even have accidental properties cannot change with respect to them. On the traditional conception, therefore, God must be completely immutable, completely beyond the reach of becoming. It does not even make sense to put him in time, since he would then have shifting relations of simultaneity with the events of the world, which is not possible. It is unlikely, however, that proponents of the temporal conception of eternity would be persuaded by this argument. For one thing, they may have misgivings about the very idea of there being timelessly eternal entities and states of affairs. Secondly, they might claim the conception of the divine nature called for by atemporalists is simply too demanding. Perhaps it *is* wrong, strictly speaking, to think of there being any change in a being whose essence is to be, and who enjoys complete sovereignty over the world. But, the temporalist might point out, the fact is that we do this with God all the time: we speak of him as learning about things as they occur, and as causing different events at different times. And although we may try to observe protocol by insisting that all of God's knowledge and activity occurs in a single, eternal act, it is not clear that this advances our understanding very much. Indeed, the temporalist may go further. He may argue that causation and knowing, or at least some knowing, are in themselves *intrinsically* temporal operations, so that if we apply these concepts to God at all, we *must* conceive of him as a temporal being. I want to address these concerns in order, beginning with the one about there being timelessly eternal things.

II. Atemporal States of Affairs

A number of reasons might be given for doubting that there is a realm of timeless entities or timeless facts about them. Some are based on misunderstandings. It may be thought, for example, that if for God there is no time, then time must somehow be unreal—an illusion, perhaps, that accompanies our own creaturely perceptions, but not a genuine aspect of the real world. And it might well be argued that this is too much to swallow; time is too central, too inexpungible from our experience to be plausibly considered an illusion. There is no reason, however, why defenders of timeless eternity need be committed to such a view. After all, no one takes the fact that God is not a spatial entity to imply that space is an illusion, so why take such a position with respect to time? Furthermore, atemporalism is not committed to the view that for God there is no time. It holds, to be precise, that God is not *in* time, that his life and experience transcend change and temporal passage. It does not follow from this that time is unreal or even that God is unfamiliar with it. Indeed, if he is both omniscient and the Creator of time, precisely the opposite would have to be the case. The only restriction is that his activity and awareness must not involve change, even though the world that is their object does. It may, of course, be argued that this is not possible, and we shall shortly be examining such arguments. But the important thing to see at this point is that an argument is needed; it is in no way obvious that the atemporalist position here is untenable.

A second reason for doubting that there are timeless states of affairs stems from the way in which defenders of timeless eternity have been prone to express their view. Boethius described timeless eternity as "the complete possession, all at once, of illimitable life," and held that the God who possesses this life comprehends "the infinite spaces of that which is past and to come . . . as though they were now in doing."[2] Following this precedent, it is not uncommon for timeless eternity to be described in terms that are at least partly temporal rather than timeless. God's experience is held to be of an "eternal present," for example, or we may be told that in eternity all of the world's history is "simultaneously present" to God. As a stepping stone to understanding timeless eternity such language is probably to be expected, and it is useful in some ways. It conveys the point that God's experience of the world is single and unchanging, that it

involves no serial presentation of events or alteration of content. It also suggests something else to which the defender of timeless eternity should be committed: that the *content* of God's experience of the world includes its temporal features, that he is aware of things in their temporality as well as in all other aspects of their being.

But to say that all of history is eternally or simultaneously *present* to God leads to implications that are not intended, and that we should not accept. It suggests, first, that besides having temporal content, God's act of experiencing the world is itself a temporal thing, that it occurs in a kind of unchanging present moment, notwithstanding the fact that it is supposed to be completely outside time. This in itself is a contradiction, to which defenders of timeless eternity need not be committed. A lot more contradictions threaten if we add that God's experience must be of all of history, which now must be conceived as *simultaneously* present to God. This makes all of history present "at once" to God's now retemporalized act of awareness, and the effect is that all of history must be held to be simultaneous. So we would have to say that the American Civil War is simultaneous with the Protestant Reformation, that yesterday's events are simultaneous with tomorrow's, etc.[3] Obviously, however, these things are false.

One way of dealing with these problems is to seek to define notions of presentness and simultaneity that would be appropriate to the timeless order and would not carry unacceptable implications.[4] But I think it is better, at least for present purposes, simply to drop the idea that history is "present" to God, in any sense other than being given to him timelessly in experience or awareness. This is not to say the events of which God is aware are not temporal, but it is to say his awareness of them is not. God creates and is aware of all of history neither simultaneously nor at different times, but eternally. His activity as Creator and Knower is unified and unchanging, but it does not occur at any present moment, not even a supposed eternal one. It simply is. To proceed in this way deprives us of some handy ways for describing timeless eternity, but it also forces us to describe the realities it involves in ways that do not threaten immediate contradiction.[5]

But are there any timeless realities? After all, the sempiternalist might urge, apart from its supposed indispensability for describing how things are with God, we would have no need of the notion of timeless reality at all. Nothing in our earthly experience, it seems, is usefully described in terms of timelessness; and since heavenly experience is not now available to us, it may well be that the timeless realities eternalists suppose pertain to it are not really there, but instead are just figments of our inability to comprehend. To this atemporalists have replied that we are in fact familiar with timeless entities, namely, those of the conceptual and mathematical realms. Such entities as propositions and numbers, they have held, are incapable of intrinsic change, and truths about them represent timelessly eternal states of affairs. Consider the fact that the number 2 is even. This, obviously, is not something we expect to change, for we do not view the number 2 as capable of change. And when we say that 2 is even, we mean to assert more than just a fact we take to hold at that particular moment. That 2 is incapable of change, according to the atemporalist, makes the number 2 as timeless a reality as any. And the fact that it is even, along with all other mathematical and conceptual facts, counts as a timelessly eternal state of affairs.[6]

The temporalist rejoinder here is that this view of things goes too far. Granted, mathematical entities and facts do not change. But, it is insisted, all this means is that these are sempiternal, or everlasting, realities, not that they are atemporal. And while "2 is even" does have import beyond the present moment, it need not be taken as reporting a timeless fact. Instead, it can be taken as *omnitemporal*—that is, as speaking about all times. We can understand "2 is even" as saying that 2 always was even, is even now, and always will be even. To do this is to understand 2 as sempiternal rather than timeless, and it accommodates the unchanging character of the fact that 2 is even. What need is there to go further than this, and commit ourselves to an ontology of timeless states of affairs? And of course the same applies to truths about Euclidean triangles, trigonometric functions, or any other conceptual entity you like. In short, there is just no need to invoke the concept of timeless eternity to deal with

conceptual realities. Any entity we might view as timelessly eternal can equally well be treated as sempiternal, and any statement we might think describes something timeless can be effectively replaced with one that is omnitemporal—which describes unchanging, but nevertheless temporal, realities.

Unfortunately, however, the replacement does not always work—a fact that emerges when we consider how the sempiternalist would have to formulate the very issues over which the he and the atemporalist disagree. Presumably, the sempiternalist would endorse the following two statements:

(a) There are no timelessly eternal states of affairs.
(b) There is no timelessly eternal God.

The atemporalist, by contrast, would be expected to reject (a) and (b), since he holds that there *are* timelessly eternal facts and a timeless God. But in fact the atemporalist *cannot* reject (a) and (b), if they are understood in the way sempiternalists *must* understand them—that is, as meaning:

(c) There never have been, are not now, and never will be any timelessly eternal states of affairs.
(d) There never has been, is not now, and never will be a timelessly eternal God.

On the contrary, defenders of timeless eternity must agree with (c) and (d), since they deny that temporal existence pertains to any timeless entity, God or otherwise. But then (c) and (d) cannot express what (a) and (b) mean. In order to capture what the disagreement is about, (a) and (b) have to be taken as atemporal statements, and cannot be replaced by omnitemporal ones. The only way the sempiternalist can express his disagreement with the atemporalist, then, is to accept the idea of there being timeless states of affairs, at least of a negative variety. And once that is done the notion of timeless states of affairs can no longer be considered suspect.

Indeed, it is a mistake to think it is even permissible to treat entities like numbers, propositions, and the like—that is, entities that are incapable of intrinsic change—as temporal. It is tempting to think of time as a matter of there being some cosmic clock "out there," beyond any specific type of change, but nevertheless ticking away inexorably the destiny of anything we can find an expression to refer to. But there is no such thing, and if there were, it would have nothing to do with the temporality of the world as we know it. In that world, things are not made subject to change by being temporal; rather, they are made temporal by being subject to change. It makes sense to treat atoms, or the heavens, or you and me as temporal beings because all of these things are subject to intrinsic changes, and because some of these changes can be used to measure others. Outside of this, the idea of becoming loses its empirical hold, and with it goes any useful notion of time.

Once this is realized, it becomes pointless to treat entities not subject to change as temporal—especially if, as we have just seen, timeless states of affairs have to be accepted anyway. Nothing about abstract entities can usefully be held to be simultaneous with anything in the world of becoming. There is nothing about any supposed career of the number 2, for example, that we are justified in claiming to be simultaneous with my writing this sentence. To be sure, relations between the number and other things can come to be and pass away, as when I think about the number during my writing. But as far as the number 2 is concerned this is only a relational, not an intrinsic change. The intrinsic change is only in me: I begin to have a thought, and later cease to have it. And, of course, that change could occur whether 2 is in time or not. Only if there are intrinsic changes in the number itself would it be correct to say 2 undergoes an alteration simultaneous with my writing this sentence or with any other genuine event. There are, however, no such changes. Hence, there is nothing about the number 2 that is simultaneous with anything that goes on in the world of genuine becoming. But if this is so, what justification could there be for claiming 2 is an entity "in time"? None, I submit, short of a conception of time that borders on outright mythology. And if that is correct, then 2 and all other abstract entities are eternal, and intrinsic facts about them must be counted as timelessly eternal states of affairs. Does it follow, as Stephen Davis has complained, that we can no longer meaningfully assert, say, that the number 7 was greater than the number

6 during the whole of the Punic Wars?[7] Of course not. Such statements are perfectly meaningful, just as it is meaningful to assert that the interior angles of a triangle total 360 degrees. It is just that they are false: numbers, and triangles, are simply not that sort of thing.

III. Eternity and Creation

The God of tradition is causally involved with the universe in what appear to be two ways. First, he is responsible for its existence. Popular accounts of this are usually quasi-deistic: God is held to have created the universe "in the beginning," in a series of phases, and then ceased activity. Thus, the universe had a beginning in time and presumably has since continued to exist on its own. But even if it is denied that the universe had a beginning in time, standard theology still makes God responsible for its existence. He must, it is claimed, have been responsible for the existence of the historical whole, since even the existence of a sempiternal universe demands an explanation. God's second causal role is as a worker of wonders. Periodically, he intervenes in history's course to produce unusual and sometimes titanic events for the sake of our well-being. Now both as Creator and as Providential Intervener, God causes specific events to occur at specific times. And it may be argued that no one can cause an event to occur at a given time without being active at that time. So if the parting of the Red Sea occurred in, say, 1500 B.C., then God would have to have been active in 1500 B.C. to cause it, and similarly for any other change he produces. If this is true, then a God who is not in time cannot create or cause anything.[8]

Why should it be, however, that in order to produce a change which occurs at t, the agent of the change must be active at t? One possibility is that causation itself is an intrinsically temporal concept, signifying an operation that must occur in time. This appears to be the position of Stephen Davis, who holds that God's activity as Creator can only be understood to occur in time, on the ground that we do not have what he calls a "usable concept of atemporal causation."[9] In fact, however, causation is not an intrinsically temporal concept at all. It could not possibly be, for one simple reason: Causation is not a process. When a cue ball strikes an object ball, thereby causing it to accelerate, there is not, between the impact and the acceleration, a third event tucked in, which is the former's causing the latter. Indeed, if there were such an event we would most likely have to invent a second sort of causation to explain its relation to the other two. But as things are there is no need, for causation is not in itself a kind of change. Rather, it signifies a relation of explanation, wherein one thing is held to account for the occurrence of another. There is nothing intrinsically either temporal or atemporal about the notion of explanation, hence to know that a causal relation exists tells us nothing whatever about whether the cause is operative in time or outside it.

If the concept of causation, taken by itself, is neutral on the issue of temporality, then whether a particular causal operation is temporal or not has to depend on how the effect is produced, and whether the agent must change in order to produce it. And where our own activity as agents is concerned, that certainly is necessary. It is worth noting here that we do not require human agents to be active at the very moment an effect is produced. There can be wide temporal gaps—as when by planting bulbs in my garden in the fall, I cause it to have daffodils in the spring. But such gaps are permissible only when my activity as agent occurs before the effect in question, and is connected to it by a continuous process. The reason for this is important: When we, as agents, cause changes in the world beyond ourselves, we have to do so indirectly, by taking advantage of natural processes that begin in us. Natural processes are, of course, temporal, and they do not permit gaps between cause and effect. So for me to cause changes in this way, there has to be a continuous natural process that begins with some doing of mine, and issues in the effect. The process need not, of course, be lengthy: When I ring a doorbell, it is so brief that my activity of pressing the button may well overlap with the sound it causes. Always, however, I have to be active at or before the time of the effect to which my action leads when I produce effects in this way.

Now, of course, it cannot be that every effect I produce as an agent is produced indirectly. If it were, each means I employ would require another, and I would never get anything done. So the doing on my part that initiates a sequence of natural change must be a *direct* product of my agency. This is a controversial topic, but we can see that at least two things would have to be true of such an activity. First, whatever makes it a manifestation of my agency would have to be intrinsic to it.[10] I would have to be active *in* the doing, rather than producing it by some further means, or by some fictitious process of "causing." Second, if this activity is supposed to initiate a process by which I produce further changes, then it is going to have to be found *in me,* since I do not have the capacity to affect the external world directly. But, of course, I am a being in time, and what that means is that even when my agency is directly exercised, I am going to have to be active in time for the exercise to occur. That is, I am going to have to *change.* As to what the fundamental activity through which I effect changes in the world is, that is part of the controversy. The most plausible candidate is probably my willing the sorts of physical exertion by which I perform voluntary bodily movements. And obviously, willing involves change. I cannot will all of my movements at once, and if I could, it would accomplish nothing. Rather, I must engage in the appropriate exertion at the appropriate time, taking advantage of the opportunities the world presents as they arise. And the same would be true no matter what events we took as direct manifestations of human agency. We would have to change in their production, and so could give rise to them only by being active in time.

We have good reasons for thinking, then, that where human agency is concerned, one can produce an effect at *t* only by being active at or before *t.* But do such reasons apply to God? The answer is that they do not. Obviously, God cannot create the world by exploiting any natural process, for there are no natural processes independent of the very world he creates. Moreover, it would be a violation of God's sovereignty to suppose his creative power was limited by available means or in any way hostage to principles external to it. Rather, God's creative activity must be viewed as direct: The results he produces are *ex nihilo.* They are not the outgrowth of changes in anything else or of any manufacturing process, but instead are direct manifestations of his agency. Yet, unlike direct manifestations of human agency, the results of God's creative activity are *not* changes in him. Rather, the world whose being is owing to God exists as a being in its own right. It cannot be identified with God; for although its existence requires an explanation his does not. And unlike God, who is simple and immaterial, the world is a material entity, composed of parts. It turns out, then, that the reasons why a human agent can produce a change at *t* only by acting at or before *t* do not apply to God. Creation cannot involve the exploitation of natural processes, and although the results produced through it are in time, they are not modifications of God.

Are there any other reasons for thinking a being who produces a temporal result must be acting in time? I can think of none, and if that is correct, then there is no reason to suppose a timelessly eternal God is precluded from being the Creator of heaven and earth. Such a being could create the entire universe in a single, unchanging, timeless act. Moreover, in the single act of creating the universe, he would be responsible for its entire existence, through all of its history. It is important to recognize this, for a lot of our tendency to believe that God, as agent, has to be temporal is owing to the fact that, from our position within the bounds of time, God often seems to be more involved in some events than in others. This is reinforced by the biblical story of Creation, which seems to make God directly responsible only for the first existence of things, and by popular conceptions of miracles as involving God occasionally bestirring himself to alter the course of history. Now, in fact, there is nothing about being timelessly eternal that would prevent God from being more directly involved in some of history than the rest. Nevertheless, this model of God's involvement in the universe is adequate neither to the needs of creation nor to divine providence. On the first point, God cannot just cause the world to exist "at *t*." Indeed, if the atemporalist view is correct, then independent of God's creating the world of change, there is no "*t*" at which he could cause it to exist. Furthermore, we have no reason to

suppose a world that requires a God to create it could somehow keep itself existing once it appears, nor can we imagine any mechanism it might use to do so. On the contrary, God must sustain the world in existence: He must be just as responsible for its surviving another instant as he is for it being here at all. Second, as for providence, a perfectly loving father, one who knows the fall of every sparrow, has to be fully and intimately involved in each aspect of the world's career. This does not prevent there being extraordinary events. If the concept of a miracle requires that there be events that are discontinuous with others as far as natural explanations go, well and good. But we should not let that lead us to believe the occurrence of the others is somehow less a manifestation of God's power. Were it not for his creative activity, nothing would be going on at all, and the most mundane events fall as much within the purview of providence as the most spectacular. Even from our own, time-bound perspective, then, God's creative involvement and concern with the world must be understood as complete and all-embracing. And this should help us to see that the Creator of heaven and earth can after all be timelessly eternal.[11]

But he cannot be temporally eternal, for several reasons. First, if, contrary to what is suggested above, there really is an absolute time "out there," uncreated by God but restrictive of his behavior, then God is not the Creator of heaven and earth, and that is that. There is a pervasive aspect of the universe he has not put there. And if we try to fix this by making him the Creator of time after all, then we give up the claim that God is essentially temporal. God could not create time unless his own being transcends it, and his act of creating it could not be temporal. Second, if time exists independently of the world then God would have had to decide when to produce the world, when to begin his activity as Creator. But what reason could there have been for creating it at one time rather than another? Nor can we avoid this problem by making the created world everlasting too, for even then God would have had to decide whether to have things occur at the times they do, or to move everything forward or backward by, say, twenty-four hours. Again, however, there could not possibly be a reason for such a choice.

This is not to say, of course, that God might not have plunged ahead. After all, he might have had good reason for creating a universe at some time or other, rather than never doing so. All the same, a God who creates in this way could not be fully rational. He would have justification for creating the world, but not for creating it "at *t.*"[12]

But the strongest reason for rejecting a temporal creator is what this notion does to God's sovereignty. An all-powerful God should be not just the producer of the universe but its complete master, the absolute ruler of everything that is not himself. To make him subject to the limitations of time flies in the face of this conception. Once launched on the enterprise of creation, at least, such a creator must busy himself with whatever tasks are at hand. If he has goals to achieve by his action, then like us he must await his opportunities, which are now limited by the stern taskmaster of becoming. And like us, his experience of his creation must be hemmed in by time: limited, in the case of the past, to memories that, however vivid, must be of events that can never be retrieved; limited, in the case of the future, to anticipations each of whose fulfillment takes literally forever to come, only to vanish like smoke. Such a God may be the master of much, but of time he is a slave. And that is a high price to pay for accepting the groundless supposition that only a temporal being can produce temporal effects.

IV Eternity and Omniscience

An omniscient God should know of every true proposition that it is true, and of every false proposition that it is false. And it is probably fair to say that when it comes to omniscience, proponents of timeless eternity have traditionally thought they had the upper hand. Suppose John mows his lawn next Saturday. If so then it would have been correct to assert now that he will. That is, the statement "John will mow his lawn next Saturday" is true. But suppose also that John's action is free, in the sense that until he decides one way or the other, there are no conditions in place that determine which way he will act. If so, then it does not appear that a temporal

being could *know,* prior to the event, what John will do. One could, of course, make a lucky guess: I might venture a prediction that John will mow his lawn next Saturday, believe it is true, and turn out to be right. But it does not follow that I *knew* what John would do; my prediction, though correct, appears to have lacked sufficient grounds.

Needless to say, the same argument applies to God if he is temporal. If the behavior of rational agents is free in the sense described— and it is often claimed that moral responsibility requires this— then no conditions obtain in advance that would enable God to predict such behavior with certainty. It seems the only way he could avoid mistakes would be by an incredible series of lucky guesses or by simply not entertaining beliefs about future free actions. In neither case would he be omniscient. So unless another way can be found for God to know about future free actions, defenders of temporal eternity must make do with a restricted notion of divine omniscience. Contrast this with the situation of a timelessly eternal God. Such a God does not know about events either before or after their occurrence, or even simultaneously with it. Rather, he knows them timelessly, in a single act of awareness whose content comprises all of history. But then free actions on our part impose no deficit of knowledge on him. A timeless God cannot be in the dark about what for us is the future, since he is directly aware of all of it. He knows, therefore, about John's mowing his lawn next Saturday because he is eternally aware of that very action. And, of course, this does not compromise John's freedom, any more than it would if next Saturday had already arrived, and you and I were watching him mow his lawn.[13]

Initially, then, it would appear defenders of timeless eternity are able to offer a more robust and satisfying account of divine omniscience. Recently, however, sempiternalists have mounted a counterattack, claiming that in fact the limitations on God's omniscience are far worse if he is timelessly eternal than if he is temporal. For suppose in fact John is mowing his lawn right now, and that I report his activity to you by asserting:

(e) John is mowing his lawn.

It would be a mistake to interpret (e) as reporting some timeless state of affairs. That is, (e) says more than that there is (timelessly) some act of lawn mowing on John's part, or even that such an act is (timelessly) located at the point in history which happens to be today. These readings fail to respect the tense of (e), which does not reduce to any timeless reality. Rather, the full force of (e) is that John's act of mowing his lawn is occurring *now,* that it is actually *present.* The situation with the other tenses is similar: If I predict John will mow his lawn again next Saturday, I am saying that act will occur after the present; and if I say he mowed it last Saturday, I am saying the act in question occurred before the present. Always, then, tensed statements are indexed to a certain temporal location *as present.* But then, it may be argued, knowing which tensed statements are true requires knowing what the present moment is. And, it is claimed, that is something a timelessly eternal God cannot know. Being outside of time, he cannot, as we would say, know what time it is. That is, he cannot know which moment in time is the present one, and hence cannot know which ones are past and which future. But then it must be that a timelessly eternal God cannot know *any* tensed proposition. He cannot know what John will do next week, what he is doing now, or what he has ever done, and the same for any other tensed state of affairs. Not an enviable position for a supposedly omniscient God, and a far worse one than simply being unable to tell about John's future free actions.[14]

A hint that there is something wrong here can be gotten from the fact that an exactly analogous argument could have been given for propositions that are spatially indexed.[15] Suppose I assert that it is raining *here.* My assertion has to mean more than that there is a rainstorm, or that rain is falling outside my study. Neither of the latter statements respects the element of perspective the word "here" introduces, an element that does not reduce to other spatial relations. And surely if God is omniscient and it is raining here, he must know that. Yet no one argues on these grounds that God must be located in space or in any way subject to its limitations. So some sort of mistake appears to have been made. But to have a hint that something is wrong and to be able to say what it is

are two different things, and the sources of the present error are not easy to locate. One possible source can, I think, be dismissed pretty quickly. It cannot be the case that when I assert (e), I am in part asserting something about myself—such as that I am in the same temporal location as John's act of lawn mowing, or that I am experiencing that act now. Any temptation to think this is the problem can be overcome simply by realizing that if in fact (e) is true—if John is now mowing his lawn—then this would have been true even if I had never lived. That would be impossible if (e) contained information about me, since it would then be rendered incorrect simply by my failing to exist. Tensed propositions involve a perspective on the world of change, just as spatially indexed propositions involve one on space; but they say nothing about anyone occupying that perspective.

But if this is not the source of the error, then what is? Here is one way in which it can begin: It might be thought that tensed propositions change their truth value, depending on whether the events they report are actually occurring. One might think, for example, that proposition (e) was false before John began mowing his lawn, is true only while he mows it, and thereafter will become false again. And one might think that only a God in time could detect changing truth values. Now, in fact, this last claim is in no way obvious. Atemporalists might well insist that here as elsewhere, there is no reason to think awareness of change requires a changing awareness, and that a God outside of time could be as much aware of truth value changes as of any others. But there is a more fundamental error here, for the fact is that tensed propositions do not change in truth value. What misleads us about this, I think, is a belief that when we employ the same *sentence* assertively on different occasions, we must be asserting the same proposition—so that if twenty-four hours ago I had also uttered the sentence "John is mowing his lawn" assertively, I would then have been asserting exactly the same proposition— namely, (e)—that I assert using the sentence now. But that is mistaken. We might express (e) more carefully as:

John is (thismoment) mowing his lawn.

This is to be distinguished from the proposition I would have asserted had I said yesterday that John was mowing his lawn. For even if I had used exactly the same words, the phrase "this moment" would yesterday have referred to a different time. This means the proposition I would have asserted yesterday—let us call it (f)—would have been indexed to a different "now," and that gives the two propositions different truth conditions. What happened yesterday is decisive for the truth of (f) but irrelevant to that of (e); and what happens today has everything to do with the truth of (e) and nothing to do with that of (f). In short, (e) and (f) count as entirely different pieces of information, and so are different propositions.

This is borne out by our attitudes when we make tensed statements. If I had asserted yesterday that John was mowing his lawn, I would have meant he was mowing it *then*. Were I wrong, I would not have claimed vindication when he began mowing it today, holding that what I said yesterday had now become true. Rather, I need to make a new statement, (e), to cover the present case. Or, suppose John also mowed his lawn two weeks ago, and that I said so at the time. When, upon seeing him mowing it today, I assert (e), you would not accuse me of repeating myself, of stating the same fact I asserted a two weeks ago. That fact was an entirely different one. The situation is similar with other tenses. If today I assert that Lincoln will be assassinated, I am not saying something that used to be true. Rather, my statement is false: Lincoln is not going to be assassinated; he already was. If, on the other hand, I report that Lincoln *was* assassinated, I am not asserting a proposition that used to be false. My assertion is true, because it is indexed to the present, and only what holds from the perspective of the present counts for its truth or falsity.

Each time I use a tensed sentence to make an assertion, then, I am asserting a *different* proposition, even if the sentences are indistinguishable.[16] Each proposition is tied to the perspective of a particular temporal moment, and different conditions determine its truth or falsity. With this in mind, consider again the idea that propositions can change truth values. It is, of course, a suspect idea from the outset. Propositions are abstract entities,

which we have seen are incapable of intrinsic change. And propositions that describe timeless states of affairs, like "2 is even," could not change truth values anyway. The state of affairs they describe will either obtain (timelessly) or not, and that is the end of the matter. So change in truth value would have to be confined to tensed propositions, and it would have to be owing to some change outside the proposition itself. But now it turns out that tensed propositions depend for their truth only on what obtains from the perspective in time to which they are indexed. It follows that tensed propositions cannot change in truth value either. Their truth conditions are defined by a perspective that is localized to a single instant. And any conditions thus defined must simply either be satisfied or not. They cannot change within the bounds of a single point in time, and nothing that occurs at any other time matters. How could it? If when I assert (e) my statement does not even concern yesterday or tomorrow, how could conditions yesterday or tomorrow have anything to do with its truth? Obviously, they could not. So even tensed propositions do not change truth values. Indeed, for all that is capable of "happening" to the truth or falsity of a proposition, there is no good reason even for taking the predicates "is true" and "is false" to be tensed predicates. On the contrary, there is every reason to think the truth or falsity of propositions, even tensed ones, is in itself a timelessly eternal state of affairs, one that is not even capable of change.

Where does this leave us on the issue of whether a God beyond time can know tensed propositions? If the above argument is correct, the truth or falsity of a tensed proposition is not an elusive thing at all. It is, rather, a timeless and unchanging state of affairs, just like the truth or falsity of a statement in mathematics. But then surely it should not be a difficult assignment for a timeless God to know a tensed proposition. What would be required, presumably, is the same thing such knowledge requires in our own case—namely, direct experience of the world of change. We have seen no reason to deny such experience to a timeless God, who traditionally has been held to have direct and unchanging awareness of the entire sweep of history. So it looks like God can know tensed propositions after all. Yet it might be thought that something is still missing. What of the point about what time it is? If tensed propositions are indexed to times, wouldn't God have to know what time it is in order to know that it is (e) rather than, say, (f) that actually describes what John is presently doing? And doesn't this require more than simply having John's action presented to him in awareness? Wouldn't God also have to know that, as opposed to all the other stages of history of which he is aware, the one in which John's act is embedded is the one that is really going on right now? And how could he know this further fact from outside of time?

The answer is that there is no such fact to be known, for there is never anything to "what time it is" beyond the events whose simultaneous occurrence constitutes any given stage of the world's history. The belief that there is more arises from a pervasive but misleading way of representing our experience of change, which underlies the above objection. It begins with our analogizing time to space: We think of the events that make up the world's history as being lined up "out there" in order of their occurrence, rather like a row of barges floating on a river. Then, to account for the fact that our experience is a changing one, we put the river in motion. We think of time itself as flowing past us, sweeping along with it a history all of which is equally real, but only some of which is present. The question what time it "really" is is then just the question, What part of history is really before us? But the question is bogus, as is this picture of temporal transition. It may be useful for some purposes to analogize time to space. But once I do, I have used time up. There is no second time to accommodate or measure any supposed flow of the first or of the events within it. Yet a second time is precisely what we demand if we insist that the truth of statement (e) requires, in addition to the event of John mowing his lawn, a further event of the mowing being present. There is no such event, and the demand for it is just one more manifestation of the myth that there is a time "out there," independent of change. The truth is quite the opposite: The presence of John's mowing his lawn is to be found in the event itself. When it is not present, it does not exist at all. As for the elusive sense of "passage" that charac-

terizes our experience of the world, it is simply a manifestation of the fact that we belong to that world: that our experience of it is not just an experience of change but also a changing experience. Admittedly, this is a difficult thing to describe, and in trying to do so we may feel almost compelled to fall back on the idea of time as a kind of quasi-space that we traverse in living out our lives. But that is a deception. Becoming is a reality; but it consists neither in our marching through time nor in time marching past us.

There is, perhaps, more that could be said about temporal transition and our awareness of it. But the above considerations are enough to show that it is not a matter of an additional change that accrues to events which are somehow already there. Rather, temporal transition lies in the phenomenon of change itself, in the fact that there are entities that undergo alteration of their characteristics. Because this is so, to be aware of the temporal features of events cannot require any more than that one be aware of the events themselves. It is a mistake, therefore, to think that in order to know which tensed proposition describes John's behavior God must, in addition to being directly aware of that behavior, know that it is "really" happening. There is no other way to be directly aware of an event than to be aware of it as really happening. The most we could require in addition is that God know the *setting* of John's behavior: which events are simultaneous with it, which come before, and which after. This, presumably, would be necessary in order to know the other tensed propositions that hold from the perspective of that setting. And to be sure, a timeless God cannot learn about relations of before and after in the way we do, by experiencing different events seriatim. But there is no more reason to think a God beyond time must be ignorant of the distribution of events within it than there is to think a God outside space cannot know the relative positions of physical objects. If he is timelessly aware of all events, then surely he is aware of how they are positioned with respect to each other.

If this is correct, then the God who is beyond time knows all there is to know about what time it is. More important, he knows each and every tensed proposition that is true, from each and every temporal perspective the entire history of the universe has to offer. Furthermore, his position in this respect is far superior to that of a temporal God. For consider again proposition (f), which we said was the proposition I would have asserted yesterday had I then claimed "John is mowing his lawn." And let us suppose (f) is (timelessly, of course) true. John, we may imagine, has a large lawn that takes two days to mow. Now we seem to have a pretty clear idea what proposition (f) is; and certainly we can know *that* (f) is true, since we can know John was mowing his lawn yesterday. Yet it may be questioned whether I could ever *assert* (f) from my present temporal vantage point. It looks as though I am confined in my assertions of tensed propositions to those which are temporally indexed to the point in time at which the assertion is made. If that is so, then even though I can always know that (f) is true, the time is forever gone when (f) could have been a *vehicle* of knowledge for me. As a temporal being, I can only grasp the world from one temporal perspective at a time, and that has to be reflected in the way my knowledge is formulated. In a way, then, I lack access to (f), even though I know it is true. And of course the same limitation would apply to a temporal God. It may not be a serious limitation in terms of the usual definition of omniscience, for it does not prevent him from knowing of each true proposition *that* it is true, and of each false one that it is false. Nevertheless, it reflects the confinement we place upon God when we make him temporally eternal. He, like us, can only see things a certain way. And if that means there are other ways which are closed to him, the result can only be a limitation on his knowing.

V. Conclusion

The case for thinking God is timelessly eternal is, then, far stronger than the case for thinking he is temporal. Timeless eternity is more in keeping with God's nature as traditionally defined, and there is no persuasive reason to think it impairs either his creative power or his ability to know. Admittedly, it is the more difficult conception. To say that God can produce and comprehend the universe in all its history in a single timeless act is to attribute to him

powers far beyond our own. And even if the attribution is justified, we have far less feel for what it would be like to *be* such a God than we do for the God of sempiternalism, who is by contrast rather comforting. His experience and abilities are very like our own, even if vastly greater, and we may find it far easier to see in a temporal God the loving father of religious tradition. Nevertheless, I think the timeless conception is to be preferred. The acceptability of a theory of God's nature cannot, after all, be a function of its anthropomorphism. Rather, we must try to understand God's nature in terms that maximize his perfection, both in himself and in his hegemony over creation. Where eternity is concerned, I think it is the timeless conception that does that. And although the task may be more difficult, there is no real reason for pessimism about finding in such a God the personal traits traditionally ascribed to him. It may be that all we need is a higher conception of those as well, a conception commensurate with a God whose ways are as far above our own as the heavens are above the earth.[17]

Notes

1. The terminology of *enduring* or *persistence* is to be preferred over that which treats God as temporally "extended." The latter suggests God is spread out in time as a physical object is in space, which is an unacceptable analogy. One consequence of it is that just as a physical object cannot exist in its entirety at a single spatial point, so God would be unable to exist at any point in time. But then he could not exist now or at any other time, which is precisely the opposite of what defenders of sempiternity wish to claim.

2. Boethius, *The Consolation of Philosophy*, Bk. V, sec. 6.

3. Cf. Richard Swinburne, *The Coherence of Theism* (New York: Oxford University Press, 1977), pp. 220–21.

4. For this approach, see Eleonore Stump and Norman Kretzmann, "Eternity," *The Journal of Philosophy* 78 (1981):429–58.

5. For further discussion see Paul Helm, *Eternal God* (New York: Oxford University Press, 1988), chap. 2.

6. William Kneale, "Time and Eternity in Theology," *Proceedings of the Aristotelian Society* 61 (1960–61): 87–108.

7. Stephen T. Davis, *Logic and the Nature of God* (Grand Rapids, Mich.: Eerdmans, 1983), Reprinted in this anthology. See previous reading.

8. Arguments of this kind are given by Stephen Davis, op. cit., Nelson Pike, *God and Timelessness* (New York: Schocken Books, 1970), pp. 104–107; and Swinburne, op. cit., p. 221.

9. *Logic and the Nature of God,*

10. This assumes that human agency does not reduce to a causal relation between passive states like desire and biological events such as the motion of a limb. I have defended this claim in a number of places. See, for example, "Intrinsic Intentionality," *Theory and Decision* 20 (1986):247–73.

11. These themes are further elaborated by Jonathan Kvanvig and myself in "Divine Conservation and the Persistence of the World," in *Divine and Human Action,* ed. T. V. Morris (Ithaca, N.Y.: Cornell University Press, 1988), pp. 13–49; and in "The Occasionalist Proselytizer: A Modified Catechism," in *Philosophical Perspectives* 5 (1991), ed. J. E. Tomberlin (Atascadero, Calif.: Ridgeview Publishing Company), pp. 587–615.

12. This argument stems from Leibniz. *The Leibniz-Clarke Correspondence,* ed., H. G. Alexander (New York: Barnes & Noble, 1956), pp. 26–27.

13. The problem of divine foreknowledge and human freedom is a difficult one, and recent discussions of it have become complicated indeed. For an excellent summary see John Martin Fischer, "Recent Work on God and Freedom," *American Philosophical Quarterly* 29 (1992):91–109.

14. Arguments like this stem from A. N. Prior, "The Formalities of Omniscience," *Philosophy* 37 (1962):114–29. See also Norman Kretzmann, "Omniscience and Immutability," *The Journal of Philosophy* 63 (1966):409–21.

15. Helm, op. cit., pp. 43–44.

16. Similar treatments of tensed sentences can be found in Richard Swinburne, "Tensed Facts," *American Philosophical Quarterly* 27 (1990):117–30; and in E. J. Lowe, "The Indexical Fallacy in McTaggart's Proof of the Unreality of Time," *Mind* 96 (1987):62–70.

17. I am grateful to my colleague Jonathan Kvanvig, and to Philip Quinn, Eleonore Stump, and Louis Pojman for helpful discussions of earlier versions of this paper.

IV.B God's Omniscience and Human Freedom

And before him no creature is hidden, but all are open and laid bare to the eyes of him with whom we have to do.

HEBREWS 4:13

The second attribute we consider here is God's omniscience, his power to know everything. Let us roughly define *knowledge* as true justified belief, in which the manner of justification is a proper one. As an illustration of this concept, let us say that if John knows some proposition *p* (e.g., the Kansas City Royals won the World Series in 1985), then (1) John believes that *p* is true; (2) *p* is true; (3) John has an adequate justification for his belief that *p* is true (e.g., he watched all seven games on television with an adequate knowledge of what was going on). We may define God's property of all-knowingness in the following way: For any proposition, God knows whether it is true or false. That is, all God's beliefs are justified and true. He holds no false beliefs at all. Certain questions immediately arise from the notion of omniscience. For example, much of our descriptive or propositional knowledge depends on knowledge by acquaintance, experiential knowledge. But experiential knowledge is particular to the individual experiencer. I cannot experience *your* taste of chocolate ice cream or feel *your* headache, so how can God be said to know our experiences if they are ours? Is his experience of our pain exactly similar to ours when he looks within us? Does he need to take on a body to experience the *kinds* of feelings that we experience?

I leave you to wrestle with these questions. For in this section I want to introduce you to the problem of omniscience in relation to human freedom. Let us define freedom of the will in this sense: An agent *S* freely does an act *A* if and only if *S* could have done otherwise in the situation. That is, although at time *t* in situation *x*, *S* does *A*, it could have been the case that *S* did some other act, for example, *B*. Given the identical antecedent conditions, *A* and *B* are both in *S*'s power as genuine alternatives. This is a different notion of freedom from that of the *compatibilist* (soft determinist), who views a free act as one that is causally determined but done voluntarily. The view that I have outlined is called the *libertarian* view of freedom of the will.

Now the problem arises when we combine the two propositions described above:

(1) God is omniscient.
(2) Humans act freely.

Let us examine how these two propositions produce a problem. If God knows that you will go to your early morning class tomorrow, are you free to stay in bed until noon? If God knows that you will do anything, are you free to do it or not to do it? For the compatibilist (one who tries to combine the notion of free action with the thesis that every action is causally determined), there is no contradiction between human freedom and God's omniscience because every action is determined whether or not God knows which actions we will perform. But for the libertarian there may be a problem in reconciling these two propositions.

Note first that reconciling freedom with knowledge isn't ordinarily a problem. I may predict during our philosophy class that you will get up at the end of class and walk out the door. Knowing a lot about you, I may have very good evidence that this is the kind of thing you are likely to do; I have a justification for my belief, which turns out to be true at the end of the hour when you fulfill my prediction. We would normally say that I knew that you would walk out the door. But this would in no way limit your freedom. You could have stayed in your seat if you had really wanted to do so. If we are really free, our free acts do not depend on whether anyone happens to know what we will do, for knowledge in itself does not cause actions. My knowing or not knowing that you will walk out the door has absolutely nothing to do with whether you will do

257

it (unless, of course, I tell you, in which case it might affect your reasons for acting). So knowledge of action and freedom to act do not ordinarily seem to conflict at all. So why shouldn't we apply all this to God and say that God's foreknowledge of what we are going to do in no way causes us to do it? God simply knows ahead of time what we are going to do; that is,

(3) God's knowledge of human action is contingent upon what humans will actually do.

This is the classical position on freedom and omniscience. Boethius and, in our first reading, Augustine argued that God's knowledge is contingent on our choices.

However, other philosophers have objected to comparing our knowledge to God's. The above contingency applies to human, finite knowledge. At time *t* I believe that you will walk out the door at time *t* + 1. You can cause it to be the case that I have a false belief by staying in your seat through the next class or even fainting and thus having to be carried out the door. But God's knowledge, these philosophers contend, is not like human knowledge in that it is not contingent but necessary. That is, we cannot bring it about by our actions that God believes any falsehood. This is essentially the position of Nelson Pike in the second of our readings. If God, who by virtue of his omniscience believes at *t* that you will walk out of your class at *t* + 1, how can you be free to stay in your seat?

Pike states the classical position as follows:

(4) God exists at *t* and believes at *t* that you would walk out of the classroom at *t* + 1, and it is in your power to refrain from walking out of the classroom.

But if this is the case, then there seem to be only three possibilities:

(5) You could have brought it about at *t* + 1 that God held a false belief;

(6) It was in your power to bring it about that God really did not believe that you would walk out of the classroom at *t* + 1 even though he did hold this belief; or

(7) It was in your power to do something that would have brought it about that any person who believed that you would walk out of the room held a false belief and hence was not God; that is to say, God does not exist.

Since (5), (6), (7) seem to contradict (1) and (2) above, which explicitly states that God is omniscient and we are free, Pike concludes that an examination of the implications of God's essential omniscience shows that it is incompatible with human freedom. Either we must understand God's omniscience differently, or God is not omniscient, or humans are not free.

In our third reading Alvin Plantinga responds to Pike's position, arguing that there really is no incompatibility between divine omniscience and human freedom. Essentially, he argues that all the options—(5), (6), and (7)—can be suitably accommodated to the traditional view of God's omniscience and human freedom. For example, (5) can be read as follows:

(5a) It was in your power at *t* + 1 to do something such that if you had done it, then a belief that God *did hold* at *t would have been* false.

But (5a) is not at all paradoxical and does not imply that it was within your power to do something that would have caused God to hold a false belief. Plantinga carries out a similar strategy with regard to (6) and (7), which you will want to examine carefully. You might also want to read Pike's response to Plantinga in his article "Divine Foreknowledge, Human Freedom and Possible Worlds" (*The Philosophical Review*, April 1977), in which he contends that the problem does not disappear with Plantinga's strategy because divine omniscience entails God's essential knowledge holding in every possible world.

IV.B.1   Divine Foreknowledge and Human Free Will

ST. AUGUSTINE

St. Augustine (354–430), Bishop of Hippo in North Africa, one of the greatest thinkers in the history of the Christian Church, argues that God's foreknowledge of human actions does not necessitate those actions. Specifically, human sin was not committed because God knew that it would happen, but God knew that it would happen because he knows how humans will choose.

We enter the dialogue with a question by Augustine's disciple, Evodius.

Chapter II

Why God's foreknowledge does not take free will away from sinners, a question troubles very many men.

Evodius: This being the case, I am disturbed more than I can tell you, as to how it can be both that God foreknows all future things, and that we do not sin by necessity. For whoever says that anything can come to pass otherwise than as God has foreknown it, is laboring with maddest impiety to do away with God's foreknowledge. Therefore God foreknew that the first man would sin; for anyone will concede this to be necessary, who agrees with me that God foreknows all things to come. This being the case, I do not say that He should not have made man, for *He* made him good, nor is the sin of him whom God himself made good anything prejudicial to God; rather indeed has He shown His goodness in making him, and shown likewise His justice in punishing him, and His mercy in forgiving him. And so I do not say that He should not have made him, but I do say this: that since He foreknew that man would sin, it was necessary that that should come to pass which God

Reprinted from *St. Augustine on Free Will,* trans. Carroll Mason Sparrow, University of Virginia Studies (The Dietz Press, 1947), by permission of the publisher.

foreknew would be. How then is the will free, where necessity seems so inevitable.

Chapter III

God's foreknowledge does not so act that we do not sin by free will.

Augustine: It is this, to be sure, that troubles you, and that you cannot understand—why these two things are not conflicting and opposed: that God has foreknowledge of all things to come, and that we sin, not by necessity, but by our own will. For, say you, if God foreknows that a man is going to sin, it is necessary that he should sin; but if it is necessary, there is then no choice of the will in sinning, but rather an inevitable and fixed necessity. By this reasoning, forsooth, you are afraid lest it should follow either that God's foreknowledge of all things to come is impiously denied; or that, if we . . . cannot deny this, we admit that man sins not by choice, but by necessity. Is there anything else that troubles you?

E. Nothing else at the moment.

A. You think, then, that the whole scheme of things that God foreknows comes to pass, not by will, but by necessity?

E. Entirely so, I think.

A. Wake up then, take a look at yourself, and tell me if you can, what sort of will you are going to have tomorrow. Will it be to sin, or not to sin?

E. I do not know.

A. Do you think that God too does not know?

E. By no means would I think that.

A. If then He knows your will of tomorrow, and foresees the future wills of all men who are or who will be, much more surely does He foresee what He is going to do regarding just and impious men.

E. Assuredly, if I say that God foreknows my own works, much more confidently can I say that

He foreknows His own works, and foresees with certainty what He is going to do.

A. Are you not then on your guard lest it be said to you that even God will do what He is going to do, not by will, but by necessity; if all things that He foreknows come to pass by necessity, not by will?

E. When I said that all those things come to pass by necessity which God has foreknown were to be, I was looking at those things alone which happen in His creation, but not those which are in God himself; for these do not happen, but eternally are.

A. God, then, is not occupied with His creation?

E. He has decreed once for all how the order of the world He has created is to be carried out, and does not administer anything by a new act of will.

A. Does God make no one happy?

E. Surely He does.

A. Then surely He does so when that person becomes happy.

E. True.

A. If, therefore, for example, you are going to be happy a year hence He is going to make you happy a year from now.

E. Yes.

A. Therefore He foreknows today that you are going to be made happy a year from now.

E. He has always foreknown it: I agree that He foreknows it now too, if it is going to be so.

7. A. Tell me, pray, are not you His creature, and will not your happiness be made in you?

E. I am indeed His creature, and in me will it come to pass that I shall be happy.

A. Therefore your happiness will come to pass in you not by will, but by necessity, God doing it.

E. His will is my necessity.

A. So, then, you will be happy against your will?

E. If I had the power to be happy I should surely be so; for even now I wish to be, and am not; because it is not I, but He that makes me happy.

A. Most excellently does the truth cry out from you. For you cannot perceive anything else to be in our power, except that which we do when we will. Wherefore nothing is so completely in our power as the will itself. For it is present with absolutely no interval, as soon as we will. And therefore we can

say rightly that we grow old not by will, but by necessity; or that we die not by will, but by necessity; and anything else like that. But who but a crazy man would say that we do not will by will?

Wherefore, although God foreknows our wills to be, it does not thereby follow that we do not will a thing by our will. You said about happiness that you could not become happy through yourself, and said it as if I would deny it. But I say, when you are going to be happy you are not going to be happy against your will, but wanting to be happy. When therefore, God foreknows your future happiness, it cannot come to pass otherwise than as He has foreknown it, else there is no foreknowledge; nevertheless we are not obliged to think what is most absurd and far removed from the truth, that you are going to be happy when you do not want to. Moreover, just as God's foreknowledge, which today is certain of your future happiness, does not take away your will for happiness when you shall have begun to be happy; so also a culpable will, if you are going to have one, will be none the less your own will because God foreknows that it is to be so.

8. For mark, I beg you, with what blindness it is said that if God has foreknown my future will, it is necessary that I will what he has foreknown, since naught can come to pass otherwise than as He has foreknown. But if it is necessary, it must be acknowledged that I will no longer by will, but by necessity. O strange unreason! How then could it not be otherwise than as God has foreknown, if that should not be a will which He foreknew would be a will? I pass over that equally monstrous thing which a little while ago I said was said by the same man: It is necessary that I so will—thus endeavoring to take away the will and to substitute necessity. For if it is necessary that he so will, how then does he will when there is no will?

But if, speaking in another way, he says that, because it is necessary that he should will, the will itself is not in his power, he is met by what you said just now when I asked you whether you are going to be happy against your will. For you answered that you would be happy now if it were in your power; saying that you wanted to, but were not yet able. Whereupon I interjected that the truth had cried out from you. For we can deny that we have a power only when what we want is not there. But when we will, if the will itself is not there, we surely do not will. But if it cannot happen that while we will we do not will, a will is certainly present to those who will; nor is anything else in their power but what is present to those who will it. Therefore our will would not be a will if it were not in our power.

Moreover, because it is in our power it is free to us. For that is not free to us that we have not, or cannot have, in our power. And so it comes about both that we do not deny that God foreknows all that is to be, and that notwithstanding we may will what

we will. For when He foreknows our will, it will be that very will that He foreknows. It will therefore be a will, because His foreknowledge is of a will. Nor can it be a will if it is not in our power. Therefore He is also foreknowing of the power. Therefore that power is not taken from me by His foreknowledge, but because of it will be more surely present to me; because He whose foreknowledge errs not has foreknown that it will be present to me.

E. Behold, I no longer deny that whatsoever God foreknows must needs come to pass, and that He so foreknows our sins that there yet remains to us a will that is free, and placed in our power. . . .

IV.B.2 God's Foreknowledge and Human Free Will Are Incompatible

NELSON PIKE

Nelson Pike (1930–   ) is professor Emeritus of philosophy at the University of California at Irvine. In this article, he argues that given commonly held theological assumptions about God's nature, no human action is free. If God exists at a given time and holds infallible beliefs concerning what agents will do in the future, those actions cannot be free because they could, then, cause it to be the case that what God believed was false.

In Part V, Section III of his *Consolatio Philosophiae,* Boethius entertained (though he later rejected) the claim that if God is omniscient, no human action is voluntary. This claim seems intuitively false. Surely, given only a doctrine describing God's *knowledge,* nothing about the voluntary status of human actions will follow. Perhaps such a conclusion would follow from a doctrine of divine omnipotence or di-

Reprinted from Nelson Pike, "Divine Omniscience and Voluntary Action," *The Philosophical Review* 74 (January 1965).

vine providence, but what connection could there be between the claim that God is *omniscient* and the claim that human actions are determined? Yet Boethius thought he saw a problem here. He thought that if one collected together just the right assumptions and principles regarding God's knowledge, one could derive the conclusion that if God exists, no human action is voluntary. Of course, Boethius did not think that all the assumptions and principles required to reach this conclusion are true (quite the contrary), but he thought it important to draw attention to them nonetheless. If a theologian is to construct a doctrine of God's knowledge which does not commit him to determinism, he must first understand that there is a way of thinking about God's knowledge which would so commit him.

In this paper, I shall argue that although his claim has a sharp counterintuitive ring, Boethius was right in thinking that there is a selection from among the various doctrines and principles clustering about the notions of knowledge, omniscience, and God which, when brought together, demand the conclusion that if God exists, no human action is voluntary. Boethius, I think, did not succeed in making explicit all of the ingredients in the problem. His suspicions were sound, but his discussion was incomplete. His argument needs to be developed. This is the task I shall undertake in the pages to follow. I should like to make clear at the outset that my purpose in rearguing this thesis is not to show that determinism is true, nor to show that God does not exist, nor to show that either determinism is true or God does not exist. Following Boethius, I shall not claim that the items needed to generate the problem are either philosophically or theologically adequate. I want to concentrate attention on the implications of a certain set of assumptions. Whether the assumptions are themselves acceptable is a question I shall not consider.

I

A. Many philosophers have held that if a statement of the form "*A* knows *X*" is true, then "*A* believes *X*" is true and "*X*" is true. As a first assumption, I shall take this partial analysis of "*A* knows *X*" to be correct. And I shall suppose that since this analysis holds for all knowledge claims, it will hold when speaking of God's knowledge. "God knows *X*" entails "God believes *X*" and "'*X*' is true."

Secondly, Boethius said that with respect to the matter of knowledge, God "cannot in anything be mistaken."[1] I shall understand this doctrine as follows. Omniscient beings hold no false beliefs. Part of what is meant when we say that a person is omniscient is that the person in question believes nothing that is false. But, further, it is part of the "essence" of God to be omniscient. This is to say that any person who is not omniscient could not be the person we usually mean to be referring to when using the name "God." To put this last point a little differently: if the person we usually mean to be referring to when using the name "God" were suddenly to lose the quality of omniscience (suppose, for example, He came to believe something false, the resulting person would no longer be God. Although we might call this second person "God" (I might call my cat "God"), the absence of the quality

of omniscience would be sufficient to guarantee that the person referred to was not the same as the person formerly called by that name. From this last doctrine it follows that the statement "If a given person is God, that person is omniscient" is an a priori truth. From this we may conclude that the statement "If a given person is God, that person holds no false beliefs" is also an a priori truth. It would be conceptually impossible for God to hold a false belief. "'*X*' is true" follows from "God believes *X*." These are all ways of expressing the same principle—the principle expressed by Boethius in the formula "God cannot in anything be mistaken."

A second principle usually associated with the notion of divine omniscience has to do with the scope or range of God's intellectual gaze. To say that a being is omniscient is to say that he knows everything. "Everything" in this statement is usually taken to cover future, as well as present and past, events and circumstances. In fact, God is usually said to have had foreknowledge of everything that has ever happened. With respect to anything that was, is, or will be the case, God knew, *from eternity,* that it would be the case.

The doctrine of God's knowing everything from eternity is very obscure. One particularly difficult question concerning this doctrine is whether it entails that with respect to everything that was, is, or will be the case, God knew *in advance* that it would be the case. In some traditional theological texts, we are told that God is *eternal* in the sense that He exists "outside of time," that is, in the sense that He bears no temporal relations to the events or circumstances of the natural world.[2] In a theology of this sort, God could not be said to have known that a given natural event was going to happen before it happened. If God knew that a given natural event was going to occur *before* it occurred, at least one of God's cognitions would then have occurred before some natural event. This, surely, would violate the idea that God bears no temporal relations to natural events.[3] On the other hand, in a considerable number of theological sources, we are told that God *has always* existed—that He existed long *before* the occurrence of any natural event. In a theology of this sort, to say that God is eternal is not to say that God exists "outside of time" (bears no temporal relations to natural events), it is to say, instead, God has existed (and will continue to exist) at each moment.[4] The doctrine of omniscience which goes with this second understanding of the notion of eternity is one in which it is affirmed that God *has always* known that what was going to happen in the natural world. John Calvin wrote as follows:

When we attribute foreknowledge to God, we mean that all things have ever been and perpetually remain before, his eyes, so that to his knowledge nothing is future or past, but all things are present; and present in such manner, that he does not merely conceive of them from ideas formed in his mind, as things remembered by us appear to our minds, but really he holds and sees them as if *(tanquam)* actually placed before him.[5]

All things are "present" to God in the sense that He "sees" them as if *(tanquam)* they were actually before Him. Further, with respect to any given natural event, not only is that event "present" to God in the sense indicated, it has *ever been and has perpetually remained* "present" to Him in that sense. This latter is the point of special interest. Whatever one thinks of the idea that God "sees" things as if "actually placed before him," Calvin would appear to be committed to the idea that God has *always known* what was going to happen in the natural world. Choose an event *(E)* and a time *(T2)* at which *E* occurred. For any time *(T1)* prior to *T2* (say, five thousand, six hundred, or eighty years prior to *T2*), God knew at *T1* that *E* would occur at *T2*. It will follow from this doctrine, of course, that with respect to any human action, God knew well in advance of its performance that the action would be performed. Calvin says, "when God created man, He foresaw what would happen concerning him." He adds, "little more than five thousand years have elapsed since the creation of the world."[6] Calvin seems to have thought that God foresaw the outcome of every human action well over five thousand years ago.

In the discussion to follow, I shall work only with this second interpretation of God's knowing everything *from eternity*. I shall assume that if a person is omniscient, that person has always known what was going to happen in the natural world—and, in particular, has always known what human actions were going to be performed. Thus, as above, assum-

ing that the attribute of omniscience is part of the "essence" of God, the statement "For any natural event (including human actions), if a given person is God, that person would always have known that that event was going to occur at the time it occurred" must be treated as an a priori truth. This is just another way of stating a point admirably put by St. Augustine when he said: "For to confess that God exists and at the same time to deny that He has foreknowledge of future things is the most manifest folly. . . . One who is not prescient of all future things is not God."[7]

B. Last Saturday afternoon, Jones mowed his lawn. Assuming that God exists and is (essentially) omniscient in the sense outlined above, it follows that (let us say) eighty years prior to last Saturday afternoon, God knew (and thus believed) that Jones would mow his lawn at that time. But from this it follows, I think, that at the time of action (last Saturday afternoon) Jones was not *able*—that is, it was not *within Jones's power*—to refrain from mowing his lawn.[8] If at the time of action, Jones had been able to refrain from mowing his lawn, then (the most obvious conclusion would seem to be) at the time of action, Jones was able to do something which would have brought it about that God held a false belief eighty years earlier. But God cannot in anything be mistaken. It is not possible that some belief of His was false. Thus, last Saturday afternoon, Jones was not able to do something which would have brought it about that God held a false belief eighty years ago. To suppose that it was would be to suppose that, at the time of action, Jones was able to do something having a conceptually incoherent description, namely something that would have brought it about that one of God's beliefs was false. Hence, given that God believed eighty years ago that Jones would mow his lawn on Saturday, if we are to assign Jones the power on Saturday to refrain from mowing his lawn, this power must not be described as the power to do something that would have rendered one of God's beliefs false. How then should we describe it vis-à-vis God and His belief? So far as I can see, there are only two other alternatives. First, we might try describing it as the power to do something that would have brought it about that God believed otherwise than He did eighty years ago; or, secondly, we might try describing it as the power to do something that would have brought it about that God (Who, by hypothesis, existed eighty years earlier) did not exist eighty years earlier—that is, as the power to do something that would have brought it about that any person who believed eighty years ago that Jones would mow his lawn on Saturday (one of whom was, by hypothesis, God) held a false belief, and thus was not God. But again, neither of these latter can be accepted. Last Saturday afternoon, Jones was not able to do something that would have brought it about that God believed otherwise than He did eighty years ago. Even if we suppose (as was suggested by Calvin) that eighty years ago God knew Jones would mow his lawn on Saturday in the sense that He "saw" Jones mowing his lawn as if this action were occurring before Him, the fact remains that God knew (and thus believed) eighty years prior to Saturday that Jones would mow his lawn. And if God held such a belief eighty years prior to Saturday, Jones did not have the power on Saturday to do something that would have made it the case that God did not hold this belief eighty years earlier. No action performed at a given time can alter the fact that a given person held a certain belief at a time prior to the time in question. This last seems to be an a priori truth. For similar reasons, the last of the above alternatives must also be rejected. On the assumption that God existed eighty years prior to Saturday, Jones on Saturday was not able to do something that would have brought it about that God did not exist eighty years prior to that time. No action performed at a given time can alter the fact that a certain person existed at a time prior to the time in question. This, too, seems to me to be an a priori truth. But if these observations are correct, then, given that Jones mowed his lawn on Saturday, and given that God exists and is (essentially) omniscient, it seems to follow that at the time of action, Jones did not have the power to refrain from mowing his lawn. The upshot of these reflections would appear to be that Jones's mowing his lawn last Saturday cannot be counted as a voluntary action. Although I do not have an analysis of what it is for action to be *voluntary,* it seems to me that a situation in which it would be wrong to assign Jones the *ability*

or *power* to do *other* than he did would be a situation in which it would also be wrong to speak of his action as voluntary. As a general remark, if God exists and is (essentially) omniscient in the sense specified above, no human action is voluntary.[9]

As the argument just presented is somewhat complex, perhaps the following schematic representation of it will be of some use.

1. "God existed at T_1" entails "If Jones did X at T_2, God believed at T_1 that Jones would do X at T_2."
2. "God believes X" entails "'X' is true."
3. It is not within one's power at a given time to do something having a description that is logically contradictory.
4. It is not within one's power at a given time to do something that would bring it about that someone who held a certain belief at a time prior to the time in question did not hold that belief at the time prior to the time in question.
5. It is not within one's power at a given time to do something that would bring it about that a person who existed at an earlier time did not exist at that earlier time.
6. If God existed at T_1 and if God believed at T_1 that Jones would do X at T_2, then if it was within Jones's power at T_2 to refrain from doing X, then (1) it was within Jones's power at T_2 to do something that would have brought it about that God held a false belief at T_1, or (2) it was within Jones's power at T_2 to do something which would have brought it about that God did not hold the belief He held at T_1, or (3) it was within Jones's power at T_2 to do something that would have brought it about that any person who believed at T_1 that Jones would do X at T_2 (one of whom was, by hypothesis, God) held a false belief and thus was not God—that is, that God (who by hypothesis existed at T_1) did not exist at T_1.
7. Alternative 1 in the consequent of item 6 is false (from 2 and 3).
8. Alternative 2 in the consequent of item 6 is false (from 4).
9. Alternative 3 in the consequent of item 6 is false (from 5).

10. Therefore, if God existed at T_1 and if God believed at T_1 that Jones would do X at T_2, then it was not within Jones's power at T_2 to refrain from doing X (from 6 through 9).

11. Therefore, if God existed at T_1, and if Jones did X at T_2, it was not within Jones's power at T_2 to refrain from doing X (from 1 and 10).

In this argument, items 1 and 2 make explicit the doctrine of God's (essential) omniscience with which I am working. Items 3, 4, and 5 express what I take to be part of the logic of the concept of ability or power as it applies to human beings. Item 6 is offered as an analytic truth. If one assigns Jones the power to refrain from doing X at T_2 (given that God believed at T_1 that he would do X at T_2), so far as I can see, one would have to describe this power in one of the three ways listed in the consequent of item 6. I do not know how to argue that these are the only alternatives, but I have been unable to find another. Item 11, when generalized for all agents and actions, and when taken together with what seems to me to be a minimal condition for the application of "voluntary action," yields the conclusion that if God exists (and is essentially omniscient in the way I have described) no human action is voluntary.

C. It is important to notice that the argument given in the preceding paragraphs avoids use of two concepts that are often prominent in discussions of determinism.

In the first place, the argument makes no mention of the *causes* of Jones's action. Say (for example, with St. Thomas)[10] that God's foreknowledge of Jones's action was, itself, the cause of the action (though I am really not sure what this means). Say, instead, that natural events or circumstances caused Jones to act. Even say that Jones's action had no cause at all. The argument outlined above remains unaffected. If eighty years prior to Saturday, God believed that Jones would mow his lawn at that time, it was not within Jones's power at the time of action to refrain from mowing his lawn. The reasoning that justifies this assertion makes no mention of a causal series preceding Jones's action.

Secondly, consider the following line of thinking. Suppose Jones mowed his lawn last Saturday.

It was then *true* eighty years ago that Jones would mow his lawn at that time. Hence, on Saturday, Jones was not able to refrain from mowing his lawn. To suppose that he was would be to suppose that he was able on Saturday to do something that would have made false a proposition that was *already true* eighty years earlier. This general kind of argument for determinism is usually associated with Leibniz, although it was anticipated in Chapter IX of Aristotle's *De Interpretatione*. It has been used since, with some modification, in Richard Taylor's article, "Fatalism."[11] This argument, like the one I have offered above, makes no use of the notion of causation. It turns, instead, on the notion of its being *true eighty years ago* that Jones would mow his lawn on Saturday.

I must confess that I share the misgivings of those contemporary philosophers who have wondered what (if any) sense can be attached to a statement of the form "It was true at T_1 that E would occur at T_2."[12] Does this statement mean that had someone believed, guessed, or asserted at T_1 that E would occur at T_2, he would have been right?[13] (I shall have something to say about this form of determinism later in this paper.) Perhaps it means that at T_1 there was sufficient evidence upon which to predict that E would occur at T_2.[14] Maybe it means neither of these. Maybe it means nothing at all.[15] The argument presented above presupposes that it makes straightforward sense to suppose that God (or just anyone) held a true belief eighty years prior to Saturday. But this is not to suppose that *what* God believed *was true eighty years prior to Saturday*. Whether (or in what sense) it was true eighty years ago that Jones would mow his lawn on Saturday is a question I shall not discuss. As far as I can see, the argument in which I am interested requires nothing in the way of a decision on this issue.

II

I now want to consider three comments on the problem of divine foreknowledge which seem to be instructively incorrect.

A. Leibniz analyzed the problem as follows:

They say that what is foreseen cannot fail to exist and they say so truly; but it follows not that what is foreseen is necessary. For necessary truth is that whereof the contrary is impossible or implies a contradiction. Now the truth which states that I shall write tomorrow is not of that nature, it is not necessary. Yet, supposing that God foresees it, it is necessary that it come to pass, that is, the consequence is necessary, namely that it exist, since it has been foreseen; for God is infallible. This is what is termed a *hypothetical necessity*. But our concern is not this necessity; it is an *absolute* necessity that is required, to be able to say that an action is necessary, that it is not contingent, that it is not the effect of free choice.[16]

The statement "God believed at T_1 that Jones would do X at T_2" (where the interval between T_1 and T_2 is, for example, eighty years) does not entail "'Jones did X at T_2' is necessary." Leibniz is surely right about this. All that will follow from the first of these statements concerning "Jones did X at T_2" is that the latter is *true,* not that it is *necessarily true.* But this observation has no real bearing on the issue at hand. The following passage from St. Augustine's formulation of the problem may help to make this point clear.

> Your trouble is this. You wonder how it can be that these two propositions are not contradictory and incompatible, namely that God has foreknowledge of all future events, and that we sin voluntarily and not by necessity. For if, you say, God foreknows that a man will sin, he must necessarily sin. But if there is necessity there is no voluntary choice of sinning, but rather fixed and unavoidable necessity.[17]

In this passage, the term "necessity" (or the phrase "by necessity") is not used to express a modal-logical concept. The term "necessity" is here used in contrast with the term "voluntary," not (as in Leibniz) in contrast with the term "contingent." If one's action is necessary (or by necessity), this is to say that one's action is not voluntary. Augustine says that if God has foreknowledge of human actions, the actions are necessary. But the form of this conditional is "P implies Q," not "P implies $N(Q)$." "Q" in the consequent of this conditional is the claim that human actions are not voluntary—that is, the one is not able, or does not have the power, to do other than he does.

Perhaps I can make this point clearer by reformulating the original problem in such a way as to make explicit the modal operators working within it. Let it be *contingently* true that Jones did X at T_2. Since God holds a belief about the outcome of each human action well in advance of its performance, it is then *contingently* true that God believed at T_1 that Jones would do X at T_2. But it follows from this that it is *contingently* true that at T_2 Jones was not able to refrain from doing X. Had he been (contingently) able to refrain from doing X at T_2, then either he was (contingently) able to do something at T_2 that would have brought it about that God held a false belief at T_1, or he was (contingently) able to do something at T_2 that would have brought it about that God believed otherwise than He did at T_1, or he was (contingently) able to do something at T_2 that would have brought it about that God did not exist at T_1. None of these latter is an aceptable alternative.

B. In *Concordia Liberi Arbitrii,* Luis de Molina wrote as follows:

> It was not that since He foreknew what would happen from those things which depend on the created will that it would happen; but, on the contrary, it was because such things would happen through the freedom of the will, that He foreknew it; and that He would foreknow the opposite if the opposite was to happen.[18]

Remarks similar to this one can be found in a great many traditional and contemporary theological texts. In fact, Molina assures us that the view expressed in this passage has always been "above controversy"—a matter of "common opinion" and unanimous consent"— not only among the Church fathers, but also, as he says, "among all catholic men."

One claim made in the above passage seems to me to be truly "above controversy." With respect to any given action foreknown by God, God would have foreknown the opposite if the opposite was to happen. If we assume the notion of omniscience outlined in the first section of this paper, and if we agree that omniscience is part of the "essence" of God, this statement is a conceptual truth. I doubt if anyone would be inclined to dispute it. Also involved in this passage, however, is at least the suggestion of a doctrine that cannot be taken as an item of "common opinion" among *all* catholic men. Molina says it is not because God foreknows what He foreknows that men act as they do: it is because men act as they do that God foreknows what He foreknows. Some theologians have rejected this claim. It seems to entail that men's actions determine God's cognitions. And this latter, I think, has been taken by some theologians to be a violation of the notion of God as self-sufficient and incapable of being affected by events of the natural world.[19] But I shall not develop this point further. Where the view put forward in the above passage seems to me to go wrong in an interesting and important way is in Molina's claim that God can have foreknowledge of things that will happen "through the freedom of the will." It is this claim that I here want to examine with care.

What exactly are we saying when we say that God can know in advance what will happen *through the freedom of the will?* I think that what Molina has in mind is this. God can know in advance that a given man is going to *choose* to perform a certain action sometime in the future. With respect to the case of Jones mowing his lawn, God knew at T_1 that Jones would *freely decide* to mow his lawn at T_2. Not only did God know at T_1 that Jones would mow his lawn at T_2, He also knew at T_1 that this action would be performed *freely*. In the words of Emil Brunner, "God knows that which will take place in freedom in the future as something which happens in freedom."[20] What God knew at T_1 is that Jones would *freely* mow his lawn at T_2.

I think that this doctrine is incoherent. If God knew (and thus believed) at T_1 that Jones would do X at T_2,[21] I think it follows that Jones was not able to do other than X at T_2 (for reasons already given). Thus, if God knew (and thus believed) at T_1 that Jones would do X at T_2, it would follow that Jones did X at T_2, but *not freely*. It does not seem to be possible that God could have believed at T_1 that Jones would freely do X at T_2. If God believed at T_1 that Jones would *do X* at T_2, Jones's action at T_2 was not free; and if God *also* believed at T_1 that Jones

would freely act at T_2, it follows that God held a false belief at T_1—which is absurd.

C. Frederich Schleiermacher commented on the problem of divine foreknowledge as follows:

> In the same way, we estimate the intimacy between two persons by the foreknowledge one has of the actions of the other, without supposing that in either case, the one or the other's freedom is thereby endangered. So even the divine foreknowledge cannot endanger freedom.[22]

St. Augustine made this same point in *De Libero Arbitrio.* He said:

> Unless I am mistaken, you would not directly compel the man to sin, though you knew beforehand that he was going to sin. Nor does your prescience in itself compel him to sin even though he was certainly going to sin, as we must assume if you have real prescience. So there is no contradiction here. Simply you know beforehand what another is going to do with his own will. Similarly God compels no man to sin, though he sees beforehand those who are going to sin by their own will.[23]

If we suppose (with Schleiermacher and Augustine) that the case of an intimate friend having foreknowledge of another's action has the same implications for determinism as the case of God's foreknowledge of human actions, I can imagine two positions which might then be taken. First, one might hold (with Schleiermacher and Augustine) that God's foreknowledge of human actions cannot entail determinism—since it is clear that an intimate friend can have foreknowledge of another's voluntary actions. Or, secondly, one might hold that an intimate friend cannot have foreknowledge of another's voluntary actions—since it is clear that God cannot have foreknowledge of such actions. This second position could take either of two forms. One might hold that since an intimate friend *can* have foreknowledge of another's actions, the actions in question cannot be voluntary. Or, alternatively, one might hold that since the other's actions *are* voluntary, the intimate friend cannot have foreknowledge of them.[24] But what I propose to argue in the remaining pages of this paper is that Schleiermacher and Augustine were mistaken in supposing that the case of an intimate friend having foreknowledge of other's actions has the same implications for determinism as the case of God's foreknowledge of human actions. What I want to suggest is that the argument I used above to show that God cannot have foreknowledge of voluntary actions cannot be used to show that an intimate friend cannot have foreknowledge of another's actions. Even if one holds that an intimate friend *can* have foreknowledge of another's voluntary actions, one ought not to think that the case is the same when dealing with the problem of divine foreknowledge.

Let Smith be an ordinary man and an intimate friend of Jones. Now, let us start by supposing that Smith believed at T_1 that Jones would do X at T_2. We make no assumption concerning the truth or falsity of Smith's belief, but assume only that Smith held it. Given only this much, there appears to be no difficulty in supposing that at T_2 Jones was able to do X and that at T_2 Jones was able to do not-X. So far as the above description of the case is concerned, it might well have been within Jones's power at T_2 to do something (namely, X) which would have brought it about that Smith held a true belief at T_1, and it might well have been within Jones's power at T_2 to do something (namely, not-X) which would have brought it about that Smith held a false belief at T_1. So much seems apparent.

Now let us suppose Smith *knew* at T_1 that Jones would do X at T_2. This is to suppose that Smith correctly believed (with evidence) at T_1 that Jones would do X at T_2. It follows, to be sure, that Jones did X at T_2. But now let us inquire about what Jones was *able* to do at T_2. I submit that there is nothing in the description of this case that requires the conclusion that it was not within Jones's power at T_2 to refrain from doing X. By hypothesis, the belief held by Smith at T_1 was true. Thus, by hypothesis, Jones did X at T_2. But even if we assume that the belief held by Smith at T_1 was *in fact* true, we can add that the belief held by Smith at T_1 *might have* turned out to be false.[25] Thus, even if we say that Jones *in fact* did X at T_2, we can add that Jones *might not* have done X at T_2—meaning by this that it was within Jones's power at T_2 to refrain from doing X. Smith held a true belief which might have turned out to be false, and, correspondingly, Jones performed an action which he was able to refrain from performing. Given that Smith correctly believed at

T_1 that Jones would do X at T_2, we can still assign Jones the *power* at T_2 to refrain from doing X. All we need add is that the power in question is one which Jones *did not exercise.*

These last reflections have no application, however, when dealing with God's foreknowledge. Assume that God (being essentially omniscient) existed at T_1, and assume that He believed at T_1 that Jones would do X at T_2. It follows, again, that Jones did X at T_2. God's beliefs are true. But now, as above, let us inquire into what Jones was *able* to do at T_2. We cannot claim now, as in the Smith case, that the belief held by God at T_1 was *in fact* true but *might have* turned out to be false. No sense of "might have" has application here. It is a conceptual truth that God's beliefs are true. Thus, we cannot claim, as in the Smith case, that Jones *in fact* acted in accordance with God's beliefs but had the *ability* to refrain from so doing. The ability to refrain from acting in accordance with one of God's beliefs would be the ability to do something that would bring it about that one of God's beliefs was false. And no one could have an ability of this description. Thus, in the case of God's foreknowledge of Jones's action at T_2, if we are to assign Jones the ability at T_2 to refrain from doing X, we must understand this ability in some way other than the way we understood it when dealing with Smith's foreknowledge. In this case, either we must say that it was the ability at T_2 to bring it about that God believed otherwise than He did at T_1; or we must say that it was the ability at T_2 to bring it about that any person who believed at T_1 that Jones would do X at T_2 (one of whom was, by hypothesis, God) held a false belief and thus was not God. But, as pointed out earlier, neither of these last alternatives can be accepted.

The important thing to be learned from the study of Smith's foreknowledge of Jones's action is that the problem of divine foreknowledge has as one of its pillars the claim the truth is *analytically* connected with God's *beliefs.* No problem of determinism arises when dealing with human knowledge of future actions. This is because truth is not analytically connected with human belief even when (as in the case of human knowledge) truth is contingently conjoined to belief. If we suppose that Smith knows at T_1 that Jones will do X at T_2, what we are supposing is that Smith believes at T_1 that Jones will do X at T_2 and (as an additional, contingent, fact) that the belief in question is true. Thus having supposed that Smith knows at T_1 that Jones will do X at T_2, when we turn to a consideration of the situation of T_2 we can infer (1) that Jones *will* do X at T_2 (since Smith's belief is true), and (2) that Jones does not have the power at T_2 to do something that would bring it about that Jones did not *believe* as he did at T_1. But paradoxical though it may seem (and it seems paradoxical only at first sight), Jones can have the power at T_2 to do something that would bring it about that Smith did not have *knowledge* at T_1. This is simply to say that Jones can have the *power* at T_2 to do something that would bring it about that the belief held by Smith at T_1 (which was, in fact, true) was (instead) false. We are required only to add that since Smith's belief was in fact true (that is, was knowledge) Jones *did not* (in fact) *exercise* that power. But when we turn to a consideration of God's foreknowledge of Jones's action at T_2 the elbowroom between belief and truth disappears and, with it, the possibility of assigning Jones even the *power* of doing other than he does at T_2. We begin by supposing that God *knows* at T_1 that Jones will do X at T_2. As above, this is to suppose that God believes at T_1 that Jones will do X at T_2, and it is to suppose that this belief is true. But it is *not* an additional, contingent fact that the belief held by God is true. "God believes X" entails "X is true." Thus, having supposed that God knows (and thus believes) at T_1 that Jones will do X at T_2, we can infer (1) that Jones *will do* X at T_2 (since God's belief is true); (2) that Jones does not have the power at T_2 to do something that would bring it about that God did not hold the belief He held at T_1, and (3) that Jones does not have the power at T_2 to do something that would bring it about that the belief held by God at T_1 was false. This last is what we could *not* infer when truth and belief were only factually connected—as in the case of Smith's knowledge. To be sure, "Smith knows at T_1 that Jones will do X at T_2" and "God knows at T_1 that Jones will do X at T_2" both entail "Jones will do X at T_2" ("A knows X" entails "'X' is true"). But this similarity between "Smith knows X" and "God knows X" is not a point of any special interest in the present discussion. As

Schleiermacher and Augustine rightly insisted (and as we discovered in our study of Smith's foreknowledge) the mere fact that someone knows in advance how another will act in the future is not enough to yield a problem of the sort we have been discussing. We begin to get a glimmer of the knot involved in the problem of divine foreknowledge when we shift attention away from the *similarities* between "Smith knows X" and "God knows X" (in particular, that they both entail "'X' is true") and concentrate instead on the logical *differences* which obtain between Smith's knowledge and God's knowledge. We get to the difference which makes the difference when, after analyzing the notion of knowledge as true belief (supported by evidence) we discover the radically dissimilar relations between truth and belief in the two cases. When truth is only factually connected with belief (as in Smith's knowledge) one can have the power (though, by hypothesis, one will not exercise it) to do something that would make the belief false. But when truth is analytically connected with belief (as in God's belief) no one can have the power to do something which would render the belief false.

To conclude: I have assumed that any statement of form "*A* knows X" entails a statement of the form "*A* believes X" as well as a statement of the form "'X' is true." I have then supposed (as an analytic truth) that if a given person is omniscient, that person (1) holds no false beliefs, and (2) holds beliefs about the outcome of human actions in advance of their performance. In addition, I have assumed that the statement "If a given person is God that person is omniscient" is an a priori statement. (This last I have labeled the doctrine of God's essential omniscience.) Given these items (plus some premises concerning what is and what is not within one's power), I have argued that if God exists, it is not within one's power to do other than he does. I have inferred from this that if God exists, no human action is voluntary.

As emphasized earlier, I do not want to claim that the assumptions underpinning the argument are acceptable. In fact, it seems to me that a theologian interested in claiming both that God is omniscient and that men have free will could deny any one (or more) of them. For example, a theologian might deny that a statement of the form "*A* knows *X* entails a statement of the form "*A* believes *X*" (some contemporary philosophers have denied this) or, alternatively, he might claim that this entailment holds in the case of human knowledge but fails in the case of God's knowledge. This latter would be to claim that when knowledge is attributed to God, the term "knowledge" bears a sense other than the one it has when knowledge is attributed to human beings. Then again, a theologian might object to the analysis of "omniscience" with which I have been working. Although I doubt if any Christian theologian would allow that an omniscient being could believe something false, he might claim that a given person could be omniscient although he did not hold beliefs about the outcome of human actions *in advance* of their performance. (This latter is the way Boethius escaped the problem.) Still again, a theologian might deny the doctrine of God's essential omniscience. He might admit that if a given person is God that person is omniscient, but he might deny that this statement formulates an a priori truth. This would be to say that although God is omniscient, He is not *essentially* omniscient. So far as I can see, within the conceptual framework of theology employing any one of these adjustments, the problem of divine foreknowledge outlined in this paper could not be formulated. There thus appears to be a rather wide range of alternatives open to the theologian at this point. It would be a mistake to think that commitment to determinism is an unavoidable implication of the Christian concept of divine omniscience.

But having arrived at this understanding, the importance of the preceding deliberations ought not to be overlooked. There is a pitfall in the doctrine of divine omniscience. That knowing involves believing (truly) is surely a tempting philosophical view (witness the many contemporary philosophers who have affirmed it). And the idea that God's attributes (including omniscience) are essentially connected to His nature, together with the idea that an omniscient being would hold no false beliefs and would hold beliefs about the outcome of human actions in advance of their performance, might be taken by some theologians as obvious candidates for inclusion in a finished Christian theology. Yet the theologian must approach these items critically. If they are embraced together, then if one affirms the existence of God, one is committed to the view that no human action is voluntary.

Notes

1. *Consolatio Philosophiae*, Bk. V, sec. 3, par. 6.
2. This position is particularly well formulated in St. Anselm's *Proslogium*, ch. xix and *Monologium*, chs. xxi–xxii; and in Frederich Schleiermacher's *The Christian Faith*, Pt. 1, sec. 2, par. 51. It is also explicit in Boethius, op. cit., secs. 4–6, and in St. Thomas' *Summa Theologica*, Pt. 1, Q. 10.
3. This point is explicit in Boethius, op. cit., secs. 4–6.
4. This position is particularly well expressed in William Paley's *Natural Theology*, ch. xxiv. It is also involved in John Calvin's discussion of predestination, *Institutes of the Christian Religion*, Bk. III, ch. xxi; and in some formulations of the first cause argument for existence of God, e.g., John Locke's *Essay Concerning Human Understanding*, Bk. IV, ch. x.
5. *Institutes of the Christian Religion*, Bk. III, ch. xxi; this passage trans. by John Allen (Philadelphia, 1813), II, 145.
6. Ibid., p. 144.
7. *City of God*, Bk. V, sec. 9.
8. The notion of someone being *able* to do something and the notion of something being *within one's power* are essentially the same. Traditional formulations of the problem of divine foreknowledge (e.g., those of Boethius and Augustine) made use of the notion of what is (and what is not) *within one's power*. But the problem is the same when framed in terms of what one is (and one is not) *able* to do. Thus, I shall treat the statements "Jones was able to do *X*," "Jones had the ability to do *X*," and "It was within Jones's power to do *X*" as equivalent. Richard Taylor, in "I Can," *Philosophical Review*, LXIX (1960), 78–89, has argued that the notion of ability or power involved in these last three statements is incapable of philosophical analysis. Be this as it may, I shall not here attempt such an analysis. In what follows I shall, however, be careful to affirm only those statements about what is (or is not) within one's power that would have to be preserved on any analysis of this notion having even the most distant claim to adequacy.
9. In Bk. II, ch. xxi, secs. 8–11 of the *Essay*, John Locke says that an agent is not *free* with respect to a given action (i.e., that an action is done "under necessity") when it is not within the agent's power to do otherwise. Locke allows a special kind of case, however, in which an action

may be *voluntary* though done under necessity. If a man chooses to do something without knowing that it is not within his power to do otherwise (e.g., if a man chooses to stay in a room without knowing that the room is locked), his action may be voluntary though he is not free to forbear it. If Locke is right in this (and I shall not argue the point one way or the other), replace "voluntary" with (let us say) "free" in the above paragraph and throughout the remainder of this paper.

10. *Summa Theologica,* Pt. 1, Q. 14, a. 8.

11. *Philosophical Review,* LXXI (1962), 56–66. Taylor argues that if an event *E* fails to occur at T$_2$, then at T$_1$ it was true that *E* would fail to occur at T$_2$. Thus, at T$_1$, a necessary condition of anyone's performing an action sufficient for the occurrence of *E* at T$_2$ is missing. Thus at T$_1$, no one could have the power to perform an action that would be sufficient for the occurrence of *E* at T$_2$. Hence, no one has the power at T$_1$ to do something sufficient for the occurrence of an event at T$_2$ that is not going to happen. The parallel between this argument and the one recited above can be seen very clearly if one reformulates Taylor's argument, pushing back the time at which it was true that *E* would not occur at T$_2$.

12. For a helpful discussion of difficulties involved here, see Rogers Albritton's "Present Truth and Future Contingency," a reply to Richard Taylor's "The Problem of Future Contingency," both in the *Philosophical Review,* LXVI (1957), 1–28.

13. Gilbert Ryle interprets it this way. See "It Was to Be," *Dilemmas* (Cambridge, 1954).

14. Richard Gale suggests this interpretation in "Endorsing Predictions," *Philosophical Review,* LXX (1961), 378–385.

15. This view is held by John Turk Saunders in "Sea Fight Tomorrow?" *Philosophical Review,* LXVII (1958), 367–378.

16. *Théodicée,* Pt. 1, sec. 37. This passage trans. by E. M. Huggard (New Haven, 1952), p. 144.

17. *De Libero Arbitrio,* Bk. III. This passage trans. by J. H. S. Burleigh, *Augustine's Earlier Writings* (Philadelphia, 1955).

18. This passage trans. by John Mourant, *Readings in the Philosophy of Religion* (New York, 1954), p. 426.

19. Cf. Boethius' *Consolatio,* Bk. V, sec. 3, par. 2.

20. *The Christian Doctrine of God,* trans. by Olive Wyon (Philadelphia, 1964), p. 262.

21. Note: no comment here about *freely* doing *X.*

22. *The Christian Faith,* Pt. 1, sec. 2, par. 55. This passage trans. by W. R. Matthew (Edinburgh, 1928), p. 228.

23. Loc. cit.

24. This last seems to be the position defended by Richard Taylor in "Deliberation and Foreknowledge," *American Philosophical Quarterly,* 1 (1964).

25. The phrase "might have" as it occurs in this sentence does not express mere *logical* possibility. I am not sure how to analyze the notion of possibility involved here, but I think it is roughly the same notion as is involved when we say, "Jones might have been killed in the accident (had it not been for the fact that at the last minute he decided not to go)."

IV.B.3 God's Foreknowledge and Human Free Will Are Compatible

ALVIN PLANTINGA

Alvin Plantinga is professor of philosophy at the University of Notre Dame. In this article he appeals to the notion of possible worlds in order to show that Pike's logic misfires and that there really is no incompatibility between divine foreknowledge and human free will.

Reprinted from Alvin Plantinga, *God, Freedom and Evil* (New York: Harper & Row, 1974), 66–72, by permission of the author.

The last argument I wish to discuss is perhaps only mildly atheological. This is the claim that God's omniscience is incompatible with *human freedom.* Many people are inclined to think that if God is omniscient, then human beings are never free. Why? Because the idea that God is omniscient implies that at any given time God knows not only what *has* taken place and what *is* taking place, but also what *will* take place. He knows the future as well as the past. But now suppose He knows that Paul will perform some trivial action tomorrow—having an orange for lunch, let's say. If God knows in advance that Paul will have an orange for lunch tomorrow, then it must be the case that he'll have an orange tomorrow; and if it *must* be the case that Paul will have an orange tomorrow, then it isn't possible that Paul will *refrain* from so doing—in which case he won't be free to refrain, and hence won't be free with respect to the action of taking the orange. So if God knows in advance that a person will perform a certain action *A*, then that person isn't free with respect to that action. But if God is omniscient, then for any person and any action he performs, God knew in advance that he'd perform that action. So if God is omniscient, no one ever performs any free actions.

This argument may initially sound plausible, but the fact is it is based upon confusion. The central portion can be stated as follows:

(49) If God knows in advance that *X* will do *A*, then it must be the case that *X* will do *A*

and

(50) If it must be the case that *X* will do *A*, then *X* is not free to refrain from *A*.

From (49) and (50) it follows that if God knows in advance that someone will take a certain action, then that person isn't free with respect to that action. But (49) bears further inspection. Why should we think it's *true*? Because, we shall be told, if God *knows* that *X* will do *A*, it *logically follows* that *X* will do *A*: it's necessary that if God knows that *p*, then *p* is true. But this defense of (49) suggests that the latter is *ambiguous*; it may mean either

(49a) Necessarily, if God knows in advance that *X* will do *A*, then indeed *X* will do *A*

or

(49b) If God knows in advance that *X* will do *A*, then it is necessary that *X* will do *A*.

The atheological argument requires the truth of (49b); but the above defense of (49) supports only (49a), not (49b). It is indeed necessarily true that if God (or anyone else) knows that a proposition *P* is true, then *P* is true; but it simply doesn't follow that if God knows *P*, then *P* is *necessarily* true. *If I know that Henry is a bachelor, then Henry is a bachelor* is a necessary truth; it does not follow that if I know

that Henry is a bachelor, then it is necessarily true that he is. I know that Henry is a bachelor: what follows is only that *Henry is married* is false; it doesn't follow that it is necessarily false.

So the claim that divine omniscience is incompatible with human freedom seems to be based upon confusion. Nelson Pike has suggested[1] an interesting revision of this old claim: he holds, not that human freedom is incompatible with God's being omniscient, but with God's being *essentially* omniscient. Recall . . . that an object *X* has a property *P* essentially if *X* has *P* in every world in which *X* exists—if, that is, it is impossible that *X* should have existed but lacked *P*. Now many theologians and philosophers have held that at least some of God's important properties are essential to him in this sense. It is plausible to hold, for example, that God is essentially omnipotent. Things could have gone differently in various ways; but if there had been no omnipotent being, then God would not have existed. *He* couldn't have been powerless or limited in power. But the same may be said for God's *omniscience*. If God is omniscient, then He is unlimited in knowledge; He knows every true proposition and believes none that are false. If He is *essentially* omniscient, furthermore, then He not only *is not* limited in knowledge; He *couldn't* have been. There is no possible world in which He exists but fails to know some truth or believes some falsehood. And Pike's claim is that this belief—the belief that God is essentially omnipotent—is inconsistent with human freedom.

To argue his case Pike considers the case of Jones who mowed his lawn at T_2—last Saturday, let's say. Now suppose that God is essentially omniscient. Then at any earlier time T_1—80 years ago, for example—God believed that Jones would mow his lawn at T_2. Since He is *essentially* omniscient, furthermore, it isn't possible that God falsely believes something; hence His having believed at T_1 that Jones would mow his lawn at T_2 entails that Jones does indeed mow his lawn at T_2. Pike's argument (in his own words) then goes as follows:

1. "God existed at T_1" entails "If Jones did *X* at T_2, God believed at T_1 that Jones would do *X* at T_2."

2. "God believes *X*" entails "*X* is true."
3. It is not within one's power at a given time to do something having a description that is logically contradictory.
4. It is not within one's power at a given time to do something that would bring it about that someone who held a certain belief at a time prior to the time in question did not hold that belief at the time prior to the time in question.
5. It is not within one's power at a given time to do something that would bring it about that a person who existed at an earlier time did not exist at that earlier time.
6. If God existed at T_1 and if God believed at T_1 that Jones would do *X* at T_2, then if it was within Jones' power at T_2 to refrain from doing *X*, then (1) it was within Jones' power at T_2 to do something that would have brought it about that God held a false belief at T_1, or (2) it was within Jones' power at T_2 to do something which would have brought it about that God did not hold the belief He held at T_1, or (3) it was within Jones' power at T_2 to do something that would have brought it about that any person who believed at T_1 that Jones would do *X* at T_2 (one of whom was, by hypothesis, God) held a false belief and thus was not God—that is, that God (who by hypothesis existed at T_1) did not exist at T_1.
7. Alternative 1 in the consequent of item 6 is false (from 2 and 3).
8. Alternative 2 in the consequent of item 6 is false (from 4).
9. Alternative 3 in the consequent of item 6 is false (from 5).
10. Therefore, if God existed at T_1 and if God believed at T_1 that Jones would do *X* at T_2, then it was not within Jones' power at T_2 to refrain from doing *X* (from 1 and 10).[2]

What about this argument? The first two premises simply make explicit part of what is involved in the idea that God is essentially omniscient; so there is no quarreling with them. Premises 3–5 also seem correct. But that complicated premise (6) warrants a closer look. What exactly does it say? I think we can understand Pike here as follows. Consider

(51) God existed at T_1, and God believed at T_1 that Jones would do *X* at T_2, and it was within Jones' power to refrain from doing *X* at T_2.

What Pike means to say, I believe, is that either (51) entails

(52) It was within Jones' power at T_2 to do something that would have brought it about that God held a false belief at T_1

or (51) entails

(53) It was with Jones' power at T_2 to do something that would have brought it about that God did not hold the belief He did hold at T_1

or it entails

(54) It was within Jones' power at T_2 to do something that would have brought it about that anyone who believed at T_1 that Jones would do *X* at T_2 (one of whom was by hypothesis God) held a false belief and thus was not God—that is, that God (who by hypothesis existed at T_1) did not exist at T_1.

[The remainder of Pike's reasoning consists in arguing that each of (52), (53), and (54) is necessarily false, if God is essentially omniscient; hence (51) is necessarily false, if God is essentially omniscient, which means that God's being essentially omniscient is incompatible with human freedom.] Now suppose we look at these one at a time. Does (51) entail (52)? No. (52) says that it was within Jones' power to do something—namely, refrain from doing *X*—such that if he had done that thing, then God *would have* held a false belief at T_1. But this does not follow from (51). If Jones had refrained from *X*, then a proposition that God *did in fact* believe would have been false; but if Jones had refrained from *X* at T_2, then God (since He is omniscient) *would not have believed at* T_1 *that Jones will do X* at T_2. What follows from (51) is not (52) but only (52'):

(52') It was within Jones' power to do something such that if he had done it, then a belief that God *did hold* at T_1 *would have been* false.

But (52′) is not at all paradoxical and in particular does not imply that it was within Jones' power to do something that would have brought it about that God held a false belief.

Perhaps we can see this more clearly if we look at it from the vantage point of possible worlds. We are told by (51) both that in the actual world God believes that Jones does X at T_2 and also that it is within Jones' power to *refrain* from doing X at T_2. Now consider any world W in which Jones *does* refrain from doing X. In *that* world, a belief that God holds in the actual world—in Kronos—is false. That is, if W had been actual, then a belief that God does *in fact* hold world have been false. But it does not follow that in W God holds a false belief. For it doesn't follow that if W had been actual, God would have believed that Jones would do X at T_2. Indeed, if God is essentially omniscient (omniscient in every world in which He exists) what follows is that in W God did *not* believe at T_1 that Jones will do X at T_2; He believed instead that Jones will *refrain* from X. So (51) by no means implies that it was within Jones' power to bring it about that God held a false belief at T_1.

What about

(53) It was within Jones' power at T_2 to do something that would have brought it about that God did not hold the belief He did hold at T_1?

Here the first problem is one of understanding. How are we to take this proposition? One way is this. What (53) says is that it was within Jones' power, at T_2, to do something such that if he had done it, then at T_1 God would have held a certain belief and also *not* held that belief. That is, (53) so understood attributes to Jones the power to bring about a contradictory state of affairs [call this interpretation (53a)]. (53a) is obviously and resoundingly false; but there is no reason whatever to think that (51) entails it. What (51) entails is rather

(53b) It was within Jones' power at T_2 to do something such that if he had done it, then God would not have held a belief that in fact he did hold.

This follows from (51) but is perfectly innocent. For suppose again that (51) is true, and consider a world W in which Jones refrains from doing X. If God is essentially omniscient, then in this world W He is omniscient and hence does not believe at T_1 that Jones will do X at T_2. So what follows from (51) is the harmless assertion that it was within Jones' power to do something such that if he had done it, then God would not have held a belief that in fact (in the actual world) He did hold. But by no stretch of the imagination does it follow that if Jones had done it, then it would have been true that God *did* hold a belief He didn't hold. Taken one way (53) is obviously false but not a consequence of (51); taken the other it is a consequence of (51) but by no means obviously false.

(54) fares no better. What it says is that it was within Jones' power at T_2 to do something such that if he had done it, then God would not have been omniscient and thus would not have been God. But this simply doesn't follow from (51). The latter does, of course, entail

(54′) It was within Jones' power to do something such that if he'd done it, then anyone who believed at T_1 that Jones would do X at T_2 would have held a false belief.

For suppose again that (51) is in fact true, and now consider one of those worlds W in which Jones refrains from doing X. In that world

(55) Anyone who believed at T_1 that Jones will do X at T_2 held a false belief

is true. That is, if W had been actual, (55) would have been true. But again in W God does not believe that Jones will do X at T_2; (55) is *true* in W but isn't relevant to God there. If Jones had refrained from X, then (55) would have been true. It does not follow that God would not have been omniscient; for in those worlds in which Jones does not do X at T_2, God does not believe at T_1 that He does.

Perhaps the following is a possible source of confusion here. If God is *essentially* omniscient, then He is omniscient in every possible world in which He exists. Accordingly there is no possible world in which He holds a false belief. Now consider any belief that God does in fact hold. It might be tempting to suppose that if He is essentially omniscient, then He holds that belief in every world in which He exists. But of course this doesn't follow. It is not essential to Him to hold the beliefs He does hold; what is essential to Him is the quite different property of holding only true beliefs. So if a belief is true in Kronos but false in some world *W,* then in Kronos God holds that belief and in *W* He does not.

Much more should be said about Pike's piece, and there remain many fascinating details. I shall leave them to you, however. And by way of con-cluding our study of natural atheology: none of the arguments we've examined has prospects for suc-cess; all are unacceptable. There are arguments we haven't considered, of course; but so far the indi-cated conclusion is that natural atheology doesn't work.

Notes

1. Nelson Pike, "Divine Omniscience and Voluntary Action," *Philosophical Review* 74 (January 1965): 27.
2. Ibid., pp. 33–34.

IV.C God's Omnipotence

Omnipotence has traditionally been seen as one of God's attributes, for if God is a being possessing all perfections, surely he must possess omnipotence as a significant perfection. But what exactly is omnipotence? Is it the ability to do just anything at all? Some philosophers, following Descartes, hold that it even includes violating logical truths. However, the implications of this view seem catastrophic for any intelligent talk of God (since all rational discussion presupposes the laws of logic). If we do not presuppose that the laws of logic apply to God, we might just as well say that God does and does not exist at the same time, for a contradiction fails to describe any state of affairs at all. Hence, the overwhelming majority of philosophers and theologians, at least since Aquinas, have not included the notion of doing the logically impossible as being part of the perfections of God. We may roughly define omnipotence as the ability to do whatever is not logically impossible. God can create a universe, but he cannot square a circle.

Still, there are problems with this definition. On the surface, at least, it does not seem contradictory to say that God could make a stone heavier than he could lift or that he could sin if he wanted to (though his being perfectly good keeps him from exercising this power). Consider the paradox of the stone argument, as formulated by Wade Savage*:

1. Either x can create a stone that x cannot lift, or x cannot create a stone that x cannot lift.
2. If x can create a stone that x cannot lift, then, necessarily, there is at least one task that x cannot perform (namely, lift the stone in question).
3. If x cannot create a stone that x cannot lift, then, necessarily, there is at least one act that x cannot perform (namely, create the stone in question).

4. Hence, there is at least one task that x cannot perform.
5. If x is an omnipotent being, then x can perform any task.
6. Therefore, x is not omnipotent.

Since x could be any being whatsoever, the paradox apparently proves that the notion of omnipotence is incoherent.

Note first that there are some things that traditional theism admits God cannot control. God cannot create free beings, capable of choosing right and wrong, without giving up his power to control them. Can God make a world that he cannot control? Can he limit his own omnipotence? Theologians are divided on this issue, some saying that God cannot give up his omnipotence, for he is *essentially* omnipotent and any such ability would be a weakness. Others disagree and say that a God who can voluntarily limit himself is more powerful than a God who cannot. For these theologians, God's omnipotence is *nonessential*.

Your response to the paradox of the stone may depend on which view of omnipotence you accept. In our readings, George Mavrodes embraces the first alternative, presupposing that God is *essentially* omnipotent and so *cannot* create a stone heavier than he can lift, because such an act turns out to be logically impossible. This solution has been criticized by Wade Savage as a case of question begging, supposing as it does that the statement "God is omnipotent" is necessarily true.

A second line of thought is taken by Harry Frankfurt, who argues that if God is able to do one impossible thing, make a stone heavier than he can lift, he can also do a second impossible thing and lift that stone. So the paradox of the stone does not show that the notion of omnipotence is incoherent.

The third line of thought, which Alvin Plantinga and Richard Swinburne take, is that God's omnipotence would enable him to create such a stone but this fact does not lessen his ability

The Philosophical Review 76 (1967), 75f.

unless he does indeed create such a stone. Swinburne is worth quoting at this point.

True, if an omnipotent being actually exercises (as opposed to merely possessing) his ability to bring about the existence of a stone too heavy for him subsequently to bring about its rising, then he will cease to be omnipotent. . . . But the omnipotence of a person at a certain time includes the ability to make himself no longer omnipotent, an ability which he may or may not choose to exercise. A person may remain omnipotent forever because he never exercises his power to create stones too heavy to lift, forces too strong to resist, or universes too wayward to control.*

Similar to the paradox of the stone but more crucial to our idea of God is the question of whether God's omnipotence gives him the power to sin! Again, Aquinas and many medieval theologians argue that such power would be pseudopower, in fact, impotence. Others, following William of Ockham, have argued that God necessarily cannot sin because sin is defined as simply being that which is opposed to God's will and God cannot oppose his own will at one and the same time. (This view presupposes a divine command theory of goodness, which we examine in Part 9.) Still others, such as Richard Swinburne, argue that an omniscient and perfectly free being cannot sin because sin necessarily involves a failure in reason or freedom.† It is not clear that Swinburne's conditions for sin are the only possible ones. In our fourth reading Nelson Pike argues that omnipotence includes the ability to sin. It is logically possible for God to do evil, but it is highly unlikely that he ever will because he always happens to will to do good. God "cannot bring himself to do evil" because that would violate a "firm and stable feature of his nature."

---

*The Coherence of Theism (Oxford: Oxford Univ. Press, 1977), 157f.

†Ibid., 202f.

IV.C.1   Is God's Power Limited?

ST. THOMAS AQUINAS

Thomas Aquinas (1225–1274), one of the greatest theologians in the Western tradition, argues that although it is difficult to explain what God's omnipotence is, it includes only those things that are logically possible. Since God contains all perfections and sinning is an imperfection, the ability to sin is not part of his omnipotence.

We proceed thus to the Third Article:

Objection 1. It seems that God is not omnipotent. For movement and passiveness belong to everything. But this is impossible for God, since He is immovable, as was said above. Therefore He is not omnipotent.

Obj. 2. Further, sin is an act of some kind. But God cannot sin, nor *deny Himself,* as it is said *2 Tim.* ii. 13. Therefore He is not omnipotent.

Obj. 3. Further, it is said of God that He manifests His omnipotence *especially by sparing and having mercy.* Therefore the greatest act possible to the divine power is to spare and have mercy. There are things much greater, however, than sparing and having mercy; for example, to create another world, and the like. Therefore God is not omnipotent.

Obj. 4. Further, upon the text, *God hath made foolish the wisdom of this world* (*I Cor.* i. 20), the *Gloss* says: *God hath made the wisdom of this world foolish* by showing those things to be possible which it judges to be impossible. Whence it seems

---

From *Summa Theologica,* part 1, in *The Basic Writings of St. Thomas Aquinas,* vol. 1, edited by Anton C. Pegis (New York: Random House, 1945), 262–64, by permission of the Anton Pegis Estate.

that nothing is to be judged possible or impossible in reference to inferior causes, as the wisdom of this world judges them; but in reference to the divine power. If God, then were omnipotent, all things would be possible; nothing, therefore, impossible. But if we take away the impossible, then we destroy also the necessary; for what necessarily exists cannot possibly not exist. Therefore, there would be nothing at all that is necessary in things if God were omnipotent. But this is an impossibility. Therefore God is not omnipotent.

On the contrary, It is said: *No word shall be impossible with God (Luke* i. 37).

I answer that, All confess that God is omnipotent; but it seems difficult to explain in what His omnipotence precisely consists. For there may be a doubt as to the precise meaning of the word "all" when we say that God can do all things. If, however, we consider the matter aright, since power is said in reference to possible things, this phrase, *God can do all things,* is rightly understood to mean that God can do all things that are possible; and for this reason He is said to be omnipotent. Now according to the Philosopher a thing is said to be possible in two ways. First, in relation to some power; thus whatever is subject to human power is said to be possible to man. Now God cannot be said to be omnipotent through being able to do all things that are possible to created nature; for the divine power extends farther than that. If, however, we were to say that God is omnipotent because He can do all things that are possible to His power, there would be a vicious circle in explaining the nature of His power. For this would be saying nothing else but that God is omnipotent because He can do all that He is able to do.

It remains, therefore, that God is called omnipotent because he can do all things that are possible absolutely; which is the second way of saying a thing is possible. For a thing is said to be possible or impossible absolutely, according to the relation in which the very terms stand to one another: possible, if the predicate is not incompatible with the subject, as that Socrates sits; and absolutely impossible when the predicate is altogether incompatible with the subject, as, for instance, that a man is an ass.

It must, however, be remembered that since every agent produces an effect like itself, to each active power there corresponds a thing possible as its proper object according to the nature of that act on which its active power is founded; for instance, the power of giving warmth is related, as to its proper object, to the being capable of being warmed. The divine being, however, upon which the nature of power in God is founded, is infinite; it is not limited to any class of being, but possesses within itself the perfection of all being. Whence, whatsoever has or can have the nature of being is numbered among the absolute possibles, in respect of which God is called omnipotent.

Now nothing is opposed to the notion of being except non-being. Therefore, that which at the same time implies being and non-being is repugnant to the notion of an absolute possible, which is subject to the divine omnipotence. For such cannot come under the divine omnipotence; not indeed because of any defect in the power of God, but because it has not the nature of a feasible or possible thing. Therefore, everything that does not imply a contradiction in terms is numbered among those possibles in respect of which God is called omnipotent; whereas whatever implies contradiction does not come within the scope of divine omnipotence, because it cannot have the aspect of possibility. Hence it is more appropriate to say that such things cannot be done, than that God cannot do them. Nor is this contrary to the word of the angel, saying: *No word shall be impossible with God (Luke* i. 37). For whatever implies a contradiction cannot be a word, because no intellect can possibly conceive such a thing.

Reply Obj. 1. God is said to be omnipotent in respect to active power, not to passive power, as was shown above. Whence the fact that He is immovable or impassible is not repugnant to His omnipotence.

Reply Obj. 2. To sin is to fall short of a perfect action; hence to be able to sin is to be able to fall short in action, which is repugnant to omnipotence. Therefore it is that God cannot sin, because of His omnipotence. Now it is true that the Philosopher says that *God can deliberately do what is evil.* But this must be understood either on a condition, the

antecedent of which is impossible—as, for instance, if we were to say that God can do evil things if He will. For there is no reason why a conditional proposition should not be true, though both the antecedent and consequent are impossible: as if one were to say: *If man is an ass, he has four feet.* Or he may be understood to mean that God can do some things which now seem to be evil: which, however, if He did them, would then be good. Or he is, perhaps, speaking after the common manner of the pagans, who thought that men became gods, like Jupiter or Mercury.

Reply Obj. 3. God's omnipotence is particularly shown in sharing and having mercy, because in this it is made manifest that God has supreme power, namely, that He freely forgives sins. For it is not for one who is bound by laws of a superior to forgive sins of his own free choice. Or, it is thus shown because by sparing and having mercy upon men, He leads them to the participation of an infinite good; which is the ultimate effect of the divine power. Or it is thus shown because, as was said above, the effect of the divine mercy is the foundation of all the divine works. For nothing is due

anyone, except because of something already given him gratuitously by God. In this way the divine omnipotence is particularly made manifest, because to it pertains the first foundation of all good things.

Reply Obj. 4. The absolute possible is not so called in reference either to higher causes, or to inferior causes, but in reference to itself. But that which is called possible in reference to some power is named possible in reference to its proximate cause. Hence those things which it belongs to God alone to do immediately—as, for example, to create, to justify, and the like—are said to be possible in reference to a higher cause. Those things, however, which are such as to be done by inferior causes, are said to be possible in reference to those inferior causes. For it is according to the condition of the proximate cause that the effect has contingency or necessity, as was shown above. Thus it is that the wisdom of the world is deemed foolish, because what is impossible to nature it judges to be impossible to God. So it is clear that the omnipotence of God does not take away from things their impossibility and necessity.

IV.C.2   Some Puzzles Concerning Omnipotence

GEORGE MAVRODES

George Mavrodes (1926–   ) is professor Emeritus of philosophy at the University of Michigan. In this reading he applies the Thomistic view of God's omnipotence to the paradox of the stone, arguing that since the paradox entails doing something contradictory, it can be resolved.

The doctrine of God's omnipotence appears to claim that God can do anything. Consequently,

Reprinted from *The Philosophical Review* 72 (1963), 221–23.

there have been attempts to refute the doctrine by giving examples of things which God cannot do; for example, He cannot draw a square circle.

Responding to objections of this type, St. Thomas pointed out that "anything" should be here construed to refer only to objects, actions, or states of affairs whose descriptions are not self-contradictory.[1] For it is only such things whose nonexistence might plausibly be attributed to a lack of power in some agent. My failure to draw a circle on the exam may indicate my lack of geometrical skill, but my failure to draw a square circle does not indicate any such lack. Therefore, the fact that it is false (or perhaps meaningless) to say that God could draw

one does no damage to the doctrine of His omnipotence.

A more involved problem, however, is posed by this type of question: can God create a stone too heavy for Him to lift? This appears to be stronger than the first problem, for it poses a dilemma. If we say that God can create a stone, then it seems that there might be such a stone. And if there might be a stone too heavy for Him to lift, then He is evidently not omnipotent. But if we deny that God can create such a stone, we seem to have given up His omnipotence already. Both answers lead us to the same conclusion.

Further, this problem does not seem obviously open to St. Thomas' solution. The form "x is able to draw a square circle" seems plainly to involve a contradiction, while "x is able to make a thing too heavy for x to lift" does not. For it may easily be true that I am able to make a boat too heavy for me to lift. So why should it not be possible for God to make a stone too heavy for Him to lift?

Despite this apparent difference, this second puzzle *is* open to essentially the same answer as the first. The dilemma fails because it consists of asking whether God can do a self-contradictory thing. And the reply that He cannot does no damage to the doctrine of omnipotence.

The specious nature of the problem may be seen in this way. God is either omnipotent or not.[2] Let us assume first that He is not. In that case the phrase "a stone too heavy for God to lift" may not be self-contradictory. And then, of course, if we assert either that God is able or that He is not able to create such a stone, we may conclude that He is not omnipotent. But this is no more than the assumption with which we began, meeting us again after our roundabout journey. If this were all that the dilemma could establish it would be trivial. To be significant it must derive this same conclusion *from the assumption that God is omnipotent;* that is, it must show that the assumption of the omnipotence of God leads to a *reductio.* But does it?

On the assumption that God is omnipotent, the phrase "a stone too heavy for God to lift" becomes self-contradictory. For it becomes "a stone which cannot be lifted by Him whose power is sufficient for lifting anything." But the "thing" described by a self-contradictory phrase is absolutely impossible and hence has nothing to do with the doctrine of omnipotence. Not being an object of power at all, its failure to exist cannot be the result of some lack in the power of God. And, interestingly, it is the very omnipotence of God which makes the existence of such a stone absolutely impossible, while it is the fact that I am finite in power which makes it possible for me to make a boat too heavy for me to lift.

But suppose that some die-hard objector takes the bit in his teeth and denies that the phrase "a stone too heavy for God to lift" is self-contradictory, even on the assumption that God is omnipotent. In other words, he contends that the description "a stone too heavy for an omnipotent God to lift" is self-coherent and therefore describes an absolutely possible object. Must I then attempt to prove the contradiction which I assume above as intuitively obvious? Not necessarily. Let me reply simply that if the objector is right in this contention, then the answer to the original question is "Yes, God can create such a stone." It may seem that this reply will force us into the original dilemma. But it does not. For now the objector can draw no damaging conclusion from this answer. And the reason is that he has just now contended that such a stone is compatible with the omnipotence of God. Therefore, from the possibility of God's creating such a stone it cannot be concluded that God is not omnipotent. The objector cannot have it both ways. The conclusion which he himself wishes to draw from an affirmative answer to the original question is itself the required proof that the descriptive phrase which appears there is self-contradictory. And "it is more appropriate to say that such things cannot be done, than that God cannot do them."[3]

The spacious nature of this problem may also be seen in a somewhat different way.[4] Suppose that some theologian is convinced by this dilemma that he must give up the doctrine of omnipotence. But he resolves to give up as little as possible, just enough to meet the argument. One way he can do so is by retaining the infinite power of God with regard to lifting, while placing a restriction on the sort of stone He is able to create. The only restriction required here, however, is that God must not be able to create a stone too heavy for Him to lift.

Beyond that the dilemma has not even suggested any necessary restriction. Our theologian has, in effect, answered the original question in the negative, and he now regretfully supposes that this has required him to give up the full doctrine of omnipotence. He is now retaining what he supposes to be the more modest remnants which he has salvaged from that doctrine.

We must ask, however, what it is which he has in fact given up. Is it the unlimited power of God to create stones? No doubt. But what stone is it which God is now precluded from creating? The stone too heavy for Him to lift, of course. But we must remember that nothing in the argument required the theologian to admit any limit on God's power with regard to the lifting of stones. He still holds that to be unlimited. And if God's power to lift is infinite, then His power to create may run to infinity also without outstripping that first power. The supposed limitation turns out to be no limitation at all, since it is specified only by reference to another power which is itself infinite. Our theologian need have no

regrets, for he has given up nothing. The doctrine of the power of God remains just what it was before.

Nothing I have said above, of course, goes to prove that God is, in fact, omnipotent. All I have intended to show is that certain arguments intended to prove that He is not omnipotent fail. They fail because they propose, as tests of God's power, putative tasks whose descriptions are self-contradictory. Such pseudo-tasks, not falling within the realm of possibility, are not objects of power at all. Hence the fact that they cannot be performed implies no limit on the power of God, and hence no defect in the doctrine of omnipotence.

Notes

1. St. Thomas Aquinas, *Summa Theologiae*, la, q. 25, a. 3.
2. I assume, of course, the existence of God, since that is not being brought in question here.
3. St. Thomas, *loc. cit.*
4. But this method rests finally on the same logical relations as the preceding one.

IV.C.3 The Logic of Omnipotence

HARRY G. FRANKFURT

Harry Frankfurt is professor of philosophy at Princeton University and the author of several works in philosophy, including an important study of René Descartes. In this essay he argues that even if Mavrodes's solution to the paradox of the stone is incorrect, the critic of omnipotence is not helped. For if God can do the impossible and create a stone heavier than he can lift, he can also do another impossible thing and lift that stone.

George Mavrodes has recently presented an analysis designed to show that, despite some appearances to the contrary, a certain well-known puzzle actually raises no serious difficulties in the notion of divine omnipotence.[1] The puzzle suggests a test of God's power—can He create a stone too heavy for Him to lift?—which, it seems, cannot fail to reveal that His power is limited. For He must, it would appear, either show His limitations by being unable to create such a stone or by being unable to lift it once He had created it.

In dealing with this puzzle, Mavrodes points out that it involves the setting of a task whose description is self-contradictory—the task of creating a stone too heavy for an omnipotent being to lift. He

From *The Philosophical Review* 73 (1964).

calls such tasks "pseudo-tasks" and he says of them: "Such pseudo-tasks, not falling within the realm of possibility, are not objects of power at all. Hence the fact that they cannot be performed implies no limit on the power of God, and hence no defect in the doctrine of omnipotence."[2] Thus his way of dealing with the puzzle relies upon the principle that an omnipotent being need not be supposed capable of performing tasks whose descriptions are self-contradictory.

Now this principle is one which Mavrodes apparently regards as self-evident, since he offers no support for it whatever except some references which indicate that it was also accepted by Saint Thomas Aquinas. I do not wish to suggest that the principle is false. Indeed, for all I know it may even be self-evident. But it happens to be a principle which has been rejected by some important philosophers.[3] Accordingly, it might be preferable to have an analysis of the puzzle in question which does not require the use of this principle. And in fact, such an analysis is easy to provide.

Suppose, then, that God's omnipotence enables Him to do even what is logically impossible and that He actually creates a stone too heavy for Him to lift. The critic of the notion of divine omnipotence is quite mistaken if he thinks that this supposition plays into his hands. What the critic wishes to claim, of course, is that when God has created a stone which He cannot lift He is then faced with a task beyond His ability and is therefore seen to be limited in power. But this claim is not justified.

For why should God not be able to perform the task in question? To be sure, it is a task—the task of lifting a stone which He cannot lift—whose description is self-contradictory. But if God is supposed capable of performing one task whose description is self-contradictory—that of creating the problematic stone in the first place—why should He not be supposed capable of performing another—that of lifting the stone? After all, is there any greater trick in performing two logically impossible tasks than there is in performing one?

If an omnipotent being can do what is logically impossible, then he can not only create situations which he cannot handle but also, since he is not bound by the limits of consistency, he can handle situations which he cannot handle.

Notes

1. George Mavrodes, "Some Puzzles Concerning Omnipotence," *The Philosophical Review* 72 (1963), 221–23.

2. *Ibid.,* p. 223.

3. Descartes, for instance, who in fact thought it blasphemous to maintain that God can do only what can be described in a logically coherent way: "The truths of mathematics . . . were established by God and entirely depend on Him, as much as do all the rest of His creatures. Actually, it would be to speak of God as a Jupiter or Saturn and to subject Him to the Styx and to the Fates, to say that these truths are independent of Him. . . . You will be told that if God established these truths He would be able to change them, as a king does his laws; to which it is necessary to reply that this is correct. . . . In general we can be quite certain that God can do whatever we are able to understand, but not that He cannot do what we are unable to understand. For it would be presumptuous to think that our imagination extends as far as His power" (letter to Mersenne, 15 April 1630). "God was as free to make it false that all the radii of a circle are equal as to refrain from creating the world" (letter to Mersenne, 27 May 1630). "I would not even dare to say that God cannot arrange that a mountain should exist without a valley, or that one and two should not make three; but I only say that He has given me a mind of such a nature that I cannot conceive a mountain without a valley or a sum of one and two which would not be three, and so on, and that such things imply contradictions in my conception" (letter to Arnauld, 29 July 1648). "As for the difficulty in conceiving how it was a matter of freedom and indifference to God to make it true that the three angles of a triangle should equal two right angles, or generally that contradictions should not be able to be together, one can easily remove it by considering that the power of God can have no limit. . . . God cannot have been determined to make it true that contradictions cannot be together, and consequently He could have been determined to make it true that contradictions cannot be together, and consequently he could have done the contrary" (letter to Mesland, 2 May 1644).

IV.C.4 Omnipotence and God's Ability to Sin

NELSON PIKE

Nelson Pike is professor of philosophy at the University of California at Irvine. Starting with an important distinction between the use of God as a title and its use as a name, Pike argues that God's omnipotence is not an essential property and that the being who is called "God" could sin if he so desired. However, "the individual that is God cannot sin in that sinning would be contrary to a firm and stable feature of his nature."

In the first chapter of the *Epistle of James* (verse 13) it is said that "God cannot be tempted by evil." This idea recurs in the confessional literature of the Christian tradition,[1] and is stated in its fullest form in the theological doctrine of God's *impeccability*.[2] God is not only free from sin, He is incapable of moral deviation. God not only does not sin, He *cannot* sin. This is generally held to be part of what is communicated in the claim that God is perfectly good. On the surface, at least, this doctrine appears to be in conflict with the traditional Christian doctrine of divine omnipotence. An omnipotent being is one that can do all things possible. But, surely, it is possible to sin. Men do this sort of thing all the time. It would thus appear that if God is perfectly good (and thus impeccable), He cannot sin; and if God is omnipotent (and thus can do all things possible), He can sin.

This argument appears to be sophistical. We are tempted to dismiss it with a single comment, viz., it involves an equivocation on the model element in the statement "God can (cannot) sin." In the long run, I think (and shall try to show) that this single remark is correct. But that's in the long run; and in the interim there is a complicated and interesting terrain that has not yet been adequately explored. In this paper I shall discuss this matter in detail. After

Reprinted from the *American Philosophical Quarterly* 6 (1969), 208–16, by permission of the author and the editor.

working through what I judge to be a number of conceptual tangles that have accumulated in this literature on this topic, I shall end by making a suggestion as to how the various senses of "God can (cannot) sin" ought to be sorted out.

I

I shall begin by identifying three assumptions that will work importantly in the discussion to follow.

First, I shall assume that within the discourse of the Christian religion, the term "God" is a descriptive expression having an identifiable meaning. It is not, e.g., a proper name. As part of this first assumption, I shall suppose, further, that "God" is a very special type of descriptive expression—what I shall call a *title*. A title is a term used to mark a certain position or value-status as does, e.g., "Caesar" in the sentence "Hadrian is Caesar." To say that Hadrian is Caesar is to say that Hadrian occupies a certain governmental position; more specifically, it is to say that Hadrian is Emperor of Rome. To affirm of some individual that He is God is to affirm that that individual occupies some special position (e.g., that He is Ruler of the Universe) or that that individual has some special value-status (e.g., that He is a being a greater than which cannot be conceived).

Secondly, I shall assume that whatever the particular semantical import of the term "God" may be (i.e., whether it means, for instance, "Ruler of the Universe," "a being than which no greater can be conceived," etc.), the attribute-terms "perfectly good," "omnipotent," "omniscient," and the like, attach to it in such a way as to make the functions "If x is God, then x is perfectly good," "If x is God, then x is omnipotent," etc., necessary truths. It is a logically necessary condition of bearing the title "God," that an individual be perfectly good, omnipotent, omniscient, and so on for all of the standard attributes traditionally assigned to the Christian God. If we could assume that in order to be Emperor (as opposed to Empress) of Rome one had to be male (rather than female), then if "*x* is Caesar" means "*x* is Emperor of Rome," then "If *x* is Caesar, then *x* is male" would have the same logical status as I am assuming for "If *x* is God, then *x* is perfectly good," "If *x* is God, then *x* is omnipotent," etc.

If there is an individual (e.g., Yahweh) who occupies the position or has the value-status marked by the term "God," then that individual is perfectly good, omnipotent, omniscient, etc. If He were not, then He could not (logically) occupy the position or have the value-status in question. However, with respect to the predicate "perfectly good," I shall assume that any individual possessing the attribute named by this phrase might not (logically) have possessed that attribute. This assumption entails that any individual who occupies the position or who has the value-status indicated by the term "God" might not (logically) have held that position or had that status. It should be noticed that this third assumption covers only a *logical* possibility. I am not assuming that there is any real (i.e., material) possibility that Yahweh (if He exists) is not perfectly good. I am assuming only that the hypothetical function "If *x* is *Yahweh,* then *x* is perfectly good" differs from the hypothetical function "If *x* is *God,* then *x* is perfectly good" in that the former, unlike the latter, does not formulate a necessary truth. With Job, one might at least *entertain* the idea that Yahweh is not perfectly good. This is at least a *consistent* conjecture even though to assert such a thing would be to deny a well-established part of the Faith.[3]

I now want to make two further preliminary comments—one about the predicate "omnipotent" and one about the concept of moral responsibility.

Preanalytically, to say that a given individual is omnipotent is to say that that individual has unlimited power. This is usually expressed in religious discourse with the phrase "infinite power." St. Thomas explicated the intuitive content of this idea as follows: "God is called omnipotent because He can do all things that are possible absolutely.[4] As traditionally understood, St. Thomas' formula must be given a relatively restricted interpretation. The permissive verb "do" in "do all things possible is usually replaced with one of a range of more specific verbs such as "create," "bring about," "effect,"

"make-to-be," "produce," etc.[5] God's omnipotence is thus to be thought of as creative-power only. It is not to be understood as the ability to *do* anything at all, e.g., it is not to be interpreted as including the ability to swim the English Channel or ride a bicycle. God is omnipotent in that He can create, bring about, effect, make-to-be, produce, etc., anything possible absolutely. For St. Thomas, something is "possible absolutely" when its description is logically consistent. Thus, on the finished analysis, God is omnipotent insofar as he can bring about any consistently describable object or state of affairs. In his article on "omnipotence" in the *Catholic Encyclopedia,*[6] J. A. McHugh analyzes the notion in this way. It seems clear from the context of this piece that McHugh meant to be reformulating St. Thomas' view of the matter. I might add that I think this restricted interpretation of the preanalytical notion of infinite power is an acurate portrayal of the way this concept works in the ordinary as well as in most of the technical (theological) discourse of the Christian religion.

Now, let us suppose that an innocent child suffers a slow and torturous death by starvation. Let it be true that this event was avoidable and that no greater good was served by its occurrence. Let it also be true that neither the child (or its parents) committed an offense for which it (or its parents) could be righteously punished. This is a consistently describable state of affairs (whether or not it ever occurred). I think it is clear that an individual that knowingly brought this state of affairs about would be morally reprehensible.

We can now formulate the problem under discussion in this paper more rigorously than above. God is omnipotent. When read hypothetically, this statement formulates a necessary truth. On the analysis of "omnipotent" with which we are working, it follows that God (if He exists) can bring about any consistently describable state of affairs. However, God is perfectly good. Again, when read hypothetically, this statement formulates a necessary truth. Further, an individual would not qualify as perfectly good if he were to act in a morally reprehensible way. Thus, the statement "God acts in a morally reprehensible way" is logically incoherent. This is to say that "God sins" is a logical contradiction.[7] Hence, some consistently describable states of affairs are such that God (being perfectly good) could not bring them about.[8] The problem, then, is this: If God is both omnipotent and perfectly good, there are at least some consistently describable states of affairs that He both can and cannot bring about. There would thus appear to be a logical conflict in the claim that God is both omnipotent and perfectly good.

I think it is worth noting that the problem just exposed is not the same as the classical theological problem of evil. The problem of evil is generally formulated as follows: Evil exists. If God exists and is omnipotent, He could have prevented evil if He had wanted to. If God exists and is perfectly good, He would have wanted to. Since evil in fact exists, it follows that God does not exist. This argument is supposed to point up a conflict between the attribute of perfect goodness and the attribute of omnipotence. But the conflict is not of a rigorous sort. So far as this argument goes, it is logically possible for there to exist a being who is both perfectly good and omnipotent. The argument is supposed to show only that since it is contingently true that evil exists, it is contingently false that omnipotence and perfect goodness are possessed by a single individual. However, the problem we are now discussing has a sharper report than this. The argument generating this latter is supposed to show that there is a direct logical conflict between the attribute of perfect goodness and the attribute of omnipotence. No contingent premiss is employed (such as, e.g., that evil exists) and the conclusion drawn is that it is logically impossible (not just contingently false) that there exists an individual who is both omnipotent and perfectly good.

II

In reply to objection 2, article 3, question 25, Part I of the *Summa Theologica,* St. Thomas Aquinas writes as follows[9]

> To sin is to fall short of a perfect action; hence to be able to sin is to be able to fall short in action, which is repugnant to omnipotence. Therefore, it is that God

cannot sin, because of his omnipotence. Now, it is true that the philosopher says that *God can deliberately do what is evil.* But this must be understood either on condition, the antecedent of which is impossible—as, for instance, if we were to say that God can do evil things if He will. For there is no reason why a conditional proposition should not be true, though both the antecedent and the consequent are impossible; as if one were to say: *If a man is an ass, he has four feet.* Or, he may be understood to mean that God can do some things which now seem to be evil: which, however, if He did them, would then be good. Or he is, perhaps, speaking after the common manner of the pagans, who thought that men became gods, like Jupiter or Mercury.

In this passage St. Thomas offers three suggestions as to how the problem we are discussing might be solved. (I do not count the suggestion made in the last sentence of this passage because it is clear that St. Thomas is not here talking about *God* but about individuals such as Jupiter or Mercury who are mistakenly thought to be God by certain misguided pagans.) Let us look at these three suggestions:

(A) St. Thomas begins with the claim that "to sin is to fall short of a perfect action." He then says that an omnipotent being cannot fall short in action. The conclusion is that God cannot sin because He is omnipotent. Essentially this same reasoning is developed in slightly more detail in the seventh chapter of St. Anselm's *Proslogium.* Anselm says:[10]

> But how art Thou omnipotent, if Thou are not capable of all things? or, if Thou canst not be corrupted and canst not lie . . . how are Thou capable of all things? Or else to be capable of these things is not power but impotence. For he who is capable of these things is capable of what is not for his good, and of what he ought not to do and the more capable of them he is, the more power have adversity and perversity against him; and the less has he himself against these.

Anselm concludes that since God is omnipotent, adversity and perversity have no power against Him and He is not capable of anything through impotence. Therefore, since God is omnipotent, He is not capable of performing morally reprehensible actions.

This argument is interesting. Both Thomas and Anselm agree that God is unable to sin. Their effort is to show that instead of being in conflict with the claim that God is omnipotent, the assignment of this inability is a direct consequence of this latter claim.

However, I think that the reasoning fails. Let us agree that to the extent that an individual is such that "adversity and perversity" can prevail against him, to that extent is he weak—*morally* weak. He is then capable of "falling short in action," i.e., of doing "what he ought not to do." So far as I can see, an individual that is able to bring about any consistently describable state of affairs might well be morally weak. I can find no conceptual difficulty in the idea of a diabolical omnipotent being. Creative-power and moral strength are readily discernible concepts. If this is right, then it does not follow from the claim that God is omnipotent that He is unable to act in a morally reprehensible way. In fact, as was set out in the original statement of the problem, quite the opposite conclusion seems to be warranted. If a being is able to bring about *any* consistently describable state of affairs, it would seem that he should be able to bring about states of affairs the production of which would be morally reprehensible. St. Thomas' first suggestion thus seems to be ineffective as a solution to the problem we are confronting. (I shall have something more to say on this topic in the fourth section of this paper.)

(B) The Philosopher says that God can deliberately do what is evil. Looking for a way of understanding this remark whereby it can be squared with his own view on the matter, St. Thomas suggests that what Aristotle may have meant is that the individual that is God can do evil *if He wants to.* Thomas adds that this last statement might be true even if it is impossible that God should want to do evil and even if it is also impossible that he can do evil. The point seems to be that although the statements "The individual that is God wants to do evil" and "The individual that is God can do evil" are false (or impossible), the conditional statement containing the first of these statements as the antecedent and the second of these statements as the consequent, might nonetheless be true.

Consider the statement: "Jones has an ace in his hand if he wants to play it." This statement has the surface grammar of a conditional, but it is not a conditional. The item mentioned in the "if . . ." clause does not condition the item described in the rest of the statement. If Jones has an ace in his hand, he has an ace in his hand whether or not he wants

to play it. What, then, does the "if . . ." clause do in this statement? I think that it serves as a way of recording a certain indeterminacy as to what will be done about (or, with respect to) the unconditional fact described in the rest of the statement. Whether or not this last remark is precisely right, the major point to be seen here is this: The statement "Jones has an ace in his hand if he wants to play it" is false if the statement "Jones has an ace in his hand" is false. We are here dealing with a use of "if . . ." that does not fit the analysis usually given conditional statements such as "I shall be nourished if I eat."

Now consider the statement: "Jones can wiggle his ear if he wants to." I think that this is another instance in which "if . . ." operates in a nonconditional capacity. If Jones has the ability to wiggle his ear, he has the ability whether or not he wants to wiggle his ear. The question of whether he wants to wiggle his ear is independent of whether he has the ability to do so. As in the case above, what the "if . . ." clause adds in this statement is not a condition on the claim that Jones has an ability. It serves as a way of recording the idea that there is some indeterminacy as to whether the ability that Jones has will be exercised. But again, I am less concerned with whether this last remark about the function of the "if . . ." clause is precisely right than I am with the relation between the truth values of "Jones can wiggle his ear if he wants to" and "Jones can wiggle his ear." In this case, as above, if Jones does not have the ability to wiggle his ear, then the statement "Jones can wiggle his ear if he wants to" is false. If the second of the above statements is false, then the first is false too.

St. Thomas says that the statement "God can sin if He wants to" is true. He adds that both the antecedent and the consequent of this conditional are "impossible." The trouble here, I think, is that "God can sin if He wants to" is not a conditional statement; and the most important point to be seen in this connection is that this statement is false if its component "God can sin" is false. But, St. Thomas clearly holds that "God can sin" is false (or impossible)—he says that God's inability to sin is a consequence of the fact that He is omnipotent. The conclusion must be that "God can sin if He wants to" is also false (or impossible). Thomas has not provided a way of understanding The Philosopher's claim that God can deliberately do what is evil. As long as St. Thomas insists that God does not have the ability to sin (which, he says, follows from the claim that God is omnipotent) he must deny that God can sin if He wants to. He must then reject The Philosopher's claim that God can deliberately do what is evil if this latter means that God can sin if He wants to.

(C) Still looking for a way of understanding the idea that God can deliberately do what is evil, St. Thomas' next suggestion is that God can do things which seem evil to us but which are such that if God did them, they would not be evil. I think that there are at least two ways of understanding this comment.

First, Thomas may be suggesting that God has the ability to bring about states of affairs that are, in fact, good, but which seem evil to us due to our limited knowledge, sympathy, moral insight, etc. However, even if we were to agree that this is true, Thomas could draw no conclusion as regards the starving-child situation described earlier. We have specified this situation in such a way that it not only *seems* evil to us, but *is* evil in fact. We have included in our description of this case that the child suffers intensely; that this suffering is not deserved and that it might have been avoided. We have added that the suffering does not contribute to a greater good. Thus, this line of reasoning does not really help with the major problem we are discussing in this paper. We still have a range of consistently describable states of affairs that God (being perfectly good) cannot bring about. We thus still have reason to think that God (being perfectly good) is not omnipotent.

Secondly, St. Thomas may be suggesting that God has the ability to bring about *any* consistently describable states of affairs (including the starving-child situation), but that if *He* were to bring about such a situation, it would no longer count as evil. Let "evil" cover any situation which is such that if one were to (knowingly) bring it about (though it is avoidable), that individual would be morally reprehensible. The view we are now considering requires that we append a special theory about the meanings of the *other* value-terms involved in our

discussion. In particular, it requires that when applied to God, the expressions "not morally reprehensible" and "perfectly good" be assigned meanings other than the ones they have when used to characterize individuals other than God. If a man were knowingly to bring about the starving-child situation, he would be morally reprehensible. He could no longer be described as perfectly good. But (so the argument goes) if God were to bring about the same situation, He might still count as perfectly good (not morally reprehensible) in the special senses of "not morally reprehensible" and "perfectly good" that apply *only* to God.

I have two comments to make about this second way of understanding St. Thomas' claim that God can do things that seem evil to us but which are such that if He did them, they would not be evil.

First, in my opinion the view we are now entertaining about the theological use of "perfectly good" and "not morally reprehensible" is one that was decisively criticized by Duns Scotus, Bishop Berkeley, and John Stuart Mill.[11] If God were to bring about circumstances such as the starving-child situation, He would be morally reprehensible and thus not perfectly good in the ordinary senses of these phrases. If we now contrive some special phrases (retaining the tabletures "not morally reprehensible" and "perfectly good") that might apply to God though He produces the situation in question, this will be of no special interest. Whatever *else* can be said of God, if He were to bring about the starving-child situation, He would not be an appropriate object of the *praise* we ordinarily convey with the phrase "perfectly good." He would be an appropriate object of the *blame* we ordinarily convey with the phrase "morally reprehensible." We might put this point as follows: If we deny that God is perfectly good in the ordinary sense of "perfectly good," and if we cover this move by introducing a technical, well-removed, sense of "perfectly good" that can apply to God though He brings about circumstances such as the starving-child situation, it may appear that we have solved the problem under discussion in this paper, but we haven't. We have eliminated conflict by agreeing that God lacks one of the "perfections," i.e., one of the qualities the possession of which makes an individual better (more praiseworthy) than he would otherwise be. Unless a being is perfectly good in the *ordinary* sense of "perfectly good," that being is not as praiseworthy as he might otherwise be. It was the sense of "perfectly good" that connects with the idea of being morally praiseworthy (in the ordinary sense) that gave rise to the problem in the first place. Surely, it is this sense of "perfectly good" that religious people have in mind when they characterize God as perfectly good.

The second remark I should like to make about this second interpretation of St. Thomas' third suggestion is that the view assigned to St. Thomas in this interpretation is one that he would most likely reject. I shall need a moment to develop this point.[12]

Consider the word "triangle" as it occurs in the discourse of geometry. Compare it with "triangle" as it is used in the discourse of carpentry or woodworking. Within the discourse of geometry, the criteria governing the use of this term are more strict than are the criteria governing its use in the discourse of carpentry. The geometrical figure is an exemplary (i.e., perfect) version of the shape embodied in the triangular block of wood. We reach an understanding of the geometrical shape by correcting imperfections (i.e., irregularities) in the shape of the triangular block. Now, let's ask whether "triangle" has the same meaning in the two cases. We might answer this question in either way. Once the relation between the criteria governing its use in the two cases is made clear, no one would be confused if we were to say that "triangle" has the same meaning in the two cases, and no one would be confused if we were to say that "triangle" has different meaning in the two cases. Regarding the relation between the criteria, the following point seems to me to be of considerable importance: If a block of wood is triangular, it has three angles that add up (roughly) to 180 degrees and its sides are (roughly) straight. *At least this much* is implied with respect to a geometrical figure when one characterizes it as a triangle. By this I mean that if one could find reasons sufficient for rejecting the claim that a given thing is a triangle as "triangle" is used in the discourse of carpentry (suppose that one of its sides is visibly curved or suppose it has four

angles), these same reasons would be sufficient for rejecting the claim that the thing in question is a triangle as "triangle" is used in the discourse of geometry. In fact, more than this can be said. If one could find slight irregularities in the shape of a thing that would cause some hesitation or prompt some reservation about whether it is a triangle as "triangle" is used in the discourse of carpentry, such irregularities would be sufficient to establish that the thing in question is not a triangle as "triangle" is used in the discourse of geometry.

According to St. Thomas, finite things are caused by God. They thus bear a "likeness" to God. God's attributes are exemplary versions of the attributes possessed by finite things. We reach whatever understanding we have of God's attributes, by removing "imperfections" that attend these qualities when possessed by finite things.[13] With respect to the predicate "good," St. Thomas writes as follows in the *Summa Theologica* (Pt. 1, Q. 6, A. 4):[14]

> Each being is called good because of the divine goodness, the first exemplar principle as well as the efficient and telic cause of all goodness. Yet it is nonetheless the case that each being is called good because of a likeness of the divine goodness by which it is denominated.

Again, in *questiones disputatae de veritate* (XXI, 4), St. Thomas says:

> Every agent is found to produce effects which resemble it. Hence, if the first goodness is the efficient cause of all things, it must imprint its likeness upon things which it produces. Thus each thing is called good because of an intrinsic goodness impressed upon it, and yet is further denominated good because of the first goodness which is the exemplar and efficient cause of all created goodness.

Shall we say that "good" has the same meaning when applied to God as it has when applied to things other than God (e.g., Socrates)? As above, it seems to me that the answer we give to this question is unimportant once we get this far into the discussion. We might say that "good" has the same meaning in the two cases, and we might say that it has different meanings in the two cases. We might even say (as St. Thomas sometimes says) that we are here dealing with a case in which "good" is "midway between" having the same meaning and having different meanings in the two cases. However, as above, the following point has importance regardless of how one answers the question about same or different meanings. When St. Thomas affirms that God is good, I think he means to be saying at *least as much* about God as one would say about, e.g., Socrates, if one were to affirm that Socrates is good. A study of "good" in nontheological contexts reveals at least the minimum implications of the corresponding predication statements relating to God. If we could find reasons sufficient for rejecting the claim that a given thing is good as "good" is used in discourse about finite agents, these same reasons would be sufficient for rejecting the claim that the thing in question is good as "good" is used in discourse about the nature of God. In fact, if we could find moral irregularities sufficient to cause hesitations or prompt reservations about whether a thing is good as "good" is used in discourse about finite agents, these irregularities would be sufficient to establish that the agent under consideration is not good as "good" is used in the discourse of theology.

So far as I can see, St. Thomas would not endorse a technical, well-removed sense of the phrase "perfectly good" that could apply to God even if God were to bring about circumstances or states of affairs the production of which would be morally reprehensible (in the ordinary sense of "morally reprehensible"). When St. Thomas says that God is good, he means to be saying that God possesses the exemplary version of the quality assigned to Socrates in the sentence "Socrates is good." This is to say that while Socrates is good, God is *perfectly* good. But on this understanding of the matter, God could not be perfectly good were He to bring about the starving-child situation described earlier. If Socrates were to bring about such a situation, we would probably refuse to describe him as "good." At the very least, we would surely have hesitations or reservations concerning his moral goodness. But if such an action would be sufficient to cause hesitations concerning an application of "good" in discourse about finite agents, this same action would be sufficient to *defeat* an application of "good" in discourse about the nature of God. In this latter context, "good" means "*perfectly* good." The logic

of this phrase will not tolerate even a minor moral irregularity.

III

I want now to discuss an approach to our problem that is very different from any of those suggested by St. Thomas. It is an approach taken by J. A. McHugh in the *Encyclopedia* article mentioned above. I think we can best get at the center of McHugh's thinking if we start with a review of that side of the problem generated by the concept of perfect goodness.

God is perfectly good. This is a necessary statement. If a being is perfectly good, that being does not bring about objects or states of affairs the production of which would be morally reprehensible. This, too, is a necessary truth. Thus, the statement "God brings about objects or states of affairs the production of which would be morally reprehensible" is logically contradictory. It follows that God cannot bring about such states of affairs. But, McHugh argues, this should not be taken as a reason for denying God's omnipotence. As St. Thomas has pointed out, a being may be omnipotent and yet not be able to do an act whose description is logically contradictory. (A being may be omnipotent though he is not able to make a round-square.) Since the claim that God acts in a morally reprehensible way is logically contradictory, God's inability to perform such acts does not constitute a limitation of power.

Consider the following argument: The term "Gid" is the title held by the most efficient of those who make only leather sandals. "Gid makes leather belts" is thus a logical contradiction. It follows that the individual that is Gid cannot make leather belts. But Gid may still be omnipotent. Though He does not have the ability to make leather belts, our analysis of "omnipotence" requires only that an omnipotent being be able to do an act whose description is logically consistent and "Gid makes leather belts" is logically inconsistent. Thus, Gid's inability to make leather belts does not constitute a limitation on his power.

I think it is plain that this last argument is deficient since its conclusion is absurd. I think, too, that in this case, two difficulties are forced pretty close to the surface.

First, the description of the kind of object that Gid is (allegedly) unable to make (viz., leather belts) is not logically contradictory. What is contradictory is the claim that *Gid makes them.* But our definition of "omnipotent" requires only that the *state of affairs* brought about be consistently describable (excluding, therefore, round squares). It does not require that a statement in which it is claimed that a given individual brings it about be consistent. Thus, if Gid does not have the ability to produce leather belts, he is not omnipotent on St. Thomas' definition of "omnipotent." If it follows from the definition of "Gid" that the individual who bears this title cannot make leather belts; and if this entails that the individual in question does not have the creative-ability to make belts, the conclusion must be that, by definition, the individual who bears this title is a limited being. I think the same kind of conclusion must be drawn in the case of God's ability to sin. If it follows from the definition of "God" that the individual bearing this title cannot bring about objects or states of affairs the production of which would be morally reprehensible; and if it follows from this that the individual bearing this title does not have the creative power necessary to bring about such states of affairs though they are consistently desirable; the conclusion is that the individual who is God is not omnipotent on the analysis of "omnipotent" that we are supposing. The fact (if it is a fact) that this creative limitation is built into the definition of "God" making "God sins" a logical contradiction does not disturb this conclusion. The upshot is, simply, that the term "God" has been so specified that an individual qualifying for this title could not be omnipotent. (Of course, this is awkward because it is also a condition of bearing this title that the individual in question be omnipotent.)

The second difficulty in the argument about Gid is this: The term "Gid" has been defined in such a way that "Gid makes leather belts" is logically contradictory. The conclusion drawn is that Gid *cannot* make belts. What this means is that if some individual makes leather belts, this is logically sufficient to assure that the individual in question does not bear the title "Gid." But it does not follow from this (as is supposed in the argument) that the individual who is Gid does not have the *ability* to make leather belts. All we can conclude is that if he does have this ability, it is one that he does not *exercise.* Thus, as is affirmed in the argument, the individual who is Gid might be omnipotent though he cannot make leather belts (and be Gid). If we suppose that he is omnipotent, we must conclude that he has the ability to make belts; but since, by hypothesis, the individual in question is Gid, we know (analytically) that he does not exercise this ability. Again, I think the same is true with respect to the argument about God's inability to sin. The term "God" has been so specified that the individual who is God *cannot* sin and be God. But it will not follow from this that the individual who is God does not have the *ability* to sin. He might have the creative power necessary to bring about states of affairs the production of which would be morally reprehensible. He is perfectly good (and thus God) insofar as He does not exercise this power.

IV

If we collect together a number of threads developed in the preceding discussions, I think we shall have enough to provide at least a tentative solution to the problem we have been discussing. I shall proceed by distinguishing three ways in which the statement "God cannot sin" might be understood.

"God cannot sin" might mean: "If a given individual sins, it follows logically that the individual does not bear the title 'God.'" In this case, the "cannot" in "cannot sin" expresses logical impossibility. The sentence as a whole might be rewritten as follows: $N(x)$ (If x is God then x does not sin.) On the assumptions we are making in this paper, this statement is true. We have supposed that the meaning of the title term "God" is such that it is a logically necessary condition of bearing this title that one be perfectly good and thus that one not perform actions that are morally reprehensible.

Secondly, "God cannot sin" might mean that if a given individual is God, that individual does not have the ability to sin, i.e., He does not have the creative power necessary to bring about states of affairs the production of which would be morally reprehensible, such as, e.g., the starving-child situation described earlier. In this case, the "cannot" in "cannot sin" does not express logical impossibility. It expresses a material concept—that of a limitation of creative-power (as in, e.g., "I cannot make leather sandals"). On St. Thomas' analysis of "omnipotence" if the individual who is God (Yahweh) cannot sin in this sense, He is not omnipotent. Further, I think there is strong reason to suspect that if the individual that is God (Yahweh) cannot sin in this sense, He is not perfectly good either. Insofar as the phrase "perfectly good" applies to the individual that is God (Yahweh) as an expression of praise—warranted by the fact that this individual does not sin—God could not be perfectly good if He does not have the ability to sin. If an individual does not have the creative-power necessary to bring about evil states of affairs, he cannot be praised (morally) for failing to bring them about. Insofar as I do not have the physical strength necessary to crush my next door neighbor with my bare hands, it is not to my credit (morally) that I do not perform this heinous act.

Thirdly, "God cannot sin" might mean that although the individual that is God (Yahweh) has the ability (i.e., the creative power necessary) to bring about states of affairs the production of which would be morally reprehensible, His nature or character is such as to provide material assurance that He will not act in this way. This is the sense in which one might say that Jones, having been reared to regard animals as sensitive and precious friends, just *cannot* be cruel to animals. Here "cannot" is not to be analyzed in terms of the notion of logical impossibility and it does not mark a limitation on Jones's physical power—he may be physically able to kick the kitten. It is used to express the idea that Jones is *strongly disposed* to be kind to animals or at least to avoid actions that would be cruel. We have a special locution in English that covers this idea. When we say that Jones cannot be cruel to animals, what we mean is that Jones cannot *bring*

himself to be cruel to animals. On this third analysis of "God cannot sin," the claim conveyed in this form of words is that the individual that is God (Yahweh) is of such character that he cannot bring himself to act in a morally reprehensible way. God is strongly disposed to perform only morally acceptable actions.

Look back for a moment over the ground we have covered.

McHugh noticed that the statement "God sins" is logically incoherent. He thus (rightly) concluded that God cannot sin. He was here affirming that the semantical import of the title term "God" is such that an individual could not (logically) bear this title and be a sinner. McHugh's conclusion ("God cannot sin") was thus intended in the first sense just mentioned. But McHugh then went on to suppose that God cannot sin in a sense of this phrase that connects with the notion of omnipotence. This is the second sense mentioned above. This conclusion was not warranted. The individual who bears the title "God" (Yahweh) might have the creative power necessary to bring about objects or states of affairs the production of which would be morally reprehensible even though "God sins" is logically contradictory. The conclusion is, simply, that if an individual bears the title "God," He does not exercise this creative-power.

St. Thomas and St. Anselm said that God cannot sin in that "adversity and perversity cannot prevail against Him." This appears to be the claim put forward in the *Epistle of James* 1:13—the claim embodied in the theological doctrine of God's impeccability—viz., "God cannot be tempted by evil." The individual that is God has a very special kind of strength—moral strength, or strength of character. He is, as we say, "above temptation." Both Thomas and Anselm concluded that God's inability to sin has a direct connection with the notion of omnipotence. It is because God is omnipotent that He is unable to sin. This line of reasoning confuses the second and third senses of the statement "God cannot sin." If we say that the individual who is God cannot sin in this second sense (i.e., in the sense that connects with the idea of creative power and thus with the standard notion of omnipotence) this is not to assign that individual strength. It is to assign Him a very definite limitation. The strength-concept in this cluster of ideas is the notion of not being able to *bring oneself* to sin. God has a special strength of character. But this latter concept is expressed in the third sense of "God cannot sin." As I argued earlier, this third sense appears to have no logical connection with the idea of having or lacking the creative power to bring about consistently describable states of affairs. It thus appears to have no logical connection to the notion of omnipotence as this latter concept is explicated by St. Thomas.

The individual that is God cannot sin and bear the title "God." The individual that is God cannot sin in that sinning would be contrary to a firm and stable feature of His nature. These claims are compatible with the idea that the individual that is God has the ability (i.e., the creative power necessary) to bring about states of affairs the production of which would be morally reprehensible. All we need add is that there is complete assurance that He will not exercise this ability and that if He did exercise this ability (which is logically possible but materially excluded), He would not bear the title "God." Further, if God is to be omnipotent in St. Thomas' sense of "omnipotent," and if God is to be perfectly good in a sense of this phrase that expresses praise for the fact that He refrains from sinful actions, this appears to be the conclusion that *must* be drawn.

Notes

1. See, for example, the *Westminister Confession,* ch. V, sect IV and the *Longer Catechism of the Eastern Church,* sects. 156–57.

2. See the *Catholic Encyclopedia* (New York, Robert Appleton Co., 1967).

3. The truth of this assumption is argued at some length by C. B. Martin in the fourth chapter of his *Religious Belief* (Ithaca, Cornell Press, 1964).

4. *Summa Theologica,* Pt. 1, Q. 25, a 3. This passage taken from *The Basic Writings of St. Thomas Aquinas,* ed. by Anton Pegis, p. 263.

5. These verbs are sometimes called "factitive verbs."

6. New York, Robert Appleton Co., 1911.

7. There is probably some distinction to be made between acting in a morally reprehensible way and sinning. However, for purposes of this discussion, I shall treat these concepts as one.

8. I am here assuming that if God brings about a given circumstance, He does so *knowingly*. God could not bring about a given circumstance by mistake. I think this follows from the idea that God is omniscient.

9. This passage is taken from *The Basic Writings of St. Thomas Aquinas,* op. cit., p. 264.

10. This passage is taken from S. N. Deane, *St. Anselm* (LaSalle, Open Court, 1958), p. 14.

11. See Scotus' *Oxford Commentary on the Sentences of Peter Lombard,* Q.II ("Man's Natural Knowledge of God"), second statement, argument IV; Berkeley's *Alcephron,* Dialogue IV, sects. 16–22 (especially sect. 17); and J. S. Mill's *An Examination of Sir William Hamilton's Philosophy,* ch. 6. What follows in this paragraph is what I think constitutes the center of these three discussions.

12. The next two paragraphs are taken almost without change from the Introduction to my book *God and Timelessness* (London, Routledge and Kegan-Paul, 1969). What I say here about the relation between "triangle" as used in the discourse of geometry and "triangle" as used in the discourse of carpentry is very much like a thesis developed by John Stuart Mill in the text mentioned above.

13. In the *Summa Theologica* (Pt. I, Q. 14, a.1) St. Thomas says: "Because perfections flowing from God to creatures exist in a higher state in God Himself, whenever a name taken from any created perfection is attributed to God, there must be separated from its signification anything that belongs to the imperfect mode proper to creatures." (Quoted from *The Basic Writings of St. Thomas Aquinas, op. cit.,* p. 136.)

14. Both of the following passages were translated by George P. Klubertanz, S. J., *Thomas Aquinas on Analogy* (Chicago, Loyola Press, 1960), p. 55. For a good analysis of St. Thomas' views on the topic of theological predication, see the whole of Klubertanz' discussion in ch. III. For an enlightening discussion of how poorly St. Thomas has been understood on this topic (even by his most illustrious interpreters) see Klubertanz' remarks in ch. I and Berkeley's discussion of St. Thomas in *Alcephron,* IV, sects. 20–22. According to Berkeley, St. Thomas' doctrine of "analogy by proportionality" is to be regarded as an expression of the view we are now discussing.

Bibliography for Part IV

Davis, Stephen T. *Logic and The Nature of God.* Grand Rapids, Mich.: Eerdmans, 1983. A very perceptive and lucid analysis of the attributes of God.

Geach, Peter. *Providence and Evil.* Cambridge, Mass.: Cambridge Univ. Press, 1977. An important work on the attributes of God.

Fischer, John Martin, ed. *God, Foreknowledge, and Freedom.* Palo Alto, Calif.: Stanford Univ. Press, 1989. An important collection of essays.

Hartshorne, Charles. *The Divine Reality.* New Haven, Conn.: Yale Univ. Press, 1948. A very good exposition of the process theological view of God and his attributes.

Kenny, Anthony, ed. *Aquinas: A Collection of Critical Essays.* New York: Doubleday, 1969. In this good collection Kenny's own essay on divine foreknowledge and human freedom stands out.

Kretzmann, Norman. "Omniscience and Immutability." *Journal of Philosophy* 63 (1966):409–21. A cogent article on the incoherence of the notion of immutability.

Pike, Nelson. *God and Time.* Ithaca, N.Y.: Cornell Univ. Press, 1970. A seminal work that has rightly played a central role in the debate on God's eternity.

Stump, Eleonore, and Norman Kretzmann. "Eternity." *Journal of Philosophy* 78 (August 1981): 429–58. A sophisticated defense of the traditional view of God's timeless eternity.

Swinburne, Richard. *The Coherence of Theism.* Oxford, Eng.: Oxford Univ. Press, 1977. A highly original work on the attributes of God, cogently argued.

Urban, Linwood, and Douglas Walton, eds. *The Power of God.* Oxford, Eng.: Oxford Univ. Press, 1978. The best available collection of articles on divine omnipotence.

Wierenga, Edward R. *The Nature of God: An Inquiry into Divine Attributes.* Ithaca, N.Y.: Cornell Univ. Press, 1989. A careful analysis of the attributes of God, cogently and insightfully argued.

Wolterstorff, Nicholas. "God Everlasting." In *God and the Good*, edited by C. Orlebeke and L. Smedes. Grand Rapids, Mich.: Eerdmans, 1975. Possibly the best defense of the thesis that God's eternity is temporal rather than timeless.

PART V

MIRACLES AND REVELATION

Wharp are miracles, and are they possible? Should miracles necessarily be defined as violations of the laws of nature? This notion has been disputed on the basis of the contention that in the Bible, which is the witness to the most significant alleged miracles in the Judeo-Christian tradition, there is no concept of nature as a closed system of law. For the Biblical writers, miracles signify simply an "extraordinary coincidence of a beneficial nature."[*]

This view is proposed by R. F. Holland in his article "The Miraculous," in which the following story is illustrative:

A child riding his toy motor-car strays on to an unguarded railway crossing near his house and a wheel of his car gets stuck down the side of one of the rails. An express train is due to pass with the signals in its favour and a curve in the track makes it impossible for the driver to stop his train in time to avoid any obstruction he might encounter on the crossing. The mother coming out of the house to look for her child sees him on the crossing and hears the train approaching. She runs forward shouting and waving. The little boy remains seated in his car looking downward engrossed in the task of pedaling it free. The brakes of the train are applied and it comes to rest a few feet from the child. The mother thanks God for the miracle; which she never ceases to think of as such, although, as she in due course learns, there was nothing supernatural about the manner in which the brakes of the train came to be applied. The driver had fainted, for a reason that had nothing to do with the presence of the child on the line, and the brakes were applied automatically as his hand ceased to exert pressure on the control lever. He fainted on this particular afternoon because his blood pressure had risen after an exceptionally heavy lunch during which he had quarrelled with a colleague, and the change in blood pressure caused a clot of blood to be dislodged and circulate. He fainted at the time when he did on the afternoon in question because this was the time at which the coagulation in his blood stream reached the brain.[†]

Was this a miracle, or was it not? It is if we define miracles in Fuller's biblical sense. It is not if we define them in an interventionist sense. We can certainly understand the woman's feeling on the matter, and perhaps in some mysterious way God had 'allowed' nature to run its course so that the little boy would be saved. Perhaps we need not be overly exclusionary but say that

---

[*]R. H. Fuller, *Interpreting the Miracle* (London, 1968), 8.
[†]*American Philosophical Quarterly*, 2 (1965).

if there is a God, each sense is valid: the *weaker* sense of an extraordinary coincidence and the *stronger* sense of a violation of the laws of nature. Nonetheless, what is philosophically interesting as well as controversial with regard to miracles is the stronger sense, that of a violation of the laws of nature by a divine force. It is this sense of miracles that we consider in this part of our work.

The most celebrated article ever written on miracles is by David Hume. In section 10 of *An Enquiry Concerning Human Understanding* he set forth an argument against belief in miracles that provoked a lively response in his day and has continued to be the subject of vigorous dispute up to the present day. The three articles that follow Hume's in our readings all deal with Hume's argument, so it is important that you read it carefully. Let us analyze it briefly. Hume begins his attack on miracles by appealing to the biases of his Scottish Presbyterian readers. He tells of a marvelous proof that Dr. Tillotson has devised against the Roman Catholic doctrine of transubstantiation, the doctrine that the body and blood of Christ are present in Holy Communion. Tillotson argues that because the evidence of the senses is of the highest rank and because it is evident that it must diminish in passing through the original witnesses to their disciples, the doctrine of transubstantiation is always contrary to the rules of reasoning and opposed to our sense experience.

1. Our evidence for the truth of transubstantiation is less than the evidence of our senses. (Even for the apostles this was the case, and their testimony must diminish in authority in passing from them to their disciples.)
2. A weaker evidence can never destroy a stronger. (That is, we are not justified in believing the weaker evidence over the stronger.)
3. Therefore, we are not warranted in believing in transubstantiation. (Even if the doctrine of transubstantiation were clearly revealed in the Scriptures, it would be against the rule of reason to give our assent to it.)

No doubt Hume's Protestant readers were delighted with such a sound refutation of the doctrine of transubstantiation. But the mischievous Hume now turns the knife on his readers. A wise person always proportions one's belief to the evidence, he goes on. One has an enormous amount of evidence for the laws of nature, so that any testimony to the contrary is to be seriously doubted. Although miracles, as violations of the laws of nature, are not logically impossible, we are never justified in believing in one. The skeleton of the argument contained in the reading goes something like this:

1. One ought to proportion one's belief to the evidence.
2. Sense perception is generally better evidence than testimony (if for no other reason than that valid testimony is based on another's sense experience).
3. Therefore, when there is a conflict between sense experience and testimony, one ought to believe according to sense perception.
4. Sense perception does not reveal any miracles to us (but rather the presumption of natural law prevails).
5. Therefore, we are never justified in believing in miracles, but we are justified in believing in the naturalness of all events.

Since we have enormous evidence in favor of the uniformity of nature, every testimony of a miracle must be weighed against that preponderance and be found wanting. But what if we believe that we personally have beheld a miracle? Aren't we justified in believing one in that case? No, for given the principle of induction (that every time we pursue an event *far enough*, we discover it to have a natural cause), we are still not justified in believing the event to be a miracle. Rather we ought to look further (*far enough*) until we discover the natural cause. The only exception to this rule (or "proof" against miracles) is if it would be even more miraculous for a miracle not to have occurred: "That no testimony is sufficient to establish a miracle, unless the testimony be of such a kind, that its falsehood would be more marvelous, than the fact, which it endeavors to establish; and even in that case there is a mutual destruction of argument, and the superior only gives us an assurance suitable to that degree of force, which remains, after deducting the inferior." The best we can hope for is an agnostic standoff in the matter.

But the criteria that would have to be fulfilled would be that (1) A sufficient number of witnesses of (2) good sense and education and (3) integrity and reputation would have to testify to a (4) public performance of the incident. Hume offers several putative examples of such cases and argues that the criteria are really not fulfilled in any of them.

One of the most vigorous critics of Hume has been Richard Swinburne, who in our second reading takes issue with him. Swinburne first inquires whether there could be evidence that a law of nature had been violated and, second, whether there could be evidence that the violation was due to a god. To satisfy the first inquiry, we would have to have good reason to believe that an event has occurred contrary to the predictions of a law that we had good reason to believe to be a law of nature; and furthermore we would have to have good reason to believe that events similar to the event would not occur in circumstances similar to those of the original occurrence. For if the event were repeatable, we would have to account for both events through the formulation of a law.

Swinburne gives as an illustration of a successful occurrence that of someone levitating (i.e., rising into the air and remaining there). If the event were sufficiently nonrepeatable and defied every attempt to work it into a lawlike framework, we would have good reason to believe that the event was a violation of the laws of nature. Here Hume seems to put the standards of justified belief too high, for given a high quality of witness, there is no reason for not believing that a violation of nature's laws had taken place.

But to be a miracle the violation of a natural law would have to be the work of a god, who is not a material object. What kind of evidence would we have to have to believe that a divine being had intervened in our world? Here Swinburne distinguishes between situations in which we do and in which we do not have sufficient circumstantial evidence to warrant our attributing the anomalous event to the work of an invisible deity. The circumstantial evidence must be strong before we are justified in believing that an event is a genuine miracle—for example, the case of Elijah's calling on Yahweh to send fire and consume his offering on Mt. Carmel (1 Kings 18). Such an event would be sufficiently analogous to normal human agency to justify our believing that a divine being caused it. But all this supposes that we do have some independent evidence for the existence of a divine being in the first place, which justifies our seeing anomalous events as genuine miracles.

Our third reading is "Miracles and Testimony" by the late J. L. Mackie of Oxford University, a man who loved Hume and exemplified his thought. In this revised Humean account of miracles, Mackie argues that the evidence for miracles will never in practice be very great. The argument is epistemological, not ontological. That is, while miracles may be logically possible (and may indeed have occurred), we are never justified in believing in one. The concept of a miracle is a coherent one, but, Mackie argues, the *double* burden of showing both that the event took place *and* that it violated the laws of nature will be extremely hard to lift, for "whatever tends to show that it would have been a violation of natural law tends for that very reason to make it most unlikely that it actually happened." Correspondingly, the deniers of miracles have two strategies of defense. They may argue that the event took place but wasn't a violation of a law of nature (the event simply followed an unknown law of nature); or they can admit that if the event had happened, it would indeed have been a violation of a law of nature, but for that reason, "there is a very strong presumption against its having happened, which it is most unlikely that any testimony will be able to outweigh."

In our final reading in this section, "Miracles and Revelation," Richard Swinburne takes up the matter of miracles where he left off in his previous article. There he argued, contra Hume, that miracles were possible. Here he argues that given the proviso that the existence of God is a plausible hypothesis or assumption, it is reasonable to expect that he would reveal himself in human history and that he would confirm the revelation by miracles (including predictive prophecy). Swinburne here sets forth the criteria that would have to be met were a religion to claim that it is based on that revelation.

V.1 Against Miracles

DAVID HUME

The reading by David Hume that follows is the most celebrated article ever written on miracles. In it Hume sets forth an argument against belief in miracles that provoked a lively response in his day and has continued to be the support of vigorous dispute up to the present day. Hume begins his attack on miracles by appealing to the biases of his Scottish Presbyterian readers. He tells of a marvelous proof that Dr. Tillotson has devised against the Roman Catholic doctrine of transubstantiation, the doctrine that the body and blood of Christ are present in Holy Communion. Tillotson argues that since the evidence of the senses is of the highest rank and since it is evident that it must diminish in passing through the original witnesses to their disciples, the doctrine of transubstantiation is always contrary to the rules of reasoning and opposed to our sense experience.

No doubt Hume's Protestant readers were delighted with such a sound refutation of the doctrine of transubstantiation. But the mischievous Hume now turns the knife on his readers. A wise person always proportions one's belief to the evidence, he goes on. One has an enormous amount of evidence for the laws of nature, so that any testimony to the contrary is to be seriously doubted. Although miracles, as violations of the laws of nature, are not logically impossible, we are never justified in believing in one. Since we have enormous evidence in favor of the uniformity of nature, every testimony of a miracle must be weighed against that preponderance and be found wanting.

Part I.

There is, in Dr. Tillotson's writings, an argument against the *real presence*, which is as concise, and

Reprinted from David Hume, *An Enquiry Concerning Human Understanding* (Oxford: Oxford Univ. Press, 1748). Footnotes edited.

elegant, and strong as any argument can possibly be supposed against a doctrine, so little worthy of a serious refutation. It is acknowledged on all hands, says that learned prelate, that the authority, either of the scripture or of tradition, is founded merely in the testimony of the apostles, who were eye-witnesses to those miracles of our Saviour, by which he proved his divine mission. Our evidence, then, for the truth of the *Christian* religion is less than the evidence for the truth of our senses; because, even in the first authors of our religion, it was no greater; and it is evident it must diminish in passing from them to their disciples; nor can any one rest such confidence in their testimony, as in the immediate object of his senses. But a weaker evidence can never destroy a stronger; and therefore, were the doctrine of the real presence ever so clearly revealed in scripture, it were directly contrary to the rules of just reasoning to give our assent to it. It contradicts sense, though both the scripture and tradition, on which it is supposed to be built, carry not such evidence with them as sense; when they are considered merely as external evidences, and are not brought home to every one's breast, by the immediate operation of the Holy Spirit.

Nothing is so convenient as a decisive argument of this kind, which must at least *silence* the most arrogant bigotry and superstition, and free us from their impertinent solicitations. I flatter myself, that I have discovered an argument of a like nature, which, if just, will, with the wise and learned, be an everlasting check to all kinds of superstitious delusion, and consequently, will be useful as long as the world endures. For so long, I presume, will the accounts of miracles and prodigies be found in all history, sacred and profane.

Though experience be our only guide in reasoning concerning matters of fact; it must be acknowledged, that this guide is not altogether infallible, but in some cases is apt to lead us into errors. One, who in our climate, should expect better weather in any week of June than in one of December, would reason justly, and conformably to experience; but it is certain, that he may happen, in the event, to find himself mistaken. However, we may observe, that, in such a case, he would have no cause to complain of experience; because it commonly informs us beforehand of the uncertainty, by that contrariety of events, which we may learn from a diligent observation. All effects follow not with like certainty from their supposed causes. Some events are found, in all countries and all ages, to have been constantly conjoined together: Others are found to have been more variable, and sometimes to disappoint our expectations; so that, in our reasonings concerning matter of fact, there are all imaginable degrees of assurance, from the highest certainty to the lowest species of moral evidence.

A wise man, therefore, proportions his belief to the evidence. In such conclusions as are founded on an infallible experience, he expects the event with the last degree of assurance, and regards his past experience as a full *proof* of the future existence of that event. In other cases, he proceeds with more caution: He weighs the opposite experiments: He considers which side is supported by the greater number of experiments: to that side he inclines, with doubt and hesitation; and when at last he fixes his judgement, the evidence exceeds not what we properly call *probability.* All probability, then, supposes an opposition of experiments and observations, where the one side is found to overbalance the other, and to produce a degree of evidence, proportioned to the superiority. A hundred instances or experiments on one side, and fifty on another, afford a doubtful expectation of any event; though a hundred uniform experiments, with only one that is contradictory, reasonably beget a pretty strong degree of assurance. In all cases, we must balance the opposite experiments, where they are opposite, and deduct the smaller number from the greater, in order to know the exact force of the superior evidence.

To apply these principles to a particular instance; we may observe, that there is no species of reasoning more common, more useful, and even necessary to human life, than that which is derived from the testimony of men, and the reports of eye-witnesses and spectators. This species of reasoning, perhaps, one may deny to be founded on the relation of cause and effect. I shall not dispute about a word. It will be sufficient to observe that our assurance in any argument of this kind is derived from no other principle than our observation of the veracity of human testimony, and of the usual conformity of facts to the reports of witnesses. It being a general maxim, that no objects have any discoverable connexion together, and that all the inferences, which we can draw from one to another, are founded merely on our experience of their constant and regular conjunction; it is evident, that we ought not to make an exception to this maxim in favour of human testimony, whose connexion with any event seems, in itself, as little necessary as any other. Were not the memory tenacious to a certain degree; had not men commonly an inclination to truth and a principle of probity; were they not sensible to shame, when detected in a falsehood: Were not these, I say, discovered by *experience* to be qualities, inherent in human nature, we should never repose the least confidence in human testimony. A man delirious, or noted for falsehood and villany, has no manner of authority with us.

And as the evidence, derived from witnesses and human testimony, is founded on past experience, so it varies with the experience, and is regarded either as a *proof* or a *probability*, according at the conjunction between any particular kind of report and any kind of object has been found to be constant or variable. There are a number of circumstances to be taken into consideration in all judgements of this kind; and the ultimate standard, by which we determine all disputes, that may arise concerning them, is always derived from experience and observation. Where this experience is not entirely uniform on any side, it is attended with an unavoidable contrariety in our judgements, and with the same opposition and mutual destruction of argument as in every other kind of evidence. We frequently hesitate concerning the reports of others. We balance the opposite circumstances, which cause any doubt or uncertainty; and when we discover a superiority on any side, we incline to it; but still with a diminution of assurance, in proportion to the force of its antagonist.

This contrariety of evidence, in the present case, may be derived from several different causes; from the opposition of contrary testimony; from the character or number of the witnesses; from the manner of their delivering their testimony; or from the union of all these circumstances. We entertain a suspicion concerning any matter of fact, when the witnesses contradict each other; when they are but few, or of a doubtful character; when they have an interest in what they affirm; when they deliver their testimony with hesitation, or on the contrary, with too violent asseverations. There are many other particulars of the same kind, which may diminish or destroy the force of any argument, derived from human testimony.

Suppose, for instance, that the fact, which the testimony endeavors to establish, partakes of the extraordinary and the marvelous; in that case, the evidence, resulting from the testimony, admits of a diminution, greater or less, in proportion as the fact is more or less unusual. The reason why we place any credit in witnesses and historians, is not derived from any *connexion,* which we perceive *a priori*, between testimony and reality, but because we are accustomed to find a conformity between them. But when the fact attested is such a one as has seldom fallen under our observation, here is a contest of two opposite experiences; of which the one destroys the other, as far as its force goes, and the superior can only operate on the mind by the force, which remains. The very same principle of experience, which gives us a certain degree of assurance in the testimony of witnesses, gives us also, in this case, another degree of assurance against the fact, which they endeavour to establish; from which contradiction there necessarily arises a counterpoise, and mutual destruction of belief and authority.

I should not believe such a story were it told me by Cato, was a proverbial saying in Rome, even during the lifetime of that philosophical patriot. The incredibility of a fact, it was allowed, might invalidate so great an authority.

The Indian prince, who refused to believe the first relations concerning the effects of frost, reasoned justly; and it naturally required very strong testimony to engage his assent to facts, that arose from a state of nature, with which he was unacquainted, and which bore so little analogy to those events, of which we had had constant and uniform experience. Though they were not contrary to his experience, they were not conformable to it.

But in order to increase the probability against the testimony of witnesses, let us suppose, that the fact, which they affirm, instead of being only marvelous, is really miraculous; and suppose also, that the testimony considered apart and in itself, amounts to an entire proof; in that case, there is proof against proof, of which the strongest must prevail, but still with a diminution of its force, in proportion to that of its antagonist.

A miracle is a violation of the laws of nature; and as a firm and unalterable experience has established these laws, the proof against a miracle, from the very nature of the fact, is as entire as any argument from experience can possibly be imagined. Why is it more than probable, that all men must die; that lead cannot, of itself, remain suspended in the air; that fire consumes wood, and is extinguished by water; unless it be, that these events are found agreeable to the laws of nature, and there is required a violation of these laws, or in other words, a miracle to prevent them? Nothing is esteemed a miracle, if it ever happen in the common course of nature. It is no miracle that a man, seemingly in good health, should die on a sudden: because such a kind of death, though more unusual than any other, has yet been frequently observed to happen. But it is a miracle, that a dead man should come to life; because that has never been observed in any age or country. There must, therefore, be a uniform experience against every miraculous event, otherwise the event would not merit that appellation. And as a uniform experience amounts to a proof, there is here a direct and full *proof,* from the nature of the fact, against the existence of any miracle; nor can such a proof be destroyed, or the miracle rendered credible, but by an opposite proof, which is superior.[1]

The plain consequence is (and it is a general maxim worthy of our attention), 'That no testimony is sufficient to establish a miracle, unless the testimony be of such a kind, that its falsehood would be more miraculous, than the fact, which it endeavours to establish; and even in that case there is a mutual destruction of arguments, and the superior only gives us an assurance suitable to that degree of force, which remains, after deducting the inferior.' When anyone tells me, that he saw a dead man restored to life, I immediately consider with myself, whether it be more probable, that this person should either deceive or be deceived, or that the fact, which he relates, should really have happened. I weigh the one miracle against the other; and according to the superiority, which I discover, I pronounce my decision, and always reject the greater miracle. If the falsehood of his testimony would be more miraculous, than the event which he relates; then, and not till then, can he pretend to command my belief or opinion.

Part II.

In the foregoing reasoning we have supposed, that the testimony, upon which a miracle is founded, may possibly amount to an entire proof, and that the falsehood of that testimony would be a real prodigy: But it is easy to show, that we have been a great deal too liberal in our concession, and that there never was a miraculous event established on so full an evidence.

For *first*, there is not to be found, in all history, any miracle attested by a sufficient number of men, of such unquestioned good-sense, education, and learning, as to secure us against all delusion in themselves; of such undoubted integrity, as to place them beyond all suspicion of any design to deceive others; of such credit and reputation in the eyes of mankind, as to have a great deal to lose in case of their being detected in any falsehood; and at the same time, attesting facts performed in such a public manner and in so celebrated a part of the world, as to render the detection unavoidable. All which circumstances are requisite to give us a full assurance in the testimony of men.

Secondly. We may observe in human nature a principle which, if strictly examined, will be found to diminish extremely the assurance, which we might, from human testimony, have, in any kind of prodigy. The maxim, by which we commonly

conduct ourselves in our reasonings, is, that the objects, of which we have no experience, resembles those, of which we have; that what we have found to be most usual is always most probable; and that where there is an opposition of arguments, we ought to give the preference to such as are founded on the greatest number of past observations. But though, in proceeding by this rule, we readily reject any fact which is unusual and incredible in an ordinary degree; yet in advancing farther, the mind observes not always the same rule; but when anything is affirmed utterly absurd and miraculous, it rather the more readily admits of such a fact, upon account of that very circumstance, which ought to destroy all its authority. The passion of *surprise* and *wonder*, arising from miracles, being an agreeable emotion, gives a sensible tendency towards the belief of those events, from which it is derived. And this goes so far, that even those who cannot enjoy this pleasure immediately, nor can believe those miraculous events, of which they are informed, yet love to partake of the satisfaction at second-hand or by rebound, and place a pride and delight in exciting the admiration of others.

With what greediness are the miraculous accounts of travellers received, their descriptions of sea and land monsters, their relations of wonderful adventures, strange men, and uncouth manners? But if the spirit of religion join itself to the love of wonder, there is an end of common sense; and human testimony, in these circumstances, loses all pretensions to authority. A religionist may be an enthusiast, and imagine he sees what has no reality: he may know his narrative to be false, and yet persevere in it, with the best intensions in the world, for the sake of promoting so holy a cause: or even where this delusion has not place, vanity, excited by so strong a temptation, operates on him more powerfully than on the rest of mankind in any other circumstances; and self-interest with equal force. His auditors may not have, and commonly have not, sufficient judgement to canvass his evidence: what judgment they have, they renounce by principle, in these sublime and mysterious subjects: or if they were ever so willing to employ it, passion and a heated imagination disturb the regularity of its operations. Their credulity increases his impudence: and his impudence over-powers their credulity.

Eloquence, when at its highest pitch, leaves little room for reason or reflection; but addressing itself entirely to the fancy or the affections, captivates the willing hearers, and subdues their understanding. Happily, this pitch it seldom attains. But what a Tully or a Demosthenes could scarcely effect over a Roman or Athenian audience, every *Capuchin*, every itinerant or stationary teacher can perform over the generality of mankind, and in a higher degree, by touching such gross and vulgar passions.

The many instances of forged miracles, and prophecies, and supernatural events, which, in all ages, have either been detected by contrary evidence, or which detect themselves by their absurdity, prove sufficiently the strong propensity of mankind to the extraordinary and the marvellous, and ought reasonably to beget a suspicion against all relations of this kind. This is our natural way of thinking, even with regard to the most common and most credible events. For instance: There is no kind of report which rises so easily, and spreads so quickly, especially in country places and provincial towns, as those concerning marriages; insomuch that two young persons of equal condition never see each other twice, but the whole neighborhood immediately join them together. The pleasure of telling a piece of news so interesting, of propagating it, and of being the first reporters of it, spreads the intelligence. And this is so well known, that no man of sense gives attention to these reports, till he find them confirmed by some greater evidence. Do not the same passions, and others still stronger, incline the generality of mankind to believe and report, with the greatest vehemence and assurance, all religious miracles.

Thirdly. It forms a strong presumption against all supernatural and miraculous relations, that they are observed chiefly to abound among ignorant and barbarous nations; or if a civilized people has ever given admission to any of them, that people will be found to have received them from ignorant and barbarous ancestors, who transmitted them with that inviolable sanction and authority, which always attend received opinions. When we peruse the first histories of all nations, we are apt to imagine

ourselves transported into some new world; where the whole frame of nature is disjointed, and every element performs its operations in a different manner, from what it does at present. Battles, revolutions, pestilence, famine and death, are never the effect of those natural causes, which we experience. Prodigies, omens, oracles, judgements, quite obscure the few natural events, that are intermingled with them. But as the former grow thinner every page, in proportion as we advance nearer the enlightened ages, we soon learn, that there is nothing mysterious or supernatural in the case, but that all proceeds from the usual propensity of mankind towards the marvellous, and that, though this inclination may at intervals receive a check from sense and learning, it can never be thoroughly extirpated from human nature.

It is strange, a judicious reader is apt to say, upon the perusal of these wonderful historians, *that such prodigious events never happen in our days.* But it is nothing strange, I hope, that men should lie in all ages. You must surely have seen instances enough of that frailty. You have yourself heard many such marvellous relations started, which, being treated with scorn by all the wise and judicious, have at last been abandoned even by the vulgar. Be assured, that those renowned lies, which have spread the flourished to such a monstrous height, arose from like beginnings; but being sown in a more proper soil, shot up at last into prodigies almost equal to those which they relate. . . .

I may add as a *fourth* reason, which diminishes the authority of prodigies, that there is no testimony for any, even those which have not been expressly detected, that is not opposed by an infinite number of witnesses; so that not only the miracle destroys the credit of testimony, but the testimony destroys itself. To make this the better understood, let us consider, that, in matters of religion, whatever is different is contrary; and that it is impossible the religions of ancient Rome, of Turkey, of Siam, and of China should, all of them, be established on any solid foundation. Every miracle, therefore, pretended to have been wrought in any of these religions (and all of them abound in miracles), as its direct scope is to establish the particular system to which it is attributed; so has it the same force, though more indirectly, to overthrow every other system. In destroying a rival system, it likewise destroys the credit of those miracles, on which that system was established; so that all the prodigies of different religions are to be regarded as contrary facts, and the evidences of these prodigies, whether weak or strong, as opposite to each other. According to this method of reasoning, when we believe any miracle of Mahomet or his successors, we have for our warrant the testimony of a few barbarous Arabians: And on the other hand, we are to regard the authority of Titus Livius, Plutarch, Tacitus, and, in short, of all the authors and witnesses, Grecian, Chinese, and Roman Catholic, who have related any miracle in their particular religion; I say, we are to regard their testimony in the same light as if they had mentioned that Mahometan miracle, and had in express terms contradicted it, with the same certainty as they have for the miracle they relate. This argument may appear over subtile and refined; but is not in reality different from the reasoning of a judge, who supposes, that the credit of two witnesses, maintaining a crime against any one, is destroyed by the testimony of two others, who affirm him to have been two hundred leagues distant, at the same instant when the crime is said to have been committed. . . .

There is also a memorable story related by Cardinal de Retz, which may well deserve our consideration. When that intriguing politician fled into Spain, to avoid the persecution of his enemies, he passed through Saragossa, the capital of Arragon, where he was shown, in the cathedral, a man, who had served seven years as a doorkeeper, and was well known to every body in town, that had ever paid his devotions at that church. He had been seen, for so long a time, wanting a leg; but recovered that limb by the rubbing of holy oil upon the stump; and the cardinal assures us that he saw him with two legs. This miracle was vouched by all the canons of the church; and the whole company in town were appealed to for a confirmation of the fact; whom the cardinal found, by their zealous devotion, to be thorough believers of the miracle. Here the relater was also contemporary to the supposed prodigy, of an incredulous and libertine character, as well as of great genius; the miracle of so

singular a nature as could scarcely admit of a counterfeit, and the witnesses very numerous, and all of them, in a manner, spectators of the fact, to which they gave their testimony. And what adds mightily to the force of the evidence, and may double our surprise on this occasion, is, that the cardinal himself, who relates the story, seems not to give any credit to it, and consequently cannot be suspected of any concurrence in the holy fraud. He considered justly, that it was not requisite, in order to reject a fact of this nature, to be able accurately to disprove the testimony, and to trace its falsehood, through all the circumstances of knavery and credulity which produced it. He knew, that, as this was commonly altogether impossible at any small distance of time and place; so was it extremely difficult, even where one was immediately present by reason of the bigotry, ignorance, cunning, and roguery of a great part of mankind. He therefore concluded, like a just reasoner, that such an evidence carried falsehood upon the very face of it, and that a miracle, supported by any human testimony, was more properly a subject of derision than of argument.

There surely never was a greater number of miracles ascribed to one person, than those, which were lately said to have been wrought in France upon the tomb of Abbé Paris, the famous Jansenist, with whose sanctity the people were so long deluded. The curing of the sick, giving hearing to the deaf, and sight to the blind, were every where talked of as the usual effects of that holy sepulchre. But what is more extraordinary; many of the miracles were immediately proved upon the spot, before judges of unquestioned integrity, attested by witnesses of credit and distinction, in a learned age, and on the most eminent theatre that is now in the world. Nor is this all: a relation of them was published and dispersed every where; nor were the *Jesuits,* though a learned body, supported by the civil magistrate, and determined enemies to those opinions, in whose favour the miracles were said to have been wrought, ever able distinctly to refute or detect them. Where shall we find such a number of circumstances, agreeing to the corroboration of one fact? And what have we to oppose to such a cloud of witnesses, but the absolute impossibility or miraculous nature of the events, which they relate? And this surely, in the eyes of all reasonable people, will alone be regarded as a sufficient refutation.

Is the consequence just, because some human testimony has the utmost force and authority in some cases, when it relates the battle of Philippi or Pharsalia for instance; that therefore all kinds of testimony must, in all cases, have equal force and authority? Suppose that the Caesarean and Pompeian factions had, each of them, claimed the victory in these battles, and that the historians of each party had uniformly ascribed the advantage to their own side; how could mankind, at this distance, have been able to determine between them? The contrariety is equally strong between the miracles related by Herodotus or Plutarch, and those delivered by Mariana, Bede, or any monkish historian.

The wise lend a very academic faith to every report which favours the passion of the reporter; whether it magnifies his country, his family, or himself, or in any other way strikes in with his natural inclinations and propensities. But what greater temptation than to appear a missionary, a prophet, an ambassador from heaven? Who would not encounter many dangers and difficulties, in order to attain so sublime a character? Or if, by the help of vanity and a heated imagination, a man has first made a convert of himself, and entered seriously into the delusion; who ever scruples to make use of pious frauds, in support of so holy and meritorious a cause?

The smallest spark may here kindle into the greatest flame; because the materials are always prepared for it. The *avidum genus auricularum*, the gazing populace, receive greedily, without examination, whatever sooths superstition, and promotes wonder.

How many stories of this nature have, in all ages, been detected and exploded in their infancy? How many more have been celebrated for a time, and have afterwards sunk into neglect and oblivion? Where such reports, therefore, fly about, the solution of the phenomenon is obvious; and we judge in conformity to regular experience and observation, when we account for it by the known and natural principles of credulity and delusion. And shall we, rather than have a recourse to so natural a solution, allow of a miraculous violation of the most established laws of nature?

I need not mention the difficulty of detecting a falsehood in any private or even public history, at the place, where it is said to happen; much more when the scene is removed to ever so small a distance. Even a court of judicature, with all the authority, accuracy, and judgement, which they can employ, find themselves often at a loss to distinguish between truth and falsehood in the most recent actions. But the matter never comes to any issue, if trusted to the common method of altercations and debate and flying rumours; especially when men's passions have taken part on either side.

In the infancy of new religions, the wise and learned commonly esteem the matter too inconsiderable to deserve their attention or regard. And when afterwards they would willingly detect the cheat, in order to undeceive the deluded multitude, the season is now past, and the records and witnesses, which might clear up the matter, have perished beyond recovery.

No means of detection remain, but those which must be drawn from the very testimony itself of the reporters: and these, though always sufficient with the judicious and knowing, are commonly too fine to fall under the comprehension of the vulgar.

Upon the whole, then, it appears, that no testimony for any kind of miracle has ever amounted to a probability, much less to a proof; and that, even supposing it amounted to a proof, it would be opposed by another proof; derived from the very nature of the fact, which it would endeavour to establish. It is experience only, which gives authority to human testimony; and it is the same experience, which assures us of the laws of nature. When, therefore, these two kinds of experience are contrary, we have nothing to do but subtract the one from the other, and embrace an opinion, either on one side or the other, with that assurance which arises from the remainder. But according to the principle here explained, this subtraction, with regard to all popular religions, amounts to an entire annihilation; and therefore we may establish it as a maxim, that no human testimony can have such force as to prove a miracle, and make it a just foundation for any such system of religion.

I beg the limitations here made may be remarked, when I say, that a miracle can never be proved, so as to be the foundation of a system of religion. For I own, that otherwise, there may possibly be miracles, or violations of the usual course of nature, of such a kind as to admit of proof from human testimony; though, perhaps, it will be impossible to find any such in all the records of history. Thus, suppose, all authors, in all languages, agree, that, from the first of January 1600, there was a total darkness over the whole earth for eight days: suppose that the tradition of this extraordinary event is still strong and lively among the people: that all travellers, who return from foreign countries, bring us accounts of the same tradition, without the least variation or contradiction: it is evident, that our present philosophers, instead of doubting the fact, ought to receive it as certain, and ought to search for the causes whence it might be derived. The decay, corruption, and dissolution of nature, is an event rendered probable by so many analogies, that any phenomenon, which seems to have a tendency towards that catastrophe, comes within the reach of human testimony, if that testimony be very extensive and uniform.

But suppose, that all the historians who treat of England, should agree, that, on the first of January 1600, Queen Elizabeth died; that both before and after her death she was seen by her physicians and the whole court, as is usual with persons of her rank; that her successor was acknowledged and proclaimed by the parliament; and that, after being interred a month, she again appeared, resumed the throne, and governed England for three years: I must confess that I should be surprised at the concurrence of so many odd circumstances, but should not have the least inclination to believe so miraculous an event. I should not doubt of her pretended death, and of those other public circumstances that followed it: I should only assert it to have been pretended, and that it neither was, nor possibly could be real. You would in vain object to me the difficulty, and almost impossibility of deceiving the world in an affair of such consequence; the wisdom and solid judgement of that renowned queen; with the little or no advantage which she could reap from so poor an artifice: All this might astonish me; but I

would still reply, that the knavery and folly of men are such common phenomena, that I should rather believe the most extraordinary events to arise from their concurrence, than admit of so signal a violation of the laws of nature.

But should this miracle be ascribed to any new system of religion; men, in all ages, have been so much imposed on by ridiculous stories of that kind, that this very circumstance would be a full proof of a cheat, and sufficient, with all men of sense, not only to make them reject the fact, but even reject it without farther examination. Though the Being to whom the miracle is ascribed, be, in this case, Almighty, it does not, upon that account, become a whit more probable; since it is impossible for us to know the attributes or actions of such a Being, otherwise than from the experience which we have of his productions, in the usual course of nature. This still reduces us to past observation, and obliges us to compare the instances of the violation of truth in the testimony of men, with those of the violation of the laws of nature by miracles, in order to judge which of them is most likely and probable. As the violations of truth are more common in the testimony concerning religious miracles, than in that concerning any other matter of fact; this must diminish very much the authority of the former testimony, and make us form a general resolution, never to lend any attention to it, with whatever specious pretence it may be covered.

Lord Bacon seems to have embraced the same principles of reasoning. 'We ought,' says he, 'to make a collection or particular history of all monsters and prodigious births or productions, and in a word of every thing new, rare, and extraordinary in nature. But this must be done with the most severe scrutiny, lest we depart from truth. Above all, every relation must be considered as suspicious, which depends in any degree upon religion, as the prodigies of Livy: And no less so, every thing that is to be found in the writers of natural magic or alchimy, or such authors, who seem, all of them, to have an unconquerable appetite for falsehood and fable.'

I am the better pleased with the method of reasoning here delivered, as I think it may serve to confound those dangerous friends or disguised enemies to the *Christian Religion*, who have undertaken to defend it by the principles of human reason. Our most holy religion is founded on *Faith*, not on reason; and it is a sure method of exposing it to put it to such a trial as it is, by no means, fitted to endure. To make this more evident, let us examine those miracles, related in scripture; and not to lose ourselves in too wide a field, let us confine ourselves to such as we find in the *Pentateuch*, which we shall examine, according to the principles of those pretended Christians, not as the word or testimony of God himself, but as the production of a mere human writer and historian. Here then we are first to consider a book, presented to us by a barbarous and ignorant people, written in an age when they were still more barbarous, and in all probability long after the facts which it relates, corroborated by no concurring testimony, and resembling those fabulous accounts, which every nation gives of its origin. Upon reading this book, we find it full of prodigies and miracles. It gives an account of a state of the world and of human nature entirely different from the present: Of our fall from that state: Of the age of man, extended to near a thousand years: Of the destruction of the world by a deluge: Of the arbitrary choice of one people, as the favorites of heaven; and that people the countrymen of the author: Of their deliverance from bondage by prodigies the most astonishing imaginable: I desire any one to lay his hand upon his heart, and after a serious consideration declare, whether he thinks that the falsehood of such a book, supported by such a testimony, would be more extraordinary and miraculous than all the miracles it relates; which is, however, necessary to make it be received, according to the measures of probability above established.

What we have said of miracles may be applied, without any variation, to prophecies; and indeed, all prophecies are real miracles, and as such only, can be admitted as proofs of any revelation. If it did not exceed the capacity of human nature to foretell future events, it would be absurd to employ any prophecy as an argument for a divine mission or authority from heaven. So that, upon the whole, we may conclude, that the *Christian Religion* not only was at first attended with miracles, but even at this day cannot be believed by any reasonable person without one. Mere reason is insufficient to convince us of its veracity: And whoever is moved by *Faith* to assent to it, is conscious of a continued miracle in his own person, which subverts all the principles of his understanding, and gives him a determination to believe what is most contrary to custom and experience.

Note

1. Sometimes an event may not, *in itself,* seem to be contrary to the laws of nature, and yet, if it were real, it might, by reason of some circumstances, be denominated a miracle; because, in *fact,* it is contrary to these laws. Thus if a person, claiming a divine authority, should command a sick person to be well, a healthful man to fall down dead, the clouds to pour rain, the winds to blow, in short, should order many natural events, which immediately follow upon his command; these might justly be esteemed miracles, because they are really, in this case, contrary to the laws of nature. For if any suspicion remain, that the event and command concurred by accident, there is no miracle and no transgression of the laws of nature. If this suspicion be removed, there is evidently a miracle, and a transgression of these laws; because nothing can be more contrary to nature than that the voice or command of a man should have such an influence. A miracle may be accurately defined, a *transgression of a law of nature by a particular volition of the Deity, or by the interposition of some invisible agent.* A miracle may either be discoverable by men or not. This alters not its nature and essence. The raising of a house or ship into the air is a visible miracle. The raising of a feather, when the wind wants ever so little of a force requisite for that purpose, is as real a miracle, though not so sensible with regard to us.

V.2 For the Possibility of Miracles

RICHARD SWINBURNE

One of the most vigorous critics of Hume has been Richard Swinburne, professor of philosophy of religion at Oxford University, who in our second reading takes issue with him. Swinburne first inquires whether there could be evidence that a law of nature had been violated and, second, whether there could be evidence that the violation was due to a god. To satisfy the first inquiry, we would have to have good reason to believe that an event has occurred contrary to the predictions of a law that we had good reason to believe to be a law of nature; and furthermore we would have to have good reason to believe that events similar to the event would not occur in circumstances similar to those of the original occurrence. For if the event were repeatable, we would have to account for both events through the formulation of a law. Swinburne's example is levitation, a person's rising into the air and remaining there.

But to be a miracle the violation of a natural law would have to be the work of a god, who is not a material object. What kind of evidence would we have to have to believe that a divine being had intervened in our world? Here Swinburne distinguishes between situations in which we do and in which we do not have sufficient circumstantial evidence to warrant our attributing the anomalous event to the work of an invisible deity. The circumstantial evidence must be strong before we are justified in believing that the event is a genuine miracle. An answer to a prayer, for example, fulfills the necessary conditions.

In this article I wish to investigate whether there could be strong historical evidence for the occurrence of miracles, and contrary to much writing

Reprinted from Richard Swinburne, "Miracles," *Philosophical Quarterly*, 18 (1968), by permission of the publisher, Basil Blackwell.

which has derived from Hume's celebrated chapter "Of Miracles," I shall argue that there could be. I understand by a miracle a violation of a law of Nature by a god, that is, a very powerful rational being who is not a material object (viz., is invisible and intangible). My definition of a miracle is thus approximately the same as Hume's: "a transgression of a law of nature by a particular volition of the Deity or by the interposition of some invisible agent."[1] It has been questioned by many biblical scholars whether this is what the biblical writers understood by the terms translated into English 'miracle'. I do not propose to enter into this controversy. Suffice it to say that many subsequent Christian theologians have understood by 'miracle' roughly what I understand by the term and that much medieval and modern apologetic which appeals to purported miracles as evidence of the truth of the Christian revelation has had a similar understanding of miracle to mine.

I shall take the question in two parts. I shall enquire first whether there could be evidence that a law of nature has been violated, and secondly, if there can be such evidence, whether there could be evidence that the violation was due to a god.

First, then, can there be evidence that a law of nature has been violated? It seems natural to understand, as Ninian Smart[2] does, by a violation of a law of nature, an occurrence of a non-repeatable counter-instance to a law of nature. Clearly, as Hume admitted, events contrary to predictions of formulae which we had good reason to believe to be laws of nature often occur. But if we have good reason to believe that they have occurred and good reason to believe that similar events would occur in similar circumstances, then we have good reason to believe that the formulae which we previously believed to be the laws of nature were not in fact such laws. Repeatable counter-instances do not violate laws of nature, they just show propositions purporting to state laws of nature to be false. But if we have good reason to believe that an event *E* has occurred contrary to predictions of a formula *L* which we have good reason to believe to be a law of nature, and we have good reason to believe that events similar to *E* would not occur in circumstances as similar as we like in any respect to those of the original occurrence, then we do not have reason to believe that *L* is not a law of nature. For any modified formula which allowed us to predict *E* would allow us to predict similar events in similar circumstances and hence, we have good reason to believe, would give false predictions. Whereas if we leave the formula *L* unmodified, it will, we have good reason to believe, give correct predictions in all other conceivable circumstances. Hence if we are to say that any law of nature is operative in the field in question we must say that it is *L*. This seems a natural thing to say rather than to say that no law of nature operates in the field. Yet *E* is contrary to the predictions of *L*. Hence, for want of a better expression, we say that *E* has violated the law of nature *L*. If the use of the word 'violated' suggests too close an analogy between laws of nature and civil or moral laws, that is unfortunate. Once we have explained, as above, what is meant by a violation of a law of nature, no subsequent confusion need arise.

The crucial question, not adequately discussed by Smart, however, is what would be good reason for believing that an event *E*, if it occurred, was a non-repeatable as opposed to a repeatable counter-instance to a formula *L* which we have on all other evidence good reason to believe to be a law of nature. The evidence that *E* is a repeatable counter-instance would be that a new formula *L* fairly well confirmed by the data as a law of nature can be set up. A formula is confirmed by data, if the data obtained so far are predicted by the formula, if new pre- dictions are successful and if the formula is a simple and coherent one relative to the collection of data.

Compatible with any finite set of data, there will always be an infinite number of possible formulae from which the data can be predicted. We can rule out many by further tests, but however many tests we make we shall still have only a finite number of data and hence an infinite number of formulae compatible with them.

But some of these formulae will be highly complex relative to the data, so that no scientist would consider that the data were evidence that those formulae were true laws of nature. Others are very simple formulae such that the data can be said to provide evidence that they are true laws of nature. Thus suppose the scientist's task is to find a formula accounting for marks on a graph, observed at $(1, 1)$, $(2, 2)$, $(3, 3)$, and $(4, 4)$, the first number of each pair being the x co-ordinate and the second the y co-ordinate. One formula which would predict these marks is $x = y$. Another one is $(x - 1)(x - 2)(x - 3)(x - 4) + x = y$. But clearly we would not regard the data as supporting the second formula. It is too clumsy a formula to explain four observations. Among simple formulae supported by the data, the simplest is the best supported and regarded, provisionally, as correct. If the formula survives further tests, that increases the evidence in its favour as a true law.

Now if for E and for all other relevant data we can construct a formula L^1 from which the data can be derived and which either makes successful predictions in other circumstances where *L* makes bad predictions, or is a fairly simple formula, so that from the fact that it can predict *E*, and *L* cannot, we have reason to believe that its predictions, if tested, would be better than those of *L* in other circumstances, then we have good reason to believe that L^1 is the true law in the field. The formula will indicate under what circumstances divergencies from *L* similar to *E* will occur. The evidence thus indicates that they will occur under these circumstances and hence that *E* is a repeatable counter-instance to the original formula *L*.

Suppose, however, that for *E* and all the other data of the field we can construct no new formula L^1 which yields more successful predictions than *L* in other examined circumstances, nor one which is fairly simple relative to the data; but for all the other data except *E* the simple formula *L* does yield good predictions. And suppose that as the data continue to accumulate, *L* remains a completely successful predictor and there remains no reason to suppose that a simple formula L^1 from which all the other data and *E* can be derived can be constructed. The evidence then indicates that the divergence from *L* will not be repeated and hence that *E* is a non-repeatable counter-instance to a law of nature *L*.

Here is an example. Suppose *E* to be the levitation (viz., rising into the air and remaining floating on it) of a certain holy person. *E* is a counter-instance to otherwise well substantiated laws of mechanics *L*. We could show *E* to be a repeatable counter-instance if we could construct a formula L^1 which predicted *E* and also successfully predicted other divergences from *L*, as well as all other tested predictions of *L*; or if we could construct L^1 which was comparatively simple relative to the data and predicted *E* and all the other tested predictions of *L*, but predicted divergences from *L* which had not yet been tested. L^1 might differ from *L* in that, according to it, under certain circumstances bodies exercise a gravitational repulsion on each other, and the circumstance in which *E* occurred was one of those circumstances. If L^1 satisfied either of the above two conditions, we would adopt it, and we would then say that under certain circumstances people do levitate and so *E* was not a counter-instance to a law of nature. However, it might be that any modification which we made to the laws of mechanics to allow them to predict *E* might not yield any more successful predictions than *L* and they be so clumsy that there was no reason to believe that their predictions not yet tested would be successful. Under these circumstances we would have good reasons to believe that the levitation of the holy person violated the laws of nature.

If the laws of nature are statistical and not deterministic, it is not in all cases so clear what counts as a counter-instance to them. How improbable does an event have to be to constitute a counter-instance to a statistical law? But this problem is a general one in the philosophy of science and does not raise any issues peculiar to the topic of miracles.

It is clear that all claims about what does or does not violate the laws of nature are corrigible. New scientific knowledge may force us to revise any such claims. But all claims to knowledge about matters of fact are corrigible, and we must reach provisional conclusions about them on the evidence available to us. We have to some extent good

evidence, about what are the laws of nature, and some of them are so well established and account for so many data that any modifications to them which we could suggest to account for the odd counter-instance would be so clumsy and *ad hoc* as to upset the whole structure of science. In such cases the evidence is strong that if the purported counter-instance occurred it was a violation of the laws of nature. There is good reason to believe that the following events, if they occurred, would be violations of the laws of nature: levitation; resurrection from the dead in full health of a man whose heart has not been beating for twenty-four hours and who was, by other criteria also, dead; water turning into wine without the assistance of chemical apparatus or catalysts; a man getting better from polio in a minute.

So then we could have the evidence that an event *E* if it occurred was a non-repeatable counter-instance to a true law of nature *L*. But Hume's argument here runs as follows. The evidence, which *ex hypothesi* is good evidence, that *L* is a true law of nature is evidence that *E* did not occur. We have certain other evidence that *E* did occur. In such circumstances, writes Hume, the wise man "weighs the opposite experiments. He considers which side is supported by the greater number of experiments."[3] Since he supposes that the evidence that *E* occurred would be that of testimony, Hume concludes "that no testimony is sufficient to establish a miracle, unless the testimony be of such a kind, that its falsehood would be more miraculous, than the fact which it endeavours to establish."[4] He considers that this condition is not in fact satisfied by any purported miracle, though he seems at times to allow that it is logically possible that it might be.

One wonders here at Hume's scale of evidence. Suppose two hundred witnesses claiming to have observed some event *E*, an event which, if it occurred, would be a non-repeatable counter-instance to a law of nature. Suppose these to be witnesses able and anxious to show that *E* did not occur if there were grounds for doing so. Would not their combined evidence give us good reason to believe that *E* occurred? Hume's answer which we can see from his discussion of two apparently equally well authenticated miracles is—No. But then, one is inclined to say, is not Hume just being bigoted, refusing to face facts? It would be virtually impossible to draw up a table showing how many witnesses and of what kind we need to establish the occurrence of an event which, if it occurred, would be a non-repeatable counter-instance to a law of nature. Each purported instance has to be considered on its merits. But certainly one feels that Hume's standards of evidence are too high. What, one wonders, would Hume himself say if he saw such an event?

But behind Hume's excessively stringent demands on evidence there may be a philosophical point which he has not fully brought out. This is a point made by Flew in justification of Hume's standards of evidence: "The justification for giving the 'scientific' thus ultimate precedence here over the 'historical' lies in the nature of the propositions concerned and in the evidence which can be displayed to sustain them . . . the candidate historical proposition will be particular, often singular, and in the past tense. . . . But just by reason of this very pastness and particularly it is no longer possible for anyone to examine the subject directly for himself . . . the law of nature will, unlike the candidate historical proposition, be a general nomological. It can thus in theory, though obviously not always in practice, be tested at any time by any person."[5]

Flew's contrast is, however, mistaken. Particularly experiments on particular occasions only give a certain and far from conclusive support to claims that a purported scientific law is true. Any person can test for the truth of a purported scientific law, but a positive result to one test will only give limited support to the claim. Exactly the same holds for purported historical truths. Anyone can examine the evidence, but a particular piece of evidence only gives limited support to the claim that the historical proposition is true. But in the historical as in the scientific case, there is no limit to the amount of evidence. We can go on and on testing for the truth of historical as well as scientific propositions. We can look for more and more data which can only be explained as effects of some specified past event, and data incompatible with its occurrence,

just as we can look for more and more data for or against the truth of some physical law. Hence the truth of the historical proposition can also "be tested at any time by any person."

What Hume seems to suppose is that the only evidence about whether an event *E* happened is the written or verbal testimony of those who would have been in a position to witness it, had it occurred. And as there will be only a finite number of such pieces of testimony, the evidence about whether or not *E* happened would be finite. But this is not the only testimony which is relevant—we need testimony about the character and competence of the original witnesses. Nor is testimony the only type of evidence. All effects of what happened at the time of the alleged occurrence of *E* are also relevant. Far more than in Hume's day we are today often in a position to assess what occurred by studying the physical traces of the event. Hume had never met Sherlock Holmes with his ability to assess what happened in the room from the way in which the furniture lay, or where the witness was yesterday from the mud on his boot. As the effects of what happened at the time of the occurrence of *E* are always with us in some form, we can always go on examining them yet more carefully. Further, we need to investigate whether *E*, if it did occur, would in fact have brought about the present effects, and whether any other cause could have brought about just these effects. To investigate these issues involves investigating which scientific laws operate (other than the law *L* of which it is claimed that *E* was a violation), and this involves doing experiments *ad lib.* Hence there is no end to the amount of new evidence which can be had. The evidence that the event *E* occurred can go on mounting up in the way that evidence that *L* is a law of nature can do. The wise man in these circumstances will surely say that he has good reason to believe that *E* occurred, but also that *L* is true law of nature and so that *E* was a violation of it.

So we could have good reason to believe that a law of nature has been violated. But for a violation of a law of nature to be a miracle, it has to be caused by a god, that is, a very powerful rational being who is not a material object. What could be evidence that it was?

To explain an event as brought about by a rational agent with intentions and purposes is to give an entirely different kind of explanation of its occurrence from an explanation by scientific laws acting on precedent causes. Our normal grounds for attributing an event to the agency of an embodied rational agent *A* is that we or others perceived *A* bringing it about *or* that it is the sort of event that *A* typically brings about and that *A*, and no one else of whom we have knowledge, was in a position to bring it about. The second kind of ground is only applicable when we have prior knowledge of the existence of *A*. In considering evidence for a violation *E* of a law of nature being due to the agency of a god, I will distinguish two cases, one where we have good reason on grounds other than the occurrence of violations of laws of nature to believe that there exists at least one god, and one where we do not.

Let us take the second case first. Suppose we have no other good reason for believing that a god exists, but an event *E* then occurs which, our evidence indicates, is a non-repeatable counter-instance to a true law of nature. Now we cannot attribute *E* to the agency of a god by seeing the god's body bring *E* about, for gods do not have bodies. But suppose that *E* occurs in ways and circumstances C strongly analogous to those in which occur events brought about by human agents, and that other violations occur in such circumstances. We would then be justified in claiming that *E* and other such violations are, like effects of human actions, brought about by agents, but ones unlike men in not being material objects. This inference would be justified because, if an analogy between effects is strong enough, we are always justified in postulating slight difference in causes to account for slight difference in effects. Thus if because of its other observable behaviour we say that light is a disturbance in a medium, then the fact that the medium, if it exists, does not, like other media, slow down material bodies passing through it, is not by itself (viz., if there are no other disanalogies) a reason for saying that the light is not a disturbance in a medium, but only for saying that the medium in which light is a disturbance has the peculiar property of not resisting the

passage of material bodies. So if, because of very strong similarity between the ways and circumstances of the occurrence of *E* and other violations of laws of nature to the ways and circumstances in which effects are produced by human agents, we postulate a similar cause—a rational agent, the fact that there are certain disanalogies (viz., we cannot point to the agent, say where his body is) does not mean that our explanation is wrong. It only means that the agent is unlike humans in not having a body. But this move is only justified if the similarities are otherwise strong. Nineteenth-century scientists eventually concluded that for light the similarities were not strong enough to outweigh the dissimilarities and justify postulating the medium with the peculiar property.

Now what similarities in the ways and circumstances C of their occurrence could there be between *E* (and other violations of laws of nature) and the effects of human actions to justify the postulation of similar causes? Suppose that *E* occurred in answer to a request. Thus *E* might be an explosion in my room, totally inexplicable by the laws of nature, when at the time of its occurrence there were in a room on the other side of the corridor men in turbans chanting "O God of the Sikhs, may there be an explosion in Swinburne's room." Suppose, too, that when *E* occurs a voice, but not the voice of an embodied agent, is heard giving reasonable reasons for granting the request. When the explosion occurs in my room, a voice emanating from no man or animal or man-made machine is heard saying "Your request is granted. He deserves a lesson." Would not all this be good reason for postulating a rational agent other than a material object who brought about *E* and the other violations, an agent powerful enough to change instantaneously by intervention the properties of things, viz., a god? Clearly if the analogy were strong enough between the ways and circumstances in which violations of laws of nature and effects of human action occur, it would be. If furthermore the prayers which were answered by miracles were prayers for certain kinds of events (e.g., relief of suffering, punishment of ill-doers) and those which were not answered by miracles were for events of different kinds, then this would show something about the character of the god. Normally, of course, the evidence adduced by theists for the occurrence of miracles is not as strong as I have indicated that very strong evidence would be. Violations are often reported as occurring subsequent to prayer for them to occur, and seldom otherwise; but voices giving reason for answering such a request are rare indeed. Whether in cases where voices are not heard but the occurrence of a violation E and of prayer for its occurrence were both well confirmed, we would be justified in concluding that the existence of a god who brought E about is a matter of whether the analogy is strong enough as it stands. The question of exactly when an analogy is strong enough to justify an inference based on it is a difficult one. But my only point here is that if the analogy were strong enough, the inference would be justified.

Suppose now that we have other evidence for the existence of a god. Then if E occurs in the circumstances C, previously described, that E is due to the activity of a god is more adequately substantiated, and the occurrence of E gives further support to the evidence for the existence of a god. But if we already have reason to believe in the existence of a god, the occurrence of E not under circumstances as similar as C to those under which human agents often bring about results, could nevertheless sometimes be justifiably attributed to his activity. Thus, if the occurrence of E is the sort of thing that the only god of whose existence we have evidence would wish to bring about if he has the character suggested by the other evidence for his existence, we can reasonably hold him responsible for the occurrence of E which would otherwise be unexplained. The healing of a faithful blind Christian contrary to the laws of nature could reasonably be attributed to the God of the Christians, if there were other evidence for his existence, whether or not the blind man or other Christians had ever prayed for that result.

For these reasons I conclude that we can have good reason to believe that a violation of a law of nature was caused by a god, and so was a miracle.

I would like to make two final points, one to tidy up the argument and the other to meet a further argument put forward by Hume which I have not previously discussed.

Entia non sunt multiplicanda praeter necessitatem.—Unless we have good reason to do so we ought not to postulate the existence of more than one god, but to suppose that the same being answers all prayers. But there could be good reason to postulate the existence of more than one god, and evidence to this effect could be provided by miracles. One way in which this could happen is that prayers for a certain kind of result, for example, shipwreck, which began "O, Neptune" were often answered, and also prayers for a different kind of result, for example, success in love, which began "O, Venus" were also often answered, but prayers for a result of the first kind beginning "O, Venus," and for a result of the second kind beginning "O, Neptune" were never answered. Evidence for the existence of one god would in general support, not oppose, evidence for the existence of a second one since, by suggesting that there is one rational being other than those whom we can see, it makes more reasonable the postulation of another one.

The second point is that there is no reason at all to suppose that Hume is in general right to claim that "every miracle . . . pretended to have been wrought in any . . . (religion) . . . as its direct scope is to establish the particular system to which it is attributed; so has it the same force, though more indirectly, to overthrow every other system. In destroying a rival system it likewise destroys the credit of those miracles on which that system was established."[6] If Hume were right to claim that evidence for the miracles of one religion was evidence against the miracles of any other, then indeed evidence for miracles in each would be poor. But in fact evidence for a miracle "wrought in one religion" is only evidence against the occurrence of a miracle "wrought in another religion" if the two miracles, if they occurred, would be evidence for propositions of the two religious systems incompatible with each other. It is hard to think of pairs of alleged miracles of this type. If there were evidence for a Roman Catholic miracle which was evidence for the doctrine of transubstantiation and evidence for a Protestant miracle which was evidence against it, here we would have a case of the conflict of evidence which, Hume claims, occurs generally with alleged miracles. But it is enough to give this example to see that most alleged miracles do not give rise to conflicts of this kind. Most alleged miracles, if they occurred, would only show the power of god or gods and their concern for the needs of men, and little else.

My main conclusion, to repeat it, is that there are no logical difficulties in supposing that there could be strong historical evidence for the occurrence of miracles. Whether there is such evidence is, of course, another matter.

Notes

1. David Hume, *An Enquiry Concerning Human Understanding*, ed. L. A. Selby-Bigge (Oxford, 2nd ed., 1902), p. 115, footnote.
2. Ninian Smart, *Philosophers and Religious Truth* (London, 1964), Ch. II.
3. Op. cit., p. 111.
4. Op. cit., p. 116.
5. Antony Flew, *Hume's Philosophy of Belief* (London, 1961), pp. 207 ff.
6. Op. cit., pp. 121ff.

V.3   Miracles and Testimony

J. L. M A C K I E

Our third reading is "Miracles and Testimony" by the late J. L. Mackie of Oxford University. In this revised Humean account of miracles, Mackie argues that the evidence for miracles will never in practice be very great. The argument is epistemological, not ontological. That is, while miracles may be logically possible (and may indeed have occurred), we are never justified in believing in one. The concept of a miracle is a coherent one, but, Mackie argues, the double burden of showing both that the event took place and that it violated the laws of nature will be extremely hard to lift, for "whatever tends to show that it would have been a violation of natural law tends for that very reason to make it most unlikely that it actually happened." Correspondingly, the deniers of miracles have two strategies of defense. They may argue that the event took place but wasn't a violation of a law of nature (the event simply followed an unknown law of nature); or they can admit that if the event had happened, it would indeed have been a violation of a law of nature, but for that reason "there is a very strong presumption against its having happened, which it is most unlikely that any testimony will be able to outweigh."*

(a) Introduction

Traditional theism, as defined in the Introduction, does not explicitly include any contrast between the natural and the supernatural. Yet there is a familiar, if vague and undeveloped, notion of the natural world in contrast with which the theistic doctrines stand out as asserting a supernatural reality. The question whether and how there can be evidence for what, if real, would be supernatural is therefore one of central significance. Besides, explicit assertions about supernatural occurrences, about miracles or divine interventions which have disrupted the natural course of events, are common in nearly all religions: alleged miracles are often cited to validate religious claims. Christianity, for example, has its share of these. In the life of Christ we have the virgin birth, the turning of water into wine, Christ's walking on the water, his healing of the sick, his raising of Lazarus from the dead, and, of course, the resurrection. The Roman Catholic church will not recognize anyone as a saint unless it is convinced that at least two miracles have been

Reprinted from *The Miracle of Theism* by J. L. Mackie (1982) by permission of Oxford University Press. Copyright © 1982 by Joan Mackie.

performed by the supposed saint, either in his or her life or after death.

The usual purpose of stories about miracles is to establish the authority of the particular figures who perform them or are associated with them, but of course these stories, with their intended interpretation, presuppose such more general religious doctrines as that of the existence of a god. We can, therefore, recognize, as one of the supports of traditional theism, an argument from miracles: that is, an argument whose main premiss is that such and such remarkable events have occurred, and whose conclusion is that a god of the traditional sort both exists and intervenes, from time to time, in the ordinary world. . . .

[Here follows a brief exposition of Hume's essay "Of Miracles".]

(b) Hume's Argument—Discussion

What Hume has been expounding are the principles for the rational acceptance of testimony, the rules that ought to govern our believing or not believing what we are told. But the rules that govern people's actual acceptance of testimony are very different. We are fairly good at detecting dishonesty, insincerity, and lack of conviction, and we readily reject what we are told by someone who betrays these defects. But we are strongly inclined simply to accept, without question, statements that are obviously assured and sincere. As Hume would say, a firm association of ideas links someone else's saying, with honest conviction, that *p*, and its being the case that *p*, and we pass automatically from the perception of the one to belief in the other. Or, as he might also have said, there is an intellectual sympathy by which we tend automatically to share what we find to be someone else's belief, analogous to sympathy in the original sense, the tendency to share what we see to be someone else's feelings. And in general this is a useful tendency. People's beliefs about ordinary matters are right, or nearly right, more often than they are wildly wrong, so that intellectual sympathy enables fairly correct information to be passed on more smoothly than it could be if we were habitually cautious and constantly checked testimony against the principles for its rational acceptance. But what is thus generally useful can sometimes be misleading, and miracle reports are a special case where we need to restrain our instinctive acceptance of honest statements, and go back to the basic rational principles which determine whether a statement is really reliable or not. Even where we are cautious, and hesitate to accept what we are told—for example by a witness in a legal case—we often do not go beyond the question 'How intrinsically reliable is this witness?', or, in detail, 'Does he seem to be honest? Does he have a motive for misleading us? Is he the sort of person who might tell plausible lies? Or is he the sort of person who, in the circumstances, might have made a mistake?' If we are satisfied on all these scores, we are inclined to believe what the witness says, without weighing very seriously the question 'How intrinsically improbable is what he has told us?' But, as Hume insists, this further question is highly relevant. His general approach to the problem of when to accept testimony is certainly sound.

Hume's case against miracles is an epistemological argument: it does not try to show that miracles never do happen or never could happen, but only that we never have good reasons for believing that they have happened. It must be clearly distinguished from the suggestion that the very concept of a miracle is incoherent. That suggestion might be spelled out as follows. A miracle is, by definition, a violation of a law of nature, and a law of nature is, by definition, a regularity—or the statement of a regularity—about what happens, about the way the world works; consequently, if some event actually occurs, no regularity which its occurrence infringes (or, no regularity-statement which it falsifies) can really be a law of nature; so this event, however unusual or surprising, cannot after all be a miracle. The two definitions together entail that whatever happens is not a miracle, that is, that miracles never happen. This, be it noted, is not Hume's argument. If it were correct, it would make Hume's argument unnecessary. Before we discuss Hume's case, then, we should consider whether there is a coherent concept of a miracle which would not thus rule out the occurrence of miracles *a priori*.

If miracles are to serve their traditional function of giving spectacular support to religious claims—whether general theistic claims, or the authority of some specific religion or some particular sect or individual teacher—the concept must not be so weakened that anything at all unusual or remarkable counts as a miracle. We must keep in the definition the notion of a violation of natural law. But then, if it is to be even possible that a miracle should occur, we must modify the definition given above of a law of nature. What we want to do is to contrast the order of nature with a possible divine or supernatural intervention. The laws of nature, we must say, describe the ways in which the world—including, of course, human beings—works when left to itself, when not interfered with. A miracle occurs when the world is not left to itself, when something distinct from the natural order as a whole intrudes into it.

This notion of ways in which the world works is coherent and by no means obscure. We know how to discover causal laws, relying on a principle of the uniformity of the course of nature—essentially the assumption that there are some laws to be found—in conjunction with suitable observations and experiments, typically varieties of controlled experiment whose underlying logic is that of Mill's 'method of difference'. Within the laws so established, we can further mark off basic laws of working from derived laws which hold only in a particular context or contingently upon the way in which something is put together. It will be a derived law that a particular clock, or clocks of a particular sort, run at such a speed, and this will hold only in certain conditions of temperature, and so on; but this law will be derived from more basic ones which describe the regular behaviour of certain kinds of material, in view of the way in which the clock is put together, and these more basic laws of materials may in turn be derived from yet more basic laws about sub-atomic particles, in view of the ways in which those materials are made up of such particles. In so far as we advance towards a knowledge of such a system of basic and derived laws, we are acquiring an understanding of ways in which the world works. As well as what we should ordinarily call causal laws, which typically concern interactions, there are similar laws with regard to the ways in which certain kinds of things simply persist through time, and certain sorts of continuous process just go on. These too, and in particular the more basic laws of these sorts, help to constitute the ways in which the world works. Thus there are several kinds of basic 'laws of working'. For our present purpose, however, it is not essential that we should even be approaching an understanding of how the world works; it is enough that we have the concept of such basic laws of working, that we know in principle what it would be to discover them. Once we have this concept, we have moved beyond the definition of laws of nature merely as (statements of) what always happens. We can see how, using this concept and using the assumption that there are some such basic laws of working to be found, we can hope to determine what the actual laws of working are by reference to a restricted range of experiments and observations. This opens up the possibility that we might determine that something *is* a basic law of working of natural objects, and yet also, independently, find that it was occasionally violated. An occasional violation does not in itself necessarily overthrow the independently established conclusion that this *is* a law of working.

Equally, there is no obscurity in the notion of intervention. Even in the natural world we have a clear understanding of how there can be for a time a closed system, in which everything that happens results from factors within that system in accordance with its laws of working, but how then something may intrude from outside it, bringing about changes that the system would not have produced of its own accord, so that things go on after this intrusion differently from how they would have gone on if the system had remained closed. All we need do, then, is to regard the whole natural world as being, for most of the time, such a closed system; we can then think of a supernatural intervention as something that intrudes into that system from outside the natural world as a whole.

If the laws by which the natural world works are deterministic, then the notion of a violation of them is quite clear-cut: such a violation would be an event which, given that the world was a closed system working in accordance with these laws, and given some actual earlier complete state of the world, simply could not have happened at all. Its occurrence would then be clear proof that either the supposed laws were not the real laws of working, or the earlier state was not as it was supposed to have been, or else the system was not closed after all. But if the basic laws of working are statistical or probabilistic, the notion of a violation of them is less precise. If something happens which, given those statistical laws and some earlier complete state of the world, is extremely improbable—in the sense of physical probability: that is, something such that there is a strong propensity or tendency for it *not* to happen—we still cannot say firmly that the laws have been violated: laws of this sort explicitly allow that what is extremely improbable may occasionally come about. Indeed it is highly probable (both physically and epistemically) that some events, each of which is very improbable, will occur at rare intervals. If tosses of a coin were governed by a statistical law that gave a 50 per cent propensity to heads at each toss, a continuous run of ten heads would be a highly improbable occurrence; but it would be highly probable that there would be some such runs in a sequence of a million tosses. Nevertheless, we can still use the contrast between the way of working of the natural world as a whole, considered as a normally closed system, and an intervention or intrusion into it. This contrast does not disappear or become unintelligible merely because we lack decisive tests for its application. We can still define a miracle as an event which would not have happened in the course of nature, and which came about only through a supernatural intrusion. The difficulty is merely that we cannot now say with certainty, simply by reference to the relevant laws and some antecedent situation, that a certain event would not have happened in the course of nature, and therefore must be such an intrusion. But we may still be able to say that it is very probable—and this is now an epistemic probability—that it would not have happened naturally, and so is likely to be such an intrusion. For if the laws made it physically improbable that it would come about, this tends to make it epistemically improbable that it did come about through those laws, if there is any other way in which it could have

come about and which is not equally improbable or more improbable. In practice the difficulty mentioned is not much of an extra difficulty. For even where we believe there to be deterministic laws and an earlier situation which together would have made an occurrence actually impossible in the course of nature, it is from our point of view at best epistemically very probable, not certain, that those are the laws and that that was the relevant antecedent situation.

Consequently, whether the laws of nature are deterministic or statistical, we can give a coherent definition of a miracle as a supernatural intrusion into the normally closed system that works in accordance with those laws, and in either case we can identify conceivable occurrences, and alleged occurrences, which if they were to occur, or have occurred, could be believed with high probability, though not known with certainty, to satisfy that definition.

However, the full concept of a miracle requires that the intrusion should be purposive, that it should fulfill the intention of a god or other supernatural being. This connection cannot be sustained by any ordinary causal theory; it presupposes a power to fulfil intentions directly, without physical means, which is highly dubious; so this requirement for a miracle will be particularly hard to confirm. On the other hand it is worth noting that successful prophecy could be regarded as a form of miracle for which there could in principle be good evidence. If someone is reliably recorded as having prophesied at t_1 an event at t_2 which could not be predicted at t_1 on any natural grounds, and the event occurs at t_2, then at any later time t_3 we can assess the evidence for the claims both that the prophecy was made at t_1 and that its accuracy cannot be explained either causally (for example, on the ground that it brought about its own fulfilment) or as accidental, and hence that it was probably miraculous.

There is, then, a coherent concept of miracles. Their possibility is not ruled out *a priori,* by definition. So we must consider whether Hume's argument shows that we never have good reason for believing that any have occurred.

Hume's general principle for the evaluation of testimony, that we have to weigh the unlikelihood of the event reported against the unlikelihood that the witness is mistaken or dishonest, is substantially correct. It is a corollary of the still more general principle of accepting whatever hypothesis gives the best overall explanation of all the available and relevant evidence. But some riders are necessary. First, the likelihood or unlikelihood, the epistemic probability or improbability, is always relative to some body of information, and may change if additional information comes in. Consequently, any specific decision in accordance with Hume's principle must be provisional. Secondly, it is one thing to decide which of the rival hypotheses in the field at any time should be provisionally accepted in the light of the evidence then available; but it is quite another to estimate the weight of this evidence, to say how well supported this favoured hypothesis is, and whether it is likely that its claims will be undermined either by additional information or by the suggesting of further alternative hypotheses. What is clearly the best-supported view of some matter at the moment may still be very insecure, and quite likely to be overthrown by some further considerations. For example, if a public opinion poll is the only evidence we have about the result of a coming election, this evidence may point, perhaps decisively, to one result rather than another; yet if the poll has reached only a small sample of the electorate, or if it was taken some time before the voting day, it will not be very reliable. There is a dimension of reliability over and above that of epistemic probability relative to the available evidence. Thirdly, Hume's description of what gives support to a prediction, or in general to a judgement about an unobserved case that would fall under some generalization, is very unsatisfactory. He seems to say that if *all* so far observed As have been Bs, then this amounts to a 'proof' that some unobserved A will be (or is, or was) a B, whereas if some observed As have been Bs, but some have not, there is only a 'probability' that an unobserved A will be a B (pp. 110–12). This mixes up the reasoning *to* a generalization with the reasoning *from* a generalization to a particular case. It is true that the premises 'All As are Bs' and 'This is an A' constitute a proof of the conclusion 'This is a B', whereas the premises '*x* per cent of As are Bs' and 'This is an A' yield—if

there is no other relevant information—a probability of *x* per cent that this is a B: they *probabilify* the conclusion to this degree, or, as we can say, the probability of the conclusion 'This is a B' relative to that evidence is *x* per cent. But the inductive argument from the observation 'All so far observed As have been Bs' to the generalization 'All As are Bs' is far from secure, and it would be most misleading to call this a proof, and therefore misleading also to describe as a proof the whole line of inference from 'All so far observed As have been Bs' to the conclusion 'This as yet unobserved A is a B'. Similarly, the inductive argument from '*x* per cent of observed As have been Bs' to the statistical generalization '*x* per cent of As are Bs' is far from secure, so that we cannot say that '*x* per cent of observed As have been Bs' even probabilifies to the degree *x* per cent the conclusion 'This as yet unobserved A is a B'. A good deal of other information and background knowledge is needed, in either case, before the generalization, whether universal or statistical, is at all well supported, and hence before the stage is properly set for either proof or probabilification about an as yet unobserved A. It is harder than Hume allows here to arrive at well-supported generalizations of either sort about how the world works.

These various qualifications together entail that what has been widely and reasonably thought to be a law of nature may not be one, perhaps in ways that are highly relevant to some supposed miracles. Our present understanding of psychosomatic illness, for example, shows that it is not contrary to the laws of nature that someone who for years has seemed, to himself as well as to others, to be paralysed should rapidly regain the use of his limbs. On the other hand, we can still be pretty confident that it is contrary to the laws of nature that a human being whose heart has stopped beating for forty-eight hours in ordinary circumstances—that is, without any special life-support systems—should come back to life, or that what is literally water should without addition or replacement turn into what is literally good-quality wine.

However, any problems there may be about establishing laws of nature are neutral between the parties to the present debate, Hume's followers and those who believe in miracles; for both these parties need the notion of a well-established law of nature. The miracle advocate needs it in order to be able to say that the alleged occurrence is a miracle, a violation of natural law by supernatural intervention, no less than Hume needs it for his argument against believing that this event has actually taken place.

It is therefore not enough for the defender of a miracle to cast doubt (as he well might) on the certainty of our knowledge of the law of nature that seems to have been violated. For he must himself say that this *is* a law of nature: otherwise the reported event will not be miraculous. That is, he must in effect *concede* to Hume that the antecedent improbability of this event is as high as it could be, hence that, apart from the testimony, we have the strongest possible grounds for believing that the alleged event did not occur. This event must, by the miracle advocate's own admission, be contrary to a genuine, not merely a supposed, law of nature, and therefore maximally improbable. It is this maximal improbability that the weight of the testimony would have to overcome.

One further improvement is needed in Hume's theory of testimony. It is well known that the agreement of two (or more) *independent* witnesses constitutes very powerful evidence. Two independent witnesses are more than twice as good as each of them on his own. The reason for this is plain. If just one witness says that *p*, one explanation of this would be that it was the case that *p* and that he has observed this, remembered it, and is now making an honest report; but there are many alternative explanations, for example that he observed something else which he mistook for its being that *p*, or is misremembering what he observed, or is telling a lie. But if two witnesses who can be shown to be quite independent of one another both say that *p*, while again one explanation is that each of them has observed this and remembered it and is reporting honestly, the alternative explanations are not now so easy. They face the question 'How has there come about this *agreement* in their reports, if it was not the case that *p*? How have the witnesses managed to misobserve to the same effect, or to misremember in the same way, or to hit upon the same lie?' It is difficult for even a single liar to keep on

telling a *consistent* false story; it is much harder for two or more liars to do so. Of course if there is any collusion between the witnesses, or if either has been influenced, directly or indirectly, by the other, or if both stories have a common source, this question is easily answered. That is why the independence of the witnesses is so important. This principle of the improbability of coincident error has two vital bearings upon the problem of miracles. On the one hand, it means that a certain sort of testimony can be more powerful evidence than Hume's discussion would suggest. On the other, it means that where we seem to have a plurality of reports, it is essential to check carefully whether they really are independent of one another; the difficulty of meeting this requirement would be an important supplement to the points made in Part II of Hume's essay. Not only in remote and barbarous times, but also in recent ones, we are usually justified in suspecting that what look like distinct reports of a remarkable occurrence arise from different strands of a single tradition between which there has already been communication.

We can now put together the various parts of our argument. Where there is some plausible testimony about the occurrence of what would appear to be a miracle, those who accept this as a miracle have the double burden of showing both that the event took place and that it violated the laws of nature. But it will be very hard to sustain this double burden. For whatever tends to show that it would have been a violation of natural law tends for that very reason to make it most unlikely that it actually happened. Correspondingly, those who deny the occurrence of a miracle have two alternative lines of defense. One is to say that the event may have occurred, but in accordance with the laws of nature. Perhaps there were unknown circumstances that made it possible; or perhaps what were thought to be the relevant laws of nature are not strictly laws; there may be as yet unknown kinds of natural causation through which this event might have come about. The other is to say that this event would indeed have violated natural law, but that for this very reason there is a very strong presumption against its having happened, which it is most unlikely that any testimony will be able to outweigh.

Usually one of these defences will be stronger than the other. For many supposedly miraculous cures, the former will be quite a likely sort of explanation, but for such feats as the bringing back to life of those who are really dead the latter will be more likely. But the *fork*, the disjunction of these two sorts of explanation, is as a whole a very powerful reply to any claim that a miracle has been performed.

However, we should distinguish two different contexts in which an alleged miracle might be discussed. One possible context would be where the parties in debate already both accept some general theistic doctrines, and the point at issue is whether a miracle has occurred which would enhance the authority of a specific sect or teacher. In this context supernatural intervention, though *prima facie* unlikely on any particular occasion, is, generally speaking, on the cards: it is not altogether outside the range of reasonable expectation for these parties. Since they agree that there is an omnipotent deity, or at any rate one or more powerful supernatural beings, they cannot find it absurd to suppose that such a being will occasionally interfere with the course of nature, and this *may* be one of these occasions. For example, if one were already a theist and a Christian, it would not be unreasonable to weigh seriously the evidence of alleged miracles as some indication whether the Jansenists or the Jesuits enjoyed more of the favour of the Almighty. But it is a very different matter if the context is that of fundamental debate about the truth of theism itself. Here one party to the debate is initially at least agnostic, and does not yet concede that there is a supernatural power at all. From this point of view the intrinsic improbability of a genuine miracle, as defined above, is very great, and one or other of the alternative explanations in our fork will always be much more likely—that is, either that the alleged event is not miraculous, or that it did not occur, that the testimony is faulty in some way.

This entails that it is pretty well impossible that reported miracles should provide a worthwhile argument for theism addressed to those who are initially inclined to atheism or even to agnosticism. Such reports can form no significant part of what, following Aquinas, we might call a *Summa contra Gentiles*, or what, following Descartes, we could describe as being addressed to infidels. Not only are such reports unable to carry any rational conviction on their own, but also they are unable even to contribute independently to the kind of accumulation or battery of arguments referred to in the Introduction. To this extent Hume is right, despite the inaccuracies we have found in his statement of the case.

One further point may be worth making. Occurrences are sometimes claimed to be literally, and not merely metaphorically, miracles, that is, to be genuine supernatural interventions into the natural order, which are not even *prima facie* violations of natural law, but at most rather unusual and unexpected, but very welcome. Thus the combination of weather conditions which facilitated the escape of the British army from Dunkirk in 1940, making the Luftwaffe less than usually effective but making it easy for ships of all sizes to cross the Channel, is sometimes called a miracle. However, even if we accepted theism, and could plausibly assume that a benevolent deity would have favoured the British rather than the Germans in 1940, this explanation would still be far less probable than that which treats it as a mere meteorological coincidence: such weather conditions can occur in the ordinary course of events. Here, even in the context of a debate among those who already accept theistic doctrines, the interpretation of the event as a miracle is much weaker than the rival natural explanation. *A fortiori,* instances of this sort are utterly without force in the context of fundamental debate about theism itself.

There is, however, a possibility which Hume's argument seems to ignore—though, as we shall see, he did not completely ignore it. The argument has been directed against the acceptance of miracles on testimony; but what, it may be objected, if one is not reduced to reliance on testimony, but has observed a miracle for oneself? Surprisingly, perhaps, this possibility does not make very much difference. The first of the above-mentioned lines of defence is still available; maybe the unexpected event that one has oneself observed did indeed occur, but in accordance with the laws of nature. Either the relevant circumstances or the operative laws were not what one has supposed them to be. But at least a part of the other line of defence is also available. Though one is not now relying literally on another witness or other witnesses, we speak not inappropriately of the evidence of our senses, and what one takes to be an observation of one's own is open to questions of the same sort as is the report of some other person. I may have misobserved what took place, as anyone knows who has even been fooled by a conjurer or 'magician,' and, though this is somewhat less likely, I may be misremembering or deceiving myself after an interval of time. And of course the corroboration of one or more independent witnesses would bring in again the testimony of others which it was the point of this objection to do without. Nevertheless, anyone who is fortunate enough to have carefully observed and carefully recorded, for himself, an apparently miraculous occurrence is no doubt rationally justified in taking it very seriously; but even here it will be in order to entertain the possibility of an alternative natural explanation.

As I said, Hume does not completely ignore this possibility. The Christian religion, he says, cannot at this day be believed by any reasonable person without a miracle. 'Mere reason is insufficient to convince us of its veracity: And whoever is moved by *Faith* to assent to it, is conscious of a continued miracle in his own person, which subverts all the principles of his understanding . . .' (p. 131). But of course this is only a joke. What the believer is conscious of in his own person, though it may be a mode of thinking that goes against 'custom and experience', and so is contrary to the ordinary rational principles of the understanding is not, as an occurrence, a violation of natural law. Rather it is all too easy to explain immediately by the automatic communication of beliefs between persons and the familiar psychological processes of wish fulfillment, and ultimately by what Hume himself was later to call 'the natural history of religion.'

V.4 Miracles and Revelation

RICHARD SWINBURNE

In our final reading in this section, Richard Swinburne takes up the matter of miracles where he left off in his previous article. There he argues, contra Hume, that miracles were possible. Here he argues that given the proviso that the existence of God is a plausible hypothesis or assumption, it is reasonable to expect that he would reveal himself in human history and that he would confirm the revelation by miracles (including predictive prophecy). Swinburne here sets forth the criteria that would have to be met were a religion to claim that it is that revelation. Although Swinburne later (in a section not included in this work) applies these criteria to

Christianity, readers are free to use them to compare the revelations as they deem appropriate.

If a man concludes that it is probable that there is a God, it follows that he has a duty to worship and obey binding on him, and so he must investigate how best to fulfill it; and that involves investigating the claims of different creeds. However, I think that the expert or the person in a parental situation may still have a duty to compare creeds, even if on his evidence it is more probable than not that there is no God. For his duty is to show to others how best to attain goals of supreme worth. He must investigate whether non-theistic ways to salvation are likely to attain that salvation. And also those dependent on him need to know as surely as they can, even if it is probable that there is no God and non-theistic ways are unlikely to attain their goal, which is the way most likely to attain its goal. Even if the agricultural biochemist believes that on balance it is improbable that more food can be got out of the land, if the people are very short of food, he still has a duty to investigate which method of fertilizing, irrigation, or crop rotation is more likely to produce an increase of yield (in the hope that his inquiries will show that one method is much more likely than any others to be successful). By analogy, if the religious investigator, who is an expert or in a parental situation, judges the goals of religion to be very worthwhile, it follows that he has a duty to pursue religious investigation even if he believes that it is not probable with respect to any one way that it will attain the goals of religion. So in these various circumstances it is a duty or at any rate a very worthwhile thing to investigate the relative probability of creeds, in order to produce a rational belief about the relative probabilities of creeds, e.g., a belief that the Christian Creed is more probable than any rival creed which justifies a different religious way. The above conclusions about the duty to investigate the comparative probabilities of creeds hold, I urge, objectively for a man who has a certain belief about how probable it is that there is a God. If he does not support his beliefs about the comparative probabilities of creeds by proper investigation, they will not be rational. . . .

The process of showing the Christian Creed to be more probable than any rival creed which justifies a different religious way can be analysed as needing three steps: first, a demonstration that it is probable to some degree on reasonably believed evidence that there is a God; secondly, a demonstration that it is more probable, if there is a God, that the other items of the Christian Creed are true than that the other items of some rival theistic creed are true; and thirdly, a demonstration that it is more probable that the Christian Creed as a whole is true than that any non-theistic religious creed is true.

The first task is the traditional task of natural theology and is far too big a subject to be discussed here. It was the subject of my earlier volume, *The Existence of God*. I concluded there that it is more probable than not that there is a God. But all that is necessary for weak belief in the Christian Creed is

a much less probable belief—say, putting it loosely, that there is a significant probability that there is a God. For, given that, there is quite a chance that salvation may be had by pursuing one of the religious ways of theistic religions, since the attainment of salvation according to these religions consists in God providing that salvation (e.g., forgiveness and life after death). The next stage is to show that if there is a God it is more likely that the other items of the Christian Creed are true than that the other items of some rival creed are true. For given that there is a God, then if the other items of the Christian Creed are more probable than the other items of rival theistic creeds, the Christian Creed as a whole (item common with other theistic creeds plus different items) will be more probable than any other theistic creed as a whole (common item plus different items). We need to show that it is more probable that God became incarnate in Christ than that Muhammad was his chief prophet; that the way to worship regularly is by attendance at the Eucharist rather than by the five daily prayer-times, and so on. The choice between religious systems in these respects turns on a judgement about which is the true revelation of God. For the grounds for believing the other items of a theistic creed—that in this way God has intervened in history, that forgiveness is available in this way, that these are the fates for men in the after-life, that this is the way to live in this life—are normally that God has revealed these truths through the mouth of some human intermediary, whom we will call his prophet. I wish therefore now to discuss the kind of considerations which are relevant to assessing such claims to revelation. The discussion will be a brief discussion to indicate the kind of considerations which need to be investigated, rather than a thorough discussion of which is the true claim to revelation. I include the discussion to indicate the kind of investigation by which faith needs to be supported.

The Evidence of Revelation

A theistic religion claims that its prophet is a special messenger of God and that what he says about the nature of reality and how men ought to live is to be believed because it comes from God. It is also sometimes claimed that the prophet and his actions have eternal significance because of his special status. The Christian claim that Jesus Christ was both God and man who by his sacrificial life redeemed the world is obviously such a claim—indeed it is by far the strongest claim for divine intervention in human history made by any of the great religions.

Theistic religions are normally prepared to allow that God has spoken to men in a limited way through prophets other than their own unique prophet. Thus Islam is prepared to allow that God spoke to men through Jesus Christ. But the point is that, according to each religion, there is truth and falsity mixed in the deliverances of prophets other than its own, and that where there is dispute the sayings of its own prophet take precedence—for what he says is true without qualification (and, perhaps also, what he does is of unrepeatable significance). If a religion claims that all prophets teach varying amounts of truth and falsity, and so purports to judge the worth of each prophet's teaching merely by considering what he says rather than the fact that he says it, that religion cannot be regarded in the traditional sense as a revealed religion, as teaching and supported by a revelation. For the grounds for believing any of what the religion asserts will not be that it has been revealed by God (for which in turn there is other evidence, including that other things which the prophet said are true); rather, the argument will always go the other way round—the grounds for believing that any of the things which a prophet teaches have been revealed by God are simply that they are true. A religion which claims a revelation in teaching claims that the prophet's message is to be believed, not because it can be known to be true independently of the prophet having said it, but because of the prophet's authority.

So then, what is the evidence for claims that some prophet is in this way a special messenger of God? The traditional view down the centuries, advocated among others by Aquinas, declared to be official Roman Catholic doctrine by the First Vatican Council and classically expounded by Paley, is that the evidence will be of various kinds but will include a central and crucial element of the miraculous.

In *Evidences of Christianity*, Paley argues that given that there is a God—who is, by definition, good—and that the human race lies in ignorance of things important for them to know, it is *a priori* to some extent to be expected that God would give a revelation to men. And what things are these important things? If the arguments of this book are correct, it is important for men to know the nature of the world and man's place in it, how they ought to live, how deep long-term happy well-being is to be achieved, how forgiveness is to be obtained from God, how God is to be worshipped and obeyed. A revelation such as the Christian revelation (as traditionally described) claims to provide knowledge on all these matters. Paley however stresses—to my mind totally disproportionately— the existence and nature of the after-life at the expense of all other elements of revelation.

Yet knowledge of all these things has great value, other than its value in preparing men for the after-life. It is good that man should understand the world, know how to live in it and how to obtain the deepest well-being this Earth can provide; it is good too that man should know how to worship and obey God and obtain forgiveness from him— all this quite independently of the consequences in an after-life for man of his doing these things. But it is also good that man know how to obtain his eternal well-being.

Men are capable of receiving such knowledge. But much of it could not to all appearances be obtained by mere reflection on the natural world. That God is three persons in one substance could hardly, if true, be known to be true by such human reflection. I claimed, in *The Existence of God*, that various phenomena, including chiefly very general and publicly observable ones such as the orderliness of nature, show the dependence of the world on a creator God. We must, I argued, suppose him to be very powerful, wise, etc., if he is to be able to bring about the existence and orderliness of the world; and considerations of simplicity involve us inferring from 'very powerful . . . etc,' to 'infinitely powerful . . . etc.' But it is hard to see how any further details of his nature could be read off from the world. I have no conclusive proof that this cannot be done. I simply appeal to the apparent impossibility of seeing how it can be done; and to the fact that nobody today thinks that it can be done, and that very few people in the past ever thought that it could be done. Likewise, mere reflection on the natural world could hardly show the details of how men ought to worship God, e.g. in the Eucharist on Sundays; or how forgiveness from God is to be obtained—through pleading the Passion of Christ. And so on.

Other such purported knowledge as is conveyed in revelations such as the Christian revelation, is purported knowledge of matters about which men produce arguments of a general philosophical character arising out of reflection on the natural world. That God is omnipotent, omniscient, etc., is, as we have seen, the subject of such argument. So too are the general principles of morality, such as that men ought to tell the truth, keep their promises, and show compassion. Now maybe all such arguments fail; it needs a detailed discussion of each case to show whether they do or not. However, I have argued in *The Existence of God* that arguments to show that there is a God omnipotent, omniscient, and perfectly free do work. And plausibly, reason can help to show claims about morality to be justified.

However, if such knowledge of the omnipotence, omniscience, etc. of God and the general principles of morality can be obtained by natural means, it is evident that some men are too stupid to obtain the knowledge—the savage argues only to a much more lowly God—and some men will never reach that knowledge because of the climate of contrary opinion in which they grow up, the climate of an atheistic authority. It is sometimes through men yielding to bad desires, either to teach things which they do not really believe (in the interests of their state or party, church or career), or not to investigate further things which they are told on authority (through fear or laziness), that men come to hold beliefs and climates of opinion develop. Hence sin plays a role in moulding belief.

So the detailed truths of creeds will either not be known at all to men or (through men's stupidity, ignorance, and sin) be known only with difficulty. Yet these are the truths which are of crucial importance if men are to make themselves good men (true

specimens of humanity), men worthy to obtain everlasting well-being. If there is a God (who is by definition good), he might to some degree be expected to intervene in history to reveal these truths which men could not discover for themselves and to give his authority to those to which reason pointed with insufficient force, for he has good reason to do this. There is also the reason to expect a revelation, not merely by teaching but by a human life, which the Christian tradition had always stressed but which Paley does not. Human sin and corruption need atonement. This is a primary reason why, on the traditional Christian doctrine, a revelation in the form of a person who lived a sacrifical life was to be expected.

So, given that there is good evidence that there is a God, there is some reason *a priori* to expect that there will be a revelation. What historical evidence would show that it had taken place on a certain occasion? It is a basic principle of confirmation theory that evidence confirms a hypothesis (i.e., adds to its probability) if and only if that evidence is more to be expected if the hypothesis is true than it would otherwise be. So given some prior probability that God would reveal himself in history, the evidence of history that he has done so will be such as is to be expected if the hypothesis is true, and not otherwise. The obvious kind of evidence, then, will be teaching such as God would be expected to give and actions such as God would be expected to do, of a kind and in circumstances in which they would not be expected to occur in the normal course of things.

What sort of teaching about the matters which man needs to know would God be expected to give through a prophet? Obviously teaching which is true and deep. Although the teaching itself must be true, it might however need to be embodied in the false historical and scientific presuppositions of the prophet's day if it is to be understood. For instance, suppose a prophet was teaching in a culture which believed that the world consisted of a flat and stationary earth surrounded by a heavenly dome in which Sun, Moon, planets, and stars moved. God wishes through the prophet to convey the message of the total dependence of the world on God. How is he to announce his message?

There seem three possible ways. The prophet might say: 'It is God who holds the flat earth still and moves round it the heavenly lights.' Or he might say: 'Whatever the true scientific description of the world, it is God who brings about that state of affairs which that description describes.' Or he might begin by giving a true scientific account of the world and then say that God brings about that world. But if he is to announce his message in the third way, the religious truth can only be announced after a complete process of scientific education. And even if he is to announce it in the second way, the message will only be understood by a people who have done quite a lot of philosophical abstraction. They would have to have understood the possible falsity of most of their common-sense science, and have got used to the abstract concepts of states of affairs which might not be describable, and descriptions which might not apply to things. If the prophet's message is to be understood by a primitive culture, it is the first way of teaching which would have to be used. And unless one thinks that divine revelation can be given only to sophisticated peoples, that means that when a divine revelation is made to a primitive people, there is a distinction to be made between the prophet's message and the scientific and historical presuppositions in terms of which it is expressed. This distinction would need to be made by a later and less primitive society which knew a bit more about science and history, in order for it to see what was the religious message clothed in the false presuppositions. And of course if the later society was not sophisticated enough, it might fail to make the distinction, and so suppose the science and history to be part of the prophet's message. This could lead to its rejecting the message on the grounds that the science and history were false (the rational reaction); or, worse (the irrational reaction) adopting the old science and history (and rejecting the alleged advances here of more recent times) on the grounds that the prophet's message was true. It will, I hope, be unnecessary to give many historical examples of such reactions.

One all too sadly obvious modern one is the example of the different reactions to Darwin's theory of evolution. Christianity has regarded the Old Testament as in a sense and to a degree licensed by Christ. He took it largely for granted in his teaching, and the Church which he founded proclaimed it (with the exception of the laws about ritual and sacrifice) as God's message. The Old Testament in telling in Genesis 1 and 2 the Creation stories seems to presuppose that animal species came into being a few thousand years ago virtually simultaneously. The theory of evolution showed that they did not. So some rejected Christianity on the grounds that it taught what was scientifically false, and others rejected the theory of evolution on the grounds that it conflicted with true religion. But it seems odd to suppose that the religious message of what is evidently a piece of poetry was concerned with the exact time and method of animal arrival on the Earth, or that that was what those who composed it were attempting to tell the world. Their message concerned, not the details of the time and method of animal arrival, but the ultimate cause of that arrival. To make the point that there is a distinction between a prophet's religious message and its scientific and historical presuppositions is not to deny that it may not always be easy to disentangle the message from the presuppositions, or to express it in more modern times. One obvious step in going about this task is for the investigator to inquire into the circumstances of the prophet's utterance and see what he was denying, and contrast this with the assumptions about more mundane matters shared by the prophet and his opponents.

So then, with this qualification, the prophet must teach what is true. Must he teach only what is true? Can there be falsity mixed with his teaching? No: the whole body of what the prophet announces as his message must be true, for the reason given earlier: that it purports to be God's announcement to man of things beyond his power to discover for himself. However, if a clear distinction could be made between the prophet's message and other things which he said but for which he did not claim any special authority, there is no reason to require that the latter be true.

The prophet's teaching must be, not merely true, but deep. Men need moral teaching and instruction about the nature of reality which is not readily available to them.

What would be the evidence that the prophet's teaching is true? First, none of what he teaches must be evidently false. His teaching on morality, for example, must not involve his telling men that they ought to do what is evidently morally wrong—the prophet who recommends cheating and child torture can be dismissed straight away. Likewise no factual teaching of the prophet must be proven false. If the prophet teaches that, whatever men do, the world will end in exactly thirty years time, and the world fails to end then; the prophet must be rejected. Secondly, such parts of the prophet's teaching as can be checked must be found to be true. Some of the prophet's moral teaching, for example, may coincide with our clear intuitions about morality. Thirdly, it may be that some parts of the prophet's teaching which do not appear obviously true to start with are found, through experience and reflection, to be true. One way in which subsequent experience could confirm a prophet's teaching would be if the sort of teaching about God, his nature, and action in history which the prophet gives makes sense of the investigator's own private and public experience, in the sense of making probable a course of experience which would not otherwise be probable. The course of a man's life, the answering of his prayers, and particular 'religious experiences' within that life might be such as the God proclaimed by the prophet would be expected to bring about. All that would be further evidence of the truth of the prophet's teaching.

All of this is independent evidence that some of what the prophet teaches is true. The fact that some of what the prophet teaches is seen to be true and deep is indeed some slight evidence that the other things which he said are true and deep. If a man says what is true on one deep matter, that is some evidence for supposing that he is a wise man, and so for supposing that what he says on other deep matters is true. But it is only slight evidence—many teachers who teach deep truths teach falsities also, and prophets who agree over one range of their teaching disagree over another range. That the moral teaching of Jesus Christ is true and deep is slender grounds for believing what he had to say about life after death.

Revelations include, and (as we have seen that Paley argued) can *a priori* be expected to include, things beyond human capacity independently to check. For example they typically assert the existence of a life after death; and they provide us with information about the sort of God who is to be worshipped in far more detail than a man could derive from examination of the created world, and they give us details of the way to worship him. Hence we need some evidence that what the prophet says is true when we cannot check independently whether it is or not. Analogy suggests the sort of evidence for which we ought to be looking. Suppose that in the days before wireless, telephones, and fast travel, a man claims to have visited a king of a distant country and to have brought back a message from him. What would show that the message comes from the king? First, the message may contain some prediction of an event of the future occurrence of which the messenger could have learnt only from the king; e.g. that the messenger's arrival would be followed by the arrival of some of the king's ships (the messenger having to all appearances travelled by land and so not having been able to meet such ships en route). Secondly, the messenger may bring some token which a man could only have obtained from the king, e.g. a precious stone of a kind only to be found in the king's country, and which is mined by the king alone and kept by him. The token might be the sort of token which people of the culture of those days traditionally gave to authenticate messages. By analogy, evidence that the prophet has his revelation from God and so is to be believed on deep matters where we have no independent means of checking, would be given, first, by his ability to predict some future event which he would have no means of predicting otherwise, i.e. by mere human powers. But any event in accordance with natural laws could be predicted by mere human powers. So this evidence needs to be evidence of an ability to predict events not in accordance with natural laws; and that, in a basically deterministic world, means violations of natural laws. The evidence would need also to suggest that the violations were brought about by God, and so were miracles. Secondly, evidence that the prophet had his revelation from God would be provided if the prophet's life was accompanied by events which, evidence suggested, were violations of natural laws produced by God in circumstances where such violations would naturally and by local convention be interpreted as vindicating the prophet's teaching. Both these further sources of evidence thus involve the occurrence of miracles.

Before taking the argument further, I need to spell out what I understand by a miracle and what would be evidence that an event was a miracle in my sense. I understand by a miracle a violation of the laws of nature, that is, a non-repeatable exception to the operation of these laws, brought about by God. Laws of nature have the form of universal statements 'all As are B,' and state how bodies behave of physical necessity. Thus Kepler's three laws of planetary motion state how the planets move. The first law states that all planets move in ellipses with the sun at one focus. If this purported law is to be a law of nature, planets must in general move as it states.

What however is to be said about an isolated exception to a purported law of nature? Suppose that one day Mars moves out of its elliptical path for a brief period and then returns to the path. There are two possibilities. This wandering of Mars may occur because of some current condition of the Universe (e.g. the proximity of Jupiter drawing Mars out of its elliptical path), such that if that condition were to be repeated the event would happen again. In this case the phenomenon is an entirely regular phenomenon. The trouble is that what might have appeared originally to be a basic law of nature proves now not to be one. It proves to be a consequence of a more fundamental law that the original purported law normally holds, but that under circumstances describable in general terms (e.g. 'when planets are close to each other') there are exceptions to it. Such repeatable exceptions to purported laws merely show that the purported laws are not basic laws of nature. The other possibility is that the exception to the law was not caused by some current condition, in such a way that if the condition were to recur the event would happen again. In this case we have a non-repeatable exception to a law of nature. But how are we to describe this event further? There are two possible moves. We may say that if there occurs an exception to a purported law of nature, the purported law can be no law. If the purported law says 'all As are B' and there is an A which is not B, then 'all As are B' is no law. The trouble with saying that is that the purported law may be a very good device for giving accurate predictions in our field of study; it may be by far the best general formula for describing what happens in the field which there is. (I understand by a general formula a formula which describes what happens in all circumstances of a certain kind, but does not mention by name particular individuals, times, or places.) To deny that the purported law is a law, when there is no more accurate general formula, just because there is an isolated exception to its operation, is to ignore its enormous ability to predict what happens in the field.

For this reason it seems not unnatural to say that the purported law is no less a law for there being a non-repeatable exception to it; and then to describe the exception as a 'violation' of the law. At any rate this is a coherent way of talking, and I think that it is what those who use such expressions as 'violation' of a law of nature are getting at. In this case we must amend our understanding of what is a law of nature. To say that a generalization 'all As are B' is a universal law of nature is to say that being A physically necessitates being B, and so that any A will be B—apart from violations.

But how do we know that some event such as the wandering of Mars from its elliptical path is a non-repeatable rather than a repeatable exception to a purported law of nature? We have grounds for believing that the exception is non-repeatable in so far as any attempt to amend the purported law of nature so that it predicted the wandering of Mars as well as all the other observed positions of Mars, would make it so complicated and *ad hoc* that we would have no grounds for trusting its future predictions. It is no good for example amending the law so that it reads: 'all planets move in ellipses with the Sun at one focus, except in years when there is a competition for the World Chess Championship between two players both of whose surnames began with *K*.' Why not? Because this proposed law mentioned properties which have no other place in physics (no other physical law invokes this sort of property) and it mentions them in an *ad hoc* way (that is, the proposed new law has the form 'so-and-so holds except under such-and-such circumstances', when the only reason for adding the exceptive clause is that otherwise the law would be incompatible with observations; the clause does not follow naturally from the theory). What we need if we are to have a more adequate law is a general formula, of which it is an entirely natural consequence that the exception to the original law occurs when it does.

In these ways we could have grounds for believing that an exception to a purported law was non-repeatable and so a violation of a natural law. Claims of this sort are of course corrigible—we could be wrong; what seemed inexplicable by natural causes might be explicable after all. But then we could be wrong about most things, including claims of the opposite kind. When I drop a piece of chalk and it falls to the ground, every one supposes that here is an event perfectly explicable by natural laws. But we could be wrong. Maybe the laws of nature are much more complicated than we suppose, and Newton's and Einstein's laws are mere approximations to the true laws of mechanics. Maybe the true laws of mechanics predict that almost always when released from the hand, chalk will fall to the ground, but not today because of a slightly abnormal distribution of distant galaxies. However although the true laws of nature predict that the chalk will rise, in fact it falls. Here is a stark violation of natural laws, but one which no one detects because of their ignorance of natural laws. 'You could be wrong' is a knife which cuts both ways. What seem to be perfectly explicable events might prove, when we come to know the laws of nature much better, to be violations. But of course this is not very likely. The reasonable man goes by the available evidence here, and also in the converse case. He supposes that what is, on all the evidence, a violation of natural laws really is one. There is good reason to suppose that events such as the following if they occurred would be violations of laws of nature: levitation, that is, a man rising in the air against gravity without the operation of magnetism or any other known physical force; res-

urrection from the dead of a man whose heart has not been beating for twenty-four hours and who counts as dead by other currently used criteria; water turning into wine without the assistance of chemical apparatus or catalysts; a man growing a new arm from the stump of an old one.

Since the occurrence of a violation of natural laws cannot be explained in the normal way, either it has no explanation or it is to be explained in a different way. The obvious explanation exists if there is a God who is responsible for the whole order of nature, including its conformity to natural laws, and who therefore can on occasion suspend the normal operation of natural laws and bring about or allow some one else to bring about events, not via this normal route. We should suppose that events have explanations if suggested explanations are at all plausible. If there is quite a bit of evidence that there is a God responsible for the natural order, then any violations are plausibly attributed to his agency and so plausibly recognized as miracles—at least so long as those violations are not ruled out by such evidence as we may have from other sources about God's character. God's permitting a law of nature to be violated is clearly necessary for this to occur if he is the author of Nature; and in the absence of evidence that any other agent had a hand in the miracle, it ought to be attributed to God's sole agency. But if there is evidence, say, that it happens after a command (as opposed to a request to God) for it to happen issued by another agent, then the miracle is to be attributed to a joint agency.

I have not considered here the kind of historical evidence needed to prove the occurrence of an event which if it occurred would be a violation, but clearly it will be of the same kind as the evidence for any other historical event. There is the evidence of one's own senses, the testimony of others (oral and written) and the evidence of traces (effects left by events, such as footprints, fingerprints, cigarette ash, etc,). I see no reason in principle why there should not be evidence of this kind to show the occurrence of a levitation or a resurrection from the dead.

Now I claimed earlier that two further kinds of evidence for the genuineness of a prophet's revelation would be provided if there was evidence of the prophet's ability to predict miracles, and if there was evidence that his teaching was vindicated by miracles. Christian theology has traditionally claimed both these further sources of evidence for the truth of what Christ said.

The life of Christ was, according to the Gospels, full of 'miracles'. Some of the 'miracle' stories are perhaps not intended to be taken literally, some of them are ill-authenticated, and some of the 'miracles' were not violations of natural laws e.g., perhaps certain cures of the mentally deranged come into this category). Yet some of the Gospel 'miracles', in particular the stories of healings of the blind and dumb and lame, seem to me to be intended to be taken literally by the Gospel writers, to be moderately well authenticated, and to be violations of natural laws, if they occurred. But the story of one 'miracle' above all, of course has dominated Christian teaching from the earliest days until the present—the story of the Resurrection of Christ. It seems to this writer that the writers of gospels and epistles intended their readers to believe that although Christ was killed on the Cross, he subsequently came to life (in a transformed body which left its tomb). If the events of the first Easter occurred in anything like the form recorded in the Gospels, there is a clear case of a violation of a natural law. As a violation of natural law, it would (for reasons already stated) be plausibly explained by the action of God intervening in human history.

Christian theology has claimed as evidence of the genuineness of Christ's revelation, his prophetic power in the sense of his ability to predict future events to be brought about by God, including Christ's crucifixion and resurrection, the establishment of the Church and the fall of Jerusalem. At any rate the resurrection, if it occurred, would have been, I have claimed, a miracle; and so if Christ had the ability to predict it, that would show some knowledge of God's purposes. I do not pronounce on the disputed issue of whether Christ did predict his Resurrection, or the other events, or whether there was anything miraculous in the latter.

Secondly, Christian theology has claimed that Christ's miracles, and above all the miracle of the Resurrection, marked God's vindication of Christ's teaching. The Resurrection meant that the sacrificial life of Jesus had not ended in disaster. If it occurred, it was the means of founding the Church and making the teaching of and about Jesus available to the world. Whatever is to be said about other purported miracles, the Resurrection (if it occurred) is for this reason reasonably interpreted as involving the divine judgement that it is good that the teaching of Jesus triumph. Since that teaching involves showing men the way to salvation, if it is good that it triumph, that must be because the way which it shows men does lead to salvation. For although God may have good reason for allowing evil to triumph, if it occurs through the free choice of men—because it is good that men should make a difference to the world through their free choice, or in accord with natural processes—as a warning to men as to the consequences of allowing such natural processes to continue; he would seem to have no reason to intervene in nature to make it triumph. Apparently, miraculous triumphing is not to be expected but for divine action and approval and therefore plausibly signifies divine action and approval. Also, Jews of the first century AD would, I suggest, readily interpret miraculous intervention to secure the triumphing of Jesus's life and teaching as evidence of a divine 'signature' on that teaching and so of its truth (and perhaps also, if Christ's death was an atoning sacrifice, as the acceptance of that sacrifice). If God gives a message to men, the right interpretation of the message is (in the absence of other considerations) the way in which it would naturally be interpreted by those who received it. For any giver of messages uses such devices as, given the conventions of his audience, will be interpreted in the right way.

Similar considerations to those about a revelation via a prophet's teaching are relevant for assessing any claim that the prophet's life was in some sense God's life, viz. that the prophet was in some sense God incarnate (although claims to such revelation are not our main concern in this chapter). A primary issue here is whether the concept of an incarnation is a coherent one at all—whether there is not some internal contradiction in the suggestion that the same individual was both God and man. If there is not, then to any claim that God has become incarnate on a particular occasion, there are relevant, first, *a priori* considerations about whether God is likely to become incarnate and under what circumstances. I noted earlier the *a priori* considerations put forward in favour of expecting God to bring about a Christian-type atonement. Then there will be evidence of two further kinds relevant to showing that God has on a particular occasion become incarnate. There will, first, be the quality of a certain prophet's human life—that it shows the kind of pattern which God would be expected to show if he accepted human limitations. It needs much argument to show what that pattern would be. But clearly, to make an atonement of the kind earlier referred to, a holy and sacrificial life is needed. Moral reflection and reflection on the prophet's life may help the investigator to see in it depths of holiness and sacrifice which are not in evidence at first sight. Yet there are many sacrificial lives lived by men on Earth. The evidence that a particular one was divine would be the testimony of the prophet himself (shown to teach true teaching by the criteria previously considered) or his accredited representative (e.g., a church); that the prophet himself could work miracles at will (not merely pray successfully for them to happen); and that his life began and ended in a way which violated natural processes. For if through the prophet's life God entered and left the world in response to the current human condition, this would require some interruption of the operation of natural processes which are concerned with the created world and planned by God from the beginning of the created world. For if the prophet's coming into the world was a natural consequence of natural laws operative throughout human history (even if made so to operate by God's original choice), his coming into the world (and so also his leaving it) would not be the result of God's spontaneous response to the mess which men had made of their lives and of the Earth. So for more than one reason, incarnation requires to be accompanied by miracle; and evidence for such miracles in connection with a holy and sacrificial life is evidence of incarnation. Claims of an incarnation typically need to be backed up by a claim to revelation in teaching (e.g. the prophet or his accredited representative—a church—teaching that the prophet was God incarnate; and there are major religions (e.g. Judaism and Islam) which claim no

incarnation and yet are to be compared with Christianity in respect of a revelation in teaching.

Brief though my discussion of revelation has been, I believe that it substantiates Paley's classical claim about revelation, especially revelation in teaching. Paley writes: 'In what way can a revelation be made, but by miracles? In none which we are able to conceive?' I have argued that Paley is right.

What a man needs to believe with respect to the claimed Christian revelation, if he is to pursue the Christian way is, we have seen, not that it is more probable than not that God revealed himself in Christ but that, if there is a God, it is more probable that he revealed himself in Christ than that he revealed himself through any other prophet with a conflicting message. If the argument of this chapter is correct, for another revelation to be more probable than the Christian revelation, it would have to be backed by a more evident miracle, or be backed by a miracle no less evident but containing more evidently true and deep teaching, or perhaps, be backed by a miracle somewhat less evident but containing teaching far more evidently true and deep. I shall come shortly to the question of how much investigation of comparative religion is necessary before a man can have a rational belief that this is so.

Paley's conclusion, after his investigation into this issue, was that no religion other than Christianity is backed by equally well-authenticated miracles. He claims that 'the only event in the history of the human species, which admits of comparison with the propagation of Christianity' is Islam. But he claims that 'Mahomet did not found his pretensions . . . upon proofs of supernatural agency, capable of being known and attested by others.'

I believe that, whatever the deficiencies of Paley's detailed historical arguments (and he wrote long before the great advances in biblical criticism in the late nineteenth century), the approach of the *Evidences* to these matters is correct. The evidence of a revelation is the plausibility to the reflective investigator of a prophet's teaching (and—if an incarnation is claimed—the holiness of his life); and some kind of miraculous divine signature symbolically affirming and forwarding the prophet's teaching and work. . . .

Bibliography for Part V

Broad, C. D. "Hume's Theory of the Credibility of Miracles." *Proceedings of the Aristotelian Society* 17 (1916–17). An insightful critique of Hume.

Flew, Antony. "Miracles." In *Encyclopedia of Philosophy*, edited by Paul Edwards. New York: Macmillan, 1966. A good survey of the problem, containing a Humean version of the attack on miracles.

Geisler, Norman L. *Miracles and Modern Thought.* Grand Rapids, Mich.: Zondervan, 1982. A clearly written apology for an evangelical position that comes to terms with major philosophical opponents. Valuable for its terse analyses, though tending to oversimplify the opposition.

Hollard, R. F. "The Miraculous." *American Philosophical Quarterly* 2 (1965): 43–51. An elaborate study and defense of the possibility of miracles, containing important distinctions.

Lewis, C. S. *Miracles* New York: Macmillan, 1947. A cogently and clearly argued defense of miracles.

Nowell-Smith, Patrick. "Miracles." In *New Essays in Philosophical Theology*, edited by Antony Flew and Alasdair MacIntyre. London: Macmillan, 1955. Attacks the concept of miracles as unscientific and, as such, incoherent.

Rowe, William. *Philosophy of Religion.* Chap. 9. Belmont: Wadsworth, 1978. A lucid introductory discussion of the overall problem.

Smart, Ninian. *Philosophers and Religious Truth.* Chap. 2. London: SCM, 1964. A defense of miracles against the charge that they are unscientific.

Swinburne, Richard. *The Concept of Miracle.* London: Macmillan, 1970. A development of the ideas contained in his articles in Part 5 of this volume.

PART VI

DEATH AND IMMORTALITY

Of all the many forms which natural religion has assumed none probably has exerted so deep and far-reaching an influence on human life as the belief in immortality and the worship of the dead; hence [a discussion] of this momentous creed and of the practical consequences which have been deduced from it can hardly fail to be at once instructive and impressive, whether we regard the record with complacency as a noble testimony to the aspiring genius of man, who claims to outlive the sun and the stars, or whether we view it with pity as a melancholy monument of fruitless labour and barren ingenuity expended in prying into that great mystery of which fools profess their knowledge and wise men confess their ignorance.*

Is there life after death? Few questions have troubled humans as deeply as this one. Is this finite, short existence of three score and ten years all that we have? Or is there reason to hope for a blessed postmortem existence where love, justice, and peace, which we now experience in fragmented forms, will unfold in all their fullness and enable human existence to find fulfillment? Are we merely mortal or blessedly immortal?

Anthropological studies reveal a widespread and ancient sense of immortality. Prehistoric societies buried their dead with food so that the deceased would not be hungry in the next life. Most cultures and religions have some version of a belief in another life, whether it be in the form of a resurrected body, a transmigrated soul, reincarnation, or an ancestral spirit present with the tribe.

Let us begin by understanding what we mean by immortality. For our purposes we do not mean living on through our works or in the memories of our loved ones; we mean a conscious afterlife in which the individual continues to exist. As a definition the Catholic one will do: "that attribute in virtue of which a being is free from death. A being is incorruptible if it does not contain within itself a principle of dissolution; it is indestructible if it can

**Sir James Frazier, *The Belief in Immortality*, vol. 1 (London: Macmillan, 1913), vii–viii.*

333

resist every external power tending to destroy or annihilate it. If the indestructible and incorruptible being is endowed with life it is called immortal. Annihilation is always possible to God by the mere withdrawal of his conserving act."*

Death for most humans is the ultimate tragedy. It is the paramount evil for it deprives us of all that we know and love on earth. Although there may be fates worse than death for some of us (living a completely evil life, being a heavy burden on others), our fear of death is profound. We want to live as long as possible (given a certain quality of life). We have a general craving for continued existence. The more life the better.

On the other hand, there is precious little direct evidence for life after death. After the brain ceases to function, a person cannot be resuscitated. We personally don't know of anyone who has come back from the dead to tell us about the next life.

So on the one hand we have a passionate longing to live again and be with our loved ones, and on the other hand there is little or no direct evidence that we shall live again. The grave seems the last environment for humankind. And yet we search for indirect evidence for immortality. We welcome any news from this possible distant clime as good news indeed, and we cannot but regard the promise of eternal life as an incentive to meet whatever a credible guide states as the necessary conditions for entry.

In the Western tradition three views have dominated this issue, one denying life after death and two affirming it. The negative view, going back to the ancient Greek atomist philosophers Democritus and Leucippus, holds that we are identical with our bodies (including our brains), so that when the body dies, so does the self. There is nothing more. We may call this view materialist monism, because it does not allow for the possibility of a soul or spiritual self that can live without the body. In our readings this view is set forth by Bertrand Russell, the eminent British philosopher who died in 1970. His argument is judged to be the most reasonable one by Antony Flew in his essay on survival.

The positive views divide into dualist and monist theories of life after death. The dualist views separate the body from the soul or self of the agent and affirm that it is the soul or self that lives forever. This view was held by the pre-Socratic philosopher Pythagoras (570–500 BC) and developed by Plato (427–347 BC). In modern philosophy it is represented by René Descartes (1596–1650). It is sometimes referred to as the Platonic-Cartesian view of immortality. These philosophers argue that we are essentially spiritual or mental beings and that our bodies are either unreal or not part of our essential selves. Death is merely the separation of our souls from our bodies, a sort of spiritual liberation. Although Plato has many arguments for this thesis, one of the most famous is found in the *Phaedo*, included in our first reading. One section is worth quoting in full:

---

*A Catholic Dictionary, edited by D. Attwater (New York: Macmillan, 1941), 261.

When the soul employs the body in any inquiry, and makes use of sight, or hearing, or any other sense—for inquiry with the body must signify inquiry with the senses—she is dragged away by the body to the things which are impermanent, changing, and the soul wanders about blindly, and becomes confused and dizzy, like a drunken man, from dealing with things that are changing. . . . [But] when the soul investigates any question by herself, she goes away to the pure and eternal, and immortal and unchangeable, to which she is intrinsically related, and so she comes to be ever with it, as soon as she is by herself, and can be so; and then she rests from her wandering and dwells with it unchangingly, for she is related to what is unchanging. And is not this state of the soul called wisdom?*

The argument may be analyzed as follows:

1. If a person's soul while in the body is capable of any activity independently of the body, then it can perform that activity in separation from the body (i.e., after death, surviving death).
2. In pure or metaphysical thinking (i.e., in contemplating the forms and their interrelationships), a person's soul performs an activity independently of the body. No observation is necessary for this investigation.
3. Therefore, a person's soul can engage in pure or metaphysical thinking in separation from the body. That is, it can and must survive death.

This is a positive argument for the existence of the soul. Unfortunately, the second premise is dubious, for it could be the case that the mind's activity is epiphenomenal, that is, dependent on the brain. Although Plato is right in saying that we need not make an empirical examination of the world in order to think analytically or metaphysically, he has not shown that analytic and metaphysical thinking can go on without a body or brain.

As far as I know, no one has offered a sound argument to *prove* that we have a soul that succeeds our physical existence. However, this is not to say that there is no evidence for this point of view. We note some below.

The second positive view on immortality is associated with the Christian tradition, namely, St. Paul's statement in 1 Corinthians 15. It is interesting to note that there is very little mention made in the Old Testament of life after death. It is at best a shadowy existence in Sheol, the place under Jerusalem where the dead lie dormant or vaguely aware, a place comparable to Hades in Greek mythology. In the New Testament, although there are references to a spiritual existence, the soul (*psyche*) is not separated from the body (*soma*); rather, the person is a holistic, unified being with the soul or self being the form of the material body (in an almost Aristotelian sense). In death the soul is not liberated from the body as from a corpse, but rather a new, glorified *body* comes into being that is somehow related to our present earthly body. The classic passage is in Paul's first letter to the Corinthians. It reads as follows:

Now if Christ be preached that he rose from the dead, how say some among you that there is no resurrection of the dead? But if there be no resurrection of the dead,

---

**Phaedo, 79 c–d, my translation.

then is Christ not risen: And if Christ be not risen, then is our preaching in vain, and your faith is also in vain. . . . Ye are still in your sins. Then they which are fallen asleep in Christ are perished. If in this life only we have hope in Christ, we are of all men most miserable.

But now is Christ risen from the dead, and become the first fruits of them that slept. For since by man came death by man also the resurrection of the dead. . . . For Christ must reign until he hath put all enemies under his feet. The last enemy that shall be destroyed is death.

But some man will say, How are the dead raised up? and with what body do they come? Thou fool, that which thou sowest is not quickened, except it die: and that which thou sowest, thou sowest not that body that shall be, but bare grain, it may chance of wheat, or so some other grain. But God giveth it a body as it hath pleased him, and to every seed his own body. All flesh is not the same flesh; but there is one kind of flesh of men, another flesh of beasts, another of fishes and another of birds. There are also celestial bodies, and bodies terrestrial: but the glory of the celestial is one, and the glory of the terrestrial is another. There is one glory of the sun, and another glory of the moon, and another glory of the stars: and one star differeth from another star in glory. So also in the resurrection of the dead. It is sown in dishonor; it is raised in glory: it is sown in weakness; it is raised in power: It is sown a natural body; it is raised a spiritual body. And so it is written, The first man Adam was made a living soul; the last Adam was made a quickening spirit. Howbeit that was not first which is spiritual, but that which is natural; and afterward that which is spiritual. The first man is of the earth, earthly: the second man is the Lord from heaven. As is the earthly, such are they also that are earthly: and as is the heavenly, such are they also that are heavenly. And as we have borne the image of the earthly, we shall also bear the image of the heavenly. Now this I say, brethren, that flesh and blood cannot inherit the kingdom of God; neither doth corruption inherit incorruption. Behold, I shew you a mystery; We shall not all sleep, but we shall all be changed. In a moment, in a twinkling of an eye, at the last trump: for the trumpet shall sound, and the dead shall be raised incorruptible, and we shall be changed. For this corruptible must put on incorruption, and this mortal must put on immortality.*

When I approach the subject of immortality in an undergraduate philosophy class, I poll the students to find out which they think is the Christian view of life after death—the view that in death the soul leaves the body and goes to heaven or the view that our bodies will be raised. Almost every student chooses the first view, which I then point out is basically Platonic and not Christian. This view is reflected in popular religion, not the least example being the bedtime prayer taught to children: "Now I lay me down to sleep, I pray the Lord my soul to keep. If I should die before I wake, I pray the Lord my soul to take." Of course, one could hold the view that there is an intermediate state in which the soul dwells disembodied, waiting for the resurrection day, at which time it will receive its new body.

Whether the notion of continued existence after death in either of these versions is a coherent thesis is a matter raised by Jeffrey Olen and Peter van Inwagen in their analyses of immortality and personal identity. Olen's article is especially important, for it contains a serious discussion of the criteria of personal identity. Given the fact that we all undergo physical and mental

---

*1 Corinthians: 15: 12–53, King James Version.

change, under what conditions can we be said to be the *same* person over time (i.e., what gives us the right to say that some person P is the same persons at t_2 as P was at some earlier time t_1)?

Olen examines two standard views on this matter, the one involving the psychological states criterion and the other involving the body (including the brain) criterion. The psychological states (or memory) criterion goes back to John Locke and states that a person is the same person if and only if he or she is psychologically continuous in character, desires, and memories. There are at least three problems with this view. First, there is no way to distinguish *apparent* memories from *genuine* remembering, so that it could be the case that someone came among us detailing the events of Napoleon's life in such a way as to cause us to believe that he had somehow gotten hold of those memories. But we would probably be reluctant to say that this person was Napoleon, especially if we already knew him to be our uncle. A second problem is that our memories (and characters and desires, for that matter) could be duplicated in other persons, so that multiple subjects could have the same "memories." We would not be able to tell which of the persons was the rememberer. Finally, there is the problem of whether the concept of memory itself makes any sense apart from a body. What kind of existence would a purely mental existence be? Would it be in time and space? If it were in space, how would it as a nonsensory entity perceive anything at all? It seems that memory and character predicates are tied to a physical existence. This leads us to consider the body criterion as the proper criterion for personal identity.

The body criterion states that a person is the same person over time if he or she is continuous with his or her body. There are problems with this criterion too, for the body changes in ways that produce states far removed from their originals. Taking this criterion literally, we would have to conclude that when a zygote divides into identical twins during the first weeks of its existence, the two resulting entities are identical to each other (rather than being exactly similar). Furthermore, we can imagine situations in which the personality of one person is transferred to another. Locke illustrates this possibility in his story of the prince and the pauper, in which the body of the prince wakes up one day with the character and all the memories and desires of the pauper. We might be inclined to say that although the prince's body was before us, we were really speaking with the pauper. We can also imagine operations in the future in which our bodies and/or brains are divided and merged with prosthetic bodies or brains. The notions of continuity and uniqueness would conflict.

When we apply these two views of personal identity to the issue of immortality, the problems are compounded. The notion of a disembodied soul implies that one's existence as a person transcends one's embodiment such that the eventual corruption of one's body need not and will not involve the cessation of one's personal existence. One will live forever. But the notion of a disembodied soul suffers from the fact that our concept of experience seems to demand a body as a necessary condition for having experiences and for making sense of personal identity. It seems that memories and the ingredients are located in the physical brain, so one is at a loss to explain how the soul stores or reduplicates them.

The notion of resurrection (or reconstitution) states that you will continue to survive your death in a new glorified body. God will reconstitute you. This is eloquently (if grandiosely) stated on Benjamin Franklin's tombstone:

> This body of B. Franklin in Christ Church
>   cemetery,
> Printer, Like the Cover of an old book,
> Its Contents torn out,
> And stript of its Lettering and Gilding,
> Lies here, Food for Worms.
> But the work shall not be lost;
> For it will, as he believed,
> Appear once more in a new and more
>   elegant Edition,
> Corrected and Improved by its Author.

But the resurrection view supposes that God will create a new being like yourself. The problem with this view, as is duly noted by Antony Flew in the fifth reading in this part, is that it does not seem all that comforting to learn that someday there will be someone just like you who will enjoy a blessed existence; for if there is no continuity between you and your future self, it is really not you but your successor (some one very similar, even exactly similar, to you, a sort of twin) who will enjoy eternal life.

Of course, many Christians believe that although there must be a body for one's full existence, it could be the case that the personality is preserved in an interim state of disembodiment between the first corruptible bodily existence and the second incorruptible bodily existence (see Richard Purtill, *Thinking About Religion*, chapter 9). But the problem remains of whether it makes sense to speak of a disembodied self.

Still, there is indirect evidence for the existence of a soul or the disembodied survival of the self. There is evidence of parapsychology and of out-of-the-body experiences. The first of these is discussed by John Hick in his article "Immortality and Resurrection" (our fourth reading). The best discussion of out-of-the-body (or near-death) experiences is found in James Moody's book *Life after Life*, in which he documents several cases of "clinically dead" persons who were revived and reported remarkably similar experiences. Moody sets down the outline of an ideal report in the following passage.

> A man is dying and, as he reaches the point of greatest physical distress, he hears himself pronounced dead by his doctor. He begins to hear an uncomfortable noise, a loud ringing or buzzing, and at the same time feels himself moving very rapidly through a long dark tunnel. After this, he suddenly finds himself outside of his own physical body, but still in the immediate physical environment, and he sees his own

body from a distance, as though he is a spectator. He watches the resuscitation attempt from the unusual vantage point and is in a state of emotional upheaval.

After a while, he collects himself and becomes more accustomed to his odd condition. He notices that he still has a "body," but one of a very different nature and with very different powers from the physical body he has left behind. Soon other things begin to happen. Others come to meet and to help him. He glimpses the spirits of relatives and friends who have already died, and a loving, warm spirit of a kind he has never encountered before—a being of light—appears before him. This being asks him a question, nonverbally, to make him evaluate his life and helps him along by showing him a panoramic, instantaneous playback of the major events of his life. At some point he finds himself approaching some sort of barrier or border, apparently representing the limit between earthly life and the next life. Yet, he finds that he must go back to the earth, that the time for his death has not yet come. At this point he resists, for by now he is taken up with his experiences in the afterlife and does not want to return. He is overwhelmed by intense feelings of joy, love, and peace. Despite his attitude, though, he somehow reunites with his physical body and lives.*

This passage is not meant to represent any one person's report but is a model or composite of the common elements found in many stories. Moody himself makes no claims for the interpretation that the patients really experienced what they claim to have experienced. There could be neurological causes for the experiences, or they could be attributed to wish fulfillment. The point is, simply, that these experiences should be considered as part of the evidence to be examined carefully—and perhaps to be followed up with further research.

Returning to Hick's article, we can say that the most important part of this essay is Hick's invitation to us to see the possibility of life after death. The case against immortality is not a clear-cut one. Hick invites us to consider a person, John Smith, who disappears from before the eyes of his friends in the United States. At the same moment, an exact replica of him appears in India. Second, imagine that instead of reappearing, Smith dies, but at the moment of his death a Smith replica appears in India. We would probably say that he had been miraculously re-created in India. Finally, suppose that Smith died and his replica reappeared in a different world altogether, a resurrection world inhabited only by resurrected people.

Hick shows that the problems of identity and continuity of persons are not intractable. We can imagine coherent (logically possible) stories of reappearances in this life, so that it is not illogical to suppose a future life involving such a reappearance. Whether Hick is correct about this you may decide by closely examining these arguments.

You will want to look carefully at Jeffrey Olen's solution to the problem of personality and immorality, for although Olen accepts a materialist view of human personality, he also accepts a functionalist view of personhood. It is conceivable, according to his account, that we live on in another life through

---

*Life After Life (New York: Bantam Books, 1976), 21f.

having another brain "programmed" with our personality and memory. Finally, Peter van Inwagen argues against the reconstitution view of Franklin and Hick, but for a version of the Christian doctrine of resurrection of the body based on God's preserving our body or an essential part of it (the brain or a part of the brain) before we die.

VI.1   Immortality of the Soul

PLATO

Plato (c. 427–347 BC), an Athenian and one of the most important philosophers who ever lived, believed that human beings were composed of two substances, a body and a soul. Of these, the true self is the soul, which lives on after the death of the body. All of Plato's writings are in the form of dialogues. In the first dialogue (from Alcibiades I*) Socrates argues with Alcibiades about the true self. The second dialogue (from the* Phaedo*) takes place in prison, where Socrates has been condemned to die. He is offered a way of escape but rejects it, arguing that it would be immoral to flee such a fate at this time and that he is certain of a better life after death.*

From *Alcibiades I*

Soc. And is self-knowledge an easy thing, and was he to be lightly esteemed who inscribed the text on the temple at Delphi? Or is self-knowledge a difficult thing, which few are able to attain?

Al. At times, I fancy, Socrates, that anybody can know himself; at other times, the task appears to be very difficult.

Soc. But whether easy or difficult, Alcibiades, still there is no other way; knowing what we are, we shall know how to take care of ourselves, and if we are ignorant we shall not know.

Reprinted from *Alcibiades I* and the *Phaedo*, translated by William Jowett (New York: Charles Scribner's Sons, 1889).

Al. That is true.

Soc. Well, then, let us see in what way the self-existent can be discovered by us; that will give us a chance to discovering our own existence, which without that we can never know.

Al. You say truly.

Soc. Come, now, I beseech you, tell me with whom you are conversing?—with whom but with me?

Al. Yes.

Soc. As I am with you?

Al. Yes.

Soc. That is to say, I, Socrates, am talking?

Al. Yes.

Soc. And I in talking use words?

Al. Certainly.

Soc. And talking and using words are, as you would say, the same?

Al. Very true.

Soc. And the user is not the same as the thing which he uses?

Al. What do you mean

Soc. I will explain: the shoemaker, for example, uses a square tool, and a circular tool, and other tools for cutting?

Al. Yes.

Soc. But the tool is not the same as the cutter and user of the tool?

Al. Of course not.

Soc. And in the same way the instrument of the harper is to be distinguished from the harper himself?

Al. He is.

Soc. Now the question which I asked was whether you conceive the user to be always different from that which he uses?

Al. I do.

Soc. Then what shall we say of the shoemaker? Does he cut with his tools only or with his hands?

Al. With his hands as well.

Soc. He uses his hands too?

Al. Yes.

Soc. And does he use his eyes in cutting leather?

Al. He does.

Soc. And we admit that the user is not the same with the things which he uses?

Al. Yes.

Soc. Then the shoemaker and the harper are to be distinguished from the hands and feet which they use?

Al. That is clear.

Soc. And does not a man use the whole body?

Al. Certainly.

Soc. And that which uses is different from that which is used?

Al. True.

Soc. Then a man is not the same as his own body?

Al. That is the inference.

Soc. What is he, then?

Al. I cannot say.

Soc. Nay, you can say that he is the user of the body.

Al. Yes.

Soc. And the user of the body is the soul?

Al. Yes, the soul.

Soc. And the soul rules?

Al. Yes.

Soc. Let me make an assertion which will, I think, be universally admitted.

Al. What is that?

Soc. That man is one of three things.

Al. What are they?

Soc. Soul, body, or the union of the two.

Al. Certainly.

Soc. But did we not say that the actual ruling principle of the body is man?

Al. Yes, we did.

Soc. And does the body rule over itself?

Al. Certainly not.

Soc. It is subject, as we were saying?

Al. Yes.

Soc. Then that is not what we are seeking?

Al. It would seem not.

Soc. But may we say that the union of the two rules over the body, and consequently that this is man?

Al. Very likely.

Soc. The most unlikely of all things: for if one of the members is subject, the two united cannot possibly rule.

Al. True.

Soc. But since neither the body, nor the union of the two, is man, either man has no real existence, or the soul is man?

Al. Just so.

Soc. Would you have a more precise proof that the soul is man?

Al. No; I think that the proof is sufficient.

Soc. If the proof, although not quite precise, is fair, that is enough for us; more precise proof will be supplied when we have discovered that which we were led to omit, from a fear that the inquiry would be too much protracted.

Al. What was that?

Soc. What I meant, when I said that absolute existence must be first considered; but now, instead of absolute existence, we have been considering the nature of individual existence, and that may be sufficient; for surely there is nothing belonging to us which has more absolute existence than the soul?

Al. There is nothing.

Soc. Then we may truly conceive that you and I are conversing with one another, soul to soul?

Al. Very true.

Soc. And that is just what I was saying—that I, Socrates, am not arguing or talking with the face of Alcibiades, but with the real Alcibiades; and that is with his soul.

Al. True. . . .

From the Phaedo

Socrates: What again shall we say of the actual acquirement of knowledge?—is the body, if invited to share in the inquiry, a hinderer or a helper? I mean to say, have sight and hearing any truth in them? Are they not, as the poets are always telling us, inaccurate witnesses? and yet, if even they are inaccurate and indistinct, what is to be said of the other senses?—for you will allow that they are the best of them?

Certainly, he replied.

Then when does the soul attain truth?—for in attempting to consider anything in company with the body she is obviously deceived.

Yes, that is true.

Then must not existence be revealed to her in thought, if at all?

Yes.

And thought is best when the mind is gathered into herself and none of these things trouble her—neither sounds nor sights nor pain nor any pleasure,—when she has as little as possible to do with the body, and has no bodily sense or feeling, but is aspiring after being?

That is true.

And in this the philosopher dishonors the body; his soul runs away from the body and desires to be alone and by herself?

That is true.

Well, but there is another thing, Simmias: Is there or is there not an absolute justice?

Assuredly there is.

And an absolute beauty and absolute good?

Of course.

But did you ever behold any of them with your eyes?

Certainly not.

Or did you ever reach them with any other bodily sense? (and I speak not of these alone, but of absolute greatness, and health, and strength, and of the essence or true nature of everything). Has the reality of them ever been perceived by you through the bodily organs? or rather, is not the nearest approach to the knowledge of their several natures made by him who so orders his intellectual vision as to have the most exact conception of the essence of that which he considers?

Certainly.

And he attains to the knowledge of them in their highest purity who goes to each of them with the mind alone, not allowing when in the act of thought the intrusion or introduction of sight or any other sense in the company of reason, but with the very light of the mind in her clearness penetrates into the very light of truth in each; he has got rid, as far as he can, of eyes and ears and of the whole body, which he conceives of only as a disturbing element, hindering the soul from the acquisition of knowledge when in company with her—is not this the sort of man who, if ever man did, is likely to attain the knowledge of existence?

There is admirable truth in that, Socrates replied Simmias.

And when they consider all this, must not true philosophers make a reflection, of which they will speak to one another in such words as these: We have found, they will say, a path of speculation which seems to bring us and the argument to the conclusion, that while we are in the body, and while the soul is mingled with this mass of evil our desire will not be satisfied, and our desire is of the truth. For the body is a source of endless trouble to us by reason of the mere requirement of food; and also is liable to diseases which overtake and impede us in the search after truth: and by filling us so full of loves, and lusts, and fears, and fancies, and idols, and every sort of folly, prevents our ever having, as people say, so much as a thought. From whence come wars, and fightings, and factions? whence but from the body and the lusts of the body? For wars are occasioned by the love of money, and money has to be acquired for the sake and in the service of the body; and in consequence of all these things the time which ought to be given to philosophy is lost. Moreover, if there is time and an inclination toward philosophy, yet the body introduces a turmoil and confusion and fear into the course of speculation, and hinders us from seeing the truth; and all experience shows that if we would have pure knowledge of anything we must be quit of the body, and the soul in herself must behold all things in themselves: then I suppose that we shall attain that which we desire, and of which we say that we are lovers, and that is wisdom; not while we live, but after death, as the argument shows; for if while in company with the body, the soul cannot have pure knowledge, one of two things seems to follow—either knowledge is not to be attained at all, or, if at all, after death. For then, and not till then, the soul will be in herself alone and without the body. In this present life, I reckon that we make the nearest approach to knowledge when we have the least possible concern or interest in the body, and are not saturated with the bodily nature, but remain pure until the hour when God himself is pleased to release us. And then the foolishness of the body will be cleared away and we shall be pure and hold converse with other pure souls, and know of ourselves the clear light everywhere; and this is surely the light of truth. For no impure thing is allowed to approach the pure. These are the sort of words, Simmias, which the true lovers of wisdom cannot help saying to one another, and thinking. You will agree with me in that?

Certainly, Socrates.

But if this is true, O my friend, then there is great hope that, going whither I go, I shall there be satisfied with that which has been the chief concern of you and me in our past lives. And now that the hour of departure is appointed to me, this is the hope with which I depart, and not I only, but every man who believes that he has his mind purified.

Certainly, replied Simmias.

And what is purification but the separation of the soul from the body, as I was saying before; the habit of the soul gathering and collecting herself into herself, out of all the courses of the body; the dwelling in her own place alone, as in another life, so also in this, as far as she can; the release of the soul from the chains of the body?

Very true, he said.

And what is that which is termed death, but this very separation and release of the soul from the body?

To be sure, he said.

And the true philosophers, and they only, study and are eager to release the soul. Is not the separation and release of the soul from the body their especial study?

That is true.

And as I was saying at first, there would be a ridiculous contradiction in men studying to live as nearly as they can in a state of death, and yet repining when death comes.

Certainly.

Then Simmias, as the true philosophers are ever studying death, to them, of all men, death is the least terrible. Look at the matter in this way: how inconsistent of them to have been always enemies of the body, and wanting to have the soul alone, and when this is granted to them, to be trembling and repining; instead of rejoicing at their departing to that place where, when they arrive, they hope to gain that which in life they loved (and this was wisdom), and at the same time to be rid of the company of their enemy. Many a man has been willing to go to the world below in the hope of seeing there an earthly love, or wife, or son, and conversing with them. And will he who is a true lover of wisdom, and is persuaded in like manner that only in the world below he can worthily enjoy her, still repine at death? Will he not depart with joy? Surely, he will, my friend, if he be a true philosopher. For he will have a firm conviction that there only, and nowhere else, he can find wisdom in her purity. And if this be true, he would be very absurd, as I was saying, if he were to fear death.

. . . .

Socrates: And were we not saying long ago that the soul when using the body as an instrument of perception, that is to say, when using the sense of sight or hearing or some other sense (for the meaning of perceiving through the body is perceiving through the senses),—were we not saying that the soul too is then dragged by the body into the region of the changeable, and wanders and is confused; the world spins round her, and she is like a drunkard when under their influence?

Very true.

But when returning into herself she reflects; then she passes into the realm of purity, and eternity, and immortality, and unchangeableness, which are her kindred, and with them she ever lives, when she is by herself and is not let or hindered; then she ceases from her erring ways, and being in communion with the unchanging is unchanging. And this state of the soul is called wisdom?

That is well and truly said, Socrates, he replied.

And to which class is the soul more nearly alike and akin, as far as may be inferred from this argument, as well as from the preceding one?

I think, Socrates, that, in the opinion of every one who follows the argument, the soul will be infinitely more like the unchangeable,—even the most stupid person will not deny that.

And the body is more like the changing?

Yes.

Yet once more consider the matter in this light: When the soul and the body are united, then nature orders the soul to rule and govern, and the body to obey and serve. Now which of these two functions is akin to the divine? and which to the mortal? Does not the divine appear to you to be that which naturally orders and rules, and the mortal that which is subject and servant?

True.

And which does the soul resemble?

The soul resembles the divine, and the body the mortal,—there can be no doubt of that, Socrates.

Then reflect, Cebes: is not the conclusion of the whole matter this,—that the soul is in the very likeness of the divine, and immortal, and intelligible, and uniform, and indissoluble, and unchangeable; and the body is in the very likeness of the human, and mortal, and unintelligible, and multiform, and dissoluble, and changeable. Can this, my dear Cebes, be denied?

No indeed.

But if this is true, then is not the body liable to speedy dissolution? and is not the soul almost or altogether indissoluble?

Certainly.

And do you further observe, that after a man is dead, the body, which is the visible part of man, and has a visible framework, which is called a corpse, and which would naturally be dissolved and decomposed and dissipated, is not dissolved or decomposed at once, but may remain for a good while, if the constitution be sound at the time of death, and the season of the year favorable? For the body when shrunk and embalmed, as is the custom in Egypt, may remain almost entire through infinite ages; and even in decay, still there are some portions, such as the bones and ligaments, which are practically indestructible. You allow that?

Yes.

And are we to suppose that the soul, which is invisible, in passing to the true Hades, which like her is invisible, and pure, and noble, and on her way to the good and wise God, whither, if God will, my soul is also soon to go,—that the soul, I repeat, if this be her nature and origin, is blown away and perishes immediately on quitting the body, as the many say? That can never be, my dear Simmias and Cebes. The truth rather is, that the soul which is pure at departing draws after her no bodily taint, having never voluntarily had connection with the body, which she is ever avoiding, herself gathered into herself (for such abstraction has been the study of her life). And what does this mean but that she has been a true disciple of philosophy, and has practiced how to die easily? And is not philosophy the practice of death?

Certainly.

The soul, I say, herself invisible, departs to the invisible world,—to the divine and immortal and rational: thither arriving, she lives in bliss and is released from the error and folly of men, their fears and wild passions and all other human ills, and forever dwells, as they say of the initiated, in company with the gods? Is not this true, Cebes?

Yes, said Cebes, beyond a doubt.

VI.2   Skepticism over Immortality of the Soul

DAVID HUME

In this brief essay the Scottish Enlightenment philosopher David Hume (1711–1776) argues that there are several reasons for doubting that a person can survive death. He questions whether the notion of a 'soul' separate from the body is coherent and whether the moral argument—that the justice of God demands that there be an afterlife wherein we are rewarded for our deeds—makes much sense. On the contrary, the physical arguments from the analogy with nature strongly suggest that the soul is mortal. Hume's opening and closing paragraphs, which seem inconsistent with the tenor of the arguments, should be read with a touch of irony. Living in eighteenth-century Calvinist Scotland, where he suffered public opprobrium for his views, Hume often mischievously threw his reader off track with statements seeming to endorse the biblical doctrine of revelation.

By the mere light of reason it seems difficult to prove the immortality of the soul; the arguments for it are commonly derived either from metaphysical topics, or moral, or physical. But in reality it is the gospel, and the gospel alone, that has brought *life and immortality to light.*

I

Metaphysical topics suppose that the soul is immaterial, and that it is impossible for thought to belong to a material substance. But just metaphysics teach us, that the notion of substance is wholly confused and imperfect; and that we have no other idea of any substance, than as an aggregate of particular qualities inhering in an unknown something. Mat-

Reprinted from David Hume, *Two Essays on Suicide and Immortality* (1777).

ter, therefore, and spirit, are at bottom equally unknown; and we cannot determine what qualities inhere in the one or in the other. They likewise teach us, that nothing can be decided *á priori* concerning any cause or effect; and that experience, being the only source of our judgments of this nature, we cannot know from any other principle, whether matter, by its structure or arrangement, may not be the cause of thought. Abstract reasonings cannot decide any question of fact or existence. But admitting a spiritual substance to be dispersed throughout the universe, like the ethereal fire of the Stoics, and to be the only inherent subject of thought, we have reason to conclude from *analogy,* that nature uses it after the manner she does the other substance, *matter.* She employs it as a kind of paste or clay; modifies it into a variety of forms and existences; dissolves after a time each modification, and from its substance erects a new form. As the same material substance may successively compose the bodies of all animals, the same spiritual substance may compose their minds: their consciousness or that system of thought which they formed during life, may be continually dissolved by death, and nothing interests them in the new modification. The most positive assertors of the mortality of the soul never denied the immortality of its substance; and that an immaterial substance, as well as a material, may lose its memory or consciousness, appears in part from experience, if the soul be immaterial. Reasoning from the common course of nature, and without supposing any new interposition of the Supreme Cause, which ought always to be excluded from philosophy, *what is incorruptible must also be ingenerable.* The soul therefore, if immortal, existed before our birth; and if the former existence noways concerned us, neither will the latter. Animals undoubtedly feel, think, love, hate, will, and even reason, though in a more imperfect manner than men: are their souls also immaterial and immortal?

II

Let us now consider the moral arguments, chiefly those derived from the justice of God, which is supposed to be further interested in the future punishment of the vicious and reward of the virtuous. But these arguments are grounded on the supposition that God has attributes beyond what he has exerted in this universe, with which alone we are acquainted. Whence do we infer the existence of these attributes? It is very safe for us to affirm, that whatever we know the Deity to have actually done is best; but it is very dangerous to affirm that he must always do what to us seems best. In how many instances would this reasoning fail us with regard to the present world? But if any purpose of nature be clear, we may affirm, that the whole scope and intention of man's creation, so far as we can judge by natural reason, is limited to the present life. With how weak a concern from the original inherent structure of the mind and passions, does he ever look further? What comparison either for steadiness or efficacy, betwixt so floating an idea and the most doubtful persuasion of any matter of fact that occurs in common life? There arise indeed in some minds some unaccountable terrors with regard to futurity; but these would quickly vanish were they not artificially fostered by precept and education. And those who foster them, what is their motive? Only to gain a livelihood, and acquire power and riches in this world. Their very zeal and industry, therefore, are an argument against them.

What cruelty, what iniquity, what injustice in nature, to confine all our concern, as well as all our knowledge, to the present life, if there be another scene still waiting us of infinitely greater consequence? Ought this barbarous deceit to be ascribed to a beneficent and wise Being? Observe with what exact proportion the task to be performed, and the performing powers, are adjusted throughout all nature. If the reason of man gives him great superiority above other animals, his necessities are proportionably multiplied upon him: his whole time, his whole capacity, activity, courage, and passion, find sufficient employment in fencing against the miseries of his present condition; and frequently, nay, almost always, are too slender for the business assigned them. A pair of shoes, perhaps, was never yet wrought to the highest degree of perfection which that commodity is capable of attaining; yet it is necessary, at least very useful, that there should be some politicians and moralists, even some geometers, poets, and philosophers among mankind. The powers of men are no more superior to their wants, considered merely in this life, than those of foxes and hares are, compared to *their* wants and to their period of existence. The inference from parity of reason is therefore obvious.

On the theory of the soul's mortality, the inferiority of women's capacity is easily accounted for. Their domestic life requires no higher faculties either of mind or body. This circumstance vanishes and becomes absolutely insignificant on the religious theory: the one sex has an equal task to perform as the other; their powers of reason and resolution ought also to have been equal, and both of them infinitely greater than at present. As every effect implies a cause, and that another, till we reach the first cause of all, which is the Deity; every thing that happens is ordained by him, and nothing can be the object of his punishment or vengeance. By what rule are punishments and rewards distributed? What is the Divine standard of merit and demerit? Shall we suppose that human sentiments have place in the Deity? How bold that hypothesis! We have no conception of any other sentiments. According to human sentiments, sense, courage, good-manners, industry, prudence, genius, etc. are essential parts of personal merits. Shall we therefore erect an elysium for poets and heroes like that of ancient mythology? Why confine all rewards to one species of virtue? Punishment, without any proper end or purpose, is inconsistent with *our* ideas of goodness and justice; and no end can be served by it after the whole scene is closed. Punishment, according to *our* conception, should bear some proportion to the offence. Why then eternal punishment for the temporary offences of so frail a creature as man? Can any one approve of Alexander's rage, who intended to exterminate a whole nation because they had seized his favorite horse Bucephalus? [1]

Heaven and hell suppose two distinct species of men, the good and the bad; but the greatest part of mankind float betwixt vice and virtue. Were one to go round the world with an intention of giving a good supper to the righteous and a sound drubbing to the wicked, he would frequently be embarrassed in his choice, and would find the merits and demerits of most men and women scarcely amount to the value of either. To suppose measures of approbation and blame different from the human confounds every thing. Whence do we learn that there is such a thing as moral distinctions, but from our own sentiments? What man who has not met with personal provocation (or what good-natured man who has) could inflict on crimes, from the sense of blame alone, even the common, legal, frivolous punishments? And does any thing steel the breast of judges and juries against the sentiments of humanity but reflection on necessity and public interest? By the Roman law, those who had been guilty of parricide, and confessed their crime, were put into a sack along with an ape, a dog, and a serpent, and thrown into the river. Death alone was the punishment of those who denied their guilt, however fully proved. A criminal was tried before Augustus, and condemned after a full conviction; but the humane emperor, when he put the last interrogatory, gave it such a turn as to lead the wretch into a denial of his guilt. "You surely (said the prince) did not kill your father?"[2] This lenity suits our natural ideas of *right* even towards the greatest of all criminals, and even though it prevents so inconsiderable a sufferance. Nay, even the most bigoted priest would naturally without reflection approve of it, provided the crime was not heresy or infidelity; for as these crimes hurt himself in his *temporal* interest and advantages, perhaps he may not be altogether so indulgent to them. The chief source of moral ideas is the reflection on the interests of human society. Ought these interests, so short, so frivolous, to be guarded by punishments eternal and infinite? The damnation of one man is an infinitely greater evil in the universe than the subversion of a thousand millions of kingdoms. Nature has rendered human infancy peculiarly frail and mortal,

as it were on purpose to refute the notion of a probationary state; the half of mankind die before they are rational creatures.

III

The physical arguments from the analogy of nature are strong for the mortality of the soul; and are really the only philosophical arguments which ought to be admitted with regard to this question, or indeed any question of fact. Where any two objects are so closely connected that all alterations which we have ever seen in the one are attended with proportionable alterations in the other; we ought to conclude, by all rules of analogy, that, when there are still greater alterations produced in the former, and it is totally dissolved, there follows a total dissolution of the latter. Sleep, a very small effect on the body, is attended with a temporary extinction, at least a great confusion in the soul. The weakness of the body and that of the mind in infancy are exactly proportioned; their vigor in manhood, their sympathetic disorder in sickness, their common gradual decay in old age. The step further seems unavoidable; their common dissolution in death. The last symptoms which the mind discovers, are disorder, weakness, insensibility, and stupidity; the forerunners of its annihilation. The further progress of the same causes increasing, the same effects totally extinguish it. Judging by the usual analogy of nature, no form can continue when transferred to a condition of life very different from the original one in which it was placed. Trees perish in the water, fishes in the air, animals in the earth. Even so small a difference as that of climate is often fatal. What reason then to imagine, that an immense alteration, such as is made on the soul by the dissolution of its body, and all its organs of thought and sensation, can be effected without the dissolution of the whole? Every thing is in common betwixt soul and body. The organs of the one are all of them the organs of the other; the existence, therefore, of the one must be dependent on the other. The souls of animals are allowed to be mortal; and these bear so near a resemblance to the souls of men, that the analogy from one to the other forms a very strong argument. Their bodies are not more resembling, yet no one rejects the argument drawn from comparative anatomy. The Metempsychosis* is therefore the only system of this kind that philosophy can hearken to.

Nothing in this world is perpetual; every thing, however, seemingly firm, is in continual flux and change: the world itself gives symptoms of frailty and dissolution. How contrary to analogy, therefore, to imagine that one single form, seeming the frailest of any, and subject to the greatest disorders, is immortal and indissoluble? What theory is that! how lightly, not to say how rashly, entertained! How to dispose of the infinite number of posthumous existences ought also to embarrass the religious theory. Every planet in every solar system, we are at liberty to imagine peopled with intelligent mortal beings, at least we can fix on no other supposition. For these then a new universe must every generation be created beyond the bounds of the present universe, or one must have been created at first so prodigiously wide as to admit of this continual influx of beings. Ought such bold suppositions to be received by any philosophy, and that merely on the pretext of a bare possibility? When it is asked, whether Agamemnon, Thersites, Hannibal, Varro, and every stupid clown that ever existed in Italy, Scythia, Bactria, or Guinea, are now alive; can any man think, that a scrutiny of nature will furnish arguments strong enough to answer so strange a question in the affirmative? The want of argument without revelation sufficiently establishes the negative. *Quanto facilius*, says Pliny,[3] *certiusque sibi quemque credere, ac specimen securitatis antigene tali sumere experimento.* Our insensibility before the composition of the body seems to natural reason a proof of a like state after dissolution. Were our horrors of annihilation an original passion, not the effect of our general love of happiness, it would rather prove the mortality of the soul: for as nature does nothing in vain, she would never give us a horror against an impossible event. She may give us a horror against an unavoidable event, provided our endeavors, as in the present case, may often remove it to some distance. Death is in the end unavoidable; yet the human species could not be preserved had not nature inspired us with an aversion towards it. All doctrines are to be suspected which are favored by our passions; and the hopes and fears which gave rise to this doctrine are very obvious.

It is an infinite advantage in every controversy to defend the negative. If the question be out of the common experienced course of nature, this circumstance is almost if not altogether decisive. By what arguments or analogies can we prove any state of existence, which no one ever saw, and which no way resembles any that ever was seen? Who will repose such trust in any pretended philosophy as to admit upon its testimony the reality of so marvellous a scene? Some new species of logic is requisite for that purpose, and some new faculties of the mind, that they may enable us to comprehend that logic.

Nothing could set in a fuller light the infinite obligations which mankind have to Divine revelation, since we find that no other medium could ascertain this great and important truth.

Notes

1. Quintus Curtius [*History of Alexander,* VI. 5.]
2. Suetonius, *The Deified Augustus,* II. 3.
3. ["But how much easier and safer for each to trust in himself, and for us to derive our idea of future tranquility from our experience of it before birth!" Pliny, *Natural History* VII. 55, tr. H. Rackham (Cambridge, Mass.: "Loeb Classical Library." 1947).]

---

*Metempsychosis: the passing of the soul at death to another body, animal or human (reincarnation).

VI.3 The Finality of Death

BERTRAND RUSSELL

*In this brief essay the eminent British philosopher
Bertrand Russell (1872–1970) outlines some of the
major objections to the idea of life after death. He
argues that it is not reasonable to believe that our
personality and memories will survive the destruction of our bodies. He claims that the inclination to
believe in immortality comes from emotional factors, notably the fear of death.*

Before we can profitably discuss whether we shall
continue to exist after death, it is well to be clear as
to the sense in which a man is the same person as
he was yesterday. Philosophers used to think that
there were definite substances, the soul and the
body, that each lasted on from day to day, that a
soul, once created, continued to exist throughout
all future time, whereas a body ceased temporarily
from death till the resurrection of the body.

The part of this doctrine which concerns the
present life is pretty certainly false. The matter of the
body is continually changing by processes of nutri-
ment and wastage. Even if it were not, atoms in
physics are no longer supposed to have continuous
existence; there is no sense in saying: this is the
same atom as the one that existed a few minutes
ago. The continuity of a human body is a matter of
appearance and behavior, not of substance.

The same thing applies to the mind. We think
and feel and act, but there is not, in addition to
thoughts and feelings and actions, a bare entity, the
mind or the soul, which does or suffers these occurrences. The mental continuity of a person is a
continuity of habit and memory: there was yesterday one person whose feelings I can remember, and
that person I regard as myself of yesterday; but, in

fact, myself of yesterday was only certain mental
occurrences which are now remembered and are
regarded as part of the person who now recollects
them. All that constitutes a person is a series of
experiences connected by memory and by certain
similarities of the sort we call habit.

If, therefore, we are to believe that a person
survives death, we must believe that the memories
and habits which constitute the person will continue to be exhibited in a new set of occurrences.

No one can prove that this will not happen. But
it is easy to see that it is very unlikely. Our memories
and habits are bound up with the structure of the
brain, in much the same way in which a river is
connected with the riverbed. The water in the river
is always changing, but it keeps to the same course
because previous rains have worn a channel. In like
manner, previous events have worn a channel in
the brain, and our thoughts flow along this channel.
This is the cause of memory and mental habits. But
the brain, as a structure, is dissolved at death, and
memory therefore may be expected to be also
dissolved. There is no more reason to think otherwise than to expect a river to persist in its old course
after an earthquake has raised a mountain where a
valley used to be.

All memory, and therefore (one may say) all
minds, depend upon a property which is very no-
ticeable in certain kinds of material structures but
exists little if at all in other kinds. This is the property
of forming habits as a result of frequent similar
occurrences. For example: a bright light makes the
pupils of the eyes contract; and if you repeatedly
flash a light in a man's eyes and beat a gong at the
same time, the gong alone will, in the end, cause
his pupils to contract. This is a fact about the brain
and nervous system—that is to say, about a certain
material structure. It will be found that exactly
similar facts explain our response to language and
our use of it, our memories and the emotions they
arouse, our moral or immoral habits of behavior,

and indeed everything that constitutes our mental personality, except the part determined by heredity. The part determined by heredity is handed on to our posterity but cannot, in the individual, survive the disintegration of the body. Thus both the hereditary and the acquired parts of a personality are, so far as our experience goes, bound up with the characteristics of certain bodily structures. We all know that memory may be obliterated by an injury to the brain, that a virtuous person may be rendered vicious by encephalitis lethargica, and, that a clever child can be turned into an idiot by lack of iodine. In view of such familiar facts, it seems scarcely probable that the mind survives the total destruction of brain structure which occurs at death.

It is not rational arguments but emotions that cause belief in a future life.

The most important of these emotions is fear of death, which is instinctive and biologically useful. If we genuinely and wholeheartedly believed in the future life, we should cease completely to fear death. The effects would be curious, and probably such as most of us would deplore. But our human and subhuman ancestors have fought and exterminated their enemies throughout many geological ages and have profited by courage; it is therefore an advantage to the victors in the struggle for life to be able, on occasion, to overcome the natural fear of death. Among animals and savages, instinctive pugnacity suffices for this purpose; but at a certain stage of development, as the Mohammedans first proved, belief in Paradise has considerable military value as reinforcing natural pugnacity. We should therefore admit that militarists are wise in encouraging the belief in immortality, always supposing that this belief does not become so profound as to produce indifference to the affairs of the world.

Another emotion which encourages the belief in survival is admiration of the excellence of man. As the Bishop of Birmingham says, "His mind is a far finer instrument than anything that had appeared earlier—he knows right and wrong. He can build Westminster Abbey. He can make an airplane. He can calculate the distance of the sun. . . . Shall, then, man at death perish utterly? Does that incomparable instrument, his mind, vanish when life ceases?"

The Bishop proceeds to argue that "the universe has been shaped and is governed by an intelligent purpose," and that it would have been unintelligent, having made man, to let him perish.

To this argument there are many answers. In the first place, it has been found, in the scientific investigation of nature, that the intrusion of moral or aesthetic values has always been an obstacle to discovery. It used to be thought that the heavenly, bodies must move in circles because the circle is the most perfect curve, that species must be immutable because God would only create what was perfect and what therefore stood in no need of improvement, that it was useless to combat epidemics except by repentance because they were sent as a punishment for sin, and so on. It has been found, however, that, so far as we can discover, nature is indifferent to our values and can only be understood by ignoring our notions of good and bad. The Universe may have a purpose, but nothing that we know suggests that, if so, this purpose has any similarity to ours.

Nor is there in this anything surprising. Dr. Barnes tells us that man "knows right and wrong". But, in fact, as anthropology shows, men's views of right and wrong have varied to such an extent that no single item has been permanent. We cannot say, therefore, that man knows right and wrong, but only that some men do. Which men? Nietzsche argued in favor of an ethic profoundly different from Christ's, and some powerful governments have accepted his teaching. If knowledge of right and wrong is to be an argument for immortality, we must first settle whether to believe Christ or Nietzsche, and then argue that Christians are immortal, but Hitler and Mussolini are not, or vice versa. The decision will obviously be made on the battlefield, not in the study. Those who have the best poison gas will have the ethic of the future and will therefore be the immortal ones.

Our feelings and beliefs on the subject of good and evil are, like everything else about us, natural facts, developed in the struggle for existence and not having any divine or supernatural origin. In one of Aesop's fables, a lion is shown pictures of huntsmen catching lions and remarks that, if he had painted them, they would have shown lions catching huntsmen. Man, says Dr. Barnes, is a fine fellow because he can make airplanes. A little while ago there was a popular song about the cleverness of flies in walking upside down on the ceiling, with the chorus: "Could Lloyd George do it? Could Mr. Baldwin do it? Could Ramsay Mac do it? Why, NO." On this basis a very telling argument could be constructed by a theologically-minded fly, which no doubt the other flies would find most convincing.

Moreover, it is only when we think abstractly that we have such a high opinion of man. Of men in the concrete, most of us think the vast majority very bad. Civilized states spend more than half their revenue on killing each other's citizens. Consider the long history of the activities inspired by moral fervor: human sacrifices, persecutions of heretics, witch-hunts, pogroms leading up to wholesale extermination by poison gases, which one at least of Dr. Barnes's episcopal colleagues must be supposed to favor, since he holds pacifism to be un-Christian. Are these abominations, and the ethical doctrines by which they are prompted, really evidence of an intelligent Creator? And can we really wish that the men who practiced them should live forever? The world in which we live can be understood as a result of muddle and accident; but if it is the outcome of deliberate purpose, the purpose must have been that of a fiend. For my part, I find accident a less painful and more plausible hypothesis.

VI.4 Immortality and Resurrection

JOHN HICK

John Hick, a British philosopher who now teaches at Claremont Graduate School, examines the Platonic notion of the immortality of the soul and argues that it is filled with problems. In its place he argues for the New Testament view of the re-creation of the psychophysical person, a holistic person who is body-soul in one. He then offers a thought experiment of "John Smith" reappearances to show that re-creation is conceivable and worthy of rational belief. In the last part of this essay Hick considers whether parapsychology can provide evidence for our survival of death.

The Immortality of the Soul

Some kind of distinction between physical body and immaterial or semimaterial soul seems to be as old as human culture; the existence of such a distinction has been indicated by the manner of burial of the earliest human skeletons yet discovered. Anthropologists offer various conjectures about the origin of the distinction: perhaps it was first suggested by memories of dead persons; by dreams of them; by the sight of reflections of oneself in water and on other bright surfaces; or by meditation upon the significance of religious rites which grew up spontaneously in face of the fact of death.

It was Plato (428/7–348/7 B.C.), the philosopher who has most deeply and lastingly influenced Western culture, who systematically developed the body–mind dichotomy and first attempted to prove the immortality of the soul.[1]

Plato argues that although the body belongs to the sensible world,[2] and shares its changing and impermanent nature, the intellect is related to the unchanging realities of which we are aware when we think not of particular good things but of Goodness itself, not of specific just acts but of Justice itself, and of the other "universals" or eternal ideas in

John H. Hick, *Philosophy of Religion*, 3d ed., copyright © 1983, pp. 122–32. Reprinted by permission of Prentice-Hall, Inc., Englewood Cliffs, N.J. Footnotes edited.

virtue of which physical things and events have their own specific characteristics. Being related to this higher and abiding realm, rather than to the evanescent world of sense, reason or the soul is immortal. Hence, one who devotes his life to the contemplation of eternal realities rather than to the gratification of the fleeting desires of the body will find at death that whereas his body turns to dust, his soul gravitates to the realm of the unchanging, there to live forever. Plato painted an awe-inspiring picture, of haunting beauty and persuasiveness, which has moved and elevated the minds of men in many different centuries and lands. Nevertheless, it is not today (as it was during the first centuries of the Christian era) the common philosophy of the West; and a demonstration of immortality which presupposes Plato's metaphysical system cannot claim to constitute a proof for the twentieth-century disbeliever.

Plato used the further argument that the only things that can suffer destruction are those that are composite, since to destroy something means to disintegrate it into its constituent parts. All material bodies are composite; the soul, however, is simple and therefore imperishable. This argument was adopted by Aquinas and has become standard in Roman Catholic theology, as in the following passage from the modern Catholic philosopher, Jacques Maritain:

> A spiritual soul cannot be corrupted, since it possesses no matter; it cannot be disintegrated, since it has no substantial parts; it cannot lose its individual unity, since it is self-subsisting, nor its internal energy, since it contains within itself all the sources of its energies. The human soul cannot die. Once it exists, it cannot disappear; it will necessarily exist for ever, endure without end. Thus, philosophic reason, put to work by a great metaphysician like Thomas Aquinas, is able to prove the immortality of the human soul in a demonstrative manner.[3]

This type of reasoning has been criticized on several grounds. Kant pointed out that although it is true that a simple substance cannot disintegrate, consciousness may nevertheless cease to exist through the diminution of its intensity to zero.[4] Modern psychology has also questioned the basic

premise that the mind is a simple entity. It seems instead to be a structure of only relative unity, normally fairly stable and tightly integrated but capable under stress of various degrees of division and dissolution. This comment from psychology makes it clear that the assumption that the soul is a simple substance is not an empirical observation but a metaphysical theory. As such, it cannot provide the basis for a general proof of immortality.

The body–soul distinction, first formulated as a philosophical doctrine in ancient Greece, was baptized into Christianity, ran through the medieval period, and entered the modern world with the public status of a self-evident truth when it was redefined in the seventeenth century by Descartes. Since World War II, however, the Cartesian mind–matter dualism, having been taken for granted for many centuries, has been strongly criticized by philosophers of the contemporary analytical school.[5] It is argued that the words that describe mental characteristics and operations—such as "intelligent," "thoughtful," "carefree," "happy," "calculating" and the like—apply in practice to types of human behaviour and to behavioral dispositions. They refer to the empirical individual, the observable human being who is born and grows and acts and feels and dies, and not to the shadowy proceedings of a mysterious "ghost in the machine." Man is thus very much what he appears to be—a creature of flesh and blood, who behaves and is capable of behaving in a characteristic range of ways—rather than a nonphysical soul incomprehensibly interacting with a physical body.

As a result of this development much mid-twentieth-century philosophy has come to see man in the way he is seen in the biblical writings, not as an eternal soul temporarily attached to a mortal body, but as a form of finite, mortal, psychophysical life. Thus, the Old Testament scholar, J. Pedersen, says of the Hebrews that for them ". . . the body is the soul in its outward form."[6] This way of thinking has led to quite a different conception of death from that found in Plato and the neo-Platonic strand in European thought.

The Re-Creation of the Psychophysical Person

Only toward the end of the Old Testament period did after-life beliefs come to have any real importance in Judaism. Previously, Hebrew religious insight had focused so fully upon God's covenant with the nation, as an organism that continued through the centuries while successive generations lived and died, that the thought of a divine purpose for the individual, a purpose that transcended this present life, developed only when the breakdown of the nation as a political entity threw into prominence the individual and the problem of his personal destiny.

When a positive conviction arose of God's purpose holding the individual in being beyond the crisis of death, this conviction took the non-Platonic form of belief in the resurrection of the body. By the turn of the eras, this had become an article of faith for one Jewish sect, the Pharisees, although it was still rejected as an innovation by the more conservative Sadducees.

The religious difference between the Platonic belief in the immortality of the soul, and the Judaic-Christian belief in the resurrection of the body is that the latter postulates a special divine act of re-creation. This produces a sense of utter dependence upon God in the hour of death, a feeling that is in accordance with the biblical understanding of man as having been formed out of "the dust of the earth,"[7] a product (as we say today) of the slow evolution of life from its lowly beginnings in the primeval slime. Hence, in the Jewish and Christian conception, death is something real and fearful. It is not thought to be like walking from one room to another, or taking off an old coat and putting on a new one. It means sheer unqualified extinction—passing out from the lighted circle of life into "death's dateless night." Only through the sovereign creative love of God can there be a new existence beyond the grave.

What does "the resurrection of the dead" mean? Saint Paul's discussion provides the basic Christian answer to this question.[8] His conception of the general resurrection (distinguished from the unique resurrection of Jesus) has nothing to do with the resuscitation of corpses in a cemetery. It concerns God's re-creation or reconstitution of the human psychophysical individual, not as the organism that has died but as a *soma pneumatikon*, a "spiritual body," inhabiting a spiritual world as the physical body inhabits our present physical world.

A major problem confronting any such doctrine is that of providing criteria of personal identity to link the earthly life and the resurrection life. Paul does not specifically consider this question, but one may, perhaps, develop his thought along lines such as the following.[9]

Suppose, first, that someone—John Smith—living in the USA were suddenly and inexplicably to disappear from before the eyes of his friends, and that at the same moment an exact replica of him were inexplicably to appear in India. The person who appears in India is exactly similar in both physical and mental characteristics to the person who disappeared in America. There is continuity of memory, complete similarity of bodily features including fingerprints, hair and eye coloration, and stomach contents, and also of beliefs, habits, emotions, and mental dispositions. Further, the "John Smith" replica thinks of himself as being the John Smith who disappeared in the USA. After all possible tests have been made and have proved positive, the factors leading his friends to accept "John Smith" as John Smith would surely prevail and would cause them to overlook even his mysterious transference from one continent to another, rather than treat "John Smith," with all John Smith's memories and other characteristics, as someone other than John Smith.

Suppose, second, that our John Smith, instead of inexplicably disappearing, dies, but that at the moment of his death a "John Smith" replica, again complete with memories and all other characteristics, appears in India. Even with the corpse on our hands we would, I think, still have to accept this "John Smith" as the John Smith who died. We would have to say that he had been miraculously re-created in another place.

Now suppose, third, that on John Smith's death the "John Smith" replica appears, not in India, but as a resurrection replica in a different world altogether, a resurrection world inhabited only by resurrected persons. This world occupies its own space distinct from that with which we are now familiar. That is to say, an object in the resurrection world is not situated at any distance or in any direction from the objects in our present world, although each object in either world is spatially related to every other object in the same world.

This supposition provides a model by which one may conceive of the divine re-creation of the embodied human personality. In this model, the element of the strange and the mysterious has been reduced to a minimum by following the view of some of the early Church Fathers that the resurrection body has the same shape as the physical body,[10] and ignoring Paul's own hint that it may be as unlike the physical body as a full grain of wheat differs from the wheat seed.[11]

What is the basis for this Judaic-Christian belief in the divine recreation or reconstitution of the human personality after death? There is, of course, an argument from authority, in that life after death is taught throughout the New Testament (although very rarely in the Old Testament). But, more basically, belief in the resurrection arises as a corollary of faith in the sovereign purpose of God, which is not restricted by death and which holds man in being beyond his natural mortality. In the words of Martin Luther, "Anyone with whom God speaks, whether in wrath or in mercy, the same is certainly immortal. The Person of God who speaks, and the Word, show that we are creatures with whom God wills to speak, right into eternity, and in an immortal manner."[12] In a similar vein it is argued that if it be God's plan to create finite persons to exist in fellowship with himself, then it contradicts both his own intention and his love for the creatures made in his image if he allows men to pass out of existence when his purpose for them remains largely unfulfilled.

It is this promised fulfillment of God's purpose for man, in which the full possibilities of human nature will be realized, that constitutes the "heaven" symbolized in the New Testament as a joyous banquet in which all and sundry rejoice together. As we saw when discussing the problem of evil, no theodicy can succeed without drawing into itself this eschatological[13] faith in an eternal, and therefore infinite, good which thus outweighs all the pains and sorrows that have been endured on the way to it.

Balancing the idea of heaven in Christian tradition is the idea of *hell*. This, too, is relevant to the problem of theodicy. For just as the reconciling of God's goodness and power with the fact of evil requires that out of the travail of history there shall come in the end an eternal good for man, so likewise it would seem to preclude man's eternal misery. The only kind of evil that is finally incompatible with God's unlimited power and love would be utterly pointless and wasted suffering, pain which is never redeemed and worked into the fulfilling of God's good purpose. Unending torment would constitute precisely such suffering; for being eternal, it could never lead to a good end beyond itself. Thus, hell as conceived by its enthusiasts, such as Augustine or Calvin, is a major part of the problem of evil! If hell is construed as eternal torment, the theological motive behind the idea is directly at variance with the urge to seek a theodicy. However, it is by no means clear that the doctrine of eternal punishment can claim a secure New Testament basis.[14] If, on the other hand, "hell" means a continuation of the purgatorial suffering often experienced in this life, and leading eventually to the high good of heaven, it no longer stands in conflict with the needs of theodicy. Again, the idea of hell may be deliteralized and valued as a *mythos*, as a powerful and pregnant symbol of the grave responsibility inherent in man's freedom in relation to his Maker.

Does Parapsychology Help?

The spiritualist movement claims that life after death has been proved by well-attested cases of communication between the living and the "dead." During the closing quarter of the nineteenth century and the decades of the present century this claim has been made the subject of careful and prolonged study by a number of responsible and competent persons.[15] This work, which may be approximately dated from the founding in London of the Society for Psychical Research in 1882, is known either by the name adopted by that society or in the United States by the name parapsychology.

Approaching the subject from the standpoint of our interest in this chapter, we may initially divide the phenomena studied by the parapsychologist into two groups. There are those phenomena that involve no reference to the idea of a life after death, chief among these being psychokinesis and extra-sensory perception (ESP) in its various forms (such as telepathy, clairvoyance, and precognition). And there are those phenomena that raise the question of personal survival after death, such as the apparitions and other sensory manifestations of dead persons and the "spirit messages" received through mediums. This division is, however, only of preliminary use, for ESP has emerged as a clue to the understanding of much that occurs in the second group. We shall begin with a brief outline of the reasons that have induced the majority of workers in this field to be willing to postulate so strange an occurrence as telepathy.

Telepathy is a name for the mysterious fact that sometimes a thought in the mind of one person apparently causes a similar thought to occur to someone else when there are no normal means of communication between them, and under circumstances such that mere coincidence seems to be excluded.

For example, one person may draw a series of pictures or diagrams on paper and somehow transmit an impression of these to someone else in another room who then draws recognizable reproductions of them. This might well be a coincidence in the case of a single successful reproduction: but can a series consist entirely of coincidences?

Experiments have been devised to measure the probability of chance coincidence in supposed cases of telepathy. In the simplest of these, cards printed in turn with five different symbols are used. A pack of fifty, consisting of ten bearing each symbol, is then thoroughly shuffled, and the sender concentrates on the cards one at a time while the receiver (who of course can see neither sender nor cards) tries to write down the correct order of symbols. This procedure is repeated, with constant reshuffling, hundreds or thousands of times. Since there are only five different symbols, a random guess would stand one chance in five of being correct. Consequently, on the assumption that only "chance" is operating, the receiver should be right in about 20 per cent of his tries, and wrong in about 80 per cent; and the longer the series, the closer should be the approach to this proportion. However, good telepathic subjects are right in a far larger number of cases than can be reconciled with random guessing. The deviation from chance expectation can be converted mathematically into "odds against chance" (increasing as the proportion of hits is maintained over a longer and longer series of tries). In this way, odds of over a million to one have been recorded. J. B. Rhine (Duke University) has reported results showing "antichance" values ranging from seven (which equals odds against chance of 100,000 to one) to eighty-two (which converts the odds against chance to billions).[16] S. G. Soal (London University) has reported positive results for precognitive telepathy with odds against chance of $10^{35} \times 5$, or of billions to one.[17] Other researchers have also recorded confirming results.[18] In the light of these reports, it is difficult to deny that some positive factor, and not merely "chance," is operating. "Telepathy" is simply a name for this unknown positive factor.

How does telepathy operate? Only negative conclusions seem to be justified to date. It can, for example, be said with reasonable certainty that telepathy does not consist in any kind of physical radiation, analogous to radio waves. For, first, telepathy is not delayed or weakened in proportion to distance, as are all known forms of radiation: and, second, there is no organ in the brain or elsewhere that can plausibly be regarded as its sending or receiving center. Telepathy appears to be a purely mental occurrence.

It is not, however, a matter of transferring or transporting a thought out of one mind into another—if, indeed, such an idea makes sense at all. The telepathized thought does not leave the sender's consciousness in order to enter that of the receiver. What happens would be better described by saying that the sender's thought gives rise to a mental "echo" in the mind of the receiver. This "echo" occurs at the unconscious level, and consequently the version of it that rises into the receiver's consciousness may be only fragmentary and may be distorted or symbolized in various ways, as in dreams.

According to one theory that has been tentatively suggested to explain telepathy, our minds are separate and mutually insulated only at the conscious (and preconscious) level. But at the deepest level of the unconscious, we are constantly influencing one another, and it is at this level that telepathy takes place.[19]

How is a telepathized thought directed to one particular receiver among so many? Apparently the thoughts are directed by some link of emotion or common interest. For example, two friends are sometimes telepathically aware of any grave crisis or shock experienced by the other, even though they are at opposite ends of the earth.

We shall turn now to the other branch of parapsychology, which has more obvious bearing upon our subject. The *Proceedings of the Society for Psychical Research* contains a large number of carefully recorded and satisfactorily attested cases of the appearance of the figure of someone who has recently died to living people (in rare instances to more than one at a time) who were, in many cases, at a distance and unaware of the death. The S.P.R. reports also establish beyond reasonable doubt that the minds that operate in the mediumistic trance, purporting to be spirits of the departed, sometimes give personal information the medium could not have acquired by normal means and at times even give information, later verified, which had not been known to any living person.

On the other hand, physical happenings, such as the "materializations" of spirit forms in a visible and tangible form, are much more doubtful. But even if we discount the entire range of physical phenomena, it remains true that the best cases of trance utterance are impressive and puzzling, and taken at face value are indicative of survival and communication after death. If, through a medium, one talks with an intelligence that gives a coherent impression of being an intimately known friend

who has died and establishes identity by a wealth of private information and indefinable personal characteristics—as has occasionally happened—then we cannot dismiss without careful trial the theory that what is taking place is the return of a consciousness from the spirit world.

However, the advance of knowledge in the other branch of parapsychology, centering upon the study of extrasensory perception, has thrown unexpected light upon this apparent commerce with the departed. For it suggests that unconscious telepathic contact between the medium and his or her client is an important and possibly a sufficient explanatory factor. This was vividly illustrated by the experience of two women who decided to test the spirits by taking into their minds, over a period of weeks, the personality and atmosphere of an entirely imaginary character in an unpublished novel written by one of the women. After thus filling their minds with the characteristics of this fictitious person, they went to a reputable medium, who proceeded to describe accurately their imaginary friend as a visitant from beyond the grave and to deliver appropriate messages from him.

An even more striking case is that of the "direct voice" medium (i.e., a medium in whose séances the voice of the communicating "spirit" is heard apparently speaking out of the air) who produced the spirit of one "Gordon Davis" who spoke in his own recognizable voice, displayed considerable knowledge about Gordon Davis, and remembered his death. This was extremely impressive until it was discovered that Gordon Davis was still alive; he was, of all ghostly occupations, a real-estate agent, and had been trying to sell a house at the time when the séance took place![20]

Such cases suggest that genuine mediums are simply persons of exceptional telepathic sensitiveness who unconsciously derive the "spirits" from their clients' minds.

In connection with "ghosts," in the sense of apparitions of the dead, it has been established that there can be "meaningful hallucinations," the source of which is almost certainly telepathic. To quote a classic and somewhat dramatic example: a woman sitting by a lake sees the figure of a man running toward the lake and throwing himself in. A few days later a man commits suicide by throwing himself into this same lake. Presumably, the explanation of the vision is that the man's thought while he was contemplating suicide had been telepathically projected onto the scene via the woman's mind.

In many of the cases recorded there is delayed action. The telepathically projected thought lingers in the recipient's unconscious mind until a suitable state of inattention to the outside world enables it to appear to his conscious mind in a dramatized form—for example, by a hallucinatory voice or vision—by means of the same mechanism that operates in dreams.

If phantoms of the living can be created by previously experienced thoughts and emotions of the person whom they represent, the parallel possibility arises that phantoms of the dead are caused by thoughts and emotions that were experienced by the person represented when he was alive. In other words, ghosts may be "psychic footprints," a kind of mental trace left behind by the dead, but not involving the presence or even the continued existence of those whom they represent.

These considerations tend away from the hopeful view that parapsychology will open a window onto another world. However, it is too early for a final verdict; and in the meantime one should be careful not to confuse absence of knowledge with knowledge of absence.

Notes

1. *Phaedo.*
2. The world known to us through our physical senses.
3. Jacques Maritain, *The Range of Reason* (London: Geoffrey Bles Ltd. and New York: Charles Scribner's Sons, 1953), p. 60.
4. Kant, *Critique of Pure Reason, Transcendental Dialectic*, "Refutation of Mendelessohn's Proof of the Permanence of the Soul."
5. Gilbert Ryle's *The Concept of Mind* (London: Hutchinson & Co., Ltd., 1949) is a classic statement of this critique.
6. *Israel* (London: Oxford Univ. Press, 1926), 1, 170.
7. Genesis 2:7; Psalm 103:14.
8. I Corinthians 15.
9. The following paragraphs are adapted, with permission, from a section of my article, "Theology and Verification," published in *Theology Today* (April, 1960) and reprinted in *The Existence of God* (New York: The Macmillan Company, 1964).
10. Irenaeus, *Against Heresies*, Book II, Chap. 34, para. 1.
11. 1 Corinthians 15:37.
12. Quoted by Emil Brunner, *Dogmatics*, II, 69.
13. From the Greek *eschaton*, end.
14. The Greek word *aionios* is used in the New Testament and is usually translated as "eternal" or "everlasting." It can bear either this meaning or the more limited meaning of "for the aeon, or age."
15. The list of presidents of the Society for Psychical Research includes the philosophers Henri Bergson, William James, Hans Driesch, Henry Sidgwick, F. C. S. Schiller, C. D. Broad, and H. H. Price; the psychologists William McDougall, Gardner Murphy, Franklin Prince, and R. H. Thouless; the physicists Sir William Crookes, Sir Oliver Lodge, Sir William Barrett, and Lord Rayleigh; and the classicist Gilbert Murray.
16. J. B. Rhine, *Extrasensory Perception* (Boston: Society for Psychical Research, 1935), Table XLIII, p. 162. See also Rhine, *New Frontiers of the Mind* (New York: Farrar and Rinehart, Inc. 1937), pp. 69f.
17. S. G. Soal, *Proceedings of the Society for Psychical Research,* XLVI, 152–98 and XLVII, 21–150. See also S. G. Soal's *The Experimental Situation in Psychical Research* (London: The Society for Psychical Research, 1947).
18. For surveys of the experimental work, see Whately Carrington, *Telepathy* (London: Methuen & Co. Ltd., 1945); G. N. M. Tyrrell, *The Personality of Man* (London: Penguin Books Ltd., 1946); S. G. Soal and F. Bateman, *Modern Experiments in Telepathy* (London: Faber & Faber Ltd. and New Haven, Conn.: Yale University Press, 1954); and for important Russian work, L. L. Vasiliev, *Experiments in Mental Suggestion*, 1962 (Church Crookham: Institute for the Study of Mental Images, 1963—English translation).
19. Whately Carrington, *Telepathy* (London: Methuen & Co. Ltd., 1945), Chaps. 6–8.
20. S. G. Soal, "A Report of Some Communications Received through Mrs. Blanche Cooper," Sec. 4, *Proceedings of the Society for Psychical Research*, XXXV, 560–89.

VI.5 Personal Identity and Life After Death

J E F F R E Y   O L E N

Jeffrey Olen (1946–   ), who teaches philosophy at the University of Wisconsin at Stevens Point, discusses the criteria of personal identity in order to determine what would have to survive our death if we were to be able to say that it is truly we who survive. Through some intriguing thought experiments, Olen builds a case for the possibility of survival. Olen has a functionalist view of personhood, believing that "the human brain is analogous to a computer." In this view, a given brain state is also a given mental state because it performs the appropriate function in the appropriate "program." That is, the human brain embodies certain abstract *descriptions. Olen argues that just as different computers can process the same information, so we could survive after death in another body as long as our personalities and memories were preserved intact.*

It is Sunday night. After a long night of hard drinking, John Badger puts on his pajamas, lowers the heat in his Wisconsin home to fifty-five degrees and climbs into bed beneath two heavy blankets. Meanwhile, in Florida, Joe Everglade kisses his wife goodnight and goes to sleep.

The next morning, two very confused men wake up. One wakes up in Wisconsin, wondering where he is and why he is wearing pajamas, lying under two heavy blankets, yet shivering from the cold. He looks out the window and sees nothing but pine trees and snow. The room is totally unfamiliar. Where is his wife? How did he get to this cold, strange place? Why does he have such a terrible hangover? He tries to spring out of bed with his usual verve but feels an unaccustomed aching in his joints. Arthritis? He wanders unsurely through

the house until he finds the bathroom. What he sees in the mirror causes him to spin around in sudden fear. But there is nobody behind him. Then the fear intensifies as he realizes that it was his reflection that had stared back at him. But it was the reflection of a man thirty years older than himself, with coarser features and a weather-beaten face.

In Florida, a man awakens with a young woman's arm around him. When she too awakens, she snuggles against him and wishes him good morning. "Who are you?" he asks. "What am I doing in your bed?" She just laughs, then tells him that he will have to hurry if he is going to get in his ten miles of jogging. From the bathroom she asks him about his coming day. None of the names or places she mentions connect with anything he can remember. He climbs out of bed, marveling at the ease with which he does so, and looks first out the window and then into the mirror over the dresser. The sun and swimming pool confound him. The handsome young man's reflection terrifies him.

Then the phone rings. The woman answers it. It is the man from Wisconsin. "What happened last night, Mary? How did I get here? How did I get to look this way?"

"Who is this?" she asks.

"Don't you recognize my voice, Mary?" But he knew that the voice was not his own. "It's Joe."

"Joe who?"

"Your husband."

She hangs up, believing it to be a crank call. When she returns to the bedroom, the man in her husband's robe asks how he got there from Wisconsin, and why he looks as he does.

Personal Identity

What happened in the above story? Who woke up in Joe Everglade's bed? Who woke up in John

Badger's? Which one is Mary's husband? Has Badger awakened with Everglade's memories and Everglade with Badger's? Or have Badger and Everglade somehow switched bodies? How are we to decide? What considerations are relevant?

To ask such questions is to raise the problem of *personal identity*. It is to ask what makes a person the same person he was the day before. It is to ask how we determine that we are dealing with the same person that we have dealt with in the past. It is to ask what constitutes personal identity over time. It is also to ask what we mean by the *same person*. And to answer this question, we must ask what we mean by the word "person."

Persons

In the previous chapter, we asked what a human being is. We asked what human beings are made of, what the nature of the human mind is, and whether human beings are part of nature or distinct from it.

To ask what a *person* is, however, is to ask a different question. Although we often use the terms "person" and "human being" interchangeably, they do not mean the same thing. If we do use them interchangeably, it is only because all the persons we know of are human beings, and because, as far as we know, whenever we are confronted with the same human being we are confronted with the same person.

But the notion of a human being is a *biological* notion. To identify something as a human being is to identify it as a member of *Homo sapiens,* a particular species of animal. It is a type of organism defined by certain physical characteristics.

The notion of a person, on the other hand, is *not* a biological one. Suppose, for instance, that we find life on another planet, and that this life is remarkably like our own. The creatures we discover communicate through a language as rich as our own, act according to moral principles, have a legal system, and engage in science and art. Suppose also that despite these cultural similarities, this form of life is biologically different from human life. In that case, these creatures would be persons, but not humans. Think, for example, of the alien in *E.T.* Since he is biologically different from us, he is not human. He is, however, a person.

What, then, is a person? Although philosophers disagree on this point, the following features are relatively noncontroversial.

First, a person is an intelligent, rational creature. Second, it is a creature capable of a peculiar sort of consciousness—self-consciousness. Third, it not only has beliefs, desires, and so forth, but it has beliefs *about* its beliefs, desires, and so forth. Fourth, it is a creature to which we ascribe moral responsibility. Persons are responsible for their actions in a way that other things are not. They are subject to moral praise and moral blame. Fifth, a person is a creature that we treat in certain ways. To treat something as a person is to treat it as a member of our own moral community. It is to grant it certain rights, both moral and legal. Sixth, a person is a creature capable of reciprocity. It is capable of treating us as members of the same moral community. Finally, a person is capable of verbal communication. It can communicate by means of a *language*, not just by barks, howls, and tail-wagging.

Since, as far as we know, only human beings meet the above conditions, only human beings are considered to be persons. But once we recognize that to be a person is not precisely the same thing that it is to be a human being, we also recognize that other creatures, such as the alien in *E.T.* is also a person. We also recognize that perhaps not all human beings are persons—human fetuses, for example, as some have argued. Certainly, in the American South before the end of the Civil War, slaves were not considered to be persons. We might also mention a remark of D'Artagnan, in Richard Lester's film version of *The Three Musketeers.* Posing as a French nobleman, he attempted to cross the English Channel with a companion. When a French official remarked that his pass was only for one person, D'Artagnan replied that he was only one person—his companion was a servant.

Moreover, once we recognize the distinction between human beings and persons, certain questions arise. Can one human being embody more than one person, either at the same time or successive times? In the example we introduced at the beginning of this chapter, has Badger's body become Everglade's and Everglade's Badger's? Can the person survive the death of the human being? Is there personal survival after the death of the body?

Concerning identity through time in general, two issues must be distinguished. First, we want to know how we can *tell* that something is the same thing we encountered previously. That is, we want to know what the *criteria* are for establishing identity through time. Second, we want to know what *makes* something the same thing it was previously. That is, we want to know what *constitutes* identity through time.

Although these issues are related, they are not the same, as the following example illustrates. We can *tell* that someone has a case of the flu by checking for certain symptoms, such as fever, lack of energy, and sore muscles. But having these symptoms does not *constitute* having a case of the flu. It is the presence of a flu virus—not the symptoms—that makes an illness a case of the flu.

We commonly use two criteria for establishing personal identity. The first is the *bodily criterion,* the second the *memory criterion.* How do we apply them?

We apply the bodily criterion in two ways. First, we go by physical resemblance. If I meet someone on the street who looks, walks, and sounds just like Mary, I assume that it is Mary. Since the body I see resembles Mary's body exactly, I assume that the person I see is Mary. But that method can sometimes fail us, as in the case of identical twins. In such cases, we can apply the bodily criterion in another way. If I can discover that there is a continuous line from one place and time to another that connects Mary's body to the body I now see, I can assume that I now see Mary. Suppose, for example, that Mary and I went to the beach together, and have been together all afternoon. In that case, I can say that the person I am now with is the person I began the day with.

There are, however, times when the bodily criterion is not available. If Mary and Jane are identical twins, and I run across one of them on the street, I may have to ask who it is. That is, I may have to rely on Mary's memory of who she is. And, if I want to make sure that I am not being fooled, I may ask a few questions. If Mary remembers things that I believe only Mary can remember, and if she remembers them as happening to *her,* and not to somebody else, then I can safely say that it really is Mary.

Generally, the bodily criterion and the memory criterion do not conflict, so we use whichever is more convenient. But what happens if they do conflict? That is what happened in our imagined story. According to the bodily criterion, each person awoke in his own bed, but with the memories of someone else. According to the memory criterion, each person awoke in the other's bed with the body of someone else. Which criterion should we take as decisive? Which is fundamental, the memory criterion or the bodily criterion?

The Constitution of Personal Identity

To ask the above questions is to ask what *constitutes* personal identity. What is it that makes me the same person I was yesterday? What makes the author of this book the same person as the baby born to Sam and Belle Olen in 1946? Answers to these questions will allow us to say which criterion is fundamental.

Perhaps the most widely discussed answer to our question comes from John Locke (1632–1704), whose discussion of the topic set the stage for all future discussions. According to Locke, the bodily criterion cannot be fundamental. Since the concept of a person is most importantly the concept of a conscious being who can be held morally and legally responsible for past actions, it is *continuity of consciousness* that constitutes personal identity. The bodily criterion is fundamental for establishing sameness of *animal,* but not sameness of *person.*

Suppose, for instance, that John Badger had been a professional thief. If the person who awoke in Badger's bed could never remember any of Badger's life as his own, but had only Everglade's memories and personality traits, while the man who awoke in Everglade's bed remembered all of Badger's crimes as his own, would we be justified in jailing the man who awoke in Badger's bed while letting the man who awoke in Everglade's go free?

Locke would say no. The person who awoke in Badger's bed was not Badger.

If we agree that it is sameness of consciousness that constitutes personal identity, we must then ask what constitutes sameness of consciousness. Some philosophers have felt that it is sameness of *mind*, where the mind is thought of as a continuing nonphysical substance. Although Locke did not deny that minds are nonphysical, he did not believe that sameness of nonphysical substance is the same thing as sameness of consciousness. If we can conceive of persons switching *physical* bodies, we can also conceive of persons switching *non*physical ones.

Then what does Locke take to be crucial for personal identity? *Memory.* It is my memory of the events of Jeffrey Olen's life as happening to *me* that makes me the person those events happened to. It is my memory of his experiences as *mine* that makes them mine.

Although Locke's answer seems at first glance a reasonable one, many philosophers have considered it inadequate. One reason for rejecting Locke's answer is that we don't remember everything that happened to us. If I don't remember anything that happened to me during a certain period, does that mean that whoever existed "in" my body then was not me? Hardly.

Another reason for rejecting Locke's answer is that memory is not always accurate. We often sincerely claim to remember things that never happened. There is a difference, then, between *genuine* memory and *apparent* memory. What marks this difference is the *truth* of the memory claim. If what I claim to remember is not true, it cannot be a case of genuine memory.

But that means that memory cannot constitute personal identity. If I claim to remember certain experiences as being my experiences, that does not make them mine, because my claim may be a case of apparent memory. If it is a case of genuine memory, that is because it is true that the remembered experiences are mine. But the memory does not *make* them mine. Rather, the fact that they are mine makes it a case of genuine memory. So Locke has the situation backward. But if memory does not constitute personal identity, what does?

Some philosophers have claimed that, regardless of Locke's views, it *must* be sameness of mind, where the mind is thought of as a continuing nonphysical entity. This entity can be thought of as the self. It is what makes us who we are. As long as the same self continues to exist, the same person continues to exist. The major problem with this answer is that it assumes the truth of mind-body dualism, a position we found good reason to reject in the previous chapter. But apart from that, there is another problem.

In one of the most famous passages in the history of philosophy, David Hume (1711–1776) argued that there is no such self—for reasons that have nothing to do with the rejection of dualism. No matter how hard we try, Hume said, we cannot discover such a self. Turning inward and examining our own consciousness, we find only individual experiences—thoughts, recollections, images, and the like. Try as we might, we cannot find a continuing self. In that case, we are justified in believing only that there are *experiences*—not that there is a continuing *experiencer*. Put another way, we have no reason to believe that there is anything persisting through time that underlies or unifies these experiences. There are just the experiences themselves.

But if we accept this view, and still require a continuing nonphysical entity for personal identity, we are forced to the conclusion that there is no such thing as personal identity. We are left, that is, with the position that the idea of a person existing through time is a mere fiction, however useful in daily life. And that is the position that Hume took. Instead of persons, he said, there are merely "bundles of ideas."

Thus, the view that personal identity requires sameness of mind can easily lead to the view that there is no personal identity. Since this conclusion seems manifestly false, we shall have to look elsewhere? But where?

The Primacy of the Bodily Criterion

If neither memory nor sameness of mind constitutes personal identity, perhaps we should accept the view that sameness of *body* does. Perhaps it is really the bodily criterion that is fundamental.

If we reflect on the problem faced by Locke's theory because of the distinction between genuine and apparent memory, it is tempting to accept the primacy of the bodily criterion. Once again, a sincere memory claim may be either genuine memory or apparent memory. How can we tell whether the claim that a previous experience was mine is genuine memory? By determining whether I was in the right place in the right time to have it. And how can we determine that? By the bodily criterion. If my *body* was there, then *I* was there. But that means that the memory criterion must rest on the bodily criterion. Also, accepting the primacy of the bodily criterion get us around Hume's problem. The self that persists through and has the experiences I call mine is my physical body.

This answer also has the advantage of being in keeping with materialism, a view accepted in the previous chapter. If human beings are purely physical, then persons must also be purely physical, whatever differences there may be between the notion of a person and the notion of a human being. But if persons are purely physical, what makes me the same person I was yesterday is no different in kind from what makes my typewriter the same typewriter it was yesterday. In both cases, we are dealing with a physical object existing through time. In the latter case, as long as we have the same physical materials (allowing for change of ribbon, change of keys, and the like) arranged in the same way, we have the same typewriter. So it is with persons. As long as we have the same physical materials (allowing for such changes as the replacement of cells) arranged in the same way, we have the same person.

Although this answer is a tempting one, it is not entirely satisfactory. Suppose that we could manage a brain transplant from one body to another. If we switched two brains, so that all the memories and personality traits of the persons involved were also switched, wouldn't we conclude that the persons, as well as their brains, had switched bodies? When such operations are performed in science-fiction stories, they are described this way.

But this possibility does not defeat the view that the bodily criterion is fundamental. It just forces us to hold that the bodily criterion must be applied to the brain, rather than the entire body. Personal identity then becomes a matter of brain identity. Same brain, same person. Unfortunately, even with this change, our answer does not seem satisfactory. Locke still seems somehow right. Let us see why.

Badger and Everglade Reconsidered

Returning to our tale of Badger and Everglade, we find that some troubling questions remain. If Mrs. Everglade continues to live with the man who awoke in her bed, might she not be committing adultery? Shouldn't she take in the man who awoke in Badger's bed? And, once again assuming that Badger was a professional thief, would justice really be served by jailing the man who awoke in his bed? However we answer these questions, one thing is certain—the two men would always feel that they had switched bodies. So, probably, would the people who knew them. Furthermore, whenever we read science-fiction stories describing such matters, we invariably accept them as stories of switched bodies. But if we accept the bodily criterion as fundamental, we are accepting the impossible, and the two men in our story, Mrs. Everglade, and their friends are mistaken in their beliefs. How, then, are we to answer our questions?

If we are unsure, it is because such questions become very tricky at this point. Their trickiness seems to rest on two points. First, cases like the Badger-Everglade case do not happen in this world. Although we are prepared to accept them in science-fiction tales, we are totally unprepared to deal with them in real life.

Second, and this is a related point, we need some way of *explaining* such extraordinary occurrences. Unless we know how the memories of Badger and Everglade came to be reversed, we will be unable to decide the answers to our questions. In the movies, it is assumed that some nonphysical substance travels from one body to another, or that there has been a brain transplant of some sort. On these assumptions, we are of course willing to describe what happens as a change of body. This description seems to follow naturally from such explanations.

What explains what happened to Badger and Everglade? We can rule out change of nonphysical substance, because of what was said in the previous chapter and earlier in this chapter. If we explain what happened as the product of a brain switch, then the bodily criterion applied to the brain allows us to say that Badger and Everglade did awaken in each other's bed, and that Mrs. Everglade would be committing adultery should she live with the man who awoke in her bed.

Are there any other possible explanations? One that comes readily to mind is hypnotism. Suppose, then, that someone had hypnotized Badger and Everglade into believing that each was the other person. In that case, we should not say that there had been a body switch. Badger and Everglade awoke in their own beds, and a wave of the hypnotist's hand could demonstrate that to everyone concerned. Their memory claims are not genuine memories, but apparent ones.

But suppose it was not a case of hypnotism? What then? At this point, many people are stumped. What else could it be? The strong temptation is to say nothing. Without a brain transplant or hypnotism or something of the sort, the case is impossible.

Suppose that we accept this conclusion. If we do, we may say the following: The memory criterion and the bodily criterion cannot really conflict. If the memories are genuine, and not apparent, then whenever I remember certain experiences as being mine, it is possible to establish that the same brain is involved in the original experiences and the memory of them. Consequently, the memory criterion and the bodily criterion are equally fundamental. The memory criterion is fundamental in the sense that consciousness determines what part of the body is central to personal identity. Because sameness of consciousness requires sameness of brain, we ultimately must apply the bodily criterion to the brain. But the bodily criterion is also fundamental, because we assume that some physical object—the brain—must remain the same if the person is to remain the same.

Multiple Personality

In recent years there have been two well-known books, both made into films, each about a woman having several radically distinct personalities—*The Three Faces of Eve* and *Sybil*. Based on actual cases, the books give detailed and fascinating accounts of the lives of the two women.

Each personality had its own memories, its own values, its own behaviour patterns, even its own name. At any given time, Eve or Sybil would assume one of these personalities. Whatever happened to her during that time would be remembered as happening only to that personality. When Eve or Sybil assumed another personality, she would either claim not to know of these experiences or claim that they had happened to someone else. The other personalities were thought of and spoken of in the third person.

Unlike science fiction and fantasy cases, the multiple-personality phenomenon is something that happens in the real world. What are we to say about it? On the one hand, we are tempted to say that each woman embodied several persons. Very often their psychiatrists spoke as though that were true. On the other hand, there is an equally strong temptation to say that each woman embodied only one person, somehow split into different personalities. Thus, we sometimes call such cases instances of *split* personality, rather than of *multiple* personality.

The first temptation is due to the fact that each woman seems to embody several distinct streams of consciousness. That is, we are led to view each woman as consisting of several persons by the *memory criterion*. The second temptation is due to the fact that each woman has only one body. That is, we are led to view each woman as one person by the *bodily criterion*. Which criterion should we accept? If there is one body but several streams of consciousness, how many persons are there? When discussing the Badger-Everglade case, we said that our answer must depend on our explanation of what happened. I think that the same thing holds for the Eve and Sybil cases.

How are such cases explained? At present, they are generally given psychoanalytic explanations. A typical psychoanalytic explanation might go like this. All of us have various aspects to our personalities. Sometimes we are forced to repress some of these aspects for one reason or another. Perhaps one of them arouses deep feelings of guilt in us; perhaps we feel we must repress it to win the love of our parents. If the repressed aspect is strong enough, and if we are unwilling to recognize it as being ours, it can cause an inner conflict resulting in a case of split or multiple personality.

This type of explanation seems to require that there is one person managing the various aspects of his or her personality. It makes the phenomenon of multiple personality seem like a strategy unconsciously adopted by *one* person to resolve inner conflict. Thus, if we accept this type of explanation, it seems that we should accept the view that the phenomenon involves one badly fractured person, rather than several persons "in" one body. So when dealing with Eve and Sybil, we should rely on the bodily criterion, not the memory criterion.

The Memory Criterion Revisited

Although the answer given above is a tidy one, it may still seem unsatisfactory. Perhaps it is a cheap trick just to dismiss the Badger-Everglade case as mere fantasy and then ignore it. After all, if we can meaningfully describe such cases in books and films, don't we have to pay some attention to them? As long as we can imagine situations in which two persons can switch bodies without a brain transplant, don't we need a theory of personal identity to cover them?

Philosophers are divided on this point. Some think that a theory of personal identity has to account only for what can happen in this world, while others think it must account for whatever can happen in any conceivable world. Then again, some do not believe that there is any conceivable world in which two persons could change bodies without a brain switch, while there are others who are not sure that such things are impossible in the actual world.

Without trying to decide the matter, I can make the following suggestion for those who demand a theory of personal identity that does not rely on the assumption that genuine memory is tied to a particular brain.

In the previous chapter, I concluded that functionalism is the theory of mind most likely to be true. To have a mind, I said, is to embody a psychology. I also said that we don't merely move our bodies, but write poetry, caress the cheek of someone we love, and perform all sorts of human actions. I might have expressed this point by saying that we are not just human beings, but persons as well. What makes a human being a person? We are persons because we embody a psychology.

If that is true, then it may also be true that we are the persons we are because of the psychologies we embody. If it is a psychology that makes a human being a person, then it is a particular psychology that makes a particular human being a particular person. Sameness of psychology constitutes sameness of person. In that case, we can agree with this much of Locke's theory—it is continuity of consciousness that constitutes personal identity. But what is continuity of consciousness, if not memory?

An answer to this question is provided by the contemporary British philosopher Anthony Quinton. At any moment, we can isolate a number of mental states belonging to the same momentary consciousness. Right now, for instance, I am simultaneously aware of the sound and sight and feel of my typewriter, plus the feel and taste of my pipe, plus a variety of other things. Such *momentary* consciousnesses belong to a continuous *series*. Each one is linked to the one before it and the one following it by certain similarities and recollections. This series is my own *continuity* of consciousness, my own *stream* of consciousness. It is this stream of consciousness that makes me the same person I was yesterday.

If we accept Quinton's theory, we can then say that the memory criterion, not the bodily criterion, is fundamental. We can also say that, even if in this world continuity of consciousness requires sameness of brain, we can conceive of worlds in which it does not. To show this, let us offer another possible explanation of the Badger-Everglade situation.

Suppose a mad computer scientist has discovered a way to reprogram human beings. Suppose that he has found a way to make us the embodiment of any psychology he likes. Suppose further that he decided to experiment on Badger and Everglade, giving Badger Everglade's psychology and Everglade Badger's and that is why the events of our story occurred. With this explanation and the considerations of the previous paragraphs, we can conclude that Badger and Everglade did change bodies. By performing his experiment, the mad scientist has made it possible for a continuing stream of consciousness to pass from one body to another. He has, in effect, performed a body transplant. . . .

Should we accept Quinton's theory? There seems to be no good reason not to. In fact, there are at least two good reasons for accepting it. First, it seems consistent with a functionalist theory of the mind. Second, it allows us to make sense of science-fiction stories while we continue to believe that in the real world to be the same person we were yesterday is to have the same brain.

Life After Death

Is it possible for the person to survive the death of the body? Is there a sense in which we can continue to live after our bodies have died? Can there be a personal life after death?

According to one popular conception of life after death, at the death of the body the soul leaves the body and travels to a realm known as heaven. Of course, this story must be taken as metaphorical. Does the soul literally leave the body? How? Out of the mouth? Ears? And how does it get to heaven? By turning left at Mars? Moreover, if the soul remains disembodied, how can it perceive anything? What does it use as sense organs? And if all souls remain disembodied, how can one soul recognize another? What is there to recognize?

As these questions might suggest, much of this popular story trades on a confusion. The soul is thought of as a translucent physical substance much like Casper the ghost, through which other objects can pass as they do through air or water. But if the soul is *really* nonphysical, it can be nothing like that.

If this story is not to be taken literally, is there some version of it that we can admit as a possibility? Is there also the possibility of personal survival through reincarnation as it is often understood—the re-embodiment of the person without memory of the former embodiment?

Materialism and the Disembodied Soul

So far, we have considered both the mind and the body as they relate to personal identity. Have we neglected the soul? It may seem that we have, but philosophers who discuss the mind-body question and personal identity generally use the terms "mind" and "soul" interchangeably. Is the practice legitimate, or is it a confusion?

The practice seems to be thoroughly legitimate. If the soul is thought to be the crucial element of the person, it is difficult to see how it could be anything but the mind. If it is our character traits, personality, thoughts, likes and dislikes, memories, and continuity of experience that makes us the persons we are, then they must belong to the soul. If they are taken to be crucial for one's personal identity, then it seems impossible to separate them from one's soul.

Moreover, people who accept some version of the popular conception of life after death noted above believe in certain continuities between earthly experiences and heavenly ones. In heaven, it is believed, we remember our earthly lives, we recognize friends and relatives, our personalities are like our earthly personalities, and we are judged by God for our actions on earth. But if we believe any of this, we must also believe that the soul cannot be separated from the mind.

If that is the case, it is difficult to accept the continued existence of a disembodied soul. Once we accept some form of materialism, we seem compelled to believe that the soul must be embodied. Does that rule out the possibility of any version of the popular story being true?

Some philosophers think that it does. Suppose, for instance, that the mind-brain identity theory is true. In that case, when the brain dies, so does the mind. Since the mind is the repository of memory and personality traits, it is identical with the soul. So when the brain dies, so does the soul.

This is a powerful argument, and it has convinced a number of people. On the other hand, it has also kept a number of people from accepting materialism of any sort. If it is felt that materialism and life after death are incompatible, and if one is firmly committed to the belief in life after death, then it is natural for one to reject materialism.

Is there a way of reconciling materialism and life after death? I think so.

Although it seems necessary that persons must be embodied, it does not seem necessary that the same person must be embodied by the same body. In our discussion of personal identity, we allowed that Badger and Everglade might have changed bodies, depending on our explanation of the story. Let us try a similar story.

Mary Brown is old and sick. She knows she will die within a couple of weeks. One morning she does die. At the same time, in some other world, a woman wakes up believing herself to be Mary. She looks around to find herself in a totally unfamiliar place. Someone is sitting next to her. This other woman looks exactly like Mary's mother, who died years earlier, and believes herself to be Mary's mother. Certainly, she knows everything about Mary that Mary's mother would know.

Before the woman believing herself to be Mary can speak, she notices some surprising things about herself. She no longer feels old or sick. Her pains are gone, and her mind is as sharp as ever. When she asks where she is, she is told heaven. She is also told that her husband, father, and numerous old friends are waiting to see her. All of them are indistinguishable from the persons they claim to be. Meanwhile, back on earth, Mary Brown is pronounced dead. Is this woman in "heaven" really Mary Brown? How could we possibly explain the phenomenon?

Suppose we put the story in a religious context. Earlier, we saw that one possible explanation of the Badger-Everglade case is that some mad computer scientist had reprogrammed the two so that each embodied the psychology of the other. Suppose we replace the mad scientist with God, and say that God had kept a body in heaven for the purpose of embodying Mary's psychology when she died, and that the person believing herself to be Mary is the new embodiment of Mary's psychology. Would this count as a genuine case of life after death?

If we accept the Badger-Everglade story, appropriately explained, as a case of two persons switching bodies, there seems no reason to deny that Mary has continued to live "in" another body. But even if we are unsure of the Badger-Everglade case, we can approach Mary Brown's this way. What is it that we want to survive after death? Isn't it our memories, our consciousness of self, our personalities, our relations with others? What does it matter whether there is some nonphysical substance that survives? If that substance has no memories of a prior life, does not recognize the soul of others who were important in that earlier life, what comfort could such a continuing existence bring? In what sense would it be the survival of the *person?* How would it be significantly different from the return of the lifeless body to the soil?

If we assume that our story is a genuine case of personal survival of the death of the body, we may wonder about another point. Is it compatible with Christian belief? According to John Hick, a contemporary British philosopher who imagined a similar story, the answer is yes. In I Corinthians 15, Paul writes of the resurrection of the body—not of the physical body, but of some spiritual body. Although one *can* think of this spiritual body as a translucent ghost-like body that leaves the physical body at death, Hick offers another interpretation.

The human being, Hick says, becomes extinct at death. It is only through God's intervention that the spiritual body comes into existence. By the resurrection of this spiritual body, we are to understand a *recreation* or *reconstitution* of the person's body in heaven. But that is precisely what happened in our story.

Thus, a materialist view of the nature of human beings is not incompatible with the Christian view of life after death. Nor, for that matter, is it incompatible with the belief that the spiritual body is nonphysical. If we can make sense of the claim that there might be such things as nonphysical bodies, then there is no reason why a nonphysical body could not embody a psychology. Remember—according to functionalism, an abstract description such as a psychology is independent of any physical description. Just as we can play chess using almost anything as chess pieces, so can a psychology be embodied by almost anything, assuming that it is complex enough. So if there can be nonphysical bodies, there can be nonphysical persons. Of course, nothing said so far assures us that the Christian story—or any other story of life after death—is true. That is another matter, to be considered in Part VII.

Reincarnation

Much of what has been said so far does, however, rule out the possibility of reincarnation as commonly understood. If human beings are purely physical, then there is no nonphysical substance that is the person that can be reincarnated in another earthly body. Moreover, even if there were such a substance, it is difficult to see how its continued existence in another body could count as the reincarnation of a particular person, *if* there is no other continuity between the old life and the new one. Once again, personal survival requires some continuity of consciousness. It is not sameness of *stuff* that constitutes personal identity, but sameness of consciousness. This requirement is often overlooked by believers in reincarnation.

But suppose that there is some continuity of consciousness in reincarnation. Suppose that memories and the rest do continue in the next incarnation, but that they are not easily accessible. Suppose, that is, that the slate is not wiped completely clean, but that what is written on it is hard to recover. In that case, the passage of the soul into a new incarnation would count as personal survival *if* there were such a soul to begin with.

Assuming, again, that there is not, what can we say about the possibility of reincarnation? To conceive of such a possibility, we must conceive of some very complicated reprogramming by God or some mad scientist or whatever. I shall leave it to you to come up with such a story, but I shall say this much. There does not seem to be any good reason to think that any such story is remotely plausible, least of all true.

The Final Word?

In this chapter we looked at two closely related questions: What constitutes personal identity? And is it possible for a person to survive the death of her own body?

The answer to the second question depended on the first. If we had concluded that the basis of personal identity is sameness of body, then we would have been forced to conclude that life after death is impossible. And there did seem to be good reason to come to these conclusions. How, we asked, could we assure that any memory claim is a case of genuine memory? Our answer was this. In the cases likely to confront us in our daily lives, we must establish some physical continuity between the person who had the original experience and the person who claims to remember it.

But the problem with this answer is that it is too limited. Because we can imagine cases like the Everglade-Badger example, and because our science-fiction tales and religious traditions offer stories of personal continuity without bodily continuity, we can say the following. Regardless of what happens in our daily lives, our concept of a person is a concept of something that does not seem tied to a particular body. Rather, our concept of a person seems to be tied to a particular stream of consciousness. If there is one continuing stream of consciousness over time, then there is one continuing person. Our question, then, was whether we can give a coherent account of continuity of consciousness from one body to another.

The answer was yes. Using the computer analogy of the functionalist, we can explain such continuity in terms of programming. If it is possible to "program" another brain to have the same psychology as the brain I now have, then it is possible for me to change bodies. And if it is possible for me to change bodies, then it is also possible for me to survive the death of my body.

VI.6   The Possibility of Resurrection

PETER VAN INWAGEN

Peter van Inwagen is professor of philosophy at Syracuse University and the author of several works in metaphysics and philosophy of religion. In this article, he argues that the Christian doctrine of the resurrection of the body is possible. In a future life, we will be able to recognize each other because we have the same bodies and because we will be able to communicate with each other. First, he argues against the notion of a reconstituted body, that God collects the atoms of a person's body at death and reassembles them in heaven. He calls this the "Aristotelian" view. Then he sets forth a hypothesis that preserves essential bodily continuity.

The real philosophical problem facing the doctrine of resurrection does not seem to me to be that there is no criterion that the men of the new age could apply to determine whether someone then alive was the same man as some man who had died before the Last Day; the problem seems to me to be that there *is* such a criterion and (given certain facts about the present age) it would, of necessity, yield the result that many men who have died in our own lifetime and earlier will not be found among those who live *after* the Last Day.

Let us consider an analogy. Suppose a certain monastery claims to have in its possession a manuscript written in St. Augustine's own hand. And suppose the monks of this monastery further claim that this manuscript was burned by Arians in the year 457. It would immediately occur to me to ask how *this* manuscript, the one I can touch, could be the very manuscript that was burned in 457. Suppose their answer to this question is that God miraculously recreated Augustine's manuscript in 458. I should respond to this answer as follows: the

Reprinted from "The Possibility of Resurrection," *International Journal for Philosophy of Religion* (1978) by permission of the publisher.

deed it describes seems quite impossible, even as an accomplishment of omnipotence. God certainly might have created a perfect duplicate of the original manuscript, but it would not be *that* one; its earliest moment of existence would have been after Augustine's death; it would never have known the impress of his hand; it would not have been a part of the furniture of the world when he was alive; and so on.

Now suppose our monks were to reply by simply asserting that the manuscript now in their possession *did* know the impress of Augustine's hand; that it *was* a part of the furniture of the world when the Saint was alive; that when God recreated or restored it, He (as an indispensable component of accomplishing this task) saw to it that the object He produced had all these properties.

I confess I should not know what to make of this. I should have to tell the monks that I did not see how what they believed could *possibly* be true. They might of course reply that their belief is a mystery, that God had *some* way of restoring the lost manuscript, but that the procedure surpasses human understanding. Now I am sometimes willing to accept such answers; for example, in the case of the doctrine of the Trinity. But there are cases in which I would never accept such an answer. For example, if there were a religion that claimed that God had created two adjacent mountains without thereby bringing into existence an intermediate valley, I should regard any attempt to defend this doctrine as a "mystery" as so much whistle-talk. After all, I can hardly expect to be able to understand the Divine Nature; but I do understand mountains and valleys. And I understand manuscripts, too. I understand them sufficiently well to be quite confident that the monks' story is impossible. Still, I wish to be reasonable. I admit that one can be mistaken about conceptual truth and falsehood. I know from experience that a proposition that *seems* to force itself irresistibly upon the mind as a conceptual truth can turn out to be false. (If I had been alive in 1890, I should doubtless have regarded the Galilean Law of the Addition of Velocities and the Unrestricted Comprehension Principle in set theory as obvious conceptual truths.) Being reasonable, therefore, I am willing to listen to any *argument* the monks might have for the conclusion that what they believe is possible. Most arguments for the conclusion that a certain proposition is possibly true take the form of a story that (the arguer hopes) the person to whom the argument is addressed will accept as possible, and which (the arguer attempts to show) entails the proposition whose modal status is in question.

Can such a story be told about the manuscript of Augustine? Suppose one of the monks is, in a very loose sense, an Aristotelian. He tells the following story (a version of a very popular tale): "Augustine's manuscript consisted of a certain 'parcel' of matter upon which a certain form had been impressed. It ceased to exist when this parcel of matter was radically deformed. To recreate it, God needed only to collect the matter (in modern terms, the atoms) that once composed it and reimpress that form upon it (in modern terms, cause these atoms to stand to one another in the same spatial and chemical relationships they previously stood in)."

This story is defective. The manuscript God creates in the story is not the manuscript that was destroyed, since the various atoms that compose the tracings of ink on its surface occupy their present positions not as a result of Augustine's activity but of God's. Thus what we have is not a manuscript in Augustine's hand. (Strictly speaking, it is not even a *manuscript*.) (Compare the following conversation: "Is that the house of blocks your daughter built this morning?" "No, I built this one after I accidentally knocked hers down. I put all the blocks just where she did, though. Don't tell her.")

I think the philosophical problems that arise in connection with the buried manuscript of St. Augustine are very like the problems that arise in connection with the doctrine of the Resurrection. If a man should be totally destroyed, then it is very hard to see how any man who comes into existence thereafter could be the *same* man. And I say this not because I have no criterion of identity I can employ

in such cases, but because I have a criterion of identity for men and it is, or *seems* to be, violated. And the popular quasi-Aristotelian story which is often supposed to establish the conceptual possibility of God's restoring to existence a man who has been totally destroyed does not lead me to think that I have got the wrong criterion or that I am misapplying the right one. The popular story, of course, is the story according to which God collects the atoms that once composed a certain man and restores them to the positions they occupied relative to one another when that man was alive; thereby (the story-teller contends) God restores the man himself. But this story, it seems to me, does not "work." The atoms of which I am composed occupy at each instant the positions they do because of the operations of certain processes within me (those processes that, taken collectively, constitute my being alive). Even when I become a corpse—provided I decay slowly and am not, say, cremated—the atoms that compose me will occupy the positions relative to one another that they do occupy *largely* because of the processes of life that *used* to go on within me: or this will be the case for at least some short period. Thus a former corpse in which the processes of life have been "started up again" may well be the very man who was once before alive, provided the processes of dissolution did not progress too far while he was a corpse. But if a man does not simply die but is totally destroyed (as in the case of cremation) then *he* can never be reconstituted, for the causal chain has been irrevocably broken. If God collects the atoms that used to constitute that man and "reassembles" them, they will occupy the positions relative to one another they occupy because of God's miracle and not because of the operation of the natural processes that, taken collectively, were the life of that man. (I should also be willing to defend the following theses: the thing such an action of God's would produce would not be a member of our species and would not speak a language or have memories of any sort, though, of course, he—or *it*—would *appear* to have these features.)

This much is analogous to the case of the burned manuscript. Possibly no one will find what I have said very convincing unless he thinks very much like me. Let me offer three arguments against an "Aristotelian" account of the Resurrection that have no analogues in the case of the manuscript, and which will perhaps be more convincing to the generality of philosophers. Arguments (a) and (b) are *ad homines*, directed against Christians who might be inclined towards the "Aristotelian" theory. Argument (c) attempts to show that the "Aristotelian" theory has an impossible consequence.

a. The atoms of which I am composed cannot be destroyed by burning or the natural processes of decay; but they *can* be destroyed, as can atomic nuclei and even subatomic particles. (Or so it would seem: the principles for identity through time for subatomic particles are very hazy; physical theory has little if anything to say on the subject.) If, in order to raise a man on the Day of Judgment, God had to collect the "building blocks"—atoms, neutrons, or what have you—of which that man had once been composed, then a wicked man could hope to escape God's wrath by seeing to it that all his "building blocks" were destroyed. But according to Christian theology, such a hope is senseless. Thus, unless the nature of the ultimate constituents of matter is different from what it appears to be, the "Aristotelian" theory is inimical to a central point of Christian theology.

b. The atoms (or what have you) of which I am composed may very well have been parts of other people at some time in the past. Thus, if the "Aristotelian" theory is true, there could be a problem on the day of resurrection about *who* is resurrected. In fact, if that theory were true, a wicked man who had read his Aquinas might hope to escape punishment in the age to come by becoming a lifelong cannibal. But again, the possibility of such a hope cannot be admitted by any Christian.

c. It is possible that none of the atoms that are now parts of me were parts of me when I was ten years old. It is therefore possible that God could collect all the atoms that were parts of me when I was ten, without destroying me, and restore them to the positions they occupied relative to one another in 1952. If the "Aristotelian" theory

were correct, this action would be sufficient for the creation of a boy who could truly say, "I am Peter van Inwagen." In fact, he and I could stand facing one another and each say truly to the other, "I am you." But this is conceptually impossible, and, therefore, the "Aristotelian" theory is *not* correct.

No story other than our "Aristotelian" story about how it might be that a man who was totally destroyed could live again seems even superficially plausible. I conclude that my initial judgment is correct and that it is absolutely impossible, even as an accomplishment of God, that a man who has been burned to ashes or been eaten by worms should ever live again. What follows from this about the Christian hope of resurrection? Very little of any interest, I think. All that follows is that if Christianity is true, then what I earlier called "certain facts about the present age" are *not* facts.

It is part of the Christian faith that all men who share in the sin of Adam must die. What does it mean to say that I must die? Just this: that one day I shall be composed entirely of non-living matter; that is, I shall be a corpse. It is not part of the Christian faith that I must at any time be totally annihilated or disintegrate. (One might note that Christ, whose story is supposed to provide the archetype for the story of each man's resurrection, became a corpse but did not, even in His human nature, cease to exist.) It is of course true that men apparently cease to exist: those who are cremated, for example. But it contradicts nothing in the creeds to suppose that this is not what really happens, and that God preserves our corpses contrary to all appearance. . . . Perhaps at the moment of each man's death, God removes his corpse and replaces it with a simulacrum which is what is burned or rots. Or perhaps God is not quite so wholesale as this: perhaps He removes for "safekeeping" only the "core person"—the brain and central nervous system—or even some special part of it. These are details.

I take it that this story shows that the resurrection is a feat an almighty being *could* accomplish. I think this is the *only* way such a being could accomplish it. Perhaps I'm wrong, but that's of little importance.

What *is* important is that God can accomplish it this way or some other. Of course one might wonder *why* God would go such lengths to make it look as if most people not only die but pass into complete nothingness. This is a difficult question. I think it can be given a plausible answer, but not apart from a discussion of the nature of religious belief. I will say just this. If corpses inexplicably disappeared no matter how carefully they were guarded, or inexplicably refused to decay and were miraculously resistant to the most persistent and ingenious attempts to destroy them, then we should be living in a world in which observable events that were *obviously* miraculous, *obviously* due to the intervention of a power beyond Nature, happened with monotonous regularity. In such a world we should all believe in the supernatural: its existence would be the best explanation for the observed phenomena. If Christianity is true, God wants us to believe in the supernatural. But experience shows us that, if there is a God, He does not do what He very well *could* do: provide us with a ceaseless torrent of public, undeniable evidence of a power outside the natural order. And perhaps it is not hard to think of good reasons for such a policy.

Bibliography for Part VI

Ducasse, Curt John. *A Critical Examination of the Belief in Life After Death*. Springfield, Ill.: Thomas, 1961. One of the most comprehensive defenses of the Platonic-Cartesian view of immortality.

Edwards, Paul, ed. *Immortality*. New York: Macmillan, 1992. The best collection of articles available. Edward's own introductory article is valuable.

Geach, Peter. *God and the Soul*. London: Routledge & Kegan Paul, 1969. An examination of the concept of the soul.

Flew, Antony. "Immortality." In *Encyclopedia of Philosophy*, edited by Paul Edwards. New York: Free Press, 1965. A helpful survey of the history of the notion of immortality and the arguments connected with it.

Johnson, Raynor. *The Imprisoned Splendor*. London: Hodder and Stoughton, 1953. A defense of reincarnation.

Lamont, Corliss. *The Illusion of Immortality*. New York: Philosophical Library, 1965. A strong attack on several arguments for immortality.

Moody, Raymond. *Life After Life*. New York: Bantam Books, 1976. A fascinating, though controversial, account of near-death experiences.

Penelhum, Terrence. *Survival and Disembodied Existence*. London: Routledge & Kegan Paul, 1970. A fine-tuned examination of the key concepts and arguments associated with both the Platonic and the reconstitution views of survival.

Perry, John. *Personal Identity and Immortality*. Indianapolis: Hackett, 1979. An excellent dialogue on the subject.

Purtill, Richard. *Thinking About Religion*. Chaps. 9 and 10. Englewood Cliffs, N.J.: Prentice Hall, 1978. A fascinating defense of the Christian notion of life after death.

Quinton, Anthony. "The Soul," *Journal of Philosophy* 59 (1962):393–409. A good survey and analysis of concepts and arguments associated with the notion of the soul.

FAITH AND REASON

One of the most important issues in the philosophy of religion is the relationship of faith to reason. Is religious belief rational? Or is faith essentially an irrational activity, or, at least, an arational one? If we cannot prove the claims of religious belief, is it nevertheless reasonable to believe these claims? For example, even if we do not have a deductive proof for the existence of God, is it nevertheless reasonable to believe that God exists? In the debate over faith and reason two opposing positions have dominated the field. The first position asserts that faith and reason are commensurable (i.e., it is rational to believe in God). The second position denies this assertion. Those holding to the first position differ among themselves over the extent of the compatibility between faith and reason. Most adherents follow Thomas Aquinas in relegating the compatibility to the 'preambles of faith' (e.g., concerning the existence of God and his nature) over against the 'articles of faith' (e.g., the doctrine of the incarnation). Few have gone as far as Immanuel Kant, who maintained complete harmony between reason and faith, that is, religious belief within the realm of reason alone.

The second position divides into two subpositions. One asserts that faith is opposed to reason and belongs in the area of irrationality (those who hold to this belief include such unlikely bedfellows as David Hume and Søren Kierkegaard). The second asserts that faith is higher than reason, is transrational. John Calvin and Karl Barth assert that a natural theology is inappropriate because it seeks to meet unbelief on its own ground (ordinary, finite reason). Revelation, however, is "self-authenticating," "carrying with it its own evidence." We may call this position the 'transrational' view of faith. Faith is not against reason but above and beyond it in its own proper domain. Actually, Kierkegaard shows that the two subpositions are compatible, for he holds that faith is both above reason (superior to it) and against reason (because human reason has been affected by sin). The irrationalist and transrationalist positions are sometimes hard to separate in the incommensurabilist's argument. Faith gets such a high value that reason seems to end up looking not simply inadequate but culpable. To use reason where faith claims the field is not only inappropriate but irreverent and faithless.

VII.A   Challenges to Faith and Responses

We begin section A with a brief debate between three Oxford University philosophers that took place in 1948. Antony Flew challenges theists to state the conditions under which they would give up their faith, arguing that unless one can state what would 'falsify' one's belief, one does not have a meaningful belief. If nothing *could* count against the belief, it does not make a serious assertion. Serious truth claims need to be tested. R. M. Hare responds by arguing that this is the wrong way of describing faith, for religious faith consists of a set of profoundly unfalsifiable assumptions—which he calls *bliks*—that govern all of a person's other beliefs. There are insane and sane *bliks*, but we cannot help having some *bliks* about the world. Religion is not subject to rational scrutiny but is beyond (and possibly against) reason. Basil Mitchell opts for a compromise position. Rational considerations enter into the debate on religious faith, but no one can say exactly when a gradual accumulation of evidence comes to count sufficiently against a believed proposition that the believer feels obliged to give it up. Rational considerations count against religious belief, but the believer will strive to see to it that they do not count decisively against it.

Our second reading is Michael Scriven's "The Presumption of Atheism." Scriven argues that unless theism can assemble reasonably clear evidence to support the thesis that God exists, rational people cannot respond even with agnosticism, let alone faith. The only proper response is atheism. Rationally, 'faith' should mean faithfulness to a reasonable commitment; and 'agnosticism' is rational only when a hypothesis and its denial both have some support, that is, when the evidence is balanced so that the thesis is about 50 percent probable. Since Scriven claims elsewhere that the arguments for the existence of God fail to give significant support, he judges theism to be wholly unfounded. The challenge of Scriven's argument to the believer is to explain how religious belief can be justified if the traditional arguments fail.

Our third reading is C. S. Lewis's "On Obstinacy in Belief." Lewis takes up the argument where Basil Mitchell leaves off in his response to Anthony Flew. Lewis distinguishes between the logic of entering into a faith relationship and the logic of fidelity once one has entered into it. There is room for speculative thinking and doubt when one is first making the decision, but once one begins to experience the relationship with God, a "logic of personal relationship" takes over. This logic may make doubt an inappropriate attitude, a sort of unfaithful suspicion that a paranoic lover may have in wondering whether to trust someone who has done nothing but good to the beloved. Lewis argues that the evidence that gradually accumulates in the believer's life is as overwhelming and self-authenticating as it is intangible and difficult to communicate to an unbeliever.

Can faith be rationally justified? Is it rationally acceptable to believe in God? This is the challenge that rationalists put to religion. Can it and should it be met? The rest of Part 7 centers around this challenge.

The readings in this part of our work exemplify the positions that we have just described. The part is divided into four sections. The first section simply introduces some of the main problems in the debate. Sections B through D are more elaborate discussions of issues central to the debate. Section B deals with pragmatic arguments for religious belief. The question asked here is, Is it sometimes morally permissible purposefully to get oneself to believe what the evidence alone doesn't warrant? Section C deals with the issue of fideism, that is, whether religious belief is a separate form of life wherein external judgments are precluded and objective reason plays a very limited role. Section D deals with a broader notion of the role of reason in assessing religious claims and centers on recent developments in the debate, namely, whether religious belief is properly basic, needing no further defense. There is considerable overlap between sections C and D, and the discussion in C is to a large degree continued in D.

VII.A.1 Theology and Falsification

ANTONY FLEW, R. M. HARE, and BASIL MITCHELL

Antony Flew (1923–   ) is professor of philosophy at York University in Canada. R. M. Hare (1919–   ) and Basil Mitchell (1917–   ) are professors of philosophy at Oxford University. In this 1948 Oxford University symposium, Flew challenges theists to state the conditions under which they would give up their faith. He contends that unless one can state what would falsify one's belief, one does not have a meaningful belief. If nothing could count against the belief, it does not make a serious assertion, for serious truth claims must be ready to undergo rational scrutiny. R. M. Hare responds by arguing that this is the wrong way of describing faith, for religious faith consists of a set of profoundly unfalsifiable assumptions—which he calls bliks—that govern all of a person's other beliefs. There are insane and sane bliks, but we cannot escape having them. Even the scientist has such fundamental assumptions. Hence religion should not be subject to the kind of rational scrutiny that Flew urges. Basil Mitchell opts for a compromise position. Rational considerations enter into the debate on faith, but no one can say exactly when a gradual accumulation of evidence becomes sufficient to overthrow religious belief. Although rational considerations count against faith, the believer will not let them count decisively against it.

From *New Essays in Philosophical Theology*, edited by Antony Flew and Alasdair MacIntyre (London: SCM Press, 1955), pp. 96–108. Copyright © 1953 by SCM Press Ltd. Reprinted by permission of Macmillan Publishing Company. Footnotes edited.

Antony Flew

Let us begin with a parable. It is a parable developed from a tale told by John Wisdom in his haunting and revelatory article 'Gods.'[1] Once upon a time two explorers came upon a clearing in the jungle. In the clearing were growing many flowers and many weeds. One explorer says, "Some gardener must tend this plot." The other disagrees, "There is no gardener." So they pitch their tents and set a watch. No gardener is ever seen. "But perhaps he is an invisible gardener." So they set up a barbed-wire fence. They electrify it. They patrol with bloodhounds. (For they remember how H. G. Wells's *The Invisible Man* could be both smelt and touched though he could not be seen.) But no shrieks ever suggest that some intruder has received a shock. No movements of the wire ever betray an invisible climber. The bloodhounds never give cry. Yet still the Believer is not convinced. "But there is a gardener, invisible, intangible, insensible to electric shocks, a gardener who has no scent and makes no sound, a gardener who comes secretly to look after the garden which he loves." At last the Sceptic despairs, "But what remains of your original assertion? Just how does what you call an invisible, intangible, eternally elusive gardener differ from an imaginary gardener or even from no gardener at all?"

In this parable we can see how what starts as an assertion, that something exists or that there is some analogy between certain complexes of phenomena, may be reduced step by step to an altogether different status, to an expression perhaps of a "picture preference." The Sceptic says there is no gardener. The Believer says there is a gardener (but invisible, etc.). One man talks about sexual behaviour. Another man prefers to talk of Aphrodite (but knows that there is not really a superhuman person additional to, and somehow responsible for, all sexual phenomena). The process of qualification may be checked at any point before the original assertion is completely withdrawn and something of that first assertion will remain (Tautology). Mr. Wells's invisible man could not, admittedly, be seen, but in all other respects he was a man like the rest of us. But though the process of qualification may be, and of course usually is checked in time, it is not always judiciously so halted. Someone may dissipate his assertion completely without noticing that he has done so. A fine brash hypothesis may thus be killed by inches, the death by a thousand qualifications.

And in this, it seems to me, lies the peculiar danger, the endemic evil, of theological utterance. Take such utterances as "God has a plan," "God created the world," "God loves us as a father loves his children." They look at first sight very much like assertions, vast cosmological assertions. Of course, this is no sure sign that they either are, or are intended to be, assertions. But let us confine ourselves to the cases where those who utter such sentences intend them to express assertions. (Merely remarking parenthetically that those who intend or interpret such utterances as crypto-commands, expressions of wishes, disguised ejaculations, concealed ethics, or as anything else but assertions, are unlikely to succeed in making them either properly orthodox or practically effective).

Now to assert that such and such is the case is necessarily equivalent to denying that such and such is not the case. Suppose then that we are in doubt as to what someone who gives vent to an utterance is asserting, or suppose that, more radically, we are sceptical as to whether he is really asserting anything at all, one way of trying to understand (or perhaps it will be to expose) his utterance is to attempt to find what he would regard as counting against, or as being incompatible with, its truth. For if the utterance is indeed an assertion, it will necessarily be equivalent to a denial of the negation of that

assertion. And anything which would count against the assertion, or which would induce the speaker to withdraw it and to admit that it had been mistaken, must be part of (or the whole of) the meaning of the negation of that assertion. And to know the meaning of the negation of an assertion, is as near as makes no matter, to know the meaning of that assertion. And if there is nothing which a putative assertion denies then there is nothing which it asserts either: and so it is not really an assertion. When the Sceptic in the parable asked the Believer, "Just how does what you call an invisible, intangible, eternally elusive gardener differ from an imaginary gardener or even from no gardener at all?" he was suggesting that the Believer's earlier statement had been eroded by qualification that it was no longer as assertion at all.

Now it often seems to people who are not religious as if there was no conceivable event or series of events the occurrence of which would be admitted by sophisticated religious people to be a sufficient reason for conceding "There wasn't a God after all" or "God does not really love us then." Someone tells us that God loves us as a father loves his children. We are reassured. But then we see a child dying of inoperable cancer of the throat. His earthly father is driven frantic in his efforts to help, but his Heavenly Father reveals no obvious sign of concern. Some qualification is made—God's love is "not a merely human love" or it is "an inscrutable love," perhaps—and we realize that such sufferings are quite compatible with the truth of the assertion that "God loves us as a father (but, of course, . . .)." We are reassured again. But then perhaps we ask: what is this assurance of God's (appropriately qualified) love worth, what is this apparent guarantee really a guarantee against? Just what would have to happen not merely (morally and wrongly) to tempt but also (logically and rightly) to entitle us to say "God does not love us" or even "God does not exist?" I therefore put to the succeeding symposiasts the simple central question, "What would have to occur or to have occurred to constitute for you a disproof of the love of, or of the existence of, God?"

R. M. Hare

I wish to make it clear that I shall not try to defend Christianity in particular, but religion in general—not because I do not believe in Christianity, but because you cannot understand what Christianity is, until you have understood what religion is.

I must begin by confessing that, on the ground marked out by Flew, he seems to me to be completely victorious. I therefore shift my ground by relating another parable. A certain lunatic is convinced that all dons want to murder him. His friends introduce him to all the mildest and most respectable dons that they can find, and after each of them has retired, they say, "You see, he doesn't really want to murder you; he spoke to you in a most cordial manner; surely you are convinced now?" But the lunatic replies "Yes, but that was only his diabolical cunning; he's really plotting against me the whole time, like the rest of them; I know it I tell you." However many kindly dons are produced, the reaction is still the same.

Now we say that such a person is deluded. But what is he deluded about? About the truth or falsity of an assertion? Let us apply Flew's test to him. There is no behaviour of dons that can be enacted which he will accept as counting against his theory; and therefore his theory, on this test, asserts nothing. But it does not follow that there is no difference between what he thinks about dons and what most of us think about them—otherwise we should not call him a lunatic and ourselves sane, and dons would have no reason to feel uneasy about his presence in Oxford.

Let us call that in which we differ from this lunatic, our respective *bliks*. He has an insane *blik* about dons; we have a sane one. It is important to realize that we have a sane one, not no *blik* at all; for there must be two sides to any argument—if he has a wrong *blik*, then those who are right about dons must have a right one. Flew has shown that a *blik* does not consist in an assertion or system of them; but nevertheless it is very important to have the right *blik*.

Let us try to imagine what it would be like to have different *bliks* about other things than dons. When I am driving my car, it sometimes occurs to me to wonder whether my movements of the steering-wheel will always continue to be followed by corresponding alterations in the direction of the car. I have never had a steering failure, though I have had skids, which must be similar. Moreover, I know enough about how the steering of my car is made, to know the sort of thing that would have to go wrong for the steering to fail—steel joints would have to part, or steel rods break, or something—but how do I know that this won't happen? The truth is, I don't know; I just have a *blik* about steel and its properties, so that normally I trust the steering of my car; but I find it not at all difficult to imagine what it would be like to lose this *blik* and acquire the opposite one. People would say I was silly about steel; but there would be no mistaking the reality of the difference between our respective *bliks*—for example, I should never go in a motor-car. Yet I should hesitate to say that the difference between us was the difference between contradictory assertions. No amount of safe arrivals or bench-tests will remove my *blik* and restore the normal one: for my *blik* is compatible with any finite number of such tests.

It was Hume who taught us that our whole commerce with the world depends upon our *blik* about the world; and that differences between *bliks* about the world cannot be settled by observation of what happens in the world. That was why, having performed the interesting experiment of doubting the ordinary man's *blik* about the world, and showing that no proof could be given to make us adopt one *blik* rather than another, he turned to backgammon to take his mind off the problem. It seems, indeed, to be impossible even to formulate as an assertion the normal *blik* about the world which makes me put my confidence in the future reliability of steel joints, in the continued ability of the road to support my car, and not gape beneath it revealing nothing below; in the general nonhomicidal tendencies of dons; in my own continued well-being (in some sense of that word that I may not now fully understand) if I continue to do what is right according to my lights; in the general likelihood of people like Hitler coming to a bad end. But perhaps a formulation less inadequate than most is to be found in the Psalms: "The earth is weak and all the inhabiters thereof: I bear up the pillars of it."

The mistake of the position which Flew selects for attack is to regard this kind of talk as some sort of *explanation*, as scientists are accustomed to use the word. As such, it would obviously be ludicrous. We no longer believe in God as an Atlas—*nous n'avons pas besoin de cette hypothèse*. But it is nevertheless true to say that, as Hume saw, without a *blik* there can be no explanation; for it is by our *bliks* that we decide what is and what is not an explanation. Suppose we believed that everything that happened, happened by pure chance. This would not of course be an assertion; for it is compatible with anything happening or not happening, and so, incidentally, is its contradictory. But if we had this belief, we should not be able to explain or predict or plan anything. Thus, although we should not be asserting anything different from those of a more normal belief, there would be a great difference between us; and this is the sort of difference that there is between those who really believe in God and those who really disbelieve in him.

The word "really" is important, and may excite suspicion. I put it in, because when people have had a good Christian upbringing, as have most of those who now profess not to believe in any sort of religion, it is very hard to discover what they really believe. The reason why they find it so easy to think that they are not religious, is that they have never got into the frame of mind of one who suffers from the doubts to which religion is the answer. Not for them the terrors of the primitive jungle. Having abandoned some of the more picturesque fringes of religion, they think that they have abandoned the whole thing—whereas in fact they still have got, and could not live without, a religion of a comfortably substantial, albeit highly sophisticated, kind, which differs from that of many "religious people" in little more than this, that "religious people" like to sing Psalms about theirs—a very natural and proper thing to do. But nevertheless there may be a big difference lying behind—the difference between two people who, though side by side, are walking in different directions. I do not know in what direction Flew is walking; perhaps he does not know either. But we have had some examples recently of various ways in which one can walk away from Christianity, and there are any number of possibilities. After all, man has not changed biologically since primitive times; it is his religion that has changed, and it can easily change again. And if you do not think that such changes make a difference, get acquainted with some Sikhs and some Mussulmans of the same Punjabi stock; you will find them quite different sorts of people.

There is an important difference between Flew's parable and my own which we have not yet noticed. The explorers do not *mind* about their garden; they discuss it with interest, but not with concern. But my lunatic, poor fellow, minds about dons; and I mind about the steering of my car; it often has people in it that I care for. It is because I mind very much about what goes on in the garden in which I find myself, that I am unable to share the explorers' detachment.

Basil Mitchell

Flew's article is searching and perceptive, but there is, I think, something odd about his conduct of the theologian's case. The theologian surely would not deny that the fact of pain counts against the assertion that God loves men. This very incompatibility generates the most intractable of theological problems—the problem of evil. So the theologian *does* recognize the fact of pain as counting against Christian doctrine. But it is true that he will not allow it—or anything—to count decisively against it; for he is committed by his faith to trust in God. His attitude is not that of the detached observer, but of the believer.

Perhaps this can be brought out by yet another parable. In time of war in an occupied country, a member of the resistance meets one night a stranger who deeply impresses him. They spend that night together in conversation. The Stranger tells the partisan that he himself is on the side of the resistance—indeed that he is in command of it, and urges the partisan to have faith in him no matter what happens. The partisan is utterly convinced at that meeting of the Stranger's sincerity and constancy and undertakes to trust him.

They never meet in conditions of intimacy again. But sometimes the Stranger is seen helping members of the resistance, and the partisan is grateful and says to his friends, "He is on our side."

Sometimes he is seen in the uniform of the police handing over patriots to the occupying power. On these occasions his friends murmur against him; but the partisan still says, "He is on our side." He still believes that, in spite of appearances, the Stranger did not deceive him. Sometimes he asks the Stranger for help and receives it. He is then thankful. Sometimes he asks and does not receive it. Then he says, "The Stranger knows best." Sometimes his friends, in exasperation, say "Well, what *would* he have to do for you to admit that you were wrong and that he is not on our side?" But the partisan refuses to answer. He will not consent to put the Stranger to the test. And sometimes his friends complain, "Well, if *that's* what you mean by his being on our side, the sooner he goes over to the other side the better."

The partisan of the parable does not allow anything to count decisively against the proposition "The Stranger is on our side." This is because he has committed himself to trust the Stranger. But he of course recognizes that the Stranger's ambiguous behaviour *does* count against what he believes about him. It is precisely this situation which constitutes the trial of his faith.

When the partisan asks for help and doesn't get it, what can he do? He can (a) conclude that the stranger is not on our side or, (b) maintain that he is on our side, but that he has reasons for withholding help.

The first he will refuse to do. How long can he uphold the second position without its becoming just silly?

I don't think one can say in advance. It will depend on the nature of the impression created by the Stranger in the first place. It will depend, too, on the manner in which he takes the Stranger's behaviour. If he blandly dismisses it as of no consequence, as having no bearing upon his belief, it will be assumed that he is thoughtless or insane. And it quite obviously won't do for him to say easily, "Oh, when used of the Stranger the phrase 'is on our side' *means* ambiguous behavior of this sort." In that case he would be like the religious man who says blandly of a terrible disaster, "It is God's will." No,

he will only be regarded as sane and reasonable in his belief, if he experiences in himself the full force of the conflict.

It is here that my parable differs from Hare's. The partisan admits that many things may and do count against his belief; whereas Hare's lunatic who has a *blik* about dons doesn't admit that anything counts against his *blik*. Nothing can count against *bliks*. Also the partisan has a reason for having in the first instance committed himself, viz. the character of the Stranger; whereas the lunatic has no reason for his *blik* about dons—because, of course, you can't have reasons for *bliks*.

This means that I agree with Flew that theological utterances must be assertions. The partisan is making an assertion when he says, "The Stranger is on our side."

Do I want to say that the partisan's belief about the Stranger is, in any sense, an explanation? I think I do. It explains and makes sense of the Stranger's behaviour; it helps to explain also the resistance movement in the context of which he appears. In each case it differs from the interpretation which the others put upon the same facts.

"God loves men" resembles "the Stranger is on our side" (and many other significant statements, e.g. historical ones) in not being conclusively falsifiable. They can both be treated in at least three different ways: (1) As provisional hypotheses to be discarded if experience tells against them; (2) As significant articles of faith; (3) As vacuous formulae (expressing, perhaps, a desire for reassurance) to which experience makes no difference and which make no difference to life.

The Christian, once he has committed himself, is precluded by his faith from taking up the first attitude: "Thou shalt not tempt the Lord thy God." He is in constant danger, as Flew has observed, of slipping into the third. But he need not; and, if he does, it is a failure in faith as well as in logic.

Note

1. *P.A.S.*, 1944–5, reprinted as Ch. X of *Logic and Language*, Vol. 1 (Blackwell, 1951), and in his *Philosophy and Psychoanalysis* (Blackwell, 1953).

VII.A.2 The Presumption of Atheism

MICHAEL SCRIVEN

Michael Scriven was professor of philosophy at the University of California at Berkeley. In this article he argues that unless theism can assemble reasonably clear evidence to support the thesis that God exists, rational people cannot respond even with agnosticism, let alone faith. The only proper response is atheism. Rationally, 'faith' should mean faithfulness to a reasonable commitment; and 'agnosticism' is rational only when a hypothesis and its denial both have some support, that is, when the evidence is balanced so that the thesis is about 50 percent probable. Since Scriven claims elsewhere that the arguments for the existence of God fail to give significant support, he judges theism to be wholly unfounded. The challenge of Scriven's argument to the believer is to explain how religious belief can be justified if the traditional arguments fail.

Faith and Reason

We must now contend with the suggestion that reason is irrelevant to the commitment to theism because this territory is the domain of another faculty: the faculty of faith. It is sometimes even hinted that it is morally wrong and certainly foolish to suggest we should be reasoning about God. For this is the domain of faith or of the "venture of faith," of the "knowledge that passeth understanding," of religious experience and mystic insight.

Now the normal meaning of *faith* is simply "confidence"; we say that we have great faith in someone or in some claim or product, meaning that we believe and act as if they were very reliable. Of such faith we can properly say that it is well founded or not, depending on the evidence for whatever it

is in which we have faith. So there is no incompatibility between this kind of faith and reason; the two are from different families and can make a very good marriage. Indeed if they do not join forces, then the resulting ill-based or inadequate confidence will probably lead to disaster. So faith, in this sense, means only a high degree of belief and may be reasonable or unreasonable.

But the term is sometimes used to mean an *alternative* to reason instead of something that should be founded on reason. Unfortunately, the mere use of the term in this way does not demonstrate that faith is a possible route to truth. It is like using the term "winning" as a synonym for "playing" instead of one possible outcome of playing. This is quaint, but it could hardly be called a satisfactory way of proving that we are winning; any time we "win" by changing the meaning of winning, the victory is merely illusory. And so it proves in this case. To use "faith" as *if* it were an alternative way to the truth cannot by-pass the crucial question whether such results really have any likelihood of being true. A rose by any other name will smell the same, and the inescapable facts about "faith" in the new sense are that it is still *applied* to a belief and is still supposed to imply *confidence in* that belief: the belief in the existence and goodness of God. So we can still ask the same old question about that belief: Is the confidence justified or misplaced? To say we "take it on faith" does not get it off parole.

Suppose someone replies that theism is a kind of belief that does not need justification by evidence. This means either that no one cares whether it is correct or not or that there is some other way of checking that it is correct besides looking at the evidence for it, that is, giving reasons for believing it. But the first alternative is false since very many people care whether there is a God or not; and the second alternative is false because any method of showing that belief is likely to be true is, by definition, a justification of that belief, that is, an appeal to reason. You certainly cannot show that a belief in God is likely to be true just by having confidence in it and by saying this is a case of knowledge "based on" faith, any more than you can win a game just by playing it and by calling that winning.

It is psychologically possible to have faith in something without any basis in fact, and once in a while you will turn out to be lucky and to have backed the right belief. This does not show you "really knew all along"; it only shows you cannot be unlucky all the time. But, in general, beliefs without foundations lead to an early grave or to an accumulation of superstitions, which are usually troublesome and always false beliefs. It is hardly possible to defend this approach just by *saying* that you have decided that in this area confidence is its own justification.

Of course, you might try to *prove* that a feeling of great confidence about certain types of propositions is a reliable indication of their truth. If you succeeded, you would indeed have shown that the belief was justified; you would have done this by justifying it. To do this you would have to show what the real facts were and show that when someone had the kind of faith we are now talking about, it usually turned out that the facts were as he believed, just as we might justify the claims of the telepath. The catch in all this is simply that you have got to show what the real facts are in some way *other* than by appealing to faith, since that would simply be assuming what you are trying to prove. And if you can show what the facts are in this other way, you do not need faith in any new sense at all; you are already perfectly entitled to confidence in any belief that you have shown to be well supported.

How are you going to show what the real facts are? You show this by any method of investigation that has itself been tested, the testing being done by still another tested method, etc., through a series of tested connections that eventually terminates in our ordinary everyday reasoning and testing procedures of logic and observation.

Is it not prejudiced to require that the validation of beliefs always involve ultimate reference to our ordinary logic and everyday-plus-scientific knowledge? May not faith (religious experience, mystic insight) give us access to some new domain of truth? It is certainly possible that it does this. But, of course, it is also possible that it lies. One can hardly accept the reports of those with faith or, indeed, the apparent revelations of one's own religious experiences on the ground that they *might* be right. So *might* be a fervent materialist who saw his interpretation as a revelation. Possibility is not veracity. It is not of the very greatest importance that we should try to find out whether we really can justify the use of the term "truth" or "knowledge" in describing the content of faith? If it is, then we must find something in that content that is known to be true in some other way, because to get off the ground we must first push off against the ground—we cannot lift ourselves by our shoelaces. If the new realm of knowledge is to be a realm of knowledge and not mythology, then it must tell us something which relates it to the kind of case that gives meaning to the term "truth." If you want to use the old word for the new events, you must show that it is applicable.

Could not the validating experience, which religious experience must have if it is to be called true, be the experience of others who also have or have had religious experiences? The religious community could, surely, provide a basis of agreement analogous to that which ultimately underlies scientific truth. Unfortunately, agreement is not the only requirement for avoiding error, for all may be in error. The difficulty for the religious community is to show that its agreement is not simply agreement about a shared mistake. If agreement were the only criterion of truth, there could never be a shared mistake; but clearly either the atheist group or the theist group shares a mistake. To decide which is wrong must involve appeal to something other than mere agreement. And, of course, it is clear that particular religious beliefs are mistaken, since religious groups do not all agree and they cannot all be right.

Might not some or all scientific beliefs be wrong too? This is conceivable, but there are crucial differences between the two kinds of belief. In the first place, any commonly agreed religious beliefs concern only one or a few entities and their properties and histories. What for convenience we are here calling "scientific belief" is actually the sum total of all conventionally founded human knowledge, much of it not part of any science, and it embraces billions upon billions of facts, each of them perpetually or frequently subject to checking by independent means, each connected with a million others. The success of *this* system of knowledge shows up every day in everything we do: we eat, and the food is not poison; we read, and the pages do not turn to dust; we slip, and the gravity does not fail to pull us down. We are not just relying on the existence of agreement about the interpretation of a certain experience among a small part of the population. We are relying directly on our extremely reliable, nearly universal, and independently tested senses, and each of us is constantly obtaining independent confirmation for claims based on these, many of these confirmations being obtained for many claims, independently of each other. It is the wildest flight of fancy to suppose that there is a body of common religious beliefs which can be set out to exhibit this degree of repeated checking by religious experiences. In fact, there is not only gross disagreement on even the most fundamental claims in the creeds of different churches, each of which is supported by appeal to religious experience or faith, but where there is agreement by many people, it is all too easily open to the criticism that it arises from the common cultural exposure of the child or the adult convert and hence is not independent in the required way.

This claim that the agreement between judges is spurious in a particular case because it only reflects previous common indoctrination of those in agreement is a serious one. It must always be met by direct disproof whenever agreement is appealed to in science, and it is. The claim that the food is not poison cannot be explained away as a myth of some subculture, for anyone, even if told nothing about the eaters in advance, will judge that the people who ate it are still well. The whole methodology of testing is committed to the doctrine that any judges who could have learned what they are expected to say about the matter they are judging are completely valueless. Now anyone exposed to religious teaching, whether a believer or not, has long known the standard for such experiences, the usual symbols, the appropriate circumstances, and so on.

These suggestions are usually very deeply implanted, so that they cannot be avoided by good intentions, and consequently members of our culture are rendered entirely incapable of being independent observers. Whenever observers are not free from previous contamination in this manner, the only way to support their claims is to examine independently testable *consequences* of the novel claims, such as predictions about the future. In the absence of these, the religious-experience gambit, whether involving literal or analogical claims, is wholly abortive.

A still more fundamental point counts against the idea that agreement among the religious can help support the idea of faith as an alternative path to truth. It is that every sane theist also believes in the claims of ordinary experience, while the reverse is not the case. Hence, the burden of proof is on the theist to show that the *further step* he wishes to take will not take him beyond the realm of truth. The two positions, of science and religion, are not symmetrical; the adherent of one of them suggests that we extend the range of allowable beliefs and yet is unable to produce the same degree of acceptance or "proving out" in the ordinary field of human activities that he insists on before believing in a new instrument or source of information. The atheist obviously cannot be shown his error in the way someone who thinks that there are no electrons can be shown his, *unless some of the arguments for the existence of God are sound.* Once again, we come back to these. If some of them work, the position of religious knowledge is secure; if they do not, nothing else will make it secure.

In sum, the idea of separating religious from scientific knowledge and making each an independent realm with its own basis in experience of quite different kinds is a counsel of despair and not a product of true sophistication, for one cannot break the connection between everyday experience and religious claims, for purposes of defending the latter, without eliminating the consequences of religion for everyday life. There is no way out of this inexorable contract: if you want to support your beliefs, you must produce some experience which can be shown to be a reliable indicator of truth, and that can be done only by showing a connection between the experience and what we know to be true in a previously established way.

So, if the criteria of religious truth are not connected with the criteria of everyday truth, then they are not criteria of truth at all and the beliefs they "establish" have no essential bearing on our lives, constitute no explanation of what we see around us, and provide no guidance for our course through time.

The Consequences If the Arguments Fail

The arguments are the only way to establish theism, and they must be judged by the usual standards of evidence—this we have argued. It will now be shown that if they fail, there is no alternative to atheism.

Against this it has commonly been held that the absence of arguments *for* the existence of something is not the same as the presence of arguments *against* its existence; so agnosticism or an option remains when the arguments fail. But insofar as this is true, it is irrelevant. It is true only if we restrict "arguments for the existence of something" to highly specific demonstrations which attempt to establish their conclusion as beyond all reasonable doubt. The absence of these is indeed compatible with the conclusion's being quite likely, which would make denial of its existence unjustified. But if we take arguments for this existence of something to include all the evidence which supports the existence claim to any significant degree, i.e., makes it at all probable, then the evidence means there is no likelihood of the existence of the entity. And this, of course, is a complete justification for the claim that the entity does not exist, provided that the entity is not one which might leave no traces (a God who is impotent or who does not care for us), and provided that we have comprehensively examined the area where such evidence would appear if there were any. Now justifying the claim that something does not exist is not quite the same as proving or having arguments that it doesn't, but it is what we are talking about. That is, we need not have a proof that God does not exist in order to justify

atheism. Atheism is obligatory in the absence of any evidence for God's existence.

Why do adults not believe in Santa Claus? Simply because they can now explain the phenomena for which Santa Claus's existence is invoked without any need for introducing a novel entity. When we were very young and naively believed our parents' stories, it was hard to see how the presents could get there on Christmas morning since the doors were locked and our parents were asleep in bed. Someone *must* have brought them down the chimney. And how could the person get to the roof without a ladder and with all those presents? Surely only by flying. And then there is a great traditional literature of stories and songs which immortalize the entity and his (horned) attendants; surely these cannot all be just products of imagination? Where there is smoke there must be fire.

Santa Claus is not a bad hypothesis at all for six-year-olds. As we grow up, no one comes forward to *prove* that such an entity does not exist. We just come to see that there is not the least reason to think he *does* exist. And so it would be entirely foolish to assert that he does, or believe that he does, or even think it likely that he does. Santa Claus is in just the same position as fairy godmothers, wicked witches, the devil, and the ether. Each of these entities has some supernatural powers, i.e., powers which contravene or go far beyond the powers that we know exist, whether it be the power to levitate a sled and reindeer or the power to cast a spell. Now even belief in something for which there is no evidence, i.e., a belief which goes *beyond* the evidence, although a lesser sin than belief in something which is *contrary* to well-established laws, is plainly irrational in that it simply amounts to attaching belief where it is not justified. So the proper alternative, when there is no evidence, is not mere suspension of belief, for example, about Santa Claus, it is *disbelief*. It most certainly is not faith.

The situation is slightly different with the Abominable Snowman, sea serpents, or even the Loch Ness monster. No "supernatural" (by which, in this context, we only mean wholly unprecedented) kinds of powers are involved. Previous discoveries have been made of creatures which had long seemed extinct, and from these we can immediately derive some likelihood of further discoveries. Footprints or disturbances for which no fully satisfactory alternative explanation has yet been discovered (although such an explanation is by no means impossible) have been seen in the Himalayan snow and the Scottish lochs. It would be credulous for the layman to believe firmly in the existence of these entities. Yet it would be equally inappropriate to say it is certain they do not exist. Here is a domain for agnosticism (though perhaps an agnosticism inclined toward skepticism). For the agnostic does not believe that a commitment either way is justified, and he is surely right about strange creatures which, while of a new *appearance*, have powers that are mere extensions, proportional to size, of those with which we are already familiar on this earth. There is some suggestive, if by no means conclusive, evidence for such entities; and the balance of general considerations is not heavily against them.

But when the assertion is made that something exists with powers that strikingly transcend the well-established generalizations we have formulated about animal capacities or reasonable extrapolations from them, then we naturally expect correspondingly better evidence before we concede that there is a serious likelihood of having to abandon those generalizations. It is entirely appropriate to demand much stronger support for claims of telepathy or levitation or miraculous cures than for new sports records or feats of memory in which previous levels of performance are merely bettered to some degree, in a way that is almost predictable. On the other hand, it is entirely prejudiced to reject all such evidence on the ground that it *must* be deceptive because it contravenes previously established generalizations. This is simply to deify the present state of science; it is the precise opposite of the experimental attitude. It is right to demand a stronger case to overthrow a strong case and to demand very strong evidence to demonstrate unprecedented powers. It is irrational to require that the evidence of these powers be just as commonplace and compelling as for the previously known powers of man or beast: one can not legislate the exceptional into the commonplace.

We can now use a set of distinctions that would previously have seemed very abstract. First, let us

distinguish a belief which is wholly without general or particular evidential support from one which can be directly disproved. The claim that a race of men lives on the moons of Jupiter or that a certain cola causes cancer of the colon is entirely unfounded but not totally impossible. The view that the ratio of a circle's circumference to its diameter can be expressed as a fraction is demonstrably untenable, as is the view that some living men are infinitely strong, or that any man is or has been unbeatable at chess, or that the FBI has wiped out the Mafia. We normally say that a claim is *well founded* if there is evidence which is best explained by this claim. We may say it is *provable* if the evidence is indubitable and the claim is very clearly required. If there is no evidence which points to this particular claim, although some general background considerations make it not too unlikely that something like this should be true (Loch Ness monster, mile record broken twice in 1980), we would say there is *some* general support for the claim. We shall say it is *wholly unfounded* (or *wholly unsupported*) if there is no evidence for it in particular and no general considerations in its favor, and *disprovable* if it implies that something would be the case that definitely is not the case.

Of course it is foolish to believe a claim that is disproved, but it is also foolish to believe a wholly unsupported claim, and it is still foolish even to treat such a claim as if it were worth serious consideration. A claim for which there is some general or some particular support cannot be dismissed, but neither can it be treated or established. The connection between evidential support and the appropriate degree of belief can be demonstrated as shown in the diagram that follows, which is quite unlike the oversimplified idea that the arrangement should be:

Provable	Theism
Disprovable	Atheism
Neither	Agnosticism

The crucial difference is that both "unfounded" and "disprovable" correlate with atheism, just as the two corresponding types of provability correlate with theism; hence the agnostic's territory is smaller than he often supposes.

Recalling that to get even a little evidential support for the existence of a Being with supernatural powers will require that the little be of very high quality (*little* does not mean "dubious"), we see that the failure of all the arguments, that is, of all the evidence, will make even agnosticism in the wide sense an indefensible exaggeration of the evidential support. And agnosticism in the narrow sense will be an exaggeration unless the arguments are strong enough to establish about a 50 percent probability for the claim of theism. Apart from the wide and narrow senses of agnosticism there is also a distinction between a positive agnostic and a negative agnostic.

A *positive agnostic* maintains that the evidence is such as to make his position the correct one and those of the theist and atheist incorrect. *Negative agnosticism* is simply the position of not accepting either theism or atheism; it does not suggest that they are both wrong—it may be just an expression of felt indecision or ignorance. The difference between negative and positive agnosticism is like the difference between a neutral who says, "I don't know who's right—maybe one of the disputants, or maybe neither," and a *third* force who says, "Neither is right, and I have a third alternative which *is* right." Obviously, the negative agnostic has not progressed as far in his thinking as the positive agnostic, in one sense, because he has not been able to decide which of the three possible positions is correct. The view of the negative agnostic cannot be right, but his position may be the right position for someone who has not thought the matter through or who lacks the capacity to do so.

In practice, an agnostic's position is often the product of an untidy mixture of factors. He may never have happened to come across an argument for either theism or atheism which struck him as compelling; a rough head counting has revealed intelligent people on either side; his nose for social stigmas indicates a slight odor of intellectual deficiency attached to theism by contemporary intellectuals and a suggestion of unnecessary boat rocking or perhaps rabid subversion attached to atheism. This makes the agnostic fence look pretty attractive; so up he climbs, to sit on top. But now we put the challenge to him. Is he incapable of thinking out an answer for himself? If so, he is intellectually inferior to those below; if not, he must descend and demonstrate the failings of the contestants before he is entitled to his perch. Agnosticism as a position is interesting and debatable; agnosticism as the absence of a position is simply a sign of the absence of intellectual activity or capacity.

Combining and Separating Arguments and Evidence

There used to be a standing joke in the Rationalist Club at Melbourne University about the theologian who said: "None of the arguments is any good by itself, but taken together they constitute an overwhelming proof." Alas for the simple approach; the instinct of the theologian was better than the formal training of the rationalists, although the error is not easily stated. There used to be a small book on the market which contained 200 "proofs" that $-1 = +1$; entertaining though these are, they do not make it one bit more likely that -1 really does equal $+1$, for they are all invalid. If you knew nothing about mathematics, even about elementary arithmetic, and the only way you could find out whether $+1$ equaled -1 was by counting the number of alleged proofs in each direction, you might reasonably conclude that it did. But if you were seriously concerned with the truth of the matter, you would want to investigate the validity of the proofs for yourself; and you would find that they were all unsound. So there is no advantage in numbers, *as far as mathematical proofs go*. They either do the whole trick or nothing at all.

The situation is different with scientific proofs, whereby we hope to do no more than show that one conclusion is so probable as to be beyond reasonable doubt. Let us suppose you are investigating a murder case. There are three clues. The first one points most strongly at North as the suspect; the second, at East; the third, at West. Obviously, you could not argue that South had been shown to be the culprit from a consideration of any one of these clues by itself. Yet there are circumstances in which you can put them all together and conclude that

South was, *without any doubt,* the murderer. Here we have a number of "proofs" (items of evidence) which separately do nothing to establish a particular conclusion but which add up to a good proof of that conclusion. How is this possible? The point about probability proofs is that they do not make the alternative explanations completely impossible and may indicate a second-best hypothesis. So, although the first clue is North's handkerchief at the scene of the crime, you also know that South is North's roommate and may have borrowed his handkerchief, while no one else could have done so without considerable difficulty. And although the second clue is that East very frequently had violent arguments with the victim and had been heard to threaten him with injury, it was also true that South stood to gain by the victim's death since he inherited his job in a public relations firm. And West's professional skill at judo, which ties in well with the victim's curiously broken neck, is not such as to make South's army training in basic karate blows an irrelevant consideration. So South is by a long way the most likely murderer. In the same way, with respect to those arguments for the existence of God which are of the probability-increasing kind, we shall have to consider not only whether they

Evidential Situation	Appropriate Attitude	Name for Appropriate Attitude in Theism Case	
1. Strictly disprovable. i.e., demonstrably incompatible with the evidence.	Rejection	Atheism	
2. Wholly unfounded, i.e., wholly lacking in general or particular support.			
3. Possessing some general or particular support; still improbable.	Skepticism but recognition as a real *possibility*; not to be wholly disregarded in comprehensive planning but to be bet *against.*	Skepticism	Agnosticism (wide sense)
4. Possessing substantial support but with substantial alternatives still open; a balance of evidence for and against; about 50 per cent probable.	Suspension of judgment. Make no commitment either way; treat each alternative as approximately equally serious.	Agnosticism (narrow sense)	
5. Possessing powerful evidential support; some difficulties or inadequacies or significant alternatives remaining; probable.	Treat as probably true; bet on.	Pragmatic theism	
6. Possessing overwhelming particular support and no basis for alternative views; beyond reasonable doubt; provable in the usual sense.	Acceptance	Theism	
7. Strictly provable, i.e., as a demonstrably necessary result of indubitable facts.			

make God's existence likely on their own but whether some of them make it a sufficiently good alternative explanation so that when we take all the arguments together it is the best overall explanation.

Obviously this can happen only if the same *hypothesis* receives support as an alternative in each case, for example, the hypothesis that South is the murderer. It would not work at all if the first clue made a secondary suspect of one man called South and the next of a cousin of the first suspect also called South. After looking at all the arguments in this kind of situation, we would not have any one candidate who was better qualified than any other; we could not even say that it was probably someone from the family of South, for as a matter of fact this is less likely than that it was one of the other three, North, East, and West.

It could be argued that the greatest confidence trick in the history of philosophy is the attempt to make the various arguments for the existence of God support each other by using the same term for the entity whose existence each is supposed to establish. In fact, almost all of them bear on entities of apparently quite different kinds, ranging from a Creator to a moral Lawgiver. The proofs must, therefore, be supplemented with a further proof or set of proofs that shows these apparently different entities to be the same if the combination trick is to work. Otherwise the arguments must be taken separately, in which case they either establish or fail to establish the existence of a number of remarkable but unrelated entities.

It can sometimes be argued that considerations of simplicity require one to adopt the hypothesis that only a single entity is involved, when the alternative is to introduce several special entities. But the circumstances in which this is legitimate are quite limited; we do not, for example, argue that simplicity requires us to assume that the murderer South is also the unknown person who stole some bonds from a bank the day before the murder. We would have to show some connection through means, opportunity, motive, or *modus operandi*, before the identification could be made at all plausible. Simplicity is a fine guide to the best hypothesis if one can only decide which hypothesis is the simpler. Although there is a greater simplicity in

terms of the number of entities involved if we say, for example, that the Creator is the moral Lawgiver, there is a greater complexity in terms of the number of explanations required, since now we must explain why and how one entity could perform these two functions. In short, we have really got to give a plausible specific reason before we can identify the two criminals or the two theological entities, since simplicity is now clearly gained by either alternative, and until we do so, any commitment to such an identification is wholly unfounded.

If only a very weak case can be made for the claim that the same entity is involved in the different arguments, the "linkage proof," it will mean that the separate arguments must be much stronger (though they need not be individually adequate) for the conclusion that God exists.

Instead of attempting to establish monotheism, one can, of course, frankly accept the arguments as separate proofs of the existence of separate beings. Roughly speaking, such a polytheist loses one god for each argument that fails and in this sense has a more vulnerable position. But the monotheist may still lose one property or power of his God for each argument that fails and thus fail altogether to establish the existence of the Being he has defined as God, Who has *all* these properties.

It is possible that monotheism owes some of its current support to the feeling that few if any of the separate arguments are without defect and hence *must* be combined for strength. But if this is so, it is surprising that more attention has not been paid to the linkage arguments, which then become crucial.

Another factor acting in favor of monotheism is the feeling that it is less difficult, in the face of the increasing success of naturalistic science, to postulate one supernatural being than several. (But it may be that only the *combination* of properties is supernatural.) To this extent there is a kind of negative justification for the widespread and curious claim that Christianity was in some sense the precursor of modern science with its allegedly unifying theories, but the causal relation is reversed. Christian theology may have been fleeing into monotheism from the shadow cast ahead of the development of Babylonian and Greek science.

VII.A.3 On Obstinacy in Belief

C. S. LEWIS

C. S. Lewis (1898–1963) was a British philosopher, theologian, and literary critic who taught at Oxford and Cambridge Universities. In this selection he traces how assent moves from the logic of specula- tion in which inquiry and doubt are appropriate, to the logic of personal relationship within faith, in which religious experience becomes self-confirm- ing and overwhelming, making doubt a sort of inattentiveness or infidelity.

Papers have more than once been read to the Socratic Club at Oxford in which a contrast was drawn between a supposedly Christian attitude and a supposedly scientific attitude to belief. We have been told that the scientist thinks it his duty to proportion the strength of his belief exactly to the evidence; to believe less as there is less evidence and to withdraw belief altogether when reliable adverse evidence turns up. We have been told that, on the contrary, the Christian regards it as positively praiseworthy to believe without evidence, or in excess of the evidence, or to maintain his belief unmodified in the teeth of steadily increasing evi- dence against it. Thus a "faith that has stood firm," which appears to mean a belief immune from all the assaults of reality, is commended.

If this were a fair statement of the case, then the co-existence within the same species of such scien- tists and such Christians, would be a very staggering phenomenon. The fact that the two classes appear to overlap, as they do, would be quite inexplicable. Certainly all discussion between creatures so differ- ent would be hopeless. The purpose of this essay is to show that things are really not quite so bad as that. The sense in which scientists proportion their

belief to the evidence and the sense in which Christians do not, both need to be defined more closely. My hope is that when this has been done, though disagreement between the two parties may remain, they will not be left staring at one another in wholly dumb and desperate incomprehension.

And first, a word about belief in general. I do not see that the state of "proportioning belief to evi- dence" is anything like so common in the scientific life as has been claimed. Scientists are mainly con- cerned not with believing things but with finding things out. And no one, to the best of my knowl- edge, uses the word "believe" about things he has found out. The doctor says he "believes" a man was poisoned before he has examined the body; after the examination, he says the man was poisoned. No one says that he believes the multiplication table. No one who catches a thief red-handed says he believes that man was stealing. The scientist, when at work, that is, when he is a scientist, is labouring to escape from belief and unbelief into knowledge. Of course he uses hypotheses or supposals. I do not think these are beliefs. We must look, then, for the scientist's behaviour about belief not to his scien- tific life but to his leisure hours.

In actual modern English usage the verb "be- lieves," except for two special usages, generally expresses a very weak degree of opinion. "Where is Tom?" "Gone to London, I believe." The speaker would be only mildly surprised if Tom had not gone to London after all. "What was the date?" "430 B.C., I believe." The speaker means that he is far from sure. It is the same with the negative if it is put in the form "I believe not." "Is Jones coming up this term?" "I believe not." But if the negative is put in a different form it then becomes one of the special usages I mentioned a moment ago. This is of course the form "I don't believe it," or the still stronger "I don't believe you." "I don't believe it" is far stronger on the negative side than "I believe" is on the positive. "Where is Mrs. Jones?" "Eloped with the butler, I believe." "I don't believe it." This, especially if said with anger, may imply a conviction which in subjective certitude might be hard to distinguish from knowledge by experience. The other special usage is "I believe" as uttered by a Christian. There is no great difficulty in making the hardened materialist understand, however little he approves, the sort of mental attitude which this "I believe" expresses. The materialist need only picture himself replying, to some report of a miracle. "I don't believe it," and then imagine this same degree of conviction on the opposite side. He knows that he cannot, there and then, produce a refutation of the miracle which would have the certainty of mathematical demonstration; but the formal possibility that the miracle might after all have occurred does not really trouble him any more than a fear that water might not be H and O. Similarly, the Christian does not necessarily claim to have demonstrative proof; but the formal possibility that God might not exist is not necessarily present in the form of the least actual doubt. Of course there are Christians who hold that such demonstrative proof exists, just as there may be materialists who hold that there is demonstrative disproof. But then, whichever of them is right (if either is) while he retained the proof or disproof would be not believing or disbelieving but knowing. We are speaking of belief and disbelief in the strongest degree but not of knowledge. Belief, in this sense, seems to me to be assent to a proposition which we think so overwhelmingly probable that there is a psychological exclusion of doubt, though not a logical exclusion of dispute.

It may be asked whether belief (and of course disbelief) of this sort ever attaches to any but theological propositions. I think that many beliefs approximate to it; that is, many probabilities seem to us so strong that the absence of logical certainty does not induce in us the least shade of doubt. The scientific beliefs of those who are not themselves scientists often have this character, especially among the uneducated. Most of our beliefs about other people are of the same sort. The scientist himself, or he who was a scientist in the laboratory, has beliefs about his wife and friends which he holds, not indeed without evidence, but with more

certitude than the evidence, if weighed in the laboratory manner, would justify. Most of my generation had a belief in the reality of the external world and of other people—if you prefer it, a disbelief in solipsism—far in excess of our strongest arguments. It may be true, as they now say, that the whole thing arose from category mistakes and was a pseudo-problem; but then we didn't know that in the twenties. Yet we managed to disbelieve in solipsism all the same.

There is, of course, no question so far of belief without evidence. We must beware of confusion between the way in which a Christian first assents to certain propositions and the way in which he afterwards adheres to them. These must be carefully distinguished. Of the second it is true, in a sense to say that Christians do recommend a certain discounting of apparent contrary evidence, and I will later attempt to explain why. But so far as I know it is not expected that a man should assent to these propositions in the first place without evidence or in the teeth of the evidence. At any rate, if anyone expects that, I certainly do not. And in fact, the man who accepts Christianity always thinks he had good evidence; whether, like Dante *fisici e metafisici argomenti*, or historical evidence, or the evidence of religious experience, or authority, or all these together. For of course authority, however we may value it in this or that particular instance, is a kind of evidence. All of our historical beliefs, most of our geographical beliefs, many of our beliefs about matters that concern us in daily life, are accepted on the authority of other human beings, whether we are Christians, Atheists, Scientists, or Men-in-the-Street.

It is not the purpose of this essay to weigh the evidence, of whatever kind, on which Christians base their belief. To do that would be to write a full-dress *apologia*. All that I need do here is to point out that, at the very worst, this evidence cannot be so weak as to warrant the view that all whom it convinces are indifferent to evidence. The history of thought seems to make this quite plain. We know, in fact, that believers are not cut off from unbelievers by any portentous inferiority of intelligence or any perverse refusal to think. Many of them have been scientists. We may suppose them to have been mistaken, but we must suppose that their error was at least plausible. We might indeed, conclude that it was, merely from the multitude and diversity of the arguments against it. For there is not one case against religion, but many. Some say, like Capaneus in Statius, that it is a projection of our primitive fears, *primus in orbe deos fecit timor*: others, with Euhemerus, that it is all a "plant" put up by wicked kings, priests, or capitalists; others, with Tylor, that it comes from dreams about the dead; others, with Frazer, that it is a by-product of agriculture; others, like Freud, that it is a complex; the moderns that it is a category mistake. I will never believe that an error against which so many and various defensive weapons have been found necessary was, from the outset, wholly lacking in plausibility. All this "post haste and rummage in the land" obviously implies a respectable enemy.

There are of course people in our own day to whom the whole situation seems altered by the doctrine of the concealed wish. They will admit that men, otherwise apparently rational, have been deceived by the arguments for religion. But they will say that they have been deceived first by their own desires and produced the arguments afterwards as a rationalisation: that these arguments have never been intrinsically even plausible, but have seemed so because they were secretly weighted by our wishes. Now I do not doubt that this sort of thing happens in thinking about religion as in thinking about other things: but as a general explanation of religious assent it seems to me quite useless. On that issue our wishes may favour either side or both. The assumption that every man would be pleased, and nothing but pleased, if only he could conclude that Christianity is true, appears to me to be simply preposterous. If Freud is right about the Oedipus complex, the universal pressure of the wish that God should not exist must be enormous, and atheism must be an admirable gratification to one of our strongest suppressed impulses. This argument, in fact, could be used on the theistic side. But I have no intention of so using it. It will not really help either party. It is fatally ambivalent. Men wish on both sides: and again, there is fear-fulfilment as well as wish-fulfilment, and hypochondriac temperaments will always tend to think true what they most

wish to be false. Thus instead of the one predicament on which our opponents sometimes concentrate there are in fact four. A man may be a Christian because he wants Christianity to be true. He may be an atheist because he wants atheism to be true. He may be an atheist because he wants Christianity to be true. He may be a Christian because he wants atheism to be true. Surely these possibilities cancel one another out? They may be of some use in analysing a particular instance of belief or disbelief, where we know the case history, but as a general explanation of either they will not help us. I do not think they overthrow the view that there is evidence both for and against the Christian propositions which fully rational minds, working honestly, can assess differently.

I therefore ask you to substitute a different and less tidy picture for that with which we began. In it, you remember, two different kinds of men, scientists, who proportioned their belief to the evidence, and Christians, who did not, were left facing one another across a chasm. The picture I should prefer is like this. All men alike, on questions which interest them, escape from the region of belief into that of knowledge when they can, and if they succeed in knowing, they no longer say they believe. The questions in which mathematicians are interested admit of treatment by a particularly clear and strict technique. Those of the scientist have their own technique, which is not quite the same. Those of the historian and the judge are different again. The mathematician's proof (at least so we laymen suppose) is by reasoning the scientist's by experiment, the historian's by documents, the judge's by concurring sworn testimony. But all these men, as men, on questions outside their own disciplines, have numerous beliefs to which they do not normally apply the methods of their own disciplines. It would indeed carry some suspicion of morbidity and even of insanity if they did. These beliefs vary in strength from weak opinion to complete subjective certitude. Specimens of such beliefs at their strongest are the Christian's "I believe" and the convinced atheist's "I don't believe a word of it." The particular subject-matter on which these two disagree does not, of course, necessarily involve such strength of belief and disbelief. There are some who moderately opine that there is, or is not, a God. But there are others whose belief or disbelief is free from doubt. And all these beliefs, weak or strong, are based on what appears to the holders to be evidence; but the strong believers or disbelievers of course think they have very strong evidence. There is no need to suppose stark unreason on either side. We need only suppose error. One side has estimated the evidence wrongly. And even so, the mistake cannot be supposed to be of a flagrant nature; otherwise the debate would not continue.

So much, then, for the way in which Christians come to assent to certain propositions. But we have now to consider something quite different; their adherence to their belief after it has once been formed. It is here that the charge of irrationality and resistance to evidence becomes really important. For it must be admitted at once that Christians do praise such an adherence as if it were meritorious; and even, in a sense, more meritorious the stronger the apparent evidence against their faith becomes. They even warn one another that such apparent contrary evidence—such "trials to faith" or "temptations to doubt"—may be expected to occur, and determine in advance to resist them. And this is certainly shockingly unlike the behaviour we all demand of the scientist or the historian in their own disciplines. There, to slur over or ignore the faintest evidence against a favourite hypothesis, is admittedly foolish and shameful. It must be exposed to every test; every doubt must be invited. But then I do not admit that a hypothesis is a belief. And if we consider the scientist not among his hypotheses in the laboratory but among the beliefs in his ordinary life, I think the contrast between him and the Christian would be weakened. If, for the first time, a doubt of his wife's fidelity crosses the scientist's mind, does he consider it his duty at once to entertain this doubt with complete impartiality, at once to evolve a series of experiments by which it can be tested, and to await the result with pure neutrality of mind? No doubt it may come to that in the end. There are unfaithful wives; there are experimental husbands. But is such a course what his brother scientists would recommend to him (all of them, I suppose, except one) as the first step he should take and the only one consistent with his honour as a

scientist? Or would they, like us, blame him for a moral flaw rather than praise him for an intellectual virtue if he did so?

This is intended, however, merely as a precaution against exaggerating the difference between Christian obstinacy in belief and the behaviour of normal people about their non-theological beliefs. I am far from suggesting that the case I have supposed is exactly parallel to the Christian obstinacy. For of course evidence of the wife's infidelity might accumulate, and presently reach a point at which the scientist would be pitiably foolish to disbelieve it. But the Christians seem to praise an adherence to the original belief which holds out against any evidence whatever. I must now try to show why such praise is in fact a logical conclusion from the original belief itself.

This can be done best by thinking for a moment of situations in which the thing is reversed. In Christianity such faith is demanded of us; but there are situations in which we demand it of others. There are times when we can do all that a fellow creature needs if only he will trust us. In getting a dog out of a trap, in extracting a thorn from a child's finger, in teaching a boy to swim or rescuing one who can't, in getting a frightened beginner over a nasty place on a mountain, the one fatal obstacle may be their distrust. We are asking them to trust us in the teeth of their senses, their imagination, and their intelligence. We ask them to believe that what is painful will relieve their pain and that what looks dangerous is their only safety. We ask them to accept apparent impossibilities: that moving the paw farther back into the trap is the way to get it out—that hurting the finger very much more will stop the finger hurting—that water which is obviously permeable will resist and support the body—that holding on to the only support within reach is not the way to avoid sinking—that to go higher and on to a more exposed ledge is the way not to fall. To support all these *incredibilia* we can rely only on the other party's confidence in us—a confidence certainly not based on demonstration, admittedly shot through with emotion, and perhaps, if we are strangers, resting on nothing but such assurance as the look of our face and the tone of our voice can supply, or even, for the dog, on our smell. Sometimes, because of their unbelief, we can do no mighty works. But if we succeed, we do so because they have maintained their faith in us against apparently contrary evidence. No one blames us for demanding such faith. No one blames them for giving it. No one says afterwards what an unintelligent dog or child or boy that must have been to trust us. If the young mountaineer were a scientist, it would not be held against him, when he came up for a fellowship, that he had once departed from Clifford's rule of evidence by entertaining a belief with strength greater than the evidence logically obliged him to.

Now to accept the Christian propositions is *ipso facto* to believe that we are to God, always, as that dog or child or bather or mountain climber was to us, only very much more so. From this it is a strictly logical conclusion that the behaviour which was appropriate to them will be appropriate to us, only very much more so. Mark: I am not saying that the strength of our original belief must by psychological necessity produce such behaviour. I am saying that the content of our original belief by logical necessity entails the proposition that such behaviour is appropriate. If human life is in fact ordered by a beneficent being whose knowledge of our real needs and of the way in which they can be satisfied infinitely exceeds our own, we must expect *a priori* that His operations will often appear to us far from beneficent and far from wise, and that it will be our highest prudence to give Him our confidence in spite of this. This expectation is increased by the fact that when we accept Christianity we are warned that apparent evidence against it will occur—evidence strong enough "to deceive if possible the very elect." Our situation is rendered tolerable by two facts. One is that we seem to ourselves, besides the apparently contrary evidence, to receive favourable evidence. Some of it is in the form of external events: as when I go to see a man, moved by what I felt to be a whim, and find he has been praying that I should come to him that day. Some of it is more like the evidence on which the mountaineer or the dog might trust his rescuer—the rescuer's voice, look, and smell. For it seems to us (though you, on your premises, must believe us deluded) that we have something like a knowledge-by-acquaintance of the Person we believe in, however

imperfect and intermittent it may be. We trust not because "a God" exists, but because *this* God exists. Or if we ourselves dare not claim to "know" Him, Christendom does, and we trust at least some of its representatives in the same way: because of the sort of people they are. The second fact is this. We think we can see already why, if our original belief is true, such trust beyond the evidence, against much apparent evidence, has to be demanded of us. For the question is not about being helped out of one trap or over one difficult place in a climb. We believe that His intention is to create a certain personal relation between Himself and us, a relation really *sui generis* but analogically describable in terms of filial or of erotic love. Complete trust is an ingredient in that relation—such trust as could have no room to grow except where there is also room for doubt. To love involves trusting the beloved beyond the evidence, even against much evidence. No man is our friend who believes in our good intentions only when they are proved. No man is our friend who will not be very slow to accept evidence against them. Such confidence, between one man and another, is in fact almost universally praised as a moral beauty, not blamed as a logical error. And the suspicious man is blamed for a meanness of character, not admired for the excellence of his logic.

There is, you see, no real parallel between Christian obstinacy in faith and the obstinacy of a bad scientist trying to preserve a hypothesis although the evidence has turned against it. Unbelievers very pardonably get the impression that an adherence to our faith is like that, because they meet Christianity, if at all, mainly in apologetic works. And there, of course, the existence and beneficence of God must appear as a speculative question like any other. Indeed, it is a speculative question as long as it is a question at all. But once it has been answered in the affirmative, you get quite a new situation. To believe that God—at least *this* God—exists is to believe that you as a person now stand in the presence of God as a Person. What would, a moment before, have been variations in opinion, now becomes variations in your personal attitude to a Person. You are no longer faced with an argument which demands your assent, but with a Person who demands your confidence. A faint analogy would be this. It is one thing to discuss *in vacuo* whether So-and-So will join us tonight, and another to discuss this when So-and-So's honour is pledged to come and some great matter depends on his coming. In the first case it would be merely reasonable, as the clock ticked on, to expect him less and less. In the second, a continued expectation far into the night would be due to our friend's character if we had found him reliable before. Which of us would not feel slightly ashamed if one moment after we had given him up he arrived with a full explanation of his delay? We should feel that we ought to have known him better.

Now of course we see, quite as clearly as you, how agonisingly two-edged all this is. A faith of this sort, if it happens to be true, is obviously what we need, and it is infinitely ruinous to lack it. But there can be faith of this sort where it is wholly ungrounded. The dog may lick the face of the man who comes to take it out of the trap; but the man may only mean to vivisect it in South Parks Road when he has done so. The ducks who come to the call "Dilly, dilly, come and be killed" have confidence in the farmer's wife, and she wrings their necks for their pains. There is that famous French story of the fire in the theatre. Panic was spreading, the spectators were just turning from an audience into a mob. At that moment a huge bearded man leaped through the orchestra on to the stage, raised his hand with a gesture full of nobility, and cried, *"Que chacun regagne sa place."* Such was the authority of his voice and bearing that everyone obeyed him. As a result they were all burned to death, while the bearded man walked quietly out through the wings to the stage door, took a cab which was waiting for someone else, and went home to bed.

That demand for our confidence which a true friend makes of us is exactly the same that a confidence trickster would make. That refusal to trust, which is sensible in reply to a confidence trickster, is ungenerous and ignoble to a friend, and deeply damaging to our relation with him. To be forewarned and therefore forearmed against apparently contrary appearance is eminently rational if our belief is true; but if our belief is a delusion, this same

forewarning and forearming would obviously be the method whereby the delusion rendered itself incurable. And yet again, to be aware of these possibilities and still to reject them is clearly the precise mode, and the only mode, in which our personal response to God can establish itself. In that sense the ambiguity is not something that conflicts with faith so much as a condition which makes faith possible. When you are asked for trust you may give it or withhold it; it is senseless to say that you will trust if you are given demonstrative certainty. There would be no room for trust if demonstration were given. When demonstration is given what will be left will be simply the sort of relation which results from having trusted, or not having trusted, before it was given.

The saying "Blessed are those that have not seen and have believed" has nothing to do with our original assent to the Christian propositions. It was not addressed to a philosopher inquiring whether God exists. It was addressed to a man who already believed that, who already had long acquaintance with a particular Person, and evidence that that Person could do very odd things, and who then refused to believe one odd thing more, often predicted by that Person and vouched for by all his closest friends. It is a rebuke not to scepticism in the philosophic sense but to the psychological quality of being "suspicious." It says in effect, "You should have known me better." There are cases between man and man where we should all, in our different way, bless those who have not seen and have believed. Our relation to those who trusted us only after we were proved innocent in court cannot be the same as our relation to those who trusted us all through.

Our opponents, then, have a perfect right to dispute with us about the grounds of our original assent. But they must not accuse us of sheer insanity if, after the assent has been given, our adherence to it is no longer proportioned to every fluctuation of the apparent evidence. They cannot of course be expected to know on what our assurance feeds, and how it revives and is always rising from its ashes. They cannot be expected to see how the *quality* of the object which we think we are beginning to know by acquaintance drives us to the view that if this were a delusion then we should have to say that the universe had produced no real thing of comparable value and that all explanations of the delusion seemed somehow less important than the thing explained. That is knowledge we cannot communicate. But they can see how the assent, of necessity, moves us from the logic of speculative thought into what might perhaps be called the logic of personal relations. What would, up till then, have been variations simply of opinion become variations of conduct by a person to a Person. *Credere Deum esse* turns into *Credere in Deum.* And *Deum* here is this God, the increasingly knowable Lord.

VII.B Pragmatic Justification of Religious Belief

In this section we have three readings, dealing with the *practical* reasonableness of religious belief. That is, even if we cannot find good evidence for religious beliefs, would it perhaps be in our interest to get ourselves to believe in these propositions anyway? And would such believing be morally permissible? In the first reading, "The Wager," the renowned French physicist and mathematician Blaise Pascal (1623–1662) argues that if we do a cost–benefit analysis of the matter, we find that it is eminently reasonable to get ourselves to believe that God exists regardless of whether we have good evidence for that belief. The argument goes something like this: Regarding the proposition 'God exists' reason is neutral. It can neither prove nor disprove it. But we must make a choice on this matter, for not to choose for God is in effect to choose against him and lose the possible benefits that belief would bring. Since these benefits promise to be infinite and the loss equally infinite, we might set forth the possibilities shown in Figure 1.

There is some sacrifice of earthly pleasures involved in belief in God, but by multiplying the various combinations we find that there is an incommensurability between A and C, on the one hand, and B and D on the other. For no matter how enormous the *finite* gain, the mere possibility of *infinite* gain will always make the latter preferable to the former. So the only relevant possibilities are A and C. Since A (believing in God) promises infinite happiness and C (not believing in God) infinite unhappiness, a rational cost–benefit analysis leaves no doubt about what we should do. We have a clear self-interested reason for believing in God.

The reader should go over this argument closely. Are there any weaknesses in it? Does it demonstrate that we all should do whatever is necessary to come to believe that God exists? Is such a belief necessary and sufficient for eternal happiness?

In the second reading in this section, "The Ethics of Belief," the British philosopher W. K. Clifford (1845–1879) assembles reason's roadblocks to such pragmatic justifications for religious belief. Clifford argues that there is an ethics to belief that makes immoral all believing without sufficient evidence. Pragmatic justifications are not justifications at all but counterfeits of genuine justifications, which must always be based on evidence.

Clifford illustrates his thesis with the example of a ship owner who sends an emigrant ship to sea. He knows that the ship is old and not well built, but he fails to have the ship inspected. Dismissing from his mind all doubts and suspicions that the vessel is not seaworthy, he trusts in Providence to care for his ship. He acquires a sincere and comfortable conviction in this way and collects his insurance money without a trace of guilt after the ship sinks and all the passengers drown.

Clifford comments that although the ship owner sincerely believed that all was well with the ship, his sincerity in no way exculpates him because "he had no right to believe on such evidence as was before him." One has an obligation to get oneself in a position in which one will believe propositions only on sufficient evidence. Furthermore, it is not a valid objection to say that the ship owner had an obligation to *act* in a certain way (viz., inspect the ship), not *believe* in a certain way.

Figure 1		*God exists*	*God does not exist*
	I believe	A. Infinite gain with minimal finite loss	B. Overall finite loss in terms of sacrifice of earthly goods
	I do not believe	C. Infinite loss with finite gain	D. Overall finite gain

The ship owner does have an obligation to inspect the ship, but the objection overlooks the function of believing in guiding action. "No man holding a strong belief on one side of a question, or even wishing to hold a belief on one side, can investigate it with such fairness and completeness as if he were really in doubt and unbiased; so that the existence of a belief not founded on fair inquiry unfits a man for the performance of this necessary duty." The general conclusion is that it is always wrong for anyone to believe anything on insufficient evidence.

The classic response to Clifford's ethics of belief is William James's "The Will to Believe" (1896), the last reading in this section. James argues that life would be greatly impoverished if we confined our beliefs to such a Scrooge-like epistemology as Clifford proposes. In everyday life, where the evidence for important propositions is often unclear, we must live by faith or cease to act at all. Although we may not make leaps of faith just anywhere, sometimes practical considerations force us to make decisions about propositions that do not have their truth value written on their faces.

In "The Sentiment of Rationality" (1879) James defines 'faith' as "a belief in something concerning which doubt is still theoretically possible; and as the test of belief is willingness to act, one may say that faith is the readiness to act in a cause the prosperous issue of which is not certified to us in advance." In "The Will to Believe" he speaks of 'belief' as a live, momentous optional hypothesis on which we cannot avoid a decision, for not to choose is in effect to choose against the hypothesis.

There is a good illustration of this notion of faith in "The Sentiment of Rationality." A mountain climber in the Alps finds himself in a position from which he can escape only by means of an enormous leap. If he tries to calculate the evidence, believing only on sufficient evidence, he will be paralyzed by emotions of fear and mistrust and hence will be lost. Without evidence that he is capable of performing this feat successfully, the climber would be better off getting himself to believe that he can and will make the leap. "In this case . . . the part of wisdom clearly is to believe what one desires; for the belief is one of the indispensable preliminary conditions of the realization of its object. *There are then cases where faith creates its own verification.*"

James claims that religion may be such an optional hypothesis for many people, and in this case one has the right to believe the better story rather than the worse. To do so, one must will to believe what the evidence alone is inadequate to support.

There are two questions, one descriptive and the other normative, that you should keep in mind when you are reading these essays. The first is whether it is possible to believe propositions at will. In what sense can we get ourselves to believe propositions that the evidence doesn't force upon us. Surely we can't believe that the world is flat or that two plus two equals five simply by willing to do so, but which propositions (if any) are subject to volitional influences? Is it psychologically impossible to make the kinds of moves that Pascal and James advise? Does it involve self-deception? If we know that the only cause for our belief in a religious proposition is our desire to believe, can we rationally continue to believe that proposition? Is there something self-defeating about volitional projects?

The second question involves the ethics of belief, stressed by Clifford. Supposing that we can get ourselves to believe or disbelieve propositions, is this morally permissible? What are the arguments for and against integrity of belief?

Note that Pascal's volitionalism is indirect, whereas James's might be interpreted as direct. In Pascal's case one must will to believe the proposition p, discover the best means to get into that state (e.g., going to church, participating in Mass, taking holy water, etc.), and act in such a way as to make the acquisition of the belief likely. In direct volitionalism one supposes that one can obtain some beliefs simply by fiat of the will.

Note that there are two different types of cases here. In one type, the truth of the proposition is something we have no control over. In the other type, the truth of the proposition is something that still has not been decided, but believing in it might help bring about the desired state of affairs (the case of the mountain climber is an example of this type). Should we have a different attitude about each of these types of cases?

You may also consider whether pragmatic justification allows one to believe decisively, in an absolute way. Many think that such belief is necessary for authentic religious faith, but pragmatic grounds alone seem to prevent complete confidence in what is assented to.

VII.B.1   The Wager

BLAISE PASCAL

In our first reading, the renowned French physicist and mathematician Blaise Pascal (1623–1662) argues that if we do a cost–benefit analysis of the matter, we find that it is eminently reasonable to get ourselves to believe that God exists regardless of whether we have good evidence for that belief. The argument goes something like this: Regarding the proposition 'God exists' reason is neutral. It can neither prove nor disprove it. But we make a choice on this matter, for not to choose for God is in effect to choose against him and lose the possible benefits that belief would bring. Since these benefits of faith promise to be infinite and the loss equally infinite, we must take a gamble on faith.

Infinite—nothing.—Our soul is cast into a body, where it finds number, time, dimension. Thereupon it reasons, and calls this nature, necessity, and can believe nothing else.

Unity joined to infinity adds nothing to it, no more than one foot to an infinite measure. The finite is annihilated in the presence of the infinite, and becomes a pure nothing. So our spirit before God, so our justice before divine justice. There is not so great disproportion between our justice and that of God, as between unity and infinity.

Reprinted from Blaise Pascal, *Thoughts,* translated by W. F. Trotter (New York: Collier & Son, 1910).

The justice of God must be vast like His compassion. Now, justice to the outcast is less vast, and ought less to offend our feelings than mercy towards the elect.

We know that there is an infinite, and are ignorant of its nature. As we know it to be false that numbers are finite, it is therefore true that there is an infinity in number. But we do not know what it is. It is false that it is even, it is false that it is odd; for the addition of a unit can make no change in its nature. Yet it is a number, and every number is odd or even (this is certainly true of every finite number). So we may well know that there is a God without knowing what He is. Is there not one substantial truth, seeing there are so many things which are not the truth itself?

We know then the existence and nature of the finite, because we also are finite and have extension. We know the existence of the infinite, and are ignorant of its nature, because it has extension like us, but not limits like us. But we know neither the existence nor the nature of God, because He has neither extension nor limits.

But by faith we know His existence; in glory we shall know His nature. Now, I have already shown that we may well know the existence of a thing, without knowing its nature.

Let us now speak according to natural lights.

If there is a God, He is infinitely incomprehensible, since, having neither parts nor limits, He has no affinity to us. We are then incapable of knowing either what He is or if He is. This being so, who will dare to undertake the decision of the question? Not we, who have no affinity to Him.

Who then will blame Christians for not being able to give a reason for their belief, since they profess a religion for which they cannot give a reason? They declare, in expounding it to the world, that it is a foolishness, *stultitiam*; and then you complain that they do not prove it! If they proved it, they would not keep their words; it is in lacking proofs, that they are not lacking in sense. "Yes, but although this excuses those who offer it as such, and takes away from them the blame of putting it forward without reason, it does not excuse those who receive it." Let us then examine this point, and say, "God is, or He is not." But to which side shall we incline? Reason can decide nothing here. There is an infinite chasm which separates us. A game is being played at the extremity of this infinite distance where heads or tails will turn up. What will you wager? According to reason, you can do neither the one thing nor the other; according to reason, you can defend neither of the propositions.

Do not then reprove for error those who have made a choice; for you know nothing about it. "No, but I blame them for having made, not this choice, but a choice; for again both he who chooses heads and he who chooses tails are equally at fault, they are both in the wrong. The true course is not to wager at all."

—Yes; but you must wager. It is not optional. You are embarked. Which will you choose then; Let us see. Since you must choose, let us see which interests you least. You have two things to lose, the true and the good; and two things to stake, your reason and your will, your knowledge and your happiness; and your nature has two things to shun, error and misery. Your reason is no more shocked in choosing one rather than the other, since you must of necessity choose. This is one point settled. But your happiness? Let us weigh the gain and the loss in wagering that God is. Let us estimate these two chances. If you gain, you gain all; if you lose, you lose nothing. Wager them without hesitation that He is.—"That is very fine. Yes, I must wager; but I may perhaps wager too much."—Let us see.

Since there is an equal risk of gain and of loss, if you had only to gain two lives, instead of one, you might still wager. But if there were three lives to gain, you would have to play (since you are under the necessity of playing), and you would be imprudent, when you are forced to play, not to chance your life to gain three at a game where there is an equal risk of loss and gain. But there is an eternity of life and happiness. And this being so, if there were an infinity of chances, of which one only would be for you, you would still be right in wagering one to win two, and you would act stupidly, being obliged to play, by refusing to stake one life against three at a game in which out of an infinity of an infinitely happy life to gain. But there is here an infinity of an infinitely happy life to gain, a chance of gain against a finite number of chances of loss, and what you stake is finite. It is all divided; wherever the infinite is and there is not an infinity of chances of loss against that of gain, there is no time to hesitate, you must give all. And thus, when one is forced to play, he must renounce reason to preserve his life, rather than risk it for infinite gain, as likely to happen as the loss of nothingness.

For it is no use to say it is uncertain if we will gain, and it is certain that we risk, and that the infinite distance between the *certainty* of what is staked and the *uncertainty* of what will be gained, equals the finite good which is certainly staked against the uncertain infinite. It is not so, as every player stakes a certainty to gain an uncertainty, and yet he stakes a finite certainty to gain a finite uncertainty, without transgressing against reason. There is not an infinite distance between the certainty staked and the uncertainty of the gain; that is untrue. In truth, there is an infinity between the certainty of gain and the certainty of loss. But the uncertainty of the gain is proportioned to the certainty of the stake according to the proportion of the chances of gain and loss. Hence it comes that, if there are as many risks on one side as on the other, the course is to play even; and then the certainty of the stake is equal to the uncertainty of the gain, so far is it from the fact that there is an infinite distance between them. And so our proposition is of infinite force, when there is the finite to stake in a game where there are equal risks of gain and loss, and the infinite to gain. This is demonstrable; and if men are capable of any truths, this is one.

"I confess it, I admit it. But still is there no means of seeing the faces of the cards?"—Yes, Scripture and the rest, &c.—"Yes, but I have my hands tied and my mouth closed; I am forced to wager, and am not free. I am not released, and am so made that I cannot believe. What then would you have me do?"

"True. But at least learn your inability to believe, since reason brings you to this, and yet you cannot believe. Endeavour then to convince yourself, not by increase of proofs of God, but by the abatement of your passions. You would like to attain faith, and do not know the way; you would like to cure yourself of unbelief, and ask the remedy for it. Learn of those who have been bound like you, and who now stake all their possessions. These are people who know the way which you would follow, and who are cured of an ill of which you would be cured. Follow the way by which they began; by acting as if they believe, taking the holy water, having masses said. &c. Even this will naturally make you believe, and deaden your acuteness.—" "But this is what I am afraid of."—And why, What have you to lose?

But to show you that this leads you there, this which will lessen the passions, which are your stumbling-blocks.

The end of this discourse.—Now what harm will befall you in taking this side? You will be faithful, honest, humble, grateful, generous, a sincere friend, truthful. Certainly you will not have those poisonous pleasures, glory and luxury; but will you not have others? I will tell you that you will thereby gain in this life, and that, at each step you take on this road, you will see so great certainty of gain, so much nothingness in what you risk, that you will at least recognize that you have wagered for something certain and infinite, for which you have given nothing.

"Ah! This discourse transports me, charms me," &c.

If this discourse pleases you and seems impressive, know that it is made by a man who has knelt, both before and after it, in prayer to that Being, infinite and without parts, before whom he lays all he has, for you also to lay before Him all you have for your own good and for His Glory, so that strength may be given to lowliness.

VII.B.2   The Ethics of Belief

W. K. CLIFFORD

In this reading the British philosopher W. K. Clifford (1845–1879) assembles reason's roadblock to pragmatic (or "wager") justifications for religious belief of the sort Pascal proposes. Clifford argues that there is an ethics to belief that makes immoral all believing without sufficient evidence. Pragmatic justifications are not justifications at all but counterfeits of genuine justifications, which must always be based on evidence.

Reprinted from W. K. Clifford, *Lectures and Essays* (London: Macmillan, 1879).

Clifford illustrates his thesis with the example of a ship owner who sends an emigrant ship to sea. He knows that the ship is old and not well built but he fails to have the ship inspected. Dismissing from his mind all doubts and suspicions that the vessel is not seaworthy, he trusts in Providence to care for his ship. He acquires a sincere and comfortable conviction in this way and collects his insurance money without a trace of guilt after the ship sinks and all the passengers drown. Clifford argues that although the ship owner sincerely believed that all was well with the ship, his sincerity in no way exculpates him because "he had no right to believe on such evidence as was before him." One has an obligation to get oneself in a position in which one will believe propositions only on sufficient evidence. His general conclusion is that it is always wrong for anyone to believe anything on insufficient evidence.

A shipowner was about to send to sea an emigrant ship. He knew that she was old, and not over-well built at the first; that she had seen many seas and climes, and often had needed repairs. Doubts had been suggested to him that possibly she was not seaworthy. These doubts preyed upon his mind and made him unhappy; he thought that perhaps he ought to have her thoroughly overhauled and refitted, even though this should put him to great expense. Before the ship sailed, however, he succeeded in overcoming these melancholy reflections. He said to himself that she had gone safely through so many voyages and weathered so many storms that it was idle to suppose she would not come safely home from this trip also. He would put his trust in Providence, which could hardly fail to protect all these unhappy families that were leaving their fatherland to seek for better times elsewhere. He would dismiss from his mind all ungenerous suspicions about the honesty of builders and contractors. In such ways he acquired a sincere and comfortable conviction that his vessel was thoroughly safe and seaworthy; he watched her departure with a light heart, and benevolent wishes for the success of the exiles in their strange new home that was to be; and he got his insurance money when she went down in midocean and told no tales.

What shall we say of him? Surely this, that he was verily guilty of the death of those men. It is admitted that he did sincerely believe in the soundness of his ship; but the sincerity of his conviction can in no wise to help him, because he had no right to believe on such evidence as was before him. He had acquired his belief not by honestly earning it in patient investigation, but by stifling his doubts. And although in the end he may have felt so sure about it that he could not think otherwise, yet inasmuch

as he had knowingly and willingly worked himself into that frame of mind, he must be held responsible for it.

Let us alter the case a little, and suppose that the ship was not unsound after all; that she made her voyage safely, and many others after it. Will that diminish the guilt of her owner? Not one jot. When an action is once done, it is right or wrong forever; no accidental failure of its good or evil fruits can possibly alter that. The man would not have been innocent, he would only have been not found out. The question of right or wrong has to do with the origin of his belief, not the matter of it; not what it was, but how he got it; not whether it turned out to be true or false, but whether he had a right to believe on such evidence as was before him.

There was once an island in which some of the inhabitants professed a religion teaching neither the doctrine of original sin nor that of eternal punishment. A suspicion got abroad that the professors of this religion had made use of unfair means to get their doctrines taught to children. They were accused of wresting the laws of their country in such a way as to remove children from the care of their natural and legal guardians; and even of stealing them away and keeping them concealed from their friends and relations. A certain number of men formed themselves into a society for the purpose of agitating the public about this matter. They published grave accusations against individual citizens of the highest position and character, and did all in their power to injure those citizens in the exercise of their professions. So great was the noise they made, that a Commission was appointed to investigate the facts; but after the Commission had carefully inquired into all the evidence that could be got, it appeared that the accused were innocent. Not only had they been accused on insufficient evidence, but the evidence of their innocence was such as the agitators might easily have obtained, if they had attempted a fair inquiry. After these disclosures the inhabitants of that country looked upon the members of the agitating society, not only as persons whose judgment was to be distrusted, but also as no longer to be counted honorable men. For although they had sincerely and conscientiously believed in the charges they had made, yet they had no right to believe on such evidence as was before them. Their sincere convictions, instead of being honestly earned by patient inquiring, were stolen by listening to the voice of prejudice and passion.

Let us vary this case also, and suppose, other things remaining as before, that a still more accurate investigation proved the accused to have been really guilty. Would this make any difference in the guilt of the accusers? Clearly not; the question is not whether their belief was true or false, but whether they entertained it on wrong grounds. They would no doubt say, "Now you see that we were right after all; next time perhaps you will believe us." And they might be believed, but they would not thereby become honorable men. They would not be innocent, they would only be not found out. Every one of them, if he chose to examine himself *in foro conscientiae*, would know that he had acquired and nourished a belief, when he had no right to believe on such evidence as was before him; and therein he would know that he had done a wrong thing.

It may be said, however, that in both of these supposed cases it is not the belief which is judged to be wrong, but the action following upon it. The shipowner might say, "I am perfectly certain that my ship is sound, but still I feel it my duty to have her examined, before trusting the lives of so many people to her." And it might be said to the agitator, "However convinced you were of the justice of your cause and the truth of your convictions, you ought not to have made a public attack upon any man's character until you had examined the evidence on both sides with the utmost patience and care."

In the first place, let us admit that, so far as it goes, this view of the case is right and necessary; right, because even when a man's belief is so fixed that he cannot think otherwise, he still has a choice in regard to the action suggested by it, and so cannot escape the duty of investigating on the ground of the strength of his convictions; and necessary, because those who are not yet capable of controlling their feelings and thoughts must have a plain rule dealing with overt acts.

But this being premised as necessary, it becomes clear that it is not sufficient, and that our previous judgment is required to supplement it. For it is not

possible so to sever the belief from the action it suggests as to condemn the one without condemning the other. No man holding a strong belief on one side of a question, or even wishing to hold a belief on one side, can investigate it with such fairness and completeness as if he were really in doubt and unbiased; so that the existence of a belief not founded on fair inquiry unfits a man for the performance of this necessary duty.

Nor is that truly a belief at all which has not some influence upon the actions of him who holds it. He who truly believes that which prompts him to an action has looked upon the action to lust after it, he has committed it already in his heart. If a belief is not realized immediately in open deeds, it is stored up for the guidance of the future. It goes to make a part of that aggregate of beliefs which is the link between sensation and action at every moment of all our lives, and which is so organized and compacted together that no part of it can be isolated from the rest, but every new addition modifies the structure of the whole. No real belief, however trifling and fragmentary it may seem, is ever truly insignificant; it prepares us to receive more of its like, confirms those which resembled it before, and weakens others; and so gradually it lays a stealthy train in our inmost thoughts, which may some day explode into overt action, and leave its stamp upon our character forever.

And no one man's belief is in any case a private matter which concerns himself alone. Our lives are guided by that general conception of the course of things which has been created by society for social purposes. Our words, our phrases, our forms and processes and modes of thought are common property, fashioned and perfected from age to age; an heirloom which every succeeding generation inherits as a precious deposit and a sacred trust to be handed on to the next one, not unchanged but enlarged and purified, with some clear marks of its proper handiwork. Into this, for good or ill, is woven every belief of every man who has speech of his fellows. An awful privilege, and an awful responsibility, that we should help to create the world in which posterity will live.

In the two supposed cases which have been considered, it has been judged wrong to believe on insufficient evidence, or to nourish belief by suppressing doubts and avoiding investigation. The reason of this judgment is not far to seek: it is that in both these cases the belief held by one man was of great importance to other men. But for as much as no belief held by one man, however seemingly trivial the belief, and however obscure the believer, is ever actually insignificant or without its effect on the fate of mankind, we have no choice but to extend our judgment to all cases of belief whatever. Belief, that sacred faculty which prompts the decisions of our will, and knits into harmonious working all the compacted energies of our being, is ours not for ourselves, but for humanity. It is rightly used on truths which have been established by long experience and waiting toil, and which have stood in the fierce light of free and fearless questioning. Then it helps to bind men together, and to strengthen and direct their common action. It is desecrated when given to unproved and unquestioned statements, for the solace and private pleasure of the believer; to add a tinsel splendor to the plain straight road of our life and display a bright mirage beyond it; or even to drown the common sorrows of our kind by a self-deception which allows them not only to cast down, but also to degrade us. Whoso would deserve well of his fellows in this matter will guard the purity of his belief with a very fanaticism of jealous care, lest at any time it should rest on an unworthy object, and catch a stain which can never be wiped away.

It is not only the leader of men, statesman, philosopher or poet, that owes this bounden duty to mankind. Every rustic who delivers in the village alehouse his slow, infrequent sentences, may help to kill or keep alive the fatal superstitions which clog his race. Every hard-worked wife of an artisan may transmit to her children beliefs which shall knit society together, or rend it in pieces. No simplicity of mind, no obscurity of station, can escape the universal duty of questioning all that we believe.

It is true that this duty is a hard one, and the doubt which comes out of it is often a very bitter thing. It leaves us bare and powerless where we thought that we were safe and strong. To know all about anything is to know how to deal with it under all circumstances. We feel much happier and more secure when we think we know precisely what to do, no matter what happens, than when we have lost our way and do not know where to turn. And if we have supposed ourselves to know all about anything, and to be capable of doing what is fit in regard to it, we naturally do not like to find that we are really ignorant and powerless, that we have to begin again at the beginning, and try to learn what the thing is and how it is to be dealt with—if indeed anything can be learned about it. It is the sense of power attached to a sense of knowledge that makes men desirous of believing, and afraid of doubting.

This sense of power is the highest and best of pleasures when the belief on which it is founded is a true belief, and has been fairly earned by investigation. For then we may justly feel that it is common property, and holds good for others as well as for ourselves. Then we may be glad, not that *I* have learned secrets by which I am safer and stronger, but that *we men* have got mastery over more of the world; and we shall be strong, not for ourselves, but in the name of Man and in his strength. But if the belief has been accepted on insufficient evidence, the pleasure is a stolen one. Not only does it deceive ourselves by giving us a sense of power which we do not really possess, but it is sinful, because it is stolen in defiance of our duty to mankind. That duty is to guard ourselves from such beliefs as from a pestilence, which may shortly master our own body and then spread to the rest of the town. What would be thought of one who, for the sake of a sweet fruit, should deliberately run the risk of bringing a plague upon his family and his neighbors?

And, as in other such cases, it is not the risk only which has to be considered; for a bad action is always bad at the time when it is done, no matter what happens afterwards. Every time we let ourselves believe for unworthy reasons, we weaken our powers of self-control, of doubting, of judicially and fairly weighing evidence. We all suffer severely enough from the maintenance and support of false beliefs and the fatally wrong actions which they lead to, and the evil born when one such belief is entertained is great and wide. But a greater and wider evil arises when the credulous character is maintained and supported, when a habit of believing for unworthy reasons is fostered and made permanent. If I steal money from any person, there may be no harm done by the mere transfer of possession; he may not feel the loss, or it may prevent him from using the money badly. But I cannot help doing this great wrong towards Man, that I make myself dishonest. What hurts society is not that it should lose its property, but that it should become a den of thieves; for then it must cease to be society. This is why we ought not to do evil that good may come; for at any rate this great evil has come, that we have done evil and are made wicked thereby. In like manner, if I let myself believe anything on insufficient evidence, there may be no great harm done by the mere belief; it may be true after all, or I may never have occasion to exhibit it in outward acts. But I cannot help doing this great wrong toward Man, that I make myself credulous. The danger to society is not merely that it should believe wrong things, though that is great enough; but that it should become credulous, and lose the habit of testing things and inquiring into them; for then it must sink back into savagery.

The harm which is done by credulity in a man is not confined to the fostering of a credulous character in others, and consequent support of false beliefs. Habitual want of care about what I believe leads to habitual want of care in others about the truth of what is told to me. Men speak the truth to one another when each reveres the truth in his own mind and in the other's mind; but how shall my friend revere the truth in my mind when I myself am careless about it, when I believe things because I want to believe them, and because they are comforting and pleasant? Will he not learn to cry, "Peace," to me, when there is no peace? By such a course I shall surround myself with a thick atmosphere of falsehood and fraud, and in that must live. It may matter little to me, in my closed castle of

sweet illusions and darling lies; but it matters much to Man that I have made my neighbors ready to deceive. The credulous man is father to the liar and the cheat; he lives in the bosom of this his family, and it is no marvel if he should become even as they are. So closely are our duties knit together, that whoso shall keep the whole law, and yet offend in one point, he is guilty of all.

To sum up: it is wrong always, everywhere and for anyone, to believe anything upon insufficient evidence.

If a man, holding a belief which he was taught in childhood or persuaded of afterwards, keeps down and pushes away any doubts which arise about it in his mind, purposely avoids the reading of books and the company of men that call in question or discuss it, and regards as impious those questions which cannot easily be asked without disturbing it—the life of that man is one long sin against mankind.

If this judgment seems harsh when applied to those simple souls who have never known better, who have been brought up from the cradle with a horror of doubt, and taught that their eternal welfare depends on what they believe, then it leads to the very serious question, Who hath made Israel to sin? . . .

Inquiry into the evidence of a doctrine is not to be made once for all, and then taken as finally settled. It is never lawful to stifle a doubt; for either it can be honestly answered by means of the inquiry already made, or else it proves that the inquiry was not complete.

"But," says one, "I am a busy man; I have no time for the long course of study which would be necessary to make me in any degree a competent judge of certain questions, or even able to understand the nature of the arguments." Then he should have no time to believe. . . .

VII.B.3 The Will to Believe

WILLIAM JAMES

The classic response to Clifford's ethics of belief is William James's "The Will to Believe" (1896), in which James argues that life would be greatly impoverished if we confined our beliefs to such a Scrooge-like epistemology as Clifford proposes. In everyday life, where the evidence for important propositions is often unclear, we must live by faith or cease to act at all. Although we may not make leaps of faith just anywhere, sometimes practical considerations force us to make decisions regarding propositions that do not have their truth value written on their faces. 'Belief' is defined as a live, momentous optional hypothesis on which we cannot avoid a decision, for not to choose is in effect to choose against the hypothesis. James claims that religion may be such an optional hypothesis for many people, and in this case one has the right to believe the better story rather than the worse. To do so, one must will to believe what the evidence alone is inadequate to support.

I

Let us give the name of hypothesis to anything that may be proposed to our belief; and just as the electricians speak of live and dead wires, let us speak of any hypothesis as either *live* or *dead*. A live hypothesis is one which appeals as a real possibility to him to whom it is proposed. If I ask you to believe in the Mahdi, the notion makes no electric connection with your nature—it refuses to scintillate with any credibility at all. As an hypothesis it is completely dead. To an Arab, however (even if he be not one of the Mahdi's followers), the hypothesis is among the mind's possibilities: It is alive. This shows that deadness and liveness in an hypothesis

Reprinted from William James, *The Will to Believe* (New York: Longmans, Green & Co., 1897).

are not intrinsic properties, but relations to the individual thinker. They are measured by his willingness to act. The maximum of liveness in an hypothesis means willingness to act irrevocably. Practically, that means belief; but there is some believing tendency wherever there is willingness to act at all.

Next, let us call the decision between two hypotheses an *option*. Options may be of several kinds. They may be first, *living* or *dead*; secondly, *forced* or *avoidable*; thirdly, *momentous* or *trivial*; and for our purposes we may call an option a *genuine* option when it is of a forced, living, and momentous kind.

1. A living option is one in which both hypotheses are live ones. If I say to you: "Be a theosophist or be a Mohammedan," it is probably a dead option, because for you neither hypothesis is likely to be alive. But if I say: "Be an agnostic or be a Christian," it is otherwise: trained as you are, each hypothesis makes some appeal, however small, to your belief.

2. Next, if I say to you: "Choose between going out with your umbrella or without it," I do not offer you a genuine option, for it is not forced. You can easily avoid it by not going out at all. Similarly, if I say, "Either love me or hate me," "Either call my theory true or call it false," your option is avoidable. You may remain indifferent to me, neither loving nor hating, and you may decline to offer any judgment as to my theory. But if I say, "Either accept this truth or go without it," I put on you a forced option, for there is no standing place outside of the alternative. Every dilemma based on a complete logical disjunction, with no possibility of not choosing, is an option of this forced kind.

3. Finally, if I were Dr. Nansen and proposed to you to join my North Pole expedition, your option would be momentous; for this would probably be your similar opportunity, and your

choice now would either exclude you from the North Pole sort of immortality altogether or put at least the chance of it into your hands. He who refuses to embrace a unique opportunity loses the prize as surely as if he tried and failed. *Per contra*, the option is trivial when the opportunity is not unique, when the stake is insignificant, or when the decision is reversible if it later proves unwise. Such trivial options abound in the scientific life. A chemist finds an hypothesis live enough to spend a year in its verification: he believes in it to that extent. But if his experiments prove inconclusive either way, he is quit for his loss of time, no vital harm being done.

It will facilitate our discussion if we keep all these distinctions well in mind.

II

The next matter to consider is the actual psychology of human opinion. When we look at certain facts, it seems as if our passional and volitional nature lay at the root of all our convictions. When we look at others, it seems as if they could do nothing when the intellect had once said its say. Let us take the latter facts up first.

Does it not seem preposterous on the very face of it to talk of our opinions being modifiable at will? Can our will either help or hinder our intellect in its perceptions of truth? Can we, by just willing it, believe that Abraham Lincoln's existence is a myth, and that the portraits of him in *McClure's Magazine* are all of some one else? Can we, by any effort of our will, or by any strength of wish that it were true, believe ourselves well and about when we are roaring with rheumatism in bed, or feel certain that the sum of the two one-dollar bills in our pocket must be a hundred dollars? We can *say* any of these things, but we are absolutely impotent to believe them; and of just such things is the whole fabric of the truths that we do believe in made up—matters of fact, immediate or remote, as Hume said, and relations between ideas, which are either there or not there for us if we see them so, and which if not there cannot be put there by any action of our own.

In Pascal's *Thoughts* there is a celebrated passage known in literature as Pascal's Wager. In it he tries to force us into Christianity by reasoning as if our concern with truth resembled our concern with the stakes in a game of chance. Translated freely his words are these: You must either believe or not believe that God is—which will you do? Your human reason cannot say. A game is going on between you and the nature of things which at the day of judgment will bring out either heads or tails. Weigh what your gains and your losses would be if you should stake all you have on heads, or God's existence: if you win in such case you gain eternal beatitude; if you lose, you lose nothing at all. If there were an infinity of chances and only one for God in this wager, still you ought to stake your all on God; for though you surely risk a finite loss by this procedure, any finite loss is reasonable, even a certain one is reasonable, if there is but the possibility of infinite gain. Go then, and take holy water, and have masses said: belief will come and stupefy your scruples. . . . Why should you not? At bottom, what have you to lose?

You probably feel that when religious faith expresses itself thus, in the language of the gaming-table, it is put to its last trumps. Surely Pascal's own personal belief in masses and holy water had far other springs; and this celebrated page of his is but an argument for others, a last desperate snatch at a weapon against the hardness of the unbelieving heart. We feel that a faith in masses and holy water adopted wilfully after such a mechanical calculation would lack the inner soul of faith's reality; and if we were ourselves in the place of the Deity, we should probably take particular pleasure in cutting off believers of this pattern from their infinite reward. It is evident that unless there be some preexisting tendency to believe in masses and holy water, the option offered to the will by Pascal is not a living option. Certainly no Turk ever took to masses and holy water on its account and even to us Protestants these means of salvation seem such foregone impossibilities that Pascal's logic, invoked for them specifically, leaves us unmoved. As well might the Mahdi write to us saying, "I am the Expected One whom God has created in his effulgence. You shall be infinitely happy if you confess me; otherwise you shall be cut off from the light of the sun. Weigh, then, your infinite gain if I am genuine against your finite sacrifice if I am not!" His logic would be that of Pascal; but he would vainly use it on us, for the hypothesis he offers us is dead. No tendency to act on it exists in us to any degree.

The talk of believing by our volition seems, then, from one point of view, simply silly. From another point of view it is worse than silly, it is vile. When one turns to the magnificent edifice of the physical sciences, and sees how it was reared; what thousands of disinterested moral lives of men lie buried in its mere foundations; what patience and postponement, what choking down of preference, what submission to the icy laws of outer fact are wrought into its very stones and mortar; how absolutely impersonal it stands in its vast augustness—then how besotted and contemptible seems every little sentimentalist who comes blowing his voluntary smoke-wreaths, and pretending to decide things from out of his private dream! Can we wonder if those bred in the rugged and manly school of science should feel like spewing such subjectivism out of their mouths? The whole system of loyalties which grow up in the schools of science go dead against its toleration; so that it is only natural that those who have caught the scientific fever should pass over to the opposite extreme, and write sometimes as if the incorruptibly truthful intellect ought positively to prefer bitterness and unacceptableness to the heart in its cup.

> It fortifies my soul to know
> That though I perish, truth is so

sings Clough, while Huxley exclaims: "My only consolation lies in the reflection that, however bad our posterity may become, so far as they hold by the plain rule of not pretending to believe what they have no reason to believe, because it may be to their advantage so to pretend [the word 'pretend' is surely here redundant], they will not have reached the lowest depths of immorality." And that delicious *enfant terrible* Clifford writes: "Belief is desecrated when given to unproved and unquestioned statements for the solace and private pleasure of the believer. . . . Whoso would deserve well of his fellows in this matter will guard the purity of his

belief with a very fanaticism of jealous care, lest at any time it should rest on an unworthy object, and catch a stain which can never be wiped away. . . . If [a] belief has been accepted on insufficient evidence [even though the belief be true, as Clifford on the same page explains] the pleasure is a stolen one. . . . It is sinful because it is stolen in defiance of our duty to mankind. That duty is to guard ourselves from such beliefs as from a pestilence which may shortly master our own body and then spread to the rest of the town. . . . It is wrong always, everywhere, and for every one, to believe anything upon insufficient evidence."

III

All this strikes one as healthy, even when expressed, as by Clifford, with somewhat too much of robustious pathos in the voice. Free will and simple wishing do seem, in the matter of our credences, to be only fifth wheels to the coach. Yet if any one should thereupon assume that intellectual insight is what remains after wish and will and sentimental preference have taken wing, or that pure reason is what then settles our opinions, he would fly quite as directly in the teeth of the facts.

It is only our already dead hypotheses that our willing nature is unable to bring to life again. But what has made them dead for us is for the most part a previous action of our willing nature of an antagonistic kind. When I say "willing nature," I do not mean only such deliberate volitions as may have set up habits of belief that we cannot now escape from—I mean all such factors of belief as fear and hope, prejudice and passion, imitation and partisanship, the circumpressure of our caste and set. As a matter of fact we find ourselves believing, we hardly know how or why. Mr. Balfour gives the name of "authority" to all those influences, born of the intellectual climate, that make hypotheses possible or impossible for us, alive or dead. Here in this room, we all of us believe in molecules and the conservation of energy, in democracy and necessary progress, in Protestant Christianity and the duty of fighting for "the doctrine of the immortal Monroe," all for no reasons worthy of the name. We see into these matters with no more inner clearness, and probably with much less, than any disbeliever in them might possess. His unconventionality would probably have some grounds to show for its conclusions; but for us, not insight, but the *prestige* of the opinions, is what makes the spark shoot from them and light up our sleeping magazines of faith. Our reason is quite satisfied, in nine hundred and ninety-nine cases out of every thousand of us, if it can find a few arguments that will do to recite in case our credulity is criticized by some one else. Our faith is faith in some one else's faith, and in the greatest matters this is the most the case. Our belief in truth itself, for instance, that there is a truth, and that our minds and it are made for each other, —what is it but a passionate affirmation of desire, in which our social system backs us up? We want to have a truth; we want to believe that our experiments and studies and discussions must put us in a continually better and better position towards it; and on this line we agree to fight out our thinking lives. But if a pyrrhonistic sceptic asks us *how we know* all this, can our logic find a reply? No! certainly it cannot. It is just one volition against another,—we willing to go in for life upon a trust or assumption which he, for his part, does not care to make.

As a rule we disbelieve all facts and theories for which we have no use. Clifford's cosmic emotions find no use for Christian feelings. Huxley belabors the bishops because there is no use for sacerdotalism in his scheme of life. Newman, on the contrary, goes over to Romanism, and finds all sorts of reasons good for staying there, because a priestly system is for him an organic need and delight. Why do so few 'scientists' even look at the evidence for telepathy, so called? Because they think, as a leading biologist, now dead, once said to me, that even if such a thing were true, scientists ought to band together to keep it suppressed and concealed. It would undo the uniformity of Nature and all sorts of other things without which scientists cannot carry on their pursuits. But if this very man had been shown something which as a scientist he might *do* with telepathy, he might not only have examined the evidence, but even have found it good enough.

This very law which the logicians would impose upon us—if I may give the name of logicians to those who would rule out our willing nature here— is based on nothing but their own natural wish to exclude all elements for which they, in their professional quality of logicians, can find no use.

Evidently, then, our non-intellectual nature does influence our convictions. There are passional tendencies and volitions which run before and others which come after belief, and it is only the latter that are too late for the fair; and they are not too late when the previous passional work has been already in their own direction. Pascal's argument, instead of being powerless, then seems a regular clincher, and is the last stroke needed to make our faith in masses and holy water complete. The state of things is evidently far from simple; and pure insight and logic, whatever they might do ideally, are not the only things that really do produce our creeds.

IV

Our next duty, having recognized this mixed up state of affairs, is to ask whether it be simply reprehensible and pathological, or whether, on the contrary, we must treat it as a normal element in making up our minds. The thesis I defend is, briefly stated, this: *Our passional nature not only lawfully may, but must, decide an option between propositions, whenever it is a genuine option that cannot by its nature be decided on intellectual grounds; for to say, under such circumstances, "Do not decide, but leave the question open," is itself a passional decision—just like deciding yes or no—and is attended with the same risk of losing the truth.* . . .

VII

One more point, small but important, and our preliminaries are done. There are two ways of looking at our duty in the matter of opinion—ways entirely different, and yet ways about whose difference the theory of knowledge seems hitherto to have shown very little concern. *We must know the truth; and we must avoid error*—these are our first and great commandments as would-be knowers; but they are not two ways of stating an identical commandment, they are two separable laws. Although it may indeed happen that when we believe the truth A, we escape as an incidental consequence from believing the falsehood B, it hardly ever happens that by merely disbelieving B we necessarily believe A. We may in escaping B fall into believing other falsehoods, C or D, just as bad as B; or we may escape B by not believing anything at all, not even A.

Believe truth! Shun error!—these, we see, are two materially different laws; and by choosing between them we may end by coloring differently our whole intellectual life. We may regard the chase for truth as paramount, and the avoidance of error as secondary; or we may, on the other hand, treat the avoidance of error as more imperative, and let truth take its chance. Clifford, in the instructive passage which I have quoted, exhorts us to the latter course. Believe nothing, he tells us, keep your mind in suspense forever, rather than by closing it on insufficient evidence incur the awful risk of believing lies. You, on the other hand, may think that the risk of being in error is a very small matter when compared with the blessings of real knowledge, and be ready to be duped many times in your investigation rather than postpone indefinitely the chance of guessing true. I myself find it impossible to go with Clifford. We must remember that these feelings of our duty about either truth or error are in any case only expressions of our passional life. Biologically considered, our minds are as ready to grind out falsehood as veracity, and he who says, "Better go without belief forever than believe a lie!" merely shows his own preponderant private horror of becoming a dupe. He may be critical of many of his desires and fears, but this fear he slavishly obeys. He cannot imagine any one questioning its binding force. For my own part, I have also a horror of being duped; but I can believe that worse things than being duped may happen to a man in this world; so Clifford's exhortation has to my ears a thoroughly fantastic sound. It is like a general informing his soldiers that it is better to keep out of battle forever than to risk a single wound. Not so are victories either over enemies or over nature gained. Our

errors are surely not such awfully solemn things. In a world where we are so certain to incur them in spite of all our caution, a certain lightness of heart seems healthier than this excessive nervousness on their behalf. At any rate, it seems the fittest thing for the empiricist philosopher.

VIII

And now, after all this introduction, let us go straight at our question. I have said, and now repeat it, that not only as a matter of fact do we find our passional nature influencing us in our opinions, but that there are some options between opinions in which this influence must be regarded both as an inevitable and as a lawful determinant of our choice.

I fear here that some of you my hearers will begin to scent danger, and lend an inhospitable ear. Two first steps of passion you have indeed had to admit as necessary—we must think so as to avoid dupery, and we must think so as to gain truth; but the surest path to those ideal consummations, you will probably consider, is from now onwards to take no further passional step.

Well, of course, I agree as far as the facts will allow. Wherever the option between losing truth and gaining it is not momentous, we can throw the chance of *gaining truth* away, and at any rate save ourselves from any chance of *believing falsehood*, by not making up our minds at all till objective evidence has come. In scientific questions, this is almost always the case; and even in human affairs in general, the need of acting is seldom so urgent that a false belief to act on is better than no belief at all. Law courts, indeed, have to decide on the best evidence attainable for the moment, because a judge's duty is to make law as well as to ascertain it, and (as a learned judge once said to me) few cases are worth spending much time over: the great thing is to have them decided on *any* acceptable principle, and got out of the way. But in our dealings with objective nature we obviously are recorders, not makers, of the truth; and decisions for the mere sake of deciding promptly and getting on to the next business would be wholly out of place. Throughout the breadth of physical nature facts are what they are quite independently of us, and seldom is there any such hurry about them that the risks of being duped by believing a premature theory need be faced. The questions here are always trivial options, the hypotheses are hardly living (at any rate not living for us spectators), the choice between believing truth or falsehood is seldom forced. The attitude of sceptical balance is therefore the absolutely wise one if we would escape mistakes. What difference, indeed, does it make to most of us whether we have or have not a theory of the Röntgen rays, whether we believe or not in mind-stuff, or have a conviction about the causality of conscious states? It makes no difference. Such options are not forced on us. On every account it is better not to make them, but still keep weighing reasons *pro et contra* with an indifferent hand.

I speak, of course, here of the purely judging mind. For purposes of discovery such indifference is to be less highly recommended, and science would be far less advanced than she is if the passionate desires of individuals to get their own faiths confirmed had been kept out of the game. See for example the sagacity which Spencer and Weismann now display. On the other hand, if you want an absolute duffer in an investigation, you must, after all, take the man who has no interest whatever in its results: he is the warranted incapable, the positive fool. The most useful investigator, because the most sensitive observer, is always he whose eager interest in one side of the question is balanced by an equally keen nervousness lest he become deceived.[1] Science has organized this nervousness into a regular *technique*, her so-called method of verification; and she has fallen so deeply in love with the method that one may even say she has ceased to care for truth by itself at all. It is only truth as technically verified that interests her. The truth of truths might come in merely affirmative form, and she would decline to touch it. Such truth as that, she might repeat with Clifford, would be stolen in defiance of her duty to mankind. Human passions, however, are stronger than technical rules. "*Le coeur a ses raisons*," as Pascal says, "*que la raison ne connait pas*";[2] and however indifferent to all but the bare rules of the game the umpire, the abstract intellect, may be, the concrete players who furnish him the materials to judge of are usually, each one of them, in love with some pet "live hypothesis" of his own. Let us agree, however, that wherever there is no forced option, the dispassionately judicial intellect with no pet hypothesis, saving us, as it does, from dupery at any rate, ought to be our ideal.

The question next arises: Are there not somewhere forced options in our speculative questions, and can we (as men who may be interested at least as much in positively gaining truth as in merely escaping dupery) always wait with impunity till the coercive evidence shall have arrived? It seems *a priori* improbable that the truth should be so nicely adjusted to our needs and powers as that. In the great boarding-house of nature, the cakes and the butter and the syrup seldom come out so even and leave the plates so clean. Indeed, we should view them with scientific suspicion if they did.

IX

Moral questions immediately present themselves as questions whose solution cannot wait for sensible proof. A moral question is a question not of what sensibly exists, but of what is good, or would be good if it did exist. Science can tell us what exists; but to compare the *worths*, both of what exists and of what does not exist, we must consult not science, but what Pascal calls our heart. . . .

Turn now from these wide questions of good to a certain class of questions of fact, questions concerning personal relations, states of mind between one man and another. *Do you like me or not?*—for example. Whether you do or not depends, in countless instances, on whether I meet you halfway, am willing to assume that you must like me, and show you trust and expectation. The previous faith on my part in your liking's existence is in such cases what makes your liking come. But if I stand aloof, and refuse to budge an inch until I have objective evidence, until you shall have done something apt, as the absolutists say, *ad extorquendum assensum meum*, ten to one your liking never comes. How many women's hearts are vanquished by the mere sanguine insistence of some man that they *must* love him! He will not consent to the hypothesis that they cannot. The desire for a certain kind of truth here brings about that special truth's existence; and so it is in innumerable cases of other sorts. . . . *And where faith in a fact can help create the fact,* that would be an insane logic which should say that faith running ahead of scientific evidence is the "lowest kind of immorality" into which a thinking being can fall. Yet such is the logic by which our scientific absolutists pretend to regulate our lives!

X

In truths dependent on our personal action, then faith based on desire is certainly a lawful and possibly an indispensable thing.

But now, it will be said, these are all childish human cases, and have nothing to do with great cosmical matters, like the question of religious faith. Let us then pass on to that. Religions differ so much in their accidents that in discussing the religious question we must make it very generic and broad. What then do we now mean by the religious hypothesis? Science says things are; morality says some things are better than other things; and religion says essentially two things.

First, she says that the best things are the more eternal things, the overlapping things, the things in the universe that throw the last stone, so to speak and say the final word. "Perfection is eternal"—this phrase of Charles Secrétan seems a good way of putting this first affirmation of religion, an affirmation which obviously cannot yet be verified scientifically at all.

The second affirmation of religion is that we are better off even now if we believe her first affirmation to be true.

Now, let us consider what the logical elements of this situation are *in case the religious hypothesis in both its branches be really true.* (Of course, we must admit that possibility at the outset. If we are to discuss the question at all, it must involve a living option. If for any of you religion be a hypothesis that

cannot, by any living possibility, be true, then you need go no farther. I speak to the "saving remnant" alone.) So proceeding, we see, first, that religion offers itself as a *momentous* option. We are supposed to gain, even now, by our belief, and to lose by our non-belief, a certain vital good. Secondly religion is a *forced* option, so far as that good goes. We cannot escape the issue by remaining sceptical and waiting for more light, because, although we do avoid error in that way *if religion be untrue,* we lose the good, *if it be true,* just as certainly as if we positively chose to disbelieve. It is as if a man should hesitate indefinitely to ask a certain woman to marry him because he was not perfectly sure that she would prove an angel after he brought her home. Would he not cut himself off from that particular angel-possibility as decisively as if he went and married some one else? Scepticism, then, is not avoidance of option; it is option of a certain particular kind of risk. *Better risk loss of truth than chance of error*—that is your faith-vetoer's exact position. He is actively playing his stake as much as the believer is; he is backing the field against the religious hypothesis, just as the believer is backing the religious hypothesis against the field. To preach scepticism to us as a duty until "sufficient evidence" for religion to be found, is tantamount therefore to telling us, when in presence of the religious hypothesis, that to yield to our fear of its being error is wiser and better than to yield to our hope that it may be true. It is not intellect against all passions, then; it is only intellect with one passion laying down its law. And by what, forsooth, is the supreme wisdom of this passion warranted? Dupery for dupery, what proof is there that dupery through hope is so much worse than dupery through fear? I, for one, can see no proof; and I simply refuse obedience to the scientist's command to imitate his kind of option, in a case where my own stake is important enough to give me the right to choose my own form of risk. If religion be true and the evidence for it be still insufficient, I do not wish, by putting your extinguisher upon my nature (which feels to me as if it had after all some business in this matter), to forfeit my sole chance in life of getting upon the winning side—that chance depending, of course, on my willingness to run the risk of acting as if my passional need of taking the world religiously might be prophetic and right.

All this is on the supposition that it really may be prophetic and right, and that, even to us who are discussing the matter, religion is a live hypothesis which may be true. Now, to most of us religion comes in a still further way that makes a veto on our active faith even more illogical. The more perfect and more eternal aspect of the universe is represented in our religions as having personal form. The universe is no longer a mere *It* to us, but a *Thou*, if we are religious; and any relation that may be possible from person to person might be possible here. For instance, although in one sense we are passive portions of the universe, in another we show a curious autonomy, as if we were small active centers on our own account. We feel, too, as if the appeal of religion to us were made to our own active goodwill, as if evidence might be forever withheld from us unless we met the hypothesis halfway to take a trivial illusion; just as a man who in a company of gentlemen made no advances, asked a warrant for every concession, and believed no one's word without proof, would cut himself off by such churlishness from all the social rewards that a more trusting spirit would earn—so here, one who should shut himself up in snarling logicality and try to make the gods extort his recognition willy-nilly, or not get it at all, might cut himself off forever from his only opportunity of making the gods' acquaintance. This feeling, forced on us we know not whence that by obstinately believing that there are gods (although not to do so would be so easy both for our logic and our life) we are doing the universe the deepest service we can, seems part of the living essence of the religious hypothesis. If the hypothesis *were* true in all its parts, including this one, then pure intellectualism, with its veto on our making willing advances, would be an absurdity; and some participation of our sympathetic nature would be logically required. I therefore, for one, cannot see my way to accepting the agnostic rules for truth-seeking, or wilfully agree to keep my willing nature out of the game. I cannot do so for this plain reason, that *a rule of thinking which would absolutely prevent me from acknowledging certain kinds of truth if those kinds of truth were really there, would*

be an irrational rule. That for me is the long and short of the formal logic of the situation, no matter what the kinds of truth might materially be.

I confess I do not see how this logic can be escaped. But sad experience makes me fear that some of you may still shrink from radically saying with me, *in abstracto*, that we have the right to believe at our own risk any hypothesis that is live enough to tempt our will. I suspect, however, that if this is so, it is because you have got away from the abstract logical point of view altogether, and are thinking (perhaps without realizing it) of some particular religious hypothesis which for you is dead. The freedom to "believe what we will" you apply to the case of some patent superstition; and the faith you think of is the faith defined by the schoolboy when he said, "Faith is when you believe something that you know ain't true." I can only repeat that this is misapprehension. *In concreto*, the freedom to believe can only cover living options which the intellect of the individual cannot by itself resolve; and living options never seem absurdities to him who has them to consider. When I look at the religious question as it really puts itself to concrete men, and when I think of all the possibilities which both practically and theoretically it involves, then this command that we shall put a stopper on our heart, instincts, and courage, and *wait*—acting of course meanwhile more or less as if religion were not true—till doomsday, or till such time as our intellect and senses working together may have raked in evidence enough—this command, I say, seems to me the queerest idol ever manufactured in the philosophic cave. Were we scholastic absolutists, there might be more excuse. If we had an infallible intellect with its objective certitudes, we might feel ourselves disloyal to such a perfect organ or knowledge in not trusting to it exclusively, in not waiting for its releasing word. But if we are empiricists, if we believe that no bell in us tolls to let us know for certain when truth is in our grasp, then it seems a piece of idle fantasticality to preach so solemnly our duty of waiting for the bell. Indeed we may wait if we will—I hope you do not think that I am denying that—but if we do so, we do so at our peril as much as if we believed. In either case we *act*, taking our life in our hands. No one of us ought to issue vetoes to the other, nor should we bandy words of abuse. We ought, on the contrary, delicately and profoundly to respect one another's mental freedom: then only shall we bring about the intellectual republic; then only shall we have that spirit of inner tolerance without which all our outer tolerance is soulless, and which is empiricism's glory; then only shall we live and let live, in speculative as well as in practical things.

I began by a reference to Fitz-James Stephen; let me end by a quotation from him. "What do you think of yourself? What do you think of the world? . . . These are questions with which all must deal as it seems good to them. They are riddles of the Sphinx, and in some way or other we must deal with them. . . . In all important transactions of life we have to take a leap in the dark. . . . If we decide to leave the riddles unanswered, that is a choice; if we waver in our answer, that, too, is a choice: but whatever choice we make, we make it at our peril. If a man chooses to turn his back altogether on God and the future no one can prevent him; no one can show beyond reasonable doubt that he is mistaken. If a man thinks otherwise and acts as he thinks, I do not see that any one can prove that he is mistaken. Each must act as he thinks best; and if he is wrong, so much the worse for him. We stand on a mountain pass in the midst of whirling snow and blinding mist, through which we get glimpses now and then of paths which may be deceptive. If we stand still we shall be frozen to death. If we take the wrong road we shall be dashed to pieces. We do not certainly know whether there is any right one. What must we do? 'Be strong and of a good courage.' Act for the best, hope for the best, and take what comes.

. . . If death ends all, we cannot meet death better. "

Notes

1. Compare Wilfrid Ward's Essay "The Wish to Believe," in his *Witnesses to the Unseen* (Macmillan & Co., 1893).

2. "The heart has its reasons which reason does not know."

3. Since belief is measured by action, he who forbids us to believe religion to be true, necessarily also forbids us to act as we should if we did believe it to be true. The whole defence of religious faith hinges upon action. If the action required or inspired by the religious hypothesis is in no way different from that dictated by the naturalistic hypothesis, then religious faith is a pure superfluity, better pruned away, and controversy about its legitimacy is a piece of idle trifling, unworthy of serious minds. I myself believe, of course, that the religious hypothesis gives to the world an expression which specifically determines our reactions, and makes them in a large part unlike what they might be on a purely naturalistic scheme of belief.

VII.C Fideism: Faith Without/Against Reason

Fideism may be called the position that holds that objective reason is simply inappropriate for religious belief. Faith does not need reason for its justification, and the attempt to apply rational categories to religion is completely out of place. Faith creates its own justification, its own criteria of internal assessment. Perhaps there are two versions of fideism. The first states that religion is bound to appear absurd when judged by the standards of theoretical reason. The second merely says that religion is an activity in which reason is properly inoperative. It is not so much against reason as above reason. The two positions are compatible. The third-century theologian Tertullian seemed to hold that religious faith was both against and beyond human reason (and perhaps St. Paul holds the same in 1 Corinthians, chapter 1), but many fideists, such as Calvin, would subscribe only to the latter position.

The Danish philosopher Søren Kierkegaard (1813–1855), father of existentialism, seems to hold to both versions of fideism. For him, faith, not reason, is the highest virtue a human can reach; faith is necessary for the deepest human fulfillment. If Kant, the rationalist, adhered to a "religion within the limits of reason alone," Kierkegaard adhered to "reason within the limitations of religion alone." He unashamedly proclaimed faith to be higher than reason in the development of essential humanness, that alone which promised eternal happiness. In a more everyday sense, Kierkegaard thought that we all live by simple faith in plans, purposes, and people. It is rarely the case in ordinary life that reason is our basic guide. Paraphrasing Hume, he might have said that "reason is and ought to be a slave to faith," for we all have an essential faith in something, and reason comes in largely as an afterthought in order to rationalize our intuitions and commitments.

No one writes more passionately about faith nor values it more highly than Kierkegaard. Whereas his predecessors had largely viewed it as a necessary evil, a distant cousin to the princely

knowledge, Kierkegaard reversed the order. Knowledge about metaphysical issues is not really desirable, because it prevents the kind of human striving that is essential for our fullest development. For him, faith is the highest virtue precisely because it is objectively uncertain; for personal growth into selfhood depends on uncertainty, risk, venturing forth over seventy thousand fathoms of ocean water. Faith is the lover's loyalty to the beloved when all the evidence is against her. Faith is the soul's deepest yearnings and hopes, which the rational part of us cannot fathom. Even if we had direct proof for theism or Christianity, we would not want it, for such objective certainty would take the venture out of the religious pilgrimage, reducing it to a set of dull mathematical certainties.

According to Kierkegaard, genuine theistic faith appears when reason reaches the end of its tether, when the individual sees that without God there is no purpose to life.

> In this manner God becomes a postulate, but not in the otiose manner in which this word is commonly understood. It becomes clear rather that the only way in which an existing individual comes into relation with God, is when the dialectical contradiction brings his passion to the point of despair and helps him to embrace God with the "category of despair" (faith). Then the postulate is so far from being arbitrary that it is precisely a life-necessity. It is then not so much that God is a postulate, as that the existing individual's postulation of God is necessary.

In the selection from *Concluding Unscientific Postscript* (1846), "Subjectivity Is Truth," included in this section, Kierkegaard argues that there is something fundamentally misguided in trying to base one's religious faith on objective evidence or reason. It is both useless (it won't work) and a bad thing (it detracts one from the essential task of growing in faith). He then goes on to develop a theory of subjectivity wherein faith finds an authentic home.

In our second reading, Robert M. Adams examines three of Kierkegaard's arguments against objective reason in religion (found in our first reading). Although he appreciates the depth of Kierkegaard's insight, he argues that the sort of fideism embraced by Kierkegaard has problems. The three arguments that Adams identifies may be described as follows:

1. The approximation argument
   A. All historical inquiry gives, at best, only approximate results.
   B. Approximate results are inadequate for religious faith (which demands certainty).
   C. Therefore, all historical inquiry is inadequate for religious faith.
2. The postponement argument
   A. One cannot have an authentic religious faith without being totally committed to the belief in question.
   B. One cannot be totally committed to any belief based on an inquiry in which one recognizes the possibility of a future need to revise the results.
   C. Therefore, authentic religious faith cannot be based on any inquiry in which one recognizes the possibility of a future need to revise the results.
   D. Since all rational inquiry recognizes the contingency of future revision, no authentic religious faith can be based on it.
3. The passion argument
   A. The most essential and valuable trait of religious faith is passion, a passion of the greatest possible intensity.
   B. An infinite passion requires objective improbability.
   C. Therefore, that which is most essential and valuable in religious faith requires objective improbability.

You should pay special attention to Adam's discussion of these points in order to determine whether his contentions undermine Kierkegaard's points. It should be noted that Adams is sympathetic to the motivation that led Kierkegaard to set forth the arguments that he did, and he recognizes that Kierkegaard's conclusion does follow from an appealing conception of religion, although Adams himself sees no need to accept that conception. Adams's article is important both for its insight into Kierkegaard's thought and for Adam's ability to translate Kierkegaard's difficult style into clear argument form.

In our third reading, we turn to the leading type of fideism in contemporary philosophy of religion. We begin with a short piece from Ludwig Wittgenstein's "Lectures on Religious Belief." Wittgenstein argues that there is something *sui generis* or special about the very linguistic framework of believers, so that the concepts they use cannot be adequately grasped by outsiders. One has to share in a form of life in order to understand the way the various concepts function in that language game. Wittgenstein ridicules one Father O'Hara for giving the impression that there is a nonperspectival, impartial way of assessing the truth value of religious assertions. Such a view, Wittgenstein believes, is absurd.

A particularly lucid interpreter and adherent of Wittgensteinian fideism is Norman Malcolm, whose article "The Groundlessness of Belief" is included as the fourth reading in this section. Malcolm contends that religious belief is in no sense a hypothesis, for it cannot be and ought not to be justified rationally. It is essentially a groundless belief like other beliefs that do not need further support, such as our belief that things don't just vanish, our belief in the uniformity of nature, and our knowledge of our own intentions.

Like other fundamental assumptions religious beliefs are not derived from other beliefs but themselves form the support for all our other beliefs. They form the framework of our inquiry on which the very process of justification depends. Hence, it does not make sense to ask for a justification of religious claims or a refutation of them from a point outside the religious framework. Science and religion are just two different language games. "Neither stands in need of justification, the one no more than the other."

Finally, Michael Martin argues that fideism is fundamentally flawed. We do have a common conceptual framework and criteria of rational assessment so that analysis and evaluation of all worldviews, including religious ones, is possible. Fideism fails to acquit itself before the bar of reason.

VII.C.1 Subjectivity Is Truth

SØREN KIERKEGAARD

Our first reading is taken from the Concluding Unscientific Postscripts, *by Danish philosopher Søren Kierkegaard (1813–1855), father of existentialism. Kierkegaard represents a radical version of fideism in which faith not only is higher than reason but, in a sense, opposes it. Faith, not reason, is the highest virtue a human can reach; faith is necessary for the deepest human fulfilment. Kierkegaard argues that there is something fundamentally misguided in trying to base one's religious faith on objective evidence or reason. It is both useless (it won't work) and a bad thing (it detracts one from the essential task of growing in faith). He then goes on to develop a theory of subjectivity wherein faith finds an authentic home. Even if we had direct proof for theism or Christianity, we would not want it, for such objective certainty would take the venture out of the religious pilgrimage, reducing it to a set of dull mathematical certainties.*

The problem we are considering is not the truth of Christianity but the individual's relation to Christianity. Our discussion is not about the scholar's systematic zeal to arrange the truths of Christianity in nice, tidy categories but about the individual's personal relationship to this doctrine, a relationship which is properly one of infinite interest to him. Simply stated, "I, Johannes Climacus, born in this city, now thirty years old, a decent fellow like most folk, suppose that there awaits me, as it awaits a maid and a professor, a highest good, which is called an eternal happiness. I have heard that Christianity is the way to that good, and so I ask, how may I establish a proper relationship to Christianity?"

From *Concluding Unscientific Postscript to the Philosophical Fragments* (1844), translated by Louis Pojman. This selection and translation was made for the first edition of this volume.

I hear an intellectual's response to this, "What outrageous presumption! What egregious egoistic vanity in this theocentric and philosophically enlightened age, which is concerned with global history, to lay such inordinate weight on one's petty self."

I tremble at such a reproof and had I not already inured myself to these kinds of responses, I would slink away like a dog with his tail between his legs. But I have no guilt whatsoever about what I am doing, for it is not I who is presumptuous, but, rather, it is Christianity itself which compels me to ask the question in this way. For Christianity places enormous significance on my little self, and upon every other self however insignificant it may seem, in that it offers each self eternal happiness on the condition that a proper relationship between itself and the individual is established.

Although I am still an outsider to faith, I can see that the only unpardonable sin against the majesty of Christianity is for an individual to take his relationship to it for granted. However modest it may seem to relate oneself in this way, Christianity considers such a casual attitude to be imprudent. So I must respectfully decline all theocentric helpers and the helpers' helpers who would seek to help me through a detached relationship to this doctrine. I would rather remain where I am with my infinite concern about my spiritual existence, with the problem of how I may become a Christian. For while it is not impossible for one with an infinite concern for his eternal happiness to achieve salvation, it is entirely impossible for one who has lost all sensitivity to the relationship to achieve such a state.

The objective problem is: Is Christianity true? The subjective problem is: What is the individual's relationship to Christianity? Quite simply, how may I, Johannes Climacus, participate in the happiness promised by Christianity? The problem concerns myself alone; partly because, if it is properly set forth, it will concern everyone in exactly the same way; and partly because all the other points of view take faith for granted, as trivial.

In order to make my problem clear, I shall first describe the objective problem and show how it should be treated. In this way the historical aspect will be given its due. After this I shall describe the subjective problem.

The Objective Problem of the Truth of Christianity.

From an objective point of view Christianity is a historical fact whose truth must be considered in a purely objective manner, for the modest scholar is far too objective not to leave himself outside—though as a matter of fact, he may count himself as a believer. 'Truth' in this objective sense may mean either (1) historical truth or (2) philosophical truth. As historical truth, the truth claims must be decided by a critical examination of the various sources in the same way we determine other historical claims. Considered philosophically, the doctrine that has been historically verified must be related to the eternal truth.

The inquiring, philosophical, and learned researcher raises the question of the truth, but not the subjective truth, that is, the truth as appropriated. The inquiring researcher is interested, but he is not infinitely, personally, and passionately interested in a way that relates his own eternal happiness to this truth. Far be it for the objective person to be so immodest, so presumptuous as that!

Such an inquirer must be in one of two states. Either he is already in faith convinced of the truth of Christianity—and in such a relationship he cannot be infinitely interested in the objective inquiry, since faith itself consists in being infinitely concerned with Christianity and regards every competing interest as a temptation; or he is not in faith but objectively considering the subject matter, and as such not in a condition of being infinitely interested in the question.

I mention this in order to draw your attention to what will be developed in the second part of this work, namely, that the problem of the truth of Christianity is never appropriately set forth in this objective manner, that is, it does not arise at all, since Christianity lies in decision. Let the scholarly

researcher work with indefatigable zeal even to the point of shortening his life in devoted service to scholarship. Let the speculative philosopher spare neither time nor effort. They are nevertheless not personally and passionately concerned. On the contrary, they wouldn't want to be but will want to develop an objective and disinterested stance. They are only concerned about objective truth, so that the question of personal appropriation is relatively unimportant, something that will follow their findings as a matter of course. In the last analysis what matters to the individual is of minor significance. Herein precisely lies the scholar's exalted equanimity as well as the comedy of his parrotlike pedantry.

The Historical Point of View.

When Christianity is considered through its historical documents, it becomes vital to get a trustworthy account of what Christian doctrine really is. If the researcher is infinitely concerned with his relationship to this truth, he will immediately despair, because it is patently clear that in historical matters the greatest certainty is still only an approximation, and an approximation is too weak for one to build his eternal happiness upon, since its incommensurability with eternal happiness prevents it from obtaining. So the scholar, having only a historical interest in the truth of Christianity, begins his work with tremendous zeal and contributes important research until his seventieth year. Then just fourteen days before his death he comes upon a new document that casts fresh light over one whole side of his inquiry. Such an objective personality is the antithesis of the restless concern of the subject who is infinitely interested in eternal happiness and who surely deserves to have a decisive answer to the question concerning that happiness.

When one raises the historical question of the truth of Christianity or of what is and what is not Christian truth, we come directly to the Holy Scriptures as the central document. The historical investigation focuses first on the Bible.

The Holy Scriptures.

It is very important that the scholar secure the highest possible reliability in his work. In this regard it is important for me not to pretend that I have learning or show that I have none, for my purpose here is more important. And that is to have it understood and remembered that even with the most impressive scholarly credentials and persistence, even if all the intelligence of all the critics met in one single head, still one would get no further than an approximation. We could never show more than that there is an incommensurability between the infinite personal concern for one's eternal happiness and the reliability of the documents.

When the Scriptures are considered as the ultimate arbiter, which determines what is and what is not Christian, it becomes imperative to secure their reliability through a critical historical investigation. So we must deal here with several issues: the canonicity of each book of the Bible, their authenticity, their integrity, the trustworthiness of the authors, and finally, we must assume a dogmatic guarantee: inspiration. When one thinks of the prodigious labors that the English are devoting to digging the tunnel under the Thames, the incredible expenditure of time and effort, and how a little accident can upset the whole project for a long time, one may be able to get some idea of what is involved in the undertaking that we are describing. How much time, what diligence, what glorious acumen, what remarkable scholarship from generation to generation have been requisitioned to accomplish this work of supreme wonder! And yet a single little dialectical doubt can suddenly touch the foundations and for a long time disturb the whole project, closing the underground way to Christianity, which one has tried to establish objectively and scientifically, instead of approaching the problem as it would be approached, above ground—subjectively.

But let us assume first that the critics have established everything that scholarly theologians in their happiest moments ever dreamed to prove about the Bible. These books and no others belong to the canon. They are authentic, complete, their authors are trustworthy—it is as though every letter were divinely inspired (one cannot say more than this, for inspiration is an object of faith and is qualitatively dialectical. It cannot be reached by a quantitative increment). Furthermore, there is not the slightest contradiction in these holy writings. For let us be

careful in formulating our hypothesis. If there is even a word that is problematic, the parenthesis of uncertainty begins again, and the critical philological enterprise will lead one astray. In general, all that is needed to cause us to question our findings is a little circumspection, the renunciation of every learned middle-term, which could in a twinkle of the eye degenerate into a hundred-year parenthesis.

And so it comes to pass that everything we hoped for with respect to the Scriptures has been firmly established. What follows from this? Has anyone who didn't previously have faith come a single step closer to faith? Of course not, not a single step closer. For faith isn't produced through academic investigations. It doesn't come directly at all, but, on the contrary, it is precisely in objective analysis that one loses the infinite personal and passionate concern that is the requisite condition for faith, its ubiquitous ingredient, wherein faith comes into existence.

Has anyone who had faith gained anything in terms of faith's strength and power? No, not the least. Rather, his prodigious learning which lies like a dragon at faith's door, threatening to devour it, will become a handicap, forcing him to put forth an even greater prodigious effort in fear and trembling in order not to fall into temptation and confuse knowledge with faith. Whereas faith had uncertainty as a useful teacher, it now finds that certainty is its most dangerous enemy. Take passion away and faith disappears, for certainty and passion are incompatible. Let an analogy throw light on this point. He who believes that God exists and providentially rules the world finds it easier to preserve his faith (and not a fantasy) in an imperfect world where passion is kept awake, than in an absolutely perfect world; for in such an ideal world faith is unthinkable. This is the reason that we are taught that in eternity faith will be annulled.

Now let us assume the opposite, that the opponents have succeeded in proving what they desired to establish regarding the Bible and did so with a certainty that transcended their wildest hopes. What then? Has the enemy abolished Christianity? Not a whit. Has he harmed the believer? Not at all. Has he won the right of being free from the responsibility of becoming a believer? By no means. Simply because these books are not by these authors, are not authentic, lack integrity, do not seem to be inspired (though this cannot be demonstrated since it is a matter of faith), it in no way follows that these authors have not existed, and above all it does not follow that Christ never existed. In so far as faith perdures, the believer is at liberty to assume it, just as free (mark well!); for if he accepted the content of faith on the basis of evidence, he would now be on the verge of giving up faith. If things ever came this far, the believer is somewhat to blame, for he invited the procedure and began to play into the hands of unbelief by attempting to prove the content of faith.

Here is the heart of the matter, and I come back to learned theology. For whose sake is the proof sought? Faith does not need it. Yes, it must regard it as an enemy. But when faith begins to feel ashamed, when like a young woman for whom love ceases to suffice, who secretly feels ashamed of her lover and must therefore have it confirmed by others that he really is quite remarkable, so likewise when faith falters and begins to lose its passion, when it begins to cease to be faith, then proof becomes necessary in order to command respect from the side of unbelief.

So when the subject of faith is treated objectively, it becomes impossible for a person to relate himself to the decision of faith with passion, let alone with infinitely concerned passion. It is a self-contradiction and as such comical to be infinitely concerned about what at best can only be an approximation. If in spite of this, we still preserve passion, we obtain fanaticism. For the person with infinite passionate concern, every relevant detail becomes something of infinite value. The error lies not in the infinite passion but in the fact that its object has become an approximation.

As soon as one takes subjectivity away—and with its subjectivity's passion—and with passion the infinite concern—it becomes impossible to make a decision—either with regard to this problem or any other; for every decision, every genuine decision, is a subjective action. A contemplator (i.e., an objective subject) experiences no infinite urge to make a decision and sees no need for a commitment anywhere. This is the falsity of objectivity and this is the problem with the Hegelian notion of mediation as the mode of transition in the continuous process, where nothing endures and where nothing is infinitely decided because the movement turns back on itself and again turns back; but the movement itself is a chimera and philosophy becomes wise afterwards. Objectively speaking, this method produces results in great supply, but it does not produce a single decisive result. This is as is expected, since decisiveness inheres in subjectivity, essentially in passion and maximally in the personal passion that is infinitely concerned about one's eternal happiness.

Christianity is spirit, spirit is inwardness, inwardness is subjectivity, subjectivity is essentially passion and at its maximum infinite personal and passionate concern about one's eternal happiness.

Becoming Subjective. Objectively we only consider the subject matter, subjectively we consider the subject and his subjectivity, and behold, subjectivity is precisely our subject matter. It must constantly be kept in mind that the subjective problem is not about some other subject matter but simply about subjectivity itself. Since the problem is about a decision, and all decisions lie in subjectivity, it follows that not a trace of objectivity remains, for at the moment that subjectivity slinks away from the pain and crisis of decision, the problem becomes to a degree objective. If the Introduction still awaits another work before a judgment can be made on the subject matter, if the philosophical system still lacks a paragraph, if the speaker still has a final argument, the decision is postponed. We do not raise the question of the truth of Christianity in the sense that when it has been decided, subjectivity is ready and willing to accept it. No, the question is about the subject's acceptance of it, and it must be regarded as an infernal illusion or a deceitful evasion which seeks to avoid the decision by taking an objective treatment of the subject matter and assumes that a subjective commitment will follow from the objective deliberation as a matter of course. On the contrary, the decision lies in subjectivity and an objective acceptance is either a pagan concept or one devoid of all meaning.

Christianity will give the single individual eternal happiness, a good that cannot be divided into parts but can only be given to one person at a time. Although we presuppose that subjectivity is available to be appropriated, a possibility that involves accepting this good, it is not a subjectivity without qualification, without a genuine understanding of the meaning of this good. Subjectivity's development or transformation, its infinite concentration in itself with regard to an eternal happiness—this highest good of Infinity, an eternal happiness—this is subjectivity's developed possibility. As such, Christianity protests against all objectivity and will infinitely concern itself only with subjectivity. If there is any Christian truth, it first arises in subjectivity. Objectively it does not arise at all. If its truth is only in a single person, then Christianity exists in him alone, and there is greater joy in heaven over this one than over all world history and philosophical systems which, as objective forces, are incommensurable with the Christian idea.

Philosophy teaches that the way to truth is to become objective, but Christianity teaches that the way is to become subjective, that is, to become a subject in truth. Lest we seem to be trading on ambiguities, let it be said clearly that Christianity aims at intensifying passion to its highest pitch but passion is subjectivity and does not exist objectively at all.

Subjective Truth, Inwardness; Truth Is Subjectivity. For an objective reflection the truth becomes an object, something objective, and thought points away from the subject. For subjective reflection the truth becomes a matter of appropriation, of inwardness, of subjectivity, and thought must penetrate deeper and still deeper into the subject and his subjectivity. Just as in objective reflection, when objectivity had come into being, subjectivity disappeared, so here the subjectivity of the subject becomes the final stage, and objectivity disappears. It is not for an instant forgotten that the subject is an existing individual, and that existence is a process of becoming, and that therefore the idea of truth being an identity of thought and being is a chimera of abstraction; this is not because the truth is not such an identity but because the believer is an existing individual for whom the truth cannot be such an identity as long as he exists as a temporal being.

If an existing subject really could transcend himself, the truth would be something complete for him, but where is this point outside of himself? The I = I is a mathematical point that does not exist, and insofar as one would take this standpoint, he will not stand in another's way. It is only momentarily that the existential subject experiences the unity of the infinite and the finite, which transcends existence, and that moment is the moment of passion. While scribbling modern philosophy is contemptuous of passion, passion remains the highest point of existence for the individual who exists in time. In passion the existential subject is made infinite in imagination's eternity, and at the same time he is himself.

All essential knowledge concerns existence, or only that knowledge that relates to existence is essential, is essential knowledge. All knowledge that is not existential, that does not involve inward reflection, is really accidental knowledge, its degree and compass are essentially a matter of no importance. This essential knowledge that relates itself essentially to the existing individual is not to be equated with the above-mentioned abstract identity between thought and being. But it means that knowledge must relate itself to the knower, who is essentially an existing individual, and therefore all essential knowledge essentially relates itself to existence, to that which exists. But all ethical and all ethical-religious knowledge has this essential relationship to the existence of the knower.

In order to elucidate the difference between the objective way of reflection and the subjective way, I shall now show how subjective reflection makes its way back into inwardness. The highest point of inwardness in an existing person is passion, for passion corresponds to truth as a paradox, and the fact that the truth becomes a paradox is grounded in its relation to an existing individual. The one corresponds to the other. By forgetting that we are existing subjects, we lose passion and truth ceases to be a paradox, but the knowing subject begins to lose his humanity and becomes fantastic and the truth likewise becomes a fantastic object for this kind of knowledge.

When the question of truth is put forward in an objective manner, reflection is directed objectively to the truth as an object to which the knower is related. The reflection is not on the relationship but on whether he is related to the truth. If that which he is related to is the truth, the subject is in the truth. When the question of truth is put forward in a subjective manner, reflection is directed subjectively to the individual's relationship. If the relation's HOW is in truth, the individual is in truth, even if the WHAT to which he is related is not true.

We may illustrate this by examining the knowledge of God. Objectively the reflection is on whether the object is the true God; subjectively reflection is on whether the individual is related to a what in such a way that his relationship in truth is a God-relationship. On which side does the truth lie? Ah, let us not lean towards mediation and say, it is on neither side but in the mediation of both of them.

The existing individual who chooses the objective way enters upon the entire approximation process that is supposed to bring God into the picture. But this in all eternity cannot be done because God is Subject and therefore exists only for the subjective individual in inwardness. The existing individual who chooses the subjective way comprehends instantly the entire dialectical difficulty involved in having to use some time, perhaps a long time, in order to find God objectively. He comprehends this dialectical difficulty in all its pain because every moment without God is a moment lost—so important is the matter of being related to God. In this way God certainly becomes a postulate but not in the useless sense in which it is often taken. It becomes the only way in which an existing individual comes into a relation with God—when the dialectical contradiction brings passion to the point of despair and helps him embrace God with the category of despair (faith). Now the postulate is far from being arbitrary or optional. It becomes a life-saving necessity, so that it is no longer simply a postulate, but rather the individual's postulation of the existence of God is a necessity.

Now the problem is to calculate on which side there is the most truth: *either* the side of one who seeks the true God objectively and pursues the approximate truth of the God-idea *or* the side of one who is driven by infinite concern for his relationship to God. No one who has not been corrupted by science can have any doubt in the matter.

If one who lives in a Christian culture goes up to God's house, the house of the true God, with a true conception of God, with knowledge of God and prays—but prays in a false spirit; and one who lives in an idolatrous land prays with the total passion of the infinite, although his eyes rest on the image of an idol; where is there most truth? The one prays in truth to God, although he worships an idol. The other prays in untruth to the true God and therefore really worships an idol.

When a person objectively inquires about the problem of immortality and another person embraces it as an uncertainty with infinite passion, where is there most truth, and who really has the greater certainty? The one has entered into an inexhaustible approximation, for certainty of immortality lies precisely in the subjectivity of the individual. The other is immortal and fights against his uncertainty.

Let us consider Socrates. Today everyone is playing with some proof or other. Some have many, some fewer. But Socrates! He put the question objectively in a hypothetical manner: "*if* there is immortality." Compared to the modern philosopher with three proofs for immortality, should we consider Socrates a doubter? Not at all. On this little *if* he risks his entire life, he dares to face death, and he has directed his life with infinite passion so that the *if* is confirmed—*if* there is immortality. Is there any better proof for life after death? But those who have the three proofs do not at all pattern their lives in conformity with the idea. If there is an immortality, it must feel disgust over their lackadaisical manner of life. Can any better refutation be given of the three proofs? These crumbs of uncertainty helped Socrates because they hastened the process along, inciting the passions. The three proofs that others have are of no help at all because they are dead to the spirit, and the fact that they need three proofs proves that they are spiritually dead. The

Socratic ignorance that Socrates held fast with the entire passion of his inwardness was an expression of the idea that eternal truth is related to an existing individual, and that this will be in the form of a paradox as long as he exists; and yet it is just possible that there is more truth in Socratic ignorance than is contained in the "objective truth" of the philosophical systems, which flirts with the spirit of the times and cuddles up to associate professors.

The objective accent falls on *what* is said; the subjective accent falls on *how* it is said. This distinction is valid even for aesthetics and shows itself in the notion that what may be objectively true may in the mouth of certain people become false. This distinction is illustrated by the saying that the difference between the older days and our day is that in the old days only a few knew the truth while in ours all know it, except that the inwardness towards it is in inverse proportion to the scope of its possession. Aesthetically the contradiction that the truth becomes error in certain mouths is best understood comically. In the ethical-religious domain the accent is again on the *how*. But this is not to be understood as referring to decorum, modulation, delivery, and so on, but to the individual's relationship to the proposition, the way he relates himself to it. Objectively it is a question simply about the content of the proposition, but subjectively it is a question of inwardness. At its maximum this inward *how* is the passion of infinity and the passion of the infinite is itself the truth. But since the passion of the infinite is exactly subjectivity, subjectivity is the truth. Objectively there is no infinite decision or commitment, and so it is objectively correct to annul the difference between good and evil as well as the law of noncontradiction and the difference between truth and untruth. Only in subjectivity is there decision and commitment, so that to seek this in objectivity is to be in error. It is the passion of infinity that brings forth decisiveness, not its content, for its content is precisely itself. In this manner the subjective *how* and subjectivity are the truth.

But the *how* that is subjectively emphasized because the subject is an existing individual is also subject to a temporal dialectic. In passion's decisive moment, where the road swings off from the way to objective knowledge, it appears that the infinite decision is ready to be made. But in that moment the existing individual finds himself in time, and the subjective *how* becomes transformed into a striving, a striving that is motivated by and is repeatedly experienced in the decisive passion of the infinite. But this is still a striving.

When subjectivity is truth, subjectivity's definition must include an expression for an opposition to objectivity, a reminder of the fork in the road, and this expression must also convey the tension of inwardness. Here is such a definition of truth: *the objective uncertainty, held fast in an appropriation process of the most passionate inwardness, is the truth*, the highest truth available for an *existing* person. There where the way swings off (and where that is cannot be discovered objectively but only subjectively), at that place objective knowledge is annulled. Objectively speaking he has only uncertainty, but precisely there the infinite passion of inwardness is intensified, and truth is precisely the adventure to choose objective uncertainty with the passion of inwardness.

When I consider nature in order to discover God, I do indeed see his omnipotence and wisdom, but I see much more that disturbs me. The result of all this is objective uncertainty, but precisely here is the place for inwardness because inwardness apprehends the objective uncertainty with the entire passion of infinity. In the case of mathematical statements objectivity is already given, but because of the nature of mathematics, the truth is existentially indifferent.

Now the above definition of truth is an equivalent description of faith. Without risk there is no faith. Faith is precisely the contradiction between the infinite passion of inwardness and objective uncertainty. If I can grasp God objectively, I do not believe, but because I cannot know God objectively, I must have faith, and if I will preserve myself in faith, I must constantly be determined to hold fast to the objective uncertainty, so as to remain out upon the ocean's deep, over seventy thousand fathoms of water, and still believe.

In the sentence 'subjectivity, inwardness is truth,' we see the essence of Socratic wisdom, whose immortal service is exactly to have recognized the essential meaning of existence, that the knower is an *existing* subject, and for this reason in his ignorance Socrates enjoyed the highest relationship to truth within the paganism. This is a truth that speculative philosophy unhappily again and again forgets: that the knower is an existing subject. It is difficult enough to recognize this fact in our objective age, long after the genius of Socrates.

When subjectivity, inwardness, is the truth, the truth becomes objectively determined as a paradox, and that it is paradoxical is made clear by the fact that subjectivity is truth, for it repels objectivity, and the expression for the objective repulsion is the intensity and measure of inwardness. The paradox is the objective uncertainty, which is the expression for the passion of inwardness, which is precisely the truth. This is the Socratic principle. The eternal, essential truth, that is, that which relates itself essentially to the individual because it concerns his existence (all other knowledge is, Socratically speaking, accidental, its degree and scope being indifferent), is a paradox. Nevertheless, the eternal truth is not essentially in itself paradoxical, but it becomes so by relating itself to an existing individual. Socratic ignorance is the expression of this objective uncertainty, the inwardness of the existential subject is the truth. To anticipate what I will develop later, Socratic ignorance is an analogy to the category of the absurd, only that there is still less objective certainty in the absurd, and therefore infinitely greater tension in its inwardness. The Socratic inwardness that involves existence is an analogy to faith, except that this inwardness is repulsed not by ignorance but by the absurd, which is infinitely deeper. Socratically the eternal, essential truth is by no means paradoxical in itself, but only by virtue of its relation to an existing individual.

Subjectivity, inwardness, is the truth. Is there a still more inward expression for this? Yes, there is. If subjectivity is seen as the truth, we may posit the opposite principle: that subjectivity is untruth, error. Socratically speaking, subjectivity is untruth if it fails to understand that subjectivity is truth and desires to understand itself objectively. But now we are presupposing that subjectivity in becoming the truth has a difficulty to overcome in as much as it is in untruth. So we must work backwards, back to inwardness. Socratically, the way back to the truth takes place through recollection, supposing that we have memories of that truth deep within us.

Let us call this untruth of the individual 'sin.' Seen from eternity the individual cannot be in sin, nor can he be eternally presupposed as having been in sin. So it must be that he becomes a sinner by coming into existence (for the beginning point is that subjectivity is untruth). He is not born as a sinner in the sense that he is sinful before he is born, but he is born in sin and as a sinner. We shall call this state *original sin.* But if existence has acquired such power over him, he is impotent to make his way back to eternity through the use of his memory (supposing that there is truth in the Platonic idea that we may discover truth through recollection). If it was already paradoxical that the eternal truth related itself to an existing individual, now it is absolutely paradoxical that it relates itself to such an individual. But the more difficult it is for him through memory to transcend existence, the more inwardness must increase in intense passion, and when it is made impossible for him, when he is held so fast in existence that the back door of recollection is forever closed to him through sin, then his inwardness will be the deepest possible.

Subjectivity is truth. Through this relationship between the eternal truth and the existing individual the paradox comes into existence. Let us now go further and suppose that the eternal truth is essentially a paradox. How does this paradox come into existence? By juxtaposing the eternal, essential truth with temporal existence. When we set them together within the truth itself, the truth becomes paradoxical. The eternal truth has come into time. This is the paradox. If the subject is hindered by sin from making his way back to eternity by looking inward through recollection, he need not trouble himself about this, for now the eternal essential truth is no longer behind him, but it is in front of him, through its being in existence or having existed, so that if the individual does not *existentially* get hold of the truth, he will never get hold of it.

It is impossible to accentuate existence more than this. When the eternal truth is related to an existing individual, truth becomes a paradox. The paradox repels the individual because of the objective uncertainty and ignorance towards inwardness. But since this paradox in itself is not paradoxical, it does not push the spirit far enough. For without risk there is no faith, and the greater the risk the greater the faith, and the more objective reliability, the less inwardness (for inwardness is precisely subjectivity). Indeed, the less objective reliability, the deeper becomes the possible inwardness. When the paradox is in itself paradoxical, it repels the individual by the power of the absurd, and the corresponding passion, which is produced in the process, is faith. But subjectivity, inwardness, is truth, for otherwise we have forgotten the Socratic contribution; but there is no more striking expression for inwardness than when the retreat from existence through recollection back to eternity is made impossible; and when the truth as paradox encounters the individual who is caught in the vice-grip of sin's anxiety and suffering, but who is also aware of the tremendous risk involved in faith—when he nevertheless makes the leap of faith—this is subjectivity at its height.

When Socrates believed in the existence of God, he held fast to an objective uncertainty in passionate inwardness, and in that contradiction, in that risk faith came into being. Now it is different. Instead of the objective uncertainty, there is objective certainty about the object—certainty that it is absurd, and it is, again, faith that holds fast to that object in passionate inwardness. Compared with the gravity of the absurd, Socratic ignorance is a joke, and compared with the strenuosity of faith in believing the paradox, Socratic existential inwardness is a Greek life of leisure.

What is the absurd? The absurd is that the eternal truth has entered time, that God has entered existence, has been born, has grown, and so on, has become precisely like any other human being, quite indistinguishable from other humans. The absurd is precisely by its objective repulsion the measure of the inwardness of faith. Suppose there is a man who desires to have faith. Let the comedy begin. He desires to obtain faith with the help of objective investigation and what the approximation process of evidential inquiry yields. What happens? With the help of the increment of evidence the absurd is transformed to something else; it becomes probable, it becomes more probable still, it becomes

perhaps highly and overwhelmingly probable. Now that there is respectable evidence for the content of his faith, he is ready to believe it, and he prides himself that his faith is not like that of the shoemaker, the tailor, and the simple folk, but comes after a long investigation. Now he prepares himself to believe it. Any proposition that is almost probable, reasonably probable, highly and overwhelmingly probable, is something that is almost known and as good as known, highly and overwhelmingly known—but it is not believed, not through faith; for the absurd is precisely faith's object and the only positive attitude possible in relation to it is faith and not knowledge.

Christianity has declared itself to be the eternal that has entered time, that has proclaimed itself as the *paradox* and demands faith's inwardness in relation to that which is a scandal to the Jews and folly to the Greeks—and as absurd to the understanding. It is impossible to say this more strongly than by saying: subjectivity is truth, and objectivity is repelled by it—by virtue of the absurd.

Subjectivity culminates in passion. Christianity is the paradox; paradox and passion belong together as a perfect match, and the paradox is perfectly suited to one whose situation is to be in the extremity of existence. Indeed, there never has been found in all the world two lovers more suited to each other than passion and paradox, and the strife between them is a lover's quarrel, when they argue about which one first aroused the other's passion. And so it is here. The existing individual by means of the paradox has come to the extremity of existence. And what is more wonderful for lovers than to be granted a long time together with each other without anything disturbing their relation except that which makes it more inwardly passionate? And this is what is granted to the unspeculative understanding between the passion and paradox, for they will dwell harmoniously together in time and be changed first in eternity.

But the speculative philosopher views things altogether differently. He believes but only to a certain degree. He puts his hand to the plow but quickly looks about for something to know. From a Christian perspective it is hard to see how he could reach the highest good in this manner.

VII.C.2 Kierkegaard's Arguments Against Objective Reasoning in Religion

ROBERT MERRIHEW ADAMS

In our second reading, Robert Merrihew Adams (1937–   ), professor of philosophy at Yale University, examines three of Kierkegaard's arguments against objective reason in religion (found in our first reading). Although he appreciates the depth of Kierkegaard's insight, he argues that the sort of fideism embraced by Kierkegaard has several problems. The three arguments that Adams identifies are called the approximation argument, the postponement argument, and the passion argument.

It is sometimes held that there is something in the nature of religious faith itself that renders it useless or undesirable to reason objectively in support of such faith, even if the reasoning should happen to have considerable plausibility. Søren Kierkegaard's *Concluding Unscientific Postscript* is probably the document most commonly cited as representative of this view. In the present essay I shall discuss three arguments for the view. I call them the Approximation Argument, the Postponement Argument, and the Passion Argument; and I suggest they can all be found in the *Postscript*. I shall try to show that the Approximation Argument is a bad argument. The other two will not be so easily disposed of, however. I believe they show that Kierkegaard's conclusion, or something like it, does indeed follow from a certain conception of religiousness—a conception which has some appeal, although for reasons which I shall briefly suggest, I am not prepared to accept it.

Kierkegaard uses the word "objective" and its cognates in several senses, most of which need not concern us here. We are interested in the sense in which he uses it when he says, "it is precisely a

misunderstanding to seek an objective assurance," and when he speaks of "an objective uncertainty held fast in the appropriation-process of the most passionate inwardness" (pp. 41, 182).[1] Let us say that a piece of reasoning, R, is *objective reasoning* just in case every (or almost every) intelligent, fair-minded, and sufficiently informed person would regard R as showing or tending to show (in the circumstances in which R is used, and to the extent claimed in R) that R's conclusion is true or probably true. Uses of "objective" and "objectively" in other contexts can be understood from their relation to this one; for example, an objective uncertainty is a proposition which cannot be shown by objective reasoning to be certainly true.

I. The Approximation Argument

"Is it possible to base an eternal happiness upon historical knowledge?" is one of the central questions in the *Postscript*, and in the *Philosophical Fragments* to which it is a "postscript." Part of Kierkegaard's answer to the question is that it is not possible to base an eternal happiness on objective reasoning about historical facts.

> For nothing is more readily evident than that the greatest attainable certainty with respect to anything historical is merely an *approximation*. And an approximation, when viewed as a basis for an eternal happiness, is wholly inadequate, since the incommensurability makes a result impossible. [p. 25]

Kierkegaard maintains that it is possible, however, to base an eternal happiness on a belief in historical facts that is independent of objective evidence for them, and that that is what one must do in order to be a Christian. This is the Approximation Argument for the proposition that Christian faith cannot be based on objective reasoning. (It is assumed that

Reprinted from *The Monist*, vol. 60, no. 2 (1977), by permission of the author and The Hegeler Institute, La Salle, Ill. Footnotes edited.

some belief about historical facts is an essential part of Christian faith, so that if religious faith cannot be based on objective historical reasoning, then Christian faith cannot be based on objective reasoning at all.) Let us examine the argument in detail.

Its first premise is Kierkegaard's claim that "the greatest attainable certainty with respect to anything historical is merely an approximation." I take him to mean that historical evidence, objectively considered, never completely excludes the possibility of error. "It goes without saying," he claims, "that it is impossible in the case of historical problems to reach an objective decision so certain that no doubt could disturb it" (p. 41). For Kierkegaard's purposes it does not matter how small the possibility of error is, so long as it is finitely small (that is, so long as it is not literally infinitesimal). He insists (p. 31) that his Approximation Argument makes no appeal to the supposition that the objective evidence for Christian historical beliefs is weaker than the objective evidence for any other historical belief. The argument turns on a claim about *all* historical evidence. The probability of error in our belief that there was an American Civil War in the nineteenth century, for instance, might be as small as 10(1/2,000,000); that would be a large enough chance of error for Kierkegaard's argument.

It might be disputed, but let us assume for the sake of argument that there is some such finitely small probability of error in the objective grounds for all historical beliefs, as Kierkegaard held. This need not keep us from saying that we "know" and it is "certain," that there was an American Civil War. For such an absurdly small possibility of error is as good as no possibility of error at all, "for all practical intents and purposes," as we might say. Such a possibility of error is too small to be worth worrying about.

But would it be too small to be worth worrying about if we had an *infinite* passionate interest in the question about the Civil War? If we have an infinite passionate interest in something, there is no limit to how important it is to us. (The nature of such an interest will be discussed more fully in section 3 below.) Kierkegaard maintains that in relation to an infinite passionate interest *no* possibility of error is too small to be worth worrying about. "In relation

to an eternal happiness, and an infinite passionate interest in its behalf (in which latter alone the former can exist), an iota is of importance, of infinite importance . . . " (p. 28). This is the basis for the second premise of the Approximation Argument, which is Kierkegaard's claim that "an approximation, when viewed as a basis for an eternal happiness, is wholly inadequate" (p. 25). "An approximation is essentially incommensurable with an infinite personal interest in an eternal happiness" (p. 26).

At this point in the argument it is important to have some understanding of Kierkegaard's conception of faith, and the way in which he thinks faith excludes doubt. Faith must be decisive; in fact it seems to consist in a sort of decision-making. "The conclusion of belief is not so much a conclusion as a resolution, and it is for this reason that belief excludes doubt." The decision of faith is a decision to disregard the possibility of error—to act on what is believed, without hedging one's bets to take account of any possibility of error.

To disregard the possibility of error is not to be unaware of it, or fail to consider it, or lack anxiety about it. Kierkegaard insists that the believer must be keenly *aware* of the risk of error. "If I wish to preserve myself in faith I must constantly be intent upon holding fast the objective uncertainty, so as to remain out upon the deep, over seventy thousand fathoms of water, still preserving my faith" (p. 182).

For Kierkegaard, then, to ask whether faith in a historical fact can be based on objective reasoning is to ask whether objective reasoning can justify one in disregarding the possibility of error which (he thinks) historical evidence always leaves. Here another aspect of Kierkegaard's conception of faith plays its part in the argument. He thinks that in all genuine religious faith the believer is *infinitely* interested in the object of his faith. And he thinks it follows that objective reasoning cannot justify him in disregarding *any* possibility of error about the object of faith, and therefore cannot lead him all the way to religious faith where a historical fact is concerned. The farthest it could lead him is to the conclusion that *if* he had only a certain finite (though very great) interest in the matter, the possibility of error would be too small to be worth worrying about and he would be justified in disregarding it. But faith disregards a possibility of error that *is* worth worrying about, since an infinite interest is involved. Thus faith requires a "leap" beyond the evidence, a leap that cannot be justified by objective reasoning (cf. p. 90).

There is something right in what Kierkegaard is saying here, but his Approximation Argument is a bad argument. He is right in holding that grounds of doubt which may be insignificant for most practical purposes can be extremely troubling for the intensity of a religious concern, and that it may require great decisiveness, or something like courage, to overcome them religiously. But he is mistaken in holding that objective reasoning could not justify one in disregarding any possibility of error about something in which one is infinitely interested.

The mistake, I believe, lies in his overlooking the fact that there are at least two different reasons one might have for disregarding a possibility of error. The first is that the possibility is too small to be worth worrying about. The second is that the risk of not disregarding the possibility of error would be greater than the risk of disregarding it. Of these two reasons only the first is ruled out by the infinite passionate interest.

I will illustrate this point with two examples, one secular and one religious. A certain woman has a very great (though not infinite) interest in her husband's love for her. She rightly judges that the objective evidence available to her renders it 99.9 percent probable that he loves her truly. The intensity of her interest is sufficient to cause her some *anxiety* over the remaining 1/1,000 chance that he loves her not; for her this chance is not too small to be worth worrying about. (Kierkegaard uses a similar example to support his Approximation Argument; see p. 511.) But she (very reasonably) wants to *disregard* the risk of error, in the sense of not hedging her bets, if he does love her. This desire is at least as strong as her desire not to be deceived if he does not love her. Objective reasoning should therefore suffice to bring her to the conclusion that she ought to disregard the risk of error, since by not disregarding it she would run 999 times as great risk of frustrating one of these desires.

Or suppose you are trying to base your eternal happiness on your relation to Jesus, and therefore have an infinite passionate interest in the question whether he declared Peter and his episcopal successors to be infallible in matters of religious doctrine. You want to be committed to whichever is the true belief on this question, disregarding any possibility of error in it. And suppose, just for the sake of argument, that objective historical evidence renders it 99 percent probable that Jesus did declare Peter and his successors to be infallible—or 99 percent probable that he did not—for our present discussion it does not matter which. The one percent chance of error is enough to make you *anxious*, in view of your infinite interest. But objective reasoning leads to the conclusion that you ought to commit yourself to the more probable opinion, *disregarding* the risk of error, if your strongest desire in the matter is to be so committed to the true opinion. For the only other way to satisfy this desire would be to commit yourself to the less probable opinion, disregarding the risk of error in it. The first way will be successful if and only if the more probable opinion is true, and the second way if and only if the less probable opinion is true. Surely it is prudent to do what gives you a 99 percent chance of satisfying your strong desire, in preference to what gives you only a 1 percent chance of satisfying it.

In this argument your strong desire to be committed to the true opinion is presupposed. The reasonableness of this desire may depend on a belief for which no probability can be established by purely historical reasoning, such as the belief that Jesus is God. But any difficulties arising from this point are distinct from those urged in the Approximation Argument, which itself presupposes the infinite passionate interest in the historical question.

There is some resemblance between my arguments in these examples and Pascal's famous Wager argument. But whereas Pascal's argument turns on weighing an infinite interest against a finite one, mine turn on weighing a large chance of success against a small one. An argument closer to Pascal's will be discussed in section 4 below.

The reader may well have noticed in the foregoing discussion some unclarity about what sort of justification is being demanded and given for religious beliefs about historical facts. There are at least two different types of question about a proposition which I might try to settle by objective reasoning: (1) Is it probable that the proposition is true? (2) In view of the evidence which I have for and against the proposition, and my interest in the matter, is it prudent for me to have faith in the truth of the proposition, disregarding the possibility of error? Correspondingly, we may distinguish two ways in which a belief can be *based on* objective reasoning. The proposition believed may be the conclusion of a piece of objective reasoning, and accepted because it is that. We may say that such a belief is *objectively probable*. Or one might hold a belief or maintain a religious faith because of a piece of objective reasoning whose conclusion is that it would be prudent, morally right, or otherwise desirable for one to hold that belief or faith. In this latter case let us say that the belief is *objectively advantageous*. It is clear that historical beliefs can be objectively probable; and in the Approximation Argument, Kierkegaard does not deny Christian historical beliefs can be objectively probable. His thesis is, in effect, that in view of an infinite passionate interest in their subject matter, they cannot be objectively advantageous, and therefore cannot be fully justified objectively even if they are objectively probable. It is this thesis that I have attempted to refute. I have not been discussing the question whether Christian historical beliefs are objectively probable.

2. The Postponement Argument

The trouble with objective historical reasoning, according to the Approximation Argument, is that it cannot yield complete certainty. But that is not Kierkegaard's only complaint against it as a basis for religious faith. He also objects that objective historical inquiry is never completely finished, so that one who seeks to base his faith on it postpones his religious commitment forever. In the process of

historical research "new difficulties arise and are overcome, and new difficulties again arise. Each generation inherits from its predecessor the illusion that the method is quite impeccable, but the learned scholars have not yet succeeded . . . and so forth. . . . The infinite personal passionate interest of the subject . . . vanishes more and more, because the decision is postponed, and postponed as following directly upon the result of the learned inquiry" (p. 28). As soon as we take "an historical document" as "our standard for the determination of Christian truth," we are "involved in a parenthesis whose conclusion is everlastingly prospective" (p. 28)— that is, we are involved in a religious digression which keeps religious commitment forever in the future.

Kierkegaard has such fears about allowing religious faith to rest on *any* empirical reasoning. The danger of postponement of commitment arises not only from the uncertainties of historical scholarship, but also in connection with the design argument for God's existence. In the *Philosophical Fragments* Kierkegaard notes some objections to the attempt to prove God's existence from evidence of "the wisdom in nature, the goodness, the wisdom in the governance of the world," and then says, "even if I began I would never finish, and would in addition have to live constantly in suspense, lest something so terrible should suddenly happen that my bit of proof would be demolished." What we have before us is a quite general sort of objection to the treatment of religious beliefs as empirically testable. On this point many analytical philosophers seem to agree with Kierkegaard. Much discussion in recent analytical philosophy of religion has proceeded from the supposition that religious beliefs are not empirically testable. I think it is far from obvious that that supposition is correct; and it is interesting to consider arguments that may be advanced to support it.

Kierkegaard's statements suggest an argument that I call the Postponement Argument. Its first premise is that one cannot have an authentic religious faith without being totally committed to it. In order to be totally committed to a belief, in the relevant sense, one must be determined not to abandon the belief under any circumstances that one recognizes as epistemically possible.

The second premise is that one cannot yet be totally committed to any belief which one bases on an inquiry in which one recognizes any possibility of a future need to revise the results. Total commitment to any belief so based will necessarily be postponed. I believe that this premise, suitably interpreted, is true. Consider the position of someone who regards himself as committed to a belief on the basis of objective evidence, but who recognizes some possibility that future discoveries will destroy the objective justification of the belief. We must ask how he is disposed to react in the event, however unlikely, that the objective basis of his belief is overthrown. Is he prepared to abandon the belief in that event? If so, he is not totally committed to the belief in the relevant sense. But if he is determined to cling to his belief even if its objective justification is taken away, then he is not basing the belief on the objective justification—or at least he is not basing it solely on the justification.

The conclusion to be drawn from these two premises is that authentic religious faith cannot be based on an inquiry in which one recognizes any possibility of a future need to revise the results. We ought to note that this conclusion embodies two important restrictions on the scope of the argument.

In the first place, we are not given an argument that authentic religious faith cannot *have* an objective justification that is subject to possible future revision. What we are given is an argument that the authentic believer's holding of his religious belief cannot *depend* entirely on such a justification.

In the second place, this conclusion applies only to those who *recognize* some epistemic possibility that the objective results which appear to support their belief may be overturned. I think it would be unreasonable to require, as part of total commitment, a determination with regard to one's response to circumstances that one does not recognize as possible at all. It may be, however, that one does not recognize such a possibility when one ought to.

Kierkegaard needs one further premise in order to arrive at the conclusion that authentic religious faith cannot without error be based on any objective empirical reasoning. This third premise is that in every objective empirical inquiry there is always, objectively considered, some epistemic possibility that the results of the inquiry will need to be revised in view of new evidence or new reasoning. I believe Kierkegaard makes this assumption; he certainly makes it with regard to historical inquiry. From this premise it follows that one is in error if in any objective empirical inquiry one does not recognize any possibility of a future need to revise the results. But if one does recognize such a possibility, then according to the conclusion already reached in the Postponement Argument, one cannot base an authentic religious faith on the inquiry.

Some philosophers might attack the third premise of this argument; and certainly it is controversial. But I am more inclined to criticize the first premise. There is undoubtedly something plausible about the claim that authentic religious faith must involve a commitment so complete that the believer is resolved not to abandon his belief under any circumstances that he regards as epistemically possible. If you are willing to abandon your ostensibly religious beliefs for the sake of objective inquiry, mightn't we justly say that objective inquiry is your real religion, the thing to which you are most deeply committed?

There is also something plausible to be said on the other side, however. It has commonly been thought to be an important part of religious ethics that one ought to be humble, teachable, open to correction, new inspiration, and growth of insight, even (and perhaps especially) in important religious beliefs. That view would have to be discarded if we were to concede to Kierkegaard that the heart of commitment in religion is an unconditional determination not to change in one's important religious beliefs. In fact I think there is something radically wrong with this conception of religious commitment. Faith ought not to be thought of as unconditional devotion to a belief. For in the first place the object of religious devotion is not a belief or attitude of one's own, but God. And in the second place it may be doubted that religious devotion to God can or should be completely unconditional. God's love for sinners is sometimes said to be completely unconditional, not being based on any excellence or merit of theirs. But religious devotion to God is generally thought to be based on His goodness and love. It is the part of the strong, not the weak, to love unconditionally. And in relation to God we are weak.

3. The Passion Argument

In Kierkegaard's statements of the Approximation Argument and the Postponement Argument it is assumed that a system of religious beliefs might be objectively probable. It is only for the sake of argument, however, that Kierkegaard allows this assumption. He really holds that religious faith, by its very nature, needs objective *im*probability. "Anything that is almost probable, or probable, or extremely and emphatically probable, is something [one] can almost know, or as good as know, or extremely and emphatically almost *know*—but it is impossible to *believe*" (p. 189). Nor will Kierkegaard countenance the suggestion that religion ought to go beyond belief to some almost-knowledge based on probability. "Faith is the highest passion in a man. There are perhaps many in every generation who do not even reach it, but no one gets further." It would be a betrayal of religion to try to go beyond faith. The suggestion that faith might be replaced by "probabilities and guarantees" is for the believer "a temptation to be resisted with all his strength" (p. 15). The attempt to establish religious beliefs on a foundation or objective probability is therefore no service to religion, but inimical to religion's true interests. The approximation to certainty which might be afforded by objective probability is rejected, not only for the reasons given in the Approximation Argument and the Postponement Argument, but also from a deeper motive, "since on the contrary it behooves us to get rid of introductory guarantees of security, proofs from consequences, and the whole mob of public pawnbrokers and guarantors, so as to permit the absurd to stand out in all its clarity—in order that the individual may believe if he wills it; I merely say that it must be strenuous in the highest degree so to believe" (p. 190).

As this last quotation indicates, Kierkegaard thinks that religious belief ought to be based on a strenuous exertion of the will—a passionate striving. His reasons for thinking that objective probability is religiously undesirable have to do with the place of passion in religion, and constitute what I call the Passion Argument. The first premise of the argument is that the most essential and the most valuable feature of religiousness is passion, indeed an infinite passion, a passion of the greatest possible intensity. The second premise is that an infinite passion requires objective improbability. And the conclusion therefore is that that which is most essential and most valuable in religiousness requires objective improbability.

My discussion of this argument will have three parts. (a) First I will try to clarify, very briefly, what it is that is supposed to be objectively improbable. (b) Then we will consider Kierkegaard's reasons for holding that infinite passion requires objective improbability. In so doing we will also gain a clearer understanding of what a Kierkegaardian infinite passion is. (c) Finally I will discuss the first premise of the argument—although issues will arise at that point which I do not pretend to be able to settle by argument.

(a) What are the beliefs whose improbability is needed by religious passion? Kierkegaard will hardly be satisfied with the improbability of just any one belief; it must surely be at least an important belief. On the other hand it would clearly be preposterous to suppose that every belief involved in Christianity must be objectively improbable. (Consider, for example, the belief that the man Jesus did indeed live.) I think that what is demanded in the Passion Argument is the objective improbability of at least one belief which must be true if the goal sought by the religious passion is to be attained.

(b) We can find in the *Postscript* suggestions of several reasons for thinking that an infinite passion needs objective improbability. The two that seem to me most interesting have to do with (i) the risks accepted and (ii) the costs paid in pursuance of a passionate interest.

(i) One reason that Kierkegaard has for valuing objective improbability is that it increases the *risk* attaching to the religious life, and risk is so essential for the expression of religious passion that "without risk there is no faith" (p. 182). About the nature of an eternal happiness, the goal of religious striving, Kierkegaard says "there is nothing to be said . . . except that it is the good which is attained by venturing everything absolutely" (p. 382).

> But what then does it mean to venture? A venture is the precise correlative of an uncertainty; when the certainty is there the venture becomes impossible. . . . If what I hope to gain by venturing is itself certain, I do not risk or venture, but make an exchange. . . . No, if I am in truth resolved to venture, in truth resolved to strive for the attainment of the highest good, the uncertainty must be there, and I must have room to move, so to speak. But the largest space I can obtain, where there is room for the most vehement gesture of the passion that embraces the infinite, is uncertainty of knowledge with respect to an eternal happiness, or the certain knowledge that the choice is in the finite sense a piece of madness: now there is room, now you can venture! [pp. 380–82]

How is it that objective improbability provides the largest space for the most vehement gesture of infinite passion? Consider two cases. (A) You plunge into a raging torrent to rescue from drowning someone you love, who is crying for help. (B) You plunge into a raging torrent in a desperate attempt to rescue someone you love, who appears to be unconscious and *may* already have drowned. In both cases you manifest a passionate interest in saving the person, risking your own life in order to do so. But I think Kierkegaard would say there is more passion in the second case than in the first. For in the second case you risk your life in what is, objectively considered, a smaller chance that you will be able to save your loved one. A greater passion is required for a more desperate attempt.

A similar assessment may be made of the following pair of cases. (A') You stake everything on your faith in the truth of Christianity, knowing that it is objectively 99 percent probable that Christianity is true. (B') You stake everything on your faith in the truth of Christianity, knowing that the truth of Christianity is, objectively, possible but so improbable that its probability is, say, as small as 10 (1/2,000,000). There is passion in both cases, but Kierkegaard will say that there is more passion in the second case than in the first. For to venture the

same stake (namely, everything) on a much smaller chance of success shows greater passion.

Acceptance of risk can thus be seen as a *measure* of the intensity of passion. I believe this provides us with one way of understanding what Kierkegaard means when he calls religious passion "infinite." An *infinite* passionate interest in x is an interest so strong that it leads one to make the greatest possible sacrifices in order to obtain x, on the smallest possible chance of success. The infinity of the passion is shown in that there is no sacrifice so great one will not make it, and no chance of success so small one will not act on it. A passion which is infinite in this sense requires, by its very nature, a situation of maximum risk for its expression.

It will doubtless be objected that this argument involves a misunderstanding of what a passionate interest is. Such an interest is a disposition. In order to have a great passionate interest it is not necessary actually to make a great sacrifice with a small chance of success; all that is necessary is to have such an intense interest that one *would* do so if an appropriate occasion should arise. It is therefore a mistake to say that there *is* more passion in case (B) than in case (A), or in (B') than in (A'). More passion is *shown* in (B) than in (A), and in (B') than in (A'); but an equal passion may exist in cases in which there is no occasion to show it.

This objection may well be correct as regards what we normally mean by "passionate interest." But that is not decisive for the argument. The crucial question is what part dispositions, possibly unactualized, ought to play in religious devotion. And here we must have a digression about the position of the *Postscript* on this question—a position that is complex at best and is not obviously consistent.

In the first place I do not think that Kierkegaard would be prepared to think of passion, or a passionate interest, as primarily a disposition that might remain unactualized. He seems to conceive of passion chiefly as an intensity in which one actually does and feels. "Passion is momentary" (p. 178), although capable of continual repetition. And what is momentarily in such a way that it must be repeated rather than protracted is presumably an occurrence rather than a disposition. It agrees with this conception of passion that Kierkegaard idealizes a life of "persistent striving," and says that the religious task is to "exercise" the God-relationship and to give "existential expression" to the religious choice (pp. 110, 364, 367).

All of this supports the view that what Kierkegaard means by "an infinite passionate interest" is a pattern of actual decision-making, in which one continually exercises and expresses one's religiousness by making the greatest possible sacrifices on the smallest possible chance of success. In order to actualize such a pattern of life one needs chances of success that are as small as possible. That is the room that is required for "the most vehement gesture" of infinite passion.

But on the other hand Kierkegaard does allow a dispositional element in the religious life, and even precisely in the making of the greatest possible sacrifices. We might suppose that if we are to make the greatest possible sacrifices in our religious devotion, we must do so by abandoning all worldly interests and devoting all of our time and attention to religion. That is what monasticism attempts to do, as Kierkegaard sees it; and (in the *Postscript*, at any rate) he rejects the attempt, contrary to what our argument to this point would have led us to expect of him. He holds that "resignation" (pp. 353, 367) or "renunciation" (pp. 362, 386) of *all* finite ends is precisely the first thing that religiousness requires; but he means a renunciation that is compatible with pursuing and enjoying finite ends (pp. 362–71). This renunciation is the practice of a sort of detachment; Kierkegaard uses the image of a dentist loosening the soft tissues around a tooth, while it is still in place in preparation for pulling it (p. 367). It is partly a matter of not treating finite things with a desperate seriousness, but with a certain coolness or humor, even while one pursues them (pp. 368, 370).

This coolness is not just a disposition. But the renunciation also has a dispositional aspect. "Now if for any individual an eternal happiness is his highest good, this will mean that all finite satisfactions are volitionally relegated to the status of what may have to be renounced in favor of an eternal happiness" (p. 350). The volitional relegation is not a disposition but an act of choice. The object of this

choice, however, appears to be a dispositional state—the state of being such that one *would* forgo any finite satisfaction *if* it were religiously necessary or advantageous to do so.

It seems clear that Kierkegaard, in the *Postscript*, is willing to admit a dispositional element at one point in the religious venture, but not at another. It is enough in most cases, he thinks, if one is *prepared* to cease for the sake of religion from pursuing some finite end; but it is not enough that one *would* hold to one's belief in the face of objective improbability. The belief must actually be improbable, although the pursuit of the finite need not actually cease. What is not clear is a reason for this disparity. The following hypothesis, admittedly somewhat speculative as interpretation of the text, is the best explanation I can offer.

The admission of a dispositional element in the religion renunciation of the finite is something to which Kierkegaard seems to be driven by the view that there is no alternative to it except idolatry. For suppose one actually ceases from all worldly pursuits and enters a monastery. In the monastery one would pursue a number of particular ends (such as getting up in the middle of the night to say the offices) which, although religious in a way ("churchy," one might say), are still finite. The absolute *telos* or end of religion is no more to be identified with them than with the ends pursued by an alderman (pp. 362–71). To pretend otherwise would be to make an idolatrous identification of the absolute end with some finite end. An existing person cannot have sacrificed everything by actually having ceased from pursuing *all* finite ends. For as long as he lives and acts he is pursuing some finite end. Therefore his renouncing *everything* finite must be at least partly dispositional.

Kierkegaard does not seem happy with this position. He regards it as of the utmost importance that the religious passion should come to expression. The problem of finding an adequate expression for a passion for an infinite end, in the face of the fact that in every concrete action one will be pursuing some finite end, is treated in the *Postscript* as the central problem of religion (see especially pp. 386–468). If the sacrifice of everything finite must remain largely dispositional, then perhaps it is all the more important to Kierkegaard that the smallness of the chance for which it is sacrificed should be fully actual, so that the infinity of the religious passion may be measured by an actuality in at least one aspect of the religious venture.

(ii) According to Kierkegaard, as I have argued, the intensity of a passion is measured in part by the smallness of the chances of success that one acts on. It can also be measured in part by its *costliness*—that is, by how much one gives up or suffers in acting on those chances. This second measure can also be made the basis of an argument for the claim that an infinite passion requires objective improbability. For the objective improbability of a religious belief, if recognized, increases the costliness of holding it. The risk involved in staking everything on an objectively improbable belief gives rise to an anxiety and mental suffering whose acceptance is itself a sacrifice. It seems to follow that if one is not staking everything on a belief one sees to be objectively improbable, one's passion is not infinite in Kierkegaard's sense, since one's sacrifice could be greater if one did adhere to an improbable belief.

Kierkegaard uses an argument similar to this. For God to give us objective knowledge of Himself, eliminating paradox from it, would be "to lower the price of the God-relationship."

> And even if God could be imagined willing, no man with passion in his heart could desire it. To a maiden genuinely in love it could never occur that she had bought her happiness too dear, but rather that she had not bought it dear enough. And just as the passion of the infinite was itself the truth, so in the case of the highest value it holds true that the price is the value, that a low price means a poor value. . . . (p. 207)

Kierkegaard here appears to hold, first, that an increase in the objective probability of religious belief would reduce its costliness, and second, that the value of a religious life is measured by its cost. I take it his reason for the second of these claims is that passion is the most valuable thing in a religious life and passion is measured by its cost. If we grant Kierkegaard the requisite conception of an infinite passion, we seem once again to have a plausible argument for the view that objective improbability is required for such a passion.

(c) We must therefore consider whether infinite passion, as Kierkegaard conceives of it, ought to be part of the religious ideal of life. Such a passion is a striving, or pattern of decision-making, in which, with the greatest possible intensity of feeling, one continually makes the greatest possible sacrifices on the smallest possible chance of success. This seems to me an impossible ideal. I doubt that any human being could have a passion of this sort, because I doubt that one could make a sacrifice so great that a greater could not be made, or have a (nonzero) chance of success so small that a smaller could not be had.

But even if Kierkegaard's ideal is impossible, one might want to try to approximate it. Intensity of passion might still be measured by the greatness of sacrifices made and the smallness of chances of success acted on, even if we cannot hope for a greatest possible or a smallest possible here. And it could be claimed that the most essential and valuable thing in religiousness is a passion that is very intense (though it cannot be infinite) by this standard—the more intense the better. This claim will not support an argument that objective improbability is absolutely required for religious passion. For a passion could presumably be very intense, involving great sacrifices and risks of some other worth, without an objectively improbable belief. But it could still be argued that objectively improbable religious beliefs enhance the value of the religious life by increasing its sacrifices and diminishing its chances of success, whereas objective probability detracts from the value of religious passion by diminishing its intensity.

The most crucial question about the Passion Argument, then, is whether maximization of sacrifice and risk are so valuable in religion as to make objective improbability a desirable characteristic of religious beliefs. Certainly much religious thought and feeling places a very high value on sacrifice and on passionate intensity. But the doctrine that it is desirable to increase without limit or to the highest possible degree (if there is one) the cost and risk of a religious life is less plausible (to say the least) than the view that *some* degree of cost and risk may add to the value of a religious life. The former doctrine would set the religious interest at enmity with all other interests, or at least with the best of them. Kierkegaard is surely right in thinking that it would be impossible to live without pursuing some finite ends. But even so it would be possible to exchange the pursuit of better finite ends for the pursuit of worse ones—for example, by exchanging the pursuit of truth, beauty, and satisfying personal relationships for the self-flagellating pursuit of pain. And a way of life would be the costlier for requiring such an exchange. Kierkegaard does not, in the *Postscript*, demand it. But the presuppositions of his Passion Argument seems to imply that such a sacrifice would be religiously desirable. Such a conception of religion is demonic. In a tolerable religious ethics some way must be found to conceive of the religious interest as inclusive rather than exclusive of the best of other interests—including, I think, the interest in having well-grounded beliefs.

4. Pascal's Wager and Kierkegaard's Leap

Ironically, Kierkegaard's views about religious passion suggest a way in which his religious beliefs could be based on objective reasoning—not on reasoning which would show them to be objectively probable, but on reasoning which shows them to be objectively advantageous. Consider the situation of a person whom Kierkegaard would regard as a genuine Christian believer. What would such a person want most of all? He would want above all else to attain the truth through Christianity. That is, he would desire both that Christianity be true and that he himself be related to it as a genuine believer. He would desire that state of affairs (which we may call *S*) so ardently that he would be willing to sacrifice everything else to obtain it, given only the smallest possible chance of success.

We can therefore construct the following argument, which has an obvious analogy to Pascal's Wager. Let us assume that there is, objectively, some chance, however small, that Christianity is

true. This is an assumption which Kierkegaard accepts (p. 31), and I think it is plausible. There are two possibilities, then: either Christianity is true, or it is false. (Others might object to so stark a disjunction, but Kierkegaard will not.) If Christianity is false it is impossible for anyone to obtain *S*, since *S* includes the truth of Christianity. It is only if Christianity is true that anything one does will help one or hinder one in obtaining *S*. And if Christianity is true, one will obtain *S* just in case one becomes a genuine Christian believer. It seems obvious that one would increase one's chances of becoming a genuine Christian believer by becoming one now (if one can), even if the truth of Christian beliefs is now objectively uncertain or improbable. Hence it would seem to be advantageous for anyone who can to become a genuine Christian believer now, if he wants *S* so much that he would be willing to sacrifice everything else for the smallest possible chance of obtaining *S*. Indeed I believe that the argument I have given for this conclusion is a piece of objective reasoning, and that Christian belief is therefore *objectively* advantageous for anyone who wants *S* as much as a Kierkegaardian genuine Christian must want it.

Of course this argument does not tend at all to show that it is objectively probable that Christianity is true. It only gives a practical, prudential reason for believing, to someone who has a certain desire. Nor does the argument do anything to prove that such an absolutely overriding desire for *S* is reasonable. It does show, however, that just as Kierkegaard's position has more logical structure than one might at first think, it is more difficult than he probably realized for him to get away entirely from objective justification.

Note

1. Søren Kierkegaard, *Concluding Unscientific Postscript*, translated by David F. Swenson; introduction, notes, and completion of translation by Walter Lowrie (Princeton, N.J.: Princeton University Press, 1941). Page references in parentheses in the body of the present paper are to this work.

VII.C.3 A Lecture on Religious Belief

LUDWIG WITTGENSTEIN

In our third reading, we turn to the leading type of fideism in contemporary philosophy of religion. Ludwig Wittgenstein (1889–1951), an Austrian-British philosopher who taught at Cambridge University, may be the most influential philosopher of the twentieth century. In this selection from his "Lectures on Religious Belief" he argues that there is something sui generis or special about the very linguistic framework of believers, so that the concepts they use cannot be adequately grasped by outsiders. One has to share in a form of life in order to understand the way the various concepts function in that language game. Wittgenstein ridicules one Father O'Hara for giving the impression that there is a nonperspectival, impartial way of assessing the truth value of religious assertions. Such a view, Wittgenstein believes, is absurd.

An Austrian general said to someone: "I shall think of you after my death, if that should be possible." We can imagine one group who would find this ludicrous, another who wouldn't.

[During the war, Wittgenstein saw consecrated bread being carried in chromium steel. This struck him as ludicrous.]

Suppose that someone believed in the Last Judgement, and I don't, does this mean that I believe the opposite to him, just that there won't be such a thing? I would say: "not at all, or not always."

Suppose I say that the body will rot, and another says "No. Particles will rejoin in a thousand years, and there will be a Resurrection of you."

If some said: "Wittgenstein, do you believe in this?" I'd say: "No." "Do you contradict the man?" I'd say: "No."

If you say this, the contradiction already lies in this.

Would you say: "I believe the opposite," or "There is no reason to suppose such a thing?" I'd say neither.

Suppose someone were a believer and said: "I believe in a Last Judgement," and I said: "Well, I'm not so sure. Possibly." You would say that there is an enormous gulf between us. If he said "There is a German aeroplane overhead," and I said "Possibly. I'm not so sure," you'd say we were fairly near.

It isn't a question of my being anywhere near him, but on an entirely different plane, which you could express by saying: "You mean something altogether different, Wittgenstein."

The difference might not show up at all in any explanation of the meaning.

Why is it that in this case I seem to be missing the entire point?

Suppose somebody made this guidance for this life: believing in the Last Judgement. Whenever he does anything, this is before his mind. In a way, how are we to know whether to say he believes this will happen or not?

Asking him is not enough. He will probably say he has proof. But he has what you might call an unshakable belief. It will show, not by reasoning or by appeal to ordinary grounds for belief, but rather by regulating for in all his life.

This is a very much stronger fact—foregoing pleasures, always appealing to this picture. This in one sense must be called the firmest of all beliefs because the man risks things on account of it, which he would not do on things which are by far better established for him. Although he distinguishes between things well-established and not well-established.

Lewy: Surely, he would say it is extremely well-established.

First, he may use "well-established" or not use it at all. He will treat this belief as an extremely

Reprinted from *Lectures and Conversations*, edited by Cyril Barrett (Berkeley: University of California Press, 1966), pp. 53–59, by permission of the publisher.

well-established, and in another way as not well-established at all.

If we have a belief, in certain cases we appeal again and again to certain grounds, and at the same time we risk pretty little—if it came to risking our lives on the ground of this belief.

There are instances where you have a faith—where you say "I believe"—and on the other hand this belief does not rest on the fact on which our ordinary everyday beliefs normally do rest.

How should we compare beliefs with each other? What would it mean to compare them?

You might say: "We compare the states of mind."

How do we compare states of mind? This obviously won't do for all occasions. First, what you say won't be taken as the measure for the firmness of a belief? But, for instance, what risks would you take?

The strength of a belief is not comparable with the intensity of a pain.

An entirely different way of comparing beliefs is seeing what sorts of grounds he will give.

A belief isn't like a momentary state of mind. "At 5 o'clock he had a very bad toothache."

Suppose you had two people, and one of them, when he had to decide which course to take, thought of retribution, and the other did not. One person might, for instance, be inclined to take everything that happened to him as a reward or punishment, and another person doesn't think of this at all.

If he is ill, he may think: "What have I done to deserve this?" This is one way of thinking of retribution. Another way is, he thinks in a general way whenever he is ashamed of himself: "This will be punished."

Take two people, one of whom talks of his behaviour and of what happens to him in terms of retribution, the other one does not. These people think entirely differently. Yet, so far, you can't say they believe different things.

Suppose someone is ill and he says: "This is a punishment," and I say: "If I'm ill, I don't think of punishment at all." If you say: "Do you believe the opposite?"—you can call it believing the opposite, but it is entirely different from what we would normally call believing the opposite.

I think differently, in a different way. I say different things to myself. I have different pictures.

It is this way: if someone said: "Wittgenstein, you don't take illness as punishment, so what do you believe?"—I'd say: "I don't have any thoughts of punishment."

There are, for instance, these entirely different ways of thinking first of all—which needn't be expressed by one person saying one thing, another person another thing.

What we call believing in a Judgement Day or not believing in a Judgement Day—The expression of belief may play an absolutely minor role.

If you ask me whether or not I believe in a Judgement Day, in the sense in which religious people have belief in it, I wouldn't say: "No. I don't believe there will be such a thing." It would seem to me utterly crazy to say this.

And then I give an explanation: "I don't believe in . . . ," but then the religious person never believes what I describe.

I can't say. I can't contradict that person.

In one sense, I understand all he says—the English words "God," "separate," etc. I understand. I could say: "I don't believe in this," and this would be true, meaning I haven't got these thoughts or anything that hangs together with them. But not that I could contradict the thing.

You might say: "Well, if you can't contradict him, that means you don't understand him. If you did understand him, then you might." That again is Greek to me. My normal technique of language leaves me. I don't know whether to say they understand one another or not.

These controversies look quite different from any normal controversies. Reasons look entirely different from normal reasons.

They are, in a way, quite inconclusive.

The point is that if there were evidence, this would in fact destroy the whole business.

Anything that I normally call evidence wouldn't in the slightest influence me.

Suppose, for instance, we knew people who foresaw the future; make forecasts for years and years ahead; and they described some sort of a Judgement Day. Queerly enough, even if there were such a thing, and even if it were more convincing than I have described but, belief in this happening wouldn't be at all a religious belief.

Suppose that I would have to forego all pleasures because of such a forecast. If I do so and so, someone will put me in fires in a thousand years, etc. I wouldn't budge. The best scientific evidence is just nothing.

A religious belief might in fact fly in the face of such a forecast, and say "No. There it will break down."

As it were, the belief as formulated on the evidence can only be the last result—in which a number of ways of thinking and acting crystallize and come together.

A man would fight for his life not to be dragged into the fire. No induction. Terror. That is, as it were, part of the substance of the belief.

That is partly why you don't get in religious controversies, the form of controversy where one person is *sure* of the thing, and the other says: 'Well, possibly.'

You might be surprised that there hasn't been opposed to those who believe in Resurrection those who say "Well, possibly."

Here believing obviously plays much more this role: suppose we said that a certain picture might play the role of constantly admonishing me, or I always think of it. Here, an enormous difference would be between those people for whom the picture is constantly in the foreground, and the others who just didn't use it at all.

Those who said: "Well, possibly it may happen and possibly not" would be on an entirely different plane.

This is partly why one would be reluctant to say: "These people rigorously hold the opinion (or view) that there is a Last Judgement." "Opinion" sounds queer.

It is for this reason that different words are used: 'dogma,' 'faith.'

We don't talk about hypothesis, or about high probability. Nor about knowing.

In a religious discourse we use such expressions as "I believe that so and so will happen," and use them differently to the way in which we use them in science.

Although, there is a great temptation to think we do. Because we do talk of evidence, and do talk of evidence by experience.

We could even talk of historic events.

It has been said that Christianity rests on an historic basis.

It has been said a thousand times by intelligent people that indubitability is not enough in this case. Even if there is as much evidence as for Napoleon. Because the indubitability wouldn't be enough to make me change my whole life.

It doesn't rest on an historic basis in the sense that the ordinary belief in historic facts could serve as a foundation.

Here we have a belief in historic facts different from a belief in ordinary historic facts. Even, they are not treated as historical, empirical, propositions.

Those people who had faith didn't apply the doubt which would ordinarily apply to *any* historical propositions. Especially propositions of a time long past, etc.

What is the criterion of reliability, dependability? Suppose you give a general description as to when you say a proposition has a reasonable weight of probability. When you call it reasonable, is this *only* to say that for it you have such and such evidence, and for others you haven't?

For instance, we don't trust the account given of an event by a drunk man.

Father O'Hara[1] is one of those people who make it a question of science.

Here we have people who treat this evidence in a different way. They base things on evidence which taken in one way would seem exceedingly flimsy. They base enormous things on this evidence. Am I to say they are unreasonable? I wouldn't call them unreasonable.

I would say, they are certainly not *reasonable*, that's obvious.

'Unreasonable' implies, with everyone rebuke.

I want to say: they don't treat this as a matter of reasonability.

Anyone who reads the Epistles will find it said not only that it is not reasonable, but that it is folly.

Not only is it not reasonable, but it doesn't pretend to be.

What seems to me ludicrous about O'Hara is his making it appear to be *reasonable*.

Why shouldn't one form of life culminate in an utterance of belief in a Last Judgement? But I couldn't either say "Yes" or "No" to the statement that there will be such a thing. Nor "Perhaps," nor "I'm not sure."

It is a statement which may not allow of any such answer.

If Mr. Lewy is religious and says he believes in a Judgement Day, I won't even know whether to say I understand him or not. I've read the same things as he's read. In a most important sense, I know what he means.

If an atheist says: "There won't be a Judgement Day," and another person says there will, do they mean the same?—Not clear what criterion or meaning the same is. They might describe the same things. You might say, this already shows that they mean the same.

We come to an island and we find beliefs there, and certain beliefs we are inclined to call religious. What I'm driving at is, that religious beliefs will not. . . . They have sentences, and there are also religious statements.

These statements would not just differ in respect to what they are about. Entirely different connections would make them into religious beliefs, and there can easily be imagined transitions where we wouldn't know for our life whether to call them religious beliefs or scientific beliefs.

You may say they reason wrongly.

In certain cases you would say they reason wrongly, meaning they contradict us. In other cases you would say they don't reason at all, or "It is an entirely different kind of reasoning." The first, you would say in the case in which they reason in a similar way to us, and make something corresponding to our blunders.

Whether a thing is a blunder or not—it is a blunder in a particular system. Just as something is a blunder in a particular game and not in another.

You could also say that where we are reasonable, they are not reasonable—meaning they don't use *reason* here.

If they do something very like one of our blunders, I would say, I don't know. It depends on further surroundings of it.

It is difficult to see, in cases in which it has all the appearances of trying to be reasonable.

I would definitely call O'Hara unreasonable. I would say, if this is religious belief, then it's all superstition.

But I would ridicule it, not by saying it is based on insufficient evidence. I would say: here is a man who is cheating himself. You can say: this man is ridiculous because he believes, and bases it on weak reasons.

The word 'God' is amongst the earliest learnt—pictures and catechisms, etc. But not the same consequences as with pictures of aunts. I wasn't shown [that which the picture pictured].

The word is used like a word representing a person. God sees, rewards, etc.

"Being shown all these things, did you understand what this word meant?" I'd say, "Yes and no. I did learn what it didn't mean. I made myself understand. I could answer questions, understand questions when they were put in different ways—and in that sense could be said to understand."

If the question arises as to the existence of a god or God, it plays an entirely different role to that of the existence of any person or object I ever heard of. One said, had to say, that one *believed* in the existence, and if one did not believe, this was regarded as something bad. Normally if I did not believe in the existence of something no one would think there was anything wrong in this. . . .

Note

1. Contribution to a Symposium on *Science and Religion* (London: Gerald Howe, 1931, pp. 107–116).

VII.C.4   The Groundlessness of Belief

NORMAN MALCOLM

Norman Malcolm (1911–1990) is a particularly lucid interpreter and adherent of Wittgensteinian fideism. Malcolm taught philosophy at Cornell University. In this reading, he contends that religious belief is in no sense a hypothesis, for it cannot be and ought not to be justified rationally. It is essentially a groundless belief like other beliefs that do not need further support, such as our belief that things don't just vanish, our belief in the uniformity of nature, and our knowledge of our own intentions.

Like other fundamental assumptions religious beliefs are not derived from other beliefs but themselves form the support for all our other beliefs. They form the framework of our inquiry on which the very process of justification depends. Hence, it does not make sense to ask for a justification of religious claims or a refutation of them from a point outside the religious framework. Science and religion are just two different language games. "Neither stands in need of justification, the one no more than the other."

I

In his final notebooks Wittgenstein wrote that it is difficult "to realize the groundlessness of our believing."[1] He was thinking of how much mere acceptance, on the basis of no evidence, forms our lives. This is obvious in the case of small children. They are told the names of things. They accept what they are told. They do not ask for grounds. A child does not demand a proof that the person who feeds him is called "Mama." Or are we to suppose that the child reasons to himself as follows: "The others present seem to know this person who is feeding me, and since they call her 'Mama' that probably is her name?" It is obvious on reflection that a child cannot consider evidence or even doubt anything until he has already learned much. As Wittgenstein puts it: "The child learns by believing the adult. Doubt comes *after* belief" (*OC*, 160).

What is more difficult to perceive is that the lives of educated, sophisticated adults are also formed by groundless beliefs. I do not mean eccentric beliefs that are out on the fringes of their lives, but fundamental beliefs. Take the belief that familiar material things (watches, shoes, chairs) do not cease to exist without some physical explanation. They don't "vanish in thin air." It is interesting that we do use that very expression: "I *know* I put the keys right here on this table. They must have vanished in thin air!" But this exclamation is hyperbole; we are not speaking in literal seriousness. I do not know of any adult who would consider, in all gravity, that the keys might have inexplicably ceased to exist.

Yet it is possible to imagine a society in which it was accepted that sometimes material things do go out of existence without having been crushed, melted, eroded, broken into pieces, burned up, eaten, or destroyed in some other way. The difference between those people and ourselves would not consist in their *saying* something that we don't say ("It vanished in thin air"), since we say it too. I conceive of these people as acting and thinking differently from ourselves in such ways as the following: If one of them could not find his wallet he would give up the search sooner than you or I would; also he would be less inclined to suppose that it was stolen. In general, what we would regard as convincing circumstantial evidence or theft those people would find less convincing. They would have less inclination to save money since it too can just disappear. They would not tend to form strong attachments to material things, animals, or other people. Generally, they would stand in a looser relation to the world than we do. The disappearance of a desired object, which would provoke us to a frantic search, they would be more inclined to accept with a shrug. Of course, their scientific theories would be different; but also their attitude toward experiment, and inference from experimental results, would be more tentative. If the repetition of a familiar chemical experiment did not yield the expected result this *could* be because one of the chemical substances had vanished.

The outlook I have sketched might be thought to be radically incoherent. I do not see that this is so. Although those people consider it to be possible that a wallet might have inexplicably ceased to exist, it is also true that they regard that as unlikely. For things that are lost usually do turn up later; or if not, their fate can often be accounted for. Those people use pretty much the same criteria of identity that we do; their reasoning would resemble ours quite a lot. Their thinking would not be incoherent. But it would be different, since they would leave room for some possibilities that we exclude.

If we compare their view that material things do sometimes go out of existence inexplicably, with our own rejection of that view, it does not appear to me that one position is supported by *better evidence* than is the other. Each position is compatible with ordinary experience. On the one hand it is true that familiar objects (watches, wallets, lawn chairs) occasionally disappear without any adequate explanation. On the other hand it happens, perhaps more frequently, that a satisfying explanation of the disappearance is discovered.

Our attitude in this matter is striking. We would not be willing to consider it as even improbable that a missing lawn chair had "just ceased to exist." We would not entertain such a suggestion. If anyone proposed it we would be sure he was joking. It is no exaggeration to say that this attitude is part of the foundations of our thinking. I do not want to say that this attitude is *un*reasonable; but rather that it is something that we do not *try* to support with grounds. It could be said to belong to "the framework" of our thinking about material things.

Wittgenstein asks: "Does anyone ever test whether this table remains in existence when no one is paying attention to it?" (*OC*, 163). The answer is: Of course not. Is this because we would not call it "a table" if that were to happen? But we do call it "a table" and none of us makes the test. Doesn't this show that we do not regard that occurrence as a possibility? People who did so regard it would seem ludicrous to us. One could imagine that they made ingenious experiments to decide the question; but this research would make us smile. Is this because experiments were conducted by our ancestors that settled the matter once and for all? I don't believe it. The principle that material things do not cease to exist without physical cause is an unreflective part of the framework within which physical investigations are made and physical explanations arrived at.

Wittgenstein suggests that the same is true of what might be called "the principle of the continuity of nature":

> Think of chemical investigations. Lavoisier makes experiments with substances in his laboratory and now concludes that this and that takes place when there is burning. He does not say that it might happen otherwise another time. He has got hold of a world-picture—not of course one that he invented: he learned it as a child. I say world-picture and not hypothesis, because it is the matter-of-course (*selbst-verständliche*) foundation for his research and as such also goes unmentioned (*OC*, 167).

> But now, what part is played by the presupposition that a substance A always reacts to a substance B in the same way, given the same circumstances? Or is that part of the definition of a substance? (*OC*, 168).

Framework principles such as the continuity of nature or the assumption that material things do not cease to exist without physical cause belong to what Wittgenstein calls a "system." He makes the following observation, which seems to me to be true: "All testing, all confirmation and disconfirmation of a hypothesis takes place already within a system. And this system is not a more or less arbitrary and doubtful point of departure for all our arguments: no, it belongs to the nature of what we call an argument. The system is not so much the point of departure, as the element in which arguments have their life" (*OC*, 105).

A "system" provides the boundaries within which we ask questions, carry out investigations, and make judgments. Hypotheses are put forth, and challenged, *within* a system. Verification, justification, the search for evidence, occur *within* a system. The framework propositions of the system are not put to the test, not backed up by evidence. This is what Wittgenstein means when he says: "Of course there is justification; but justification comes to an end" (*OC*, 192); and when he asks: "Doesn't testing come to an end?" (*OC*, 164); and when he remarks that "whenever we test anything we are already presupposing something that is not tested" (*OC*, 163).

That this is so is not to be attributed to human weakness. It is a conceptual requirement that our inquiries and proofs stay within boundaries. Think, for example, of the activity of calculating a number. Some steps in a calculation we will check for correctness, but others we won't: for example, that 4 + 4 = 8. More accurately, some beginners might check it, but grown-ups won't. Similarly, some grown-ups would want to determine by calculation whether $25 \times 25 = 625$, whereas others would regard that as laughable. Thus the boundaries of the system within which *you* calculate may not be exactly the same as *mine*. But we do calculate; and, as Wittgenstein remarks, "In certain circumstances . . . we regard a calculation as sufficiently checked. What gives us a right to do so? . . . Somewhere we must be finished with justification, and then there remains the proposition that *this* is how we calculate" (*OC*, 212). If someone did not accept any boundaries for calculating this would mean that he had not learned *that* language-game: "If someone supposed that *all* our calculations were uncertain and that we could rely on none of them (justifying himself by saying that mistakes are always possible) perhaps we would say he was crazy. But can we say he is in error? Does he not just react differently? We rely on calculations, he doesn't; we are sure, he isn't" (*OC*, 217). We are taught, or we absorb, the systems within which we raise doubts, make inquiries, draw conclusions. We grow into a framework. We don't question it. We accept it trustingly. But

this acceptance is not a consequence of reflection. We do not decide to accept framework propositions. We do not decide that we live on the earth, any more than we decide to learn our native tongue. We do come to adhere to a framework proposition, in the sense that it forms the way we think. The framework propositions that we accept, grow into, are not idiosyncrasies but common ways of speaking and thinking that are pressed on us by our human community. For our acceptances to have been withheld would have meant that we had not learned how to count, to measure, to use names, to play games, or even to *talk*. Wittgenstein remarks that "a language-game is only possible if one trusts something." Not *can*, but *does* trust something (*OC*, 509). I think he means by this trust or acceptance what he calls belief "in the sense of religious belief" (*OC*, 459). What does he mean by belief "in the sense of religious belief?" He explicitly distinguishes it from *conjecture* (*Vermutung*: ibid.) I think this means that there is nothing tentative about it; it is not adopted as a hypothesis that might later be withdrawn in the light of new evidence. This also makes explicit an important feature of Wittgenstein's understanding of belief, in the sense of "religious belief," namely, that it does not rise or fall on the basis of evidence or grounds: it is "groundless."

II

In our Western academic philosophy, religious belief is commonly regarded as unreasonable and is viewed with condescension or even contempt. It is said that religion is a refuge for those who because of weakness of intellect or character are unable to confront the stern realities of the world. The objective, mature, *strong* attitude is to hold beliefs solely on the basis of *evidence*.

It appears to me that philosophical thinking is greatly influenced by this veneration of evidence. We have an aversion to statements, reports, declarations, beliefs, that are not based on grounds. There are many illustrations of this philosophical bent.

For example, in regard to a person's report that he has an image of the Eiffel Tower we have an inclination to think that the image must *resemble* the Eiffel Tower. How else could the person declare so confidently what his image is of? *How could he know*?

Another example: A memory-report or memory-belief must be based, we think, on some mental *datum* that is equipped with various features to match the corresponding features of the memory-belief. This datum will include an image that provides the *content* of the belief, and a peculiar feeling that makes one refer the image to a *past* happening, and another feeling that makes one believe that the image is an *accurate* portrayal of the past happening, and still another feeling that informs one that it was *oneself* who witnessed the past happening. The presence of these various features makes memory-beliefs thoroughly reasonable.

Another illustration: If interrupted in speaking one can usually give a confident account, later on of what one had been *about* to say. How is this possible? Must not one remember a *feeling of tendency to say just those words*? This is one's basis for knowing what one had been about to say. It justifies one's account.

Still another example: After dining at a friend's house you announce your intention to go home. How do you know your intention? One theory proposes that you are presently aware of a particular mental state or bodily feeling which, as you recall from your past experience, has been highly correlated with the behavior of going home; so you infer that *that* is what you are going to do now. A second theory holds that you must be aware of some definite mental state or event which reveals itself, not by experience but *intrinsically*, as the intention to go home. Your awareness of that mental item *informs* you of what action you will take.

Yet another illustration: This is the instructive case of the man who, since birth, has been immune to sensations of bodily pain. On his thirtieth birthday he is kicked in the shins and for the first time he responds by crying out, hopping around on one foot, holding his leg, and exclaiming, "The pain is terrible!" We have an overwhelming inclination to wonder, "How could he tell, *this first time*, that what

he felt was *pain*?" Of course, the implication is that *after* the first time there would be *no* problem. Why not? Because his first experience with pain would provide him with a sample that would be preserved in memory; thereafter he would be equipped to determine whether any sensation he feels is or isn't pain; he would just compare it with the memory-sample to see whether the two match! Thus he will have a justification for believing that what he feels is pain. But the *first time* he will not have this justification. This is why the case is so puzzling. Could it be that this first time he *infers* that he is in pain from his own behavior?

A final illustration: Consider the fact that after a comparatively few examples and bits of instruction a person can go on to carry out a task, apply a word correctly in the future, continue a numerical series from an initial segment, distinguish grammatical from ungrammatical constructions, solve arithmetical problems, and so on. These correct performances will be dealing with new and different examples, situations, combinations. The performance output will be far more varied than the instruction input. How is this possible? What carries the person from the meager instruction to his rich performance? The explanation has to be that an effect of his training was that he abstracted the Idea, perceived the Common Nature, "internalized" the Rule, grasped the Structure. What else could bridge the gap between the poverty of instruction and the wealth of performance? Thus we postulate an intervening mental act or state which removes the inequality and restores the balance.

My illustrations belong to what could be called the *pathology* of philosophy. Wittgenstein speaks of a "general disease of thinking" which attempts to explain occurrences of discernment, recognition, or understanding, by postulating mental states or processes from which those occurrences flow "as from a reservoir" (*BB*, p. 143). These mental intermediaries are assumed to contribute to the causation of the various cognitive performances. More significantly for my present purpose, they are supposed to *justify* them; they provide our *grounds* for saying or doing this rather than that; they *explain how we know*. The Image, or Cognitive State, or Feeling, or Idea, or Sample, or Rule, or Structure, *tells* us. It is like a road map or a signpost. It guides our course.

What is "pathological" about these explanatory constructions and pseudoscientific inferences? Two things at least. First, the movement of thought that demands these intermediaries is circular and empty, unless it provides criteria for determining their presence and nature *other than* the occurrence of the phenomena they are postulated to explain—and, of course, no such criteria are forthcoming. Second, there is the great criticism by Wittgenstein of this movement of philosophical thought: namely, his point that no matter what kind of state, process paradigm, sample, structure, or rule, is conceived as giving us the necessary guidance, *it* could be taken, or understood, as indicating a *different* direction from the one in which we actually did go. The assumed intermediary Idea, Structure, or Rule, does not and cannot reveal that because of it we went in the only direction it was reasonable to go. Thus the internalized intermediary we are tempted to invoke to bridge the gap between training and performance, as being that which shows us what we must do or say if we are to be rational, cannot do the job it was invented to do. It cannot fill the epistemological gap. It cannot provide the bridge of justification. It cannot put to rest the How-do-we-know? question. Why not? Because it cannot tell us how *it itself* is to be taken, understood, applied. Wittgenstein puts the point briefly and powerfully: "Don't always think that you read off your words from facts; that you portray these in words according to rules. For even so you would have to apply the rule in the particular case without guidance" (*PI*, 292). Without guidance! Like Wittgenstein's signpost arrow that cannot tell us whether to go in the direction of the arrow tip or in the opposite direction, so too the Images, Ideas, Cognitive Structures, or Rules, that we philosophers imagine as devices for guidance, cannot interpret themselves to us. The signpost does not tell the traveler how to read it. A second signpost might tell him how to read the first one; we can imagine such a case. But this can't go on. If the traveler is to continue his journey he will have to do something on his own, without guidance.

The parable of the traveler speaks for *all* of the language-games we learn and practice; even those

in which there is the most disciplined instruction and the most rigorous standards of conformity. Suppose that a pupil has been given thorough training in some procedure, whether it is drawing patterns, building fences, or proving theorems. But then he has to carry on by himself in new situations. How does he know what to do? Wittgenstein presents the following dialogue: "'However you instruct him in the continuation of a pattern—how can he *know* how he is to continue by himself?'—Well, how do *I* know?—If that means 'Have I grounds?', the answer is: the grounds will soon give out. And then I shall act, without grounds" (*PI*, 211). Grounds come to an end. Answers to How-do-we-know? questions come to an end. Evidence comes to an end. We must speak, act, live, without evidence. This is so, not just on the fringes of life and language, but at the center of our most regularized activities. We do learn rules and learn to follow them. But our training was in the past! We had to leave it behind and proceed on our own.

It is an immensely important fact of nature that as people carry on an activity in which they have received a common training, they do largely agree with one another, accepting the same examples and analogies, taking the same steps. We agree in what to say, in how to apply language. We agree in our responses to particular cases.

As Wittgenstein says: "That is not agreement in opinions but in form of life" (*PI*, 241). We cannot explain this agreement by saying that we are just doing what the rules tell us—for our agreement in applying rules, formulae, and signposts is what gives them their meaning.

One of the primary pathologies of philosophy is the feeling that we must *justify* our language-games. We want to establish them as well-grounded. But we should consider here Wittgenstein's remark that a language-game "is not based on grounds. It is there—like our life" (*OC*, 559).

Within a language-game there is justification and lack of justification, evidence and proof, mistakes and groundless opinions, good and bad reasoning, correct measurements and incorrect ones. One cannot properly apply these terms to a language-game itself. It may, however, be said to be "groundless," not in the sense of a groundless opinion, but in the sense that we accept it, we live it. We can say, "This is what we do. This is how we are."

In this sense religion is groundless; and so is chemistry. Within each of these two systems of thought and action there is controversy and argument. Within each there are advances and recessions of insight into the secrets of nature or the spiritual condition of humankind and the demands of the Creator, Savior, Judge, Source. Within the framework of each system there is criticism, explanation, justification. But we should not expect that there might be some sort of rational justification of the framework itself.

A chemist will sometimes employ induction. Does he have evidence for a Law of Induction? Wittgenstein observes that it would strike him as nonsense to say, "I know that the Law of Induction is true." ("Imagine such a statement made in a law court.") It would be more correct to say, "I believe in the Law of Induction" (*OC*, 500). This way of putting it is better because it shows that the attitude toward induction is belief in the sense of "religious" belief—that is to say, an acceptance which is not conjecture or surmise and for which there is no reason—it is a groundless acceptance.

It is intellectually troubling for us to conceive that a whole system of thought might be groundless, might have no rational justification. We realize easily enough, however, that grounds soon give out—that we cannot go on giving reasons for our reasons. There arises from this realization the conception of a reason that is *self-justifying*—something whose credentials as a reason cannot be questioned.

This metaphysical conception makes its presence felt at many points—for example, as an explanation of how a person can tell what his mental image is *of*. We feel that the following remarks, imagined by Wittgenstein, are exactly right: "The image must be more similar to its object than any picture. For however similar I make the picture to what it is supposed to represent, it can always be the picture of something else. But it is essential to the image that it is the image of *this* and of nothing else" (*PI*, 389). A pen and ink drawing represents

the Eiffel Tower; but it could represent a mine shaft or a new type of automobile jack. Nothing prevents this drawing from being taken as a representation of something other than the Eiffel Tower. But my mental image of the Eiffel Tower is *necessarily* an image of the Eiffel Tower. Therefore it must be a "remarkable" kind of picture. As Wittgenstein observes: "Thus one might come to regard the image as a super-picture" (*ibid.*). Yet we have no intelligible conception of how a super-picture would differ from an ordinary picture. It would seem that it has to be a *super-likeness*—but what does this mean?

There is a familiar linguistic practice in which one person *tells* another what his image is of (or what he intends to do, or what he was about to say) and no question is raised of how the first one knows that what he says is true. This question is imposed from outside, artificially, by the philosophical craving for justification. We can see here the significance of these remarks: "It isn't a question of explaining a language-game by means of our experiences, but of noting a language-game" (*PI*, 655). "Look on the language-game as the *primary* thing" (*PI*, 656). Within a system of thinking and acting there occurs, *up to a point*, investigation and criticism of the reasons and justifications that are employed in that system. This inquiry into whether a reason is good or adequate cannot, as said, go on endlessly. We stop it. We bring it to an end. We come upon something that *satisfies* us. It is as if we made a decision or issued an edict: "*This* is an adequate reason!" (or explanation, or justification). Thereby we fix a boundary of our language-game.

There is nothing wrong with this. How else could we have disciplines, systems, games? But our fear of groundlessness makes us conceive that we are under some logical compulsion to terminate at *those particular* stopping points. We imagine that we have confronted the self-evident reason, the self-justifying explanation, the picture or symbol whose meaning cannot be questioned. This obscures from us the *human* aspect of our concepts—the fact that what we call "a reason," "evidence," "explanation," "justification," is what appeals to and satisfies *us*.

III

The desire to provide a rational foundation for a form of life is especially prominent in the philosophy of religion, where there is an intense preoccupation with purported proofs of the existence of God. In American universities there must be hundreds of courses in which these proofs are the main topic. We can be sure that nearly always the critical verdict is that the proofs are invalid and consequently that, up to the present time at least, religious belief has received no rational justification.

Well, of course not! The obsessive concern with the proofs reveals the assumption that in order for religious belief to be intellectually respectable it *ought* to have a rational justification. *That* is the misunderstanding. It is like the idea that we are not justified in relying on memory until memory has been proved reliable.

Roger Trigg makes the following remark: "To say that someone acts in a certain way because of his belief in God does seem to be more than a redescription of his action. . . . It is to give a *reason* for it. The belief is distinct from the commitment which may follow it, and is the justification for it."[2] It is evident from other remarks that by "belief in God" Trigg means "belief in the existence of God" or "belief that God exists." Presumably by the *acts* and *commitments* of a religious person Trigg refers to such things as prayer, worship, confession, thanksgiving, partaking of sacraments, and participation in the life of a religious group.

For myself I have great difficulty with the notion of belief in *the existence* of God, whereas the idea of belief *in* God is to me intelligible. If a man did not ever pray for help or forgiveness, or have any inclination toward it; nor ever felt that it is "a good and joyful thing" to thank God for the blessings of this life; nor was ever concerned about his failure to comply with divine commandments—then, it seems clear to me, he could not be said to believe in God. Belief in God is not an all or none thing; it can be more or less; it can wax and wane. But belief in God in any degree does require, as I understand the words, some religious action, some commitment, or if not, at least a bad conscience.

According to Trigg, if I take him correctly, a man who was entirely devoid of any inclination toward religious action or conscience, might believe in *the existence* of God. What would be the marks of this? Would it be that the man knows some theology, can recite the Creeds, is well-read in Scripture? Or is his belief in the existence of God something different from this? If so, what? What would be the difference between a man who knows some articles of faith, heresies, scriptural writings, and in addition believes in the existence of God, and one who knows these things but does not believe in the existence of God? I assume that both of them are indifferent to the acts and commitments of religious life.

I do not comprehend this notion of belief in *the existence* of God which is thought to be distinct from belief *in* God. It seems to me to be an artificial construction of philosophy, another illustration of the craving for justification.

Religion is a form of life; it is language embedded in action—what Wittgenstein calls a "language-game." Science is another. Neither stands in need of justification, the one no more than the other.

Present-day academic philosophers are far more prone to challenge the credentials of religion than of science, probably for a number of reasons. One may be the illusion that science can justify its own framework. Another is the fact that science is a vastly greater force in our culture. Still another may be the fact that by and large religion is to university people an alien form of life. They do not participate in it and do not understand what it is all about.

Their nonunderstanding is of an interesting nature. It derives, at least in part, from the inclination of academics to suppose that their employment as scholars demands of them the most severe objectivity and dispassionateness. For an academic philosopher to become a religious believer would be a stain on his professional competence! Here I will quote from Nietzsche, who was commenting on the relation of the German scholar of his day to religious belief; yet his remarks continue to have a nice appropriateness for the American and British scholars of our own day:

Pious or even merely church-going people seldom realize *how much* good will, one might even say wilfulness, it requires nowadays for a German scholar to take the problem of religion seriously; his whole trade . . . disposes him to a superior, almost good-natured merriment in regard to religion, sometimes mixed with a mild contempt directed at the "uncleanliness" of spirit which he presupposes wherever one still belongs to the church. It is only with the aid of history (thus *not* from his personal experience) that the scholar succeeds in summoning up a reverent seriousness and a certain shy respect towards religion; but if he intensifies his feelings towards it even to the point of feeling grateful to it, he has still in his own person not got so much as a single step closer to that which still exists as church or piety; perhaps the reverse. The practical indifference to religious things in which he was born and raised is as a rule sublimated in him into a caution and cleanliness which avoids contact with religious people and things. . . . Every age has its own divine kind of naïvety for the invention of which other ages may envy it—and how much naïvety, venerable, childlike and boundlessly stupid naïvety there is in the scholar's belief in his superiority, in the good conscience of his tolerance, in the simple unsuspecting certainty with which his instinct treats the religious man as an inferior and lower type which he himself has grown beyond and above.[3]

Notes

1. Ludwig Wittgenstein, *On Certainty*, ed. G. E. M. Anscombe and G. H. von Wright; English translation by D. Paul and G. E. M. Anscombe (Oxford, 1969), paragraph 166. Henceforth I include references to this work in the text, employing the abbreviation "*OC*" followed by paragraph number. References to Wittgenstein's *The Blue and Brown Books* (Oxford, 1958) are indicated in the text by "*BB*" followed by page number. References to his *Philosophical Investigations*, ed. G. E. M. Anscombe and R. Rhees; English translation by Anscombe (Oxford, 1967) are indicated by "*PI*" followed by paragraph number. In *OC* and *PI*, I have mainly used the translations of Paul and Anscombe but with some departures.

2. *Reason and Commitment* (Cambridge, 1973), p. 75.

3. Friedrich Nietzsche, *Beyond Good and Evil*, trans. R. J. Hollingdale, para. 58.

VII.C.5 A Critique of Fideism

MICHAEL MARTIN

Michael Martin (1932–   ) is professor of philosophy at Boston University and author of several works in philosophy of science and philosophy of religion, including Atheism: A Philosophical Justification *(1990) from which this essay is taken.*

While Martin agrees with the fideists, notably Wittgenstein and Malcolm, that one must understand a religion before one can understand or criticize it, he thinks that even an atheist can have sufficient understanding to analyze and evaluate the arguments embedded in religious forms of life. He argues that fideism fails as an argument for religious belief.

Reprinted from *Atheism: A Philosophical Justification* (Philadelphia: Temple University Press, 1990) by permission of the publisher. © 1990 Temple University Press. Footnotes deleted.

According to Wittgensteinian fideism, religious discourse is embedded in a form of life and has its own rules and logic. It can only be understood and evaluated in its own terms, and any attempt to impose standards on such discourse from the outside—for example, from science—is quite inappropriate. Since religious discourse is a separate unique language game different from that of science, religious statements, unlike scientific ones, are not empirically testable. To demand that they be is a serious misunderstanding of that form of discourse. On this view of the language game of religion, religious discourse is rational and intelligible when judged in its own terms, which are the only appropriate ones. Because the meaning of a term varies from one language game to another, to understand religious language one must see it from within the religious language game itself. In general, a philosopher's task is not to criticize a form of life or its language but to describe both and, where necessary, to eliminate philosophical puzzlement concerning the operation of the language. In particular, a philosopher of religion's job is to describe the use of religious discourse and eliminate any perplexities that may result from it.

Now, there are some aspects of the Wittgensteinian point of view with which even its severest critics can sympathize; for example, that it is important to get inside a religious practice to understand it. But from this admission the major and most controversial views of Wittgensteinian fideism do not follow.

First of all, the basis for distinguishing one form of life from another, one language game from another, is unclear. For example, consider the practices of astrology and fortunetelling by reading palms, tea leaves, and so on. Do these constitute forms of life with their own language games? What about political practices? Does each political group and its practice constitute a different form of life with its own language game? Did the Nazis have their own form of life with its own language game? In the case of religion, is there only one religious language game, or are there many? Is there one for each religion? One for each denomination or sect within each religion? The differences between Buddhism and Christianity are so vast that one strongly suspects that the Wittgensteinian fideist would have to say that these constitute different forms of life involving different language games. But if this is granted, must one not also admit that the practices of different Christian denominations differ in fundamental ways? Consider, for example, Roman Catholicism, Mormonism, and Christian Science. Would not a Wittgensteinian fideist have to say that in these cases there are different religious forms of life involving different language games? But if one goes this far, would not one have to say that different Protestant denominations such as the Methodist and the Baptist, and even different sects within each, have different religious language games? Yet since for Wittgensteinian fideism the same terms in different language games have different meanings, this seems to have the absurd consequence that

members of one Baptist sect would not be able to understand members of another Baptist sect.

Second, since each form of life is governed by its own standards, there could be no external criticism. Yet this has unacceptable consequences. Suppose that astrology and fortunetelling by reading palms or tea leaves constitute separate forms of life. It would follow that these practices must not be judged by outside standards despite the fact that they seem to be based on false or at least dubious assumptions. Suppose that each political practice constitutes a separate form of life. If so, external criticism of a practice such as Nazism would be impossible.

Suppose each religious form of life is governed by its own standards. Then there could be no external standards that could be used in criticizing a religious form of life. However, this has unfortunate consequences. Some religious denominations practice sexual and racial discrimination; for instance, the Mormon church excluded blacks from positions in the church hierarchy, and it still excludes women. It is not implausible to suppose that most enlightened people today believe that this practice and the beliefs on which it rests are wrong. Yet if Mormonism is a separate form of life, there can be no external criticism of its practices.

Despite what Wittgensteinian fideists say, external criticism is not only possible but essential. If Wittgensteinian fideists are correct, there would be something contradictory or incoherent in the claim, "This is an ongoing religious form of life that is irrational." But there is not. Indeed, even participants in a religion sometimes find its doctrines incoherent, its major arguments resting on dubious premises, and some of its practices morally questionable. In fact, there seems to be no good reason why a religious form of life or, for that matter, any form of life could not be evaluated externally and found wanting. Although insight into a form of life may be gained by taking the participants' perspective, one cannot rest content with this, for the participants may be blind to the problems with their own practices and beliefs, and the perspective of an outsider may be necessary if these are to be detected.

Wittgensteinian fideism also has paradoxical implications concerning the truth of religious utterances within a language game. If Jones says "There is no God" within the Buddhist's language game, and Smith says "There is a God" within the Christian language game, the Wittgensteinian fideist would seem to be holding that both statements are true. Since they seem to contradict one another, how can that be? The answer a Wittgensteinian fideist would give is that the meaning of a religious utterance is relative to the language game to which it belongs. So despite appearances to the contrary, what Jones denies in our example is not what Smith affirms. The Wittgensteinian fideist seems committed to believing it is an illusion that a Roman Catholic who says the pope is infallible contradicts a Baptist who says the pope is not infallible. One tends to think otherwise because one does not realize that the meanings of religious utterances are relative to different language games.

Why should we accept the view of language and meaning presupposed by this view? There seems to be no good reason for the thesis that the meaning of language is radically contextual and that it is impossible to communicate across practices or ways of life. Indeed, it makes nonsense of the debates not only between Christians and non-Christians, but between defenders of different Christian denominations. For on this view, despite the long and bitter arguments, there is no real disagreement; the debating parties are on different tracks talking past one another. Such a view, although perhaps not impossible, seems highly unlikely.

Surely a more plausible view of these examples is that the Christian and non-Christian are really disagreeing and that the Catholic and Baptist are talking about the same thing; in other words, that there are a common language and common categories. As Kai Nielsen has argued:

> There is no "religious language" and "scientific language." There is rather the international notation of mathematics and logic; and English, French, Spanish and the like. In short, "religious discourse" and "scientific discourse" are part of the same overall conceptual structure. Moreover, in that conceptual structure there is a large amount of discourse, which is neither religious nor scientific, that is constantly being utilized by both the religious man and the scientist when they make religious and scientific claims. In short, they share a number of key categories.

What Nielsen says about the scientist and the religious person can be said with equal validity about the Christian and non-Christian, the Catholic and Baptist. Religious language is not completely compartmentalized from other languages, and the language of one religion denomination, or sect is not completely compartmentalized from the languages of others.

Norman Malcolm's approach to religious faith is a typical example of Wittgensteinian fideism. A pupil of Wittgenstein and one of his most sensitive commentators, Malcolm argues in "The Groundlessness of Belief" that many of our fundamental beliefs are merely the framework within which questions are posed and our inquiries are carried out. For example, the belief that "material things (watches, shoes, chairs) do not cease to exist without some physical explanation" is a groundless belief that provides part of the framework of our entire system of beliefs. Suppose one's keys are lost. According to Malcolm, no one in our society would seriously consider that the keys vanished into thin air, but one could imagine a society in which people did believe that. In such a society, Malcolm says, science, people's attitudes toward money, and many other things would differ from ours. People would have a different framework. However, Malcolm insists that our belief that material things do not vanish into thin air is not based on better evidence than the contrary belief of people in that other society. We are not even willing to consider the suggestion that something just ceased to exist, he says. The belief that things do not cease to exist without physical cause "is an unreflective part of the framework within which physical investigations are made and physical explanations arrived at."

Malcolm maintains that religious belief is groundless in the same way. Both it and religious practice are embedded in a form of life in which, because of common training, there is wide agreement. Within the religious language game there is justification, evidence, and proof, but there is no justification of the language game itself. As Malcolm puts it, when pressed for a justification of the religious language game we can only say, "This is what we do. This is how we are." Malcolm is opposed to the common belief that unless one can give a rational proof for the existence of God, a belief in God is irrational. This is as much a misunderstanding as is the supposition that one must have a rational proof in order to have a justified belief that things don't vanish into thin air. According to Malcolm, people's belief in God and the actions that accompany it, such as praying for help or forgiveness and complying with divine commandments, are simply what religious people do, and they need no more justification than does the scientific form of life.

Malcolm's defense of religious faith is unacceptable. The analogy he draws between belief in God (G) and belief that material objects do not vanish into thin air (M) is not compelling. First of all, there are in our society no sane people, other than professional philosophical skeptics, who question M, and it is in fact hard to see how they could. What kind of reason could they give? But there are many people who do question G and give plausible reasons for their disbelief. Further, some people who now question G at one time did not. Even some people who accept G find it problematic and difficult to defend. It is significant that only professional philosophers attempted to defend M in the light of skeptical arguments and that even philosophical skeptics do not seriously question M in their everyday life. But it is not only professional philosophical skeptics who question G. Many ordinary people have either given up their belief in God or believe with difficulty.

In fact, one may agree with Malcolm that we have certain groundless beliefs that provide a framework for questions and inquiries and yet deny that any religious beliefs are groundless, for a particular mode of justification that is embedded within some language game may itself need justification in terms of some more basic mode of justification. For example, it is common practice to appeal to the authority of a dictionary to settle questions about the meaning of a word. However, this practice itself needs justification—for example, justification based on inductive evidence of the

reliability of lexicographers in determining the meaning of words. Malcolm must show that the religious mode is autonomous, that it does not need to be justified by some more fundamental mode of justification. To do this would require his giving an adequate account of religious language. This he has not done.

Moreover, despite what Malcolm says, there does seem to be better evidence for M than for ~M. Consequently, there is good reason to suppose that M is not a groundless belief. There is good inductive evidence for M of the following kind. In the vast majority of cases where things have seemed to disappear into thin air—the vanished cards of the magician, the ships and planes missing in the so-called Bermuda triangle—either we know what happened or we have plausible explanations. But what about the small number of cases for which we have no plausible explanations? Aside from their not yet having been explained, these cases do not seem to be significantly different from those that initially seemed unexplainable but now have an explanation. It is therefore a reasonable inductive conclusion that these cases also have an explanation, although it is as yet unknown. However, if M is not groundless, the analogy between the groundlessness of M and the groundlessness of G collapses.

Malcolm seems to assume that people in our culture believe M and people in other cultures believe ~M without good reason. I have just suggested that there are inductive reasons for preferring M over ~M. However, even if there were no inductive reasons for preferring M over ~M, the choice would not be arbitrary. There is good reason to reject ~M, for its acceptance as a working hypothesis would prevent us from ever discovering an explanation if one is available. Thus working on the assumption that there is always an explanation for apparent disappearance into thin air does not block inquiry, whereas working on the assumption that sometimes there is no explanation would block inquiry. Consequently, rejecting ~M and accepting M is vindicated on practical grounds.

As we have seen, Malcolm seems to reject all grounds for belief in God. On the other hand, he does say that *within* a language game there is justification, evidence, and proof. But it is unclear how this suggestion is to be understood and how it relates to the thesis that belief in God is groundless. On one interpretation, Malcolm can be taken to be suggesting that belief in God and perhaps other religious beliefs as well are groundless within the religious language game, while other religious beliefs are proved or justified in terms of these groundless beliefs. On this reading, his position is a type of religious foundationalism: Some basic beliefs are not based on any other beliefs, and all other beliefs are based on these. On a second interpretation, Malcolm can be understood as suggesting that some of the standard arguments for the existence of God—for example, the teleological argument—are sound *within* the religious language game but not when external standards are applied. On a third interpretation, he can be taken as suggesting that proofs very different from the standard ones have a special relevance within certain religious language games but not within others. For example, in some fundamentalist Christian language games a proof

consists in simply citing Scripture; in others a proof consists in citing the pronouncements of some religious leader.

The problems with the first interpretation need not detain us here, since religious foundationalism is considered in detail below.* It is difficult to understand the second interpretation, since it is not clear how an argument could be both sound and unsound. This view may, however, rest on an assumption we have already rejected: that the meaning of religious language is radically contextual and compartmentalized. The third interpretation has many problems, not the least of which is that the use of scriptural citation as proof allows conflicting religious theses to be proved, as does appeal to different religious leaders.

I must conclude that as an approach to religious faith, Wittgensteinian fideism is no more successful than traditional and existential ones.

---

*See reading VII.D.3, "A Critique of Plantinga's Reformed Epistemology."

VII.D   Rationality and Justified Religious Belief

In this section we are concerned with the contemporary discussion of the relationship of reason to religious belief. In the theoretical or epistemological sense (over against the pragmatic sense) of rationality, is it rational to believe religious propositions? Specifically, is it rational to believe that God exists? These readings offer various interpretations of the notion of rationality and show how they apply to theistic belief.

In the first reading, "Rational Theistic Belief Without Proof," John Hick discusses the relevancy of the proofs or arguments for theistic beliefs that we studied in Part 1. He argues that the proofs are largely irrelevant to religion. They are neither sufficient nor necessary for the religious life. Not only do the so-called proofs for the existence of God fail to accomplish what they set out to do, but even if they did demonstrate what they purported to demonstrate, this would at best only force our notional assent. They would not bring about the deep devotion and sense of worship necessary for a full religious life. Furthermore, they are not necessary because believers have something *better*, an intense, coercive, indubitable experience, which convinces them of the reality of the being in question. For believers, God is not a hypothesis brought in ex machina to explain the world but a living presence, closer to them than the air they breathe.

Nonetheless, believers are not irrational in believing in God. Hick describes a notion of person-relativeness of evidence, such that it might be rational for one person, A, on the evidence E_1, which A has, to believe some proposition p, whereas it may be clearly irrational for B to believe that same p given the evidence E_2, which B has. Religious individuals base their belief upon certain evidence that comes through religious experience that nonreligious individuals do not have as part of their data. Although the believers cannot demonstrate that they are right, they can show that it is reasonable for them to believe that God exists, given their experience.

At this point Hick develops a notion of religious experience analogous to our claim that we experience an external world. Neither proposition can be proved, but both are natural beliefs. The main difference between the two kinds of experience is that virtually everyone agrees on the reality of an external world, but only a relatively small minority of humankind experience compelling religious experience. Should this undermine the argument from religious experience? Not necessarily, for it may be the case that the few have access to a higher reality. They cannot easily be dismissed as insane or simply hallucinating, for the "general intelligence and exceptionally high moral quality of the great religious figures clashes with any analysis of their experience in terms of abnormal psychology."

At the end of his article Hick applies his thesis about the sense of the presence of God to the problem of the plurality of religions. He suggests that there is a convergence of religious experience, indicating the existence of a common higher reality.

In our next reading, Alvin Plantinga carries on Hick's argument, arguing that the evidentialist objections to theism (such as those put forth by W. K. Clifford earlier in this book) fail to make their case, for the evidentialists have yet to set forth unambiguous criteria to account for all the clear cases of justified beliefs that would exclude the belief in God. Plantinga outlines the position of the foundationalist-evidentialist as one that claims that all justified beliefs must either be properly basic by virtue of fulfilling certain criteria or be based on other beliefs. This eventually results in a treelike construction with properly basic beliefs resting at the bottom, or the foundation. According to classic foundationalism,

A proposition *p* is properly basic for a person *S* if and only if *p* is either self-evident to *S* or incorrigible for *S* or evident to the senses for *S*.

Self-evident propositions are those that a person just sees as true immediately, such as that one plus two equals three or that a contradiction cannot be true. Incorrigible propositions are those about one's states of consciousness in which one cannot mistakenly believe what is not true, such as 'I think, therefore I am' or 'I am in pain.' Aquinas and John Locke add a third type of proposition, that which is evident to the senses, such as 'I see a tree.' The goal of the classical foundationalist is to protect our belief systems from error by allowing only solid or absolutely certain beliefs to make up the foundation of our belief systems. Plantinga shows that there are many beliefs that we seem to be justified in holding that do not fit into any of these three categories, such as memory beliefs (e.g., 'I ate breakfast this morning'), belief in an external world, and belief in other minds. These beliefs are not dependent on other beliefs, yet neither are they self-evident, incorrigible, or evident to the senses.

Having shown the looseness of what we can accept as properly basic, Plantinga next shows that the Protestant Reformers saw belief in God as properly basic. He asks us to consider this as a legitimate option and examines possible objections to it. His claim is that belief in God is properly basic and that none of the objections to this view succeed. Note that although Plantinga's position may resemble the fideist position in that it does not appeal to evidence to support theism, it differs from it in being open to consideration of the claims of reason. If the atheologian could assemble a clear and cogent case against theism, the rational believer would have to revise his or her religious beliefs. In this sense, Plantinga's reformed epistemology might be considered a version of soft rationalism, a type of rationalism that makes no claims to having exact criteria for what is to count as rationally acceptable but is open to evidence and argument.

In our third reading Michael Martin analyzes foundationalism in general as well as Plantinga's attempt to place belief in God in the foundations of a noetic structure. He argues that Plantinga's arguments against classical foundationalism are weak, so that it isn't clear that his thesis escapes their criticism. Furthermore, on Plantinga's formulation virtually anyone could justify any belief system, simply placing it in the foundation of his or her noetic structure.

In the fourth reading, "Can Religious Belief Be Rational?", I argue that a coherentist approach to religion may have a better chance of justifying religious belief than a foundationalist approach. That is, rather than view our beliefs in terms of the foundationalist model, in which one belief is supported by more basic beliefs until we get to foundational beliefs for which there is no further evidence, it might be better to see our belief systems in terms of a web or network of beliefs mutually supporting each other. Although some beliefs may be privileged or more self-evident than others, few beliefs can be sustained independently of the whole system or large parts of it.

Furthermore, there is a certain person-relativeness in every person's noetic structure. Each of us has had a different, complex history of evidence gathering and belief formation, so that intersubjective belief comparison and evaluation become difficult. What is rational for you to believe, given your framework, may not be rational for me to believe, given my framework. That is, we find ourselves assessing evidence within various worldviews, from interpretive perspectives, so that it is difficult to communicate across worldviews. Nevertheless, there are core experiences and criteria of rationality that are common to all (or nearly all) humans and that can provide a common measure for attempting to arrive at optimally rational positions. That is, although it is difficult to be critically rational about religious beliefs and experiences, it is possible, and the rationally religious person seeks to scrutinize all of his or her beliefs and revise those beliefs as fresh experience is made available. So communication and a sharing of our reasons for our various belief systems is possible in spite of the high degree of relativity in those systems.

In the final reading, "Faith Without Belief?" I examine the relationship between belief and faith and argue that religious faith can exist and flourish in the absence of belief. One may not be able to believe in God because of an insufficiency of evidence, but one may still live committed to a theistic worldview in hope. I argue that this is an authentic religious position, too often neglected in the literature.

VII.D.1   Rational Theistic Belief Without Proof

JOHN HICK

In this reading John Hick, professor of philosophy at Claremont Graduate School, argues that the so-called proofs for the existence of God are largely irrelevant to religion. They are neither sufficient nor necessary for the religious life. Not only do they fail to accomplish what they set out to do, but even if they did accomplish it, this would at best only force our notional assent. They would not bring about the deep devotion and sense of worship necessary for a full religious life. Furthermore, they are not necessary because believers have something better, an intense, coercive, indubitable experience, which convinces them of the reality of the being in question. For believers, God is not a hypothesis brought in ex machina to explain the world but a living presence, closer to them than the air they breathe.

Nonetheless, believers are not irrational in believing in God. Hick describes a notion of person-relativeness of evidence, so that it might be rational for one person, A, on the evidence E1, which A has, to believe some proposition p, whereas it may be clearly irrational for B to believe that same p given the evidence E2, which B has. Religious individuals base their belief on certain evidence that comes through religious experience that nonreligious individuals do not have as part of their data.

Hick goes on to develop a notion of religious experience analogous to our claim that we experience an external world. At the end of his article Hick applies his thesis about the sense of the presence of God to the problem of the plurality of religions. He suggests that there is a convergence of religious experience, indicating the existence of a common higher reality.

(a) The religious rejection of the theistic arguments

We have seen that the major theistic arguments are all open to serious philosophical objections. Indeed we have in each case concluded, in agreement with the majority of contemporary philosophers, that these arguments fail to do what they profess to do. Neither those which undertake strictly to demonstrate the existence of an absolute Being, nor those which profess to show divine existence to be probable, are able to fulfil their promise. We have seen that it is impossible to demonstrate the reality of God by *a priori* reasoning, since such reasoning is confined to the realm of concepts; impossible to demonstrate it by *a posteriori* reasoning, since this would have to include a premise begging the very question at issue; and impossible to establish it as in a greater or lesser degree probable, since the notion of probability lacks any clear meaning in this context. A philosopher unacquainted with modern developments in theology might well assume that theologians would, *ex officio*, be supporters of the theistic proofs and would regard as a fatal blow this

Reprinted from John Hick, *Arguments for the Existence of God* (Macmillan, London and Basingstoke, 1971) by permission of the publisher. Footnotes edited.

conclusion that there can be neither a strict demonstration of God's existence nor a valid probability argument for it. In fact however such an assumption would be true only of certain theological schools. It is true of the more traditional Roman Catholic theology, of sections of conservative Protestantism, and of most of those Protestant apologists who continue to work within the tradition of nineteenth-century idealism. It has never been true, on the other hand, of Jewish religious thought; and it is not true of that central stream of contemporary Protestant theology which has been influenced by the 'neo-orthodox' movement, the revival of Reformation studies and the 'existentialism' of Kierkegaard and his successors; or of the most significant contemporary Roman Catholic thinkers, who are on this issue (as on so many others) in advance of the official teaching of the magisterium. Accordingly we have now to take note of this theological rejection of the theistic proofs, ranging from a complete lack of concern for them to a positive repudiation of them as being religiously irrelevant or even harmful. There are several different considerations to be evaluated.

1. It has often been pointed out that for the man of faith, as he is depicted in the Bible, no theistic proofs are necessary. Philosophers in the rationalist tradition, holding that to know means to be able to prove, have been shocked to find that in the Bible, which is supposed to be the basis of Western religion, no attempt whatever is made to demonstrate the existence of God. Instead of professing to establish the divine reality by philosophical reasoning the Bible throughout takes this for granted. Indeed to the biblical writers it would have seemed absurd to try to establish by logical argumentation that God exists. For they were convinced that they were already having to do with him and he with them in all the affairs of their lives. They did not think of God as an inferred entity but as an experienced reality. Many of the biblical writers were (sometimes, though doubtless not all times) as vividly conscious of being in God's presence as they were of living in a material world. It is impossible to read their pages without realising that to them God was not a proposition completing a syllogism, or an idea adopted by the mind, but the supreme experiential reality. It

would be as sensible for a husband to desire a philosophical proof of the existence of the wife and family who contribute so much of the meaning and value of his life as for the man of faith to seek for a proof of the existence of the God within whose purpose he believes that he lives and moves and has his being.

As Cook Wilson wrote:

> If we think of the existence of our friends; it is the 'direct knowledge' which we want: merely inferential knowledge seems a poor affair. To most men it would be as surprising as unwelcome to hear it could not be directly known whether there were such existences as their friends, and that it was only a matter of (probable) empirical argument and inference from facts which are directly known. And even if we convince ourselves on reflection that this is really the case, our actions prove that we have a confidence in the existence of our friends which can't be derived from an empirical argument (which can never be certain) for a man will risk his life for his friend. We don't want merely inferred friends. Could we possibly be satisfied with an inferred God?

In other words the man of faith has no need of theistic proofs; for he has something which for him is much better. However it does not follow from this that there may not be others who do need a theistic proof, nor does it follow that there are in fact no such proofs. All that has been said about the irrelevance of proofs to the life of faith may well be true, and yet it might still be the case that there are valid arguments capable of establishing the existence of God to those who stand outside the life of faith.

2. It has also often been pointed out that the God whose existence each of the traditional theistic proofs professes to establish is only an abstraction from and a pale shadow of the living God who is the putative object of biblical faith. A First Cause of the Universe might or might not be a deity to whom an unqualified devotion, love and trust would be appropriate; Aquina's *Et hoc omnes intelligunt Deum* ('and this all understand to be God') is not the last step in a logical argument but merely an exercise of the custom of overlooking a gap in the argument at this point. A Necessary Being, and indeed a being who is metaphysically absolute in every respect—omnipotent, omniscient, eternal, uncreated—might be morally good or evil. As H. D.

Aitken has remarked, 'Logically, there is no reason why an almighty and omniscient being might not be a perfect stinker.' A divine Designer of the world whose nature is read off from the appearances of nature might, as Hume showed, be finite or infinite, perfect or imperfect, omniscient or fallible, and might indeed be not one being but a veritable pantheon. It is only by going beyond what is proved, or claimed to have been proved, and identifying the First Cause, Necessary Being, or Mind behind Nature with the God of biblical faith that these proofs could ever properly impel to worship. By themselves and without supplementation of content and infusion of emotional life from religious traditions and experiences transcending the proofs themselves they would never lead to the life of faith.

The ontological argument on the other hand is in this respect in a different category. If it succeeds it establishes the reality of a being so perfect in every way that no more perfect can be conceived. Clearly if such a being is not worthy of worship none ever could be. It would therefore seem that, unlike the other proofs, the ontological argument, if it were logically sound, would present the relatively few persons who are capable of appreciating such abstract reasoning with a rational ground for worship. On the other hand, however, whilst this is the argument that would accomplish most if it succeeded it is also the argument which is most absolutely incapable of succeeding; for it is, as we have seen, inextricably involved in the fallacy of professing to deduce existence from a concept.

3. It is argued by some religious writers that a logical demonstration of the existence of God would be a form of coercion and would as such be incompatible with God's evident intention to treat his human creatures as free and responsible persons. A great deal of twentieth-century theology emphasises that God as the infinite personal reality, having made man as person in his own image, always treats men as persons, respecting their relative freedom and autonomy. He does not override the human mind by revealing himself in overwhelming majesty and power, but always approaches us in ways that leave room for an uncompelled response of human faith. Even God's own entry into our earthly history, it is said, was in an 'incognito' that could be penetrated only by the eyes of faith. As Pascal put it, 'willing to appear openly to those who seek him with all their heart and to be hidden from those who flee from him with all their heart, he so regulates the knowledge of himself that he has given indications of himself which are visible to those who seek him and not to those who do not seek him. There is enough light for those to see who only desire to see, and enough obscurity for those who have a contrary disposition.' God's self-revealing actions are accordingly always so mediated through the events of our temporal experience that men only become aware of the divine presence by interpreting and responding to these events in the way which we call religious faith. For if God were to disclose himself to us in the coercive manner in which our physical environment obtrudes itself we should be dwarfed to nothingness by the infinite power thus irresistibly breaking open the privacy of our souls. Further, we should be spiritually blinded by God's perfect holiness and paralysed by his infinite energy; 'for human kind cannot bear very much reality.' Such a direct, unmediated confrontation breaking in upon us and shattering the frail autonomy of our finite nature would leave no ground for a free human response of trust, self-commitment and obedience. There could be no call for a man to venture upon a dawning consciousness of God's reality and thus to receive this consciousness as an authentic part of his own personal existence precisely because it has not been injected into him or clamped upon him by magisterial exercise of divine omnipotence.

The basic principle invoked here is that for the sake of creating a personal relationship of love and trust with his human creatures God does not force an awareness of himself upon them. And (according to the view which we are considering) it is only a further application of the same principle to add that a logically compelling demonstration of God's existence would likewise frustrate this purpose. For men—or at least those of them who are capable of following the proof—could then be forced to know that God is real. Thus Alasdair MacIntyre, when a Christian apologist, wrote: 'For if we could produce logically cogent arguments we should produce the kind of certitude that leaves no room for decision;

where proof is in place, decision is not. We do not decide to accept Euclid's conclusions; we merely look to the rigour of his arguments. If the existence of God were demonstrable we should be as bereft of the possibility of making a free decision to love God as we should be if every utterance of doubt or unbelief was answered by thunderbolts from heaven.' This is the 'religious coercion' objection to the theistic proofs.

To what extent is it a sound objection? We may accept the theological doctrine that for God to force men to know him by the coercion of logic would be incompatible with his purpose of winning the voluntary response and worship of free moral beings. But the question still remains whether the theistic proofs could ever do this. Could a verbal proof of divine existence compel a consciousness of God comparable in coerciveness with a direct manifestation of his divine majesty and power? Could anyone be moved and shaken in their whole being by the demonstration of a proposition, as men have been by a numinous experience of overpowering impressiveness? Would the things that have just been said about an overwhelming display of divine glory really apply to verbal demonstrations—that infinite power would be irresistibly breaking in upon the privacy of our souls and that we should be blinded by God's perfect holiness and paralysed by his infinite energy? Indeed could a form of words, culminating in the proposition that 'God exists,' ever have power by itself to produce more than what Newman calls a notional assent in our minds?

It is of course true that the effect of purely rational considerations such as those which are brought to bear in the theistic proofs are much greater in some minds than in others. The more rational the mind the more considerable is the effect to be expected. In many persons—indeed taking mankind as a whole, in the great majority—the effect of a theistic proof, even when no logical flaw is found in it, would be virtually nil! But in more sophisticated minds the effect must be greater, and it is at least theoretically possible that there are minds so rational that purely logical considerations can move them as effectively as the evidence of their senses. It is therefore conceivable that some-

one who is initially agnostic might be presented with a philosophical proof of divine existence—say the ontological argument, with its definition of God as that than which no more perfect can be conceived—and might as a result be led to worship the being whose reality has thus been demonstrated to him. This seems to be possible; but I believe that even in such a case there must, in addition to an intelligent appreciation of the argument, be a distinctively religious response to the idea of God which the argument presents. Some propensity to respond to unlimited perfection as holy and as rightly claiming a response of unqualified worship and devotion must operate, over and above the purely intellectual capacity for logical calculation. For we can conceive of a purely or merely logical mind, a kind of human calculating machine, which is at the same time devoid of the capacity for numinous feeling and worshipping response. Such a being might infer that God exists but be no more existentially interested in this conclusion than many people are in, say, the fact that the Shasta Dam is 602 feet high. It therefore seems that when the acceptance of a theistic proof leads to worship, a religious reaction occurs which turns what would otherwise be a purely abstract conclusion into an immensely significant and moving fact. In Newman's terminology, when a notional assent to the proposition that God exists becomes a real assent, equivalent to an actual living belief and faith in God, there has been a free human response to an idea which could instead have been rejected by being held at the notional level. In other words, a verbal proof of God's existence cannot by itself break down our human freedom; it can only lead to a notional assent which has little or no positive religious value or substance.

I conclude, then, that the theological objections to the theistic proofs are considerably less strong than the philosophical ones; and that theologians who reject natural theology would therefore do well to do so primarily on philosophical rather than on theological grounds. These philosophical reasons are, as we have seen, very strong; and we therefore now have to consider whether, in the absence of any theistic proofs, it can nevertheless be rational to believe in the existence of God.

(b) Can there be rational theistic belief without proofs?

During the period dominated by the traditional theistic arguments the existence of God was often treated by philosophers as something to be discovered through reasoning. It was seen as the conclusion of an inference; and the question of the rationality of the belief was equated with that of the soundness of the inference. But from a religious point of view, as we have already seen, there has always been something very odd about this approach. The situation which it envisages is that of people standing outside the realm of faith, for whom the apologist is trying to build a bridge of rational inference to carry them over the frontier into that realm. But of course this is not the way in which religious faith has originally or typically or normally come about. When the cosmological, ontological, teleological and moral arguments were developed, theistic belief was already a functioning part of an immemorially established and developing form of human life. The claims of religion are claims made by individuals and communities on the basis of their experience—and experience which is none the less their own for occurring within an inherited framework of ideas. We are not dealing with a merely conceivable metaphysical hypothesis which someone has speculatively invented but which hardly anyone seriously believes. We are concerned, rather, with convictions born out of experience and reflection and living within actual communities of faith and practice. Historically, then, the philosophical proofs of God have normally entered in to support and confirm but not to create belief. Accordingly the proper philosophical approach would seem to be a probing of the actual foundations and structure of a living and operative belief rather than of theoretical and non-operative arguments subsequently formulated for holding those beliefs. The question is not whether it is possible to prove, starting from zero, that God exists; the question is whether the religious man, given the distinctively religious form of human existence in which he participates, is properly entitled as a rational person to believe what he does believe?

At this point we must consider what we mean by a rational belief. If by a belief we mean a proposition believed, then what we are to be concerned with here are not rational beliefs but rational believings. Propositions can be well-formed or ill-formed, and they can be true or false, but they cannot be rational or irrational. It is *people* who are rational or irrational, and derivatively their states and their actions, including their acts and states of believing. Further, apart from the believing of analytic propositions, which are true by definition and are therefore rationally believed by anyone who understands them, the rationality of acts (or states) of believing has to be assessed separately in each case. For it is a function of the relation between the proposition believed and the evidence on the basis of which the believer believes it. It might conceivably be rational for Mr. X to believe p but not rational for Mr. Y to believe p, because in relation to the data available to Mr. X p is worthy of belief but not in relation to the data available to Mr. Y. Thus the question of the rationality of belief in the reality of God is the question of the rationality of a particular person's believing given the data that he is using; or that of the believing of a class of people who share the same body of data. Or putting the same point the other way round, any assessing of the belief-worthiness of the proposition that God exists must be an assessing of it in relation to particular ranges of data.

Now there is one area of data or evidence which is normally available to those who believe in God, and that provides a very important part of the ground of their believing, but which is normally not available to and therefore not taken into account by those who do not so believe; and this is religious experience. It seems that the religious man is in part basing his believing upon certain data of religious experience which the non-religious man is not using because he does not have them. Thus our question resolves itself into one about the theist's right, given his distinctively religious experience, to be certain that God exists. It is the question of the rationality or irrationality, the well-groundedness or ill-groundedness, of the religious man's claim to know God. The theist cannot hope to prove that God exists; but despite this it may nevertheless be possible for him to show it to be wholly reasonable for him to believe that God exists.

What is at issue here is not whether it is rational for someone else, who does not participate in the distinctively religious mode of experience, to believe in God on the basis of the religious man's reports. I am not proposing any kind of 'argument from religious experience' by which God is inferred as the cause of the special experiences described by mystics and other religious persons. It is not the non-religious man's theoretical use of someone else's reported religious experience that is to be considered, but the religious man's own practical use of it. The question is whether he is acting rationally in trusting his own experience and in proceeding to live on the basis of it.

In order to investigate this question we must consider what counts as rational belief in an analogous case. The analogy that I propose is that between the religious person's claim to be conscious of God and any man's claim to be conscious of the physical world as an environment, existing independently of himself, of which he must take account.

In each instance a realm of putatively cognitive experience is taken to be veridical and is acted upon as such, even though its veridical character cannot be logically demonstrated. So far as sense experience is concerned this has emerged both from the failure of Descartes' attempt to provide a theoretical guarantee that our senses relate us to a real material environment, and from the success of Hume's attempt to show that our normal non-solipsist belief in an objective world of enduring objects around us in space is neither a product of, nor justifiable by, philosophical reasoning but is what has been called in some expositions of Hume's thought (though the term does not seem to have been used by Hume himself) a natural belief. It is a belief which naturally and indeed inevitably arises in the normal human mind in response to normal human perceptual experience. It is a belief on the basis of which we live and the rejection of which, in favour of a serious adoption of the solipsist alternative, would so disorient our relationship to other persons within a common material environment that we should be accounted insane. Our

insanity would consist in the fact that we should no longer regard other people as independent centres of consciousness, with their own purposes and wills, with whom interpersonal relationships are possible. We should instead be living in a one-person world.

It is thus a basic truth in, or a presupposition of, our language that it is rational or sane to believe in the reality of the external world that we inhabit in common with other people, and irrational or insane not to do so.

What are the features of our sense experience in virtue of which we all take this view? They would seem to be twofold: the givenness or the involuntary character of this form of cognitive experience, and the fact that we can and do act successfully in terms of our belief in an external world. That is to say, being built and circumstanced as we are we cannot help initially believing as we do, and our belief is not contradicted, but on the contrary continuously confirmed, by our continuing experience. These characteristics jointly constitute a sufficient reason to trust and live on the basis of our perceptual experience in the absence of any positive reason to distrust it; and our inability to exclude the theoretical possibility of our experience as a whole being purely subjective does not constitute such a reason. This seems to be the principle on which, implicitly, we proceed. And it is, by definition, rational to proceed in this way. That is to say, this is the way in which all human beings do proceed and have proceeded, apart from a very small minority who have for that very reason been labelled by the majority as insane. This habitual acceptance of our perceptual experience is thus, we may say, part of our operative concept of human rationality.

We can therefore now ask whether a like principle may be invoked on behalf of a parallel response to religious experience. 'Religious experience' is of course a highly elastic concept. Let us restrict attention, for our present purpose, to the theistic 'sense of the presence of God,' the putative awareness of a transcendent divine Mind within whose field of consciousness we exist and with whom therefore we stand in a relationship of mutual awareness. This sense of 'living in the divine presence' does not take the form of a direct vision of God, but of experiencing events in history and in our own personal life as the medium of God's dealings with us. Thus religious differs from non-religious experience, not as the awareness of a different world, but as a different way of experiencing the same world. Events which can be experienced as having a purely natural significance are experienced by the religious mind as having also and at the same time religious significance and as mediating the presence and activity of God.

It is possible to study this type of religious experience either in its strongest instances, in the primary and seminal religious figures, or in its much weaker instances in ordinary adherents of the traditions originated by the great exemplars of faith. Since we are interested in the question of the claims which religious experience justifies it is appropriate to look at that experience in its strongest and purest forms. A description of this will accordingly apply only very partially to the ordinary rank-and-file believer either of today or in the past.

If then we consider the sense of living in the divine presence as this was expressed by, for example, Jesus of Nazareth, or by St. Paul, St. Francis, St. Anselm or the great prophets of the Old Testament, we find that their 'awareness of God' was so vivid that he was as indubitable a factor in their experience as was their physical environment. They could no more help believing in the reality of God than in the reality of the material world and of their human neighbours. Many of the pages of the Bible resound with the sense of God's presence as a building might reverberate from the tread of some gigantic being walking through it. God was known to the prophets and apostles as a dynamic will interacting with their own wills; a sheerly given personal reality, as inescapably to be reckoned with as destructive storm and life-giving sunshine, the fixed contours of the land, or the hatred of their enemies and the friendship of their neighbours.

Our question concerns, then, one whose 'experience of God' has this compelling quality, so that he is no more inclined to doubt its veridical character than to doubt the evidence of his senses. Is it rational for him to take the former, as it is certainly rational for him to take the latter, as reliably cognitive of an aspect of his total environment and

thus as knowledge in terms of which to act? Are the two features noted above in our sense experience—its givenness, or involuntary character, and the fact that we can successfully act in terms of it—also found here? It seems that they are. The sense of the presence of God reported by the great religious figures has a similar involuntary and compelling quality; and as they proceed to live on the basis of it they are sustained and confirmed by their further experiences in the conviction that they are living in relation, not to illusion, but to reality. It therefore seems prima facie, that the religious man *is* entitled to trust his religious experience and to proceed to conduct his life in terms of it.

The analogy operating within this argument is between our normal acceptance of our sense experiences as perception of an objective external world, and a corresponding acceptance of the religious experience of 'living in God's presence' as the awareness of a divine reality external to our own minds. In each case there is a solipsist alternative in which one can affirm *solus ipse* to the exclusion of the transcendent—in the one case denying a physical environment transcending our own private consciousness and in the other case denying a divine Mind transcending our own private consciousness. It should be noted that this analogy is not grounded in the perception of particular material objects and does not turn upon the contrast between veridical and illusory sense perceptions, but is grounded in our awareness of an objective external world as such and turns upon the contrast between this and a theoretically possible solipsist interpretation of the same stream of conscious experience.

(c) Religious and perceptual belief

Having thus set forth the analogy fairly boldly and starkly I now want to qualify it by exploring various differences between religious and sensory experience. The resulting picture will be more complex than the first rough outline presented so far; and yet its force as supporting the rationality of theistic faith will not, I think, in the end have been undermined.

The most obvious difference is that everyone has and cannot help having sense experiences, whereas not everyone has religious experiences, at any rate of the very vivid and distinct kind to which we have been referring. As bodily beings existing in a material environment, we cannot help interacting consciously with that environment. That is to say, we cannot help 'having' a stream of sense experiences; and we cannot help accepting this as the perception of a material world around us in space. When we open our eyes in daylight we cannot but receive the visual experiences that come to us; and likewise with the other senses. And the world which we thus perceive is not plastic to our wishes but presents itself to us as it is, whether we like it or not. Needless to say, our senses do not coerce us in any sense of the word 'coerce' that implies unwillingness on our part, as when a policeman coerces an unwilling suspect to accompany him to the police station. Sense experience is coercive in the sense that we cannot when sane believe that our material environment is not broadly as we perceive it to be, and that if we did momentarily persuade ourselves that what we experience is not there we should quickly be penalised by the environment and indeed, if we persisted, destroyed by it.

In contrast to this we are not obliged to interact consciously with a spiritual environment. Indeed it is a commonplace of much contemporary theology that God does not force an awareness of himself upon mankind but leaves us free to know him by an uncompelled response of faith. And yet once a man has allowed himself freely to become conscious of God—it is important to note—that experience is, at its top levels of intensity, coercive. It creates the situation of the person who *cannot help* believing in the reality of God. The apostle, prophet or saint may be so vividly aware of God that he can no more doubt the veracity of his religious awareness than of his sense experience. During the periods when he is living consciously in the presence of God, when God is to him the divine Thou, the question whether God exists simply does not arise. Our cognitive freedom in relation to God is not to be found at this point but at the prior stage of our coming to be aware of him. The individual's own free receptivity and responsiveness plays an essential part in his dawning consciousness of God; but once he *has* become conscious of God that consciousness can possess a coercive and indubitable quality.

It is a consequence of this situation that whereas everyone perceives and cannot help perceiving the physical world, by no means everyone experiences the presence of God. Indeed only rather few people experience religiously in the vivid and coercive way reported by the great biblical figures. And this fact immediately suggests a sceptical question. Since those who enjoy a compelling religious experience form such a small minority of mankind, ought we not to suspect that they are suffering from a delusion comparable with that of the paranoiac who hears threatening voices from the walls or the alcoholic who sees green snakes?

This is of course a possible judgment to make. But this judgment should not be made *a priori*, in the absence of specific grounds such as we have in the other cases mentioned. And it would in fact be difficult to point to adequate evidence to support this hypothesis. On the contrary the general intelligence and exceptionally high moral quality of the great religious figures clashes with any analysis of their experience in terms of abnormal psychology. Such analyses are not indicated, as is the parallel view of paranoiacs and alcoholics, by evidence of general disorientation to reality or of incapacity to live a productive and satisfying life. On the contrary, Jesus of Nazareth, for example, has been regarded by hundreds of millions of people as the fulfilment of the ideal possibilities of human nature. A more reasonable negative position would therefore seem to be the agnostic one that whilst it is proper for the religious man himself, given his distinctive mode of experience, to believe firmly in the reality of God, one does not oneself share that experience and therefore has no ground upon which to hold that belief. Theism is then not positively denied, but is on the other hand consciously and deliberately not affirmed. This agnostic position must be accepted by the theist as a proper one. For if it is reasonable for one man, on the basis of his distinctively religious experience, to affirm the reality of God it must also be reasonable for another man, in the absence of any such experience, not to affirm the reality of God.

The next question that must be raised is the closely connected one of the relation between rational belief and truth. I suggested earlier that, strictly, one should speak of rational believings rather than of rational beliefs. But nevertheless it is sometimes convenient to use the latter phrase, which we may then understand as follows. By a rational belief we shall mean a belief which it is rational for the one who holds it to hold, given the data available to him. Clearly such beliefs are not necessarily or always true. It is sometimes rational for an individual to have, on the basis of incomplete data, a belief which is in fact false. For example, it was once rational for people to believe that the sun revolves round the earth; for it was apparently perceived to do so, and the additional theoretical and observational data were not yet available from which it has since been inferred that it is the earth which revolves round the sun. If, then, a belief may be rational and yet false, may not the religious man's belief be of this kind? May it not be that when the data of religious experience are supplemented in the believer's mind by further data provided by the sciences of psychology or sociology, it ceases to be rational for him to believe in God? Might it not then be rational for him instead to believe that his 'experience of the presence of God' is to be understood as an effect of a buried infancy memory of his father as a benevolent higher power; or of the pressure upon him of the human social organism of which he is a cell; or in accordance with some other naturalistic theory of the nature of religion?

Certainly this is possible. Indeed we must say, more generally, that all our beliefs, other than our acceptance of logically self-certifying propositions, are in principle open to revision or retraction in the light of new data. It is always conceivable that something which it is now rational for us to believe, it may one day not be rational for us to believe. But the difference which this general principle properly makes to our present believing varies from a maximum in relation to beliefs involving a considerable theoretical element, such as the higher-level hypotheses of the sciences, to a minimum in relation to perceptual beliefs, such as the belief that I now see a sheet of paper before me. And I have argued that so far as the great primary religious figures are concerned, belief in the reality of God is closer to the latter in that it is analogous to belief in the reality of the perceived material world. It is not an explanatory hypothesis, logically comparable with those developed in the sciences, but a perceptual belief. God was not, for Amos or Jeremiah or Jesus of Nazareth, an inferred entity but an experienced personal presence. If this is so, it is appropriate that the religious man's belief in the reality of God should be no more provisional than his belief in the reality of the physical world. The situation is in each case that given the experience which he has and which is part of him, he cannot help accepting as 'there' such aspects of his environment as he experiences. He cannot help believing either in the reality of the material world which he is conscious of inhabiting, or of the personal divine presence which is overwhelmingly evident to him and to which his mode of living is a free response. And I have been suggesting that it is as reasonable for him to hold and to act upon the one belief as the other.

VII.D.2 Religious Belief Without Evidence

ALVIN PLANTINGA

Alvin Plantinga, professor of philosophy at the University of Notre Dame, argues that it is rational to believe in God in spite of the lack of evidence for such belief. Those (like W. K. Clifford) who insist that we must have evidence for all our beliefs simply fail to make their case, for the evidentialists have yet to set forth unambiguous criteria to account for all the clear cases of justified beliefs that would exclude the belief in God. Plantinga outlines the position of the foundationalist-evidentialist as one that claims that all justified beliefs must either be properly basic by virtue of fulfilling certain criteria or be based on other beliefs. This eventually results in a treelike construction with properly basic beliefs resting at the bottom.

Plantinga shows that there are many beliefs that we seem to be justified in holding that do not fit into the foundationalist framework, such as memory beliefs (e.g., 'I ate breakfast this morning'), belief in an external world, and belief in other minds. These beliefs are not dependent on other beliefs, yet neither are they self-evident, incorrigible, or evident to the senses.

Having shown the looseness of what we can accept as properly basic, Plantinga next shows that the Protestant Reformers saw belief in God as properly basic. He asks us to consider this as a legitimate option and examines possible objections to it.

What I mean to discuss, in this paper, is the question, Is belief in God rational? That is to say, I wish to discuss the question "Is it rational, or reasonable, or rationally acceptable, to believe in God?" I mean to *discuss* this question, not answer it. My initial aim

is not to argue that religious belief *is* rational (although I think it is) but to try to understand this question.

The first thing to note is that I have stated the question misleadingly. What I really want to discuss is whether it is rational to believe that God exists—that there is such a person as God. Of course there is an important difference between believing that God exists and believing *in* God. To believe that God exists is just to accept a certain proposition—the proposition that there really is such a person as God—as true. According to the book of James (2:19) the devils believe this proposition, and they tremble. To believe *in* God, however, is to trust him, to commit your life to him, to make his purposes your own. The devils do not do that. So there is a difference between believing in God and believing that he exists; for purposes of economy, however, I shall use the phrase 'belief in God' as a synonym for 'belief that God exists.'

Our question, therefore, is whether belief in God is rational. This question is widely asked and widely answered. Many philosophers—most prominently, those in the great tradition of natural theology—have argued that belief in God *is* rational; they have typically done so by providing what they took to be *demonstrations* or *proofs* of God's existence. Many others have argued that belief in God is *ir*rational. If we call those of the first group 'natural theologians,' perhaps we should call those of the second 'natural atheologians.' (That would at any rate be kinder than calling them 'unnatural theologians.') J. L. Mackie, for example, opens his statement of the problem of evil as follows: "I think, however, that a more telling criticism can be made by way of the traditional problem of evil. Here it can be shown, not merely that religious beliefs lack rational support, but that they are positively irrational. . . . " And a very large number of philosophers take it that a central question—perhaps *the* central question—of philosophy of religion is the question whether religious belief in general and belief in God in particular is rationally acceptable.

Now an apparently straightforward and promising way to approach this question would be to take a definition of rationality and see whether belief in God conforms to it. The chief difficulty with this appealing course, however, is that no such definition of rationality seems to be available. If there *were* such a definition, it would set out some conditions for a belief's being rationally acceptable—conditions that are severally necessary and jointly sufficient. That is, each of the conditions would have to be met by a belief that is rationally acceptable; and if a belief met all the conditions, then it would follow that it is rationally acceptable. But it is monumentally difficult to find any non-trivial necessary conditions at all. Surely, for example, we cannot insist that S's belief that p is rational only if it is *true*. For consider Newton's belief that if x, y and z are moving colinearly, then the motion of z with respect to x is the sum of the motions of y with respect to x and z with respect to y. No doubt Newton was rational in accepting this belief; yet it was false, at least if contemporary physicists are to be trusted. And if they aren't—that is, if they are wrong in contradicting Newton—then *they* exemplify what I'm speaking of; they rationally believe a proposition which, as it turns out, is false.

Nor can we say that a belief is rationally acceptable only if it is possibly true, not necessarily false in the broadly logical sense. For example, I might do the sum of $735 + 421 + 9,216$ several times and get the same answer: 10,362. I am then rational in believing that $735 + 421 + 9,216 = 10,362$, even though the fact is I've made the same error each time—failed to carry a '1' from the first column—and thus believe what is necessarily false. Or I might be a mathematical neophyte who hears from his teacher that every continuous function is differentiable. I need not be irrational in believing this, despite the fact that it is necessarily false. Examples of this sort can be multiplied.

So this question presents something of an initial enigma in that it is by no means easy to say what it is for a belief to be rational. And the fact is those philosophers who ask this question about belief in God do not typically try to answer it by giving necessary and sufficient conditions for rational belief. Instead, they typically ask whether the believer has *evidence* or *sufficient evidence* for his belief; or they may try to argue that in fact there is sufficient evidence for the proposition that there is *no* God; but in any case they try to answer this question by finding evidence for or against theistic belief. Philosophers who think there are sound arguments for the existence of God—the natural theologians—claim there is good evidence *for* this proposition; philosophers who believe that there are sound arguments for the non-existence of God naturally claim that there is evidence *against* this proposition. But they concur in holding that belief in God is rational only if there is, on balance, a preponderance of evidence for it—or less radically, only if there is not, on balance, a preponderance of evidence against it.

The nineteenth-century philosopher W. K. Clifford provides a splendid if somewhat strident example of the view that the believer in God must have evidence if he is not to be irrational. Here he does not discriminate against religious belief; he apparently holds that a belief of any sort at all is rationally acceptable only if there is sufficient evidence for it. And he goes on to insist that it is wicked, immoral, monstrous, and perhaps even impolite to accept a belief for which one does not have sufficient evidence:

> Whoso would deserve well of his fellows in this matter will guard the purity of his belief with a very fanaticism of jealous care, lest at any time it should rest on an unworthy object, and catch a stain which can never be wiped away.

He adds that if a

> belief has been accepted on insufficient evidence, the pleasure is a stolen one. Not only does it deceive ourselves by giving us a sense of power which we do not really possess, but it is sinful, because it is stolen in defiance of our duty to mankind. That duty is to guard ourselves from such beliefs as from a pestilence which may shortly master our body and spread to the rest of the town.

And finally:

> To sum up: it is wrong always, everywhere, and for anyone to believe anything upon insufficient evidence.

(It is not hard to detect, in these quotations, the "tone of robustious pathos" with which William James credits him.) Clifford finds it utterly obvious, furthermore, that those who believe in God do indeed so believe on insufficient evidence and thus deserve the above abuse. A believer in God is, on his view, at best a harmless pest and at worst a menace to society; in either case he should be discouraged.

Now there are some initial problems with Clifford's claim. For example, he doesn't tell us how *much* evidence is sufficient. More important, the notion of evidence is about as difficult as that of rationality: What is evidence? How do you know when you have some? How do you know when you have sufficient or enough? Suppose, furthermore, that a person thinks he has sufficient evidence for a proposition *p* when in fact he does not—would he then be irrational in believing *p*? Presumably a person can have sufficient evidence for what is false—else either Newton did not have sufficient evidence for his physical beliefs or contemporary physicists don't have enough for *theirs*. Suppose, then, that a person has sufficient evidence for the false proposition that he has sufficient evidence for *p*. Is he then irrational in believing *p*? Presumably not; but if not, having sufficient evidence is not, contrary to Clifford's claim, a necessary condition for believing *p* rationally.

But suppose we temporarily concede that these initial difficulties can be resolved and take a deeper look at Clifford's position. What is essential to it is the claim that we must evaluate the rationality of belief in God by examining its relation to *other* propositions. We are directed to estimate its rationally by determining whether we have evidence for it—whether we know, or at any rate rationally believe, some other propositions which stand in the appropriate relation to the proposition in question. And belief in God is rational, or reasonable, or rationally acceptable, on this view, only if there are other propositions with respect to which it is thus evident.

According to the Cliffordian position, then, there is a set of propositions *E* such that my belief in God is rational if and only if it is evident with respect to *E*—if and only if *E* constitutes, on balance,

evidence for it. But what propositions are to be found in *E*? Do we know that belief in God is not itself in *E*? If it *is*, of course, then it is certainly evident with respect to *E*. How does a proposition get into *E* anyway? How do we decide which propositions are the ones such that my belief in God is rational if and only if it is evident with respect to them? Should we say that *E* contains the propositions that I *know*? But then, for our question to be interesting, we should first have to argue or agree that I don't know that God exists—that I only *believe* it, whether rationally or irrationally. This position is widely taken for granted, and indeed taken for granted by theists as well as others. But why should the latter concede that he doesn't know that God exists—that at best he rationally believes it? The Bible regularly speaks of *knowledge* in this context—not just rational or well-founded belief. Of course it is true that the believer has *faith*—faith in God, faith in what He reveals, faith that God exists—but this by no means settles the issue. The question is whether he doesn't also *know* that God exists. Indeed, according to the Heidelberg Catechism, knowledge is an essential element of faith, so that one has true faith that *p* only if he knows that *p*:

> True faith is not only a certain (i.e., sure) knowledge whereby I hold for truth all that God has revealed in His word, but also a deep-rooted assurance created in me by the Holy Spirit through the gospel that not only others but I too have had my sins forgiven, have been made forever right with God and have been granted salvation. (Q 21)

So from this point of view a man has true faith that *p* only if he knows that *p* and also meets a certain further condition: roughly (where *p* is a universal proposition) that of accepting the universal instantiation of *p* with respect to himself. Now of course the theist may be unwilling to concede that he does not have true faith that God exists; accordingly he may be unwilling to concede—initially, at any rate—that he does not know, but only believes that God exists.

[After a discussion of other attacks on theism from an evidentialist perspective, Plantinga turns to the foundationalist theory of knowledge, beginning with the classical version of that doctrine, held by Aquinas, Descartes, Locke, Clifford, and many others.]

[Both] Aquinas and the evidentialist objector [to theism] concur in holding that belief in God is rationally acceptable only if there is evidence for it—if, that is, it is probable with respect to some body of propositions that constitutes the evidence. And here we can get a better understanding of Aquinas and the evidentialist objector if we see them as accepting some version of *classical foundationalism*. This is a *picture* or total way of looking at faith, knowledge, justified belief, rationality, and allied topics. This picture has been enormously popular in Western thought; and despite a substantial opposing groundswell, I think it remains the dominant way of thinking about these topics. According to the foundationalist some propositions are properly basic and some are not; those that are not are rationally accepted only on the basis of *evidence*, where the evidence must trace back, ultimately, to what *is* properly basic. The existence of God, furthermore, is not among the propositions that are properly basic; hence a person is rational in accepting theistic belief only if he has evidence for it. The vast majority of those in the western world who have thought about our topic have accepted some form of classical foundationalism. The evidentialist objection to belief in God, furthermore, is obviously rooted in this way of looking at things. So suppose we try to achieve a deeper understanding of it.

Earlier I said the first thing to see about the evidentialist objection is that it is a *normative* contention or claim. The same thing must be said about foundationalism; this thesis is a normative thesis, a thesis about how a system of beliefs *ought* to be structured, a thesis about the properties of a correct, or acceptable, or rightly structured system of beliefs. According to the foundationalist there are norms, or duties, or obligations with respect to belief just as there are with respect to actions. To conform to these duties and obligations is to be rational; to fail to measure up to them is to be irrational. To be rational, then, is to exercise one's epistemic powers *properly*—to exercise them in such a way as to go contrary to none of the norms for such exercise. . . .

I think we can understand foundationalism more fully if we introduce the idea of a *noetic structure*. A person's noetic structure is the set of propositions he believes, together with certain epistemic relations that hold among him and these propositions. As we have seen, some of my beliefs may be based upon others; it may be that there are a pair of propositions A and B such that I believe B, and believe A *on the basis of* B. An account of a person's noetic structure, then, would specify which of his beliefs are basic and which nonbasic. Of course it is abstractly possible that *none* of his beliefs is basic; perhaps he holds just three beliefs, A, B, and C, and believes each of them on the basis of the other two. We might think this improper or irrational, but that is not to say it could not be done. And it is also possible that *all* of his beliefs are basic; perhaps he believes a lot of propositions but does not believe any of them on the basis of any others. In the typical case however, a noetic structure will include both basic and nonbasic beliefs. It may be useful to give some examples of beliefs that are often basic for a person. Suppose I seem to see a tree; I have that characteristic sort of experience that goes with perceiving a tree. I may then believe the proposition that I see a tree. It is *possible* that I believe that proposition *on the basis of* the proposition that I seem to see a tree; in the typical case, however, I will not believe the former on the basis of the latter because in the typical case I will not believe the latter at all. I will not be paying any attention to my experience but will be concentrating on the tree. Of course I *can* turn my attention to my experience, notice how things look to me, and acquire the belief that I seem to see something that looks like *that*; and if you challenge my claim that I see a tree, perhaps I *will* thus turn my attention to my experience. But in the typical case I will not believe that I see a tree on the basis of a proposition about my experience; for I believe A on the basis of B only if I believe B, and in the typical case where I perceive a tree I do not believe (or entertain) any propositions about my experience. Typically I take such a proposition as basic. Similarly, I believe I had breakfast this morning; this too is basic for me. I do not believe this proposition on the basis of some proposition about my experience—for example, that I seem to remember having had breakfast. In the typical case I will not have even considered *that* question—the question whether I *seem* to remember having had breakfast; instead I simply believe that I had breakfast; I take it as a basic.

Second, an account of a noetic structure will include what we might call an index of *degree* of belief. I hold some of my beliefs much more firmly than others. I believe both that $2 + 1 = 3$ and that London, England, is north of Saskatoon, Saskatchewan; but I believe the former more resolutely than the latter. Some beliefs I hold with maximum firmness; others I do in fact accept, but in a much more tentative way. . . .

Third, a somewhat vaguer notion: an account of S's noetic structure would include something like an index of *depth of ingression*. Some of my beliefs are, we might say, on the periphery of my noetic structure. I accept them, and may even accept them firmly, but I could give them up without much change elsewhere in my noetic structure. I believe there are some large boulders on the top of the Grand Teton. If I come to give up this belief (say by climbing it and not finding any), that change need not have extensive reverberations throughout the rest of my noetic structure; it could be accommodated with minimal alteration elsewhere. So its depth of ingression into my noetic structure is not great. On the other hand, if I were to come to believe that there simply is no such thing as the Grand Teton, or no mountains at all, or no such thing as the state of Wyoming, that would have much greater reverberations. And suppose I were to come to think there had not been much of a past (that the world was created just five minutes ago, complete with all its apparent memories and traces of the past) or that there were not any other persons: these changes would have even greater reverberations; these beliefs of mine have great depth of ingression into my noetic structure. . . .

Now foundationalism is best construed, I think, as a thesis about *rational* noetic structures. A noetic structure is rational if it could be the noetic structure of a person who was completely rational. To be completely rational, as I am here using the term, is not to believe only what is true, or to believe all the logical consequences of what one believes, or

to believe all necessary truths with equal firmness, or to be uninfluenced by emotion in forming belief; it is, instead, to do the right thing with respect to one's believings. It is to violate no epistemic duties. From this point of view, a rational person is one whose believings meet the appropriate standards; to criticize a person as irrational is to criticize her for failing to fulfill these duties or responsibilities, for failing to conform to the relevant norms or standards. To draw the ethical analogy, the irrational is the impermissible; the rational is the permissible. . . .

A rational noetic structure, then, is one that could be the noetic structure of a wholly rational person; and foundationalism, as I say, is a thesis about such noetic structures. We may think of the foundationalist as beginning with the observation that some of our beliefs are based upon others. According to the foundationalist a rational noetic structure will *have a foundation*—a set of beliefs not accepted on the basis of others; in a rational noetic structure some beliefs will be basic. Nonbasic beliefs, of course, will be accepted on the basis of other beliefs, which may be accepted on the basis of still other beliefs, and so on until the foundations are reached. In a rational noetic structure, therefore, every nonbasic belief is ultimately accepted on the basis of basic beliefs. . . .

According to the foundationalist, therefore, every rational noetic structure has a foundation, and all nonbasic beliefs are ultimately accepted on the basis of beliefs in the foundations. But a belief cannot properly be accepted on the basis of just *any* other belief; in a rational noetic structure, A will be accepted on the basis of B only if B *supports* A or is a member of a set of beliefs that together support A. It is not clear just what this relation—call it the "supports" relation—is; and different foundationalists propose different candidates. Presumably, however, it lies in the neighborhood of *evidence*; if A supports B, then A is evidence for B, or makes B evident; or perhaps B is likely or probable with respect to B. This relation admits of degrees. My belief that Feike can swim is supported by my knowledge that nine out of ten Frisians can swim and Feike is a Frisian; it is supported more strongly by my knowledge that the evening paper contains a picture of Feike triumphantly finishing first in the fifteen-hundred meter freestyle in the 1980 summer Olympics. And the foundationalist holds, sensibly enough, that in a rational noetic structure the strength of a nonbasic belief will depend upon the degree of support from foundational beliefs. . . .

By way of summary, then, let us say that according to foundationalism: (1) in a rational noetic structure the believed-on-the-basis-of relation is asymmetric and irreflexive, (2) a rational noetic structure has a foundation, and (3) in a rational noetic structure nonbasic belief is proportional in strength to support from the foundations.

Conditions of Proper Basicality

Next we note a further and fundamental feature of classic varieties of foundationalism: they all lay down certain conditions of proper basicality. From the foundationalist point of view not just any kind of belief can be found in the foundations of a rational noetic structure; a belief to be properly basic (that is, basic in a rational noetic structure) must meet certain conditions. It must be capable of functioning foundationally, capable of bearing its share of the weight of the whole noetic structure. Thus Thomas Aquinas, as we have seen, holds that a proposition is properly basic for a person only if it is self-evident to him or "evident to the senses."

Suppose we take a brief look at self-evidence. Under what conditions does a proposition have it? What kinds of propositions are self-evident? Examples would include very simple arithmetical truths such as

(1) 2 + 1 = 3;

simple truths of logic such as

(2) No man is both married and unmarried;

perhaps the generalizations of simple truths of logic, such as

(3) For any proposition p the conjunction of p with its denial is false;

and certain propositions expressing identity and diversity; for example,

(4) Redness is distinct from greenness,
(5) The property of being prime is distinct from the property of being composite,

and

(6) The proposition *all* men are *mortal* is distinct from the proposition *all mortals are men.*

· ·

Still other candidates—candidates which may be less than entirely uncontroversial—come from many other areas; for example,

(7) If p is necessarily true and p entails q, then q is necessarily true,
(8) If e^1 occurs before e^2 and e^2 occurs before e^3, then e^1 occurs before e^3,

and

(9) It is wrong to cause unnecessary (and unwanted) pain just for the fun of it.

What is it that characterizes these propositions? According to the tradition the outstanding characteristic of a self-evident proposition is that one simply sees it to be true upon grasping or understanding it. Understanding a self-evident proposition is sufficient for apprehending its truth. Of course this notion must be relativized to *persons;* what is self-evident to you might not be to me. Very simple arithmetical truths will be self-evident to nearly all of us, but a truth like 17 + 18 = 35 may be self-evident only to some. And of course a proposition is self-evident to a person only if he does in fact grasp it, so a proposition will not be self-evident to those who do not apprehend the concepts it involves. As Aquinas says, some propositions are self-evident only to the learned; his example is the truth that immaterial substances do not occupy space. Among those propositions whose concepts not everyone grasps, some are such that anyone who *did* grasp them would see their truth; for example,

(10) A model of a first-order theory T assigns truth to the axioms of T.

Others—17 + 13 = 30, for example—may be such that some but not all of those who apprehend them also see that they are true.

But how shall we understand this "seeing that they are true?" Those who speak of self-evidence explicitly turn to this visual metaphor and expressly explain self-evidence by reference to vision. There are two important aspects to the metaphor and two corresponding components to the idea of self-evidence. First, there is the *epistemic* component: a proposition *p* is self-evident to a person *S* only if *S* has *immediate* knowledge of *p*—that is, knows *p*, and does not know *p* on the basis of his knowledge of other propositions. Consider a simple arithmetic truth such as *2 + 1 = 3* and compare it with one like *24 × 24 = 576*. I know each of these propositions, and I know the second but not the first on the basis of computation, which is a kind of inference. So I have immediate knowledge of the first but not the second.

But there is also a phenomenological component. Consider again our two propositions; the first but not the second has about it a kind of luminous aura or glow when you bring it to mind or consider it. Locke speaks, in this connection, of an "evident luster"; a self-evident proposition, he says, displays a kind of "clarity and brightness to the attentive mind." Descartes speaks instead of "clarity and distinctness"; each, I think, is referring to the same phenomenological feature. And this feature is connected with another: upon understanding a proposition of this sort one feels a strong inclination to accept it; this luminous obviousness seems to compel or at least impel assent. Aquinas and Locke, indeed, held that a person, or at any rate a normal, well-formed human being, finds it impossible to withhold assent when considering a self-evident proposition. The phenomenological component of the idea of self-evidence, then, seems to have a double aspect: there is the luminous aura that *2 + 1 = 3* displays, and there is also an experienced tendency to accept or believe it. Perhaps, indeed, the luminous aura *just is* the experienced impulsion toward acceptance; perhaps these are the very same thing. In that case the phenomenological component would not have the double aspect I suggested it did have; in either case, however, we

must recognize this phenomenological aspect of self-evidence.

Aquinas therefore holds that self-evident propositions are properly basic. I think he means to add that propositions "evident to the senses" are also properly basic. By this latter term I think he means to refer to *perceptual* propositions—propositions whose truth or falsehood we can determine by looking or employing some other sense. He has in mind, I think, such propositions as

(11) There is a tree before me,

(12) I am wearing shoes,

and

(13) That tree's leaves are yellow.

So Aquinas holds that a proposition is properly basic if and only if it is either self-evident or evident to the senses. Other foundationalists have insisted that propositions basic in a rational noetic structure must be *certain* in some important sense. Thus it is plausible to see Descartes as holding that the foundations of a rational noetic structure include, not such propositions as (11)–(13), but more cautious claims—claims about one's own mental life; for example,

(14) It seems to me that I see a tree,

(15) I seem to see something green,

or, as Professor Chisholm puts it,

(16) I am appeared greenly to.

Propositions of this latter sort seem to enjoy a kind of immunity from error not enjoyed by those of the former. I could be mistaken in thinking I see a pink rat; perhaps I am hallucinating or the victim of an illusion. But it is at the least very much harder to see that I could be mistaken in believing that I *seem* to see a pink rat, in believing that I am appeared pinkly (or pink ratly) to. Suppose we say that a proposition with respect to which I enjoy this sort of immunity from error is incorrigible for me; then perhaps Descartes means to hold that a proposition is properly basic for *S* only if it is either self-evident or incorrigible for *S*.

By way of explicit definition:

(17) *p* is incorrigible for *S* if and only if (a) it is not possible that *S* believes *p* and *p* be false, and (b) it is not possible that *S* believe ~*p* and *p* be true.

· ·

Here we have a further characteristic of foundationalism: the claim that not just any proposition is properly basic. Ancient and medieval foundationalists tended to hold that a proposition is properly basic for a person only if it is either self-evident or evident to the senses: modern foundationalists—Descartes, Locke, Leibniz, and the like—tended to hold that a proposition is properly basic for *S* only if either self-evident or incorrigible for *S*. Of course this is a historical generalization and is thus perilous; but perhaps it is worth the risk. And now let us say that a *classical foundationalist* is any one who is either an ancient and medieval or a modern foundationalist.

The Collapse of Foundationalism

Now suppose we return to the main question: Why should not belief in God be among the foundations of my noetic structure? The answer, on the part of the classical foundationalist, was that even if this belief is *true*, it does not have the characteristics a proposition must have to deserve a place in the foundations. There is no room in the foundations for a proposition that can be rationally accepted only on the basis of other propositions. The only properly basic propositions are those that are self-evident or incorrigible or evident to the senses. Since the proposition that God exists is none of the above, it is not properly basic for anyone; that is, no well-formed, rational noetic structure contains this proposition in its foundations. But now we must take a closer look at this fundamental principle of classical foundationalism:

(18) A proposition *p* is properly basic for a person *S* if and only if *p* is either self-evident to *S* or incorrigible for *S* or evident to the senses for *S*.

(18) contains two claims: first, a proposition is properly basic *if* it is self-evident, incorrigible, or

evident to the senses, and, second, a proposition is properly basic *only if* it meets this condition. The first seems true enough; suppose we concede it. But what is to be said for the second? Is there any reason to accept it? Why does the foundationalist accept it? Why does he think the theist ought to?

We should note first that if this thesis, and the correlative foundationalist thesis that a proposition is rationally acceptable only if it follows from or is probable with respect to what is properly basic—if these claims are true, then enormous quantities of what we all in fact believe are irrational. One crucial lesson to be learned from the development of modern philosophy—Descartes through Hume, roughly—is just this: relative to propositions that are self-evident and incorrigible, most of the beliefs that form the stock in trade of ordinary everyday life are not probable—at any rate there is no reason to think they are probable. Consider all those propositions that entail, say, that there are enduring physical objects, or that there are persons distinct from myself, or that the world has existed for more than five minutes: none of these propositions, I think, is more probable than not with respect to what is self-evident or incorrigible for me; at any rate no one has given good reason to think any of them is. And now suppose we add to the foundations propositions that are evident to the senses, thereby moving from modern to ancient and medieval foundationalism. Then propositions entailing the existence of material objects will of course be probable with respect to the foundations, because included therein. But the same cannot be said either for propositions about the past or for propositions entailing the existence of persons distinct from myself; as before, these will not be probable with respect to what is properly basic.

And does not this show that the thesis in question is false? The contention is that

(19) *A* is properly basic for me only if *A* is self-evident or incorrigible or evident to the senses for me.

But many propositions that do not meet these conditions *are* properly basic for me. I believe, for example, that I had lunch this noon. I do not believe this proposition on the basis of other propositions;

I take it as basic; it is in the foundations of my noetic structure. Furthermore, I am entirely rational in so taking it, even though this proposition is neither self-evident nor evident to the senses nor incorrigible for me. Of course this may not convince the foundationalist; he may think that in fact I do *not* take that proposition as basic, or perhaps he will bite the bullet and maintain that if I really *do* take it as basic, then the fact is I *am*, so far forth, irrational.

Perhaps the following will be more convincing. According to the classical foundationalist (call him *F*) a person *S* is rational in accepting (19) only if either (19) is properly basic (self-evident or incorrigible or evident to the senses) for him, or he believes (19) on the basis of propositions that are properly basic for him and support (19). Now presumably if *F* knows of some support for (19) from propositions that are self-evident or evident to the senses or incorrigible, he will be able to provide a good argument—deductive, inductive, probabilistic or whatever—whose premises are self-evident or evident to the senses or incorrigible and whose conclusion is (19). So far as I know, no foundationalist has provided such an argument. It therefore appears that the foundationalist does not know of any support for (19) from propositions that are (on his account) properly basic. So if he is to be rational in accepting (19), he must (on his own account) accept it as basic. But according to (19) itself, (19) is properly basic for *F* only if (19) is self-evident or incorrigible or evident to the senses for him. Clearly (19) meets none of these conditions. Hence it is not properly basic for *F*. But then *F* is self-referentially inconsistent in accepting (19); he accepts (19) as basic, despite the fact that (19) does not meet the condition for proper basicality that (19) itself lays down.

Furthermore, (19) is either false or such that in accepting it the foundationalist is violating his epistemic responsibilities. For *F* does not know of any argument or evidence for (19). Hence if it is true, he will be violating his epistemic responsibilities in accepting it. So (19) is either false or such that *F* cannot rationally accept it. Still further, if the theist were to accept (19) at the foundationalist's urging but without argument, he would be adding to his noetic structure a proposition that is either false or

such that in accepting it he violates his noetic responsibilities. But if there is such a thing as the ethics of belief, surely it will proscribe believing a proposition one knows to be either false or such that one ought not to believe it. Accordingly, I ought not to accept (19) in the absence of argument from premises that meet the condition it lays down. The same goes for the foundationalist: if he cannot find such an argument for (19), he ought to give it up. Furthermore, he ought not to urge and I ought not to accept any objection to theistic belief that crucially depends upon a proposition that is true only if I ought not to believe it. . . .

Now we could canvass revisions of (19), and later I shall look into the proper procedure for discovering and justifying such criteria for proper basicality. It is evident, however, that classical foundationalism is bankrupt, and insofar as the evidentialist objection is rooted in classical foundationalism, it is poorly rooted indeed.

Of course the evidentialist objection *need* not presuppose classical foundationalism; someone who accepted quite a different version of foundationalism could no doubt urge this objection. But in order to evaluate it, we should have to see what criterion of proper basicality was being invoked. In the absence of such specification the objection remains at best a promissory note. So far as the present discussion goes, then, the next move is up to the evidentialist objector. He must specify a criterion for proper basicality that is free from self-referential difficulties, rules out belief in God as properly basic, and is such that there is some reason to think it is true. . . .

The Reformed Objection to Natural Theology

Suppose we think of natural theology as the attempt to prove or demonstrate the existence of God. This enterprise has a long and impressive history—a history stretching back to the dawn of Christendom and boasting among its adherents many of the truly great thinkers of the Western world. One thinks, for example, of Anselm, Aquinas, Scotus, and Ockham, of Descartes, Spinoza, and Leibniz. Recently—since the time of Kant, perhaps—the tradition of natural theology has not been as overwhelming as it once was; yet it continues to have able defenders both within and without officially Catholic philosophy.

Many Christians, however, have been less than totally impressed. In particular Reformed or Calvinist theologians have for the most part taken a dim view of this enterprise. A few Reformed thinkers—B. B. Warfield, for example—endorse the theistic proofs, but for the most part the Reformed attitude has ranged from tepid endorsement, through indifference, to suspicion, hostility, and outright accusations of blasphemy. And this stance is initially puzzling. It looks a little like the attitude some Christians adopt toward faith healing: it can't be done, but even if it could it shouldn't be. What exactly, or even approximately, do these sons and daughters of the Reformation have against proving the existence of God? What *could* they have against it? What could be less objectionable to any but the most obdurate atheist?

The Objection Initially Stated

By way of answering this question, I want to consider three representative Reformed thinkers. Let us begin with the nineteenth-century Dutch theologian Herman Bavinck:

> A distinct natural theology, obtained apart from any revelation, merely through observation and study of the universe in which man lives, does not exist. . . .
>
> Scripture urges us to behold heaven and earth, birds and ants, flowers and lilies, in order that we may see and recognize God in them. "Lift up your eyes on high, and see who hath created these." Is. 40:26. Scripture does not reason in the abstract. It does not make God the conclusion of a syllogism, leaving it to us whether we think the argument holds or not. But it speaks with authority. Both theologically and religiously it proceeds from God as the starting point.
>
> We receive the impression that belief in the existence of God is based entirely upon these proofs. But indeed that would be "a wretched faith, which, before it invokes God, must first prove his existence." The contrary, however, is the truth. There is not a single object the existence of which we hesitate to accept until definite proofs are furnished. Of the existence of self, of the world round about us, of logical and moral laws, etc.,

we are so deeply convinced because of the indelible impressions which all these things make upon our consciousness that we need no arguments or demonstration. Spontaneously, altogether involuntarily: without any constraint or coercion, we accept that existence. Now the same is true in regard to the existence of God. The so-called proofs are by no means the final grounds of our most certain conviction that God exists. This certainty is established only by faith; that is, by the spontaneous testimony which forces itself upon us from every side.

According to Bavinck, then, belief in the existence of God is not based upon proofs or arguments. By "argument" here I think he means arguments in the style of natural theology—the sort given by Aquinas and Scotus and later by Descartes, Leibniz, Clarke, and others. And what he means to say, I think, is that Christians do not *need* such arguments. Do not need them for what?

Here I think Bavinck means to hold two things. First, arguments or proofs are not, in general, the source of the believer's confidence in God. Typically the believer does not believe in God on the basis of arguments; nor does he believe such truths as that God has created the world on the basis of arguments. Second, argument is not needed for *rational justification*; the believer is entirely within his epistemic right in believing, for example, that God has created the world, even if he has no argument at all for that conclusion. The believer does not need natural theology in order to achieve rationality or epistemic propriety in believing; his belief in God can be perfectly rational even if he knows of no cogent argument, deductive or inductive, for the existence of God—indeed, even if there is no such argument.

Bavinck has three further points. First he means to add, I think, that we cannot come to knowledge of God on the basis of argument; the arguments of natural theology just do not work. (And he follows this passage with a more or less traditional attempt to refute the theistic proofs, including an endorsement of some of Kant's fashionable confusions about the ontological argument.) Second, Scripture "proceeds from God as the starting point," and so should the believer. There is nothing by way of proofs or arguments for God's existence in the Bible; that is simply presupposed. The same should be true of the Christian believer then; he should *start* from belief in God rather than from the premises of some argument whose conclusion is that God exists. What is it that makes those premises a better starting point anyway? And third, Bavinck points out that belief in God relevantly resembles belief in the existence of the self and of the external world—and, we might add, belief in other minds and the past. In none of these areas do we typically *have* proof or arguments, or *need* proofs or arguments.

Suppose we turn next to John Calvin, who is as good a Calvinist as any. According to Calvin God has implanted in us all an innate tendency, or *nisus*, or disposition to believe in him:

'There is within the human mind, and indeed by natural instinct, an awareness of divinity.' This we take to be beyond controversy. To prevent anyone from taking refuge in the pretense of ignorance, God himself has implanted in all men a certain understanding of his divine majesty. Ever renewing its memory, he repeatedly sheds fresh drops. Since, therefore, men one and all perceive that there is a God and that he is their Maker, they are condemned by their own testimony because they have failed to honor him and to consecrate their lives to his will. If ignorance of God is to be looked for anywhere, surely one is most likely to find an example of it among the more backward folk and those more remote from civilization. Yet there is, as the eminent pagan says, no nation so barbarous, no people so savage, that they have not a deep-seated conviction that there is a God. So deeply does the common conception occupy the minds of all, so tenaciously does it inhere in the hearts of all! Therefore, since from the beginning of the world there has been no region, no city, in short, no household, that could do without religion, there lies in this a tacit confession of a sense of deity inscribed in the hearts of all.

Indeed, the perversity of the impious, who though they struggle furiously are unable to extricate themselves from the fear of God, is abundant testimony that this conviction, namely, that *there is some God*, is naturally inborn in all, and is fixed deep within, as it were in the very marrow. . . . From this we conclude *that it is not a doctrine that must first be learned in school*, but one of which each of us is master from his mother's womb and which nature itself permits no one to forget.

Calvin's claim, then, is that God has created us in such a way that we have a strong tendency or inclination toward belief in him. This tendency has been in part overlaid or suppressed by sin. Were it not for the existence of sin in the world, human beings would believe in God to the same degree and with the same natural spontaneity that we believe in the existence of other persons, an external world, or the past. This is the natural human condition; it is because of our presently unnatural sinful condition that many of us find belief in God difficult or absurd. The fact is, Calvin thinks, one who does not believe in God is in an epistemically substandard position—rather like a man who does not believe that his wife exists, or thinks she is like a cleverly constructed robot and has no thoughts, feelings, or consciousness.

Although this disposition to believe in God is partially suppressed, it is nonetheless universally present. And it is triggered or actuated by a widely realized condition:

Lest anyone, then, be excluded from access to happiness, he not only sowed in men's minds that seed of religion of which we have spoken, but revealed himself and daily discloses himself in the whole workmanship of the universe. As a consequence, men cannot open their eyes without being compelled to see him.

Like Kant, Calvin is especially impressed in this connection, by the marvelous compages of the starry heavens above:

Even the common folk and the most untutored, who have been taught only by the aid of the eyes, cannot be unaware of the excellence of divine art, for it reveals itself in this innumerable and yet distinct and well-ordered variety of the heavenly host.

And Calvin's claim is that one who accedes to this tendency and in these circumstances accepts the belief that God has created the world—perhaps upon beholding the starry heavens, or the splendid majesty of the mountains, or the intricate, articulate beauty of a tiny flower—is entirely within his epistemic rights in so doing. It is not that such a person is justified or rational in so believing by virtue of having an implicit argument—some version of the teleological argument, say. No; he does not need any argument for justification or rationality. His belief need not be based on any other propositions at all; under these conditions he is perfectly rational in accepting belief in God in the utter absence of any argument, deductive or inductive. Indeed, a person in these conditions, says Calvin, *knows* that God exists.

Elsewhere Calvin speaks of "arguments from reason" or rational arguments:

The prophets and apostles do not boast either of their keenness or of anything that obtains credit for them as they speak; nor do they dwell upon rational proofs. Rather, they bring forward God's holy name, that by it the whole world may be brought into obedience to him. Now we ought to see how apparent it is not only by plausible opinion but by clear truth that they do not call upon God's name heedlessly or falsely. If we desire to provide in the best way for our consciences—that they may not be perpetually beset by the instability of doubt or vacillation, and that they may not also boggle at the smallest quibbles—we ought to seek our conviction in a higher place than human reasons, judgments, or conjectures, that is, in the secret testimony of the Spirit. (book 1, chapter 7, p. 78)

Here the subject for discussion is not belief in the existence of God, but belief that God is the author of the Scriptures; I think it is clear, however, that Calvin would say the same thing about belief in God's existence. The Christian does not *need* natural theology, either as the source of his confidence or to justify his belief. Furthermore, the Christian *ought* not to believe on the basis of argument; if he does, his faith is likely to be "unstable and wavering," the "subject of perpetual doubt." If my belief in God is based on argument, then if I am to be properly rational, epistemically responsible, I shall have to keep checking the philosophical journals to see whether, say, Anthony Flew has finally come up with a good objection to my favorite argument. This could be bothersome and time-consuming; and what do I do if someone does find a flaw in my argument? Stop going to church? From Calvin's point of view believing in the existence of God on the basis of rational argument is like believing in the existence of your spouse on the basis of the analogical argument for other minds—whimsical at best and unlikely to delight the person concerned. . . .

Karl Barth joins Calvin and Bavinck in holding that the believer in God is entirely within his epistemic rights in believing as he does even if he does not know of any good theistic argument. They all hold that belief in God is *properly basic*—that is, such that it is rational to accept it without accepting it on the basis of any other proposition or beliefs at all. In fact, they think the Christian ought not to accept belief in God on the basis of argument; to do so is to run the risk of a faith that is unstable and wavering, subject to all the wayward whim and fancy of the latest academic fashion. What the Reformers held was that a believer is entirely rational, entirely within his epistemic rights, in *starting with* belief in God, in accepting it as basic, and in taking it as premise for argument to other conclusions.

In rejecting natural theology, therefore, these Reformed thinkers mean to say first of all that the propriety or rightness of belief in God in no way depends upon the success or availability of the sort of theistic arguments that form the natural theologian's stock in trade. I think this is their central claim here, and their central insight. As these Reformed thinkers see things, one who takes belief in God as basic is not thereby violating any epistemic duties or revealing a defect in his noetic structure; quite the reverse. The correct or proper way to believe in God, they thought, was not on the basis of arguments from natural theology or anywhere else; the correct way is to take belief in God as basic.

I spoke earlier of classical foundationalism, a view that incorporates the following three theses:

(1) In every rational noetic structure there is a set of beliefs taken as basic—that is, not accepted on the basis of any other beliefs,

(2) In a rational noetic structure nonbasic belief is proportional to support from the foundations,

and

(3) In a rational noetic structure basic beliefs will be self-evident or incorrigible or evident to the senses.

Now I think these three Reformed thinkers should be understood as rejecting classical foundationalism. They may have been inclined to accept (1); they show no objection to (2); but they were utterly at odds with the idea that the foundations of a rational noetic structure can at most include propositions that are self-evident or evident to the senses or incorrigible. In particular, they were prepared to insist that a rational noetic structure can include belief in God as basic. As Bavinck put it, "Scripture

. . . does not make God the conclusion of a syllogism, leaving it to us whether we think the argument holds or not. But it speaks with authority. Both theologically and religiously it proceeds from God as the starting point." And of course Bavinck means to say that we must emulate Scripture here.

In the passages I quoted earlier, Calvin claims the believer does not need argument—does not need it, among other things, for epistemic respectability. We may understand him as holding, I think, that a rational noetic structure may very well contain belief in God among its foundations. Indeed, he means to go further, and in two separate directions. In the first place he thinks a Christian *ought* not believe in God on the basis of other propositions; a proper and well-formed Christian noetic structure will *in fact* have belief in God among its foundations. And in the second place Calvin claims that one who takes belief in God as basic can *know* that God exists. Calvin holds that one can *rationally accept* belief in God as basic; he also claims that one can *know* that God exists even if he has no argument, even if he does not believe on the basis of other propositions. A foundationalist is likely to hold that some properly basic beliefs are such that anyone who accepts them *knows* them. More exactly, he is likely to hold that among the beliefs properly basic for a person *S*, some are such that if *S* accepts them, *S* knows them. He could go on to say that *other* properly basic beliefs cannot be known if taken as basic, but only rationally believed; and he might think of the existence of God as a case in point. Calvin will have none of this; as he sees it, one needs no arguments to know that God exists. . . .

Is Belief in God Properly Basic?

The Great Pumpkin Objection

It is tempting to raise the following sort of question. If belief in God is properly basic, why cannot *just any* belief be properly basic? Could we not say the same for any bizarre aberration we can think of? What about voodoo or astrology? What about the belief that the Great Pumpkin returns every Hallow-

een? Could I properly take *that* as a basic? Suppose I believe that if I flap my arms with sufficient vigor, I can take off and fly about the room; could I defend myself against the charge of irrationality by claiming this belief is basic? If we say that belief in God is properly basic, will we not be committed to holding that just anything, or nearly anything, can properly be taken as basic, thus throwing wide the gates to irrationalism and superstition?

Certainly not. According to the Reformed epistemologist certain beliefs are properly basic in certain circumstances; those same beliefs may *not* be properly basic in other circumstances. Consider the belief that I see a tree: this belief is properly basic in circumstances that are hard to describe in detail, but include my being appeared to in a certain characteristic way; that same belief is not properly basic in circumstances including, say, my knowledge that I am sitting in the living room listening to music with my eyes closed. What the Reformed epistemologist holds is that there are widely realized circumstances in which belief in God is properly basic; but why should that be thought to commit him to the idea that just about *any* belief is properly basic in any circumstances, or even to the vastly weaker claim that for any belief there are circumstances in which it is properly basic? Is it just that he rejects the criteria for proper basicality purveyed by classical foundationalism? But why should *that* be thought to commit him to such tolerance of irrationality? Consider an analogy. In the palmy days of positivism the positivists went about confidently wielding their verifiability criterion and declaring meaningless much that was clearly meaningful. Now suppose someone rejected a formulation of that criterion—the one to be found in the second edition of A. J. Ayer's *Language, Truth and Logic*, for example. Would that mean she was committed to holding that

(1) T' was brillig; and the slithy toves did gyre and gymble in the wabe,

contrary to appearances, makes good sense? Of course not. But then the same goes for the Reformed epistemologist: the fact that he rejects the criterion of proper basicality purveyed by classical foundationalism does not mean that he is committed to supposing just anything is properly basic.

But what then is the problem? Is it that the Reformed epistemologist not only rejects those criteria for proper basicality but seems in no hurry to produce what he takes to be a better substitute? If he has no such criterion, how can he fairly reject belief in the Great Pumpkin as properly basic?

This objection betrays an important misconception. How *do* we rightly arrive at or develop criteria for meaningfulness, or justified belief, or proper basicality? Where do they come from? Must one have such a criterion before one can sensibly make any judgments—positive or negative—about proper basicality? Surely not. Suppose I do not know of a satisfactory substitute for the criteria proposed by classical foundationalism; I am nevertheless entirely within my epistemic rights in holding that certain propositions in certain conditions are not properly basic.

Some propositions seem self-evident when in fact they are not; that is the lesson of some of the Russell paradoxes. Nevertheless it would be irrational to take as basic the denial of a proposition that seems self-evident to you. Similarly, suppose it seems to you that you see a tree; you would then be irrational in taking as basic the proposition that you do not see a tree or that there are no trees; in the same way, even if I do not know of some illuminating criterion of meaning, I can quite properly declare (1) (above) meaningless.

And this raises an important question—one Roderick Chisholm has taught us to ask. What is the status of criteria for knowledge, or proper basicality, or justified belief? Typically these are universal statements. The modern foundationalist's criterion for proper basicality, for example, is doubly universal:

(2) For any proposition *A* and person *S*, *A* is properly basic for *S* if and only if *A* is incorrigible for *S* or self-evident to *S*.

But how could one know a thing like that? What are its credentials? Clearly enough, (2) is not self-evident or just obviously true. But if it is not, how does one arrive at it? What sorts of arguments would be appropriate? Of course a foundationalist might find (2) so appealing he simply takes it to be true, neither offering argument for it nor accepting it on the basis of other things he believes. If he does so, however, his noetic structure will be self-referentially incoherent. (2) itself is neither self-evident nor incorrigible; hence if he accepts (2) as basic, the modern foundationalist violates in accepting it the condition of proper basicality he himself lays down. On the other hand, perhaps the foundationalist will try to produce some argument for it from premises that are self-evident or incorrigible: it is exceeding hard to see, however, what such an argument might be like. And until he has produced such arguments, what shall the rest of us do—we who do not find (2) at all obvious or compelling? How could he use (2) to show us that belief in God, for example, is not properly basic? Why should we believe (2) or pay it any attention?

The fact is, I think, that neither (2) nor any other revealing necessary and sufficient condition for proper basicality follows from clearly self-evident premises by clearly acceptable arguments. And hence the proper way to arrive at such a criterion is, broadly speaking, *inductive*. We must assemble examples of beliefs and conditions such that the former are obviously properly basic in the latter, and examples of beliefs and conditions such that the former are obviously *not* properly basic in the latter. We must then frame hypotheses as to the necessary and sufficient conditions of proper basicality and test these hypotheses by reference to those examples. Under the right conditions, for example, it is clearly rational to believe that you see a human person before you: a being who has thoughts and feelings, who knows and believes things, who makes decisions and acts. It is clear, furthermore, that you are under no obligation to reason to this belief from others you hold; under those conditions that belief is properly basic for you. But then (2) must be mistaken; the belief in question, under those circumstances, is properly basic, though neither self-evident nor incorrigible for you. Similarly, you may seem to remember that you had breakfast this morning, and perhaps you know of no reason to suppose your memory is playing you tricks. If so, you are entirely justified in taking that belief as basic. Of course it is not properly basic on the criteria offered by classical foundationalists, but that fact counts not against you but against those criteria. . . .

Accordingly, criteria for proper basicality must be reached from below rather than above; they should not be presented *ex cathedra* but argued to and tested by a relevant set of examples. But there is no reason to assume, in advance, that everyone will agree on the examples. The Christian will of course suppose that belief in God is entirely proper and rational; if he does not accept this belief on the basis of other propositions, he will conclude that it is basic for him and quite properly so. Followers of Bertrand Russell and Madelyn Murray O'Hare may disagree; but how is that relevant? Must my criteria, or those of the Christian community, conform to their examples? Surely not. The Christian community is responsible to *its* set of examples, not to theirs. . . .

So, the Reformed epistemologist can properly hold that belief in the Great Pumpkin is not properly basic, even though he holds that belief in God is properly basic and even if he has no full-fledged criterion of proper basicality. Of course he is committed to supposing that there is a relevant *difference* between belief in God and belief in the Great Pumpkin if he holds that the former but not the latter is properly basic. But this should prove no great embarrassment; there are plenty of candidates. These candidates are to be found in the neighborhood of the conditions that justify and ground belief in God—conditions I shall discuss in the next section. Thus, for example, the Reformed epistemologist may concur with Calvin in holding that God has implanted in us a natural tendency to see his hand in the world around us; the same cannot be said for the Great Pumpkin, there being no Great Pumpkin and no natural tendency to accept beliefs about the Great Pumpkin.

VII.D.3 A Critique of Plantinga's Religious Epistemology

MICHAEL MARTIN

Michael Martin is professor of philosophy at Boston University and author of several works in philosophy of science and philosophy of religion, including Atheism: A Philosophical Justification *(1990), from which this essay is taken.*

In this essay Martin analyzes Plantinga's arguments for proper basicality and argues that they fail, that his arguments against classical foundationalism are weak, that his logic leads to an extreme relativism, and that his own foundationalism has serious problems.

Religious Beliefs and Basic Beliefs

One recent attempt to justify religious beliefs argues that some religious beliefs—for example, the belief that God exists—should be considered as basic beliefs that form the foundations of all other beliefs. The best-known advocate of this position is Alvin Plantinga, whose theory is based on a critique of classical foundationalism.

Foundationalism

Foundationalism was once a widely accepted view in epistemology; and although it has undergone modifications, it still has many advocates. The motivation for the view seems compelling. If we try to justify all our beliefs in terms of other beliefs, the justification generates an infinite regress or vicious circularity. Therefore, there must be some beliefs that do not need to be justified by other beliefs. Because they form the foundation of all knowledge, these are called basic beliefs, and the statements expressing them are called basic statements.

Foundationalism is usually considered a normative theory. It sets standards of what are properly basic beliefs and standards of how nonbasic beliefs are to be related to basic ones. Not every belief could be basic and not every relation could link nonbasic beliefs to basic ones. According to the classical normative account of foundationalism, if one believes that a self-evident statement P is true because of the statement's self-evidence, then P is a properly basic one. According to this view, if a statement is self-evident, no conscious inference or calculation is required to determine its truth; one can merely look at it and know immediately that it is true. For example, certain simple and true statements of mathematics (2 + 2 = 4) and logic (either p or ~p) are self-evidently true to almost everyone, while some more complex statements of mathematics and logic are self-evidently true only to some. Consequently, statements such as 2 + 2 = 4 are considered basic statements for almost everyone while the more complex statements are basic only to some.

In addition to self-evident statements, classical foundationalists held that beliefs based on direct perception are properly basic and the statements expressing such beliefs—sometimes called statements that are evident to the senses—were considered basic statements. Some foundationalists included, in the class of statements that are evident to the senses, ones about observed physical objects (There is a blue bird in the tree). However, in modern times it has been more common for foundationalists to restrict statements that are evident to the senses to ones about immediate sense impressions (I seem to see a blue bird in the tree, or I am being appeared to bluely, or perhaps, Here now blue sense datum). According to the classical foundationalist account, statements that are evident to the senses are incorrigible; that is, one can not believe such statements and be mistaken.

Denying that any statement is incorrigible, many contemporary epistemologists, although sympathetic with the foundationalist program, have maintained that statements that are evident to the senses are either initially credible or self-warranted. Moreover, some contemporary foundationalists have argued that memory statements, such as "I remember having breakfast ten minutes ago" should be included in the class of properly basic statements. Classical foundationalism also maintained that nonbasic beliefs had to be justified in terms of basic beliefs. Thus in order for a person P's nonbasic statement NS_1 (Other people have minds) to be justified, it would either have to follow logically from P's set of basic statement BS_1 & BS_2 & . . . BS_n or be probable relative to that set of statements. However, those contemporary foundationalists who maintain that properly basic statements are only initially credible allow that it is possible that a person P's basic statement BS_1 could be shown to be false if it conflicted with many of the well-supported nonbasic statements NS_1 & NS_2 & . . . NS_n of P. In addition, some have argued that deductive and inductive principles of inference must be supplemented with other principles of derivation. Consequently, a person P's nonbasic statement NS_1 is justified only if it follows from P's set of basic statements or is probable relative to this set or is justified relative to this set by means of certain special epistemic principles.

Plantinga's Critique of Foundationalism

Plantinga characterizes foundationalism as follows:

> Ancient and medieval foundationalists tended to hold that a proposition is properly basic for a person only if it is either self-evident or evident to the senses: modern foundationalists—Descartes, Locke, Leibniz, and the like—tended to hold that a proposition is properly basic for *S* only if either self-evident or incorrigible for *S*. Let us now say that a *classical foundationalist* is any one who is either an ancient and medieval or a modern foundationalist.

He defines properly basic statements in terms of this understanding of foundationalism. Consider:

(1) A proposition p is properly basic for a person S if and only if p is self-evident to S, or incorrigible, or evident to the senses.

Plantinga gives two basic arguments against foundationalism so understood. (a) He maintains that many of the statements we know to be true cannot be justified in foundationalist terms. These statements are not properly basic according to the definition given above, nor can they be justified by either deductive or inductive inference from properly basic statements. As examples of such statements Plantinga cites "Other people have minds" and "The world existed five minutes ago." To be sure, he says, such statements are basic for most people in a descriptive sense. According to classical foundationalists, however, they should not be, since they are not self-evident, not incorrigible, and not evident to the senses. According to Plantinga, examples such as these show that there is something very wrong with classical foundationalism.

(b) Plantinga argues also that foundationalists are unable to justify (1) in their own terms; that is, they have not shown that (1) follows from properly basic statements or is probable relative to these. Moreover, (1) is not itself self-evident or incorrigible or evident to the senses. Consequently, he argues, a foundationalist who accepts (1) is being "self-referentially inconsistent"; such a person accepts a statement that does not meet the person's own conditions for being properly basic. Thus he concludes that classical foundationalism is "bankrupt."

Belief in God as Properly Basic

Following a long line of reformed thinkers—that is, thinkers influenced by the doctrines of John Calvin, Plantinga contends that traditional arguments for the existence of God are not needed for rational belief. He cites with approval Calvin's claim that God created humans in such a way that they have a strong tendency to believe in God. According to Plantinga, Calvin maintained:

> Were it not for the existence of sin in the world, human beings would believe in God to the same degree and with the same natural spontaneity that we believe in the existence of other persons, an external world, or the past. This is the natural human condition; it is because of our presently unnatural sinful condition that many of us find belief in God difficult or absurd. The fact is, Calvin thinks, one who does not believe in God is in an epistemically substandard position—rather like

a man who does not believe that his wife exists, or thinks she is like a cleverly constructed robot and has no thoughts, feelings, or consciousness.

Although this natural tendency to believe in God may be partially suppressed, Plantinga argues, it is triggered by "a widely realizable condition." For example, it may be triggered "in beholding the starry heavens, or the splendid majesty of the mountains, or the intricate, articulate beauty of a tiny flower." This natural tendency to accept God in these circumstances is perfectly rational. No argument for God is needed. Plantinga maintains that the best interpretation of Calvin's views, as well as those of the reformed thinkers he cites, is that they rejected classical foundationalism and maintained that belief in God can itself be a properly basic belief.

Surprisingly, Plantinga insists that although belief in God and belief about God's attributes and actions are properly basic, for reformed epistemologists this does not mean that there are no justifying circumstances or that they are without grounds. The circumstances that trigger the natural tendency to believe in God and to believe certain things about God provide the justifying circumstances for belief. So although beliefs about God are properly basic, they are not groundless.

How can we understand this? Plantinga draws an analogy between basic statements of religion and basic statements of perceptual belief and memory. A perceptual belief, he says, is taken as properly basic only under certain circumstances. For example, if I know that I am wearing rose-tinted glasses, then I am not justified in saying that the statement "I see a rose-colored wall before me" is properly basic; and if I know that my memory is unreliable, I am not justified in saying that the statement "I remember that I had breakfast" is properly basic. Although Plantinga admits that these conditions may be hard to specify, he maintains that their presence is necessary in order to claim that a perceptual or memory statement is basic. Similarly, he maintains that not every statement about God that is not based on argument or evidence should be considered properly basic. A statement is properly basic only in the right circumstances. What circumstances are right? Plantinga gives no general account, but in addition to the triggering condition mentioned above, the right conditions include reading the Bible, having done something wrong, and being in grave danger. Thus if one is reading the Bible and believes that God is speaking to one, then the belief is properly basic.

Furthermore, Plantinga insists that although reformed epistemologists allow belief in God as a properly basic belief, this does not mean they must allow that anything at all can be a basic belief. To be sure, he admits that he and other reformed epistemologists have not supplied us with any criterion of what is properly basic. He argues, however, that this is not necessary. One can know that some beliefs in some circumstances are not properly basic without having an explicitly formulated criterion of basicness. Thus Plantinga says that reformed epistemologists can correctly maintain that belief in voodoo or astrology or the Great Pumpkin is not a basic belief.

How is one to arrive at a criterion for being properly basic? According to Plantinga the route is "broadly speaking, *inductive.*" He adds, "We must assemble examples of beliefs and conditions such that the former are obviously properly basic in the latter. . . . We must frame hypotheses as to the necessary and sufficient conditions of proper basicality and test these hypotheses by reference to these examples."

He argues that, using this procedure,

the Christian will of course suppose that belief in God is entirely proper and rational; if he does not accept this belief on the basis of other propositions, he will conclude that it is basic for him and quite properly so. Followers of Russell and Madelyn Murray O'Hair [sic] may disagree; but how is that relevant? Must my criteria, or those of the Christian community, conform to their examples? Surely not. The Christian community is responsible to *its* set of examples, not to theirs.

Evaluation of Plantinga's Critique of Foundationalism

Recall that Plantinga argues that classical foundationalists are being self-referentially inconsistent. But as James Tomberlin has pointed out, since what is self-evident is relative to persons, a classical foundationalist (CF) could argue that (1) is self-evi-

dent and that if Plantinga were sufficiently attentive, the truth of (1) would become clear to him. Tomberlin argues that this response is similar to Calvin's view that in beholding the starry heavens, the properly attuned theist senses the existence of God. As Tomberlin puts it: "If the theist may be so attuned, why can't the classical foundationalist enjoy a similar relation to (1)? No, I do not think that Plantinga has precluded CF's rejoinder; and consequently he has not proved that (1) fails to be self-evident to the classical foundationalist."

However, even if Plantinga can show that (1) is not self-evident for classical foundationalists, he has not shown that (1) could not be deductively or inductively inferred from statements that are self-evident or incorrigible or evident to the senses. As Philip Quinn has argued, the classical foundationalist can use the broadly inductive procedures suggested by Plantinga to arrive at (1). Since the community of classical foundationalists is responsible for its own set of examples of properly basic beliefs and the conditions that justify them, it would not be surprising that the hypothesis they came up with in order to account for their examples would be (1).

Furthermore, even if Plantinga has refuted classical foundationalism, this would hardly dispose of foundationalism. Contemporary foundationalism has seriously modified the classical theory, and it is not at all clear that in the light of these modifications, Plantinga's critique could be sustained. Recall that one of his criticisms was that a statement such as "The world existed five minutes ago" could not be justified on classical foundationalist grounds. Since contemporary foundationalists include memory statements in the class of basic statements, there would not seem to be any particular problem in justifying such a statement, for "I remember having my breakfast ten minutes ago" can be a properly basic statement. Furthermore, if basic statements only have to be initially credible and not self-evident or incorrigible or evident to the senses, the criticism of self-referential inconsistency is much easier to meet. It is not at all implausible to suppose that a criterion of basicality in term of initial credibility is itself either initially credible or based on statements that are.

Plantinga is aware that there is more to foundationalism than the classical formulation of it. He says:

> Of course the evidentialist objection *need* not presuppose classical foundationalism; someone who accepted a different version of foundationalism could no doubt urge this objection. But in order to evaluate it, we should have to see what criterion of properly basic was being invoked. In the absence of such specification the objection remains at best a promissory note. So far as the present discussion goes, then, the next move is up to the evidentialist objector.

Many contemporary foundationalist theories have been constructed on nonclassical lines. Indeed, it may be safe to say that few contemporary foundationalists accept the classical view or even take it seriously. Moreover, these contemporary versions are hardly promissory notes, as Plantinga must be aware. Indeed, his refutation of classical foundationalism has just about as much relevance for contemporary foundationalism as a refutation of the emotive theory in ethics has for contemporary ethical noncognitivism. The next move, therefore, does not seem to be up to contemporary foundationalists. Plantinga must go on to show that his critique has relevance to the contemporary foundationalist program and that, given the best contemporary formulations of foundationalism, beliefs about God can be basic statements. This he has yet to do.

The Trouble with Reformed Foundationalism

What can one say about Plantinga's ingenious attempt to save theism from the charge of irrationality by making beliefs about God basic?

(1) Plantinga's claim that his proposal would not allow just any belief to become a basic belief is misleading. It is true that it would not allow just any belief to become a basic belief *from the point of view of Reformed epistemologists.* However it would seem to allow any belief at all to become basic from the point of view of *some* community. Although reformed epistemologists would not have to accept voodoo beliefs as rational, voodoo followers would be able to claim that insofar as they are basic in the voodoo community they are ra-

tional and, moreover, that reformed thought was irrational in this community. Indeed, Plantinga's proposal would generate many different communities that could *legitimately* claim that their basic beliefs are rational and that these beliefs conflict with basic beliefs of other communities. Among the communities generated might be devil worshipers, flat earthers, and believers in fairies just so long as belief in the devil, the flatness of the earth, and fairies was basic in the respective communities.

(2) On this view the rationality of any belief is absurdly easy to obtain. The cherished belief that is held without reason by *any* group could be considered properly basic by the group's members. There would be no way to make a critical evaluation of any beliefs so considered. The community's most cherished beliefs and the conditions that, according to the community, correctly trigger such beliefs would be accepted uncritically by the members of the community as just so many more examples of basic beliefs and justifying conditions. The more philosophical members of the community could go on to propose hypotheses as to the necessary and sufficient conditions for inclusion in this set. Perhaps, using this inductive procedure, a criterion could be formulated. However, what examples the hypotheses must account for would be decided by the community. As Plantinga says, each community would be responsible only to its own set of examples in formulating a criterion, and each would decide what is to be included in this set.

(3) Plantinga seems to suppose that there is a consensus in the Christian community about what beliefs are basic and what conditions justify these beliefs. But this is not so. Some Christians believe in God on the basis of the traditional arguments or on the basis of religious experiences; their belief in God is not basic. There would, then, certainly be no agreement in the Christian community over whether belief in God is basic or nonbasic. More important, there would be no agreement on whether doctrinal beliefs concerning the authority of the pope, the makeup of the Trinity, the nature of Christ, the means of salvation, and so on were true, let alone basic. Some Christian sects would hold certain doctrinal beliefs to be basic and rational; others would hold the same beliefs to be irrational and,

indeed, the gravest of heresies. Moreover, there would be no agreement over the conditions for basic belief. Some Christians might believe that a belief is properly basic when it is triggered by listening to the pope. Others would violently disagree. Even where there was agreement over the right conditions, these would seem to justify conflicting basic beliefs and, consequently, conflicting religious sects founded on them. For example, a woman named Jones, the founder of sect S_1, might read the Bible and be impressed that God is speaking to her and telling her *that* p, a man named Smith, the founder of sect S_2, might read the Bible and be impressed that God is speaking to him and telling him that ~p. So Jones's belief that p and Smith's belief that ~p would both be properly basic. One might wonder how this differs from the doctrinal disputes that have gone on for centuries among Christian sects and persist to this day. The difference is that on Plantinga's proposal each sect could *justifiably* claim that its belief, for which there might be no evidence or argument, was completely rational.

(4) So long as belief that there is no God was basic for them, atheists could also justify the claim that belief in God is irrational relative to their basic beliefs and the conditions that trigger them without critically evaluating any of the usual reasons for believing in God. Just as theistic belief might be triggered by viewing the starry heavens above and reading the Bible, so atheistic beliefs might be triggered by viewing the massacre of innocent children below and reading the writings of Robert Ingersoll. Theists may disagree, but is that relevant? To paraphrase Plantinga: Must atheists' criteria conform to the Christian communities' criteria? Surely not. The atheistic community is responsible to *its* set of examples, not to theirs.

(5) There may not at present be any clear criterion for what can be a basic belief, but belief in God seems peculiarly inappropriate for inclusion in the class since there are clear disanalogies between it and the basic beliefs allowable by classical foundationalism. For example, in his critique of classical foundationalism, Plantinga has suggested that belief in other minds and the external world should be considered basic. There are many plausible alternatives to belief in an all-good, all-powerful, all-knowing God, but there are few, if any, plausible alternatives to belief in other minds and the external world. Moreover, even if one disagrees with these arguments that seem to provide evidence against the existence of God, surely one must attempt to meet them. Although there are many skeptical arguments against belief in other minds and the external world, there are in contrast no seriously accepted arguments purporting to show that there are no other minds or no external world. In this world, atheism and agnosticism are live options for many intelligent people; solipsism is an option only for the mentally ill.

(6) As we have seen, Plantinga, following Calvin, says that some conditions that trigger belief in God or particular beliefs about God also justify these beliefs and that, although these beliefs concerning God are basic; they are not groundless. Although Plantinga gave no general account of what these justifying conditions are, he presented some examples of what he meant and likened these justifying conditions to those of properly basic perceptual and memory statements. The problem here is the weakness of the analogy. As Plantinga points out, before we take a perceptual or memory belief as properly basic we must have evidence that our perception or memory is not faulty. Part of the justification for believing that our perception or memory is not faulty is that in general it agrees with the perception or memory of our epistemological peers—that is, our equals in intelligence, perspicacity, honesty, thoroughness, and other relevant epistemic virtues, as well as with our other experiences. For example, unless my perceptions generally agreed with other perceivers with normal eyesight in normal circumstances and with my nonvisual experience—for example, that I feel something solid when I reach out—there would be no justification for supposing that my belief that I see a rose-colored wall in front of me is properly basic. Plantinga admits that if I know my memory is unreliable, my belief that I had breakfast should not be taken as properly basic. However, one

knows that one's memory is reliable by determining whether it coheres with the memory reports of other people whose memory is normal and with one's other experiences.

As we have already seen, lack of agreement is commonplace in religious contexts. Different beliefs are triggered in different people when they behold the starry heavens or when they read the Bible. Beholding the starry heavens can trigger a pantheistic belief or a purely aesthetic response without any religious component. Sometimes no particular response or belief at all is triggered. From what we know about the variations of religious belief, it is likely that people would not have theistic beliefs when they beheld the starry heavens if they had been raised in nontheistic environments. Similarly, a variety of beliefs and responses are triggered when the Bible is read. Some people are puzzled and confused by the contradictions, others become skeptical of the biblical stories, others believe that God is speaking to them and has appointed them as his spokesperson, others believe God is speaking to them but has appointed no one as His spokesperson. In short, there is no consensus in the Christian community, let alone among Bible readers generally. So unlike perception and memory, there are no grounds for claiming that a belief in God is properly basic since the conditions that trigger it yield widespread disagreement among epistemological peers.

(7) Part of the trouble with Plantinga's account of basic belief is the assumption he makes concerning what it means to say that a person accepts one proposition on the basis of accepting another. According to Michael Levine, Plantinga understands the relation in this way:

(A) For any person S, and distinct propositions p and q, S believes q on the basis of p only if S entertains p, S accepts p, S infers q from p, and S accepts q.

Contemporary foundationalists do not accept (A) as a correct account of the relation of accepting one proposition on the basis of another. The following seems more in accord with contemporary understanding:

(B) For any person S and distinct propositions p and q, if S believes q, and S *would cite p if* queried under optimal conditions about his reasons for believing in q, then S believes q on the basis of p.

On (B) it seems unlikely that any nonepistemologically deficient person—for example, a normal adult—would be unable to cite any reason for believing in God if this person did believe in God. Consequently, Plantinga's claim that "the mature theist does not typically accept belief in God . . . as a conclusion from other things that he believes" is irrelevant if his claim is understood in terms of (A) and probably false if understood in terms of (B).

(8) Finally, to consider belief in God as a basic belief seems completely out of keeping with the spirit and intention of foundationalism. Whatever else it was and whatever its problems, foundationalism was an attempt to provide critical tools for objectively appraising knowledge claims and provide a nonrelativistic basis for knowledge. Plantinga's foundationalism is radically relativistic and puts any belief beyond rational appraisal once it is declared basic.

The Trouble with Foundationalism

So far in my critique of Plantinga's attempt to incorporate beliefs in or about God into the set of properly basic beliefs that form the foundation of knowledge, I have uncritically accepted the idea that the structure of knowledge must have a foundation in terms of basic beliefs. But as Laurence BonJour has recently shown, there is a serious problem with any foundationalist account of knowledge.

According to all foundationalist accounts, basic statements are justified noninferentially. For example, contemporary foundationalists who hold a moderate position maintain that properly basic statements, although not incorrigible or self-evident, are highly justified without inductive or deductive support. But it may be asked, where does this justification come from? As BonJour argues, a basic constraint on any standards or justification for empirical knowledge is that there is a good reason for thinking that those standards lead to truth. So if basic beliefs are to provide a foundation for knowledge for the moderate foundationalist, then whatever the criterion for being properly basic, it must provide a good reason for supposing that basic beliefs are true. Further, such a criterion must provide grounds for the person who holds a basic belief to suppose that it is true. Thus moderate foundationalism must hold that for any person P, basic belief B, and criterion of being properly basic ϕ, in order for P to be justified in holding properly basic belief B, P must be justified in believing the premises of the following justifying argument:

(1) B has feature ϕ.
(2) <u>Beliefs having feature ϕ are likely to be true.</u>
(3) Therefore, B is highly likely to be true.

Although, as BonJour argues, it might be possible that one of the two premises in the above argument could be known to be true on an *a priori* basis, it does not seem possible that both premises could be known *a priori*. Once this is granted, it follows that B is not basic after all, since B's justification would depend on some other empirical belief. But if B is properly basic, its justification cannot depend on any other empirical belief. BonJour goes on to meet objections to his argument showing that a coherent account of the structure of empirical knowledge can be developed to overcome this problem of foundationalism and that the objections usually raised against the coherence theory can be answered. Surely any defender of foundationalism must meet BonJour's challenge.

As we have seen, when Plantinga proposes that belief about God can be considered properly basic, he admits that he did not have any criterion for being properly basic. But BonJour's argument tends to show that whatever criterion Plantinga might offer, there will be a problem for reformed foundationalism. If BonJour is correct, whatever this criterion is, it will have to provide a good reason for

supposing that properly basic beliefs are true, and this will involve knowledge of further empirical beliefs. In order to defend his position, Plantinga must refute BonJour's argument.

Conclusion

In Chapter 1 it was argued that there was a strong presumption that belief in God should be based on epistemic reasons. Some theists disagree, maintaining that religious belief is basic or should be based on faith. The conclusion here is that this argument fails. Although not all theories of faith have been examined here, the ones that were are representative enough to give us confidence that all such arguments will fail.

In a way Aquinas seems to agree with our position. He maintains that belief in the existence of God should be based on epistemic reasons; and, as we shall see in Chapter 14, he believed the arguments he produced provided such reasons. However, he believed that certain Christian dogmas were not provable by means of argument and must be based on faith. But even here he thought that one could have good epistemic reason to believe that these dogmas were revealed by God. He was wrong, however, to suppose that they were. Kierkegaard's view that faith in God should be based on absurdities and improbabilities was rejected, since the arguments he used to support this view were unsound and, in any case, his view led to fanaticism. Wittgensteinian fideism was also rejected, since it led to absurdities and presupposed an indefensible view of meaning and language.

Plantinga's reformed foundationalism has some interesting similarities to the doctrine that belief in God should be based on faith, but should not be identified with it. To be sure, his view is similar to that of Aquinas, who maintains that particular Christian doctrines, although not themselves based on reason, are rational. The basic difference between the Aquinas and Plantinga positions is that Aquinas attempts to provide epistemic reasons that would persuade all rational beings to accept certain propositions as revealed truths. Plantinga provides no such reason other than the argument that belief in God is basic and some such beliefs, including belief in God, are completely rational. Thus Plantinga's views differ markedly from those of Kierkegaard, who forsook any appeal to rationality in justifying religious belief. Plantinga's views also differ in important respects from Wittgensteinian fideism. While Wittgensteinian fideism appeals to ordinary religious practice and language to justify belief in God, Plantinga appeals to theoretical considerations from epistemology. Nevertheless, Plantinga's reformed foundationalism should be rejected since his arguments against classical foundationalism are weak, the logic of his position leads to a radical and absurd relativism, and foundationalism in general has serious problems.

VII.D.4 Can Religious Belief Be Rational?

L O U I S P. P O J M A N

In this essay I argue for a thoroughly rationalist conception of faith within a coherentist framework. First I outline an ethics of belief that makes rational believing a duty, and then I explain a person-relative notion of belief using a coherentist model. Rather than view our beliefs in terms of the foundationalist model, in which one belief is supported by more basic beliefs until we get to foundational beliefs for which there is no further evidence, it might be better to see our belief systems in terms of a web or network of beliefs mutually supporting each other. Although some beliefs may be more self-evident than others, few beliefs can be sustained independently of the whole system or large parts of it. Furthermore, there is a certain person-relativeness in every person's noetic structure. Each of us has had a different, complex history of evidence gathering and belief formation, so that intersubjective belief comparison and evaluation becomes difficult. Nevertheless, there are core experiences and criteria of rationality that are common to all humans and that can provide a common measure for attempting to arrive at optimally rational positions.

Introduction

In this essay, I argue for a thoroughly rationalistic faith. I argue that religious faith has a moral dimension underlying it, so that any faith that is not rational for a person to hold may also be immoral. I outline a notion of an ethics of belief that makes rational believing a *prima facie* moral duty and casts moral censure at leaps of faith beyond the evidence. Then I outline a coherentist strategy for justifying religious belief within the bounds of reason.*

Nearly every Christian theologian has demurred from the idea of a wholly rational faith. The Catholic tradition, stemming from Thomas Aquinas, avers that the subset of doctrines, the preambles, are in accordance with reason but that such doctrines as the incarnation and the trinity are beyond its pale. On the other side of the spectrum we have the antirationalists, who believe that the key to religious belief is a miracle of faith "which subverts all the principles of understanding," as Hume skeptically but Hamann and Kierkegaard approvingly put it. (It's a fascinating intellectual anecdote in the history of philosophy that Hamann discovered Hume's

---

*More accurately, my proposal calls for the defense of theism via *abductive* reasoning, reasoning to the best explanation, rather than via a simple coherence model. I reject pure coherentism for the usual reasons that it lacks criteria to rule out fairy tales and absurd theories (such that a Great Pumpkin created the Universe), putting too much weight on the criterion of consistency and mutual support. Abduction seeks to satisfy a plurality of criteria, such as explanatory power, fruitfulness, predictability, and simplicity, which we usually use in arriving at explanations of phenomena, but since more than one value is involved, it is normally difficult to decide between two theories where different values are weighted differently. Hence the role for intuition and understanding.

dictum and set it forth in his writings as the essence of faith, where it was read by Kierkegaard, who thought Hamann had originated it and applauded him for his brilliant insight.) For Tertullian, Hamann, Kierkegaard, and Shestov the very irrationality of Christianity is reason for embracing it. If God is wholly other, we should expect his truth to seem contradictory to sinful human minds. Modern fideists, following some remarks by Wittgenstein, claim that religious belief is groundless and not subject to rational scrutiny. Somewhere in between these opposing positions is the reformed view (that of Calvin, Warfield, and Bavinck) of natural theology as somehow an irreverent activity. As Barth puts it, to reason about faith is to assume the standpoint of unbelief; it "makes reason a judge over Christ." Most recently, a well-argued version of this position has been developed by Alvin Plantinga, which claims that belief in God may be properly basic to the foundations of one's noetic structure, as justified as our belief that there are other minds or as any of our immediate empirical or memory beliefs (e.g., the memory belief that I had breakfast this morning).[1]

Although I have learned much from Plantinga and have sympathy for a great deal in his position, especially since he has modified it lately to include the notion that reason could inform faith's stance, I find two problems with his position, which I have tried to remedy:

(1) The criteria of proper basicality for Plantinga seems so open-ended that virtually any worldview, no matter how implausible to thoughtful people, could be justified. Although honest people will certainly differ about what is properly basic, one should suspect or even not fully accept one's own beliefs as basic if they fail to win support from the consensus of rationally informed people or epistemologists as basic or evidential. There are limits to what can count as properly basic, and although exact criteria are hard to come by, not everything can properly be part of the foundations of a noetic structure. As far as I understand the logic of Plantinga's position, there are no epistemically neutral criteria that would eliminate anyone's favorite insane belief. Here his position reminds one of Hare's famous paranoid student who had a *blik*

(read "properly basic belief") that all dons were out to harm him.

(2) Second, I doubt that theoretical beliefs such as the existence of a divine creator of the universe fit as well into a foundationalist view of epistemology as they do into a coherentist framework. Would we believe in God if the concept had no support at all from our beliefs about the world's having a cause, a design or order, if we didn't have testimony of various encounters with the divine, if there were no claims to miraculous events confirming divine authority? Theistic belief does not stand unsupported, alone and in isolation, but as part and parcel of many other considerations that together help us make sense of the world. Although a great many of our core beliefs cannot easily be traced back to their origins or justificatory basis, we can still offer considerations for them, showing that they are supported by other beliefs in an all-encompassing network of beliefs. Our noetic structure may well be more in the metaphorical shape of a web than in the shape of a house with a foundation. It is the very foundational metaphor that makes Plantinga's views so implausible to some of us.

The Ethics of Belief

First let me state why there are ethical duties to believe according to the best evidence available. Often the beliefs that we have affect the well-being of others. Suppose that you are a physician who is consulted about certain symptoms. You prescribe a drug that you have a hunch will help the patient, but your diagnosis is wrong and the patient dies. When examiners inquire into the situation, they discover that you hadn't kept up on your medicine and that your mistake would have been easily prevented had you been aware of side effects of the drug in question (and had you not misdiagnosed the symptoms). Since you could have had correct beliefs about these matters had you read the latest literature in the area, which was abundantly available, you are rightly judged to be culpably ignorant. You had an obligation to keep up with the literature. At bottom, an ethic of belief may reduce to an ethic of investigation and openness to criticism, but the point is that we are responsible for many of the beliefs that we have and that, as guides to actions, eventually result in action that may harm or help our fellow humans.

Of course, the duty to believe according to the best evidence is not our only moral duty, and perhaps there are times when another duty overrides it, but it is a duty that ought to be taken with the utmost seriousness, more than most thinkers have afforded it. Besides, how confident can we be of our beliefs if we know deep down that they are not backed up by good evidence?

If we apply this to religious belief, we can see that it is also important that we follow the best reasons in forming our belief states. Since the best justified beliefs have the best chance of being true and hence reliable, we should seek to justify even our most personal religious beliefs or doubt them. It would seem that a morally good God who created us as rational would honor doxastic honesty even if it led to unbelief.[2]

Rationality and Conceptual Frameworks

Sometimes it is claimed that we use a clear-cut decision-making process, similar to the one used in mathematics and empirical science, when we arrive at justified belief or truth. A person has a duty to believe exactly according to the available evidence. Hence there is no excuse for anyone to believe anything on insufficient evidence. Such is the case of Descartes and logical positivism, which is echoed in Clifford's classical formula, "It is wrong always, everywhere, and for anyone to believe anything on insufficient evidence." Laying aside the criticism that the statement itself is self-referentially incoherent (it doesn't give us sufficient evidence for believing itself), the problem is that different data will count as evidence to different degrees according to the background beliefs a person has. The contribution of Polanyi, Popper, and Wittgenstein has been to demonstrate the power of perspectivism, the thesis that the way we evaluate or even pick out evidence is determined by our prior picture of

the world, which itself is made up of a loosely connected and mutually supporting network of propositions. Do the farmer, the real estate dealer, and the landscape artist on looking at a field see the same field?

The nonperspectivist position, seen in Plato, Aquinas, Descartes, Locke, Clifford, and Chisholm, seems damaged beyond repair. However, the reaction has been to claim that since what is basic is the conceptual (fiduciary) framework, no interchange between worldviews is possible. As Karl Barth says, "Belief can only preach to unbelief." No argument is possible. We may call this reaction to the postcritical critique of rationalism "hard-perspectivism."

The nonperspectivist writes as though arriving at the truth were a matter of impartial evaluation of the evidence, and the hard-perspectivist writes as though no meaningful communication were possible. The worldviews (*Weltanschauungen*) are discontinuous. As fideists often say, "The believer and unbeliever live in different worlds."[3] There is an infinite qualitative distinction existing between various forms of life that no amount of argument or discussion can bridge. For hard-perspectivists, including Wittgensteinian fideists, reason can only have intramural significance. There are no bridges between worldviews.

However, hard-perspectivism is not the only possible reaction to the postcritical revolution. One may accept the insight that our manner of evaluating evidence is strongly affected by our conceptual frameworks without opting for a view that precludes communication across worldviews. One may recognize the depth of a conceptual framework and still maintain that communication between frameworks is possible and that reason may have an intermural as well as intramural significance in the process. Such a view has been called soft-perspectivist. The soft-perspectivist is under no illusion regarding the difficulty of effecting a massive shift in the total evaluation of an immense range of data, of producing new patterns of feeling and acting in persons, but he or she is confident that the program is viable. One of the reasons given in support of this is that there is something like a core rationality common to every human culture, especially with regard to practical life. Certain rules of inference (deductive and inductive) have virtually universal application. Certain assumptions (basic beliefs) seem common to every culture (e.g., that there are other minds, that there is time, that things move, that perceptions are generally to be trusted). Through sympathetic imagination one can attain some understanding of another's conceptual system; through disappointment one can begin to suspect weakness in one's own world-view and thus seek for a more adequate explanation. It is not my purpose here to produce a full defense of a soft-perspective position, but only to indicate its plausibility. The assumption on which this essay is written is that the case for soft-perspectivism can be made. And if it is true, then it is possible for reason to play a significant role in the examination, revision, and rejection of one's current beliefs and in the acquisition of new beliefs.

Does Rationality Imply a Neutrality That Is Incompatible with Religious Faith?

We may say that postcritical rationalists of the soft-perspectivist variety are individuals who seek to support all their beliefs (especially their convictions)[4] with good reasons. They attempt to evaluate the evidence as impartially as possible, to accept the challenge of answering criticisms, and to remain open to the possibility that they might be wrong and may need to revise, reexamine, or reject any one of their beliefs (at least those not involving broadly logical necessity). This character description of the rationalist is often interpreted to mean that rationalists must be neutral and detached with regard to their beliefs.[5] This is a mistake. It is a confusion between *impartiality* and *neutrality*. Both concepts imply conflict situations (e.g., war, a competitive sport, a legal trial, an argument), but to be neutral signifies not taking sides, doing nothing to influence the outcome, remaining passive in the fray; whereas impartiality *involves* one in the conflict in that it calls for a judgment in favor of the party that is right. To the extent that one party is right or wrong (measured by objective criteria) neutrality and impartiality are incompatible concepts. To be neutral is to detach oneself from the struggle; to be impartial (rational) is to commit oneself to a position—though not partially (i.e., unfairly or arbitrarily) but in accordance with an objective standard. The model of the neutral person is an atheist who is indifferent about football watching a game between Notre Dame and Southern Methodist. The model of the partial or prejudiced person is the coach who, on any given dispute, predictably judges his team to be in the right and the other to be in the wrong and for whom it is an axiom that any judgment by a referee against his team is, at best, of dubious merit. The model of the impartial person is the referee in the game, who, knowing that his wife has just bet their life savings on the underdog, Southern Methodist, still manages to call what any reasonable spectator would judge to be a fair game. He does not let his wants or self-interest enter into the judgment he makes.

To be rational does not lessen the passion involved in religious beliefs. Rational believers, who believe that they have good grounds for believing that a perfect being exists, are not less likely to trust that being absolutely than believers who do not think that they have reasons. Likewise, persons who live in hope of God's existence may be as passionate about their commitment as persons who entertain no doubts. In fact the rational hoper or believer will probably judge it to be irrational not to be absolutely committed to such a being. Hence the charge leveled against the rationalist by Kierkegaard and others that rational inquiry cools the passions seems unfounded.

However, nonrationalists have a slightly different but related argument at hand. They may argue that if there were sufficient evidence available, it might be the case that one might be both religious and rational. But there is not sufficient evidence; hence the very search for evidence simply detracts believers from worship and passionate service, leading them on a wild-goose chase for evidence that does not exist. The believer is involved in cool calculation instead of passionate commitment, questioning instead of obeying.

There are at least two responses to this charge. First of all, how does the nonrationalist know that there is not sufficient evidence for a religious claim? How does the nonrationalist know that not merely a demonstrative proof but even a cumulative case with some force is impossible? It would seem reasonable to expect that a good God would not leave his creatures wholly in the dark about so important a matter. The nonrationalist's answer (that of Calvin and Kierkegaard, and suggested by Plantinga) that sin has destroyed the use of reason or our ability to see God seem unduly ad hoc and inadequate. It would seem that little children in nontheistic cultures should manifest some theistic tendencies on this view, for which there is no evidence. Second, why cannot the search for truth itself be a way of worshipping God? A passionate act of service? Again one would expect the possession of well-founded beliefs to be God's will for us. Is the person who in doubt prays, "God, if you exist, please show me better evidence," any less passionate a worshipper than the person who worships without doubts?

A word is in order about the relation of the emotions and passions to religious belief. The claims of a religion cannot but move a person. Anyone who does not see the importance of its claims either does not have a sense of selfhood or does not understand what is being said, for a religion claims to explain who and why one is and what one can expect to become. It claims to make sense out of the world. For example, to entertain the proposition that a personal, loving Creator exists is to entertain a proposition whose implications affect every part of a person's understanding of self and world. If the proposition is true, the world is personal rather than mechanistic, friendly rather than strange, purposeful rather than simply a vortex of chance and necessity. If it is not true, a different set of entailments follow that are likely to lead to different patterns of feeling and action. If Judeo-Christian theism is accepted, the believer has an additional reason for being a moral person, for treating fellow humans with equal respect. It is because God has created all persons in his image, as infinitely precious, destined to enjoy his fellowship forever. Theism can provide a more adequate metaphysical basis for morality. Hence it can be both descriptively and prescriptively significant.

Toward a Theory of Rationality

It is often said that rational persons tailor the strength of their beliefs to the strength of the evidence. The trouble with this remark is that it is notoriously difficult to give sense to any discussion of discovering objective criteria for what is to count as evidence and to what extent it is to count. One of my criticisms of Swinburne's usually perceptive work is that he tries to apply the concept of probabilities to worldviews, as though we somehow could identify evidential wholes without comparing them to other outcomes.

Deciding *what* is to count as evidence for something else in part depends on a whole network of other considerations, and deciding *to what extent* something is to count as evidence involves weighing procedures that are subjective. Two judges may have the same evidence before them and come to different verdicts. Two equally rational persons may have the same evidence about the claims of a religion and still arrive at different conclusions in the matter. It would seem that the prescription to tailor one's beliefs according to the evidence is either empty or a shorthand for something more complex. I think that it is the latter. Let me illustrate what I think it signifies.

Consider any situation in which our self-interest may conflict with the truth. Take the case of three German wives who are suddenly confronted with evidence that their husbands have been unfaithful. Their surnames are Uberglaubig, Misstrauisch, and Wahrnehmen. Each is disturbed about the evidence and makes further inquiries. Mrs. Uberglaubig is soon finished and finds herself rejecting all the evidence, maintaining resolutely her husband's fidelity. Others, even relatives of Mr. Uberglaubig, are surprised by her credulity, for the evidence against Mr. Uberglaubig is the sort that would lead most people to conclude that he was unfaithful. No matter how much evidence is adduced, Mrs. Uberglaubig is unchanged in her judgment. She seems to have a fixation about her husband's fidelity. Mrs. Misstrauisch seems to suffer from an opposite weakness. If Mrs. Uberglaubig overbelieves, she seems to underbelieve. She suspects the worst and even though others who know Mr. Misstrauisch deem the evidence against him weak (especially in comparison to the evidence presented against Mr. Uberglaubig), she is convinced that her husband is unfaithful. No evidence seems to be sufficient to reassure her. It is as though the very suggestion of infidelity were enough to stir up doubts and disbelief. Mrs. Wahrnehmen also considers the evidence, which is considerable, and comes to a judgment, though with some reservations. Suppose she finds herself believing that her husband is faithful. Others may differ in their assessment of the situation, but Mrs. Wahrnehmen is willing and able to discuss the matter, give her grounds, and considers the objections of others. Perhaps we can say that she is more self-aware, more self-controlled, and more self-secure than the other women. She seems to have the capacity to separate her judgment from her hopes, wants, and fears in a way that the other two women do not.

This should provide some clue to what it means to be rational. It does not necessarily mean having true beliefs (though we would say that rationality tends toward truth), for it might just turn out that by luck Mr. Wahrnehmen is indeed an adulterer and Mr. Uberglaubig innocent. Still, we would want to say that Mrs. Wahrnehmen was justified in her beliefs but Mrs. Uberglaubig was not.

What does characterize rational judgment are two properties, one being *intention* and the other being *capacity-behavioral*. First, rationality involves an intention to seek the truth or the possession of a high regard for the truth, especially when there may be a conflict between it and one's wishes. It involves a healthy abhorrence of being deceived combined with a parallel desire to have knowledge in matters vital to one's life. Mrs. Wahrnehmen and Mrs. Misstrauisch care about the truth in a way that Mrs. Uberglaubig does not. But secondly, it involves a skill or behavioral capacity to judge impartially, to examine the evidence objectively, to know what sort of things count in coming to a considered judgment. It is as though Mrs. Wahrnehmen alone were able to see clearly through the fog of emotion and self-interest, focusing on some ideal standard of evidence. Of course, there is no such simple standard of evidence, any more than there is for the art critic in making a judgment on the authenticity

of a work of art. Still, the metaphor of the ideal standard may be useful. It draws attention to the objective feature in rational judgment, a feature that is internalized in the person of the expert. Like learning to discriminate between works of art or with regard to criminal evidence, rationality is a learned trait that calls for a long apprenticeship (a lifetime?) under the cooperative tutelage of other rational persons. Some people with little formal education seem to learn this better than some "well-educated" people, but despite this uncomfortable observation, I would like to believe that it is the job of education to train people to judge impartially over a broad range of human experience.

As a skill combined with an intention, rationality may seem to be in a shaky situation. How do we decide who has the skill or who has the right combination of traits? There is no certain way, but judge we must in this life, and the basis of our judgment will be manifestations of behavior that we classify as truth directed, noticing that persons with this skill seek out evidence and pay attention to criticism and counterclaims, that they usually support their judgment with recognizable good reasons, that they revise and reject their beliefs in the light of new information. These criteria are not foolproof, and it seems impossible to give an exact account of the process involved in rational decision or belief, but this seems to be the case with any skill. In the end rationality seems more like a set of trained intuitions than anything else.

Let us carry our story a little further. Suppose now Mrs. Wahrnehmen receives some new information to the effect that her husband has been unfaithful. Suppose it becomes known to others who were previously convinced by her arguments acquitting her husband, and suppose that the new evidence infirms many of those arguments, so that the third parties now come to believe that Mr. Wahrnehmen is an adulterer. Should Mrs. Wahrnehmen give up her belief? Perhaps not. At least, it may not be a good thing to give it up at once. If she has worked out a theory to account for a great many of her husband's actions, she might better cling to her theory and work out some ad hoc hypotheses to account for this evidence. This principle of clinging to one's theory in spite of adverse evidence is what Peirce debunkingly and Lakatos approvingly call the principle of tenacity.[6] It receives special attention in Lakatos's treatment of a progressive research program. In science, theoretical change often comes as a result of persevering with a rather vaguely formulated hypothesis (a core hypothesis), which the researcher will hold on to in spite of a good many setbacks. Scientists must be ready to persevere (at least for a time) even in the face of their own doubts and their recognition of the validity of their opponents' objections. If maximum fruitfulness of the experiment is to be attained, it must endure through many modifications as new evidence comes in. As Basil Mitchell has pointed out, a scientific thesis is like a growing infant, which "could be killed by premature antisepsis." The biographies of eminent scientists and scholars are replete with instances of going it alone in the face of massive intellectual opposition and finally overturning a general verdict. Hence researchers cushion the core hypothesis against the blows and shocks that might otherwise force them to give it up. They invent ad hoc explanations in the hope of saving the core hypothesis. They surround the core hypothesis with a battery of such hypotheses, and as the ad hoc hypotheses fall, they invent new ones. Mitchell compares this process to a criminal network, in which the mastermind (core hypothesis) always manages to escape detection and punishment "by sacrificing some of his less essential underlings, unless or until the final day of reckoning comes and his entire empire collapses."[7]

Admittedly, each ad hoc hypothesis weakens the system, but the core hypothesis may nevertheless turn out to approximate a true or adequate theory. But the more ad hoc hypotheses it becomes necessary to invent, the less plausibility attaches to the core hypothesis, until the time comes when the researcher is forced to give up the core hypothesis and conclude that the whole project has outlived its usefulness. In Lakato's words, "it has become a degenerative research project."[8] No one can say exactly when that time comes in a particular project, but every experimental scientist fears it and, meanwhile, lives in hope that the current project will bear fruit.

Let us apply this paradigm to rational religious believers. Once they find themselves with a deep conviction, they have a precedent or model in science for clinging to it tenaciously, experimenting with it, drawing out all its implications, and surrounding it with tentative ad hoc or auxiliary explanations in order to cushion it from premature antisepsis. Nevertheless, if the analogy with the scientist holds, they must recognize that the time may come when they are forced to abandon their conviction because of the enormous accumulation of counterevidence. Such rational persons probably cannot say exactly when and how this might happen, and they do not expect it to happen, but they acknowledge the possibility of its happening. There is no clear decision procedure that tells us when we have crossed over the fine line between plausibility and implausibility, but suddenly the realization hits us that we now disbelieve theory *A* and believe theory *B*, whereas up to this point the reverse was true. Conversions or paradigm switches occur every day in the minds of both the highly rational and the less rational. There is also a middle zone where a person considering two seemingly incompatible explanatory theories can find something plausible in each of them, so that the person cannot be said to believe either one. Still, such individuals may place their hope in one theory and live by it in an experimental faith, keeping themselves open to new evidence and maintaining the dialogue with those who differ so as not to slip into a state of self-deception. The whole matter of double vision and experimental faith is quite complicated, but often we can see the world in more than one way and yet find our moral bearings. What I want to emphasize is the Kierkegaardian point (used in an un-Kierkegaardian manner) that more important than *what* one believes is the manner in which one believes, the *how* of believing, the openness of mind, the willingness to discuss the reasons for one's belief, the carefulness of one's examination of new and conflicting evidence, one's commitment to follow the argument and not simply one's emotions, one's training as a rational person that enables one to recognize what is to count as a good argument.

This leads me to say a few things about the role and mode of argument in rationality. One problem that has plagued discussion in philosophy of religion through the ages is that the way philosophers have written has implied that unless one had a deductive proof for a religious thesis, one had no justification for it. The result of this narrow view of argument in religious matters has pushed those who believe in religion to the point of conceding too much, that is, that religion is not rational. This is one of the main reasons for the incommensurabilist position. I think that this is a mistake. Our concept of argument must be broadened from mere deductive and strict inductive argument to include non–rule-governed judgments. What I have in mind is the sort of intuitive judgment illustrated by the art critic in assessing an authentic work of art, the chicken sexer in identifying the sex of the baby chicks without knowing or being able to tell us how he knows the chick's sexual identity, or the water diviner in discovering underground springs without knowing how he does so. Another example of non–rule-governed reasoning is a child's invention of new sentences. The child follows rules which seem to be programmed into her, but she does not do it consciously and cannot tell us what the rules are. Later, however, she may be able to do so.

Perhaps even more typical of everyday non-rule-governed reasoning is the process whereby judges or juries make judgments when the evidence is ambiguous or there is considerable evidence on both sides of an issue. In weighing pros and cons and assessing conflicting evidence, the judge or jury does not normally go through standard logical procedures to arrive at a verdict. They rely on intangible and intuitive weighing procedures. It is hard to see how the deductive and strict inductive schemes of argument can account for our judgments when we have good reasons for and against a conclusion. Nor is it easy to see how deductive and strict inductive reasoning account for the decisions experts make in distinguishing the valuable from the mediocre. They cannot formalize their judgment, and we may not be able to offer an account of it, but we would still recognize it as valid and importantly rational. Perhaps we ought generally to aim at formalizing our judgments as carefully as possible, using the traditional forms of reasoning, but it is not always necessary or possible to do this.

We can be said to be rational because we typically arrive at decisions and judgments that other rational creatures would regard as a fair estimation of the evidence (this excuses the occasional idiosyncratic judgment), because we attempt to face the challenge of our opponent with the grounds of our beliefs, and because we are honest about the deficiencies of our positions. It is a whole family of considerations that leads us to an overall conclusion about whether another person is rational and not simply whether or not the person is able to provide sound deductive or inductive arguments. Of course, induction plays a strong role in our relying on another's judgments. It is because we have generally found that people of this sort usually make reliable judgments in cases of such-and-such a type that we are ready to take their intuitions as credible.

A great deal more needs to be said about non–rule-governed judgments, but this discussion at least shows that something broader than the standard moves is needed in an account of rational argument. There is a need to recognize the important role that intuition plays in reasoning itself or, at least, in the reasoning of the trained person. This is what the Greeks called *phronesis* ("wise insight") and *ortho logos* ("correct thinking"), and it should be given greater emphasis in modern philosophy.

Is a Rational Account of Religion Compatible with the Biblical Picture of Faith?

Let me turn finally to the important objection that the position that I have outlined distorts the biblical notion of faith. Biblical faith is, the critic affirms, believing against or without sufficient evidence. As Hick points out, there is little deductive reasoning in the Scriptures, but the Holy of Holies is taken as the starting point of all thinking.[9]

But the claim that this is the sole meaning of faith in the Bible seems an unwarranted generalization. Actually, several different but related concepts of faith are found in the Bible, including loyalty, trust, fear, and obedience, as well as propositional belief.

What we have called rational faith seems duly accounted for in the miracles and prophecy of the Bible, especially in the Old Testament, which in part serve as evidence for the Hebrew faith. When Elijah, in 1 Kings 18, competes with the priests of Baal on Mt. Carmel to determine which god is more powerful, we are given a concrete scientific testing of competing hypotheses. When John the Baptist's disciples come to ask Jesus if he is the Messiah, Jesus does not rebuke them for seeking grounds for their beliefs but immediately "cures many diseases and plagues and evil spirits" and opens the eyes of the blind; only after this does he answer them, "Go and tell John what you have seen and heard; the blind receive their sight, the lame walk, lepers are cleansed, and the deaf hear, the dead are raised up, the poor have the good news preached to them" (Luke 7:20–22). When Jesus does chide his disciples for unbelief, it seems to be for good reasons. "Don't you remember what the Scriptures demand? Don't you trust me in spite of my being with you so long and having proved my reliability over and over?" What the Scriptures deny is *sight*. We cannot see God directly and live, for there is another dimension to his reality, but we can see him *indirectly* through his works (Rom. 1:20f). When Thomas doubts good evidence (viz., the witness of his fellow disciples and the words of Jesus' prophecy), he is given evidence, the point being not that evidence is contrary to faith but that dependence on too much outward evidence may get in the way of inward discernment. There is just enough evidence to satisfy a person passionately concerned but not enough to produce a comfortable proof.

Usually, nonrationalists make their point about the antipathy between faith and reason in the Bible by pointing to Abraham's reliance on God even to the point of being willing to kill his son Isaac. Abraham, the father of faith, is put forth as the paradigm of believing against all evidence. As Kierkegaard puts it, "Abraham believed by virtue of the absurd," despite the impossibility of the promise to give him a son when he was old or to bring him back after he was sacrificed. He believed God would somehow bring it about that Isaac would live despite the fact that he was going to kill him. The reader will recall the story. God tells Abraham to go to Mt. Moriah and sacrifice Isaac in order to prove his love for God. Abraham proceeds to carry out the command, but at the last moment an angel stops him, showing him a lamb in the thicket to be used for the offering. The story of Abraham and Isaac has usually been taken as the height of religious faith: believing God when it really affects one's deepest earthly commitments. It is taken to prove that faith is irrational, that faith involves believing against all standards of rationality.

Of course, many Old Testament scholars dismiss the literalness of the story and interpret it within the context of Middle Eastern child sacrifice. The story, according to these scholars, provides the pictorial grounds for breaking with the custom. But even leaving aside this plausible explanation, we might contend that Abraham's action can be seen as rational given his noetic framework. One can imagine him replying to a friendly skeptic years after the incident in the following manner:

I heard a voice. It was the same voice (or so I believed) that commanded me years before to leave my country, my kindred, and my father's house to venture forth into the unknown. It was the same voice that promised me that I would prosper. I hearkened, and though the evidence seemed weak, the promise was fulfilled. It was the same voice that promised me a son in my old age and Sarah's old age, when childbearing was thought to be impossible. Yet it happened. My trust was vindicated. My whole existence has been predicated on the reality of that voice. I already became an exception by hearkening unto it the first time. I have never regretted it. This last call was in a tone similar to the other calls. The voice was unmistakable. To deny its authenticity would be to deny the authenticity of the others. In doing so, I should be admitting that my whole life has been founded on an illusion. But I don't believe that it has, and I prefer to take the risk of obeying what I take to be the voice of God and disobey certain norms than to obey the norms and miss the possibility of any absolute relation to the Absolute. And what's more, I'm ready to recommend that all people who feel so called by a higher power do exactly as I have done.

It seems to me that even if we accept the story of Abraham's offering his son as a sacrifice at face value, we can give it an interpretation not inconsistent with the commensurabilist's position. Abraham has had inductive evidence that following the voice is the best way to live. We can generalize the principle on which Abraham acted to be as follows:

> If one acts on a type of intuition *I* in an area of experience *E*, over a period of time *t* and with remarkable success, and no other information is relevant or overriding, one can be said to have good reason for following that intuition (*I$_n$*, an instance of type *I*) the next time it presents itself in an *E*-type situation.

Given the cultural context of Abraham's life, his actions seem amenable to a rationalist account. Of course, what this shows is that given enough background data, almost any proposition could be considered *rational* for an individual believer. Irrationality would occur if Abraham neglected counterevidence at his disposal.

My point in all this has not been to prove that the Bible contains a fully developed philosophy of faith and reason but simply to indicate that it seems far closer to the commensurabilist's position than the fideist might imagine. My impression is that the Scriptures pay a great deal of attention to evidence, acts of deliverance, and the testimony of the saints and prophets who hear God's voice and sometimes even get a vision of his splendor.

Let me end this article on a conciliatory note. I can appreciate the criticism of someone who feels that my approach overemphasizes the rational and intellectual aspects of believing at the expense of the emotional and volitional aspects, the feelings of divine presence and inner certainty and devotion. I do not want to deny the importance of these feelings. My point has been simply that they are compatible with a rationalist perspective. Further thought on the matter may reveal that my approach to religion as an experimental faith in a viable hypothesis fails to get at the heart of religious commitment. But even so, the general quest for justification may not be inappropriate. Complex as religious phenomena are, profound as the feelings are, at some point religious experience needs to be scrutinized honestly and carefully by the believer him- or herself. When Barth and Bultmann protest that God does not need to justify himself before man, the proper response is to echo Karl Jasper's reply to Bultmann: "I do not say that God has to justify himself, but that everything that appears in the world and claims to be God's word, God's act, God's revelation, has to justify itself."[10] This outline of a commensurabilist position with regard to religious belief is intended as a small step in doing just that.

Notes

1. The most complete version of Plantinga's views is his essay "Reason and Belief in God," in *Faith and Rationality*, edited by Alvin Plantinga and Nicholas Wolterstorff (Notre Dame, Ind.: Univ. of Notre Dame Press, 1983).

2. See my book, *Religious Belief and the Will* (London: Routledge & Kegan Paul, 1986), part 2, chap. 2.

3. Alvin Plantinga suggests that the believer and the unbeliever have different conceptions of reason. Op. cit., 91.

4. I follow McClendon and Smith's definition of *conviction* here as "a persistent belief such that if *X* has a conviction, it will not be easily relinquished without making *X* a significantly different person than before." James McClendon and James Smith, *Understanding Religious Convictions* (Notre Dame, Ind.: Univ. of Notre Dame Press, 1975), 7.

5. Even McClendon and Smith make this mistake in their usually reliable work. Ibid., 108.

6. Basil Mitchell, "Faith and Reason: A False Antithesis?" *Religious Studies* 16 (June 1980): I. Lakatos, "Falsification and Methodology of Scientific Research Programs," in *Criticism and the Growth of Knowledge*, edited by I. Lakatos and A. Musgrave (Cambridge, Mass.: Cambridge Univ. Press, 1970) 91–196.

7. Mitchell, op. cit.

8. Lakatos, op. cit., 118.

9. John Hick, *Arguments for the Existence of God* (New York: Macmillan, 1971), chap. 7.

10. Quoted in John Macquarrie, *Twentieth Century Religious Thought* (New York: Harper & Row, 1966), 334.

VII.D.5   Faith Without Belief?

LOUIS P. POJMAN

A bio-sketch of Louis Pojman appears in II. 6.

For many religious people there is a problem of doubting various credal statements contained in their religions. Often propositional beliefs are looked upon as necessary conditions for salvation. This causes great anxiety in doubters and raises the question of the importance of belief in religion and in life in general. It is a question that has been neglected in philosophy of religion and theology. In this paper I shall explore the question of the importance of belief as a religious attitude and suggest that there is at least one other attitude which may be adequate for religious faith even in the absence of belief.

It is worth noting, by way of conclusion, that the mature believer, the mature theist, does not typically accept belief in God tentatively, or hypothetically, or until something better comes along. Nor, I think, does he accept it as a conclusion from other things he believes; he accepts it as basic, as a part of the foundations of his noetic structure. The mature theist *commits* himself to belief in God: this means that he accepts belief in God as basic (Alvin Plantinga, "Is Belief in God Rational?").

Entombed in a secure prison, thinking our situation quite hopeless, we may find unutterable joy in the information that there is, after all, the slimmest possibility of escape. Hope provides comfort, and hope does not always require probability. But we must believe that what we hope for is at least possible (Gretchen Weirob in John Perry's *A Dialogue on Personal Identity and Immortality*).

For many religious people there is a problem of doubting various credal statements contained in their religions. Often propositional beliefs are

Reprinted from *Faith and Philosophy*; vol. 3, no. 2 April 1986. Endnotes edited.

looked upon as a necessary, though not sufficient condition, for salvation. This causes great anxiety in doubters and raises the question of the importance of belief in religion and in life in general. It is a question that has been neglected in philosophy of religion and Christian theology. In this paper I shall explore the question of the importance of belief as a religious attitude and suggest that there is at least one other attitude which may be adequate for religious faith even in the absence of belief, that attitude being hope. I shall develop a concept of faith as hope as an alternative to the usual notion that makes propositional belief that God exists a necessary condition for faith, as Plantinga implies in the quotation above. Finally, I shall deal with objections to this position as set forth by Gary Gutting in his recent book, *Religious Belief and Religious Skepticism*. For simplicity's sake I shall concentrate on the most important proposition in Western religious creeds, that which states that God exists (defined broadly as a benevolent, supreme Being, who is responsible for the creation of the universe), but the analysis could be applied *mutatis mutandis* to many other important propositions in religion (e.g., the Incarnation and the doctrine of the Trinity).

Many reflective religious people find themselves at one time or another doubting God's existence. If they have studied the alleged proofs for God's existence, they may become convinced that these "proofs" do not work as probative but, at best, simply point to the possibility of an intelligent force that influences the universe. For many of these people God's existence is not self-evident, nor is it properly basic for them. They are troubled by the lack of evidence for God's existence and believe that the move made by some philosophers to set it into the foundations of one's noetic structure is not acceptable for them. Their prayer is, "God, if you exist, show me better evidence." Although they would like to believe with confidence that God exists and are tempted to take the Pascalian-Jamesian line of acquiring this belief by getting themselves into a context where viewing selective evidence will cause belief, they resist this temptation as unethical. They adhere to an ethics of belief that prevents them from manipulating their noetic structure in such ways as to cause a belief that the evidence alone does not warrant. Such a maneuver would constitute a breach in their concern for having the best justified beliefs, a concern that puts a high premium on impartial regard for evidence. They also have the prudential concern of worrying about the possible bad effect such belief manipulations might have on their belief-forming mechanisms. It may even be that some of these doubters have tried but failed to get themselves to believe by using auto-suggestion or getting themselves into a favorable context as Pascal suggests.

I. The Importance of Belief

Being unable to believe either because of the lack of evidence or because of moral compunctions against acquiring beliefs through volitional means, these people have the unwelcome prospect of being denied the benefits of religious faith altogether or, at least, of being designated "immature theists," since faith with belief is generally regarded by orthodoxy as the sole manner of being a genuine believer with the benefits of salvation. The question immediately arises, What is so important about believing anyway? May there not be other propositional attitudes that are equally as effective as believing or, at least, adequate for the essential benefits of religion?

The traditional virtues of the attitude of belief have been (1) its ability to give intellectual and emotional surcease to the pain and insecurity of doubt and (2) its action-guiding function. Both of these virtues are ably discussed in C. S. Peirce's essay "The Fixation of Belief." According to Peirce, doubt is a type of pain, which, as such, is necessary as a warning mechanism to make us aware of the need for evidence. It is, like all pain, undesirable in itself, and a state from which we seek release. "Doubt is an uneasy and dissatisfied state from

which we struggle to free ourselves and pass into the state of belief; while the latter is a calm and satisfying state which we do not wish to avoid, or to change to a belief in anything else. On the contrary, we cling tenaciously, not merely to believing, but to believing just what we [already] believe."

Furthermore, argues Peirce, beliefs are action guides, directing our desires and shaping our actions. It is important to arrive at beliefs, because unless we do so, we cannot act. Beliefs are necessary conditions for actions. Let us look a little closer at these two theses.

Turning to the first thesis, why is belief restful or relief-ful, whereas doubt is anxiety ridden and stressful? Perhaps it is because in many cases, unless we have a conviction, we cannot act with abandon and singlemindedness. If we doubt our course, the doubt may deflect us from our goal. The runner who believes the prize to be uncertain may flag in his zeal. Furthermore, there may seem to be something unstable and unreliable about a doubter. The doubter, who wavers in his beliefs, "is like a wave of the sea driven with the wind and tossed. . . . A double minded man is unstable in all his ways" (Epistle of James 1:6, 8). One cannot imagine, the objection continues, a lover who doubts the beloved, a guerrilla fighter who doubts his cause, a successful businessman who doubts the free enterprise system, a skillful gambler who doubts his luck or a successful musician who wonders about her talent while performing. Doubt is the hobgoblin against every successful venture.

Contrast the doubter with the "mature believer," who confidently asserts, "I know whom I have believeth," or "The testimony of the Spirit is superior to all reason. . . . [It] is an undeniable truth, that they who have been inwardly taught by the Spirit feel an entire acquiescence in the Scripture, and that it is self-authenticating, carrying with it its own evidence, and ought not to be made the subject of demonstration and argument from reason. . . . We feel the firmest conviction that we hold an invincible truth."[1] Such absolute confidence certainly does offer a pleasant feeling of security, as well as a sense of rest from the further search for truth on this issue.

But, while doubt may be painful, it may be a wholesome suffering that causes us to recheck our propositional states, which may lead to greater accuracy and approximation of the truth. It is true that the runner who doubts may flag in zeal, but it is equally true that doubt may deflect him from the wrong course. In any case, we can learn to live gracefully with necessary pain, and it may be necessary for many religious people to learn to live gracefully with doubt, using it to probe deeper into ultimate questions. The suffering of doubt may be a cross that a disciple must learn to bear.

Turning to Peirce's second reason for having beliefs, i.e., that they are action-guiding, we can agree that this is an important aspect of fixing a belief. However, we need not agree with him that a belief is a necessary condition for action; at least it is not necessary to believe that a proposition is true in order to act on it. For many actions belief that the state of affairs in question will occur is not a necessary condition. I may act on the mere possibility of something being the case without actually believing that it will be the case. I can believe that a hypothesis is the best among a series of weak hypotheses and worth following through without believing that it is true. I can believe that it is worthwhile to bet on a horse that is underrated at 10 to 1 odds when I have only $10 and need $100 soon and have no other way of getting it. I can bet on the horse, risk everything on it and still not believe that it will win. I only need to believe that it is a worthwhile action to bet in this way, given my overall set of goals and beliefs about reaching these goals. Likewise, I can attempt to swim five miles to shore after my ship has sunk, in hope of reaching the shore, without believing that I can or will reach the shore safely. Finally, Columbus' sailors need not have believed that the earth was round in order to have embarked from Spain to sail to the New World. They simply had to believe that the risk was worth taking.

When the evidence is perceived as weak, too weak to produce belief in the veracious person, and where the ethics of belief forbids mind manipulations or acquiring beliefs volitionally, but where the consequences are great, the best a person can do is live belief-lessly according to the hypothesis in question. That is, we may be justified in doing a cost-benefit analysis in order to determine whether the proposition is worth following for the possible consequences. For example. I may have two incompatible goals at some moment and need to decide which one to aim at. Suppose that I determine that goal A has a probability index of 0.4, whereas goal B has one of 0.6, making it positively probable. Although B has a better chance of being reached than A, I might still be justified in aiming at goal A rather than B. I would be justified in doing so just in case I desired A sufficiently more than B—if, for example, I give A a preference value of 0.7 and B only a value of 0.4. Of course, we usually do not give exact quantified indices and preference values to possible courses of action, but we do make rough approximations of this type very often. When a graduate student accepts a challenging job with a questionable future over a more secure job with less challenge, a decision process has often gone on which has weighed subjective probabilities and strengths of desires. If I believe that there is only slight chance that there is a bomb in the briefcase on the other side of the room, I do not need to make a formal cost-benefit assessment of the matter in order to act swiftly. I leave the room because the stakes are very high, even though I may not be convinced that there really is a bomb in the briefcase. It seems that our sub-conscious is constantly making rough cost-benefit assessments in the various situations in which we find ourselves, maximizing expected utility.

If my analysis is correct, positively believing in the existence of objects in question may not be as important as we have sometimes been led to suppose. We may be guided by weak probabilities, and the distressing doubt that we feel may often be redemptive, causing us to check our evidence, justify our beliefs, and obtain more accurate beliefs.

II. Faith as Hope

We have argued that it is not necessary to believe that a proposition is positively probable in order to act on it. The perception of its possibility is often sufficient to incite activity. One such alternative propositional attitude to belief is hope (or, negatively, fear). In the next section (A) I shall examine the concept of hope. In Section B I shall compare it with its close relatives: 'belief-in,' 'trust,' 'living-as-if' and 'optimism.' Then, in Part III of this paper I shall apply the analysis of hope to religious faith, showing that faith need not be belief-ful, but may be an expression of hope.[2]

A. An Analysis of Hope

Let us begin with some examples of expressions of hope.

1. Mary hopes to get an A in her History course.
2. John hopes that Mary will marry him.
3. Mary hopes that Happy Dancer will win the Kentucky Derby next week.
4. John hopes that the Yankees won their game yesterday.
5. Mary hopes that the sun is shining in Dallas today for her sister's wedding.
6. Although John desires a cigarette, he hopes that he will not give in to his desire.

If we look closely at these examples of hoping, we can pick out certain necessary features of the concept of hope. First of all, hope involves belief in the possibility of a state of affairs obtaining. We cannot hope for what we believe to be impossible. If Mary hopes to get an A in History, she must believe that it is possible that she get one in that course, and if she hopes that Happy Dancer will win the Kentucky Derby, we must believe that it is possible that he will win. The Oxford English Dictionary defines 'hope' as an 'expectation of something desired,' but this seems too strong. Expectation implies belief that something will occur, but we may hope even when we do not expect the object of desire to obtain, as when John hopes that Mary will marry him but realizes that the odds are greatly against it or when Mary hopes that Happy Dancer will win the Kentucky Derby although she accepts the official odds against it. I may likewise hope to win a lottery but not expect to do so. Belief that the object of desire will obtain is not necessary for hope. It is enough

that the hoper believe that the proposition in question is not impossible. What separates hope from belief is that in believing one necessarily believes that the proposition is true (has a subjective probability index of greater than .5), whereas in hoping this is not necessary.

Secondly, hope precludes certainty. John will not be certain that Mary will marry him or that the Yankees won the game yesterday. There must be an apparent possibility of the states of affairs not obtaining. We would think it odd to say, "John knows that the Yankees won the game yesterday, for he was at the game, but he still hopes that the Yankees won the game yesterday." "For hope that is seen is not hope: for what a man seeth, why doth he yet hope for" (Epistle to the Romans 8:24). Hope entails uncertainty, a subjective probability index greater than 0 but less than 1.

Thirdly, hope entails desire for the state of affairs in question to obtain or the proposition to be true. In all of the above cases a propositional content can be seen as the object of desire. The state of affairs envisaged evokes a pro-attitude. The subject wants some proposition p to be true. It matters not whether the state of affairs is past (case 4), present (cases 5 and 6) or future (cases 1–3), though it generally turns out—because of the role hope plays in goal orientation—that the state of affairs will be a future situation.

Hope is to be distinguished from its near relatives, other pro-attitudes, especially from wishing. In wishing for something one need not even believe that it is possible. Mary can wish that she had never been born but she cannot hope this. I may wish I were smarter than I am, but I cannot now hope that. After John discovers that the Yankees lost the game yesterday, he may wish that his favorite team had won, but he can no longer hope for it. Furthermore, we can wish for possible things which we are not ready to do anything about because the cost–benefit analysis shows that the possible benefit is not worth the risk involved. I might wish to make an extra $100 this week, but I may conclude that the loss of my free time in working overtime is not worth the extra money. Here I cannot be said to hope to make the extra $100, though I might wish that it were somehow possible to have the requisite extra time to do so.

This brings us to our fourth characteristic of hope. If one hopes for *p*, one will be disposed to do what one can to bring *p* about, if there is anything that one can do to bring it about. In hoping, unlike wishing, there will be a tendency to try to bring about the state of affairs if there is anything that can be done to bring it about. In the examples above cases 1, 2 and 6 are situations where the hoper can make a difference, whereas there is nothing he or she can do to bring about the desired result in cases 3 through 5. In this, hoping seems more reflective than wishing or merely having a desire. It is closer to having a want-on-balance, having considered the alternatives, as in case 6, where John has three desires but only one hope. (1) He wants to smoke, (2) he wants to stop smoking, and (3) he has a second order desire, in that he wants his second desire to win out over his first. He will try to bring it about that he will be successful in this. In this case it would be odd for John to speak of two hopes, that of having a cigarette and that of not smoking. John's full-blooded hope is to lick the habit, beginning by refraining from taking the cigarette.

In this sense hoping (where something can be done to bring about the state of affairs) is similar to intending where the agent desires that some state of affairs obtain and will try to bring it about. The difference between this dimension of hope and intending is that in intending to do action *A* one must believe that one will succeed, whereas no such requirement is necessary in hoping. If I intend to get an A in History, I must believe that I will, but I may hope to get an A without believing that I will be successful. Hope stands mid way between wishing and intending. In the former category, I may not believe that *p* is possible and in the latter, I must believe that I will probably bring it about. In hope I must believe that it is possible, but I need not believe that I will be able to bring it about.

A more difficult question is whether one can have incompatible hopes. Muyskens, in his important study *The Sufficiency of Hope*, follows Aquinas in denying that we can have conflicting preferences on balance. We may have conflicting wishes but not hopes.

> If S hopes for *p*, either S prefers *p* on balance or S believes that he does not prefer anything that opposes his desire for *p*. The following formulation of this necessary condition is most perspicuous: It is not the case that *p* is not preferred by S on balance, or that S believes that *q*, which he prefers on balance, is incompatible with *p* (p. 18).

But why can't we have incompatible hopes, even as we have incompatible desires? It may not be rational to have them, but we are not talking about justified hopes, simply about having hopes. Can I not hope to travel to Greece this summer and also hope to finish my manuscript, which I can only do if I stay home from Greece? Perhaps the full analysis of this state is something like the following. I desire both to go to Greece and to finish my manuscript, but since there are many other contingencies that may prevent either of these from happening (e.g., I may have to teach summer school in order to earn some money or go in for an operation, either of which will prevent me from realizing either of my desires about going to Greece or finishing my manuscript) or prevent one of these from happening (e.g., I may not have enough money to go to Greece, or I may have my contract cancelled and so lose my motivation for writing my manuscript), I may be said to have a disjunctive hope: I hope either to go to Greece this summer or write my manuscript. It would be odd to say, under these circumstances, "I hope both to write the manuscript and go to Greece this summer, but I know that I cannot do both."

There may be a tendency to emphasize the desiderative aspect of hope and maintain that incompatible hopes are possible, as incompatible desires are. Hoping does not entail belief, but a mere pro-attitude. I cannot believe that *p* and *q* where they are incompatible (and I realize it), but I can desire both. Because hope does not necessitate belief, it may seem that we cannot rule out the possibility of incompatible hopes. However, the key phrase here is 'desiring on balance,' which connotes a more reflective or intentional stance. If hope is closely allied to intention, as I have argued, it would seem to rule out incompatible hopes in the sense that if someone realizes that he hopes for two separate states of affairs, he must give up one in order to try to bring about the other. It seems to me that this attitude carries over to situations where one is powerless to affect the outcome. Mary may unreflectively hope that Happy Dancer wins the race and that Slippery Heels wins the same race, but when she realizes that these horses are running in the same race, she must give up one of her hopes or at least hope something like the following: that either Happy Dancer or Slippery Heels will win, or, if Happy Dancer does not win, that Slippery Heels will.

It may be objected that we can have incompatible hopes but that they are vain, ill-advised, foolish or whatever. This seems to call for a normative notion of hoping, separating rational hopes from irrational ones; where hopes are incompatible at least one hope is irrational. Mary may believe that she hopes to get an A in History but also hope to go to a party on the two nights preceding the exam. We want to say that such hope is irrational or imprudent. Mary should realize that it is virtually impossible for her to get an A in history without studying the two nights before the exam. If Mary were more rational, she would reflect on her incompatible hopes and decide on one of these hopes to the exclusion of the other. If hope is made up of a desiderative and an estimative factor, we may call hope unjustified or irrational just in case we can call either of its components unjustified or irrational. If John hopes to square the circle, we want to say that since the belief in question is irrational, the hope is also. If Mary hopes to party instead of studying, but has long term goals which entail good grades, which in turn entail studying instead of partying, then we can speak of Mary having irrational hopes.

It may be countered that what is irrational about Mary is not her hoping but her believing that there is a chance of getting an A without studying. Or we may say that Mary really doesn't hope to get an A. She is self-deceived about her attitude and really only wishes to get the A. If hope has the intentional dimension that I have argued for, either of these

redescriptions of Mary's state seem preferable to saying that Mary has consciously incompatible, though irrational, hopes. The issue is difficult, but I am inclined to hold to the irrational/rational distinction regarding hoping. Since hoping has an estimative (doxastic) and desiderative component, if one of these is irrational, the whole (i.e., the hope itself) may be irrational. At the very least we can say that a hope is irrational if the agent should know that the object in question is either certain or impossible. If John hopes he is God or Mary hopes to be forgiven by John after John has made it clear that he has freely forgiven her, their hopes are irrational. There is also the phenomenon of something being so close to impossible or certain that hoping may be irrational, as when an average person hopes to live to 200 or an average high school football player with no great athletic promise hopes to make the pros and gives up all else in order to do this.

If we can apply the rational-irrational distinction to hopes, can we also speak of morally unjustified and justified hopes? Are there moral constraints to hoping? J. P. Day denies, but Muyskens affirms, that there are such. We may have morally unacceptable hopes in a way that we cannot have immoral beliefs. This is because hope statements involve desire in a way that beliefs do not. Consider the difference between:

1. I believe that the US and the USSR will annihilate the world in a nuclear war.

and

2. I hope that the US and the USSR will annihilate the world in a nuclear war.

Beliefs may be formed through a culpable lack of attention and thus have a moral dimension, but the belief itself cannot be judged moral or immoral. Hopes can. Having certain hopes, like having certain desires, shows bad character in a more fundamental way than belief acquisition does. But the most important difference is that the belief may be evidential and justified while the affective state of hoping is still inappropriate. We ought not allow ourselves to give in to such malicious desires.

B. Hope and Other Propositional Attitudes

We have argued that hoping need not involve a subject's actually believing a proposition, but only that the proposition could be or could become true. In believing a proposition, the doxastic state has a subjective probability index of greater than 0.5, but in hoping that p is true, one need not believe that the proposition has that high an index.[3] John need not believe that Mary will marry him in order to hope that she will, nor need he believe that the Yankees have won the baseball game in order to hope that they have.

But if hoping does not entail belief-that so-and-so is the case, does it, at least, entail belief-in, a relationship of trust? Believing-in or trusting is a relational attitude. 'S trusts X' or 'S trusts in X' or 'S believes in X' indicates a sense of dependency and willingness to run a risk (however small) because of the positive valuation on the object in question. Some instances of hope do entail believing-in the object of hope. Consider case 3 (Mary hopes that Happy Dancer will win the Kentucky Derby next week). What would it mean to say that Mary believed-in Happy Dancer in this context? She must act or be disposed to act in some way as to manifest trust in Happy Dancer. She may bet on Happy Dancer without believing that he will win the race, but she cannot hope that Happy Dancer will win the race without being inclined to take some action in appropriate circumstances. The most likely action would be to bet on Happy Dancer, if she is able to do so, and the degree to which she hopes in Happy Dancer may be to some degree measured by how much she would bet on Happy Dancer. Of course, she may not bet on Happy Dancer, just in case her desire is sufficiently weak, or she has compunctions against gambling, or her estimation of Happy Dancer's chances are too low to warrant a risk. We can weakly hope (all things considered) without acting when there are countervailing desires (e.g., the desire not to risk one's hard earned money on a long shot). There is a fine line where our desire for something ceases to be a weak hope (with some inclination to act) and becomes a mere wish.

Although because of the desiderative nature of hope, there will be some inclination or tendency for the subject to believe-in or trust the object of hope, there are cases where there is nothing one can do (e.g., when I hope that the Yankees won their game yesterday or that the sun will shine in Dallas today for my sister's wedding) or where the hope is so weak that it is easily overridden by other considerations (e.g., when I hedge my bet, when I hope the sun will shine but take an umbrella or hope to live a long life but take out an expensive life insurance policy or hope that the enemy will not attack but keep my powder dry).

Here we need to make a distinction between ordinary hope or weak hope and a deep hope. Consider Mary's situation as she hopes in Happy Dancer. She may only believe that Happy Dancer has a 1 in 10 chance of winning the Kentucky Derby, but she may judge this to be significantly better than the official odds of 100 to 1 against him. Suppose that she has only $10 but wants desperately to enter a special professional training program next week which will cost $1000. She has no hope of getting the money elsewhere but sees that if she wins on Happy Dancer, she will get the required amount. Since she believes that the real odds are better than the official odds and that winning will enable her to get into the training program, she bets her $10 on the horse. She both hopes and trusts in Happy Dancer, though she never really believes that he will win. We might call these cases where one is disposed to risk something significant on the possibility of the proposition's being or becoming true, 'deep' or 'profound hope' and cases where the person hopes against belief, against the available evidence and is even ready to risk something significant, 'desperate hope.' Desperate hope is a species of deep or profound hope. In all cases of profound hope hoping entails trusting in the object of hope. There are rational and irrational, moral and immoral profound hopes. A morally acceptable, rational, profound, desperate hope is exemplified by a version of William James's classical mountain climber, who cannot believe but only hopes that he will be successful in jumping across the gorge.[4]

Sometimes it is thought that belief-in statements entail existential belief-that statements. That is, belief-in some object x presupposes that one believe-that x exists or will exist.[5] But this seems to be incorrect. The object need not be realizable, nor need the subject believe that he will realize it. All that is necessary is that the individual believe that there is some possibility of realizing it. A scientist may risk his reputation and spend enormous time and energy on a hypothesis that involves the possible existence of an entity which may not exist or which is far different from his tentative description of it.

If belief-in, or trusting, can be analyzed in terms of commitment to a course of action or a disposition to act, then it seems that we do not need to believe-that x exists in order to believe-in or deeply hope in the existence of x. We can live in profound hope, trusting in the object of hope. In ordinary hope we may not act according to the proposition in question, but may hedge our bet, as I have indicated above. But in profound hope (and especially in desperate hope) the desire for the object is so great that the subject is ready to act even in the light of very little evidence or subjective probability that the object in question will be realized. In such hope enormous risk is warranted by the strength of the desire and the felt need. The person lives *as if* the proposition were true or would become so. Columbus' sailors live on the hypothesis that the world is round, even though they doubt it. The explorer hopes to find the Fountain of Youth, even though he has doubts that such a fountain exists. A seriously sick woman can act in desperation, writing to an unknown person (who may not exist) for a wonder drug which in fact does not exist, but which she has heard about from misinformed friends.

We can imagine a situation where Mary has merely heard a rumor about some horse running in the Kentucky Derby at ridiculously low odds. She isn't sure that she has the name right, but in despair she goes to the local bookmaker in order to place her bet on Happy Dancer. She may doubt whether Happy Dancer exists and doubts the ill-reputed bookmaker who assures her that there is such a horse (suppose that she has good grounds for her suspicions). We may, nevertheless, say that she

trusts that there is, that she lives *as if* there is such a horse. She lives in profound, desperate hope.

Genuinely living *as if* must be distinguished from pretending. You can pretend and act as though you love your neighbors, for you may believe that it is good policy to give this impression; but in genuinely profound hope the intentional state is different from that of pretending.

Finally, we should examine the relationship between hoping and optimism. If John hopes to marry Mary, must he be optimistic about this possibility? Can we imagine John hopeful with regard to marrying her and still pessimistic about its occurrence? We can imagine him hoping desperately, against hope, as it were, and we can imagine an alternative between hope and despair (distinguishing desperation from despair by the fact that despair tends to paralyze or cause inaction, whereas desperation tends to cause action). If we mean by pessimistic 'a low estimation of the chances of realizing the state of affairs,' then we certainly can be hopeful and pessimistic, but if we mean 'a psychological state of resigning or despairing of realizing the state of affairs,' then we cannot be hopeful and pessimistic. Resignation, despairing and fearing, as Day has shown, are all contraries to hope. I think, in fact, the terms 'optimistic' and 'pessimistic' are ambiguous in this way, so that we may be able to conjoin pessimistic with hopeful if we are emphasizing the estimative aspect of pessimism or optimism. It is possible, then, to be a hopeful pessimist, while living *as if* a proposition were true. Indeed, one can live *as if* a proposition were true without hope, in a desperate way, trusting, but not deeming the outcome significantly possible. Profound hope, then, is a species of faith, but it is not identical with it. Normally, however, the profound hoper will tend to envision the best outcome, even while realizing the objective factors that count against it. He won't be dominated by the objectively low probabilities of success.

We conclude, then, that hoping is distinguished from believing in that it involves a strong volitional or affective aspect in a way believing does not and that, as such, it is subject to moral assessment in a way that believing is not. Hoping is desiderative, but is more inclined to action than mere wishing.

Profound hope is distinguished from ordinary hope by the intensity of the desire and willingness to take great risk towards obtaining one's goal, and desperate hope is a type of profound hope where the estimative aspect is low. Hope is not identical with optimism, if optimism is defined as estimative. A hoper may see that the odds are objectively against him and yet profoundly try to realize a state of affairs. Nevertheless, in spite of the intensity of desire, the moral hoper will continue to keep his mind open to fresh argument and evidence which could either incline him towards belief-ful hope or abandoning one hope for another.

III. Profound Hope and Religious Faith

Can we apply this analysis of profound hope to religious faith without loss? Can we have religious faith in a religion like Christianity without believing that the object of faith exists? Let me tell a story in order to have some data for our analysis. Suppose Aaron and Moses both have an obligation to defend Israel from the Canaanites, who are seen as a present danger. The question is whether or not Israel should launch a preemptive strike against the neighboring tribe or whether there is still room for negotiations. One morning Moses sincerely reports that he has been appeared to by God, who has commanded him to annihilate the Canaanites because of their wickedness and idolatry. He has no doubts about the reality of the revelation, claims that it was self-authenticating, and tries to convince Aaron to help him prepare for war. Aaron must make a decision whether or not to support Moses, for he doubts whether God exists, let alone whether he has revealed himself to his brother. However, he doubts these things only weakly, deeming it possible that Yahweh exists and has so revealed himself to Moses. He wonders at the clouds by day and the fire in the distance by night which Moses claims are God's means of leading his people to their destination. Aaron is agnostic about both the existence of Yahweh and the revelation to Moses. Since he would like it to be the case that a benevolent guide for Israel exists, he might be tempted to take William James's advice and get himself to believe the requi-

site propositions by willing to believe them: but we may suppose that he does not believe that volitional believing is possible for him or morally acceptable. His only option is to live *as if* the proposition in question were true. He assists Moses in every way in carrying out the campaign against the Canaanites. He proclaims the need for his people to fight against the enemy, and if he sounds more convinced than he really is, he judges this deception to be justified. True, he may not act out of spontaneous abandon as Moses does. On the other hand, his scrupulous doubt may help him to notice problems and evidence which might otherwise be neglected, to which the true believer is impervious. This awareness may signal danger which may be avoided, thus saving the tribe from disaster. Doubt may have as many virtues as belief, though they may be different ones.

Moses and Aaron do not act out of entirely different noetic structures.

Moses entirely believes what Aaron only hopes for. Moses acts because he believes that *p* and that it is a good thing that *p*. Aaron acts because he believes that it would be a good thing if *p*, that *p* is possible and that it is rational and morally permissible to hope that *p*. He exemplifies what we have called living *as if* God exists and has revealed himself to Israel. He lives in profound hope (and if he estimates the chances of God's existing to be very low, he also lives in desperate hope). He identifies an ideal state of affairs, believes it to be possible, though not probable, and being a hopeful person, plumps for the better scenario, rather than the worse. He lives experimentally with theism, in an experimental faith in which he continues to keep his mind open to, and to search for, new evidence which would either confirm or disconfirm the hypothesis on which his hopeful faith is based. While the hoper may live in a deep or even desperate hope, his eye, if he holds to an ethics of hope, is always on the evidence so that there may come a time when the available evidence (or his subjective probability estimate) becomes too low to sustain faith.

My analysis suggests that the difference between faith and belief is more radical than has usually been supposed. Usually, it is assumed that faith is a special type of belief, one in which, in addition to belief in the existence of the religious object, one trusts in it and allows its influence to dominate one's life. To have faith in God is to believe that he exists and to commit one's life to him. This seems to have New Testament backing, especially in the Epistle to the Hebrews (chapter 11), where we read that unless we believe that God exists, we can neither come to God nor please him. However, as prominent as this view has been in Western thought (note its presence in the quotation by Plantinga at the beginning of this paper), I suggest that it is an illicit entailment and that the writer of the letter to the Hebrews either had an overly behavioral interpretation of belief or was engaging in religious rhetoric, for I see no good reason to exclude the possibility of coming to God in hope rather than belief. On my analysis one may alter the passage "Lord, I believe, help Thou my unbelief" to read: "Lord, I hope in you; if you exist, please give me better evidence." To believe that God exists is to believe that there is a being with certain necessary properties such as omnipotence, omniscience, omnibenevolence and being the maker of heaven and earth. But to believe-in God implies only that one regards such a being as possibly existing and that one is committed to live *as if* such a being does exist. Whether it is rational to commit oneself in this way depends on the outcome of an analysis of comparative values in relationship to probable outcomes. It is the sort of assessment that goes on in any cost-benefit analysis.

It may usually be the case that those who believe *in* God also believe *that* God exists, but there is no entailment between the two states. One might believe that God exists without believing in God, and one might believe in God without believing that God exists, either as an atheist (who finds the proposition 'God exists' as genuinely possible and decides to live by it) or as an agnostic (who finds the God-hypothesis worth living in accordance with). Often, it has been supposed that there can be no hypothetical element in religious commitment and that to treat God's existence as such is to violate the very essence of religious faith. Supposedly, the hypothetical stance is inadequate to produce the requisite commitment and unreserved worship which religion demands. But if this is true of traditional religious beliefs, I see no need to accept it as the only valid type of faith. An *experimental faith* that is open to new evidence is also an option. In this regard, my analysis has in common with William James the notion of theism being a live option (an hypothesis that is momentous and which the subject sees as calling for a decision). It agrees with James that it would be good thing if theism and Christianity were true and can accept James's own rejection of the necessity of sufficient evidence for the proposition that Christianity is true before we can have faith. "If religion be true and the evidence for it be still insufficient, I do not wish, by putting [the rationalist's] extinguisher upon my nature . . . to forfeit my sole chance in life of getting upon the winning side."[6] I would also agree with James against Pascal that there is a psychological aspect to the decision of choosing religion which must supplement the merely calculative. While an atheist (who does not rule out the possibility of God's existence) may be persuaded of the logic of Pascal's Wager, he might not be moved by it. James is right when he says that the hypothesis in question must be a psychologically "live hypothesis." My analysis differs from James's in that I don't think it is necessary to get oneself to believe that the hypothesis is true in order to choose it in a profound way. One can have faith in God and Christianity without belief. Aaron is just as much in faith as Moses. There are different types of faith.

Belief-that may be overrated in regard to explanatory hypotheses that involve worldviews such as religions, political theories, and metaphysical systems. It is important to come as close as possible to a fit between the best objective evidence and the degree with which one believes propositions, but, admittedly, this is a person-relative experience. My analysis presupposes that it makes sense to speak of proportioning the strength of one's belief (which I separate from the value of one's belief to the individual, the depth of ingress of the belief) to the evidence, but it accepts intuitive beliefs as themselves prima facie evidence for themselves and their entailments. Ultimately, if someone counts her intuitions as evidence more than we do, all we can do is try to get her to see that she really has counter-evidence or intuitions which should lessen the strength of her apparent intuitive beliefs. There may be a more objective notion of proportioning one's beliefs to the evidence, but my analysis is content with this weaker thesis. It is possible that the belief that God exists is properly basic for some people, but, by the same standard, it may be that the belief that the Devil is really God is properly basic for others, given their noetic structure. For many of us neither are properly basic.

If my analysis is correct, agnosticism and even an interested type of atheism are possible religious positions. Doubt about God's existence, immortality, the Incarnation, or the Trinity, though agonizing in the extreme at times, may be necessary for some intellectually honest people. If there is an obligation to seek to have true or justified beliefs, then what God desires is not sycophantic struggling to get oneself to manipulate one's mind to believe what seems implausible on a clear look at the evidence, but a doxastic morality that allows the mind to be impartially shaped by the evidence.

If this is the case, then an interesting implication follows. Sometimes, as in the Athanasian Creed or Evangelical theologies and sermons, religious people have asserted that a belief that certain propositions are true is a necessary condition for eternal salvation. We will be judged by whether or not we have believed these propositions (e.g., those contained in the doctrine of the Trinity, the Incarnation, and so forth). Pascal and others believed this so strongly that they advocated that you should "pretend you believe" in order to get yourself to believe what you don't believe by an impartial look at the evidence. But if we have ethical duties to have the best justified beliefs possible in important matters, and if those duties include a duty to acquire beliefs through impartial investigation of the evidence, then it would seem that we cannot be judged unrighteous for not believing in these propositions, if we justifiably find the evidence inadequate. It would follow that there is a moral basis even to religious believing, so that a moral God could not judge us merely on the basis of the beliefs we have. What we can be judged for is how well we have responded to criticism of our beliefs, including our religious beliefs, how faithful we have been to the truth as we have seen it. On this basis it might well be the case that in heaven (or purgatory) Calvin, Barth, Billy Graham and Jerry Falwell may have to be rehabilitated by taking catechism lessons in the ethics of belief from such archangels as David Hume and Bertrand Russell.

IV. Is Experimental Faith Adequate for Religious Belief?

In philosophical literature I know of only one serious set of objections to the position that I have set forth. It has to do with the alleged inadequacy of any sort of tentativeness or nontenacity in religious believing. Experimental faith lacks the ultimate commitment that is necessary for an adequate religious faith. This objection is given its best expression by Gary Gutting in his incisive work *Religious Belief and Religious Skepticism*, in which he distinguishes between "interim assent" and "decisive assent." Decisive assent terminates the process of inquiry into the truth of the core propositions, whereas interim assent keeps the inquiry going.[7] In decisive assent one ends the search for justifying reasons and becomes wholly concerned with understanding the implications of what one believes. In interim assent one accepts the propositions in question without terminating the search for their truth. While there may be a difference between Gutting's notion of interim assent and what I have been calling experimental faith or hopeful commitment,—the former but not the latter presupposing, at least, weak belief—much of his attack on interim assent is applicable to my account. On Gutting's account such faith is inadequate for religious life.

Essentially, interim assent is inadequate for genuine religious belief because of the way religious belief functions in the life of the believer. Gutting gives three reasons for thinking that religious faith demands decisive assent and prohibits interim assent. (1) Religious belief is a (relative) end of a quest for "emotional and intellectual satisfaction." "Any religious belief worthy of the name must surely call for and legitimate a longing for God as the all-dominative longing of the believer's life, the believer's 'master passion.' By contrast, the life of a believer who gave only interim assent to God's reality . . . could be rightly dominated not by the longing for God but, at best, only by the longing to know whether or not God exists." (p. 106) (2) Religious belief requires total commitment to the implications of what is believed and this is incompatible with continuing reflection on its truth. Believers must often make fundamental sacrifices, which only decisive assent would allow. (3) Merely interim assent is inconsistent with the typically religious attitude toward nonbelief, which sees nonbelief as intrinsically bad. Interim assent has not the singlemindedness of decisive assent and cannot "proclaim the ideal of its belief as 'the one thing needful.'" (p. 108)

My first reaction to Gutting's insistence that decisive faith is a necessary condition for adequate religious belief is to say that perhaps there is something morally repugnant about "adequate" religious belief, since it seems to demand a premature closure of inquiry. If there were good objective grounds for theism, the mandate might be understandable. Since there doesn't seem to be that kind of requisite evidence, the closure seems unwarranted. Even if experimental faith failed to give what Gutting deems the necessary conditions for adequate religious belief, this doesn't mean that experimental faith is a less valid position. It might mean that traditional religious belief is not the only meaningful possibility for intelligent persons. Perhaps traditionally necessary conditions are not the necessary conditions that we would want to use to define an adequate faith for today. It might be the case, for example, that traditional religions have under-emphasized the role of an ethics of belief and assumed that a rigid set of beliefs was necessary for genuine faith. If my analysis is correct, too much emphasis may have been placed on credal affirmation in the past.

Gutting's analysis of the inferiority of interim assent has other problems. Regarding his first point that "any religious belief worthy of the name must surely call for and legitimate a longing for God as the all dominating longing of the believer's life" and

that interim assent fails here, we may demur at two points. (a) Not every religion makes this longing the dominant passion. Buddhism doesn't. Neither does Sikhism or Quakerism. On what independent grounds does Gutting exclude these religions as "worthy religious beliefs," except by begging the question? (b) Even if Gutting is right, however, I see no reason for concluding that the person who hopes in God cannot be dominated by this passion, even while questing for truth. To have faith in God, in the sense I have described, is to long for God passionately, to live *as if* God exists. But why is this incompatible with seeking the best evidence on the matter, of admitting that one only weakly believes this (or is agnostic on the matter)? Doesn't the believing Biblical scholar have to inquire impartially into the evidence for important events upon which is faith is based? I think that it is a rather narrow notion of "passionate longing" which rules out impartial inquiry. The hoper in God worships with passion and commitment; only he or she acknowledges and is committed to doxastic integrity, to continuing the dialogue with those who differ, and regards engaging in the dialogue as one aspect of worship. Otherwise, how is it possible for the person of faith to find honest "intellectual satisfaction," which Gutting acknowledges as a necessary condition for adequate religion?

Gutting's second criticism of interim assent is that it precludes the sort of unconditional commitment necessary for decisive action and fundamental sacrifices. It is true, as our discussion of Peirce and our parable of Aaron and Moses show, that the doubter's steps are tripped by obstacles over which the true believer hurdles with the greatest of ease. The question is whether this sort of commitment is of the essence of genuine religion. The same imperviousness to difficulty has led to some of the greatest intolerance and fanaticism the world has known. We can rightly spot it as evil in fanatical Nazis or Shiite Moslems following the Ayatollah Khoumeni, but we sometimes miss it in ourselves. Gutting may have in mind the martyrs who are willing to die for belief in the Incarnation or the existence of God, and perhaps the hoper in God will not be as willing to die as the believer. But the hoper in God may, nevertheless, be willing to live and die for the moral principles which he sees tied up with the essence of the religious faith and which express much of the importance of believing in God in the first place. The hoper in God may question whether we have any reason to believe that a morally adequate religion or God's will demand that people give their lives for the proposition that God exists. If God is all-powerful and benevolent, surely, he could insure that the witness to his existence is not lost.

The third criticism that Gutting makes of interim assent is that it does not allow for the deep conviction that belief in God is the "one thing needful," that it is an unspeakably sad thing not to believe that God exists. Gutting is saying that it is the relationship with God, trust in Him, that is needful, but he implies that this entails believing that God exists. "For the believer, the world would be a better place if everyone could see his way to accepting the believer's faith," but interim assent must allow "equal value" to opposing beliefs, an essential element in continuing discussion. But this objection misses the point that the manner of holding a belief may be as important as the belief itself. If everyone in the world came to believe that God existed by manipulating their minds, it might well turn out that these belief states were disconnected from the rest of their noetic structure and represented a deep character flaw. It is not clear that honest doubt is less a state of reverence for God than fearful prohibition of doubt.

Gutting and I agree that belief in God can make a profound difference in the way we live and that theism, which is at the basis of Judaism and Christianity, is greatly inspiring and can motivate to high moral action. My point is that one need not be a full-fledged believer *that* God exists in order to draw inspiration from this insight. One can live imaginatively in hope, letting the thought of the possibility of a benevolent Being motivate one to a more dedicated and worshipful moral life.

Notes

1. John Calvin, *Institutes of the Christian Religion*, Philadelphia: Westminster Press, 1960. Book I, Ch 7, pp. 79f.

2. Much of my analysis has been influenced by James Muyskens' excellent study, *The Sufficiency of Hope*, Philadelphia: Temple University Press, 1979.

3. While it is controversial whether 'belief that' statements involve probability estimates, I think a plausible case for this can be made based on the fact that we believe propositions to various degrees. If we can set numbers from 0 to 1, indicating absolute disbelief and absolute conviction, with 0.5 as withholding belief or suspending judgment, we can roughly fix the degree of other belief-states on a continuum between these points. All that is needed is an arbitrary measure and the notion of 'believing that p to a greater degree than that q.' Muyskens' counter-example that a gambler can believe that the odds are 100:1 against his winning and yet believe that he will win can be accommodated by making a distinction between objective inductive evidence and subjective probability, which is simply a function of a belief state. Cf. Muyskens, op. cit., p. 38.

4. William James, "The Sentiment of Rationality" in *Essays in Pragmatism*, ed., Alburey Castell. New York: Hafners Publishing Company, 1948.

5. Gary Gutting, *Religious Belief and Religious Skepticism*, Notre Dame: University of Notre Dame Press. 1982, p. 105. In correspondence, Gutting says that he has sympathy for my approach and that "I am merely pointing out the incompatibility of interim assent with faith as it has been traditionally regarded." Letter dated October 6. 1983.

6. William James, *The Will to Believe*, New York: Dover, 1897; p. 19.

7. Gary Gutting, op. cit.

Bibliography for Part VII

Crosson, Frederick, ed. *The Autonomy of Religious Belief.* Notre Dame, Ind.: Univ. of Notre Dame Press, 1981. A valuable set of articles on fideism, especially those of Phillips and Nielsen.

Davis, Stephen. *Faith, Skepticism and Evidence.* Lewisburg, Pa.: Bucknell Univ. Press, 1978. Examines the concepts discussed in this section.

Delaney, C. F., ed. *Rationality and Religious Belief.* Notre Dame, Ind.: Univ. of Notre Dame Press, 1978. A good collection of essays on faith and reason.

Flew, Antony. *The Presumption of Atheism.* New York: Harper & Row, 1976. Part 1, chap. 1, 2, and 5 are relevant to the discussion.

Jordan, Jeff, ed. *Gambling on God: Essays on Pascal's Wager,* Lanham, MD: Rowman & Littlefield, 1994.

Kellenberger, J. *Religious Discovery, Faith and Knowledge.* Englewood Cliffs, N.J.: Prentice Hall, 1972. A lucid defense of a moderate fideist position.

Mackie, J. L. *The Miracle of Theism: Arguments for and Against the Existence of God.* Oxford, Eng.: Clarendon Press, 1982. Probably the best defense of atheism in recent years, taking into consideration every major argument in the field.

Mavrodes, George. *Belief in God.* New York: Random House, 1970. A clear presentation of religious epistemology.

Mitchell, Basil. *The Justification of Religious Belief.* London: Macmillan, 1973. A good discussion of the cumulative case for theism.

Phillips, D. Z. *Religion Without Explanation.* Oxford, Eng.: Basil Blackwell, 1976. A valuable study by one of the foremost Wittgensteinian philosophers.

Plantinga, Alvin, and Nicholas Wolterstorff, eds. *Faith and Rationality.* Notre Dame, Ind.: Univ. of Notre Dame Press, 1983. A valuable collection from a reformed Christian perspective.

Pojman, Louis. *Religious Belief and the Will.* London: Routledge & Kegan Paul, 1986. Contains a history of the subjects, faith and reason.

Swinburne, Richard. *Faith and Reason.* Oxford, Eng.: Clarendon Press, 1981. One of the best studies of the subject in recent years.

PART VIII

RELIGIOUS PLURALISM

Is there only one way to God? If God exists, why hasn't he revealed himself in all times and places to all nations and people? Or has he done so, but through different faiths, through different symbols, and different interpretations of himself? Are all religions simply different paths to the same Ultimate Reality?

In the last twenty years or so, the question of religious pluralism has become a burning issue among philosophers of religion and theologians. On the one side are the *pluralists,* those who hold that all religions or all major religions are different paths to the same God, or Ultimate Reality. On the other side are the *exclusivists,* who argue that there is only one way to God. Pluralist philosophers like John Hick (see our first reading) believe that the major religions—Judaism, Christianity, Hinduism, Buddhism, and Islam—are different paths to the same Ultimate Reality. To use Kant's metaphors, the Ultimate Reality is the *noumenon,* the Holy that is beyond our finite capacity to understand; the individual religions, however, are the *phenomena,* the earthly appearances of God's presence or interpretations of God. The Buddhist parable of the six blind men is sometimes used to illustrate this point:

> Once upon a time a group of religious seekers from different traditions came together and began to discuss the nature of God. Offering quite different answers, they began quarreling among themselves as to who was right and who wrong. Finally, when no hope for a reconciliation was in sight, they called in the Buddha and asked him to tell them who was right. The Buddha proceeded to tell the following story.
>
> There was once a king who asked his servants to bring him all the blind people in a town and an elephant. Six blind men and an elephant were soon set before him. The king instructed the blind men to feel the animal and describe the elephant. "An elephant is like a large waterpot," said the first who touched the elephant's head. "Your Majesty, he's wrong," said the second, as he touched an ear. "An elephant is like a fan." "No," insisted a third, "an elephant is like a snake," as he held his trunk. "On the contrary, you're all mistaken," said a fourth, as he held the tusks, "An elephant is like two prongs of a plow." The fifth man demurred and said, "It is quite clear that an elephant is like a pillar," as he grasped the animal's rear leg. "You're all mistaken," insisted the sixth. "An elephant is a long snake," and he held up the tail. Then they all began to shout at each other about their convictions of the nature of an elephant.
>
> The Buddha told the story and commented, "How can you be so sure of what you cannot see. We are all like blind people in this world. We cannot see God. Each of you may be partly right, yet none completely so."

The religious pluralist calls on us to give up our claims to exclusivity and accept the thesis that many paths lead to God and to salvation or liberation. As Lord Krishna says in the *Bhagavad Gītā,* "In whatever way men approach me, I am gracious to them; men everywhere follow my path."

On the other side of the debate are exclusivists. They believe that only one way leads to God or salvation. Whereas Hinduism, reflected in the words of Lord Krishna (above), has tended to be pluralistic, Christianity and Islam have tended to exclusivity. In the Gospel of John, Jesus says, "I am the way, the truth, and the life, no man cometh to the Father but by me." And Peter says in the Book of Acts, "Neither is there salvation in any other; for there is none other name under heaven given among men, whereby we must be saved." The inspiration of the missionary movement within Christianity and Islam has been to bring salvation to those who would otherwise be lost.

Christians and Muslims have historically rejected pluralism. If Christ or Mohammed is the unique way to God, the other creeds must be erroneous since they deny these claims. Since Muslims and Christians believe that they have good reasons for their beliefs, why should they give them up? Why should they give up their claim to exclusivity? One consideration given by the pluralists is that it is an empirical fact that people generally adhere to the religion of their geographical location, of their native culture; thus, Indians are likely to be Hindus, Tibetans Buddhists, Israelis Jews, Arabs Muslims, and Europeans and Americans Christians. If we recognize the accidentality of our religious preference, shouldn't we give up the claim to exclusivity?

The exclusivist responds that one may give up a certain certainty as he or she recognizes that other traditions have different beliefs, but if on reexamination of one's position, one still finds oneself adhering to one's position, then the person may have done all reason can ask. No doubt we should engage in interreligious dialogue, but that is in itself no guarantee that one religion is closer to the truth than the others or that it is God's special revelation.

In our readings, Alvin Plantinga defends religious exclusivity. He argues that religious exclusivity is not (or need not be) morally or epistemically improper and that a certain exclusivity is present no matter what we believe. That is, suppose the pluralist believes that all the major religions are equally good paths to God. In that case, the pluralist is an *exclusivist* with regard to that belief, judging the religious exclusivist as holding to a false belief. Believing anything implies that those who believe the contrary of what you believe, are wrong. So we are all inevitably exclusivist in one way or another. Plantinga discusses these points under the topics of rationality and irrationality.

David Basinger, in the third reading, attempts to reconcile Hick's religious pluralism with the reformed exclusivism of Plantinga. He argues that, properly understood, the two positions are compatible, both offering valid insights on the diversity of religious phenomena.

In our fourth reading Paul Tillich approaches religious faith from a broader perspective than either Hick or Plantinga, defining faith as ultimate concern common to all humans. The goal of faith is to have the Ultimate, God, for one's proper object of devotion. The ultimate is beyond the God of religion or worldviews but is approached only through religions or worldviews.

In our final reading, Joseph Runzo identifies six different responses to the relationship between one's religion and other religions. He defends religious relativism, which holds that first-order truth-claims about reality are relative to the worldview of a particular culture.

VIII.1 Religious Pluralism and Ultimate Reality

JOHN HICK

John Hick (1922–   ), until his recent retirement, was professor of religion at Claremont Graduate School. He is one of the most distinguished philosophers of religion and the most prominent contemporary advocate of religious pluralism. In this essay from his path-breaking work, God and the Universe of Faiths *(1973), Hick sets forth the thesis that God historically revealed himself (or itself) through various individuals in various situations where geographic isolation prevented a common revelation to all humanity. Each major religion has been a different interpretation of the same Ultimate Reality, to the same salvation. Now the time has come to engage in interreligious dialogue so that we may discover our common bonds and realize that other religious people participate in Ultimate Reality as validly as we do within our religion, "for all these exist in time, as ways through time to eternity."*

Let me begin by proposing a working definition of religion as an understanding of the universe, together with an appropriate way of living within it, which involves reference beyond the natural world to God or gods or to the Absolute or to a transcendent order or process. Such a definition includes such theistic faiths as Judaism, Christianity, Islam, Sikhism; the theistic Hinduism of the Bhagavad Gītā; the semi-theistic faith of Mahayana Buddhism and the non-theistic faiths of Theravada Buddhism and non-theistic Hinduism. It does not however include purely naturalistic systems of belief, such as communism and humanism, immensely important though these are today as alternatives to religious life.

When we look back into the past we find that religion has been a virtually universal dimension of human life—so much so that man has been defined as the religious animal. For he has displayed an innate tendency to experience his environment as being religiously as well as naturally significant, and to feel required to live in it as such. To quote the anthropologist, Raymond Firth, "religion is universal in human societies."[1] "In every human community on earth today," says Wilfred Cantwell Smith, "there exists something that we, as sophisticated observers, may term religion, or a religion. And we are able to see it in each case as the latest development in a continuous tradition that goes back, we can now affirm, for at least one hundred thousand years."[2] In the life of primitive man this religious tendency is expressed in a belief in sacred objects endowed with *mana,* and in a multitude of nature and ancestral spirits needing to be carefully propitiated. The divine was here crudely apprehended as a plurality of quasi-animal forces which could to some extent be controlled by ritualistic and magical procedures. This represents the simplest beginning of man's awareness of the transcendent in the infancy of the human race—an infancy which is also to some extent still available for study in the life of primitive tribes today.

The development of religion and religions begins to emerge into the light of recorded history as the third millennium B.C. moves towards the period around 2000 B.C. There are two main regions of the earth in which civilisation seems first to have arisen and in which religions first took a shape that is at least dimly discernible to us as we peer back through the mists of time—these being Mesopotamia in the Near East and the Indus valley of northern India. In Mesopotamia men lived in nomadic shepherd tribes, each worshipping its own god. Then the tribes gradually coalesced into nation states, the former tribal gods becoming ranked in hierarchies (some however being lost by amalgamation in the process) dominated by great national deities such as Marduk of Babylon, the Sumerian Ishtar, Amon

Reprinted from John Hick, *God and the Universe of Faiths* (London: The Macmillan Press, Ltd., 1973). Copyright © 1973 Macmillan. Reprinted by permission.

of Thebes, Jahweh of Israel, the Greek Zeus, and so on. Further east in the Indus valley there was likewise a wealth of gods and goddesses, though apparently not so much tribal or national in character as expressive of the basic forces of nature, above all fertility. The many deities of the Near East and of India expressed man's awareness of the divine at the dawn of documentary history, some four thousand years ago. It is perhaps worth stressing that the picture was by no means a wholly pleasant one. The tribal and national gods were often martial and cruel, sometimes requiring human sacrifices. And although rather little is known about the very early, pre-Aryan Indian deities, it is certain that later Indian deities have vividly symbolised the cruel and destructive as well as the beneficent aspects of nature.

These early developments in the two cradles of civilisation, Mesopotamia and the Indus valley, can be described as the growth of natural religion, prior to any special intrusions of divine revelation or illumination. Primitive spirit-worship expressed man's fears of unknown forces; his reverence for nature deities expressed his sense of dependence upon realities greater than himself; and his tribal gods expressed the unity and continuity of his group over against other groups. One can in fact discern all sorts of causal connections between the forms which early religion took and the material circumstances of man's life, indicating the large part played by the human element within the history of religion. For example, Trevor Ling points out that life in ancient India (apart from the Punjab immediately prior to the Aryan invasions) was agricultural and was organised in small village units; and suggests that "among agricultural peoples, aware of the fertile earth which brings forth from itself and nourishes its progeny upon its broad bosom, it is the mother-principle which seems important."[3] Accordingly God the Mother, and a variety of more specialised female deities, have always held a prominent place in Indian religious thought and mythology. This contrasts with the characteristically male expression of deity in the Semitic religions, which had their origins among nomadic, pastoral, herd-keeping peoples in the Near East. The divine was known to the desert-dwelling herds-

men who founded the Israelite tradition as God the King and Father; and this conception has continued both in later Judaism and in Christianity, and was renewed out of the desert experience of Mohammed in the Islamic religion. Such regional variations in our human ways of conceiving the divine have persisted through time into the developed world faiths that we know today. The typical western conception of God is still predominantly in terms of the male principle of power and authority; and in the typical Indian conceptions of deity the female principle still plays a distinctly larger part than in the west.

Here then was the natural condition of man's religious life: religion without revelation. But sometime around 800 B.C. there began what has been called the golden age of religious creativity. This consisted in a remarkable series of revelatory experiences occurring during the next five hundred or so years in different parts of the world, experiences which deepened and purified men's conception of the ultimate, and which religious faith can only attribute to the pressure of the divine Spirit upon the human spirit. First came the early Jewish prophets, Amos, Hosea and first Isaiah, declaring that they had heard the Word of the Lord claiming their obedience and demanding a new level of righteousness and justice in the life of Israel. Then in Persia the great prophet Zoroaster appeared; China produced Lao-tzu and then Confucius; in India the Upanishads were written, and Gotama the Buddha lived, and Mahavira, the founder of the Jain religion and, probably about the end of this period, the writing of the Bhagavad Gītā,[4] and Greece produced Pythagoras and then, ending this golden age, Socrates and Plato. Then after the gap of some three hundred years came Jesus of Nazareth and the emergence of Christianity; and after another gap the prophet Mohammed and the rise of Islam.

The suggestion that we must consider is that these were all moments of divine revelation. But let us ask, in order to test this thought, whether we should not expect God to make his revelation in a single mighty act, rather than to produce a number of different, and therefore presumably partial, revelations at different times and places? I think that in seeing the answer to this question we receive an important clue to the place of the religions of the world in the divine purpose. For when we remember the facts of history and geography we realise that in the period we are speaking of, between two and three thousand years ago, it was not possible for God to reveal himself through any human mediation to all mankind. A world-wide revelation might be possible today, thanks to the inventions of printing, and even more of radio, TV and communication satellites. But in the technology of the ancient world this was not possible. Although on a time scale of centuries and millennia there has been a slow diffusion and interaction of cultures, particularly within the vast Euro-Asian land mass, yet the more striking fact for our present purpose is the fragmented character of the ancient world. Communications between the different groups of humanity was then so limited and slow that for all practical purposes men inhabited different worlds. For the most part people in Europe, in India, in Arabia, in Africa, in China were unaware of the others' existence. And as the world was fragmented, so was its religious life. If there was to be a revelation of the divine reality to mankind it had to be a pluriform revelation, a series of revealing experiences occurring independently within the different streams of human history. And since religion and culture were one, the great creative moments of revelation and illumination have influenced the development of the various cultures, giving them the coherence and impetus to expand into larger units, thus creating the vast, many-sided historical entities which we call the world religions.

Each of these religio-cultural complexes has expanded until it touched the boundaries of another such complex spreading out from another centre. Thus each major occasion of divine revelation has slowly transformed the primitive and national religions within the sphere of its influence into what we now know as the world faiths. The early Dravidian and Aryan polytheisms of India were drawn through the religious experience and thought of the Brahmins into what the west calls Hinduism. The national and mystery cults of the mediterranean world and then of northern Europe were drawn by influences stemming from the life and teaching of Christ into what has become Chris-

tianity. The early polytheism of the Arab peoples has been transformed under the influence of Mohammed and his message into Islam. Great areas of Southeast Asia, of China, Tibet and Japan were drawn into the spreading Buddhist movement. None of these expansions from different centres of revelation has of course been simple and uncontested, and a number of alternatives which proved less durable have perished or been absorbed in the process—for example, Mithraism has disappeared altogether; and Zoroastrianism, whilst it greatly influenced the development of the Judaic-Christian tradition, and has to that extent been absorbed, only survives directly today on a small scale in Parseeism.

Seen in this historical context these movements of faith—the Judaic-Christian, the Buddhist, the Hindu, the Muslim—are not essentially rivals. They began at different times and in different places, and each expanded outwards into the surrounding world of primitive natural religion until most of the world was drawn up into one or other of the great revealed faiths. And once this global pattern had become established it has ever since remained fairly stable. It is true that the process of establishment involved conflict in the case of Islam's entry into India and the virtual expulsion of Buddhism from India in the medieval period, and in the case of Islam's advance into Europe and then its retreat at the end of the medieval period. But since the frontiers of the different world faiths became more or less fixed there has been little penetration of one faith into societies moulded by another. The most successful missionary efforts of the great faiths continue to this day to be "downwards" into the remaining world of relatively primitive religions rather than "sideways" into territories dominated by another world faith. For example, as between Christianity and Islam there has been little more than rather rare individual conversions; but both faiths have successful missions in Africa. Again, the Christian population of the Indian subcontinent, after more than two centuries of missionary effort, is only about 2.7 per cent; but on the other hand the Christian missions in the South Pacific are fairly successful. Thus the general picture, so far as the great world religions is concerned, is that each has gone through an early period of geographical expansion, converting a region of the world from its more primitive religious state, and has thereafter continued in a comparatively settled condition within more of less stable boundaries.

Now it is of course possible to see this entire development from the primitive forms of religion up to and including the great world faiths as the history of man's most persistent illusion, growing from crude fantasies into sophisticated metaphysical speculations. But from the standpoint of religious faith the only reasonable hypothesis is that this historical picture represents a movement of divine self-revelation to mankind. This hypothesis offers a general answer to the question of the relation between the different world religions and of the truths which they embody. It suggests to us that the same divine reality has always been self-revealingly active towards mankind, and that the differences of human response are related to different human circumstances. These circumstances—ethnic, geographical, climatic, economic, sociological, historical—have produced the existing differentiations of human culture, and within each main cultural region the response to the divine has taken its own characteristic forms. In each case the post-primitive response has been initiated by some spiritually outstanding individual or succession of individuals, developing in the course of time into one of the great religio-cultural phenomena which we call the world religions. Thus Islam embodies the main response of the Arabic peoples to the divine reality; Hinduism, the main (though not the only) response of the peoples of India; Buddhism, the main response of the peoples of South-east Asia and parts of northern Asia; Christianity, the main response of the European peoples, both within Europe itself and in their emigrations to the Americas and Australasia.

Thus it is, I think, intelligible historically why the revelation of the divine reality to man, and the disclosure of the divine will for human life, had to occur separately within the different streams of human life. We can see how these revelations took different forms related to the different mentalities of the peoples to whom they came and developed within these different cultures into the vast and many-sided historical phenomena of the world religions.

But let us now ask whether this is intelligible theologically. What about the conflicting truth-claims of the different faiths? Is the divine nature personal or non-personal; does deity become incarnate in the world; are human beings born again and again on earth; is the Bible, or the Koran, or the Bhagavad Gītā the Word of God? If what Christianity says in answer to these questions is true, must not what Hinduism says be to a large extent false? If what Buddhism says is true, must not what Islam says be largely false?

Let us begin with the recognition, which is made in all the main religious traditions, that the ultimate divine reality is infinite and as such transcends the grasp of the human mind. God, to use our Christian term, is infinite. He is not a thing, a part of the universe, existing alongside other things; nor is he a being falling under a certain kind. And therefore he cannot be defined or encompassed by human thought. We cannot draw boundaries around his nature and say that he is this and no more. If we could fully define God, describing his inner being and his outer limits, this would not be God. The God whom our minds can penetrate and whom our thoughts can circumnavigate is merely a finite and partial image of God.

From this it follows that the different encounters with the transcendent within the different religious traditions may all be encounters with the one infinite reality; though with partially different and overlapping aspects of that reality. This is a very familiar thought in Indian religious literature. We read, for example, in the ancient Rig-Vedas, dating back to perhaps as much as a thousand years before Christ:

> They call it Indra, Mitra, Varuna, and Agni
> And also heavenly, beautiful Garutman:
> The real is one, though sages name it variously.[5]

We might translate this thought into the terms of the faiths represented today in Britain:

> They call it Jahweh, Allah, Krishna, Param Atma,
> And also holy, blessed Trinity:

The real is one, though sages name it differently.

And in the Bhagavad Gītā the Lord Krishna, the personal God of love, says, "However men approach me, even so do I accept them: for, on all sides, whatever path they may choose is mine."[6]

Again, there is the parable of the blind men and the elephant, said to have been told by the Buddha. An elephant was brought to a group of blind men who had never encountered such an animal before. One felt a leg and reported that an elephant is a great living pillar. Another felt the trunk and reported that an elephant is a great snake. Another felt the tusk and reported than an elephant is like a sharp ploughshare. And so on. And then they all quarrelled together, each claiming that his own account was the truth and therefore all the others false. In fact of course they were all true, but each referring only to one aspect of the total reality and all expressed in very imperfect analogies.

Now the possibility, indeed the probability, that we have seriously to consider is that many different accounts of the divine reality may be true, though all expressed in imperfect human analogies, but that none is "the truth, the whole truth, and nothing but the truth." May it not be that the different concepts of God, as Jahweh, Allah, Krishna, Param Atma, Holy Trinity, and so on: and likewise the different concepts of the hidden structure of reality, as the eternal emanation of Brahman or as an immense cosmic process culminating in Nirvana, are all images of the divine, each expressing some aspect or range of aspects and yet none by itself fully and exhaustively corresponding to the infinite nature of the ultimate reality?

Two immediate qualifications however to this hypothesis. First, the idea that we are considering is not that any and every conception of God or of the transcendent is valid, still less all equally valid; but that every conception of the divine which has come out of a great revelatory religious experience and has been tested though a long tradition of worship, and has sustained human faith over centuries of time and in millions of lives, is likely to represent a genuine encounter with the divine reality. And second, the parable of the blind men and the ele-

phant is of course only a parable and like most parables it is designed to make one point and must not be pressed as an analogy at other points. The suggestion is not that the different encounters with the divine which lie at the basis of the great religious traditions are responses to different *parts* of the divine. They are rather encounters from different historical and cultural standpoints with the same infinite divine reality and as such they lead to differently focused awareness of the reality. The indications of this are most evident in worship and prayer. What is said about God in the theological treatises of the different faiths is indeed often widely different. But it is in prayer that a belief in God comes alive and does its main work. And when we turn from abstract theology to the living stuff of worship we meet again and again the overlap and confluence of faiths.

Here, for example, is a Muslim prayer at the feast of Ramadan:

> Praise be to God, Lord of creation, Source of all livelihood, who orders the morning, Lord of majesty and honour, of grace and beneficence. He who is so far that he may not be seen and so near that he witnesses the secret things. Blessed be he and for ever exalted.[7]

And here is a Sikh creed used at the morning prayer:

> There is but one God. He is all that is.
> He is the Creator of all things and He is all-pervasive.
> He is without fear and without enmity.
> He is timeless, unborn and self-existent.
> He is the Enlightener
> And can be realised by grace of Himself alone.
> He was in the beginning; He was in all ages.
> The True One is, was, O Nanak, and shall forever be.[8]

And here again is a verse from the Koran:

> To God belongs the praise. Lord of the heavens and Lord of the earth, the Lord of all being. His is the dominion in the heavens and in the earth: he is the Almighty, the All-wise.[9]

Turning now to the Hindu idea of the many incarnations of God, here is a verse from the Rāmāyana:

> Seers and sages, saints and hermits, fix on Him
>   their reverent gaze,
> And in faint and trembling accents, holy scrip-
>   ture hymns His praise.
> He the omnipresent spirit, lord of heaven and
>   earth and hell,
> To redeem His people, freely has vouchsafed
>   with men to dwell.[10]

And from the rich literature of devotional song here is a Bhakti hymn of the Vaishnavite branch of Hinduism:

> Now all my days with joy I'll fill, full to the
>   brim
> With all my heart to Vitthal cling, and only
>   Him.
> He will sweep utterly away all dole and care;
> And all in sunder shall I rend illusion's snare.
> O altogether dear is He, and He alone,
> For all my burden He will take to be His own.
> Lo, all the sorrow of the world will straight-
>   way cease,
> And all unending now shall be the reign of
>   peace.[11]

And a Muslim mystical verse:

> Love came a guest
> Within my breast,
> My soul was spread,
> Love banqueted.[12]

And finally another Hindu (Vaishnavite) devotional hymn:

> O save me, save me, Mightiest,
>   Save me and set me free.
> O let the love that fills my breast
>   Cling to thee lovingly.
> Grant me to taste how sweet thou art;
>   Grant me but this, I pray.
> And never shall my love depart
>   Or turn from thee away.
> Then I thy name shall magnify
>   And tell thy praise abroad,

> For very love and gladness I
>   Shall dance before my God.[13]

Such prayers and hymns as these must express, surely, diverse encounters with the same divine reality. These encounters have taken place within different human cultures by people of different ways of thought and feeling, with different histories and different frameworks of philosophical thought, and have developed into different systems of theology embodied in different religious structures and organisations. These resulting large-scale religio-cultural phenomena are what we call the religions of the world. But must there not lie behind them the same infinite divine reality, and may not our divisions into Christian, Hindu, Muslim, Jew, and so on, and all that goes with them, accordingly represent secondary, human, historical developments?

There is a further problem, however, which now arises. I have been speaking so far of the ultimate reality in a variety of terms—the Father, Son and Spirit of Christianity, the Jahweh of Judaism, the Allah of Islam, and so on—but always thus far in theistic terms, as a personal God under one name or another. But what of the non-theistic religions? What of the non-theistic Hinduism according to which the ultimate reality, Brahman, is not He but It; and what about Buddhism, which in one form is agnostic concerning the existence of God even though in another form it has come to worship the Buddha himself? Can these non-theistic faiths be seen as encounters with the same divine reality that is encountered in theistic religion?

Speaking very tentatively, I think it is possible that the sense of the divine as non-personal may indeed reflect an aspect of the same infinite reality that is encountered as personal in theistic religious experience. The question can be pursued both as a matter of pure theology and in relation to religious experience. Theologically, the Hindu distinction between Nirguna Brahman and Saguna Brahman is important and should be adopted into western religious thought. Detaching the distinction, then from its Hindu context we may say that Nirguna God is the eternal self-existent divine reality, beyond the scope of all human categories, including personality; and Saguna God is God in relation to his creation and with the attributes which express this relationship, such as personality, omnipotence, goodness, love and omniscience. Thus the one ultimate reality is both Nirguna and non-personal, and Saguna and personal, in a duality which is in principle acceptable to human understanding. When we turn to men's religious awareness of God we are speaking of Saguna God, God in relation to man. And here the larger traditions of both east and west report a dual experience of the divine as personal and as other than personal. It will be a sufficient reminder of the strand of personal relationship with the divine in Hinduism to mention Iswaru, the personal God who represents the Absolute as known and worshipped by finite persons. It should also be remembered that the characterisation of Brahman as *satcitananda,* absolute being, consciousness and bliss, is not far from the conception of infinitely transcendent personal life. Thus there is both the thought and the experience of the personal divine within Hinduism. But there is likewise the thought and the experience of God as other than personal within Christianity. Rudolph Otto describes this strand in the mysticism of Meister Eckhart. He says:

The divine, which on the one hand is conceived in symbols taken from the social sphere, as Lord, King, Father, Judge—a person in relation to persons—is on the other hand denoted in dynamic symbols as the power of life, as light and life, as spirit ebbing and flowing, as truth, knowledge, essential justice and holiness, a glowing fire that penetrates and pervades. It is characterized as the principle of a renewed, supernatural Life, mediating and giving itself, breaking forth in the living man as his nova vita, as the content of his life and being. What is here insisted upon is not so much an immanent God, as an "experienced" God, known as an inward principle of the power of new being and life. Eckhart knows this *deuteros theos* besides the personal God . . .[14]

Let me now try to draw the threads together and to project them into the future. I have been suggesting that Christianity is a way of salvation which, beginning some two thousand years ago, has become the principal way of salvation in three continents. The other great faiths are likewise of salvation, providing the principal path to the divine reality for other large sections of humanity. I have also suggested that the idea that Jesus proclaimed

himself as God incarnate, and as the sole point of saving contact between God and man, is without adequate historical foundation and represents a doctrine developed by the church. We should therefore not infer, from the christian experience of redemption through Christ, that salvation cannot be experienced in any other way. The alternative possibility is that the ultimate divine reality—in our christian terms, God—has always been pressing in upon the human spirit, but in ways which leave men free to open or close themselves to the divine presence. Human life has developed along characteristically different lines in the main areas of civilisation, and these differences have naturally entered into the ways in which men have apprehended and responded to God. For the great religious figures through whose experience divine revelation has come have each been conditioned by a particular history and culture. One can hardly imagine Gotama the Buddha except in the setting of the India of his time, or Jesus the Christ except against the background of Old Testament Judaism, or Mohammed except in the setting of Arabia. And human history and culture have likewise shaped the development of the webs of religious creeds, practices and organisations which we know as the great world faiths.

It is thus possible to consider the hypothesis that they are all, at their experiential roots, in contact with the same ultimate reality, but that their differing experiences of that reality, interacting over the centuries with the different thought-forms of different cultures, have led to increasing differentiation and contrasting elaboration—so that Hinduism, for example, is a very different phenomenon from Christianity, and very different ways of conceiving and experiencing the divine occur within them.

However, now that the religious traditions are consciously interacting with each other in the "one world" of today, in mutual observation and dialogue, it is possible that their future developments may be on gradually converging courses. For during the next few centuries they will no doubt continue to change, and it may be that they will grow closer together, and even that one day such names as "Christianity," "Buddhism," "Islam," "Hinduism," will no longer describe the then current configurations of men's religious experience and belief. I am not here thinking of the extinction of human religiousness in a universal wave of secularisation. This is of course a possible future; and indeed many think it the most likely future to come about. But if man is an indelibly religious animal he will always, even in his secular cultures, experience a sense of the transcendent by which he will be both troubled and uplifted. The future I am thinking of is accordingly one in which what we now call the different religions will constitute the past history of different emphases and variations within a global religious life. I do not mean that all men everywhere will be overtly religious, any more than they are today. I mean rather that the discoveries now taking place by men of different faiths of central common ground, hitherto largely concealed by the variety of cultural forms in which it was expressed, may eventually render obsolete the sense of belonging to rival ideological communities. Not that all religious men will think alike, or worship in the same way or experience the divine identically. On the contrary, so long as there is a rich variety of human cultures— and let us hope there will always be this—we should expect there to be correspondingly different forms of religious cult, ritual and organisation, conceptualised in different theological doctrines. And so long as there is a wide spectrum of human psychological types—and again let us hope that there will always be this—we should expect there to be correspondingly different emphases between, for example, the sense of the divine as just and as merciful, between *karma* and *bhakti;* or between worship as formal and communal and worship as free and personal. Thus we may expect the different world faiths to continue as religio-cultural phenomena, though phenomena which are increasingly influencing one another's development. The relation between them will then perhaps be somewhat like that now obtaining between the different denominations of Christianity in Europe or the United States. That is to say, there will in most countries be a dominant religious tradition, with other traditions present in varying strengths, but with considerable awareness on all hands of what they have in common; with some degree of osmosis of membership through their institutional walls; with a large degree

of practical cooperation; and even conceivably with some interchange of ministry.

Beyond this the ultimate unity of faiths will be an eschatological unity in which each is both fulfilled and transcended—fulfilled in so far as it is true, transcended in so far as it is less than the whole truth. And indeed even such fulfilling must be a transcending; for the function of a religion is to bring us to a right relationship with the ultimate divine reality, to awareness of our true nature and our place in the Whole, into the presence of God. In the eternal life there is no longer any place for religions; the pilgrim has no need of a way after he has finally arrived. In St. John's vision of the heavenly city at the end of our christian scriptures it is said that there is no temple—no christian church or chapel, no jewish synagogue, no hindu or buddhist temple, no muslim mosque, no sikh gurdwara. . . . For all these exist in time, as ways through time to eternity.

Notes

1. *Elements of Social Organization,* 3rd ed. (London: Tavistock Publications, 1969) p. 216.

2. *The Meaning and End of Religion* (New York: Mentor Books, 1963) p. 22.

3. *A History of Religion East and West* (London: Macmillan and New York: St. Martin's Press, 1968) p. 27.

4. The dating of the Bhagavad Gītā has been a matter of much debate; but R. C. Zaehner in his recent monumental critical edition says that "One would probably not be going far wrong if one dated it as some time between the fifth and second centuries B.C." *The Bhagavad Gītā* (Oxford: Clarendon Press, 1969) p. 7.

5. I 164.

6. IV II.

7. Kenneth Cragg, *Alive to God: Muslim and Christian Prayer* (London and New York: Oxford University Press, 1970) p. 65.

8. Harbans Singh, *Guru Nanak and Origins of the Sikh Faith* (Bombay, London and New York: Asia Publishing House, 1969), pp. 96–7.

9. *Alive to God,* p. 61 (Surah of the Kneeling, v. 35).

10. *Sacred Books of the World,* edited by A. C. Bouquet (London: Pelican Books, 1954) p. 226 (The Rāmāyana of Tulsi Das, Canto 1, Chandha 2, translated by F. S. Growse).

11. Ibid., p. 245 (A Hymn of Namdev, translated by Nicol MacNicol).

12. *Alive to God,* p. 79 (From Ibn Hazm, "The Ring of the Dove").

13. *Sacred Books of the World,* p. 246 (A Hymn of Tukaram).

14. Rudolph Otto, *Mysticism East and West,* trans. Bertha L. Bracey and Richenda C. Payne (New York: Meridian Books, 1957), p. 131.

VIII.2 A Defense of Religious Exclusivism

ALVIN PLANTINGA

Alvin Plantinga (1932–   ) is professor of philosophy of religion at the University of Notre Dame and one of the leading religious thinkers of our day. In this defense of religious exclusivism, he argues for three theses: (1) The religious exclusivist is not necessarily guilty of any moral wrongdoing; (2) the religious exclusivist is not necessarily guilty of any epistemic fault; (3) some exclusivism in our beliefs is inevitable. If a person truly believes his or her creed, it may be wrong to expect him or her to treat all religions as equally good ways to God or even ways to God simpliciter. Nevertheless, Plantinga agrees that the knowledge of other religions is something to be sought, which may lessen our assurance in our own belief.

When I was a graduate student at Yale, the philosophy department prided itself on diversity, and it was indeed diverse. There were idealists, pragmatists, phenomenologists, existentialists, Whiteheadians, historians of philosophy, a token positivist, and what could only be described as observers of the passing intellectual seene. In some ways, this was indeed something to take pride in; a student could behold and encounter real, live representatives of many of the main traditions in philosophy. However, it also had an unintended and unhappy side effect. If anyone raised a philosophical question inside, but particularly outside, of class, the typical response would be to catalog some of the various

different answers the world has seen: There is the Aristotelian answer, the existentialist answer, the Cartesian answer, Heidegger's answer, perhaps the Buddhist answer, and so on. But the question "What is the truth about this matter?" was often greeted with disdain as unduly naive. There are all these different answers, all endorsed by people of great intellectual power and great dedication to philosophy; for every argument *for* one of these positions, there is another *against* it; would it not be excessively naive, or perhaps arbitrary, to suppose that one of these is in fact true, the others being false? Or, if even there really is a truth of the matter, so that one of them is true and conflicting ones false, wouldn't it be merely arbitrary, in the face of this embarrassment of riches, to *endorse* one of them as the truth, consigning the others to falsehood? How could you possibly know which was true?

A similar attitude is sometimes urged with respect to the impressive variety of religions the world displays. There are theistic religions but also at least some nontheistic religions (or perhaps nontheistic strands) among the enormous variety of religions going under the names Hinduism and Buddhism; among the theistic religions, there are strands of Hinduism and Buddhism and American Indian religion as well as Islam, Judaism, and Christianity; and all differ significantly from each other. Isn't it somehow arbitrary, or irrational, or unjustified, or unwarranted, or even oppressive and imperialistic to endorse one of these as opposed to all the others? According to Jean Bodin, "each is refuted by all";[1] must we not agree? It is in this neighborhood that the so-called problem of pluralism arises. Of course, many concerns and problems can come

This essay appeared in print for the first time in the previous edition of this text. Reprinted by permission of Alvin Plantinga. Endnotes edited.

under this rubric; the specific problem I mean to discuss can be thought of as follows. To put it in an internal and personal way, I find myself with religious beliefs, and religious beliefs that I realize aren't shared by nearly everyone else. For example, I believe both

(1) The world was created by God, an almighty, all-knowing, and perfectly good personal being (one that holds beliefs; has aims, plans, and intentions; and can act to accomplish these aims).

(2) Human beings require salvation, and God has provided a unique way of salvation through the incarnation, life, sacrificial death, and resurrection of his divine son.

Now there are many who do not believe these things. First, there are those who agree with me on (1) but not (2): They are non-Christian theistic religions. Second, there are those who don't accept either (1) or (2) but nonetheless do believe that there is something beyond the natural world, a something such that human well-being and salvation depend upon standing in a right relation to it. Third, in the West and since the Enlightenment, anyway, there are people—*naturalists,* we may call them—who don't believe any of these three things. And my problem is this: When I become really aware of these other ways of looking at the world, these other ways of responding religiously to the world, what must or should I do? What is the right sort of attitude to take? What sort of impact should this awareness have on the beliefs I hold and the strength with which I hold them? My question is this: How should I think about the great religious diversity the world in fact displays? Can I sensibly remain an adherent of just one of these religions, rejecting the others? And here I am thinking specifically of *beliefs.* Of course, there is a great deal more to any religion or religious practice than just belief, and I don't for a moment mean to deny it. But belief is a crucially important part of most religions; it is a crucially important part of *my* religion; and the question I mean to ask here is, What does the awareness of religious diversity mean or should mean for my religious beliefs?

Some speak here of a *new* awareness of religious diversity and speak of this new awareness as constituting (for us in the West) a crisis, a revolution, an intellectual development of the same magnitude as the Copernican revolution of the sixteenth century and the alleged discovery of evolution and our animal origins in the nineteenth.[2] No doubt there is at least some truth to this. Of course, the fact is all along many Western Christians and Jews have known that there are other religions and that not nearly everyone shares *their* religion. The ancient Israelites—some of the prophets, say—were clearly aware of Canaanite religion; and the apostle Paul said that he preached "Christ crucified, a stumbling block to Jews and folly to the Greeks" (1 Corinthians 1:23). Other early Christians, the Christian martyrs, say, must have suspected that not everyone believed as they did; and the chruch fathers, in offering defenses of Christianity, were certainly apprised of this fact. Thomas Aquinas, again, was clearly aware of those to whom he addressed the *Summa Contra Gentiles;* and the fact that there are non-Christian religions would have come as no surprise to the Jesuit missionaries of the sixteenth and seventeenth centuries or to the Methodist missionaries of the nineteenth. To come to more recent times, when I was a child, *The Banner,* the official publication of my church, contained a small column for children; it was written by "Uncle Dick" who exhorted us to save our nickels and send them to our Indian cousins at the Navaho mission in New Mexico. Both we and our elders knew that the Navahos had or had had a religion different from Christianity, and part of the point of sending the nickels was to try to rectify that situation.

Still, in recent years, probably more of us Christian Westerners have become aware of the world's religious diversity; we have probably learned more about people of other religious persuasions, and we have come to see that they display what looks like real piety, devoutness, and spirtuality. What is new, perhaps, is a more widespread sympathy for other religions, a tendency to see them as more valuable, as containing more by way of truth, and a new feeling of solidarity with their practitioners.

Now there are several possible reactions to awareness of religious diversity. One is to continue to believe what you have all along believed; you learn about this diversity but continue to believe— that is, take to be true—such propositions as (1) and (2) above, consequently taking to be false any beliefs, religious or otherwise, that are incompatible with (1) and (2). Following current practice, I will call this *exclusivism;* the exclusivist holds that the tenets or some of the tenets of *one* religion— Christianity, let's say—are in fact true; he adds, naturally enough, that any propositions, including other religious beliefs, that are incompatible with those tenets are false. And there is a fairly widespread apprehension that there is something seriously wrong with exclusivism. It is irrational, or egotistical and unjustified,[3] or intellectually arrogant,[4] or elitist,[5] or a manifestation of harmful pride,[6] or even oppressive and imperialistic.[7] The claim is that exclusivism as such is or involves a vice of some sort: It is wrong or deplorable. It is this claim I want to examine. I propose to argue that exclusivism need not involve either epistemic or moral failure and that, furthermore, something like it is wholly unavoidable, given our human condition.

These objections, of course, are not to the *truth* of (1) or (2) or any other proposition someone might accept in this exclusivist way (although objections of that sort are also put forward); they are instead directed to the *propriety or rightness* of exclusivism. There are initially two different kinds of indictments of exclusivism: broadly moral, or ethical, indictments and other broadly intellectual, or epistemic, indictments. These overlap in interesting ways as we will see below. But initially, anyway, we can take some of the complaints about exclusivism as *intellectual* criticisms: It is *irrational* or *unjustified* to think in an exclusivistic way. The other large body of complaint is moral: There is something *morally* suspect about exclusivism—it is arbitrary, or intellectually arrogant, or imperialistic. As Joseph Runzo suggests, exclusivism is "neither tolerable nor any longer intellectually honest in the context of our contemporary knowledge of other faiths."[8] I want to consider both kinds of claims or criticisms; I propose to argue that the

exclusivist as such is not necessarily guilty of any of these charges.

Moral Objections to Exclusivism

I turn to the moral complaints: that the exclusivist is intellectually arrogant, or egotistical or self-servingly arbitrary, or dishonest, or imperialistic, or oppressive. But first, I provide three qualifications. An exclusivist, like anyone else, will probably be guilty of some or of all of these things to at least some degree, perhaps particularly the first two. The question, however, is whether she is guilty of these things just by virtue of being an exclusivist. Second, I will use the term *exclusivism* in such a way that you don't count as an exclusivist unless you are rather fully aware of other faiths, have had their existence and their claims called to your attention with some force and perhaps fairly frequently, and have to some degree reflected on the problem of pluralism, asking yourself such questions as whether it is or could be really true that the Lord has revealed Himself and His programs to us Christians, say, in a way in which He hasn't revealed Himself to those of other faiths. Thus, my grandmother, for example, would not have counted as an exclusivist. She had, of course, *heard* of the heathen, as she called them, but the idea that perhaps Christians could learn from them, and learn from them with respect to religious matters, had not so much as entered her head; and the fact that it *hadn't* entered her head, I take it, was not a matter of moral dereliction on her part. This same would go for a Buddhist or Hindu peasant. These people are not, I think, properly charged with arrogance or other moral flaws in believing as they do.

Third, suppose I am an exclusivist with respect to (1), for example, but nonculpably believe, like Aquinas, say, that I have a knock-down, drag-out argument, a demonstration or conclusive proof of the proposition that there is such a person as God; and suppose I think further (and nonculpably) that if those who don't believe (1) were to be apprised of this argument (and had the ability and training necessary to grasp it and were to think about the argument fairly and reflectively), *they* too would come to believe (1)? Then I could hardly be charged with these moral faults. My condition would be like that of Gödel, let's say, upon having recognized that he had a proof for the incompleteness of arithmetic. True, many of his colleagues and peers didn't believe that arithmetic was incomplete, and some believed that it *was* complete; but presumably Gödel wasn't arbitrary or egotistical in believing that arithmetic is in fact incomplete. Furthermore, he would not have been at fault had he nonculpably but *mistakenly* believed that he had found such a proof. Accordingly, I will use the term *exclusivist* in such a way that you don't count as an exclusivist if you nonculpably think you know of a demonstration or conclusive argument for the beliefs with respect to which you are an exclusivist, or even if you nonculpably think you know of an argument that would convince all or most intelligent and honest people of the truth of that proposition. So an exclusivist, as I use the term, not only believes something like (1) or (2) and thinks false any proposition incompatible with it; she also meets a further condition C that is hard to state precisely and in detail (and in fact any attempt to do so would involve a long and presently irrelevant discussion of *ceteris paribus* clauses). Suffice it to say that C includes (a) being rather fully aware of other religions, (b) knowing that there is much that at the least looks like genuine piety and devoutness in them, and (c) believing that you know of no arguments that would necessarily convince all or most honest and intelligent dissenters.

Given these qualifications then, why should we think that an exclusivist is properly charged with these moral faults? I will deal first and most briefly with charges of oppression and imperialism: I think we must say that they are on the face of it wholly implausible. I daresay there are some among you who reject some of the things I believe; I do not believe that you are thereby oppressing me, even if you do not believe you have an argument that would convince me. It is conceivable that exclusivism might in some way *contribute* to oppression, but it isn't in itself oppressive.

The more important moral charge is that there is a sort of self-serving arbitrariness, an arrogance or egotism, in accepting such propositions as (1) or

(2) under condition C; exclusivism is guilty of some serious moral fault or flaw. According to Wilfred Cantwell Smith, ". . . except at the cost of insensitivity or delinquency, it is morally not possible actually to go out into the world and say to devout, intelligent, fellow human beings: '. . . we believe that we know God and we are right; you believe that you know God, and you are totally wrong.'"[9]

So what can the exclusivist have to say for himself? Well, it must be conceded immediately that if he believes (1) or (2), then he must also believe that those who believe something incompatible with them are mistaken and believe what is false. That's no more than simple logic. Furthermore, he must also believe that those who do not believe as he does—those who believe neither (1) nor (2), whether or not they believe their negations—*fail* to believe something that is deep and important and that he *does* believe. He must therefore see himself as *privileged* with respect to those others—those others of both kinds. There is something of great value, he must think, that *he* has and *they* lack. They are ignorant of something—something of great importance—of which he has knowledge. But does this make him properly subject to the above censure?

I think the answer must be no. Or if the answer is yes, then I think we have here a genuine moral dilemma; for in our earthly life here below, as my Sunday School teacher used to say, there is no real alternative; there is no reflective attitude that is not open to the same strictures. These charges of arrogance are a philosophical tar baby: Get close enough to them to use them against the exclusivist and you are likely to find them stuck fast to yourself. How so? Well, as an exclusivist, I realize that I can't convince others that they should believe as I do, but I nonetheless continue to believe as I do. The charge is that I am, as a result, arrogant or egotistical, arbitrarily preferring my way of doing things to other ways.[10] But what are my alternatives with respect to a proposition like (1)? There seem to be three choices. I can continue to hold it; I can withhold it, in Roderick Chisholm's sense, believing neither it nor its denial, and I can accept its denial. Consider the third way, a way taken by those pluralists who, like John Hick, hold that such propositions as (1) and (2) and their colleagues from other faiths are literally false, although in some way still valid responses to the Real. This seems to me to be no advance at all with respect to the arrogance or egotism problem; this is not a way out. For if I do this, I will then be in the very same condition as I am now: I will believe many propositions others don't believe and will be in condition *C* with respect to those propositions. For I will then believe the denials of (1) and (2) (as well as the denials of many other propositions explicitly accepted by those of other faiths). Many others, of course, do not believe the denials of (1) and (2) and in fact believe (1) and (2). Further, I will not know of any arguments that can be counted on to persuade those who do believe (1) or (2) (or propositions accepted by the adherents of other religions). I am therefore in the condition of believing propositions that many others do not believe and furthermore am in condition *C*. If, in the case of those who believe (1) and (2), that is sufficient for intellectual arrogance or egotism, the same goes for those who believe their denials.

So consider the second option: I can instead *withhold* the proposition in question. I can say to myself: "The right course here, given that I can't or couldn't convince these others of what *I* believe, is to believe neither these propositions nor their denials." The pluralist objector to exclusivism can say that the right course, under condition *C*, is to abstain from believing the offending proposition and also abstain from believing its denial; call him, therefore, "the abstemious pluralist." But does he thus really avoid the condition that, on the part of the exclusivist, leads to the charges of egotism and arrogance in this way? Think, for a moment, about disagreement. Disagreement, fundamentally, is a matter of adopting conflicting propositional attitudes with respect to a given proposition. In the simplest and most familiar case, I disagree with you if there is some proposition *p* such that I believe *p* and you believe –*p*. But that's just the simplest case; there are also others. The one that is presently of interest is this: I believe *p* and you withhold it, fail to believe it. Call the first kind of disagreement "contradicting"; call the second "dissenting."

My claim is that if contradicting others (under the condition *C* spelled out above) is arrogant and egotistical, so is dissenting (under that same condition). Suppose you believe some proposition *p* but I don't; perhaps you believe that it is wrong to discriminate against people simply on the grounds of race, but I, recognizing that there are many people who disagree with you, do not believe this proposition. I don't disbelieve it either, of course, but in the circumstances I think the right thing to do is to abstain from belief. Then am I not implicitly condemning your attitude, your *believing* the proposition, as somehow improper—naive, perhaps, or unjustified, or in some other way less than optimal? I am implicitly saying that my attitude is the superior one; I think my course of action here is the right one and yours somehow wrong, inadequate, improper, in the circumstances at best second-rate. Of course, I realize that there is no question, here, of *showing* you that your attitude is wrong or improper or naive; so am I not guilty of intellectual arrogance? Of a sort of egotism, thinking I know better than you, arrogating to myself a privileged status with respect to you? The problem for the exclusivist was that she was obliged to think she possessed a truth missed by many others; the problem for the abstemious pluralist is that he is obliged to think that he possesses a virtue others don't or acts rightly where others don't. If, in condition *C*, one is arrogant by way of believing a proposition others don't, isn't one equally, under those reflective conditions, arrogant by way of withholding a proposition others don't?

Perhaps you will respond by saying that the abstemious pluralist gets into trouble, falls into arrogance, by way of implicitly saying or believing that his way of proceeding is better or wiser than other ways pursued by other people; and perhaps he can escape by abstaining from *that* view as well. Can't he escape the problem by refraining from believing that racial bigotry is wrong and also refraining from holding the view that it is *better,* under the conditions that obtain, to withhold that proposition than to assert and believe it? Well, yes he can; then he has no *reason* for his abstention; he doesn't believe that abstention is better or more appropriate; he simply does abstain. Does this get him off the egotistical hook? Perhaps. But then he can't, in consistency, also hold that there is something wrong with *not* abstaining, with coming right out and *believing* that bigotry is wrong; he loses his objection to the exclusivist. Accordingly, this way out is not available for the abstemious pluralist who accuses the exclusivist of arrogance and egotism.

Indeed, I think we can show that the abstemious pluralist who brings charges of intellectual arrogance against exclusivism is hoist with his own petard, holds a position that in a certain way is self-referentially inconsistent in the circumstances. For he believes

(3) If *S* knows that others don't believe *p* and that he is in condition *C* with respect to *p*, then *S* should not believe *p*.

This or something like it is the ground of the charges he brings against the exclusivist. But the abstemious pluralist realizes that many do not accept (3); and I suppose he also realizes that it is unlikely that he can find arguments for (3) that will convince them; hence, he knows that condition *C* obtains. Given his acceptance of (3), therefore, the right course for him is to abstain from believing (3). Under the conditions that do in fact obtain—namely, his knowledge that others don't accept it and that condition *C* obtains—he can't properly accept it.

I am therefore inclined to think that one can't, in the circumstances, properly hold (3) or any other proposition that will do the job. One can't find here some principle on the basis of which to hold that the exclusivist is doing the wrong thing, suffers from some moral fault—that is, one can't find such a principle that doesn't, as we might put it, fall victim to itself.

So the abstemious pluralist is hoist with his own petard; but even apart from this dialectical argument (which in any event some will think unduly cute), aren't the charges unconvincing and implausible? I must concede that there are a variety of ways in which I can be and have been intellectually arrogant and egotistic; I have certainly fallen into this vice in the past and no doubt am not free of it now. But am I really arrogant and egotistic just by virtue of believing what I know others don't believe, where I can't

show them that I am right? Suppose I think the matter over, consider the objections as carefully as I can, realize that I am finite and furthermore a sinner, certainly no better than those with whom I disagree; but suppose it still seems clear to me that the proposition in question is true. Can I really be behaving immorally in continuing to believe it? I am dead sure that it is wrong to try to advance my career by telling lies about my colleagues; I realize there are those who disagree; I also realize that in all likelihood there is no way I can find to show them that they are wrong; nonetheless I think they *are* wrong. If I think this after careful reflection, if I consider the claims of those who disagree as sympathetically as I can, if I try my level best to ascertain the truth here, and it *still* seems to me sleazy, wrong, and despicable to lie about my colleagues to advance my career, could I really be doing what is immoral by continuing to believe as before? I can't see how. If, after careful reflection and thought, you find yourself convinced that the right propositional attitude to take to (1) and (2) in the face of the facts of religious pluralism is abstention from belief, how could you properly be taxed with egotism, either for so believing or for so abstaining? Even if you knew others did not agree with you?

Epistemic Objections to Exclusivism

I turn now to *epistemic* objections to exclusivism. There are many different specifically epistemic virtues and a corresponding plethora of epistemic vices. The ones with which the exclusivist is most frequently charged, however, are *irrationality* and *lack of justification* in holding his exclusivist beliefs. The claim is that as an exclusivist he holds unjustified beliefs and/or irrational beliefs. Better, *he* is unjustified or irrational in holding these beliefs. I will therefore consider those two claims, and I will argue that the exclusivist views need not be either unjustified or irrational. I will then turn to the question whether his beliefs could have *warrant*—that property, whatever precisely it is, that distinguishes knowledge from mere true belief—and whether they could have enough warrant for knowledge.

Justification

The pluralist objector sometimes claims that to hold exclusivist views, in condition *C,* is *unjustified—epistemically* unjustified. Is this true? And what does he mean when he makes this claim? As even a brief glance at the contemporary epistemological literature will show, justification is a protean and multifarious notion. There are, I think, substantially two possibilities as to what he means. The central core of the notion, its beating heart, the paradigmatic center to which most of the myriad contemporary variations are related by way of analogical extension and family resemblance, is the notion of *being within one's intellectual rights,* having violated no intellectual or cognitive duties or obligations in the formation and sustenance of the belief in question. This is the palimpsest, going back to René Descartes and especially John Locke, that underlies the multitudinous battery of contemporary inscriptions. There is no space to argue that point here; but chances are, when the pluralist objector to exclusivism claims that the latter is unjustified, it is some notion lying in this neighborhood that he has in mind. (Here we should note the very close connection between the moral objections to exclusivism and the objection that exclusivism is epistemically unjustified.)

The duties involved, naturally enough, would be specifically *epistemic* duties: perhaps a duty to proportion degree of belief to (propositional) evidence from what is *certain,* that is, self-evident or incorrigible, as with Locke, or perhaps to try one's best to get into and stay in the right relation to the truth, as with Chisholm, the leading contemporary champion of the justificationist tradition with respect to knowledge. But at present there is widespread (and as I see it, correct) agreement that there is no duty of the Lockean kind. Perhaps there is one of the Chisholmian kind; but isn't the exclusivist conforming to that duty if, after the sort of careful, indeed prayerful consideration I mentioned in the response to the moral objection, it still seems to him strongly that (1), say, is true and he accordingly still believes it? It is therefore very hard to see that the exclusivist is necessarily unjustified in this way.

The second possibility for understanding the charge—the charge that exclusivism is epistemically unjustified—has to do with the oft-repeated claim that exclusivism is intellectually *arbitrary.* Perhaps the idea is that there is an intellectual duty to treat similar cases similarly; the exclusivist violates this duty by arbitrarily choosing to believe (for the moment going along with the fiction that we *choose* beliefs of this sort) (1) and (2) in the face of the plurality of conflicting religious beliefs the world presents. But suppose there is such a duty. Clearly you do not violate it if you nonculpably think the beliefs in question are *not* on a par. And as an exclusivist, I *do* think (nonculpably, I hope) that they are not on a par: I think (1) and (2) *true* and those incompatible with either of them *false.*

The rejoinder, of course, will be that it is not alethic parity (their having the same truth value) that is at issue: it is *epistemic* parity that counts. What kind of epistemic parity? What would be relevant, here, I should think, would be *internal* or internalist epistemic parity: parity with respect to what is internally available to the believer. What is internally available to the believer includes, for example, detectable relationships between the belief in question and other beliefs you hold; so internal parity would include parity of propositional evidence. What is internally available to the believer also includes the *phenomenology* that goes with the beliefs in question: the *sensuous* phenomenology but also the nonsensuous phenomenology involved, for example, in the belief's just having the feel of being *right.* But once more, then, (1) and (2) are not on an internal par, for the exclusivist, with beliefs that are incompatible with them. (1) and (2), after all, seem to me to be true; they have for me the phenomenology that accompanies that seeming. The same cannot be said for propositions incompatible with them. If, furthermore, John Calvin is right in thinking that there is such a thing as the *Sensus Divinitatis* and the Internal Testimony of the Holy Spirit, then perhaps (1) and (2) are produced in me by those belief-producing processes and have for me the phenomenology that goes with them; the same is not true for propositions incompatible with them.

But then the next rejoinder: Isn't it probably true that those who reject (1) and (2) in favor of other beliefs have propositional evidence for their beliefs that is on a par with mine for my beliefs? And isn't it also probably true that the same or similar phenomenology accompanies their beliefs as accompanies mine? So that those beliefs really are epistemically and internally on a par with (1) and (2), and the exclusivist is still treating like cases differently? I don't think so; I think there really are arguments available for (1), at least, that are not available for its competitors. And as for similar phenomenology, this is not easy to say; it is not easy to look into the breast of another; the secrets of the human heart are hard to fathom; it is hard indeed to discover this sort of thing even with respect to someone you know really well. I am prepared, however, to stipulate both sorts of parity. Let's agree for purposes of argument that these beliefs are on an epistemic par in the sense that those of a different religious tradition have the same sort of internally available markers—evidence, phenomenology and the like—for their beliefs as I have for (1) and (2). What follows?

Return to the case of moral belief. King David took Bathsheba, made her pregnant, and then, after the failure of various stratagems to get her husband Uriah to think the baby was his, arranged for him to be killed. The prophet Nathan came to David and told him a story about a rich man and a poor man. The rich man had many flocks and herds; the poor man had only a single ewe lamb, which grew up with his children, "ate at his table, drank from his cup, lay in his bosom, and was like a daughter to him." The rich man had unexpected guests. Rather than slaughter one of his own sheep, he took the poor man's single ewe lamb, slaughtered it, and served it to his guests. David exploded in anger: "The man who did this deserves to die!" Then, in one of the most riveting passages in all the Bible, Nathan turns to David and declares, "You are that man!" And then David sees what he has done.

My interest here is in David's reaction to the story. I agree with David: Such injustice is utterly and despicably wrong; there are really no words for it. I believe that such an action is wrong, and I believe that the proposition that it *isn't* wrong—either because really *nothing* is wrong, or because even if *some* things are wrong, *this* isn't—is false. As a matter of fact, there isn't a lot I believe more strongly. I recognize, however, that there are those who disagree with me; and once more, I doubt that I could find an argument to show them that I am right and they wrong. Further, for all I know, their conflicting beliefs have for them the same internally available epistemic markers, the same phenomenology, as mine have for me. Am I then being arbitrary, treating similar cases differently in continuing to hold, as I do, that in fact that kind of behavior *is* dreadfully wrong? I don't think so. Am I wrong in thinking racial bigotry despicable, even though I know that there are others who disagree, and even if I think they have the same internal markers for their beliefs as I have for mine? I don't think so. I believe in serious actualism, the view that no objects have properties in worlds in which they do not exist, not even nonexistence. Others do not believe this, and perhaps the internal markers of their dissenting views have for them the same quality as my views have for me. Am I being arbitrary in continuing to think as I do? I can't see how.

And the reason here is this: in each of these cases, the believer in question doesn't really think the beliefs in question *are* on a relevant epistemic par. She may agree that she and those who dissent are equally convinced of the truth of their belief and even that they are internally on a par, that the internally available markers are similar, or relevantly similar. But she must still think that there is an important epistemic difference, she thinks that somehow the other person has *made a mistake,* or *has a blind spot,* or hasn't been wholly attentive, or hasn't received some grace she has, or is in some way epistemically less fortunate. And, of course, the pluralist critic is in no better case. He thinks the thing to do when there is internal epistemic parity is to withhold judgment; he knows that there are others who don't think so, and for all he knows that belief has internal parity with his; if he continues in that belief, therefore, he will be in the same condition as the exclusivist; and if he doesn't continue in this belief, he no longer has an objection to the exclusivist.

But couldn't I be wrong? Of course I could! But I don't avoid that risk by withholding all religious (or philosophical or moral) beliefs; I can go wrong that way as well as any other, treating all religions, or all philosophical thoughts, or all moral views as on a par. Again, there is no safe haven here, no way to avoid risk. In particular, you won't reach a safe haven by trying to take the same attitude toward all the historically available patterns of belief and withholding; for in so doing, you adopt a particular pattern of belief and withholding, one incompatible with some adopted by others. "You pays your money and you takes your choice," realizing that you, like anyone else, can be desperately wrong. But what else can you do? You don't really have an alternative. And how can you do better than believe and withhold according to what, after serious and responsible consideration, seems to you to be the right pattern of belief and withholding?

Irrationality

I therefore can't see how it can be sensibly maintained that the exclusivist is unjustified in his exclusivist views; but perhaps, as is sometimes claimed, he or his view is *irrational.* Irrationality, however, is many things to many people; so there is a prior question: What is it to be irrational? More exactly, precisely what quality is it that the objector is attributing to the exclusivist (in condition *C*) when the former says the latter's exclusivist beliefs are irrational? Since the charge is never developed at all fully, it isn't easy to say. So suppose we simply consider the main varieties of irrationality (or, if you prefer, the main senses of "irrational") and ask whether any of them attach to the exclusivist just by virtue of being an exclusivist. I believe there are substantially five varieties of rationality, five distinct but analogically connected senses of the term *rational;* fortunately not all of them require detailed consideration.

Aristotelian rationality. This is the sense in which man is a rational animal, one that has *ratio,* one that can look before and after, can hold beliefs, make inferences and is capable of knowledge. This is perhaps the basic sense, the one of which the others are analogical extensions. It is also, presumably

irrelevant in the present context; at any rate I hope the objector does not mean to hold that an exclusivist will by that token no longer be a rational animal.

The deliverances of reason. To be rational in the Aristotelian sense is to possess reason: the power or thinking, believing, inferring, reasoning, knowing. Aristotelian rationality is thus *generic.* But there is an important more specific sense lurking in the neighborhood; this is the sense that goes with reason taken more narrowly, as the source of a priori knowledge and belief. An important use of *rational* analogically connected with the first has to do with reason taken in this more narrow way. It is by reason thus construed that we know *self-evident* beliefs— beliefs so obvious that you can't so much as grasp them without seeing that they couldn't be false. These will be among the *deliverances of reason.* Of course there are other beliefs—$38 \times 39 = 1482$, for example—that are not self-evident but are a consequence of self-evident beliefs by way of arguments that are self-evidently valid; these too are among the deliverances of reason. So say that the deliverances of reason is the set of those propositions that are self-evident for us human beings, closed under self-evident consequence. This yields another sense of rationality: a belief is *rational* if it is among the deliverances of reason and *irrational* if it is contrary to the deliverances of reason. (A belief can therefore be neither rational nor irrational, in this sense.) This sense of *rational* is an analogical extension of the fundamental sense, but it is itself extended by analogy to still other senses. Thus, we can broaden the category of reason to include memory, experience, induction, probability, and whatever else goes into science; this is the sense of the term when reason is sometimes contrasted with faith. And we can also soften the requirement for self-evidence, recognizing both that self-evidence or a priori warrant is a matter of degree and that there are many propositions that have a priori warrant, but are not such that no one who understands them can fail to believe them.[17]

Is the exclusivist irrational in *these* senses? I think not; at any rate, the question whether he is isn't the question at issue. His exclusivist beliefs are irrational in these senses only if there is a good argument from the deliverances of reason (taken broadly) to the denials of what he believes. I do not believe that there are any such arguments. Presumably, the same goes for the pluralist objector: at any rate, his objection is not that (1) and (2) are demonstrably false or even that there are good arguments against them from the deliverances of reason; his objection is instead that there is something wrong or subpar with believing them in condition *C.* This sense too, then, is irrelevant to our present concerns.

The deontological sense. This sense of the term has to do with intellectual *requirement,* or *duty,* or *obligation;* a person's belief is irrational in this sense if in forming or holding it she violates such a duty. This is the sense of *irrational* in which according to many contemporary evidentialist objectors to theistic belief, those who believe in God without propositional evidence are irrational. Irrationality in this sense is a matter of failing to conform to intellectual or epistemic duties; the analogical connection with the first, Aristotelian sense is that these duties are thought to be among the deliverances of reason (and hence among the deliverances of the power by virtue of which human beings are rational in the Aristotelian sense). But we have already considered whether the exclusivist is flouting duties; we need say no more about the matter here. As we say, the exclusivist is not necessarily irrational in this sense either.

Zweckrationalität. A common and very important notion of rationality is *means—end rationality*— what our continental cousins, following Max Weber, sometimes call *Zweckrationalität,* the sort of rationality displayed by your actions if they are well calculated to achieve your goals. (Again, the analogical connection with the first sense is clear: The calculation in question requires the power by virtue of which we are rational in Aristotle's sense.) Clearly, there is a whole constellation of notions lurking in the nearby bushes: What would *in fact* contribute to your goals? What you *take* it would contribute to your goals? What you *would* take it would contribute to your goals if you were sufficiently acute, or knew enough, or weren't distracted by lust, greed, pride, ambition, and the like?

What you would take it would contribute to your goals if you weren't thus distracted and were also to reflect sufficiently? and so on. This notion of rationality has assumed enormous importance in the last 150 years or so. (Among its laurels, for example, is the complete domination of the development of the discipline of economics.) Rationality thus construed is a matter of knowing how to get what you want; it is the cunning of reason. Is the exclusivist properly charged with irrationality in this sense? Does his believing in the way he does interfere with his attaining some of his goals, or is it a markedly inferior way of attaining those goals?

An initial *caveat:* It isn't clear that this notion of rationality applies to belief at all. It isn't clear that in *believing* something, I am acting to achieve some goal. If believing is an action at all, it is very far from being the paradigmatic kind of action taken to achieve some end; we don't have a choice as to whether to have beliefs, and we don't have a lot of choice with respect to which beliefs we have. But suppose we set this *caveat* aside and stipulate for purposes of argument that we have sufficient control over our beliefs for them to qualify as actions. Would the exclusivist's beliefs then be irrational in this sense? Well, that depends upon what his goals *are;* if among his goals for religious belief is, for example, not believing anything not believed by someone else, then indeed it would be. But, of course, he needn't have *that* goal. If I do have an end or goal in holding such beliefs as (1) and (2), it would presumably be that of believing the truth on this exceedingly important matter or perhaps that of trying to get in touch as adequately as possible with God, or more broadly with the deepest reality. And if (1) and (2) are *true,* believing them will be a way of doing exactly that. It is only if they are *not* true, then, that believing them could sensibly be thought to be irrational in this means–ends sense. Because the objector does not propose to take as a premise the proposition that (1) and (2) are false—he holds only that there is some flaw involved in *believing* them—this also is presumably not what he means.

Rationality as sanity and proper function. One in the grip of pathological confusion, or flight of ideas, or certain kinds of agnosia, or the manic phase of manic-depressive psychosis will often be said to be irrational; the episode may pass, after which he has regained rationality. Here *rationality* means absence of dysfunction, disorder, impairment, or pathology with respect to rational faculties. So this variety of rationality is again analogically related to Aristotelian rationality; a person is rational in this sense when no malfunction obstructs her use of the faculties by virtue of the possession of which she is rational in the Aristotelian sense. Rationality as sanity does not require possession of particularly exalted rational faculties; it requires only normality (in the nonstatistical sense) or health, or proper function. This use of the term, naturally enough, is prominent in psychiatric discussions—Oliver Sack's male patient who mistook his wife for a hat, for example, was thus irrational. This fifth and final sense of rationality is itself a family of analogically related senses. The fundamental sense here is that of sanity and proper function, but there are other closely related senses. Thus, we may say that a belief (in certain circumstances) is irrational, not because no sane person would hold it, but because no person who was sane and had also undergone a certain course of education would hold it or because no person who was sane and furthermore was as intelligent as we and our friends would hold it; alternatively and more briefly, the idea is not merely that no one who was functioning properly in those circumstances would hold it, but rather no one who was functioning *optimally,* as well or nearly as well as human beings ordinarily do (leaving aside the occasional great genius) would hold it. And this sense of rationality leads directly to the notion of *warrant;* I turn now to that notion; in treating it, we will also treat *ambulando*—this fifth kind of irrationality.

Warrant

So we come to the third version of the epistemic objection: that at any rate the exclusivist doesn't have warrant, or anyway *much* warrant (enough warrant for knowledge) for his exclusivistic views. Many pluralists—for example, Hick, Runzo, and Cantwell Smith—unite in declaring that, at any rate,

the exclusivist certainly can't *know* that his exclusivistic views are true. But is this really true? I will argue briefly that it is not. At any rate, from the perspective of each of the major contemporary accounts of knowledge, it may very well be that the exclusivist knows (1) or (2) or both. First, consider the two main internalistic accounts of knowledge: the justified true belief accounts and the coherentist accounts. As I have already argued, it seems clear that a theist, a believer in (1) could certainly be *justified* (in the primary sense) in believing as she does: she could be flouting no intellectual or cognitive duties or obligations. But then on the most straightforward justified true belief account of knowledge, she can also *know* that it is true—if, that is, it *can* be true. More exactly, what must be possible is that both the exclusivist is justified in believing (1) and/or (2) and they be true. Presumably, the pluralist does not mean to dispute this possibility.

For concreteness, consider the account of justification given by the classical foundationalist Chisholm. On this view, a belief has warrant for me to the extent that accepting it is apt for the fulfillment of my epistemic duty, which (roughly speaking) is that of trying to get and remain in the right relation to the truth. But if after the most careful, thorough, open, and prayerful consideration, it still seems to me—perhaps more strongly than ever—that (1) and (2) are true, then clearly accepting them has great aptness for the fulfillment of that duty.

A similarly brief argument can be given with respect to *coherentism,* the view that what constitutes warrant is coherence with some body of belief. We must distinguish two varieties of coherentism. On the one hand, it might be held that what is required is coherence with some or all of the other beliefs I actually hold; on the other, that what is required is coherence with my *verific* noetic structure (Keith Lehrer's term): the set of beliefs that remains when all the false ones are deleted or replaced by their contradictories. But surely a coherent set of beliefs could include both (1) and (2) together with the beliefs involved in being in condition *C;* what would be required, perhaps, would be that the set of beliefs contain some explanation of why it is that others do not believe as I do. And if (1) and (2) *are* true, then surely (and a fortiori) there can be coherent verific noetic structures that include them. Hence, neither of these versions of coherentism rule out the possibility that the exclusivist in condition *C* could know (1) and/or (2).

And now consider the main externalist accounts. The most popular externalist account at present would be one or another version of *reliabilism*. And there is an oft-repeated pluralistic argument that seems to be designed to appeal to reliabilist intuitions. The conclusion of this argument is not always clear, but here is its premise, in Hick's words:

> For it is evident that in some ninety-nine percent of cases the religion which an individual professes and to which he or she adheres depends upon the accidents of birth. Someone born to Buddhist parents in Thailand is very likely to be a Buddhist, someone born to Muslim parents in Saudi Arabia to be a Muslim, someone born to Christian parents in Mexico to be a Christian, and so on.

As a matter of sociological fact, this may be right. Furthermore, it can certainly produce a sense of intellectual vertigo. But what is one to do with this fact, if fact it is, and what follows from it? Does it follow, for example, that I ought not to accept the religious views that I have been brought up to ac- cept, or the ones that I find myself inclined to accept, or the ones that seem to me to be true? Or that the belief producing processes that have produced those beliefs in me are unreliable? Surely not. Furthermore, self-referential problems once more loom; this argument is another philosophical tar baby.

For suppose we concede that if I had been born of Muslim parents in Morocco rather than Christian parents in Michigan, my beliefs would have been quite different. (For one thing, I probably wouldn't believe that I was born in Michigan.) The same goes for the pluralist. Pluralism isn't and hasn't been widely popular in the world at large; if the pluralist had been born in Madagascar, or medieval France, he probably wouldn't have been a pluralist. Does it follow that he shouldn't be a pluralist or that his pluralist beliefs are produced in him by an unreliable belief producing process? I doubt it. Suppose I hold the following, or something similar:

(4) If *S*'s religious or philosophical beliefs are such that if *S* had been born elsewhere and elsewhen, she wouldn't have held them, then those beliefs are produced by unreliable belief producing mechanisms and hence have no warrant.

Once more I will be hoist with my own petard. For in all probability, someone born in Mexico to Christian parents wouldn't believe (4) itself. No matter what philosophical and religious beliefs we hold and withhold (so it seems), there are places and times such that if we have been born there and then, then we would not have displayed the pattern of holding and withholding of religious and philosophical beliefs we *do* display. As I said, this can indeed be vertiginous; but what can we make of it? What can we infer from it about what has warrant and how we should conduct our intellectual lives? That's not easy to say. Can we infer *anything at all* about what has warrant or how we should conduct our intellectual lives? Not obviously.

To return to reliabilism then: For simplicity, let's take the version of reliabilism according to which *S* knows *p* if the belief that *p* is produced in *S* by a reliable belief producing mechanism or process. I don't have the space here to go into this matter in sufficient detail, but it seems pretty clear that if (1) and (2) are true, then it *could be* that the beliefs that (1) and (2) be produced in me by a reliable belief-producing process. For either we are thinking of *concrete* belief producing processes, like your memory or John's powers of a priori reasoning (tokens as opposed to types), or else we are thinking of *types* of belief producing processes (type reliabilism). The problem with the latter is that there are an enormous number of *different* types of belief producing processes for any given belief, some of which are reliable and some of which are not; the problem (and a horrifying problem it is) is to say which of these is the type the reliability of which determines whether the belief in question has warrant. So the first (token reliabilism) is a better way of stating reliabilism. But then clearly enough if (1) or (2) *are* true, they could be produced in me by a reliable belief-producing process. Calvin's *Sensus Divinitatis,* for example, could be working in the exclusivist in such a way as to reliably produce the belief that (1) is true; Calvin's Internal Testimony of the Holy Spirit could do the same for (2). If (1) and (2) are true, therefore, then from a reliabilist perspective there is no reason whatever to think that the exclusivist might not know that they are true.

There is another brand of externalism which seems to me to be closer to the truth than reliabilism: call it *(faute de mieux)* "proper functionalism." This view can be stated to a first approximation as follows: *S* knows *p* if (1) the belief that *p* is produced in *S* by cognitive faculties that are functioning properly (working as they ought to work, suffering from no dysfunction), (2) the cognitive environment in which *p* is produced is appropriate for those faculties, (3) the purpose of the module of the epistemic faculties producing the belief in question is to produce true beliefs (alternatively, the module of the design plan governing the production of *p* is aimed at the production of true beliefs), and (4) the objective probability of a belief's being true, given that it is produced under those conditions, is high. All of this needs explanation, of course; for present purposes, perhaps, we can collapse the account into the first condition. But then clearly it *could* be, if (1) and (2) are true, that they are produced in me by cognitive faculties functioning properly under condition *C*. For suppose (1) is true. Then it is surely possible that God has created us human beings with something like Calvin's *Sensus Divinitatis,* a belief producing process that in a wide variety of circumstances functions properly to produce (1) or some very similar belief. Furthermore it is also possible that in response to the human condition of sin and misery, God has provided for us human beings a means of salvation, which he has revealed in the Bible. Still further, perhaps he has arranged for us to come to believe what he means to teach there by way of the operation of something like the Internal Testimony of the Holy Spirit of which Calvin speaks. So on this view, too, if (1) and (2) are true, it is certainly possible that the exclusivist *know* that they are. We can be sure that the exclusivist's views are irrational in this sense, then, only if they are false; but the pluralist objector does not mean to claim that they *are* false; this version of the objection, therefore, also fails. The exclusivist isn't necessarily irrational, and indeed might *know* that (1) and (2) are true, if indeed they *are* true.

All this seems right. But don't the realities of religious pluralism count for anything at all? Is there nothing at all to the claims of the pluralists? Could that really be right? Of course not. For many or most exclusivists, I think, an awareness of the enormous variety of human religious response functions as a *defeater* for such beliefs as (1) and (2)—an *undercutting* defeater, as opposed to a rebutting defeater. It calls into question, to some degree or other, the sources of one's belief in (1) or (2). It doesn't or needn't do so by way of an *argument;* and indeed there isn't a very powerful argument from the proposition that many apparently devout people around the world dissent from (1) and (2) to the conclusion that (1) and (2) are false. Instead, it works more directly; it directly reduces the level of confidence or degree of belief in the proposition in question. From a Christian perspective, this situation of religious pluralism and our awareness of it is itself a manifestation of our miserable human condition; and it may deprive us of some of the comfort and peace the Lord has promised his followers. It can also deprive the exclusivist of the *knowledge* that (1) and (2) are true, if even they *are* true and he *believes* that they are. Because degree of warrant depends in part on degree of belief, it is possible, though not necessary, that knowledge of the facts of religious pluralism should reduce an exclusivist's degree of belief and hence of warrant for (1) and (2) in such a way as to deprive him of knowledge of (1) and (2). He might be such that if he *hadn't* known the facts of pluralism, then he would have known (1) and (2), but now that he *does* know those facts, he doesn't know (1) and (2). In this way, he may come to know less by knowing more.

Things *could* go this way with the exclusivist. On the other hand, they *needn't* go this way. Consider once more the moral parallel. Perhaps you have always believed it deeply wrong for a counselor to use his position of trust to seduce a client. Perhaps you discover that others disagree; they think it more like a minor peccadillo, like running a red light when there's no traffic; and you realize that possibly these people have the same internal markers for their beliefs that you have for yours. You think the matter over more fully, imaginatively re-create and rehearse such situations, become more aware of just what is involved in such a situation (the breach of trust, the breaking of implied prom-ises, the injustice and unfairness, the nasty irony of a situation in which someone comes to a counselor seeking help but receives only hurt), and come to believe even more fully that such an action is wrong—and indeed to have more warrant for that belief. But something similar can happen in the case of religious beliefs. A fresh or heightened awareness of the facts of religious pluralism could bring about a reappraisal of one's religious life, a reawakening, a new or renewed and deepened grasp and appre-hension of (1) and (2). From Calvin's perspective, it could serve as an occasion for a renewed and more powerful working of the belief-producing processes by which we come to apprehend (1) and (2). In that way, knowledge of the facts of pluralism could initially serve as a defeater, but in the long run have precisely the opposite effect.

Notes

1. *Colloquium Heptaplomeres de Rerum Sub-limium Arcanis Abditis,* written by 1593 but first publish-ed in 1857. English translation by Marion Kuntz (Princeton, N.J.: Princeton Univ. Press, 1975), p. 256.

2. Joseph Runzo: "Today, the impressive piety and evident rationality of the belief systems of other religious traditions, inescapably confronts Christians with a crisis—and a potential revolution." "God, Commitment, and Other Faiths: Pluralism vs. Relativism," *Faith and Philoso-phy* 5, no. 4 (October 1988):343f. (Reading VIII.5 in this book.)

3. Gary Gutting: "Applying these considerations to religious belief, we seem led to the conclusion that, because believers have many epistemic peers who do not share their belief in God . . ., they have no right to maintain their belief without a justification. If they do so, they are guilty of epistemological egoism." *Religious Belief and Religious Skepticism* (Notre Dame, Ind.: Univ. of Notre Dame Press, 1982), p. 90 (but see the following pages for an important qualification).

4. Wilfred Cantwell Smith: "Here my submission is that on this front the traditional doctrinal position of the Church has in fact militated against its traditional moral position, and has in fact encouraged Christians to ap-proach other men immorally. Christ has taught us humil-ity, but we have approached them with arrogance. . . . This charge of arrogance is a serious one." *Religious Diversity* (New York: Harper & Row, 1976), p. 13.

5. Runzo: "Ethically, Religious Exclusivism has the morally repugnant result of making those who have privi-leged knowledge, or who are intellectually astute, a reli-gious elite, while penalizing those who happen to have no access to the putatively correct religious view, or who are incapable of advanced understanding." Op. cit., p. 348.

6. John Hick: "But natural pride, despite its positive contribution to human life, becomes harmful when it is elevated to the level of dogma and is built into the belief system of a religious community. This happens when its sense of its own validity and worth is expressed in doc-trines implying an exclusive or a decisively superior ac-cess to the truth or the power to save." "Religious Pluralism and Absolute Claims," *Religious Pluralism* (Notre Dame, Ind.: Univ. of Notre Dame Press, 1984), p. 197.

7. John Cobb: "I agree with the liberal theists that even in Pannenberg's case, the quest for an absolute as a basis for understanding reflects the long tradition of Chris-tian imperialism and triumphalism rather than the plural-istic spirit." "The Meaning of Pluralism for Christian Self-Understanding," *Religious Pluralism,* ed. Leroy Rouner (Notre Dame, Ind.: Univ. of Notre Dame Press, 1984), p. 171.

8. "God, Commitment, and Other Faiths: Pluralism vs. Relativism" *Faith and Philosophy* 5, no. 4 (October 1988):357.

9. Smith, op. cit., p. 14.

10. John Hick: ". . . the only reason for treating one's tradition differently from others is the very human but not very cogent reason that it is one's own!" *An Interpretation of Religion,* loc. cit.

11. *An Interpretation of Religion* (New Haven, Conn.: Yale Univ. Press, 1989), p. 2.

VIII.3   Hick's Religious Pluralism and "Reformed Epistemology"— A Middle Ground

DAVID BASINGER

David Basinger is professor of philosophy at Roberts Wesleyan College in Rochester, New York, and the author of several works in the philosophy of religion.

The purpose of this discussion is to analyze comparatively the influential argument for religious pluralism offered by John Hick and the argument for religious exclusivism (sectarianism) which can be generated by proponents of what has come to be labeled 'Reformed Epistemology.' I argue that while Hick and the Reformed exclusivist appear to be giving us incompatible responses to the same question about the true nature of 'religious' reality, they are actually responding to related, but distinct questions, each of which must be considered by those desiring to give a religious explanation for the phenomenon of religious diversity. Moreover, I conclude that the insights of neither ought to be emphasized at the expense of the other.

No one denies that the basic tenets of many religious perspectives are, if taken literally, quite incompatible. The salvific claims of some forms of Judeo-Christian thought, for example, condemn the proponents of all other perspectives to hell, while the incompatible salvific claims of some forms of Islamic thought do the same.

Such incompatibility is normally explained in one of three basic ways. The non-theist argues that all religious claims are false, the product perhaps of wish fulfillment. The religious pluralist argues that the basic claims of at least all of the major world religions are more or less accurate descriptions of the same reality. Finally, the religious exclusivist argues that the tenets of only one religion (or some

Reprinted from *Faith and Philosophy* Vol. 5:4, October 1988 by permission. Endnotes deleted.

limited number of religions) are to any significant degree accurate descriptions of reality.

The purpose of this discussion is to analyze comparatively the influential argument for religious pluralism offered by John Hick and the argument for religious exclusivism which can be (and perhaps has been) generated by proponents of what has come to be labeled 'Reformed Epistemology.' I shall argue that while Hick and the Reformed epistemologist appear to be giving us incompatible responses to the same question about the true nature of 'religious' reality, they are actually responding to related, but distinct questions, each of which must be considered by those desiring to give a religious explanation for the phenomenon of religious diversity. Moreover, I shall conclude that the insights offered by both Hick and the Reformed epistemologist are of value and, accordingly, that those of neither ought to be emphasized at the expense of the other.

John Hick's Theological Pluralism

Hick's contention is not that different religions make no conflicting truth claims. In fact, he believes that "the differences of belief between (and within) the traditions are legion," and has often in great detail discussed them. His basic claim, rather, is that such differences are best seen as "different ways of conceiving and experiencing the one ultimate divine Reality."

However, if the various religions are really "responses to a single ultimate transcendent Reality," how then do we account for such significant differences? The best explanation, we are told, is the assumption that "the limitless divine reality has been thought and experienced by different human mentalities forming and formed by different intellectual frameworks and devotional techniques."

Or, as Hick has stated the point elsewhere, the best explanation is the assumption that the correspondingly different ways of responding to divine reality "owe their differences to the modes of thinking, perceiving and feeling which have developed within the different patterns of human existence embodied in the various cultures of the earth." Each "constitutes a valid context of salvation/liberation; but none constitutes the one and only such context."

But why accept such a pluralistic explanation? Why not hold, rather, that there is no higher Reality beyond us and thus that all religious claims are false—i.e., why not opt for naturalism? Or why not adopt the exclusivistic contention that the religious claims of only one perspective are true?

Hick does not reject naturalism because he sees it to be an untenable position. It is certainly *possible,* he tells us, that the "entire realm of [religious] experience is delusory or hallucinatory, simply a human projection, and not in any way or degree a result of the presence of a greater divine reality." In fact, since the "universe of which we are part is religiously ambiguous," it is not even *unreasonable or implausible* "to interpret any aspect of it, including our religious experience, in non-religious as well as religious ways."

However, he is quick to add, "it is perfectly reasonable and sane for us to trust our experience"—including our religious experience—"as generally cognitive of reality except when we have some reason to doubt it." Moreover, "the mere theoretical possibility that any or all [religious experience] may be illusory does not count as a reason to doubt it." Nor is religious experience overturned by the fact that the great religious figures of the past, including Jesus, held a number of beliefs which we today reject as arising from the now outmoded science of their day, or by the fact that some people find "it impossible to accept that the profound dimension of pain and suffering is the measure of the cost of creation through creaturely freedom."

He acknowledges that those who have "no positive ground for religious belief within their own experience" often do see such factors as "insuperable barriers" to religious belief. But given the am-

biguous nature of the evidence, he argues, it cannot be demonstrated that all rational people must see it this way. That is, belief in a supernatural realm can't be shown to be any less plausible than disbelief. Accordingly, he concludes, "those who actually participate in this field of religious experience are fully entitled, as sane and rational persons, to take the risk of trusting their own experience together with that of their tradition, and of proceeding to live and to believe on the basis of it, rather than taking the alternative risk of distrusting it and so—for the time being at least—turning their backs on God."

But why choose pluralism as the best religious hypothesis? Why does Hick believe we ought not be exclusivists? It is not because he sees exclusivism as incoherent. It is certainly possible, he grants, that "one particular 'Ptolomaic' religious vision does correspond uniquely with how things are." Nor does Hick claim to have some privileged "cosmic vantage point from which [he can] observe both the divine reality in itself and the different partial human awarenesses of that reality." But when we individually consider the evidence in the case, he argues, the result is less ambiguous. When "we start from the phenomenological fact of the various forms of religious experience, and we seek an hypothesis which will make sense of this realm of phenomena" from a religious point of view, "the theory that most naturally suggests itself postulates a divine Reality which is itself limitless, exceeding the scope of human conceptuality and language, but which is humanly thought and experienced in various conditioned and limited ways."

What is this evidence which makes the pluralistic hypothesis so "considerably more probable" than exclusivism? For one thing, Hick informs us, a credible religious hypothesis must account for the fact, "evident to ordinary people (even though not always taken into account by theologians) that in the great majority of cases—say 98 to 99 percent—the religion in which a person believes and to which he adheres depends upon where he was born." Moreover, a credible hypothesis must account for the fact that within all of the major religious traditions, "basically the same salvific process is taking place, namely the transformation of human existence from self-centeredness to Reality-centeredness." And while pluralism "illuminates" these otherwise baffling facts, the strict exclusivist's view "has come to seem increasingly implausible and unrealistic."

But even more importantly, he maintains, a credible religious hypothesis must account for the fact, of which "we have become irreversibly aware in the present century, as the result of anthropological, sociological and psychological studies and the work of philosophy of language, that there is no one universal and invariable" pattern for interpreting human experience, but rather a range of significantly different patterns or conceptual schemes "which have developed within the major cultural streams." And when considered in light of this, Hick concludes, a "pluralistic theory becomes inevitable."

The Reformed Objection

There are two basic ways in which Hick's pluralistic position can be critiqued. One "appropriate critical response," according to Hick himself, "would be to offer a better [religious] hypothesis." That is, one way to challenge Hick is to claim that the evidence he cites is better explained by some form of exclusivism.

But there is another, potentially more powerful type of objection, one which finds its roots in the currently popular 'Reformed Epistemology' being championed by philosophers such as Alvin Plantinga. I will first briefly outline Plantinga's latest version of this epistemological approach and then discuss its impact on Hick's position.

According to Plantinga, it has been widely held since the Enlightenment that if theistic beliefs—e.g., religious hypotheses—are to be considered rational, they must be based on propositional evidence. It is not enough for the theist just to refute objections to any such belief. The theist "must also have something like an argument for the belief, or some positive reason to think that the belief is true." But this is incorrect, Plantinga maintains. There are beliefs which acquire their warrant propositionally—i.e., have warrant conferred on them by an evidential line of reasoning from other beliefs. And

for such beliefs, it may well be true that proponents need something like an argument for their veridicality.

However, there are also, he tells us, *basic* beliefs which are not based on propositional evidence and, thus, do not require propositional warrant. In fact, *if* such beliefs can be affirmed "without either violating an epistemic duty or displaying some kind of noetic defect," they can be considered *properly basic*. And, according to Plantinga, many theistic beliefs can be properly basic: "Under widely realized conditions it is perfectly rational, reasonable, intellectually respectable and acceptable to believe [certain theistic tenets] without believing [them] on the basis of [propositional] evidence."

But what are such conditions? Under what conditions can a belief have positive epistemic status if it is not conferred by other propositions whose epistemic status is not in question? The answer, Plantinga informs us, lies in an analysis of belief formation.

[We have] cognitive faculties designed to enable us to achieve true beliefs with respect to a wide variety of propositions—propositions about our immediate environment, about our interior lives, about the thoughts and experiences of other persons, about our universe at large, about right and wrong, about the whole realm of *abstracta*—numbers, properties, propositions, states of affairs, possible worlds and their like, about modality— what is necessary and possible—and about [ourselves]. These faculties work in such a way that under the appropriate circumstances we form the appropriate belief. More exactly, the appropriate belief is *formed in us;* in the typical case we do not *decide* to hold or form the belief in question, but simply find ourselves with it. Upon considering an instance of *modus ponens*, I find myself believing its corresponding conditional; upon being appeared to in the familiar way, I find myself holding the belief that there is a large tree before me; upon being asked what I had for breakfast, I reflect for a moment and find myself with the belief that what I had was eggs on toast. In these and other cases I do not *decide* what to believe; I don't total up the evidence (I'm being appeared to redly; on most occasions when thus appeared to I am in the presence of something red, so most probably in this case I am) and make a decision as to what seems best supported; I simply find myself believing.

And from a theistic point of view, Plantinga continues, the same is true in the religious realm. Just as it is true that when our senses or memory are functioning properly, "appropriate belief is formed in us," so it is that God has created us with faculties which will, "when they are working the way they were designed to work by the being who designed and created us and them," produce true theistic beliefs. Moreover, if these faculties are functioning properly, a basic belief thus formed has "positive epistemic status to the degree [the individual in question finds herself] inclined to accept it."

What, though, of the alleged counter-evidence to such theistic beliefs? What, for example, of all the arguments the conclusion of which is that God does not exist? Can they all be dismissed as irrelevant? Not immediately, answers Plantinga. We must seriously consider potential defeaters of our basic beliefs. With respect to the belief that God exists, for example, we must seriously consider the claim that religious belief is mere wish fulfillment and the claim that God's existence is incompatible with (or at least improbable given) the amount of evil in the world.

But to undercut such defeaters, he continues, we need not engage in positive apologetics: produce propositional evidence for our beliefs. We need only engage in *negative* apologetics: refute such arguments. Moreover, it is Plantinga's conviction that such defeaters do normally exist. "The non-propositional warrant enjoyed by [a person's] belief in God, for example, [seems] itself sufficient to turn back the challenge offered by some alleged defeaters"—e.g., the claim that theistic belief is mere wish fulfillment. And other defeaters such as the "problem of evil," he tell us, can be undercut by identifying validity or soundness problems or even by appealing to the fact that "experts think it unsound or that the experts are evenly divided as to its soundness."

Do Plantinga or other proponents of this Reformed epistemology maintain that their exclusivistic religious hypotheses are properly basic and can thus be 'defended' in the manner just outlined? I am not *certain* that they do. However, when Plantinga, for example, claims that "God exists" is for most adult theists properly basic, he appears to have in mind a classical Christian conception of the divine—i.e., a being who is the triune, omnipotent, omniscient, perfectly good, *ex nihilo* creator of the universe. In fact, given his recent claim that "the internal testimony of the Holy Spirit . . . is a source of reliable and perfectly acceptable beliefs about what is communicated [by God] in Scripture," and the manner in which most who make such a claim view the truth claims of the other world religions, it would appear that Plantinga's 'basic' conception of God is quite exclusive.

However, even if no Reformed epistemologist actually does affirm an exclusivistic hypothesis she claims is properly basic, it is obvious that the Reformed analysis of belief justification can be used to critique Hick's line of reasoning. Hick claims that an objective inductive assessment of the relevant evidence makes his pluralistic thesis a more plausible religious explanation than any of the competing exclusivistic hypotheses. But a Reformed exclusivist could easily argue that this approach to the issue is misguided. My affirmation of an exclusivistic Christian perspective, such an argument might begin, is not evidential in nature. It is, rather, simply a belief I have found formed in me, much like the belief that I am seeing a tree in front of me or the belief that killing innocent children is wrong.

Now, of course, I must seriously consider the allegedly formidable defeaters with which pluralists such as Hick have presented me. I must consider the fact, for example, that the exclusive beliefs simply formed in most people are not similar to mine, but rather tend to mirror those beliefs found in the cultures in which such people have been raised. But I do not agree with Hick that this fact is best explained by a pluralistic hypothesis. I attribute this phenomenon to other factors such as the epistemic blindness with which most of humanity has been plagued since the fall.

Moreover, to defend my position—to maintain justifiably (rationally) that I am right and Hick is wrong—I need not, as Hick seems to suggest, produce objective 'proof' that his hypothesis is weaker than mine. That is, I need not produce 'evidence' that would lead most rational people to agree with me. That would be to involve myself in Classical Foundationalism, which is increasingly being recognized as a bankrupt epistemological methodology. All I need do is undercut Hick's defeaters—i.e., show that his challenge does not require me to abandon my exclusivity thesis. And this I can easily do. For Hick has not demonstrated that my thesis is self-contradictory. And it is extremely doubtful that there exists any other nonquestion-begging criterion for plausibility by which he could even attempt to demonstrate that my thesis is less plausible (less probable) than his.

Hick, of course, believes firmly that his hypothesis makes the most sense. But why should this bother me? By his own admission, many individuals firmly believe that, given the amount of seemingly gratuitous evil in the world, God's nonexistence is by far most plausible. Yet this does not keep him from affirming theism. He simply reserves the right to see things differently and continues to believe. And there is no reason why I cannot do the same.

Moreover, even if what others believed were relevant, by Hick's own admission, the majority of theists doubt that his thesis is true. Or, at the very least, I could rightly maintain that "the experts are evenly divided as to its soundness." Thus, given the criteria for defeater assessment which we Reformed exclusivists affirm, Hick's defeaters are clearly undercut. And, accordingly, I remain perfectly justified in continuing to hold that my exclusivity thesis is correct and, therefore, that all incompatible competing hypotheses are false.

A Middle Ground

It is tempting to see Hick and the Reformed exclusivist as espousing incompatible approaches to the question of religious diversity. If Hick is correct—if the issue is primarily evidential in nature—then the Reformed exclusivist is misguided and vice versa. But this, I believe, is an inaccurate assessment of the situation. There are two equally important, but distinct, questions which arise in this context, and Hick and the Reformed exclusivist, it seems to me, each *primarily* address only one.

The Reformed exclusivist is primarily interested in the following question:

Q1: Under what conditions is an individual within her epistemic rights (is she rational) in affirm-

ing one of the many mutually exclusive religious diversity hypotheses?

In response, as we have seen, the Reformed exclusivist argues (or at least could argue) that a person need not grant that her religious hypothesis (belief) requires propositional (evidential) warrant. She is within her epistemic rights in maintaining that it is a *basic* belief. And if she does so, then to preserve rationality, she is not required to 'prove' in some objective manner that her hypothesis is most plausible. She is fulfilling all epistemic requirements solely by defending her hypothesis against claims that it is less plausible than competitors.

It seems to me that the Reformed exclusivist is basically right on this point. I do believe, for reasons mentioned later in this essay, that attempts by any knowledgeable exclusivist to define her hypothesis will ultimately require her to enter the realm of positive apologetics—i.e., will require her to engage in a comparative analysis of her exclusivistic beliefs. But I wholeheartedly agree with the Reformed exclusivist's contention that to preserve rationality, she need not actually demonstrate that her hypothesis is most plausible. She need ultimately only defend herself against the claim that a thoughtful assessment of the matter makes the affirmation of some incompatible perspective—i.e., pluralism or some incompatible exclusivistic perspective—the only rational option. And this, I believe, she can clearly do.

What this means, of course, is that if Hick is actually arguing that pluralism is the only rational option, then I think he is wrong. And his claim that pluralism "is considerably more probable" than exclusivism does, it must be granted, make it appear as if he believes pluralism to be the only hypothesis a knowledgeable theist can justifiably affirm.

But Hick never actually calls his opponents irrational in this context. That is, while Hick clearly believes that sincere, knowledgeable exclusivists are *wrong,* he has never to my knowledge claimed that they are guilty of violating the basic epistemic rules governing rational belief. Accordingly, it seems best to assume that Q1—a concern with what can be rationally affirmed—is not Hick's primary interest in this context.

But what then is it with which Hick is concerned? As we have seen, Q1 is defensive in nature. It asks for identification of conditions under which we can justifiably continue to affirm a belief we *already* hold. But *why* hold the specific religious beliefs we desire to defend? Why, specifically, choose to defend religious pluralism rather than exclusivism or vice versa? Or, to state this question of 'belief origin' more formally:

Q2: Given that an individual can be within her epistemic rights (can be rational) in affirming either exclusivism or pluralism, upon what basis should her actual choice be made?

This is the type of question in which I believe Hick is primarily interested.

Now, it might be tempting for a Reformed exclusivist to contend that she is exempt from the consideration of Q2. As I see it, she might begin, this question is based on the assumption that individuals consciously choose their religious belief systems. But the exclusivistic hypothesis which I affirm was not the result of a conscious attempt to choose the most plausible option. I have simply discovered this exclusivistic hypothesis formed in me in much the same fashion I find my visual and moral beliefs just formed in me. And thus Hick's question is simply irrelevant to my position.

But such a response will not do. There is no reason to deny that Reformed exclusivists do have, let's say, a Calvinistic religious hypothesis just formed in them. However, although almost everyone in every culture does in the appropriate context have similar 'tree-beliefs' just formed in them, there is no such unanimity within the religious realm. As Hick rightly points out, the religious belief that the overwhelming majority of people in any given culture find just formed in them is the dominant hypothesis of that culture or subculture. Moreover, the dominant religious hypotheses in most of these cultures are exclusivistic—i.e., incompatible with one another.

Accordingly, it seems to me that Hick can rightly be interpreted as offering the following challenge to the knowledgeable Reformed exclusivist (the exclusivist aware of pervasive religious diversity): I will grant that your exclusivistic beliefs were not originally the product of conscious deliberation. But given that most sincere theists initially go through a type of religious belief-forming process similar to yours and yet usually find formed in themselves the dominant exclusivistic hypotheses of their own culture, upon what basis can you justifiably continue to claim that the hypothesis you affirm has some special status just because you found it formed in you? Or, to state the question somewhat differently, Hick's analysis of religious diversity challenges knowledgeable Reformed exclusivists to ask themselves why they now believe that their religious belief-forming mechanisms are functioning properly while the analogous mechanisms in all others are faulty.

Some Reformed exclusivists, as we have seen, have a ready response. Because of 'the fall,' they maintain, most individuals suffer from religious epistemic blindness—i.e., do not possess properly functioning religious belief-forming mechanisms. Only our mechanisms are trustworthy. However, every exclusivistic religious tradition can—and many do—make such claims. Hence, an analogous Hickian question again faces knowledgeable Reformed exclusivists: Why do you believe that only those religious belief-forming mechanisms which produce exclusivistic beliefs compatible with yours do not suffer from epistemic blindness?

Reformed exclusivists cannot at this point argue that they have found this belief just formed in them for it is *now* the reliability of the belief-forming mechanism, itself, which is being questioned. Nor, since they are anti-foundationalists, can Reformed exclusivists argue that the evidence demonstrates conclusively that their religious position is correct. So upon what then can they base their crucial belief that their belief-forming mechanisms *alone* produce true beliefs?

They must, it seems to me, ultimately fall back on the contention that their belief-forming mechanisms can alone be trusted because that set of beliefs thus generated appears to them to form the most plausible religious explanatory hypothesis available. But to respond in this fashion brings them into basic methodological agreement with Hick's position on Q2. That is, it appears that knowledgeable Reformed exclusivists must ultimately maintain with Hick that when attempting to discover which of the many self-consistent hypotheses that *can* rationally be affirmed is the one that *ought* to be affirmed, a person must finally decide which hypothesis she believes best explains the phenomena. Or, to state this important point differently yet, what Hick's analysis of religious diversity demonstrates, I believe, is that even for those knowledgeable Reformed exclusivists who claim to find their religious perspectives just formed in them, a conscious choice among competing religious hypotheses is ultimately called for.

This is not to say, it must again be emphasized, that such Reformed exclusivists must attempt to 'prove' their choice is best. But, given the culturally relative nature of religious belief-forming mechanisms, a simple appeal to such a mechanism seems inadequate as a basis for such exclusivists to continue to affirm their perspective. It seems rather that knowledgeable exclusivists must ultimately make a conscious decision whether to retain the religious hypothesis that has been formed in them or choose another. And it further appears that they should feel some prima facie obligation to consider the available options—consciously consider the nature of the various religious hypotheses formed in people—before doing so.

Now, of course, to agree that such a comparative analysis should be undertaken is not to say that Hick's pluralistic hypothesis, is, in fact, the most plausible alternative. I agree with the Reformed exclusivist that 'plausibility' is a very subjective concept. Thus, I doubt that the serious consideration of the competing explanatory hypotheses for religious phenomena, even by knowledgeable open-minded individuals, will produce consensus.

However, I do not see this as in any sense diminishing the importance of engaging in the type of comparative analysis suggested. For even if such comparative assessment will not lead to consensus, it will produce two significant benefits. First, only by such assessment, I feel, can a person acquire 'ownership' of her religious hypothesis. That is, only by such an assessment can she insure herself that her belief is not solely the product of environmental conditioning. Second, such an assessment should lead all concerned to be more tolerant of those with whom they ultimately disagree. And in an age where radical religious exclusivism again threatens world peace, I believe such tolerance to be of inestimable value.

This does not mean, let me again emphasize in closing, that the consideration of Q1—the consideration of the conditions under which a religious hypothesis can be rationally affirmed—is unimportant or even less important than the consideration of Q2. It is crucial that we recognize who must actually shoulder the 'burden of proof' in this context. And we need to thank Reformed exclusivists for helping us think more clearly about this matter. But I fear that a preoccupation with Q1 can keep us from seeing the importance of Q2— the consideration of the basis upon which we choose the hypothesis to be defended—and the comparative assessments of hypotheses to which such consideration leads us. And we need to thank pluralists such as Hick for drawing our attention to this fact.

VIII.4   Faith as Ultimate Concern

PAUL TILLICH

Paul Tillich (1886–1965), one of the most influential Christian thinkers of our time, fled his native Germany for the United States when Hitler came to power. He taught theology at Union Theological Seminary, Harvard University, and the University of Chicago Divinity School. In this essay, Tillich applies existentialist insights to the religious dimension and analyzes faith as ultimate concern, a state of being common to each human. The proper object of our deepest concern is the Ultimate, God. But God for Tillich is a mysterious Ground of all being, beyond the personal God of theism. In this sense, Tillich argues all religions and all worldviews contain religious value.

What Faith Is

1. Faith as Ultimate Concern

Faith is the state of being ultimately concerned: the dynamics of faith are the dynamics of man's ultimate concern. Man, like every living being, is concerned about many things, above all about those which condition his very existence, such as food and shelter. But man, in contrast to other living beings, has spiritual concerns—cognitive, aesthetic, social, political. Some of them are urgent, often extremely urgent, and each of them as well as the vital concerns can claim ultimacy for a human life or the life of a social group. If it claims ultimacy it demands the total surrender of him who accepts this claim, and it promises total fulfillment even if all other claims have to be subjected to it or rejected in its name. If a national group makes the life and growth of the nation its ultimate concern, it demands that all other concerns, economic well-be-

ing, health and life, family, aesthetic and cognitive truth, justice and humanity, be sacrificed. The extreme nationalisms of our century are laboratories for the study of what ultimate concern means in all aspects of human existence, including the smallest concern of one's daily life. Everything is centered in the only god, the nation—a god who certainly proves to be a demon, but who shows clearly the unconditional character of an ultimate concern.

But it is not only the unconditional demand made by that which is one's ultimate concern, it is also the promise of ultimate fulfillment which is accepted in the act of faith. The content of this promise is not necessarily defined. It can be expressed in indefinite symbols or in concrete symbols which cannot be taken literally, like the "greatness" of one's nation in which one participates even if one has died for it, or the conquest of mankind by the "saving race," etc. In each of these cases it is "ultimate fulfillment" that is promised, and it is exclusion from such fulfillment which is threatened if the unconditional demand is not obeyed.

An example—and more than an example—is the faith manifest in the religion of the Old Testament. It also has the character of ultimate concern in demand, threat and promise. The content of this concern is not the nation—although Jewish nationalism has sometimes tried to distort it into that—but the content is the God of justice, who, because he represents justice for everybody and every nation, is called the universal God, the God of the universe. He is the ultimate concern of every pious Jew, and therefore in his name the great commandment is given: "You shall love the Lord your God with all your heart, and with all your soul, and with all your might" (Deut. 6:5). This is what ultimate concern means and from these words the term "ultimate concern" is derived. They state unambiguously the character of genuine faith, the demand of total surrender to the subject of ultimate concern. The Old Testament is full of commands which make the nature of this surrender concrete, and it is full of promises and threats in relation to it. Here also are the promises of symbolic indefiniteness, although they center around fulfillment of the national and individual life, and the threat is the exclusion from such fulfillment through national extinction and individual catastrophe. Faith, for the men of the Old Testament, is the state of being ultimately and unconditionally concerned about Jahweh and about what he represents in demand, threat and promise.

Another example—almost a counter-example, yet nevertheless equally revealing—is the ultimate concern with "success" and with social standing and economic power. It is the god of many people in the highly competitive Western culture and it does what every ultimate concern must do: it demands unconditional surrender to its laws even if the price is the sacrifice of genuine human relations, personal conviction, and creative *eros*. Its threat is social and economic defeat, and its promise—indefinite as all such promises— the fulfillment of one's being. It is the breakdown of this kind of faith which characterizes and makes religiously important most contemporary literature. Not false calculations but a misplaced faith is revealed in novels like *Point of No Return*. When fulfilled, the promise of this faith proves to be empty.

Faith is the state of being ultimately concerned. The content matters infinitely for the life of the believer, but it does not matter for the formal definition of faith. And this is the first step we have to make in order to understand the dynamics of faith.

2. Faith as a Centered Act

Faith as ultimate concern is an act of the total personality. It happens in the center of the personal life and includes all its elements. Faith is the most centered act of the human mind. It is not a movement of a special section of a special function of man's total being. They all are united in the act of faith. But faith is not the sum total of their impacts. It transcends every special impact as well as the totality of them and it has itself a decisive impact on each of them.

Since faith is an act of the personality as a whole, it participates in the dynamics of personal life. These dynamics have been described in many ways, especially in the recent developments of analytic psychology. Thinking in polarities, their tensions and their possible conflicts, is a common characteristic of most of them. This makes the psychology of personality highly dynamic and requires a dynamic theory of faith as the most personal of all personal acts. The first and decisive polarity in analytic psychology is that between the so-called unconscious and the conscious. Faith as an act of the total personality is not imaginable without the participation of the unconscious elements in the personality structure. They are always present and decide largely about the content of faith. But, on the other hand, faith is a conscious act and the unconscious elements participate in the creation of faith only if they are taken into the personal center which transcends each of them. If this does not happen, if unconscious forces determine the mental status without a centered act, faith does not occur, and compulsions take its place. For faith is a matter of freedom. Freedom is nothing more than the possibility of centered personal acts. The frequent discussion in which faith and freedom are contrasted could be helped by the insight that faith is a free, namely, centered act of the personality. In this respect freedom and faith are identical.

Also important for the understanding of faith is the polarity between what Freud and his school call ego and superego. The concept of the superego is quite ambiguous. On the one hand, it is the basis of all cultural life because it restricts the uninhibited actualization of the always-driving libido; on the other hand, it cuts off man's vital forces, and produces disgust about the whole system of cultural restrictions, and brings about a neurotic state of mind. From this point of view, the symbols of faith are considered to be expressions of the superego or, more concretely, to be an expression of the father image which gives content to the superego. Responsible for this inadequate theory of the superego is Freud's naturalistic negation of norms and principles. If the superego is not established through valid principles, it becomes a suppressive tyrant. But real faith, even if it uses the father image for its expression, transforms this image into a principle of truth and justice to be defended even against the "father." Faith and culture can be affirmed only if the superego represents the norms and principles of reality.

This leads to the question of how faith as a personal, centered act is related to the rational structure of man's personality which is manifest in his meaningful language, in his ability to know the true and to do the good, in his sense of beauty and justice. All this, and not only his possibility to analyze, to calculate and to argue, makes him a rational being. But in spite of this larger concept of reason we must deny that man's essential nature is identical with the rational character of his mind. Man is able to decide for or against reason, he is able to create beyond reason or to destroy below reason. This power is the power of his self, the center of self-relatedness in which all elements of his being are united. Faith is not an act of any of his rational functions, as it is not an act of the unconscious, but it is an act is which both the rational and the nonrational elements of his being are transcended.

Faith as the embracing and centered act of the personality is "ecstatic." It transcends both the drives of the nonrational unconscious and the structures of the rational conscious. It transcends them, but it does not destroy them. The ecstatic character of faith does not exclude its rational character although it is not identical with it, and it includes nonrational strivings without being identical with them. In the ecstasy of faith there is an awareness of truth and of ethical value; there are also past loves and hates, conflicts and reunions, individual and collective influences. "Ecstasy" means "standing outside of oneself"—without ceasing to be oneself—with all the elements which are united in the personal center.

A further polarity in these elements, relevant for the understanding of faith, is the tension between the cognitive function of man's personal life, on the one hand, and emotion and will, on the other hand. In a later discussion I will try to show that many distortions of the meaning of faith are rooted in the attempt to subsume faith to the one or the other of these functions. At this point it must be stated as

sharply and insistently as possible that in every act of faith there is cognitive affirmation, not as the result of an independent process of inquiry but as an inseparable element in a total act of acceptance and surrender. This also excludes the idea that faith is the result of an independent act of "will to believe." There is certainly affirmation by the will of what concerns one ultimately, but faith is not a creation of the will. In the ecstasy of faith the will to accept and to surrender is an element, but not the cause. And this is true also of feeling. Faith is not an emotional outburst: this is not the meaning of ecstasy. Certainly, emotion is in it, as in every act of man's spiritual life. But emotion does not produce faith. Faith has a cognitive content and is an act of the will. It is the unity of every element in the centered self. Of course, the unity of all elements in the act of faith does not prevent one or the other element from dominating in a special form of faith. It dominates the character of faith but it does not create the act of faith.

This also answers the question of a possible psychology of faith. Everything that happens in man's personal being can become an object of psychology. And it is rather important for both the philosopher of religion and the practical minister to know how the act of faith is embedded in the totality of psychological processes. But in contrast to this justified and desirable form of a psychology of faith there is another one which tries to derive faith from something that is not faith but is most frequently fear. The presupposition of this method is that fear or something else from which faith is derived is more original and basic than faith. But this presupposition cannot be proved. On the contrary, one can prove that in the scientific method which leads to such consequences faith is already effective. Faith precedes all attempts to derive it from something else, because these attempts are themselves based on faith.

3. The Source of Faith

We have described the act of faith and its relation to the dynamics of personality. Faith is a total and centered act of the personal self, the act of unconditional, infinite and ultimate concern. The question now arises: what is the source of this all-embracing and all-transcending concern? The word "concern" points to two sides of a relationship, the relation between the one who is concerned and his concern. In both respects we have to imagine man's situation in itself and in his world. The reality of man's ultimate concern reveals something about his being, namely, that he is able to transcend the flux of relative and transitory experiences of his ordinary life. Man's experiences, feelings, thoughts are conditioned and finite. They not only come and go, but their content is of finite and conditional concern—unless they are elevated to unconditional validity. But this presupposes the general possibility of doing so; it presupposes the element of infinity in man. Man is able to understand in an immediate personal and central act the meaning of the ultimate, the unconditional, the absolute, the infinite. This alone makes faith a human potentiality.

Human potentialities are powers that drive toward actualization. Man is driven toward faith by his awareness of the infinite to which he belongs, but which he does not own like a possession. This is in abstract terms what concretely appears as the "restlessness of the heart" within the flux of life.

The unconditional concern which is faith is the concern about the unconditional. The infinite passion, as faith has been described, is the passion for the infinite. Or, to use our first term, the ultimate concern is concern about what is experienced as ultimate. In this way we have turned from the subjective meaning of faith as a centered act of the personality to its objective meaning, to what is meant in the act of faith. It would not help at this point of our analysis to call that which is meant in the act of faith "God" or "a god." For at this step we ask: What in the idea of God constitutes divinity? The answer is: It is the element of the unconditional and of ultimacy. This carries the quality of divinity. If this is seen, one can understand why almost every thing "in heaven and on earth" has received ultimacy in the history of human religion. But we also can understand that a critical principle was and is at work in man's religious consciousness, namely, that which is really ultimate over against what

claims to be ultimate but is only preliminary, transitory, finite.

The term "ultimate concern" unites the subjective and the objective side of the act of faith—the *fides qua creditur* (the Faith through which one believes) and the *fides quae creditur* (the faith which is believed). The first is the classical term for the centered act of the personality, the ultimate concern. The second is the classical term for that toward which this act is directed, the ultimate itself, expressed in symbols of the divine. This distinction is very important, but not ultimately so, for the one side cannot be without the other. There is no faith without a content toward which it is directed. There is always something meant in the act of faith. And there is no way of having the content of faith except in the act of faith. All speaking about divine matters which is not done in the state of ultimate concern is meaningless. Because that which is meant in the act of faith cannot be approached in any other way than through an act of faith.

In terms like ultimate, unconditional, infinite, absolute, the difference between subjectivity and objectivity is overcome. The ultimate of the act of faith and the ultimate that is meant in the act of faith are one and the same. This is symbolically expressed by the mystics when they say that their knowledge of God is the knowledge God has of himself; and it is expressed by Paul when he says (I Cor. 13) that he will know as he is known, namely, by God. God never can be object without being at the same time subject. Even a successful prayer is, according to Paul (Rom. 8), not possible without God as Spirit praying within us. The same experience expressed in abstract language is the disappearance of the ordinary subject-object scheme in the experience of the ultimate, the unconditional. In the act of faith that which is the source of this act is present beyond the cleavage of subject and object. It is present as both and beyond both.

This character of faith gives an additional criterion for distinguishing true and false ultimacy. The finite which claims infinity without having it (as, e.g., a nation or success) is not able to transcend the subject-object scheme. It remains an object which the believer looks at as a subject. He can approach it with ordinary knowledge and subject it to ordinary handling. There are, of course, many degrees in the endless realm of false ultimacies. The nation is nearer to true ultimacy than is success. Nationalistic ecstasy can produce a state in which the subject is almost swallowed by the object. But after a period the subject emerges again, disappointed radically and totally, and by looking at the nation in a skeptical and calculating way does injustice even to its justified claims. The more idolatrous a faith the less it is able to overcome the cleavage between subject and object. For that is the difference between true and idolatrous faith. In true faith the ultimate concern is a concern about the truly ultimate; while in idolatrous faith preliminary, finite realities are elevated to the rank of ultimacy. The inescapable consequence of idolatrous faith is "existential disappointment," a disappointment which penetrates into the very existence of man! This is the dynamics of idolatrous faith: that it is faith, and as such, the centered act of a personality; that the centering point is something which is more or less on to the periphery; and that, therefore, the act of faith leads to a loss of the center and to a disruption of the personality. The ecstatic character of even an idolatrous faith can hide this consequence only for a certain time. But finally it breaks into the open.

Symbols of Faith

1. The Meaning of Symbol

Man's ultimate concern must be expressed symbolically, because symbolic language alone is able to express the ultimate. This statement demands explanation in several respects. In spite of the manifold research about the meaning and function of symbols which is going on in contemporary philosophy, every writer who uses the term "symbol" must explain his understanding of it.

Symbols have one characteristic in common with signs; they point beyond themselves to something else. The red sign at the street corner points to the order to stop the movements of cars at certain intervals. A red light and the stopping of cars have essentially no relation to each other, but conventionally they are united as long as the convention

lasts. The same is true of letters and numbers and partly even words. They point beyond themselves to sounds and meanings. They are given this special function by convention within a nation or by international conventions, as the mathematical signs. Sometimes such signs are called symbols; but this is unfortunate because it makes the distinction between signs and symbols more difficult. Decisive is the fact that signs do not participate in the reality of that to which they point, while symbols do. Therefore, signs can be replaced for reasons of expediency or convention, while symbols cannot.

This leads to the second characteristic of the symbol: It participates in that to which it points: the flag participates in the power and dignity of the nation for which it stands. Therefore, it cannot be replaced except after an historic catastrophe that changes the reality of the nation which it symbolizes. An attack on the flag is felt as an attack on the majesty of the group in which it is acknowledged. Such an attack is considered blasphemy.

The third characteristic of a symbol is that it opens up levels of reality which otherwise are closed for us. All arts create symbols for a level of reality which cannot be reached in any other way. A picture and a poem reveal elements of reality which cannot be approached scientifically. In the creative work of art we encounter reality in a dimension which is closed for us without such works. The symbol's fourth characteristic not only opens up dimension and elements of reality which otherwise would remain unapproachable but also unlocks dimensions and elements of our soul which correspond to the dimensions and elements of reality. A great play gives us not only a new vision of the human scene, but it opens up hidden depths of our own being. Thus we are able to receive what the play reveals to us in reality. There are within us dimensions of which we cannot become aware except through symbols, as melodies and rhythms in music.

Symbols cannot be produced intentionally—this is the fifth characteristic. They grow out of the individual or collective unconscious and cannot function without being accepted by the unconscious dimension of our being. Symbols which have an especially social function, as political and religious symbols, are created or at least accepted by the collective unconscious of the group in which they appear.

The sixth and last characteristics of the symbol is a consequence of the fact that symbols cannot be invented. Like living beings, they grow and they die. They grow when the situation is ripe for them, and they die when the situation changes. The symbol of the "king" grew in a special period of history, and it died in most parts of the world in our period. Symbols do not grow because people are longing for them, and they do not die because of scientific or practical criticism. They die because they no longer produce response in the group where they originally found expression.

These are the main characteristics of every symbol. Genuine symbols are created in several spheres of man's cultural creativity. We have mentioned already the political and the artistic realm. We could add history and, above all, religion, whose symbols will be our particular concern.

2. Religious Symbols

We have discussed the meaning of symbols generally because, as we said, man's ultimate concern must be expressed symbolically! One may ask: Why can it not be expressed directly and properly? If money, success or the nation is someone's ultimate concern, can this not be said in a direct way without symbolic language? Is it not only in those cases in which the content of the ultimate concern is called "God" that we are in the realm of symbols? The answer is that everything which is a matter of unconditional concern is made into a god. If the nation is someone's ultimate concern, the name of the nation becomes a sacred name and the nation receives divine qualities which far surpass the reality of the being and functioning of the nation. The nation then stands for and symbolizes the true ultimate, but in an idolatrous way. Success as ultimate concern is not the national desire of actualizing potentialities, but is readiness to sacrifice all other values of life for the sake of a position of power and social predominance. The anxiety about not being a success is an idolatrous form of the anxiety

about divine condemnation. Success is grace; lack of success, ultimmate judgment. In this way concepts designating ordinary realities become idolatrous symbols of ultimate concern.

The reason for this transformation of concepts into symbols is the character of ultimacy and the nature of faith. That which is the true ultimate transcends the realm of finite reality infinitely. Therefore, no finite reality can express it directly and properly. Religiously speaking, God transcends his own name. This is why the use of his name easily becomes an abuse or a blasphemy. Whatever we say about that which concerns us ultimately, whether or not we call it God, has a symbolic meaning. It points beyond itself while participating in that to which it points. In no other way can faith express itself adequately. The language of faith is the language of symbols. If faith were what we have shown that it is not, such an assertion could not be made. But faith, understood as the state of being ultimately concerned, has no language other than symbols. When saying this I always expect the question: Only a symbol? He who asks this question shows that he has not understood the difference between signs and symbols nor the power of symbolic language, which surpasses in quality and strength the power of any nonsymbolic language. One should never say "only a symbol," but one should say "not less than a symbol." With this in mind we can now describe the different kinds of symbols of faith.

The fundamental symbol of our ultimate concern is God. It is always present in any act of faith, even if the act of faith includes the denial of God. Where there is ultimate concern, God can be denied only in the name of God. One God can deny the other one. Ultimate concern cannot deny its own character as ultimate. Therefore, it affirms what is meant by the word "God." Atheism, consequently, can only mean the attempt to remove any ultimate concern—to remain unconcerned about the meaning of one's existence. Indifference toward the ultimate question is the only imaginable form of atheism. Whether it is possible is a problem which must remain unsolved at this point. In any case, he who denies God as a matter of ultimate concern affirms God, because he affirms ultimacy in his concern. God is the fundamental symbol for what concerns us ultimately. Again it would be completely wrong to ask: So God is nothing but a symbol? Because the next question has to be: A symbol for what? And then the answer would be: For God! God is symbol for God. This means that in the notion of God we must distinguish two elements: the element of ultimacy, which is a matter of immediate experience and not symbolic in itself, and the element of concreteness, which is taken from our ordinary experience and symbolically applied to God. The man whose ultimate concern is a sacred tree has both the ultimacy of concern and the concreteness of the tree which symbolizes his relation to the ultimate. The man who adores Apollo is ultimately concerned, but not in an abstract way. His ultimate concern is symbolized in the divine figure of Apollo. The man who glorifies Yahweh, the God of the Old Testament, has both an ultimate concern and a concrete image of what concerns him ultimately. This is the meaning of the seemingly cryptic statement that God is the symbol of God. In this qualified sense God is the fundamental and universal content of faith.

It is obvious that such an understanding of the meaning of God makes the discussions about the existence or nonexistence of God meaningless. It is meaningless to question the ultimacy of an ultimate concern. This element in the idea of God is in itself certain. The symbolic expression of this element varies endlessly through the whole history of mankind. Here again it would be meaningless to ask whether one or another of the figures in which an ultimate concern is symbolized does "exist." If "existence" refers to something which can be found within the whole of reality, no divine being exists. The question is not this, but: which of the innumerable symbols of faith is most adequate to the meaning of faith? In other words, which symbol of ultimacy expresses the ultimate without idolatrous elements? This is the problem, and not the so-called "existence of God"—which is in itself an impossible combination of words. God as the ultimate in man's ultimate concern is more certain than any other certainty, even that of oneself. God as symbolized in a divine figure is a matter of daring faith, of courage and risk.

God is the basic symbol of faith, but not the only one. All the qualities we attribute to him, power, love, justice, are taken from finite experiences and applied symbolically to that which is beyond finitude and infinity. If faith calls God "almighty," it uses the human experience of power in order to symbolize the content of its infinite concern, but it does not describe a highest being who can do as he pleases. So it is with all the other qualities and with all the actions, past, present and future, which men attribute to God. They are symbols, taken from our daily experience, and not information about what God did once upon a time or will do sometime in the future. Faith is not the belief in such stories, but it is the acceptance of symbols that express our ultimate concern in terms of divine actions.

Another group of symbols of faith are manifestations of the divine in things and events, in persons and communities, in words and documents. This whole realm of sacred objects is a treasure of symbols. Holy things are not holy in themselves, but they point beyond themselves to the source of all holiness, that which is of ultimate concern.

3. Symbols and Myths

The symbols of faith do not appear in isolation. They are united in "stories of the gods," which is the meaning of the Greek word "mythos"—myth. The gods are individualized figures, analogous to human personalities, sexually differentiated, descending from each other, related to each other in love and struggle, producing world and man, acting in time and space. They participate in human greatness and misery, in creative and destructive works. They give to man cultural and religious traditions, and defend these sacred rites. They help and threaten the human race, especially some families, tribes or nations. They appear in epiphanies and incarnations, establish sacred places, rites and persons, and thus create a cult. But they themselves are under the command and threat of a fate which is beyond everything that is. This is mythology as developed most impressively in ancient Greece. But many of these characteristics can be found in every mythology. Usually the mythological gods are not equals. There is a hierarchy, at the top of which is a ruling god, as in Greece; or a trinity of them, as in India; or a duality of them, as in Persia. There are savior-gods who mediate between the highest gods and man, sometimes sharing the suffering and death of man in spite of their essential immortality. This is the world of the myth, great and strange, always changing but fundamentally the same: man's ultimate concern symbolized in divine figures and actions. Myths are symbols of faith combined in stories about divine-human encounters.

Myths are always present in every act of faith, because the language of faith is the symbol. They are also attacked, criticized and transcended in each of the great religions of mankind. The reason for this criticism is the very nature of the myth. It uses material from our ordinary experience. It puts the stories of the gods into the framework of time and space although it belongs to the nature of the ultimate to be beyond time and space. Above all, it divides the divine into several figures, removing ultimacy from each of them without removing their claim to ultimacy. This inescapably leads to conflicts of ultimate claims, able to destroy life, society, and consciousness.

The criticism of the myth first rejects the division of the divine and goes beyond it to one God, although in different ways according to the different types of religion. Even one God is an object of mythological language, and if spoken about is drawn into the frame work of time and space. Even he loses his ultimacy if made to be the content of concrete concern. Consequently, the criticism of the myth does not end with the rejection of the polytheistic mythology.

Monotheism also falls under the criticism of the myth. It needs, as one says today, "demythologization." This word has been used in connection with the elaboration of the mythical elements in stories and symbols of the Bible, both of the Old and the New Testaments—stories like those of the Paradise, of the fall of Adam, of the great Flood, of the Exodus from Egypt, of the virgin birth of the Messiah, of many of his miracles, of his resurrection and ascension, of his expected return as the judge of the universe. In short, all the stories in which divine-human interactions are told are considered as mythological in character, and objects of demythologization. What does this negative and artificial term mean? It must be accepted and supported if it points to the necessity of recognizing a symbol as a symbol and a myth as a myth. It must be attacked and rejected if it means the removal of symbols and myths altogether. Such an attempt is the third step in the criticism of the myth. It is an attempt which never can be successful, because symbol and myth are forms of the human consciousness which are always present. One can replace one myth by another, but one cannot remove the myth from man's spiritual life. For the myth is the combination of symbols of our ultimate concern.

A myth which is understood as a myth, but not removed or replaced, can be called a "broken myth." Christianity denies by its very nature any unbroken myth, because its presupposition is the first commandment: the affirmation of the ultimate as ultimate and the rejection of any kind of idolatry. All mythological elements in the Bible, and doctrine and liturgy should be recognized as mythological, but they should be maintained in their symbolic form and not be replaced by scientific substitutes. For there is no substitute for the use of symbols and myths: they are the language of faith.

The radical criticism of the myth is due to the fact that the primitive mythological consciousness resists the attempt to interpret the myth of myth. It is afraid of every act of demythologization. It believes that the broken myth is deprived of its truth and of its convincing power. Those who live in an unbroken mythological world feel safe and certain. They resist, often fanatically, any attempt to introduce an element of uncertainty by "breaking the myth," namely, by making conscious its symbolic character. Such resistance is supported by authoritarian systems, religious or political, in order to give security to the people under their control and unchallenged power to those who exercise the control. The resistance against demythologization expresses itself in "literalism." The symbols and myths are understood in their immediate meaning. The material, taken from nature and history, is used in its proper sense. The character of the symbol to point beyond itself to something else is disregarded.

Creation is taken as a magic act which happened once upon a time. The fall of Adam is localized on a special geographical point and attributed to a human individual. The virgin birth of the Messiah is understood in biological terms, resurrection and ascension as physical events, the second coming of the Christ as a telluric, or cosmic, catastrophe. The presupposition of such literalism is that God is a being, acting in time and space, dwelling in a special place, affecting the course of events and being affected by them like any other being in the universe. Literalism deprives God of his ultimacy and, religiously speaking, of his majesty. It draws him down to the level of that which is not ultimate, the finite and conditional. In the last analysis it is not rational criticism of the myth which is decisive but the inner religious criticism. Faith, if it takes its symbols literally, becomes idolatrous! It calls something ultimate which is less than ultimate. Faith, conscious of the symbolic character of its symbols, gives God the honor which is due him.

One should distinguish two stages of literalism, the natural and the reactive. The natural stage of literalism is that in which the mythical and the literal are indistinguishable. The primitive period of individuals and groups consists in the inability to separate the creations of symbolic imagination from the facts which can be verified through observation and experiment. This stage has a full right of its own and should not be disturbed, either in individuals or in groups, up to the moment when man's questioning mind breaks the natural acceptance of the mythological visions as literal. If, however, this moment has come, two ways are possible. The one is to replace the unbroken by the broken myth. It is the objectively demanded way, although it is impossible for many people who prefer the repression of their questions to the uncertainty which appears with the breaking of the myth. They are forced into the second stage of literalism, the conscious one, which is aware of the questions but represses them, half consciously, half unconsciously. The tool of repression is usually an acknowledged authority with sacred qualities like the Church or the Bible,

to which one owes unconditional surrender. This stage is still justifiable, if the questioning power is very weak and can easily be answered. It is unjustifiable if a mature mind is broken in its personal center by political or psychological methods, split in his unity, and hurt in his integrity. The enemy of a critical theology is not natural literalism but conscious literalism with repression of and aggression toward autonomous thought.

Symbols of faith cannot be replaced by other symbols, such as artistic ones, and they cannot be removed by scientific criticism. They have a genuine standing in the human mind, just as science and art have. Their symbolic character is their truth and their power. Nothing less than symbols and myths can express our ultimate concern.

One more question arises, namely, whether myths are able to express every kind of ultimate concern. For example, Christian theologians argue that the word "myth" should be reserved for natural myths in which repetitive natural processes, such as the seasons, are understood in their ultimate meaning. They believe that if the world is seen as a historical process with beginning, end and center, as in Christianity and Judaism, the term "myth" should not be used. This would radically reduce the realm in which the term would be applicable. Myth could not be understood as the language of our ultimate concern, but only as a discarded idiom of this language. Yet history proves that there are not only natural myths but also historical myths. If the earth is seen as the battleground of two divine powers, as in ancient Persia, this is an historical myth. If the God of creation selects and guides a nation through history toward an end which transcends all history, this is an historical myth. If the Christ—a transcendent, divine being—appears in the fullness of time, lives, dies and is resurrected, this is an historical myth. Christianity is superior to those religions which are bound to a natural myth. But Christianity speaks the mythological language like every other religion. It is a broken myth, but it is a myth; otherwise Christianity would not be an expression of ultimate concern.

VIII.5   God, Commitment, and Other Faiths: Pluralism Versus Relativism

J O S E P H   R U N Z O

Joseph Runzo is professor of philosophy at Chapman University in Orange, California, and the author of several works in the philosophy of religion. He has written this abstract of his article:

This paper addresses the challenge of the problem of religious pluralism: how can we remain fully committed to our most basic truth-claims about God, and yet take full account of the claims of other world religious traditions? Six possible responses to this problem are delineated and assessed. Among the possible responses, certain strengths are identified in Inclusivism, though it is rejected. Focusing then on Religious Pluralism and Religious Relativism, these two views are extensively compared and contrasted. Finally, Christian Relativism is defended on the grounds that it best incorporates the strengths, without the salient weaknesses, of other possible responses to the conflicting truth-claims of the world religions.

Crises in religion historically precipitate revolutions in religious thought. Today, the impressive piety and evident rationality of the belief systems of *other* religious traditions, inescapably confronts Christians with a crisis—and a potential revolution. How should Christians respond responsibly to the conflicting claims of other faiths? More pointedly, should Christians abjure traditional claims to the one truth and the one way to salvation? As even Descartes (rather quaintly) observes in his *Discourse on Method,*

> . . . I further recognised in the course of my travels that all those whose sentiments are very contrary to ours are yet not necessarily barbarians or savages, but may be possessed of reason in as great or even a greater degree than ourselves. I also considered how very different the self-same man, identical in mind and spirit, may become, according as he is brought up from

childhood amongst the French or Germans, or has passed his whole life amongst Chinese or cannibals.

Religious beliefs, like many philosophical orientations, seem largely an accident of birth. If you are born in India, you are likely to be a Hindu; if born in France, you are likely to be a Christian. Moreover, on their own grounds, Buddhists and Muslims and adherents of other great religious faiths, seem rationally justified in their beliefs. This raises the *problem of religious pluralism:* the mutually conflicting systems of truth-claims of the world's religions, if taken separately, appear rationally justified—but are they *correct?* Is only one system of religious truth-claims correct, is more than one system correct, or are all religious systems mistaken?

Descartes, concluding from the diversity of opinion which he observed that "it is much more custom and example that persuade us than any certain knowledge," attempts to arrive at a method for attaining certainty, despite the fact that "there is nothing imaginable so strange or so little credible that it has not been maintained by one philosopher or other." Likewise, is there one correct religious system, and can we know what it is? Or is the search for universal or certain truth in religious matters as overambitious as Descartes was philosophically overly ambitious?

A major problem with the desire for a comforting certainty in religious matters is identified in Tillich's observation that the church has become all too insular: "theologians have become careless in safeguarding their idea of a personal God from slipping into 'henotheistic' mythology (the belief in *one* god who, however, remains particular and bound to a particular group)." But if henotheism poses a danger on one side, a too ready acceptance of pluralism in religion poses a danger on the other side. For an uncritical pluralism undermines the strength of commitment of faith. How then can we

Reprinted from *Faith and Philosophy* Vol. 5:4, October 1988 by permission. Endnotes deleted.

both remain fully committed to our most basic truth-claims about God, and at the same time take full account of religious pluralism? Christians today must be responsive to other faiths, but responsive *within* the Christian vision expressed in the Vatican II Declaration *Nostra Aetate:* ". . . all peoples comprise a single community, and have a single origin . . . God . . . One also is their final goal: God."

After explaining why the problem of religious pluralism is a problem of conflicting *truth*-claims, I will set out six possible responses, religious and nonreligious, to the conflicting truth-claims of the world's religions. Then I will assess each response in turn from an external, religious (but not necessarily Christian) point of view, ultimately focusing on the Pluralist and Relativist responses. I will end by defending the Relativist response from an internal, Christian perspective, and explain how it incorporates strengths, without some of the salient weaknesses, of other possible responses to the conflicting truth-claims of the world religions.

I

In the *Dynamics of Faith,* Tillich suggests that "The conflict between religions is not a conflict between forms of belief, but it is a conflict between expressions of our ultimate concern . . . . All decisions of faith are existential, not thoeretical, decisions." It *would* be a gross distortion of faith to reduce it to merely theoretical concerns or to questions of belief. But in avoiding this intellectualist distortion of faith Tillich is mistaken to suggest that the conflict between religions is not a conflict between truth-claims. True, a religious way of life importantly involves such elements as ritual and symbols, and a moral ordering of one's life. But our beliefs, or more comprehensively, our worldviews—i.e., the total cognitive web of our interrelated concepts, beliefs, and processes of rational thought—determine the very nature of our ultimate concern. For all experience, understanding, and praxis—whether it concerns the mundane or the *mysterium tremendum*—is structured by our worldviews. Consequently, conflicts between religious traditions fundamentally stem from conflicts of belief, con-

flicts over specific claims about how meaning and value are to be achieved, and what is the desired telos for humankind.

In assessing the conflict of truth-claims among world religions it must be kept in mind that a religion is not itself true or false any more than any other human institution such as art, government, or law, is in and of itself true or false. A total institution—aesthetic, political, legal, or religious—is only more or less expedient, only more or less effective in meeting its intended goals. What is true or false, and what is most fundamentally in conflict between such systems, are the underlying, specific truth-claims within the systems. Now, in the conflict of religious truth-claims, all of the world's major religions agree that the divine, or the Absolute, or the Real, is One, transcends the natural order, and is ultimately inexpressible. As *Ecclesiastes* puts it, God "has put eternity into man's mind, yet so that he cannot find out what God has done from the beginning to the end." (Eccles. 3:11, RSV) But though they have this general point of agreement, and though each religious tradition includes truth-claims and even scriptural material which is expendable, there is a fundamental or "vital core" of beliefs in each religion which is definitive of that very tradition. And it is particular elements of this "vital core" of beliefs that are incompatible among world religions.

For instance, there is no intractable conflict between claims in the Muslim tradition that Mahdis will periodically appear to revive faith in God, and orthodox Christian claims that Jesus represents the final prophetic revelation of God. For Christians could come to accept, and Sunnis could come to reject, further prophetic revelations from God *via* Mahdis, without impugning the respective orthodox status of Jesus or Mohammed. But traditionally it *is* essential to monotheistic traditions, like Christianity, Islam, Judaism and Ramanujan Hinduism, that the correct human perception of the divine is the perception of a personal deity. In contrast, on a Hinayana (Theravada) Buddhist view, God does not exist, and in much of the Hindu tradition, the notion of a personal deity is talk about an illusory state of affairs bound to this life. Or, to take another trenchant conflict among religious truth-claims, consider some of the diverse notions of the relation of humanity to Ultimate Reality. In Hinayana Buddhism there is no real question of one's relation to ultimate reality, for the goal of liberation is the complete extinction of the ego; in Islam the basic human relation to God is one of slave to master; in orthodox Judaism the central relation is one of a servant to his or her God.

Thus, because they make essentially different truth-claims, different religious traditions are structured by *essentially* different worldviews, offering *essentially* different paths to what is perceived as Ultimate Reality. Since a person's worldview, then, is inherently constitutive of their religious way of life, the question is whether the differences in *truth-claims* among the world religions, and the consequent differences in the (putative) paths to Ultimate Reality, are significant or ultimately irrelevant.

We can also see that the conflict among the world religions is fundamentally a conflict of *truth-claims* if we consider the meaning of "faith" and of "religion." Faith is the more encompassing notion. Faith can be either religious or non-religious: we speak of faith in the progress of science or in the inevitableness of dialectical materialism, as much as of Christian or Muslim faith. Therefore, I will use the term "faith" to refer to a person's fundamental commitment to any worldview, a commitment which is a total dispositional state of the person involving affective, conative, and cognitive elements.

Religion, on the other hand, involves a particular form of faith, focused within a specific religious tradition. To distinguish religious from non-religious faith, I will define a religion or religious tradition as a set of symbols and rituals, myths and stories, concepts and truth-claims, which a community believes gives ultimate meaning to life, *via* its connection to a transcendent God or Ultimate Reality *beyond* the natural order. Thus religion is a *human* construct (or institution) which fundamentally involves beliefs at two levels: (I) it involves the meta-belief that the religion in question does indeed refer to a transcendent reality which gives meaning to life, and (II) it involves specific beliefs— including vital core beliefs—about the nature of that ultimate reality and the way in which it gives

meaning to life. The first sort of belief, (I), is shared by the world religions. The second sort of belief, (II), is the point of conflict among the world religions.

II

There are six possible responses, religious and non-religious, to the conflicting truth-claims of vital core beliefs among the world religions:

1. *Atheism:* all religions are mistaken.
2. *Religious Exclusivism:* only one world religion is correct, and all others are mistaken.
3. *Religious Inclusivism:* only one world religion is fully correct, but other world religions participate in or partially reveal some of the truth of the one correct religion.
4. *Religious Subjectivism:* each world religion is correct, and each is correct insofar as it is best for the individual who adheres to it.
5. *Religious Pluralism:* ultimately all world religions are correct, each offering a different, salvific path and partial perspective *vis-a-vis* the one Ultimate Reality.
6. *Religious Relativism:* at least one, and probably more than one, world religion is correct, and the correctness of a religion is relative to the worldview(s) of its community of adherents.

One obvious response to the conflicting truth-claims of the world's religions is the Atheist response, (1). It is not most plausible, given the enormity of the conflict among truth-claims, that all religious traditions are simply false in different ways, rather than that one is correct, or that *several* are correct in different ways? In the absence of a generally acceptable deductive proof or inductive proof with a high probability, for the existence of God or the Absolute, there is no incontrovertible reply to this query. Indeed, there are important sociological and psychological arguments, like those of Feuerbach and Freud, which lend support to the Atheist response.

At stake here is the basic religious presupposition that only reference to a transcendent divine or ultimate reality gives ultimate meaning to human life. This meta-belief (I) is supported in the various religious traditions by appeals to religious experience, purported transformations of people's lives, the claimed necessity of a "leap of faith," and so on. These are internal considerations which will not, of course, prove that the Atheist response (1) must be mistaken. But in this discussion we can set aside the Atheist response if we take the basic religious meta-belief (I) as a presupposition.

Turning to the second response, Exclusivism in its strongest form is exemplified by the traditional Roman Catholic dogma, *Extra ecclesiam nulla salus.* Exclusivism is the view that salvation can only be found either (as in the dogma just cited) inside a particular *institutional* structure, or on the basis of a specified tradition of religious beliefs, symbols, and rituals—e.g., as Karl Barth says of Christianity, "the Christian religion is true, because it has pleased God, who alone can be the judge in this matter, to affirm it to be the true religion." But such unqualified Exclusivism seems untenable in the face of the problem of religious pluralism. In Ernst Troeltsch's words, regarding Christianity,

> a study of the non-Christian religions convinced me more and more that their naive claims to absolute validity are also genuinely such. I found Buddhism and Brahminism especially to be really humane and spiritual religions, capable of appealing in precisely the same way to the inner certitude and devotion of their followers as Christianity, . . .

Principal considerations against Exclusivism within *any* religious tradition include the following: Historically, it is largely a matter of geographical accident whether one grows up as a Hindu or Buddhist, Christian or Muslim, etc. Theologically, a strict reading of Exclusivism condemns the vast majority of humanity to perdition, which certainly appears contrary to the notion of a loving God, as well as seeming to contradict the idea of an Absolute which is the telos of all humankind. Ethically, Religious Exclusivism has the morally repugnant result of making those who have privileged knowledge, or who are intellectually astute, a religious elite, while penalizing those who happen to have no access to the putatively correct religious views, or who are incapable of advanced understanding. Sociologically, Exclusivism is a concomitant of sectarianism, serving as a rationale for enforcing discipline and communal cohesion. Epistemologically, one could not *know* with certainty that there is only one correct set of religious truth-claims or only one institutional structure providing a path to salvation—a consideration exacerbated by the fact that all religions at some point make Exclusivist claims. And religiously, Exclusivism is highly presumptuous, ignoring the fact that religious truth-claims are human constructs, human attempts to know Ultimate Reality, subject to the limitations and fallibility of the human mind.

It is of course possible that the Exclusivism of some particular religious tradition is correct. But given these weighty considerations against Exclusivism, we must turn to responses (3)–(6), responses that hold that in some form each of the great world religions is at least in part correctly directed toward the divine or Absolute. The problem is how to avoid the serious moral, theological, empirical, and epistemological deficiencies of Exclusivism without dissipating the very cohesiveness and vitality of one's own religious tradition which Exclusivism properly seeks to protect.

III

A natural alternative to take to meet these concerns is Inclusivism. This has become an especially prominent view in Roman Catholic theology since Vatican II. Religious Inclusivists jointly hold two theses: That other religions convey part of the truth about Ultimate Reality and the relation of humanity to Ultimate Reality, but that only one's own tradition most fully provides an understanding of Ultimate Reality, and most adequately provides a path to salvation. Thus, *Nostra Aetate* states both that "The Catholic Church rejects nothing which is true and holy in [other] religions," and that the cross of Christ "is the sign of God's all-embracing love" and "the fountain from which every grace flows."

From these foundations, Christian Inclusivism has been developed in considerable detail by Karl Rahner, who suggests that those in the non-Christian traditions can be "anonymous" Christians.

Since, Rahner suggests, " we have to keep in mind . . . the necessity of Christian faith *and* the universal salvific will of God's love and omnipotence,"

we can only reconcile them by saying that somehow all men must be capable of being members of the Church; and this capacity must not be understood merely in the sense of an abstract and purely logical possibility, but as a real and historically concrete one.

In the same vein, R. C. Zaehner offers an historical argument for Inclusivism:

The drive towards the integration of . . . the personal and the collective, has been characteristic of the most original thinkers in [all religions] during the first two-thirds of the twentieth century. . . . This unity in diversity is the birthright of the Catholic Church . . . all the other religions, in their historical development, grow into 'other Catholic Churches' . . . [For while one God] is the inspiration of all religions and peculiar to none . . . The only religion that has from the beginning been both communal and individual is Christianity.

Inclusivism is typically based on the notion that one's own religion most fully possesses a particular element which is most essential to religion. Zaehner looks to the integration of the personal and collective; Kant holds that true religiosity is identical to the moral life; Schleiermacher proposes that underlying genuine religion is "the feeling of absolute dependence"; Rudolph Otto emphasizes a numinous sense of the holy, a sense of the *mysterium tremendum; Nostra Aetate* declares that "from ancient times down to the present, there has existed among diverse peoples a certain perception of that hidden power which hovers over the course of things and over the events of human life"; and John Baillie suggests that all humans have a knowledge of God through a felt presence of the divine such that all people "already believe in him."

That other religious traditions, in accordance with the religious meta-belief (I), might provide some apprehension of Ultimate Reality, is not at issue here. Rather, Inclusivism supposes that a *particular* sort of apprehension and understanding of Ultimate Reality is elemental to all religion. However, in the first place we could not *know* that all humans have the same sort of elemental apprehension of Ultimate Reality. Second, the empirical evidence supports precisely the opposite supposi-

tion. Even in the broadest terms, the notion of an elemental apprehension of Ultimate Reality is understood in *personal* terms in the monotheistic traditions, while it is *non-personal* in Confucianism and in Hindu and Buddhist traditions. And third, each religion tends to see itself as the culmination of *the* elemental apprehension of Ultimate Reality: "other religions can have their own fulfillment theology. Sri Aurobindo sees the world religious process converging on Mother India rather than the Cosmic Christ, and Sir Muhammad Iqbal sees it converging upon a kind of ideal Islam."

So when Rahner, for example, says that the Christian has, "other things being equal, a still greater chance of salvation than someone who is merely an anonymous Christian," this can only be a statement of faith, not one of certain knowledge. Yet the strength of Inclusivism *is* this unequivocal faith—*within* an acceptance of other traditions—that one's own religion is salvific. Inclusivism expresses an appropriate religious disposition. But Inclusivism ultimately fails as a warranted epistemological thesis. This failure leads us to the pluralistic types of responses to the problem of religious pluralism.

IV

Subjectivism, Pluralism, and Relativism are all pluralistic responses to the conflicting truth-claims of world religions. All three views share a basic *idealist epistemology:* i.e., they share the basic assumption that the world we experience and understand is not the world independent of our perceiving but a world at least in part structured by our minds. Thus these pluralistic views share the epistemic view expressed in the Kantian dictum that "[sensible] intuitions without concepts are blind," a view sometimes expressed in the contemporary notion that all experiencing is experiencing-*as.* But further, they share the assumption that there is more than one set of human concepts—more than one worldview—which is valid for understanding the world. Thus they share the sort of *pluralist* epistemology expressed by William James in *The Varieties of Religious Experience:* "why in the name of common sense need we assume that only one . . . system of ideas can be true? The obvious outcome of our total experience is that the world can be handled according to many systems of ideas, . . ." The three pluralistic religious responses all hold that one's perception of religious truth is in some sense relative to one's worldview. Typically this view is supported on the grounds of the ineluctable enculturation or the historicity of all thought and experience, or, as in the Whorf hypothesis, by suggesting a necessary connection between language, which varies from community to community, and truth, which consequently varies.

The most radical of the pluralistic responses to the conflicting truth-claims of the world religions is Subjectivism, where religious truth and salvation are literally as varied as individuals are diverse. As a general view in epistemology, subjectivism is a form of relativism about truth. It is the extreme epistemological position that truth is relative to each individual's idiosyncratic worldview. Thus, on a Religious Subjectivist's view, religion is a radically private affair, often understood as purely a matter of one's individual relation to the divine or Absolute. But subjectivism, and therefore Religious Subjectivism, is conceptually incoherent. Truth-bearers are statements or propositions. Statements or propositions are comprised of concepts. And precisely what Wittgenstein's "private-language" argument demonstrates is that concepts are social constructions and cannot be purely private, individual understandings. Thus, since statements and propositions are comprised of concepts, and concepts are social constructs, truth cannot be idiosyncratically individualistic. Religious Subjectivism, then, must be rejected.

The two remaining pluralistic views, Religious Pluralism and Religious Relativism, are often conflated. John Hick offers a concise description of Pluralism as the view that "There is not merely one way but a plurality of ways of salvation or liberation . . . taking place in different ways within the contexts of all the great religious traditions." Pluralism holds that there is only one Ultimate Reality, but that Ultimate Reality is properly, though only partially, understood in different ways. Following a metaphor which Hick employs, just as the historian does not

have direct access to figures of history, and consequently different historians develop different perspectives on historical figures like Genghis Khan or Sun Yat-Sen because of historians' different methods of inquiry, cultural backgrounds, etc., so too, different religious traditions or different theologies, not having direct access to the divine, offer different encultured "images" of the one Ultimate Reality. On the Pluralist account, there is no ultimate conflict between these different perspectives, since there still remains one set of truths, even if those truths are imperfectly and only partially understood within each perspective. Religious Pluralism, then, focuses on the viability of different religious *perspectives* on Ultimate Reality.

Religious Relativism, in contrast, is directly a thesis about differences of religious *truth-claims.* The Religious Relativist minimally holds the general epistemic view, which I shall designate as "conceptual relativism," that first-order truth-claims about reality—e.g., that persons or that subatomic particles or that God exists—are relative to the worldview of a particular society. More precisely, a conceptual relativist definitively holds that, corresponding to differences of worldview, there are mutually incompatible, yet individually adequate, sets of conceptual-schema-relative truths. Thus for the Religious Relativist, unlike the Pluralist, truth itself is relative and plural.

However, Religious Pluralism and Religious Relativism do share two underlying Kantian theses. They share the Kantian metaphysical division (though the Kantian terminology may not be employed) between noumena and phenomena, distinguishing between God in Himself or the Absolute in itself, and God or the Absolute as humanly experienced. And as we have seen, they share the Kantian epistemic notion that all experience, and so all religious experience, is structured by the (culturally and historically conditioned) worldview of the percipient. Thus, Religious Pluralism and Religious Relativism hold that differences of religious perception cannot just be treated as a matter of some people simply being wrong about the nature of the divine Reality, but rather that such differences of perception are inherent to religious perception and conception. Given these points of fundamental agreement, which position, Pluralism or Relativism, better accounts for the conflicting truth-claims of the world religions?

V

An important exponent of Religious Pluralism is Wilfred Cantwell Smith. Cantwell Smith argues that the notions of "religion" and of "a religion" are obsolete. He holds that only God and humanity are "givens"—global universals—and that the centrality given to religion is misguided and the conception of a religion as a belief system mistaken. Rather than starting from a particular religious tradition and then considering God and humanity, one should start from God and humanity and consider particular religious traditions from this global perspective. Smith reaches the Pluralist conclusion that the one truth about the religious life of humankind is conveyed in the various Buddhist, Christian, Islamic, and so on, forms.

Quite correctly, I think, Smith is attempting to circumvent the obstacles which *religion* often places between humans and their response to the divine. But there are several problems with his approach. First, he suggests replacing the world-view(s) of particular religious traditions with another world-view on which it is presupposed that God and humanity are givens in the experience of all humans. This is neither a neutral world-view, nor one which will be shared by all religious persons. Many adherents of particular religious world-views would reject the generalized approach to the divine Cantwell Smith proposes as so amorphous that it fails to capture *their* religious beliefs. Second, Smith's position rests on the dubious thesis, which we have already addressed, that there *is* a universal, innate experience or conception of the divine. Smith himself effectively argues against *Christian* Exclusivism by asking: "how could one possibly know?" that only the Christian faith is correct. But the same argument is equally applicable to Smith's own position: how could one possibly *know* that there is a global, innate apprehension or "givenness" of God and humanity? If anything, the evidence most strongly supports the conclusion that all

humankind does not share the same innate concept or primal experience of Ultimate Reality, much less of the nature of God, or even of humanity, *per se*.

John Hick has developed another, rather impressive and comprehensive, Pluralist approach, in part by following out a key aspect of Cantwell Smith's work, *viz.* the rejection of the idea that a religion is fundamentally a set of beliefs. Proposing instead that religion definitively concerns "the transformation of human existence from self-centeredness to Reality-centeredness," Hick essentially argues that the apparently conflicting truth-claims of the world's religions are, in the final analysis, irrelevant, and that the world religions can be reconciled, and the integrity of each preserved, through this more fundamental shared goal of moving from self- to Reality-centeredness.

Hick explicitly employs the two Kantian theses underlying both Pluralism and Relativism. He employs the Kantian thesis that all experience is structured by the mind by suggesting that specific forms of religious awareness "are formed by the presence of the divine Reality, . . . coming to consciousness in terms of the different sets of religious concepts and structures of religious meaning that operate within the different religious traditions", i.e., as divine *personae* (e.g., Yahweh, Allah, etc.) for theists and *as* divine *impersonae* (e.g., Brahman, the Dharma, the Tao, etc.) for non-theists. Regarding the phenomenal/noumenal distinction, he supports the distinction between personal and non-personal divine phenomena and the Eternal noumenon, on the basis of what he takes to be strong inductive evidence from religious experience. And indeed we do find consistent differentiation in the world religions between Ultimate Reality as we experience it and as it is in itself. There is the Hindu distinction between *saguna* Brahman and *nirguna* Brahman; the Jewish Cabalistic distinction between the God of the Bible and En Soph; and in the Christian tradition, Eckhart's distinction between God *qua* Trinity and the Godhead itself, and more recently, Tillich's notion of "the God above the God of theism," and so on.

Hick does allow for the logical possibility that only one religion might be correct, but he thinks that the overwhelming facts of religious diversity make Religious Pluralism the most plausible response to the conflicting truth-claims of world religions. A comprehensive Religious Pluralism like Hick's fully confronts the diversity of religious truth-claims. As such, it is an admirable and helpful response to the challenge which these conflicting claims presents. But even so, Religious Pluralism has significant shortcomings.

VI

Religious Pluralism fails to adequately account for the necessary, central role of cognition in religious faith. Hick suggests that differences of belief among the world religions are

> of great philosophical importance as elements within our respective theories about the universe; but they are not of great *religious*, i.e. soteriological, importance. For different groups can hold incompatible sets of theories all of which constitute intellectual frameworks within which the process of salvation/liberation can proceed.

Of course, even incompatible theories can serve as guides to the same religious goal. But from this it neither follows that systems of belief and theory are irrelevant to guiding one to that goal, nor that it is unimportant which *particular* belief system one holds for reaching that end. Rather, the cognitive content of religious faith is essential for providing a coherent and sufficiently comprehensive view of reality as a basis for purposive action and an effective, directive guide to "salvation/liberation." Further, the *specific* cognitive content of one's faith is of paramount importance since it is precisely what delimits one's *specific* path to salvation/liberation. And the specific path to salvation/liberation is not just a means to an end but is itself an integral part of the goal of salvation/liberation. This is expressed in the New Testament in the idea that the Kingdom of God is not future but begins in the lives of those who enter the new covenant now: "asked by the Pharisees when the kingdom was coming, he [Jesus] answered them, 'The kingdom of God is not coming with signs to be observed; . . . the kindgom of God is in the midst of you.'" (Luke 17:20–21), RSV) Consequently, since the specific path to salvation/libera-

tion is itself part of that very salvation/liberation, a specific religious worldview is importantly constitutive of what makes a way of life a (particular) *religious* way of life.

Indeed, it would seem that specific religious cognitive content is essential to making it meaningful even to be committed at all to a religious way of life. True, de-emphasizing specific doctrines—such as the idea that the Christ-event is the definitive self-revelation of the divine—makes it easier to reconcile apparently conflicting religious truth-claims, especially the notion of a personal God with the notion of a non-personal Absolute. But the more such specific doctrines are set aside, the more questionable it becomes whether a *religious,* as opposed to a non-religious, commitment is what gives life ultimate significance. Insofar as the specificity of religious doctrines is de-emphasized, the basic religious meta-belief (I) that religion does indeed refer to a transcendent Reality which gives meaning to life becomes less plausible. The plausibility of (I) rests in large part on the evidence of religious experience. But as any hypothesis about the nature of reality is made more indefinite, the available inductive evidence to support that hypothesis is not increased, as for example Hick's defense of Religious Pluralism seems to suggest, but decreased. For evidence for an indefinite hypothesis is correspondingly indefinite or ambiguous.

Another difficulty with Religious Pluralism is this. Exactly what a recognition of pluralism in general seems to acknowledge is that humans, and human conceptions, fundamentally differ. But then, to the extent that the differences of human conception embedded in the world religions are regarded as inconsequential, the dignity of the individual and the value of each distinct community of faith is lessened.

To see how this applies to Christianity, consider Maurice Wiles' observation that, "there are two fundamental characteristics of the conception of God . . . it must be a profoundly personal concept, . . . And secondly it is God in relation to us with which we have to do." The Christian understanding that the universe is under the providence of a God who has revealed Himself as a personal being— One who understands and loves humanity—is and must be a conception of God as He manifests Himself *to us.* Yet this conception of an essentially *personal* God is not incidental but central to both corporate and individual Christian faith. Hick attempts to account for this by suggesting that among the world religions the Real is experienced as *either* personal or non-personal. While this Religious Pluralist view properly acknowledges that theistic understanding is an understanding of Ultimate Reality not *an sich* but *as* it confronts us in history, it obviates the significance of the Christian understanding of a personal God as *somehow* correctly revealing the nature of Ultimate Reality in itself. A personal reality might have non-personal aspects, but it could not be identical to something which is non-personal. Hence, this Pluralist account entails that the monotheist's experience of a *personal* divine reality *cannot,* to that extent, correctly represent the nature of the Real in itself.

Finally, Religious Pluralism is deficient insofar as it unintentionally undermines the sense of the reality of God. It is part of the fundamental metabelief (I) of religion that the God or the Absolute of which humans speak is real and not a metaphysical illusion or psychological delusion. But if the God of which monotheists speak is only an "image," only a perspective on an unknowable, noumenal reality, then the God history will not be a real God. I will address this last point more fully below.

These deficiencies must be met if a pluralistic resolution to the conflicting truth-claims of the world religions is to be successful. Yet despite these shortcomings, Religious Pluralism has an obvious strength which must be retained for any successful pluralistic resolution. Religious Pluralism offers a reconciliation of the disparate world religious traditions which avoids the theologically unacceptable and epistemically unsupportable religious imperialism which we find in Exclusivism, and even in Inclusivism.

VII

If, then, we reject the religious imperialism of the Exclusivist and Inclusivist views that one's own tradition must be either the sole or at least the fullest arbiter of truth about the divine, we have two choices about how to deal with the irreducible plurality of religious conception and experience. We can either take the approach of Pluralism, treat the incompatible beliefs among differing religious worldviews as ultimately inessential, and conclude that the great world religions simply offer different perspectives on Ultimate Reality. Or we can accept the doctrines which adherents of different world religions so ardently profess and passionately follow as *essential* to their faith. I have suggested that the former approach runs the danger of undermining the basic religious meta-belief (I), and reducing the substance of religious worldviews to vacuity, obviating just those differences in the path to salvation/liberation which give significance to each individual religious tradition. If I am right about this, we are led to conclude that different religions have different constitutive sets of truth-claims, and that— while these sets of core truth-claims are mutually incompatible—each set of truth-claims is probably adequate in itself.

This is the Religious Relativist response to the problem of religious pluralism. Granted, the different religious worldviews among the world's great religious traditions are complementary insofar as they have a commonality in the religious experiences and perceptions of humankind. But different religious worldviews are, ultimately, irreducibly plural, with features that are incompatible if not contradictory *vis-a-vis* other religious worldviews. Further, corresponding to each distinct religious worldview, there is a different set of possible religious *experiences.* For what can be experienced depends on what *can be* real or unreal, and what can be real—i.e., what is possible—is determined by the percipient's worldview. This means that each distinct religious worldview delineates a distinct possible divine reality—though just to the extent that religious worldviews "overlap," characteristics of these distinct possible divine realities will overlap.

For instance, monotheistic truth-claims will be most directly about God *as* humans experience Him, for they are most directly above divine reality *relative to* a particular theistic worldview. But then each theology, as a product of human constructive reasoning, will delimit only one *possible* divine reality. There will be other *contrasting*—though not totally mutually exclusive—valid theologies, held by other sincere women and men of faith, delimiting other possible divine phenomenal realities.

Importantly, on this Religious Relativist account, "The" God of history, delimited by the strictures of a particular theology is *not,* if He exists, somehow unreal *vis-a-vis* the noumenal. God *qua* noumenal lies "behind," so to speak, the possible plurality of real phenomenal divine realities, delimited by different monotheistic worldviews. But noumenal and phenomenal reality are two different categories of reality. And just as there is nothing unreal about nuclear weapons or pains or piano concertos because they are part of phenomenal reality, "The" God of history, "The" God one confronts, is not less real, if He exists, just because He is not in the category of the noumenal. What could be *more* real than that which we do experience? And to try to transcend our experience for something putatively "untainted" by human thought is not only the worst sort of degenerate Platonism, it is to turn away from the means we *do* have in experience for understanding the divine and our own humanity in relation to the divine.

Among the possible responses to the problem of religious pluralism, this Religious Relativist account of a possible plurality of phenomenal divine realities seems to offer the best explanation of the differing experiences and incompatible conceptions of the great religious traditions. The Atheist response to the problem of religious pluralism is ruled out if we presuppose the religious meta-belief (I). Religious Exclusivism is neither tolerable nor any longer intellectually honest in the context of our contemporary knowledge of other faiths. Religious Subjectivism is conceptually incoherent. Religious Inclusivism does not go far enough toward solving the problem of religious pluralism. And Religious Pluralism has serious deficiencies which Religious Relativism avoids.

First, Religious Relativism reasserts the central role which cognition has in a religious life. The path to salvation is itself part of the salvific process. And one's religious worldview, as a guide for attitudes and actions, is inseparable from the path. Moreover, if all experience is conceptualized, then one will quite literally not be able to have any experience of the divine without a worldview which, e.g., enables one to experience the world *as* under the providence of God, or *as* an environment for working out one's *Karma*, etc. But then, as Religious Relativism asserts, *specific* truth-claims are essential to a religious tradition and way of life, and the conflict among the claims of the world religions cannot be resolved by de-emphasizing those conflicting claims.

Second, it follows from this that Religious Relativism treats adherents of each religious tradition with fullest dignity. Regarding Christianity, we could say, as the Pluralist must, that the doctrine of the Incarnation cannot be taken literally and cannot mean for *any* Christian that Jesus uniquely manifests the presence of God. Or, we can allow that on *some* worldviews this would be a perfectly rational view, delineating a world where Jesus *is* the definitive self-manifestation of God. Ironically, we fall back into a certain measure of the old absolutism that undergirds Exclusivism if we take the inflexible, even though Pluralist, first course. In contrast, Relativism not only allows with Pluralism that the world's great religions could have the same telos, it allows for the likelihood that more than one of the conflicting sets of *specific* truth-claims, which adherents of the differing world religions themselves regard as vital to their faith, is correct.

Third, that it is essential for the direct object of theological conception to be a *real* God seems to leave a Pluralist view like Hick's caught between two problematic options. As in his earlier work, the God of theology can be characterized as an "image" of God. But then the God of theology does not have the ontological status of an existent entity with causal properties in the phenomenal world. This will unintentionally reduce the sense of the reality of God, for what theology would then be most directly referring to would not be *God,* but a human *idea* of the noumenal. So to speak about *God,* would be to speak about something noumenal about which we can only know that we do not know its true character. In contrast, on Religious Relativism the God of theology can be a *real* God, not just a conception of or perspective on the divine. God *qua* phenomenal is not just, in Tillich's phrase, "a symbol for God."

On the other hand, the Pluralist might hold, as Hick does in his more recent work, that the divine phenomena just *are* the divine noumenon *as* experienced by humans via their particular religio-cultural perspectives. While this does indicate a more substantive ontological status for divine personae and impersonae, it threatens to collapse the phenomena/noumena distinction and runs counter to the basic idealist epistemology which underlies both Pluralism and Relativism. First, this suggests that the divine noumenon is itself experienced. One can postulate an unexperienced divine noumenon, and one can talk about divine phenomena which are (putatively) experienced. But this cannot amount to talk about the same thing—even if in different ways—for that would effectively be to eliminate the divine noumenon. And given an idealist epistemology, one cannot claim that the divine noumenon *is* experienced insofar as it appears to us in various ways, *even though* we cannot characterize the noumenal. For the conceptualization of all experience implies that what we experience can, in principle, be characterized.

Second, that a particular divine phenomenon somehow manifests the divine noumenon is a matter of faith. And while it could be a matter of reasonable faith for an individual to claim that the divine phenomenon which *they* experience somehow manifests Ultimate Reality in itself, it would not make sense to say that it was a matter of one's *faith* that the various divine phenomena, which adherents of all the great world religions feel that they experience, all *do* manifest Ultimate Reality. Rather this would amount to a hypothesis or theory about the world religions. And I do not see how we could know that this hypothesis is true; how could we know that the divine phenomena of all the great world religions *are* (or most probably are) the divine noumenon *as* experienced by humans? One's faith warrants one's own religious commitment; it cannot warrant the mutually conflicting commitments of others.

In contrast, on a Religious Relativist account, what is putatively experienced is not the noumenal Ultimate Reality, but e.g., the *real* God of history. Now, I do think that it is a mistake to suppose that one can *know* that specific claims which we make about phenomenal divine reality are also true of the divine noumenon, since this would obviate the very point of the noumena/phenomena distinction. But I think it is perfectly sensible to make the bare claim that there *is* a noumenal—*whatever* its character—which, so to speak, "lies behind" the phenomenal reality which we experience. Presumably there is no one-to-one correspondence between phenomena and noumena and hence no *direct* check from our successes and failures to the nature of the noumenal. But the greater the correspondence between our conception of the phenomenal and the character of the noumenal (whatever it is), the more our purposive activity, carried out within phenomenal reality as *we* understand it, will be successful and the closer—in principle—our understanding of the phenomenal will correspond to the noumenal. For the monotheist it is a matter of faith that, in this manner, one's *own* experience of the presence of "The" God of history does increase, on the whole, one's understanding of God in Himself.

VIII

One obvious point of resistance to this Religious Relativist account is the notion that there may be more than one phenomenal reality, and more than one phenomenal divine reality. But this notion initially seems strange only because we are used to thinking in terms of that one possible world which *we* regard as *the* (unique) actual world. Commonly, we treat any other conception of the actual world as simply false or mistaken. But if one accepts the idea that phenomenal reality is relative to a worldview, and that therefore there is a plurality of actual worlds corresponding to the plurality of distinct worldviews, that does not undermine or alter what *we* call the actual world—i.e., the world delimited by *our* schemas.

Recognizing that others might be responding to a different phenomenal God is like recognizing that others might rationally claim to discern a cyclical recurrence of events in history where you discern none. One can accept that there *could* be states of affairs which others but not you experience, without thereby committing yourself to the existence of any *particular* such state of affairs. To have faith in only one real (phenomenal) God is to say that for *oneself* there is only one real God who lives and moves and has His being; for others there may be other real entities which are "The" God of *their* history. But just as any actual event or state of affairs is by definition an event or state of affairs in *your* actual world, any actual event which you acknowledge as an act of God is an act of the real God who confronts *you* within (your) history.

IX

Frank Whaling raises another possible objection to both Pluralism and Relativism. Whaling argues that these views avoid "the necessity of theological ordering of any sort," and that they have "the appearance of being a somewhat abstract exercise in the theology of religion, rather than a summing-up of where the Christian community around the world actually *is*." The second, descriptive point, that Christians do not currently tend to be Religious Pluralists or Relativists, misses the question of whether Christians *ought* to move toward Pluralism or Relativism in the face of the challenge of the conflicting truth-claims of the world religions. But with respect to the first point, it *would* be a serious defect of any pluralistic response to the world religions if diverse religious truth-claims cannot be compared and assessed. Here Pluralism and Relativism offer two quite different approaches.

Pluralists most naturally approach the apparently conflicting truth-claims of world religions from the perspective of a "global theology." That is, the Pluralist fundamentally attempts to look at religious traditions from an external, or inclusive point of view. But the unavoidable historicity and the inherent enculturation of our thought obviate the very possibility of being able to assume this purported global perspective. There can be no such thing as a "neutral" or "objective" perspective in

either religious or non-religious matters. Hence, any attempt to assess other faiths from a genuinely global perspective is inherently impossible.

Religious Relativism, on the other hand, avoids this difficulty by suggesting an internal approach to assessing other faiths. Relativism, more fundamentally than Pluralism, recognizes the inextricably socio-historical conditioning of one's perspective, and hence fundamentally recognizes that judgments about *other* faiths will necessarily be made from the point of view of one's *own* faith. This is simply to acknowledge an inherent condition of the human mind, and does not entail falling back into the religious imperialism we found in Exclusivism and Inclusivism. For there are general meta-criteria that can be applied across worldviews to assess the acceptability of a worldview. These criteria include the internal coherence of a worldview, its comprehensiveness, thoroughness of explanation (e.g., that it does not depend on ad hoc hypotheses), the efficaciousness of the worldview in producing its intended end, considerations of parsimony, and so on. Thus Relativism, while not attempting to assume the stance of an impossible "neutral" global theology, can employ these meta-criteria to assess other faiths and so meet Whaling's objection. Further, this gives Relativism a strength that we observed in Religious Inclusivism. Religious Relativism, while recognizing that salvation *could* come to others in other traditions, supports the strength of commitment to one's own tradition.

X

While the Pluralist attempts to solve the problem of religious pluralism by setting aside conflicting truth-claims and emphasizing a universality and unity to all religions, the Religious Relativist can resolve the problem of religious pluralism by accepting these conflicting truth-claims as an appropriate manifestation of divine/human interaction. In the spirit of the Leibnizian notion that not just the quantity of good, but the *variety* of good things makes this "the best of all possible worlds"—the world that a good God would create—we *should* expect correct religious beliefs and veridical religious experiences to be as richly varied as human needs and human individuality. Contrary to the Pluralist conception, an ultimate uniformity of the central elements of all religious traditions is not an ultimate value. Where Pluralism tends to homogenize religion, if one believes that God indeed has providence over the world, then precisely what the evidence of the world we find ourselves in indicates is that a diversity of religious truth-claims is intrinsically valuable, and divinely valued. Rather than a problem to be solved, the conflicting truth-claims of the great religious traditions, and even conflicting systems *within* traditions, can be accepted as a profound indication of God's manifest love and delight in the diverse worlds of His creatures.

That our religious beliefs have a correlation to the transcendent divine reality is a matter of faith. Since our perception and understanding are ineluctably limited to our worldview, even if what we believe is true about God *qua* phenomenal turns out to be true also of God *qua* noumenal, we could never *know* that that was so. We cannot *know* that we possess the requisite conceptual resources to apply to God in Himself, or *know* that we have formed ideas which are true of God *qua* noumenal, or *know* that our ideas do properly refer to the noumenal God. But just because we cannot know these things to be true *vis-a-vis* the noumenal God, this clearly does not entail that they are not the case.

I do not see how it could be shown that it is *impossible* that our concepts or beliefs do in fact correctly refer to the noumenal. Quite the contrary, it is a matter of reasonable faith that Christian religious experience and theological conception *do* provide the basis for proper reference and proper talk about God in Himself. Yet to acknowledge that we cannot transcend our worldviews, and that they in turn are inescapably structured by our limiting socio-historical perspective, is to recognize the fundamental fallibility and finitude of even our noblest conceptions and highest values. There is thus a religiously appropriate humbleness which Religious Relativism brings to our claims to religious truth.

Faced with the inescapable challenge of the claims of other faiths, it may now be time for Christians to move toward a Christian Relativism. A Christian Relativism would combine the strengths of Exclusivism and Inclusivism, and of Pluralism, without their respective disadvantages. A Christian Relativism would enable us to say, on the one hand, that salvation through Christ is definitive, without committing us, on the other hand, to the unsupportable view that salvation is exclusively Christian. A Christian Relativism would sustain Christian commitment and support Christian claims to truth, without claiming to be the only truth.

Bibliography for Part VIII

Dean, Thomas, ed. *Religious Pluralism and Truth: Essays on Cross-Cultural Philosophy of Religion* (SUNY Press, 1995).

Heim, S. Mark. *Salvations: Truth and Difference in Religion* (Orbis, 1993).

Hick, John. *God and the Universe of Faiths.* London: Macmillan, 1973. A pioneer work in the area from which our first reading is taken.

———, advisory ed. *Religious Pluralism.* A special issue of *Faith and Philosophy* 5, no. 4 (October 1988). Contains important essays by John Hick, Joseph Runzo, William Alston, and others.

Hick, John, and Paul Knitter, eds. *The Myth of Christian Uniqueness: Towards a Pluralistic Theology of Religions* (Orbis, 1987).

———. *An Interpretation of Religion: Human Responses to the Transcendent* (Yale, 1989).

Ogden, Schubert. *Is There Only One True Religion or Are There Many?* (SMU Press, 1992).

———. *Doing Theology Today* (Trinity Press, 1996).

Smith, Wilfred Cantwell. *Towards a World Theology*. Philadelphia: Westminster, 1981. An important work in religious pluralism.

Yandell, Keith. "Religious Experience and Rational Appraisal." *Religious Studies* 8 (June 1974). Seeks a middle ground between pluralism and exclusivism.

PART IX

RELIGION AND ETHICS

In examining the relationship of religion to ethics, we find two problems, which are indicated by the following questions: (1) Does morality depend on religion? and (2) Are religious ethics essentially different from secular ethics? These questions are related, but they are not the same. Unlike many religions of the ancient world, Judaism and Christianity are ethical monotheisms. They not only promise salvation to the faithful but tie ethical responsibility into the matrix of salvation in a very close way, by making the moral life either a necessary condition for God's favor or a consequence of it.

The question is whether moral standards themselves depend on God for their validity or whether there is an autonomy of ethics so that even God is subject to the moral order. As Socrates asks in our first reading, taken from the *Euthyphro*, "Do the gods love holiness because it is holy, or is it holy because the gods love it?" According to one theory, called the divine command theory, ethical principles are simply the commands of God. They derive their validity from God's commanding them, and they *mean* 'commanded by God.' Without God, there would be no universally valid morality. As Dostoevsky wrote in *The Brothers Karamazov*, "If God doesn't exist, everything is permissible." Many interpret the writings of Nietzsche as representing such a nihilistic ethics, a worldview in which there is no God (or in which he is "dead," irrelevant to life).

The opposing viewpoint is that ethical values are autonomous and that even God must keep the moral law, which exists independently of him—as logical laws do. God, of course, *knows* what is right—better than we do—but in principle we act morally for the same reasons that God does. We both follow moral reasons that are independent of God. If there is no God, on this account, nothing is changed. Morality is left intact, and if we choose to be moral, we have the very same duties we would have as theists.

The motivation for the divine command theory is to preserve or do justice to the omnipotence or sovereignty of God. God somehow is thought to be less sovereign or necessary to our lives if he is not the source of morality. When the believer asks what the will of God is, it is a direct appeal to a personal will, not to an independently existing rule.

561

One problem with the divine command theory is that it would seem to make the attribution of 'goodness' to God redundant. When we say 'God is good,' we think that we are stating a property to God, but if 'good' simply meant 'what God commands or wills,' then we are not attributing any property to God. Our statement merely means 'God wills what God wills,' which is a tautology. A second problem is that if God's arbitrary fiat (in the sense of not being based on reasons) is the sole arbiter of right and wrong, it would seem to be logically possible for such "heinous" acts as rape, killing of the innocent for the fun of it, and gratuitous cruelty to become morally good actions—if God suddenly decided to command us to do these things. But then, wouldn't morality be reduced to the right of the powerful, Nietzsche's 'might make right?'

The second problem in the relationship between religion and morality is the degree to which religious morality and nonreligious morality are in *content* and *form* similar to each other. According to Immanuel Kant, who held to the autonomy of ethics, there could be no difference between valid religious ethics and valid philosophical ethics. God and humanity each have to obey the same rational principles, and reason is sufficient to guide us to these principles. But some utilitarians, such as Patrick Nowell-Smith in our readings, have argued that religious ethics are essentially deontological (based on rules without decisive regard for consequences), whereas secular ethics, at their best, are teleological, based on what will produce the best overall consequences. Nowell-Smith argues that this shows the superiority of secular ethics over religious ethics.

In our final reading, George Mavrodes argues that philosophers like Nowell-Smith who set forth secular moral theories not only are mistaken about the weaknesses of religious ethics but also fail to realize that their own systems are woefully lacking in resources for moral living. Something "puzzling" haunts them. For one thing, they cannot give an adequate answer to the question, Why be moral at times when cheating will go undetected and I will not suffer any bad consequences from it? Values in the secular world are not deep as they are in a Platonic or Christian or religious worldview.

Who is closer to the truth, Nowell-Smith or Mavrodes? A close study of their arguments will repay your efforts.

IX.1 Morality and Religion

P L A T O

We have already encountered the writings of Plato (427–347 BC) in our readings on immortality. Here we see his mentor, Socrates, engaged in a dialogue with the self-righteously religious Euthyphro, who is going to court to report his father for having killed a slave. In the course of the discussion Socrates raises the question that is known as the question of the divine command theory of ethics: Is the good good because God loves it, or does God love the good because it is good?

Socrates. But shall we . . . say that whatever all the gods hate is unholy, and whatever they all love is holy: while whatever some of them love, and others hate, is either both or neither? Do you wish us now to define holiness and unholiness in this manner?

Euthyphro. Why not, Socrates?

Socr. There is no reason why I should not, Euthyphro. It is for you to consider whether that definition will help you to instruct me as you promised.

Euth. Well, I should say that holiness is what all the gods love, and that unholiness is what they all hate.

Socr. Are we to examine this definition, Euthyphro, and see if it is a good one? Or are we to be content to accept the bare assertions of other men, or of ourselves, without asking any questions? Or must we examine the assertions?

Euth. We must examine them. But for my part I think that the definition is right this time.

Socr. We shall know that better in a little while, my good friend. Now consider this question. Do the gods love holiness because it is holy, or is it holy because they love it?

Euth. I do not understand you, Socrates.

Socr. I will try to explain myself: we speak of a thing being carried and carrying, and being led and

leading, and being seen and seeing; and you understand that all such expressions mean different things, and what the difference is.

Euth. Yes, I think I understand.

Socr. And we talk of a thing being loved, and, which is different, of a thing loving?

Euth. Of course.

Socr. Now tell me: is a thing which is being carried in a state of being carried, because it is carried, or for some other reason?

Euth. No, because it is carried.

Socr. And a thing is in a state of being led, because it is led, and of being seen, because it is seen?

Euth. Certainly.

Socr. Then a thing is not seen because it is in a state of being seen; it is in a state of being seen because it is seen; and a thing is not led because it is in a state of being led; it is in a state of being led because it is led: and a thing is not carried because it is in a state of being carried; it is in a state of being carried because it is carried. Is my meaning clear now, Euthyphro? I mean this: if anything becomes, or is affected, it does not become because it is in a state of becoming; it is in a state of becoming because it becomes; and it is not affected because it is in a state of being affected; it is in a state of being affected because it is affected. Do you not agree?

Euth. I do.

Socr. Is not that which is being loved in a state, either of becoming, or of being affected in some way by something?

Euth. Certainly.

Socr. Then the same is true here as in the former cases. A thing is not loved by those who love it because it is in a state of being loved. It is in a state of being loved because they love it.

Euth. Necessarily.

Socr. Well, then, Euthyphro, what do we say about holiness? Is it not loved by all the gods, according to your definition?

Reprinted from the *Euthyphro*, translated by William Jowett (New York: Charles Scribner's Sons, 1889).

Euth. Yes.

Socr. Because it is holy, or for some other reason?

Euth. No, because it is holy.

Socr. Then it is loved by the gods because it is holy; it is not holy because it is loved by them?

Euth. It seems so.

Socr. But then what is pleasing to the gods is pleasing to them, and is in a state of being loved by them, because they love it?

Euth. Of course.

Socr. Then holiness is not what is pleasing to the gods, and what is pleasing to the gods is not holy, as you say, Euthyphro. They are different things.

Euth. And why, Socrates?

Socr. Because we are agreed that the gods love holiness because it is holy; and that it is not holy because they love it. Is not this so?

Euth. Yes.

Socr. And that what is pleasing to the gods because they love it, is pleasing to them by reason of this same love; and that they do not love it because it is pleasing to them.

Euth. True.

Socr. Then, my dear Euthyphro, holiness, and what is pleasing to the gods, are different things. If the gods had loved holiness because it is holy, they would also have loved what is pleasing to them because it is pleasing to them; but if what is pleasing to them had been pleasing to them because they loved it, then holiness too would have been holiness, because they loved it. But now you see that they are opposite things, and wholly different from each other. For the one is of a sort to be loved because it is loved: while the other is loved, because it is of a sort to be loved. My question, Euthyphro, was, What is holiness? But it turns out that you have not explained to me the essence of holiness; you have been content to mention an attribute which belongs to it, namely, that all the gods love it. You have not yet told me what is its essence. Do not, if you please, keep from me what holiness is; begin again and tell me that. Never mind whether the gods love it, or whether it has other attributes: we shall not differ on that point. Do your best to make it clear to me what is holiness and what is unholiness.

IX.2   Morality: Religious and Secular

PATRICK NOWELL-SMITH

Patrick Nowell-Smith is a British philosopher who teaches at York University in Canada. He is a utilitarian—that is, he believes that ethics ought to maximize the welfare of society or happiness in it. He argues in this section that religious ethics are essentially deontological (based on rules without decisive regard for consequences), whereas secular ethics, at their best (viz., utilitarianism), are teleological and aim at producing the best overall consequences. Nowell-Smith argues that this shows the superiority of secular ethics over religious ethics.

Reprinted from "Morality: Religious and Secular," in *The Rationalist Annual*, 1961 (London: Pemberton Publishing Co., 1961) by permission of the author.

The central thesis of this paper is that religious morality is infantile. I am well aware that this will sound absurd. To suggest that Aquinas and Kant—to say nothing of millions of Christians of lesser genius—never grew up is surely to put oneself out of court as a philosopher to be taken seriously. My thesis is not so crude as that; I shall try to show that, in the moralities of adult Christians, there are elements which can be set apart from the rest and are, indeed, inconsistent with them, that these elements can properly be called "religious" and that just these elements are infantile.

I shall start by making some assumptions that I take to be common ground between Christians and secular humanists. I propose to say almost nothing about the content of morality; that love, sympathy, loyalty, and consideration are virtues, and that their opposites, malice, cruelty, treachery, and callousness, are vices, are propositions that I shall assume without proof. One can't do everything at the same time, and my job now is not to refute Thrasymachus. Secondly, I propose to occupy, as common ground, some much more debatable territory; I shall assume in broad outline the metaphysical view of the nature of man that we have inherited from Plato and Aristotle. The basis of this tradition is that there is something called "Eudaimonia" or "The Good Life," that this consists in fulfilling to the highest possible degree the nature of Man, and that the nature of Man is to be a rational, social animal. Love, I shall assume, is the supreme virtue because the life of love is, in the end, the only life that is fully rational and fully social. My concern will be, not with the content of morality, but with its form or structure, with the ways in which the manifold concepts and affirmations of which a moral system is composed hang together; not with rival views of what conduct is moral and what is immoral, but with rival views of what morality *is*.

This contrast between form and content is not difficult to grasp, but experience has taught me that it is often ignored. When they discover that I have moral views but no religious beliefs, people often ask me this question: "Where do you get your moral ideas from?" Faced with this question, my habit is to take it literally and to answer it truthfully. "From my father and mother," I say, "from the companions of my boyhood and manhood, from teachers and from books, from my own reflections on the experience I have had of the sayings and doings of myself and others, an experience similar in countless ways to that of other people born of middle-class English parents some forty-five years ago, but in its totality unique." This boring and autobiographical answer never satisfies the questioner; for, though it is the right answer to the question he actually asked, it is not, as I very well knew, the answer to the question he really had in mind. He did not want to know *from* whom I learnt my moral views; he wanted to know what *authority* I have for holding them. But why, if this is what he wanted to know, did he not ask me? He has confused two different questions; and it is natural enough that he should have confused them, since it is often the case that to point to the source of an opinion or claim is to show the authority on which it is based. We appeal to the dictionary to vindicate an assertion about the spelling of a word, and the policeman's production of a warrant signed by a magistrate is a necessary and sufficient condition of his authority to enter my house. But even a dictionary can make mistakes, and one may doubt whether one *ought* to admit the policeman even after his legal title to enter has been satisfactorily made out. "He certainly has a legal right," one might say, "but even so, things being as they are, ought I to admit him?"

Those who put this question to me have made an assumption that they have not examined because they have not reflected sufficiently on the form of morality. They have simply assumed that just as the legal propriety of an action is established by showing it to emanate from an authoritative source, so also the moral propriety of an action must be established in the same way; that legal rightness has the same form as moral rightness, and may therefore be used to shed light on it. This assumption made, they naturally suppose that, even when I agree with them—for example, about the immorality of murder—I have no right to hold this impeccable view unless I can show that I have received it from an authoritative source. My autobiographical answer clearly fails to do this. My parents may have had a right to my obedience, but no right to make the moral law. Morality, on this view, is an affair of being commanded to behave in certain ways by some person who has a right to issue such commands; and once this premise is granted, it is said with some reason that only God has such a right. Morality must be based on religion, and a morality not so based, or one based on the wrong religion, lacks all validity.

It is this premise, that being moral consists in obedience to commands, that I deny. There is an argument, familiar to philosophers but of which the force is not always appreciated, which shows that this premise cannot be right. Suppose that I have satisfied myself that God has commanded me to do this or that thing—in itself a large supposition, but I will waive objections on this score in order to come quickly to the main point—it still makes *sense* for me to ask whether or not I *ought* to do it. God, let us say, is an omnipotent, omniscient creator of the universe. Such a creator might have evil intentions and might command me to do wrong; and if that were the case though it would be imprudent to disobey, it would not be wrong. There is nothing in the idea of an omnipotent, omniscient creator which by itself, entails his goodness or his right to command, unless we are prepared to assent to Hobbes' phrase, "God, who by right, *that is by irresistible power,* commandeth all things." Unless we accept Hobbes' consistent but repugnant equation of God's right with his might, we must be persuaded *independently* of his goodness before we admit his right to command. We must judge for ourselves whether the Bible is the inspired word of a just and benevolent God or a curious amalgam of profound wisdom and gross superstition. To judge this is to make a moral decision, so that in the end, so far from morality being based on religion, religion is based on morality.

Before passing to my main theme, I must add two cautions about what this argument does *not* prove. It does not prove that we should in no case take authority as a guide. Suppose that a man's aim is to make money on the Stock Exchange. He decides that it would be most profitable to invest his money in company A; but his broker prefers company B. He will usually be well advised to accept the verdict of his broker, even if the broker is, as they often are, inarticulate in giving his reasons. He might decide to put all his financial affairs in the hands of a broker, and to do nothing but what the broker tells him to do. But *this* decision, even if it is the only financial decision he ever makes in his life, is still his own. In much the same way, a man might decide to put his conscience wholly into the hands of a priest or a Church, to make no moral decisions of his own but always to do what the priest tells him. Even he, though he makes but one moral decision in his life, must make and continually renew that one. Those who accept the authority of a priest or a Church on what to do are, in accepting that authority, deciding for themselves. They may not fully comprehend that this is so; but that is another matter.

Secondly, to deny that morality need or can have an external nonmoral basis on which to stand is by no means to deny that it can have an internal basis, in the sense of one or a few moral beliefs that are fundamental to the other beliefs of the system. A man's views on gambling or sex or business ethics may (though they need not) form a coherent system in which some views are held *because* certain other views are held. Utilitarianism is an example of such a system in which all moral rules are to be judged by their tendency to promote human happiness. A moral system of this kind is like a system of geometry in which some propositions appear as axioms, others as theorems owing their place in the system to their derivability from the axioms. Few of us are so rationalistic as to hold all our moral beliefs in this way, but to move towards this goal is to begin to think seriously about morals.

1. In any system of morality we can distinguish between its content and its form. By its "content" I mean the actual commands and prohibitions it contains, the characteristics it lists as virtues and as vices; by its "form" I mean the sort of propositions it contains and the ways in which these are thought of as connected with each other. The basic distinction here is between a teleological morality in which moral rules are considered to be subordinate to ends, to be rules *for* achieving ends and consequently to be judged by their tendency to promote those ends, and a deontological system in which moral rules are thought of as absolute, as categorical imperatives in no way depending for their validity on the good or bad consequences of obedience, and in which moral goodness is thought to lie in conformity to these rules for their own sake. The first of these ways of looking at morality as a whole derives from the Greeks, so I shall call it the Greek view of morality; it can be summed up in the slogan "the Sabbath was made for man, not man for the Sabbath." The second, deriving from Jewish sources, I shall call the Hebrew view. This involves a serious oversimplification, since we find deontological elements in the Greek New Testament and teleological elements in the Hebrew Old Testament; but, taken broadly, the contrast between the deontological character of the Old and the teleological character of the New Testaments is as

striking as the difference of language. I shall also indulge in another serious oversimplification in speaking of Christianity as a morality of the Hebrew type while it is, of course, an amalgam of both with different elements predominating in different versions. This oversimplification would be quite unjustifiable if my task were to give an account of Christian morality; but it is legitimate here because my task is to contrast those elements in the Christian tradition which secular humanists accept with those which they reject, and these are broadly coterminous with the Greek and the Hebrew elements in Christianity respectively.

How there can be these two radically different ways of looking at morality, one which sees it as a set of recipes to be followed for the achievement of ends, the other which sees it as a set of commands to be obeyed, can best be understood if we consider the way in which we learn what it is to be moral. For a man's morality is a set of habits of choice, of characteristic responses to his environment, in particular to his social environment, the people among whom he lives; and habits are learnt in childhood. Growing up morally is learning to cope with the world into which we find ourselves pitched, and especially to cope with our relations with other human beings. In the course of living we learn to reflect on our responses, to find in some of them sources of satisfaction, in others of regret, and "coping with the world" means coping with it in a manner ultimately satisfactory to ourselves. Philosophers such as Aristotle and Hobbes who boldly and crudely identified "good" with "object of desire" may have made a technical mistake; but they were certainly on the right lines. If men had no desires and aversions, if they felt no joy and no remorse, if they were totally indifferent to everything in the universe, there would be no such thing as choice and we should have no concept of morality, of good and evil.

The baby is born with some desires, not many; others it acquires as time goes on. Learning to cope with the world is learning how to satisfy and to modify these desires in a world that is partly propitious and partly hostile. For the world does not leap to gratify my desires like an assiduous flunkey; I do not get fed by being hungry. My desires are incompatible with each other and they come into conflict with those of other people. We have to learn both to bend the world to our wills and to bend our wills to the world. A man's morality is the way in which, in important matters, he does this.

Men are by nature rational and social animals, but only potentially so; they become actually rational and social only in a suitable environment, an environment in which they learn to speak a language. Learning how to cope with one's environment goes on side by side with learning to talk. The child's concepts, the meanings which, at every stage, words have for him, change as his horizon becomes wider, as he learns to grasp ideas that are more and more complicated, more and more remote from the primitive actions and passions that initially constitute his entire conscious life. It is not therefore surprising that the *form* of his morality, the meanings which moral words have and the ways in which they hang together, reflect at each stage the kind of experience he has. To babies who cannot yet talk we cannot, without serious error, attribute any thoughts at all; but though they cannot think, they can certainly feel, experience pleasure and pain, satisfaction and frustration. It is in these preverbal experiences that the origin of the ideas of "good" and "bad," even of "right" and "wrong," must be found; for their later development I turn to Piaget. My case for saying that religious morality is infantile cannot be conclusively made out without a much more detailed study of Piaget's researches than I have space for; I shall concentrate on a few points that seem to me to bear directly on the issue between the religious morality of law and the secular morality of purpose.

Piaget made a detailed study of the attitudes of children of different ages to the game of marbles, and he found three distinct stages. A very small child handles the marbles and throws them about as his humor takes him; he is playing, but not playing a *game*; for there are no rules governing his actions, no question of anything being done right or wrong. Towards the end of this stage he will, to some extent, be playing according to rules; for he will imitate older children who are playing a rule-governed game. But the child himself is not conscious of obeying rules; he has not yet grasped the concept of a "rule," of what a rule *is*. We may call this the premoral attitude to rules.

The second type of attitude is exhibited by children from five to nine. During this stage, says Piaget, "the rules are regarded as sacred and inviolable, emanating from adults and lasting for ever. Every suggested alteration in the rules strikes the child as a transgression." Piaget calls this attitude to rules "heteronomous" to mark the fact that the children regard the rules as coming, as indeed they do, from the outside, as being imposed on them by others. We might also call this the "deontological stage," to mark the fact that the rules are not questioned; they just *are* the rules of marbles, and that's that. At this stage the child has the concept of a rule, he knows what a rule is; but he has not yet asked what a rule is *for*. This deontological character is obviously connected with the unchangeability of the rules. Like laws in a primitive society, they are thought of as having been handed down from time immemorial, as much a part of the natural order of things as sunrise and sunset. The child may chafe at obedience and may sometimes disobey; but he does not question the authority of the rules.

Finally, at the third stage, the child begins to learn what the rules are for, what the point of having any rules is, and why it is better to have this rule rather than that. "The rule," says Piaget, "is now looked upon as a law due to mutual consent, which you must respect if you want to be loyal, but which it is permissible to alter on condition of enlisting the general opinion on your side." He calls this type of attitude "autonomous" to mark the fact that the children now regard themselves, collectively, as the authors of the rules. This is not to say that they falsely suppose themselves to have invented them; they know well enough that they received them from older children. But they are the authors in the sense of being the final authorities; what tradition gave them they can change; from "this is how we learnt to play" they no longer pass unquestioningly to "this is how we ought to play." We might also call this stage "teleological" to mark the fact that the rules are no longer regarded as sacred, as worthy of obedience simply because they are what they are, but as serving a purpose, as rules for playing a game that they want to play. Rules there must certainly be; and in one sense they are sacred enough. Every player must abide by them; he cannot pick and choose But in another sense there is nothing sacred about them;

they are, and are known to be, a *mere* device, to be molded and adapted in the light of the purpose which they are understood by all the players to serve.

To illustrate the transition between the second and the third stages I should like to refer to a case from my own experience. Last summer I was with one other adult and four children on a picnic and the children wanted to play rounders. We had to play according to the rules they had learnt at school because those just were the rules of rounders. This involved having two teams, and you can well imagine that, with only three players in each team, the game quickly ran on the rocks. When I suggested adapting the rules to our circumstances all the children were scandalized at first. But the two older children soon came round to the idea that, situated as we were, we should have to change the rules or not play at all and to the idea that it would not be wicked to change the rules. The two younger children were troubled, one might say, in their consciences about the idea of changing the rules. In Piaget's words, they thought of an alteration of rules as a transgression against them, having as yet no grasp of the distinction between an alteration of the rules by common consent to achieve a common purpose and the unilateral breach or defiance of them. In the eyes of these younger children we were not proposing to play a slightly different game, one better adapted to our situation; we were proposing to play the old game, but to play it wrong, almost dishonestly.

In another of Piaget's researches, this time directly concerned with moral attitudes, he told the children pairs of stories in each of which a child does something in some sense "bad" and asked which of the children was naughtier, which deserved most punishment. In one such story a child accidentally breaks fifteen cups while opening a door, and in the companion story breaks one cup while stealing jam. The replies of the very young children are mixed, some saying that the first child was naughtier; older children are unanimous in calling the second child naughtier. They have got beyond the primitive level of assessing moral guilt by the extent of the damage done.

Some of the youngest children do not recognize an act as wrong unless it is actually found out and punished, and we may call these last two points taken together "moral realism," because they display an attitude of mind that makes questions of morality questions of external fact. The inner state of the culprit—his motives and intentions—have nothing to do with it. To break crockery is wrong; therefore to break more crockery is more wrong. Moral laws are like laws of Nature, and Nature gives no marks for good or bad intentions and accepts no excuses. The fire will burn you if you touch it, however careful you were to avoid it. But if you are careless and, by good luck, avoid it, you will not be burnt; for Nature gives no bad marks for carelessness either. In the same way, if you lie and are pun- ished, that is bad; but if you lie and are not punished, that is not bad at all. The fact that retribution did not follow *shows* that the lie was not, in this case, wrong.

2. I want now to compare the religious with the secular attitude towards the moral system which, in its content, both Christians and Humanists accept. I shall try to show that the religious attitude retains these characteristics of deontology, heteronomy and realism which are proper and indeed necessary in the development of a child, but not proper to an adult: But I must repeat the caution with which I began. The views which I called "moral realism," which make intentions irrelevant, were expressed by very young children. No doubt many of these children were Christians and I do not wish to suggest that they never grew up, that they never adopted a more mature and enlightened attitude. This would be absurd. My thesis is rather that these childish attitudes survive in the moral attitudes of adult Christians—and of some secular moralists—as an alien element, like an outcrop of igneous rock in an alluvial plain. When Freud says of someone that he is fixated at the oral stage of sexuality he does not mean that he still sucks his thumb; he means rather that some of his characteristic attitudes and behavior patterns can be seen as an adult substitute for thumb sucking. In the same way, I suggest that some elements characteristic of Christian morality are substitutes for childish attitudes. In the course of this comparison I shall try to show how these infantile attitudes belong to a stage that is a *necessary stage* on the way to the fully adult, a stage which we must have passed through in order to reach maturity.

It needs little reflection to see that deontology and heteronomy are strongly marked features of all religious moralities. First for deontology. For some Christians the fundamental sin, the fount and origin of all sin, is disobedience to God. It is not the nature of the act of murder or of perjury that makes it wrong; it is the fact that such acts are transgressions of God's commands. On the other hand, good acts are not good in themselves, good in their own nature, but good only as acts of obedience to God. "I give no alms only to satisfy the hunger of my brother, but to accomplish the will and command of my God; I draw not my purse for his sake that demands it, but his that enjoined it" (Sir Thomas Browne, *Religio Medici* II, 2). Here charity itself is held to be good *only because* God has told us to be charitable. It is difficult not to see in this a reflection of the small child's attitude towards his parents and the other authorities from whom he learns what it is right to do. In the first instance little Tommy learns that it is wrong to pull his sister's hair, not because it hurts her, but because Mummy forbids it.

The idea of heteronomy is also strongly marked in Christian morality. "Not as I will, but as thou wilt." The demand made by Christianity is that of surren- dering self, not in the ordinary sense of being unselfish, of loving our neighbor and even our enemy. It is the total surrender of the *will* that is required; Abraham must be prepared to sacrifice Isaac at God's command, and I take this to mean that we must be prepared to sacrifice our most deeply felt moral concerns if God should require us to do so. If we dare to ask why, the only answer is "Have faith"; and faith is an essentially heteronomous idea; for it is not a reasoned trust in someone in whom we have good grounds for reposing trust; it is blind faith, utter submission of our own reason and will.

Now, to the small child morality is necessarily deontological and heteronomous in form; he must learn *that* certain actions are right and others wrong before he can begin to ask *why* they are, and he learns this from other people. The child has his own spontaneous springs of action; there are things he wants to do off his own bat; morality is a curb, at first nothing but a curb on his own volition. He comes up against parental discipline, even if only in the form of the giving and withdrawing of love, long before he can have any compassion, long before he has any conception of others as sentient beings. When he begins to learn language, words like "bad" must mean simply "what hurts me; what I don't like"; through the mechanism of parental discipline they come to mean "what adults forbid and punish me for." It is only because actions which cause suffering to others figure so largely among parental prohibitions that the child learns to connect the word "bad" with them at all.

If we consider the foundations of Christian ethics in more detail we shall find in them moral realism as well. Christianity makes much of charity and the love of our neighbor; but it does not say, as the Greeks did, that this is good because it is what befits the social animal, Man. We ought to be charitable because this is laid on us as a duty and because this state of the soul is the proper state for it during its transient mortal life. We must be charitable because (we are told) only so can we arrive at the soul's goal, the right relation to God. This fundamental isolation of the individual soul with God seems clearly to reflect what one supposes must be the state of mind of the small baby for whom, at the dawn of consciousness, there is only himself on the one side and the collective world of adults, represented largely by his parents, on the other, for whom the idea of others as individuals, as beings like himself, does not yet exist.

This impression is increased when we consider some accounts of what this right relationship between the soul and God is. Granted that to achieve this is the object of right living, just *what* relationship is it that we are to try to achieve? The terms of the relation are an omnipotent creator and his impotent creature, and between such terms the only relation possible is one of utter one-sided dependence, in which the only attitude proper to the creature must be one of adoration, a blend of love and fear. Surely this is just how the world must appear to the young child; for he really *is* impotent, wholly dependent on beings whose ways he cannot understand, beings sometimes loving, sometimes angry, but always omnipotent, always capricious—in short, gods. "As for Dr. Wulicke himself personally, he had all the awful mystery, duplicity, obstinacy, and jealousy of the Old Testament God. He was as rightful in his smiles as in his anger."[1]

Consider in this connection the ideas of original sin and grace. Every son of Adam is, of his own nature, utterly corrupt, redeemable only by divine grace. Once more, the conditions in which the child learns morality provide an obvious source for this remarkable conception. Parents are not only omniscient and omnipotent; they are also necessarily and always morally in the right. This must be so, since they are, as the child sees it, the authors of the moral law. Morality, the idea of something being right or wrong, enters the horizon of the child only at those points at which he has, so to speak, a dispute with authority, only on those occasions on which he is told or made to do something that he does not spontaneously want to do. From these premises that, at the time when the meanings of "right" and "wrong" are being learnt, the child must disagree with its parents and that they must be right he naturally passes to the conclusion that he must always be wrong. To have the sense of actual sin is to have the sense that one has, on this occasion, done wrong; to have the sense of original sin is simply to feel that one must be always and inevitably wrong. This sense of sin has often been deliberately and cruelly fostered; John Bunyan is not the only man to have left on record the agony of his childhood; but the point I wish to make is that the infantile counterpart of the sense of sin is a necessity at a certain stage of moral development, the stage at which moral words are being learnt and moral rules accepted as necessarily what parents say they are.

On the other side of the picture there is the doctrine of grace. Each individual soul is either saved or damned; but its fate, at least according to some versions, is wholly out of its own control. In these extreme versions, grace is absolutely necessary and wholly sufficient for salvation; and grace is the *free* gift of God. As far as the creature is concerned, there is absolutely nothing that he can do or even try to do either to merit or to obtain it.[2] From his point of view the giving or withholding of the means of salvation must be wholly capricious.

Once more, this is how parental discipline must seem to the child who cannot yet understand its aims and motives. Consider, for example, how even the most careful and consistent parents react towards what they call the clumsiness of a child. He knocks things over; he fumbles with his buttons.

Though most parents do not think of themselves as punishing a child for such things, their behavior is, from the child's point of view, indistinguishable from punishment. They display more irritation when the child knocks over a valuable vase than when he knocks over a cheap cup, when the button-fumbling happens to occur at a moment when they are in a hurry than when it does not. If a father takes from a small child something that is dangerous to play with or stops him hurting himself by a movement necessarily rough, that to the child is indistinguishable from punishment; it is a thwarting of his inclination for no reason that he can see. Children often say things that they know to be untrue; sometimes they are reprimanded for lying, sometimes complimented on their imagination. How can the child know under which heading, the good or the bad, a piece of invention will come, except by observing whether it is punished or rewarded? The child, by this time, is beginning to make efforts to try to please his parents, to do what, in his childish mind, he thinks right. The parents, not being expert child psychologists, will often fail to notice this; more often they will disregard it. To the child, therefore, there is little correlation between his own intentions and the reactions he evokes from the adult world. Salvation in the form of parental smiles and damnation in the form of parental frowns will come to him, like grace, in a manner that both seems and is wholly unconnected with any inwardly felt guilt. The mystery of God's ways to Man is the mystery of a father's ways to his children.

This characterization of religious morality as essentially infantile may seem to be unnecessary; for do not Christians themselves liken their relationship to God as that of child to father? In so doing they do not seem to me always to realize how incompatible this father–child relationship is with the Greek conception of the good life which they recognize as one of the sources of their moral doctrine. Aristotle says that children, like animals, have no share in the good life (a remark which always sounds so odd when people translate it as "children have no share in happiness"), and the reason he gives is that children do not *act*. This is a deep furrow to begin to plough at this stage—what is meant by "action"; but briefly it is motion that is self-initiated and responsible. The prime difference between the adult and the child is that the adult has freedom to choose for himself and has, what goes with freedom, responsibility for his actions. In the life of a child there is always, in the last resort, the parent or some substitute for a parent to turn to. The father is responsible at law for the actions of his child; he will undo what harm the child has done; he will put things right, will save the child from the consequences of his mistakes. To pass from childhood into adulthood is essentially to pass from dependence into freedom, and the price we pay is responsibility. As adults we make our own choices and must accept their consequences; the shield that in our childish petulance we once thought so irksome is no longer there to protect us. To many of us this is a matter of life-long regret, and we search endlessly for a father substitute. Surely "they" will get us out of the mess; there ought to be a law; why doesn't somebody. . . . These, in this godless age, are the common secular substitutes; religion, when it is not a patent substitute, is only a more profound, a more insinuating one.

3. The postulation of a god as the author of the moral law solves no more problems in ethics than the postulation of a god as first cause solves problems in metaphysics. Nor need we base morality, as I have done, on the metaphysical conception of Man as a rational, social animal, though we shall do so if we care to maintain the link with the old meaning of the word "humanist." To me, as a philosopher, some systematic view of the whole of my experience, some metaphysic, is essential, and this conception of the nature of Man makes more sense of my experience than any other I know. But I certainly should not argue that *because* the species Man has such and such a nature, *therefore* each and every man ought to act in such and such ways. In trying to sketch a humanist morality I shall start simply with the idea that a morality is a set of habits of choice ultimately determined by the question "What life is most satisfactory to me as a whole?" and I start with this because I simply do not *understand* the suggestion that I ought to do anything that does not fit into this conception. Outside this context the word "ought" has for me no meaning; and here at least I should expect Christians to agree with me.

If we start in this way, inquiries into my own nature and into the nature of Man at once become relevant. For my nature is such that there are some things that are impossible for me to do. Some hopes must be illusory, and nothing but frustration could come of indulging them. I could not, for example, become an operatic tenor or a test cricketer. Inquiries into the nature of Man are relevant in two ways; first, because I have to live as a man among men, secondly, because all men are to some degree alike and some of my limitations are common to us all. None of us can fly or witness past events. It is only insofar as men are alike that we can even begin to lay down rules as to how they should (all) behave; for it is only insofar as they are alike that they will find satisfaction and frustration in the same things. Prominent among the similarities among men are the animal appetites, the desire for the love and companionship of their own species, and the ability to think; and it is these three similarities that make us all "moral" beings. Morality consists largely, if not quite wholly, in the attempt to realize these common elements in our nature in a coherent way, and we have found that this cannot be done without adopting moral rules and codes of law. Humanism does not imply the rejection of all moral rules, but it does imply the rejection of a deontological attitude towards them. Even Piaget's older children could not have played marbles without rules; but they treated them as adaptable, as subservient to the purpose of playing a game, which is what they wanted to do. They treated the rules as a wise man treats his motor car, not as an object of veneration but as a convenience.

This, I suggest, is how we, as adults, should regard moral rules. They are necessary, in the first place, because one man's aim in life often conflicts with the aims of others and because most of our aims involve the cooperation of others, so that, even for purely selfish reasons, we must conform to rules to which others also conform. Most moral rules, from that prohibiting murder to that enjoining punctuality, exist for this purpose. But morality is not wholly an affair of regulating our dealings with others; each man has within himself desires of many different kinds which cannot all be fully satisfied; he must establish an order of priorities. Here I think almost all moralists, from Plato to D. H. Lawrence,

have gone astray; for they have overemphasized the extent to which men are like each other and consequently been led to embrace the illusory concept of a "best life" that is the same for all of us. Plato thought this was a life dominated by the pursuit of knowledge, Lawrence one dominated by the pursuit of sensual experience and animal activity. I do not happen to enjoy lying naked on the grass; but I should not wish to force my preference for intellectual endeavor on anyone who did. Why should we not, within the framework of uniformity required for any life to be satisfactory to anyone at all, seek satisfaction in our own different ways?

The word "morality" is usually understood in a sense narrower than that in which I have been using it, to refer to just this necessary framework, to the rules to which we must all conform in order to make our aims, however diverse, realizable in a world which we all have to share. In Hobbes' words, the sphere of morality is limited to "those qualities of mankind that concern their living together in peace and unity" (*Leviathan*, ch. xi). If this is the purpose of moral rules, we must be willing to keep them under review and to discard or modify those that, in the light of experience, we find unnecessary or obstructive. But they must retain a certain inflexibility, since, in our casual contacts, it is important that people should be reliable, should conform so closely to a publicly agreed code that, even if we do not know them as individuals, we know what to expect of them. "That men perform their covenants made" is an adequate summary of morality in this limited sense.

But, though morality in this sense is necessary, it is not all. Rules belong to the superficial periphery of life. Like the multiplication table and other thought-saving dodges, they exist to free us for more important activities. It is beyond the power of any man to regulate all his dealings with all the people with whom he comes in casual contact by love; for love requires a depth of understanding that cannot be achieved except in close intimacy. Rules have no place in marriage or in friendship. This does not mean that a man must keep his word in business but may break promises made to his wife or to a friend; it is rather that the notion of keeping a promise made to a wife or friend from a sense of duty is utterly out of place, utterly foreign to the spirit of their mutual relationship. For what the sense of duty requires of us is always the commission or omission of specific acts.

That friends should be loyal to one another I take for granted; but we cannot set out a list of acts that they should avoid as disloyal with the sort of precision (itself none too great) with which we could list the things a man should not do in business. Too much will depend on the particular circumstances and the particular natures of the people concerned. Rules must, of their very nature, be general; that is their virtue and their defect. They lay down what is to be done or not done in *all* situations of a certain general kind, and they do this because their function is to ensure reliability in the absence of personal knowledge. But however large we make the book of rules, however detailed we try to make its provisions, its complexity cannot reach to that of a close personal relationship. Here what matters is not the commission or omission of specific acts but the spirit of the relationship as a whole. A man thinks, not of what his obligation to his wife or his friend requires of him, but of what it is best for his wife or his friend that he should do. A personal relationship does indeed consist of specific acts; the spirit that exists between husband and wife or between friends is nothing over and above the specific things they do together. But each specific act, like each brush stroke in a picture or each note in a symphony, is good or bad only as it affects the quality of the relationship as a whole. The life of love is, like a work of art, not a means to an end, but an end in itself. For this reason in all close human relationships there should be a flexibility in our attitude to rules characteristic to the expert artist, craftsman, or games player

The expert moves quickly, deftly, and to the untutored eye, even carelessly. It takes me hours to prune an apple tree, and I have to do it book in hand; the expert goes over the tree in a few minutes, snipping here and slashing there, with the abandonment of a small boy who has neither knowledge of pruning nor intention to prune. Indeed, to someone who does not know what he is about, his movements must seem more like those of Piaget's youngest children who just threw the marbles about. But the similarity is superficial. For one thing, the master craftsman's movements do mostly follow the book

for all that he never refers to it; and for another he does know what he is about and it is just this knowledge that entitles him to flout the rules when it is suitable to do so. No apple tree is exactly like the drawing in the book, and expertise lies in knowing when and how to deviate from its instructions.

This analogy must not be pressed too far. The conduct of life is more complicated and more difficult than any such task as pruning a tree and few of us could claim, without improper pride, the master craftsman's licence. But I should like to press it some way, to suggest that, in all important matters, our chief consideration should be, not to conform to any code of rules, but simply how we can produce the best results; that we should so act that we can say in retrospect, not "I did right," but "I did what befitted the pattern of life I have set myself as a goal."

As a philosopher, I cannot but speak in abstract generalities, and it is central to my thesis that at this point the philosopher must give way to the novelist. Tolstoy, Thomas Mann, and Forster have given us many examples of the contrast between the rule-bound and the teleological attitudes to life. But I should like to end by descending one level, not to the particular, but to the relatively specific, and to consider as an example one moral rule, the prohibition of adultery.

By "adultery" I understand the act of sexual intercourse with someone other than one's spouse. It is expressly forbidden in the Bible, absolutely and without regard to circumstances; it is a crime in some countries and many would make it a crime in this. Until very recently it was almost the only ground for civil divorce. A marriage is supposed to be a life-long union. It could be entirely devoid of love—some married couples have not spoken to each other for years, communicating by means of a blackboard; yet no grounds for divorce existed. Or the husband might insist on sexual intercourse with his wife against her will and yet commit no sin. But let him once go out, get drunk, and have a prostitute and the whole scene changes. He has sinned; his wife has a legal remedy and, in the eyes of many who are not Christians but have been brought up in a vaguely Christian tradition, he has now done a serious wrong. This is a rule-and-act morality according to which what is wrong is a specific act; and it is wrong in all circumstances even, for example, if the wife is devoid of jealousy or so devoid of love that she would rather have her husband lie in any bed but hers.

If we look at this rule against adultery from a teleological standpoint it must appear wholly different. A humanist may, of course, reject the whole conception of monogamy; but if, like myself, he retains it, he will do so only because he believes that the life-long union of a man and a woman in the intimacy of marriage is a supreme form of love. Copulation has its part to play in such a union; but, for the species Man, it cannot be its essence. If someone who holds this view still thinks adultery is wrong, he will do so because it appears to him to be an act of disloyalty, an act likely to break the union which he values. Two consequences follow from this. The first is that if a marriage is, for whatever reason, devoid of love, there is now no union to break; so neither adultery nor any other act can break it. The second is that since adultery is now held to be wrong, not in itself, but only as an act of disloyalty, it will not be wrong when it is *not* an act of disloyalty. An adultery committed with the full knowledge and consent of the spouse will not be wrong at all. A so-called "platonic" friendship, even

too assiduous an attendance at the local pub or sewing circle, anything that tends to weaken the bonds of love between the partners will be far more damaging to the marriage and consequently far more deeply immoral. Just *what* specific acts are immoral must, on this view, depend on the particular circumstances and the particular people concerned. Christians also insist on the uniqueness of individual people; but since law is, of its nature, general, this insistence seems wholly incompatible with the morality of law to which they are also committed.

Notes

1. Thomas Mann, *Buddenbrooks*, referring to the headmaster whom Hanno and Kai nicknamed "The Lord God." The whole chapter, Part XI, ch. 2, illustrates this point.

2. This is, I know, heretical: yet I cannot see in the subtle palliatives offered by Catholic theologians anything but evasions, vain attempts to graft a more enlightened moral outlook on to a theological tree which will not bear them. The reformers seem to me to have been right in the sense that they were restoring the original doctrine of the church.

IX.3 Religion and the Queerness of Morality

GEORGE MAVRODES

George Mavrodes is professor of philosophy at the University of Michigan. In this reading, he defends the need for belief in God in ethics. He criticizes Bertrand Russell's secular view of ethics as puzzling, for if there is no God, secular ethics suffers from a serious inadequacy: It cannot satisfactorily answer the question, Why should I be moral all of the time? For, on its account, the common goods at which morality aims

are often just those goods that we sacrifice in carrying out our moral obligation. Why should we sacrifice our welfare for moral duty?

Another oddity about secular ethics is that it is superficial, not deeply rooted. It seems to lack the metaphysical basis that a Platonic or Judeo-Christian worldview affords. Values and obligations are not as deep in a secular world. Mavrodes outlines how a religious morality can meet these desiderata, and, if we are inclined to believe that morality is not queer, how it can provide some evidence for the religious worldview.

Reprinted from George I. Mavrodes, "Religion and the Queerness of Morality," in *Rationality, Religious Belief and Moral Commitment: Essays in the Philosophy of Religion*, edited by Robert Audi and William J. Wainwright. Copyright © 1986 by Cornell University. Used by permission of the publisher, Cor-

Many arguments for the existence of God may be construed as claiming that there is some feature of the world that would somehow make no sense unless there was something else that had a stronger version of that feature or some analogue of it. So, for example, the cosmological line of argument may be thought of as centering upon the claim that the way in which the world exists (called "contingent" existence) would be incomprehensible unless there were something else—that is, God—that had a stronger grip upon existence (that is, "necessary" existence).

Now, a number of thinkers have held a view something like this with respect to morality. They have claimed that in some important way morality is dependent upon religion—dependent, that is, in such a way that if religion were to fail, morality would fail also. And they have held that the dependence was more than psychological, that is, if religion were to fail, it would somehow be *proper* (perhaps logically or perhaps in some other way) for morality to fail also. One way of expressing this theme is by Dostoevsky's "If there is no God, then everything is permitted," a sentiment that in this century has been prominently echoed by Sartre. But perhaps the most substantial philosophical thinker of the modern period to espouse this view, though in a rather idiosyncratic way, was Immanuel Kant, who held that the existence of God was a necessary postulate of 'practical' (that is, moral) reason.

On the other hand, it has recently been popular for moral philosophers to deny this theme and to maintain that the dependence of morality on religion is, at best, merely psychological. Were religion to fail, so they apparently hold, this would grant no sanction for the failure of morality. For morality stands on its own feet, whatever those feet may turn out to be.

Now, the suggestion that morality somehow depends on religion is rather attractive to me. It is this suggestion that I wish to explore in this paper, even though it seems unusually difficult to formulate clearly the features of this suggestion that make it attractive. I will begin by mentioning briefly some aspects that I will not discuss.

First, beyond this paragraph I will not discuss the claim that morality cannot survive psychologically without the support of religious belief. At least in the short run, this proposal seems to me false. For there certainly seem to be people who reject religious belief, at least in the ordinary sense, but who apparently have a concern with morality and who try to live a moral life. Whether the proposal may have more force if it is understood in a broader way, as applying to whole cultures, epochs, and so forth, I do not know.

Second, I will not discuss the attempt to define some or all moral terms by the use of religious terms, or vice versa. But this should not be taken as implying any judgment about this project.

Third, beyond this paragraph I shall not discuss the suggestion that moral statements may be entailed by religious statements and so may be "justified" by religious doctrines or beliefs. It is popular now to hold that no such alleged entailment can be valid. But the reason usually cited for this view is the more general doctrine that moral statements cannot be validly deduced from nonmoral statements, a doctrine usually traced to Hume. Now, to my mind the most important problem raised by this general doctrine is that of finding some interpretation of it that is both significant and not plainly false. If it is taken to mean merely that there is *some* set of statements that entails no moral statement, then it strikes me as probably true, but trivial. At any rate, we should then need another reason to suppose that religious statements fall in this category. If, on the other hand, it is taken to mean that one can divide the domain of statements into two classes, the moral and the nonmoral, and that none of the latter entail any of the former, then it is false. I, at any rate, do not know a version of this doctrine that seems relevant to the religious case and that has any reasonable likelihood of being true. But I am not concerned on this occasion with the possibly useful project of deducing morality from religion, and so I will not pursue it further. My interest is closer to a move in the other direction, that of deducing religion from morality. (I am not quite satisfied with this way of putting it and will try to explain this dissatisfaction later on.)

For the remainder of this discussion. then, my project is as follows. I will outline one rather common nonreligious view of the world, calling attention to what I take to be its most relevant features. Then I shall try to portray some sense of the odd status that morality would have in a world of that sort. I shall be hoping, of course, that you will notice that this odd status is not the one that you recognize morality to have in the actual world. But it will perhaps be obvious that the "worldview" amendments required would move substantially toward a religious position.

First, then, the nonreligious view. I take a short and powerful statement of it from a 1903 essay by Bertrand Russell, "A Free Man's Worship."

> That man is the product of causes which had no prevision of the end they were achieving; that his origin, his growth, his hopes and fears, his loves and his beliefs are but the outcome of accidental collocations of atoms; that no fire, no heroism, no intensity of thought and feeling, can preserve an individual life beyond the grave; that all the labors of the ages, all the devotion, all the inspiration, all the noonday brightness of human genius, are destined to extinction in the vast death of the solar system, and that the whole temple of man's achievement must inevitably be buried beneath the debris of a universe in ruins—all these things, if not quite beyond dispute, are yet so nearly certain that no philosophy which rejects them can hope to stand. Only within the scaffolding of these truths, only on the firm foundation of unyielding despair, can the soul's habitation henceforth be safely built.[1]

For convenience, I will call a world that satisfies the description given here a "Russellian world." But we are primarily interested in what the status of morality would be in the actual world if that world should turn out to be Russellian. I shall therefore sometimes augment the description of a Russellian world with obvious features of the actual world.

What are the most relevant features of a Russellian world? The following strike me as especially important: (1) Such phenomena as minds, mental activities, consciousness, and so forth are the products of entities and causes that give no indication of being mental themselves. In Russell's words, the causes are "accidental collocations of atoms" with "no prevision of the end they were achieving." Though not stated explicitly by Russell, we might add the doctrine, a commonplace in modern science, that mental phenomena—and indeed life itself—are comparative latecomers in the long history of the earth. (2) Human life is bounded by physical death and each individual comes to a permanent end at his physical death. We might add to this the observation that the span of human life is

comparatively short, enough so that in some cases we can, with fair confidence, predict the major consequences of certain actions insofar as they will affect a given individual throughout his whole remaining life. (3) Not only each individual but also the human race as a species is doomed to extinction "beneath the debris of a universe in ruins."

So much, then, for the main features of a Russellian world. Because the notion of benefits and goods plays an important part in the remainder of my discussion, I want to introduce one further technical expression—"Russellian benefit." A Russellian benefit is one that could accrue to a person in a Russellian world. A contented old age would be, I suppose, a Russellian benefit, as would a thrill of sexual pleasure or a good reputation. Going to heaven when one dies, though a benefit, is not a Russellian benefit. Russellian benefits are only the benefits possible in a Russellian world. But one can have Russellian benefits even if the world is not Russellian. In such a case there might, however, also be other benefits, such as going to heaven.

Could the actual world be Russellian? Well, I take it to be an important feature of the actual world that human beings exist in it and that in it their actions fall, at least sometimes, within the sphere of morality—that is, they have moral obligations to act (or to refrain from acting) in certain ways. And if they do not act in those ways, then they are properly subject to a special and peculiar sort of adverse judgment (unless it happens that there are special circumstances that serve to excuse their failure to fulfill the obligations). People who do not fulfill their obligations are not merely stupid or weak or unlucky; they are morally reprehensible.

Now, I do not have much to say in an illuminating manner about the notion of moral obligation, but I could perhaps make a few preliminary observations about how I understand this notion. First, I take it that morality includes, or results in, judgments of the form "N ought to do (or to avoid doing) ____" or "It is N's duty to do (or to avoid doing) ____." That is, morality ascribes to particular people an obligation to do a certain thing on a certain occasion. No doubt morality includes other things as well—general moral rules, for example. I shall, however, focus on judgments of the sort just mentioned, and when I speak without further qualification of someone's having an obligation I intend it to be understood in terms of such a judgment.

Second, many authors distinguish prima facie obligations from obligations "all things considered." Probably this is a useful distinction. For the most part, however, I intend to ignore prima facie obligations and to focus upon our obligations all things considered, what we might call our "final obligations." These are the obligations that a particular person has in some concrete circumstance at a particular place and time, when all the aspects of the situation have been taken into account. It identifies the action that, if not done, will properly subject the person to the special adverse judgment.

Finally, it is, I think, a striking feature of moral obligations that a person's being unwilling to fulfill the obligation is irrelevant to having the obligation and is also irrelevant to the adverse judgment in case the obligation is not fulfilled. Perhaps even more important is the fact that, at least for some obligations, it is also irrelevant in both these ways for one to point out that he does not see how fulfilling the obligations can do him any good. In fact, unless we are greatly mistaken about our obligations, it seems clear that in a Russellian world there are an appreciable number of cases in which fulfilling an obligation would result in a loss of good to ourselves. On the most prosaic level, this must be true of some cases of repaying a debt, keeping a promise, refraining from stealing, and so on. And it must also be true of those rarer but more striking cases of obligation to risk death or serious injury in the performance of a duty. People have, of course, differed as to what is good for humans. But so far as I can see, the point I have been making will hold for any candidate that is plausible in a Russellian world. Pleasure, happiness, esteem, contentment, self-realization, knowledge—all of these can suffer from the fulfillment of a moral obligation.

It is not, however, a *necessary* truth that some of our obligations are such that their fulfillment will yield no net benefit, within Russellian limits, to their fulfiller. It is not contradictory to maintain that, for every obligation that I have, a corresponding benefit awaits me within the confines of this world and this life. While such a contention would not be contradictory, however, it would nevertheless be false. I discuss below one version of this contention.

At present it must suffice to say that a person who accepts this claim will probably find the remainder of what I have to say correspondingly less plausible.

Well, where are we now? I claim that in the actual world we have some obligations that, when we fulfill them, will confer on us no net Russellian benefit—in fact, they will result in a Russellian loss. If the world is Russellian, then Russellian benefits and losses are the only benefits and losses, and also then we have moral obligations whose fulfillment will result in a net loss of good to the one who fulfills them. I suggest, however, that it would be very strange to have such obligations—strange not simply in the sense of being unexpected or surprising but in some deeper way. I do not suggest that it is strange in the sense of having a straightforward logical defect, of being self-contradictory to claim that we have such obligations. Perhaps the best thing to say is that were it a fact that we had such obligations, then the world that included such a fact would be absurd—we would be living in a crazy world.

Now, whatever success I may have in this paper will in large part be a function of my success (or lack thereof) in getting across a sense of that absurdity, that queerness. On some accounts of morality, in a Russellian world there would not be the strangeness that I allege. Perhaps, then, I can convey some of that strangeness by mentioning those views of morality that would eliminate it. In fact, I believe that a good bit of their appeal is just the fact that they do get rid of this queerness.

First, I suspect that morality will not be queer in the way I suggest, even in a Russellian world, if judgments about obligations are properly to be analyzed in terms of the speaker rather than in terms of the subject of the judgment. And I more than suspect that this will be the case if such judgments are analyzed in terms of the speaker's attitude or feeling toward some action, and/or his attempt or inclination to incite a similar attitude in someone else. It may be, of course, that there is something odd about the supposition that human beings, consciousness, and so forth, could arise at all in a Russellian world. A person who was impressed by that oddity might he attracted toward some "teleological" line of reasoning in the direction of a more religious view. But I think that this oddity is not the one I am touching on here. Once given the existence of human beings with capabilities for feelings and attitudes, there does not seem to be anything further that is queer in the supposition that a speaker might have an attitude toward some action, might express that attitude, and might attempt (or succeed) in inciting someone else to have a similar attitude. Anyone, therefore, who can be satisfied with such an analysis will probably not be troubled by the queerness that I allege.

Second, for similar reasons, this queerness will also be dissipated by any account that understands judgments about obligations purely in terms of the feelings, attitudes, and so forth of the subject of the judgment. For, given again that there are human beings with consciousness, it does not seem to be any additional oddity that the subject of a moral judgment might have feelings or attitudes about an actual or prospective action of his own. The assumption that morality is to be understood in this way takes many forms. In a closely related area, for example, it appears as the assumption—so common now that it can pass almost unnoticed—that guilt could not be anything other than guilt *feelings*, and that the "problem" of guilt is just the problem generated by such feelings.

In connection with our topic here, however, we might look at the way in which this sort of analysis enters into one plausible-sounding explanation of morality in a Russellian world, an explanation that has a scientific flavor. The existence of morality in a Russellian world, it may be said, is not at all absurd because its existence there can be given a perfectly straightforward explanation: morality has a survival value for a species such as ours because it makes possible continued cooperation and things of that sort. So it is no more absurd that people have moral obligations than it is absurd that they have opposable thumbs.

I think that this line of explanation will work only if one analyzes obligations into feelings, or beliefs. I think it is plausible (though I am not sure it is correct) to suppose that everyone's having feelings of moral obligation might have survival value for a species such as Man, given of course that these feelings were attached to patterns of action that contributed to such survival. And if that is so, then it is not implausible to suppose that there may be a survival value for the species even in a moral feeling that leads to the death of the individual who

has it. So far so good. But this observation, even if true, is not relevant to the queerness with which I am here concerned. For I have not suggested that the existence of moral feelings would be absurd in a Russellian world; it is rather the existence of moral *obligations* that is absurd, and I think it important to make the distinction. It is quite possible, it seems to me, for one to feel (or to believe) that he has a certain obligation without actually having it, and also vice versa. Now, beliefs and feelings will presumably have some effect upon actions, and this effect may possibly contribute to the survival of the species. But, so far as I can see, the addition of actual moral obligations to these moral beliefs and feelings will make no further contribution to action nor will the actual obligations have an effect upon action in the absence of the corresponding feelings and beliefs. So it seems that neither with nor without the appropriate feelings will moral obligations contribute to the survival of the species. Consequently, an "evolutionary" approach such as this cannot serve to explain the existence of moral obligations, unless one rejects my distinction and equates the obligations with the feelings.

And finally, I think that morality will not be queer in the way I allege, or at least it will not be as queer as I think, if it should be the case that every obligation yields a Russellian benefit to the one who fulfills it. Given the caveat expressed earlier, one can perhaps make some sense out of the notion of a Russellian good or benefit for a sentient organism in a Russellian world. And one could, I suppose, without further queerness imagine that such an organism might aim toward achieving such goods. And we could further suppose that there were certain actions—those that were "obligations"—that would, in contrast with other actions, actually yield such benefits to the organism that performed them. And finally, it might not be too implausible to claim that an organism that failed to perform such an action was defective in some way and that some adverse judgment was appropriate.

Morality, however, seems to require us to hold that certain organisms (namely, human beings) have in addition to their ordinary properties and relations another special relation to certain actions. This relation is that of being "obligated" to perform those actions. And some of those actions are pretty clearly such that they will yield only Russellian losses to the one who performs them. Nevertheless, we are supposed to hold that a person who does not perform an action to which he is thus related is defective in some serious and important way and an adverse judgment is appropriate against him. And that certainly does seem odd.

The recognition of this oddity—or perhaps better, this absurdity—is not simply a resolution to concern ourselves only with what "pays." Here the position of Kant is especially suggestive. He held that a truly moral action is undertaken purely out of respect for the moral law and with no concern at all for reward. There seems to be no room at all here for any worry about what will "pay." But he also held that the moral enterprise needs, in a deep and radical way, the postulate of a God who can, and will, make happiness correspond to virtue. This postulate is "necessary" for practical reason. Perhaps we could put this Kantian demand in the language I have been using here, saying that the moral enterprise would make no sense in a world in which that correspondence ultimately failed.

I suspect that what we have in Kant is the recognition that there cannot be, in any "reasonable" way, a moral demand upon me, unless reality itself is committed to morality in some deep way. It makes sense only if there is a moral demand on the world too and only if reality will in the end satisfy that demand. This theme of the deep grounding of morality is one to which I return briefly near the end of this paper.

The oddity we have been considering is, I suspect, the most important root of the celebrated and somewhat confused question, "Why should I be moral?" Characteristically, I think, the person who asks that question is asking to have the queerness of that situation illuminated. From time to time there are philosophers who make an attempt to argue—perhaps only a halfhearted attempt—that being moral really is in one's interest after all. Kurt Baier, it seems to me, proposes a reply of this sort. He says:

> Moralities are systems of principles whose acceptance by everyone as overruling the dictates of self-interest is in the interest of everyone alike though following the rules of a morality is not of course identical with following self-interest. . . .

The answer to our question "Why should we be moral?" is therefore as follows. We should be moral because being moral is following rules designed to overrule self-interest whenever it is in the interest of everyone alike that everyone should set aside his interest.[2]

As I say, this seems to be an argument to the effect that it really is in everyone's interest to be moral. I suppose that Baier is here probably talking about Russellian interests. At least, we must interpret him in that way if his argument is to be applicable in this context, and I will proceed on that assumption. But how exactly is the argument to be made out?

It appears here to begin with a premise something like

(A) It is in everyone's best interest (including mine, presumably) for everyone (including me) to be moral.

This premise itself appears to be supported earlier by reference to Hobbes. As I understand it, the idea is that without morality people will live in a "state of nature," and life will be nasty, brutish, and short. Well, perhaps so. At any rate, let us accept (A) for the moment. From (A) we can derive

(B) It is in my best interest for everyone (including me) to be moral.

And from (B) perhaps one derives

(C) It is in my best interest for me to be moral.

And (C) may be taken to answer the question, "Why should I be moral?" Furthermore, if (C) is true, then moral obligation will at least not have the sort of queerness that I have been alleging.

Unfortunately, however, the argument outlined above is invalid. The derivation of (B) from (A) *may* be all right, but the derivation of (C) from (B) is invalid. What does follow from (B) is

(C')It is in my best interest for me to be moral *if everyone else is moral.*

The argument thus serves to show that it is in a given person's interest to be moral only on the assumption that everyone else in the world is moral. It might, of course, be difficult to find someone ready to make that assumption.

There is, however, something more of interest in this argument. I said that the derivation of (B) from (A) may be all right. But in fact is it? If it is not all right, then this argument would fail even if everyone else in the world were moral. Now (A) can be interpreted as referring to "everyone's best interest" ("the interest of everyone alike," in Baier's own words) either collectively or distributively; that is, it may be taken as referring to the best interest of the whole group considered as a single unit, or as referring to the best interest of each individual in the group. But if (A) is interpreted in the collective sense, then (B) does not follow from it. It may not be in *my* best interest for everyone to act morally, even if it is in the best interest of the group as a whole, for the interest of the group as a whole may be advanced by the sacrificing of my interest. On this interpretation of (A), then, the argument will not answer the question "Why should I be moral?" even on the supposition that everyone else is moral.

If (A) is interpreted in the distributive sense, on the other hand, then (B) does follow from it, and the foregoing objection is not applicable. But another objection arises. Though (A) in the collective sense has some plausibility, it is hard to imagine that it is true in the distributive sense. Hobbes may have been right in supposing that life in the state of nature would be short, etc. But some lives are short anyway. In fact, some lives are short just because the demands of morality are observed. Such a life is not bound to have been shorter in the state of nature. Nor is it bound to have been less happy, less pleasurable, and so forth. In fact, does it not seem obvious that *my* best Russellian interest will be further advanced in a situation in which everyone else acts morally but I act immorally (in selected cases) than it will be in case everyone, including me, acts morally? It certainly seems so. It can, of course, be observed that if I act immorally then so will other people, perhaps reducing my benefits. In the present state of the world that is certainly true. But in the present state of the world it is also true, as I observed earlier, that many other people will act immorally *anyway,* regardless of what I do.

A more realistic approach is taken by Richard Brandt.[3] He asks, "Is it *reasonable* for me to do my duty if it conflicts seriously with my personal welfare?" After distinguishing several possible senses of this question, he chooses a single one to discuss further, presumably a sense that he thinks important. As reformulated, the question is now: "Given that doing x is my duty and that doing some conflicting

act y will maximize my personal welfare, will the performance of x instead of y satisfy my reflective preferences better?" And the conclusion to which he comes is that "the correct answer may vary from one person to another. It depends on what kind of person one is, what one cares about." And within Russellian limits Brandt must surely be right in this. But he goes on to say, "It is, of course, no defense of one's failure to do one's duty, before others or society, to say that doing so is not 'reasonable' for one in this sense." And this is just to bring the queer element back in. It is to suppose that besides "the kind of person" I am and my particular pattern of "cares" and interests there is something else, my duty, which may go against these and in any case properly overrides them. And one feels that there must be some sense of "reasonable" in which one can ask whether a world in which that is true is a reasonable world, whether such a world makes any sense.

This completes my survey of some ethical or metaethical views that would eliminate or minimize this sort of queerness of morality. I turn now to another sort of view, stronger I think than any of these others, which accepts that queerness but goes no further. And one who holds this view will also hold, I think, that the question "Why should I be moral?" must be rejected in one way or another. A person who holds this view will say that it is simply a fact that we have the moral obligations that we do have, and that is all there is to it. If they sometimes result in a loss of good, then that too is just a fact. These may be puzzling or surprising facts, but there are lots of puzzling and surprising things about the world. In a Russellian world, morality will be, I suppose, an "emergent" phenomenon; it will be a feature of certain effects though it is not a feature of their causes. But the wetness of water is an emergent feature, too. It is not a property of either hydrogen or oxygen. And there is really nothing more to be said; somewhere we must come to an end of reasons and explanations. We have our duties. We can fulfill them and be moral, or we can ignore them and be immoral. If all that is crazy and absurd— well, so be it. Who are we to say that the world is not crazy and absurd?

Such a view was once suggested by William Alston in a criticism of Hasting Rashdall's moral argument for God's existence. Alston attributed to

Rashdall the view that "God is required as a locus for the moral law." But Alston then went on to ask, "Why could it not just be an ultimate fact about the universe that kindness is good and cruelty bad? This seems to have been Plato's view." And if we rephrase Alston's query slightly to refer to obligations, we might be tempted to say, "Why not indeed?"

I say that this is perhaps the strongest reply against me. Since it involves no argument, there is no argument to be refuted. And I have already said that, so far as I can see, its central contention is not self-contradictory. Nor do I think of any other useful argument to the effect that the world is not absurd and crazy in this way. The reference to Plato, however, might be worth following for a moment. Perhaps Plato did think that goodness, or some such thing related to morality, was an ultimate fact about the world. But a Platonic world is not very close to a Russellian world. Plato was not a Christian, of course, but his worldview has very often been taken to be congenial (especially congenial compared to some other philosophical views) to a religious understanding of the world. He would not have been satisfied, I think, with Russell's "accidental collocations of atoms," nor would he have taken the force of the grave to be "so nearly certain." The idea of the Good seems to play a metaphysical role in his thought. It is somehow fundamental to what *is* as well as to what ought to be, much more fundamental to reality than are the atoms. A Platonic man, therefore, who sets himself to live in accordance with the Good aligns himself with what is deepest and most basic in existence. Or to put it another way, we might say that whatever values a Platonic world imposes on a man are values to which the Platonic world itself is committed, through and through.

Not so, of course, for a Russellian world. Values and obligations cannot be deep in such a world. They have a grip only upon surface phenomena, probably only upon man. What is deep in a Russellian world must be such things as matter and energy, or perhaps natural law, chance, or chaos. If it really were a fact that one had obligations in a Russellian world, then something would be laid upon man that might cost a man everything but that went no further than man. And that difference from a Platonic world seems to make all the difference.

This discussion suggests, I think, that there are two related ways in which morality is queer in a Russellian world. Or maybe they are better construed as two aspects of the queerness we have been exploring. In most of the preceding discussion I have been focusing on the strangeness of an overriding demand that does not seem to conduce to the *good* of the person on whom it is laid. (In fact, it does not even promise his good.) Here, however, we focus on the fact that this demand—radical enough in the human life on which it is laid—is *superficial* in a Russellian world. Something that reaches close to the heart of my own life, perhaps even demanding the sacrifice of that life, is not deep at all in the world in which (on a Russellian view) that life is lived. And that, too, seems absurd.

This brings to an end the major part of my discussion. If I have been successful at all you will have shared with me to some extent in the sense of the queerness of morality, its absurdity in a Russellian world. If you also share the conviction that it cannot in the end be absurd in that way, then perhaps you will also be attracted to some religious view of the world. Perhaps you also will say that morality must have some deeper grip upon the world than a Russellian view allows. And, consequently, things like mind and purpose must also be deeper in the real world than they would be in a Russellian world. They must be more original, more controlling. The accidental collocation of atoms cannot be either primeval or final, nor can the grave be an end. But or course that would be only a beginning, a sketch waiting to be filled in.

We cannot here do much to fill it in further. But I should like to close with a final, and rather tentative suggestion, as to a direction in which one might move in thinking about the place of morality in the world. It is suggested to me by certain elements in my own religion, Christianity.

I come more and more to think that morality, while a fact, is a twisted and distorted fact. Or perhaps better, that it is a barely recognizable version of another fact, a version adapted to a twisted and distorted world. It is something like, I suppose, the way in which the pine that grows at timberline, wind blasted and twisted low against the rock, is a version of the tall and symmetrical tree that grows lower on the slopes. I think it may be that the related notions of sacrifice and gift represent (or come close to representing) the fact, that is, the pattern of life, whose distorted version we know here as morality. Imagine a situation, an "economy" if you will, in which no one ever buys or trades for or seizes any good thing. But whatever good he enjoys is either one which he himself has created or else one which he receives as a free and unconditional gift. And as soon as he has tasted it and seen that it is good he stands ready to give it away in his turn as soon as the opportunity arises. In such a place, if one were to speak either of his rights or his duties, his remark might be met with puzzled laughter as his hearers struggled to recall an ancient world in which those terms referred to something important.

We have, of course, even now some occasions that tend in this direction. Within some families perhaps, or even in a regiment in desperate battle, people may for a time pass largely beyond morality and live lives of gift and sacrifice. On those occasions nothing would be lost if the moral concepts and the moral language were to disappear. But it is probably not possible that such situations and occasions should be more than rare exceptions in the daily life of the present world. Christianity, however, which tells us that the present world is "fallen" and hence leads us to expect a distortion in its important features, also tells us that one day the redemption of the world will be complete and that then all things shall be made new. And it seems to me to suggest an

"economy" more akin to that of gift and sacrifice than to that of rights and duties. If something like that should be true, then perhaps morality, like the Marxist state, is destined to wither away (unless perchance it should happen to survive in hell).

Christianity, then, I think is related to the queerness or morality in one way and perhaps in two. In the first instance, it provides a view of the world in which morality is not an absurdity. It gives morality a deeper place in the world than does a Russellian view and thus permits it to "make sense." But in the second instance, it perhaps suggests that morality is not the deepest thing, that it is provisional and transitory, that it is due to serve its use and then to pass away in favor of something richer and deeper. Perhaps we can say that it begins by inverting the quotation with which I began and by telling us that, since God exists, not everything is permitted; but it may also go on to tell us that, since God exists, in the end there shall be no occasion for any prohibition.

Notes

1. Bertrand Russell, *Mysticism and Logic* (New York: Barnes & Noble, 1917), pp. 47–48.
2. Kurt Baier, *The Moral Point of View* (Ithaca: Cornell University Press, 1958), p. 314.
3. Richard Brandt, *Ethical Theory* (Englewood Cliffs, N.J.: Prentice Hall, 1959), pp. 375–78.

Bibliography for Part IX

Hare, John E. *The Moral Gap.* Oxford Univ. Press, 1996.

Helm, Paul, ed. *The Divine Command Theory of Ethics.* Oxford, Eng.: Oxford Univ. Press, 1979. This work contains a good selection of the latest material on the subject.

Kierkegaard, Søren. *Fear and Trembling,* translated by Howard V. Hong and Edna H. Hong. Princeton, N.J.: Princeton Univ. Press, 1983. A classic work on the relation of religion to morality.

Nielson, Kai. *Ethics Without God.* London: Pemberton Books, 1973. A clearly written description of humanistic ethics.

Outka, Gene, and J. P. Reeder, eds. *Religion and Morality: A Collection of Essays.* New York: Anchor Books, 1973. A good collection of essays.

Pojman, Louis, "Ethics: Religious and Secular," *The Modern Schoolman,* Vol. 70 (Nov. 1992), pp. 1–30.

Quinn, Philip. *Divine Commands and Moral Requirements.* Oxford, Eng.: Clarendon Press, 1978. An incisive treatise on the subject.